Stanley Gibbons Commonwealth Stamp

Leeward Islands

2nd edition 2012

STANLEY GIBBONS LTD
London and Ringwood

By Appointment to Her Majesty The Queen
Stanley Gibbons Ltd, London
Philatelists

Published by Stanley Gibbons Ltd
Editorial, Publications Sales Offices
and Distribution Centre:
7 Parkside, Christchurch Road, Ringwood,
Hants BH24 3SH

© Stanley Gibbons Ltd 2012

Copyright Notice

The contents of this Catalogue, including the numbering system and illustrations, are fully protected by copyright. No part of this publication may be reproduced, stored in a retrieval system, or transmitted in any form or by any means, electronic, mechanical, photocopying, recording or otherwise, without the prior permission of Stanley Gibbons Limited. Requests for such permission should be addressed to the Catalogue Editor. This Catalogue is sold on condition that it is not, by way of trade or otherwise, lent, re-sold, hired out, circulated or otherwise disposed of other than in its complete, original and unaltered form and without a similar condition including this condition being imposed on the subsequent purchaser.

British Library Cataloguing in
Publication Data.
A catalogue record for this book is available from the British Library.

Errors and omissions excepted
the colour reproduction of stamps is only as accurate as the printing process will allow.

ISBN-10: 0-85259-848-3
ISBN-13: 978-0-85259-848-1

Item No. R 2989-12

Printed by
GraphyCems, Spain

Contents

Stanley Gibbons Holdings Plc	**iv**
Complete List of Parts	**v**
General Philatelic Information	**vi**
Prices	vi
Guarantee	vii
Condition Guide	ix
Acknowledgements	ix
The Catalogue in General	**x**
Contacting the editor	x
Technical matters	xi
Abbreviations	**xxii**
Features Listing	**xxiii**
Glossary	**xxv**
Guide to Entries	**xxx**
Anguilla	**1**
Stamp Booklets	27
Antigua	**29**
Antigua and Barbuda	45
Stamp Booklets	118
Barbuda	118
Stamp Booklets	147
Redonda	147
British Virgin Islands	**148**
Official Stamps	177
Leeward Islands	**178**
Montserrat	**182**
Stamp Booklets	217
Official Stamps	**217**
St. Kitts-Nevis	**221**
St. Christopher	**221**
Revenue Stamps	221
Nevis	222
St. Kitts-Nevis	223
St. Christopher, Nevis and Anguilla	225
Official Stamps	233
St. Kitts	**233**
Stamp Booklets	261
Official Stamps	261
Nevis	**261**
Stamp Booklets	311
Official Stamps	311

Stanley Gibbons Holdings Plc

Stanley Gibbons Limited, Stanley Gibbons Auctions
399 Strand, London WC2R 0LX
Tel: +44 (0)207 836 8444
Fax: +44 (0)207 836 7342
E-mail: help@stanleygibbons.com
Website: www.stanleygibbons.com
for all departments, Auction and Specialist Stamp Departments.

Open Monday–Friday 9.30 a.m. to 5 p.m. Shop. Open Monday–Friday 9 a.m. to 5.30 p.m. and Saturday 9.30 a.m. to 5.30 p.m.

Stanley Gibbons Publications Gibbons Stamp Monthly and Philatelic Exporter
7 Parkside, Christchurch Road, Ringwood, Hampshire BH24 3SH.
Tel: +44 (0)1425 472363
Fax: +44 (0)1425 470247
E-mail: help@stanleygibbons.com
Publications Mail Order.
FREEPHONE 0800 611622

Monday–Friday 8.30 a.m. to 5 p.m.

Stanley Gibbons (Guernsey) Limited
18–20 Le Bordage, St Peter Port, Guernsey GY1 1DE.
Tel: +44 (0)1481 708270
Fax: +44 (0)1481 708279
E-mail: investment@stanleygibbons.com

Stanley Gibbons (Jersey) Limited
18 Hill Street, St Helier, Jersey, Channel Islands JE2 4UA.
Tel: +44 (0)1534 766711
Fax: +44 (0)1534 766177
E-mail: investment@stanleygibbons.com

Stanley Gibbons (Asia) Limited
Level 10
Central Building
1-3 Pedder Street
Hong Kong
Tel: +852 3975 2988
E-mail: ganandappa@stanleygibbons.com

Benham Collectibles Limited
Unit K, Concept Court, Shearway Business Park
Folkestone Kent CT19 4RG
E-mail: benham@benham.com

Fraser's
(a division of Stanley Gibbons Ltd)
399 Strand, London WC2R 0LX
Autographs, photographs, letters and documents
Tel: +44 (0)207 836 8444
Fax: +44 (0)207 836 7342
E-mail: sales@frasersautographs.com
Website: www.frasersautographs.com

Monday–Friday 9 a.m. to 5.30 p.m. and Saturday 10 a.m. to 4 p.m.

Stanley Gibbons Publications Overseas Representation
Stanley Gibbons Publications are represented overseas by the following

Australia *Renniks Publications PTY LTD*
Unit 3 37-39 Green Street, Banksmeadow, NSW 2019, Australia
Tel: +612 9695 7055
Website: www.renniks.com

Canada *Unitrade Associates*
99 Floral Parkway, Toronto, Ontario M6L 2C4, Canada
Tel: +1 416 242 5900
Website: www.unitradeassoc.com

Germany *Schaubek Verlag Leipzig*
Am Glaeschen 23, D-04420
Markranstaedt, Germany
Tel: +49 34 205 67823
Website: www.schaubek.de

Italy *Ernesto Marini S.R.L.*
V. Struppa, 300, Genova, 16165, Italy
Tel: +3901 0247-3530
Website: www.ernestomarini.it

Japan *Japan Philatelic*
PO Box 2, Suginami-Minami, Tokyo 168-8081, Japan
Tel: +81 3330 41641
Website: www.yushu.co.jp

Netherlands (also covers Belgium Denmark, Finland & France)
Uitgeverij Davo BV
PO Box 411, Ak Deventer, 7400
Netherlands
Tel: +315 7050 2700
Website: www.davo.nl

New Zealand *House of Stamps*
PO Box 12, Paraparaumu, New Zealand
Tel: +61 6364 8270
Website: www.houseofstamps.co.nz

New Zealand *Philatelic Distributors*
PO Box 863
15 Mount Edgecumbe Street
New Plymouth 4615, New Zealand
Tel: +6 46 758 65 68
Website: www.stampcollecta.com

Norway *SKANFIL A/S*
SPANAV. 52 / BOKS 2030
N-5504 HAUGESUND, Norway
Tel: +47-52703940
E-mail: magne@skanfil.no

Singapore *C S Philatelic Agency*
Peninsula Shopping Centre #04-29
3 Coleman Street, 179804, Singapore
Tel: +65 6337-1859
Website: www.cs.com.sg

South Africa *Peter Bale Philatelics*
P O Box 3719, Honeydew,
2040, South Africa
Tel: +27 11 462 2463
Tel: +27 82 330 3925
E-mail: balep@iafrica.com

Sweden *Chr Winther Sorensen AB*
Box 43, S-310 20 Knaered, Sweden
Tel: +46 43050743
Website: www.collectia.se

USA *Regency Superior Ltd*
229 North Euclid Avenue
Saint Louis, Missouri 63108, USA

PO Box 8277, St Louis,
MO 63156-8277, USA
Toll Free Tel: (800) 782-0066
Tel: (314) 361-5699
Website: www.RegencySuperior.com
Email: info@regencysuperior.com

We have catalogues to suit every aspect of stamp collecting

Our catalogues cover stamps issued from across the globe - from the Penny Black to the latest issues. Whether you're a specialist in a certain reign or a thematic collector, we should have something to suit your needs. All catalogues include the famous SG numbering system, making it as easy as possible to find the stamp you're looking for.

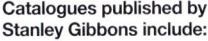

Catalogues published by Stanley Gibbons include:

1 Commonwealth & British Empire Stamps 1840–1970 (114th edition, 2012)

Stamps of the World 2012
- Volume 1 A–Char
- Volume 2 Chil–Geo
- Volume 3 Ger–Ja
- Volume 4 Je–New R
- Volume 5 New S–Sin
- Volume 6 Sir–Z

Commonwealth Country Catalogues
Australia and Dependencies (7th edition, 2011)
Bangladesh, Pakistan & Sri Lanka (2nd edition, 2012)
Belize, Guyana, Trinidad & Tobago (1st edition, 2009)
Brunei, Malaysia & Singapore (3rd edition, 2009)
Canada (4th edition, 2011)
Cyprus, Gibraltar & Malta (3rd edition, 2011)
East Africa with Egypt and Sudan (2nd edition, 2010)
Eastern Pacific (2nd edition, 2011)
Falkland Islands (5th edition, 2012)
Hong Kong (3rd edition, 2010)
India (including Convention and Feudatory States) (3rd edition, 2009)
Indian Ocean (2nd edition, 2012)
Ireland (5th edition, 2012)
Leeward Islands (2nd edition, 2012)
New Zealand (4th edition, 2010)
Northern Caribbean, Bahamas & Bermuda (2nd edition, 2009)
St. Helena & Dependencies (4th edition, 2011)
Southern and Central Africa (1st combined edition, 2011)
West Africa (1st edition, 2009)
Western Pacific (2nd edition, 2009)
Windward Islands and Barbados (1st edition, 2007)

Foreign Countries
2 **Austria & Hungary** (7th edition, 2009)
3 **Balkans** (5th edition, 2009)
4 **Benelux** (6th edition, 2010)
5 **Czech Republic, Slovakia & Poland** (7th edition, 2012)
6 **France** (7th edition, 2010)
7 **Germany** (9th edition, 2011)
8 **Italy & Switzerland** (7th edition, 2010)
9 **Portugal & Spain** (6th edition, 2011)
10 **Russia** (6th edition, 2008)
11 **Scandinavia** (6th edition, 2008)
12 **Africa since Independence A-E** (2nd edition, 1983)
13 **Africa since Independence F-M** (1st edition, 1981)
14 **Africa since Independence N-Z** (1st edition, 1981)
15 **Central America** (3rd edition, 2007)
16 **Central Asia** (4th edition, 2006)
17 **China** (9th edition, 2012)
18 **Japan & Korea** (5th edition, 2008)
19 **Middle East** (7th edition, 2009)
20 **South America** (4th edition, 2008)
21 **South-East Asia** (4th edition, 2004)
22 **United States of America** (7th edition, 2010)

Thematic Catalogues
Stanley Gibbons Catalogues for use with *Stamps of the World*.
Collect Aircraft on Stamps (2nd edition, 2009)
Collect Birds on Stamps (5th edition, 2003)
Collect Chess on Stamps (2nd edition, 1999)
Collect Fish on Stamps (1st edition, 1999)
Collect Motor Vehicles on Stamps (1st edition, 2004)

Great Britain Catalogues
Collect British Stamps (63rd edition, 2012)
Great Britain Concise Stamp Catalogue (26th edition, 2011)
Volume 1 *Queen Victoria* (16th edition, 2012)
Volume 2 *King Edward VII to King George VI* (13th edition, 2009)
Volume 3 *Queen Elizabeth II Pre-decimal issues* (12th edition, 2011)
Volume 4 *Queen Elizabeth II Decimal Definitive Issues – Part 1* (10th edition, 2008)
Queen Elizabeth II Decimal Definitive Issues – Part 2 (10th edition, 2010)
Volume 5 *Queen Elizabeth II Decimal Special Issues* (3rd edition, 1998 with 1998-99 and 2000/1 Supplements)

Other publications
Africa Simplified Volume 1 (1st edition, 2011)
Asia Simplified Volume 1 (1st edition, 2010)
Antarctica (including Australian and British Antarctic Territories, French Southern and Antarctic Territories and Ross Dependency) (1st edition, 2010)
Collect Channel Islands and Isle of Man Stamps (27th edition, 2012)
Commonwealth Simplified (4th edition, 2010)
Enjoy Stamp Collecting (7th edition, 2006)
Great Britain Numbers Issued (3rd edition, 2008)
How to Identify Stamps (4th edition, 2007)
North America Combined (1st edition, 2010)
Philatelic Terms Illustrated (4th edition, 2003)
United Nations (also including International Organizations based in Switzerland and UNESCO) (1st edition, 2010)
Western Europe Simplified (2nd edition, 2012)

Visit stanleygibbons.com to find out more about our full range of philatelic literature

Stanley Gibbons Publications
7 Parkside, Christchurch Road, Ringwood, Hampshire BH24 3SH
UK: 0800 611 622 Int: +44 1425 363 | orders@stanleygibbons.co.uk

www.stanleygibbons.com

General Philatelic Information and Guidelines to the Scope of Stanley Gibbons Commonwealth Catalogues

These notes reflect current practice in compiling the Stanley Gibbons Commonwealth Catalogues.

The Stanley Gibbons Stamp Catalogue has a very long history and the vast quantity of information it contains has been carefully built up by successive generations through the work of countless individuals. Philately is never static and the Catalogue has evolved and developed over the years. These notes relate to the current criteria upon which a stamp may be listed or priced. These criteria have developed over time and may have differed somewhat in the early years of this catalogue. These notes are not intended to suggest that we plan to make wholesale changes to the listing of classic issues in order to bring them into line with today's listing policy, they are designed to inform catalogue users as to the policies currently in operation.

PRICES

The prices quoted in this Catalogue are the estimated selling prices of Stanley Gibbons Ltd at the time of publication. They are, unless it is specifically stated otherwise, for examples in fine condition for the issue concerned. Superb examples are worth more; those of a lower quality considerably less.

All prices are subject to change without prior notice and Stanley Gibbons Ltd may from time to time offer stamps below catalogue price. Individual low value stamps sold at 399 Strand are liable to an additional handling charge. Purchasers of new issues should note the prices charged for them contain an element for the service rendered and so may exceed the prices shown when the stamps are subsequently catalogued. Postage and handling charges are extra.

No guarantee is given to supply all stamps priced, since it is not possible to keep every catalogued item in stock. Commemorative issues may, at times, only be available in complete sets and not as individual values.

Quotation of prices. The prices in the left-hand column are for unused stamps and those in the right-hand column are for used.

A dagger (†) denotes that the item listed does not exist in that condition and a blank, or dash, that it exists, or may exist, but we are unable to quote a price.

Prices are expressed in pounds and pence sterling. One pound comprises 100 pence (£1 = 100p).

The method of notation is as follows: pence in numerals (e.g. 10 denotes ten pence); pounds and pence, up to £100, in numerals (e.g. 4.25 denotes four pounds and twenty-five pence); prices above £100 are expressed in whole pounds with the '£' sign shown.

Unused stamps. Great Britain and Commonwealth: the prices for unused stamps of Queen Victoria to King George V are for lightly hinged examples. Unused prices for King Edward VIII, King George VI and Queen Elizabeth issues are for unmounted mint.

Some stamps from the King George VI period are often difficult to find in unmounted mint condition. In such instances we would expect that collectors would need to pay a high proportion of the price quoted to obtain mounted mint examples. Generally speaking lightly mounted mint stamps from this reign, issued before 1945, are in considerable demand.

Used stamps. The used prices are normally for stamps postally used but may be for stamps cancelled-to-order where this practice exists.

A pen-cancellation on early issues can sometimes correctly denote postal use. Instances are individually noted in the Catalogue in explanation of the used price given.

Prices quoted for bisects on cover or large piece are for those dated during the period officially authorised.

Stamps not sold unused to the public (e.g. some official stamps) are priced used only.

The use of 'unified' designs, that is stamps inscribed for both postal and fiscal purposes, results in a number of stamps of very high face value. In some instances these may not have been primarily intended for postal purposes, but if they are so inscribed we include them. We only price such items used, however, where there is evidence of normal postal usage.

Cover prices. To assist collectors, cover prices are quoted for issues up to 1945 at the beginning of each country.

The system gives a general guide in the form of a factor by which the corresponding used price of the basic loose stamp should be multiplied when found in fine average condition on cover.

Care is needed in applying the factors and they relate to a cover which bears a single of the denomination listed; if more than one denomination is present the most highly priced attracts the multiplier and the remainder are priced at the simple figure for used singles in arriving at a total.

The cover should be of non-philatelic origin; bearing the correct postal rate for the period and distance involved and cancelled with the markings normal to the offices concerned. Purely philatelic items have a cover value only slightly greater than the catalogue value for the corresponding used stamps. This applies generally to those high-value stamps used philatelically rather than in the normal course of commerce. Low-value stamps, e.g. ¼d. and ½d., are desirable when used as a single rate on cover and merit an increase in 'multiplier' value.

First day covers in the period up to 1945 are not within the scope of the system and the multiplier should not be used. As a special category of philatelic usage, with wide variations in valuation according to scarcity, they require separate treatment.

Oversized covers, difficult to accommodate on an album page, should be reckoned as worth little more than the corresponding value of the used stamps. The condition of a cover also affects its value. Except for 'wreck covers', serious damage or soiling reduce the value where the postal markings and stamps are ordinary ones. Conversely, visual appeal adds to the value and this can include freshness of appearance, important addresses, old-fashioned but legible handwriting, historic town-names, etc.

The multipliers are a base on which further value would be added to take account of the cover's postal historical importance in demonstrating such things as unusual, scarce or emergency cancels, interesting routes, significant postal markings, combination usage, the development of postal rates, and so on.

Minimum price. The minimum catalogue price quoted is 10p. For individual stamps prices between 10p. and 95p. are provided as a guide for catalogue users. The lowest price charged for individual stamps or sets purchased from Stanley Gibbons Ltd is £1

Set prices. Set prices are generally for one of each value, excluding shades and varieties, but including major colour changes. Where there are alternative shades, etc., the cheapest is usually included. The number of stamps in the set is always stated for clarity. The prices for sets containing *se-tenant* pieces are based on the prices quoted for such combinations, and not on those for the individual stamps.

Varieties. Where plate or cylinder varieties are priced in used condition the price quoted is for a fine used example with the cancellation well clear of the listed flaw.

Specimen stamps. The pricing of these items is explained under that heading.

Stamp booklets. Prices are for complete assembled booklets in fine condition with those issued before 1945 showing normal wear and tear. Incomplete booklets and those which have been 'exploded' will, in general, be worth less than the figure quoted.

Repricing. Collectors will be aware that the market factors of supply and demand directly influence the prices quoted in this Catalogue. Whatever the scarcity of a particular stamp, if there is no one in the market who wishes to buy it cannot be expected to achieve a high price. Conversely, the same item actively sought by numerous potential buyers may cause the price to rise.

All the prices in this Catalogue are examined during the preparation of each new edition by the expert staff of Stanley Gibbons and repriced as necessary. They take many factors into account, including supply and demand, and are in close touch with the international stamp market and the auction world.

Commonwealth cover prices and advice on postal history material originally provided by Edward B Proud.

GUARANTEE

All stamps are guaranteed originals in the following terms:

If not as described, and returned by the purchaser, we undertake to refund the price paid to us in the original transaction. If any stamp is certified as genuine by the Expert Committee of the Royal Philatelic Society, London, or by BPA Expertising Ltd, the purchaser shall not be entitled to make any claim against us for any error, omission or mistake in such certificate.

Consumers' statutory rights are not affected by the above guarantee.

The recognised Expert Committees in this country are those of the Royal Philatelic Society, 41 Devonshire Place, London W1G, 6JY, and BPA Expertising Ltd, PO Box 1141, Guildford, Surrey GU5 0WR. They do not undertake valuations under any circumstances and fees are payable for their services.

Information and Guidelines

MARGINS ON IMPERFORATE STAMPS

| Superb | Very fine | Fine | Average | Poor |

GUM

| Unmounted | Very lightly mounted | Lightly mounted | Mounted/ large part original gum (o.g.). | Heavily mounted small part o.g. |

CENTRING

| Superb | Very fine | Fine | Average | Poor |

CANCELLATIONS

| Superb | Very fine | Fine | Average | Poor |

| Superb | Very fine |

| Fine | Average | Poor |

Information and Guidelines

CONDITION GUIDE

To assist collectors in assessing the true value of items they are considering buying or in reviewing stamps already in their collections, we now offer a more detailed guide to the condition of stamps on which this catalogue's prices are based.

For a stamp to be described as 'Fine', it should be sound in all respects, without creases, bends, wrinkles, pin holes, thins or tears. If perforated, all perforation 'teeth' should be intact, it should not suffer from fading, rubbing or toning and it should be of clean, fresh appearance.

Margins on imperforate stamps: These should be even on all sides and should be at least as wide as half the distance between that stamp and the next. To have one or more margins of less than this width, would normally preclude a stamp from being described as 'Fine'. Some early stamps were positioned very close together on the printing plate and in such cases 'Fine' margins would necessarily be narrow. On the other hand, some plates were laid down to give a substantial gap between individual stamps and in such cases margins would be expected to be much wider.

An 'average' four-margin example would have a narrower margin on one or more sides and should be priced accordingly, while a stamp with wider, yet even, margins than 'Fine' would merit the description 'Very Fine' or 'Superb' and, if available, would command a price in excess of that quoted in the catalogue.

Gum: Since the prices for stamps of King Edward VIII, King George VI and Queen Elizabeth are for 'unmounted' or 'never hinged' mint, even stamps from these reigns which have been very lightly mounted should be available at a discount from catalogue price, the more obvious the hinge marks, the greater the discount.

Catalogue prices for stamps issued prior to King Edward VIII's reign are for mounted mint, so unmounted examples would be worth a premium. Hinge marks on 20th century stamps should not be too obtrusive, and should be at least in the lightly mounted category. For 19th century stamps more obvious hinging would be acceptable, but stamps should still carry a large part of their original gum—'Large part o.g.'—in order to be described as 'Fine'.

Centring: Ideally, the stamp's image should appear in the exact centre of the perforated area, giving equal margins on all sides. 'Fine' centring would be close to this ideal with any deviation having an effect on the value of the stamp. As in the case of the margins on imperforate stamps, it should be borne in mind that the space between some early stamps was very narrow, so it was very difficult to achieve accurate perforation, especially when the technology was in its infancy. Thus, poor centring would have a less damaging effect on the value of a 19th century stamp than on a 20th century example, but the premium put on a perfectly centred specimen would be greater.

Cancellations: Early cancellation devices were designed to 'obliterate' the stamp in order to prevent it being reused and this is still an important objective for today's postal administrations. Stamp collectors, on the other hand, prefer postmarks to be lightly applied, clear, and to leave as much as possible of the design visible. Dated, circular cancellations have long been 'the postmark of choice', but the definition of a 'Fine' cancellation will depend upon the types of cancellation in use at the time a stamp was current—it is clearly illogical to seek a circular datestamp on a Penny Black.

'Fine', by definition, will be superior to 'Average', so, in terms of cancellation quality, if one begins by identifying what 'Average' looks like, then one will be half way to identifying 'Fine'. The illustrations will give some guidance on mid-19th century and mid-20th century cancellations of Great Britain, but types of cancellation in general use in each country and in each period will determine the appearance of 'Fine'.

As for the factors discussed above, anything less than 'Fine' will result in a downgrading of the stamp concerned, while a very fine or superb cancellation will be worth a premium.

Combining the factors: To merit the description 'Fine', a stamp should be fine in every respect, but a small deficiency in one area might be made up for in another by a factor meriting an 'Extremely Fine' description.

Some early issues are so seldom found in what would normally be considered to be 'Fine' condition, the catalogue prices are for a slightly lower grade, with 'Fine' examples being worth a premium. In such cases a note to this effect is given in the catalogue, while elsewhere premiums are given for well-centred, lightly cancelled examples.

Stamps graded at less than fine remain collectable and, in the case of more highly priced stamps, will continue to hold a value. Nevertheless, buyers should always bear condition in mind.

ACKNOWLEDGEMENTS

We are grateful to individual collectors, members of the philatelic trade and specialist societies and study circles for their assistance in improving and extending the Stanley Gibbons range of catalogues. The addresses of societies and study circles relevant to this volume is:

British West Indies Study Circle
Membership Secretary: Mr S. Jarvis
5 Redbridge Drive, Andover
Hampshire SP10 2LF

British Caribbean Philatelic Study Group
Overseas Director: Mr D.N. Druett
Pennymead Auctions, 1 Brewerton Street
Knaresborough, North Yorkshire HG5 8AZ

Information and Guidelines

The Catalogue in General

Contents. The Catalogue is confined to adhesive postage stamps, including miniature sheets. For particular categories the rules are:
(a) Revenue (fiscal) stamps or telegraph stamps are listed only where they have been expressly authorised for postal duty.
(b) Stamps issued only precancelled are included, but normally issued stamps available additionally with precancel have no separate precancel listing unless the face value is changed.
(c) Stamps prepared for use but not issued, hitherto accorded full listing, are nowadays foot-noted with a price (where possible).
(d) Bisects (trisects, etc.) are only listed where such usage was officially authorised.
(e) Stamps issued only on first day covers or in presentation packs and not available separately are not listed but may be priced in a footnote.
(f) New printings are only included in this Catalogue where they show a major philatelic variety, such as a change in shade, watermark or paper. Stamps which exist with or without imprint dates are listed separately; changes in imprint dates are mentioned in footnotes.
(g) Official and unofficial reprints are dealt with by footnote.
(h) Stamps from imperforate printings of modern issues which occur perforated are covered by footnotes, but are listed where widely available for postal use.

Exclusions. The following are excluded:
(a) non-postal revenue or fiscal stamps;
(b) postage stamps used fiscally (although prices are now given for some fiscally used high values);
(c) local carriage labels and private local issues;
(d) bogus or phantom stamps;
(e) railway or airline letter fee stamps, bus or road transport company labels or the stamps of private postal companies operating under licence from the national authority;
(f) cut-outs;
(g) all types of non-postal labels and souvenirs;
(h) documentary labels for the postal service, e.g. registration, recorded delivery, air-mail etiquettes, etc.;
(i) privately applied embellishments to official issues and privately commissioned items generally;
(j) stamps for training postal officers.
(k) Telegraph stamps

Full listing. 'Full listing' confers our recognition and implies allotting a catalogue number and (wherever possible) a price quotation.

In judging status for inclusion in the catalogue broad considerations are applied to stamps. They must be issued by a legitimate postal authority, recognised by the government concerned, and must be adhesives valid for proper postal use in the class of service for which they are inscribed. Stamps, with the exception of such categories as postage dues and officials, must be available to the general public, at face value, in reasonable quantities without any artificial restrictions being imposed on their distribution.

For errors and varieties the criterion is legitimate (albeit inadvertent) sale through a postal administration in the normal course of business. Details of provenance are always important; printers' waste and deliberately manufactured material are excluded.

Certificates. In assessing unlisted items due weight is given to Certificates from recognised Expert Committees and, where appropriate, we will usually ask to see them.

Date of issue. Where local issue dates differ from dates of release by agencies, 'date of issue' is the local date. Fortuitous stray usage before the officially intended date is disregarded in listing.

Catalogue numbers. Stamps of each country are catalogued chronologically by date of issue. Subsidiary classes are placed at the end of the country, as separate lists, with a distinguishing letter prefix to the catalogue number, e.g. D for postage due, O for official and E for express delivery stamps.

The catalogue number appears in the extreme left-column. The boldface Type numbers in the next column are merely cross-references to illustrations.

Once published in the Catalogue, numbers are changed as little as possible; really serious renumbering is reserved for the occasions when a complete country or an entire issue is being rewritten. The edition first affected includes cross-reference tables of old and new numbers.

Our catalogue numbers are universally recognised in specifying stamps and as a hallmark of status.

Illustrations. Stamps are illustrated at three-quarters linear size. Stamps not illustrated are the same size and format as the value shown, unless otherwise indicated. Stamps issued only as miniature sheets have the stamp alone illustrated but sheet size is also quoted. Overprints, surcharges, watermarks and postmarks are normally actual size. Illustrations of varieties are often enlarged to show the detail. Stamp booklet covers are illustrated half-size, unless otherwise indicated.

Designers. Designers' names are quoted where known, though space precludes naming every individual concerned in the production of a set. In particular, photographers supplying material are usually named only where they also make an active contribution in the design stage; posed photographs of reigning monarchs are, however, an exception to this rule.

CONTACTING THE CATALOGUE EDITOR

The editor is always interested in hearing from people who have new information which will improve or correct the Catalogue. As a general rule he must see and examine the actual stamps before they can be considered for listing; photographs or photocopies are insufficient evidence.

Submissions should be made in writing to the Catalogue Editor, Stanley Gibbons Publications at the Ringwood office. The cost of return postage for items submitted is appreciated, and this should include the registration fee if required.

Where information is solicited purely for the benefit of the enquirer, the editor cannot undertake to reply if the answer is already contained in these published notes or if return postage is omitted. Written communications are greatly preferred to enquiries by telephone or e-mail and the editor regrets that he or his staff cannot see personal callers without a prior appointment being made. Correspondence may be subject to delay during the production period of each new edition.

The editor welcomes close contact with study circles and is interested, too, in finding reliable local correspondents who will verify and supplement official information in countries where this is deficient.

We regret we do not give opinions as to the genuineness of stamps, nor do we identify stamps or number them by our Catalogue.

TECHNICAL MATTERS

The meanings of the technical terms used in the catalogue will be found in our *Philatelic Terms Illustrated*.

References below to (more specialised) listings are to be taken to indicate, as appropriate, the Stanley Gibbons *Great Britain Specialised Catalogue* in five volumes or the *Great Britain Concise Catalogue*.

1. Printing

Printing errors. Errors in printing are of major interest to the Catalogue. Authenticated items meriting consideration would include: background, centre or frame inverted or omitted; centre or subject transposed; error of colour; error or omission of value; double prints and impressions; printed both sides; and so on. Designs *tête-bêche*, whether intentionally or by accident, are listable. *Se-tenant* arrangements of stamps are recognised in the listings or footnotes. Gutter pairs (a pair of stamps separated by blank margin) are not included in this volume. Colours only partially omitted are not listed. Stamps with embossing omitted are reserved for our more specialised listings.

Printing varieties. Listing is accorded to major changes in the printing base which lead to completely new types. In recess-printing this could be a design re-engraved; in photogravure or photolithography a screen altered in whole or in part. It can also encompass flat-bed and rotary printing if the results are readily distinguishable.

To be considered at all, varieties must be constant.

Early stamps, produced by primitive methods, were prone to numerous imperfections; the lists reflect this, recognising re-entries, retouches, broken frames, misshapen letters, and so on. Printing technology has, however, radically improved over the years, during which time photogravure and lithography have become predominant. Varieties nowadays are more in the nature of flaws and these, being too specialised for this general catalogue, are almost always outside the scope.

In no catalogue, however, do we list such items as: dry prints, kiss prints, doctor-blade flaws, colour shifts or registration flaws (unless they lead to the complete omission of a colour from an individual stamp), lithographic ring flaws, and so on. Neither do we recognise fortuitous happenings like paper creases or confetti flaws.

Overprints (and surcharges). Overprints of different types qualify for separate listing. These include overprints in different colours; overprints from different printing processes such as litho and typo; overprints in totally different typefaces, etc. Major errors in machine-printed overprints are important and listable. They include: overprint inverted or omitted; overprint double (treble, etc.); overprint diagonal; overprint double, one inverted; pairs with one overprint omitted, e.g. from a radical shift to an adjoining stamp; error of colour; error of type fount; letters inverted or omitted, etc. If the overprint is handstamped, few of these would qualify and a distinction is drawn. We continue, however, to list pairs of stamps where one has a handstamped overprint and the other has not.

Varieties occurring in overprints will often take the form of broken letters, slight differences in spacing, rising spaces, etc. Only the most important would be considered for listing or footnote mention.

Sheet positions. If space permits we quote sheet positions of listed varieties and authenticated data is solicited for this purpose.

De La Rue plates. The Catalogue classifies the general plates used by De La Rue for printing British Colonial stamps as follows:

VICTORIAN KEY TYPE

Die I

1. The ball of decoration on the second point of the crown appears as a dark mass of lines.
2. Dark vertical shading separates the front hair from the bun.
3. The vertical line of colour outlining the front of the throat stops at the sixth line of shading on the neck.
4. The white space in the coil of the hair above the curl is roughly the shape of a pin's head.

Die II

1. There are very few lines of colour in the ball and it appears almost white.
2. A white vertical strand of hair appears in place of the dark shading.

Information and Guidelines

3. The line stops at the eighth line of shading.
4. The white space is oblong, with a line of colour partially dividing it at the left end.

Plates numbered 1 and 2 are both Die I. Plates 3 and 4 are Die II.

GEORGIAN KEY TYPE

Die I

A. The second (thick) line below the name of the country is cut slanting, conforming roughly to the shape of the crown on each side.
B. The labels of solid colour bearing the words "POSTAGE" and "& REVENUE" are square at the inner top corners.
C. There is a projecting "bud" on the outer spiral of the ornament in each of the lower corners.

Die II

A. The second line is cut vertically on each side of the crown.
B. The labels curve inwards at the top.
C. There is no "bud" in this position.

Unless otherwise stated in the lists, all stamps with watermark Multiple Crown CA (w **8**) are Die I while those with watermark Multiple Crown Script CA (w **9**) are Die II. The Georgian Die II was introduced in April 1921 and was used for Plates 10 to 22 and 26 to 28. Plates 23 to 25 were made from Die I by mistake.

2. Paper

All stamps listed are deemed to be on (ordinary) paper of the wove type and white in colour; only departures from this are normally mentioned.

Types. Where classification so requires we distinguish such other types of paper as, for example, vertically and horizontally laid; wove and laid bâtonné; card(board); carton; cartridge; glazed; granite; native; pelure; porous; quadrillé; ribbed; rice; and silk thread.

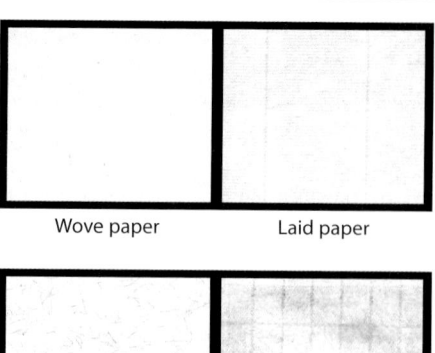

Wove paper   Laid paper

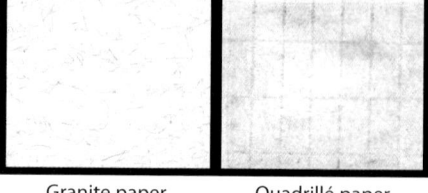

Granite paper   Quadrillé paper

Burelé band

The various makeshifts for normal paper are listed as appropriate. The varieties of double paper and joined paper are recognised. The security device of a printed burelé band on the back of a stamp, as in early Queensland, qualifies for listing.

Descriptive terms. The fact that a paper is handmade (and thus probably of uneven thickness) is mentioned where necessary. Such descriptive terms as "hard" and "soft"; "smooth" and "rough"; "thick", "medium" and "thin" are applied where there is philatelic merit in classifying papers.

Coloured, very white and toned papers. A coloured paper is one that is coloured right through (front and back of the stamp). In the Catalogue the colour of the paper is given in italics, thus:

black/*rose* = black design on rose paper.

Papers have been made specially white in recent years by, for example, a very heavy coating of chalk. We do not classify shades of whiteness of paper as distinct varieties. There does exist, however, a type of paper from early days called toned. This is off-white, often brownish or buffish, but it cannot be assigned any definite colour. A toning effect brought on by climate, incorrect storage or gum staining is disregarded here, as this was not the state of the paper when issued.

"Ordinary" and "Chalk-surfaced" papers. The availability of many postage stamps for revenue purposes made necessary some safeguard against the illegitimate re-use of stamps with removable cancellations. This was at first secured by using fugitive inks and later by printing on paper surfaced by coatings containing either chalk or china clay, both of which made it difficult to remove any form of obliteration without damaging the stamp design.

This catalogue lists these chalk-surfaced paper varieties from their introduction in 1905. Where no indication is given, the paper is "ordinary".

The "traditional" method of indentifying chalk-surfaced papers has been that, when touched with a silver wire, a black mark is left on the paper, and the listings in this catalogue are based on that test. However, the test itself is now largely discredited, for, although the mark can be removed by a soft rubber, some damage to the stamp will result from its use.

The difference between chalk-surfaced and pre-war ordinary papers is fairly clear: chalk-surfaced papers being smoother to the touch and showing a characteristic sheen when light is reflected off their surface. Under good magnification tiny bubbles or pock marks can be seen on the surface of the stamp and at the tips of the perforations the surfacing appears "broken". Traces of paper fibres are evident on the surface of ordinary paper and the ink shows a degree of absorption into it.

Initial chalk-surfaced paper printings by De La Rue had a thinner coating than subsequently became the norm. The characteristics described above are less pronounced in these printings.

During and after the Second World War, substitute papers replaced the chalk-surfaced papers, these do not react to the silver test and are therefore classed as "ordinary", although differentiating them without recourse to it is more difficult, for, although the characteristics of the chalk-surfaced paper remained the same, some of the ordinary papers appear much smoother than earlier papers and many do not show the watermark clearly. Experience is the only solution to identifying these, and comparison with stamps whose paper type is without question will be of great help.

Another type of paper, known as "thin striated" was used only for the Bahamas 1s. and 5s. (Nos. 155a, 156a, 171 and 174) and for several stamps of the Malayan states. Hitherto these have been described as "chalk-surfaced" since they gave some reaction to the silver test, but they are much thinner than usual chalk-surfaced papers, with the watermark showing clearly. Stamps on this paper show a slightly 'ribbed' effect when the stamp is held up to the light. Again, comparison with a known striated paper stamp, such as the 1941 Straits Settlements Die II 2c. orange (No. 294) will prove invaluable in separating these papers.

Glazed paper. In 1969 the Crown Agents introduced a new general-purpose paper for use in conjunction with all current printing processes. It generally has a marked glossy surface but the degree varies according to the process used, being more marked in recess-printing stamps. As it does not respond to the silver test this presents a further test where previous printings were on chalky paper. A change of paper to the glazed variety merits separate listing.

Green and yellow papers. Issues of the First World War and immediate postwar period occur on green and yellow papers and these are given separate Catalogue listing. The original coloured papers (coloured throughout) gave way to surface-coloured papers, the stamps having "white backs"; other stamps show one colour on the front and a different one at the back. Because of the numerous variations a grouping of colours is adopted as follows:

Yellow papers
(1) The original *yellow* paper (throughout), usually bright in colour. The gum is often sparse, of harsh consistency and dull-looking. Used 1912–1920.
(2) The *white-backs*. Used 1913–1914.
(3) A bright lemon paper. The colour must have a pronounced greenish tinge, different from the "yellow" in (1). As a rule, the gum on stamps using this lemon paper is plentiful, smooth and shiny, and the watermark shows distinctly. Care is needed with stamps printed in green on yellow paper (1) as it may appear that the paper is this lemon. Used 1914–1916.
(4) An experimental *orange-buff* paper. The colour must have a distinct brownish tinge. It is not to be confused with a muddy yellow (1) nor the misleading appearance (on the surface) of stamps printed in red on yellow paper where an engraved plate has been insufficiently wiped. Used 1918–1921.
(5) An experimental *buff* paper. This lacks the brownish tinge of (4) and the brightness of the yellow shades. The gum is shiny when compared with the matt type used on (4). Used 1919–1920.
(6) A *pale yellow* paper that has a creamy tone to the yellow. Used from 1920 onwards.

Green papers
(7) The original "green" paper, varying considerably through shades of blue-green and yellow-green, the front and back sometimes differing. Used 1912–1916.
(8) The *white backs*. Used 1913–1914.
(9) A paper blue-green on the surface with *pale olive* back. The back must be markedly paler than the front and this and the pronounced olive tinge to the back distinguish it from (7). Used 1916–1920.
(10) Paper with a vivid green surface, commonly called *emerald-green*; it has the olive back of (9). Used 1920.
(11) Paper with *emerald-green* both back and front. Used from 1920 onwards.

3. Perforation and Rouletting
Perforation gauge. The gauge of a perforation is the number of holes in a length of 2 cm. For correct classification the size of the holes (large or small) may need to be distinguished; in a few cases the actual number of holes on each edge of the stamp needs to be quoted.

Measurement. The Gibbons *Instanta* gauge is the standard for measuring perforations. The stamp is viewed against a dark background with the transparent gauge put on top of it. Though the gauge measures to decimal accuracy, perforations read from it are generally quoted in the Catalogue to the nearest half. For example:

Just over perf $12\frac{3}{4}$ to just under $13\frac{1}{4}$ = perf 13
Perf $13\frac{1}{4}$ exactly, rounded up = perf $13\frac{1}{2}$
Just over perf $13\frac{1}{4}$ to just under $13\frac{3}{4}$ = perf $13\frac{1}{2}$
Perf $13\frac{3}{4}$ exactly, rounded up = perf 14

However, where classification depends on it, actual quarter-perforations are quoted.

Notation. Where no perforation is quoted for an issue it is imperforate. Perforations are usually abbreviated (and spoken) as follows, though sometimes they may be spelled out for clarity. This notation for rectangular stamps (the majority) applies to diamond shapes if "top" is read as the edge to the top right.

P 14: perforated alike on all sides (read: "perf 14").
P 14×15: the first figure refers to top and bottom, the second to left and right sides (read: "perf 14 by 15"). This is a compound perforation. For an upright triangular stamp the first figure refers to the two sloping sides and second to the base. In inverted

triangulars the base is first and the second figure to the sloping sides.

P 14–15: perforation measuring anything between 14 and 15: the holes are irregularly spaced, thus the gauge may vary along a single line or even along a single edge of the stamp (read: "perf 14 to 15").

P 14 *irregular*: perforated 14 from a worn perforator, giving badly aligned holes irregularly spaced (read: "irregular perf 14").

P *comp(ound)* 14×15: two gauges in use but not necessarily on opposite sides of the stamp. It could be one side in one gauge and three in the other; or two adjacent sides with the same gauge. (Read: "perf compound of 14 and 15".) For three gauges or more, abbreviated as "P 12, 14½, 15 or compound" for example.

P 14, 14½: perforated approximately 14¼ (read: "perf 14 or 14½"). It does *not* mean two stamps, one perf 14 and the other perf 14½. This obsolescent notation is gradually being replaced in the Catalogue.

Imperf: imperforate (not perforated)

Imperf×P 14: imperforate at top ad bottom and perf 14 at sides.

P 14×*imperf*: perf 14 at top and bottom and imperforate at sides.

Such headings as "P 13×14 (*vert*) and P 14×13 (*horiz*)" indicate which perforations apply to which stamp format—vertical or horizontal.

Some stamps are additionally perforated so that a label or tab is detachable; others have been perforated for use as two halves. Listings are normally for whole stamps, unless stated otherwise.

Imperf×perf

Other terms. Perforation almost always gives circular holes; where other shapes have been used they are specified, e.g. square holes; lozenge perf. Interrupted perfs are brought about by the omission of pins at regular intervals. Perforations merely simulated by being printed as part of the design are of course ignored. With few exceptions, privately applied perforations are not listed.

In the 19th century perforations are often described as clean cut (clean, sharply incised holes), intermediate or rough (rough holes, imperfectly cut, often the result of blunt pins).

Perforation errors and varieties. Authenticated errors, where a stamp normally perforated is accidentally issued imperforate, are listed provided no traces of perforation (blind holes or indentations) remain. They must be provided as pairs, both stamps wholly imperforate, and are only priced in that form.

Stamps imperforate between stamp and sheet margin are not listed in this catalogue, but such errors on Great Britain stamps will be found in the *Great Britain Specialised Catalogue*.

Pairs described as "imperforate between" have the line of perforations between the two stamps omitted.

Imperf between (horiz pair): a horizontal pair of stamps with perfs all around the edges but none between the stamps.

Imperf between (vert pair): a vertical pair of stamps with perfs all around the edges but none between the stamps.

Imperf between (vertical pair)   Imperf horizontally (vertical pair)

Where several of the rows have escaped perforation the resulting varieties are listable. Thus:

Imperf vert (horiz pair): a horizontal pair of stamps perforated top and bottom; all three vertical directions are imperf—the two outer edges and between the stamps.

Imperf horiz (vert pair): a vertical pair perforated at left and right edges; all three horizontal directions are imperf—the top, bottom and between the stamps.

Straight edges. Large sheets cut up before issue to post offices can cause stamps with straight edges, i.e. imperf on one side or on two sides at right angles. They are not usually listable in this condition and are worth less than corresponding stamps properly perforated all round. This does not, however, apply to certain stamps, mainly from coils and booklets, where straight edges on various sides are the manufacturing norm affecting every stamp. The listings and notes make clear which sides are correctly imperf.

Malfunction. Varieties of double, misplaced or partial perforation caused by error or machine malfunction are not listable, neither are freaks, such as perforations placed diagonally from paper folds, nor missing holes caused by broken pins.

Types of perforating. Where necessary for classification, perforation types are distinguished. These include:

Line perforation from one line of pins punching single rows of holes at a time.

Comb perforation from pins disposed across the sheet in comb formation, punching out holes at three sides of the stamp a row at a time.

Harrow perforation applied to a whole pane or sheet at one stroke.

Rotary perforation from toothed wheels operating across a sheet, then crosswise.

Sewing machine perforation. The resultant condition,

clean-cut or rough, is distinguished where required.
Pin-perforation is the commonly applied term for pin-roulette in which, instead of being punched out, round holes are pricked by sharp-pointed pins and no paper is removed.
Mixed perforation occurs when stamps with defective perforations are re-perforated in a different gauge.

Punctured stamps. Perforation holes can be punched into the face of the stamp. Patterns of small holes, often in the shape of initial letters, are privately applied devices against pilferage. These (perfins) are outside the scope except for Australia, Canada, Cape of Good Hope, Papua and Sudan where they were used as official stamps by the national administration. Identification devices, when officially inspired, are listed or noted; they can be shapes, or letters or words formed from holes, sometimes converting one class of stamp into another.

Rouletting. In rouletting the paper is cut, for ease of separation, but none is removed. The gauge is measured, when needed, as for perforations. Traditional French terms descriptive of the type of cut are often used and types include:

Arc roulette (percé en arc). Cuts are minute, spaced arcs, each roughly a semicircle.
Cross roulette (percé en croix). Cuts are tiny diagonal crosses.
Line roulette (percé en ligne or en ligne droite). Short straight cuts parallel to the frame of the stamp. The commonest basic roulette. Where not further described, "roulette" means this type.
Rouletted in colour or coloured roulette (percé en lignes colorées or en lignes de couleur). Cuts with coloured edges, arising from notched rule inked simultaneously with the printing plate.
Saw-tooth roulette (percé en scie). Cuts applied zigzag fashion to resemble the teeth of a saw.
Serpentine roulette (percé en serpentin). Cuts as sharply wavy lines.
Zigzag roulette (percé en zigzags). Short straight cuts at angles in alternate directions, producing sharp points on separation. US usage favours "serrate(d) roulette" for this type.
Pin-roulette (originally *percé en points* and now *perforés trous d'epingle*) is commonly called pin-perforation in English.

4. Gum

All stamps listed are assumed to have gum of some kind; if they were issued without gum this is stated. Original gum (o.g.) means that which was present on the stamp as issued to the public. Deleterious climates and the presence of certain chemicals can cause gum to crack and, with early stamps, even make the paper deteriorate. Unscrupulous fakers are adept in removing it and regumming the stamp to meet the unreasoning demand often made for "full o.g." in cases where such a thing is virtually impossible.

The gum normally used on stamps has been gum arabric until the late 1960s when synthetic adhesives were introduced. Harrison and Sons Ltd for instance use *polyvinyl alcohol,* known to philatelists as PVA. This is almost invisible except for a slight yellowish tinge which was incorporated to make it possible to see that the stamps have been gummed. It has advantages in hot countries, as stamps do not curl and sheets are less likely to stick together. Gum arabic and PVA are not distinguished in the lists except that where a stamp exists with both forms this is indicated in footnotes. Our more specialised catalogues provide separate listing of gums for Great Britain.

Self-adhesive stamps are issued on backing paper, from which they are peeled before affixing to mail. Unused examples are priced as for backing paper intact, in which condition they are recommended to be kept. Used examples are best collected on cover or on piece.

5. Watermarks

Stamps are on unwatermarked paper except where the heading to the set says otherwise.

Detection. Watermarks are detected for Catalogue description by one of four methods: (1) holding stamps to the light; (2) laying stamps face down on a dark background; (3) adding a few drops of petroleum ether 40/60 to the stamp laid face down in a watermark tray; (4) by use of the Stanley Gibbons Detectamark, or other equipment, which work by revealing the thinning of the paper at the watermark. (Note that petroleum ether is highly inflammable in use and can damage photogravure stamps.)

Listable types. Stamps occurring on both watermarked and unwatermarked papers are different types and both receive full listing.

Single watermarks (devices occurring once on every stamp) can be modified in size and shape as between different issues; the types are noted but not usually separately listed. Fortuitous absence of watermark from a single stamp or its gross displacement would not be listable.

To overcome registration difficulties the device may be repeated at close intervals *(a multiple watermark)*, single stamps thus showing parts of several devices. Similarly, a *large sheet watermark* (or *all-over watermark*) covering numerous stamps can be used. We give informative notes and illustrations for them. The designs may be such that numbers of stamps in the sheet automatically lack watermark: this is not a listable variety. Multiple and all-over watermarks sometimes undergo modifications, but if the various types are difficult to distinguish from single stamps notes are given but not separate listings.

Papermakers' watermarks are noted where known but not listed separately, since most stamps in the sheet will lack them. Sheet watermarks which are nothing more than officially adopted papermakers' watermarks are, however, given normal listing.

Marginal watermarks, falling outside the pane of stamps, are ignored except where misplacement caused the adjoining row to be affected, in which case they may be footnoted.

Watermark errors and varieties. Watermark errors are recognised as of major importance. They comprise stamps intended to be on unwatermarked paper but issued watermarked by mistake, or stamps printed on paper with the wrong watermark. Varieties showing letters omitted from the watermark are also included, but broken or deformed bits on the dandy roll are not listed unless they represent repairs.

Watermark positions. The diagram shows how watermark position is described in the Catalogue. Paper has a side intended for printing and watermarks are usually impressed so that they read normally when looked through from that printed side. However, since philatelists customarily detect watermarks by looking at the back of the stamp the watermark diagram also makes clear what is actually seen.

Information and Guidelines

Illustrations in the Catalogue are of watermarks in normal positions (from the front of the stamps) and are actual size where possible.

Differences in watermark position are collectable varieties. This Catalogue now lists inverted, sideways inverted and reversed watermark varieties on Commonwealth stamps from the 1860s onwards except where the watermark position is completely haphazard.

Great Britain inverted and sideways inverted watermarks can be found in the *Great Britain Specialised Catalogue* and the *Great Britain Concise Catalogue*.

Where a watermark comes indiscriminately in various positions our policy is to cover this by a general note: we do not give separate listings because the watermark position in these circumstances has no particular philatelic importance.

AS DESCRIBED (Read through front of stamp)		AS SEEN DURING WATERMARK DETECTION (Stamp face down and back examined)
GvR	Normal	ЯvƆ
ЯʌƆ	Inverted	ƆʌЯ
ЯvƆ	Reversed	GvR
ƆʌЯ	Reversed and Inverted	ЯʌƆ
GvR (sideways)	Sideways	ƆvЯ (sideways)
GvR (sideways)	Sideways Inverted	ЯvƆ (sideways)

Standard types of watermark. Some watermarks have been used generally for various British possessions rather than exclusively for a single colony. To avoid repetition the Catalogue classifies 11 general types, as under, with references in the headings throughout the listings being given either in words or in the form ("W w **9**") (meaning "watermark type w **9**"). In those cases where watermark illustrations appear in the listings themselves, the respective reference reads, for example, W **153**, thus indicating that the watermark will be found in the normal sequence of illustrations as (type) **153**.

The general types are as follows, with an example of each quoted.

W	Description	Example
w **1**	Large Star	St. Helena No. 1
w **2**	Small Star	Turks Is. No. 4
w **3**	Broad (pointed) Star	Grenada No. 24
w **4**	Crown (over) CC, small stamp	Antigua No. 13
w **5**	Crown (over) CC, large stamp	Antigua No. 31
w **6**	Crown (over) CA, small stamp	Antigua No. 21
w **7**	Crown CA (CA over Crown), large stamp	Sierra Leone No. 54
w **8**	Multiple Crown CA	Antigua No. 41
w **9**	Multiple Script CA	Seychelles No. 158
w **9**a	do. Error	Seychelles No. 158a
w **9**b	do. Error	Seychelles No. 158b
w **10**	V over Crown	N.S.W. No. 327
w **11**	Crown over A	N.S.W. No. 347

CC in these watermarks is an abbreviation for "Crown Colonies" and CA for "Crown Agents". Watermarks w **1**, w **2** and w **3** are on stamps printed by Perkins, Bacon; w **4** onwards on stamps from De La Rue and other printers.

w **1**
Large Star

w **2** w **3**
Small Star Broad-pointed Star

Watermark w **1**, *Large Star*, measures 15 to 16 mm across the star from point to point and about 27 mm from centre to centre vertically between stars in the sheet. It was made for long stamps like Ceylon 1857 and St. Helena 1856.

Watermark w **2**, *Small Star* is of similar design but measures 12 to 13½mm from point to point and 24 mm from centre to centre vertically. It was for use with ordinary-size stamps such as Grenada 1863–71.

When the Large Star watermark was used with the smaller stamps it only occasionally comes in the centre of the paper. It is frequently so misplaced as to show portions of two stars above and below and this eccentricity will very often help in determining the watermark.

Watermark w **3**, *Broad-pointed Star*, resembles w **1** but the points are broader.

Information and Guidelines

w **4**
Crown (over) CC

w **5**
Crown (over) CC

Two *Crown (over) CC* watermarks were used: w **4** was for stamps of ordinary size and w **5** for those of larger size.

w **6**
Crown (over) CA

w **7**
CA over Crown

Two watermarks of *Crown CA* type were used, w **6** being for stamps of ordinary size. The other, w **7**, is properly described as *CA over Crown*. It was specially made for paper on which it was intended to print long fiscal stamps: that some were used postally accounts for the appearance of w **7** in the Catalogue. The watermark occupies twice the space of the ordinary Crown CA watermark, w **6**. Stamps of normal size printed on paper with w **7** watermark show it *sideways*; it takes a horizontal pair of stamps to show the entire watermark.

w **8**
Multiple Crown CA

w **9**
Multiple Script CA

Multiple watermarks began in 1904 with w **8**, *Multiple Crown CA*, changed from 1921 to w **9**, *Multiple Script CA*. On stamps of ordinary size portions of two or three watermarks appear and on the large-sized stamps a greater number can be observed. The change to letters in script character with w **9** was accompanied by a Crown of distinctly different shape.

It seems likely that there were at least two dandy rolls for each Crown Agents watermark in use at any one time with a reserve roll being employed when the normal one was withdrawn for maintenance or repair.

of Mult Crown CA and the Mult Script CA been with one or other of the letters omitted experien impressions. It is possible that most the Script a the reserve rolls as they have only until 1951. ain issues. The MCA watermark

During the 192 ems during the early 1920s and on one of the Crown. period from the early 1940s found on certain issues. must also have occurred and consists of an oval bastituted Crown has been with a circle positioned betwaller than the normal upper line of the Crown's base is, two upright ovals and right-hand circles at the top and upper ends. The the centre circle. as are the left
e cross over

Substituted Crown

The *Multiple Script CA* watermark, w **9**, is known with two errors, recurring among the 1950–52 printings of several territories. In the first a crown has fallen away from the dandy-roll that impresses the watermark into the paper pulp. It gives w **9a**, *Crown missing*, but this omission has been found in both "Crown only" (*illustrated*) and "Crown CA" rows. The resulting faulty paper was used for Bahamas, Johore, Seychelles and the postage due stamps of nine colonies

w **9a**: Error, Crown missing

w **9b**: Error, St. Edward's Crown

When the omission was noticed a second mishap occurred, which was to insert a wrong crown in the space, giving w **9b**, St. Edward's Crown. This produced varieties in Bahamas, Perlis, St. Kitts-Nevis and Singapore and the incorrect crown likewise occurs in (Crown only) and (Crown CA) rows.

xvii

Information and Guidelines

w 10
V over Crown

w 11
Crown over A

Resuming the usual types, two watermarks found in issues of Australian States are: w 10, V over Crown, and w 11, Crown over A.

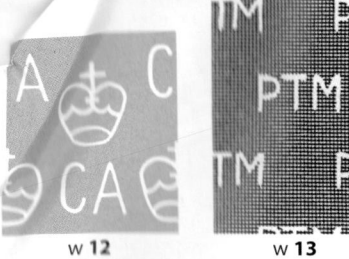

w 12
Multiple St. Edward's Crown Block CA

w 13
Multiple PTM

The *Multiple St. Edward's Crown Block CA* watermark, w 12, was introduced in 1957 and besides the change in the Crown (from that used in Multiple Crown Script CA, w 9) the letters reverted to block capitals. The new watermark began to appear sideways in 1966 and these stamps are generally listed as separate sets.

The watermark w 13, *Multiple PTM*, was introduced for new Malaysian issues in November 1961.

w 14
Multiple Crown CA Diagonal

By 1974 the two dandy-rolls the "upright" and the "sideways" for w 12 were wearing out; the Crown Agents therefore discontinued using the sideways watermark one and retained the other only as a stand-by. A new dandy-roll with the pattern of w 14. *Multiple Crown CA Diagonal*, was introduced and first saw use with some Churchill Centenary issues.

The new watermark had the design arranged in gradually spiralling rows. It is improved in design to allow smooth passage over the paper (the gaps between letters and rows had caused jolts in previous dandy-rolls) and the sharp corners and angles, where fibres used to accumulate, have been eliminated by rounding.

This watermark had no "normal" sideways position amongst the different printers using it. To avoid confusion our more specialised listings do not rely on such terms as "sideways inverted" but describe the direction in which the watermark points.

w 15
Multiple POST OFFICE

During 1981 w 15. *Multiple POST OFFICE* was introduced for certain issues prepared by Philatelists Ltd, acting for various countries in the Indian Ocean, Pacific and West Indies.

w 16
Multiple Crown Script CA Diagonal

A new Crown Agents watermark was introduced during 1985, w 16, *Multiple Crown Script CA Diagonal*. This was very similar to the previous w 14, but showed "CA" in script rather than block letters. It was first used on the omnibus series of stamps commemorating the Life and Times of Queen Elizabeth the Queen Mother.

w 17
Multiple CARTOR

Watermark w 17, Multiple CARTOR, was used from 1985 for issues printed by this French firm for countries which did not normally use the Crown Agents watermark.

w **18**

In 2008, following the closure of the Crown Agents Stamp Bureau, a new Multiple Crowns watermark, w **18** was introduced

In recent years the use of watermarks has, to a small extent, been superseded by fluorescent security markings. These are often more visible from the reverse of the stamp (Cook Islands from 1970 onwards), but have occurred printed over the design (Hong Kong Nos. 415/30). In 1982 the Crown Agents introduced a new stock paper, without watermark, known as "C-Kurity" on which a fluorescent pattern of blue rosettes is visible on the reverse, beneath the gum. This paper was used for issues from Gambia and Norfolk Island.

6. Colours

Stamps in two or three colours have these named in order of appearance, from the centre moving outwards. Four colours or more are usually listed as multicoloured.

In compound colour names the second is the predominant one, thus:

orange-red = a red tending towards orange;
red-orange = an orange containing more red than usual.

Standard colours used. The 200 colours most used for stamp identification are given in the Stanley Gibbons Stamp Colour Key. The Catalogue has used the Stamp Colour Key as standard for describing new issues for some years. The names are also introduced as lists are rewritten, though exceptions are made for those early issues where traditional names have become universally established.

Determining colours. When comparing actual stamps with colour samples in the Stamp Colour Key, view in a good north daylight (or its best substitute; fluorescent "colour matching" light). Sunshine is not recommended. Choose a solid portion of the stamp design; if available, marginal markings such as solid bars of colour or colour check dots are helpful. Shading lines in the design can be misleading as they appear lighter than solid colour. Postmarked portions of a stamp appear darker than normal. If more than one colour is present, mask off the extraneous ones as the eye tends to mix them.

Errors of colour. Major colour errors in stamps or overprints which qualify for listing are: wrong colours; one colour inverted in relation to the rest; albinos (colourless impressions), where these have Expert Committee certificates; colours completely omitted, but only on unused stamps (if found on used stamps the information is footnoted) and with good credentials, missing colours being frequently faked.

Colours only partially omitted are not recognised, Colour shifts, however spectacular, are not listed.

Shades. Shades in philately refer to variations in the intensity of a colour or the presence of differing amounts of other colours. They are particularly significant when they can be linked to specific printings. In general, shades need to be quite marked to fall within the scope of this Catalogue; it does not favour nowadays listing the often numerous shades of a stamp, but chooses a single applicable colour name which will indicate particular groups of outstanding shades. Furthermore, the listings refer to colours as issued; they may deteriorate into something different through the passage of time.

Modern colour printing by lithography is prone to marked differences of shade, even within a single run, and variations can occur within the same sheet. Such shades are not listed.

Aniline colours. An aniline colour meant originally one derived from coal-tar; it now refers more widely to colour of a particular brightness suffused on the surface of a stamp and showing through clearly on the back.

Colours of overprints and surcharges. All overprints and surcharges are in black unless stated otherwise in the heading or after the description of the stamp.

7. Specimen Stamps

Originally, stamps overprinted SPECIMEN were circulated to postmasters or kept in official records, but after the establishment of the Universal Postal Union supplies were sent to Berne for distribution to the postal administrations of member countries.

During the period 1884 to 1928 most of the stamps of British Crown Colonies required for this purpose were overprinted SPECIMEN in various shapes and sizes by their printers from typeset formes. Some locally produced provisionals were handstamped locally, as were sets prepared for presentation. From 1928 stamps were punched with holes forming the word SPECIMEN, each firm of printers using a different machine or machines. From 1948 the stamps supplied for UPU distribution were no longer punctured.

Stamps of some other Commonwealth territories were overprinted or handstamped locally, while stamps of Great Britain and those overprinted for use in overseas postal agencies (mostly of the higher denominations) bore SPECIMEN overprints and handstamps applied by the Inland Revenue or the Post Office.

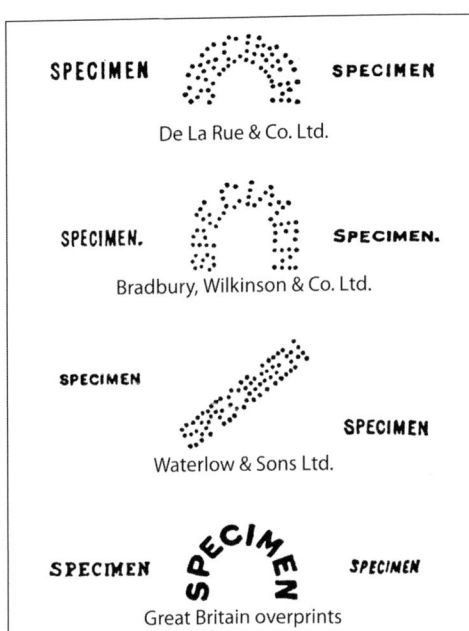

Some of the commoner types of overprints or punctures are illustrated here. Collectors are warned that dangerous forgeries of the punctured type exist.

The *Stanley Gibbons Commonwealth Catalogues* record those Specimen overprints or perforations intended for distribution by the UPU to member countries. In addition the Specimen overprints of Australia and its dependent territories, which were sold to collectors by the Post Office, are also included.

Various Perkins Bacon issues exist obliterated with a "CANCELLED" within an oval of bars handstamp.

Perkins Bacon "CANCELLED" Handstamp

This was applied to six examples of those issues available in 1861 which were then given to members of Sir Rowland Hill's family. 75 different stamps (including four from Chile) are recorded with this handstamp although others may possibly exist. The unauthorised gift of these "CANCELLED" stamps to the Hill family was a major factor in the loss of the Agent General for the Crown Colonies (the forerunner of the Crown Agents) contracts by Perkins Bacon in the following year. Where examples of these scarce items are known to be in private hands the catalogue provides a price.

For full details of these stamps see *CANCELLED by Perkins Bacon* by Peter Jaffé (published by Spink in 1998).

All other Specimens are outside the scope of this volume.

Specimens are not quoted in Great Britain as they are fully listed in the Stanley Gibbons *Great Britain Specialised Catalogue*.

In specifying type of specimen for individual high-value stamps, "H/S" means handstamped, "Optd" is overprinted and "Perf" is punctured. Some sets occur mixed, e.g. "Optd/Perf". If unspecified, the type is apparent from the date or it is the same as for the lower values quoted as a set.

Prices. Prices for stamps up to £1 are quoted in sets; higher values are priced singly. Where specimens exist in more than one type the price quoted is for the cheapest. Specimen stamps have rarely survived even as pairs; these and strips of three, four or five are worth considerably more than singles.

8. Luminescence

Machines which sort mail electronically have been introduced in recent years. In consequence some countries have issued stamps on flourescent or phosphorescent papers, while others have marked their stamps with phosphor bands.

The various papers can only be distinguished by ultraviolet lamps emitting particular wavelengths. They are separately listed only when the stamps have some other means of distinguishing them, visible without the use of these lamps. Where this is not so, the papers are recorded in footnotes or headings.

For this catalogue we do not consider it appropriate that collectors be compelled to have the use of an ultraviolet lamp before being able to identify stamps by our listings. Some experience will also be found necessary in interpreting the results given by ultraviolet. Collectors using the lamps, nevertheless, should exercise great care in their use as exposure to their light is potentially dangerous to the eyes.

Phosphor bands are listable, since they are visible to the naked eye (by holding stamps at an angle to the light and looking along them, the bands appear dark). Stamps existing with or without phosphor bands or with differing numbers of bands are given separate listings. Varieties such as double bands, bands omitted, misplaced or printed on the back are not listed.

Detailed descriptions appear at appropriate places in the listings in explanation of luminescent papers; see, for example, Australia above No. 363, Canada above Nos. 472 and 611, Cook Is. above 249, etc.

For Great Britain, where since 1959 phosphors have played a prominent and intricate part in stamp issues, the main notes above Nos. 599 and 723 should be studied, as well as the footnotes to individual listings where appropriate. In general the classification is as follows.

Stamps with phosphor bands are those where a separate cylinder applies the phosphor after the stamps are printed. Issues with "all-over" phosphor have the "band" covering the entire stamp. Parts of the stamp covered by phosphor bands, or the entire surface for "all-over" phosphor versions, appear matt. Stamps on phosphorised paper have the phosphor added to the paper coating before the stamps are printed. Issues on this paper have a completely shiny surface.

Further particularisation of phosphor – their methods of printing and the colours they exhibit under ultraviolet – is outside the scope. The more specialised listings should be consulted for this information.

9. Coil Stamps

Stamps issued only in coil form are given full listing. If stamps are issued in both sheets and coils the coil stamps are listed separately only where there is some feature (e.g. perforation or watermark sideways) by which singles can be distinguished. Coil stamps containing different stamps *se-tenant* are also listed.

Coil join pairs are too random and too easily faked to permit of listing; similarly ignored are coil stamps which have accidentally suffered an extra row of perforations from the claw mechanism in a malfunctioning vending machine.

10. Stamp Booklets

Stamp booklets are now listed in this catalogue.

Single stamps from booklets are listed if they are distinguishable in some way (such as watermark or perforation) from similar sheet stamps.

Booklet panes are listed where they contain stamps of different denominations *se-tenant*, where stamp-size labels are included, or where such panes are otherwise identifiable. Booklet panes are placed in the listing under the lowest denomination present.

Particular perforations (straight edges) are covered by appropriate notes.

11. Miniature Sheets and Sheetlets

We distinguish between "miniature sheets" and "sheetlets" and this affects the catalogue numbering. An item in sheet form that is postally valid, containing a single stamp, pair, block or set of stamps, with wide, inscribed and/or decorative margins, is a miniature sheet if it is sold at post offices as an indivisible entity. As such the Catalogue allots a single MS number and describes what stamps make it up. The sheetlet or small sheet differs in that the individual stamps are intended to be purchased separately for postal purposes. For sheetlets, all the component postage stamps are numbered individually and the composition explained in a footnote. Note that the definitions refer to post office sale—not how items may be subsequently offered by stamp dealers.

12. Forgeries and Fakes

Forgeries. Where space permits, notes are considered if they can give a concise description that will permit unequivocal detection of a forgery. Generalised warnings, lacking detail, are not nowadays inserted, since their value to the collector is problematic.

Forged cancellations have also been applied to genuine stamps. This catalogue includes notes regarding those manufactured by "Madame Joseph", together with the cancellation dates known to exist. It should be remembered that these dates also exist as genuine cancellations.

For full details of these see *Madame Joseph Forged Postmarks* by Derek Worboys (published by the Royal Philatelic Society London and the British Philatelic Trust in 1994) or *Madame Joseph Revisited* by Brian Cartwright (published by the Royal Philatelic Society London in 2005).

Fakes. Unwitting fakes are numerous, particularly "new shades" which are colour changelings brought about by exposure to sunlight, soaking in water contaminated with dyes from adherent paper, contact with oil and dirt from a pocketbook, and so on. Fraudulent operators, in addition, can offer to arrange: removal of hinge marks; repairs of thins on white or coloured papers; replacement of missing margins or perforations; reperforating in true or false gauges; removal of fiscal cancellations; rejoining of severed pairs, strips and blocks; and (a major hazard) regumming. Collectors can only be urged to purchase from reputable sources and to insist upon Expert Committee certification where there is any kind of doubt.

The Catalogue can consider footnotes about fakes where these are specific enough to assist in detection.

Features Listing

Area	Feature	Collect British Stamps	Stamps of the World	Thematic Catalogues	Comprehensive Catalogue, Parts 1-22 (including Commonwealth and British Empire Stamps and country catalogues)	Great Britain Concise	Specialised catalogues
Design and Description	Shade varieties				√	√	√
Design and Description	Type number	√	√		√	√	√
Illustrations	Multiple stamps from set illustrated	√			√	√	√
Illustrations	A Stamp from each set illustrated in full colour (where possible, otherwise mono)	√	√	√	√	√	√
Price	Catalogue used price	√	√	√	√	√	√
Price	Catalogue unused price	√	√	√	√	√	√
Price	Price - booklet panes				√	√	√
Price	Price - shade varieties				√	√	√
Price	On cover and on piece price				√	√	√
Price	Detailed GB pricing breakdown	√			√	√	√
Print and Paper	Basic printing process information	√	√	√	√	√	√
Print and Paper	Detailed printing process information, e.g. Mill sheets				√		√
Print and Paper	Paper information				√		√
Print and Paper	Detailed perforation information	√			√	√	√
Print and Paper	Details of research findings relating to printing processes and history						√
Print and Paper	Paper colour	√	√		√	√	√
Print and Paper	Paper description to aid identification				√	√	√
Print and Paper	Paper type				√	√	√
Print and Paper	Ordinary or chalk-surfaced paper				√	√	√
Print and Paper	Embossing omitted note						√
Print and Paper	Essays, Die Proofs, Plate Descriptions and Proofs, Colour Trials information						√
Print and Paper	Glazed paper				√	√	√
Print and Paper	Gum details				√		√
Print and Paper	Luminescence/Phosphor bands - general coverage	√			√	√	√
Print and Paper	Luminescence/Phosphor bands - specialised coverage						√
Print and Paper	Overprints and surcharges - including colour information	√	√	√	√	√	√
Print and Paper	Perforation/Imperforate information	√	√		√	√	√
Print and Paper	Perforation errors and varieties				√	√	√
Print and Paper	Print quantities				√		√
Print and Paper	Printing errors				√		√
Print and Paper	Printing flaws						√
Print and Paper	Printing varieties				√	√	√
Print and Paper	Punctured stamps - where official				√		
Print and Paper	Sheet positions				√	√	√
Print and Paper	Specialised plate number information						√
Print and Paper	Specimen overprints (only for Commonwealth & GB)				√	√	√
Print and Paper	Underprints					√	√
Print and Paper	Visible Plate numbers	√			√	√	√
Print and Paper	Yellow and Green paper listings				√		√
Index	Design index	√			√	√	

International Philatelic Glossary

English	French	German	Spanish	Italian
Agate	Agate	Achat	Agata	Agata
Air stamp	Timbre de la poste aérienne	Flugpostmarke	Sello de correo aéreo	Francobollo per posta aerea
Apple Green	Vert-pomme	Apfelgrün	Verde manzana	Verde mela
Barred	Annulé par barres	Balkenentwertung	Anulado con barras	Sbarrato
Bisected	Timbre coupé	Halbiert	Partido en dos	Frazionato
Bistre	Bistre	Bister	Bistre	Bistro
Bistre-brown	Brun-bistre	Bisterbraun	Castaño bistre	Bruno-bistro
Black	Noir	Schwarz	Negro	Nero
Blackish Brown	Brun-noir	Schwärzlichbraun	Castaño negruzco	Bruno nerastro
Blackish Green	Vert foncé	Schwärzlichgrün	Verde negruzco	Verde nerastro
Blackish Olive	Olive foncé	Schwärzlicholiv	Oliva negruzco	Oliva nerastro
Block of four	Bloc de quatre	Viererblock	Bloque de cuatro	Bloco di quattro
Blue	Bleu	Blau	Azul	Azzurro
Blue-green	Vert-bleu	Blaugrün	Verde azul	Verde azzuro
Bluish Violet	Violet bleuâtre	Bläulichviolett	Violeta azulado	Violtto azzurrastro
Booklet	Carnet	Heft	Cuadernillo	Libretto
Bright Blue	Bleu vif	Lebhaftblau	Azul vivo	Azzurro vivo
Bright Green	Vert vif	Lebhaftgrün	Verde vivo	Verde vivo
Bright Purple	Mauve vif	Lebhaftpurpur	Púrpura vivo	Porpora vivo
Bronze Green	Vert-bronze	Bronzegrün	Verde bronce	Verde bronzo
Brown	Brun	Braun	Castaño	Bruno
Brown-lake	Carmin-brun	Braunlack	Laca castaño	Lacca bruno
Brown-purple	Pourpre-brun	Braunpurpur	Púrpura castaño	Porpora bruno
Brown-red	Rouge-brun	Braunrot	Rojo castaño	Rosso bruno
Buff	Chamois	Sämisch	Anteado	Camoscio
Cancellation	Oblitération	Entwertung	Cancelación	Annullamento
Cancelled	Annulé	Gestempelt	Cancelado	Annullato
Carmine	Carmin	Karmin	Carmín	Carminio
Carmine-red	Rouge-carmin	Karminrot	Rojo carmín	Rosso carminio
Centred	Centré	Zentriert	Centrado	Centrato
Cerise	Rouge-cerise	Kirschrot	Color de ceresa	Color Ciliegia
Chalk-surfaced paper	Papier couché	Kreidepapier	Papel estucado	Carta gessata
Chalky Blue	Bleu terne	Kreideblau	Azul turbio	Azzurro smorto
Charity stamp	Timbre de bienfaisance	Wohltätigkeitsmarke	Sello de beneficenza	Francobollo di beneficenza
Chestnut	Marron	Kastanienbraun	Castaño rojo	Marrone
Chocolate	Chocolat	Schokolade	Chocolate	Cioccolato
Cinnamon	Cannelle	Zimtbraun	Canela	Cannella
Claret	Grenat	Weinrot	Rojo vinoso	Vinaccia
Cobalt	Cobalt	Kobalt	Cobalto	Cobalto
Colour	Couleur	Farbe	Color	Colore
Comb-perforation	Dentelure en peigne	Kammzähnung, Reihenzähnung	Dentado de peine	Dentellatura e pettine
Commemorative stamp	Timbre commémoratif	Gedenkmarke	Sello conmemorativo	Francobollo commemorativo
Crimson	Cramoisi	Karmesin	Carmesí	Cremisi
Deep Blue	Blue foncé	Dunkelblau	Azul oscuro	Azzurro scuro
Deep bluish Green	Vert-bleu foncé	Dunkelbläulichgrün	Verde azulado oscuro	Verde azzurro scuro

International Philatelic Glossary

English	French	German	Spanish	Italian
Design	Dessin	Markenbild	Diseño	Disegno
Die	Matrice	Urstempel. Type, Platte	Cuño	Conio, Matrice
Double	Double	Doppelt	Doble	Doppio
Drab	Olive terne	Trüboliv	Oliva turbio	Oliva smorto
Dull Green	Vert terne	Trübgrün	Verde turbio	Verde smorto
Dull purple	Mauve terne	Trübpurpur	Púrpura turbio	Porpora smorto
Embossing	Impression en relief	Prägedruck	Impresión en relieve	Impressione a relievo
Emerald	Vert-eméraude	Smaragdgrün	Esmeralda	Smeraldo
Engraved	Gravé	Graviert	Grabado	Inciso
Error	Erreur	Fehler, Fehldruck	Error	Errore
Essay	Essai	Probedruck	Ensayo	Saggio
Express letter stamp	Timbre pour lettres par exprès	Eilmarke	Sello de urgencia	Francobollo per espresso
Fiscal stamp	Timbre fiscal	Stempelmarke	Sello fiscal	Francobollo fiscale
Flesh	Chair	Fleischfarben	Carne	Carnicino
Forgery	Faux, Falsification	Fälschung	Falsificación	Falso, Falsificazione
Frame	Cadre	Rahmen	Marco	Cornice
Granite paper	Papier avec fragments de fils de soie	Faserpapier	Papel con filamentos	Carto con fili di seta
Green	Vert	Grün	Verde	Verde
Greenish Blue	Bleu verdâtre	Grünlichblau	Azul verdoso	Azzurro verdastro
Greenish Yellow	Jaune-vert	Grünlichgelb	Amarillo verdoso	Giallo verdastro
Grey	Gris	Grau	Gris	Grigio
Grey-blue	Bleu-gris	Graublau	Azul gris	Azzurro grigio
Grey-green	Vert gris	Graugrün	Verde gris	Verde grigio
Gum	Gomme	Gummi	Goma	Gomma
Gutter	Interpanneau	Zwischensteg	Espacio blanco entre dos grupos	Ponte
Imperforate	Non-dentelé	Geschnitten	Sin dentar	Non dentellato
Indigo	Indigo	Indigo	Azul indigo	Indaco
Inscription	Inscription	Inschrift	Inscripción	Dicitura
Inverted	Renversé	Kopfstehend	Invertido	Capovolto
Issue	Émission	Ausgabe	Emisión	Emissione
Laid	Vergé	Gestreift	Listado	Vergato
Lake	Lie de vin	Lackfarbe	Laca	Lacca
Lake-brown	Brun-carmin	Lackbraun	Castaño laca	Bruno lacca
Lavender	Bleu-lavande	Lavendel	Color de alhucema	Lavanda
Lemon	Jaune-citron	Zitrongelb	Limón	Limone
Light Blue	Bleu clair	Hellblau	Azul claro	Azzurro chiaro
Lilac	Lilas	Lila	Lila	Lilla
Line perforation	Dentelure en lignes	Linienzähnung	Dentado en linea	Dentellatura lineare
Lithography	Lithographie	Steindruck	Litografía	Litografia
Local	Timbre de poste locale	Lokalpostmarke	Emisión local	Emissione locale
Lozenge roulette	Percé en losanges	Rautenförmiger Durchstich	Picadura en rombos	Perforazione a losanghe
Magenta	Magenta	Magentarot	Magenta	Magenta
Margin	Marge	Rand	Borde	Margine
Maroon	Marron pourpré	Dunkelrotpurpur	Púrpura rojo oscuro	Marrone rossastro
Mauve	Mauve	Malvenfarbe	Malva	Malva
Multicoloured	Polychrome	Mehrfarbig	Multicolores	Policromo
Myrtle Green	Vert myrte	Myrtengrün	Verde mirto	Verde mirto
New Blue	Bleu ciel vif	Neublau	Azul nuevo	Azzurro nuovo
Newspaper stamp	Timbre pour journaux	Zeitungsmarke	Sello para periódicos	Francobollo per giornali

International Philatelic Glossary

English	French	German	Spanish	Italian
Obliteration	Oblitération	Abstempelung	Matasello	Annullamento
Obsolete	Hors (de) cours	Ausser Kurs	Fuera de curso	Fuori corso
Ochre	Ocre	Ocker	Ocre	Ocra
Official stamp	Timbre de service	Dienstmarke	Sello de servicio	Francobollo di
Olive-brown	Brun-olive	Olivbraun	Castaño oliva	Bruno oliva
Olive-green	Vert-olive	Olivgrün	Verde oliva	Verde oliva
Olive-grey	Gris-olive	Olivgrau	Gris oliva	Grigio oliva
Olive-yellow	Jaune-olive	Olivgelb	Amarillo oliva	Giallo oliva
Orange	Orange	Orange	Naranja	Arancio
Orange-brown	Brun-orange	Orangebraun	Castaño naranja	Bruno arancio
Orange-red	Rouge-orange	Orangerot	Rojo naranja	Rosso arancio
Orange-yellow	Jaune-orange	Orangegelb	Amarillo naranja	Giallo arancio
Overprint	Surcharge	Aufdruck	Sobrecarga	Soprastampa
Pair	Paire	Paar	Pareja	Coppia
Pale	Pâle	Blass	Pálido	Pallido
Pane	Panneau	Gruppe	Grupo	Gruppo
Paper	Papier	Papier	Papel	Carta
Parcel post stamp	Timbre pour colis postaux	Paketmarke	Sello para paquete postal	Francobollo per pacchi postali
Pen-cancelled	Oblitéré à plume	Federzugentwertung	Cancelado a pluma	Annullato a penna
Percé en arc	Percé en arc	Bogenförmiger Durchstich	Picadura en forma de arco	Perforazione ad arco
Percé en scie	Percé en scie	Bogenförmiger Durchstich	Picado en sierra	Foratura a sega
Perforated	Dentelé	Gezähnt	Dentado	Dentellato
Perforation	Dentelure	Zähnung	Dentar	Dentellatura
Photogravure	Photogravure, Héliogravure	Rastertiefdruck	Fotograbado	Rotocalco
Pin perforation	Percé en points	In Punkten durchstochen	Horadado con alfileres	Perforato a punti
Plate	Planche	Platte	Plancha	Lastra, Tavola
Plum	Prune	Pflaumenfarbe	Color de ciruela	Prugna
Postage Due stamp	Timbre-taxe	Portomarke	Sello de tasa	Segnatasse
Postage stamp	Timbre-poste	Briefmarke, Freimarke, Postmarke	Sello de correos	Francobollo postale
Postal fiscal stamp	Timbre fiscal-postal	Stempelmarke als Postmarke verwendet	Sello fiscal-postal	Fiscale postale
Postmark	Oblitération postale	Poststempel	Matasello	Bollo
Printing	Impression, Tirage	Druck	Impresión	Stampa, Tiratura
Proof	Épreuve	Druckprobe	Prueba de impresión	Prova
Provisionals	Timbres provisoires	Provisorische Marken. Provisorien	Provisionales	Provvisori
Prussian Blue	Bleu de Prusse	Preussischblau	Azul de Prusia	Azzurro di Prussia
Purple	Pourpre	Purpur	Púrpura	Porpora
Purple-brown	Brun-pourpre	Purpurbraun	Castaño púrpura	Bruno porpora
Recess-printing	Impression en taille douce	Tiefdruck	Grabado	Incisione
Red	Rouge	Rot	Rojo	Rosso
Red-brown	Brun-rouge	Rotbraun	Castaño rojizo	Bruno rosso
Reddish Lilac	Lilas rougeâtre	Rötlichlila	Lila rojizo	Lilla rossastro
Reddish Purple	Poupre-rouge	Rölichpurpur	Púrpura rojizo	Porpora rossastro
Reddish Violet	Violet rougeâtre	Rötlichviolett	Violeta rojizo	Violetto rossastro
Red-orange	Orange rougeâtre	Rotorange	Naranja rojizo	Arancio rosso
Registration stamp	Timbre pour lettre chargée (recommandée)	Einschreibemarke	Sello de certificado lettere	Francobollo per raccomandate
Reprint	Réimpression	Neudruck	Reimpresión	Ristampa
Reversed	Retourné	Umgekehrt	Invertido	Rovesciato

International Philatelic Glossary

English	French	German	Spanish	Italian
Rose	Rose	Rosa	Rosa	Rosa
Rose-red	Rouge rosé	Rosarot	Rojo rosado	Rosso rosa
Rosine	Rose vif	Lebhaftrosa	Rosa vivo	Rosa vivo
Roulette	Perçage	Durchstich	Picadura	Foratura
Rouletted	Percé	Durchstochen	Picado	Forato
Royal Blue	Bleu-roi	Königblau	Azul real	Azzurro reale
Sage green	Vert-sauge	Salbeigrün	Verde salvia	Verde salvia
Salmon	Saumon	Lachs	Salmón	Salmone
Scarlet	Écarlate	Scharlach	Escarlata	Scarlatto
Sepia	Sépia	Sepia	Sepia	Seppia
Serpentine roulette	Percé en serpentin	Schlangenliniger Durchstich	Picado a serpentina	Perforazione a serpentina
Shade	Nuance	Tönung	Tono	Gradazione de colore
Sheet	Feuille	Bogen	Hoja	Foglio
Slate	Ardoise	Schiefer	Pizarra	Ardesia
Slate-blue	Bleu-ardoise	Schieferblau	Azul pizarra	Azzurro ardesia
Slate-green	Vert-ardoise	Schiefergrün	Verde pizarra	Verde ardesia
Slate-lilac	Lilas-gris	Schierferlila	Lila pizarra	Lilla ardesia
Slate-purple	Mauve-gris	Schieferpurpur	Púrpura pizarra	Porpora ardesia
Slate-violet	Violet-gris	Schieferviolett	Violeta pizarra	Violetto ardesia
Special delivery stamp	Timbre pour exprès	Eilmarke	Sello de urgencia	Francobollo per espressi
Specimen	Spécimen	Muster	Muestra	Saggio
Steel Blue	Bleu acier	Stahlblau	Azul acero	Azzurro acciaio
Strip	Bande	Streifen	Tira	Striscia
Surcharge	Surcharge	Aufdruck	Sobrecarga	Soprastampa
Tête-bêche	Tête-bêche	Kehrdruck	Tête-bêche	Tête-bêche
Tinted paper	Papier teinté	Getöntes Papier	Papel coloreado	Carta tinta
Too-late stamp	Timbre pour lettres en retard	Verspätungsmarke	Sello para cartas retardadas	Francobollo per le lettere in ritardo
Turquoise-blue	Bleu-turquoise	Türkisblau	Azul turquesa	Azzurro turchese
Turquoise-green	Vert-turquoise	Türkisgrün	Verde turquesa	Verde turchese
Typography	Typographie	Buchdruck	Tipografia	Tipografia
Ultramarine	Outremer	Ultramarin	Ultramar	Oltremare
Unused	Neuf	Ungebraucht	Nuevo	Nuovo
Used	Oblitéré, Usé	Gebraucht	Usado	Usato
Venetian Red	Rouge-brun terne	Venezianischrot	Rojo veneciano	Rosso veneziano
Vermilion	Vermillon	Zinnober	Cinabrio	Vermiglione
Violet	Violet	Violett	Violeta	Violetto
Violet-blue	Bleu-violet	Violettblau	Azul violeta	Azzurro violetto
Watermark	Filigrane	Wasserzeichen	Filigrana	Filigrana
Watermark sideways	Filigrane couché	Wasserzeichen liegend	Filigrana acostado	Filigrana coricata
Wove paper	Papier ordinaire, Papier uni	Einfaches Papier	Papel avitelado	Carta unita
Yellow	Jaune	Gelb	Amarillo	Giallo
Yellow-brown	Brun-jaune	Gelbbraun	Castaño amarillo	Bruno giallo
Yellow-green	Vert-jaune	Gelbgrün	Verde amarillo	Verde giallo
Yellow-olive	Olive-jaunâtre	Gelboliv	Oliva amarillo	Oliva giallastro
Yellow-orange	Orange jaunâtre	Gelborange	Naranja amarillo	Arancio giallastro
Zig-zag roulette	Percé en zigzag	Sägezahnartiger Durchstich	Picado en zigzag	Perforazione a zigzag

About Us

Our History
Edward Stanley Gibbons started trading postage stamps in his father's chemist shop in 1856. Since then we have been at the forefront of stamp collecting for over 150 years. We hold the Royal Warrant, offer unsurpassed expertise and quality and provide collectors with the peace of mind of a certificate of authenticity on all of our stamps. If you think of stamp collecting, you think of Stanley Gibbons and we are proud to uphold that tradition for you.

399 Strand
Our world famous stamp shop is a collector's paradise, with all of our latest catalogues, albums and accessories and, of course, our unrivalled stockholding of postage stamps.
www.stanleygibbons.com   shop@stanleygibbons.co.uk   +44 (0)20 7836 8444

Specialist Stamp Sales
For the collector that appreciates the value of collecting the highest quality examples, Stanley Gibbons is the only choice. Our extensive range is unrivalled in terms of quality and quantity, with specialist stamps available from all over the world.
www.stanleygibbons.com/stamps   shop@stanleygibbons.co.uk   +44 (0)20 7836 8444

Stanley Gibbons Auctions and Valuations
Sell your collection or individual rare items through our prestigious public auctions or our regular postal auctions and benefit from the excellent prices being realised at auction currently. We also provide an unparalleled valuation service.
www.stanleygibbons.com/auctions   auctions@stanleygibbons.co.uk   +44 (0)20 7836 8444

Stanley Gibbons Publications
The world's first stamp catalogue was printed by Stanley Gibbons in 1865 and we haven't looked back since! Our catalogues are trusted worldwide as the industry standard and we print several titles each year. We also publish consumer and trade magazines, Gibbons Stamp Monthly and Philatelic Exporter to bring you news, views and insights into all things philatelic. Never miss an issue by subscribing today and benefit from exclusive subscriber offers each month.
www.stanleygibbons.com/shop   orders@stanleygibbons.co.uk   +44 (0)1425 472 363

Stanley Gibbons Investments
The Stanley Gibbons Investment Department offers a unique range of investment propositions that have consistently outperformed more traditional forms of investment, from capital protected products with unlimited upside to portfolios made up of the world's rarest stamps and autographs.
www.stanleygibbons.com/investment   investment@stanleygibbons.co.uk   +44 (0)1481 708 270

Fraser's Autographs
Autographs, manuscripts and memorabilia from Henry VIII to current day. We have over 60,000 items in stock, including movie stars, musicians, sport stars, historical figures and royalty. Fraser's is the UK's market leading autograph dealer and has been dealing in high quality autographed material since 1978.
www.frasersautographs.com   sales@frasersautographs.co.uk   +44 (0)20 7557 4404

stanleygibbons.com
Our website offers the complete philatelic service. Whether you are looking to buy stamps, invest, read news articles, browse our online stamp catalogue or find new issues, you are just one click away from anything you desire in the world of stamp collecting at stanleygibbons.com. Happy browsing!
www.stanleygibbons.com

Guide to Entries

Ⓐ Country of Issue – When a country changes its name, the catalogue listing changes to reflect the name change, for example Namibia was formerly known as South West Africa, the stamps in Southern Africa are all listed under Namibia, but split into South West Africa and then Namibia.

Ⓑ Country Information – Brief geographical and historical details for the issuing country.

Ⓒ Currency – Details of the currency, and dates of earliest use where applicable, on the face value of the stamps.

Ⓓ Illustration – Generally, the first stamp in the set. Stamp illustrations are reduced to 75%, with overprints and surcharges shown actual size.

Ⓔ Illustration or Type Number – These numbers are used to help identify stamps, either in the listing, type column, design line or footnote, usually the first value in a set. These type numbers are in a bold type face – **123**; when bracketed (**123**) an overprint or a surcharge is indicated. Some type numbers include a lower-case letter – **123a**, this indicates they have been added to an existing set.

Ⓕ Date of issue – This is the date that the stamp/set of stamps was issued by the post office and was available for purchase. When a set of definitive stamps has been issued over several years the Year Date given is for the earliest issue. Commemorative sets are listed in chronological order. Stamps of the same design, or issue are usually grouped together, for example some of the New Zealand landscapes definitive series were first issued in 2003 but the set includes stamps issued to May 2007.

Ⓖ Number Prefix – Stamps other than definitives and commemoratives have a prefix letter before the catalogue number.
Their use is explained in the text: some examples are A for airmail, D for postage due and O for official stamps.

Ⓗ Footnote – Further information on background or key facts on issues.

Ⓘ Stanley Gibbons Catalogue number – This is a unique number for each stamp to help the collector identify stamps in the listing. The Stanley Gibbons numbering system is universally recognized as definitive.
   Where insufficient numbers have been left to provide for additional stamps to a listing, some stamps will have a suffix letter after the catalogue number (for example 214a). If numbers have been left for additions to a set and not used they will be left vacant.
   The separate type numbers (in bold) refer to illustrations (see **E**).

Ⓙ Colour – If a stamp is printed in three or fewer colours then the colours are listed, working from the centre of the stamp outwards (see **R**).

Ⓚ Design line – Further details on design variations

Ⓛ Key Type – Indicates a design type on which the stamp is based. These are the bold figures found below each illustration, for example listed in Cameroon, in the West Africa catalogue, is the Key type A and B showing the ex-Kaiser's yacht *Hohenzollern*. The type numbers are also given in bold in the second column of figures alongside the stamp description to indicate the design of each stamp. Where an issue comprises stamps of similar design, the corresponding type number should be taken as indicating the general design. Where there are blanks in the type number column it means that the type of the corresponding stamp is that shown by the number in the type column of the same issue. A dash (–) in the type column means that the stamp is not illustrated. Where type numbers refer to stamps of another country, e.g. where stamps of one country are overprinted for use in another, this is always made clear in the text.

Ⓜ Coloured Papers – Stamps printed on coloured paper are shown – e.g. "brown/*yellow*" indicates brown printed on yellow paper.

Ⓝ Surcharges and Overprints – Usually described in the headings. Any actual wordings are shown in bold type. Descriptions clarify words and figures used in the overprint. Stamps with the same overprints in different colours are not listed separately. Numbers in brackets after the descriptions are the catalogue numbers of the non-overprinted stamps. The words "inscribed" or "inscription" refer to the wording incorporated in the design of a stamp and not surcharges or overprints.

Ⓞ Face value – This refers to the value of each stamp and is the price it was sold for at the Post Office when issued. Some modern stamps do not have their values in figures but instead it is shown as a letter, for example Great Britain use 1st or 2nd on their stamps as opposed to the actual value.

Ⓟ Catalogue Value – Mint/Unused. Prices quoted for Queen Victoria to King George V stamps are for lightly hinged examples.

Ⓠ Catalogue Value – Used. Prices generally refer to fine postally used examples. For certain issues they are for cancelled-to-order.

Prices
Prices are given in pence and pounds. Stamps worth £100 and over are shown in whole pounds:

Shown in Catalogue as	Explanation
10	10 pence
1.75	£1.75
15.00	£15
£150	£150
£2300	£2300

Prices assume stamps are in 'fine condition'; we may ask more for superb and less for those of lower quality. The minimum catalogue price quoted is 10p and is intended as a guide for catalogue users. The lowest price for individual stamps purchased from Stanley Gibbons is £1.
   Prices quoted are for the cheapest variety of that particular stamp. Differences of watermark, perforation, or other details, often increase the value. Prices quoted for mint issues are for single examples, unless otherwise stated. Those in *se-tenant* pairs, strips, blocks or sheets may be worth more. Where no prices are listed it is either because the stamps are not known to exist (usually shown by a †) in that particular condition, or, more usually, because there is no reliable information on which to base their value.
All prices are subject to change without prior notice and we cannot guarantee to supply all stamps as priced. Prices quoted in advertisements are also subject to change without prior notice.

Ⓡ Multicoloured – Nearly all modern stamps are multicoloured (more than three colours); this is indicated in the heading, with a description of the stamp given in the listing.

Ⓢ Perforations – Please see page xiii for a detailed explanation of perforations.

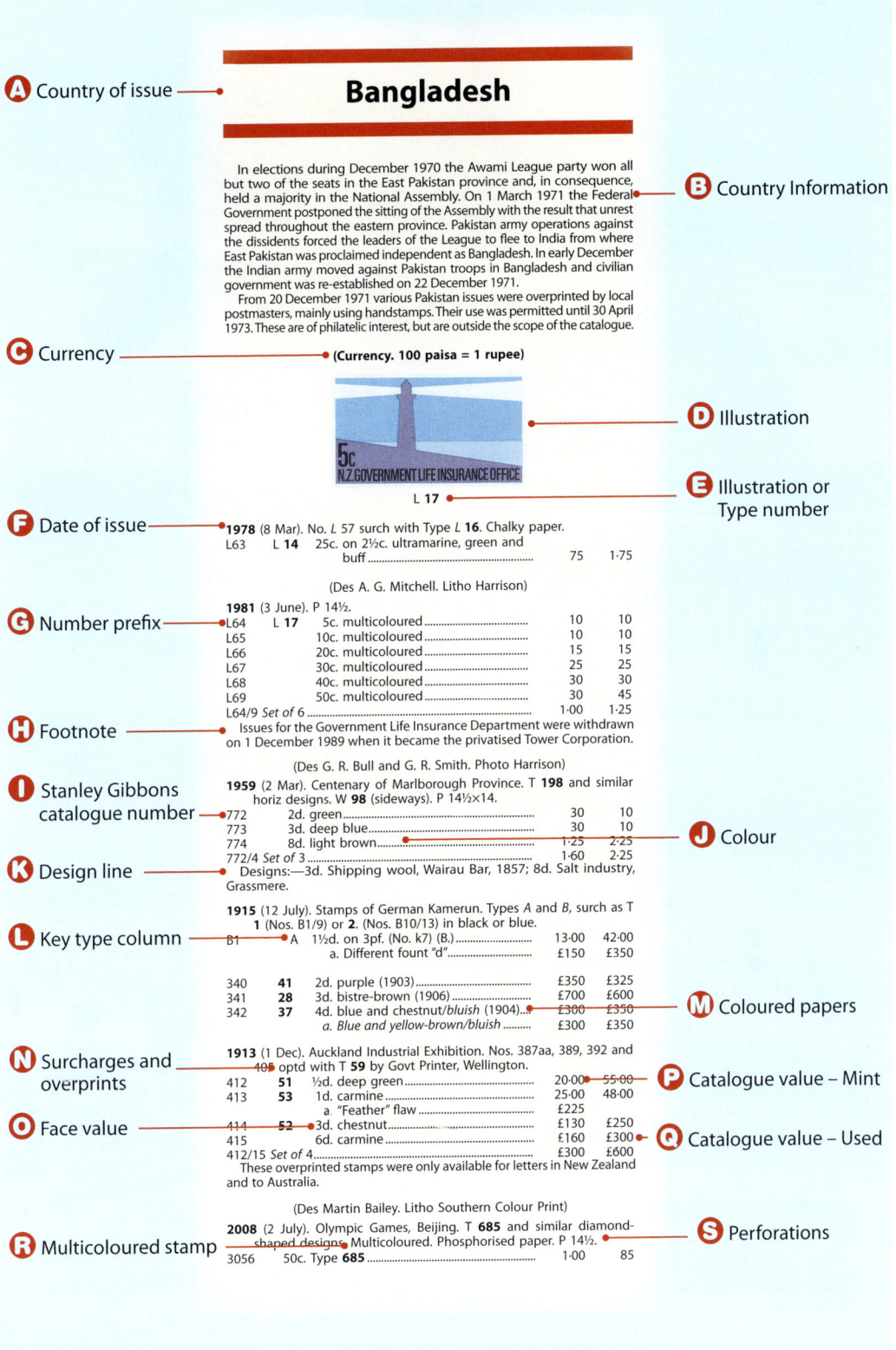

THE WORLD OF STAMP COLLECTING IN YOUR HANDS

- The UK's biggest selling stamp magazine • Consistently over 150 pages per issue
- Written by stamp collectors for stamp collectors • Monthly colour catalogue supplement
- Philatelic news from around the world • Dedicated GB stamp section
- Regular offers exclusively for subscribers

FREE SAMPLE

For your **FREE** sample, contact us by:

Telephone: +44(0)1425 472 363
Email: orders@stanleygibbons.co.uk
Post: Stanley Gibbons Limited, 7 Parkside, Christchurch Road, Ringwood, Hampshire, BH24 3SH

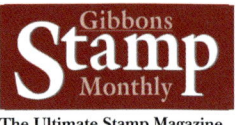
The Ultimate Stamp Magazine

For more information please visit
www.gibbonsstampmonthly.com

Anguilla

Following the grant of Associated Statehood to St. Christopher, Nevis and Anguilla, on 27 February 1967 the population of Anguilla agitated for independence and the St. Kitts-Nevis authorities left the island on 30 May 1967. Nos. 1/16 were issued by the Island Council and were accepted for international mail. On 7 July 1969 the Anguilla post office was officially recognised by the Government of St. Christopher, Nevis and Anguilla and normal postal communications via St. Christopher were resumed. By the Anguilla Act of 21 July 1971, Anguilla was restored to direct British control.

A degree of internal self-government with an Executive Council was introduced on 10 February 1976 and the links with St. Kitts-Nevis were officially severed on 18 December 1980.

(Currency. 100 cents = 1 Eastern Carribean dollar)

Independent Anguilla
(1)

2 Mahogany Tree, The Quarter

1967 (4 Sept). Nos. 129/44 of St. Kitts-Nevis optd as T **1**, by Island Press Inc, St. Thomas, U.S. Virgin Islands.

1	½c. New lighthouse, Sombrero	60·00	26·00
2	1c. Loading sugar cane, St. Kitts	75·00	11·00
3	2c. Pall Mall Square, Basseterre	70·00	2·25
4	3c. Gateway, Brimstone Hill Fort, St. Kitts	70·00	6·00
	w. Wmk inverted	—	48·00
5	4c. Nelson's Spring, Nevis	75·00	6·50
6	5c. Grammar School, St. Kitts	£275	32·00
7	6c. Crater, Mt. Misery, St. Kitts	£120	17·00
8	10c. Hibiscus	70·00	9·50
9	15c. Sea Island cotton, Nevis	£140	15·00
10	20c. Boat building, Anguilla	£300	22·00
11	25c. White-crowned Pigeon	£225	38·00
	w. Wmk inverted	£300	75·00
12	50c. St. George's Church Tower, Basseterre	£4250	£750
13	60c. Alexander Hamilton	£5000	£1500
14	$1 Map of St. Kitts-Nevis	£3750	£650
15	$2.50 Map of Anguilla	£2750	£425
16	$5 Arms of St. Christopher, Nevis and Anguilla	£3000	£450
1/16 Set of 16		£18000	£3500

Owing to the limited stocks available for overprinting, the sale of the above stamps was personally controlled by the Postmaster and no orders from the trade were accepted.

(Des John Lister Ltd. Litho A. & M.)

1967 (27 Nov)–**68**. T **2** and similar horiz designs. P 12½×13.

17	1c. dull green, bistre-brown and pale orange	10	1·00
18	2c. bluish green and black (21.3.68)	10	3·00
19	3c. black and light emerald (10.2.68)	10	10
20	4c. cobalt-blue and black (10.2.68)	10	10
21	5c. multicoloured	10	10
22	6c. light vermilion and black (21.3.68)	10	10
23	10c. multicoloured	15	10
24	15c. multicoloured (10.2.68)	2·50	20
25	20c. multicoloured	1·25	2·75
26	25c. multicoloured	60	20
27	40c. apple green, light greenish blue and black	1·00	25
28	60c. multicoloured (10.2.68)	4·50	4·75
29	$1 multicoloured	1·75	3·25
30	$2.50 multicoloured (21.3.68)	2·00	7·50
31	$5 multicoloured (10.2.68)	3·00	4·25
17/31 Set of 15		15·00	25·00

Designs:—2c. Sombrero Lighthouse; 3c. St. Mary's Church; 4c. Valley Police Station; 5c. Old Plantation House, Mt. Fortune; 6c. Valley Post Office; 10c. Methodist Church, West End; 15c. Wall-Blake Airport; 20c. Beech A90 King Air aircraft over Sandy Ground; 25c. Island Harbour; 40c. Map of Anguilla; 60c. Hermit Crab and Starfish; $1 Hibiscus; $2.50, Local scene; $5, Spiny Lobster.

17 Yachts in Lagoon

(Des John Lister Ltd. Litho A.& M.)

1968 (11 May). Anguillan Ships. T **17** and similar horiz designs. Multicoloured. P 14.

32	10c. Type **17**	35	10
33	15c. Boat on beach	40	10
34	25c. Warspite (schooner)	55	15
35	40c. Atlantic Star (schooner)	65	20
32/35 Set of 4		1·75	50

18 Purple-throated Carib

(Des John Lister Ltd. Litho A. & M.)

1968 (8 July). Anguillan Birds. T **18** and similar multicoloured designs. P 14.

36	10c. Type **18**	65	15
37	15c. Bananaquit	80	20
38	25c. Black-necked Stilt (horiz)	85	20
39	40c. Royal Tern (horiz)	90	30
36/39 Set of 4		3·00	75

19 Guides' Badge and Anniversary Years

(Des John Lister Ltd. Litho A. & M.)

1968 (14 Oct). 35th Anniv of Anguillan Girl Guides. T **19** and similar multicoloured designs. P 13½×13½ (10, 25c.) or 13½×13 (others).

40	10c. Type **19**	10	10
41	15c. Badge and silhouettes of Guides (vert)	15	10
42	25c. Guides' badge and Headquarters	20	15
43	40c. Association and Proficiency badges (vert)	25	15
40/43 Set of 4		65	45

20 The Three Kings

(Des John Lister Ltd. Litho A. & M.)

1968 (18 Nov). Christmas. T **20** and similar designs. P 13.

44	1c. black and cerise	10	10
45	10c. black and light greenish blue	10	10
46	15c. black and chestnut	15	10
47	40c. black and blue	15	10
48	50c. black and dull green	20	15
44/48 Set of 5		60	50

Designs: Vert—10c. The Wise Men; 15c. Holy Family and manger. Horiz—40c. The Shepherds; 50c. Holy Family and donkey.

21 Bagging Salt

INDEPENDENCE JANUARY, 1969
(21a)

(Des John Lister Ltd. Litho A. & M.)

1969 (4 Jan). Anguillan Salt Industry. T **21** and similar horiz designs. Multicoloured. P 13.

49	10c. Type **21**	25	10

ANGUILLA

50	15c. Packing salt	30	10
51	40c. Salt pond	35	10
52	50c. Loading salt	35	10
49/52 Set of 4		1·10	35

1969 (17 Jan*). Expiration of Interim Agreement on Status of Anguilla. Nos. 17/24 and 26/7 optd with T **21a**.

52a	1c. dull green, bistre-brown and pale orange	10	40
52b	2c. bluish green and black	10	40
52c	3c. black and light emerald	10	40
52d	4c. cobalt-blue and black	10	40
52e	5c. multicoloured	10	20
52f	6c. light vermilion and black	10	20
52g	10c. multicoloured	10	30
52h	15c. multicoloured	90	30
52i	25c. multicoloured	80	30
52j	40c. apple green, light greenish blue and black	1·00	40
52a/j Set of 10		3·00	3·00

*Earliest known postmark date. The remaining values of the 1967–68 series, Nos. 17/31, also come with this overprint. The complete set exists on large first day covers postmarked 9 January 1969. The values listed above have been reported used on commercial mail from Anguilla.

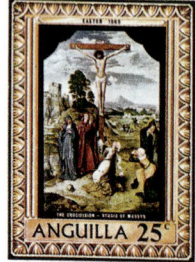

22 "The Crucifixion"
(Studio of Massys)

(Des John Lister Ltd. Litho Format)

1969 (31 Mar). Easter Commemoration. T **22** and similar vert design. P 13½.

53	25c. multicoloured	25	15
54	40c. multicoloured	35	15

Design:—10c. "The Last Supper" (ascribed to Roberti).

23 Amaryllis

(Des John Lister Ltd. Litho Format)

1969 (10 June). Flowers of the Caribbean. T **23** and similar horiz designs. Multicoloured. P 14.

55	10c. Type **23**	15	20
56	15c. Bougainvillea	15	25
57	40c. Hibiscus	20	50
58	50c. Cattleya orchid	1·00	1·60
55/58 Set of 4		1·40	2·25

24 Superb Gaza, Channelled Turban,
Chestnut Turban and Carved Star Shell

(Des John Lister Ltd. Litho A. & M.)

1969 (22 Sept). Sea Shells. T **24** and similar horiz designs. Multicoloured. P 14.

59	10c. Type **24**	20	20
60	15c. American Thorny Oyster	20	20
61	40c. Scotch, Royal and Smooth Scotch Bonnets	30	30
62	50c. Atlantic Trumpet Triton	40	30
59/62 Set of 4		1·00	90

(25)   (26)   (27)

(28)   (29)

1969 (1 Oct). Christmas. Nos. 17, 25/8 optd with T **25/29**.

63	1c. dull green, bistre-brown and light orange	10	10
64	20c. multicoloured	20	10
65	25c. multicoloured	20	10
66	40c. apple-green, light greenish blue and black	25	15
67	60c. multicoloured	40	20
63/67 Set of 5		1·00	55

30 Spotted Goatfish   31 "Morning Glory"

(Des John Lister Ltd. Litho A. & M.)

1969 (1 Dec). Fish. T **30** and similar horiz designs. Multicoloured. P 14.

68	10c. Type **30**	45	15
69	15c. Blue-striped Grunt	60	15
70	40c. Nassau Grouper	75	20
71	50c. Banded Butterflyfish	80	20
68/71 Set of 4		2·40	65

(Des John Lister Ltd. Litho A. & M.)

1970 (23 Feb). Flowers. T **31** and similar vert designs. Multicoloured. P 14.

72	10c. Type **31**	25	10
73	15c. Blue Petrea	35	10
74	40c. Hibiscus	50	20
75	50c. "Flame Tree"	60	25
72/75 Set of 4		1·50	55

32 "The Crucifixion" (Masaccio)   33 Scout Badge and Map

(Des John Lister Ltd. Litho Format)

1970 (26 Mar). Easter. T **32** and similar multicoloured designs. P 13½.

76	10c. "The Ascent to Calvary" (Tiepolo) (horiz)	15	10
77	20c. Type **32**	20	10
78	40c. "Deposition" (Rosso Fiorentino)	25	15
79	60c. "The Ascent to Calvary" (Murillo) (horiz)	25	15
76/79 Set of 4		75	45

(Des John Lister Ltd. Litho A. & M.)

1970 (10 Aug). 40th Anniv of Scouting in Anguilla. T **33** and similar horiz designs. Multicoloured. P 13.

80	10c. Type **33**	15	20
81	15c. Scout camp and cubs practising first-aid	20	20
82	40c. Monkey Bridge	25	30
83	50c. Scout H.Q. Building and Lord Baden-Powell	35	40
80/83 Set of 4		85	85

ANGUILLA

34 Boatbuilding

(Des John Lister Ltd. Litho Format)

1970 (23 Nov). Various horiz designs as T **34**. Multicoloured. P 14.
84	1c. Type **34**..	30	40
85	2c. Road Construction.............................	30	40
86	3c. Quay, Blowing Point.........................	30	20
87	4c. Broadcaster, Radio Anguilla............	30	50
88	5c. Cottage Hospital Extension..............	40	50
89	6c. Valley Secondary School...................	30	50
90	10c. Hotel Extension.................................	30	30
91	15c. Sandy Ground....................................	30	30
92	20c. Supermarket and Cinema................	70	30
93	25c. Bananas and Mangoes.....................	35	1·00
94	40c. Wall Blake Airport.............................	4·00	3·25
95	60c. Sandy Ground Jetty..........................	65	3·50
96	$1 Administration Buildings..................	1·25	1·40
97	$2.50 Livestock...	1·50	4·00
98	$5 Sandy Hill Bay.....................................	3·25	3·75
84/98 Set of 15...		13·00	18·00

35 "The Adoration of the Shepherds" (Reni)
36 "Ecce Homo" (detail, Correggio)

(Des John Lister Ltd. Litho Questa)

1970 (11 Dec). Christmas. T **35** and similar vert designs. Multicoloured. P 13½.
99	1c. Type **35**...	10	15
100	20c. "The Virgin and Child" (Gozzoli)......	30	20
101	25c. "Mystic Nativity" (detail, Botticelli)...	30	25
102	40c. "The Santa Margherita Madonna" (detail, Mazzola)...........................	40	25
103	50c. "The Adoration of the Magi" (detail, Tiepolo).....................................	40	25
99/103 Set of 5..		1·25	1·00

(Des John Lister Ltd. Litho Format)

1971 (29 Mar). Easter. T **36** and similar designs. P 13½.
104	10c. multicoloured...................................	25	10
105	15c. multicoloured...................................	25	10
106	40c. multicoloured...................................	30	10
107	50c. multicoloured...................................	30	15
104/7 Set 4..		1·00	30

Designs: *Vert*—15c. "Christ appearing to St. Peter" (detail, Carracci). *Horiz*—40c. "Angels weeping over the Dead Christ" (detail, Guercino); 50c. "The Supper at Emmaus" (detail, Caravaggio).

37 *Hypolimnas misippus*
38 *Magnanime* and *Aimable* in Battle

(Des John Lister Ltd. Litho Questa)

1971 (21 June). Butterflies. T **37** and similar horiz designs. Multicoloured. P 14×14½.
108	10c. Type **37**...	1·60	70
109	15c. *Junonia evarete*................................	1·60	80
110	40c. *Agraulis vanillae*..............................	2·00	1·25
111	50c. *Danaus plexippus*............................	2·00	1·50
108/11 Set of 4..		6·50	3·75

(Des John Lister Ltd. Litho Format)

1971 (30 Aug). Sea-battles of the West Indies. T **38** and similar vert designs. Multicoloured. P 14.
112	10c. Type **38**...	1·10	1·40
	a. Horiz strip of 5. Nos. 112/16......	6·50	7·75
113	15c. H.M.S. *Duke*, *Glorieux* and H.M.S. *Agamemnon*...................................	1·25	1·60
114	25c. H.M.S. *Formidable* and H.M.S. *Namur* against *Ville de Paris*......................	1·50	1·75
115	40c. H.M.S. *Canada*..................................	1·60	1·90
116	50c. H.M.S. *St. Albans* and wreck of *Hector*....	1·75	2·00
112/16 Set of 5..		6·50	7·75

Nos. 112/16 were issued in horizontal *se-tenant* strips within the sheet, to form a composite design in the order listed.

ADMINISTRATION BY BRITISH COMMISSIONER

 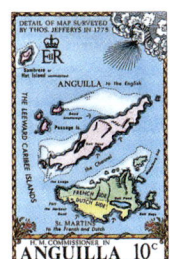

39 "The Ansidei Madonna" (detail, Raphael)
40 Map of Anguilla and St. Martins by Thomas Jefferys (1775)

(Des John Lister Ltd. Litho Questa)

1971 (29 Nov). Christmas. T **39** and similar vert designs. P 13½.
117	20c. multicoloured...................................	30	30
118	25c. multicoloured...................................	30	30
119	40c. multicoloured...................................	35	40
120	50c. multicoloured...................................	40	70
117/20 Set of 4..		1·25	1·50

Designs:—25c. "Mystic Nativity" (detail, Botticelli); 40c. "Adoration of the Shepherds" (detail; ascr to Murillo); 50c. "The Madonna of the Iris" (detail; ascr to Dürer).

(Litho Format)

1972 (24 Jan). Maps. T **40** and similar multicoloured designs showing maps by the cartographers given. P 14.
121	10c. Type **40**...	25	10
122	15c. Samuel Fahlberg (1814)...................	35	15
123	40c. Thomas Jefferys (1775) (*horiz*).......	50	25
124	50c. Capt. E. Barnett (1847) (*horiz*)........	60	25
121/4 Set of 4..		1·50	65

41 "Jesus Buffeted"
42 Loblolly Tree

(Des John Lister Ltd. Litho Format)

1972 (14 Mar). Easter. Stained Glass Windows from Church of St. Michael, Bray, Berkshire. T **41** and similar vert designs. Multicoloured. P 14×13½.
125	10c. Type **41**...	25	25
	a. Horiz strip of 5. Nos. 125/9........	1·40	1·40
126	15c. "The Way of Sorrows"......................	30	30
127	25c. "The Crucifixion"...............................	30	30

ANGUILLA

128	40c. "Descent from the Cross"		35	35
129	50c. "The Burial"		40	40
125/9 Set of 5			1·40	1·40

Nos. 125/9 were printed horizontally *se-tenant* within the sheet.

(Litho Questa ($10), Format (others))

1972 (30 Oct)–**75**. T **42** and similar multicoloured designs (horiz, except 2, 4 and 6c.). P 13½.

130	1c. Spear fishing		10	40
131	2c. Type **42**		10	40
132	3c. Sandy Ground		10	40
133	4c. Ferry at Blowing Point		1·75	20
134	5c. Agriculture		15	1·00
135	6c. St. Mary's Church		25	20
136	10c. St. Gerard's Church		25	40
137	15c. Cottage Hospital extension		25	30
138	20c. Public library		30	35
139	25c. Sunset at Blowing Point		40	2·00
140	40c. Boat building		5·00	1·50
141	60c. Hibiscus		4·00	4·00
142	$1 Magnificent Frigate Bird		10·00	8·00
143	$2.50 Frangipani		5·00	10·00
144	$5 Brown Pelican		17·00	17·00
144a	$10 Green-back turtle (20.5.75)		16·00	18·00
130/44a Set of 16			55·00	55·00

43 *Malcolm Miller* (schooner) and Common Dolphin

(Des (from photograph by D. Groves) and photo Harrison)

1972 (20 Nov). Royal Silver Wedding. Multicoloured; background colour given. W w **12**. P 14×14½.

145	**43**	25c. yellow-olive (*shades*)	50	75
146		40c. chocolate	50	75
		w. Wmk inverted	1·25	

44 Flight into Egypt    **45** "The Betrayal of Christ"

(Des John Lister Ltd. Litho Questa)

1972 (4 Dec). Christmas. T **44** and similar vert designs. Multicoloured. P 13½.

147	1c. Type **44**	10	10
148	20c. Star of Bethlehem	20	20
	a. Vert strip of 4. Nos. 148/51	75	85
149	25c. Holy Family	20	20
150	40c. Arrival of the Magi	20	25
151	50c. Adoration of the Magi	25	25
147/51 Set of 5		75	85

Nos. 148/51 were printed vertically *se-tenant* within a sheet of 20 stamps.

(Des John Lister Ltd. Litho Questa)

1973 (26 Mar). Easter. T **45** and similar vert designs. Multicoloured; bottom panel in gold and black. P 13½.

152	1c. Type **45**	10	10
153	10c. "The Man of Sorrows"	10	10
	a. Vert strip of 5. Nos. 153/7	55	70
154	20c. "Christ bearing the Cross"	10	15
155	25c. "The Crucifixion"	15	15
156	40c. "The Descent from the Cross"	15	15
157	50c. "The Resurrection"	15	20
152/7 Set of 6		55	70
MS158 140×141 mm. Nos. 152/7. Bottom panel in gold and mauve		70	80

Nos. 153/7 were printed within one sheet, vertically *se-tenant*.

46 Santa Maria   **47** Princess Anne and Captain Mark Phillips

(Des John Lister Ltd. Litho Questa)

1973 (10 Sept). Columbus Discovers the West Indies. T **46** and similar horiz designs. Multicoloured. P 13½.

159	1c. Type **46**	10	10
160	20c. Early map	1·50	1·25
	a. Horiz strip of 4. Nos. 160/3	6·75	6·00
161	40c. Map of voyages	1·60	1·40
162	70c. Sighting land	1·90	1·75
163	$1.20 Landing of Columbus	2·50	2·25
159/63 Set of 5		6·75	6·00
MS164 193×93 mm. Nos. 159/63		6·75	7·00

Nos. 160/3 were printed horizontally *se-tenant* within the sheet.

(Des PAD Studio. Litho Questa)

1973 (14 Nov). Royal Wedding. Centre multicoloured. W w **12** (sideways). P 13½.

165	**47**	60c. turquoise-green	20	15
166		$1.20 deep mauve	30	15

48 "The Adoration of the Shepherds" (Reni)

(Des John Lister Ltd. Litho Questa)

1973 (2 Dec). Christmas. T **48** and similar horiz designs. Multicoloured. P 13½.

167	1c. Type **48**	10	10
168	10c. "The Madonna and Child with Saints Jerome and Dominic" (Lippi)	10	10
	a. Horiz strip of 5. Nos. 168/72	75	75
169	20c. "The Nativity" (Master of Brunswick)	15	15
170	25c. "Madonna of the Meadow" (Bellini)	15	15
171	40c. "Virgin and Child" (Cima)	20	20
172	50c. "Adoration of the Kings" (Geertgen)	20	20
167/72 Set of 6		75	75
MS173 148×149 mm. Nos. 167/72		80	1·60

Nos. 168/72 were printed within the sheet, horizontally *se-tenant*.

49 "The Crucifixion" (Raphael)

(Des John Lister Ltd. Litho Questa)

1974 (30 Mar). Easter. T **49** and similar vert designs showing various details of Raphael's "Crucifixion". P 13½.

174	1c. multicoloured	10	10
175	15c. multicoloured	10	10
	a. Vert strip of 5. Nos. 175/9	70	70
176	20c. multicoloured	15	15

177	25c. multicoloured		15	15
178	40c. multicoloured		15	15
179	$1 multicoloured		20	25
174/9 Set of 6			70	70
MS180 123×141 mm. Nos. 174/9			1·00	1·25

Nos. 175/9 were printed vertically *se-tenant* within one sheet.

50 Churchill making "Victory" Sign

(Des John Lister Ltd. Litho Questa)

1974 (24 June). Birth Centenary of Sir Winston Churchill. T **50** and similar horiz designs. Multicoloured. P 13½.

181	1c. Type **50**		10	10
182	20c. Churchill with Roosevelt		20	20
	a. Horiz strip of 5. Nos. 182/6		1·40	1·50
183	25c. Wartime broadcast		20	20
184	40c. Birthplace, Blenheim Palace		30	30
185	60c. Churchill's statue		30	35
186	$1.20 Country residence, Chartwell		45	55
181/6 Set of 6			1·40	1·50
MS187 195×96 mm. Nos. 181/6			1·40	2·50

Nos. 182/6 were printed horizontally *se-tenant* within the sheet.

51 U.P.U. Emblem

(Des John Lister Ltd. Litho Questa)

1974 (27 Aug). Centenary of Universal Postal Union. P 13½*.

188	**51**	1c. black and bright blue	10	10
189		20c. black and pale orange	15	15
		a. Horiz strip of 5. Nos. 189/93	1·10	1·40
190		25c. black and light yellow	15	15
191		40c. black and bright mauve	20	25
192		60c. black and light emerald	30	40
193		$1.20 black and light blue	50	60
188/93 Set of 6			1·10	1·40
MS194 195×96 mm. Nos. 188/93			1·25	2·25

Nos. 189/93 were printed horizontally *se-tenant* within the sheet.

*In No. **MS**194 the lower row of three stamps, 40c., 60c. and $1.20 values, are line-perforated 15 at foot, the remaining 3 stamps being comb-perforated 13½.

52 Anguillan pointing to Star   **53** "Mary, John and Mary Magdalene" (Matthias Grunewald)

(Litho Questa)

1974 (16 Dec). Christmas. T **52** and similar horiz designs. Multicoloured. P 14.

195	1c. Type **52**		10	10
196	20c. Child in Manger		10	20
	a. Horiz strip of 5. Nos. 196/200		70	70
197	25c. King's offering		10	20
198	40c. Star over Map of Anguilla		15	20
199	60c. Family looking at star		15	20
200	$1.20 Angels of Peace		20	30
195/200 Set of 6			1·00	2·00

MS201 177×85 mm. Nos. 195/200			1·10	1·75

Nos. 196/200 were printed horizontally *se-tenant* within the sheet.

(Litho Questa)

1975 (25 Mar). Easter. T **53** and similar multicoloured designs showing details of the Isenheim altarpiece. P 14.

202	1c. Type **53**		10	10
203	10c. "The Crucifixion"		15	15
	a. Horiz strip of 5. Nos. 203/7		80	1·25
204	15c. "St. John the Baptist"		15	15
205	20c. "St. Sebastian and Angels"		15	20
206	$1 "The Entombment"		20	35
207	$1.50 "St. Anthony the Hermit"		25	45
202/7 Set of 6			80	1·25
MS208 134×127 mm. Nos. 202/7. Imperf			1·00	2·00

Nos. 203/7 were printed horizontally *se-tenant* within the sheet.

54 Statue of Liberty   **55** "Madonna Child and the Infant John the Baptist" (Raphael)

(Des John Lister Ltd. Litho Questa)

1975 (10 Nov). Bicentenary of American Revolution. T **54** and similar horiz designs. Multicoloured. P 13½*.

209	1c. Type **54**		10	10
210	10c. The Capitol		20	10
	a. Horiz strip of 5. Nos. 210/14		1·60	1·25
211	15c. "Congress voting for Independence" (Pine and Savage)		30	15
212	20c. Washington and map		30	15
213	$1 Boston Tea Party		45	40
214	$1.50 Bicentenary logo		50	60
209/14 Set of 6			1·60	1·25
MS215 198×97 mm. Nos. 209/14			1·25	2·50

Nos. 210/14 were printed horizontally *se-tenant* within the sheet.

*In No. **MS**215 the lower row of three stamps, 20c., $1 and $1.50 values, are line-perforated 15 at foot, the remaining 3 stamps being comb-perforated 13½.

(Des John Lister Ltd. Litho Questa)

1975 (8 Dec). Christmas. T **55** and similar vert designs showing the "Madonna and Child". Multicoloured. P 13½.

216	1c. Type **55**		10	10
217	10c. Cima		15	15
	a. Horiz strip of 5. Nos. 217/21		1·25	1·00
218	15c. Dolci		20	15
219	20c. Dürer		20	20
220	$1 Bellini		35	25
221	$1.50 Botticelli		45	35
216/21 Set of 6			1·25	1·00
MS222 130×145 mm. Nos. 216/21			2·00	2·25

Nos. 217/21 were printed horizontally *se-tenant* within the sheet.

EXECUTIVE COUNCIL

NEW CONSTITUTION 1976

(**56**)   **57** Almond

57a Italic second "O" in "CONSTITUTION". Occurs on Row 2/2 (Nos. 226, 228, 232, 235, 239), Row 3/2 (Nos. 230/1, 233/4, 236/8), Row 4/5 (Nos. 223/5, 240) or Row 5/2 (Nos. 225, 227, 229).

1976 (10 Feb–July). New Constitution. Nos. 130 etc. optd with T **56** or surch also.

223	1c. Spear fishing	30	50
	a. Italic "O"	3·00	
224	2c. on 1c. Spear fishing	30	50
	a. Italic "O"	3·00	
225	2c. Type **42** (1.7.76)	7·50	1·75
	a. Italic "O"	22·00	
226	3c. on 40c. Boat building	75	70
	a. "3c" omitted	£500	
	b. Typo. "3c"*	13·00	14·00
	c. Italic "O"	5·50	
227	4c. Ferry at Blowing Point	1·00	1·00
	a. Italic "O"	8·50	
228	5c. on 40c. Boat building	30	60
	a. Italic "O"	3·00	
229	6c. St. Mary's Church	30	60
	a. Italic "O"	3·00	
230	10c. on 20c. Public Library	30	50
	a. Italic "O"	3·00	
231	10c. St. Gerard's Church (1.7.76)	9·50	4·75
	a. Italic "O"	25·00	
232	15c. Cottage Hospital extension	30	1·25
	a. Italic "O"	3·00	
233	20c. Public Library	30	50
	a. Italic "O"	3·00	
234	25c. Sunset at Blowing Point	30	50
	a. Italic "O"	3·00	
235	40c. Boat building	1·00	70
	a. Italic "O"	7·00	
236	60c. Hibiscus	70	70
	a. Italic "O"	4·75	
237	$1 Magnificent Frigate Bird	6·50	2·25
	a. Italic "O"	24·00	
238	$2.50 Frangipani	2·25	2·25
	a. Italic "O"	11·00	
239	$5 Brown Pelican	8·00	10·00
	a. Italic "O"	29·00	
240	$10 Green-back turtle	3·00	6·00
	a. Italic "O"	17·00	
223/40 Set of 18		38·00	32·00

*Nos. 226a/b occur on R. 5/2, the "3c" having been omitted during the normal litho surcharging.

(Des John Lister Ltd. Litho Questa)

1976 (16 Feb). Flowering Trees. T **57** and similar horiz designs. Multicoloured. P 13½.

241	1c. Type **57**	10	10
242	10c. Autograph	20	20
	a. Horiz strip of 5. Nos. 242/6	1·25	1·50
243	15c. Calabash	20	20
244	20c. Cordia	20	20
245	$1 Papaya	30	45
246	$1.50 Flamboyant	35	55
241/6 Set of 6		1·25	1·50
MS247 194×99 mm. Nos. 241/6		1·50	2·00

Nos. 242/6 were printed horizontally se-tenant within the sheet.

58 The Three Marys   59 French Ships approaching Anguilla

(Litho Questa)

1976 (5 Apr). Easter. T **58** and similar multicoloured designs showing portions of the Altar Frontal Tapestry, Rheinau. P 13½.

248	1c. Type **58**	10	10
249	10c. The Crucifixion	10	10
	a. Horiz strip of 5. Nos. 249/53	1·75	1·75
250	15c. Two Soldiers	15	15
251	20c. The Annunciation	15	15
252	$1 The complete tapestry (horiz)	65	65
253	$1.50 The Risen Christ	80	80
248/53 Set of 6		1·75	1·75
MS254 138×130 mm. Nos. 248/53. Imperf		1·75	2·10

Nos. 249/53 were printed horizontally se-tenant within the sheet.

(Des John Lister Ltd. Litho Questa)

1976 (8 Nov). Battle for Anguilla, 1796. T **59** and similar horiz designs. Multicoloured. P 13½.

255	1c. Type **59**	10	10
256	3c. *Margaret* (sloop) leaving Anguilla	1·25	35
	a. Horiz strip of 5. Nos. 256/60	7·50	4·25
257	15c. Capture of Le Desius	1·50	55
258	25c. La Vaillante forced aground	1·50	80
259	$1 H.M.S. *Lapwing*	2·00	1·25
260	$1.50 Le Desius burning	2·25	1·75
255/60 Set of 6		7·50	4·25
MS261 205×103 mm. Nos. 255/60		7·50	6·00

Nos. 256/60 were printed horizontally se-tenant within the sheet.

60 "Christmas Carnival" (A. Richardson)

(Litho Questa)

1976 (22 Nov). Christmas. T **60** and similar horiz designs showing children's paintings. Multicoloured. P 13½.

262	1c. Type **60**	10	10
263	3c. Dreams of Christmas Gifts" (J. Connor)	10	10
	a. Horiz strip of 5. Nos. 263/7	1·00	1·10
264	15c. "Carolling" (P. Richardson)	15	15
265	25c. "Candle-light Procession" (A. Mussington)	20	20
266	$1 "Going to Church" (B. Franklin)	30	30
267	$1.50 "Coming Home for Christmas" (E. Gumbs)	40	40
262/7 Set of 6		1·00	1·10
MS268 232×147 mm. Nos. 262/7		1·50	1·75

Nos. 263/7 were printed horizontally se-tenant within the sheet.

61 Prince Charles and H.M.S. *Minerva* (frigate)

(Des John Lister Ltd. Litho Questa)

1977 (9 Feb). Silver Jubilee. T **61** and similar horiz designs. Multicoloured. P 13½.

269	25c. Type **61**	15	10
270	40c. Prince Philip landing at Road Bay, 1964	15	10
271	$1.20 Coronation scene	20	20
272	$2.50 Coronation regalia and map of Anguilla	25	30
269/72 Set of 4		65	55
MS273 145×96 mm. Nos. 269/72		65	90

62 Yellow-crowned Night Heron

(Des John Lister Ltd. Litho Questa)

1977 (18 Apr)–**78**. T **62** and similar horiz designs. Multicoloured. P 13½.

274	1c. Type **62**	30	1·25
275	2c. Great Barracuda	30	2·75
276	3c. Queen or Pink Conch	2·00	3·75
277	4c. Spanish Bayonet	40	70
278	5c. Honeycomb Trunkfish	1·50	30
279	6c. Cable and Wireless Building	30	30
280	10c. American Kestrel (20.2.78)	5·50	4·00
281	15c. Ground Orchid (20.2.78)	3·50	1·75
282	20c. Stop-light Parrotfish (20.2.78)	3·50	75
283	22c. Lobster fishing boat (20.2.78)	50	60

284	35c. Boat race (20.2.78)		1·40	70
285	50c. Sea Bean (20.2.78)		90	50
286	$1 Sandy Island (20.2.78)		60	50
287	$2.50 Manchineel (20.2.78)		1·00	1·00
288	$5 Ground Lizard (20.2.78)		2·00	2·00
289	$10 Red-billed Tropic Bird		9·00	4·50
274/89 Set of 16			30·00	23·00

No. 290 is left vacant.

63 "The Crucifixion" (Massys)

(Des John Lister Ltd. Litho Questa)

1977 (25 Apr). Easter. T **63** and similar horiz designs showing paintings by Castagno ($1.50) or Ugolino (others). Multicoloured. P 13½.

291	1c. Type **63**		10	10
292	3c. "The Betrayal"		10	10
	a. Horiz strip of 5. Nos. 292/6		1·25	1·25
293	22c. "The Way to Calvary"		20	20
294	30c. "The Deposition"		25	25
295	$1 "The Resurrection"		40	40
296	$1.50 "The Crucifixion"		45	45
291/6 Set of 6			1·25	1·25
MS297 192×126 mm. Nos. 291/6			1·60	1·75

Nos. 292/6 were printed horizontally *se-tenant* within the sheet.

ROYAL VISIT TO WEST INDIES

(64)

65 "Le Chapeau de Paille"

1977 (26 Oct). Royal Visit. Nos. 269/MS273 optd with T **64**.

298	25c. Type **61**		10	10
299	40c. Prince Philip landing at Road Bay, 1964.		10	15
300	$1.20 Coronation scene		20	25
301	$2.50 Coronation regalia and map of Anguilla		25	35
298/301 Set of 4			60	75
MS302 145×96 mm. Nos. 298/301			80	60

(Des John Lister Ltd. Litho Questa)

1977 (1 Nov). 400th Birth Anniv of Rubens. T **65** and similar vert designs. Multicoloured. P 13½.

303	25c. Type **65**		15	15
304	40c. "Helene Fourment and her Two Children"		20	25
305	$1.20 "Rubens and his Wife"		60	65
306	$2.50 "Marchesa Brigida Spinola-Doria"		75	95
303/6 Set of 4			1·50	1·75
MS307 93×145 mm. Nos. 303/6			2·00	2·10

Each value was issued in sheets of 5 stamps and 1 label.

EASTER 1978

(66) (67)

1977 (14 Nov). Christmas. Nos. 262/8 with old date blocked out and additionally inscr "1977", some surch also as T **66**.

308	1c. Type **60**		10	10
309	5c. on 3c. "Dreams of Christmas Gifts"		10	10
	a. Horiz strip of 5. Nos. 309/13		1·75	1·75
310	12c. on 15c. "Carolling"		15	15
311	18c. on 25c. "Candle-light Procession"		20	20
312	$1 "Going to Church"		45	45
313	$2.50 on $1.50 "Coming Home for Christmas"		90	90
308/13 Set of 6			1·75	1·75
MS314 232×147 mm. Nos. 308/13			2·50	2·50

1978 (6 Mar). Easter. Nos. 303/7 optd with T **67**, in gold.

315	25c. Type **65**		15	20
316	40c. "Helene Fourment and her Two Children"		15	20
317	$1.20 "Rubens and his Wife"		35	40
318	$2.50 "Marchesa Brigida Spinola-Doria"		45	60
315/18 Set of 4			1·00	1·25
MS319 93×145 mm. Nos. 315/18			1·25	1·50

68 Coronation Coach at Admiralty Arch (69) (70)

(Des John Lister Ltd. Litho Questa)

1978 (6 Apr). 25th Anniv of Coronation. T **68** and similar horiz designs. Multicoloured. P 14.

320	22c. Buckingham Palace		10	10
321	50c. Type **68**		10	10
322	$1.50 Balcony scene		15	15
323	$2.50 Royal coat of arms		25	25
320/3 Set of 4			50	50
MS324 138×92 mm. Nos. 320/3			60	60

1978 (14 Aug). Anniversaries. Nos. 283/8 optd as T **69** or surch as T **70**.

325	22c. Lobster fishing boat		25	15
	a. Opt double		£150	
	b. "C" omitted from "SECONDARY"		4·50	
326	35c. Boat race		35	20
	a. "C" omitted from "SECONDARY"		4·75	
327	50c. Sea Bean		35	30
	a. "I" omitted from "METHODIST"		4·75	
328	$1 Sandy Island		40	40
	a. "I" omitted from "METHODIST"		5·00	
329	$1.20 on $5 Ground Lizard		45	45
	a. "I" omitted from "METHODIST"		5·50	
330	$1.50 on $2.50 Manchineel		50	55
	a. "C" omitted from "SECONDARY"		6·50	
325/30 Set of 6			2·10	1·75

The 22, 35c. and $1.50 values commemorate the 25th anniversary of Valley Secondary School; the other values commemorate the Centenary of Road Methodist Church.

Nos. 325b, 326a and 330a occur on R. 4/1 and Nos. 327a, 328a and 329a on R. 2/4.

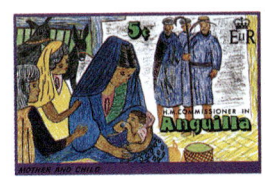

71 Mother and Child

(Des and litho Questa)

1978 (11 Dec). Christmas. Children's Paintings. T **71** and similar horiz designs. Multicoloured. P 13½.

331	5c. Type **71**		10	10
332	12c. Christmas masquerade		15	10
333	18c. Christmas dinner		15	10
334	22c. Serenading		15	10
335	$1 Child in manger		35	20
336	$2.50 Family going to church		55	40
331/6 Set of 6			1·25	70
MS337 191×101 mm. Nos. 331/6			1·25	1·75

1979 (15 Jan). International Year of the Child. As Nos. 331/7 but additionally inscr with emblem and "1979 INTERNATIONAL YEAR OF THE CHILD". Borders in different colours.

338	5c. Type **71**		10	10
339	12c. Christmas masquerade		10	10
340	18c. Christmas dinner		10	10
341	22c. Serenading		10	10
342	$1 Child in manger		30	30
343	$2.50 Family going to church		50	50

ANGUILLA

338/43	Set of 6	1·00	1·00
MS344	205×112 mm. Nos. 338/43	1·75	2·50

12 CENTS

(72)

1979 (12 Feb). Nos. 274/7 and 279/80 surch as T **72**.

345	12c. on 2c. Great Barracuda	50	50
346	14c. on 4c. Spanish Bayonet	40	50
	a. Surch inverted	35·00	
347	18c. on 3c. Queen or Pink Conch	1·00	55
348	25c. on 6c. Cable and Wireless Building	55	50
349	38c. on 10c. American Kestrel	2·50	70
350	40c. on 1c. Type **62**	2·75	70
345/50	Set of 6	7·00	3·00

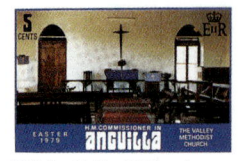

73 Valley Methodist Church

(Des John Lister Ltd. Litho Questa)

1979 (30 Mar). Easter. Church Interiors. T **73** and similar horiz designs. Multicoloured. P 14.

351	5c. Type **73**	10	10
	a. Horiz strip of 6. Nos. 351/6	1·25	1·25
352	12c. St. Mary's Anglican Church, The Valley	10	10
353	18c. St. Gerard's Roman Catholic Church, The Valley	15	15
354	22c. Road Methodist Church	15	15
355	$1.50 St. Augustine's Anglican Church, East End	40	40
356	$2.50 West End Methodist Church	50	50
351/6	Set of 6	1·25	1·25
MS357	190×105 mm. Nos. 351/6	1·50	2·25

Nos. 351/6 were printed together horizontally *se-tenant*, within the sheet.

74 Cape of Good Hope 1d. "Woodblock" of 1881

(Des Stanley Gibbons Ltd. Litho Questa)

1979 (23 Apr). Death Centenary of Sir Rowland Hill. T **74** and similar horiz designs showing stamps. Multicoloured. P 14.

358	1c. Type **74**	10	10
359	1c. U.S.A. inverted Jenny of 1918	10	10
360	22c. Penny Black ("V.R. Official")	15	15
361	35c. Germany 2m. *Graf Zeppelin* of 1928	20	20
362	$1.50 U.S.A. $5 Columbus of 1893	40	60
363	$2.50 Great Britain £5 orange of 1882	60	95
358/63	Set of 6	1·25	1·75
MS364	187×123 mm. Nos. 358/63	1·25	2·40

75 Wright *Flyer I* (1st powered flight, 1903)

(Des John Lister Ltd. Litho Questa)

1979 (21 May). History of Powered Flight. T **75** and similar horiz designs. Multicoloured. P 14.

365	5c. Type **75**	20	10
366	12c. Louis Blériot at Dover after Channel crossing, 1909	25	10
367	18c. Vickers FB-27 Vimy (1st non-stop crossing of Atlantic, 1919)	30	15
368	22c. Ryan NYP Special *Spirit of St. Louis* (1st solo Atlantic flight by Charles Lindbergh, 1927)	30	20
369	$1.50 Airship LZ-127 *Graf Zeppelin*, 1928	65	60
370	$2.50 Concorde, 1979	3·50	90
365/70	Set of 6	4·75	1·75
MS371	200×113 mm. Nos. 365/70	4·25	3·25

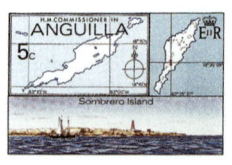

76 Sombrero Island

(Des John Lister Ltd. Litho Questa)

1979 (20 Aug). Outer Islands. T **76** and similar horiz designs. Multicoloured. P 14.

372	5c. Type **76**	15	10
373	12c. Anguillita Island	15	10
374	18c. Sandy Island	15	15
375	25c. Prickly Pear Cays	15	15
376	$1 Dog Island	40	40
377	$2.50 Scrub Island	60	70
372/7	Set of 6	1·40	1·40
MS378	180×91 mm. Nos. 372/7	2·75	2·25

77 Red Poinsettia

(Des John Lister Ltd. Litho Format)

1979 (22 Oct). Christmas. Flowers. T **77** and similar diamond-shaped designs. Multicoloured. P 14½.

379	22c. Type **77**	15	20
380	35c. Kalanchoe	20	30
381	$1.50 Cream Poinsettia	40	50
382	$2.50 White Poinsettia	60	70
379/82	Set of 4	1·25	1·50
MS383	146×164 mm. Nos. 379/82	1·75	2·25

78 Exhibition Scene

(Des R. Granger Barrett. Litho Format)

1979 (10 Dec). "London 1980" International Stamp Exhibition (1st issue). T **78** and similar horiz designs. Multicoloured. P 13.

384	35c. Type **78**	15	20
	a. Perf 14½	15	20
385	50c. Earls Court Exhibition Centre	15	25
	a. Perf 14½	20	25
386	$1.50 Penny Black and Two penny Blue stamps	25	60
	a. Perf 14½	30	60
387	$2.50 Exhibition logo	45	95
	a. Perf 14½	50	95
384/7	Set of 4	90	1·75
MS388	150×94 mm. Nos. 384/7	1·40	2·00
	a. Perf 14½	1·40	2·00

Nos. 384a/7a come from booklets and also exist from uncut booklet sheets of 10.

See also Nos. 407/10.

ANGUILLA

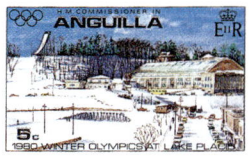

79 Games Site

(Des John Lister Ltd. Litho Format)

1980 (14 Jan). Winter Olympic Games, Lake Placid, U.S.A. T **79** and similar horiz designs. Multicoloured. P 13.

389	5c. Type **79**		10	10
390	18c. Ice-hockey		20	10
391	35c. Ice-skating		20	20
392	50c. Bobsleighing		20	20
393	$1 Skiing		20	35
394	$2.50 Luge-tobogganing		40	80
389/94 Set of 6			1·10	1·60
MS395 136×128 mm. Nos. 389/94			1·00	2·00

Nos. 389/94 also exist perforated 14½ (*Price for set of 6 £1.10 mint, £1.50 used*) from additional sheetlets of 10. Stamps perforated 13 are from normal sheets of 40.

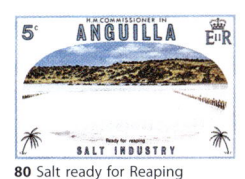

80 Salt ready for Reaping

75th Anniversary Rotary 1980
(82)

50th Anniversary Scouting 1980
(81)

(Des John Lister Ltd. Litho Questa)

1980 (14 Apr). Salt Industry. T **80** and similar horiz. designs. Multicoloured. P 14.

396	5c. Type **80**		10	10
397	12c. Tallying salt		10	10
398	18c. Unloading salt flats		15	15
399	22c. Salt storage heap		15	15
400	$1 Salt for bagging and grinding		30	40
401	$2.50 Loading salt for export		50	70
396/401 Set of 6			1·10	1·40
MS402 180×92 mm. Nos. 396/401			1·10	1·75

Nos. 396/7, 398/9 and 400/1 were each printed in the same sheet, but with the values in separate panes.

1980 (16 Apr). Anniversaries. Nos. 280, 282 and 287/8 optd with T **81** (10c., $2.50) or **82** (others).

403	10c. American Kestrel		1·75	20
404	20c. Stop-light Parrotfish		1·00	20
405	$2.50 Manchineel		1·75	1·50
406	$5 Ground Lizard		2·50	2·50
403/6 Set of 4			6·25	4·00

Commemorations:—10c., $2.50, 50th anniversary of Anguilla Scout Movement; others, 75th anniversary of Rotary International.

83 Palace of Westminster and Great Britain 1970 9d. "Philympia" Commemorative

84 Queen Elizabeth the Queen Mother

(Des Stamp Magazine. Litho Rosenbaum Bros, Vienna)

1980 (6 May). "London 1980" International Stamp Exhibition (2nd issue). T **83** and similar horiz designs showing famous landmarks and various international stamp exhibition commemorative stamps. Multicoloured. P 13½.

407	50c. Type **83**		55	75
408	$1.50 City Hall, Toronto and Canada 1978 $1.50, "CAPEX"		85	1·25
409	$2.50 Statue of Liberty and U.S.A. 1976 13c. "Interphil"		1·10	1·60
407/9 Set of 3			2·25	3·25
MS410 157×130 mm. Nos. 407/9			2·25	3·00

(Des R. Granger Barrett from photograph by N. Parkinson. Litho Rosenbaum Bros, Vienna)

1980 (4 Aug). 80th Birthday of Queen Elizabeth the Queen Mother. P 13½.

411	**84**	35c. multicoloured	70	40
412		50c. multicoloured	85	50
413		$1.50 multicoloured	1·25	1·50
414		$3 multicoloured	2·00	2·50
411/14 Set of 4			4·25	4·25
MS415 160×110 mm. Nos. 411/14			4·75	4·75

85 Brown Pelicans

SEPARATION 1980
(86)

(Des John Lister Ltd. Litho Questa)

1980 (13 Nov). Christmas. Birds. T **85** and similar vert designs. Multicoloured. P 13½.

416	5c. Type **85**		45	10
417	22c. Great Blue Heron		1·00	20
418	$1.50 Barn Swallow		2·00	60
419	$3 Ruby-throated Hummingbird		2·25	1·40
416/19 Set of 4			5·00	2·10
MS420 126×160 mm. Nos. 416/19			10·00	7·50

1980 (18 Dec). Separation of Anguilla from St. Kitts-Nevis. Nos. 274, 277, 279/89, 341 and 418/19 optd as T **86** or surch also.

421	1c. Type **62**		20	80
422	2c. on 4c. Spanish Bayonet		20	80
423	5c. on 15c. Ground orchid		1·75	80
424	5c. on $1.50 Barn Swallow		1·75	80
425	5c. on $3 Ruby-throated Hummingbird		1·75	80
426	10c. American Kestrel		2·25	80
427	12c. on $1 Sandy Island		30	80
428	14c. on $2.50 Manchineel		30	80
429	15c. Ground orchid		2·00	80
430	18c. on $5 Ground Lizard		35	80
431	20c. Stop-light Parrotfish		35	80
432	22c. Lobster fishing boat		35	80
433	25c. on 15c. Ground orchid		2·00	85
434	35c. Boat race		35	85
435	38c. on 22c. Serenading		35	85
436	40c. on 1c. Type **62**		1·00	85
437	50c. Sea Bean		40	95
438	$1 Sandy Island		50	1·25
439	$2.50 Manchineel		1·25	3·00
440	$5 Ground Lizard		2·25	4·00
441	$10 Red-billed Tropic Bird		5·00	6·00
442	$10 on 6c. Cable and Wireless Building		5·00	6·00
421/42 Set of 22			26·00	30·00

87 First Petition for Separation, 1825

(Des John Lister Ltd. Litho Format)

1980 (22 Dec). Separation of Anguilla from St. Kitts-Nevis. T **87** and similar horiz designs. Multicoloured. P 14.

443	18c. Type **87**		10	10
444	22c. Referendum ballot paper, 1967		15	10
445	35c. Airport blockade, 1967		40	15
446	50c. Anguilla flag		70	30
447	$1 Separation celebrations, 1980		40	45
443/7 Set of 5			1·60	1·00
MS448 178×92 mm. Nos. 443/7			1·40	1·25

ANGUILLA

Nos. 443/4 and 445/6 were each printed in the same sheet with the two values in separate panes.

88 "Nelson's Dockyard"
(R. Granger Barrett)

(Litho Rosenbaum Bros, Vienna)

1981 (2 Mar). 175th Death Anniv of Lord Nelson. Paintings. T **88** and similar horiz designs. Multicoloured. P 14.

449	22c. Type **88**	2·50	50
450	35c. "Ships in which Nelson served" (Nicholas Pocock)	2·50	70
451	50c. H.M.S. *Victory* (Monamy Swaine)	3·00	1·50
452	$3 "Battle of Trafalgar" (Clarkson Stanfield)	3·75	6·50
449/52	Set of 4	10·50	8·25
MS453	82×63 mm. $5 "Horatio Nelson" (L. F. Abbott) and coat of arms	3·00	3·25

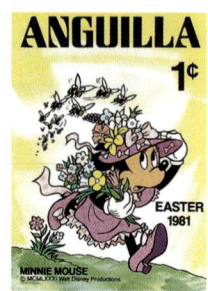

89 Minnie Mouse being chased by Bees

(Litho Questa)

1981 (30 Mar). Easter. Walt Disney Cartoon Characters. T **89** and similar vert designs. Multicoloured. P 13½×14.

454	1c. Type **89**	10	10
455	2c. Pluto laughing at Mickey Mouse	10	10
456	3c. Minnie Mouse tying ribbon round Pluto's neck	10	10
457	5c. Minnie Mouse confronted by love-struck bird who fancies her bonnet	10	10
458	7c. Dewey and Huey admiring themselves in mirror	10	10
459	9c. Horace Horsecollar and Clarabelle Cow out for a stroll	10	10
460	10c. Daisy Duck with hat full of Easter eggs	10	10
461	$2 Goofy unwrapping Easter hat	1·40	1·40
462	$3 Donald Duck in his Easter finery	1·60	1·60
454/62	Set of 9	3·25	3·25
MS463	134×108 mm. $5 Chip and Dale making off with hat	3·50	3·50

90 Prince Charles, Lady Diana Spencer and St. Paul's Cathedral

Extra flagstaff at right of Windsor Castle (R. 1/5 of each pane)

(Des R. Granger Barrett. Litho Rosenbaum Bros, Vienna)

1981 (15 June). Royal Wedding. T **90** and similar horiz designs showing Prince Charles, Lady Diana Spencer and buildings. Multicoloured. P 14.

(a) No wmk.

464	50c. Type **90**	15	20
465	$2.50 Althorp	30	50
466	$3 Windsor Castle	35	60
	a. Extra flagstaff	9·00	
464/6	Set of 3	70	1·10
MS467	90×72 mm. $5 Buckingham Palace	1·25	1·50

*(b) Booklet stamps. W w **15** (sideways*)*

468	50c. Type **90**	25	45
	a. Booklet pane of 4	75	
	ab. Black printed twice	7·50	
	w. Wmk reading upwards	25	
	wa. Booklet pane of 4	75	
469	$3 As No. 466	40	85
	a. Booklet pane of 4	1·40	
	ab. Black printed twice	7·50	
	w. Wmk reading upwards	40	
	wa. Booklet pane of 4	1·40	

*On Nos. 468/9 the normal sideways watermark reads downwards.

Nos. 464/6 also exist from additional sheetlets of two stamps and one label with changed background colours (*Price for set of 3 80p mint or used*).

Nos. 468/9 come from $14 stamp booklets. Nos. 468ab and 469ab show the black features of the portraits strengthened by a further printing applied by typography. This is particularly visible on the Prince's suit and on the couple's hair.

91 Children playing in Tree

(Des Susan Csomer. Litho Rosenbaum Bros, Vienna)

1981 (31 July–30 Sept). 35th Anniv of U.N.I.C.E.F. T **91** and similar horiz designs. Multicoloured. P 14.

470	5c. Type **91**	20	30
471	10c. Children playing by pool	20	30
472	15c. Children playing musical instruments	20	30
473	$3 Children playing with pets (30 Sept)	2·50	3·00
470/3	Set of 4	2·75	3·50
MS474	78×106 mm. $4 Children playing football (*vert*) (30 Sept)	3·50	5·00

(Litho Questa)

1981 (2 Nov). Christmas. Horiz designs as T **89** showing scenes from Walt Disney's cartoon film "The Night before Christmas". P 13½.

475	1c. multicoloured	10	10
476	2c. multicoloured	10	10
477	3c. multicoloured	10	10
478	5c. multicoloured	15	10
479	7c. multicoloured	15	10
480	10c. multicoloured	15	10
481	12c. multicoloured	15	10
482	$2 multicoloured	3·75	1·25
483	$3 multicoloured	3·75	1·60
475/83	Set of 9	7·50	3·00
MS484	130×105 mm. $5 multicoloured	5·50	3·50

92 Red Grouper   (93)

(Des R. Granger Barrett. Litho Questa)

1982 (1 Jan). Horiz designs as T **92**. Multicoloured. P 13½x 14.

485	1c. Type **92**	15	1·25
486	5c. Ferry service, Blowing Point	30	1·25
487	10c. Island dinghies	20	60
488	15c. Majorettes	20	60
489	20c. Launching boat, Sandy Hill	40	60
490	25c. Corals	1·50	60
491	30c. Little Bay cliffs	30	75
492	35c. Fountain Cave interior	1·50	80
493	40c. Sunset over Sandy Island	30	75
494	45c. Landing at Sombrero	50	80
495	60c. Seine fishing	3·25	3·25
496	75c. Boat race at sunset, Sandy Ground	1·00	2·00
497	$1 Bagging lobster at Island Harbour	2·25	2·00
498	$5 Brown Pelicans	17·00	14·00
499	$7.50 Hibiscus	11·00	16·00
500	$10 Queen Triggerfish	17·00	16·00
485/500	Set of 16	50·00	55·00

1982 (22 Mar). No. 494 surch with T **93**.

501	50c. on 45c. Landing at Sombrero	50	35

ANGUILLA

94 Anthurium and *Heliconius charithonia*

95 Lady Diana Spencer in 1961

(Des R. Granger Barrett. Litho Questa)
1982 (5 Apr). Easter. Flowers and Butterflies. T **94** and similar vert designs. Multicoloured. P 14.
502	10c. Type **94**.......................................	1·10	15
503	35c. Bird of Paradise and *Junonia evarete*......	2·00	40
504	75c. Allamanda and *Danaus plexippus*........	2·25	70
505	$3 Orchid Tree and *Biblis hyperia*............	3·50	2·25
502/5 Set of 4		8·00	3·25
MS506 65×79 mm. $5 Amaryllis and *Dryas julia*.........		2·75	3·50

(Des R. Granger Barrett. Litho Ueberreuter)
1982 (17 May–30 Aug). 21st Birthday of Princess of Wales. T **95** and similar vert designs. Multicoloured. P 14.
507	10c. Type **95**..	50	20
	a. Booklet pane of 4 (30 Aug)............	1·75	
508	30c. Lady Diana Spencer in 1968................	1·75	25
509	40c. Lady Diana in 1970...........................	50	30
	a. Booklet pane of 4 (30 Aug)............	1·75	
510	60c. Lady Diana in 1974...........................	55	35
	a. Booklet pane of 4 (30 Aug)............	2·00	
511	$2 Lady Diana in 1981............................	80	1·10
	a. Booklet pane of 4 (30 Aug)............	3·00	
512	$3 Lady Diana in 1981 (*different*)	5·50	1·40
507/12 Set of 6..		8·50	3·25
MS513 72×90 mm. $5 Princess of Wales.....................		7·50	3·00
MS514 125×125 mm. As Nos. 507/12, but with buff borders...		9·50	7·00

96 Pitching Tent

(Litho Ueberreuter)
1982 (5 July). 75th Anniv of Boy Scout Movement. T **96** and similar horiz designs. Multicoloured. P 14.
515	10c. Type **96**..	45	20
516	35c. Scout band....................................	85	50
517	75c. Yachting.......................................	1·25	90
518	$3 On parade......................................	3·00	2·75
515/18 Set of 4		5·00	4·00
MS519 90×72 mm. $5 Cooking..............................		4·50	4·00

(Litho Format)
1982 (3 Aug). World Cup Football Championship, Spain. Horiz designs as T **89** showing scenes from Walt Disney's cartoon film "Bedknobs and Broomsticks". P 11.
520	1c. multicoloured.................................	10	10
521	3c. multicoloured.................................	10	10
522	4c. multicoloured.................................	10	10
523	5c. multicoloured.................................	10	10
524	7c. multicoloured.................................	10	10
525	9c. multicoloured.................................	10	10
526	10c. multicoloured.................................	10	10
527	$2.50 multicoloured................................	2·50	1·75
528	$3 multicoloured................................	2·50	2·00
520/8 Set of 9		5·00	4·00
MS529 126×101 mm. $5 mult. P 14×13½.................		9·00	8·50

COMMONWEALTH GAMES 1982

(**97**)

1982 (18 Oct). Commonwealth Games, Brisbane. Nos. 487, 495/6 and 498 optd with T **97**.
530	10c. Island dinghies..............................	15	25
	a. "S" omitted from "GAMES"............	2·75	
531	60c. Seine fishing.................................	45	60
	a. "S" omitted from "GAMES"............	4·00	
532	75c. Boat race at sunset, Sandy Ground	60	80
	a. "S" omitted from "GAMES"............	4·75	
533	$5 Brown Pelicans................................	3·25	3·75
	a. "S" omitted from "GAMES"............	20·00	
530/3 Set of 4		4·00	4·75

The "S" omitted variety occurs on R. 2/2 of the right-hand pane for all values.

(Litho Questa)
1982 (29 Nov). Birth Centenary of A. A. Milne (author). Horiz designs as T **89** showing scenes from various "Winnie the Pooh" stories. P 14×13½.
534	1c. multicoloured................................	25	20
535	2c. multicoloured................................	25	20
536	3c. multicoloured................................	25	20
537	5c. multicoloured................................	35	20
538	7c. multicoloured................................	35	25
539	10c. multicoloured................................	50	15
540	12c. multicoloured................................	60	20
541	20c. multicoloured................................	90	25
542	$5 multicoloured................................	9·00	9·50
534/42 Set of 9		11·00	10·00
MS543 120×93 mm. $5 multicoloured......................		7·50	9·00

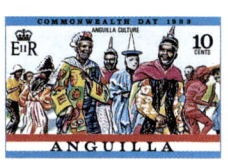

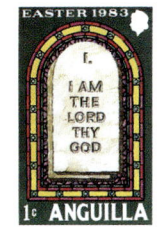

98 Culture

99 "I am the Lord Thy God"

(Des R. Granger Barrett. Litho Ueberreuter)
1983 (28 Feb). Commonwealth Day. T **98** and similar horiz designs. Multicoloured. P 14.
544	10c. Type **98**..	10	15
545	35c. Anguilla and British flags	30	30
546	75c. Economic co-operation	60	1·00
547	$2.50 Salt industry (salt pond)	3·75	5·25
544/7 Set of 4		4·25	6·00
MS548 76×61 mm. $5 World map showing position of Commonwealth countries		2·50	2·50

(Litho Questa)
1983 (31 Mar). Easter. The Ten Commandments. T **99** and similar vert designs. Multicoloured. P 14.
549	1c. Type **99**..	10	10
550	2c. "Thou shalt not make any graven image"..	10	10
551	3c. "Thou shalt not take My Name in vain"	10	10
552	10c. "Remember the Sabbath Day"............	25	10
553	35c. "Honour thy father and mother".........	65	20
554	60c. "Thou shalt not kill"........................	1·00	40
555	75c. "Thou shalt not commit adultery"........	1·25	50
556	$2 "Thou shalt not steal"......................	2·75	1·50
557	$2.50 "Thou shalt not bear false witness".....	3·00	1·50
558	$5 "Thou shalt not covet".....................	4·25	2·75
549/58 Set of 10		12·00	6·50
MS559 126×102 mm. $5 "Moses receiving the Tablets" (16th-century woodcut)..................		2·75	3·00

100 Leatherback Turtle

101 Montgolfier Hot Air Balloon, 1783

11

(Des R. Granger Barrett. Litho Questa)

1983 (10 Aug). Endangered Species. Turtles. T **100** and similar horiz designs. Multicoloured. P 13½.

560	10c. Type **100**	4·00	80
	a. Perf 12	6·00	1·50
561	35c. Hawksbill Turtle	7·00	1·25
	a. Perf 12	10·00	3·25
562	75c. Green Turtle	8·00	3·50
	a. Perf 12	11·00	7·00
563	$1 Loggerhead Turtle	9·00	7·50
	a. Perf 12	13·00	8·50
560/3 Set of 4		25·00	11·50
560a/3a Set of 4		35·00	18·00
MS564 93×72 mm. $5 Leatherback Turtle (*different*)		22·00	4·00

(Des R. Granger Barrett. Litho Questa)

1983 (22 Aug). Bicentenary of Manned Flight. T **101** and similar vert designs. Multicoloured. P 13½.

565	10c. Type **101**	50	50
566	60c. Blanchard and Jeffries crossing English Channel by balloon, 1785	1·25	85
567	$1 Henri Giffard's steam-powered dirigible airship, 1852	1·75	1·50
568	$2.50 Otto Lilienthal and biplane glider, 1890–96	3·00	3·00
565/8 Set of 4		6·00	5·25
MS569 72×90 mm. $5 Wilbur Wright flying round Statue of Liberty, 1909		2·75	3·50

102 Boys' Brigade Band and Flag

(Des R. Granger Barrett. Litho Questa)

1983 (12 Sept). Centenary of Boys' Brigade. T **102** and similar horiz design. Multicoloured. P 13½.

570	10c. Type **102**	50	15
571	$5 Brigade members marching	3·50	2·75
MS572 96×115 mm. Nos. 570/1		3·25	4·50

150TH ANNIVERSARY ABOLITION OF SLAVERY ACT
(**103**)

1983 (24 Oct). 150th Anniv of the Abolition of Slavery (1st issue). Nos. 487, 493 and 497/8 optd with T **103**.

573	10c. Island dinghies	20	10
	a. Opt inverted	38·00	
574	40c. Sunset over Sandy Island	30	25
575	$1 Bagging lobster at Island Harbour	80	50
576	$5 Brown Pelicans	10·00	2·75
573/6 Set of 4		10·00	3·25

See also Nos. 616/24.

104 Jiminy on Clock (*Cricket on the Hearth*)

(Litho Format)

1983 (14 Nov). Christmas. Walt Disney Cartoon Characters. T **104** and similar vert designs depicting scenes from Dickens' Christmas stories. Multicoloured. P 13½.

577	1c. Type **104**	10	10
578	2c. Jiminy with fiddle (*Cricket on the Hearth*)	10	10
579	3c. Jiminy among toys (*Cricket on the Hearth*)	10	10
580	4c. Mickey as Bob Cratchit (*A Christmas Carol*)	10	10
581	5c. Donald Duck as Scrooge (*A Christmas Carol*)	10	10
582	6c. Minnie and Goofy in *The Chimes*	10	10
583	10c. Goofy sees an imp appearing from bells (*The Chimes*)	10	10
584	$2 Donald Duck as Mr. Pickwick (*The Pickwick Papers*)	3·50	2·75
585	$3 Disney characters as Pickwickians (*The Pickwick Papers*)	4·00	2·25
577/85 Set of 9		7·50	5·50
MS586 130×104 mm. $5 Donald Duck as Mr. Pickwick with gifts (*The Pickwick Papers*)		10·00	11·00

105 100 Metres Race

(Litho Questa)

1984 (20 Feb–24 Apr). Olympic Games, Los Angeles. T **105** and similar horiz designs showing Mickey Mouse in Decathlon events. Multicoloured.

A. Inscr "1984 Los Angeles". P 14×13½.

587A	1c. Type **105**	10	10
588A	2c. Long jumping	10	10
589A	3c. Shot-putting	10	10
590A	4c. High jumping	10	10
591A	5c. 400 metres race	10	10
592A	6c. Hurdling	10	10
593A	10c. Discus-throwing	10	10
594A	$1 Pole-vaulting	3·25	1·25
595A	$4 Javelin-throwing	6·00	3·50
587A/95A Set of 9		9·00	4·75
MS596A 117×93 mm. $5 1500 metres race		7·50	4·50

B. Inscr "1984 Olympics Los Angeles" and Olympic emblem. P 14×13½ (No. **MS**596B) or 12 (others) (24 Apr)

587B	1c. Type **105**	10	10
588B	2c. Long jumping	10	10
589B	3c. Shot-putting	10	10
590B	4c. High jumping	10	10
591B	5c. 400 metres race	10	10
592B	6c. Hurdling	10	10
593B	10c. Discus-throwing	10	10
594B	$1 Pole-vaulting	3·75	3·00
595B	$4 Javelin-throwing	7·50	8·50
587B/95B Set of 9		10·50	11·00
MS596B 117×93 mm. $5 1500 metres race		8·00	4·50

Nos. 587B/95B were each printed in small sheets of 6 stamps including one se-tenant stamp-size label in position 2.

106 "Justice"

(Des and litho Questa)

1984 (19 Apr). Easter. T **106** and similar vert designs showing details from "La Stanza della Segnatura" by Raphael. Multicoloured. P 13½×14.

597	10c. Type **106**	15	10
598	25c. "Poetry"	20	20
599	35c. "Philosophy"	30	30
600	40c. "Theology"	30	30
601	$1 "Abraham and Paul"	85	95
602	$2 "Moses and Matthew"	1·60	2·25
603	$3 "John and David"	2·25	3·00
604	$4 "Peter and Adam"	2·50	3·00
597/604 Set of 8		7·25	9·00
MS605 83×110 mm. $5 "Astronomy"		3·00	3·00

35c

(107)

1984 (24 Apr–17 May). Nos. 485 491 and 498/500 surch as T **107**.
606	25c. on $7.50 Hibiscus (17 May)	65	35
607	35c. on 30c. Little Bay cliffs	50	40
608	60c. on 1c. Type **92**	55	45
609	$2.50 on $5 Brown Pelicans	3·00	1·50
	a. Surch at left with decimal point*	22·00	
610	$2.50 on $10 Queen Triggerfish	1·75	1·50
	a. Surch at right without decimal point*	22·00	
606/10 Set of 5		5·75	3·75

*The surcharge on No. 609 shows the figures at right of the design and without a decimal point. On No. 610 they are to the left and include a decimal point. No. 609a shows, in error, the surcharge for No. 610 and No. 610a that intended for No. 609.

108 Australia 1913 1d. Kangaroo Stamp

(Des K. Cato. Litho Leigh-Mardon Ltd, Melbourne)

1984 (16 July). "Ausipex 84" International Stamp Exhibition, Melbourne. T **108** and similar horiz designs showing Australian stamps. Multicoloured. P 13½×14.
611	10c. Type **108**	40	30
612	75c. 1914 6d. Laughing Kookaburra	1·50	1·25
613	$1 1932 2d. Sydney Harbour Bridge	2·00	1·75
614	$2.50 1938 10s. King George VI	2·25	4·00
611/14 Set of 4		5·50	6·50
MS615 95×86 mm. $5 £1 Bass and £2 Admiral King		5·00	7·00

109 Thomas Fowell Buxton

(Des R. Granger Barrett. Litho Questa)

1984 (1 Aug). 150th Anniv of Abolition of Slavery (2nd issue). T **109** and similar horiz designs. Multicoloured. P 14.
616	10c. Type **109**	15	10
617	25c. Abraham Lincoln	30	25
618	35c. Henri Christophe	40	35
619	60c. Thomas Clarkson	60	50
620	75c. William Wilberforce	70	60
621	$1 Olaudah Equiano	80	70
622	$2.50 General Charles Gordon	1·75	1·60
623	$5 Granville Sharp	3·00	3·00
616/23 Set of 8		7·00	6·50
MS624 150×121 mm. Nos. 616/23. P 12		7·50	10·00

U.P.U. CONGRESS HAMBURG 1984
(110)

PRINCE HENRY BIRTH 15.9.84
(111)

1984 (13 Aug). Universal Postal Union Congress, Hamburg. Nos. 486/7 and 498 optd as T **110** or surch also (No. 626).
625	5c. Ferry services, Blowing Point	30	10
626	20c. on 10c. Island dinghies	30	15
627	$5 Brown Pelicans	5·50	3·50
625/7 Set of 3		5·50	3·50

1984 (31 Oct). Birth of Prince Henry. Nos. 507/14 optd as T **111**.
628	10c. Type **95**	20	10
	a. Booklet pane of 4	70	
629	30c. Lady Diana Spencer in 1968	40	25
630	40c. Lady Diana in 1970	20	30
	a. Booklet pane of 4	75	
631	60c. Lady Diana in 1974	30	45
	a. Booklet pane of 4	1·10	
632	$2 Lady Diana in 1981	75	1·25
	a. Booklet pane of 4	2·75	
633	$3 Lady Diana in 1981 (*different*)	1·25	1·75
628/33 Set of 6		2·75	3·75
MS634 72×90 mm. $5 Princess of Wales		2·00	3·00
MS635 125×125 mm. As Nos. 628/33, but with buff borders		2·00	4·00

On No. MS634 the lines of overprint are larger, being placed vertically each side of the portrait.

112 Christmas in Sweden

(Litho Questa)

1984 (12 Nov). Christmas. Walt Disney Cartoon Characters. T **112** and similar horiz designs showing national scenes. Multicoloured. P 12 ($2) or 14×13½ (others).
636	1c. Type **112**	10	10
637	2c. Italy	10	10
638	3c. Holland	10	10
639	4c. Mexico	10	10
640	5c. Spain	10	10
641	10c. Disneyland, U.S.A	10	10
642	$1 Japan	3·00	2·00
643	$2 Anguilla	4·00	4·50
644	$4 Germany	6·50	7·50
636/44 Set of 9		12·00	13·00
MS645 126×102 mm. $5 England		7·00	5·00

No. 643 was printed in sheetlets of 8 stamps.

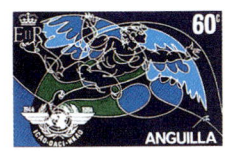

113 Icarus in Flight

(Des H. Herni (60c.), S. Diouf (75c.), adapted R. Granger Barrett. Litho Ueberreuter)

1984 (3 Dec). 40th Anniv of International Civil Aviation Organization. T **113** and similar multicoloured designs. P 14.
646	60c. Type **113**	60	75
647	75c. "Solar Princess" (abstract)	80	90
648	$2.50 I.C.A.O. emblem (*vert*)	2·25	3·00
646/8 Set of 3		3·25	4·25
MS649 65×49 mm. $5 Map of air routes serving Anguilla		3·00	4·50

114 Barn Swallow

(Litho Questa)

1985 (29 Apr). Birth Bicentenary of John J. Audubon (ornithologist). T **114** and similar multicoloured designs. P 14.
650	10c. Type **114**	1·25	75
651	60c. American Wood Stork	1·75	1·50
652	75c. Roseate Tern	1·75	1·50
653	$5 Osprey	4·75	6·50
650/3 Set of 4		8·50	9·25

ANGUILLA

MS654 Two sheets, each 73×103 mm. (a) $4 Western Tanager (*horiz*); (b) $4 Solitary Vireo (*horiz*) Set of 2 sheets .... 10·00 6·00

Nos. 650/3 were each issued in sheetlets of five stamps and one stamp-size label, which appears in the centre of the bottom row.

115 The Queen Mother visiting King's College Hospital, London

116 White-tailed Tropic Bird

(Des J.W. Litho Questa)

1985 (2 July). Life and Times of Queen Elizabeth the Queen Mother. T **115** and. similar vert designs. Multicoloured. P 14.
655	10c. Type **115**	10	10
656	$2 The Queen Mother inspecting Royal Marine Volunteer Cadets, Deal	80	1·25
657	$3 The Queen Mother outside Clarence House	1·10	1·50
655/7 Set of 3		1·75	2·50
MS658 56×85 mm. $5 At Ascot, 1979		1·75	2·50

Nos. 655/7 also exist perforated 12×12½ from additional sheetlets of five stamps and one label (*Price for set of 3 £1.75 mint, £2.50 used*).

(Des R. Granger Barrett. Litho Questa)

1985 (22 July)–**86**. Birds. T **116** and similar horiz designs. Multicoloured. P 13½×14.
659	5c. Brown Pelican (11.11.85)	1·75	1·75
660	10c. Mourning Dove (11.11.85)	1·75	1·75
661	15c. Magnificent Frigate Bird (inscr "Man-o-War") (11.11.85)	1·75	1·75
662	20c. Antillean Crested Hummingbird (11.11.85)	1·75	1·75
663	25c. Type **116**	1·75	1·75
664	30c. Caribbean Elaenia (11.11.85)	1·75	1·75
665	35c. Black-whiskered Vireo (11.11.85)	7·50	5·50
665a	35c. Lesser Antillean Bullfinch (10.3.86)	6·00	3·00
666	40c. Yellow-crowned Night Heron (11.11.85)	2·00	1·75
667	45c. Pearly-eyed Thrasher (30.9.85)	1·75	1·75
668	50c. Laughing Gull (30.9.85)	1·75	1·75
669	65c. Brown Booby	1·75	1·75
670	80c. Grey Kingbird (30.9.85)	2·25	3·00
671	$1 Audubon's Shearwater (30.9.85)	2·25	3·00
672	$1.35 Roseate Tern	2·00	3·00
673	$2.50 Bananaquit (11.11.85)	6·00	8·50
674	$5 Belted Kingfisher	5·00	8·50
675	$10 Green Heron (30.9.85)	7·00	11·00
659/75 Set of 18		50·00	55·00

GIRL GUIDES 75TH ANNIVERSARY 1910–1985

(**117**)

1985 (14 Oct). 75th Anniv of Girl Guide Movement. Nos. 486, 491, 496 and 498 optd with T **117**.
676	5c. Ferry service, Blowing Point	30	30
677	30c. Little Bay cliffs	40	35
678	75c. Boat race at sunset, Sandy Ground	60	85
679	$5 Brown Pelicans	10·00	10·00
	a. Opt double	95·00	
676/9 Set of 4		10·00	10·50

118 Goofy as Huckleberry Finn Fishing

(Des Walt Disney Productions. Litho Questa)

1985 (11 Nov). 150th Birth Anniv of Mark Twain (author). T **118** and similar horiz designs showing Walt Disney cartoon characters in scenes from *Huckleberry Finn*. Multicoloured. P 12 ($1) or 14×13½ (others).
680	10c. Type **118**	70	20
681	60c. Pete as Pap surprising Huck	2·25	85
682	$1 "Multiplication tables"	2·75	1·25
683	$3 The Duke reciting Shakespeare	4·00	4·00
680/3 Set of 4		8·75	5·75
MS684 127×102 mm. $5 "In school but out"		8·50	8·00

No. 682 was printed in sheetlets of 8 stamps.

119 Hansel and Gretel (Mickey and Minnie Mouse) awakening in Forest

(Des Walt Disney Productions. Litho Questa)

1985 (11 Nov). Birth Bicentenaries of Grimm Brothers (folklorists). T **119** and similar horiz designs showing Walt Disney cartoon characters in scenes from *Hansel and Gretel*. Multicoloured. P 12 (90c.) or 14×13½ (others).
685	5c. Type **119**	55	55
686	50c. Hansel and Gretel find the gingerbread house	1·50	60
687	90c. Hansel and Gretel meeting the Witch	2·00	1·00
688	$4 Hansel and Gretel captured by the Witch	3·50	5·00
685/8 Set of 4		6·75	6·50
MS689 126×101 mm. $5 Hansel and Gretel riding on swan		8·00	9·00

No. 687 was printed in sheetlets of 8 stamps.

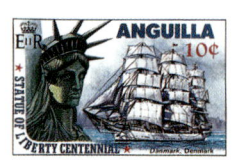

120 Statue of Liberty and *Danmark* (Denmark)

(Litho Format)

1985 (14 Nov). Centenary of the Statue of Liberty (1986). T **120** and similar multicoloured designs showing the Statue of Liberty and cadet ships. P 15.
690	10c. Type **120**	1·00	85
691	20c. *Eagle* (U.S.A.)	1·25	90
692	60c. *Amerigo Vespucci* (Italy)	1·60	1·50
693	75c. Sir Winston Churchill (Great Britain)	1·60	1·50
694	$2 *Nippon Maru* (Japan)	1·75	4·00
695	$2.50 *Gorch Fock* (West Germany)	1·75	4·00
690/5 Set of 6		8·00	11·50
MS696 96×69 mm. $5 Statue of Liberty (*vert*)		7·50	4·50

80TH ANNIVERSARY ROTARY 1985

(**121**)

INTERNATIONAL YOUTH YEAR

(**122**)

1985 (18 Nov). 80th Anniv of Rotary (10, 35c.) and International Youth Year (others). Nos. 487, 491 and 497 surch or optd as T **121** (10c., 35c.) or **122** (others).
697	10c. Island dinghies	30	25
698	35c. on 30c. Little Bay cliffs	60	45
699	$1 Bagging lobster at Island Harbour	1·50	1·25
700	$5 on 30c. Little Bay cliffs	4·25	5·25
697/700 Set of 4		6·00	6·50

123 Johannes Hevelius (astronomer) and Mayan Temple Observatory

(Des W. Hanson. Litho Questa)

1986 (17 Mar). Appearance of Halley's Comet. T **123** and similar horiz designs. Multicoloured. P. 14.

701	5c. Type **123**	55	55
702	10c. "Viking Lander" space vehicle on Mars, 1976	55	55
703	60c. Comet in 1664 (from *Theatri Cosmicum*, 1668)	1·50	85
704	$4 Comet over Mississippi riverboat, 1835 (150th birth anniv of Mark Twain)	4·50	5·00
701/4	Set of 4	6·50	6·25
MS705	101×70 mm. $5 Halley's Comet over Anguilla	4·50	6·00

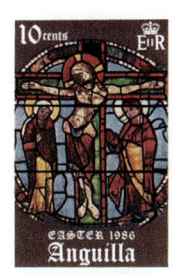

124 The Crucifixion

(Des R. Granger Barrett. Litho Questa)

1986 (27 Mar). Easter. T **124** and similar designs showing stained glass windows from Chartres Cathedral. P 14×13½.

706	10c. multicoloured	20	20
707	25c. multicoloured	35	35
708	45c. multicoloured	65	65
709	$4 multicoloured	3·75	5·00
706/9	Set of 4	4·50	5·50
MS710	93×75 mm. $5 multicoloured (*horiz*). P 13½×14	6·00	8·50

125 Princess Elizabeth inspecting Guards, 1946

AMERIPEX 1986
(**126**)

(Litho Questa)

1986 (21 Apr). 60th Birthday of Queen Elizabeth II. T **125** and similar vert designs. P. 14.

711	20c. black and yellow	40	20
712	$2 multicoloured	1·75	1·50
713	$3 multicoloured	1·75	1·75
711/13	Set of 3	3·50	3·00
MS714	120×85 mm. $5 black and grey-brown	2·75	3·75

Designs:—$2 Queen at Garter Ceremony; $3 At Trooping the Colour; $5 Duke and Duchess of York with baby Princess Elizabeth, 1926.

1986 (22 May). "Ameripex" International Stamp Exhibition, Chicago. Nos. 659, 667, 671, 673 and 675 optd with T **126**.

715	5c. Brown Pelican	60	1·00
716	45c. Pearly-eyed Thrasher	1·25	50
717	$1 Audubon's Shearwater	2·00	1·25
718	$2.50 Bananaquit	2·75	3·25
719	$10 Green Heron	6·50	9·50
715/19	Set of 5	11·50	14·00

127 Prince Andrew and Miss Sarah Ferguson

(Des and litho Questa)

1986 (23 July). Royal Wedding. T **127** and similar vert designs. Multicoloured. P. 14.

720	10c. Type **127**	50	15
	a. Perf 12	60	15
721	35c. Prince Andrew	85	35
	a. Perf 12	95	35
722	$2 Miss Sarah Ferguson	2·25	1·50
	a. Perf 12	2·25	1·60
723	$3 Prince Andrew and Miss Sarah Ferguson (*different*)	2·50	2·00
	a. Perf 12	2·75	2·25
720/3	Set of 4	5·50	3·50
MS724	119×90 mm. $6 Westminster Abbey	5·50	6·50
	a. Perf 12	5·50	7·00

INTERNATIONAL YEAR OF PEACE

(**128**)

1986 (29 Sept). International Peace Year. Nos. 616/24 optd with T **128**.

725	10c. Type **109**	90	60
726	25c. Abraham Lincoln	1·25	50
727	35c. Henri Christophe	1·40	55
728	60c. Thomas Clarkson	2·00	80
729	75c. William Wilberforce	2·00	1·00
730	$1 Olaudah Equiano	2·00	1·25
731	$2.50 General Gordon	3·75	4·75
732	$5 Granville Sharp	4·25	7·00
725/32	Set of 8	16·00	16·00
MS733	150×121 mm. Nos. 725/32	15·00	17·00

129 Trading Sloop

130 Christopher Columbus with Astrolabe

(Des R. Granger Barrett. Litho Questa)

1986 (25 Nov). Christmas. Ships. T **129** and similar multicoloured designs. P. 14.

734	10c. Type **129**	1·75	60
735	45c. *Lady Rodney* (cargo liner)	3·25	1·10
736	80c. *West Derby* (19th-century sailing ship)	4·25	2·50
737	$3 *Warspite* (local sloop)	8·50	10·00
734/7	Set of 4	16·00	12·50
MS738	130×100 mm. $6 Boat race day (*vert*)	18·00	20·00

(Des Mary Walters. Litho Questa)

1986 (22 Dec). 500th Anniv of Discovery of America (1992) (1st issue). T **130** and similar multicoloured designs. P. 14.

739	5c. Type **130**	60	60
740	10c. Columbus on board ship	1·00	60
741	35c. *Santa Maria*	2·10	1·10
742	80c. King Ferdinand and Queen Isabella of Spain (*horiz*)	1·50	1·75

ANGUILLA

743	$4 Caribbean Indians smoking tobacco (*horiz*)	3·25	5·00
739/43	Set of 5	7·50	8·00

MS744 Two sheets, each 96×66 mm. (a) $5 Caribbean Manatee (*horiz*). (b) $5 Dragon Tree Set of 2 sheets .... 15·00   17·00

See also Nos. 902/6.

131 *Danaus plexippus*

(Des R. Vigurs. Litho Questa)

1987 (14 Apr). Easter. Butterflies. T **131** and similar horiz designs. Multicoloured. P 14.

745	10c. Type **131**	1·50	70
746	80c. *Anartia jatrophae*	4·00	2·75
747	$1 *Heliconius charithonia*	4·25	2·75
748	$2 *Junonia evarete*	7·00	8·50
745/8	Set of 4	15·00	13·00

MS749 90×69 mm. $6 *Dryas julia* .... 11·00   13·00

132 Old Goose Iron and Modern Electric Iron   (**133**)

(Des R. Vigurs. Litho Questa)

1987 (25 May). 20th Anniv of Separation from St. Kitts-Nevis. T **132** and similar horiz designs. Multicoloured. P 14.

750	10c. Type **132**	70	40
751	35c. Old East End School and Albena Lake-Hodge Comprehensive College	75	45
752	45c. Past and present markets	85	50
753	80c. Previous sailing ferry and new motor ferry, Blowing Point	2·50	1·25
754	$1 Original mobile office and new telephone exchange	2·50	1·40
755	$2 Open-air meeting, Burrowes Park, and House of Assembly in session	2·75	3·25
750/5	Set of 6	9·50	6·50

MS756 159×127 mm. Nos. 750/5 .... 13·00   16·00

1987 (13 June). "Capex '87" International Stamp Exhibition, Toronto. Nos. 665a, 667, 670 and 675 optd with T **133** in red.

757	35c. Lesser Antillean Bullfinch	2·50	1·00
758	45c. Pearly-eyed Thrasher	2·50	1·00
759	80c. Grey Kingbird	3·75	1·50
760	$10 Green Heron	12·00	14·00
757/60	Set of 4	19·00	16·00

20 YEARS OF PROGRESS

1967 – 1987
(**134**)

1987 (4 Sept). 20th Anniv of Independence. Nos. 659, 661/4 and 665a/75 optd as T **134** in red or surch additionally in black (No. 762).

761	5c. Brown Pelican	3·25	3·25
762	10c. on 15c. Magnificent Frigate Bird	3·25	3·25
763	15c. Magnificent Frigate Bird	3·25	3·25
764	20c. Antillean Crested Hummingbird	3·25	3·25
765	25c. Type **116**	3·25	3·25
766	30c. Caribbean Elaenia	3·25	3·25
767	35c. Lesser Antillean Bullfinch	3·25	3·25
768	40c. Yellow-crowned Night Heron	3·25	3·25
769	45c. Pearly-eyed Thrasher	3·25	3·25
	a. Opt double, one albino	45·00	
770	50c. Laughing Gull	3·25	3·25
771	65c. Brown Booby	3·50	3·50
772	80c. Grey Kingbird	3·50	3·50
773	$1 Audubon's Shearwater	3·50	3·50
774	$1.35 Roseate Tern	4·00	4·25
775	$2.50 Bananaquit	5·00	7·00
776	$5 Belted Kingfisher	7·00	9·50
777	$10 Green Heron	9·00	12·00

761/77	Set of 17	60·00	65·00

135 Wicket Keeper and Game in Progress

(Des R. Granger Barrett. Litho Questa)

1987 (5 Oct). Cricket World Cup. T **135** and similar horiz designs. Multicoloured. P 13½×14.

778	10c. Type **135**	2·50	80
779	35c. Batsman and local Anguilla team	2·50	70
780	45c. Batsman and game in progress	3·00	75
781	$2.50 Bowler and game in progress	6·00	9·00
778/81	Set of 4	12·50	10·00

MS782 100×75 mm. $6 Batsman and game in progress (*different*) .... 16·00   17·00

136 West Indian Top Shell

(Des R. Granger Barrett. Litho Questa)

1987. Christmas. Sea Shells and Crabs. T **136** and similar horiz designs. Multicoloured. P 13½×14.

783	10c. Type **136**	1·75	55
784	35c. Ghost Crab	2·50	60
785	50c. Spiny Caribbean Vase	3·25	1·40
786	$2 Great Land Crab	6·50	8·50
783/6	Set of 4	12·50	10·00

MS787 101×75 mm. $6 Queen or Pink Conch .... 14·00   15·00

40TH WEDDING ANNIVERSARY

H.M. QUEEN ELIZABETH II

H.R.H. THE DUKE OF EDINBURGH
(**137**)

1987 (16 Dec). Royal Ruby Wedding. Nos. 665a, 671/2 and 675 optd with T **137** in carmine.

788	35c. Lesser Antillean Bullfinch	1·50	55
789	$1 Audubon's Shearwater	2·25	80
790	$1.35 Roseate Tern	2·50	90
791	$10 Green Heron	6·50	10·00
788/91	Set of 4	11·50	11·00

138 *Crinum erubescens*   **139** Relay Racing

(Des R. Vigurs. Litho Questa)

1988 (28 Mar). Easter. Lilies. T **138** and similar vert designs. Multicoloured. P 14×13½.

792	30c. Type **138**	70	25
793	45c. Spider Lily	70	25
794	$1 *Crinum macowanii*	2·00	85
795	$2.50 Day Lily	2·00	3·00
792/5	Set of 4	4·75	4·00

MS796 100×75 mm. $6 Easter Lily .... 2·75   4·50

(Des R. Vigurs. Litho Questa)

1988 (25 July). Olympic Games, Seoul. T **139** and similar vert designs. Multicoloured. P 14×13½.

797	35c. Type **139**	45	30
798	45c. Windsurfing	55	45
799	50c. Tennis	1·50	1·10
800	80c. Basketball	6·50	2·75
797/800 *Set of 4*		8·00	4·25
MS801 104×78 mm. $6 Athletics		3·00	4·50

140 Common Sea Fan

(Des R. Vigurs. Litho Questa)

1988 (28 Nov). Christmas. Marine Life. T **140** and similar horiz designs. Multicoloured. P 13½×14.

802	35c. Type **140**	1·00	30
803	80c. Coral Crab	1·75	70
804	$1 Grooved Brain Coral	2·00	1·00
805	$1.60 Queen Triggerfish	2·75	3·25
802/5 *Set of 4*		6·75	4·75
MS806 103×78 mm. $6 West Indies Spiny Lobster		3·00	4·50

H.R.H. PRINCESS ALEXANDRA'S VISIT NOVEMBER 1988
(**141**)

1988 (14 Dec). Visit of Princess Alexandra. Nos. 665a, 670/1 and 673 optd with T **141**.

807	35c. Lesser Antillean Bullfinch	3·00	70
808	80c. Grey Kingbird	4·00	1·40
809	$1 Audubon's Shearwater	4·00	1·60
810	$2.50 Bananaquit	6·00	6·00
807/10 *Set of 4*		15·00	8·75

142 Wood Slave

143 "Christ Crowned with Thorns" (detail) (Bosch)

(Des R. Vigurs. Litho Questa)

1988 (20 Feb). Lizards. T **142** and similar horiz designs. Multicoloured. P 13½×14.

811	45c. Type **142**	1·75	50
812	80c. Slippery Back	2·50	85
813	$2.50 *Iguana delicatissima*	4·50	4·75
811/13 *Set of 3*		7·50	5·50
MS814 101×75 mm. $6 Tree Lizard		14·00	4·75

(Des R. Vigurs. Litho Questa)

1989 (23 Mar). Easter. Religious Paintings. T **143** and similar vert designs. Multicoloured. P 14×13½.

815	35c. Type **143**	80	25
816	80c. "Christ bearing the Cross" (detail) (Gerard David)	1·25	75
817	$1 "The Deposition" (detail) (Gerard David)	1·40	80
818	$1.60 "Pietà" (detail) (Rogier van der Weyden)	2·00	2·75
815/18 *Set of 4*		5·00	4·00
MS819 103×77 mm. $6 "Crucified Christ with the Virgin Mary and Saints" (detail) (Raphael)		2·75	4·25

144 University Arms

(**145**) 20th ANNIVERSARY MOON LANDING

(Des R. Vigurs. Litho Questa)

1989 (24 Apr). 40th Anniv of University of the West Indies. P 14×13½.

820	**144**	$5 multicoloured	4·50	5·00

1989 (31 July). 20th Anniv of First Manned Landing on Moon. Nos. 670/2 and 674 optd with T **145**.

821	80c. Grey Kingbird	3·25	90
822	$1 Audubon's Shearwater	3·25	1·00
823	$1.35 Roseate Tern	3·75	1·75
824	$5 Belted Kingfisher	9·00	12·00
821/4 *Set of 4*		17·00	14·00

146 Lone Star House, 1930

(Des J. Vigurs. Litho Questa)

1989 (11 Dec). Christmas. Historic Houses. T **146** and similar horiz designs. Multicoloured. P 13½×14.

825	5c. Type **146**	50	1·50
826	35c. Whitehouse, 1906	1·00	45
827	45c. Hodges House	1·10	50
828	80c. Warden's Place	1·75	1·75
825/8 *Set of 4*		3·75	3·75
MS829 102×77 mm. $6 Wallblake House, 1787		4·25	6·50

147 Bigeye ("Blear Eye")

148 The Last Supper

(Des J. Vigurs. Litho Questa)

1990 (2 Apr)–**92**. Fish. T **147** and similar horiz designs. Multicoloured. P 13½×14.

A. Without imprint date at foot.

830A	5c. Type **147**	1·25	1·50
831A	10c. Long-spined Squirrelfish ("Redman")	1·25	1·50
832A	15c. Stop-light Parrotfish ("Speckletail")	80	60
833A	25c. Blue-striped Grunt	1·00	80
834A	30c. Yellow Jack	1·00	80
835A	35c. Red Hind	3·00	1·25
836A	40c. Spotted Goatfish	1·25	80
837A	45c. Queen Triggerfish ("Old Wife")	1·25	60
838A	50c. Coney ("Butter Fish")	1·25	80
839A	65c. Smooth Trunkfish ("Shell Fish")	1·75	1·00
840A	80c. Yellow-tailed Snapper	1·50	90
841A	$1 Banded Butterflyfish ("Katy")	1·50	1·00
842A	$1.35 Nassau Grouper	2·25	1·25
843A	$2.50 Blue Tang ("Doctor Fish")	2·50	3·75
844A	$5 Queen Angelfish	3·00	6·00
845A	$10 Great Barracuda	4·75	9·00
830A/45A *Set of 16*		26·00	29·00

ANGUILLA

B. With imprint date (10.6.92).

830B	5c. Type **147**		75	1·00
831B	10c. Long-spined Squirrelfish ("Redman")		75	1·00
835B	35c. Red Hind		1·00	75
830B/5B	Set of 3		2·25	2·50

(Des M. Pollard. Litho Questa)

1990 (2 Apr). Easter. T **148** and similar vert designs. Multicoloured. P 14×13½.

846	35c. Type **148**	1·25	40
847	45c. The Trial	1·25	40
848	$1.35 The Crucifixion	3·00	2·25
849	$2.50 The Empty Tomb	3·50	5·00
846/9	Set of 4	8·00	7·25
MS850	114×84 mm. $6 The Resurrection	12·00	14·00

149 G.B. 1840 Penny Black

WORLD CUP FOOTBALL CHAMPIONSHIPS 1990

(**150**)

(Litho Questa)

1990 (30 Apr). "Stamp World London 90" International Stamp Exhibition. T **149** and similar multicoloured designs showing stamps. P 14.

851	25c. Type **149**	1·25	35
852	50c. G.B. 1840 Twopenny Blue	1·75	50
853	$1.50 Cape of Good Hope 1861 1d. "woodblock" (*horiz*)	3·00	3·25
854	$2.50 G.B. 1882 £5 (*horiz*)	3·50	4·25
851/4	Set of 4	8·50	7·50
MS855	86×71 mm. $6 Penny Black and Twopence Blue (*horiz*)	13·00	16·00

1990 (24 Sept). Anniversaries and Events. Nos. 841A/4A optd as T **150**.

856	$1 Banded Butterflyfish (optd "EXPO '90")	1·75	1·25
857	$1.35 Nassau Grouper (optd "1990 INTERNATIONAL LITERACY YEAR")	1·75	1·25
858	$2.50 Blue Tang (optd with T **150**)	7·00	7·00
859	$5 Queen Angelfish (optd "90TH BIRTHDAY H.M. THE QUEEN MOTHER")	12·00	12·00
856/9	Set of 4	20·00	19·00

151 Mermaid Flag

(Des R. Vigurs. Litho Questa)

1990 (5 Nov). Island Flags. T **151** and similar horiz designs. Multicoloured. P 13½×14.

860	50c. Type **151**	2·25	70
861	80c. New Anguilla official flag	2·75	1·00
862	$1 Three Dolphins flag	3·00	1·25
863	$5 Governor's official flag	7·50	10·00
860/3	Set of 4	14·00	11·50

152 Laughing Gulls

1991 (**153**)

(Des R. Vigurs. Litho Questa)

1990 (26 Nov). Christmas. Sea Birds. T **152** and similar horiz designs. Multicoloured. P 13½×14.

864	10c. Type **152**	60	50
865	35c. Brown Booby	1·00	50
866	$1.50 Bridled Tern	2·00	2·00
867	$3.50 Brown Pelican	3·25	5·50
864/7	Set of 4	6·25	7·75
MS868	101×76 mm. $6 Little Tern	9·50	12·00

1991 (30 Apr). Easter. Nos. 846/50 optd with T **153**.

869	35c. Type **148**	1·50	60
870	45c. The Trial	1·60	60
871	$1.35 The Crucifixion	3·00	2·00
872	$2.50 The Empty Tomb	4·25	7·50
869/72	Set of 4	9·25	9·50
MS873	114×84 mm. $6 The Resurrection	13·00	16·00

On No. **MS873** the "1990" inscription on the sheet margin has also been obliterated.

154 Angel

155 Angels with Palm Branches outside St. Gerard's Church

(Des Michele Lavalette. Litho Questa)

1991 (16 Dec). Christmas. T **154** and similar designs. P 14×13½ (5c., 35c.) or 13½×14 (others).

874	5c. dull violet, chestnut and black	1·00	1·00
875	35c. multicoloured	2·50	55
876	80c. multicoloured	2·50	2·25
877	$1 multicoloured	3·50	2·25
874/7	Set of 4	8·50	5·25
MS878	131×97 mm. $5 mult. P 13½×14	13·00	15·00

Designs: *Vert*—35c. Father Christmas. *Horiz*—80c. Church and house; $1 Palm trees at night; $5 Anguilla village.

(Des Lucia Butler. Litho Questa)

1992 (21 Apr). Easter. T **155** and similar multicoloured designs. P 13½×14 (80c., $5) or 14×13½ (others).

879	35c. Type **155**	1·40	45
880	45c. Angels singing outside Methodist Church	1·60	45
881	80c. Village (*horiz*)	2·75	90
882	$1 Congregation going to St. Mary's Church	2·75	1·25
883	$5 Dinghy regatta (*horiz*)	7·00	11·00
879/83	Set of 5	14·00	12·50

$1.60
(**156**)

1992 (10 June). As No. 834, but with imprint date, surch with T **156**.

884	$1.60 on 30c. Yellow Jack	3·25	2·50

157 Anguillan Flags

(Litho Questa)

1992 (10 Aug). 25th Anniv of Separation from St. Kitts-Nevis. T **157** and similar square designs. Multicoloured. P 14.

885	80c. Type **157**	3·25	1·50
886	$1 Present official seal	3·25	1·75
887	$1.60 Anguillan flags at airport	5·00	4·00
888	$2 Royal Commissioner's official seal	5·00	6·00
885/8	Set of 4	15·00	12·00
MS889	116×117 mm. $10 "Independent Anguilla" overprinted stamps of 1967 (85×85 *mm*)	16·00	18·00

18

158 Dinghy Race

(Des Michele Lavalette. Litho Questa)

1992 (12 Oct). Sailing Dinghy Racing. T **158** and similar designs. P 13½×14 (horiz) or 14×13½ (vert).

890	20c. multicoloured	2·00	1·00
891	35c. multicoloured	2·50	75
892	45c. multicoloured	2·75	75
893	80c. multicoloured	3·50	5·00
	a. Vert pair. Nos. 893/4	7·00	10·00
894	80c. black and pale azure	3·50	5·00
895	$1 multicoloured	3·50	3·00
890/5	*Set of 6*	16·00	14·00
MS896	129×30 mm. $6 multicoloured	11·00	13·00

Designs: *Vert*—35c. Stylized poster 80c. (No. 893) *Blue Bird* in race; 80c. (No. 894) Construction drawings of Blue Bird by Douglas Pyle; $1 Stylized poster (*different*). *Horiz* (as T **158**)—45c. Dinghies on beach. (97×32 *mm*)—$6 Composite design as 20 and 45c. values.

Nos. 893/4 were printed together, *se-tenant*, in vertical pairs throughout the sheet.

159 Mucka Jumbie on Stilts

(Litho Questa)

1992 (7 Dec). Christmas. Local Traditions. T **159** and similar horiz designs. Multicoloured. P 14.

897	20c. Type **159**	1·25	40
898	70c. Masqueraders	2·50	60
899	$1.05 Baking in old style oven	2·75	1·25
900	$2.40 Collecting presents from Christmas tree	5·50	7·00
897/900	*Set of 4*	11·00	8·25
MS901	128×101 $5 As No. 900	4·00	6·50

No. **MS**901 also contains labels in designs as Nos. 897/9, but without face values.

160 Columbus landing in New World

161 "Kite Flying" (Kyle Brooks)

(Des Michele Lavalette. Litho Questa)

1992 (15 Dec). 500th Anniv of Discovery of America by Columbus (2nd issue). T **160** and similar designs. P 14.

902	80c. multicoloured	3·25	1·25
903	$1 brownish black and yellow-brown	3·25	1·25
904	$2 multicoloured	5·00	5·00
905	$3 multicoloured	5·50	7·00
902/5	*Set of 4*	15·00	13·00
MS906	78×54 mm. $6 multicoloured	15·00	14·00

Designs: *Vert*—$1 Christopher Columbus; $6 Columbus and map of West Indies. *Horiz*—$2 Fleet of Columbus; $3 *Pinto*.

(Litho Questa)

1993 (29 Mar). Easter. Children's Paintings. T **161** and similar vert designs. Multicoloured. P 14.

907	20c. Type **161**	2·00	75
908	45c. "Clifftop Village Service" (Kara Connor)	2·50	70
909	80c. Morning Devotion on Sombrero (Junior Carty)	3·25	1·40
910	$1.50 Hill Top Church Service" (Leana Harris)	4·50	7·00
907/10	*Set of 4*	11·00	8·75

MS911	90×110 *mm*. $5 "Good Friday Kites" (Marvin Hazel and Kyle Brooks) (39×53 *mm*)	5·50	7·50

162 Salt Picking

163 Lord Great Chamberlain presenting Spurs of Chivalry to Queen

(Des Penny Slinger. Litho Questa)

1993 (23 June). Traditional Industries. T **162** and similar horiz designs. Multicoloured. P 14.

912	20c. Type **162**	4·00	1·25
913	80c. Tobacco growing	2·75	1·25
914	$1 Cotton picking	2·75	1·25
915	$2 Harvesting sugar cane	5·00	7·00
912/15	*Set of 4*	13·00	9·75
MS916	111×85 mm. $6 Fishing	12·00	14·00

(Des John Lister Ltd. Litho Questa)

1993 (16 Aug). 40th Anniv of Coronation. T **163** and similar vert designs. Multicoloured. P 14.

917	80c. Type **163**	2·50	80
918	$1 The Benediction	2·75	90
919	$2 Queen Elizabeth II in Coronation robes	3·50	3·50
920	$3 St. Edward's Crown	4·00	4·50
917/20	*Set of 4*	11·50	8·75
MS921	114×95 mm. $6 The Queen and Prince Philip in Coronation coach	14·00	15·00

164 Carnival Pan Player

(Des Penny Slinger. Litho Questa)

1993 (23 Aug). Anguilla Carnival. T **164** and similar horiz designs. Multicoloured. P 13½×14.

922	20c. Type **164**	1·00	50
923	45c. Revellers dressed as pirates	1·50	40
924	80c. Revellers dressed as stars	2·50	80
925	$1 Mas dancing	2·75	3·25
926	$2 Masked couple	3·75	4·75
927	$3 Revellers dressed as commandos	4·25	6·00
922/7	*Set of 6*	14·00	14·00
MS928	123×94 mm. $5 Revellers in fantasy costumes	13·00	15·00

165 Mucka Jumbies Carnival Characters

(Litho Questa)

1993 (7 Dec). Christmas. T **165** and similar multicoloured designs. P 14×13½.

929	20c. Type **165**	1·25	80
930	35c. Local carol singers	1·60	70
931	45c. Christmas home baking	1·75	70

ANGUILLA

932	$3 Decorating Christmas tree	5·50	7·50
929/32	Set of 4	9·00	8·75
MS933	123×118 mm. $4 Mucka Jumbies and carol singers (58½×47 mm). P 14	3·50	5·00

166 Travelling Branch Mail Van at Sandy Ground

167 Princess Alexandra, 1988

(Litho Questa)

1994 (11 Feb). Delivering the Mail. T **166** and similar multicoloured designs. P 14.

934	20c. Type **166**	2·25	80
935	45c. *Betsy R* (mail schooner) at The Forest (vert)	2·75	80
936	80c. Mail van at old Post Office	3·25	1·60
937	$1 Jeep on beach, Island Harbour (vert)	3·25	1·60
938	$4 New Post Office	5·00	8·00
934/8	Set of 5	15·00	11·50

(Litho Questa)

1994 (18 Feb). Royal Visitors. T **167** and similar vert designs. Multicoloured. P 14.

939	45c. Type **167**	2·00	1·00
940	50c. Princess Alice, 1960	2·00	1·00
941	80c. Prince Philip, 1993	3·00	1·50
942	$1 Prince Charles, 1973	3·00	1·75
943	$2 Queen Elizabeth II, 1994	4·50	5·50
939/43	Set of 5	13·00	9·75
MS944	162×90 mm. Nos. 939/43	14·00	15·00

168 "The Crucifixion"

169 Cameroun Player and Pontiac Silverdome, Detroit

(Litho Questa)

1994 (6 Apr). Easter. Stained-glass Windows. T **168** and similar vert designs. Multicoloured. P 14×15.

945	20c. Type **168**	1·25	60
946	45c. "The Empty Tomb"	1·60	45
947	80c. "The Resurrection"	2·25	90
948	$3 "Risen Christ with Disciples"	5·00	8·50
945/8	Set of 4	9·00	9·50

(Des R. Vigurs. Litho Questa)

1994 (3 Oct). World Cup Football Championship, U.S.A. T **169** and similar horiz designs. Multicoloured. P 14.

949	20c. Type **169**	1·00	50
950	70c. Argentine player and Foxboro Stadium, Boston	1·75	70
951	$1.80 Italian player and RFK Memorial Stadium, Washington	2·75	3·25
952	$2.40 German player and Soldier Field, Chicago	3·75	4·75
949/52	Set of 4	8·25	8·25
MS953	112×85 mm. $6 American and Colombian players	13·00	14·00

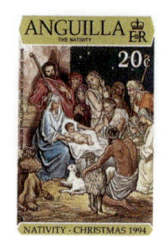

170 "The Nativity" (Gustave Doré)

(Des R. Vigurs. Litho Questa)

1994 (22 Nov). Christmas. Religious Paintings. T **170** and similar vert designs. Multicoloured. P 14.

954	20c. Type **170**	1·00	80
955	30c. "The Wise Men guided by the Star" (Doré)	1·25	80
956	35c. "The Annunciation" (Doré)	1·25	80
957	45c. "Adoration of the Shepherds" (detail) (Poussin)	1·40	80
958	$2.40 "The Flight into Egypt" (Doré)	5·00	7·25
954/8	Set of 5	9·00	9·50

171 Pair of Zenaida Doves

(Des R. Vigurs. Litho Questa)

1995 (10 Apr). Easter. Zenaida Doves. T **171** and similar horiz designs. Multicoloured. P 13½×14.

959	20c. Type **171**	65	40
960	45c. Dove on branch	85	50
961	50c. Guarding nest	90	55
962	$5 With chicks	5·50	7·00
959/62	Set of 4	7·00	7·50

172 Trygve Lie (first Secretary-General) and General Assembly

(Des R. Vigurs. Litho Questa)

1995 (26 June). 50th Anniv of United Nations. T **172** and similar multicoloured designs. P 14×13½ (vert) or 13½×14 (others).

963	20c. Type **172**	30	30
964	80c. Flag and building showing "50"	60	65
965	$1 Dag Hammarskjold and U Thant (former Secretary-Generals) and U.N. Charter	70	75
966	$5 U.N. Building (vert)	4·00	7·00
963/6	Set of 4	5·00	7·75

173 Anniversary Emblem and Map of Anguilla

(Des R. Vigurs. Litho Questa)

1995 (15 Aug). 25th Anniv of Caribbean Development Bank. T **173** and similar horiz design. Multicoloured. P 3½×14.

967	45c. Type **173**	1·75	2·00
	a. Horiz pair. Nos. 967/8	5·50	6·50

| 968 | $5 Bank building and launches | 3·75 | 4·50 |

Nos. 967/8 were printed together, *se-tenant*, in horizontal pairs throughout sheets of 10.

174 Blue Whale

(Litho Questa)

1995 (24 Nov). Endangered Species. Whales. T **174** and similar multicoloured designs. P 14×13½ (45c.) or 13½×14 (others).

969	20c. Type **174**	2·50	85
970	45c. Right Whale (*vert*)	2·75	75
971	$1 Sperm Whale	3·25	1·75
972	$5 Humpback Whale	8·50	9·00
969/72	Set of 4	15·00	11·00

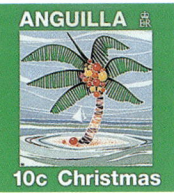

175 Palm Tree  **176** Deep Water Gorgonia

(Litho Questa)

1995 (12 Dec). Christmas. T **175** and similar square designs. Multicoloured. P 14½.

973	10c. Type **175**	1·00	1·00
974	25c. Balloons and fish	1·40	60
975	45c.	1·75	60
976	$5	10·00	11·00
973/6	Set of 4	13·00	12·00

(Des Michele Lavalette. Litho Cot Printery Ltd, Barbados)

1996 (21 June). Corals. T **176** and similar horiz designs. Multicoloured. P 14×14½.

977	20c. Type **176**	1·75	80
978	80c. Common Sea Fan	2·75	1·00
979	$5 Venus Sea Fern	8·00	10·00
977/9	Set of 3	11·00	10·50

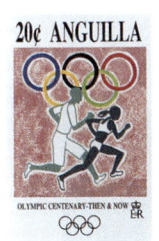

177 Running  **178** Siege of Sandy Hill Fort

(Des Iris Lewis. Litho Cot Printery Ltd, Barbados)

1996 (12 Dec). Olympic Games, Atlanta. T **177** and similar vert designs. Multicoloured. P 14.

980	20c. Type **177**	1·00	60
981	80c. Javelin throwing and wheelchair basketball	3·50	1·50
982	$1 High jumping and hurdles	1·50	1·50
983	$3.50 Olympic rings and torch with Greek and American flags	6·00	6·00
980/3	Set of 4	11·00	8·75

(Des Iris Lewis. Litho Cot Printery Ltd, Barbados)

1996 (12 Dec). Bicentenary of the Battle for Anguilla. T **178** and similar multicoloured designs. P 14.

984	60c. Type **178**	1·50	1·25
985	75c. French troops destroying church (*horiz*)	1·50	1·25
986	$1.50 Naval battle (*horiz*)	3·25	3·00
987	$4 French troops landing at Rendezvous Bay	4·50	6·00
984/7	Set of 4	9·75	10·50

179 Gooseberry

(Des Michele Lavalette. Litho Questa)

1997 (30 Apr). Fruit. T **179** and similar horiz designs. Multicoloured. P 14.

988	10c. Type **179**	60	85
989	20c. West Indian Cherry	70	40
990	40c. Tamarind	85	30
991	50c. Pomme-surette	90	40
992	60c. Sea Almond	1·00	55
993	75c. Sea Grape	1·25	85
994	80c. Banana	1·25	85
995	$1 Genip	1·50	1·00
996	$1.10 Coco Plum	1·50	1·60
997	$1.25 Pope	2·00	2·25
998	$1.50 Pawpaw	2·00	2·25
999	$2 Sugar Apple	2·75	3·25
1000	$3 Soursop	3·50	4·00
1001	$4 Pomegranate	4·50	4·75
1002	$5 Cashew	5·50	6·50
1003	$10 Mango	8·50	9·50
998/1003	Set of 16	35·00	35·00

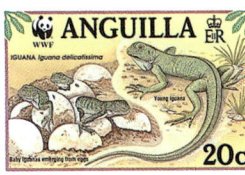

180 West Indian Iguanas hatching

1997 (13 Oct). Endangered Species. West Indian Iguanas. T **180** and similar horiz designs. Multicoloured. Litho. P 13½×14.

1004	20c. Type **180**	1·75	1·50
	a. Strip of 4. Nos. 1004/7	8·25	8·00
1005	50c. On rock	2·00	1·60
1006	75c. On branch	2·25	2·00
1007	$3 Head of West Indian Iguana	3·25	4·00
1004/7	Set of 4	8·25	8·00

Nos. 1004/7 were printed together, *se-tenant*, in horizontal and vertical strips of 4 throughout the sheet.

181 "Juluca, Rainbow Deity"  **182** Diana, Princess of Wales

(Des Clair Twaron and N. Graulke. Litho Cot Printery Ltd, Barbados)

1997 (17 Nov). Ancient Stone Carvings from Fountain Cavern. T **181** and similar horiz designs. Multicoloured. P 14×14½.

1008	30c. Type **181**	75	35
1009	$1.25 "Lizard with front legs extended"	1·50	1·00
1010	$2.25 "Chief"	2·50	2·75
1011	$2.75 "Jocahu, the Creator"	3·00	3·50
1008/11	Set of 4	7·00	7·00

(Des R. Vigurs. Litho Questa)

1998 (14 Apr). Diana, Princess of Wales Commemoration. T **182** and similar vert designs. Multicoloured. P 14×13½.

1012	15c. Type **182**	2·00	1·25
	a. Strip of 4. Nos. 1012/15	10·00	8·00
1013	$1 Wearing yellow blouse	2·75	1·60
1014	$1.90 Wearing tiara	3·00	3·00

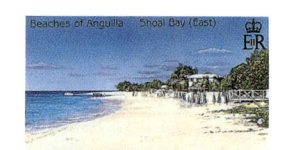

ANGUILLA

1015	$2.25 Wearing blue short-sleeved Red Cross blouse	3·25	3·25
1012/15	Set of 4	10·00	8·00

Nos. 1012/15 were printed together, *se-tenant*, in horizontal and vertical strips of 4 throughout the sheet.

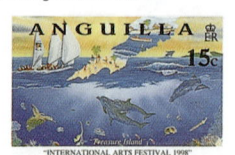

183 "Treasure Island" (Valarie Alix)

(Litho Cot Printery Ltd, Barbados)

1998 (24 Aug). International Arts Festival. T **183** and similar multicoloured designs. P 14.

1016	15c. Type **183**	60	60
1017	30c. "Posing in the Light" (Melsadis Fleming) (*vert*)	60	40
1018	$1 "Pescadores de Anguilla" (Juan Garcia) (*vert*)	90	80
1019	$1.50 "Fresh Catch" (Verna Hart)	1·25	1·75
1020	$1.90 "The Bell Tower of St. Mary's" (Ricky Racardo Edwards) (*vert*)	1·50	2·25
1016/20	Set of 5	4·25	5·25

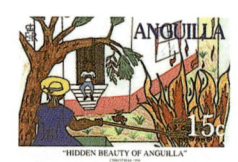

184 Roasting Corn-cobs on Fire

(Litho Cot Printery Ltd, Barbados)

1998 (18 Nov). Christmas. "Hidden Beauty of Anguilla". T **184** and similar horiz designs showing children's paintings. Multicoloured. P 14.

1021	15c. Type **184**	35	30
1022	$1 Fresh fruit and market stallholder	80	50
1023	$1.50 Underwater scene	1·00	1·25
1024	$3 Cacti and view of sea	1·60	2·50
1021/4	Set of 4	3·25	4·00

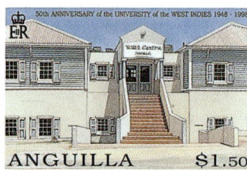

185 University of West Indies Centre, Anguilla

(Des R. Vigurs. Litho Cartor)

1998 (31 Dec). 50th Anniv of University of West Indies. T **185** and similar horiz design. Multicoloured. P 13½.

1025	$1.50 Type **185**	1·00	1·00
1026	$1.90 Man with torch and University arms	1·40	2·00

Nos. 1025/6 are on fluorescent paper. A printing on ordinary paper disappeared in transit and was not issued in Anguilla.

186 Sopwith Camel and Bristol F2B Fighters

(Des R. Vigurs. Litho Cartor)

1998 (31 Dec). 80th Anniv of Royal Air Force. T **186** and similar horiz designs. Multicoloured. P 13½.

1027	30c. Type **186**	1·25	60
1028	$1 Supermarine Spitfire Mk II and Hawker Hurricane Mk I	2·25	90
1029	$1.50 Avro Lancaster	2·50	2·25
1030	$1.90 Panavia Tornado F3 and Harrier GR7	3·00	3·50
1027/30	Set of 4	8·00	6·50

Nos. 1027/30 are on fluorescent paper. A printing on ordinary paper disappeared in transit and was not issued in Anguilla.

187 Saturn 5 Rocket and "Apollo 11" Command Module

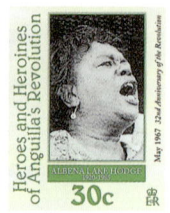

188 Albena Lake Hodge

(Des R. Vigurs. Litho Cartor)

1999 (6 May). 30th Anniv of First Manned Landing on Moon. T **187** and similar horiz designs. Multicoloured. P 13½.

1031	30c. Type **187**	55	35
1032	$1 Astronaut Edwin Aldrin, Lunar Module *Eagle* and first footprint on Moon	1·00	70
1033	$1.50 Lunar Module leaving Moon's surface	1·00	1·00
1034	$1.90 Recovery of Command Module	1·40	2·00
1031/4	Set of 4	3·50	3·50

(Litho Cot Printery Ltd, Barbados)

1999 (5 July). Anguillan Heroes and Heroines (1st series). T **188** and similar vert designs. Each black, light green and cream. P 14½×14.

1035	30c. Type **188**	40	30
1036	$1 Collins O. Hodge	80	65
1037	$1.50 Edwin Wallace Rey	1·00	1·25
1038	$1.90 Walter G. Hodge	1·25	2·00
1035/8	Set of 4	3·00	3·75

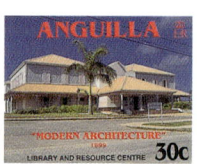

189 Library and Resource Centre

(Litho Cot Printery Ltd, Barbados)

1999 (16 Nov). Modern Architecture. T **189** and similar horiz designs. Multicoloured. P 14×14½.

1039	30c. Type **189**	45	35
1040	65c. Parliamentary building and Court House	75	70
1041	$1 Caribbean Commercial Bank	1·00	90
1042	$1.50 Police Headquarters	3·00	2·25
1043	$1.90 Post Office	2·00	3·00
1039/43	Set of 5	6·50	6·50

190 Beach Barbecue and Fireworks

(Litho Cartor)

1999 (13 Dec). Christmas and New Millennium. T **190** and similar horiz designs. Multicoloured. P 13½.

1044	30c. Type **190**	70	30
1045	$1 Musicians around globe	1·50	55
1046	$1.50 Family at Christmas dinner	2·25	1·75
1047	$1.90 Celebrations around decorated shrub	2·75	3·50
1044/7	Set of 4	6·50	5·50

191 Shoal Bay (East)

ANGUILLA

(Litho Cartor)

2000 (12 Jan*). Beaches. T **191** and similar horiz designs. Multicoloured. P 12.

1048	15c. Type **191**	40	60
1049	30c. Maundys Bay	45	30
1050	$1 Rendezvous Bay	90	60
1051	$1.50 Meads Bay	1·25	1·25
1052	$1.90 Little Bay	1·50	2·25
1053	$2 Sandy Ground	1·50	2·25
1048/53 Set of 6		5·50	6·50
MS1054 144×144 mm. Nos. 1048/53		5·00	6·00

*It was intended that Nos. 1048/54 would be released on 31 December 1999, but supplies were delayed on their way to Anguilla.

For No. **MS**1054 with "The Stamp Show 2000" on bottom margin see No. **MS**1064.

192 Toy Banjo (Casey Reid)

(Litho Cartor)

2000 (5 Apr). Easter. Indigenous Toys. T **192** and similar multicoloured designs. P 13½.

1055	25c. Type **192**	40	30
1056	30c. Spinning top (Johniela Harrigan)	40	30
1057	$1.50 Catapult (Akeem Rogers)	1·10	1·10
1058	$1.90 Roller (Melisa Mussington)	1·40	1·75
1059	$2.50 Killy Ban (trap) (Casey Reid)	1·75	2·25
1055/9 Set of 5		4·50	5·00
MS1060 145×185 mm. 75c. Rag Doll (Jahia Esposito) (vert); $1 Kite (Jawed Maynard) (vert); $1.25, Cricket ball (Jevon Lake) (vert); $4 Pond boat (Corvel Fleming) (vert)		4·75	5·50

193 Lanville Harrigan

(Des A. Melville-Brown. Litho Cartor)

2000 (5 May). West Indies Cricket Tour and 100th Test Match at Lord's. T **193** and similar multicoloured designs. P 13½.

1061	$2 Type **193**	2·25	2·25
1062	$4 Cardigan Connor	3·25	4·50
MS1063 119×102 mm. $6 Lord's Cricket Ground (horiz)		9·50	9·00

(Litho Cartor)

2000 (22 May). "The Stamp Show 2000" International Stamp Exhibition, London. Beaches. As No. **MS**1054 but with exhibition logo on bottom margin. Multicoloured. P 12.

MS1064 144×144 mm. Nos. 1048/53 .... 4·75 6·00

Stamps in No. **MS**1064 show "2000" imprint date instead of "1999".

194 Prince William and Royal Family after Trooping the Colour

(Des R. Vigurs. Litho Cartor)

2000 (20 July). 18th Birthday of Prince William. T **194** and similar multicoloured designs. P 13½.

1065	30c. Type **194**	1·75	50
1066	$1 Prince and Princess of Wales with sons	2·50	85
1067	$1.90 With Prince Charles and Prince Harry	3·00	3·00
1068	$2.25 Skiing with father and brother	3·50	3·50
1065/8 Set of 4		9·75	7·00
MS1069 125×95 mm. $8 Prince William as pupil at Eton (vert)		8·00	9·00

195 Queen Elizabeth the Queen Mother and Prince William

(Litho Cartor)

2000 (4 Aug). 100th Birthday of Queen Elizabeth the Queen Mother. T **195** and similar horiz designs showing different portraits. Multicoloured. P 13½.

1070	30c. Type **195**	65	40
1071	$1.50 Island scene	1·50	1·00
1072	$1.90 Clarence House	1·75	1·60
1073	$5 Castle of Mey	3·25	4·00
1070/3 Set of 4		6·50	6·25

196 "Anguilla Montage" (Weme Caster)

197 Dried Flower Arrangement

(Litho Cot Printery Ltd, Barbados)

2000 (21 Sept). International Arts Festival. T **196** and similar horiz designs. Multicoloured. P 14.

1074	15c. Type **196**	30	40
1075	30c. "Serenity" (Damien Carty)	35	35
1076	65c. "Inter Island Cargo" (Paula Walden)	55	45
1077	$1.50 "Rainbow City where Spirits find Form" (Fiona Percy)	1·25	1·50
1078	$1.90 "Sailing Silver Seas" (Valerie Carpenter)	1·40	2·00
1074/8 Set of 5		3·50	4·25
MS1079 75×100 mm. $7 "Historic Anguilla" (Melsadis Fleming) (42×28 mm)		4·75	6·00

(Litho Cartor)

2000 (22 Nov). Christmas. Flower and Garden Show. T **197** and similar vert designs showing different floral arrangements. P 13½.

1080	15c. multicoloured	25	25
1081	25c. multicoloured	30	25
1082	30c. multicoloured	30	25
1083	$1 multicoloured	80	60
1084	$1.50 multicoloured	1·25	1·50
1085	$1.90 multicoloured	1·50	2·50
1080/5 Set of 6		4·00	4·75

198 Winning Primary School Football Team (Bank Sponsorship)

(Litho Cartor)

2000 (27 Nov). 15th Anniv of National Bank of Anguilla. T **198** and similar multicoloured designs. P 13½.

1086	30c. Type **198**	30	25
1087	$1 De-Chan (yacht) (Bank sponsorship) (vert)	70	60
1088	$1.50 Bank crest (vert)	1·25	1·50
1089	$1.90 New Bank Headquarters	1·50	2·25
1086/9 Set of 4		3·25	4·25

ANGUILLA

199 Ebenezer Methodist Church in 19th Century

(Litho Cartor)

2000 (4 Dec). 170th Anniv of Ebenezer Methodist Church. T **199** and similar horiz design. P 13½.
1090	30c. reddish brown and black	30	20
1091	$1.90 multicoloured	1·50	2·00

Design:—$1.90, Church in 2000.

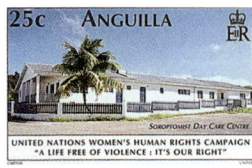

200 Soroptomist Day Care Centre

(Litho Cartor)

2001 (8 Mar). United Nations Women's Human Rights Campaign. T **200** and similar multicoloured designs. P 13½.
1092	25c. Type **200**	30	30
1093	30c. Britannia Idalia Gumbs (Anguillan politician) (*vert*)	30	30
1094	$2.25 "Caribbean Woman II" (Leisel Renee Jobity) (*vert*)	1·60	2·25
1092/4 Set of 3		2·00	2·50

201 John Paul Jones and U.S.S. *Ranger* (frigate)

(Des R. Vigurs. Litho Cartor)

2001 (11 June). 225th Anniv of American War of Independence. T **201** and similar horiz designs. Multicoloured. P 13½.
1095	30c. Type **201**	1·75	80
1096	$1 George Washington and Battle of Yorktown	2·50	1·25
1097	$1.50 Thomas Jefferson and submission of Declaration of Independence to Congress	2·75	3·00
1098	$1.90 John Adams and the signing of the Treaty of Paris	3·00	4·00
1095/8 Set of 4		9·00	8·00

202 Bahama Pintail

203 "Children encircling Globe" (Urska Golob)

(Des R. Vigurs. Litho Cartor)

2001 (6 Aug). Anguillian Birds. T **202** and similar multicoloured designs. P 13½.
1099	30c. Type **202**	1·00	65
1100	$1 Black-faced grassquit (*vert*)	1·50	1·00
1101	$1.50 Common noddy	2·00	1·60
1102	$2 Black-necked stilt (*vert*)	2·50	2·50
1103	$3 Kentish plover ("Snowy Plover")	3·50	4·00
1100/3 Set of 4		9·50	8·75

MS1104	124×88 mm. 25c. Snowy egret; 65c. Red-billed tropic bird; $1.35 Greater yellowlegs; $2.25 Sooty tern	6·50	6·50

(Litho Cartor)

2001 (9 Oct). U.N. Year of Dialogue among Civilisations. P 13½×13.
1105	**203** $1.90 multicoloured	1·60	2·25

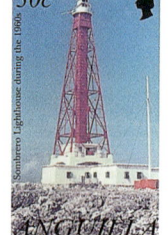

204 Triangle

205 Sombrero Lighthouse, 1962

(Litho Cartor)

2001 (5 Nov). Christmas. Indigenous Musical Instruments. T **204** and similar multicoloured designs. P 13½.
1106	15c. Type **204**	25	30
1107	25c. Maracas	35	35
1108	30c. Guiro (*vert*)	35	35
1109	$1.50 Marimba	1·25	1·25
1110	$1.90 Tambu (hand drum) (*vert*)	1·50	1·75
1111	$2.50 Bass Pan	2·00	2·50
1106/11 Set of 6		5·00	5·75
MS1112	110×176 mm. 75c. Banjo (*vert*); $1 Quatro (*vert*); $1.25 Ukelele (*vert*); $3 Cello (*vert*)	5·00	6·00

(Litho Cartor)

2002 (2 Apr). Commissioning of New Sombrero Lighthouse. T **205** and similar multicoloured designs. P 13½.
1113	30c. Type **205**	1·00	65
1114	$1.50 Old and new lighthouses (*horiz*)	2·00	1·75
1115	$1.90 New, fully-automated lighthouse, 2001	2·50	3·00
1113/15 Set of 3		5·00	4·75

206 Anguillaus of all ages

(Des Jo-Anne Mason. Litho Cartor)

2002 (28 May). 20th Anniv of Social Security Board. T **206** and similar designs. Multicoloured (except 30c.). P 13½.
1116	30c. Artist, entertainer and sportsmen (dull ultramarine and dull violet-blue)	40	30
1117	75c. Type **206**	70	65
1118	$2.50 Anguillan workers (*horiz*)	2·25	3·50
1116/18 Set of 3		3·00	4·00

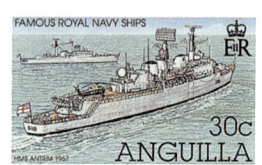

207 H.M.S. *Antrim* (destroyer), 1967

(Des R. Vigurs. Litho Cartor)

2002 (14 June). Ships of the Royal Navy. T **207** and similar multicoloured designs. P 13½.
1119	30c. Type **207**	1·25	65
1120	50c. H.M.S. *Formidable* (aircraft carrier), 1939	1·75	85

1121	$1.50 H.M.S. *Dreadnought* (battleship), 1906		2·50	2·00
1122	$2 H.M.S. *Warrior* (ironclad), 1860		3·00	4·00
1119/22	Set of 4		7·75	6·75
MS1123	102×77 mm. $7 H.M.S. *Ark Royal* (aircraft carrier), 1981 (*vert*)		8·00	9·00

208 Princess Elizabeth with Prince Charles

(Des R. Vigurs. Litho Cartor)

2002 (14 Oct). Golden Jubilee. T **208** and similar vert designs. Multicoloured. P 13½.

1124	30c. Type **208**	75	45
1125	$1.50 Queen Elizabeth wearing white coat	1·40	1·10
1126	$1.90 Queen Elizabeth in evening dress	2·00	1·75
1127	$5 Wearing yellow hat and coat	4·75	6·00
1124/7 Set of 4		8·00	8·50
MS1128 106×75 mm. $8 Queen Elizabeth sitting at desk		10·00	11·00

209 Valley Health Centre

(Litho Cartor)

2002 (9 Nov). Centenary of Pan American Health Organization. T **209** and similar horiz design. Multicoloured. P 13½.

1129	30c. Type **209**	45	40
1130	$1.50 Centenary of P.A.H.O. logo	1·25	1·60

210 *Finance* (sloop)  **211** Stone Pestle

(Des R. Vigurs. Litho DLR)

2003 (10 June). Past Sailing Vessels of Anguilla. T **210** and similar horiz designs. Multicoloured. P 14.

1131	15c. Type **210**	50	40
1132	30c. *Tiny Gull*	60	30
1133	65c. *Lady Laurel* (schooner)	80	40
1134	75c. *Spitfire* (gaff rigged sloop)	80	40
1135	$1 *Liberator* (schooner)	1·00	50
1136	$1.35 *Excelsior* (schooner)	1·25	70
1137	$1.50 *Rose Millecent*	1·50	1·00
1138	$1.90 *Betsy R.* (sloop)	1·75	1·10
1139	$2 *Sunbeam R.* (sloop)	2·00	1·60
1140	$2.25 *New London*	2·25	2·25
1141	$3 *Ismay* (schooner)	2·75	3·00
1142	$10 *Warspite* (schooner)	7·50	8·50
1131/42 Set of 12		20·00	18·00

(Litho Cartor)

2003 (18 Aug). Artifacts of Anguilla. T **211** and similar vert designs. Multicoloured. P 13½.

1143	30c. Type **211**	50	25
1144	$1 Frog worked shell ornament	1·00	75
1145	$1.50 Pottery	1·25	1·25
1146	$1.90 Mask worked shell ornament	1·50	2·00
1143/6 Set of 4		3·75	3·75

212 Frangipani Beach Club

(Litho Cartor)

2003 (3 Nov). Hotels of Anguilla. T **212** and similar horiz designs. Multicoloured. P 13½.

1147	75c. Type **212**	70	45
1148	$1 Pimms, Cap Juluca	85	55
1149	$1.35 Cocoloba Beach Resort	1·00	1·00
1150	$1.50 Malliouhana Hotel	1·25	1·10
1151	$1.90 Carimar Beach Club	1·40	1·40
1152	$3 Covecastles	2·00	3·00
1147/52 Set of 6		6·50	6·75

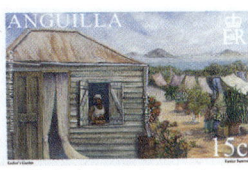

213 "Eudice's Garden" (Eunice Summer)

(Litho Cartor)

2004 (23 Aug). International Arts Festival. T **213** and similar multicoloured designs. P 13½.

1153	15c. Type **213**	50	40
1154	30c. "Hammocks" (Lisa Davenport)	60	30
1155	$1 "Conched Out" (Richard Shaffett)	1·00	70
1156	$1.50 "Islands Rhythms." (Carol Garvin)	1·40	1·25
1157	$1.90 "Party at the Beach" (Jean-Pierre Ballagny)	1·75	1·75
1158	$3 "Shoal Bay before Luis" (Jacqueline Mariethoz)	2·50	3·25
1153/8 Set of 6		7·00	7·00

214 Athlete (400 Metres)  **215** Goat

(Litho Cartor)

2004 (20 Sept). Olympic Games, Athens. T **214** and similar multicoloured designs. P 13½.

1159	30c. Type **214**	60	30
1160	$1 Laser dinghies (sailing)	1·00	60
1161	$1.50 Gymnastics (rings)	1·40	1·25
1162	$1.90 The Acropolis, Athens, Pierre de Coubertin (founder of modern Olympics) and Dimetrios Vikelas (first IOC President) (*horiz*)	1·75	2·25
1159/62 Set of 4		4·25	4·00

(Litho Cartor)

2004 (4 Oct). Goats of Anguilla. T **215** and similar multicoloured designs. P 13½.

1163	30c. Type **215**	60	30
1164	50c. Black and white goat	70	35
1165	$1 Black and tan goat (*vert*)	1·00	60
1166	$1.50 Chestnut goat	1·40	1·25
1167	$1.90 Chestnut and white goat (*vert*)	1·75	2·00
1168	$2.25 Two kids	2·00	2·50
1163/8 Set of 6		6·75	6·25

ANGUILLA

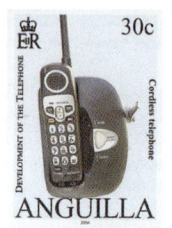

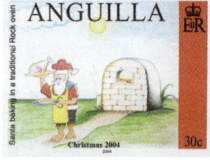

216 Cordless Telephone

217 Santa baking in Traditional Rock Oven

(Litho Cartor)

2004 (8 Nov). Development of the Telephone. T **216** and similar multicoloured designs. P 13×13½ ($1.90) or 13½×13 (others).
1169	30c. Type **216**	40	30
1170	$1 Touch tone telephone	1·00	70
1171	$1.50 Cellular phone	1·40	1·40
1172	$1.90 Circular dial telephone (horiz)	1·75	1·75
1173	$3.80 Magneto telephone	3·50	5·00
1169/73 Set of 5		7·25	8·25

(Litho Cartor)

2004 (15 Nov). Christmas. T **217** and similar horiz designs. Multicoloured. P 13×13½.
1174	30c. Type **217**	45	25
1175	$1.50 Santa climbing coconut tree	1·40	1·40
1176	$1.90 Santa's String Band	1·60	1·60
1177	$3.80 Santa delivering gifts by donkey	3·00	4·50
1174/7 Set of 4		5·50	7·00
MS1178 107×76 mm. $8 Santa delivering gifts by boat		6·50	8·00

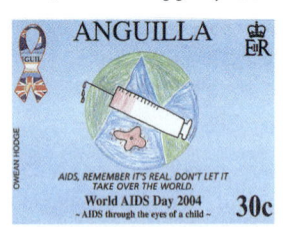

218 "AIDS, Remember it's Real. Don't let it take over the World" (Owean Hodge)

(Litho Cartor)

2005 (18 Jan). World AIDS Day 2004—"AIDS through the Eyes of a Child". T **218** and similar horiz designs showing children's paintings. Multicoloured. P 13.
1179	30c. Type **218**	45	30
1180	$1.50 "Arm Yourself against AIDS" (Lydia Fleming)	1·50	1·50
1181	$1.90 "AIDS is Your Concern" (Nina Rodriguez)	1·75	2·00
1179/81 Set of 3		3·25	3·50
MS1182 144×144 mm. 15c. Classroom (Kenswick Richardson); 75c. Dancer, Schoolgirl, Teacher, Smoker (Toniquewah Ruan); $1 Girls and Tree (Elizabeth Anne Orchard); $2 "Even I can get AIDS" (Tricia Watty-Beard)		3·00	3·50

219 Arms of Anguilla and Rotary Emblem

220 Grey Dog

(Litho BDT)

2005 (23 Mar). Centenary of Rotary International and 25th Anniv of Anguilla Rotary Club. T **219** and similar vert designs. Multicoloured. P 15×14.
1183	30c. Type **219**	40	30
1184	$1 Brown pelican and palm tree (District 7020)	1·25	85
1185	$1.50 Paul Harris (founder)	1·40	1·40
1186	$1.90 Children on slide (School Playground Project)	1·60	2·00
1183/6 Set of 4		4·25	4·00

(Litho BDT)

2005 (1 June). Dogs of Anguilla. T **220** and similar multicoloured designs. P 14×15 (horiz) or 15×14 (vert).
1187	30c. Type **220**	65	40
1188	$1.50 Black and tan dog with puppy (vert)	1·75	1·40
1189	$1.90 Black and tan dog (vert)	2·00	2·00
1190	$2.25 Tan dog	2·50	2·75
1187/90 Set of 4		6·25	6·00

221 Air Anguilla Cessna 402

(Litho Cartor)

2006 (13 Mar). Early Airlines. T **221** and similar horiz designs. Multicoloured. P 13½.
1191	30c. Type **221**	65	40
1192	40c. LIAT DHC Dash 8	70	55
1193	60c. Winair Foxtrot DHC Twin Otter	1·00	80
1194	$1 Anguilla Airways Piper Aztec	1·50	1·00
1195	$1.50 St. Thomas Air Transport Piper Aztec	2·00	1·75
1196	$1.90 Carib Air Service Piper Aztec	2·25	2·50
1191/6 Set of 6		7·25	6·25

222 Appias drusillia

(Litho Cartor)

2006 (9 Oct). Butterflies. T **222** and similar horiz designs. Multicoloured. P 13½.
1197	30c. Type **222**	65	40
1198	$1.50 Danaus plexippus megalippe	1·75	1·40
1199	$1.90 Phoebis sennae	2·25	2·25
1200	$2.75 Papilio demoleus	3·50	4·00
1197/200 Set of 4		7·25	7·25

No. **MS**1201 is left for miniature sheet not yet received.

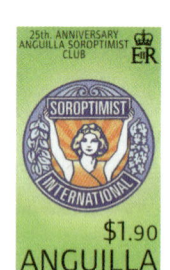

223 Soroptimist International Logo

224 St. Bruno (Carthusian founder)

2007 (29 Jan). 25th Anniv (2006) of Anguilla Soroptimist Club. T **223** and similar vert design. Multicoloured. Litho. P 13½.
1202	$1.90 Type **223**	1·75	1·90
1203	$2.75 Alecia Ballin	2·75	3·25

2007 (19 Mar). Bronze Devotional Medallions. T **224** and similar vert designs showing medallions from Spanish ship El Buen Consejo, sunk in 1772 off Anguilla coast. Multicoloured. Litho. P 13½.
1204	30c. Type **224**	40	30
1205	$1.50 Our Lady of Sorrows	1·40	1·40
1206	$1.90 Five Wounds of Jesus	1·60	1·75
1207	$2.75 Virgin and Child	2·50	3·25
1204/7 Set of 4		5·50	6·00

225 Hyacinth Carty

2008 (18 July). 40th Anniv of the Revolution (independence from St. Kitts-Nevis). T **225** and similar vert designs. Multicoloured. Litho. P 13½.
1208	30c. Type **225**	40	30
1209	$1 Edward Duncan	1·00	80
1210	$1.50 Connell Harrigan	1·40	1·40
1211	$1.90 Reverend Leonard Carty	1·75	1·75
1212	$2.25 Jeremiah Gumbs	2·00	2·50
1213	$3.75 Atlin Harrigan	3·50	4·50
1208/13	Set of 6	9·00	10·00

226 White-painted House with Gabled Roof and Lean-to

(Des Darryl Thompson ($1), Susan Croft ($1.50) or Melsadis Fleming (others). Litho B.D.T)

2008 (6 Oct). Historical Architecture. Local Houses of the 1930s–1960s. T **226** and similar horiz designs. Multicoloured. P 14×15.
1214	30c. Type **226**	40	30
1215	$1 House with gabled roof and lean-to at back	1·00	65
1216	$1.25 House with double hipped roof and flight of steps	1·25	1·00
1217	$1.50 House on seashore with hipped roof	1·50	1·10
1218	$1.90 House with double gabled roof	1·90	1·75
1219	$2.40 House with double gabled roof and verandah	2·50	2·75
1220	$2.75 House with hipped roof and verandah	3·00	3·50
1221	$3.75 House with gabled roof and flight of steps	4·50	5·00
1214/21	Set of 8	14·00	14·50

227 Three Legged Pot

228 *Tabebuia heterophylla*

(Litho Cartor)

2009 (6 Jul). Traditional Household Items. T **227** and similar horiz designs. Multicoloured. P 13½.
1222	30c. Type **227**	40	30
1223	$1 Mortar and pestle	1·10	70
1224	$1.50 Gas and coal irons	1·60	1·25
1225	$1.90 Oil and gas lamps	2·00	1·75
1226	$2 Coal pots	2·25	2·50
1227	$2.25 Enamel and aluminium utensils (wrongly inscr 'USTENSILS')	3·25	3·50
1222/27	Set of 6	9·50	9·00

(Des Jo-Anne Mason. Litho)

2009 (1 Dec). Wild Flowers. T **228** and similar vert designs. Multicoloured. P 13½.
1228	30c. Type **228**	55	50
1229	$1 *Argemone mexicana*	1·25	1·00
1230	$1.50 *Catharanthus roseus*	1·60	1·50
1231	$1.90 *Datura stramonium*	2·00	2·00
1232	$2 *Centrosema virginianum*	2·50	2·50
1233	$2.25 *Tetramicra canaliculata*	3·00	3·50
1228/33	Set of 6	10·00	10·00

STAMP BOOKLETS

1977 (9 Feb). Silver Jubilee. Multicoloured cover showing Crown and map of Anguilla. Stapled.
SB1 $8.70 booklet containing 25c., 40c., $120 and $2.50 (Nos. 269/72), each in pair .... 1·75
    a. Stamps with margin at right .... 3·50
No. SB1 was produced from normal sheets and can be found stapled at the left or the right. A further printing was later produced from specially prepared sheets, so that stamps from Booklet No. SB1a occur with small vertical margins at the right of each pair, in addition to the binding margin at left.

1978. 25th Anniv of Coronation. Multicoloured cover, 105×38 mm, showing Royal coat-of-arms and map of Anguilla. Stapled.
SB2 $9.44 booklet containing 22c., 50c., $1.50 and $2.50 (Nos. 320/3), each in pair .... 1·75
    a. Stamps with margin at right .... 2·00
No. SB2 exists with three different scenes on the back cover. A second printing of No. SB2 exists with a sheet arrangement as described for No. SB1a.

1979. Death Centenary of Sir Rowland Hill. Multicoloured cover, 104×39 mm, showing design from "Mulready" envelope on the front and coral beaches on the back. Stapled.
SB3 $9.18 booklet containing 1c.×2, 22c, 35c., $1.50 and $2.50 (Nos. 358/63), each in pair .... 2·75
No. SB3 exists with three different scenes on the back cover.

1980. "London 1980" International Stamp Exhibition. Three multicoloured covers, each 109×39 mm, showing designs from Anguilla stamps, eiher No. 384 385 or 387, on front and different views of Anguilla on the back. Stapled.
SB4 $9.70 booklet (any cover) containing 35c., 50c., $1.50 and $2.50 (Nos. 384a/7a), each in pair .... 2·50
Set of 3 different cover designs .... 7·00

1981 (15 June). Royal Wedding. Multicoloured covers, each 105×65 mm, showing Prince of Wales emblem on front and local scene on back. Stapled.
SB5 $14 booklet containing two panes of 4 (either Nos. 468a, 469a or Nos. 468wa, 469wa) .... 2·00
No. SB5 exists with three different scenes on the back cover.

1982 (30 Aug). 21st Birthday of Princess of Wales. Multicoloured cover, 105×65 mm, showing Prince of Wales emblem on front and coral beach on back. Stapled.
SB6 $12.40 booklet containing four panes of 4 (Nos. 507a, 509a, 510a, 511a) .... 7·00

1984 (31 Oct). Birth of Prince Henry. Booklet No. SB6 optd "PRINCE HENRY BIRTH 15.9.84" on cover.
SB7 $12.40 booklet containing four panes of 4 (Nos. 628a, 630a, 631a, 632a) .... 7·50

1996 (5 June). Black on salmon cover, 105×71 mm, showing flag and map of Anguilla. Stamps attached by selvedge.
SB8 $5 booklet containing Nos. 894 and 959, each ×5 .... 4·00
It is understood that fourteen other combinations of contents with 20c. and 80c. face values exist.

1998 (13 Mar). Cover as No. SB8, but surch "EC $9.00".
SB9 $9 booklet containing Nos. 792 and 998, each×5 .... 6·00
It is understood that other combinations of contents with 30c. and $1.50 face values exist.

1998 (12 Nov). Multicoloured cover, 105×71 mm, showing outline map of Anguilla and flag emblem. Stamps attached by selvedge.
SB10 $6.50 booklet containing Nos. 1017/18, each×5, plus 5 printed labels .... 3·50
It is understood that other combinations of contents with 30c. and $1 face values exist.

1999 (25 May). Multicoloured cover, 103×72 mm, showing new General Post Office. Stamps attached by selvedge.
SB11 $6.50 booklet containing Nos. 1027/8, each ×5, plus 5 labels from sheet gutters .... 3·50

STANLEY GIBBONS

Commonwealth Department
Recently offered from our ever changing stock

Antigua SG 105ab

1938-51 1s frame printed double, one albino. Only a few examples recorded.

Leeward Islands SG 114cw

1938-51 £1 perf 13, wmk inverted. Only one sheet of 60 existed.

St Kitts Nevis SG 107b

1954-63 1c imperforate vertically. Only two examples known to us.

If you would like to receive our bi-monthly illustrated list, contact
Pauline MacBroom on 020 7557 4450 or by email at pmacbroom@stanleygibbons.com
or Brian Lucas on 020 7557 4418 or by email at blucas@stanleygibbons.com

Stanley Gibbons Limited, 399 Strand, London WC2R 0LX
Tel: 020 7836 8444   Fax: 020 7557 4499

To view all of our stock 24 hours a day visit **www.stanleygibbons.com**

Antigua

It is believed that the first postmaster for Antigua was appointed under Edward Dummer's scheme in 1706. After the failure of his service, control of the overseas mails passed to the British G.P.O. Mail services before 1850 were somewhat haphazard, until St. John's was made a branch office of the British G.P.O. in 1850. A second office, at English Harbour, opened in 1857.

The stamps of Great Britain were used between May 1858 and the end of April 1860, when the island postal service became the responsibility of the local colonial authorities. In the interim period, between the take-over and the appearance of Antiguan stamps, the crowned-circle handstamps were again utilised and No. CC1 can be found used as late as 1869.

CC 1 — PAID AT ANTIGUA
CC 3 — PAID AT ENGLISH HARBOUR

ST. JOHN'S
CROWNED-CIRCLE HANDSTAMPS

CC1	CC **1** ANTIGUA (St. John's) (9.3.1850) (R.)	Price on cover	£650

Stamps of GREAT BRITAIN cancelled "A 02"

1858–60.
Z1	1d. rose-red (1857), P 14	£650
Z2	2d. blue (1855), P 14 (Plate No. 6)	£1400
Z3	2d. blue (1858) (Plate Nos. 7, 8, 9)	£900
Z4	4d. rose (1857)	£600
Z5	6d. lilac (1856)	£180
Z6	1s. green (1856)	£2750

ENGLISH HARBOUR
CROWNED-CIRCLE HANDSTAMPS

CC2	CC **3** ENGLISH HARBOUR (10.12.1857)	Price on cover	£8500

Stamps of GREAT BRITAIN cancelled "A 18"

1858–60.
Z6a	1d. rose red (1857)	
Z7	2d. blue (1858) (Plate No. 7)	£6000
Z8	4d. rose (1857)	£6000
Z9	6d. lilac	£2000
Z10	1s. green (1856)	

PRICES FOR STAMPS ON COVER TO 1945

No. 1	from × 10
Nos. 2/4	†
Nos. 5/10	from × 20
Nos. 13/14	from × 30
No. 15	from × 60
Nos. 16/18	from × 50
Nos. 19/23	from × 12
No. 24	from × 50
Nos. 25/30	from × 10
Nos. 31/51	from × 4
Nos. 52/4	from × 10
Nos. 55/61	from × 4
Nos. 62/80	from × 3
Nos. 81/90	from × 4
Nos. 91/4	from × 5
Nos. 95/7	from × 4
Nos. 98/109	from × 3

CROWN COLONY

1 — ANTIGUA ONE PENNY
3 — ANTIGUA FOUR PENCE

(Eng C. Jeens after drawing by Edward Corbould. Recess P.B.)

1862 (Aug). No wmk.

(a) Rough perf 14 to 16
1	**1**	6d. blue-green	£800	£550

(b) P 11 to 12½
| 2 | **1** | 6d. blue-green | £7500 | |

(c) P 14 to 16×11 to 12½
| 3 | **1** | 6d. blue-green | £3250 | |

(d) P 14 to 16 compound with 11 to 12½
| 4 | **1** | 6d. blue-green | £3250 | |

Nos. 2/4 may be trial perforations. They are not known used.

1863 (Jan)–**67**. Wmk Small Star. W **w 2** (sideways on 6d.). Rough perf 14 to 16.

5	**1**	1d. rosy mauve	£130	70·00
6		1d. dull rose (1864)	£120	55·00
		a. Imperf between (vert pair)	£30000	
7		1d. vermilion (1867)	£250	30·00
		a. Imperf between (horiz pair)	£30000	
		b. Wmk sideways	£250	42·00
8		6d. green (*shades*)	£650	26·00
		a. Wmk upright	—	£170
9		6d. dark green	£700	26·00
10		6d. yellow-green	£4000	95·00

Caution is needed in buying No. 10 as some of the shades of No. 8 verge on yellow-green.

The 1d. rosy mauve exists showing trial perforations of 11 to 12½ and 14 to 16 (*Price*, £8500 *unused*).

(Recess D.L.R. from P.B. plates)

1872. Wmk Crown CC. P 12½.

13	**1**	1d. lake	£180	17·00
		w. Wmk inverted	£275	80·00
		x. Wmk reversed	£180	17·00
		y. Wmk inverted and reversed		
14		1d. scarlet	£200	24·00
		w. Wmk inverted	£200	60·00
		x. Wmk reversed	—	32·00
15		6d. blue-green	£500	11·00
		w. Wmk inverted	—	£100
		x. Wmk reversed	£500	14·00
		y. Wmk inverted and reversed	—	£120

1876. Wmk Crown CC. P 14.

16	**1**	1d. lake	£200	11·00
		a. Bisected (½d.) (1883) (on cover)	†	£7500
		x. Wmk reversed	—	38·00
17		1d. lake-rose	£200	11·00
		w. Wmk inverted	£350	90·00
		x. Wmk reversed	—	35·00
		y. Wmk inverted and reversed		
18		6d. blue-green	£350	21·00
		w. Wmk inverted	†	£120
		x. Wmk reversed	£350	22·00
		y. Wmk inverted and reversed	£500	80·00

(Recess (T **1**); typo (T **3**) De La Rue & Co).

1879. Wmk Crown CC. P 14.

19	**3**	2½d. red-brown	£600	£170
		a. Large "2" in "2½" with slanting foot	£10000	£2500
20		4d. blue	£250	15·00

Top left triangle detached
(Pl 2 R. 3/3 of right pane)

1882. Wmk Crown CA. P 14.

21	**3**	½d. dull green	3·75	17·00
		a. Top left triangle detached	£300	£500
22		2½d. red-brown	£190	55·00
		a. Top left triangle detached		
		b. Large "2" in "2½" with slanting foot	£3250	£1200
23		4d. blue	£275	15·00
		a. Top left triangle detached	—	£750

1884. Wmk Crown CA. P 12.

24	**1**	1d. carmine-red	55·00	16·00
		w. Wmk inverted		
		y. Wmk inverted and reversed		

The 1d. scarlet is a colour changeling.

ANTIGUA

1884–87. Wmk Crown CA. P 14.
25	**1**	1d. carmine-red	2·25	3·75
		x. Wmk reversed	—	23·00
		y. Wmk inverted and reversed		
26		1d. rose	60·00	12·00
27	**3**	2½d. ultramarine (1887)	7·00	14·00
		a. Large "2" in "2½" with slanting foot	£160	£250
		b. Top left triangle detached	£400	£475
28		4d. chestnut (1887)	2·25	3·00
		a. Top left triangle detached	£350	£375
29	**1**	6d. deep green	60·00	£120
30	**3**	1s. mauve (1886)	£160	£140
		a. Top left triangle detached	£2000	
25/30		Set of 5	£200	£250
27s, 28s, 30s Optd "SPECIMEN" Set of 3			£150	

Nos. 25 and 26 postmarked "A 12" in place of "A 02" were used in St. Christopher.

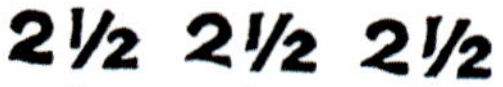

2½   2½   2½
 A   B   C

The variety "Large '2' in '2½' with slanting foot" occurs on R. 7/1 of the duty plate on all printings. At this position the "NN" of "PENNY" also sustained damage in about 1882, leaving three vertical strokes shortened. A and B (above) represent two states of the flaw at R. 7/1. Head plate 2, first used for Antigua in 1886, was a double-pane plate of 120, but the same 60-set duty plate remained in use, the variety thus occurring on R. 7/1 of each pane. A very similar flaw (C above) appeared at R. 3/1 of the duty plate (on which the "NN" was undamaged) early in the life of No. 27 and thus occurs on both panes of that stamp.

From 31 October 1890 until July 1903 Leeward Islands general issues were used. Subsequently both general issues and the following separate issues were in concurrent use until July 1956, when the general Leeward Islands stamps were withdrawn.

4    5

(Typo D.L.R.)

1903 (July)–**07.** Wmk Crown CC. Ordinary paper. P 14.
31	**4**	½d. grey-black and grey-green	3·75	6·50
32		1d. grey-black and rose-red	10·00	1·25
		w. Wmk inverted	†	£325
33		2d. dull purple and brown	7·50	25·00
34		2½d. grey-black and blue	13·00	20·00
		a. Chalk-surfaced paper (1907)	40·00	70·00
35		3d. grey-green and orange-brown	11·00	20·00
36		6d. purple and drab	32·00	55·00
		w. Wmk inverted	£190	
37		1s. blue and dull purple	55·00	65·00
		a. Chalk-surfaced paper (1907)	75·00	£140
38		2s. grey-green and pale violet	90·00	£110
39		2s.6d. grey-black and purple	27·00	65·00
40	**5**	5s. grey-green and violet	£110	£150
		a. Chalk-surfaced paper (1907)	£180	£225
31/40		Set of 10	£325	£475
31s/40s Optd "SPECIMEN" Set of 10			£200	

1908–17. Wmk Mult Crown CA. Chalk-surfaced paper (2d., 3d. to 2s.). P 14.
41	**4**	½d. green	4·50	4·75
		w. Wmk inverted		
42		½d. blue-green (1917)	7·00	7·00
43		1d. red (1909)	11·00	2·25
44		1d. scarlet (5.8.15)	7·50	3·25
		w. Wmk inverted		
45		2d. dull purple and brown (1912)	4·75	32·00
46		2½d. ultramarine	21·00	16·00
		a. Blue	32·00	24·00
47		3d. grey-green and orange-brown (1912)	6·50	19·00
48		6d. purple and drab (1911)	7·50	40·00
49		1s. blue and dull purple	23·00	70·00
50		2s. grey-green and violet (1912)	£110	£130
41/50		Set of 8	£170	£275
41s, 43s, 46s Optd "SPECIMEN" Set of 3			80·00	

1913. As T **5**, but portrait of George V. Wmk Mult Crown CA. Chalk-surfaced paper. P 14.
51		5s. grey-green and violet	95·00	£150
		s. Optd "SPECIMEN"	85·00	

WAR STAMP
(**7**)

1916 (Sept)–**17.** No. 41 optd in London with T **7**.
52	**4**	½d. green (Bk.)	4·00	2·75
53		½d. green (R.) (1.10.17)	1·50	2·50

1918 (July). Optd with T **7**. Wmk Mult Crown CA. P 14.
54	**4**	1½d. orange	1·00	1·25
52s/4s Optd "SPECIMEN" Set of 3			£100	

8

(Typo D.L.R.)

1921–29. P 14.

(a) Wmk Mult Crown CA. Chalk-surfaced paper
55	**8**	3d. purple/*pale yellow*	4·50	13·00
56		4d. grey-black and red/*pale yellow* (1922)	2·25	5·50
57		1s. black/*emerald*	4·25	9·00
		y. Wmk inverted and reversed	£375	
58		2s. purple and blue/*blue*	13·00	28·00
59		2s.6d. black and red/*blue*	17·00	65·00
60		5s. green and red/*pale yellow* (1922)	8·50	50·00
61		£1 purple and black/*red* (1922)	£250	£350
55/61 Set of 7			£275	£450
55s/61s Optd "SPECIMEN" Set of 7			£200	

(b) Wmk Mult Script CA. Chalk-surfaced paper (3d. to 4s.)
62	**8**	½d. dull green	3·00	50
63		1d. carmine-red	4·25	50
64		1d. bright violet (1923)	6·50	1·50
		a. *Mauve*	19·00	7·00
65		1d. bright scarlet (1929)	35·00	4·25
67		1½d. dull orange (1922)	5·50	7·00
68		1½d. carmine-red (1926)	9·00	1·75
69		1½d. pale red-brown (1929)	3·00	60
70		2d. grey	4·00	70
		a. Wmk sideways	†	£3250
71		2½d. bright blue	7·50	17·00
72		2½d. orange-yellow (1923)	2·50	17·00
73		2½d. ultramarine (1927)	12·00	4·50
74		3d. purple/*pale yellow* (1925)	11·00	8·50
75		6d. dull and bright purple (1922)	7·00	4·75
76		1s. black/*emerald* (1929)	6·00	4·00
77		2s. purple and blue/*blue* (1927)	11·00	65·00
78		2s.6d. black and red/*blue* (1927)	48·00	35·00
79		3s. green and violet (1922)	50·00	£100
80		4s. grey-black and red (1922)	50·00	75·00
62/80 Set of 16			£200	£300
62s/80s Optd or Perf (Nos. 65, 69, 76) "SPECIMEN" Set of 18			£425	

9 Old Dockyard, English Harbour

10 Government House, St. John's

11 Nelson's *Victory*

12 Sir Thomas Warner's *Concepcion*

(Des Mrs. J. Goodwin (5s.), Waterlow (others). Recess Waterlow)

1932 (27 Jan). Tercentenary. Wmk Mult Script CA. P 12½.
81	**9**	½d. green	4·50	7·50
82		1d. scarlet	6·00	7·50

83		1½d. brown		3·75	4·75
84	10	2d. grey		7·50	26·00
85		2½d. deep blue		7·50	8·50
86		3d. orange		7·50	12·00
87	11	6d. violet		15·00	12·00
88		1s. olive-green		20·00	32·00
89		2s.6d. claret		55·00	75·00
90	12	5s. black and chocolate		£110	£140
81/90 Set of 10				£200	£300
81s/90s Perf "SPECIMEN" Set of 10					£225

Examples of all values are known showing a forged St. John's postmark dated "MY 18 1932".

13 Windsor Castle

Diagonal line by turret (Plate 2A R. 10/1 and 10/2)

Dot to left of chapel (Plate 2B R. 8/3)

Dot by flagstaff (Plate 4 R. 8/4)

(Des H. Fleury. Recess D.L.R.)

1935 (6 May). Silver Jubilee. Wmk Mult Script CA. P 13½×14.

91	13	1d. deep blue and carmine		3·00	4·00
		f. Diagonal line by turret		£100	
92		1½d. ultramarine and grey		2·75	1·50
93		2½d. brown and deep blue		7·00	1·60
		g. Dot to left of chapel		£225	£225
94		1s. slate and purple		8·50	17·00
		a. Frame printed double, one albino		£1900	
		h. Dot by flagstaff		£375	
91/94 Set of 4				19·00	22·00
91s/4s Perf "SPECIMEN" Set of 4					£110

14 King George VI and Queen Elizabeth

(Des D.L.R. Recess B.W.)

1937 (12 May). Coronation. Wmk Mult Script CA. P 11×11½.

95	14	1d. carmine		70	2·75
96		1½d. yellow-brown		60	2·50
97		2½d. blue		2·25	3·00
95/7 Set of 3				3·25	7·50
95s/97s Perf "SPECIMEN" Set of 3					95·00

15 English Harbour  **16** Nelson's Dockyard

16a Fort James  **16b** St. John's Harbour

(Recess Waterlow)

1938 (15 Nov)–**51**. Wmk Mult Script CA. P 12½.

98	15	½d. green		40	1·25
99	16	1d. scarlet		3·50	2·50
		a. Red (8.42 and 11.47)		5·50	3·00
100		1½d. chocolate-brown		8·50	2·25
		a. Dull reddish brown (12.43)		2·75	4·00
		b. Lake-brown (7.49)		32·00	14·00
101	15	2d. grey		1·00	1·00
		a. Slate-grey (6.51)		9·50	6·50
102	16	2½d. deep ultramarine		1·25	80
103	16a	3d. orange		1·25	1·00
104	16b	6d. violet		4·50	1·25
105		1s. black and brown		6·00	2·00
		a. Black and red-brown (7.49)		32·00	11·00
		ab. Frame ptd double, one albino		£6000	
106	16a	2s.6d. brown-purple		50·00	19·00
		a. Maroon (8.42)		35·00	19·00
107	16b	5s. olive-green		15·00	12·00
108	16a	10s. magenta (1.4.48)		21·00	35·00
109	–	£1 slate-green (1.4.48)		42·00	65·00
98/109 Set of 12				£120	£130
98s/109s Perf "SPECIMEN" Set of 12					£250

17 Houses of Parliament, London

(Des and recess D.L.R.)

1946 (1 Nov). Victory. Wmk Mult Script CA. P 13½×14.

110	17	1½d. brown		30	10
111		3d. red-orange		30	50
110s/11s Perf "SPECIMEN" Set of 2					90·00

18 King George VI and Queen Elizabeth  **19**

(Des and photo Waterlow (T **18**). Design recess; name typo B.W. (T **19**))

1949 (3 Jan). Royal Silver Wedding. Wmk Mult Script CA.

112	18	2½d. ultramarine (P 14×15)		50	2·75
113	19	5s. grey-olive (P 11½×11)		15·00	12·00

ANTIGUA

20 Hermes, Globe and Forms of Transport
21 Hemispheres, Jet-powered Vickers Viking Airliner and Steamer 
22 Hermes and Globe 
23 U.P.U. Monument 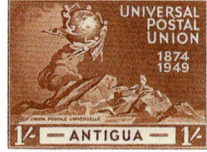

(Recess Waterlow (T **20**, **23**). Designs recess, name typo B.W. (T **21/2**).)
1949 (10 Oct). 75th Anniv of Universal Postal Union. Wmk Mult Script CA.

114	**20**	2½d. ultramarine (P 13½–14)	40	75
115	**21**	3d. orange (P 11×11½)	2·00	3·25
116	**22**	6d. purple (P 11×11½)	45	3·00
117	**23**	1s. red-brown (P 13½–14)	45	1·25
114/17 Set of 4			3·00	7·50

(New Currency. 100 cents = 1 West Indian, later Eastern Caribbean, dollar)

24 Arms of University
25 Princess Alice 

(Recess Waterlow)
1951 (16 Feb). Inauguration of B.W.I. University College. Wmk Mult Script CA. P 14×14½.

118	**24**	3c. black and brown	55	1·75
119	**25**	12c. black and violet	1·00	2·00

26 Queen Elizabeth II
27 Martello Tower 

(Des and eng B.W. Recess D.L.R.)
1953. (2 June). Coronation. Wmk Mult Script CA. P 13½×13.

120	**26**	2c. black and deep yellow-green	30	75

(Recess Waterlow until 1961, then D.L.R.)
1953 (2 Nov)–**62**. Designs previously used for King George VI issue, but with portrait of Queen Elizabeth II as in T **27**. Wmk Mult Script CA. P 13×13½ (horiz) or 13½×13 (vert).

120a	**16a**	½c. brown (3.7.56)	40	40
121	**15**	1c. slate-grey	30	1·75
		a. Slate (7.11.61)	3·00	3·50
122	**16**	2c. green	30	10
123		3c. black and orange-yellow	40	20
		a. Black and yellow-orange (5.12.61)	3·50	2·75
124	**15**	4c. scarlet	1·25	10
		a. Brown-red (11.12.62)	1·25	50
125	**16**	5c. black and slate-lilac	2·50	40
126	**16a**	6c. yellow-ochre	2·25	10
		a. Dull yellow-ochre (5.12.61)	8·50	2·75
127	**27**	8c. deep blue	2·50	10
128	**16b**	12c. violet	2·25	10
129		24c. black and chocolate	5·00	15
130	**27**	48c. purple and deep blue	10·00	2·75
131	**16a**	60c. maroon	7·50	80
132	**16b**	$1.20 olive green	4·25	70
		a. Yellowish olive (10.8.55)	3·75	1·00
133	**16**	$2.40 bright reddish purple	17·00	12·00
134	**16a**	$4.80 slate-blue	23·00	27·00
120a/134 Set of 15			70·00	42·00

See also Nos. 149/58.

28 Federation Map
(29) COMMEMORATION ANTIGUA CONSTITUTION 1960

(Recess B.W.)
1958 (22 Apr). Inauguration of British Caribbean Federation. W w **12**. P 11½×11.

135	**28**	3c. deep green	1·25	30
136		6c. blue	1·40	2·75
137		12c. scarlet	1·60	75
135/137 Set of 3			3·75	3·50

MINISTERIAL GOVERNMENT

1960 (1 Jan). New Constitution. Nos. 123 and 128 optd with T **29**.

138		3c. black and orange-yellow (R)	15	15
139		12c. violet	15	15

30 Nelson's Dockyard and Admiral Nelson
31 Stamp of 1862 and R.M.S.P. *Solent I* at English Harbour 

(Recess B.W.)
1961 (14 Nov). Restoration of Nelson's Dockyard. W w **12**. P 11½×11.

140	**30**	20c. purple and brown	1·60	1·60
141		30c. green and blue	1·75	2·25

(Des A. W. Money. Recess B.W.)
1962 (1 Aug). Stamp Centenary. W w **12**. P 13½.

142	**31**	3c. purple and deep green	90	10
143		10c. blue and deep green	1·00	10
144		12c. deep sepia and deep green	1·10	10
145		50c. orange-brown and deep green	1·50	2·25
142/145 Set of 4			4·00	2·25

32 Protein Foods
33 Red Cross Emblem 

(Des M. Goaman. Photo Harrison)
1963 (4 June). Freedom from Hunger. W w **12**. P 14×14½.

146	**32**	12c. bluish green	15	15

(Des V. Whiteley. Litho B.W.)
1963 (2 Sept). Red Cross Centenary. W w **12**. P 13½.

147	**33**	3c. red and black	30	1·00
148		12c. red and blue	45	1·25

(Recess D.L.R.)
1963 (16 Sept)–**65**. As 1953–61 but wmk w **12**.

149	**16a**	½c. brown (13.4.65)	2·75	75
150	**15**	1c. slate (13.4.65)	1·50	1·00
151	**16**	2c. green	70	30
152		3c. black and yellow-orange	45	20
153	**15**	4c. brown-red	30	2·25
154	**16**	5c. black and slate-lilac	20	10
		a. Black and reddish violet (15.1.65)	20	10
155	**16a**	6c. yellow-ochre	60	30
156	**27**	8c. deep blue	30	20
157	**16b**	12c. violet	1·25	20
158		24c. black and deep chocolate	6·50	70
		a. Black and chocolate-brown (28.4.65)	8·50	3·50
149/158 Set of 10			13·00	5·50

ANTIGUA

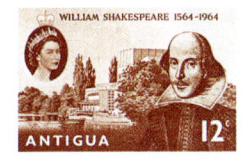

34 Shakespeare and Memorial Theatre, Stratford-upon-Avon

(Des R. Granger Barrett. Photo Harrison)

1964 (23 April). 400th Birth Anniv of William Shakespeare. W w **12**. P 14×14½.

164	**34**	12c. orange-brown	30	10
		w. Wmk inverted	80·00	

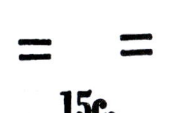

(35) **36** I.T.U. Emblem

1965 (1 April). No. 157 surch with T **35**.

165		15c. on 12c. violet	10	10

(Des M. Goaman. Litho Enschedé)

1965. I.T.U. Centenary. W w **12**. P 11×11½.

166	**36**	2c. light blue and light red	25	15
167		50c. orange-yellow and ultramarine	75	1·25

37 I.C.Y. Emblem

(Des V. Whiteley. Litho Harrison)

1965 (25 Oct). International Co-operation Year. W w **12**. P 14½.

168	**37**	4c. reddish purple and turquoise-green	20	10
169		15c. deep bluish green and lavender	30	20

38 Sir Winston Churchill, and St. Paul's Cathedral in Wartime

(Des Jennifer Toombs. Photo Harrison)

1966 (24 Jan). Churchill Commemoration. Printed in black, cerise and gold and with background in colours stated. W w **12**. P 14.

170	**38**	½c. new blue	10	1·75
		a. Value omitted	£750	
171		4c. deep green	65	10
172		25c. brown	1·50	45
173		35c. bluish violet	1·50	55
170/3	Set of 4		3·25	2·50

No. 170a was caused by misplacement of the gold and also shows "ANTIGUA" moved to the right.

39 Queen Elizabeth II and Duke of Edinburgh

(Des H. Baxter. Litho B.W.)

1966 (4 Feb). Royal Visit. W w **12**. P 11×12.

174	**39**	6c. black and ultramarine	1·50	1·10
175		15c. black and magenta	1·50	1·40

40 Footballer's Legs, Ball and Jules Rimet Cup

(Des V. Whiteley. Litho Harrison)

1966 (1 July). World Cup Football Championship. W w **12** (sideways). P 14.

176	**40**	6c. violet, yellow-green, lake and yellow-brown	20	75
177		35c. chocolate, blue-green, lake and yellow-brown	60	25

41 W.H.O. Building

(Des M. Goaman. Litho Harrison)

1966 (20 Sept). Inauguration of W.H.O. Headquarters, Geneva. W w **12** (sideways). P 14.

178	**41**	2c. black, yellow-green and light blue	20	25
179		15c. black, light purple and yellow-brown	1·25	25

42 Nelson's Dockyard

(Des, eng and recess B.W.)

1966 (1 Nov)–**70**. Horiz designs as T **42**. W w **12**. Ordinary paper. P 11½×11.

180	½c. green and turquoise-blue	10	1·25
	a. Perf 13½ (24.6.69)	10	2·50
181	1c. purple and cerise	10	30
	a. Perf 13½ (24.6.69)	10	1·50
	ab. Glazed paper (30.9.69)	75	20
182	2c. slate-blue and yellow-orange	10	20
	a. Perf 13½ (24.6.69)	10	75
	ab. Glazed paper (30.9.69)	1·25	10
183	3c. rose-red and black	30	30
	a. Perf 13½ (24.6.69)	15	15
184	4c. slate-violet and brown	1·75	10
	a. Perf 13½ (24.6.69)	15	30
	ab. Glazed paper (6.4.70)	16·00	2·75
185	5c. ultramarine and yellow-olive	10	10
	a. Perf 13½ (24.6.69)	15	10
	ab. Glazed paper (30.9.69)	40	10
186	6c. salmon and purple	1·75	30
	a. Perf 13½ (24.6.69)	15	1·00
187	10c. emerald and rose-red	15	15
	a. Perf 13½ (24.6.69)	15	15
	ab. Glazed paper (30.9.69)	4·00	10
188	15c. brown and new blue	1·75	10
	a. Perf 13½ (*glazed paper*) (30.9.69)	55	10
189	25c. slate-blue and sepia	35	20
	a. Perf 13½ (*glazed paper*) (30.9.69)	45	10
190	35c. cerise and blackish brown	1·50	55
	a. Perf 13½ (*glazed paper*) (30.9.69)	60	1·00
191	50c. dull green and black	3·25	2·50
	a. Perf 13½ (*glazed paper*) (30.9.69)	70	2·25
192	75c. greenish blue and ultramarine	4·25	2·50
193	$1 cerise and yellow-olive	11·00	2·50
	a. Carmine and yellow-olive (14.5.68)	42·00	16·00
	b. Perf 13½ (*glazed paper*) (30.9.69)	1·25	5·00
194	$2.50 black and cerise	10·00	8·50
	a. Perf 13½ (*glazed paper*) (30.9.69)	1·50	8·00
195	$5 olive-green and slate-violet	12·00	6·50
	a. Perf 13½ (*glazed paper*) (30.9.69)	12·00	24·00
180/195	Set of 16	42·00	23·00
180a/195a	Set of 15	16·00	40·00

ANTIGUA

Designs:—1c. Old Post Office, St. John's; 2c. Health Centre; 3c. Teachers' Training College; 4c. Martello Tower, Barbuda; 5c. Ruins of Officers' Quarters, Shirley Heights; 6c. Government House, Barbuda; 10c. Princess Margaret School; 15c. Air Terminal building; 25c. General Post Office; 35c. Clarence House; 50c. Government House, St. John's; 75c. Administration Building; $1, Courthouse, St. John's; $2.50, Magistrates' Court; $5, St. John's Cathedral.

54 "Education"

55 "Science"

56 "Culture"

(Des Jennifer Toombs. Litho Harrison)

1966 (1 Dec). 20th Anniv of U.N.E.S.C.O. W w **12** (sideways). P 14.

196	**54**	4c. slate-violet, red, yellow and orange	20	10
197	**55**	25c. orange-yellow, violet and deep olive	45	10
198	**56**	$1 black, bright purple and orange	90	2·25
196/198 Set of 3			1·40	2·25

ASSOCIATED STATEHOOD

57 State Flag and Maps

(Des W. D. Cribbs. Photo Harrison)

1967 (27 Feb). Statehood. T **57** and similar horiz designs. Multicoloured. W w **12** (sideways*). P 14.

199		4c. Type **57**	10	10
200		15c. State Flag	10	20
		w. Wmk Crown to right of CA	1·75	
201		25c. Premier's Office and State Flag	10	25
202		35c. As 15c.	15	25
199/202 Set of 4			40	70

*The normal sideways watermark shows Crown to left of CA, as seen from the back of the stamp.

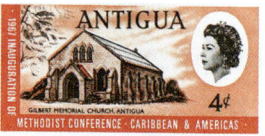

60 Gilbert Memorial Church

(Des G. Drummond (from sketches by W. D. Cribbs). Photo Harrison)

1967 (18 May). Attainment of Autonomy by the Methodist Church. T **60** and similar horiz designs. W w **12**. P 14½×13½.

203	4c. black and orange-red	10	10
204	25c. black and bright green	15	15
205	35c. black and bright blue	15	15
203/205 Set of 3		35	35

Designs:—25c. Nathaniel Gilbert's House; 35c. Caribbean and Central American map.

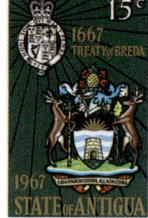

63 Coat of Arms  **64** Susan Constant (settlers' ship)

(Des V. Whiteley (from sketches by W. D. Cribbs). Photo Harrison)

1967 (21 July). 300th Anniv of Treaty of Breda and Grant of New Arms. W w **12** (sideways*). P 14½×14.

206	**63**	15c. multicoloured	15	10
		w. Wmk Crown to right of CA	10·00	10·00
207		35c. multicoloured	15	10

*The normal sideways watermark shows Crown to left of CA, as seen from the back of the stamp.

(Des and recess B.W.)

1967 (14 Dec). 300th Anniv of Barbuda Settlement. T **64** and similar horiz design. W w **12**. P 11½×11.

208	**64**	4c. deep ultramarine	45	10
209	–	6c. purple	45	1·25
210	**64**	25c. emerald	50	20
211	–	35c. black	55	25
208/11 Set of 4			1·75	1·50

Design:—6, 35c. Risen's map of 1665.

66 Tracking Station  **70** Limbo-dancing

(Des G. Vasarhelyi. Photo Harrison)

1968 (29 Mar). N.A.S.A. Apollo Project. Inauguration of Dow Hill Tracking Station. T **66** and similar vert designs in deep blue, orange yellow and black. W w **12** (sideways). P 14½×14.

212	4c. Type **66**	10	10
213	15c. Antenna and spacecraft taking off	20	10
214	25c. Spacecraft approaching Moon	20	10
215	50c. Re-entry of space capsule	30	40
212/215 Set of 4		70	60

(Des and photo Harrison)

1968 (1 July). Tourism. T **70** and similar horiz designs. Multicoloured. W w **12**. P 14½×14.

216	½c. Type **70**	10	50
217	15c. Water-skiing and bathers	30	10
218	25c. Yachts and beach	30	10
219	35c. Underwater swimming	30	10
220	50c. Type **70**	35	1·25
216/220 Set of 5		1·25	1·75

74 Old Harbour in 1768 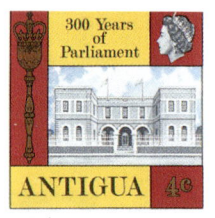 **78** Parliament Buildings

(Des R. Granger Barrett. Recess B.W.)

1968 (31 Oct). Opening of St. John's Deep Water Harbour. T **74** and similar horiz designs. W w **12**. P 13.

221	2c. light blue and carmine	10	40
222	15c. light yellow-green and sepia	35	10
223	25c. olive-yellow and blue	40	10
224	35c. salmon and emerald	50	10

225	$1 black		90	2·00
221/225	Set of 5		2·00	2·25

Designs:—15c. Old Harbour in 1829; 25c. Freighter and chart of New Harbour; 35c. New Harbour, 1968; $1, Type **74**.

(Des R. Granger Barrett. Photo Harrison)

1969 (3 Feb). Tercentenary of Parliament. T **78** and similar square designs. Multicoloured. W w **12** (sideways). P 12½.

226	4c. Type **78**		10	10
227	15c. Antigua Mace and bearer		20	10
228	25c. House of Representatives' Room		20	10
229	50c. Coat of arms and Seal of Antigua		30	1·60
226/229	Set of 4		70	1·75

82 Freight Transport

(Des Jennifer Toombs. Litho D.L.R.)

1969 (14 Apr). 1st Anniv of CARIFTA (Caribbean Free Trade Area). T **82** and similar design. W w **12** (sideways on 4c., 15c). P 13.

230	4c. black and reddish purple		10	10
231	15c. black and turquoise-blue		20	30
232	25c. chocolate, black and yellow-ochre		25	30
233	35c. chocolate, black and yellow-brown		25	30
230/233	Set of 4		70	90

Designs: *Horiz*—4, 15c. Type **82**. *Vert*—25, 35c. Crate of cargo.
Nos. 234 to 248 are redundant.

84 Island of Redonda (Chart)

(Des R. Granger Barrett. Photo Enschedé)

1969 (1 Aug). Centenary of Redonda Phosphate Industry. T **84** and similar horiz design. W w **12** (sideways). P 13×13½.

249	15c. Type **84**		20	10
250	25c. Redonda from the sea		20	10
251	50c. Type **84**		45	75
249/251	Set of 3		75	85

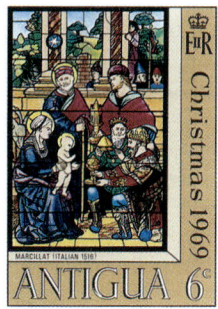

86 "The Adoration of the Magi" (Marcillat)

(88)

(Des adapted by V. Whiteley. Litho Enschedé)

1969 (15 Oct). Christmas. Stained-glass Windows. T **86** and similar vert design. Multicoloured. W w **12** (sideways*). P 13×14.

252	6c. Type **86**		10	10
253	10c. "The Nativity" (unknown German artist, 15th-century)		10	10
254	35c. Type **86**		25	10
255	50c. As 10c.		50	40
	w. Wmk Crown to right of CA		20·00	
252/255	Set of 4		85	60

*The normal sideways watermark shows Crown to left of CA, as seen from the back of the stamp.

1970 (2 Jan). No. 189 surch with T **88**.

256	20c. on 25c. slate-blue and sepia		10	10

89 Coat of Arms **90** Sikorsky S-38 Flying Boat

(Des and photo Harrison)

1970 (30 Jan)–**73**. Coil Stamps. W w **12**. P 14½×14.

A. Chalk-surfaced paper. Wmk upright (30.1.70)

257A	**89**	5c. blue	10	40
258A		10c. emerald	10	35
259A		25c. crimson	20	35
257A/259A	Set of 3		35	1·00

B. Glazed paper. Wmk sideways (5.3.73)

257B	**89**	5c. blue	1·25	2·50
258B		10c. emerald	1·25	2·50
259B		25c. crimson	1·75	2·25
257B/9B	Set of 3		3·75	6·50

These stamps were issued on Multiple Crown CA Diagonal paper in 1975.

(Des R. Granger Barrett. Litho J.W.)

1970 (16 Feb). 40th Anniv of Antiguan Air Services. T **90** and similar designs. Multicoloured. W w **12** (sideways). P 14½.

260	5c. Type **90**		50	10
261	20c. Dormer Do-X flying boat		80	10
262	35c. Hawker Siddeley H.S. 748		1·00	10
263	50c. Douglas C-124C Globemaster II		1·00	1·50
264	75c. Vickers Super VC-10		1·25	2·00
260/264	Set of 5		4·00	3·50

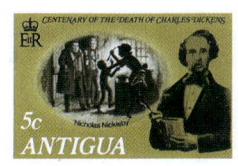

91 Dickens and Scene from *Nicholas Nickleby*

(Des Jennifer Toombs. Litho Walsall)

1970 (19 May). Death Centenary of Charles Dickens. T **91** and similar horiz designs. W w **12** (sideways). P 14.

265	5c. bistre, sepia and black		10	10
266	20c. light turquoise-blue, sepia and black		20	10
267	35c. violet-blue, sepia and black		30	10
268	$1 rosine, sepia and black		75	80
265/268	Set of 4		1·25	1·00

Designs:—20c. Dickens and Scene from *Pickwick Papers*; 35c. Dickens and Scene from *Oliver Twist*; $1 Dickens and Scene from *David Copperfield*.

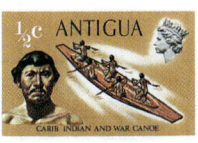

92 Carib Indian and War Canoe **93** "The Small Passion" (detail) (Dürer)

(Des J.W. Litho Questa)

1970 (19 Aug)–**75**. Horiz designs as T **92**. Multicoloured. Toned paper. W w **12** (sideways*). P 14.

269	½c. Type **92**		10	1·50
270	1c. Columbus and *Nina*		30	1·50
271	2c. Sir Thomas Warner's emblem and *Conception*		40	3·25
	a. Whiter paper (20.10.75)		1·50	3·25
272	3c. Viscount Hood and H.M.S. *Barfleur*		40	1·75
	w. Wmk Crown to right of CA		3·75	3·75
273	4c. Sir George Rodney and H.M.S. *Formidable*		40	3·00
274	5c. Nelson and H.M.S. *Boreas*		50	40
275	6c. William IV and H.M.S. *Pegasus*		1·75	4·25
276	10c. "Blackbeard" and pirate ketch		80	20
277	15c. Captain Collingwood and H.M.S. *Pelican*		11·00	1·00
278	20c. Nelson and H.M.S. *Victory*		1·25	40

279	25c. *Solent I* (paddle-steamer)		1·25	40
280	35c. George V (when Prince George) and H.M.S. *Canada* (screw corvette)		2·25	80
281	50c. H.M.S. *Renown* (battle cruiser)		4·00	6·00
282	75c. *Federal Maple* (freighter)		5·00	6·00
283	$1 *Sol Quest* (yacht) and class emblem		5·00	2·00
284	$2.50 H.M.S. *London* (destroyer)		8·00	7·50
285	$5 *Pathfinder* (tug)		2·50	6·00
269/285 Set of 17			40·00	40·00

*The normal sideways watermark shows Crown to left of CA *as seen from the back of the stamp*.

Stamps in these designs were issued with upright watermark between 1972 and 1974 and the $5 value was issued with a change of watermark in 1975.

(Des G. Drummond. Recess and litho D.L.R.)

1970 (28 Oct). Christmas. T **93** and similar vert design. W w **12**. P 13½×14.

286	**93**	3c. black and turquoise-blue	10	10
287	–	10c. dull purple and pink	10	10
288	**93**	35c. black and rose-red	30	10
289	–	50c. black and lilac	45	50
286/289 Set of 4			85	70

Design:—10c., 50c. "Adoration of the Magi" (detail) (Dürer).

94 4th King's Own Regt, 1759

95 Market Woman casting Vote

(Des P. W. Kingsland. Litho Questa)

1970 (14 Dec). Military Uniforms (1st series). T **94** and similar vert designs. Multicoloured. W w **12**. P 14×13½.

290	½c. Type **94**	10	10
291	10c. 4th West India Regiment, 18.04	65	10
292	20c. 60th Regiment, The Royal American, 1809	1·00	10
293	35c. 93rd Regiment, Sutherland Highlanders, 1826–34	1·25	10
294	75c. 3rd West India Regiment, 1851	1·75	2·00
290/294 Set of 5		4·25	2·10
MS295 128×146 mm. Nos. 290/4		5·50	11·00

(Des Sylvia Goaman. Photo Harrison)

1971 (1 Feb). 20th Anniversary of Adult Suffrage. T **95** and similar vert designs. W w **12** (sideways). P 14½×14.

296	5c. brown	10	10
297	20c. deep olive	10	10
298	35c. reddish purple	10	10
299	50c. ultramarine	15	30
296/9 Set of 4		30	40

People voting:—20c. Executive; 35c. Housewife; 50c. Artisan.

96 "The Last Supper"

97 "Madonna and Child" (detail, Veronese)

(Des Jennifer Toombs. Litho Questa)

1971 (7 Apr). Easter. Works by Dürer. T **96** and similar vert designs. W w **12**. P 14×13½.

300	5c. black, grey and scarlet	10	10
301	35c. black, grey and bluish violet	10	10
302	75c. black, grey and gold	20	30
300/2 Set of 3		30	35

Designs:—35c. The Crucifixion; 75c. The Resurrection.

(Des J. W. Litho Questa)

1971 (12 July). Military Uniforms (2nd series). Multicoloured designs as T **94**. W w **12**. P 13½.

303	½c. Private, 12th Regiment, The Suffolk (1704)	10	10
	w. Wmk inverted	60·00	
304	10c. Grenadier, 38th Regiment, South Staffs (1751)	35	10
305	20c. Light Company, 5th Regiment, Royal Northumberland Fusiliers (1778)	50	10
306	35c. Private, 48th Regiment, The Northamptonshire (1793)	60	10
307	75c. Private, 15th Regiment, East Yorks (1805)	1·00	3·00
	w. Wmk inverted	3·25	
303/7 Set of 5		2·25	3·00
MS308 127×144 mm. Nos. 303/7		4·50	6·50

(Des Jennifer Toombs. Litho Questa)

1971 (4 Oct). Christmas. T **97** and similar vert design. Multicoloured. W w **12**. P 13½.

309	3c. Type **97**	10	10
310	5c. "Adoration of the Shepherds" (detail, Veronese)	10	10
311	35c. Type **97**	25	10
312	50c. As 5c.	40	30
309/12 Set of 4		70	40

(Des J.W. Litho Questa)

1972 (1 July). Military Uniforms (3rd series). Multicoloured designs as T **94**. W w **12** (sideways). P 14×13½.

313	½c. Battalion Company Officer, 25th Foot, 1815	10	10
314	10c. Sergeant, 14th Foot, 1837	70	10
315	20c. Private, 67th Foot, 1853	1·25	15
316	35c. Officer, Royal Artillery, 1854	1·40	20
317	75c. Private, 29th Foot, 1870	1·75	4·00
313/17 Set of 5		4·75	4·00
MS318 125×141 mm. Nos. 313/17		7·00	8·50

98 Reticulated Cowrie-Helmet

(Des J.W. Litho Questa)

1972 (1 Aug). Shells. T **98** and similar horiz designs. Multicoloured. W w **12** (sideways). P 14½.

319	3c. Type **98**	50	10
320	5c. Measled Cowrie	50	10
321	35c. West Indian Fighting Conch	1·40	15
322	50c. Hawk-wing Conch	1·60	3·00
319/22 Set of 4		3·50	3·00

1972 (2 Nov)–**74**. As No. 269 etc., but W w **12** (upright) and whiter paper.

323	½c. Type **92**	20	50
324	1c. Columbus and *Nina* (2.1.74)	50	1·25
325	3c. Viscount Hood and H.M.S. *Barfleur* (2.1.74)	1·00	1·25
326	4c. Sir George Rodney and H.M.S. *Formidable* (2.1.74)	65	2·00
327	5c. Nelson and H.M.S. *Boreas* (2.1.74)	70	40
328	6c. William IV and H.M.S. *Pegasus* (2.1.74)	1·00	2·75
329	10c. "Blackbeard" and pirate ketch (2.1.74)	70	60
330	15c. Collingwood and H.M.S. *Pelican*	7·50	90
	w. Wmk inverted	90·00	
331	75c. *Federal Maple* (freighter)	7·50	3·00
332	$1 *Sol Quest* (yacht) and class emblem	3·00	1·75
333	$2.50 H.M.S. *London* (destroyer) (25.2.74)	2·75	6·50
334	$5 *Pathfinder* (tug)	4·00	10·00
323/34 Set of 12		26·00	26·00

See also No. 426.

99 St. John's Cathedral, Side View

ANTIGUA

(Des J.W. Litho Format)
1972 (6 Nov). Christmas and 125th Anniversary of St. John's Cathedral. T **99** and similar horiz designs. Multicoloured. W w **12**. P 14.

335	35c. Type **99**		20	10
336	50c. Cathedral interior		25	25
337	75c. St. John's Cathedral		30	60
335/7 Set of 3			65	80
MS338 165×102 mm. Nos. 335/7. P 15			65	1·00

100 Floral Pattern

(Des (from photograph by D. Groves) and photo Harrison)
1972 (20 Nov). Royal Silver Wedding. Multicoloured; background colour given. W w **12**. P 14×14½.

339	**100**	20c. bright blue	15	15
340		35c. turquoise-blue	15	15
		w. Wmk inverted	13·00	

101 Batsman and Map

(Des G. Vasarhelyi. Litho Questa)
1972 (15 Dec). 50th Anniv of Rising Sun Cricket Club. T **101** and similar horiz designs. Multicoloured. W w **12**. P 13½.

341	5c. Type **101**	55	15
	w. Wmk inverted	3·75	
342	35c. Batsman and wicket-keeper	65	10
343	$1 Club badge	1·00	2·25
341/3 Set of 3		2·00	2·25
MS344 88×130 mm. Nos. 341/3		3·25	7·50
	w. Wmk inverted	75·00	

102 Yacht and Map
103 "Episcopal Coat of Arms" 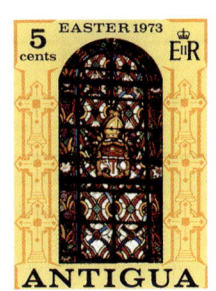

(Des M. and G. Shamir. Litho Format)
1972 (29 Dec). Sailing Week and Inauguration of Tourist Office, New York. T **102** and similar square designs. Multicoloured. W w **12**. P 14½.

345	35c. Type **102**	15	10
346	50c. Yachts	20	15
347	75c. St. John's G.P.O.	25	25
348	$1 Statue of Liberty	25	25
345/8 Set of 4		75	65
MS349 100×94 mm. Nos. 346, 348		75	1·25

(Des PAD Studio. Litho Format)
1973 (16 Apr). Easter. T **103** and similar vert designs showing stained-glass windows from St. John's Cathedral. Multicoloured. W w **12** (sideways*). P 13½.

350	5c. Type **103**	10	10
351	35c. "The Crucifixion"	15	10
352	75c. "Arms of 1st Bishop of Antigua"	25	30
	w. Wmk Crown to right of CA	12·00	
350/2 Set of 3		40	35

*The normal sideways watermark shows Crown to left of CA on the 75c., and to right of CA on the others, *as seen from the back of the stamp.*

(Des J.W. Litho Questa)
1973 (1 July). Military Uniforms (4th series). Multicoloured designs as T **94**. W w **12** (sideways*). P 13½.

353	½c. Private, Zacharia Tiffin's Regiment of Foot, 1701	10	10
354	10c. Private, 63rd Regiment of Foot, 1759	40	10
355	20c. Light Company Officer, 35th Regiment of Foot, 1828	50	15
	w. Wmk Crown to right of CA	7·50	
356	35c. Private, 2nd West India Regiment, 1853	65	15
357	75c. Sergeant, 49th Regiment, 1858	1·00	1·25
353/7 Set of 5		2·25	1·50
MS358 127×145 mm. Nos. 353/7		3·75	3·25

*The normal sideways watermark shows Crown to right of CA on the 35 and 75c., and to left of CA on the others, *as seen from the back of the stamp.*

104 Butterfly Costumes

(Des G. Vasarhelyi. Litho Format)
1973 (30 July). Carnival. T **104** and similar horiz designs. Multicoloured. P 13½.

359	5c. Type **104**	10	10
360	20c. Carnival street scene	15	10
361	35c. Carnival troupe	20	10
362	75c. Carnival Queen	30	30
359/62 Set of 4		65	35
MS363 134×95 mm. Nos. 359/62		65	1·00

105 "Virgin of the Milk Porridge" (Gerard David)
106 Princess Anne and Captain Mark Phillips 

(Des G. Vasarhelyi. Litho Format)
1973 (15 Oct). Christmas. T **105** and similar vert designs. Multicoloured. P 14½.

364	3c. Type **105**	10	10
365	5c. "Adoration of the Magi" (Stomer)	10	10
366	20c. "The Granducal Madonna" (Raphael)	15	10
367	35c. "Nativity with God the Father and Holy Ghost" (Battista)	20	10
368	$1 "Madonna and Child" (Murillo)	40	60
364/8 Set of 5		75	70
MS369 130×128 mm. Nos. 364/8		1·10	1·75

(Des G. Drummond. Litho Format)
1973 (14 Nov). Royal Wedding. T **106** and similar horiz design. P 13½.

370	**106**	35c. multicoloured	10	10
371	–	$2 multicoloured	25	25
MS372 78×100 mm. Nos. 370/1			50	40

The $2 is as T **106** but has a different border.
Nos. 370/1 were each issued in small sheets of five stamps and one stamp-size label.

(**107**) HONEYMOON VISIT DECEMBER 16th 1973

1973 (15 Dec). Honeymoon Visit of Princess Anne and Captain Phillips. Nos. 370/**MS**372 optd with T **107** by lithography.*

373	**106**	35c. multicoloured	15	10
		a. Typo opt	1·50	1·50
374	–	$2 multicoloured	30	30

ANTIGUA

a. Typo opt	2·25	2·25
MS375 78×100 mm. Nos. 373/4	55	55
a. Typo opt	8·50	12·00

*The litho overprints can be distinguished from the typo by the latter being less clear, less intense, and showing through on the reverse.

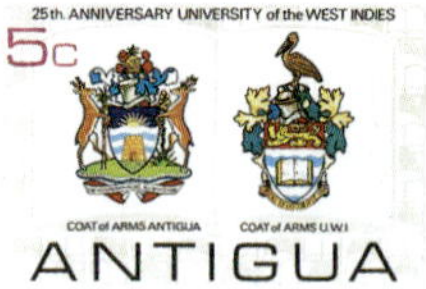

108 Coats of Arms of Antigua and University

(Des PAD Studio. Litho D.L.R.)

1974 (18 Feb). 25th Anniv of University of West Indies. T **108** and similar horiz designs. Multicoloured. W w **12**. P 13.

376	5c. Type **108**	15	10
377	20c. Extra-mural art	20	10
378	35c. Antigua campus	20	10
379	75c. Antigua chancellor	25	35
376/9 Set of 4		70	40

(Des J.W. Litho Questa)

1974 (1 May). Military Uniforms (5th series). Multicoloured designs as T **94**. W w **12** (sideways*). P 13½.

380	½c. Officer, 59th Foot, 1797	10	10
381	10c. Gunner, Royal Artillery, 1800	35	10
	a. Error. Wmk T **55** of Malawi	60·00	
382	20c. Private, 1st West India Regiment, 1830.	50	10
383	35c. Officer, 92nd Foot, 1843	60	10
384	75c. Private, 23rd Foot, 1846	75	2·25
380/4 Set of 5		3·00	2·25
MS385 127×145 mm. Nos. 380/4		2·25	2·50

*The normal sideways watermark shows Crown to right of CA on the 20c., and to left of CA on the others, *as seen from the back of the stamp.*

109 English Postman, Mailcoach and Westland Dragonfly Helicopter

110 Traditional Player

(Des G. Vasarhelyi. Litho Format)

1974 (15 July). Centenary of Universal Postal Union. T **109** and similar horiz designs. Multicoloured. P 14½.

386	½c. Type **109**	10	20
387	1c. Bellman, mail steamer *Orinoco* and satellite	10	20
388	2c. Train guard, post-bus and hydrofoil	10	20
389	5c. Swiss messenger, Wells Fargo coach and Concorde	60	50
390	20c. Postilion, Japanese postmen and carrier pigeon	35	10
391	35c. Antiguan postman, Sikorsky S-88 flying boat and tracking station	45	15
392	$1 Medieval courier, American express train and Boeing 747-100	1·75	2·00
386/92 Set of 7		3·00	3·00
MS393 141×164 mm. Nos. 386/92 plus label. P 13		3·00	2·50

On the ½c. "English" is spelt "Enlish", and on the 2c. "Postal" is spelt "Fostal".

(Des C. Abbott. Litho Questa)

1974 (1 Aug). Antiguan Steel Bands. T **110** and similar designs. W w **12** (sideways on 5c., 75c. and **MS**398). P 13.

394	5c. rose-red, carmine and black	10	10
395	20c. brown-ochre, chestnut and black	10	10
396	35c. light sage-green, blue-green and black	10	10
397	75c. dull blue, dull ultramarine and black	20	1·10
394/7 Set of 4		30	1·25
MS398 115×108 mm. Nos. 394/7		35	1·25

Designs: *Horiz*—20c. Traditional band; 35c. Modern band. *Vert*—75c. Modern player.

111 Footballers

EARTHQUAKE RELIEF
(112)

(Des G. Vasarhelyi. Litho Format)

1974 (23 Sept). World Cup Football Championship. T **111** and similar vert designs showing footballers. P 14½.

399	**111**	5c. multicoloured	10	10
400	–	35c. multicoloured	15	10
401	–	75c. multicoloured	30	30
402	–	$1 multicoloured	35	40
399/402 Set of 4			70	70
MS403 135×130 mm. Nos. 399/402 plus two labels. P 13.			85	90

Nos. 399/402 were each issued in small sheets of five stamps and one stamp-size label.

1974 (16 Oct). Earthquake Relief Fund. Nos. 400/2 and 397 optd with T **112**, No. 397 surch also.

404	35c. multicoloured	20	10
405	75c. multicoloured	30	30
406	$1 multicoloured	40	40
407	$5 on 75c. dull blue, dull ultram and black	1·25	2·25
404/7 Set of 4		2·00	2·75

113 Churchill as Schoolboy and School College Building, Harrow

114 "Madonna of the trees" (Bellini)

(Des V. Whiteley. Litho Format)

1974 (20 Oct). Birth Centenary of Sir Winston Churchill. T **113** and similar horiz designs. Multicoloured. P 14½.

408	5c. Type **113**	15	10
409	35c. Churchill and St. Paul's Cathedral	20	10
410	75c. Coat of arms and catafalque	30	65
411	$1 Churchill, "reward" notice and South African escape route	45	1·00
408/11 Set of 4		1·00	1·50
MS412 107×82 mm. Nos. 408/11. P 13		1·00	1·50

(Des M. Shamir. Litho Format)

1974 (18 Nov). Christmas. T **114** and similar vert designs showing "Madonna and Child" by the artists given. Multicoloured. P 14½.

413	½c. Type **114**	10	10
414	1c. Raphael	10	10
415	2c. Van der Weyden	10	10
416	3c. Giorgione	10	10
417	5c. Mantegna	10	10
418	20c. Vivarini	20	10
419	35c. Montagna	30	10
420	75c. Lorenzo Costa	55	1·10
413/20 Set of 8		1·25	1·50
MS421 139×126 mm. Nos. 417/20. P 13		1·00	1·40

$10
(115)

1975 (14 Jan). Nos. 331 and 390/2 surch as T **115**.

422	50c. on 20c. multicoloured	1·25	2·00
423	$2.50 on 35c. multicoloured	2·00	5·50
424	$5 on $1 multicoloured	6·50	7·00
425	$10 on 75c. multicoloured	2·00	7·50
422/5 Set of 4		10·50	20·00

1975 (21 Jan). As No. 334, but W w **14** (sideways).

426	$5 *Pathfinder* (tug)	3·00	10·00

ANTIGUA

116 Carib War Canoe, English Harbour, 1300

(Des G. Drummond. Litho Format)

1975 (17 Mar). Nelson's Dockyard. T **116** and similar horiz designs. Multicoloured. P 14½.

427	5c. Type **116**	20	10
428	15c. Ship of the line, English Harbour, 1770	80	15
429	35c. H.M.S. *Boreas* at anchor, and Lord Nelson, 1787	1·00	15
430	50c. Yachts during "Sailing Week", 1974	1·00	1·50
431	$1 Yacht Anchorage, Old Dockyard, 1970	1·00	2·25
427/31	*Set of 5*	3·50	3·75
MS432	130×134 mm. As Nos. 427/31, but in larger format, 43×28 mm. P 13½	3·00	2·00

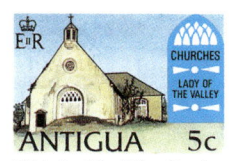

117 Lady of the Valley Church

(Des R. Vigurs. Litho Format)

1975 (19 May). Antiguan Churches. T **117** and similar horiz designs. Multicoloured. P 14½.

433	5c. Type **117**	10	10
434	20c. Gilbert Memorial	10	10
435	35c. Grace Hill Moravian	15	10
436	50c. St. Phillips	20	20
437	$1 Ebenezer Methodist	35	50
433/7	*Set of 5*	65	75
MS438	91×101 mm. Nos. 435/7. P 13	65	1·25

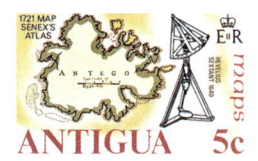

118 Map of 1721 and Sextant of 1640

(Des PAD Studio. Litho Questa)

1975 (21 July). Maps of Antigua. T **118** and similar horiz designs. Multicoloured. W w **14** (sideways). P 14.

439	5c. Type **118**	30	15
440	20c. Map of 1775 and galleon	55	15
441	35c. Maps of 1775 and 1955	70	15
442	$1 1973 maps of Antigua and English Harbour	1·40	2·25
439/42	*Set of 4*	2·75	2·25
MS443	130×89 mm. Nos. 439/42	3·00	3·25

119 Scout Bugler

(Des G. Vasarhelyi. Litho Questa)

1975 (26 Aug). World Scout Jamboree, Norway. T **119** and similar horiz designs. Multicoloured. P 14.

444	15c. Type **119**	25	15
445	20c. Scouts in camp	30	15
446	35c. "Lord Baden-Powell" (D. Jagger)	50	20
447	$2 Scout dancers from Dahomey	1·50	2·25
444/7	*Set of 4*	2·25	2·50
MS448	145×107 mm. Nos. 444/7	2·75	3·50

120 *Eurema elathea*

121 "Madonna and Child" (Correggio)

(Des G. Vasarhelyi. Litho Questa)

1975 (30 Oct). Butterflies. T **120** and similar horiz designs. Multicoloured. P 14.

449	½c. Type **120**	10	30
450	1c. *Danaus plexippus*	10	30
451	2c. *Phoebis philea*	15	30
452	5c. *Hypolimnas misippus*	30	10
453	20c. *Eurema proterpia*	1·00	40
454	35c. *Battus polydamas*	1·50	50
455	$2 *Cynthia cardui*	4·25	9·00
449/55	*Set of 7*	6·50	10·00
MS456	147×94 mm. Nos 452/5	6·00	11·00

No. 452 is incorrectly captioned "Marpesia petreus thetys".

(Des G. Vasarhelyi. Litho Questa)

1975 (17 Nov). Christmas. T **121** and similar vert designs showing "Madonna and Child". Multicoloured. P 14.

457	½c. Type **121**	10	10
458	1c. El Greco	10	10
459	2c. Dürer	10	10
460	3c. Antonello	10	10
461	5c. Bellini	10	10
462	10c. Dürer (*different*)	10	10
463	35c. Bellini (*different*)	40	10
464	$2 Dürer (*different*)	1·00	1·00
457/64	*Set of 8*	1·50	1·10
MS465	138×119 mm. Nos. 461/4	1·50	1·60

122 Vivian Richards

123 Antillean Crested Hummingbird

(Des G. Vasarhelyi. Litho Format)

1975 (15 Dec). World Cup Cricket Winners. T **122** and similar multicoloured designs. P 13½.

466	5c. Type **122**	1·25	20
467	35c. Andy Roberts	2·25	60
468	$2 West Indies team (*horiz*)	4·25	8·00
466/8	*Set of 3*	7·00	8·00

(Des G. Vasarhelyi. Litho Format)

1976 (19 Jan)–**78**. Various multicoloured designs as T **123**. P 13½ ($2.50, $5 and $10) or 14½ (others).

A. Without imprint (19.1.76).

469A	½c. Type **123**	40	50
470A	1c. Imperial Amazon	1·40	50
471A	2c. Zenaida Dove	1·40	50
472A	3c. Loggerhead Kingbird	1·40	60
473A	4c. Red-necked Pigeon	1·10	2·25
474A	5c. Rufous-throated Solitaire	2·00	10
475A	6c. Orchid Tree	30	2·00
476A	10c. Bougainvillea	30	10
477A	15c. Geiger Tree	35	10
478A	20c. Flamboyant	35	35
479A	25c. Hibiscus	40	15
480A	35c. Flame of the Wood	40	40
481A	50c. Cannon at Fort James	55	60
482A	75c. Premier's Office	60	2·00

ANTIGUA

483A	$1 Potworks Dam	75	1·00
484A	$2.50 Irrigation Scheme, Diamond Estate (44×28 *mm*)	1·00	5·00
485A	$5 Government House (44×28 *mm*)	1·50	6·00
486A	$10 Coolidge Airport (44×28 *mm*)	3·75	8·00
469A/86A	Set of 18	16·00	26·00

B. With imprint date at foot (1978)

469B	½c. Type **123**	70	1·25
470B	1c. Imperial Amazon	1·50	1·25
471B	2c. Zenaida Dove	1·50	1·25
472B	3c. Loggerhead Kingbird	1·50	1·25
473B	4c. Red-necked Pigeon	1·75	1·50
474B	5c. Rufous-throated Solitaire	2·00	1·00
475B	6c. Orchid Tree	30	1·50
476B	10c. Bougainvillea	30	40
477B	15c. Geiger Tree	30	40
478B	20c. Flamboyant	30	1·25
479B	25c. Hibiscus	35	50
480B	35c. Flame of the Wood	35	50
481B	50c. Cannon at Fort James	50	1·25
482B	75c. Premier's Office	55	1·50
483B	$1 Potworks Dam	75	1·60
484B	$2.50 Irrigation Scheme, Diamond Estate (44×28 *mm*)	1·75	6·50
485B	$5 Government House (44×28 *mm*)	1·50	7·50
486B	$10 Coolidge Airport (44×28 *mm*)	6·00	9·50
469B/86B	Set of 18	19·00	35·00

Nos. 469A, 472B, 473B, 474B, 475A/B, 476A/B, 477A, 478B, 479A/B, 480B, 481A/B, 482A/B, 483A, 484A/B, 485A/B and 486A/B exist imperforate from stock dispersed by the liquidator of Format International Security Printers Ltd.

124 Privates, Clark's Illinois Regt

125 High Jump

(Des J. W. Litho Format)

1976 (17 Mar). Bicentenary of American Revolution. T **124** and similar vert designs. Multicoloured. P 14½.

487	½c. Type **124**	10	10
488	1c. Riflemen, Pennsylvania Militia	10	10
489	2c. Powder horn	10	10
	a. Imperf (pair)	£160	
490	5c. Water bottle	10	10
491	35c. American flags	40	10
492	$1 *Montgomery* (American brig)	75	30
493	$5 *Ranger* (privateer sloop)	1·50	1·75
487/93	Set of 7	2·50	2·00
MS494	71×84 mm. $2.50 Congress flag. P 13	1·00	1·40

(Des J. W. Litho Format)

1976 (17 July). Olympic Games, Montreal. T **125** and similar horiz designs. P 14½.

495	½c. orange-brown, bistre-yellow and black	10	10
496	1c. light reddish violet, bright blue and black	10	10
497	2c. light green and black	10	10
498	15c. bright blue and black	15	10
499	30c. olive brown, yellow-ochre and black	20	15
500	$1 red-orange, Venetian red and black	40	40
501	$2 rosine and black	60	80
495/501	Set of 7	1·25	1·40
MS502	88×138 mm. Nos. 498/501. P 13½	1·75	1·25

Designs:—1c. Boxing; 2c. Pole vault; 15c. Swimming; 30c. Running; $1 Cycling; $2 Shot put.

126 Water Skiing

(Des J. W. Litho Questa)

1976 (26 Aug). Water Sports. T **126** and similar horiz designs. Multicoloured. P 14.

503	½c. Type **126**	10	10
504	1c. Sailing	10	10
505	2c. Snorkelling	10	10
506	20c. Deep sea fishing	50	10
507	50c. Scuba diving	75	35
508	$2 Swimming	1·25	1·25
503/8	Set of 6	2·25	1·60
MS509	89×114 mm. Nos. 506/8	1·75	1·75

127 French Angelfish

128 The Annunciation

(Des G. Drummond. Litho Questa)

1976 (4 Oct). Fish. T **127** and similar horiz designs. Multicoloured. W w **14** (sideways). P 13½.

510	15c. Type **127**	40	15
511	30c. Yellow-finned Grouper	55	30
512	50c. Yellow-tailed Snapper	70	50
513	90c. Shy Hamlet	90	1·50
510/13	Set of 4	2·25	2·25

(Des J.W. Litho Walsall)

1976 (15 Nov). Christmas. T **128** and similar vert designs. Multicoloured. P 13½.

514	8c. Type **128**	10	10
515	10c. Holy Family	10	10
516	15c. The Magi	10	10
517	50c. The Shepherds	20	25
518	$1 Epiphany scene	30	50
514/18	Set of 5	60	75

129 Mercury and U.P.U. Emblem

130 Royal Family

(Des BG Studio. Litho Questa)

1976 (28 Dec). Special Events, 1976. T **129** and similar horiz designs. Multicoloured. P 14.

519	½c. Type **129**	10	10
520	1c. Alfred Nobel	10	10
521	10c. Space satellite	30	10
522	50c. Viv Richards and Andy Roberts	3·50	1·75
523	$1 Bell and telephones	1·00	2·00
524	$2 Yacht *Freelance*	2·25	4·50
519/24	Set of 6	6·50	7·50
MS525	127×101 mm. Nos. 521/4	7·50	13·00

Events:—½c. 25th Anniv of U.N. Postal Administration; 1c. 75th Anniv of Nobel Prize; 10c. "Viking" Space Mission; 50c. Cricketing achievements; $1 Telephone Centenary; $2 "Operation Sail", U.S. Bicentennial.

(Des J. W. Litho Questa (Nos. 526/31) Manufactured by Walsall (Nos. 532/3))

1977 (7 Feb–26 Sept). Silver Jubilee. T **130** and similar vert designs. Multicoloured.

(a) Sheet stamps. P 14 (7 Feb).

526	10c. Type **130**	10	10
527	30c. Royal Visit, 1966	10	10
528	50c. The Queen enthroned	15	15
529	90c. The Queen after Coronation	15	25

530	$2.50 Queen and Prince Charles	30	55
526/30	Set of 5	60	95
MS531	116×78 mm. $5 Queen and Prince Philip	65	85
	a. Error. Imperf	£375	

(b) Booklet stamps. Roul 5×imperf (50c.) or imperf ($5). Self adhesive (26 Sept)

532	50c. Design as No. 529 (24×42 mm)	35	75
	a. Booklet pane of 6	1·75	
533	$5 Design as stamp from No. MS531 (24×42 mm)	2·00	3·75
	a. Booklet pane of 1	2·00	

*No. 532 was separated by various combinations of rotary knife (giving a straight edge) and roulette. No. 533 exists only with straight edges.

Stamps as Nos. 526/30 but perforated 11½×12, come from sheets of 5 stamps and 1 label. These were not placed on sale by the Antigua Post Office.

131 Making Camp **132** Carnival Costume

(Des J.W. Litho Questa)

1977 (23 May). Caribbean Scout Jamboree, Jamaica. T **131** and similar horiz designs. Multicoloured. P 14.

534	½c. Type **131**	10	10
535	1c. Hiking	10	10
536	2c. Rock-climbing	10	10
537	10c. Cutting logs	15	10
538	30c. Map and sign reading	40	10
539	50c. First aid	65	25
540	$2 Rafting	1·25	2·50
534/40	Set of 7	2·25	2·75
MS541	127×114 mm. Nos. 538/40	3·00	4·00

1977. Coil Stamps. As Nos. 257/9, but W w **14** (inverted on 10c.). P 14½×14.

541a	**89** 5c. blue	5·00	
541b	10c. emerald	—	2·00
541c	25c. crimson	9·00	

(Des C. Abbott. Litho Walsall)

1977 (18 July). 21st Anniv of Carnival. T **132** and similar vert designs. Multicoloured. P 14.

542	10c. Type **132**	10	10
543	30c. Carnival Queen	25	10
544	50c. Butterfly costume	30	15
545	90c. Queen of the band	40	25
546	$1 Calypso King and Queen	40	30
542/6	Set of 5	1·25	70
MS547	140×120 mm. Nos. 542/6	1·10	1·60

ROYAL VISIT 28th OCTOBER 1977 (**133**)

134 "Virgin and Child Enthroned" (Tura)

1977 (17 Oct). Royal Visit. Nos. 526/531 optd with T **133**. P 14.

548	10c. Type **130**	10	10
549	30c. Royal Visit, 1966	15	10
550	50c. The Queen enthroned	20	10
551	90c. The Queen after Coronation	30	20
552	$2.50 Queen and Prince Charles	50	35
548/52	Set of 5	1·00	65
MS553	116×78 mm. $5 Queen and Prince Philip	1·00	1·00
	a. Opt double	55·00	

Nos. 548/52 also exist perf 11½×12 (*Price for set of 5 80p mint or used*) from additional sheetlets of five stamps and one label.

(Des M. Shamir. Litho Questa)

1977 (21 Nov). Christmas. T **134** and similar vert designs showing "Virgin and Child" by the artists given. Multicoloured. P 14.

554	½c. Type **134**	10	20
555	1c. Crivelli	10	20
556	2c. Lotto	10	20
557	8c. Pontormo	15	10
558	10c. Tura	15	10
559	25c. Lotto (*different*)	30	10
560	$2 Crivelli (*different*)	85	1·00
554/60	Set of 7	1·50	1·50
MS561	144×118 mm. Nos. 557/60	1·75	2·75

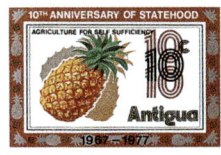

135 Pineapple

(Des and litho J. W.)

1977 (29 Dec). Tenth Anniv of Statehood. T **135** and similar horiz designs. Multicoloured. P 13.

562	10c. Type **135**	10	10
563	15c. State flag	60	20
564	50c. Police band	2·50	80
565	90c. Premier V. C. Bird	55	80
566	$2 State Coat of Arms	90	2·00
562/6	Set of 5	4·25	3·50
MS567	126×99 mm. Nos. 563/6. P 14	3·50	3·00

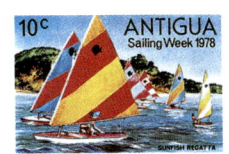

136 Wright Glider III, 1902 **137** Sunfish Regatta

(Des PAD Studio. Litho Questa)

1978 (23 Mar). 75th Anniv of Powered Flight. T **136** and similar multicoloured designs. P 14.

568	½c. Type **136**	10	10
569	1c. Wright *Flyer I*, 1903	10	10
570	2c. Launch system and engine	10	10
571	10c. Orville Wright (*vert*)	30	10
572	50c. Wright *Flyer III*, 1905	60	15
573	90c. Wilbur Wright (*vert*)	80	30
574	$2 Wright Type B, 1910	1·00	80
568/74	Set of 7	2·50	1·25
MS575	90×75 mm. $2.50, Wright *Flyer I* on launch system	1·25	2·75

(Des G. Drummond. Litho Format)

1978 (27 Apr). Sailing Week. T **137** and similar horiz designs. Multicoloured. P 15.

576	10c. Type **137**	20	10
577	50c. Fishing and work boat race	35	20
578	90c. Curtain Bluff race	60	35
579	$2 Power boat rally	1·10	1·25
576/9	Set of 4	2·00	1·75
MS580	110×77 mm. $2.50, Guadeloupe-Antigua race	1·50	1·75

Nos. 576/9 exist imperforate from stock dispersed by the liquidator of Format International Security Printers Ltd.

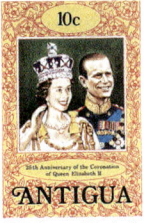

138 Queen Elizabeth and Prince Philip **139** Glass Coach

ANTIGUA

(Des J.W. Litho Questa (Nos. 581/6) Manufactured by Walsall (Nos. 587/9))

1978 (2 June). 25th Anniv of Coronation. Multicoloured. P 14.

(a) Sheet stamps. Vert designs as T 138.

581	10c. Type **138**	10	10
582	30c. Crowning	10	10
583	50c. Coronation procession	15	10
584	90c. Queen seated in St. Edward's Chair	20	15
585	$2.50 Queen wearing Imperial State Crown	40	40
581/5 Set of 5		65	65
MS586 114×104 mm. $5 Queen and Prince Philip		80	80

(b) Booklet stamps. Horiz design as T 139 showing State Coaches. Imperf ($5) or roul 5×imperf.* Self-adhesive.

587	25c. Type **139**	15	30
	a. Booklet pane. Nos. 587/8×3	1·25	
588	50c. Irish State Coach	25	50
589	$5 Coronation Coach	1·75	3·00
	a. Booklet pane of 1	1·75	
587/9 Set of 3		2·00	3·50

Nos. 581/5 also exist perf 12 (*Price for set of 5 65p mint or used*) from additional sheetlets of three stamps and one label. These stamps have changed background colours.

*Nos. 587/8 were separated by various combinations of rotary knife (giving a straight edge) and roulette. No. 589 exists only with straight edges.

140 Player running with Ball

141 Petrea

(Des BG Studio. Litho Format)

1978 (17 Aug). World Cup Football Championship, Argentina. T **140** and similar vert designs. Multicoloured. P 14½.

590	10c. Type **140**	15	10
591	15c. Players in front of goal	15	10
592	$3 Referee and player	1·50	1·75
590/2 Set of 3		1·50	1·75
MS593 126×88 mm. 25c. Player crouching with ball; 30c. Players heading ball; 50c. Players running with ball; $2 Goalkeeper diving. (*All horiz*)		3·25	2·50

Nos. 590/2 were each printed in small sheets of 6 including 1 *se-tenant* stamp-size label.

Nos. 590/2 exist imperforate from stock dispersed by the liquidator of Format International Security Printers Ltd.

(Des G. Drummond. Litho Questa)

1978 (5 Oct). Flowers. T **141** and similar vert designs. Multicoloured. P 14.

594	25c. Type **141**	20	10
595	50c. Sunflower	30	20
596	90c. Frangipani	50	30
597	$2 Passion Flower	90	60
594/7 Set of 4		1·75	2·25
MS598 118×85 mm. $2.50, Hibiscus		1·40	1·60

142 "St Ildefonso receiving the Chasuble from the Virgin" (Rubens)

143 1d. Stamp of 1863

(Des BG Studio. Litho Questa)

1978 (30 Oct). Christmas Paintings. T **142** and similar horiz designs. Multicoloured. P 14.

599	8c. Type **142**	10	10
600	25c. "The Flight of St. Barbara" (Rubens)	20	10
601	$2 "Madonna and Child, with St. Joseph, John the Baptist and Donor" (Sebastiano del Piombo*)	65	55
599/601 Set of 3		80	60
MS602 170×113 mm. $4 "The Annunciation" (Rubens)		1·25	1·50

*The work is incorrectly attributed to Rubens on the stamp.

(Des G. Vasarhelyi. Litho Questa)

1979 (12 Feb). Death Centenary of Sir Rowland Hill. T **143** and similar vert designs. Multicoloured. P 14.

603	25c. Type **143**	10	10
604	50c. Penny Black	20	15
605	$1 Stage-coach and woman posting letter, circa 1840	30	20
606	$2 Modern mail transport	1·10	60
603/6 Set of 4		1·50	85
MS607 108×82 mm. $2.50, Sir Rowland Hill		80	90

Nos. 603/6 also exist perf 12 (*Price for set of 4 £1.50 mint or used*) from additional sheetlets of five stamps and one label.

144 "The Deposition from the Cross" (painting)

145 Toy Yacht and Child's Hand

(Des BG Studio. Litho Questa)

1979 (15 Mar). Easter. Works by Dürer. T **144** and similar vert designs. Multicoloured. P 14.

608	10c. multicoloured	10	10
609	50c. multicoloured	35	20
610	$4 black, magenta and greenish yellow	1·00	90
608/10 Set of 3		1·25	1·00
MS611 114×99 mm. $2.50, multicoloured		80	80

Designs:—50c., $2.50, "Christ on the Cross—The Passion" (wood engravings) (*both different*); $4 "Man of Sorrows with Hands Raised" (wood engraving).

(Des M. Rubin. Litho Questa)

1979 (9 Apr). International Year of the Child. T **145** and similar vert designs showing toys and hands of children of different races. Multicoloured. P 14.

612	25c. Type **145**	10	10
613	50c. Rocket	25	15
614	90c. Car	40	25
615	$2 Train	1·00	90
612/15 Set of 4		1·60	1·25
MS616 80×112 mm. $5 Aeroplane		1·10	1·10

146 Yellow Jack

147 Cook's Birthplace, Marton

(Des P. Powell. Litho Questa)

1979 (14 May). Fish. T **146** and similar horiz designs. Multicoloured. P 14½×14.

617	30c. Type **146**	35	15
618	50c. Blue-finned Tuna	40	25
619	90c. Sailfish	60	40
620	$3 Wahoo	1·50	1·75
617/20 Set of 4		2·50	2·25
MS621 122×75 mm. $2.50, Great Barracuda		1·50	1·40

(Des J.W. Litho Questa)

1979 (2 July). Death Bicentenary of Captain Cook. T **147** and similar vert designs. Multicoloured. P 14.

622	25c. Type **147**	65	25
623	50c. H.M.S. *Endeavour*	1·25	60

624	90c. Marine chronometer	75	80
625	$3 Landing at Botany Bay	1·75	3·00
622/5 Set of 4		4·00	4·00
MS626 110×85 mm. $2.50, H.M.S. *Resolution*		2·25	1·50

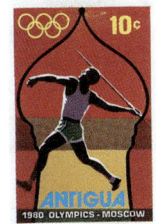

148 The Holy Family

149 Javelin Throwing

(Des J.W. Litho Questa)

1979 (1 Oct). Christmas. T **148** and similar vert designs. Multicoloured. P 14.

627	8c. Type **148**	10	10
628	25c. Virgin and Child on Ass	15	10
629	50c. Shepherd and star	25	35
630	$4 Wise Men with gifts	85	2·50
627/30 Set of 4		1·25	2·50
MS631 113×94 mm. $3 Angel with trumpet. P 12		1·00	1·50

(Des Design Images Inc. Litho Questa)

1980 (18 Feb). Olympic Games, Moscow. T **149** and similar multicoloured designs. P 14.

632	10c. Type **149**	20	10
633	25c. Running	20	10
634	$1 Pole vaulting	50	50
635	$2 Hurdling	70	1·75
632/5 Set of 4		1·40	2·25
MS636 127×96 mm. $3 Boxing (*horiz*)		80	90

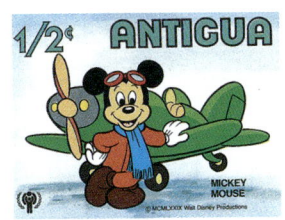

150 Mickey Mouse and Aeroplane

(Litho Format)

1980 (24 Mar). International Year of the Child (1979). Walt Disney Cartoon Characters. T **150** and similar multicoloured designs showing characters and transport. P 11.

637	½c. Type **150**	10	10
638	1c. Donald Duck driving car	10	10
639	2c. Goofy driving taxi	10	10
640	3c. Mickey Mouse on motorcycle with Minnie Mouse in sidecar	10	10
641	4c. Huey, Dewey and Louie riding cycle	10	10
642	5c. Grandma Duck, chickens and pickup truck	10	10
643	10c. Mickey Mouse driving jeep (*vert*)	10	10
644	$1 Chip and Dale in sailing boat	2·00	2·00
645	$4 Donald Duck riding toy train (*vert*)	4·00	6·50
637/45 Set of 9		5·50	7·50
MS646 101×127 mm. $2.50, Goofy flying biplane. P 14×13½		4·50	3·25

See also Nos. 671/80.

LONDON 1980

(**151**)

1980 (6 May). "London 1980" International Stamp Exhibition. Nos. 603/6 optd with T **151**. P 12.

647	25c. Type **143**	25	15
648	50c. Penny Black	35	35
649	$1 Stage-coach and woman posting letter, *circa* 1840	60	70
650	$2 Modern mail transport	3·25	3·00
647/50 Set of 4		4·00	3·75

152 "David" (statue, Donatello)

153 Rotary International 75th Anniversary Emblem and Headquarters, U.S.A.

(Des J.W. Litho Questa)

1980 (23 June). Famous Works of Art. T **152** and similar multicoloured designs. P 13½.

651	10c. Type **152**	10	10
652	30c. "The Birth of Venus" (painting, Sandro Botticelli) (*horiz*)	30	15
653	50c. "Reclining Couple" (sarcophagus, Cerveteri) (*horiz*)	40	40
654	90c. "The Garden of Earthly Delights" (painting, Hieronymus Bosch) (*horiz*)	55	65
655	$1 "Portinari Altarpiece" (painting, Hugo van der Goes) (*horiz*)	65	75
656	$4 "Eleanora of Toledo and her Son Giovanni de'Medici" (painting, Agnolo Bronzino)	1·75	3·00
651/6 Set of 6		3·25	4·50
MS657 99×124 mm. $5 "The Holy Family" (painting, Rembrandt)		2·50	1·75

(Des G. Vasarhelyi. Litho Questa)

1980 (21 July). 75th Anniv of Rotary International. T **153** and similar horiz designs. Multicoloured. P 14.

658	30c. Type **153**	30	30
659	50c. Rotary anniversary emblem and Antigua Rotary Club banner	40	50
660	90c. Map of Antigua and Rotary emblem	60	70
661	$3 Paul P. Harris (founder) and Rotary emblem	2·00	3·50
658/61 Set of 4		3·00	4·25
MS662 102×78 mm. $5 Antiguan flags and Rotary emblems		1·25	2·00

154 Queen Elizabeth the Queen Mother

155 Ringed Kingfisher

(Des G. Vasarhelyi. Litho Questa)

1980 (4 Aug). 80th Birthday of Queen Elizabeth the Queen Mother. P 14.

663	**154** 10c. multicoloured	40	10
664	$2.50 multicoloured	1·00	1·75
MS665 68×90 mm. **154** $3 multicoloured. P 12		1·40	2·25

(Des Jennifer Toombs. Litho Questa)

1980 (3 Nov). Birds. T **155** and similar vert designs. Multicoloured. P 14.

666	10c. Type **155**	70	30
667	30c. Plain Pigeon	1·00	50
668	$1 Green-throated Carib	1·50	2·00
669	$2 Black-necked Stilt	2·00	4·00
666/9 Set of 4		4·75	5·50
MS670 73×73 mm. $2.50, Roseate Tern		7·00	6·00

(Litho Format)

1980 (23 Dec). Christmas. Scenes from Walt Disney's Cartoon Film "Sleeping Beauty". Horiz designs as T **150**. P 11.

671	½c. multicoloured	10	10
672	1c. multicoloured	10	10
673	2c. multicoloured	10	10

ANTIGUA

674	4c. multicoloured		10	10
675	8c. multicoloured		10	10
676	10c. multicoloured		15	10
677	25c. multicoloured		20	20
678	$2 multicoloured		2·25	2·25
679	$2.50 multicoloured		2·50	2·50
671/9	*Set of 9*		4·75	4·75
MS680	126×101 mm. $4 multicoloured (*vert*) P 13½×14		5·00	3·25

156 Diesel locomotive No. 15

(Des G. Drummond. Litho Questa)

1981 (12 Jan). Sugar Cane Railway Locomotives. T **156** and similar horiz designs. Multicoloured. P 14.

681	25c. Type **156**		15	15
682	50c. Narrow-gauge steam locomotive		30	30
683	90c. Diesel locomotives Nos. 1 and 10		55	60
684	$3 Steam locomotive hauling sugar cane		2·00	2·25
681/4	*Set of 4*		2·75	3·00
MS685	82×111 mm. $2.50, Antigua sugar factory, railway yard and sheds		1·75	1·75

"INDEPENDENCE 1981"
(157)

1981 (31 Mar). Independence. Optd with T **157**.

A. On Nos. 475A, 478A, 480A and 484A/6A.

686A	6c. Orchid Tree		60	1·00
688A	20c. Flamboyant		60	60
690A	35c. Flame of the Wood		1·25	1·25
694A	$2.50 Irrigation Scheme, Diamond Estate		2·00	4·25
695A	$5 Government House		3·50	8·00
696A	$10 Coolidge Airport		6·50	12·00
686A/96A	*Set of 6*		13·00	24·00

B. On Nos. 4751B/61B and 478B/86B

686B	6c. Orchid Tree		10	50
687B	10c. Bougainvillea		10	10
688B	20c. Flamboyant		10	10
689B	25c. Hibiscus		15	15
690B	35c. Flame of the Wood		20	20
691B	50c. Cannon at Fort James		35	45
692B	75c. Premier's Office		40	60
693B	$1 Potworks Dam		55	75
694B	$2.50 Irrigation Scheme, Diamond Estate		75	2·00
695B	$5 Government House		1·40	3·50
696B	$10 Coolidge Airport		3·25	6·00
686B/96B	*Set of 11*		6·50	13·00

158 "Pipes of Pan"

159 Prince Charles and Lady Diana Spencer

(Des J.W. Litho Questa)

1981 (5 May). Birth Centenary of Picasso. T **158** and similar vert designs. Multicoloured. P 14.

697	10c. Type **158**		10	10
698	50c. "Seated Harlequin"		30	30
699	90c. "Paulo as Harlequin"		55	55
700	$4 "Mother and Child"		2·00	2·00
697/700	*Set of 4*		2·50	2·50
MS701	115×140 mm. $5 "Three Musicians" (detail)		1·75	2·75

(Des J.W. Litho Questa)

1981 (23 June). Royal Wedding (1st issue). T **159** and similar vert designs. Multicoloured. P 14.

702	25c. Type **159**		10	10
703	50c. Glamis Castle		10	10
704	$4 Prince Charles skiing		80	80
702/4	*Set of 3*		80	80
MS705	96×82 mm. $5 Glass Coach		80	80

Nos. 702/4 also exist perforated 12 (*Price for set of 3 80p mint or used*) from additional sheetlets of five stamps and one label. These stamps have changed background colours.

160 Prince of Wales at Investiture, 1969

(Manufactured by Walsall)

1981 (23 June). Royal Wedding (2nd issue). T **160** and similar vert designs. Multicoloured ($5) or black and flesh (others). Self-adhesive. Roul 5×imperf*.

706	25c. Type **160**		15	25
	a. Booklet pane. Nos. 706/11		1·50	
707	25c. Prince Charles as baby, 1948		15	25
708	$1 Prince Charles at R.A.F. College, Cranwell, 1971		25	50
709	$1 Prince Charles attending Hill House School, 1956		25	50
710	$2 Prince Charles and Lady Diana Spencer		50	75
711	$2 Prince Charles at Trinity College, 1967		50	75
712	$5 Prince Charles and Lady Diana (*different*)		1·00	1·50
	a. Booklet pane of 1		1·00	
706/12	*Set of 7*		2·50	4·00

*The 25c. to $2 values were each separated by various combinations of rotary knife (giving a straight edge) and roulette. The $5 value exists only with straight edges. Nos. 706/12 were only issued in $11.50 stamp booklets.

161 Irene Joshua (founder)

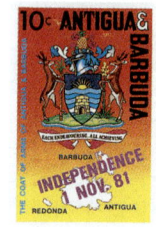

162 Antigua and Barbuda Coat of Arms

(Des M. Diamond. Litho Format)

1981 (28 Oct). 50th Anniv of Antigua Girl Guide Movement. T **161** and similar horiz designs. Multicoloured. P 14½.

713	10c. Type **161**		15	10
714	50c. Campfire sing-song		45	35
715	90c. Sailing		75	65
716	$2.50 Animal tending		1·50	2·00
713/16	*Set of 4*		2·50	2·75
MS717	110×85 mm. $5 Raising the flag		4·50	3·00

INDEPENDENT

Nos. 718/22 and 733 onwards are inscribed "ANTIGUA & BARBUDA".

(Des E. Henry. Litho Format)

1981 (1 Nov). Independence. T **162** and similar multicoloured designs. P 14½.

718	10c. Type **162**		25	10
719	50c. Pineapple, Antigua flag and map		2·00	60
720	90c. Prime Minister Vere Bird		55	55
721	$2.50 St. John's Cathedral (38×25 *mm*)		1·50	3·50
718/21	*Set of 4*		3·75	4·25
MS722	105×79 mm. $5 Map of Antigua and Barbuda (42×42 *mm*)		4·50	2·75

163 "Holy Night" (Jacques Stella)

164 Swimming

(Des Clover Mill. Litho Format)

1981 (16 Nov). Christmas. Paintings. T **163** and similar vert designs. Multicoloured. P 14½.

723	8c. Type **163**	15	10
724	30c. "Mary with Child" (Julius Schnorr von Carolfeld)	40	15
725	$1 "Virgin and Child" (Alonso Cano)	75	90
726	$3 "Virgin and Child" (Lorenzo di Credi)	1·10	3·75
723/6	Set of 4	2·25	4·25
MS727	77×111 mm. $5 "Holy Family" (Pieter von Avon)	2·50	4·50

(Des M. Diamond. Litho Format)

1981 (1 Dec). International Year for Disabled Persons. Sport for the Disabled. T **164** and similar horiz designs. Multicoloured. P 15.

728	10c. Type **164**	10	10
729	50c. Discus throwing	20	30
730	90c. Archery	40	55
731	$2 Baseball	1·00	1·40
728/31	Set of 4	1·50	2·10
MS732	108×84 mm. $4 Basketball	5·00	2·75

165 Scene from Football Match

166 Airbus Industrie A300

(Des Clover Mill. Litho Questa)

1982 (15 Apr). World Cup Football Championship, Spain. T **165** and similar horiz designs showing scenes from different matches. P 14.

733	10c. multicoloured	30	10
734	50c. multicoloured	60	35
735	90c. multicoloured	1·10	70
736	$4 multicoloured	3·00	3·50
733/6	Set of 4	4·50	4·25
MS737	75×92 mm. $5 multicoloured	6·00	10·00

Nos. 733/6 also exist perforated 12 (*Price for set of 4, £4.50 mint or used*) from additional sheetlets of five stamps and one label. These stamps have changed inscription colours.

(Des Clover Mill. Litho Format)

1982 (17 June). Coolidge International Airport. T **166** and similar multicoloured designs. P 14½.

738	10c. Type **166**	10	10
739	50c. Hawker Siddeley H.S. 748	30	30
740	90c. de Havilland DHC-6 Twin Otter	60	60
741	$2.50 Britten Norman Islander	1·75	1·75
738/41	Set of 4	2·50	2·50
MS742	99×73 mm. $5 Boeing 747-100 (*horiz*)	2·75	4·00

167 Cordia

(Des G. Drummond. Litho Questa)

1982 (28 June). Death Centenary of Charles Darwin. Fauna and Flora. T **167** and similar multicoloured designs. P 15.

743	10c. Type **167**	30	10
744	50c. Small Indian Mongoose (*horiz*)	70	40
745	90c. Corallita	1·10	75
746	$3 Mexican Bulldog Bat (*horiz*)	2·50	3·25
743/6	Set of 4	4·25	4·00
MS747	107×85 mm. $5 Caribbean Monk Seal	7·50	8·00

168 Queen's House, Greenwich

169 Princess of Wales

(Des PAD Studio. Litho Questa)

1982 (1 July). 21st Birthday of Princess of Wales. T **168/9** and similar vert design. Multicoloured. P 14½×14.

748	90c. Type **168**	45	45
749	$1 Prince and Princess of Wales	65	50
750	$4 Princess Diana (*different*)	3·00	2·00
748/50	Set of 3	3·50	2·75
MS751	102×75 mm. $5 Type **169**	3·75	2·50

Nos. 748/50 also exist in sheetlets of 5 stamps and 1 label.

170 Boy Scouts decorating Streets for Independence Parade

ROYAL BABY 21.6.82
(**171**)

(Des J.W. Litho Questa)

1982 (15 July). 75th Anniv of Boy Scout Movement. T **170** and similar horiz designs. Multicoloured. P 14.

752	10c. Type **170**	25	10
753	50c. Boy Scout giving helping hand during street parade	50	40
754	90c. Boy Scouts attending Princess Margaret at Independence Ceremony	80	75
755	$2.20 Cub Scout giving directions to tourists	1·50	2·75
752/5	Set of 4	2·75	3·50
MS756	102×72 mm. $5 Lord Baden-Powell	4·50	5·50

1982 (30 Aug). Birth of Prince William of Wales. Nos. 748/51 optd with T **171**.

757	90c. Type **168**	45	45
758	$1 Prince and Princess of Wales	50	50
759	$4 Princess Diana (*different*)	1·50	1·50
757/9	Set of 3	2·25	2·25
MS760	102×75 mm. $5 Type **169**	2·40	2·50

Nos. 757/9 also exist in sheetlets of 5 stamps and 1 label.

172 Roosevelt in 1940

(Des PAD Studio. Litho Format)

1982 (20 Sept). Birth Centenary of Franklin D. Roosevelt (Nos. 761, 763 765/6 and MS767), and 250th Birth Anniv of George Washington (others). T **172** and similar multicoloured designs. P 15.

761	10c. Type **172**	20	10
762	25c. Washington as blacksmith	45	15
763	45c. Churchill, Roosevelt and Stalin at Yalta Conference	1·75	40
764	60c. Washington crossing the Delaware (*vert*)	1·00	40
765	$1 "Roosevelt Special" train (*vert*)	1·75	90

ANTIGUA AND BARBUDA

766	$3 Portrait of Roosevelt (vert)	1·40	2·40
761/6	Set of 6	6·00	3·75
MS767	92×87 mm. $4 Roosevelt and Wife	2·00	1·75
MS768	92×87 mm. $4 Portrait of Washington (vert)	2·00	1·75

No. MS768 exists imperforate from stock dispersed by the liquidator of Format International Security Printers Ltd.

173 "Annunciation"

(Des Design Images. Litho Questa)

1982 (Nov). Christmas. Religious Paintings by Raphael. T **173** and similar horiz designs. Multicoloured. P 14×13½.

769	10c. Type **173**	10	10
770	30c. "Adoration of the Magi"	15	15
771	$1 "Presentation at the Temple"	50	40
772	$4 "Coronation of the Virgin"	1·75	1·90
769/72	Set of 4	2·25	2·25
MS773	95×124 mm. $5 "Marriage of the Virgin"	2·75	2·50

174 Tritons and Dolphins

175 Pineapple Produce

(Des Design Images. Litho Format)

1983 (28 Jan). 500th Birth Anniv of Raphael. Details from "Galatea" Fresco. T **174** and similar multicoloured designs. P 14½.

774	45c. Type **174**	20	25
775	50c. Sea Nymph carried off by Triton	25	30
776	60c. Winged angel steering Dolphins (horiz)	30	35
777	$4 Cupids shooting arrows (horiz)	1·60	2·00
774/7	Set of 4	2·10	2·50
MS778	101×125 mm. $5 Galatea pulled along by Dolphins	1·50	2·25

(Des Artists International. Litho Questa)

1983 (14 Mar). Commonwealth Day. T **175** and similar horiz designs. Multicoloured. P 14.

779	25c. Type **175**	15	15
780	45c. Carnival	20	25
781	60c. Tourism	30	35
782	$3 Airport	1·00	1·50
779/82	Set of 4	1·50	2·00

176 T.V. Satellite Coverage of Royal Wedding

(Des PAD Studio. Litho Questa)

1983 (5 Apr). World Communications Year. T **176** and similar horiz designs. Multicoloured. P 14.

783	15c. Type **176**	40	20
784	50c. Police communications	2·25	1·50
785	60c. House-to-train telephone call	2·25	1·50
786	$3 Satellite earth station with planets Jupiter and Saturn	4·75	5·00
783/6	Set of 4	8·50	7·50
MS787	100×90 mm. $5 "Comsat" satellite over West Indies	2·00	3·75

177 Bottle-nosed Dolphin

(Des D. Miller. Litho Format)

1983 (9 May). Whales. T **177** and similar horiz designs. Multicoloured. P 14½.

788	15c. Type **177**	85	20
789	50c. Fin Whale	1·75	1·25
790	60c. Bowhead Whale	2·00	1·25
791	$3 Spectacled Porpoise	3·75	4·25
788/91	Set of 4	7·50	6·25
MS792	122×101 mm. $5 Narwhal	8·50	6·00

Nos. 788/92 exist imperforate from stock dispersed by the liquidator of Format International Security Printers Ltd.

178 Cashew Nut

(Des J.W. Litho Questa)

1983 (11 July)–**85**. Fruits and Flowers. T **178** and similar horiz designs. Multicoloured. P 14.

793	1c. Type **178**	15	1·25
	a. Perf 12 (3.85)	20	1·00
794	2c. Passion Fruit	15	1·25
	a. Perf 12 (3.85)	20	1·00
795	3c. Mango	15	1·25
	a. Perf 12 (3.85)	20	1·00
796	5c. Grapefruit	20	1·25
	a. Perf 12 (3.85)	30	1·00
797	10c. Pawpaw	50	20
	a. Perf 12 (3.85)	30	20
798	15c. Breadfruit	75	20
	a. Perf 12 (3.85)	75	20
799	20c. Coconut	50	20
	a. Perf 12 (3.85)	60	20
800	25c. Oleander	75	30
	a. Perf 12 (3.85)	75	20
801	30c. Banana	60	40
	a. Perf 12 (3.85)	75	30
802	40c. Pineapple	70	40
	a. Perf 12 (3.85)	75	30
803	45c. Cordia	80	55
	a. Perf 12 (3.85)	85	40
804	50c. Cassia	90	60
	a. Perf 12 (3.85)	1·25	50
805	60c. Poui	1·50	1·00
	a. Perf 12 (3.85)	1·75	1·10
806	$1 Frangipani	2·25	1·75
	a. Perf 12 (3.85)	2·00	1·50
807	$2 Flamboyant	3·75	4·00
	a. Perf 12 (12.85)	3·50	4·50
808	$2.50 Lemon	3·75	6·50
	a. Perf 12 (12.85)	4·50	6·00
809	$5 Lignum Vitae	5·00	13·00
	a. Perf 12 (12.85)	7·00	13·00
810	$10 National flag and coat of arms	8·00	17·00
	a. Perf 12 (3.85)	11·00	18·00
793/810	Set of 18	27·00	45·00
793a/810a	Set of 18	32·00	45·00

179 Dornier Do X Flying Boat

(Des W. Wright. Litho Format)

1983 (15 Aug). Bicentenary of Manned Flight. T **179** and similar horiz designs. Multicoloured. P 14½.

811	30c. Type **179**	1·00	30
812	50c. Supermarine S6B seaplane	1·25	60

813	60c. Curtiss F-9C Sparrowhawk biplane and airship U.S.S. *Akron*............	1·40	85
814	$4 Hot-air balloon *Pro Juventute*............	3·25	6·00
811/14	Set of 4	6·25	7·00
MS815	80×105 mm. $5 Airship LZ-127 *Graf Zeppelin*...	1·75	2·25

180 "Sibyls and Angels" (detail) (Raphael)

(Des W. Wright. Litho Format)

1983 (4 Oct). Christmas. 500th Birth Anniv of Raphael. T **180** and similar designs. P 13½.

816	10c. multicoloured	30	20
817	30c. multicoloured	65	35
818	$1 multicoloured	1·50	1·25
819	$4 multicoloured	2·50	5·00
816/19	Set of 4	4·00	6·25
MS820	101×131 mm. $5 multicoloured	1·50	2·25

Designs: *Horiz*—10c. to $4 Different details from "Sibyls and Angels". *Vert*—$5 "The Vision of Ezekiel".

Nos. 816/20 exist imperforate from stock dispersed by the liquidator of Format International Security Printers Ltd.

181 John Wesley (founder)

182 Discus

(Des M. Diamond. Litho Questa)

1983 (7 Nov). Bicentenary of Methodist Church (1984). T **181** and similar vert designs. Multicoloured. P 14.

821	15c. Type **181**	25	15
822	50c. Nathaniel Gilbert (founder in Antigua)	70	50
823	60c. St. John Methodist Church steeple	75	65
824	$3 Ebenezer Methodist Church, St. John's .	2·00	4·00
821/4	Set of 4	3·25	4·75

(Des Artists International. Litho Format)

1984 (9 Jan). Olympic Games, Los Angeles. T **182** and similar vert designs. Multicoloured. P 14½.

825	25c. Type **182**	20	15
826	50c. Gymnastics	35	30
827	90c. Hurdling	65	70
828	$3 Cycling	2·50	4·25
825/8	Set of 4	3·25	4·75
MS829	82×67 mm. $5 Volleyball	2·75	3·00

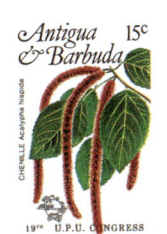

183 *Booker Vanguard* (freighter)   **184** Chenille

(Des Artists International. Litho Format)

1984 (14 June). Ships. T **183** and similar multicoloured designs. P 15.

830	45c. Type **183**	1·00	55
831	50c. *Canberra* (liner)	1·25	80
832	60c. Yachts	1·50	1·00
833	$4 *Fairwind* (cargo liner)	3·00	7·00
830/3	Set of 4	6·00	8·50
MS834	107×80 mm. $5 18th-century British man-o-war (vert)	1·75	3·50

Nos. 830/4 exist imperforate from stock dispersed by the liquidator of Format International Security Printers Ltd.

(Des J.W. Litho Format)

1984 (19 June). Universal Postal Union Congress, Hamburg. T **184** and similar vert designs showing flowers. Multicoloured. P 15.

835	15c. Type **184**	40	15
836	50c. Shell Flower	75	70
837	60c. Anthurium	75	1·10
838	$3 Angels Trumpet	2·25	6·50
835/8	Set of 4	3·75	7·50
MS839	100×75 mm. $5 Crown of Thorns	1·50	3·25

Nos. 835/9 exist imperforate from stock dispersed by the liquidator of Format International Security Printers Ltd.

(**185**)   (**186**)

1984 (25 June).

*(a) Nos. 702/5 surch with T **185***

840	$2 on 25c. Type **159**	2·50	2·50
841	$2 on 50c. Glamis Castle	2·50	2·50
842	$2 on $4 Prince Charles skiing	2·50	2·50
840/2	Set of 3	6·75	6·75
MS843	96×82 mm. $2 on $5 Glass Coach	4·00	4·00

*(b) Nos. 748/51 surch with T **186***

844	$2 on 90c. Type **168** (Gold)*	2·50	2·50
845	$2 on $1 Prince and Princess of Wales (Gold)*	2·50	2·50
846	$2 on $4 Princess Diana (*different*) (Gold)*	2·50	2·50
844/6	Set of 3	6·75	6·75
MS847	102×75 mm. $2 on $5 Type **169** (Gold)	4·00	4·00

*(c) Nos. 757/60 surch with T **186***

848	$2 on 90c. Type **168** (Gold)*	2·00	2·00
849	$2 on $1 Prince and Princess of Wales (Gold)*	2·00	2·00
850	$2 on $4 Princess Diana (*different*) (Gold)*	2·00	2·00
848/50	Set of 3	5·50	5·50
MS851	102×75 mm. $2 on $5 Type **169** (Gold)	4·00	4·00

*(d) Nos. 779/82 surch as T **185***

852	$2 on 25c. Type **175**	2·75	1·25
853	$2 on 45c. Carnival	2·75	1·25
854	$2 on 60c. Tourism	2·75	1·25
855	$2 on $3 Airport	2·75	1·25
852/5	Set of 4	10·00	4·50

*Nos. 844/6 and 848/50 also exist with similar surcharges in gold or silver on the sheetlets of five stamps and 1 label (*price for set of 3 as Nos. 844/6, £6 mint or used*) (*price for set of 3 as Nos. 848/50, £6 mint or used*).

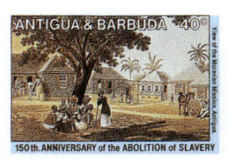

187 Abraham Lincoln   **188** View of Moravian Mission

(Des Liane Fried. Litho Questa)

1984 (18 July). Presidents of the United States of America. T **187** and similar vert designs. Multicoloured. P 14.

856	10c. Type **187**	15	10
857	20c. Harry Truman	20	15
858	30c. Dwight Eisenhower	30	25
859	40c. Ronald Reagan	50	30

ANTIGUA AND BARBUDA

860	90c. Gettysburg Address, 1863	90	75
861	$1.10 Formation of N.A.T.O., 1949	2·00	1·25
862	$1.50 Eisenhower during Second World War	1·60	1·75
863	$2 Reagan and Caribbean Basin Initiative	1·75	2·00
856/63 Set of 8		6·50	6·00

(Des and litho Questa)

1984 (1 Aug). 150th Anniv of Abolition of Slavery. T **188** and similar horiz designs. Multicoloured. P 14.

864	40c. Type **188**	90	50
865	50c. Antigua Courthouse, 1823	1·00	65
866	60c. Planting sugar-cane, Monks Hill	1·10	75
867	$3 Boiling house, Delaps' estate	4·25	6·00
864/7 Set of 4		6·50	7·00
MS868 95×70 mm. $5 Loading sugar, Willoughby Bay		6·50	4·75

189 Rufous-sided Towhee

190 Grass-skiing

(Des Jennifer Toombs. Litho Format)

1984 (15 Aug). Songbirds. T **189** and similar vert designs. Multicoloured. P 15.

869	40c. Type **189**	1·25	85
870	50c. Parula Warbler	1·40	1·10
871	60c. House Wren	1·50	1·50
872	$2 Ruby-crowned Kinglet	2·00	3·75
873	$3 Common Flicker	2·75	5·00
869/73 Set of 5		8·00	11·00
MS874 76×76 mm. $5 Yellow-breasted Chat		2·50	6·00

(Des Bonny Redecker. Litho Questa)

1984 (21 Sept). "Ausipex" International Stamp Exhibition, Melbourne. Australian Sports. T **190** and similar vert designs. Multicoloured. P 14½.

875	$1 Type **190**	1·25	1·50
876	$5 Australian Football	3·25	4·75
MS877 108×78 mm. $5 Boomerang-throwing		2·00	3·50

191 "The Virgin and Infant with Angels and Cherubs" (Correggio)

192 "The Blue Dancers" (Degas)

(Litho Format)

1984 (4 Oct). 450th Death Anniv of Correggio (painter). T **191** and similar vert designs. Multicoloured. P 15.

878	25c. Type **191**	40	20
879	60c. "The Four Saints"	80	50
880	90c. "St. Catherine"	1·10	90
881	$3 "The Campori Madonna"	2·25	4·25
878/81 Set of 4		4·00	5·25
MS882 90×60 mm. $5 "St. John the Baptist"		1·75	2·75

(Litho Format)

1984 (4 Oct). 150th Birth Anniv of Edgar Degas (painter). T **192** and similar multicoloured designs. P 15.

883	15c. Type **192**	35	15
884	50c. "The Pink Dancers"	80	60
885	70c. "Two Dancers"	1·10	85
886	$4 "Dancers at the Bar"	2·50	4·75
883/6 Set of 4		4·25	5·75
MS887 90×60 mm. $5 "The Folk Dancers" (40×27 mm)		2·00	2·75

193 Sir Winston Churchill

194 Donald Duck fishing

(Des J. Iskowitz. Litho Format)

1984 (19 Nov). Famous People. T **193** and similar multicoloured designs. P 15.

888	60c. Type **193**	1·10	1·50
889	60c. Mahatma Gandhi	1·10	1·50
890	60c. John F. Kennedy	1·10	1·50
891	60c. Mao Tse-tung	1·10	1·50
892	$1 Churchill with General De Gaulle, Paris, 1944 (horiz)	1·25	1·75
893	$1 Gandhi leaving London by train, 1931 (horiz)	1·25	1·75
894	$1 Kennedy with Chancellor Adenauer and Mayor Brandt, Berlin, 1963 (horiz)	1·25	1·75
895	$1 Mao Tse-tung with Lin Piao, Peking, 1969 (horiz)	1·25	1·75
888/95 Set of 8		8·50	11·50
MS896 114×80 mm. $5 Flags of Great Britain, India, the United States and China		9·50	8·00

Nos. 888 and 890/5 exist imperforate from stock dispersed by the liquidator of Format International Security Printers Ltd.

(Litho Format)

1984 (26 Nov). Christmas. 50th Birthday of Donald Duck. T **194** and similar multicoloured designs showing Walt Disney cartoon characters. P 11.

897	1c. Type **194**	10	10
898	2c. Donald Duck lying on beach	10	10
899	3c. Donald Duck and nephews with fishing rods and fishes	10	10
900	4c. Donald Duck and nephews in boat	10	10
901	5c. Wearing diving masks	10	10
902	10c. In deckchairs reading books	10	10
903	$1 With toy shark's fin	2·25	1·25
904	$2 In sailing boat	2·50	3·00
905	$5 Attempting to propel boat	4·00	6·00
897/905 Set of 9		8·00	9·50
MS906 Two sheets, each 125×100 mm. (a) $5 Nephews with crayon and paintbrushes (horiz). P 14×13½. (b) $5 Donald Duck in deckchair. P 13½×14 Set of 2 sheets		7·50	13·00

No. 904 was printed in sheetlets of 8 stamps.
Nos. 897/905 exist imperforate from stock dispersed by the liquidator of Format International Security Printers Ltd.

195 Torch from Statue in Madison Square Park, 1885

(Des J. Iskowitz. Litho Format)

1985 (7 Jan). Centenary of the Statue of Liberty (1986) (1st issue). T **195** and similar multicoloured designs. P 15.

907	25c. Type **195**	30	20
908	30c. Statue of Liberty and scaffolding ("Restoration and Renewal") (vert)	30	20
909	50c. Frederic Bartholdi (sculptor) supervising construction, 1876	40	40
910	90c. Close-up of Statue	60	75
911	$1 Statue and cadet ship ("Operation Sail", 1976) (vert)	1·60	1·40
912	$3 Dedication ceremony, 1886	1·75	1·75
907/12 Set of 6		4·50	5·50
MS913 110×80 mm. $5 Port of New York		3·75	3·75

See also Nos. 1110/19.

196 Arawak Pot Sherd and Indians making Clay Utensils

(Des N. Waldman. Litho Format)

1985 (21 Jan). Native American Artefacts. T **196** and similar designs. Multicoloured. P 15.

914	15c. Type **196**	15	10
915	50c. Arawak body design and Arawak Indians tattooing	30	40
916	60c. Head of the god "Yocahu" and Indians harvesting manioc	40	50
917	$3 Carib war club and Carib Indians going into battle	1·25	2·50
914/17 Set of 4		1·90	3·25
MS918 97×68 mm. $5 Taino Indians worshipping stone idol		1·50	2·50

197 Triumph 2hp "Jap", 1903

(Des BG Studio. Litho Questa)

1985 (7 Mar). Centenary of the Motorcycle. T **197** and similar horiz designs. Multicoloured. P 14.

919	10c. Type **197**	65	15
920	30c. Indian "Arrow", 1949	1·10	40
921	60c. BMW "R100RS", 1976	1·60	1·25
922	$4 Harley-Davidson "Model II", 1916	5·50	9·00
919/22 Set of 4		8·00	9·75
MS923 90×93 mm. $5 Laverda "Jota", 1975		5·50	7·00

198 Slavonian Grebe

(Litho Questa)

1985 (25 Mar). Birth Bicentenary of John J. Audubon (ornithologist) (lst issue). T **198** and similar multicoloured designs showing original paintings. P 14.

924	90c. Type **198**	1·75	1·25
925	$1 British Storm Petrel	2·00	1·25
926	$1.50 Great Blue Heron	2·50	3·25
927	$3 Double-crested Cormorant	3·75	6·00
924/7 Set of 4		9·00	10·50
MS928 103×72 mm. $5 White-tailed Tropic Bird (vert)		7·00	6·00

Nos. 924/7 were each issued in sheetlets of five stamps and one stamp-size label, which appears in the centre of the bottom row. See also Nos. 990/4.

199 *Anaea cyanea*

(Des R. Sauber. Litho Questa)

1985 (16 Apr). Butterflies. T **199** and similar horiz designs. Multicoloured. P 14.

929	25c. Type **199**	1·00	30
930	60c. *Leodonta dysoni*	2·25	1·25
931	90c. *Junea doraete*	2·75	1·50
932	$4 *Prepona pylene*	7·50	10·50
929/32 Set of 4		12·00	12·00
MS933 132×105 mm. $5 *Caerois gerdtrudtus*		4·50	6·50

200 Cessna 172D Skyhawk   **201** Maimonides

(Des A. DiLorenzo. Litho Questa)

1985 (30 Apr). 40th Anniv of International Civil Aviation Organization. T **200** and similar horiz designs. Multicoloured. P 14.

934	30c. Type **200**	1·25	30
935	90c. Fokker D.VII	2·75	1·25
936	$1.50 SPAD VII	3·75	3·25
937	$3 Boeing 747-100	5·50	7·50
934/7 Set of 4		12·00	11·00
MS938 97×83 mm. $5 de Havilland DHC-6 Twin Otter		4·50	6·50

(Des and litho Questa)

1985 (17 June). 850th Birth Anniv of Maimonides (physician, philosopher and scholar). P 14.

939	**201**	$2 bright green	4·25	3·25
MS940 70×84 mm. **201** $5 reddish brown			7·00	4·50

No. 939 was printed in sheetlets of 6 stamps.

202 Young Farmers with Produce   **203** The Queen Mother attending Church

(Des Susan David. Litho Questa)

1985 (1 July). International Youth Year. T **202** and similar horiz designs. Multicoloured. P 14.

941	25c. Type **202**	25	20
942	50c. Hotel management trainees	40	50
943	60c. Girls with goat and boys with football ("Environment")	1·00	70
944	$3 Windsurfing ("Leisure")	2·75	5·50
941/4 Set of 4		4·00	6·25
MS945 102×72 mm. $5 Young people with Antiguan flags		2·75	3·25

(Des J.W. Litho Questa)

1985 (10 July). Life and Times Queen Elizabeth the Queen Mother. T **203** and similar vert designs. Multicoloured. P 14.

946	$1 Type **203**	45	60
947	$1.50 Watching children playing in London garden	60	85
948	$2.50 The Queen Mother in 1979	90	1·40
946/8 Set of 3		1·75	2·50
MS949 56×85 mm. $5 With Prince Edward at Royal Wedding, 1981		5·50	3·00

Stamps as Nos. 946/8, but with face values of 90c., $1 and $3, exist from additional sheetlets of 5 plus a label issued 13 January 1986. These also have changed background colours and are perforated 12×12½ (*price for set of 3 stamps £2 mint*).

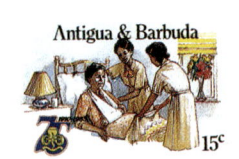

204 Magnificent Frigate Bird   **205** Girl Guides Nursing

ANTIGUA AND BARBUDA

(Des Mary Walters. Litho Questa)

1985 (1 Aug). Marine Life. T **204** and similar vert designs. Multicoloured. P 14.

950	15c. Type **204**	1·00	30
951	45c. Brain Coral	2·00	95
952	60c. Cushion Star	2·25	1·75
953	$3 Spotted Moray	7·00	9·00
950/3	Set of 4	11·00	11·00
MS954	110×80 mm. $5 Elkhorn Coral	9·00	7·00

(Des Y. Berry. Litho Questa)

1985 (22 Aug). 75th Anniv of Girl Guide Movement. T **205** and similar horiz designs. Multicoloured. P 14.

955	15c. Type **205**	75	20
956	45c. Open-air Girl Guide meeting	1·40	60
957	60c. Lord and Lady Baden-Powell	1·75	90
958	$3 Girl Guides gathering flowers	4·25	4·50
955/8	Set of 4	7·50	5·75
MS959	67×96 mm. $5 Barn Swallow (Nature study)	6·50	8·50

206 Bass Trombone   **207** Flags of Great Britain and Antigua

(Des Susan David. Litho Questa)

1985 (26 Aug). 300th Birth Anniv of Johann Sebastian Bach (composer). T **206** and similar vert designs. P 14.

960	25c. multicoloured	1·40	55
961	50c. multicoloured	1·75	1·10
962	$1 multicoloured	3·25	1·75
963	$3 multicoloured	6·00	7·00
960/3	Set of 4	11·00	9·50
MS964	104×73 mm. $5 black and brownish grey	4·50	4·75

Designs:—50c. English horn; $1 Violino piccolo; $3 Bass rackett; $5 Johann Sebastian Bach.

(Des Mary Walters. Litho Format)

1985 (24 Oct). Royal Visit. T **207** and similar multicoloured designs. P 14½.

965	60c. Type **207**	1·00	65
966	$1 Queen Elizabeth II (vert)	1·50	1·25
967	$4 Royal Yacht *Britannia*	3·25	7·00
965/7	Set of 3	5·25	7·00
MS968	110×83 mm. $5 Map of Antigua	3·00	3·25

(Des Walt Disney Productions. Litho Questa)

1985 (4 Nov). 150th Birth Anniv of Mark Twain (author). Horiz designs as T **118** of Anguilla showing Walt Disney cartoon characters in scenes from "Roughing It". Multicoloured. P 14×13½.

969	25c. Donald Duck and Mickey Mouse meeting Indians	1·00	20
970	50c. Mickey Mouse, Donald Duck and Goofy canoeing	1·50	55
971	$1.10 Goofy as Pony Express rider	2·50	2·25
972	$1.50 Donald Duck and Goofy hunting buffalo	3·00	3·75
973	$2 Mickey Mouse and silver mine	3·50	4·50
969/73	Set of 5	10·50	9·25
MS974	127×101 mm. $5 Mickey Mouse driving stagecoach	8·00	7·50

(Des Walt Disney Productions. Litho Questa)

1985 (11 Nov). Birth Bicentenaries of Grimm Brothers (folklorists). Horiz designs as T **119** of Anguilla showing Walt Disney cartoon characters in scenes from, "Spindle, Shuttle and Needle". Multicoloured. P 14×13½.

975	30c. The Prince (Mickey Mouse) searches for a bride	1·25	40
	a. Error. Wmk w **16**	95·00	
976	60c. The Prince finds the Orphan Girl (Minnie Mouse)	1·75	80
977	70c. The Spindle finds the Prince	2·00	1·40
978	$1 The Needle tidies the Girl's House	2·50	1·75
979	$3 The Prince proposes	4·75	7·50
975/9	Set of 5	11·00	10·00
MS980	125×101 mm. $5 The Orphan Girl and spinning wheel on Prince's horse	8·00	7·50

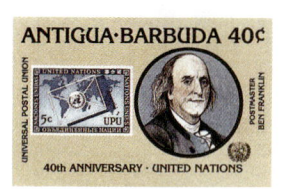

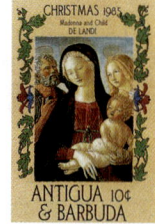

208 Benjamin Franklin and U.N. (New York) 1953 U.P.U. 5c. Stamp

209 "Madonna and Child" (De Landi)

(Litho Walsall)

1985 (18 Nov). 40th Anniv of United Nations Organization. T **208** and similar multicoloured designs showing United Nations (New York) stamps. P 13½×14.

981	40c. Type **208**	1·00	70
982	$1 George Washington Carver (agricultural chemist) and 1982 Nature Conservation 28c. stamp	2·00	2·00
983	$3 Charles Lindbergh (aviator) and 1978 I.C.A.O. 25c. stamp	4·75	7·50
981/3	Set of 3	7·00	9·00
MS984	101×77 mm. $5 Marc Chagall (artist) (vert). P 14×13½	6·50	4·75

(Des Mary Walters. Litho Format)

1985 (30 Dec). Christmas. Religious Paintings. T **209** and similar vert designs. Multicoloured. P 15.

985	10c. Type **209**	30	15
986	25c. "Madonna and Child" (Berlinghiero)	55	25
987	60c. "The Nativity" (Fra Angelico)	70	60
988	$4 "Presentation in the Temple" (Gio-vanni di Paolo)	1·75	4·25
985/8	Set of 4	3·00	4·75
MS989	113×81 mm. $5 "The Nativity" (Antoniazzo Romano)	3·00	3·75

No. **MS**989 exists imperforate from stock dispersed by the liquidator of Format International Security Printers Ltd.

(Litho Questa)

1986 (6 Jan). Birth Bicentenary of John J. Audubon (ornithologist) (2nd issue). Horiz designs as T **198** showing original paintings. Multicoloured. P 12.

990	60c. Mallard	2·25	1·50
991	90c. North American Black Duck	2·75	2·00
992	$1.50 Pintail	3·50	4·50
993	$3 American Wigeon	4·75	6·50
990/3	Set of 4	12·00	13·00
MS994	102×73 mm. $5 American Eider. P 14	7·00	5·50

Nos. 990/3 were issued in sheetlets of 5 as Nos. 924/7.

210 Football, Boots and Trophy   **211** Tug

Des M. Dank. Litho Questa

1986 (17 Mar). World Cup Football Championship, Mexico. T **210** and similar multicoloured designs. P 14.

995	30c. Type **210**	1·50	40
996	60c. Goalkeeper (vert)	2·00	85
997	$1 Referee blowing whistle (vert)	2·50	1·75
998	$4 Ball in net	6·50	7·00
995/8	Set of 4	11·00	11·00
MS999	87×76 mm. $5 Two players competing for ball	8·50	7·50

(Des W. Hanson. Litho Questa)

1986 (24 Mar). Appearance of Halley's Comet (1st issue). Horiz designs as T **123** of Anguilla. Multicoloured. P 14.

1000	5c. Edmond Halley and Old Greenwich Observatory	30	20
1001	10c. Messerschmitt Me 163B Komet (fighter aircraft), 1944	30	15

1002	60c. Montezuma (Aztec Emperor) and Comet in 1517 (from "Historias de las Indias de Neuva Espana")	1·50	70
1003	$4 Pocahontas saving Capt. John Smith and Comet in 1607	4·50	5·50
1000/3	Set of 4	6·00	6·00
MS1004	101×70 mm. $5 Halley's Comet over English Harbour, Antigua	3·50	3·75

See also Nos. 1047/51.

(Litho Questa)

1986 (21 Apr). 60th Birthday of Queen Elizabeth II. Vert designs as T **125** of Anguilla. P 14.

1005	60c. black and yellow	30	35
1006	$1 multicoloured	50	55
1007	$4 multicoloured	1·40	1·90
1005/7	Set of 3	2·00	2·50
MS1008	120×85 mm. $5 black and grey-brown	2·00	3·00

Designs:—60c. Wedding photograph, 1947; $1 Queen at Trooping the Colour; $4 In Scotland; $5 Queen Mary and Princess Elizabeth, 1927.

(Des A. DiLorenzo. Litho Questa)

1986 (15 May). Local Boats. T **211** and similar vert designs. Multicoloured. P 14.

1009	30c. Type **211**	25	20
1010	60c. Game fishing boat	45	35
1011	$1 Yacht	75	60
1012	$4 Lugger with auxiliary sail	2·50	3·25
1009/12	Set of 4	3·50	4·00
MS1013	108×78 mm. $5 Boats under construction	3·00	4·00

212 "Hiawatha" Express

213 Prince Andrew and Miss Sarah Ferguson

(Des W. Wright. Litho Format)

1986 (22 May). "Ameripex '86" International Stamp Exhibition, Chicago. Famous American Trains. T **212** and similar horiz designs. Multicoloured. P 15.

1014	25c. Type **212**	1·25	50
1015	50c. "Grand Canyon" express	1·50	80
1016	$1 "Powhattan Arrow" express	1·75	1·75
1017	$3 "Empire State" express	3·00	6·00
1014/17	Set of 4	6·75	9·00
MS1018	116×87 mm. $5 Southern Pacific "Daylight" express	6·00	11·00

Nos. 1014/18 exist imperforate from stock dispersed by the liquidator of Format International Security Printers Ltd.

(Des and litho Questa)

1986 (1 July). Royal Wedding. T **213** and similar vert designs. Multicoloured. P 14.

1019	45c. Type **213**	70	35
1020	60c. Prince Andrew	80	45
1021	$4 Prince Andrew with Prince Philip	2·75	3·50
1019/21	Set of 3	3·75	3·75
MS1022	88×88 mm. $5 Prince Andrew and Miss Sarah Ferguson (different)	5·00	4·50

214 Fly-specked Cerith

215 *Nymphaea ampla* (Water Lily)

(Des L. Birmingham. Litho Format)

1986 (6 Aug). Sea Shells. T **214** and similar multicoloured designs. P 15.

1023	15c. Type **214**	75	50
1024	45c. Smooth Scotch Bonnet	1·75	1·25
1025	60c. West Indian Crown Conch	2·00	2·00
1026	$3 Ciboney Murex	5·50	10·00
1023/6	Set of 4	9·00	12·50
MS1027	109×75 mm. $5 Colourful Atlantic Moon (horiz)	7·50	8·50

(Des Mary Walters. Litho Format)

1986 (25 Aug). Flowers. T **215** and similar horiz designs. Multicoloured. P 15.

1028	10c. Type **215**	20	15
1029	15c. Queen of the Night	20	15
1030	50c. Cup of Gold	55	55
1031	60c. Beach Morning Glory	70	70
1032	70c. Golden Trumpet	80	80
1033	$1 Air Plant	90	1·10
1034	$3 Purple Wreath	1·75	3·00
1035	$4 Zephyr Lily	2·00	3·75
1028/35	Set of 8	6·50	9·00
MS1036	Two sheets, each 102×72 mm. (a) $4 Dozakie. (b) $5 Four O'Clock Flower Set of 2 sheets	5·00	7·50

Nos. 1028/35 exist imperforate from stock dispersed by the liquidator of Format International Security Printers Ltd.

(216)

217 *Hygrocybe occidentalis* var. *scarletina*

1986 (15 Sept). World Cup Football Championship Winners, Mexico. Nos. 995/9 optd as T **216** in gold.

1037	30c. Type **210**	1·25	40
1038	60c. Goalkeeper (vert)	1·75	75
1039	$1 Referee blowing whistle (vert)	2·25	1·10
1040	$4 Ball in net	5·50	4·50
1037/40	Set of 4	7·75	6·00
MS1041	87×76 mm. $5 Two players competing for ball	5·50	4·00

The overprint on the horizontal designs is in two lines.

(Litho Format)

1986 (15 Sept). Mushrooms. T **217** and similar vert designs. Multicoloured. P 15.

1042	10c. Type **217**	30	25
1043	50c. *Trogia buccinalis*	70	55
1044	$1 *Collybia subpruinosa*	1·00	1·25
1045	$4 *Leucocoprinus brebissonii*	2·50	4·50
1042/5	Set of 4	4·00	6·00
MS1046	102×82 mm $5 *Pyrrhoglossum pyrrhum*	13·00	11·00

An unissued 3$ and examples of No. 1045 with the face value shown as "4$" exist from stock dispersed by the liquidator of Format International Security Printers Ltd.

(218)

219 Auburn "Speedster" (1933)

1986 (15 Oct). Appearance of Halley's Comet (2nd issue). Nos. 1000/4 optd with T **218** (in silver on $5).

1047	5c. Edmond Halley and Old Greenwich Observatory	20	10
1048	10c. Messerschmltt Me 163B Komet (fighter aircraft), 1944	50	10
1049	60c. Montezuma (Aztec Emperor) and Comet in 1517 (from "Historias de las Indias de Neuva Espana")	1·25	65
1050	$4 Pocahontas saving Capt. John Smith and Comet in 1607	4·50	4·00
1047/50	Set of 4	5·75	4·25
MS1051	101×70 mm. $5 Halley's Comet over English Harbour, Antigua	6·00	6·50

ANTIGUA AND BARBUDA

(Des J. Martin. Litho Questa)

1986 (20 Oct). Centenary of First Benz Motor Car. T **219** and similar horiz designs. Multicoloured. P 14.

1052	10c. Type **219**	20	10
1053	15c. Mercury "Sable" (1986)	25	10
1054	50c. Cadillac (1959)	60	30
1055	60c. Studebaker (1950)	75	45
1056	70c. Lagonda "V-12" (1939)	85	55
1057	$1 Adler "Standard" (1930)	1·25	75
1058	$3 DKW (1956)	2·50	2·50
1059	$4 Mercedes "500K" (1936)	3·00	3·00
1052/9	Set of 8	8·50	7·00

MS1060 Two sheets, each 99×70 mm. (a) $5 Daimler (1896). (b) $5 Mercedes "Knight" (1921) *Set of 2 sheets* .... 9·00 6·50

220 Young Mickey Mouse playing Santa Claus

221 Arms of Antigua

(Des Walt Disney Co. Litho Format)

1986 (4 Nov). Christmas. T **220** and similar horiz designs showing Walt Disney cartoon characters as babies. Multicoloured. P 11.

1061	25c. Type **220**	60	35
1062	30c. Mickey and Minnie Mouse building snowman	70	40
1063	40c. Aunt Matilda and Goofy baking	75	45
1064	60c. Goofy and Pluto	1·00	85
1065	70c. Pluto, Donald and Daisy Duck carol singing	1·10	1·00
1066	$1.50 Donald Duck, Mickey Mouse and Pluto stringing popcorn	1·75	2·50
1067	$3 Grandma Duck and Minnie Mouse	3·00	4·50
1068	$4 Donald Duck and Pete	3·25	4·50
1061/8	Set of 8	11·00	13·00

MS1069 Two sheets, each 127×102 mm. P 14×13½. (a) $5 Goofy, Donald and Minnie Mouse playing reindeer. (b) $5 Mickey Mouse, Donald and Daisy Duck playing with toys. *Set of 2 sheets* .... 13·00 14·00

1986 (25 Nov). Coil stamps. T **221** and similar vert design. Litho. P 14.

1070	10c. new blue	1·00	1·00
1071	25c. orange-vermilion	1·00	1·00

Design:—25c. Flag of Antigua.

222 *Canada I* (1981)

223 Bridled Burrfish

(Des J. Iskowitz. Litho Format)

1987 (5 Feb). America's Cup Yachting Championship. T **222** and similar multicoloured designs. P 15.

1072	30c. Type **222**	45	20
1073	60c. *Gretel II* (1970)	60	50
1074	$1 *Sceptre* (1958)	85	1·00
1075	$3 *Vigilant* (1893)	1·75	3·00
1072/5	Set of 4	3·25	4·25

MS1076 113×84 mm. $5 *Australia II* defeating *Liberty* (1983) (*horiz*) .... 4·00 5·00

Nos. 1072/6 exist imperforate from stock dispersed by the liquidator of Format International Security Printers Ltd.

(Des G. Drummond. Litho Questa)

1987 (23 Feb). Marine Life. T **223** and similar horiz designs. Multicoloured. P 14.

1077	15c. Type **223**	2·50	50
1078	30c. Common Noddy	5·00	60
1079	40c. Nassau Grouper	3·00	70
1080	50c. Laughing Gull	6·00	1·50
1081	60c. French Angelfish	3·50	1·50
1082	$1 Porkfish	3·50	1·75
1083	$2 Royal Tern	8·00	6·00
1084	$3 Sooty Tern	8·00	8·00
1077/84	Set of 8	35·00	18·00

MS1085 Two sheets, each 120×94 mm. (a) $5 Banded Butterflyfish. (b) $5 Brown Booby *Set of 2 sheets* .... 17·00 14·00

Nos. 1078, 1080 and 1083/5 are without the World Wildlife Fund logo shown on Type **223**.

224 Handball

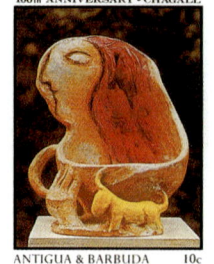

225 "The Profile"

(Litho Questa)

1987 (23 Mar). Olympic Games, Seoul (1988) (1st issue). T **224** and similar horiz designs. Multicoloured. P 14.

1086	10c. Type **224**	60	10
1087	60c. Fencing	85	35
1088	$1 Gymnastics	1·00	80
1089	$3 Football	2·25	4·00
1086/9	Set of 4	4·25	4·75

MS1090 100×72 mm. $5 Boxing gloves .... 3·00 4·25

See also Nos. 1222/6.

(Litho Questa)

1987 (30 Mar). Birth Centenary of Marc Chagall (artist). T **225** and similar multicoloured designs. P 13½×14.

1091	10c. Type **225**	30	15
1092	30c. "Portrait of the Artist's Sister"	45	30
1093	40c. "Bride with Fan"	50	40
1094	60c. "David in Profile"	55	45
1095	90c. "Fiancee with Bouquet"	75	60
1096	$1 "Self Portrait with Brushes"	75	65
1097	$3 "The Walk"	1·75	2·25
1098	$4 "Three Candles"	2·00	2·50
1091/8	Set of 8	6·25	6·50

MS1099 Two sheets, each 110×95 mm. (a) $5 "Fall of Icarus" (104×89 *mm*). (b) $5 "Myth of Orpheus" (104×89 *mm*). Imperf *Set of 2 sheets* .... 6·50 6·00

226 *Spirit of Australia* (fastest powerboat), 1978

227 Lee Iacocca at Unveiling of Restored Statue

(Des W. Wright. Litho Format)

1987 (9 Apr). Milestones of Transportation. T **226** and similar horiz designs. Multicoloured. P 15.

1100	10c. Type **226**	80	40
1101	15c. Werner von Siemens's electric locomotive, 1879	1·50	50
1102	30c. U.S.S. *Triton* (first submerged circumnavigation), 1960	1·25	50
1103	50c. Trevithick's steam carriage (first passenger-carrying vehicle), 1801	1·75	60
1104	60c. U.S.S. *New Jersey* (battleship), 1942	1·75	85
1105	70c. Draisine bicycle, 1818	2·00	1·00
1106	90c. *United States* (liner) (holder of Blue Riband), 1952	1·75	1·00
1107	$1.50 Cierva C.4 (first autogyro), 1923	1·75	2·75
1108	$2 Curtiss NC-4 flying boat (first transatlantic flight), 1919	2·00	3·00
1109	$3 *Queen Elizabeth 2* (liner), 1969	3·50	4·50
1100/9	Set of 10	16·00	13·50

Nos. 1100/9 exist imperforate from stock dispersed by the liquidator of Format International Security Printers Ltd.

(Litho Questa)

1987 (23 Apr). Centenary of Statue of Liberty (1986) (2nd issue). T **227** and similar multicoloured designs. P 14.

1110	15c. Type **227**	15	15
1111	30c. Statue at sunset (side view)	20	20
1112	45c. Aerial view of head	30	30
1113	50c. Lee Iacocca and torch	35	35
1114	60c. Workmen inside head of Statue (*horiz*)	35	35
1115	90c. Restoration work (*horiz*)	50	50
1116	$1 Head of Statue	55	55
1117	$2 Statue at sunset (front view)	1·00	1·50
1118	$3 Inspecting restoration work (*horiz*)	1·00	2·00
1119	$5 Statue at night	1·75	3·50
1110/19 Set of 10		5·50	8·00

228 Grace Kelly

229 Scouts around Camp Fire and Red Kangaroo

(Des Lynda Bruscheni. Litho Questa)

1987 (11 May). Entertainers. T **228** and similar vert designs. Multicoloured. P 14.

1120	15c. Type **228**	90	40
1121	30c. Marilyn Monroe	2·75	80
1122	45c. Orson Welles	90	60
1123	50c. Judy Garland	90	65
1124	60c. John Lennon	4·25	1·25
1125	$1 Rock Hudson	1·40	1·10
1126	$2 John Wayne	2·50	2·00
1127	$3 Elvis Presley	10·00	4·50
1120/7 Set of 8		21·00	10·00

(Litho Format)

1987 (25 May). 16th World Scout Jamboree, Australia. T **229** and similar horiz designs. Multicoloured. P 15.

1128	10c. Type **229**	65	20
1129	60c. Scouts canoeing and Blue-winged Kookaburra	1·25	80
1130	$1 Scouts on assault course and Ring-tailed Rock Wallaby	1·00	85
1131	$3 Field kitchen and Koala	1·50	4·25
1128/31 Set of 4		4·00	5·50
MS1132 103×78 mm. $5 Flags of Antigua, Australia and Scout Movement		3·25	3·50

Nos. 1128/32 exist imperforate from stock dispersed by the liquidator of Format International Security Printers Ltd.

230 Whistling Frog

(Des B. Burndock. Litho Questa)

1987 (15 June). "Capex '87" International Stamp Exhibition, Toronto. Reptiles and Amphibians. T **230** and similar horiz designs. Multicoloured. P 14.

1133	30c. Type **230**	55	20
1134	60c. Croaking Lizard	75	40
1135	$1 Antiguan Anole	1·00	70
1136	$3 Red-footed Tortoise	2·00	3·00
1133/6 Set of 4		3·75	3·75
MS1137 106×76 mm. $5 Ground Lizard		2·25	2·75

(**231**)

1987 (9 Sept). 10th Death Anniv of Elvis Presley (entertainer). No. 1127 optd with T **231**.

1138	$3 Elvis Presley	8·00	4·75

232 House of Burgesses, Virginia ("Freedom of Speech")

233 "Madonna and Child" (Bernardo Daddi)

(Des and litho Questa)

1987 (16 Nov). Bicentenary of U.S. Constitution. T **232** and similar multicoloured designs. P 14.

1139	15c. Type **232**	10	10
1140	45c. State Seal, Connecticut	20	25
1141	60c. State Seal, Delaware	25	35
1142	$4 Gouverneur Morris (Pennsylvania delegate) (*vert*)	1·75	2·25
1139/42 Set of 4		2·10	2·75
MS1143 105×75 mm. $5 Roger Sherman (Connecticut delegate) (*vert*)		2·00	2·75

Nos. 1139/42 were each issued in sheetlets of five stamps and one stamp-size label, which appears in the centre of the bottom row.

(Litho Questa)

1987 (1 Dec). Christmas. Religious Paintings. T **233** and similar vert designs. Multicoloured. P 14.

1144	45c. Type **233**	50	15
1145	60c. "St. Joseph" (detail, "The Nativity") (Sano di Pietro)	65	30
1146	$1 "Virgin Mary" (detail, "The Nativity") (Sano di Pietro)	85	55
1147	$4 "Music-making Angel" (Melozzo da Forli)	2·25	3·50
1144/7 Set of 4		3·75	4·00
MS1148 99×70 mm. $5 "The Flight into Egypt" (Sano di Pietro)		2·25	2·75

234 Wedding Photograph, 1947

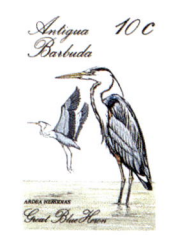

235 Great Blue Heron

(Des and litho Questa)

1988 (8 Feb). Royal Ruby Wedding. T **234** and similar vert designs. P 14.

1149	25c. deep brown, black and bright new blue	30	15
1150	60c. multicoloured	60	40
1151	$2 deep brown, black and light green	1·10	1·10
1152	$3 multicoloured	1·50	1·60
1149/52 Set of 4		3·25	3·00
MS1153 102×77 mm. $5 multicoloured		2·50	2·75

Designs:—60c. Queen Elizabeth II; $2 Princess Elizabeth and Prince Philip with Prince Charles at his christening, 1948; $3 Queen Elizabeth (from photo by Tim Graham), 1980; $5 Royal Family, 1952.

(Des W. Wright. Litho Questa)

1988 (1 Mar). Birds of Antigua. T **235** and similar multicoloured designs. P 14.

1154	10c. Type **235**	50	40
1155	15c. Ringed Kingfisher (*horiz*)	55	40
1156	50c. Bananaquit (*horiz*)	1·00	50
1157	60c. Purple Gallinule (*horiz*)	1·00	50
1158	70c. Blue-hooded Euphonia (*horiz*)	1·10	55
1159	$1 Brown-throated Conure ("Caribbean Parakeet")	1·40	75
1160	$3 Troupial (*horiz*)	2·50	3·50

ANTIGUA AND BARBUDA

1161	$4 Purple-throated Carib (horiz)	2·50	3·50
1154/61	Set of 8	9·50	9·00

MS1162 Two sheets, each 115×86 mm. (a) $5 Greater Flamingo. (b) $5 Brown Pelican Set of 2 sheets .... 4·50   5·50

236 First Aid at Daycare Centre, Antigua

(Des G. Vasarhelyi. Litho Format)

1988 (10 Mar). Salvation Army's Community Service. T **236** and similar horiz designs. Multicoloured. P 14×13½.

1163	25c. Type 236	80	65
1164	30c. Giving penicillin injection, Indonesia	80	65
1165	40c. Children at daycare centre, Bolivia	90	75
1166	45c. Rehabilitation of the handicapped, India	90	75
1167	50c. Training blind man, Kenya	1·00	1·25
1168	60c. Weighing baby, Ghana	1·00	1·25
1169	$1 Training typist, Zambia	1·40	1·75
1170	$2 Emergency food kitchen, Sri Lanka	2·00	3·50
1163/70	Set of 8	8·00	9·50

MS1171 152×83 mm. $5 General Eva Burrows .... 3·75   4·50

237 Columbus' Second Fleet, 1493

238 "Bust of Christ"

(Des I. MacLaury. Litho Questa)

1988 (16 Mar–16 May). 500th Anniv of Discovery of America by Columbus (1992) (1st issue). T **237** and similar horiz designs. Multicoloured. P 14.

1172	10c. Type 237	80	40
1173	30c. Painos Indian village and fleet (16.5)	80	45
1174	45c. Santa Mariagalante (flagship) and Painos village (16.5)	1·25	45
1175	60c. Painos Indians offering Columbus fruit and vegetables (16.5)	80	50
1176	90c. Painos Indian and Columbus with Scarlet Macaw	2·50	1·00
1177	$1 Columbus landing on island	1·75	1·00
1178	$3 Spanish soldier and fleet	2·50	3·25
1179	$4 Fleet under sail (16.5)	2·75	3·25
1172/9	Set of 8	12·00	9·25

MS1180 Two sheets, each 110×80 mm. (a) $5 Queen Isabella's cross. (b) $5 Gold coin of Ferdinand and Isabella (16.5) Set of 2 sheets .... 6·50   7·00

See also Nos. 1267/71, 1360/8, 1503/11, 1654/60 and 1670/1.

(Litho Questa)

1988 (11 Apr). 500th Birth Anniv of Titian. T **238** and similar vert designs showing paintings. Multicoloured. P 13½×14.

1181	30c. Type 238	40	20
1182	40c. "Scourging of Christ"	45	25
1183	45c. "Madonna in Glory with Saints"	45	25
1184	50c. "The Averoldi Polyptych" (detail)	45	35
1185	$1 "Christ Crowned with Thorns"	70	55
1186	$2 "Christ Mocked"	1·10	1·25
1187	$3 "Christ and Simon of Cyrene"	1·50	1·75
1188	$4 "Crucifixion with Virgin and Saints"	1·75	2·25
1181/8	Set of 8	6·25	6·25

MS1189 Two sheets, each 110×95 mm. (a) $5 "Ecce Homo" (detail). (b) $5 "Noli me Tangere" (detail) Set of 2 sheets .... 5·50   7·50

239 Two Yachts rounding Buoy

(Des G. Drummond. Litho Format)

1988 (18 Apr). Sailing Week. T **239** and similar horiz designs. Multicoloured. P 15.

1190	30c. Type 239	35	20
1191	60c. Three yachts	50	40
1192	$1 British yacht underway	60	55
1193	$3 Three yachts (different)	1·10	2·50
1190/3	Set of 4	2·25	3·25

MS1194 103×92 mm. $5 Two yachts .... 1·75   3·25

Nos. 1190/4 exist imperforate from stock dispersed by the liquidator of Format International Security Printers Ltd.

240 Mickey Mouse and Diver with Porpoise

(241)

(Des Walt Disney Co. Litho Questa)

1988 (3 May). Disney EPCOT Centre, Orlando, Florida. T **240** and similar multicoloured designs showing cartoon characters and exhibits. P 14×13½ (horiz) or 13½×14 (vert).

1195	1c. Type 240	10	10
1196	2c. Goofy and Mickey Mouse with futuristic car (vert)	10	10
1197	3c. Mickey Mouse and Goofy as Atlas (vert)	10	10
1198	4c. Mickey Mouse and Edaphosaurus (prehistoric reptile)	10	10
1199	5c. Mickey Mouse at Journey into Imagination exhibit	15	10
1200	10c. Mickey Mouse collecting vegetables (vert)	20	10
1201	25c. Type 240	55	25
1202	30c. As 2c	55	25
1203	40c. As 3c	60	30
1204	60c. As 4c	85	50
1205	70c. As 5c	95	60
1206	$1.50 As 10c	2·00	2·00
1207	$3 Goofy and Mickey Mouse with robot (vert)	2·50	2·75
1208	$4 Mickey Mouse and Clarabelle at Horizons exhibit	2·50	2·75
1195/1208	Set of 14	10·00	9·00

MS1209 Two sheets, each 125×99 mm. (a) $5 Mickey Mouse and monorail (vert). (b) $5 Mickey Mouse flying over EPCOT Centre Set of 2 sheets .... 7·00   6·50

1988 (9 May). Stamp Exhibitions. Nos. 1083/5 optd as T **241** showing various emblems.

1210	$2 Royal Tern (optd T 241, Prague)	7·00	3·50
1211	$3 Sooty Tern (optd "INDEPENDENCE 40", Israel)	7·00	4·00

MS1212 Two sheets, each 120×94 mm. (a) $5 Banded Butterflyfish (optd "OLYMPHILEX '88", Seoul). (b) $5 Brown Booby (optd "FINLANDIA 88", Helsinki) Set of 2 sheets .... 23·00   14·00

242 Jacaranda

243 Gymnastics

ANTIGUA AND BARBUDA

(Des Mary Walters. Litho Questa)

1988 (16 May). Flowering Trees. T **242** and similar vert designs. Multicoloured. P 14.

1213	10c. Type **242**	30	20
1214	30c. Cordia	40	20
1215	50c. Orchid Tree	60	40
1216	90c. Flamboyant	70	50
1217	$1 African Tulip Tree	75	55
1218	$2 Potato Tree	1·40	1·60
1219	$3 Crepe Myrtle	1·60	2·00
1220	$4 Pitch Apple	1·75	2·75
1213/20 Set of 8		6·75	7·50

MS1221 Two sheets, each 106×76 mm. (a) $5 Cassia. (b) $5 Chinaberry *Set of 2 sheets* .... 5·00 6·00

(Des J. Martin. Litho Questa)

1988 (10 June). Olympic Games, Seoul (2nd issue). T **243** and similar multicoloured designs. P 14.

1222	40c. Type **243**	30	25
1223	60c. Weightlifting	40	30
1224	$1 Water polo (*horiz*)	80	50
1225	$3 Boxing (*horiz*)	1·50	2·25
1222/5 Set of 4		2·75	3·00

MS1226 114×80 mm. $5 Runner with Olympic torch.. 2·00 3·00

244 *Danaus plexippus*

(Des S. Heimann. Litho Questa)

1988 (29 Aug)–**90**. Caribbean Butterflies. T **244** and similar horiz designs. Multicoloured. P 14.

1227	1c. Type **144**	60	1·25
1228	2c. *Greta diaphanus*	70	1·25
1229	3c. *Calisto archebates*	70	1·25
1230	5c. *Hamadryas feronia*	85	1·25
1231	10c. *Mestra dorcas*	1·00	30
1232	15c. *Hypolimnas misippus*	1·50	30
1233	20c. *Dione juno*	1·60	30
1234	25c. *Heliconius charithonia*	1·60	30
1235	30c. *Eurema pyro*	1·60	30
1236	40c. *Papilio androgeus*	1·60	30
1237	45c. *Anteos maerula*	1·60	30
1238	50c. *Aphrissa orbis*	1·75	45
1239	60c. *Astraptes xagua*	2·00	60
1240	$1 *Heliopetes arsalte*	2·25	1·00
1241	$2 *Polites baracoa*	3·25	3·75
1242	$2.50 *Phocides pigmalion*	4·00	5·00
1243	$5 *Prepona amphitoe*	5·50	8·00
1244	$10 *Oarisma nanus*	7·50	12·00
1244a	$20 *Parides lycimenes* (19.2.90)	17·00	22·00
1227/44a Set of 19		50·00	55·00

245 President Kennedy and Family **246** Minnie Mouse carol singing

(Des J. Iskowitz. Litho Questa)

1988 (23 Nov). 25th Death Anniv of John F. Kennedy (American statesman). T **245** and similar horiz designs, each showing different inset portrait. Multicoloured. P 14.

1245	1c. Type **245**	10	10
1246	2c. Kennedy commanding *PT 109*	10	10
1247	3c. Funeral cortege	10	10
1248	4c. In motorcade, Mexico City	10	10
1249	30c. As 1c.	35	15
1250	60c. As 4c.	1·00	40
1251	$1 As 3c.	1·10	75
1252	$4 As 2c.	3·00	3·50
1245/52 Set of 8		5·25	4·25

MS1253 105×75 mm. $5 Kennedy taking presidential oath of office .... 2·50 3·25

(Des Walt Disney Co. Litho Questa)

1988 (1 Dec). Christmas. "Mickey's Christmas Chorale". T **246** and similar multicoloured designs showing Walt Disney cartoon characters. P 13½×14.

1254	10c. Type **246**	40	30
1255	25c. Pluto	55	45
1256	30c. Mickey Mouse playing ukelele	55	45
1257	70c. Donald Duck and nephew	90	80
1258	$1 Mordie and Ferdie carol singing	90	1·00
	a. Sheetlet. Nos. 1258/65	6·50	7·25
1259	$1 Goofy carol singing	90	1·00
1260	$1 Chip n' Dale sliding off roof	90	1·00
1261	$1 Two of Donald Duck's nephews at window	90	1·00
1262	$1 As 10c.	90	1·00
1263	$1 As 25c.	90	1·00
1264	$1 As 30c.	90	1·00
1265	$1 As 70c.	90	1·00
1254/65 Set of 12		8·75	9·00

MS1266 Two sheets, each 127×102 mm. (a) $7 Donald Duck playing trumpet and Mickey and Minnie Mouse in carriage. P 13½×14. (b) $7 Mickey Mouse and friends singing carols on roller skates (*horiz*). P 14×13½ *Set of 2 sheets* .... 8·50 8·50

Nos. 1258/65 were printed together, *se-tenant* as a composite design, in sheetlets of eight.

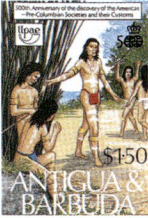

247 Arawak Warriors **248** de Havilland Comet 4 Airliner

(Des D. Miller. Litho Questa)

1989 (16 May). 500th Anniv of Discovery of America by Columbus (1992) (2nd issue). Pre-Columbian Arawak Society. T **247** and similar vert designs. Multicoloured. P 14.

1267	$1.50 Type **247**	1·10	1·40
	a. Horiz strip of 4. Nos. 1267/70	4·00	5·00
1268	$1.50 Whip dancers	1·10	1·40
1269	$1.50 Whip dancers and chief with pineapple	1·10	1·40
1270	$1.50 Family and camp fire	1·10	1·40
1267/70 Set of 4		4·00	5·00

MS1271 71×84 mm. $6 Arawak chief .... 2·75 3·00

Nos. 1267/70 were printed together, *se-tenant*, in horizontal strips of 4 throughout the sheet, each strip forming a composite design.

(Des W. Wright. Litho Questa)

1989 (29 May). 50th Anniv of First Jet Flight. T **248** and similar horiz designs. Multicoloured. P 14.

1272	10c. Type **248**	90	45
1273	30c. Messerschmitt Me 262 fighter	1·50	45
1274	40c. Boeing 707 airliner	1·50	45
1275	60c. Canadair CL-13 Sabre ("F-86 Sabre") fighter	1·90	55
1276	$1 Lockheed F-104 Starfighter	2·25	1·10
1277	$2 Douglas DC-10 airliner	3·00	3·00
1278	$3 Boeing 747-300/400 airliner	3·25	4·50
1279	$4 McDonnell Douglas F-4 Phantom II fighter	3·25	4·50
1272/9 Set of 8		16·00	13·50

MS1280 Two sheets, each 114×83 mm. (a) $7 Grumman F-14A Tomcat fighter. (b) $7 Concorde airliner *Set of 2 sheets* .... 11·00 13·00

249 *Festivale*

(Des W. Wright. Litho Questa)

1989 (20 June). Caribbean Cruise Ships. T **249** and similar horiz designs. Multicoloured. P 14.

1281	25c. Type **249**	2·00	50

ANTIGUA AND BARBUDA

1282	45c. *Southward*	2·25	50
1283	50c. *Sagafjord*	2·25	50
1284	60e. *Daphne*	2·25	60
1285	75c. *Cunard Countess*	2·50	1·00
1286	90c. *Song of America*	2·75	1·10
1287	$3 *Island Princess*	4·25	5·50
1288	$4 *Galileo*	4·25	6·00
1281/8 Set of 8		20·00	14·00

MS1289 (a) 113×87 mm. $6 *Norway*. (b) 111×82 mm. $6 *Oceanic*Set of 2 sheets .... 7·50 11·00

250 "Fish swimming by Duck half-submerged in Stream"

(Litho Questa)

1989 (1 July). Japanese Art. Paintings by Hiroshige. T **250** and similar horiz designs. Multicoloured. P 14×13½.

1290	25c. Type **250**	1·00	50
1291	45c. "Crane and Wave"	1·25	50
1292	50c. "Sparrows and Morning Glories"	1·40	50
1293	60c. "Crested Blackbird and Flowering Cherry"	1·50	60
1294	$1 "Great Knot sitting among Water Grass"	1·75	80
1295	$2 "Goose on a Bank of Water"	2·50	2·50
1296	$3 "Black Paradise Flycatcher and Blossoms"	3·00	3·00
1297	$4 "Sleepy Owl perched on a Pine Branch"	3·00	3·00
1290/7 Set of 8		14·00	10·00

MS1298 Two sheets, each 102×75 mm. (a) $5 "Bullfinch flying near a Clematis Branch". (b) $5 "Titmouse on a Cherry Branch" *Set of 2 sheets* .... 9·00 9·50

Nos. 1290/7 were each printed in sheetlets of 10 containing two horizontal strips of 5 stamps separated by printed labels commemorating Emperor Hirohito.

251 Mickey and Minnie Mouse in Helicopter over River Seine

(Des Walt Disney Company. Litho Questa)

1989 (7 July). "Philexfrance 89" International Stamp Exhibition, Paris. T **251** and similar multicoloured designs showing Walt Disney cartoon characters in Paris. P 14×13½.

1299	1c. Type **251**	10	10
1300	2c. Goofy and Mickey Mouse passing Arc de Triomphe	10	10
1301	3c. Mickey Mouse painting picture of Notre Dame	10	10
1302	4c. Mickey and Minnie Mouse with Pluto leaving Metro station	10	10
1303	5c. Minnie Mouse as model in fashion show	10	10
1304	10c. Daisy Duck, Minnie Mouse and Clarabelle as Folies Bergere dancers	10	10
1305	$5 Mickey and Minnie Mouse shopping in street market	7·00	7·00
1306	$6 Mickey and Minnie Mouse, Jose Carioca and Donald Duck at pavement cafe	7·00	7·00
1299/1306 Set of 8		13·00	13·00

MS1307 Two sheets, each 127×101 mm. (a) $5 Mickey and Minnie Mouse in hot air balloon. P 14×13½. (b) $5 Mickey Mouse at Pompidou Centre cafe (*vert*) P 13½×14 *Set of 2 sheets* .... 11·00 13·00

252 Goalkeeper **253** *Mycena pura*

(Des D. Bruckner. Litho B.D.T.)

1989 (21 Aug). World Cup Football Championship, Italy (1990). T **252** and similar multicoloured designs. P 14.

1308	15c. Type **252**	85	30
1309	25c. Goalkeeper moving towards ball	90	30
1310	$1 Goalkeeper reaching for ball	1·50	1·25
1311	$4 Goalkeeper saving goal	3·00	5·00
1308/11 Set of 4		5·50	6·25

MS1312 Two sheets, each 75×105 mm. (a) $5 Three players competing for ball (*horiz*). (b) $5 Ball and players' legs (*horiz*) *Set of 2 sheets* .... 7·00 10·00

(Litho Questa)

1989 (12 Oct). Fungi. T **253** and similar multicoloured designs. P 14.

1313	10c. Type **253**	75	50
1314	25c. *Psathyrella tuberculata* (*vert*)	1·10	40
1315	50c. *Psilocybe cubensis*	1·50	60
1316	60c. *Leptonia caeruleocapitata* (*vert*)	1·50	70
1317	75c. *Xeromphalina tenuipes* (*vert*)	1·75	1·10
1318	$1 *Chlorophyllum molybdites* (*vert*)	1·75	1·25
1319	$3 *Marasmius haematocephalus*	2·75	3·75
1320	$4 *Cantharellus cinnabarinus*	2·75	3·75
1313/20 Set of 8		12·00	11·00

MS1321 Two sheets, each 88×62 mm. (a) $6 *Leucopaxillus gracillimus* (*vert*). (b) $6 *Volvariella volvacea*Set of 2 sheets .... 13·00 15·00

254 Desmarest's Hutia **255** Goofy and Old Printing Press

(Des J. Barbaris. Litho B.D.T.)

1989 (19 Oct). Local Fauna. T **254** and similar multicoloured designs. P 14.

1322	25c. Type **254**	80	50
1323	45c. Caribbean Monk Seal	2·50	1·00
1324	60c. Mustache Bat (*vert*)	1·50	1·00
1325	$4 American Manatee (*vert*)	3·50	5·50
1322/5 Set of 4		7·50	7·25

MS1326 113×87 mm. $5 West Indies Giant Rice Rat .... 7·00 9·00

(Des Walt Disney Co. Litho Questa)

1989 (2 Nov). "American Philately". T **255** and similar multicoloured designs, each showing Walt Disney cartoon characters with stamps and the logo of the American Philatelic Society. P 13½×14.

1327	1c. Type **255**	10	10
1328	2c. Donald Duck cancelling first day cover for Mickey Mouse	10	10
1329	3c. Donald Duck's nephews reading recruiting poster for Pony Express riders	10	10
1330	4c. Morty and Ferdie as early radio broadcasters	10	10
1331	5c. Donald Duck and water buffalo watching television	10	10
1332	10c. Donald Duck with stamp album	10	10
1333	$4 Daisy Duck with computer system	4·75	6·00
1334	$6 Donald's nephews with stereo radio, trumpet and guitar	6·00	7·00

1327/34	Set of 8	10·00	12·00

MS1335 Two sheets, each 127×102 mm. (a) $5 Donald's nephews donating stamps to charity. P 13½×14. (b) $5 Minnie Mouse flying mailplane upside down (*horiz*). P 14×13½ Set of 2 sheets............ 11·00 13·00

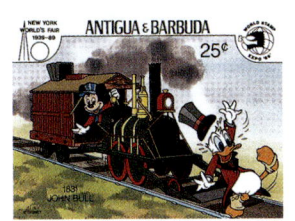

256 Mickey Mouse and Donald Duck with Camden and Amboy Locomotive *John Bull*, 1831

(Des Walt Disney Co. Litho Questa)

1989 (17 Nov). "World Stamp Expo '89" International Stamp Exhibition, Washington (1st issue). T **256** and similar multicoloured designs showing Walt Disney cartoon characters and locomotives. P 14×13½.

1336	25c. Type **256**	90	50
1337	45c. Mickey Mouse and friends with *Atlantic*, 1832	1·10	50
1338	50c. Mickey Mouse and Goofy with *William Crooks*, 1861	1·10	50
1339	60c. Mickey Mouse and Goofy with *Minnetonka*, 1869	1·10	65
1340	$1 Chip n' Dale with *Thatcher Perkins*, 1863	1·40	75
1341	$2 Mickey and Minnie Mouse with *Pioneer*, 1848	2·25	2·25
1342	$3 Mickey Mouse and Donald Duck with cog railway locomotive *Peppersass*, 1869	3·00	4·00
1343	$4 Mickey Mouse with Huey, Dewey and Louie aboard N.Y. World's Fair *Gimbels Flyer*, 1939	3·25	4·00
1336/43	Set of 8	13·00	12·00

MS1344 Two sheets, each 127×101 mm. (a) $6 Mickey Mouse and locomotive *Thomas Jefferson*, 1835 (*vert*). P 13½×14. (b) $6 Mickey Mouse and friends at Central Pacific "Golden Spike" ceremony, 1869. P 14×13½ Set of 2 sheets .... 8·50 10·00

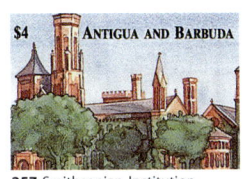

257 Smithsonian Institution, Washington

(Des Design Element. Litho Questa)

1989 (17 Nov). "World Stamp Expo '89" International Stamp Exhibition, Washington (2nd issue). Sheet 78×61 mm. P 14.

MS1345 **257** $4 multicoloured............................ 1·75 2·25

258 Launch of "Apollo 11"

(Des J. Iskowitz. Litho B.D.T.)

1989 (24 Nov). 20th Anniv of First Manned Landing on Moon. T **258** and similar multicoloured designs. P 14.

1346	10c. Type **258**	50	30
1347	45c. Aldrin on Moon	1·25	30
1348	$1 Module *Eagle* over Moon (*horiz*)	1·75	1·10
1349	$4 Recovery of "Apollo 11" crew after splashdown (*horiz*)	2·75	5·00
1346/9	Set of 4	5·50	6·00

MS1350 107×77 mm. $5 Astronaut Neil Armstrong...... 4·50 5·50

259 "The Small Cowper Madonna" (Raphael)

260 Star-eyed Hermit Crab

(Litho Questa)

1989 (11 Dec). Christmas. Paintings by Raphael and Giotto. T **259** and similar vert designs. Multicoloured. P 14.

1351	10c. Type **259**	30	15
1352	25c. "Madonna of the Goldfinch" (Raphael)..	45	20
1353	30c. "The Alba Madonna" (Raphael)	45	20
1354	50c. Saint (detail, "Bologna Altarpiece") (Giotto)	65	30
1355	60c. Angel (detail, "Bologna Altarpiece") (Giotto)	70	35
1356	70c. Angel slaying serpent (detail, "Bologna Altarpiece") (Giotto)	80	40
1357	$4 Evangelist (detail, "Bologna Altarpiece") (Giotto)	3·00	4·50
1358	$5 Madonna of Foligno" (detail) (Raphael).	3·00	4·50
1351/8	Set of 8	8·50	9·50

MS1359 Two sheets, each 71×96 mm. (a) $5 "The Marriage of the Virgin" (detail) (Raphael). (b) $5 Madonna and Child (detail, "Bologna Altarpiece") (Giotto) Set of 2 sheets.................................. 9·00 12·00

(Des Mary Walters. Litho Questa)

1990 (26 Mar). 500th Anniv of Discovery of America by Columbus (1992) (3rd issue). New World Natural History – Marine Life. T **260** and similar vert designs. Multicoloured. P 14.

1360	10c. Type **260**	45	20
1361	20c. Spiny Lobster	65	25
1362	25c. Magnificent Banded Fanworm	65	25
1363	45c. Cannonball Jellyfish	80	40
1364	60c. Red-spiny Sea Star	1·00	60
1365	$2 Peppermint Shrimp	2·00	2·50
1366	$3 Coral Crab	2·25	3·75
1367	$4 Branching Fire Coral	2·25	3·75
1360/7	Set of 8	9·00	10·50

MS1368 Two sheets, each 100×69 mm. (a) $5 Common Sea Fan. (b) $5 Portuguese Man-of-war Set of 2 sheets... 8·00 9·00

261 *Vanilla mexicana*

262 Queen Victoria and Queen Elizabeth II

(Des Mary Walters. Litho Questa)

1990 (17 Apr). "EXPO 90" International Garden and Greenery Exhibition, Osaka. Orchids. T **261** and similar vert designs. Multicoloured. P 14.

1369	15c. Type **261**	75	50
1370	45c. *Epidendrum ibaguense*	1·10	50
1371	50c. *Epidendrum secundum*	1·25	55
1372	60c. *Maxillaria conferta*	1·40	55
1373	$1 *Oncidium altissimum*	1·50	1·00
1374	$2 *Spiranthes lanceolata*	2·00	2·50
1375	$3 *Tonopsis utricularioides*	2·25	3·50
1376	$5 *Epidendrum nocturnum*	3·25	4·50
1369/76	Set of 8	12·00	12·00

MS1377 Two sheets, each 102×70 mm. (a) $6 *Octomeria graminifolia*. (b) $6 *Rodriguezia lanceolata* Set of 2 sheets .... 6·50 8·00

ANTIGUA AND BARBUDA

(Des M. Pollard. Litho B.D.T)

1990 (3 May). 150th Anniv of the Penny Black. T **262** and similar horiz designs. P 14½×14.

1378	**262**	45c. blue-green	1·25	40
1379	–	60c. magenta	1·50	65
1380	–	$5 ultramarine	3·75	5·50
1378/80	Set of 3		6·00	6·00
MS1381	102×80 mm. $6 blackish purple		5·00	6·50

Designs:—60c., $5 As Type **262**, but with different backgrounds.

263 Britannia (mail paddle-steamer), 1840

(Des M. Pollard. Litho B.D.T)

1990 (3 May). "Stamp World London 90" International Stamp Exhibition. T **263** and similar horiz designs. P 13½.

1382	50c. deep grey-green and scarlet-vermilion	1·25	35
1383	75c. purple-brown and scarlet-vermilion	1·50	90
1384	$4 deep ultramarine and scarlet-vermilion	4·00	5·50
1382/4	Set of 3	6·00	6·00
MS1385	104×81 mm. $6 brownish black and scarlet-vermilion	4·50	6·00

Designs:—75c. Travelling Post Office sorting van, 1892; $4 Short S.23 Empire "C" Class flying boat *Centaurus*, 1938; $6 Post Office underground railway, London, 1927.

264 Flamefish

265 "Voyager 2" passing Saturn

(Des G. Drummond. Litho Questa)

1990 (21 May). Reef Fish. T **264** and similar horiz designs. Multicoloured. P 14.

1386	10c. Type **264**	65	55
1387	15c. Coney	80	55
1388	50c. Long-spined Squirrelfish	1·25	60
1389	60c. Sergeant Major	1·25	60
1390	$1 Yellow-tailed Snapper	1·50	85
1391	$2 Rock Beauty	2·25	2·75
1392	$3 Spanish Hogfish	2·75	3·75
1393	$4 Striped Parrotfish	2·75	3·75
1386/93	Set of 8	12·00	12·00
MS1394	Two sheets, each 99×70 mm. (a) $5 Black-barred Soldierfish. (b) $5 Four-eyed Butterflyfish Set of 2 sheets	10·00	11·00

(Des K. Gromell. Litho B.D.T)

1990 (11 June). Achievements in Space. T **265** and similar square designs. Multicoloured. P 14.

1395	45c. Type **265**	1·10	85
	a. Sheetlet. Nos. 1395/1414	20·00	15·00
1396	45c. "Pioneer 11" photographing Saturn	1·10	85
1397	45c. Astronaut in transporter	1·10	85
1398	45c. Space shuttle *Columbia*	1·10	85
1399	45c. "Apollo 10" command module on parachutes	1·10	85
1400	45c. "Skylab" space station	1·10	85
1401	45c. Astronaut Edward White in space	1·10	85
1402	45c. "Apollo" spacecraft on joint mission	1·10	85
1403	45c. "Soyuz" spacecraft on joint mission	1·10	85
1404	45c. "Mariner 1" passing Venus	1·10	85
1405	45c. "Gemini 4" capsule	1·10	85
1406	45c. "Sputnik 1"	1·10	85
1407	45c. Hubble space telescope	1·10	85
1408	45c. North American X-15	1·10	85
1409	45c. Bell XS-1 airplane	1·10	85
1410	45c. "Apollo 17" astronaut and lunar rock formation	1·10	85
1411	45c. Lunar Rover	1·10	85
1412	45c. "Apollo 14" lunar module	1·10	85
1413	45c. Astronaut Buzz Aldrin on Moon	1·10	85
1414	45c. Soviet "Lunokhod" lunar vehicle	1·10	85
1395/1414	Set of 20	20·00	15·00

Nos. 1395/1414 were printed together, *se-tenant*, in sheetlets of 20 forming a composite design.

266 Queen Mother in Evening Dress

267 Mickey Mouse as Animator

(Des D. Miller. Litho Questa)

1990 (27 Aug). 90th Birthday of Queen Elizabeth the Queen Mother. T **266** and similar vert designs showing recent photographs of the Queen Mother. P 14.

1415	15c. multicoloured	55	20
1416	35c. multicoloured	75	25
1417	75c. multicoloured	1·00	85
1418	$3 multicoloured	2·50	3·50
1415/18	Set of 4	3·50	4·00
MS1419	67×98 mm. $6 multicoloured	4·00	4·50

(Des Walt Disney Co. Litho Questa)

1990 (3 Sept). Mickey Mouse in Hollywood. T **267** and similar horiz designs showing Walt Disney cartoon characters. Multicoloured. P 14×13½.

1420	25c. Type **267**	60	25
1421	45c. Minnie Mouse learning lines while being dressed	80	25
1422	50c. Mickey Mouse with clapper board	90	30
1423	60c. Daisy Duck making-up Mickey Mouse	1·00	35
1424	$1 Clarabelle Cow as Cleopatra	1·25	70
1425	$2 Mickey Mouse directing Goofy and Donald Duck	1·75	2·25
1426	$3 Mickey Mouse directing Goofy as birdman	2·25	3·50
1427	$4 Donald Duck and Mickey Mouse editing film	2·25	3·50
1420/7	Set of 8	9·50	9·25
MS1428	Two sheets, each 132×95 mm. (a) $5 Minnie Mouse, Daisy Duck and Clarabelle as musical stars. (b) $5 Mickey Mouse on set as director Set of 2 sheets	7·00	9·00

268 Men's 20 Kilometres Walk

269 Huey and Dewey asleep (*Christmas Stories*)

(Des B. Grout. Litho Questa)

1990 (1 Oct). Olympic Games, Barcelona (1992) (1st issue). T **268** and similar vert designs. Multicoloured. P 14.

1429	50c. Type **268**	75	40
1430	75c. Triple jump	1·00	75
1431	$1 Men's 10,000 metres	1·25	85
1432	$5 Javelin	3·50	6·00
1429/32	Set of 4	6·00	6·75
MS1433	100×70 mm. $6 Athlete lighting Olympic flame at Los Angeles Olympics	5·50	7·00

See also Nos. 1553/61 and 1609/17.

(Des Walt Disney Co. Litho Questa)

1990 (15 Oct). International Literacy Year. T **269** and similar vert designs showing Walt Disney cartoon characters illustrating works by Charles Dickens. Multicoloured. P 13½×14.

1434	15c. Type **269**	65	35
1435	45c. Donald Duck as Poor Jo looking at grave (*Bleak House*)	1·00	45
1436	50c. Dewey as Oliver asking for more (*Oliver Twist*)	1·10	50
1437	60c. Daisy Duck as The Marchioness (*Old Curiosity Shop*)	1·25	55

1438	$1 Little Nell giving nosegay to her grandfather (*Little Nell*)	1·40	85
1439	$2 Scrooge McDuck as Mr. Pickwick (*Pickwick Papers*)	2·00	2·50
1440	$3 Minnie Mouse as Florence and Mickey Mouse as Paul (*Dombey and Son*)	2·25	3·50
1441	$5 Minnie Mouse as Jenny Wren (*Our Mutual Friend*)	2·75	4·50
1434/41	Set of 8	11·00	12·00
MS1442	Two sheets, each 126×102 mm. (a) $6 Artful Dodger picking pocket (*Oliver Twist*). (b) $6 Unexpected arrivals at Mr. Peggoty's (*David Copperfield*) Set of 2 sheets	10·00	12·00

(270) Winners West Germany 1 Argentina 0

271 Pearly-eyed Thrasher

1990 (11 Nov). World Cup Football Championship Winners, Italy. Nos. 1308/12 optd as T **270** by Questa.

1443	15c. Type **252**	75	40
1444	25c. Goalkeeper moving towards ball	75	40
1445	$1 Goalkeeper reaching for ball	1·50	1·60
1446	$4 Goalkeeper saving goal	3·25	5·50
1443/6	Set of 4	5·50	7·25
MS1447	Two sheets, each 75×105 mm. (a) $5 Three players competing for ball (*horiz*). (b) $5 Ball and players' legs (*horiz*) Set of 2 sheets	9·50	11·00

The overprint on No. **MS**1447 is larger and thicker, 31×13 mm.

(Des Jennifer Toombs. Litho B.D.T.)

1990 (19 Nov). Birds. T **271** and similar horiz designs. Multicoloured. P 14.

1448	10c. Type **271**	55	30
1449	25c. Purple-throated Carib	60	35
1450	50c. Yellowthroat	75	40
1451	60c. American Kestrel	1·00	70
1452	$1 Yellow-bellied Sapsucker	1·25	80
1453	$2 Purple Gallinule	2·25	2·50
1454	$3 Yellow-crowned Night Heron	2·50	3·25
1455	$4 Blue-hooded Euphonia	2·50	3·50
1448/55	Set of 8	10·50	10·50
MS1456	Two sheets, each 76×60 mm. (a) $6 Brown Pelican. (b) $6 Magnificent Frigate Bird Set of 2 sheets	14·00	16·00

272 "Madonna and Child with Saints" (detail, Sebastiano del Piombo)

(Litho Questa)

1990 (10 Dec). Christmas. Paintings by Renaissance Masters. T **272** and similar multicoloured designs. P 14×13½ (horiz) or 13½×14 (vert).

1457	25c. Type **272**	80	30
1458	30c. "Virgin and Child with Angels" (detail, Grünewald) (*vert*)	90	30
1459	40c. "The Holy Family and a Shepherd" (detail, Titian)	1·00	30
1460	60c. "Virgin and Child" (detail, Lippi) (*vert*)	1·40	40
1461	$1 "Jesus, St. John and Two Angels" (Rubens)	2·00	70
1462	$2 "Adoration of the Shepherds" (detail, Vincenzo Catena)	2·50	2·75
1463	$4 "Adoration of the Magi" (detail, Giorgione)	4·00	5·50
1464	$5 "Virgin and Child adored by Warrior" (detail, Vincenzo Catena)	4·00	5·50
1457/64	Set of 8	15·00	14·00
MS1465	Two sheets, each 71×101 mm. (a) $6 "Allegory of the Blessings of Jacob" (detail, Rubens) (*vert*). (b) $6 "Adoration of the Magi" (detail, Fra Angelico) (*vert*) Set of 2 sheets	7·00	8·50

273 "Rape of the Daughters of Leucippus" (detail)

(Litho Questa)

1991 (21 Jan). 350th Death Anniv of Rubens. T **273** and similar horiz designs. Multicoloured. P 14×13½.

1466	25c. Type **273**	1·00	40
1467	45c. "Bacchanal" (detail)	1·50	45
1468	50c. "Rape of the Sabine Women" (detail)	1·50	50
1469	60c. "Battle of the Amazons" (detail)	1·60	65
1470	$1 "Rape of the Sabine Women" (different detail)	2·00	1·00
1471	$2 "Bacchanal" (different detail)	2·50	2·50
1472	$3 "Rape of the Sabine Women" (different detail)	3·50	4·25
1473	$4 "Bacchanal" (different detail)	3·50	5·25
1466/73	Set of 8	16·00	13·50
MS1474	Two sheets, each 101×71 mm. (a) $6 "Rape of Hippodameia" (detail). (b) $6 "Battle of the Amazons" (different detail) Set of 2 sheets	8·50	10·00

274 U.S. Troops cross into Germany, 1944

(Des W. Wright. Litho B.D.T.)

1991 (11 Mar). 50th Anniv of Second World War. T **274** and similar horiz designs. Multicoloured. P 14.

1475	10c. Type **274**	1·10	65
1476	15c. Axis surrender in North Africa, 1943	1·25	50
1477	25c. U.S. tanks invade Kwajalein, 1944	1·25	50
1478	45c. Roosevelt and Churchill meet at Casablanca, 1943	2·75	70
1479	50c. Marshal Badoglio, Prime Minister of Italian anti-fascist government, 1943	1·50	70
1480	$1 Lord Mountbatten, Supreme Allied Commander South-east Asia, 1943	3·25	1·50
1481	$2 Greek victory at Koritza, 1940	2·25	2·75
1482	$4 Anglo-Soviet mutual assistance pact, 1941	3·25	4·25
1483	$5 Operation Torch landings, 1942	3·50	4·25
1475/83	Set of 9	18·00	14·00
MS1484	Two sheets, each 108×80 mm. (a) $6 Japanese attack Pearl Harbor, 1941. (b) $6 U.S.A.A.F. daylight raid on Schweinfurt, 1943 Set of 2 sheets	11·00	12·00

275 Locomotive *Prince Regent*, Middleton Colliery, 1812

(Des W. Hanson Studio. Litho Walsall)

1991 (18 Mar). Cog Railways. T **275** and similar multicoloured designs. P 14.

1485	25c. Type **275**	1·25	55
1486	30c. Snowdon Mountain Railway	1·25	55
1487	40c. First railcar at Hell Gate, Manitou and Pike's Peak Railway, U.S.A.	1·40	65
1488	60c. P.N.K.A. rack railway, Java	1·60	70
1489	$1 Green Mountain Railway, Maine, 1883	2·00	1·00
1490	$2 Rack locomotive *Pike's Peak*, 1891	3·00	3·00
1491	$4 Vitznau-Rigi Railway, Switzerland, and Mt Rigi hotel local post stamp	3·75	4·75
1492	$5 Leopoldina Railway, Brazil	3·75	4·75
1485/92	Set of 8	16·00	14·50

ANTIGUA AND BARBUDA

MS1493 Two sheets, each 100×70 mm. (a) $6 Electric towing locomotives, Panama Canal. (b) $6 Gornergracht Railway, Switzerland (*vert*) Set of 2 sheets. ... 12·00 13·00

276 *Heliconius charithonia*

(Des T. Pedersen. Litho B.D.T.)

1991 (15 Apr). Butterflies. T **276** and similar multicoloured designs. P 14.

1494	10c. Type **276**	65	50
1495	35c. Marpesia petreus	1·10	50
1496	50c. Anartia amathea	1·25	60
1497	75c. Siproeta stelenes	1·50	1·00
1498	$1 Battus polydamas	1·75	1·10
1499	$2 Historis odius	2·25	2·75
1500	$4 Hypolimnas misippus	3·25	4·25
1501	$5 Hamadryas feronia	3·25	4·25
1494/1501 Set of 8		13·50	13·50

MS1502 Two sheets. (a) 73×100 mm. $6 *Vanessa cardui* caterpillar (*vert*). (b) 100×73 mm. $6 *Danaus plexippus* caterpillar (*vert*) Set of 2 sheets ... 14·00 16·00

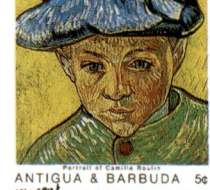

277 Hanno the Phoenician, 450 B.C.

278 "Camille Roulin" (Van Gogh)

(Des T. Agans. Litho Questa)

1991 (22 Apr). 500th Anniv of Discovery of America by Columbus (1992) (4th issue). History of Exploration. T **277** and similar designs. P 14.

1503	10c. multicoloured	70	40
1504	15c. multicoloured	80	40
1505	45c. multicoloured	1·25	50
1506	60c. multicoloured	1·40	60
1507	$1 multicoloured	1·75	85
1508	$2 multicoloured	2·25	2·75
1509	$4 multicoloured	3·00	4·00
1510	$5 multicoloured	3·00	4·00
1503/10 Set of 8		13·00	12·00

MS1511 Two sheets, each 106×76 mm. (a) $6 black and Indian red. (b) $6 black and Indian red Set of 2 sheets ... 7·00 9·00

Designs: *Horiz*—15c. Pytheas the Greek, 325 B.C.; 45c. Erik the Red discovering Greenland, 985 A.D.; 60c. Leif Eriksson reaching Vinland, 1000 A.D.; $1 Scylax the Greek in the Indian Ocean, 518 A.D.; $2 Marco Polo sailing to the Orient, 1259 A.D.; $4 Ship of Queen Hatshepsut of Egypt, 1493 B.C.; $5 St. Brendan's coracle, 500 A.D. *Vert*—$6 (No. **MS**1511a) Engraving of Columbus as Admiral; $6 (No. **MS**1511b) Engraving of Columbus bare-headed.

(Litho Walsall)

1991 (13 May). Death Centenary of Vincent van Gogh (artist) (1990). T **278** and similar multicoloured designs. P 13½.

1512	5c. Type **278**	70	85
1513	10c. "Armand Roulin"	70	60
1514	15c. "Young Peasant Woman with Straw Hat sitting in the Wheat"	85	50
1515	25c. "Adeline Ravoux"	1·00	50
1516	30c. "The Schoolboy"	1·00	50
1517	40c. "Doctor Gachet"	1·10	50
1518	50c. "Portrait of a Man"	1·25	50
1519	75c. "Two Children"	1·75	80
1520	$2 "The Postman Joseph Roulin"	2·75	2·75
1521	$3 "The Seated Zouave"	3·75	4·00
1522	$4 "L'Arlésienne"	4·00	4·50
1523	$5 "Self-Portrait, November/December 1888"	4·00	4·50
1512/23 Set of 12		20·00	18·00

MS1524 Three sheets, each 102×76 mm. (a) $5 "Farmhouse in Provence" (*horiz*). (b) $5 "Flowering Garden" (*horiz*). (c) $6 "The Bridge at Trinquetaille" (*horiz*). Imperf Set of 3 sheets ... 16·00 18·00

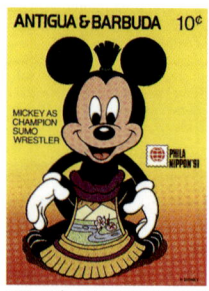

279 Mickey Mouse as Champion Sumo Wrestler

(Des Walt Disney Co. Litho Questa)

1991 (20 June). "Phila Nippon '91" International Stamp Exhibition, Tokyo. T **279** and similar multicoloured designs showing Walt Disney cartoon characters participating in martial arts. P 13½×14 (*vert*) or 14×13½ (*horiz*).

1525	10c. Type **279**	80	20
1526	15c. Goofy using the tonfa (*horiz*)	90	25
1527	45c. Donald Duck as a Ninja (*horiz*)	1·60	50
1528	60c. Mickey armed for Kung fu	2·00	65
1529	$1 Goofy with Kendo sword	2·50	1·25
1530	$2 Mickey and Donald demonstrating Aikido (*horiz*)	3·00	3·00
1531	$4 Mickey and Donald in Judo bout (*horiz*)	4·00	5·00
1532	$5 Mickey performing Yabusame (mounted archery)	4·00	5·00
1525/32 Set of 8		17·00	14·00

MS1533 Two sheets, each 127×102 mm. (a) $6 Mickey delivering Karate kick (*horiz*). (b) $6 Mickey demonstrating Tamashiwara Set of 2 sheets ... 10·00 12·00

280 Queen Elizabeth and Prince Philip in 1976

281 Daisy Duck teeing-off

(Des D. Miller. Litho Walsall)

1991 (8 July). 65th Birthday of Queen Elizabeth II. T **280** and similar horiz designs. Multicoloured. P 14.

1534	15c. Type **280**	40	10
1535	20c. The Queen and Prince Philip in Portugal, 1985	40	10
1536	$2 Queen Elizabeth II	1·75	1·50
1537	$4 The Queen and Prince Philip at Ascot, 1986	2·75	3·25
1534/7 Set of 4		4·75	4·50

MS1538 68×90 mm. $4 The Queen at National Theatre, 1986, and Prince Philip ... 3·50 4·00

(Des D. Miller. Litho Walsall)

1991 (8 July). 10th Wedding Anniv of Prince and Princess of Wales. Horiz designs as T **280**. Multicoloured. P 14.

1539	10c. Prince and Princess of Wales at party, 1986	50	10
1540	40c. Separate portraits of Prince, Princess and sons	1·00	25
1541	$1 Prince Henry and Prince William	1·25	70
1542	$5 Princess Diana in Australia and Prince Charles in Hungary	4·50	4·50
1539/42 Set of 4		6·50	5·00

MS1543 68×90 mm. $4 Prince Charles in Hackney and Princess and sons in Majorca, 1987 ... 5·50 5·50

(Des Walt Disney Co. Litho Questa)

1991 (7 Aug). Golf. T **281** and similar multicoloured designs showing Walt Disney cartoon characters. P 13½×14.

1544	10c. Type **281**	70	50
1545	15c. Goofy playing ball from under trees	75	50
1546	45c. Mickey Mouse playing deflected shot	1·25	50
1547	60c. Mickey hacking divot out of fairway	1·50	65
1548	$1 Donald Duck playing ball out of pond	1·75	1·10
1549	$2 Minnie Mouse hitting ball over pond	2·50	2·75
1550	$4 Donald in a bunker	3·25	4·00
1551	$5 Goofy trying snooker shot into hole	3·25	4·00
1544/51 Set of 8		13·50	12·50

MS1552 Two sheets, each 127×102 mm. (a) $6 Grandma Duck in senior tournament. P 13½×14. (b) $6 Mickey and Minnie Mouse on course (*horiz*). P 14×13½ *Set of 2 sheets* .... 10·00 12·00

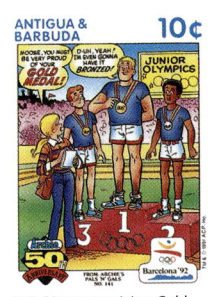

282 Moose receiving Gold Medal

(Des Archie Comic Publications Inc. Litho Questa)

1991 (19 Aug). 50th Anniv of Archie Comics, and Olympic Games, Barcelona (1992) (2nd issue). T **282** and similar multicoloured designs. P 14×13½ (vert) or 13½×14 (horiz).

1553	10c. Type **282**	55	40
1554	25c. Archie playing polo on a motorcycle (*horiz*)	85	40
1555	40c. Archie and Betty at fencing class	1·10	45
1556	60c. Archie joining girls' volleyball team	1·40	65
1557	$1 Archie with tennis ball in his mouth	1·75	1·10
1558	$2 Archie running marathon	2·50	3·00
1559	$4 Archie judging women's gymnastics (*horiz*)	3·75	4·50
1560	$5 Archie watching the cheer-leaders	3·75	4·50
1553/60 Set of 8		14·00	13·50

MS1561 Two sheets, each 128×102 mm. (a) $6 Archie heading football. (b) $6 Archie catching baseball (*horiz*) *Set of 2 sheets* .... 11·00 13·00

283 Presidents De Gaulle and Kennedy, 1961

(Des. J. Iskowitz. Litho Questa)

1991 (11 Sept). Birth Centenary of Charles de Gaulle (French statesman). T **283** and similar multicoloured designs. P 14.

1562	10c. Type **283**	80	50
1563	15c. General De Gaulle with Pres. Roosevelt, 1945 (*vert*)	80	50
1564	45c. Pres. De Gaulle with Chancellor Adenauer, 1962 (*vert*)	1·25	50
1565	60c. De Gaulle at Arc de Triomphe, Liberation of Paris, 1944 (*vert*)	1·50	65
1566	$1 General De Gaulle crossing the Rhine, 1945	1·75	1·25
1567	$2 General De Gaulle in Algiers, 1944	2·50	3·00
1568	$4 Presidents De Gaulle and Eisenhower, 1960	3·25	4·50
1569	$5 De Gaulle returning from Germany, 1968 (*vert*)	3·25	4·50
1562/9 Set of 8		13·50	14·00

MS1570 Two sheets. (a) 76×106 mm. $6 De Gaulle with crowd. (b) 106×76 mm. $6 De Gaulle and Churchill at Casablanca, 1943 *Set of 2 sheets* .... 15·00 13·00

284 Parliament Building and Map

(Litho Questa)

1991 (28 Oct). 10th Anniv of Independence. T **284** and similar horiz design. P 14.
| 1571 | **284** | 10c. multicoloured | 75 | 50 |

MS1572 87×97 mm. $6 Old Post Office, St. Johns, and stamps of 1862 and 1981 (50×37 *mm*) .... 6·00 7·50

285 Germans celebrating Reunification

(Des L. Fried (Nos. 1573, 1576, 1580, **MS**1583a), W. Hanson Studio (Nos. 1574, 1577 1581, **MS**1583b), J. Iskowitz (Nos. 1575, 1582) or W. Wright (others). Litho Questa)

1991 (9 Dec). Anniversaries and Events. T **285** and similar multicoloured designs. P 14.

1573	25c. Type **285**	30	30
1574	75c. Cubs erecting tent	70	50
1575	$1.50 *Don Giovanni* and Mozart	5·50	3·00
1576	$2 Chariot driver and Gate at night	1·10	2·00
1577	$2 Lord Baden-Powell and members of 3rd Antigua Methodist cub pack (*vert*)	3·25	2·75
1578	$2 Lilienthals signature and glider *Flugzeug Nr. 5*	3·50	2·75
1579	$2.50 Driver in Class P36 steam locomotive (*vert*)	6·50	4·00
1580	$3 Statues from podium	1·75	3·25
1581	$3.50 Cubs and camp fire	2·50	3·25
1582	$4 St. Peter's Cathedral, Salzburg	10·00	7·50
1573/82 Set of 10		32·00	26·00

MS1583 Two sheets. (a) 100×72 mm. $4 Detail of chariot and helmet; (b) 89×117 mm. $5 Antiguan flag and Jamboree emblem (*vert*) *Set of 2 sheets* ...... 9·00 11·00
Anniversaries and Events:—Nos. 1573, 1576, 1580, **MS**1583a, Bicentenary of Brandenburg Gate, Germany Nos. 1574, 1577, 1581, **MS**1583b, 17th World Scout Jamboree, Korea; Nos. 1575, 1582, Death bicentenary of Mozart; No. 1578, Centenary of Otto Lilienthal's gliding experiments; No. 1579, Centenary of Trans–Siberian Railway.

286 *Nimitz* Class Carrier and *Ticonderoga* Class Cruiser

287 "The Annunciation" (Fra Angelico)

(Des L. Birmingham. Litho Questa)

1991 (9 Dec). 50th Anniv of Japanese Attack on Pearl Harbor. T **286** and similar horiz designs. Multicoloured. P 14½.

1585	$1 Type **286**	2·50	1·75
	a. Sheetlet. Nos. 1585/94	23·00	16·00
1586	$1 Tourist launch	2·50	1·75
1587	$1 U.S.S. *Arizona* memorial	2·50	1·75
1588	$1 Wreaths on water and aircraft	2·50	1·75
1589	$1 White Tern	2·50	1·75
1590	$1 Mitsubishi A6M Zero-Sen fighters over Pearl City	2·50	1·75
1591	$1 Mitsubishi A6M Zero-Sen fighters attacking	2·50	1·75
1592	$1 Battleship Row in flames	2·50	1·75
1593	$1 U.S.S. *Nevada* (battleship) underway	2·50	1·75

ANTIGUA AND BARBUDA

1594	$1 Mitsubishi A6M Zero-Sen fighters returning to carriers	2·50	1·75
1585/94	Set of 10	23·00	16·00

Nos. 1585/94 were printed together, *se-tenant*, in sheetlets of 10 with the stamps arranged in two horizontal strips of 5 separated by a gutter showing the wreck of U.S.S. *Arizona*.

(Litho Walsall)

1991 (12 Dec). Christmas. Religious Paintings by Fra Angelico. T **287** and similar vert designs. Multicoloured. P 12.

1595	10c. Type **287**	40	30
1596	30c. "Nativity"	65	30
1597	40c. "Adoration of the Magi"	75	30
1598	60c. "Presentation in the Temple"	1·00	45
1599	$1 "Circumcision"	1·25	65
1600	$3 "Flight into Egypt"	2·50	3·50
1601	$4 "Massacre of the Innocents"	2·50	4·00
1602	$5 "Christ teaching in the Temple"	2·50	4·00
1595/1602	Set of 8	10·50	12·00
MS1603	Two sheets, each 102×127 mm. (a) $6 "Adoration of the Magi" (Cook Tondo). (b) $6 "Adoration of the Magi" (*different*). P 14 Set of 2 sheets	13·00	14·00

288 Queen Elizabeth II and Bird Sanctuary

289 Mickey Mouse awarding Swimming Gold Medal to Mermaid

(Des D. Miller. Litho Questa)

1992 (27 Feb). 40th Anniv of Queen Elizabeth II's Accession. T **288** and similar horiz designs. Multicoloured. P 14.

1604	10c. Type **288**	1·25	40
1605	30c. Nelson's Dockyard	1·50	40
1606	$1 Ruins on Shirley Heights	1·50	70
1607	$5 Beach and palm trees	3·00	4·25
1604/7	Set of 4	6·50	5·00
MS1608	Two sheets, each 75×98 mm. (a) $6 Beach. (b) $6 Hillside foliage Set of 2 sheets	8·50	9·00

(Des Walt Disney Co. Litho B.D.T.)

1992 (16 Mar). Olympic Games, Barcelona (3rd issue). T **289** and similar multicoloured designs showing Walt Disney cartoon characters. P 13.

1609	10c. Type **289**	70	30
1610	15c. Huey, Dewey and Louie with kayak	80	30
1611	30c. Donald Duck and Uncle Scrooge in yacht	1·00	35
1612	50c. Donald and horse playing water polo	1·40	50
1613	$1 Big Pete weightlifting	2·00	85
1614	$2 Donald and Goofy fencing	3·00	3·00
1615	$4 Mickey and Donald playing volleyball	4·00	4·50
1616	$5 Goofy vaulting	4·00	4·50
1609/16	Set of 8	15·00	13·00
MS1617	Four sheets, each 123×98 mm. (a) $6 Mickey playing football. (b) $6 Mickey playing basketball (*horiz*). (c) $6 Minnie Mouse on uneven parallel bars (*horiz*). (d) $6 Mickey, Goofy and Donald judging gymnastics (*horiz*) Set of 4 sheets	14·00	15·00

290 Pteranodon

291 "Supper at Emmaus" (Caravaggio)

(Des R. Frank. Litho Walsall)

1992 (6 Apr). Prehistoric Animals. T **290** and similar multicoloured designs. P 14.

1618	10c. Type **290**	65	40
1619	15c. Brachiosaurus	65	40
1620	30c. Tyrannosaurus Rex	85	40
1621	50c. Parasaurolophus	1·00	50
1622	$1 Deinonychus (*horiz*)	1·50	1·00
1623	$2 Triceratops (*horiz*)	2·00	2·00
1624	$4 Protoceratops hatching (*horiz*)	2·25	3·25
1625	$5 Stegosaurus (*horiz*)	2·25	3·25
1618/25	Set of 8	10·00	10·00
MS1626	Two sheets, each 100×70 mm. (a) $6 Apatosaurus (*horiz*). (b) $6 Allosaurus (*horiz*) Set of 2 sheets	8·50	9·50

(Litho Questa)

1992 (15 Apr). Easter. Religious Paintings. T **291** and similar multicoloured designs. P 14×13½.

1627	10c. Type **291**	65	25
1628	15c. "Vision of St. Peter" (Zurbarán)	80	25
1629	30c. "Christ driving the Money-changers from the Temple" (Tiepolo)	1·25	40
1630	40c. "Martyrdom of St. Bartholomew" (detail) (Ribera)	1·40	50
1631	$1 "Christ driving the Money-changers from the Temple" (detail) (Tiepolo)	2·25	1·00
1632	$2 "Crucifixion" (detail) (Altdorfer)	3·25	3·00
1633	$4 "The Deposition" (detail) (Fra Angelico)	4·25	5·00
1634	$5 "The Deposition" (*different detail*) (Fra Angelico)	4·25	5·00
1627/34	Set of 8	16·00	14·00
MS1635	Two sheets. (a) 102×71 mm. $6 "The Last Supper" (detail) (Masip). P 14×13½. (b) 71×102 mm. $6 "Crucifixion" (detail) (*vert*) (Altdorfer). P 13½×14 Set of 2 sheets	9·50	12·00

292 "The Miracle at the Well" (Alonso Cano)

293 *Amanita caesarea*

(Litho B.D.T.)

1992 (11 May). "Granada '92" International Stamp Exhibition, Spain. Spanish Paintings. T **292** and similar multicoloured designs. P 13×13½ (vert) or 13½×13 (horiz).

1636	10c. Type **292**	50	30
1637	15c. "The Poet Luis de Goingora y Argote" (Velázquez)	65	30
1638	30c. "The Painter Francisco Goya" (Vincente López Portana)	85	40
1639	40c. "María de las Nieves Michaela Fourdinier" (Luis Paret y Alcázar)	95	50
1640	$1 "Carlos III eating before his Court" (Alcázar) (*horiz*)	1·75	1·25
1641	$2 "Rain Shower in Granada" (Antonio Munoz Degrain) (*horiz*)	2·50	2·75
1642	$4 "Sarah Bernhardt" (Santiago Rusinol i Prats)	3·50	4·00
1643	$5 "The Hermitage Garden" (Joaquim Mir Trinxet)	3·50	4·00
1636/43	Set of 8	13·00	12·00
MS1644	Two sheets, each 120×95 mm. (a) $6 "The Ascent of Monsieur Bouclé's Montgolfier Balloon in the Gardens of Aranjuez" (Antonio Carnicero) (112×87 *mm*). (b) $6 "Olympus: Battle with the Giants" (Francisco Bayeu y Subias) (112×87 *mm*). Imperf Set of 2 sheets	15·00	16·00

(Litho Walsall)

1992 (18 May). Fungi. T **293** and similar vert designs. Multicoloured. P 14.

1645	10c. Type **293**	70	40
1646	15c. *Collybia fusipes*	85	40
1647	30c. *Boletus aereus*	1·25	40
1648	40c. *Laccaria amethystina*	1·25	50
1649	$1 *Russula virescens*	2·00	1·25

ANTIGUA AND BARBUDA

1650	$2 *Tricholoma equestre* ("*Tricholoma auratum*")	2·75	2·75
1651	$4 *Calocybe gambosa*	3·50	4·00
1652	$5 *Lentinus tigrinus* ("*Panus tigrinus*")	3·50	4·00
1645/52 Set of 8		14·00	12·00
MS1653 Two sheets, each 100×70 mm. (a) $6 *Clavariadelphus truncatus*. (b) $6 *Auricularia auricula-judae* Set of 2 sheets		12·00	13·00

294 Memorial Cross and Huts, San Salvador

(Des R. Jung. Litho Questa)

1992 (25 May). 500th Anniv of Discovery of America by Columbus (5th issue). World Columbian Stamp "Expo '92", Chicago. T **294** and similar horiz designs. Multicoloured. P 14.

1654	15c. Type **294**	30	25
1655	30c. Martin Pinzon with telescope	55	25
1656	40c. Christopher Columbus	80	35
1657	$1 Pinta	2·75	1·50
1658	$2 Nina	3·00	3·00
1659	$4 Santa Maria	3·75	6·00
1654/9 Set of 6		10·00	10·00
MS1660 Two sheets, each 108×76 mm. (a) $6 Ship and map of West Indies. (b) $6 Sea monster Set of 2 sheets		10·00	12·00

295 Antillean Crested Hummingbird and Wild Plantain

296 Columbus meeting Amerindians

(Des J. Papeo. Litho Walsall)

1992 (10 Aug). "Genova '92" International Thematic Stamp Exhibition. Hummingbirds and Plants. T **295** and similar horiz designs. Multicoloured. P 14.

1661	10c. Type **295**	45	50
1662	25c. Green Mango and Parrot's Plantain	60	40
1663	45c. Purple-throated Carib and Lobster Claws	80	45
1664	60c. Antillean Mango and Coral Plant	90	55
1665	$1 Vervain Hummingbird and Cardinal's Guard	1·40	85
1666	$2 Ruffus-breasted Hermit and Heliconia	2·00	2·00
1667	$4 Blue-headed Hummingbird and Red Ginger	3·00	3·75
1668	$5 Green-throated Carib and Ornamental Banana	3·00	3·75
1661/8 Set of 8		11·00	11·00
MS1669 Two sheets, each 100×70 mm. (a) $6 Bee Hummingbird and Jungle Flame. (b) $6 Western Streamertail and Bignonia Set of 2 sheets		10·00	12·00

(Des F. Paul ($1), J. Esquino ($2). Litho Questa)

1992 (24 Aug). 500th Anniv of Discovery of America by Columbus (6th issue). Organization of East Caribbean States. T **296** and similar vert design. Multicoloured. P 14½.

1670	$1 Type **296**	85	65
1671	$2 Ships approaching island	1·40	1·60

297 Ts'ai Lun and Paper

(Des L. Fried. Litho Questa)

1992 (19 Oct). Inventors and Inventions. T **297** and similar horiz designs. Multicoloured. P 14.

1672	10c. Type **297**	25	25
1673	25c. Igor Sikorsky and *Bolshoi Baltiskii* (first four-engined airplane)	1·75	40
1674	30c. Alexander Graham Bell and early telephone	55	45
1675	40c. Johannes Gutenberg and early printing press	55	45
1676	60c. James Watt and stationary steam engine	4·00	1·25
1677	$1 Anton van Leeuwenhoek and early microscope	2·00	1·60
1678	$4 Louis Braille and hands reading braille	5·00	5·50
1679	$5 Galileo and telescope	5·00	5·50
1672/9 Set of 8		17·00	14·00
MS1680 Two sheets, each 100×73 mm. (a) $6 Edison and Latimer's phonograph. (b) $6 *Clermont* (first commercial paddle-steamer) Set of 2 sheets		9·50	12·00

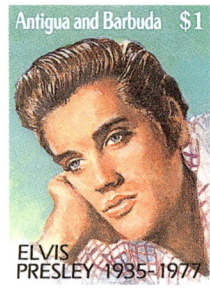

298 Elvis looking Pensive

(Des J. Iskowitz. Litho Questa)

1992 (26 Oct). 15th Death Anniv of Elvis Presley. T **298** and similar vert designs. Multicoloured. P 14.

1681	$1 Type **298**	1·90	1·25
	a. Sheetlet. Nos. 1681/9	15·00	10·00
1682	$1 Wearing black and yellow striped shirt	1·90	1·25
1683	$1 Singing into microphone	1·90	1·25
1684	$1 Wearing wide-brimmed hat	1·90	1·25
1685	$1 With microphone in right hand	1·90	1·25
1686	$1 In Army uniform	1·90	1·25
1687	$1 Wearing pink shirt	1·90	1·25
1688	$1 In yellow shirt	1·90	1·25
1689	$1 In jacket and bow tie	1·90	1·25
1681/9 Set of 9		15·00	10·00

Nos. 1681/9 were printed together, *se-tenant*, in sheetlets of 9.

299 Madison Square Gardens

(Des Kerri Schiff. Litho Questa)

1992 (28 Oct). Postage Stamp Mega Event, New York. Sheet 100×70 mm. P 14.

MS1690 **299** $6 multicoloured		4·50	6·00

300 "Virgin and Child with Angels" (detail) (School of Piero della Francesca)

301 Russian Cosmonauts

63

ANTIGUA AND BARBUDA

(Litho Questa)

1992 (16 Nov). Christmas. T **300** and similar vert designs showing details of the Holy Child from various paintings. Multicoloured. P 13½.

1691	10c. Type **300**	60	30
1692	25c. "Madonna degli Alberelli" (Giovanni Bellini)	90	30
1693	30c. "Madonna and Child with St. Anthony Abbot and St. Sigismund" (Neroccio)	95	30
1694	40c. "Madonna and the Grand Duke" (Raphael)	1·00	30
1695	60c. "The Nativity" (Georges de La Tour)	1·50	60
1696	$1 "Holy Family" (Jacob Jordaens)	1·75	1·00
1697	$4 "Madonna and Child Enthroned" (Magaritone)	3·75	4·75
1698	$5 "Madonna and Child on a Curved Throne" (Byzantine school)	3·75	4·75
1691/8	Set of 8	13·50	11·00

MS1699 Two sheets, each 76×102 mm. (a) $6 "Madonna and Child" (Domenco Ghirlando). (b) $6 "The Holy Family" (Pontormo) Set of 2 sheets ... 9·50 12·00

(Des W. Wright and L. Fried (Nos. 1700, 1711, **MS**1714a), W. Wright and W. Hanson (Nos. 1701, 1713, **MS**1714b), W. Wright (others). Litho Questa)

1992 (14 Dec). Anniversaries and Events. T **301** and similar multicoloured designs. P 14.

1700	10c. Type **301**	80	60
1701	40c. Airship LZ-127 *Graf Zeppelin*, 1929	1·75	65
1702	45c. Bishop Daniel Davis	50	40
1703	75c. Konrad Adenauer making speech	65	65
1704	$1 Bus Mosbacher and *Weatherly* (yacht)	1·25	1·25
1705	$1.50 Rain forest	1·75	1·75
1706	$2 Tiger	7·00	4·00
1707	$2 National flag, plant and emblem (*horiz*)	5·50	3·00
1708	$2 Members of Community Players company (*horiz*)	2·00	3·00
1709	$2.25 Women carrying pots	2·00	3·00
1710	$3 Lions Club emblem	2·25	3·25
1711	$4 Chinese rocket on launch tower	4·25	5·00
1712	$4 West German and N.A.T.O. flags	5·50	5·50
1713	$6 Hugo Eckener (airship pioneer)	5·00	6·00
1700/13	Set of 14	35·00	35·00

MS1714 Four sheets, each 100×71 mm. (a) $6 Projected European space station. (b) $6 Airship LZ-129 *Hindenburg*, 1936 (c) $6 Brandenburg Gate on German flag. (d) $6 *Danaus plexippus* (butterfly) Set of 4 sheets ... 23·00 25·00

Anniversaries and Events:— Nos. 1700, 1711, **MS**1714a, International Space Year; Nos. 1701, 1713, **MS**1714b, 75th death anniv of Count Ferdinand von Zeppelin; No. 1702, 150th anniv of Anglican Diocese of North-eastern Caribbean and Aruba; Nos. 1703, 1712, **MS**1714c, 25th death anniv of Konrad Adenauer (German statesman); Nos. 1705/6, **MS**1714d, Earth Summit '92, Rio; No. 1707, 50th anniv of Inter-American Institute for Agricultural Co-operation; No. 1708, 40th anniv of Cultural Development; No. 1709, United Nations World Health Organization Projects; No. 1710, 75th anniv of International Association of Lions Clubs.

302 Boy Hiker resting  **303** Goofy playing Golf

(Litho Questa)

1993 (6 Jan). Hummel Figurines. T **302** and similar vert designs. Multicoloured. P 14.

1715	15c. Type **302**	35	15
1716	30c. Girl sitting on fence	55	25
1717	40c. Boy hunter	65	35
1718	50c. Boy with umbrella	75	45
1719	$1 Hikers at signpost	1·25	75
1720	$2 Boy hiker with pack and stick	1·75	2·25
1721	$4 Girl with young child and goat	2·75	3·50
1722	$5 Boy whistling	2·75	3·50
1715/22	Set of 8	9·75	10·00

MS1723 Two sheets, each 97×122 mm. (a) $1.50×4, As Nos. 1715/18. (b) $1.50×4, As Nos. 1719/22 Set of 2 sheets ... 13·00 14·00

(Des Euro-Disney, Paris. Litho Questa)

1993 (22 Feb). Opening of Euro-Disney Resort, Paris. T **303** and similar multicoloured designs. P 14×13½.

1724	10c. Type **303**	80	30
1725	25c. Chip and Dale at Davy Crockett's Campground	1·00	30
1726	30c. Donald Duck at the Cheyenne Hotel	1·00	35
1727	40c. Goofy at the Santa Fe Hotel	1·10	35
1728	$1 Mickey and Minnie Mouse at the New York Hotel	2·25	1·25
1729	$2 Mickey, Minnie and Goofy in car	2·75	2·75
1730	$4 Goofy at Pirates of the Caribbean	4·00	5·00
1731	$5 Donald at Adventureland	4·00	5·00
1724/31	Set of 8	15·00	12·00

MS1732 Four sheets, each 127×102 mm. (a) $6 Mickey in bellboy outfit. P 14×13½. (b) $6 Mickey on star (*vert*). P 13½×14. (c) $6 Mickey on opening poster (*vert*). P 13½×14. (d) $6 Mickey and balloons on opening poster (*vert*). P 13½×14 Set of 4 sheets ... 16·00 18·00

304 Cardinal's Guard

(Des Dot Barlowe. Litho Questa)

1993 (15 Mar). Flowers. T **304** and similar vert designs. Multicoloured. P 14.

1733	15c. Type **304**	1·00	40
1734	25c. Giant Granadilla	1·10	40
1735	30c. Spider Flower	1·10	40
1736	40c. Gold Vine	1·25	40
1737	$1 Frangipani	2·00	1·25
1738	$2 Bougainvillea	2·75	2·75
1739	$4 Yellow Oleander	3·75	4·50
1740	$5 Spicy Jatropha	3·75	4·50
1733/40	Set of 8	15·00	13·00

MS1741 Two sheets, each 100×70 mm. (a) $6 Bird Lime Tree. (b) $6 Fairy Lily Set of 2 sheets ... 9·00 12·00

305 "The Destiny of Marie de' Medici" (upper detail) (Rubens)

(Litho Walsall)

1993 (22 Mar). Bicentenary of the Louvre, Paris. Paintings by Peter Paul Rubens. T **305** and similar vert designs. Multicoloured. P 12.

1742	$1 Type **305**	95	85
	a. Sheetlet. Nos. 1742/9	7·00	6·00
1743	$1 "The Birth of Marie de' Medici"	95	85
1744	$1 "The Education of Marie de' Medici"	95	85
1745	$1 "The Destiny of Marie de' Medici" (lower detail)	95	85
1746	$1 "Henry VI receiving the Portrait of Marie"	95	85
1747	$1 "The Meeting of the King and Marie at Lyons"	95	85
1748	$1 "The Marriage by Proxy"	95	85
1749	$1 "The Birth of Louis XIII"	95	85
1750	$1 "The Capture of Juliers"	95	85
	a. Sheetlet. Nos. 1750/7	7·00	6·00
1751	$1 "The Exchange of the Princesses"	95	85
1752	$1 "The Regency"	95	85
1753	$1 "The Majority of Louis XIII"	95	85

ANTIGUA AND BARBUDA

1754	$1 "The Flight from Blois"	95	85
1755	$1 "The Treaty of Angouléme"	95	85
1756	$1 "The Peace of Angers"	95	85
1757	$1 "The Reconciliation of Louis and Marie de' Medici"	95	85
1742/57	Set of 16	14·00	12·00
MS1758	70×100 mm. $6 "Helene Fourment with a Coach" (52×85 mm). P 14½	5·50	7·00

Nos. 1742/9 and 1750/7 depict details from "The Story of Marie de' Medici" and were each printed together, *se-tenant*, in sheetlets of 8 stamps and one centre label.

306 St. Lucia Amazon

(Des D. Burkhardt. Litho Questa)

1993 (5 Apr). Endangered Species. T **306** and similar horiz designs. Multicoloured. P 14.

1759	$1 Type **306**	90	90
	a. Sheetlet. Nos. 1759/70	9·50	9·50
1760	$1 Cahow	90	90
1761	$1 Swallow-tailed Kite	90	90
1762	$1 Everglade Kite	90	90
1763	$1 Imperial Amazon	90	90
1764	$1 Humpback Whale	90	90
1765	$1 Plain Pigeon	90	90
1766	$1 St. Vincent Amazon	90	90
1767	$1 Puerto Rican Amazon	90	90
1768	$1 Leatherback Turtle	90	90
1769	$1 American Crocodile	90	90
1770	$1 Hawksbill Turtle	90	90
1759/70	Set of 12	9·50	9·50
MS1771	Two sheets, each 100×70 mm. (a) $6 As No. 1764. (b) $6 West Indian manatee Set of 2 sheets	8·00	10·00

Nos. 1759/70 were printed together, *se-tenant*, in sheetlets of 12 with the background forming a composite design.

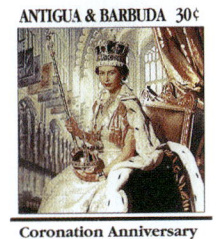

307 Queen Elizabeth II at Coronation (photograph by Cecil Beaton)

308 Princess Margaret and Antony Armstrong-Jones

(Des Kerri Schiff. Litho Questa)

1993 (2 June). 40th Anniv of Coronation (1st issue). T **307** and similar vert designs. P 13½×14.

1772	30c. multicoloured	60	60
	a. Sheetlet. Nos. 1772/5×2	8·75	
1773	40c. multicoloured	70	70
1774	$2 indigo and black	1·75	2·00
1775	$4 multicoloured	2·25	2·50
1772/5	Set of 4	4·75	5·00
MS1776	70×100 mm. $6 multicoloured. P 14	5·00	6·00

Designs:—40c. Queen Elizabeth the Queen Mother's Crown, 1937; $2 Procession of heralds; $4 Queen Elizabeth II and Prince Edward. (28½×42½ mm)—$6 "Queen Elizabeth II" (detail) (Dennis Fildes).

Nos. 1772/5 were printed together in sheetlets of 8, containing two *se-tenant* blocks of 4.

(Litho Questa)

1993 (2 June). 40th Anniv of Coronation (2nd issue). T **308** and similar vert designs. P 13½×14.

1777/1808	$1×32 either grey and black or mult	29·00	30·00

Nos. 1777/1808 were printed in four *se-tenant* sheetlets of 9 (3×3) containing eight stamps and one bottom centre label, each sheetlet showing views from a decade of the reign.

309 Edward Stanley Gibbons and Catalogue of 1865

310 Paul Gascoigne

(Des Kerri Schiff (Nos. 1809/14), D. Keren (No. **MS**1815). Litho Questa)

1993 (14 June). Famous Professional Philatelists (1st series). T **309** and similar horiz designs. P 14.

1809	$1.50 agate, black and green	1·75	1·50
1810	$1.50 multicoloured	1·75	1·50
1811	$1.50 multicoloured	1·75	1·50
1812	$1.50 multicoloured	1·75	1·50
1813	$1.50 multicoloured	1·75	1·50
1814	$1.50 multicoloured	1·75	1·50
1809/14	Set of 6	9·50	8·00
MS1815	98×69 mm. $3 black; $3 black	5·50	6·50

Designs:—No. 1810, Theodore Champion and France 1849 1f. stamp; No. 1811, J. Walter Scott and U.S.A. 1918 24c. "Inverted Jenny" error; No. 1812, Hugo Michel and Bavaria 1849 1k. stamp; No. 1813, Alberto and Giulio Bolaffi with Sardinia 1851 5c. stamp; No. 1814, Richard Borek and Brunswick 1865 1gr. stamp; No. **MS**1815, Front pages of *Mekeel's Weekly Stamp News* in 1891 (misdated 1890) and 1993.

See also No. 1957.

(Des Rosemary DeFiglio. Litho Questa)

1993 (30 July). World Cup Football Championship, U.S.A. (1st issue). T **310** and similar vert designs showing English players. Multicoloured. P 14.

1816	$2 Type **310**	1·50	1·40
1817	$2 David Platt	1·50	1·40
1818	$2 Martin Peters	1·50	1·40
1819	$2 John Barnes	1·50	1·40
1820	$2 Gary Lineker	1·50	1·40
1821	$2 Geoff Hurst	1·50	1·40
1822	$2 Bobby Charlton	1·50	1·40
1823	$2 Bryan Robson	1·50	1·40
1824	$2 Bobby Moore	1·50	1·40
1825	$2 Nobby Stiles	1·50	1·40
1826	$2 Gordon Banks	1·50	1·40
1827	$2 Peter Shilton	1·50	1·40
1816/27	Set of 12	16·00	15·00
MS1828	Two sheets, each 135×109 mm. (a) $6 Bobby Moore holding World Cup (b) $6 Gary Lineker and Bobby Robson Set of 2 sheets	9·00	11·00

See also Nos. 2039/45.

311 Grand Inspector W. Heath

312 Hugo Eckener and Dr. W. Beckers with Airship LZ-127 *Graf Zeppelin* over Lake George, New York

(Des Kerri Schiff (Nos. 1830, 1837, 1840, 1844, **MS**1847b and **MS**1847e). Litho Questa)

1993 (16 Aug). Anniversaries and Events. T **311** and similar designs. Deep blue-green and black (No. **MS**1847c) or multicoloured (others). P 14.

1829	10c. Type **311**	2·50	1·00
1830	15c. Rodnina and Oulanov (U.S.S.R.) (pairs figure skating) (*horiz*)	1·25	50
1831	30c. Present Masonic Hall, St. John's (*horiz*)	2·75	1·00
1832	30c. Willy Brandt with Helmut Schmidt and George Leber (*horiz*)	70	40
1833	30c. "Cat and Bird" (Picasso) (*horiz*)	70	40
1834	40c. Previous Masonic Hall, St. John's (*horiz*)	2·75	1·00
1835	40c. "Fish on a Newspaper" (Picasso) (*horiz*)	70	50

65

ANTIGUA AND BARBUDA

1836	40c. Early astronomical equipment	70	50
1837	40c. Prince Naruhito and engagement photographs (*horiz*)	70	50
1838	60c. Grand Inspector J. Jeffery	4·00	1·25
1839	$1 "Woman Combing her Hair" (W. Slewinski) (*horiz*)	1·25	1·25
1840	$3 Masako Owada and engagement photographs (*horiz*)	2·50	3·00
1841	$3 "Artist's Wife with Cat" (Konrad Kryzanowski) (*horiz*)	2·50	3·00
1842	$4 Willy Brandt and protest march (*horiz*)	3·00	3·50
1843	$4 Galaxy	3·00	3·50
1844	$5 Alberto Tomba (Italy) (giant slalom) (*horiz*)	3·00	3·50
1845	$5 "Dying Bull" (Picasso) (*horiz*)	3·00	3·50
1846	$5 Pres. Clinton and family (*horiz*)	3·00	3·50
1829/46 Set of 18		35·00	28·00

MS1847 Seven sheets. (a) 106×75 mm. $5 Copernicus. (b) 106×75 mm. $6 Womens' 1500 metre speed skating medallists (*horiz*). (c) 106×75 mm. $6 Willy Brandt at Warsaw Ghetto Memorial (*horiz*). (d) 106×75 mm. $6 "Woman with a Dog" (detail) (Picasso) (*horiz*). (e) 106×75 mm. $6 Masako Owada. (f) 70×100 mm. $6 "General Confusion" (S. I. Witkiewicz). (g) 106×75 mm. $6 Pres. Clinton taking the Oath (42½×57 mm) Set of 7 sheets .... 28·00 30·00

Anniversaries and Events:—Nos. 1829, 1831, 1834, 1838, 150th anniv of St. John's Masonic Lodge No. 492; Nos. 1830, 1844, **MS**1847b, Winter Olympic Games '94, Lillehammer; Nos. 1832, 1842, **MS**1847c, 80th birth anniv of Willy Brandt (German politician); Nos. 1833, 1835 1845, **MS**1847d, 20th death anniv of Picasso (artist); Nos. 1836, 1843 **MS**1847a, 450th death anniv of Copernicus (astronomer); Nos. 1837, 1840, **MS**1847e, Marriage of Crown Prince Naruhito of Japan; Nos. 1839, 1841, **MS**1847f, "Polska '93" International Stamp Exhibition, Poznan; Nos. 1846, **MS**1847g, Inauguration of U.S. President William Clinton.

(Des W. Hanson. Litho Questa)

1993 (16 Aug–11 Oct). Aviation Anniversaries. T **312** and similar multicoloured designs. P 14.

1848	30c. Type **312**	1·00	70
1849	40c. Chicago World's Fair from *Graf Zeppelin*	1·00	1·00
1850	40c. Gloster Whittle E28/39, 1941 (11 Oct)	1·00	1·00
1851	40c. George Washington writing balloon mail letter (*vert*) (11 Oct)	1·00	1·00
1852	$4 Pres. Wilson and Curtiss JN-4 'Jenny' (11 Oct)	3·75	4·50
1853	$5 Airship LZ-129 *Hindenburg* over Ebbets Field baseball stadium, 1937	3·75	4·50
1854	$5 Gloster Meteor in dogfight (11 Oct)	3·75	4·50
1848/54 Set of 7		14·00	15·00

MS1855 Three sheets. (a) 86×105 mm. $6 Hugo Eckener (*vert*). (b) 105×86 mm. $6 Consolidated PBY-5 Catalina flying boat (57×42½ mm). (c) 105×86 mm. $6 Alexander Hamilton, Washington and John Jay watching Blanchard's balloon, 1793 (*horiz*) Set of 3 sheets .... 16·00 18·00

Anniversaries:—Nos. 1848/9, 1853, **MS**1855a, 125th birth anniv of Hugo Eckener (airship commander); Nos. 1850 1854, **MS**1855b, 75th anniv of Royal Air Force; Nos. 1851/2, **MS**1855c, Bicent of First Airmail Flight.

313 Lincoln Continental

314 *The Musical Farmer*, 1932

(Des W. Hanson. Litho Questa)

1993 (11 Oct). Centenaries of Henry Ford's First Petrol Engine (Nos. 1856, 1858, **MS**1860a) and Karl Benz's First Four-wheeled Car (others). T **313** and similar horiz designs. Multicoloured. P 14.

1856	30c. Type **313**	1·00	75
1857	40c. Mercedes racing car, 1914	1·00	75
1858	$4 Ford "GT40", 1966	4·00	4·50
1859	$5 Mercedes Benz "gull-wing" coupe, 1954	4·00	4·50
1856/9 Set of 4		9·00	9·50

MS1860 Two sheets. (a) 114×87 mm. $6 Ford's Mustang emblem. (b) 87×114 mm. $6 Germany 1936 12pf. Benz and U.S.A. 1968 12c. Ford stamps Set of 2 sheets .... 9·00 12·00

(Des Rosemary DeFiglio. Litho Questa)

1993 (25 Oct). Mickey Mouse Film Posters. T **314** and similar vert designs. Multicoloured. P 13½×14.

1861	10c. Type **314**	75	30
1862	15c. *Little Whirlwind*, 1941	85	35
1863	30e. *Pluto's Dream House*, 1940	1·00	40
1864	40c. *Gulliver Mickey*, 1934	1·00	40
1865	50c. *Alpine Climbers*, 1936	1·00	50
1866	$1 *Mr. Mouse Takes a Trip*, 1940	1·50	1·00
1867	$2 *The Nifty Nineties*, 1941	2·25	2·50
1868	$4 *Mickey Down Under*, 1948	3·25	4·50
1869	$5 *The Pointer*, 1939	3·25	4·50
1861/9 Set of 9		13·00	13·00

MS1870 Two sheets, each 125×105 mm. (a) $6 *The Simple Things*, 1953 (b) $6 *The Prince and the Pauper*, 1990 Set of 2 sheets .... 11·00 14·00

315 Marie and Fritz with Christmas Tree

(Des Alvin White Studio. Litho Questa)

1993 (8 Nov). Christmas. Mickey's Nutcracker. T **315** and similar multicoloured designs showing Walt Disney cartoon characters in scenes from *The Nutcracker*. P 14×13½.

1871	10c. Type **315**	75	40
1872	15c. Marie receives Nutcracker from Godfather Drosselmeir	80	40
1873	20c. Fritz breaks Nutcracker	80	40
1874	30c. Nutcracker with sword	90	40
1875	40c. Nutcracker and Marie in the snow	95	40
1876	50c. Marie and the Prince meet Sugar Plum Fairy	1·00	60
1877	60c. Marie and Prince in Crystal Hall	1·00	60
1878	$3 Huey, Dewey and Louie as Cossack dancers	3·25	4·00
1879	$6 Mother Ginger and her puppets	4·50	6·50
1871/9 Set of 9		12·50	12·00

MS1880 Two sheets, each 127×102 mm. (a) $6 Marie and Prince in sleigh. P 14×13½. (b) $6 The Prince in sword fight (*vert*). P 13½×14 Set of 2 sheets .... 9·00 12·00

316 "Hannah and Samuel" (Rembrandt)

(Des Kerri Schiff. Litho Questa)

1993 (22 Nov). Famous Paintings by Rembrandt and Matisse. T **316** and similar vert designs. Multicoloured. P 13½×14.

1881	15c. Type **316**	40	30
1882	15c. "Guitarist" (Matisse)	40	30
1883	30c. "The Jewish Bride" (Rembrandt)	55	30
1884	40c. "Jacob wrestling with the Angel" (Rembrandt)	60	30
1885	60c. "Interior with a Goldfish Bowl" (Matisse)	80	50
1886	$1 "Mlle Yvonne Landsberg" (Matisse)	1·25	80
1887	$4 "The Toboggan" (Matisse)	3·00	4·25
1888	$5 "Moses with the Tablets of the Law" (Rembrandt)	3·00	4·25
1881/8 Set of 8		9·50	12·00

MS1889 Two sheets. (a) 124×99 mm. $6 "The Blinding of Samson by the Philistines" (detail) (Rembrandt). (b) 99×124 mm. $6 "The Three Sisters" (detail) (Matisse) Set of 2 sheets .... 10·00 11·00

ANTIGUA AND BARBUDA

317 Hong Kong 1981 $1 Golden Threadfin Bream Stamp and Sampans, Shau Kei Wan

(Des W. Hanson. Litho Questa)

1994 (18 Feb). "Hong Kong '94" International Stamp Exhibition (1st issue). T **317** and similar horiz design. Multicoloured. P 14.
1890	40c. Type **317**	80	80
	a. Horiz pair. Nos. 1890/1	1·60	1·60
1891	40c. Antigua 1990 $2 Rock Beauty stamp and sampans Shau Kei Wan	80	80

Nos. 1890/1 were printed together, *se-tenant*, in horizontal pairs throughout the sheet with the centre part of each pair forming a composite design.

318 Terracotta Warriors

(Des Kerri Schiff. Litho Questa)

1994 (18 Feb). "Hong Kong '94" International Stamp Exhibition (2nd issue). Qin Dynasty Terracotta Figures. T **318** and similar horiz designs. Multicoloured. P 14.
1892	40c. Type **318**	60	60
	a. Sheetlet. Nos. 1892/7	3·25	3·25
1893	40c. Cavalryman and horse	60	60
1894	40c. Warriors in armour	60	60
1895	40c. Painted bronze chariot and team	60	60
1896	40c. Pekingese dog	60	60
1897	40c. Warriors with horses	60	60
1892/7 Set of 6		3·25	3·25

Nos. 1892/7 were printed together, *se-tenant*, in sheetlets of 6.

319 Mickey Mouse in Junk    **320** Sumatran Rhinoceros lying down

(Litho Questa)

1994 (18 Feb). "Hong Kong '94" International Stamp Exhibition (3rd issue). T **319** and similar multicoloured designs showing Walt Disney cartoon characters. P 13½×14.
1898	10c. Type **319**	70	30
1899	15c. Minnie Mouse as mandarin	75	35
1900	30c. Donald and Daisy Duck on houseboat	90	45
1901	50c. Mickey holding bird in cage	1·10	60
1902	$1 Pluto and ornamental dog	1·75	1·00
1903	$2 Minnie and Daisy celebrating Bun Festival	2·50	2·50
1904	$4 Goofy making noodles	3·50	4·50
1905	$5 Goofy pulling Mickey in rickshaw	3·50	4·50
1898/1905 Set of 8		13·00	13·00

MS1906 Two sheets, each 133×109 mm. (a) $5 Mickey and Donald on harbour ferry (*horiz*). (b) $5 Mickey in traditional dragon dance (*horiz*). P 14×13½ Set of 2 sheets .... 7·00   9·00

(Litho Questa)

1994 (1 Mar). Centenary of Sierra Club (environmental protection society) (1992). Endangered Species. T **320** and similar multicoloured designs. P 14.
1907	$1.50 Type **320**	1·25	1·25
	a. Sheetlet. Nos. 1907/14	8·50	8·50
1908	$1.50 Sumatran Rhinoceros feeding	1·25	1·25
1909	$1.50 Ring-tailed Lemur on ground	1·25	1·25
1910	$1.50 Ring-tailed Lemur on branch	1·25	1·25
1911	$1.50 Red-fronted Brown Lemur on branch	1·25	1·25
1912	$1.50 Head of Red-fronted Brown Lemur	1·25	1·25
1913	$1.50 Head of Red-fronted Brown Lemur in front of trunk	1·25	1·25
1914	$1.50 Sierra Club Centennial emblem (black, buff and deep blue-green)	80	80
	a. Sheetlet. Nos. 1914/21	8·50	8·50
1915	$1.50 Head of Bactrian Camel	1·25	1·25
1916	$1.50 Bactrian Camel	1·25	1·25
1917	$1.50 African Elephant drinking	1·25	1·25
1918	$1.50 Head of African Elephant	1·25	1·25
1919	$1.50 Leopard sitting upright	1·25	1·25
1920	$1.50 Leopard in grass (emblem at right)	1·25	1·25
1921	$1.50 Leopard in grass (emblem at left)	1·25	1·25
1907/21 Set of 15		17·00	17·00

MS1922 Four sheets. (a) 100×70 mm. $1.50, Sumatran Rhinoceros (*horiz*). (b) 70×100 mm. $1.50, Ring-tailed Lemur (*horiz*). (c) 70×100 mm. $1.50, Bactrian Camel (*horiz*). (d) 100×70 mm. $1.50, African Elephant (*horiz*) Set of 4 sheets .... 6·00   8·00

Nos. 1907/14 and 1914/21 were printed together, *se-tenant*, in sheetlets of 8 with each sheetlet containing No. 1914 at bottom right.

321 West Highland White Terrier    **322** *Spiranthes lanceolata*

(Des Jennifer Toombs. Litho Questa)

1994 (5 Apr). Dogs of the World. Chinese New Year ("Year of the Dog"). T **321** and similar horiz designs. Multicoloured. P 14×14½.
1923	50c. Type **321**	75	65
	a. Sheetlet. Nos. 1923/34	8·00	7·00
1924	50c. Beagle	75	65
1925	50c. Scottish Terrier	75	65
1926	50c. Pekingese	75	65
1927	50c. Dachshund	75	65
1928	50c. Yorkshire Terrier	75	65
1929	50c. Pomeranian	75	65
1930	50c. Poodle	75	65
1931	50c. Shetland Sheepdog	75	65
1932	50c. Pug	75	65
1933	50c. Shih Tzu	75	65
1934	50c. Chihuahua	75	65
1935	75c. Mastiff	75	65
	a. Sheetlet. Nos. 1935/46	8·00	7·00
1936	75c. Border Collie	75	65
1937	75c. Samoyed	75	65
1938	75c. Airedale Terrier	75	65
1939	75c. English Setter	75	65
1940	75c. Rough Collie	75	65
1941	75c. Newfoundland	75	65
1942	75c. Weimarana	75	65
1943	75c. English Springer Spaniel	75	65
1944	75c. Dalmatian	75	65
1945	75c. Boxer	75	65
1946	75c. Old English Sheepdog	75	65
1923/46 Set of 24		16·00	14·00

MS1947 Two sheets, each 93×58 mm. (a) $6 Welsh Corgi. (b) $6 Labrador Retriever Set of 2 sheets .... 9·00   12·00

Nos. 1923/34 and 1935/46 were printed together, *se-tenant*, in sheetlets of 12.

(Litho Questa)

1994 (11 Apr). Orchids. T **322** and similar vert designs. Multicoloured. P 14.
1948	10c. Type **322**	70	60
1949	20c. *Ionopsis utricularioides*	1·00	50
1950	30c. *Tetramicra canaliculata*	1·25	50
1951	50c. *Oncidium picturatum*	2·00	1·25
1952	$1 *Epidendrum difforme*	3·00	2·75
1953	$2 *Epidendrum ciliare*	4·00	4·25
1954	$4 *Epidendrum ibaguense*	4·00	4·25
1955	$5 *Epidendrum nocturnum*	4·00	4·25
1948/55 Set of 8		15·00	13·00

MS1956 Two sheets, each 100×73 mm. (a) $6 *Rodriguezia lanceolata*. (b) $6 *Encyclia cochleata* Set of 2 sheets .... 9·00   12·00

ANTIGUA AND BARBUDA

323 Hermann E. Sieger, Germany 1931 1m. Zeppelin Stamp and Airship LZ-127 *Graf Zeppelin*

324 *Danaus plexippus*

(Litho Questa)

1994 (6 June). Famous Professional Philatelists (2nd series). P 14.
1957	**323**	$1.50 multicoloured	3·00	2·50

(Des B. Hargreaves. Litho Questa)

1994 (27 June). Butterflies. T **324** and similar vert designs. Multicoloured. P 14.
1958	10c. Type **324**	85	75
1959	15c. *Appias drusilla*	1·00	45
1960	30c. *Eurema Lisa*	1·25	55
1961	40c. *Anaea troglodyta*	1·25	60
1962	$1 *Urbanus proteus*	2·00	1·25
1963	$2 *Junonia evarete*	2·75	2·75
1964	$4 *Battus polydamas*	3·50	4·50
1965	$5 *Heliconius charitonia*	3·50	4·50
1958/65 *Set of 8*		15·00	13·00
MS1966 Two sheets, each 102×72 mm. (a) $6 *Phoebis sennae*. (b) $6 *Hemiargus hanno*Set of 2 sheets		9·00	12·00

No. 1959 is inscribed "Appisa drusilla" and No. 1965 'Heliconius charitonius", both in error.

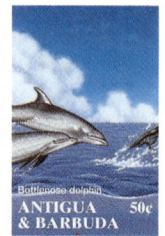

325 Bottlenose Dolphin

326 Edwin Aldrin (astronaut)

(Des J. Genzo. Litho Questa)

1994 (21 July). Marine Life. T **325** and similar multicoloured designs. P 14.
1967	50c. Type **325**	75	75
	a. Sheetlet. Nos. 1967/75	6·00	6·00
1968	50c. Killer Whale	75	75
1969	50c. Spinner Dolphin	75	75
1970	50c. Oceanic Sunfish	75	75
1971	50c. Caribbean Reef Shark and Short Fin Pilot Whale	75	75
1972	50c. Copper-banded Butterflyfish	75	75
1973	50c. Mosaic Moray	75	75
1974	50c. Clown Triggerfish	75	75
1975	50c. Red Lobster	75	75
1967/75 *Set of 9*		6·00	6·00
MS1976 Two sheets, each 106×76 mm. (a) $6 Seahorse. (b) $6 Swordfish ("Blue Marlin") (*horiz*) *Set of 2 sheets*		11·00	12·00

Nos. 1967/75 were printed together, *se-tenant*, in sheetlets of 9.

(Des W. Hanson. Litho Questa)

1994 (4 Aug). 25th Anniv of First Moon Landing. T **326** and similar horiz designs. Multicoloured. P 14.
1977	$1.50 Type **326**	2·00	1·50
	a. Sheetlet. Nos. 1977/82	11·00	8·00
1978	$1.50 First lunar footprint	2·00	1·50
1979	$1.50 Neil Armstrong (astronaut)	2·00	1·50
1980	$1.50 Aldrin stepping onto Moon	2·00	1·50
1981	$1.50 Aldrin and equipment	2·00	1·50
1982	$1.50 Aldrin and U.S.A. flag	2·00	1·50
1983	$1.50 Aldrin at Tranquility Base	2·00	1·50
	a. Sheetlet. Nos. 1983/8	11·00	8·00
1984	$1.50 Moon plaque	2·00	1·50
1985	$1.50 *Eagle* leaving Moon	2·00	1·50
1986	$1.50 Command module in lunar orbit	2·00	1·50
1987	$1.50 First day cover of U.S.A 1969 10c. First Man on Moon stamp	2·00	1·50
1988	$1.50 Pres. Nixon and astronauts	2·00	1·50
1977/88 *Set of 12*		22·00	16·00
MS1989 72×102 mm. $6 Armstrong and Aldrin with postal official		5·00	4·00

Nos. 1977/82 and 1983/8 were printed together, *se-tenant*, in sheetlets of 6.

327 Edwin Moses (U.S.A.) (400 metres hurdles), 1984

(Des Kerri Schiff. Litho Questa)

1994 (4 Aug). Centenary of International Olympic Committee. Gold Medal Winners. T **327** and similar horiz designs. Multicoloured. P 14.
1990	50c. Type **327**	40	30
1991	$1.50 Steffi Graf (Germany) (tennis), 1988	2·00	1·75
MS1992 79×110 mm. $6 Johann Olav Koss (Norway) (500, 1500 and 10,000 metre speed skating), 1994		5·00	5·50

328 Antiguan Family

(Litho Questa)

1994 (4 Aug). International Year of the Family. P 14.
1993	**328**	90c. multicoloured	1·00	1·00

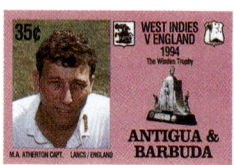

329 Mike Atherton (England) and Wisden Trophy

(Des A. Melville-Brown. Litho Questa)

1994 (4 Aug). Centenary of First English Cricket Tour to the West Indies (1995). T **329** and similar multicoloured designs. P 14.
1994	35c. Type **329**	1·25	65
1995	75c. Viv Richards (West Indies) (*vert*)	2·00	1·25
1996	$1.20 Richie Richardson (West Indies) and Wisden Trophy	2·75	2·50
1994/6 *Set of 3*		5·50	4·00
MS1997 80×100 mm. $3 English team, 1895 (black and grey-brown)		2·50	3·00

330 Entrance Bridge, Songgwangsa Temple

(Des Kerri Schiff. Litho Questa (Nos. 1998, 2007/9), B.D.T. (Nos. 1999/2006))

1994 (4 Aug). "Philakorea '94" International Stamp Exhibition, Seoul. T **330** and similar multicoloured designs. P 13½ (Nos. 1999/2006) or 14 (others).
1998	40c. Type **330**	50	40
1999	75c. Long-necked bottle	70	75
	a. Sheetlet. Nos. 1999/2006	5·50	6·00
2000	75c. Punch'ong ware jar with floral decoration	70	75

2001	75c. Punch'ong ware jar with blue dragon pattern		70	75
2002	75c. Ewer in shape of bamboo shoot		70	75
2003	75c. Punch'ong ware green jar		70	75
2004	75c. Pear-shaped bottle		70	75
2005	75c. Porcelain jar with brown dragon pattern		70	75
2006	75c. Porcelain jar with floral pattern		70	75
2007	90c. Song-op Folk Village, Cheju		70	75
2008	$3 Port Sogwipo		1·75	2·25
1998/2008 Set of 11			7·75	8·50
MS2009 104×71 mm. $4 Ox herder playing flute (vert)			3·25	4·00

Nos. 1999/2006, each 24×47 mm, were printed together, se-tenant, in sheetlets of 8.

331 Short S.25 Sunderland Flying Boat

332 Travis Tritt

(Des J. Batchelor. Litho Questa)

1994 (4 Aug). 50th Anniv of D-Day. T **331** and similar horiz designs. Multicoloured. P 14.

2010	40c. Type **331**		1·25	40
2011	$2 Lockheed P-38 Lightning fighters attacking train		3·00	2·75
2012	$3 Martin B-26 Marauder bombers		3·25	3·75
2010/12 Set of 3			6·75	6·25
MS2013 108×78 mm. $6 Hawker Typhoon fighter bomber			6·75	6·25

(Des J. Iskowitz. Litho Questa)

1994 (18 Aug). Stars of Country and Western Music. T **332** and similar multicoloured designs. P 14.

2014	75c. Type **332**		70	70
	a. Sheetlet. Nos. 2014/21		5·00	5·00
2015	75c. Dwight Yoakam		70	70
2016	75c. Billy Ray Cyrus		70	70
2017	75c. Alan Jackson		70	70
2018	75c. Garth Brooks		70	70
2019	75c. Vince Gill		70	70
2020	75c. Clint Black		70	70
2021	75c. Eddie Rabbit		70	70
2022	75c. Patsy Cline		70	70
	a. Sheetlet. Nos. 2022/9		5·00	5·00
2023	75c. Tanya Tucker		70	70
2024	75c. Dolly Parton		70	70
2025	75c. Anne Murray		70	70
2026	75c. Tammy Wynette		70	70
2027	75c. Loretta Lynn		70	70
2028	75c. Reba McEntire		70	70
2029	75c. Skeeter Davis		70	70
2030	75c. Hank Snow		70	70
	a. Sheetlet. Nos. 2030/7		5·00	5·00
2031	75c. Gene Autry		70	70
2032	75c. Jimmie Rodgers		70	70
2033	75c. Ernest Tubb		70	70
2034	75c. Eddy Arnold		70	70
2035	75c. Willie Nelson		70	70
2036	75c. Johnny Cash		70	70
2037	75c. George Jones		70	70
2014/37 Set of 24			14·00	14·00
MS2038 Three sheets. (a) 100×70 mm. $6 Hank Williams Jr. (b) 100×70 mm. $6 Hank Williams Sr. (c) 70×100 mm. $6 Kitty Wells (horiz) Set of 3 sheets			15·00	15·00

Nos. 2014/21, 2022/9 and 2030/7 were printed together, se-tenant, in sheetlets of 8.

333 Hugo Sanchez (Mexico)

(Litho B.D.T.)

1994 (19 Sept). World Cup Football Championship, U.S.A. (2nd issue). T **333** and similar multicoloured designs. P 14.

2039	15c. Type **333**		75	30
2040	35c. Jürgen Klinsmann (Germany)		1·25	45
2041	65c. Antiguan player		1·50	55
2042	$1.20 Cobi Jones (U.S.A.)		2·00	1·75
2043	$4 Roberto Baggio (Italy)		3·25	4·00
2044	$5 Bwalya Kalusha (Zambia)		3·25	4·00
2039/44 Set of 6			11·00	10·00
MS2045 Two sheets. (a) 72×105 mm. $6 Maldive Islands player (vert). (b) 107×78 mm. $6 World Cup trophy (vert) Set of 2 sheets			8·50	9·00

No. 2040 is inscribed "Klinsman" in error.

334 Sir Shridath Ramphal

(Litho Questa)

1994 (26 Sept). First Recipients of Order of the Caribbean Community. T **334** and similar horiz designs. Multicoloured. P 14.

2046	65c. Type **334**		50	40
2047	90c. William Demas		65	60
2048	$1.20 Derek Walcott		2·50	1·75
2046/8 Set of 3			3·25	2·50

335 Pair of Magnificent Frigate Birds

336 "Virgin and Child by the Fireside" (Robert Campin)

(Des Tracy Pedersen. Litho Questa)

1994 (12 Dec). Birds. T **335** and similar multicoloured designs. P 14.

2049	10c. Type **335**		60	45
2050	15c. Bridled Quail Dove		70	40
2051	30c. Magnificent Frigate Bird chick hatching		1·00	70
2052	40c. Purple-throated Carib (vert)		1·00	70
2053	$1 Male Magnificent Frigate Bird in courtship display (vert)		1·40	1·40
2054	$1 Broad-winged Hawk (vert)		1·40	1·40
2055	$3 Young Magnificent Frigate Bird		2·50	3·25
2056	$4 Yellow Warbler		2·75	3·25
2049/56 Set of 8			10·00	10·50
MS2057 Two sheets. (a) 70×100 mm. $6 Female Magnificent Frigate Bird (vert). (b) 100×70 mm. $6 Black-billed Whistling Duck ducklings Set of 2 sheets			8·00	9·00

Nos. 2049, 2051, 2053 and 2055 also show the W.W.F. Panda emblem.

(Litho Questa)

1994 (12 Dec). Christmas. Religious Paintings. T **336** and similar vert designs. Multicoloured. P 13½×14.

2058	15c. Type **336**		80	30
2059	35c. "The Reading Madonna" (Giorgione)		1·10	30
2060	40c. "Madonna and Child" (Giovanni Bellini)		1·25	30
2061	45c. "Litta Madonna" (Da Vinci)		1·25	30
2062	65c. "The Virgin and Child under the Apple Tree" (Lucas Cranach the Elder)		1·60	55
2063	75c. "Madonna and Child" (Master of the Female Half-lengths)		1·75	70
2064	$1.20 "An Allegory of the Church" (Alessandro Allori)		2·25	2·00
2065	$5 "Madonna and Child wreathed with Flowers" (Jacob Jordaens)		3·75	5·50
2058/65 Set of 8			13·00	9·00

ANTIGUA AND BARBUDA

MS2066 Two sheets. (a) 123×88 mm. $6 "Madonna and Child with Commissioners" (detail) (Palma Vecchio). (b) 88×123 mm. $6 "The Virgin Enthroned with Child" (detail) (Bohemian master) Set of 2 sheets .... 13·00 9·00

337 Magnificent Frigate Bird

338 Head of Pachycephalosaurus

(Des W. Wright. Litho China Security Ptg Ltd, Hong Kong)

1995 (6 Feb). Birds. T **337** and similar vert designs. Multicoloured. P 15×14.

2067	15c. Type **337**	45	20
2068	25c. Blue-hooded Euphonia	60	20
2069	35c. Eastern Meadowlark	70	20
2070	40c. Red-billed Tropic Bird	75	20
2071	45c. Greater Flamingo	75	25
2072	60c. Yellow-faced Grassquit	1·00	30
2073	65c. Yellow-billed Cuckoo	1·00	30
2074	70c. Purple-throated Carib	1·00	35
2075	75c. Bananaquit	1·00	35
2076	90c. Painted Bunting	1·10	40
2077	$1.20 Red-legged Honeycreeper	1·50	65
2078	$2 Northern Jacana	2·50	1·75
2079	$5 Greater Antillean Bullfinch	4·00	4·25
2080	$10 Caribbean Elaenia	7·00	8·00
2081	$20 Brown Trembler	11·00	15·00
2067/81	Set of 15	30·00	29·00

(Des B. Regal. Litho Questa)

1995 (15 May). Prehistoric Animals. T **338** and similar multicoloured designs. P 14.

2082	15c. Type **338**	60	60
2083	20c. Head of Afrovenator	60	60
2084	65c. Centrosaurus	85	80
2085	75c. Kronosaurus (horiz)	85	85
	a. Sheetlet. Nos. 2085/96	9·50	9·50
2086	75c. Ichthyosaurus (horiz)	85	85
2087	75c. Plesiosaurus (horiz)	85	85
2088	75c. Archelon (horiz)	85	85
2089	75c. Pair of Tyrannosaurus (horiz)	85	85
2090	75c. Tyrannosaurus (horiz)	85	85
2091	75c. Parasaurolophus (horiz)	85	85
2092	75c. Pair of Parasaurolophus (horiz)	85	85
2093	75c. Oviraptor (horiz)	85	85
2094	75c. Protoceratops with eggs (horiz)	85	85
2095	75c. Pteranodon and Protoceratops (horiz)	85	85
2096	75c. Pair of Protoceratops (horiz)	85	85
2097	90c. Pentaceratops drinking	1·00	1·00
2098	$1.20 Head of Tarbosaurus	1·25	1·25
2099	$5 Head of Styracosaurus	3·50	4·50
2082/99	Set of 18	16·00	17·00

MS2100 Two sheets, each 101×70 mm. (a) $6 Head of Corythosaurus (horiz). (b) $6 Head of Carnotaurus (horiz) Set of 2 sheets .... 11·00 13·00

Nos. 2085/96 were printed together, se-tenant, in sheetlets of 12.

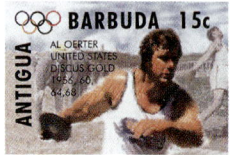

339 Al Oerter (U.S.A.) (discus – 1956, 1960, 1964, 1968)

(Des R. Sauber. Litho B.D.T.)

1995 (6 June). Olympic Games, Atlanta (1996). Previous Gold Medal Winners (1st issue). T **339** and similar multicoloured designs. P 14.

2101	15c. Type **339**	60	30
2102	20c. Greg Louganis (U.S.A.) (diving – 1984, 1988)	60	30
2103	65c. Naim Suleymanoglu (Turkey) (weightlifting – 1988)	75	50
2104	90c. Louise Ritter (U.S.A.) (high jump – 1988)	1·00	70
2105	$1.20 Nadia Comaneci (Rumania) (gymnastics – 1976)	2·00	1·40
2106	$5 Olga Bondarenko (Russia) (10,000 metres – 1988)	3·25	5·00
2101/6	Set of 6	6·75	7·50

MS2107 Two sheets, each 106×76 mm. (a) $6 United States crew (eight-oared shell – 1964). (b) $6 Lutz Hessilch (Germany) (cycling – 1988) (vert) Set of 2 sheets .... 11·00 12·00

No. 2106 is inscribed "BOLDARENKO" in error. See also Nos. 2302/23.

340 Map of Berlin showing Russian Advance

(Des W. Wright. Litho Questa)

1995 (20 July). 50th Anniv of End of Second World War in Europe. T **340** and similar multicoloured designs. P 14.

2108	$1.20 Type **340**	1·50	1·25
	a. Sheetlet. Nos. 2108/15	11·00	9·00
2109	$1.20 Russian tank and infantry	1·50	1·25
2110	$1.20 Street fighting in Berlin	1·50	1·25
2111	$1.20 German tank exploding	1·50	1·25
2112	$1.20 Russian air raid	1·50	1·25
2113	$1.20 German troops surrendering	1·50	1·25
2114	$1.20 Hoisting the Soviet flag on the Reichstag	1·50	1·25
2115	$1.20 Captured German standards	1·50	1·25
2108/15	Set of 8	11·00	9·00

MS2116 104×74 mm. $6 Gen. Konev (vert) .... 4·50 5·50

Nos. 2108/15 were printed together, se-tenant, in sheetlets of 8 with the stamps arranged in two horizontal strips of 4 separated by a gutter showing a German soldier in the ruins of Berlin.

341 Signatures and Earl of Halifax

(Des L. Fried. Litho Questa)

1995 (20 July). 50th Anniv of United Nations. T **341** and similar vert designs. Multicoloured. P 14.

2117	75c. Type **341**	70	1·00
	a. Horiz strip of 3. Nos. 2117/19	1·90	2·75
2118	90c. Virgnia Gildersleeve	70	1·00
2119	$1.20 Harold Stassen	70	1·00
2117/19	Set of 3	1·90	2·75

MS2120 100×70 mm. $6 Pres. Franklin D. Roosevelt .... 3·50 4·25

Nos. 2117/19 were printed together in sheets of 9 (3×3) containing three se-tenant horizontal strips, each forming a composite design.

342 Woman buying Produce from Market

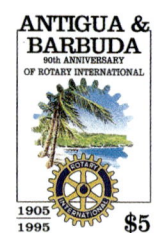

343 Beach and Rotary Emblem

(Des L. Fried. Litho Questa)

1995 (20 July). 50th Anniv of Food and Agriculture Organization. T **342** and similar vert designs. Multicoloured. P 14.

2121	75c. Type **342**	70	1·00
	a. Horiz strip of 3. Nos. 2121/3	1·90	2·75

2122	90c. Women shopping	70	1·00
2123	$1.20 Women talking	70	1·00
2121/3	Set of 3	1·90	2·75
MS2124	100×70 mm. $6 Tractor	3·00	3·75

Nos. 2121/3 were printed together in sheets of 9 (3×3) containing three *se-tenant* horizontal strips, each forming a composite design.

(Litho Questa)

1995 (20 July). 90th Anniv of Rotary International. T **343** and similar vert design. Multicoloured. P 14.

2125	$5 Type **343**	3·50	4·00
MS2126	74×104 mm. $6 National flag and emblem	3·50	4·00

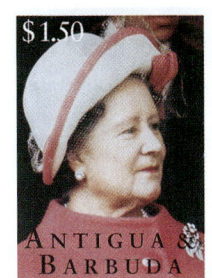

344 Queen Elizabeth the Queen Mother

(Litho Questa)

1995 (20 July)–**02**. 95th Birthday of Queen Elizabeth the Queen Mother. T **344** and similar vert designs. P 13½×14.

2127	$1.50 orange-brown, pale brown and black	1·50	1·50
	a. Sheetlet. Nos. 2127/30×2	10·00	
	ab. Sheetlet. As No. 2127a, but with top margin additionally inscr "IN MEMORIAM 1900-2002" (11.6.02)	10·00	
2128	$1.50 multicoloured	1·50	1·50
2129	$1.50 multicoloured	1·50	1·50
2130	$1.50 multicoloured	1·50	1·50
2127/30	Set of 4	5·50	5·50
MS2131	102×127 mm. $6 multicoloured	5·50	5·50
	a. Additionally inscr "IN MEMORIAM 1900-2002" on margin (11.6.02)	5·50	5·50

Designs:—No. 2127, Queen Elizabeth the Queen Mother (pastel drawing); No. 2128, Type **344**; No. 2129, At desk (oil painting); No 2130, Wearing green dress; No. MS2131, Wearing blue dress.

Nos. 2128/30 were printed together in sheetlets of 8, containing two *se-tenant* horizontal strips of 4.

Nos. 2127a and **MS**2131 were re-issued in 2002 with additional memorial inscription and black frames on the margins.

(Des J. Batchelor. Litho Questa)

1995 (20 July). 50th Anniv of End of Second World War in the Pacific. Horiz designs as T **93b** of Nevis. Multicoloured. P 14.

2132	$1.20 Gen. Chiang Kai-shek and Chinese guerrillas	1·10	1·25
	a. Sheetlet. Nos. 2132/7	6·00	6·75
2133	$1.20 Gen. Douglas MacArthur and beach landing	1·10	1·25
2134	$1.20 Gen. Claire Chennault and U.S. fighter aircraft	1·10	1·25
2135	$1.20 Brig. Orde Wingate and supply drop	1·10	1·25
2136	$1.20 Gen. Joseph Stilwell and U.S. supply plane	1·10	1·25
2137	$1.20 Field-Marshal Bill Slim and loading cow into plane	1·10	1·25
2132/7	Set of 6	6·00	6·75
MS2138	108×76 mm. $3 Admiral Nimitz and aircraft carrier	2·75	3·50

Nos. 2132/7 were printed together, *se-tenant*, in sheetlets of 6 with the stamps arranged in two horizontal strips of 3 separated by a gutter showing Japanese soldiers surrendering.

345 Family ("Caring")

1995 (31 July). Tourism. Sheet 95×72 mm, containing T **345** and similar horiz designs. Multicoloured. Litho. P 14.

MS2139	$2 Type **345**; $2 Market trader ("Marketing"); $2 Workers and housewife ("Working"); $2 Leisure pursuits ("Enjoying Life")	5·50	7·00

346 Purple-throated Carib

(Des Tracy Pedersen. Litho Questa)

1995 (31 Aug). Birds. T **346** and similar vert designs. Multicoloured. P 14.

2140	75c. Type **346**	1·10	1·00
	a. Sheetlet. Nos. 2140/51	12·00	11·00
2141	75c. Antillean Crested Hummingbird	1·10	1·00
2142	75c. Bananaquit	1·10	1·00
2143	75c. Mangrove Cuckoo	1·10	1·00
2144	75c. Troupial	1·10	1·00
2145	75c. Green-throated Carib	1·10	1·00
2146	75c. Yellow Warbler	1·10	1·00
2147	75c. Blue-hooded Euphonia	1·10	1·00
2148	75c. Scaly-breasted Thrasher	1·10	1·00
2149	75c. Burrowing Owl	1·10	1·00
2150	75c. Carib Grackle	1·10	1·00
2151	75c. Adelaide's Warbler	1·10	1·00
2152	75c. Ring-necked Duck	1·10	1·00
	a. Sheetlet. Nos. 2152/63	12·00	11·00
2153	75c. Ruddy Duck	1·10	1·00
2154	75c. Green-winged Teal	1·10	1·00
2155	75c. Wood Duck	1·10	1·00
2156	75c. Hooded Merganser	1·10	1·00
2157	75c. Lesser Scaup	1·10	1·00
2158	75c. Black-billed Whistling Duck ("West Indian Tree Duck")	1·10	1·00
2159	75c. Fulvous Whistling Duck	1·10	1·00
2160	75c. Bahama Pintail	1·10	1·00
2161	75c. Shoveler	1·10	1·00
2162	75c. Masked Duck	1·10	1·00
2163	75c. American Wigeon	1·10	1·00
2140/63	Set of 24	24·00	22·00
MS2164	Two sheets, each 104×74 mm. (a) $6 Head of Purple Gallinule. (b) $6 Heads of Blue-winged Teals Set of 2 sheets	13·00	13·00

Nos. 2140/51 and 2152/63 were printed together, *se-tenant*, in sheetlets of 12 with the background forming a composite design.

347 Original Church, 1845

348 Mining Bees

(Litho Questa)

1995 (4 Sept). 150th Anniv of Greenbay Moravian Church. T **347** and similar vert designs. Multicoloured. P 14.

2165	20c. Type **347**	70	30
2166	60c. Church in 1967	1·00	40
2167	75c. Present church	1·25	50
2168	90c. Revd. John Buckley (first minister of African descent)	1·40	60
2169	$1.20 Bishop John Ephraim Knight (longest-serving minister)	1·75	1·75
2170	$2 As 75c.	2·75	3·50
2165/70	Set of 6	8·00	6·25
MS2171	110×81 mm. $6 Front of present church	4·50	6·00

(Des Y. Lee. Litho Questa)

1995 (7 Sept). Bees. T **348** and similar horiz designs. Multicoloured. P 14.

2172	90c. Type **348**	1·00	70
2173	$1.20 Solitary Bee	1·40	90
2174	$1.65 Leaf-cutter Bee	2·00	2·00

ANTIGUA AND BARBUDA

2175	$1.75 Honey Bees	2·00	2·00
2172/5	Set of 4	5·75	5·00
MS2176	110×80 mm. $6 Solitary Mining Bee	4·00	5·00

349 Narcissus

(Des Y. Lee. Litho Questa)

1995 (7 Sept). Flowers. T **349** and similar vert designs. Multicoloured. P 14.

2177	75c. Type **349**	80	80
	a. Sheetlet. Nos. 2177/88	8·50	8·50
2178	75c. Camellia	80	80
2179	75c. Iris	80	80
2180	75c. Tulip	80	80
2181	75c. Poppy	80	80
2182	75c. Peony	80	80
2183	75c. Magnolia	80	80
2184	75c. Oriental Lily	80	80
2185	75c. Rose	80	80
2186	75c. Pansy	80	80
2187	75c. Hydrangea	80	80
2188	75c. Azalea	80	80
2177/88	Set of 12	8·50	8·50
MS2189	80×110 mm. $6 Calla Lily	4·00	5·00

Nos. 2177/88 were printed together, *se-tenant*, in sheetlets of 12.
No. 2186 is inscribed "Pansie" in error.

350 Somali

(Des Y. Lee. Litho Questa)

1995 (7 Sept). Cats. T **350** and similar multicoloured designs. P 14.

2190	45c. Type **350**	80	60
	a. Sheetlet. Nos. 2190/201	8·50	6·50
2191	45c. Persian and butterflies	80	60
2192	45c. Devon Rex	80	60
2193	45c. Turkish Angora	80	60
2194	45c. Himalayan	80	60
2195	45c. Maine Coon	80	60
2196	45c. Ginger non-pedigree	80	60
2197	45c. American Wirehair	80	60
2198	45c. British Shorthair	80	60
2199	45c. American Curl	80	60
2200	45c. Black non-pedigree and butterfly	80	60
2201	45c. Birman	80	60
2190/2201	Set of 12	8·50	6·50
MS2202	104×74 mm. $6 Siberian kitten (*vert*)	7·50	7·50

Nos. 2190/2201 were printed together, *se-tenant*, in sheetlets of 12, with the backgrounds forming a composite design.

351 The Explorer Tent

1995 (5 Oct). 18th World Scout Jamboree, Netherlands. Tents. T **351** and similar multicoloured designs. Litho. P 14.

2203	$1.20 Type **351**	1·60	1·60
	a. Horiz strip of 3. Nos. 2203/5	4·25	4·25
2204	$1.20 Camper tent	1·60	1·60
2205	$1.20 Wall tent	1·60	1·60
2206	$1.20 Trail tarp	1·60	1·60
	a. Horiz strip of 3. Nos. 2206/8	4·25	4·25
2207	$1.20 Miner's tent	1·60	1·60
2208	$1.20 Voyager tent	1·60	1·60
2203/8	Set of 6	8·50	8·50
MS2209	Two sheets, each 76×106 mm. (a) $6 Scout and camp fire. (b) $6 Scout with back pack (*vert*) Set of 2 sheets	8·50	10·00

Nos. 2203/5 and 2206/8 were printed together, *se-tenant*, as horizontal strips of 3 in sheets of 9.

352 Trans-Gabon Diesel-electric Train

(Des B. Regal. Litho Questa)

1995 (23 Oct). Trains of the World. T **352** and similar multicoloured designs. P 14.

2210	35c. Type **352**	1·00	65
2211	65c. Canadian Pacific diesel-electric locomotive	1·50	90
2212	75c. Santa Fe Railway diesel-electric locomotive, U.S.A.	1·60	1·00
2213	90c. High Speed Train, Great Britain	1·60	1·00
2214	$1.20 TGV express train, France	1·60	1·60
2215	$1.20 Diesel-electric locomotive, Australia	1·60	1·60
	a. Sheetlet. Nos. 2215/23	11·50	11·50
2216	$1.20 Pendolino "ETR 450" electric train, Italy	1·60	1·60
2217	$1.20 Diesel-electric locomotive, Thailand	1·60	1·60
2218	$1.20 Pennsylvania Railroad Type K4 steam locomotive, U.S.A.	1·60	1·60
2219	$1.20 Beyer-Garratt steam locomotive, East African Railways	1·60	1·60
2220	$1.20 Natal Govt steam locomotive	1·60	1·60
2221	$1.20 Rail gun, American Civil War	1·60	1·60
2222	$1.20 Locomotive *Lion* (red livery), Great Britain	1·60	1·60
2223	$1.20 William Hedley's *Puffing Billy* (green livery), Great Britain	1·60	1·60
2224	$6 Amtrak high speed diesel locomotive, U.S.A.	3·75	4·50
2210/24	Set of 15	21·00	21·00
MS2225	Two sheets, each 110×80 mm. (a) $6 Locomotive *Iron Rooster*, China (*vert*). (b) $6 "Indian-Pacific" diesel-electric locomotive, Australia (*vert*) Set of 2 sheets	14·00	14·00

Nos. 2215/23 were printed together, *se-tenant*, in sheetlets of 9.

353 Dag Hammarskjöld (1961 Peace)

(Des B. Regal. Litho Walsall)

1995 (8 Nov). Centenary of Nobel Prize Trust Fund. T **353** and similar multicoloured designs. P 14.

2226	$1 Type **353**	1·10	1·10
	a. Sheetlet. Nos. 2226/34	9·00	9·00
2227	$1 Georg Wittig (1979 Chemistry)	1·10	1·10
2228	$1 Wilhelm Ostwald (1909 Chemistry)	1·10	1·10
2229	$1 Robert Koch (1905 Medicine)	1·10	1·10
2230	$1 Karl Ziegler (1963 Chemistry)	1·10	1·10
2231	$1 Alexander Fleming (1945 Medicine)	1·10	1·10
2232	$1 Hermann Staudinger (1953 Chemistry)	1·10	1·10
2233	$1 Manfred Eigen (1967 Chemistry)	1·10	1·10
2234	$1 Arno Penzias (1978 Physics)	1·10	1·10
2235	$1 Shmuel Agnon (1966 Literature)	1·10	1·10
	a. Sheetlet. Nos. 2235/43	9·00	9·00
2236	$1 Rudyard Kipling (1907 Literature)	1·10	1·10
2237	$1 Aleksandr Solzhenitsyn (1970 Literature)	1·10	1·10
2238	$1 Jack Steinberger (1988 Physics)	1·10	1·10
2239	$1 Andrei Sakharov (1975 Peace)	1·10	1·10
2240	$1 Otto Stern (1943 Physics)	1·10	1·10
2241	$1 John Steinbeck (1962 Literature)	1·10	1·10
2242	$1 Nadine Gordimer (1991 Literature)	1·10	1·10
2243	$1 William Faulkner (1949 Literature)	1·10	1·10
2226/43	Set of 18	18·00	18·00
MS2244	Two sheets, each 100×70 mm. (a) $6 Elie Wiesel (1986 Peace) (*vert*). (b) $6 The Dalai Lama (1989 Peace) (*vert*) Set of 2 sheets	9·00	10·00

Nos. 2226/34 and 2235/43 were printed together, *se-tenant*, in sheetlets of 9.

ANTIGUA AND BARBUDA

354 Elvis Presley

355 John Lennon and Signature

1995 (8 Dec). 60th Birth Anniv of Elvis Presley. T **354** and similar vert designs. Multicoloured. Litho. P 13½×14.

2245	$1 Type **354**	1·25	95
	a. Sheetlet. Nos. 2245/53	10·00	8·50
2246	$1 Holding microphone in right hand	1·25	95
2247	$1 In blue shirt and with neck of guitar	1·25	95
2248	$1 Wearing blue shirt and smiling	1·25	95
2249	$1 On wedding day	1·25	95
2250	$1 In army uniform	1·25	95
2251	$1 Wearing red shirt	1·25	95
2252	$1 Wearing white shirt	1·25	95
2253	$1 In white shirt with microphone	1·25	95
2245/53 Set of 9		10·00	8·50
MS2254 101×71 mm. $6 "Ghost" image of Elvis amongst the stars		7·50	5·50

Nos. 2245/54 were printed together, *se-tenant*, in sheetlets of 9.

(Litho Questa)

1995 (8 Dec). 15th Death Anniv of John Lennon (entertainer). T **355** and similar vert designs. Multicoloured. P 14.

2255	45c. Type **355**	50	40
2256	50c. In beard and spectacles	50	50
2257	65c. Wearing sunglasses	55	55
2258	75c. In cap with heart badge	65	65
2255/8 Set of 4		2·00	1·90
MS2259 103×73 mm. $6 As 75c.		5·50	6·50

Nos. 2255/8 were each issued in numbered sheets of 16 which have enlarged illustrated left-hand margins.

"Hurricane Relief" (**356**)

357 "Rest on the Flight into Egypt" (Paolo Veronese)

1995 (14 Dec). Hurricane Relief. Nos. 2203/9 optd as T **356**.

2260	$1.20 Type **351**	1·25	1·25
	a. Horiz strip of 3. Nos. 2260/2	3·25	3·25
2261	$1.20 Camper tent	1·25	1·25
2262	$1.20 Wall tent	1·25	1·25
2263	$1.20 Trail tarp	1·25	1·25
	a. Horiz strip of 3. Nos. 2263/5	3·25	3·25
2264	$1.20 Miner's tent	1·25	1·25
2265	$1.20 Voyager tent	1·25	1·25
2260/5 Set of 6		6·50	6·50
MS2266 Two sheets, each 76×106 mm. (a) $6 Scout and camp fire. (b) $6 Scout with back pack (*vert*) Set of 2 sheets		12·00	15·00

The overprints on No. **MS**2266 are larger, 12½×5 mm or 5×12½ mm on the vertical design.

(Litho Questa)

1995 (18 Dec). Christmas. Religious Paintings. T **357** and similar vert designs. Multicoloured. P 13½×14.

2267	15c. Type **357**	35	30
2268	35c. "Madonna and Child" (Van Dyck)	50	40
2269	65c. "Sacred Conversation Piece" (Veronese)	70	50
2270	75c. "Vision of St. Anthony" (Van Dyck)	80	60
2271	90c. "Virgin and Child" (Van Eyck)	90	65
2272	$6 "The Immaculate Conception" (Giovanni Tiepolo)	3·25	4·75
2267/72 Set of 6		6·00	6·50
MS2273 Two sheets. (a) 101×127 mm. $5 "Christ appearing to his Mother" (detail) (Van der Weyden). (b) 127×101 mm. $6 "The Infant Jesus and the Young St. John" (Murillo) Set of 2 sheets		8·00	9·00

358 *Hygrophoropsis aurantiaca*

359 H.M.S. *Resolution* (Cook)

(Des D. Burkhart. Litho Questa)

1996 (22 Apr). Fungi. T **358** and similar vert designs. Multicoloured. P 14.

2274	75c. Type **358**	60	70
	a. horiz strip of 4. Nos. 2274/7	2·25	2·50
2275	75c. *Hygrophorus bakerensis*	60	70
2276	75c. *Hygrophorus conicus*	60	70
2277	75c. *Hygrophorus miniatus* (*Hygracybe miniata*)	60	70
2278	75c. *Suillus brevipes*	60	70
	a. Horiz strip of 4. Nos. 2278/81	2·25	2·50
2279	75c. *Suillus luteus*	60	70
2280	75c. *Suillus granulatus*	60	70
2281	75c. *Suillus caerulescens*	60	70
2274/81 Set of 8		4·50	5·00
MS2282 Two sheets, each 105×75 mm. (a) $6 *Conocybefilaris*. (b) $6 *Hygrocybe flavescens* Set of 2 sheets		7·00	8·00

Nos. 2274/7 and 2278/81 were each printed together in sheetlets of 12 containing three horizontal *se-tenant* strips.

(Litho B.D.T.)

1996 (25 Apr). Sailing Ships. T **359** and similar horiz designs. Multicoloured. P 14.

2283	15c. Type **359**	1·25	75
2284	25c. *Mayflower* (Pilgrim Fathers)	1·25	65
2285	45c. *Santa Maria* (Columbus)	1·50	65
2286	75c. *Aemilia* (Dutch galleon)	1·50	1·50
2287	75c. *Sovereign of the Seas* (English galleon)	1·50	1·50
2288	90c. H.M.S. *Victory* (Nelson)	1·75	1·25
2289	$1.20 As No. 2286	1·75	1·60
	a. Sheetlet. Nos. 2289/94	9·50	9·50
2290	$1.20 As No. 2287	1·75	1·60
2291	$1.20 *Royal Louis* (French galleon)	1·75	1·60
2292	$1.20 H.M.S. *Royal George* (ship of the line)	1·75	1·60
2293	$1.20 *Le Protecteur* (French frigate)	1·75	1·60
2294	$1.20 As No. 2288	1·75	1·60
2295	$1.50 As No. 2285	1·75	1·60
	a. Sheetlet. Nos. 2295/2300	9·50	9·50
2296	$1.50 *Vitoria* (Magellan)	1·75	1·75
2297	$1.50 *Golden Hind* (Drake)	1·75	1·75
2298	$1.50 As No. 2284	1·75	1·75
2299	$1.50 *Griffin* (La Salle)	1·75	1·75
2300	$1.50 Type **359**	1·75	1·75
2283/2300 Set of 18		27·00	24·00
MS2301 Two sheets. (a) 102×72 mm. $6 U.S.S. *Constitution* (frigate); (b) 98×67 mm. $6 *Grande Hermine* (Cartier) Set of 2 sheets		10·00	11·00

Nos. 2289/94 and 2295/2300 were each printed together, *se-tenant*, in sheetlets of 6.

360 Florence Griffith Joyner (U.S.A.) (Gold – track, 1988)

361 Black Skimmer

ANTIGUA AND BARBUDA

(Des R. Martin. Litho Questa)

1996 (6 May). Olympic Games, Atlanta. Previous Medal Winners (2nd issue). T **360** and similar multicoloured designs. P 14.

2302	65c. Type **360**	60	60
2303	75c. Olympic Stadium, Seoul (1988) (*horiz*)	65	65
2304	90c. Allison Jolly and Lynne Jewell (U.S.A.) (Gold – yachting, 1988) (*horiz*)	75	70
2305	90c. Wolfgang Nordwig (Germany) (Gold – pole vaulting, 1972)	75	75
	a. Sheetlet. Nos. 2305/13	6·25	6·25
2306	90c. Shirley Strong (Great Britain) (Silver – 100 metres hurdles, 1984)	75	75
2307	90c. Sergei Bubka (Russia) (Gold – pole vault, 1988)	75	75
2308	90c. Filbet Bayi (Tanzania) (Silver – 3000 metres steeplechase, 1980)	75	75
2309	90c. Victor Saneyev (Russia) (Gold – triple jump, 1968, 1972, 1976)	75	75
2310	90c. Silke Renk (Germany) (Gold – javelin, 1992)	75	75
2311	90c. Daley Thompson (Great Britain) (Gold – decathlon, 1980, 1984)	75	75
2312	90c. Robert Richards (U.S.A.) (Gold – pole vault, 1952, 1956)	75	75
2313	90c. Parry O'Brien (U.S.A.) (Gold – shot put, 1952, 1956)	75	75
2314	90c. Ingrid Kramer (Germany) (Gold – Women's platform diving, 1960)	75	75
	a. Sheetlet. Nos. 2314/22	6·25	6·25
2315	90c. Kelly McCormick (U.S.A.) (Silver – Women's springboard diving, 1984)	75	75
2316	90c. Gary Tobian (U.S.A.) (Gold – Men's springboard diving, 1960)	75	75
2317	90c. Greg Louganis (U.S.A.) (Gold – Men's diving, 1984 and 1988)	75	75
2318	90c. Michelle Mitchell (U.S.A.) (Silver – Women's platform diving, 1984 and 1988)	75	75
2319	90c. Zhou Jihong (China) (Gold – Women's platform diving, 1984)	75	75
2320	90c. Wendy Wyland (U.S.A.) (Bronze – Women's platform diving, 1984)	75	75
2321	90c. Xu Yanmei (China) (Gold – Women's platform diving, 1988)	75	75
2322	90c. Fu Mingxia (China) (Gold – Women's platform diving, 1992)	75	75
2323	$1.20 2000 metre tandem cycle race (*horiz*)	1·00	1·00
2302/23 Set of 22		14·00	15·00

MS2324 Two sheets, each 106×76 mm. (a) $5 Bill Toomey (U.S.A.) (Gold–Decathlon, 1968) (*horiz*). (b) $6 Mark Lenzi (U.S.A.) (Gold–Men's springboard diving 1992) *Set of 2 sheets* .... 7·50   8·00

Nos. 2305/13 and 2314/22 were each printed together, *se-tenant*, in sheetlets of 9, with the backgrounds forming composite designs.

1996 (13 May). Sea Birds. T **361** and similar horiz designs. Multicoloured. Litho. P 14.

2325	75c. Type **361**	90	90
	a. Vert strip of 4. Nos. 2325/8	3·25	3·25
2326	75c. Black-capped Petrel	90	90
2327	75c. Sooty Tern	90	90
2328	75c. Royal Tern	90	90
2329	75c. Pomarine Skua ("Pomarine Jaegger")	90	90
	a. Vert strip of 4. Nos. 2329/32	3·25	3·25
2330	75c. White-tailed Tropic Bird	90	90
2331	75c. Northern Gannet	90	90
2332	75c. Laughing Gull	90	90
2325/32 Set of 8		6·50	6·50

MS2333 Two sheets, each 105×75 mm. (a) $5 Great Frigate Bird. (b) $6 Brown Pelican *Set of 2 sheets* ...... 8·00   9·00

Nos. 2325/8 and 2329/32 were each printed together, *se-tenant*, in vertical strips of 4 throughout sheets of 12.

362 Mickey and Goofy on Elephant (*Around the World in Eighty Days*)

(Litho Questa)

1996 (6 June). Novels of Jules Verne. T **362** and similar horiz designs showing Walt Disney cartoon characters in scenes from the books. Multicoloured. P 14×13½.

2334	1c. Type **362**	15	25
2335	2c. Mickey, Donald and Goofy entering cave (*A Journey to the Centre of the Earth*)	20	25
2336	5c. Mickey and Minnie driving postcart (*Michel Strogoff*)	35	25
2337	10c. Mickey and Goofy in space rocket (*From the Earth to the Moon*)	50	20
2338	15c. Mickey and Goofy in balloon (*Five Weeks in a Balloon*)	50	20
2339	20c. Mickey and Goofy in China (*Around the World in Eighty Days*)	50	20
2340	$1 Mickey, Goofy and Pluto on island (*The Mysterious Island*)	2·25	85
2341	$2 Mickey, Pluto, Goofy and Donald on Moon (*From the Earth to the Moon*)	2·75	2·75
2342	$3 Mickey being lifted by bird (*Captain Grant's Children*)	3·25	3·50
2343	$5 Mickey with seal and squid (*Twenty Thousand Leagues Under the Sea*)	4·25	5·00
2334/43 Set of 10		13·00	12·00

MS2344 Two sheets, each 124×99 mm. (a) $6 Mickey on *Nautilus* (*Twenty Thousand Leagues Under the Sea*). (b) $6 Mickey and Donald on raft (*A Journey to the Centre of the Earth*) *Set of 2 sheets* .... 12·50   12·50

363 Bruce Lee   **364** Queen Elizabeth II

1996 (13 June). "CHINA '96" 9th Asian International Stamp Exhibition, Peking. Bruce Lee (actor). T **363** and similar vert designs. Multicoloured. Litho. P 14.

2345	75c. Type **363**	60	70
	a. Sheetlet. Nos. 2345/53	4·75	5·75
2346	75c. Bruce Lee in white shirt and red tie	60	70
2347	75c. In plaid jacket and tie	60	70
2348	75c. In mask and uniform	60	70
2349	75c. Bare-chested	60	70
2350	75c. In mandarin jacket	60	70
2351	75c. In brown jumper	60	70
2352	75c. In fawn shirt	60	70
2353	75c. Shouting	60	70
2345/53 Set of 9		4·75	5·75

MS2354 76×106 mm. $5 Bruce Lee .... 3·75   4·00

Nos 2345/53 were printed together, *se-tenant*, in numbered sheetlets of 9 with enlarged illustrated left-hand margin.

(Litho Questa)

1996 (17 July). 70th Birthday of Queen Elizabeth II. T **364** and similar vert designs. Multicoloured. P 13½×14.

2355	$2 Type **364**	1·25	1·50
	a. Strip of 3. Nos. 2355/7	3·25	4·00
2356	$2 With bouquet	1·25	1·50
2357	$2 In garter robes	1·25	1·50
2355/7 Set of 3		3·25	4·00

MS2358 96×111 mm. $6 Wearing white dress .... 5·50   6·00

Nos. 2355/7 were printed together, *se-tenant*, in horizontal and vertical strips of 3 throughout sheets of 9.

365 Ancient Egyptian Cavalryman   **366** Girl in Red Sari

1996 (24 July). Cavalry through the Ages. T **365** and similar multicoloured designs. Litho. P 14.

2359	60c. Type **365**	50	55
	a. Block of 4. Nos. 2359/62	1·75	2·00

2360	60c. 13th-century English knight		50	55
2361	60c. 16th-century Spanish lancer		50	55
2362	60c. 18th-century Chinese cavalryman		50	55
2359/62 Set of 4			1·75	2·00
MS2363 100×70 mm. $6 19th-century French cuirassier (vert)			3·25	3·75

Nos. 2359/62 were printed together, *se-tenant*, in blocks of four within sheets of 16.

(Litho Questa)

1996 (30 July). 50th Anniv of U.N.I.C.E.F. T **366** and similar vert designs. Multicoloured. P 14.

2364	75c. Type **366**	60	60
2365	90c. South American mother and child	70	70
2366	$1.20 Nurse with child	90	1·00
2364/6 Set of 3		2·00	2·10
MS2367 114×74 mm. $6 Chinese child		3·25	3·75

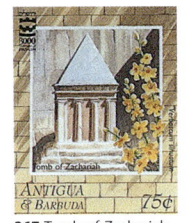

367 Tomb of Zachariah and *Verbascum sinuatum*

(Des Jennifer Toombs. Litho Questa)

1996 (30 July). 3000th Anniv of Jerusalem. T **367** and similar vert designs. Multicoloured. P 14½.

2368	75c. Type **367**	75	65
2369	90c. Pool of Siloam and *Hyacinthus orientalis*	85	75
2370	$1.20 Hurva Synagogue and *Ranunculus asiaticus*	1·25	1·10
2368/70 Set of 3		2·50	2·25
MS2371 66×80 mm. $6 Model of Herod's Temple and *Cercis siliquastrum*		6·50	6·00

368 Kate Smith

(Des J. Iskowitz. Litho Questa)

1996 (30 July). Centenary of Radio. Entertainers. T **368** and similar vert designs. P 13½.

2372	65c. Type **368**	50	50
2373	75c. Dinah Shore	60	60
2374	90c. Rudy Vallee	75	70
2375	$1.20 Bing Crosby	1·10	1·00
2372/5 Set of 4		2·75	2·50
MS2376 72×104 mm. $6 Jo Stafford (28×42 *mm*). P 14		3·25	3·75

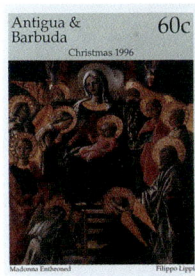

369 "Madonna Enthroned"

370 Robert Preston (*The Music Man*)

(Litho Questa)

1996 (25 Nov). Christmas. Religious Paintings by Filippo Lippi. T **369** and similar vert designs. Multicoloured. P 13½×14.

2377	60c. Type **369**	80	40
2378	90c. "Adoration of the Child and Saints"	1·00	55
2379	$1 "The Annunciation"	1·10	90
2380	$1.20 "Birth of the Virgin"	1·25	1·25
2381	$1.60 "Adoration of the Child"	1·60	1·90
2382	$1.75 "Madonna and Child"	1·90	2·50
2377/82 Set of 6		7·00	6·75
MS2383 Two sheets, each 76×106 mm. (a) $6 "Madonna and Child" (*different*). (b) $6 "The Circumcision" Set of 2 sheets		11·00	12·00

(Des J. Iskowitz. Litho Questa)

1997 (17 Feb). Broadway Musical Stars. T **370** and similar vert designs. Multicoloured. P 13½×14.

2384	$1 Type **370**	90	90
	a. Sheetlet. Nos. 2384/92	7·25	7·25
2385	$1 Michael Crawford (*Phantom of the Opera*)	90	90
2386	$1 Zero Mostel (*Fiddler on the Roof*)	90	90
2387	$1 Patti Lupone (*Evita*)	90	90
2388	$1 Raul Julia (*Threepenny Opera*)	90	90
2389	$1 Mary Martin (*South Pacific*)	90	90
2390	$1 Carol Channing (*Hello Dolly*)	90	90
2391	$1 Yul Brynner (*The King and I*)	90	90
2392	$1 Julie Andrews (*My Fair Lady*)	90	90
2384/92 Set of 9		7·25	7·25
MS2393 106×76 mm. $6 Mickey Rooney (*Sugar Babies*)		4·00	5·00

Nos. 2384/92 were printed together, *se-tenant*, in sheetlets of 9 with the backgrounds forming a composite design.

371 Goofy and Wilbur

(Litho Questa)

1997 (17 Feb). Walt Disney Cartoon Characters. T **371** and similar multicoloured designs. P 14×13½.

2394	1c. Type **371**	10	10
2395	2c. Donald and Goofy in boxing ring	10	10
2396	5c. Donald, Panchito and Jose Carioca	10	10
2397	10c. Mickey and Goofy playing chess	20	15
2398	15c. Chip and Dale with acorns	20	15
2399	20c. Pluto and Mickey	20	15
2400	$1 Daisy and Minnie eating ice-cream	90	75
2401	$2 Daisy and Minnie at dressing table	1·50	1·75
2402	$3 Gus Goose and Donald	2·00	2·50
2394/402 Set of 9		4·75	5·00
MS2403 Two sheets. (a) 102×127 mm. $6 Goofy. P 14×13½. (b) 127×102 mm. $6 Donald Duck playing guitar (*vert*). P 13½×14 Set of 2 sheets		8·50	9·00

372 Charlie Chaplin as Young Man

373 *Charaxes porthos*

(Des J. Iskowitz. Litho Questa)

1997 (24 Feb). 20th Death Anniv of Charlie Chaplin (film star). T **372** and similar vert designs. Multicoloured. P 13½×14.

2404	$1 Type **372**	80	70
	a. Sheetlet. Nos. 2404/12	6·50	5·75
2405	$1 Pulling face	80	70
2406	$1 Looking over shoulder	80	70
2407	$1 In cap	80	70
2408	$1 In front of star	80	70

ANTIGUA AND BARBUDA

2409	$1 In *The Great Dictator*		80	70
2410	$1 With movie camera and megaphone		80	70
2411	$1 Standing in front of camera lens		80	70
2412	$1 Putting on make-up		80	70
2404/12 Set of 9			6·50	5·75
MS2413 76×106 mm. $6 Charlie Chaplin			4·00	4·25

Nos. 2404/12 were printed together, *se-tenant*, in sheetlets of 9 with the backgrounds forming a composite design.

(Des T. Wood. Litho Questa)

1997 (10 Mar). Butterflies. T **373** and similar multicoloured designs. P 14.

2414	90c. Type **373**	80	50
2415	$1.10 *Charaxes protoclea protoclea*	80	80
	a. Sheetlet. Nos. 2415/23	6·50	6·50
2416	$1.10 *Byblia ilithyia*	80	80
2417	$1.10 Black-headed Bush Shrike ("Tchagra" (bird))	80	80
2418	$1.10 *Charaxes nobilis*	80	80
2419	$1.10 *Pseudacraea boisduvali trimeni*	80	80
2420	$1.10 *Charaxes smaragdalis*	80	80
2421	$1.10 *Charaxes lasti*	80	80
2422	$1.10 *Pseudacrea poggei*	80	80
2423	$1.10 *Graphium colonna*	80	80
2424	$1.10 Carmine Bee Eater (bird)	80	80
	a. Sheetlet. Nos. 2424/32	6·50	6·50
2425	$1.10 *Pseudacraea eurytus*	80	80
2426	$1.10 *Hypolimnas monteironis*	80	80
2427	$1.10 *Charaxes anticlea*	80	80
2428	$1.10 *Graphium leonidas*	80	80
2429	$1.10 *Graphium illyris*	80	80
2430	$1.10 *Nephronia argia*	80	80
2431	$1.10 *Gamphium policenes*	80	80
2432	$1.10 *Papilio dardanus*	80	80
2433	$1.20 *Aethiopana honorius*	80	80
2434	$1.60 *Charaxes hadrianus*	1·25	1·10
2435	$1.75 *Precis westermanni*	1·25	1·40
2414/35 Set of 22		16·00	16·00

MS2436 Three sheets, each 106×76 mm. (a) $6 *Charaxes lactitinctus* (horiz). (b) $6 *Eupheadra neophron*. (c) $6 *Euxanthe tiberius* (horiz) *Set of 3 sheets* .... 11·00 13·00

Nos. 2415/23 and 2424/32 were each printed together, *se-tenant*, in sheetlets of 9 with the backgrounds forming composite designs.

No. 2430 is inscribed "Nepheronia argia" in error.

374 Convent of the Companions of Jesus, Morelia, Mexico

(Des M. Freedman and Dena Rubin. Litho Questa)

1997 (10 Apr). 50th Anniv of U.N.E.S.C.O. T **374** and similar multicoloured designs. P 14×13½ (horiz) or 13½×14 (vert).

2437	60c. Type **374**	70	35
2438	90c. Fortress at San Lorenzo, Panama (*vert*)	80	50
2439	$1 Canaima National Park, Venezuela (*vert*)	80	55
2440	$1.10 Aerial view of church with tower, Guanajuato, Mexico (*vert*)	80	90
	a. Sheetlet. Nos. 2440/7 and central label	5·75	6·50
2441	$1.10 Church facade, Guanajuato, Mexico (*vert*)	80	90
2442	$1.10 Aerial view of churches with domes, Guanajuato, Mexico (*vert*)	80	90
2443	$1.10 Jesuit Missions of the Chiquitos, Bolivia (*vert*)	80	90
2444	$1.10 Huascaran National Park, Peru (*vert*)	80	90
2445	$1.10 Jesuit Missions of La Santisima, Paraguay (*vert*)	80	90
2446	$1.10 Cartagena, Colombia (*vert*)	80	90
2447	$1.10 Fortification, Havana, Cuba (*vert*)	80	90
2448	$1.20 As No. 2444 (*vert*)	85	90
2449	$1.60 Church of San Francisco, Guatemala (*vert*)	1·25	1·40
2450	$1.65 Tikal National Park, Guatemala	1·50	1·60
	a. Sheetlet. Nos. 2450/4 and label	6·75	7·25
2451	$1.65 Rio Platano Reserve, Honduras	1·50	1·60
2452	$1.65 Ruins of Copan, Honduras	1·50	1·60
2453	$1.65 Antigua ruins, Guatemala	1·50	1·60
2454	$1.65 Teotihuacan, Mexico	1·50	1·60
2455	$1.75 Santo Domingo, Dominican Republic (*vert*)	1·75	1·90
2437/55 Set of 19		18·00	19·00

MS2456 Two sheets, each 127×102 mm. (a) $6 Tikal National Park, Guatemala. (b) $6 Teotihuacan pyramid, Mexico *Set of 2 sheets* .... 9·00 9·50

Nos. 2440/7 and 2450/4 were each printed, *se-tenant*, in sheetlets of 8 and 5 with a label.

No. 2446 is inscribed "Columbia" in error.

375 Red Bishop

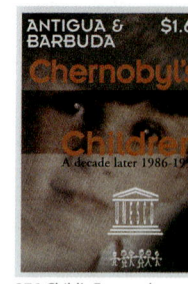

376 Child's Face and U.N.E.S.C.O. Emblem

1997 (24 Apr). Endangered Species. T **375** and similar vert designs. Multicoloured. Litho. P 14.

2457	$1.20 Type **375**	1·40	1·40
	a. Sheetlet. Nos. 2457/62	7·50	7·50
2458	$1.20 Yellow Baboon	1·40	1·40
2459	$1.20 Superb Starling	1·40	1·40
2460	$1.20 Ratel	1·40	1·40
2461	$1.20 Hunting Dog	1·40	1·40
2462	$1.20 Serval	1·40	1·40
2463	$1.65 Okapi	1·40	1·40
	a. Sheetlet. Nos. 2463/8	7·50	7·50
2464	$1.65 Giant Forest Squirrel	1·40	1·40
2465	$1.65 Lesser Masked Weaver	1·40	1·40
2466	$1.65 Small-spotted Genet	1·40	1·40
2467	$1.65 Yellow-billed Stork	1·40	1·40
2468	$1.65 Red-headed Agama	1·40	1·40
2457/68 Set of 12		15·00	15·00

MS2469 Three sheets, each 106×76 mm. (a) $6 South African Crowned Crane. (b) $6 Bat-eared Fox. (c) $6 Malachite Kingfisher *Set of 3 sheets* .... 15·00 16·00

Nos. 2457/62 and 2463/8 were each printed together, *se-tenant*, in sheetlets of 6 with the backgrounds forming composite designs.

(Litho Questa)

1997 (12 June). 10th Anniv of Chernobyl Nuclear Disaster. T **376** and similar vert design. Multicoloured. P 13½.

2470	$1.65 Type **376**	1·40	1·50
2471	$2 As Type **376**, but inscribed "CHABAD'S CHILDREN OF CHERNOBYL" at foot	1·75	2·00

377 Paul Harris and James Grant

(Des J. Iskowitz, Litho Questa)

1997 (12 June). 50th Death Anniv of Paul Harris (founder of Rotary International). T **377** and similar horiz design. Multicoloured. P 14.

2472	$1.75 Type **377**	1·25	1·50

MS2473 78×107 mm. $6 Group study exchange, New Zealand .... 3·75 4·25

378 Queen Elizabeth II

(Litho Questa)

1997 (12 June). Golden Wedding of Queen Elizabeth and Prince Philip. T **378** and similar horiz designs. Multicoloured. P 14.

2474	$1 Type **378**	1·10	1·10
	a. Sheetlet. Nos. 2474/9	6·00	6·00
2475	$1 Royal coat of arms	1·10	1·10

ANTIGUA AND BARBUDA

2476	$1 Queen Elizabeth and Prince Philip at reception		1·10	1·10
2477	$1 Queen Elizabeth and Prince Philip in landau		1·10	1·10
2478	$1 Balmoral		1·10	1·10
2479	$1 Prince Philip		1·10	1·10
2474/9 Set of 6			6·00	6·00
MS2480 100×71 mm. $6 Queen Elizabeth with Prince Philip in naval uniform			4·25	4·50

Nos. 2474/9 were printed together, *se-tenant*, in sheetlets of 6.

379 Kaiser Wilhelm I and Heinrich von Stephan

380 The Ugly Sisters and their Mother

(Des J. Iskowitz. Litho Questa)

1997 (12 June). "Pacific '97" International Stamp Exhibition, San Francisco. Death Centenary of Heinrich von Stephan (founder of the U.P.U.). T **379** and similar horiz designs. P 14.

2481	$1.75 dull blue	1·25	1·40
	a. Sheetlet. Nos. 2481/3	3·25	3·75
2482	$1.75 chestnut	1·25	1·40
2483	$1.75 deep magenta	1·25	1·40
2481/3 Set of 3		3·25	3·75
MS2484 82×119 mm. $6 violet		3·75	4·50

Designs: No. 2481, Type **379**; 2482, Von Stephan and Mercury; No. 2483, Carrier pigeon and loft; No. **MS**2484, Von Stephan and 15th-century Basle messenger.

Nos. 2481/3 were printed together, *se-tenant*, in sheetlets of 3 with enlarged right-hand margin.

No. 2483 is inscribed "PIDGEON" in error.

(Des R. Sauber. Litho Questa)

1997 (12 June). 175th Anniv of Brothers Grimm's Third Collection of Fairy Tales. Cinderella. T **380** and similar vert designs. Multicoloured. P 13½×14.

2485	$1.75 Type **380**	1·60	1·60
	a. Sheetlet. Nos. 2485/7	4·25	4·25
2486	$1.75 Cinderella and her Fairy Godmother	1·60	1·60
2487	$1.75 Cinderella and the Prince	1·60	1·60
2485/7 Set of 3		4·25	4·25
MS2488 124×96 mm. $6 Cinderella trying on slipper		4·25	4·50

Nos. 2485/7 were printed together, *se-tenant*, in sheetlets of 3 with illustrated margins.

381 *Marasmius rotula*

382 *Odontoglossum cervantesii*

(Des D. Burkhart, Litho Questa)

1997 (12 Aug). Fungi. T **381** and similar horiz designs. Multicoloured. P 14.

2489	45c. Type **381**	50	30
2490	65c. *Cantharellus cibarius*	60	40
2491	70c. *Lepiota cristata*	60	40
2492	90c. *Auricularia mesenterica*	70	50
2493	$1 *Pholiota alnicola*	75	55
2494	$1.65 *Leccinum aurantiacum*	1·10	1·25
2495	$1.75 *Entoloma serrulatum*	1·25	1·40
	a. Sheetlet. Nos. 2495/2500	6·75	7·50
2496	$1.75 *Panaeolus sphinctrinus*	1·25	1·40
2497	$1.75 *Volvariella bombycina*	1·25	1·40
2498	$1.75 *Conocybe percincta*	1·25	1·40
2499	$1.75 *Pluteus cervinus*	1·25	1·40
2500	$1.75 *Russula foetens*	1·25	1·40
2489/2500 Set of 12		10·50	10·50
MS2501 Two sheets, each 106×76 mm. (a) $6 *Amanita cothurnata*. (b) $6 *Panellus serotinus* Set of 2 sheets		7·50	8·50

Nos. 2495/2500 were printed together, *se-tenant*, in sheetlets of 6.

(Des T. Wood. Litho Questa)

1997 (19 Aug). Orchids of the World. T **382** and similar vert designs. Multicoloured. P 14.

2502	45c. Type **382**	60	30
2503	65c. *Phalaenopsis* Medford Star	70	40
2504	75c. *Vanda* Motes Resplendent	75	45
2505	90c. *Odontonia* Debutante	80	50
2506	$1 *Iwanagaara* Apple Blossom	90	70
2507	$1.65 *Cattleya* Sophia Martin	1·25	1·25
	a. Sheetlet. Nos. 2507/14	9·00	9·00
2508	$1.65 Dogface Butterfly	1·25	1·25
2509	$1.65 *Laeliocattleya* Mini Purple	1·25	1·25
2510	$1.65 *Cymbidium* Showgirl	1·25	1·25
2511	$1.65 *Brassolaeliocattleya* Dorothy Bertsch	1·25	1·25
2512	$1.65 *Disa blackii*	1·25	1·25
2513	$1.65 *Paphiopedilum leeanum*	1·25	1·25
2514	$1.65 *Paphiopedilum macranthum*	1·25	1·25
2515	$1.65 *Brassocattleya* Angel Lace	1·25	1·25
	a. Sheetlet. Nos. 2515/22	9·00	9·00
2516	$1.65 *Saphrolae liocattleya* Precious Stones	1·25	1·25
2517	$1.65 Orange Theope Butterfly	1·25	1·25
2518	$1.65 *Promenaea xanthina*	1·25	1·25
2519	$1.65 *Lycaste macrobulbon*	1·25	1·25
2520	$1.65 *Amestella philippinensis*	1·25	1·25
2521	$1.65 *Masdevallia* Machu Picchu	1·25	1·25
2522	$1.65 *Phalaenopsis* Zuma Urchin	1·25	1·25
2523	$2 *Dendrobium victoria-reginae*	1·60	1·60
2502/23 Set of 22		23·00	22·00
MS2524 Two sheets, each 76×106 mm. (a) $6 *Miltonia* Seine. (b) $6 *Paphiopedilum gratrixanum* Set of 2 sheets		8·00	9·00

Nos. 2507/14 and 2515/22 were each printed together, *se-tenant*, in sheetlets of 8 with the backgrounds forming composite designs.

383 Maradona holding World Cup Trophy, 1986

(Litho Questa)

1997 (16 Oct). World Cup Football Championship, France (1998). T **383** and multicoloured designs. P 14×13½.

2525	60c. multicoloured	50	35
2526	75c. agate	60	45
2527	90c. multicoloured	70	50
2528	$1 agate	75	75
	a. Sheetlet. Nos. 2528/35 and central label	5·50	5·50
2529	$1 agate	75	75
2530	$1 agate	75	75
2531	$1 grey-black	75	75
2532	$1 agate	75	75
2533	$1 agate	75	75
2534	$1 agate	75	75
2535	$1 agate	75	75
2536	$1.20 multicoloured	75	75
2537	$1.65 multicoloured	1·10	1·25
2538	$1.75 multicoloured	1·10	1·40
2525/38 Set of 14		9·75	10·25
MS2539 Two sheets, each 102×127 mm. $6 multicoloured. P 13½×14. (b) $6 multicoloured. P 14×13½ Set of 2 sheets		7·50	8·50

Designs: Horiz—No. 2526, Fritzwalter, West Germany, 1954; No. 2527, Zoff, Italy, 1982; No. 2536, Moore, England, 1966; No. 2537, Alberto, Brazil, 1970; No. 2538, Matthaus, West Germany, 1990; No. **MS**2539(b), West German players celebrating, 1990. Vert–No. 2528, Ademir, Brazil, 1950; No. 2529, Eusebio, Portugal, 1966; No. 2530, Fontaine, France, 1958; No. 2531, Schillaci, Italy, 1990; No. 2532, Leonidas, Brazil, 1938; No. 2533, Stabile, Argentina, 1930; No. 2534, Nejedly, Czechoslovakia, 1934; No. 2535, Muller, West Germany, 1970; No. **MS**2539 (a), Bebeto, Brazil.

Nos. 2528/35 were printed together, *se-tenant*, in sheetlets of 8 stamps and a central label.

ANTIGUA AND BARBUDA

384 Scottish Fold Kitten

385 Original Drawing by Richard Trevithick, 1803

(Des R. Martin. Litho Questa)

1997 (27 Oct). Cats and Dogs. T **384** and similar multicoloured designs. P 14.

2540	$1.65 Type **384**	1·50	1·25
	a. Sheetlet. Nos. 2540/5	8·00	6·75
2541	$1.65 Japanese Bobtail	1·50	1·25
2542	$1.65 Tabby Manx	1·50	1·25
2543	$1.65 Bicolor American Shorthair	1·50	1·25
2544	$1.65 Sorrel Abyssinian	1·50	1·25
2545	$1.65 Himalayan Blue Point	1·50	1·25
2546	$1.65 Dachshund	1·50	1·25
	a. Sheetlet. Nos. 2546/51	8·00	6·75
2547	$1.65 Staffordshire Terrier	1·50	1·25
2548	$1.65 Shar-pei	1·50	1·25
2549	$1.65 Beagle	1·50	1·25
2550	$1.65 Norfolk Terrier	1·50	1·25
2551	$1.65 Golden Retriever	1·50	1·25
2540/51	Set of 12	16·00	13·50

MS2552 Two sheets, each 107×77 mm. (a) $6 Red Tabby (*vert*). (b) $6 Siberian Husky (*vert*) Set of 2 sheets .... 8·50 9·00

Nos. 2540/5 and 2546/51 were each printed together, *se-tenant*, in sheetlets of 6.

1997 (10 Nov). Railway Locomotives of the World. T **385** and similar horiz designs. Each blackish brown. Litho. P 14.

2553	$1.65 Type **385**	1·50	1·25
	a. Sheetlet. Nos. 2553/8	8·00	6·75
2554	$1.65 William Hedley's *Puffing Billy*, (1813–14)	1·50	1·25
2555	$1.65 Crampton locomotive of French Nord Railway, 1858	1·50	1·25
2556	$1.65 Lawrence Machine Shop locomotive, U.S.A., 1860	1·50	1·25
2557	$1.65 Natchez and Hamburg Railway steam locomotive *Mississippi*, U.S.A., 1834	1·50	1·25
2558	$1.65 Bury "Coppernob" locomotive, Furness Railway, 1846	1·50	1·25
2559	$1.65 David Joy's *Jenny Lind*, 1847	1·50	1·25
	a. Sheetlet. Nos. 2559/64	8·00	6·75
2560	$1.65 Schenectady Atlantic locomotive, U.S.A., 1899	1·50	1·25
2561	$1.65 Kitson Class 1800 tank locomotive, Japan 1881	1·50	1·25
2562	$1.65 Pennsylvania Railroad express freight	1·50	1·25
2563	$1.65 Karl Golsdorfs 4 cylinder locomotive, Austria	1·50	1·25
2564	$1.65 Series "E" locomotive, Russia, 1930	1·50	1·25
2553/64	Set of 12	16·00	13·50

MS2565 Two sheets, each 72×100 mm. (a) $6 George Stephenson "Patentee" type locomotive, 1843. (b) $6 Brunel's trestle bridge over River Lyhber, Cornwall Set of 2 sheets .... 8·00 9·00

Nos. 2553/8 and 2559/64 were each printed together, *se-tenant*, in sheetlets of 6.

No. 2554 is dated "1860" in error.

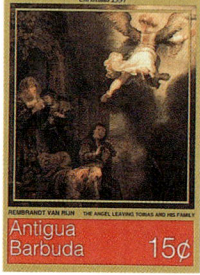

386 "The Angel leaving Tobias and his Family" (Rembrandt)

387 Diana, Princess of Wales

(Litho B.D.T.)

1997 (2 Dec). Christmas. Religious Paintings. T **386** and similar multicoloured designs. P 14.

2566	15c. Type **386**	30	15
2567	25c. "The Resurrection" (Martin Knoller)	40	20
2568	60c. "Astronomy" (Raphael)	60	40
2569	75c. "Music-making Angel" (Melozzo da Forli)	70	55
2570	90c. "Amor" (Parmigianino)	80	60
2571	$1.20 "Madonna and Child with Saints" (Rosso Fiorentino)	1·00	1·25
2566/71	Set of 6	3·50	2·75

MS2572 Two sheets, each 105×96 mm. (a) $6 "The Wedding of Tobias" (Gianantonio and Francesco Guardi) (*horiz*). (b) $6 "The Portinari Altarpiece" (Hugo van der Goes) (*horiz*) Set of 2 sheets .... 7·50 8·50

(Litho Questa)

1998 (19 Jan). Diana, Princess of Wales Commemoration. T **387** and similar vert designs. Multicoloured (except Nos. 2574, 2581/2 and **MS**2585b). P 14.

2573	$1.65 Type **387**	1·10	1·10
	a. Sheetlet. Nos. 2573/8	6·00	6·00
2574	$1.65 Wearing hoop earrings (rose-carm and black)	1·10	1·10
2575	$1.65 Carrying bouquet	1·10	1·10
2576	$1.65 Wearing floral hat	1·10	1·10
2577	$1.65 With Prince Harry	1·10	1·10
2578	$1.65 Wearing white jacket	1·10	1·10
2579	$1.65 In kitchen	1·10	1·10
	a. Sheetlet. Nos. 2579/84	6·00	6·00
2580	$1.65 Wearing black and white dress	1·10	1·10
2581	$1.65 Wearing hat (orge-brown & black)	1·10	1·10
2582	$1.65 Wearing floral print dress (lake-brown and black)	1·10	1·10
2583	$1.65 Dancing with John Travolta	1·10	1·10
2584	$1.65 Wearing white hat and jacket	1·10	1·10
2573/84	Set of 12	12·00	12·00

MS2585 Two sheets, each 70×100 mm. (a) $6 Wearing red jumper. (b) $6 Wearing black dress for papal audience (lake-brown and black) Set of 2 sheets .... 7·50 8·00

Nos. 2573/8 and 2579/84 were each printed together, *se-tenant*, in sheetlets of 6.

388 Yellow Damselfish

(Litho B.D.T.)

1998 (19 Feb). Fish. T **388** and similar horiz designs. Multicoloured. P 14.

2586	75c. Type **388**	55	40
2587	90c. Barred Hamlet	65	50
2588	$1 Yellow-tailed Damselfish ("Jewelfish")	70	55
2589	$1.20 Blue-headed Wrasse	75	60
2590	$1.50 Queen Angelfish	85	85
2591	$1.65 Jackknife-fish	95	95
	a. Sheetlet. Nos. 2591/6	5·00	5·00
2592	$1.65 Spot-finned Hogfish	95	95
2593	$1.65 Sergeant Major	95	95
2594	$1.65 Neon Goby	95	95
2595	$1.65 Jawfish	95	95
2596	$1.65 Flamefish	95	95
2597	$1.65 Rock Beauty	95	95
	a. Sheetlet. Nos. 2597/602	5·00	5·00
2598	$1.65 Yellow-tailed Snapper	95	95
2599	$1.65 Creole Wrasse	95	95
2600	$1.65 Slender Filefish	95	95
2601	$1.65 Long-spined Squirrelfish	95	95
2602	$1.65 Royal Gramma ("Fairy Basslet")	95	95
2603	$1.75 Queen Triggerfish	1·00	1·10
2586/2603	Set of 18	14·00	14·00

MS2604 Two sheets, each 80×110 mm. (a) $6 Porkfish. (b) $6 Black-capped Basslet Set of 2 sheets .... 8·00 9·00

Nos. 2591/6 and 2597/2602 were each printed together, *se-tenant*, in sheetlets of 6 with the backgrounds forming composite designs.

389 First Church and Manse, 1822–40

(Litho B.D.T.)

1998 (16 Mar). 175th Anniv of Cedar Hall Moravian Church. T **389** and similar horiz designs. Multicoloured. P 14.

2605	20c. Type **389**	20	20
2606	45c. Cedar Hall School, 1840	35	30
2607	75c. Hugh A. King, minister 1945–53	55	45
2608	90c. Present Church building	65	50
2609	$1.20 Water tank, 1822	75	75
2610	$2 Former Manse, demolished 1978	1·25	2·00
2605/10 Set of 6		3·25	3·75
MS2611 100×70 mm. $6 Present church building (*different*) (50×37 *mm*)		3·25	4·25

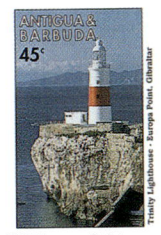

390 Europa Point Lighthouse, Gibraltar

(Des M. Friedman. Litho Questa)

1998 (20 Apr). Lighthouses of the World. T **390** and similar multicoloured designs. P 14.

2612	45c. Type **390**	65	40
2613	65c. Tierra del Fuego, Argentina (*horiz*)	75	55
2614	75c. Point Loma, California, U.S.A. (*horiz*)	80	55
2615	90c. Groenpoint, Cape Town, South Africa	90	60
2616	$1 Youghal, Cork, Ireland	1·00	90
2617	$1.20 Launceston, Tasmania, Australia	1·10	1·10
2618	$1.65 Point Abino, Ontario, Canada (*horiz*)	1·40	1·75
2619	$1.75 Great Inagua, Bahamas	1·50	2·00
2612/19 Set of 8		7·25	7·00
MS2620 99×70 mm. $6 Cape Hatteras, North Carolina, U.S.A.		5·50	6·00

No. 2613 is inscribed "Terra Del Fuego" in error.

391 Pooh and Tigger (January)

392 Miss Nellie Robinson (founder)

(Des Walt Disney Co. Litho)

1998 (11 May). Through the Year with Winnie the Pooh. T **391** and similar vert designs. Multicoloured. P 13½×14.

2621	$1 Type **391**	1·00	1·00
	a. Sheetlet. Nos. 2621/6	5·50	5·50
2622	$1 Pooh and Piglet indoors (February)	1·00	1·00
2623	$1 Piglet hang-gliding with scarf (March)	1·00	1·00
2624	$1 Tigger, Pooh and Piglet on pond (April)	1·00	1·00
2625	$1 Kanga and Roo with posy of flowers (May)	1·00	1·00
2626	$1 Pooh on balloon and Owl (June)	1·00	1·00
2627	$1 Pooh, Eeyore, Tigger and Piglet gazing at stars (July)	1·00	1·00
	a. Sheetlet. Nos. 2627/32	5·50	5·50
2628	$1 Pooh and Piglet by stream (August)	1·00	1·00
2629	$1 Christopher Robin going to school (September)	1·00	1·00
2630	$1 Eeyore in fallen leaves (October)	1·00	1·00
2631	$1 Pooh and Rabbit gathering pumpkins (November)	1·00	1·00
2632	$1 Pooh and Piglet skiing (December)	1·00	1·00
2621/32 Set of 12		11·00	11·00
MS2633 Four sheets, each 126×101 mm. (a) $6 Pooh, Rabbit and Piglet with blanket (Spring). (b) $6 Pooh by pond (Summer). (c) $6 Pooh sweeping fallen leaves (Autumn). (d) $6 Pooh and Eeyore on ice (Winter) Set of 4 sheets		16·00	16·00

Nos. 2621/6 and 2627/32 were each printed together, *se-tenant*, in sheetlets of 6.

(Des M. Friedman. Litho B.D.T)

1998 (23 July). Centenary of Thomas Oliver Robinson Memorial School. T **392** and similar designs. P 14.

2634	20c. brown-olive and black	20	20
2635	45c. multicoloured	40	25
2636	65c. brown-olive and black	55	50
2637	75c. multicoloured	60	60
2638	90c. multicoloured	70	65
2639	$1.20 red-brown, brown-olive and black	90	1·40
2634/9 Set of 6		3·00	3·25
MS2640 106×76 mm. $6 olive-brown		3·25	4·00

Designs: *Horiz*—45c. School photo, 1985: 65c. Former school building, 1930–49: 75c. Children with Mrs. Natalie Hurst (present headmistress): $1.20, Present school building, 1950. *Vert*—90c. Miss Ina Loving (former teacher); $6 Miss Nellie Robinson (*different*).

393 Spotted Eagle Ray

(Des. B. Steadman (Nos. 2641/65 and **MS**2678a), R. Martin (others). Litho Questa)

1998 (17 Aug). International Year of the Ocean. T **393** and similar horiz designs. Multicoloured. P 14.

2641/65	40c.×25 Type **393**; Manta Ray: Hawksbill Turtle; Jellyfish; Queen Angelfish; Octopus; Emperor Angelfish; Regal Angelfish; Porkfish; Racoon Butterflyfish; Atlantic Barracuda; Sea Horse; Nautilus; Trumpetfish; White Tip Shark; Sunken Spanish galleon; Black Tip Shark; Long nosed Butterflyfish; Green Moray Eel; Captain Nemo; Treasure chest; Hammerhead Shark; Divers; Lionfish; Clown Fish		
	a. Sheetlet. Nos. 2641/65	7·00	8·00
2666/77	75c.×12 Maroon-tailed Conure; Cocoi Heron; Common Tern; Rainbow Lorikeet; Saddleback Butterflyfish; Goatfish and Cat Shark; Blue Shark and Stingray; Majestic Snapper; Nassau Grouper; Black-cap Gramma and Blue Tang; Stingrays; Stingrays and Giant Starfish		
	a. Sheetlet. Nos. 2666/77	7·00	8·00
2641/77 Set of 37		14·00	16·00
MS2678 Two sheets. (a) 68×98 mm. $6 Humpback Whale. (b) 98×68 mm. $6 Fiddler Ray *Set of 2 sheets*		9·00	9·50

Nos. 2641/65 and 2666/77 were each printed together, *se-tenant*, in sheetlets of 25 or 12, with the backgrounds forming composite designs.

394 *Savannah* (paddle-steamer)

395 Flags of Antigua and CARICOM

(Des. L. Schwinger. Litho Questa)

1998 (18 Aug). Ships of the World. T **394** and similar multicoloured designs. P 14½.

2679	$1.75 Type **394**	1·50	1·50
	a. Sheetlet. Nos. 2679/81	4·00	4·00
2680	$1.75 Viking longship	1·50	1·50
2681	$1.75 Greek galley	1·50	1·50
2682	$1.75 Sailing clipper	1·50	1·50
	a. Sheetlet. Nos. 2682/4	4·00	4·00
2683	$1.75 Dhow	1·50	1·50
2684	$1.75 Fishing catboat	1·50	1·50
2679/84 Set of 6		8·00	8·00
MS2685 Three sheets each 100×70 mm. (a) $6 13th-century English warship (41×22 *mm*). (b) $6 Sailing dory (24×41 *mm*). (c) $6 Baltimore clipper (41×22 *mm*). P 14 *Set of 3 sheets*		13·00	14·00

Nos. 2679/81 and 2682/4 were printed together, *se-tenant*, in sheetlets of 3 with enlarged illustrated left-hand margins.

ANTIGUA AND BARBUDA

(Des R. Sauber. Litho Cartor)

1998 (20 Aug). 25th Anniv of Caribbean Community. P 13½.
2686	**395**	$1 multicoloured	1·25	1·25

396 Ford, 1896

1998 (1 Sept). Classic Cars. T **396** and similar horiz designs. Multicoloured. Litho. P 14.
2687	$1.65 Type **396**		1·10	1·10
	a. Sheetlet. Nos. 2687/92		6·00	6·00
2688	$1.65 Ford A, 1903		1·10	1·10
2689	$1.65 Ford T, 1928		1·10	1·10
2690	$1.65 Ford T, 1922		1·10	1·10
2691	$1.65 Ford Blackhawk, 1929		1·10	1·10
2692	$1.65 Ford Sedan, 1934		1·10	1·10
2693	$1.65 Torpedo, 1911		1·10	1·10
	a. Sheetlet. Nos. 2693/8		6·00	6·00
2694	$1.65 Mercedes 22, 1913		1·10	1·10
2695	$1.65 Rover, 1920		1·10	1·10
2696	$1.65 Mercedes-Benz 1956		1·10	1·10
2697	$1.65 Packard V-12, 1934		1·10	1·10
2698	$1.65 Opel, 1924		1·10	1·10
2687/98 Set of 12			12·00	12·00

MS2699 Two sheets, each 70×100 mm. (a) $6 Ford, 1908 (60×40 mm). (b) $6 Ford, 1929 (60×40 mm). P 14×14½ Set of 2 sheets .... 7·50 8·00

Nos. 2687/92 and 2693/8 were each printed together, *se-tenant*, in sheetlets of 6.

397 Lockheed-Boeing General Dynamics Yf-22

398 Karl Benz internal-combustion engine)

(Des E. Nisbet. Litho Questa)

1998 (22 Sept). Modern Aircraft. T **397** and similar horiz designs. Multicoloured. P 14.
2700	$1.65 Type **397**		1·25	1·25
	a. Sheetlet. Nos. 2700/5		6·75	6·75
2701	$1.65 Dassault-Breguet Rafale BO 1		1·25	1·25
2702	$1.65 MiG 29		1·25	1·25
2703	$1.65 Dassault-Breguet Mirage 2000D		1·25	1·25
2704	$1.65 Rockwell B-1B "Lancer"		1·25	1·25
2705	$1.65 McDonnell-Douglas C-17A		1·25	1·25
2706	$1.65 Space Shuttle		1·25	1·25
	a. Sheetlet. Nos. 2706/11		6·75	6·75
2707	$1.65 SAAB "Grippen"		1·25	1·25
2708	$1.65 Eurofighter EF-2000		1·25	1·25
2709	$1.65 Sukhoi SU 27		1·25	1·25
2710	$1.65 Northrop B-2		1·25	1·25
2711	$1.65 Lockheed F-117 "Nighthawk"		1·25	1·25
2700/11 Set of 12			13·50	13·50

MS2712 Two sheets, each 110×85 mm. (a) $6 F18 Hornet. (b) $6 Sukhoi SU 35 Set of 2 sheets .... 8·50 9·00

Nos. 2700/5 and 2706/11 were each printed together, *se-tenant*, in sheetlets of 6.

No. **MS**2712b is inscribed "Sukhi" in error.

1998 (10 Nov). Millennium Series. Famous People of the Twentieth Century. Inventors. T **398** and similar multicoloured designs. Litho. P 14.
2713	$1 Type **398**		1·00	1·00
	a. Sheetlet. Nos. 2713/20		7·25	7·25
2714	$1 Early Benz car and Mercedes-Benz racing car (53×38 mm)		1·00	1·00
2715	$1 Atom bomb mushroom cloud (53×38 mm)		1·00	1·00
2716	$1 Albert Einstein (theory of relativity)		1·00	1·00
2717	$1 Leopold Godowsky Jr. and Leopold Damrosch Mannes (Kodachrome film)		1·00	1·00
2718	$1 Camera and transparencies (53×38 mm)		1·00	1·00
2719	$1 Heinkel He 178 (first turbo jet plane) (53×38 mm)		1·00	1·00
2720	$1 Dr. Hans Pabst von Ohain (jet turbine engine)		1·00	1·00
2721	$1 Rudolf Diesel (diesel engine)		1·00	1·00
	a. Sheetlet. Nos. 2721/8		7·25	7·25
2722	$1 Early Diesel engine and forms of transport (53×38 mm)		1·00	1·00
2723	$1 Zeppelin airship (53×38 mm)		1·00	1·00
2724	$1 Count Ferdinand von Zeppelin (airship pioneer)		1·00	1·00
2725	$1 Wilhelm Conrad Rontgen (X-rays)		1·00	1·00
2726	$1 X-ray of hand (53×38 mm)		1·00	1·00
2727	$1 Launch of Saturn Rocket (53×38 mm)		1·00	1·00
2728	$1 Wernher von Braun (rocket research)		1·00	1·00
2713/28 Set of 16			14·50	14·50

MS2729 Two sheets, each 106×76 mm. (a) $6 Hans Geiger (Geiger counter). (b) $6 William Shockley (research into semi-conductors) Set of 2 sheets .... 9·50 10·00

Nos. 2713/20 and 2721/8 were each printed together, *se-tenant*, in sheetlets of 8 with enlarged illustrated margins. No. 2713 is inscribed "CARL BENZ" in error.

399 Stylised Americas

400 "Figures on the Seashore"

(Litho Questa)

1998 (18 Nov). 50th Anniv to of Organization of American States. P 13½×14.
2730	**399**	$1 multicoloured	80	90

(Des Diana Catherines. Litho Questa)

1998 (18 Nov). 25th Death Anniv of Pablo Picasso (painter). T **400** and similar multicoloured designs. P 14½.
2731	$1.20 Type **400**		75	70
2732	$1.65 "Three Figures under a Tree" (vert)		85	1·00
2733	$1.75 "Two Women running on the Beach"		95	1·25
2731/3 Set of 3			2·25	2·75

MS2734 126×102 mm. $6 "Bullfight" .... 3·25 3·75

401 Dino 246 GT-GTS

(Des F. Rivera. Litho Questa)

1998 (18 Nov). Birth Centenary of Enzo Ferrari (car manufacturer). T **401** and similar horiz designs. Multicoloured. P 14.
2735	$1.75 Type **401**		2·25	2·25
	a. Sheetlet. Nos. 2735/7		6·00	6·00
2736	$1.75 Front view of Dino 246 GT-GTS		2·25	2·25
2737	$1.75 365 GT4 BB		2·25	2·25
2735/7 Set of 3			6·00	6·00

MS2738 104×72 mm. $6 Dino 246 GT-GTS (91×34 mm). P 14×14½ .... 6·00 6·00

Nos. 2735/7 were printed together, *se-tenant*, in sheetlets of 3.

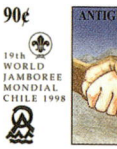

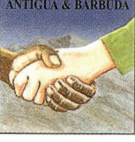

402 Scout Handshake

403 Mahatma Gandhi

(Des G. Bibby. Litho Questa)

1998 (18 Nov). 19th World Scout Jamboree, Chile. T **402** and similar horiz designs. Multicoloured. P 14.

2739	90c. Type **402**	60	55
2740	$1 Scouts hiking	75	90
2741	$1.20 Scout salute	90	1·25
2739/41	Set of 3	2·00	2·40
MS2742	68×98 mm. $6 Lord Baden-Powell	3·25	3·75

(Des M. Leboeuf. Litho Questa)

1998 (18 Nov). 50th Death Anniv of Mahatma Gandhi. T **403** and similar vert designs. Multicoloured. P 14.

2743	90c. Type **403**	1·00	60
2744	$1 Gandhi seated	1·25	85
2745	$1.20 As young man	1·60	1·25
2746	$1.65 At primary school in Rajkot, aged 7	2·25	2·25
2743/6	Set of 4	5·50	4·50
MS2747	100×70 mm. $6 Gandhi with staff	4·00	4·25

404 McDonnell Douglas Phantom F-GR1

405 Diana, Princess of Wales

(Des D. Miller. Litho Questa)

1998 (18 Nov). 80th Anniv of Royal Air Force. T **404** and similar horiz designs. P 14.

2748	$1.75 Type **404**	1·60	1·60
	a. Sheetlet. Nos. 2748/51	5·75	5·75
2749	$1.75 Two Sepecat Jaguar GR1As	1·60	1·60
2750	$1.75 Panavia Tornado F3	1·60	1·60
2751	$1.75 McDonnell Douglas Phantom F-GR2	1·60	1·60
2748/51	Set of 4	5·75	5·75
MS2752	Two sheets, each 90×68 mm. (a) $6 Golden Eagle (bird) and Bristol F2B Fighter. (b) $6 Hawker Hurricane and EF-2000 Eurofighter Set of 2 sheets	10·00	10·00

Nos. 2748/51 were printed together, *se-tenant*, in sheetlets of 4 with enlarged illustrated margins.

(Litho Questa)

1998 (24 Nov). 1st Death Anniv of Diana, Princess of Wales. P 14½×14.

2753	**405** $1.20 multicoloured	1·00	1·00
	a. Sheetlet of 6	5·00	

No. 2753 was printed in sheetlets of 6 with an enlarged illustrated right margin.

406 Brown Pelican

407 Border Collie

(Litho Questa)

1998 (24 Nov). Sea Birds of the World. T **406** and similar horiz designs. Multicoloured. P 14.

2754	15c. Type **406**	30	20
2755	25c. Dunlin	40	20
2756	45c. Atlantic Puffin	50	25
2757	75c. King Eider	65	70
	a. Sheetlet. Nos. 2757/68	7·00	7·50
2758	75c. Inca Tern	65	70
2759	75c. Little Auk ("Dovekie")	65	70
2760	75c. Ross's Gull	65	70
2761	75c. Common Noddy ("Brown Noddy")	65	70
2762	75c. Marbled Murrelet	65	70
2763	75c. Northern Gannet	65	70
2764	75c. Razorbill	65	70
2765	75c. Long-tailed Skua ("Long-tailed Jaeger")	65	70
2766	75c. Black Guillemot	65	70
2767	75c. Whimbrel	65	70
2768	75c. Oystercatcher	30	35
2769	90c. Pied Cormorant	65	70
2754/69	Set of 16	8·50	8·50
MS2770	Two sheets, each 100×70 mm. (a) $6 Black Skimmer. (b) $6 Wandering Albatross Set of 2 sheets	8·00	9·00

Nos. 2757/68 were printed together, *se-tenant*, in sheetlets of 12 with the backgrounds forming a composite design.

No. 2760 is inscribed "ROSS' BULL" in error.

(Litho B.D.T.)

1998 (10 Dec). Christmas. Dogs. T **407** and similar horiz designs. Multicoloured. P 13½×14.

2771	15c. Type **407**	45	25
2772	25c. Dalmatian	55	25
2773	65c. Weimaraner	90	50
2774	75c. Scottish Terrier	95	50
2775	90c. Long-haired Dachshund	1·10	55
2776	$1.20 Golden Retriever	1·40	1·25
2777	$2 Pekingese	2·00	2·50
2771/7	Set of 7	6·50	5·25
MS2778	Two sheets, each 75×66 mm. (a) $6 Dalmatian. (b) $6 Jack Russell Terrier Set of 2 sheets	8·50	9·00

408 Mickey Mouse sailing

(Litho Questa)

1999 (11 Jan). 70th Birthday of Mickey Mouse. T **408** and similar multicoloured designs showing Walt Disney characters participating in water sports. P 13½×14.

2779	$1 Type **408**	95	95
	a. Sheetlet. Nos. 2779/84	5·00	5·00
2780	$1 Mickey and Goofy sailing	95	95
2781	$1 Goofy windsurfing	95	95
2782	$1 Mickey sailing and seagull	95	95
2783	$1 Goofy sailing	95	95
2784	$1 Mickey windsurfing	95	95
2785	$1 Goofy running with surfboard	95	95
	a. Sheetlet. Nos. 2785/90	5·00	5·00
2786	$1 Mickey surfing	95	95
2787	$1 Donald Duck holding surfboard	95	95
2788	$1 Donald on surfboard (face value at right)	95	95
2789	$1 Minnie Mouse surfing in green shorts	95	95
2790	$1 Goofy surfing	95	95
2791	$1 Goofy in purple shorts waterskiing	95	95
	a. Sheetlet. Nos. 2791/6	5·00	5·00
2792	$1 Mickey waterskiing	95	95
2793	$1 Goofy waterskiing with Mickey	95	95
2794	$1 Donald on surfboard (face value at left)	95	95
2795	$1 Goofy in yellow shorts waterskiing	95	95
2796	$1 Minnie in pink shorts surfing	95	95
2779/96	Set of 18	15·00	15·00
MS2797	Four sheets, each 127×102 mm. (a) $6 Goofy (*horiz*). P 14×13½. (b) $6 Donald Duck. P 13½×14. (c) $6 Minnie Mouse. P 13½×14. (d) $6 Mickey Mouse. P 13½×14 Set of 4 sheets	15·00	16·00

Nos. 2779/84, 2785/90 and 2791/6 were each printed together, *se-tenant*, in sheetlets of 6 with illustrated top margins.

409 Hell's Gate Steel Orchestra, 1996

410 Tulips

(Litho Questa)

1999 (1 Feb). 50th Anniv of Hell's Gate Steel Orchestra. T **409** and similar multicoloured designs. P 14.

2798	20c. Type **409**	25	20
2799	60c. Orchestra members, New York, 1992	50	40

ANTIGUA AND BARBUDA

2800	75c. Orchestra members with steel drums, 1950	60	50
2801	90c. Eustace Henry, 1964	70	55
2802	$1.20 Alston Henry playing double tenor	1·00	1·40
2798/2802 Set of 5		2·75	2·75
MS2803 Two sheets. (a) 100×70 mm. $4 Orchestra members, 1950 (vert). (b) 70×100 mm. $4 Eustace Henry, 1964 (vert) Set of 2 sheets		5·50	6·50

(Des S. Stines. Litho Questa)

1999 (19 Apr). Flowers. T **410** and similar multicoloured designs. P 14.

2804	60c. Type **410**	40	30
2805	75c. Fuschia	50	35
2806	90c. Morning Glory (horiz)	60	60
	a. Sheetlet. Nos. 2806/14	4·75	4·75
2807	90c. Geranium (horiz)	60	60
2808	90c. Blue Hibiscus (horiz)	60	60
2809	90c. Marigolds (horiz)	60	60
2810	90c. Sunflower (horiz)	60	60
2811	90c. Impatiens (horiz)	60	60
2812	90c. Petunia (horiz)	60	60
2813	90c. Pansy (horiz)	60	60
2814	90c. Saucer Magnolia (horiz)	60	60
2815	$1 Primrose (horiz)	70	70
	a. Sheetlet. Nos. 2815/23	5·75	5·75
2816	$1 Bleeding Heart (horiz)	70	70
2817	$1 Pink Dogwood (horiz)	70	70
2818	$1 Peony (horiz)	70	70
2819	$1 Rose (horiz)	70	70
2820	$1 Hellebores (horiz)	70	70
2821	$1 Lily (horiz)	70	70
2822	$1 Violet (horiz)	70	70
2823	$1 Cherry Blossom (horiz)	70	70
2824	$1.20 Calla Lily	75	75
2825	$1.65 Sweet Pea	90	1·10
2804/25 Set of 22		12·50	12·50

MS2826 Two sheets. (a) 76×106 mm. $6 Sangria Lily. (b) 106×76 mm. $6 Zinnias Set of 2 sheets .... 7·50 8·00

Nos. 2806/14 and 2815/23 were each printed together, se-tenant, in sheetlets of 9, forming composite designs.

411 Elle Macpherson

412 "Luna 2" Moon Probe

1999 (26 Apr). "Australia'99" International Stamp Exhibition, Melbourne (1st issue). Elle Macpherson (model). T **411** and similar vert designs. Multicoloured. Litho. P 13½.

2827	$1.20 Type **411**	1·00	1·00
	a. Sheetlet. Nos. 2827/34	7·00	7·00
2828	$1.20 Lying on couch	1·00	1·00
2829	$1.20 In swimsuit	1·00	1·00
2830	$1.20 Looking over shoulder	1·00	1·00
2831	$1.20 Wearing cream shirt	1·00	1·00
2832	$1.20 Wearing stetson	1·00	1·00
2833	$1.20 Wearing black T-shirt	1·00	1·00
2834	$1.20 Holding tree branch	1·00	1·00
2827/34 Set of 8		7·00	7·00

Nos. 2827/34 were printed together, se-tenant, in sheetlets of 8 with enlarged illustrated margin at right.

See also Nos. 2875/93.

1999 (6 May). Satellites and Spacecraft. T **412** and similar multicoloured designs. Litho. P 14.

2835	$1.65 Type **412**	1·10	1·10
	a. Sheetlet. Nos. 2835/40	6·00	6·00
2836	$1.65 "Mariner 2" space probe	1·10	1·10
2837	$1.65 Giotto space probe	1·10	1·10
2838	$1.65 Rosat satellite	1·10	1·10
2839	$1.65 International Ultraviolet Explorer	1·10	1·10
2840	$1.65 Ulysses space probe	1·10	1·10
2841	$1.65 "Mariner 10" space probe	1·10	1·10
	a. Sheetlet. Nos. 2841/46	6·00	6·00
2842	$1.65 "Luna 9" Moon probe	1·10	1·10
2843	$1.65 Advanced X-ray Astrophysics Facility	1·10	1·10
2844	$1.65 Magellan space probe	1·10	1·10
2845	$1.65 "Pioneer-Venus 2" space probe	1·10	1·10
2846	$1.65 Infra-red Astronomy Satellite	1·10	1·10
2835/46 Set of 12		12·00	12·00

MS2847 Two sheets, each 106×76 mm. (a) $6 "Salyut 1" space station (horiz). (b) $6 "MIR" space station (horiz) Set of 2 sheets .... 7·50 8·00

Nos. 2835/40 and 2841/46 were each printed together, se-tenant, in sheetlets of 6, with the backgrounds forming composite designs and enlarged illustrated margins at left and foot.

413 John Glenn entering "Mercury" Capsule, 1962

414 Brachiosaurus

(Des F. Rivera and Spotlight Design. Litho Questa)

1999 (6 May). John Glenn's Return to Space. T **413** and similar vert designs. Multicoloured. P 14½×14.

2848	$1.75 Type **413**	1·25	1·25
	a. Sheetlet. Nos. 2848/51	4·50	4·50
2849	$1.75 Glenn in "Mercury" mission spacesuit	1·25	1·25
2850	$1.75 Fitting helmet for "Mercury" mission	1·25	1·25
2851	$1.75 Outside pressure chamber	1·25	1·25
2848/51 Set of 4		4·50	4·50

Nos. 2848/51 were printed together, se-tenant, as a horizontal strip of 4, with the remainder of the sheetlet depicting "Mercury" and Discovery astronauts.

(Des Zina Saunders. Litho Questa)

1999 (25 May). Prehistoric Animals. T **414** and similar multicoloured designs. P 14.

2852	65c. Type **414**	65	40
2853	75c. Oviraptor (vert)	70	40
2854	$1 Homotherium	80	45
2855	$1.20 Macrauchenia (vert)	90	60
2856	$1.65 Struthiomimus	1·00	1·00
	a. Sheetlet. Nos. 2856/64	8·00	8·00
2857	$1.65 Corythosaurus	1·00	1·00
2858	$1.65 Dsungaripterus	1·00	1·00
2859	$1.65 Compsognathus	1·00	1·00
2860	$1.65 Prosaurolophus	1·00	1·00
2861	$1.65 Montanoceratops	1·00	1·00
2862	$1.65 Stegosaurus	1·00	1·00
2863	$1.65 Deinonychus	1·00	1·00
2864	$1.65 Ouranosaurus	1·00	1·00
2865	$1.65 Leptictidium	1·00	1·00
	a. Sheetlet. Nos. 2865/73	8·00	8·00
2866	$1.65 Ictitherium	1·00	1·00
2867	$1.65 Plesictis	1·00	1·00
2868	$1.65 Hemicyon	1·00	1·00
2869	$1.65 Diacodexis	1·00	1·00
2870	$1.65 Stylinodon	1·00	1·00
2871	$1.65 Kanuites	1·00	1·00
2872	$1.65 Chriacus	1·00	1·00
2873	$1.65 Argyrolagus	1·00	1·00
2852/73 Set of 22		19·00	18·00

MS2874 Two sheets each 110×85 mm. (a) $6 Eurhinodelphis. (b)$6 Pteranodon Set of 2 sheets .... 7·50 8·00

Nos. 2856/64 and 2865/73 were each printed together, se-tenant, in sheetlets of 9, with the backgrounds forming composite designs and enlarged, inscribed margins at left.

415 Two White Kittens

(Des D. Miller. Litho Questa)

1999 (25 May). "Australia '99" International Stamp Exhibition, Melbourne (2nd issue). Cats. T **415** and similar vert designs. Multicoloured. P 14½×14.

2875	35c. Type **415**	40	30
2876	45c. Kitten with string	50	35
2877	60c. Two kittens under blanket	60	50
2878	75c. Two kittens in basket	70	55
2879	90c. Kitten with ball	80	55

82

2880	$1 White kitten	90	80
2881	$1.65 Two kittens playing	1·10	1·10
	a. Sheetlet. Nos. 2881/6	6·00	6·00
2882	$1.65 Black and white kitten	1·10	1·10
2883	$1.65 Black kitten and sleeping cream kitten	1·10	1·10
2884	$1.65 White kitten with green string	1·10	1·10
2885	$1.65 Two sleeping kittens	1·10	1·10
2886	$1.65 White kitten with black tip to tail	1·10	1·10
2887	$1.65 Kitten with red string	1·10	1·10
	a. Sheetlet. Nos. 2887/92	6·00	6·00
2888	$1.65 Two long-haired kittens	1·10	1·10
2889	$1.65 Ginger kitten	1·10	1·10
2890	$1.65 Kitten playing with mouse	1·10	1·10
2891	$1.65 Kitten asleep on blue cushion	1·10	1·10
2892	$1.65 Tabby kitten	1·10	1·10
2875/92 Set of 18		15·00	14·50

MS2893 Two sheets, each 70×100 mm. (a) $6 Cat carrying kitten in mouth. (b) $6 Kitten in tree *Set of 2 sheets* .... 8·50 9·00

Nos. 2881/6 and 2887/92 were each printed together, *se-tenant* in sheetlets of 6.

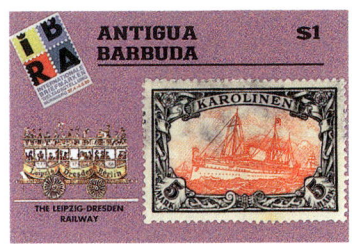

416 Early Leipzig–Dresden Railway Carriage and Caroline Islands 1901 Yacht Type 5m. Stamp

(Litho Questa)

1999 (24 June). "iBRA '99" International Stamp Exhibition, Nuremberg. T **416** and similar horiz designs. Multicoloured. P 14.

2894	$1 Type **416**	70	60
2895	$1.20 *Gölsdorf* steam locomotive and Caroline Islands 1901 Yacht type 1m.	80	70
2896	$1.65 Early Leipzig–Dresden Railway carriage and Caroline Islands 1899 optd on Germany 20pf	1·00	1·10
2897	$1.90 *Gölsdorf* steam locomotive and Caroline Islands 1901 Yacht type 5pf. and 20pf.	1·40	2·00
2894/7 Set of 4		3·50	4·00

MS2898 165×110 mm. $6 Registration label for Ponape, Caroline Islands. P 14×14½ .... 3·25 3·75

417 "People on Balcony of Sazaido" (Hokusai)  **418** Sophie Rhys-Jones

(Des R. Sauber. Litho Questa)

1999 (24 June). 150th Death Anniv of Katsushika Hokusai (Japanese artist). T **417** and similar multicoloured designs. P 13½.

2899	$1.65 Type **417**	1·00	1·00
	a. Sheetlet. Nos. 2899/904	5·50	5·50
2900	$1.65 "Nakahara in Sagami Province"	1·00	1·00
2901	$1.65 "Defensive Positions" (two wrestlers)	1·00	1·00
2902	$1.65 "Defensive Positions" (three wrestlers)	1·00	1·00
2903	$1.65 "Mount Fuji in Clear Weather"	1·00	1·00
2904	$1.65 "Nihonbashi in Edo"	1·00	1·00
2905	$1.65 "Asakusa Honganji"	1·00	1·00
	a. Sheetlet. Nos. 2905/10	5·50	5·50
2906	$1.65 "Dawn at Isawa in Kai Province"	1·00	1·00
2907	$1.65 "Samurai with Bow and Arrow" (with arrows on ground)	1·00	1·00
2908	$1.65 "Samurai with Bow and Arrow" (trees in background)	1·00	1·00
2909	$1.65 "Kajikazawa in Kai Province"	1·00	1·00
2910	$1.65 "A Great Wave"	1·00	1·00
2899/2910 Set of 12		11·00	11·00

MS2911 Two sheets, each 100×71 mm. (a) $6 "A Netsuke Workshop" (*vert*). (b) $6 "Gotenyama at Shinagawa on Tokaido Highway" (*vert*) *Set of 2 sheets* .... 7·50 8·00

Nos. 2899/904 and 2905/10 were each printed together, *se-tenant*, in sheetlets of 6.

No. 2903 is inscribed "MOUNT FUGI" in error.

1999 (24 June). Royal Wedding. T **418** and similar multicoloured designs. Litho. P 13½.

2912	$3 Type **418**	1·75	2·00
	a. Sheetlet. Nos. 2912/14	4·75	5·50
2913	$3 Sophie and Prince Edward	1·75	2·00
2914	$3 Prince Edward	1·75	2·00
2912/14 Set of 3		4·75	5·50

MS2915 108×78 mm. $6 Prince Edward with Sophie Rhys-Jones and Windsor Castle (*horiz*) .... 3·50 4·00

Nos. 2912/14 were printed together, *se-tenant*, in sheetlets of 3 with enlarged illustrated margins.

419 Three Children  **420** Crampton Type Railway Locomotive, 1855–69

1999 (24 June). 10th Anniv of United Nations Rights of the Child Convention. T **419** and similar vert designs. Multicoloured. Litho. P 14.

2916	$3 Type **419**	1·75	2·00
	a. Sheetlet. Nos. 2916/18	4·75	5·50
2917	$3 Adult hand holding child's hand	1·75	2·00
2918	$3 Dove and U.N. Headquarters	1·75	2·00
2916/18 Set of 3		4·75	5·00

MS2919 112×70 mm. $6 Dove .... 3·25 3·75

Nos. 2916/18 were printed together, *se-tenant*, in sheetlets of 3, forming a composite design.

(Litho Questa)

1999 (24 June). "PhilexFrance '99" International Stamp Exhibition, Paris. Railway Locomotives. Two sheets, each 106×81 mm containing T **420** and similar design. Multicoloured. P 14×13½.

MS2920 (a) $6 Type **420**. (b) $6 Compound type No. 232-U1 steam locomotive, 1949 *Set of 2 sheets* .... 7·50 8·00

421 Three Archangels from *Faust*  **422** *Missa Ferdie* (fishing launch)

(Des J. Iskowitz. Litho Questa)

1999 (24 June). 250th Birth Anniv of Johann von Goethe (German writer). T **421** and similar designs. P 14.

2921	$1.75 purple, bright magenta and black	1·10	1·25
	a. Sheetlet. Nos. 2921/3	3·00	3·25
2922	$1.75 dull ultramarine, bluish violet and black	1·10	1·25
2923	$1.75 light green and black	1·10	1·25
2921/3 Set of 3		3·00	3·25

MS2924 79×107 mm. $6 black and reddish brown .... 3·25 3·75

Designs: *Horiz*—No. 2921, Type **421**; No. 2922, Von Goethe and Von Schiller; No. 2923, Faust reclining with spirits. *Vert*—No. **MS**2924, Wolfgang von Goethe.

Nos. 2921/3 were printed together, *se-tenant*, in sheetlets of 3 with enlarged illustrated margins.

(Litho Questa)

1999 (24 June). Local Ships and Boats. T **422** and similar horiz designs. Multicoloured. P 13×11.

2925	25c. Type **422**	25	25
	a. Sheetlet. Nos. 2925/9	2·50	
2926	45c. Yachts in 32nd Annual Antigua International Sailing Week	40	30
2927	60c. *Jolly Roger* (tourist ship)	50	40
2928	90c. *Freewinds* (cruise liner) (10th anniv of first visit)	70	60
2929	$1.20 *Monarch of the Seas* (cruise liner)	95	1·25
2925/9 Set of 5		2·50	2·50

ANTIGUA AND BARBUDA

MS2930 98×62 mm. $4 *Freewinds* (11th anniv of maiden voyage) (50×37 *mm*). P 14 .... 2·75 3·25

Nos. 2925/9 were either printed together, *se-tenant*, in sheetlets of 5 or as larger sheets of one value with the stamps in rows divided by horizontal gutters carrying inscriptions.

423 Fiery Jewel (butterfly)

424 "Madonna and Child in Wreath of Flowers" (Rubens)

(Litho B.D.T.)

1999 (16 Aug). Butterflies. T **423** and similar multicoloured designs. P 14.

2931	65c. Type **423**	70	45
2932	75c. Hewitson's Blue Hairstreak	80	55
2933	$1 California Dog Face (*horiz*)	90	90
	a. Sheetlet. Nos. 2933/41	7·25	7·25
2934	$1 Small Copper (*horiz*)	90	90
2935	$1 Zebra Swallowtail (*horiz*)	90	90
2936	$1 White "M" Hairstreak (*horiz*)	90	90
2937	$1 Old World Swallowtail (*horiz*)	90	90
2938	$1 Buckeye (*horiz*)	90	90
2939	$1 Apollo (*horiz*)	90	90
2940	$1 Sonoran Blue (*horiz*)	90	90
2941	$1 Purple Emperor (*horiz*)	90	90
2942	$1.20 Scarce Bamboo Page (*horiz*)	1·00	1·00
2943	$1.65 Paris Peacock (*horiz*)	1·25	1·50
2931/43	Set of 13	10·50	10·50

MS2944 Two sheets. (a) 85×110 mm. $6 Monarch. (b) 110×85 mm. $6 Cairns Birdwing (*horiz*) Set of 2 sheets .... 9·00 9·50

Nos. 2933/41 were printed together, *se-tenant*, in sheetlets of 9, forming a composite design.

(Litho Questa)

1999 (23 Nov). Christmas. Religious Paintings. T **424** and similar vert designs. P 13½×14.

2945	15c. multicoloured	25	15
2946	25c. black, stone and yellow	30	15
2947	45c. multicoloured	50	25
2948	60c. multicoloured	60	30
2949	$2 multicoloured	1·75	1·75
2950	$4 black, stone and yellow	3·00	4·00
2945/50	Set of 6	5·75	6·00

MS2951 76×106 mm. $6 multicoloured .... 4·00 4·25

Designs:—25c. "Shroud of Christ held by Two Angels" (Dürer); 45c. "Madonna and Child enthroned between Two Saints" (Raphael); 60c. "Holy Family with Lamb" (Raphael); $2 "The Transfiguration" (Raphael); $4 "Three Putti holding Coat of Arms" (Dürer); $6 "Coronation of St. Catharine" (Rubens).

425 Katharine Hepburn (actress)

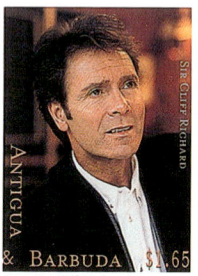

426 Sir Cliff Richard

(Des J. Iskowitz. Litho Questa)

2000 (18 Jan). Senior Celebrities of the 20th Century. T **425** and similar horiz designs. Multicoloured. P 14.

2952	90c. Type **425**	85	85
	a. Sheetlet. Nos. 2952/63	9·00	9·00
2953	90c. Martha Graham (dancer)	85	85
2954	90c. Eubie Blake (jazz pianist)	85	85
2955	90c. Agatha Christie (novelist)	85	85
2956	90c. Eudora Welty (American novelist)	85	85
2957	90c. Helen Hayes (actress)	85	85
2958	90c. Vladimir Horowitz (concert pianist)	85	85
2959	90c. Katharine Graham (newspaper publisher)	85	85
2960	90c. Pablo Casals (cellist)	85	85
2961	90c. Pete Seeger (folk singer)	85	85
2962	90c. Andres Segovia (guitarist)	85	85
2963	90c. Frank Lloyd Wright (architect)	85	85
2952/63	Set of 12	9·00	9·00

Nos. 2952/63 were printed together, *se-tenant*, in sheetlets of 12.

(Des J. Corbett. Litho Cartor)

2000 (18 Jan). 60th Birthday of Sir Cliff Richard (entertainer). P 13½.

2964	**426**	$1.65 multicoloured	1·25	1·25
		a. Sheetlet of 6	5·50	

No. 2964 was printed in sheetlets of 6 with an enlarged illustrated right margin.

427 Charlie Chaplin

(Litho Questa)

2000 (18 Jan). Charlie Chaplin (actor and director) Commemoration. T **427** and similar vert designs showing film scenes. Multicoloured. P 13½×14.

2965	$1.65 Standing in street (*Modern Times*)	95	95
	a. Sheetlet. Nos. 2965/70	5·00	5·00
2966	$1.65 Hugging man (*The Gold Rush*)	95	95
2967	$1.65 Type **427**	95	95
2968	$1.65 Wielding tools (*Modern Times*)	95	95
2969	$1.65 With hands on hips (*The Gold Rush*)	95	95
2970	$1.65 Wearing cape (*The Gold Rush*)	95	95
2965/70	Set of 6	5·00	5·00

Nos. 2965/70 were printed together, *se-tenant*, in sheetlets of 6 with enlarged illustrated top and right margins.

428 Streamertail

429 "Arthur Goodwin"

(Des D. Burkhart. Litho Questa)

2000 (17 Apr). "The Stamp Show 2000" International Stamp Exhibition, London. Birds of the Caribbean. T **428** and similar multicoloured designs. P 14.

2971	75c. Type **428**	50	35
2972	90c. Yellow-bellied Sapsucker	60	40
2973	$1.20 Rufous-tailed Jacamar	75	75
2974	$1.20 Scarlet Macaw	75	75
	a. Sheetlet. Nos. 2974/81	5·50	5·50
2975	$1.20 Yellow-crowned ("fronted") Amazon	75	75
2976	$1.20 Golden Conure ("Queen-of-Bavaria")	75	75
2977	$1.20 Nanday Conure	75	75
2978	$1.20 Jamaican Tody	75	75
2979	$1.20 Smooth-billed Ani	75	75
2980	$1.20 Puerto Rican Woodpecker	75	75
2981	$1.20 Ruby-throated Hummingbird	75	75
2982	$1.20 Scaly-breasted Ground Dove	75	75
	a. Sheetlet. Nos. 2982/9	5·50	5·50
2983	$1.20 American Wood Stork	75	75
2984	$1.20 Saffron Finch	75	75
2985	$1.20 Green-backed Heron	75	75

ANTIGUA AND BARBUDA

2986	$1.20 Lovely Cotinga	75	75
2987	$1.20 St. Vincent Amazon ("Parrot")	75	75
2988	$1.20 Cuban Grassquit	75	75
2989	$1.20 Red-winged Blackbird	75	75
2990	$2 Spectacled Owl	1·40	1·50
2971/90	Set of 20	13·00	13·50

MS2991 Two sheets, each 80×106 mm. (a) $6 Vermillion Flycatcher (50×37 mm). P 14×13½. (b) $6 Red-capped Manakin (37×50 mm). P 13½×14 Set of 2 sheets .... 9·50 10·00

Nos. 2974/81 and 2982/9 were each printed together, se-tenant, in sheetlets of 8 with the backgrounds forming composite designs.

No. 2981 is inscribed "Arhilochus colubria" in error.

(Litho Questa)

2000 (15 May). 400th Birth Anniv of Sir Anthony Van Dyck (Flemish painter). T **429** and similar vert designs. Multicoloured. P 13½×14.

2992	$1.20 Type **429**	75	75
	a. Sheetlet. Nos. 2992/7	4·00	4·00
2993	$1.20 "Sir Thomas Wharton"	75	75
2994	$1.20 "Mary Villiers, Daughter of Duke of Buckingham"	75	75
2995	$1.20 "Christina Bruce, Countess of Devonshire"	75	75
2996	$1.20 "James Hamilton, Duke of Hamilton"	75	75
2997	$1.20 "Henry Danvers, Earl of Danby"	75	75
2998	$1.20 "Marie de Raet, Wife of Philippe le Roy"	75	75
	a. Sheetlet. Nos. 2998/3003	4·00	4·00
2999	$1.20 "Jacomo de Cachiopin"	75	75
3000	$1.20 "Princess Henrietta of Lorraine attended by a Page"	75	75
3001	$1.20 "Portrait of a Man"	75	75
3002	$1.20 "Portrait of a Woman"	75	75
3003	$1.20 "Philippe le Roy, Seigneur de Ravels"	75	75
3004	$1.20 "Charles I in State Robes"	75	75
	a. Sheetlet. Nos. 3004/9	4·00	4·00
3005	$1.20 "Queen Henrietta Maria" (in white dress)	75	75
3006	$1.20 "Queen Henrietta Maria with Sir Jeffrey Hudson"	75	75
3007	$1.20 "Charles I in Armour"	75	75
3008	$1.20 "Queen Henrietta Maria in Profile facing right"	75	75
3009	$1.20 "Queen Henrietta Maria" (in black dress)	75	75
2992/3009	Set of 18	12·00	12·00

MS3010 Six sheets. (a) 102×128 mm. $5 "Charles I on Horseback". (b) 102×128 mm. $5 "Charles I Hunting". (c) 128×102 mm. $5 "Charles I with Queen Henrietta Maria". (d) 128×102 mm. $5 "Charles I" (from Three Aspects portrait). (e) 102×128 mm. $6 "William, Lord Russell". (f) 102×128 mm. $6 "Two Sons of Duke of Lennox" Set of 6 sheets .... 20·00 22·00

Nos. 2992/7, 2998/3003 and 3004/9 were each printed together, se-tenant, in sheetlets of 6 with illustrated margins.

No. 2994 is inscribed "Mary Villers", No. 3002 "Portrait of a Women", No. 3005 "Henrieta Maria" and No. **MS**3010f "Duke of Lenox", all in error.

430 Eupolea miniszeki (butterfly)   **431** Boxer

(Des R. Sauber. Litho Questa)

2000 (29 May). Butterflies. T **430** and similar multicoloured designs. P 14.

3011	$1.65 Type **430**	90	90
	a. Sheetlet. Nos. 3011/16	5·00	5·00
3012	$1.65 Heliconius doris	90	90
3013	$1.65 Evenus coronata	90	90
3014	$1.65 Papilio anchisiades	90	90
3015	$1.65 Syrmatia dorilas	90	90
3016	$1.65 Morpho patroclus	90	90
3017	$1.65 Mesosemia loruhama	90	90
	a. Sheetlet. Nos. 3017/22	5·00	5·00
3018	$1.65 Bia actorion	90	90
3019	$1.65 Anteos clorinde	90	90
3020	$1.65 Menander menande	90	90
3021	$1.65 Catasticta manco	90	90
3022	$1.65 Urania leilus	90	90
3023	$1.65 Theope eudocia (vert)	90	90
	a. Sheetlet. Nos. 3023/8	5·00	5·00
3024	$1.65 Uranus sloanus (vert)	90	90
3025	$1.65 Helicopis cupido (vert)	90	90
3026	$1.65 Papilio velovis (vert)	90	90
3027	$1.65 Graphium androcles (vert)	90	90
3028	$1.65 Mesene phareus (vert)	90	90
3011/28	Set of 18	15·00	15·00

MS3029 Three sheets. (a) 110×85 mm. $6 Graphium encelades. (b) 110×85 mm. $6 Graphium milon. (c) 85×110 mm. $6 Hemiargus isola (vert) Set of 3 sheets   13·00 14·00

Nos. 3011/16, 3017/22 and 3023/8 were each printed together, se-tenant, in sheetlets of 6 with the backgrounds forming composite designs extending on to enlarged margins.

(Des Irina Lyampe. Litho Questa)

2000 (29 May). Cats and Dogs. T **431** and similar multicoloured designs. P 14.

3030	90c. Type **431**	75	45
3031	$1 Alaskan Malamute	85	70
3032	$1.65 Bearded Collie	1·10	1·10
	a. Sheetlet. Nos. 3032/7	6·00	6·00
3033	$1.65 Cardigan Welsh Corgi	1·10	1·10
3034	$1.65 Saluki (red)	1·10	1·10
3035	$1.65 Basset Hound	1·10	1·10
3036	$1.65 White Standard Poodle	1·10	1·10
3037	$1.65 Boston Terrier	1·10	1·10
3038	$1.65 Long-haired blue and white cat (horiz)	1·10	1·10
	a. Sheetlet. Nos. 3038/43	6·00	6·00
3039	$1.65 Snow Shoe (horiz)	1·10	1·10
3040	$1.65 Persian (horiz)	1·10	1·10
3041	$1.65 Chocolate Lynx Point (horiz)	1·10	1·10
3042	$1.65 Brown and White Sphynx (horiz)	1·10	1·10
3043	$1.65 White Tortoiseshell (horiz)	1·10	1·10
3044	$2 Wirehaired Pointer	1·40	1·40
3045	$4 Saluki (black)	2·50	3·00
3030/45	Set of 16	17·00	17·00

MS3046 Two sheets. (a) 106×71 mm. $6 Cavalier King Charles Spaniel. (b) 111×81 mm. $6 Lavender Tortie Set of 2 sheets .... 12·00 12·00

Nos. 3032/7 (dogs) and 3038/43 (cats) were each printed together, se-tenant, in sheetlets of 6 with enlarged illustrated left margins.

432 Epidendrum pseudepidendrum   **433** Prince William

(Des T. Wood. Litho Questa)

2000 (29 May). Flowers of the Caribbean. T **432** and similar vert designs. Multicoloured. P 14.

3047	45c. Type **432**	85	35
3048	65c. Odontoglossum cervantesii	1·00	50
3049	75c. Cattleya dowiana	1·00	50
3050	90c. Beloperone guttata	1·00	50
3051	$1 Colliandra haematocephala	1·00	70
3052	$1.20 Brassavola nodosa	1·00	80
3053	$1.65 Pseudocalymna alliaceum	1·10	1·10
	a. Sheetlet. Nos. 3053/8	6·00	6·00
3054	$1.65 Datura candida	1·10	1·10
3055	$1.65 Ipomoea tuberosa	1·10	1·10
3056	$1.65 Allamanda cathartica	1·10	1·10
3057	$1.65 Aspasia epidendroides	1·10	1·10
3058	$1.65 Maxillaria cucullata	1·10	1·10
3059	$1.65 Anthurium andreanum	1·10	1·10
	a. Sheetlet. Nos. 3059/64	6·00	6·00
3060	$1.65 Doxantha unguiscati	1·10	1·10
3061	$1.65 Hibiscus rosa-sinensis	1·10	1·10
3062	$1.65 Canna indica	1·10	1·10
3063	$1.65 Heliconius umilis	1·10	1·10
3064	$1.65 Strelitzia reginae	1·10	1·10
3065	$1.65 Masdevallia coccinea	1·10	1·10
	a. Sheetlet. Nos. 3065/70	6·00	6·00
3066	$1.65 Paphinia cristata	1·10	1·10
3067	$1.65 Vanilla planifolia	1·10	1·10
3068	$1.65 Cattleya forbesii	1·10	1·10
3069	$1.65 Lycaste skinneri	1·10	1·10
3070	$1.65 Cattleya percivaliana	1·10	1·10
3047/70	Set of 24	23·00	21·00

ANTIGUA AND BARBUDA

MS3071 Three sheets, each 74×103 mm. (a) $6 *Cattleya leopoldiie.* (b) $6 *Strelitzia reginae.* (c) $6 *Rossioglossum grande*Set of 3 sheets .... 13·00 14·00

Nos. 3053/8, 3059/64 and 3065/70 were each printed together, se-tenant in sheetlets of 6 with illustrated margins.

No. 3061 is inscribed "rosa-sensensis" and No. **MS**3071b "regenae", both in error.

(Litho Questa)

2000 (21 June). 18th Birthday of Prince William. T **433** and similar vert designs. Multicoloured. P 14.

3072	$1.65 Prince William waving	1·40	1·40
	a. Sheetlet. Nos. 3072/5	5·00	5·00
3073	$1.65 Wearing Eton school uniform	1·40	1·40
3074	$1.65 Wearing grey suit	1·40	1·40
3075	$1.65 Type **433**	1·40	1·40
3072/5	Set of 4	5·00	5·00

MS3076 100×80 mm. $6 Princess Diana with Princes William and Harry (37×50 mm). P 13½×14 .... 4·25 4·50

Nos. 3072/5 were printed together, se-tenant, in sheetlets of 4.

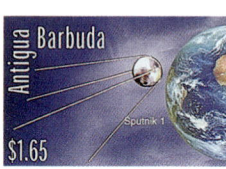

434 "Sputnik I"

435 Alexei Leonov (Commander of "Soyuz 19")

(Des Lollini. Litho B.D.T.)

2000 (26 June). "EXPO 2000" World Stamp Exhibition, Anaheim, U.S.A. Space Satellites. T **434** and similar horiz designs. P 14.

3077	$1.65 Type **434**	1·10	1·10
	a. Sheetlet. Nos. 3077/82	6·00	6·00
3078	$1.65 "Explorer I"	1·10	1·10
3079	$1.65 "Mars Express"	1·10	1·10
3080	$1.65 "Lunik I Solnik"	1·10	1·10
3081	$1.65 "Ranger 7"	1·10	1·10
3082	$1.65 "Mariner 4"	1·10	1·10
3083	$1.65 "Mariner 10"	1·10	1·10
	a. Sheetlet. Nos. 3083/8	6·00	6·00
3084	$1.65 "Soho"	1·10	1·10
3085	$1.65 "Mariner 2"	1·10	1·10
3086	$1.65 "Giotto"	1·10	1·10
3087	$1.65 "Exosat"	1·10	1·10
3088	$1.65 "Pioneer Venus"	1·10	1·10
3077/88	Set of 12	12·00	12·00

MS3089 Two sheets, each 106×76 mm. (a) $6 "Vostok I". (b) $6 Hubble Space Telescope Set of 2 sheets .... 8·50 9·50

Nos. 3077/82 and 3083/8 were each printed together, se-tenant, in sheetlets of 6 with the backgrounds forming composite designs and with enlarged illustrated bottom margins.

(Des B. Pevsner. Litho B.D.T.)

2000 (26 June). 25th Anniv of "Apollo-Soyuz" Joint Project. T **435** and similar vert designs. Multicoloured. P 14.

3090	$3 Type **435**	1·75	2·00
	a. Sheetlet. Nos. 3090/2	4·75	5·50
3091	$3 "Soyuz 19"	1·75	2·00
3092	$3 Valeri Kubasov ("Soyuz 19" engineer)	1·75	2·00
3090/2	Set of 3	4·75	5·50

MS3093 71×88 mm. $6 Alexei Leonov and Thomas Stafford (Commander of "Apollo 18") .... 3·25 3·75

Nos. 3090/2 were printed together, se-tenant, in sheetlets of 3 with enlarged illustrated and inscribed margins.

436 Anna Karina in *Une Femme est Une Femme*, 1961

(Des R. Sauber. Litho B.D.T.)

2000 (26 June). 50th Anniv of Berlin Film Festival. T **436** and similar vert designs showing actors, directors and film scenes. Multicoloured. P 14.

3094	$1.65 Type **436**	1·00	1·00
	a. Sheetlet. Nos. 3094/9	5·50	5·50
3095	$1.65 *Carmen Jones*, 1955	1·00	1·00
3096	$1.65 *Die Ratten*, 1955	1·00	1·00
3097	$1.65 *Die Vier Im Jeep*, 1951	1·00	1·00
3098	$1.65 Sidney Poitier in *Lilies of the Field*, 1963	1·00	1·00
3099	$1.65 *Invitation to the Dance*, 1956	1·00	1·00
3094/9	Set of 6	5·50	5·50

MS3100 97×103 mm. $6 Kate Winslet in *Sense and Sensibility*, 1996 .... 3·25 3·75

Nos. 3094/9 were printed together, se-tenant, in sheetlets of 6 with an enlarged illustrated and inscribed left margin showing the Berlin Bear Award.

No. 3096 is inscribed "GOLDER BERLIN BEAR" and No. **MS**3100 shows the award date "1966", both in error.

437 George Stephenson and *Locomotion No. 1*, 1825

(Des J. Iskowitz. Litho B.D.T.)

2000 (26 June). 175th Anniv of Stockton and Darlington Line (first public railway). T **437** and similar horiz design. Multicoloured. P 14.

3101	$3 Type **437**	2·50	2·50
	a. Sheetlet. Nos. 3101/2	5·00	5·00
3102	$3 Camden and Amboy Railroad locomotive *John Bull*, 1831	2·50	2·50

Nos. 3101/2 were printed together, se-tenant, in sheetlets of 2 with enlarged illustrated and inscribed top and left margins.

438 Statue of Johann Sebastian Bach

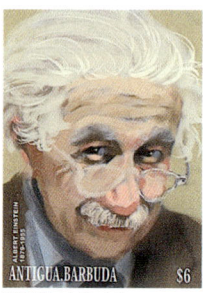

439 Albert Einstein

(Des R. Rundo. Litho B.D.T.)

2000 (26 June). 250th Death Anniv of Johann Sebastian Bach (German composer). Sheet 77×88 mm. P 14.
MS3103 **438** $6 multicoloured .... 4·00 4·50

(Des R. Sauber. Litho B.D.T.)

2000 (26 June). Election of Albert Einstein (mathematical physicist) as Time Magazine "Man of the Century". Sheet 117×91 mm. P 14.
MS3104 **439** $6 multicoloured .... 3·75 4·25

440 LZ-1 Airship, 1900

(Des G. Capasso. Litho B.D.T.)

2000 (26 June). Centenary of First Zeppelin Flight. T **440** and similar horiz designs. P 13½.

3105	$3 grey-brown, black and light violet-blue	2·50	2·50
	a. Sheetlet. Nos. 3105/7	6·75	6·75
3106	$3 grey-brown, black and light violet-blue	2·50	2·50
3107	$3 multicoloured	2·50	2·50
3105/7	Set of 3	6·75	6·75

MS3108 93×66 mm. $6 multicoloured. P 14 .... 3·75 4·00

Designs: (As T **440**)—No. 3106, LZ-2, 1906; No. 3107, LZ-3, 1906. (50×37 mm)—No. **MS**3108, LZ-7 *Deutschland*, 1910.

Nos. 3105/7 were printed together, *se-tenant*, in sheetlets of 3, with the backgrounds forming a composite design and with enlarged illustrated margins.

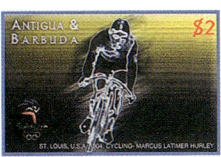

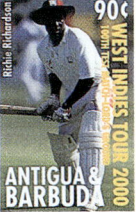

441 Marcus Latimer Hurley (cycling), St. Louis (1904)

442 Richie Richardson

(Litho B.D.T.)

2000 (26 June). Olympic Games, Sydney. T **441** and similar horiz designs. Multicoloured. P 14.

3109	$2 Type **441**	2·25	2·25
	a. Sheetlet. Nos. 3109/12	8·00	8·00
3110	$2 Diving	2·25	2·25
3111	$2 Flaminio Stadium, Rome (1960) and Italian flag	2·25	2·25
3112	$2 Ancient Greek javelin thrower	2·25	2·25
3109/12	Set of 4	8·00	8·00

Nos. 3109/12 were printed together, *se-tenant*, in sheetlets of 4 (2×2), with the horizontal rows separated by a gutter margin showing Sydney landmarks and athlete with Olympic Torch.

(Des A. Melville-Brown. Litho B.D.T.)

2000 (26 June). West Indies Cricket Tour and 100th Test Match at Lord's. T **442** and similar multicoloured designs. P 14.

3113	90c. Type **442**	1·50	70
3114	$5 Viv Richards	5·50	6·00
MS3115	121×104 mm. $6 Lord's Cricket Ground (*horiz*)	5·50	6·00

No. 3114 is inscribed "Viv Richard" in error.

443 Outreach Programme at Sunshine Home for Girls

444 Lady Elizabeth Bowes-Lyon as Young Girl

(Litho Questa)

2000 (13 July). Girls Brigade. T **443** and similar multicoloured designs. P 14.

3116	20c. Type **443**	25	20
3117	60c. Ullida Rawlins Gill (International Vice President) (*vert*)	50	35
3118	75c. Officers and girls	60	45
3119	90c. Girl with flag (*vert*)	80	55
3120	$1.20 Members of 8th Antigua Company with flag (*vert*)	1·10	1·40
3116/20	Set of 5	3·00	2·75
MS3121	102×124 mm. $5 Girls Brigade badge (*vert*)	3·25	3·75

(Litho Questa)

2000 (4 Aug)–**01**. "Queen Elizabeth the Queen Mother's Century". T **444** and similar vert designs. P 14.

3122	$2 multicoloured	1·75	1·75
	a. Sheetlet. Nos. 3122/5 (cenral label inscr "100th")	6·25	6·25
	ab. Sheetlet Nos. 3122/5 (central label inscr "101st") (17.12.01)	6·25	6·25
3123	$2 black and gold	1·75	1·75
3124	$2 black and gold	1·75	1·75
3125	$2 multicoloured	1·75	1·75
3122/5	Set of 4	6·25	6·25
MS3126	153×157 mm. $6 mult. P 13½×14	4·00	4·25
	a Inscr "Good Health and Happiness to Her Majesty the Queen Mother on her 101st birthday" (17.12.01)	4·50	4·75

Designs: (As Type **444**)—No. 3122 Type **444**; No. 3123, Queen Elizabeth in 1940; No. 3124, Queen Mother with Princess Anne, 1951; No. 3125, Queen Mother in Canada, 1989. (37×50 mm)—No. **MS**3126, Queen Mother inspecting guard of honour.

Nos. 3122/5 were printed together, *se-tenant*, as a sheetlet of four stamps and a central label with inscribed and embossed margins. No. **MS**3126 also shows the Royal Arms embossed in gold.

A $20 value embossed on gold foil also exists from a limited printing. The sheetlet and miniature sheet were re-issued in 2001 with changed label and inscription (No. 3122ab), or the embossed gold coat of arms at the bottom left of miniature sheet replaced by a commemorative inscription for the Queen Mother's 101st birthday (No. **MS**3126a).

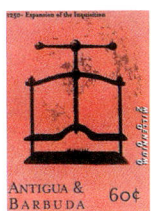

445 Thumbscrew (Expansion of Inquisition, 1250)

446 "Admonishing the Court Ladies" (attr Ku K'ai-Chih)

(Des E. Moreiro. Litho Cartor)

2000 (21 Aug). New Millennium. People and Events of Thirteenth Century (1250–1300). T **445** and similar multicoloured designs (except No. 3127). P 12½.

3127	60c. Type **445** (black and rose-red)	90	90
	a. Sheetlet. Nos. 3127/43	14·00	14·00
3128	60c. Chartres Cathedral (completed, 1260)	90	90
3129	60c. Donor's sculpture, Naumberg (completed, 1260)	90	90
3130	60c. Delegates (Simon de Montfort's Parliament, 1261)	90	90
3131	60c. "Maestà (Cimabue) (painted 1270)	90	90
3132	60c. Marco Polo (departure from Venice, 1271)	90	90
3133	60c. "Divine Wind" (Kamikaze wind saves Japan from invasion, 1274)	90	90
3134	60c. St. Thomas Aquinas (died 1274)	90	90
3135	60c. Arezzo Cathedral (completed 1277)	90	90
3136	60c. Margrethe ("The Maid of Norway") (crowned Queen of Scotland, 1286)	90	90
3137	60c. Jewish refugees (Expulsion of Jews from England, 1290)	90	90
3138	60c. Muslim horseman (capture of Acre, 1291)	90	90
3139	60c. Moshe de Leon (compiles *The Zohar*, 1291)	90	90
3140	60c. Knights in combat (German Civil War, 1292–98)	90	90
3141	60c. Kublai Khan (died 1294)	90	90
3142	60c. Dante (writes *La Vita Nuova*, 1295) (59×39 mm)	90	90
3143	60c. Autumn Colours on Quiao and Hua Mountains" (Zhan Mengfu) (painted 1296)	90	90
3127/43	Set of 17	14·00	14·00

Nos. 3127/43 were printed together, *se-tenant*, in sheetlets of 17 including a central label (59×39 mm) and inscribed left margin.

(Litho Cartor)

2000 (21 Aug). New Millennium. Two Thousand Years of Chinese Paintings. T **446** and similar multicoloured designs. P 12½.

3144	25c. Type **446**	40	40
	a. Sheetlet. Nos. 3144/60	6·00	6·00
3145	25c. Ink on silk drawing from Zhan Jadashan	40	40
3146	25c. Ink and colour on silk drawing from Mawangdui Tomb	40	40
3147	25c. "Scholars collating Texts" (attr Yang Zihua)	40	40
3148	25c. "Spring Outing" (attr Zhan Ziqian)	40	40
3149	25c. "Portrait of the Emperors" (attr Yen Liben)	40	40
3150	25c. "Sailing Boats and Riverside Mansion" (attr Li Sixun)	40	40
3151	25c. "Two Horses and Groom" (Han Kan)	40	40
3152	25c. "King's Portrait" (attr Wu Daozi)	40	40
3153	25c. "Court Ladies wearing Flowered Headdresses" (attr Zhou Fang)	40	40
3154	25c. "Distant Mountain Forest" (mountain) (Juran)	40	40
3155	25c. "Mount Kuanglu" (Jiang Hao)	40	40
3156	25c. "Pheasant and Small Birds" (Huang Jucai)	40	40
3157	25c. "Deer among Red Maples" (anon)	40	40
3158	25c. "Distant Mountain Forest" (river and fields) (Juran)	40	40

ANTIGUA AND BARBUDA

3159	25c. "Literary Gathering" (Han Huang) (57×39 mm)	40	40
3160	25c. "Birds and Insects" (Huang Quan)	40	40
3144/60	Set of 17	6·00	6·00

Nos. 3144/60 were printed together, *se-tenant*, in sheetlets of 17 including a central label (59×39 mm) and inscribed left margin.

No. 3148 is inscribed "SPRINTING", No. 3150 "MASION" and No. 3153 "HEADRESSES", all in error.

447 King Donald III of Scotland   **448** Agouti

(Des R. Sauber. Litho Questa)

2000 (21 Aug). Monarchs of the Millennium. T **447** and similar vert designs. P 13½×14.

3161	$1.65 brownish black, stone and chocolate	1·50	1·50
	a. Sheetlet. Nos. 3161/6	8·00	8·00
3162	$1.65 brownish black, stone and chocolate	1·50	1·50
3163	$1.65 brownish black, stone and chocolate	1·50	1·50
3164	$1.65 brownish black, stone and chocolate	1·50	1·50
3165	$1.65 brownish black, stone and chocolate	1·50	1·50
3166	$1.65 brownish black, stone and chocolate	1·50	1·50
3167	$1.65 multicoloured	1·50	1·50
	a. Sheetlet. Nos. 3167/72	8·00	8·00
3168	$1.65 multicoloured	1·50	1·50
3169	$1.65 multicoloured	1·50	1·50
3170	$1.65 multicoloured	1·50	1·50
3171	$1.65 multicoloured	1·50	1·50
3172	$1.65 multicoloured	1·50	1·50
3161/72	Set of 12	16·00	16·00

MS3173 Two sheets, each 115×135 mm. (a) $6 multicoloured. (b) $6 multicoloured *Set of 2 sheets* . . . . 8·50 9·50

Designs—No. 3161, Type **447**; No. 3162, King Duncan I of Scotland; No. 3163, King Duncan II of Scotland; No. 3164, King Macbeth of Scotland; No. 3165, King Malcolm III of Scotland; No. 3166, King Edgar of Scotland; No. 3167, King Charles I of England and Scotland; No. 3168, King Charles II of England and Scotland; No. 3169 Prince Charles Edward Stuart 'Bonnie Prince Charlie', incorrectly captioned as King George III of Great Britain; No. 3170, King James II of England and VII of Scotland; No. 3171, King James II of Scotland; No. 3172, King James III of Scotland; No. **MS**3173a, King Robert I of Scotland; No. **MS**3173b, Queen Anne of Great Britain.

Nos. 3161/6 and 3167/72 were each printed, *se-tenant*, in sheetlets of 6 with enlarged illustrated top margins.

(Des R. Sauber. Litho Questa)

2000 (21 Aug). Popes of the Millennium. Vert designs as T **447**. Each brownish black, olive-yellow and blackish olive. P 13½×14.

3174	$1.65 Alexander VI (bare-headed)	1·50	1·50
	a. Sheetlet. Nos. 3174/9	8·00	8·00
3175	$1.65 Benedict XIII	1·50	1·50
3176	$1.65 Boniface IX	1·50	1·50
3177	$1.65 Alexander VI (wearing cap)	1·50	1·50
3178	$1.65 Clement VIII	1·50	1·50
3179	$1.65 Clement VI	1·50	1·50
3180	$1.65 John Paul II	1·50	1·50
	a. Sheetlet. Nos. 3180/5	8·00	8·00
3181	$1.65 Benedict XV	1·50	1·50
3182	$1.65 John XXIII	1·50	1·50
3183	$1.65 Pius XI	1·50	1·50
3184	$1.65 Pius XII	1·50	1·50
3185	$1.65 Paul VI	1·50	1·50
3174/85	Set of 12	16·00	16·00

MS3186 Two sheets, each 115×135 mm. (a) $6 Pius II (brownish black, olive-yellow and black). (b) $6 Pius VII (brownish black, olive-yellow and black) *Set of 2 sheets* . . . . 9·00 9·50

Nos. 3174/9 and 3180/5 were each printed together, *se-tenant*, in sheetlets of 6 with enlarged illustrated top margins.

No. 3181 is inscribed "BENIDICT XV" in error.

(Des Francisco Roman Company. Litho Walsall)

2000 (25 Sept). Fauna of the Rain Forest. T **448** and similar multicoloured designs. P 14.

3187	75c. Type **448**	60	45
3188	90c. Capybara	70	50
3189	$1.20 Basilisk Lizard	80	70
3190	$1.65 Green Violetear	1·10	1·10
	a. Sheetlet. Nos. 3190/5	6·00	6·00
3191	$1.65 Harpy Eagle	1·10	1·10
3192	$1.65 Three-toed Sloth	1·10	1·10
3193	$1.65 White Uakari Monkey	1·10	1·10
3194	$1.65 Anteater	1·10	1·10
3195	$1.65 Coati	1·10	1·10
3196	$1.75 Red-eyed Tree Frog	1·10	1·10
	a. Sheetlet. Nos. 3196/201	6·00	6·00
3197	$1.75 Black Spider Monkey	1·10	1·10
3198	$1.75 Emerald Toucanet	1·10	1·10
3199	$1.75 Kinkajou	1·10	1·10
3200	$1.75 Spectacled Bear	1·10	1·10
3201	$1.75 Tapir	1·10	1·10
3202	$2 Heliconid Butterfly	1·25	1·40
3187/202	Set of 16	15·00	14·50

MS3203 Two sheets. (a) 90×65 mm. $6 Keel-billed Toucan (horiz). (b) 65×90 mm. $6 Scarlet Macaw *Set of 2 sheets* . . . . 10·00 11·00

Nos. 3190/5 and 3196/201 were printed together, *se-tenant*, in sheetlets of 6, forming composite designs.

449 "Sea Cliff" Submarine

(Des R. Martin. Litho Questa)

2000 (2 Oct). Submarines. T **449** and similar horiz designs. Multicoloured. P 14.

3204	65c. Type **449**	85	45
3205	75c. "Beaver Mark IV"	1·00	50
3206	90c. "Reef Ranger"	1·10	50
3207	$1 "Cubmarine"	1·25	70
3208	$1.20 "Alvin"	1·40	80
3209	$2 HMS *Revenge*	2·00	2·00
	a. Sheetlet. Nos. 3209/14	11·00	11·00
3210	$2 *Walrus*, Netherlands	2·00	2·00
3211	$2 USS *Los Angeles*	2·00	2·00
3212	$2 *Daphne*, France	2·00	2·00
3213	$2 USS *Ohio*	2·00	2·00
3214	$2 USS *Skipjack*	2·00	2·00
3215	$3 "*Argus*", Russia	2·50	2·75
3204/15	Set of 12	18·00	16·00

MS3216 Two sheets, each 107×84 mm. (a) $6 "Trieste". (b) $6 Type **209** U-boat, Germany . . . . 10·00 11·00

Nos. 3209/14 were printed together, *se-tenant*, in sheetlets of 6 with the backgrounds forming a composite design and an enlarged top margin.

450 German Lookout

(Des R. Sauber. Litho Questa)

2000 (16 Oct). 60th Anniv of Battle of Britain. T **450** and similar horiz designs. Multicoloured (except No. 3222). P 14.

3217	$1.20 Type **450**	1·50	1·50
	a. Sheetlet. Nos. 3217/24	11·00	11·00
3218	$1.20 Children's evacuation train	1·50	1·50
3219	$1.20 Evacuating hospital patients	1·50	1·50
3220	$1.20 Hawker Hurricane (fighter)	1·50	1·50
3221	$1.20 Rescue team	1·50	1·50
3222	$1.20 Churchill cartoon (black)	1·50	1·50
3223	$1.20 King George VI and Queen Elizabeth inspecting bomb damage	1·50	1·50
3224	$1.20 Barrage balloon above Tower Bridge	1·50	1·50
3225	$1.20 Bristol Blenheim (bomber)	1·50	1·50
	a. Sheetlet. Nos. 3225/32	11·00	11·00
3226	$1.20 Prime Minister Winston Churchill	1·50	1·50
3227	$1.20 Bristol Blenheim and barrage balloons	1·50	1·50
3228	$1.20 Heinkel (fighter)	1·50	1·50
3229	$1.20 Supermarine Spitfire (fighter)	1·50	1·50
3230	$1.20 German rescue launch	1·50	1·50
3231	$1.20 Messerschmitt 109 (fighter)	1·50	1·50
3232	$1.20 R.A.F. rescue launch	1·50	1·50
3217/32	Set of 16	22·00	22·00

MS3233 Two sheets, each 90×60 mm. (a) $6 Junkers 87B (dive bomber). (b) $6 Supermarine Spitfires at dusk . . . . 12·00 13·00

Nos. 3217/24 and 3225/32 were each printed together in sheetlets of 8, with the two horizontal *se-tenant* rows separated by a gutter margin showing scenes from the Battle of Britain.
No. **MS**3233 (a) is inscribed "JUNKERS 878" in error.

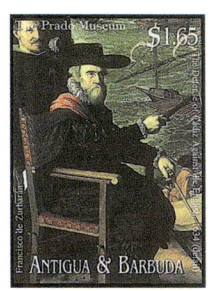

451 "The Defence of Cadiz" (Zurbarán)

(Des D. Keren. Litho Walsall)

2000 (6 Nov). "Espana 2000" International Stamp Exhibition, Madrid. Paintings from the Prado Museum. T **451** and similar multicoloured designs. P 12.

3234	$1.65 Type **451**		1·25	1·25
	a. Sheetlet. Nos 3234/9		6·75	6·75
3235	$1.65 "The Defence of Cadiz" (General and galleys)		1·25	1·25
3236	$1.65 "The Defence of Cadiz" (officers)		1·25	1·25
3237	$1.65 "Vulcan's Forge" (Vulcan) (Velázquez)		1·25	1·25
3238	$1.65 "Vulcan's Forge" (working metal)		1·25	1·25
3239	$1.65 "Vulcan's Forge" (workers with hammers)		1·25	1·25
3240	$1.65 "Family Portrait" (three men) (Adriaen Key)		1·25	1·25
	a. Sheetlet. Nos. 3240/5		6·75	6·75
3241	$1.65 "Family Portrait" (one man)		1·25	1·25
3242	$1.65 "Family Portrait" (three women)		1·25	1·25
3243	$1.65 "The Devotion of Rudolf I" (horseman with lantern) (Rubens and Jan Wildens)		1·25	1·25
3244	$1.65 "The Devotion of Rudolf I" (priest on horseback)		1·25	1·25
3245	$1.65 "The Devotion of Rudolf I" (huntsman)		1·25	1·25
3246	$1.65 "The Concert" (lute player) (Vincente González)		1·25	1·25
	a. Sheetlet. Nos. 3246/51		6·75	6·75
3247	$1.65 "The Concert" (lady with fan)		1·25	1·25
3248	$1.65 "The Concert" (two gentlemen)		1·25	1·25
3249	$1.65 "The Adoration of the Magi" (Wise Man) (Juan Maino)		1·25	1·25
3250	$1.65 "The Adoration of the Magi" (two Wise Men)		1·25	1·25
3251	$1.65 "The Adoration of the Magi" (Holy Family)		1·25	1·25
3234/51	Set of 18		20·00	20·00
MS3252	Three sheets. (a) 115×90 mm $6 "The Deliverance of St Peter" (José de Ribera) (horiz). (b) 110×90 mm $6 "The Fan Seller" (José del Castillo). (c) 110×90 mm $6 "Family in a Garden" (Jan van Kessel the Younger) Set of 3 sheets		11·00	13·00

Nos. 3234/9, 3240/5 and 3246/51 were each printed together, *se-tenant*, in sheetlets of 6, with enlarged top margins.
Nos. 3246/8 are inscribed "Gonzlez" with No. 3248 additionally inscribed "Francisco Rizi", all in error.

452 Two Angels

(Des I. Fantini. Litho B.D.T.)

2000 (5 Dec). Christmas and Holy Year. T **452** and similar vert designs. Multicoloured. P 14.

3253	25c. Type **452**		20	15
3254	45c. Heads of two angels looking down		35	25
3255	90c. Heads of two angels, one looking up		60	40
3256	$1.75 Type **452**		1·25	1·50
	a. Sheetlet. Nos. 3256/9		4·50	5·50
3257	$1.75 As 45c		1·25	1·50
3258	$1.75 As 90c		1·25	1·50
3259	$1.75 As $5		1·25	1·50
3260	$5 Two angels with drapery		3·00	3·75
3253/60	Set of 8		8·00	9·50
MS3261	110×120 mm. $6 Holy Child		3·50	4·00

Nos. 3256/9 were printed together, *se-tenant*, in sheetlets of 4 with enlarged illustrated left margin.

453 "Dr. Ephraim Bueno" (Rembrandt)

(Litho Questa)

2000 (18 Dec). Bicentenary of Rijksmuseum, Amsterdam. Dutch Paintings. T **453** and similar vert designs. Multicoloured. P 13½.

3262	$1 Type **453**		85	85
	a. Sheetlet. Nos. 3262/7		4·50	4·50
3263	$1 "Woman writing a Letter" (Frans van Meris de Oude)		85	85
3264	$1 "Mary Magdalen" (Jan van Scorel)		85	85
3265	$1 "Anna Coddle" (Maerten van Heemskerck)		85	85
3266	$1 "Cleopatra's Banquet" (Gerard Lairesse)		85	85
3267	$1 "Titus in Friar's Habit" (Rembrandt)		85	85
3268	$1.20 "Saskia" (Rembrandt)		90	90
	a. Sheetlet. Nos. 3268/73		4·75	4·75
3269	$1.20 "In the Month of July" (Paul Joseph Constantin Gabriël)		90	90
3270	$1.20 "Maria Trip" (Rembrandt)		90	90
3271	$1.20 "Still Life with Flowers" (Jan van Huysum)		90	90
3272	$1.20 "Haesje van Cleyburgh" (Rembrandt)		90	90
3273	$1.20 "Girl in a White Kimono" (George Hendrick Breitner)		90	90
3274	$1.65 "Man and Woman at a Spinning Wheel" (Pieter Pietersz)		1·10	1·10
	a. Sheetlet. Nos. 3274/9		6·00	6·00
3275	$1.65 "Self-portrait" (Rembrandt)		1·10	1·10
3276	$1.65 "Jeremiah lamenting the Destruction of Jerusalem" (Rembrandt)		1·10	1·10
3277	$1.65 "The Jewish Bride" (Rembrandt)		1·10	1·10
3278	$1.65 "Anna accused by Tobit of stealing a Kid" (Rembrandt)		1·10	1·10
3279	$1.65 "The Prophetess Anna" (Rembrandt)		1·10	1·10
3262/79	Set of 18		15·00	15·00
MS3280	Three sheets, each 118×88 mm. (a) $6 "Doubting Thomas" (Hendrick ter Brugghen); (b) $6 "Still Life with Cheeses" (Floris van Dijck); (c) $6 "Isaac Blessing Jacob" (Govert Flinck) Set of 3 sheets		11·00	13·00

Nos. 3262/7, 3268/73 and 3274/9 were each printed together, *se-tenant*, in sheetlets of 6 with inscribed and illustrated margins.

454 "Starmie No. 121"

(Des D. Klein. Litho Questa)

2001 (19 Feb). Characters from "Pokémon" (children's cartoon series). T **454** and similar horiz designs. Multicoloured. P 13½.

3281	$1.75 Type **454**		1·10	1·10
	a. Sheetlet. Nos. 3281/6		6·00	6·00
3282	$1.75 "Misty"		1·10	1·10
3283	$1.75 "Brock"		1·10	1·10
3284	$1.75 "Geodude No. 74"		1·10	1·10

ANTIGUA AND BARBUDA

3285	$1.75 "Krabby No. 98"		1·10	1·10
3286	$1.75 "Ash"		1·10	1·10
3281/6	Set of 6		6·00	6·00
MS3287	74×114 mm. $6 "Charizard No. 6"		3·25	3·50

Nos. 3281/6 were printed together, *se-tenant*, in sheetlets of 6 with enlarged illustrated margins.

455 Blue-toothed Entoloma

456 Map and Graphs

(Des D. Burkhart. Litho Cartor)

2001 (26 Mar). "Hong Kong 2001" Stamp Exhibition. Tropical Fungi. T **455** and similar vert designs. Multicoloured. P 13½.

3288	25c. Type **455**		45	30
3289	90c. Common Morel		90	50
3290	$1 Red Cage Fungus		1·00	70
3291	$1.65 Copper Trumpet		1·10	1·10
	a. Sheetlet. Nos. 3291/6		6·00	6·00
3292	$1.65 Field Mushroom ("Meadow Mushroom")		1·10	1·10
3293	$1.65 Green Gill ("Green-gilled Parasol")		1·10	1·10
3294	$1.65 The Panther		1·10	1·10
3295	$1.65 Death Cap		1·10	1·10
3296	$1.65 Royal Boletus ("King Bolete")		1·10	1·10
3297	$1.65 Lilac Fairy Helmet ("Lilac Bonnet")		1·10	1·10
	a. Sheetlet. Nos. 3297/302		6·00	6·00
3298	$1.65 Silky Volvar		1·10	1·10
3299	$1.65 Agrocybe Mushroom ("Poplar Field Cap")		1·10	1·10
3300	$1.65 Saint George's Mushroom		1·10	1·10
3301	$1.65 Red-stemmed Tough Shank		1·10	1·10
3302	$1.65 Fly Agaric		1·10	1·10
3303	$1.75 Common Fawn Agaric ("Fawn Shield-Cap")		1·25	1·50
3288/303	Set of 16		15·00	14·50
MS3304	Two sheets, each 70×90 mm. (a) $6 Yellow Parasol. (b) $6 Mutagen Milk Cap Set of 2 sheets		8·50	9·50

Nos. 3291/6 and 3297/302 were each printed together, *se-tenant*, in sheetlets of 6. with the backgrounds forming composite designs continued on to the sheet margins.

(Litho Questa)

2001 (2 Apr). Population and Housing Census. T **456** and similar square designs, each showing map and different form of graph. P 14.

3305	15c. multicoloured		15	15
3306	25c. multicoloured		20	20
3307	65c. multicoloured		55	55
3308	90c. multicoloured		70	70
3305/8	Set of 4		1·40	1·40
MS3309	55×50 mm. $6 multicoloured (Map and census logo)		5·50	6·00

457 "Yuna (Bath-house Women)" (detail)

458 Lucille Ball leaning on Mantelpiece

(Litho Questa)

2001 (28 May). "PHILANIPPON 2001" International Stamp Exhibition, Tokyo. Traditional Japanese Paintings. T **457** and similar vert designs. Multicoloured. P 14.

3310	45c. Type **457**		50	30
3311	60c. "Yuna (Bath-house Women)" (different detail)		60	50
3312	65c. "Yuna (Bath-house Women)" (different detail)		60	50
3313	75c. "The Hikone Screen" (detail)		70	50
3314	$1 "The Hikone Screen" (different detail)		75	60
3315	$1.20 "The Hikone Screen" (different detail)		80	70
3316	$1.65 Galleon and Dutch merchants with horse		95	95
	a. Sheetlet. Nos. 3316/19		3·50	3·50
3317	$1.65 Galleon and merchants with tiger		95	95
3318	$1.65 Merchants unpacking goods		95	95
3319	$1.65 Merchants with parasol and horse		95	95
3320	$1.65 Women packing food		95	95
	a. Sheetlet. Nos. 3320/5		5·00	5·00
3321	$1.65 Picnic under the cherry tree		95	95
3322	$1.65 Palanquins and resting bearers		95	95
3323	$1.65 Women dancing		95	95
3324	$1.65 Three samurai		95	95
3325	$1.65 One samurai		95	95
3310/25	Set of 16		12·00	11·50
MS3326	Three sheets, each 80×110 mm. (a) $6 "Harunobu Suzuki" (Shiba Kokani) (38×50 *mm*). (b) $6 "Daruma" (Tsujo Kako) (38×50 *mm*). (c) $6 "Visiting a Shrine on a Rainy Night" (Harunobu Suziki) (38×50 *mm*). P 14×13½ Set of 3 sheets		9·50	11·00

Nos. 3316/19 ("The Namban Screen" by Kano Nizen) and Nos. 3320/5 ("Merry-making under the Cherry Blossoms" by Kano Naganobu) were each printed together, *se-tenant*, as sheetlets of 4 or 6 with both sheetlets forming the entire painting.

(Litho Questa)

2001 (5 Mar). Scenes from *I Love Lucy* (American TV comedy series). Eight sheets each containing multicoloured design as T **458**. P 14×13½ (No. **MS**3327 (h)) or 13½×14 (others).

MS3327 (a) 118×92 mm. $6 Type **458**. (b) 98×120 mm. $6 Desi Arnaz laughing. (c) 93×130 mm. $6 William Frawley at table. (d) 114×145 mm. $6 Lucille Ball with William Frawley (e) 114×145 mm. $6 Lucille Ball in blue dress (f) 119×111 mm. $6 Lucille Ball sitting at table. (g) 128×100 mm. $6 Lucille Ball as scarecrow. (h) 93×125 mm. $6 William Frawley shouting at Desi Arnaz (*horiz*) Set of 8 sheets ... 22·00 24·00

459 Hintleya burtii

(Des Artworks Studio. Litho Walsall)

2001 (11 June). Caribbean Orchids. T **459** and similar multicoloured designs. P 14.

3328	45c. Type **459**		50	25
3329	75c. *Neomoovea irrovata*		65	45
3330	90c. *Comparettia speciosa*		70	50
3331	$1 *Cyprepedium crapeanum*		80	70
3332	$1.20 *Trichoceuos muralis* (vert)		90	90
	a. Sheetlet. Nos. 3332/7		4·50	4·50
3333	$1.20 *Dracula rampira* (vert)		90	90
3334	$1.20 *Psychopsis papilio* (vert)		90	90
3335	$1.20 *Lycaste clenningiana* (vert)		90	90
3336	$1.20 *Telipogon nevuosus* (vert)		90	90
3337	$1.20 *Masclecallia ayahbacana* (vert)		90	90
3338	$1.65 *Cattleya dowiana* (vert)		1·10	1·10
	a. Sheetlet. Nos. 3338/43		6·00	6·00
3339	$1.65 *Dendiobium cruentum* (vert)		1·10	1·10
3340	$1.65 *Bulbophyllum lobbi* (vert)		1·10	1·10
3341	$1.65 *Chysis laevis* (vert)		1·10	1·10
3342	$1.65 *Ancistrochilus rothschildicanus* (vert)		1·10	1·10
3343	$1.65 *Angraecum sororium* (vert)		1·10	1·10
3344	$1.65 *Rhyncholaelia glanca* (vert)		1·10	1·10
	a. Sheetlet. Nos. 3344/9		6·00	6·00
3345	$1.65 *Oncidium barbatum* (vert)		1·10	1·10
3346	$1.65 *Phaius tankervillege* (vert)		1·10	1·10
3347	$1.65 *Ghies brechtiana* (vert)		1·10	1·10
3348	$1.65 *Angraecum leonis* (vert)		1·10	1·10
3349	$1.65 *Cycnoches loddigesti* (vert)		1·10	1·10
3328/49	Set of 22		19·00	18·00
MS3350	Two sheets. (a) 68×104 mm $6 *Symphalossum sanquinem* (vert). (b) 104×68 mm $6 *Trichopilia fragrans* (vert) Set of 2 sheets		8·50	9·50

ANTIGUA AND BARBUDA

Nos. 3332/7, 3338/43 and 3344/9 were each printed together, se-tenant, in sheetlets of 6 with enlarged and inscribed right margins.

460 Yellowtail Damselfish

(Des T. Wood. Litho Walsall)

2001 (11 June). Tropical Marine Life. T **460** and similar multicoloured designs. P 14.

3351	25c. Type **460**	35	25
3352	45c. Indigo Hamlet	55	30
3353	65c. Great White Shark	70	40
3354	90c. Bottle-nose Dolphin	80	65
3355	90c. Palette Surgeonfish	80	65
3356	$1 Octopus	80	65
3357	$1.20 Common Dolphin	90	90
	a. Sheetlet. Nos. 3357/62	4·50	4·50
3358	$1.20 Franklin's Gull	90	90
3359	$1.20 Rock Beauty	90	90
3360	$1.20 Bicoloured Angelfish	90	90
3361	$1.20 Beaugregory	90	90
3362	$1.20 Banded Butterflyfish	90	90
3363	$1.20 Common Tern	90	90
	a. Sheetlet. Nos. 3363/8	4·50	4·50
3364	$1.20 Flying Fish	90	90
3365	$1.20 Queen Angelfish	90	90
3366	$1.20 Blue-striped Grunt	90	90
3367	$1.20 Porkfish	90	90
3368	$1.20 Blue Tang	90	90
3369	$1.65 Red-footed Booby	1·10	1·10
	a. Sheetlet. Nos. 3369/74	6·00	6·00
3370	$1.65 Bottle-nose Dolphin	1·10	1·10
3371	$1.65 Hawksbill Turtle	1·10	1·10
3372	$1.65 Monk Seal	1·10	1·10
3373	$1.65 Great White Shark (inscr "Bull Shark")	1·10	1·10
3374	$1.65 Lemon Shark	1·10	1·10
3375	$1.65 Dugong	1·10	1·10
	a. Sheetlet. Nos. 3375/80	6·00	6·00
3376	$1.65 White-tailed Tropicbird	1·10	1·10
3377	$1.65 Bull Shark	1·10	1·10
3378	$1.65 Manta Ray	1·10	1·10
3379	$1.65 Green Turtle	1·10	1·10
3380	$1.65 Spanish Grunt	1·10	1·10
3351/80 Set of 30		25·00	24·00
MS3381 Four sheets. (a) 68×98 mm. $5 Sailfish. (b) 68×98 mm. $5 Brown Pelican and Beaugregory (vert). (c) 98×68 mm. $6 Queen Triggerfish. (d) 96×68 mm. $6 Hawksbill Turtle Set of 4 sheets		18·00	19·00

Nos. 3357/62, 3363/8, 3369/74 and 3375/80 were each printed together, se-tenant, in sheetlets of 6, with illustrated margins, the backgrounds forming composite designs.

461 Freewinds (liner) and Police Band, Antigua

462 Young Queen Victoria in Blue Dress

(Litho Questa)

2001 (15 June). Work of Freewinds (Church of Scientology flagship) in Caribbean. T **461** and similar horiz designs. Multicoloured. P 14.

3382	30c. Type **461**	40	30
3383	45c. At anchor off St. Barthélemy	45	30
3384	75c. At sunset	70	60
3385	90c. Off Bonaire	90	90
3386	$1.50 Freewinds anchored off Bequia	1·25	1·40
3382/6 Set of 5		3·25	3·25
MS3387 Two sheets, each 85×60 mm. (a) $4 Freewinds alongside quay, Curaçao. (b) $4 Decorated with lights Set of 2 sheets		5·50	6·00

(Des R. Rundo. Litho Questa)

2001 (3 July). Death Centenary of Queen Victoria. T **462** and similar vert designs. Multicoloured. P 14.

3388	$2 Type **462**	1·40	1·60
	a. Sheetlet. Nos. 3388/91	5·00	5·75
3389	$2 Queen Victoria wearing red head-dress	1·40	1·60
3390	$2 Queen Victoria with jewelled hair ornament	1·40	1·60
3391	$2 Queen Victoria, after Chalon, in brooch	1·40	1·60
3388/91 Set of 4		5·00	5·75
MS3392 70×82 mm. $5 Queen Victoria in old age		3·00	3·75

Nos. 3388/91 were printed together, se-tenant, in sheetlets of 4, with an enlarged inscribed top margin.

463 "Water Lilies"

(Litho Questa)

2001 (3 July). 75th Death Anniv of Claude-Oscar Monet (French painter). T **463** and similar multicoloured designs. P 13½.

3393	$2 Type **463**	1·50	1·50
	a. Sheetlet. Nos. 3393/6	5·50	5·50
3394	$2 "Rose Portals, Giverny"	1·50	1·50
3395	$2 "Water Lily Pond, Harmony in Green"	1·50	1·50
3396	$2 "Artist's Garden, Irises"	1·50	1·50
3393/6 Set of 4		5·50	5·50
MS3397 136×111 mm. $5 "Jerusalem Artichoke Flowers" (vert)		3·25	3·75

Nos. 3393/6 were printed together, se-tenant, in sheetlets of 4 with an enlarged top margin showing a photograph of the artist.

No. 3396 is inscribed "Artists's" in error.

464 Duchess of York with Baby Princess Elizabeth (1926)

465 Verdi in Top Hat

(Des J. Iskowitz. Litho Questa)

2001 (3 July). 75th Birthday of Queen Elizabeth II. T **464** and similar multicoloured designs. P 14.

3398	$1 Type **464**	1·25	1·25
	a. Sheetlet. Nos 3398/403	6·75	6·75
3399	$1 Queen in Coronation robes (1953)	1·25	1·25
3400	$1 Young Princess Elizabeth (1938)	1·25	1·25
3401	$1 Queen Elizabeth in Garter robes (1956)	1·25	1·25
3402	$1 Princess Elizabeth with pony (1939)	1·25	1·25
3403	$1 Queen Elizabeth in red dress and pearls (1985)	1·25	1·25
3398/403 Set of 6		6·75	6·75
MS3404 90×72 mm. $6 Princess Elizabeth and Queen Elizabeth (1940)		4·50	5·00

Nos. 3398/403 were printed together, se-tenant, in sheetlets of 6 containing two vertical strips of three separated by a large illustrated gutter.

(Des T Wood. Litho Questa)

2001 (3 July). Death Centenary of Giuseppe Verdi (Italian composer). T **465** and similar vert designs. Multicoloured. P 14.

3405	$2 Type **465**	2·75	2·75
	a. Sheetlet. Nos. 3405/8	10·00	10·00
3406	$2 Don Carlos and part of opera score	2·75	2·75
3407	$2 Conductor and score for Aida	2·75	2·75
3408	$2 Musicians and score for Rigoletto	2·75	2·75
3405/8 Set of 4		10·00	10·00

ANTIGUA AND BARBUDA

MS3409	77×117 mm. $5 Verdi in evening dress	6·50	6·50

Nos. 3405/8 were printed together, *se-tenant*, in sheetlets of 4, the backgrounds forming a composite design which continues onto the sheetlet margins.

466 "Georges-Henri Manuel"

467 Marlene Dietrich smoking

(Litho Questa)

2001 (3 July). Death Centenary of Henri de Toulouse-Lautrec (French painter). T **466** and similar vert designs. Multicoloured. P 13½×14.

3410	$2 Type **466**	1·75	1·75
	a. Sheetlet. Nos. 3410/13	6·25	6·25
3411	$2 "Louis Pascal"	1·75	1·75
3412	$2 "Romain Coolus"	1·75	1·75
3413	$2 "Monsieur Fourcade"	1·75	1·75
3410/13	Set of 4	6·25	6·25
MS3414	67×84 mm. $5 "Dancing at the Moulin de la Galette"	5·00	5·00

Nos. 3410/13 were printed together, *se-tenant*, in sheetlets of 4 with enlarged illustrated right and top margins.

No. 3412 is inscribed "ROMAN" in error.

(Des D. Klein. Litho Questa)

2001 (3 July). Birth Centenary of Marlene Dietrich (actress and singer). T **467** and similar vert designs. P 13½×14.

3415	$2 black, dull purple and deep claret	1·50	1·50
	a. Sheetlet. Nos. 3415/18	5·50	5·50
3416	$2 black, dull purple and deep claret	1·50	1·50
3417	$2 multicoloured	1·50	1·50
3418	$2 black, dull purple and deep claret	1·50	1·50
3415/18	Set of 4	5·50	5·50

Designs:—No. 3415, Type **467**; No. 3416, Marlene Dietrich, in evening dress, sitting on settee; No. 3417, In black dress; No. 3418, Sitting on piano. Nos. 3415/18 were printed together, *se-tenant*, in sheetlets of 4 with further portraits in the enlarged margins.

468 Collared Peccary

(Des R. Martin. Litho Questa)

2001 (10 Sept). Vanishing Fauna of the Caribbean. T **468** and similar multicoloured designs. P 14.

3419	25c. Type **468**	45	30
3420	30c. Baird's Tapir	45	30
3421	45c. Agouti	60	30
3422	75c. Bananaquit	1·25	55
3423	90c. Six-banded Armadillo	1·00	55
3424	$1 Roseate Spoonbill	1·50	80
3425	$1.80 Mouse Opossum	2·00	2·00
	a. Sheetlet. Nos. 3425/30	11·00	11·00
3426	$1.80 Magnificent Black Frigate Bird	2·00	2·00
3427	$1.80 Northern Jacana	2·00	2·00
3428	$1.80 Painted Bunting	2·00	2·00
3429	$1.80 Haitian Solenodon	2·00	2·00
3430	$1.80 St. Lucia Iguana	2·00	2·00
3431	$2.50 West Indian Iguana	2·75	2·75
	a. Sheetlet. Nos. 3431/4	10·00	10·00
3432	$2.50 Scarlet Macaw	2·75	2·75
3433	$2.50 Cotton-topped Tamarin	2·75	2·75
3434	$2.50 Kinkajou	2·75	2·75
3419/34	Set of 16	25·00	23·00
MS3435	Two sheets. (a) 117×85 mm. $6 Ocelot (vert). (b) 162×116 mm. $6 King Vulture (vert) Set of 2 sheets	14·00	15·00

Nos. 3425/30 and 3431/4 were printed together, *se-tenant*, in sheetlets of 6 and 4, with illustrated margins.

469 Sara Crewe *The Little Princess* reading a Letter

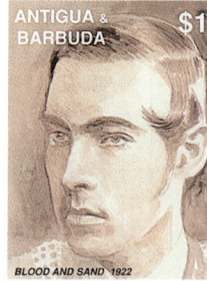

470 Rudolph Valentino in *Blood and Sand*, 1922

(Litho Questa)

2001 (2 Oct). Shirley Temple Films. T **469** and similar multicoloured designs showing film scenes. P 13½×14 (vert) or 14×13½ (horiz).

(a) The Little Princess

3436	$1.50 Type **469**	95	95
	a. Sheetlet. Nos. 3436/41	5·25	5·25
3437	$1.50 Sara in pink dressing gown	95	95
3438	$1.50 Sara cuddling doll	95	95
3439	$1.50 Sara as Princess on throne	95	95
3440	$1.50 Sara talking to man in frock coat	95	95
3441	$1.50 Sara blowing out candles	95	95
3442	$1.80 Sara with Father (*horiz*)	1·10	1·10
	a. Sheetlet. Nos. 3442/5	4·00	4·00
3443	$1.80 Sara scrubbing floor (*horiz*)	1·10	1·10
3444	$1.80 Sara and friend with Headmistress (*horiz*)	1·10	1·10
3445	$1.80 Sara with Queen Victoria (*horiz*)	1·10	1·10
3436/45	Set of 10	9·00	9·00
MS3446	106×76 mm. $6 Sara with wounded Father	3·25	3·75

Nos. 3436/41, 3442/5, 3447/52 and 3453/6 were each printed together, *se-tenant*, in sheetlets of 4 or 6, with enlarged illustrated margins.

(b) Baby, Take a Bow

3447	$1.65 Shirley in dancing class (*horiz*)	95	95
	a. Sheetlet. Nos. 3447/52	5·25	
3448	$1.65 Shirley cuddling Father (*horiz*)	95	95
3449	$1.65 Shirley at bedtime with parents (*horiz*)	95	95
3450	$1.65 Shirley in yellow dress with Father (*horiz*)	95	95
3451	$1.65 Shirley and Father at Christmas party (*horiz*)	95	95
3452	$1.65 Shirley and gangster looking in cradle (*horiz*)	95	95
3453	$1.65 Shirley in spotted dress	95	95
	a. Sheetlet. Nos. 3453/6	3·50	3·50
3454	$1.65 Shirley on steps with gangster	95	95
3455	$1.65 Shirley with gangster holding gun	95	95
3456	$1.65 Shirley with Mother	95	95
3447/56	Set of 10	8·50	8·50
MS3457	106×76 mm. $6 Shirley in spotted dress	3·25	3·75

(Des J. Iskowitz. Litho Questa)

2001 (2 Oct). 75th Death Anniv of Rudolph Valentino (Italian film actor). T **470** and similar vert designs. P 13½.

3458	$1 grey-brown and black	75	75
	a. Sheetlet. Nos. 3458/63	4·00	4·00
3459	$1 lilac and black	75	75
3460	$1 yellow-brown and black	75	75
3461	$1 red-brown and black	75	75
3462	$1 brown-red and black	75	75
3463	$1 slate-lilac and black	75	75
3464	$1 multicoloured	75	75
	a. Sheetlet. Nos. 3464/9	4·00	4·00
3465	$1 multicoloured	75	75
3466	$1 multicoloured	75	75
3467	$1 multicoloured	75	75
3468	$1 multicoloured	75	75
3469	$1 multicoloured	75	75
3458/69	Set of 12	8·00	8·00
MS3470	Two sheets. (a) 90×125 mm. $6 multicoloured. (b) 68×95 mm. $6 multicoloured Set of 2 sheets	7·50	8·50

Designs:—No. 3458, Type **470**; No. 3459, In *Eyes of Youth* with Clara Kimbal Young, 1919; No. 3460, In *All Night Long* with Carmel Meyers, 1918; No. 3461, Valentino in 1926; No. 3462, In *Camille* with Alla Nazimova, 1921; No. 3463, In *Cobra* with Nita Naldi, 1925; No. 3464, In *The Son of the Sheik* with Vilma Banky, 1926; No. 3465, In *The Young Rajah*, 1922; No. 3466, In *The Eagle* with Vilma Banky, 1925; No. 3467, In *The Sheik* with Agnes Ayres, 1921; No. 3468, In *A Sainted Devil*, 1924; No. 3469, In *Monsieur Beaucaire*, 1924; No. **MS**3470, (a) Valentino with Natacha Rambova. (b) In *The Four Horsemen of the Apocalypse*, 1921 Nos. 3458/63 and 3464/9 were each printed together, *se-tenant*, in sheetlets of 6, with enlarged illustrated margins. Nos. 3464 and 3466 are inscribed "BLANKY" and No. 3467 "AYERS", all in error.

ANTIGUA AND BARBUDA

471 Queen Elizabeth

472 Melvin Calvin, 1961

(Des R. Silvers. Litho Questa)

2001 (29 Oct). Golden Jubilee (1st issue). P 14.
3471	**471**	$1 multicoloured...................................	1·50	1·50

No. 3471 was printed in sheetlets of 8, containing two vertical rows of four, separated by a large illustrated central gutter. Both the stamp and the illustration on the central gutter are made up of a collage of miniature flower photographs.

(Des Irina Lyampe. Litho Questa)

2001 (29 Nov). Centenary of Nobel Prizes. Chemistry Winners (except No. **MS**3483c). T **472** and similar vert designs. Multicoloured. P 14.
3472	$1.50 Type **472**...................................	1·25	1·25
	a. Sheetlet. Nos. 3472/7................	6·75	6·75
3473	$1.50 Linus Pauling, 1954.................	1·25	1·25
3474	$1.50 Vincent du Vigneaud, 1955....	1·25	1·25
3475	$1.50 Richard Synge, 1952................	1·25	1·25
3476	$1.50 Archer Martin, 1952.................	1·25	1·25
3477	$1.50 Alfred Werner, 1913.................	1·25	1·25
3478	$1.50 Robert Curl Jr., 1996................	1·25	1·25
	a. Sheetlet. Nos. 3478/83...............	6·75	6·75
3479	$1.50 Alan Heeger, 2000....................	1·25	1·25
3480	$1.50 Michael Smith, 1993................	1·25	1·25
3481	$1.50 Sidney Altman, 1989...............	1·25	1·25
3482	$1.50 Elias Corey, 1990.....................	1·25	1·25
3483	$1.50 William Giauque, 1949............	1·25	1·25
3472/83 Set of 12...		13·50	13·50
MS3484 Three sheets, each 107×75 mm. (a) $6 Ernest Rutherford, 1908. (b) $6 Ernst Fischer, 1973. (c) $6 American volunteers, International Red Cross (Peace Prize, 1944) Set of 3 sheets.........................		12·50	13·00

Nos. 3472/7 and 3478/83 were each printed together, se-tenant, in sheetlets of 6, with an enlarged right margin showing a portrait of Alfred Nobel.

473 "Madonna and Child with Angels" (Filippo Lippi)

474 Final between Uruguay and Brazil, Brazil 1950

(Litho Questa)

2001 (4 Dec). Christmas. Italian Religious Paintings. T **473** and similar vert designs. Multicoloured. P 14.
3485	25c. Type **473**...................................	35	20
3486	45c. "Madonna of Corneto Tarquinia" (Lippi)....	55	25
3487	50c. "Madonna and Child" (Domenico Ghirlandaio)............	60	30
3488	75c. "Madonna and Child" (Lippi)......	1·00	55
3489	$4 "Madonna Delceppo" (Lippi)........	5·00	6·00
3485/9 Set of 5...		6·75	6·50
MS3490 106×136 mm. $6 "Madonna enthroned with Angels and Saints" (Lippi).............		4·50	5·00

(Des D. Miller. Litho Questa)

2001 (17 Dec). World Cup Football Championship, Japan and Korea (2002). T **474** and similar vert designs. Multicoloured. P 14.
3491	$1.50 Type **474**...............................	95	95
	a. Sheetlet. Nos. 3491/6................	5·25	5·25
3492	$1.50 Ferenc Puskas (Hungary), Switzerland 1954.................	95	95
3493	$1.50 Raymond Kopa (France), Sweden 1958.	95	95
3494	$1.50 Mauro (Brazil), Chile 1962..........	95	95
3495	$1.50 Gordon Banks (England), England 1966	95	95
3496	$1.50 Pelé (Brazil), Mexico 1970...........	95	95
3497	$1.50 Daniel Passarella (Argentina), Argentina 1978..........	95	95
	a. Sheetlet. Nos. 3497/502............	5·25	5·25
3498	$1.50 Karl-Heinz Rummenigge (Germany), Spain 1982............	95	95
3499	$1.50 World Cup Trophy, Mexico 1986..............	95	95
3500	$1.50 Diego Maradona (Argentina), Italy 1990..........	95	95
3501	$1.50 Roger Milla (Cameroun), USA 1994.......	95	95
3502	$1.50 Zinedine Zidane (France), France 1998..	95	95
3491/502 Set of 12..		10·50	10·50
MS3503 Two sheets, each 88×75 mm. (a) $6 Detail of Jules Rimet Trophy, Uruguay, 1930. (b) $6 Detail of World Cup Trophy, Japan/Korea 2002 Set of 2 sheets.....		7·50	8·50

Nos. 3491/6 and 3497/502 were each printed together, se-tenant, in sheetlets of 6, with enlarged illustrated margins.

No. 3500 is inscribed "Deigo" in error.

475 Battle of Nashville, 1864

476 Queen Elizabeth presenting Rosettes

(Des R. Sauber. Litho Questa)

2002 (28 Jan). American Civil War. T **475** and similar multicoloured designs. P 14½.
3504	45c. Type **475**...................................	85	85
	a. Sheetlet. Nos. 3504/21...............	15·00	15·00
3505	45c. Capture of Atlanta, 1864..............	85	85
3506	45c. Battle of Spotsylvania, 1864........	85	85
3507	45c. Battle of The Wilderness, 1864....	85	85
3508	45c. Battle of Chickamauga Creek, 1863......	85	85
3509	45c. Battle of Gettysburg, 1863...........	85	85
3510	45c. Lee and Jackson at Chancellorsville, 1863............	85	85
3511	45c. Battle of Fredericksburg, 1862.....	85	85
3512	45c. Battle of Antietam, 1862...............	85	85
3513	45c. Second Battle of Bull Run, 1862..	85	85
3514	45c. Battle of Five Forks, 1865.............	85	85
3515	45c. Seven Days' Battles, 1862............	85	85
3516	45c. First Battle of Bull Run, 1861........	85	85
3517	45c. Battle of Shiloh, 1862....................	85	85
3518	45c. Battle of Seven Pines, 1862..........	85	85
3519	45c. Bombardment of Fort Sumter, 1861.......	85	85
3520	45c. Battle of Chattanooga, 1863........	85	85
3521	45c. Grant and Lee at Appomattox, 1865.......	85	85
3522	50c. General Ulysses S. Grant (vert)...	1·00	1·00
	a. Sheetlet. Nos. 3522/33...............	11·00	11·00
3523	50c. President Abraham Lincoln (vert)........	1·00	1·00
3524	50c. President Jefferson Davis (vert)...	1·00	1·00
3525	50c. General Robert E. Lee (vert).........	1·00	1·00
3526	50c. General George Custer (vert).......	1·00	1·00
3527	50c. Admiral Andrew Hull Foote (vert)	1·00	1·00
3528	50c. General "Stonewall" Jackson (vert)....	1·00	1·00
3529	50c. General Jeb Stuart (vert)..............	1·00	1·00
3530	50c. General George Meade (vert).......	1·00	1·00
3531	50c. General Philip Sheridan (vert)......	1·00	1·00
3532	50c. General James Longstreet (vert).	1·00	1·00
3533	50c. General John Mosby (vert)...........	1·00	1·00
3504/33 Set of 30..		26·00	26·00
MS3534 Two sheets, each 105×76 mm. (a) $6 Confederate ironclad Merrimack attacking Cumberland (Federal sloop) (51×38 mm). P 13½×14. (b) $6 Monitor (Federal ironclad) Set of 2 sheets.....		13·00	14·00

Nos. 3504/21 and 3522/33 were each printed together, se-tenant, in sheetlets of 18 or 12, with enlarged top margins.

(Des D. Miller. Litho Questa)

2002 (6 Feb). Golden Jubilee (2nd issue). T **476** and similar square designs. Multicoloured. P 14½.
3535	$2 Type **476**...................................	2·50	2·50
	a. Sheetlet. Nos. 3535/8................	9·00	9·00
3536	$2 Queen Elizabeth at garden party...	2·50	2·50
3537	$2 Queen Elizabeth in evening dress..	2·50	2·50
3538	$2 Queen Elizabeth in cream coat.....	2·50	2·50
3535/8 Set of 4...		9·00	9·00
MS3539 76×108 mm. $6 Princesses Elizabeth and Margaret as bridesmaids......		4·50	5·00

Nos. 3535/8 were printed together, se-tenant, in sheetlets of 4, with an illustrated left margin.

ANTIGUA AND BARBUDA

477 U. S. Flag as Statue of Liberty and Antigua & Barbuda Flag

480 Community Players wearing Straw Hats

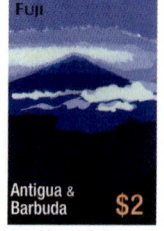

481 Mount Fuji, Japan

(Des M. Friedman. Litho Cartor)

2002 (11 Feb). "United We Stand". Support for Victims of 11 September 2001 Terrorist Attacks. P 13½.
3540	**477**	$2 multicoloured	1·25	1·40

No. 3540 was printed in sheetlets of 4, with an illustrated left margin.

478 Sir Vivian Richards waving Bat

479 Thick-billed Parrot

(Des M. Friedman. Litho Cartor)

2002 (7 Mar). 50th Birthday of Sir Vivian Richards (West Indian cricketer). T **478** and similar vert designs. Multicoloured. P 13½.

3541	25c. Type **478**	1·40	55
3542	30c. Sir Vivian Richards receiving presentation from Antigua Cricket Association	1·40	55
3543	50c. Sir Vivian Richards wearing sash	1·75	65
3544	75c. Sir Vivian Richards batting	2·00	90
3545	$1.50 Sir Vivian Richards and Lady Richards	3·25	3·50
3546	$1.80 Sir Vivian Richards with enlarged action photograph of himself	3·50	4·00
3541/6 *Set of 6*		12·00	9·00
MS3547 Two sheets, each 68×95 mm. (a) $6 Sir Vivian Richards with guard of honour. (b) $6 Sir Vivian Richards in Indian traditional dress *Set of 2 sheets*		16·00	16·00

(Des Jennifer Toombs. Litho Questa)

2002 (8 Apr). Flora and Fauna. T **479** and similar horiz designs. Multicoloured. P 14.

3548	50c. Type **479**	1·00	55
3549	75c. Lesser long-nosed bat	1·00	60
3550	90c. Quetzal	1·25	1·25
	a. Sheetlet. Nos. 3550/8	10·00	10·00
3551	90c. Two-toed sloth	1·25	1·25
3552	90c. Lovely cotinga	1·25	1·25
3553	90c. *Pseudolycaena marsyas* (butterfly)	1·25	1·25
3554	90c. Magenta-throated woodstar	1·25	1·25
3555	90c. *Automeris rubrescens* (moth)	1·25	1·25
3556	90c. *Bufo periglenes* (toad)	1·25	1·25
3557	90c. Collared peccary	1·25	1·25
3558	90c. Tamandua anteater	1·25	1·25
3559	$1 St. Lucia parrot	1·25	1·25
	a. Sheetlet. Nos. 3559/67	10·00	10·00
3560	$1 Cuban kite	1·25	1·25
3561	$1 West Indian whistling-duck	1·25	1·25
3562	$1 *Eurema amelia* (butterfly)	1·25	1·25
3563	$1 Scarlet ibis	1·25	1·25
3564	$1 Black-capped petrel	1·25	1·25
3565	$1 *Cnemidophorus vanzoi* (lizard)	1·25	1·25
3566	$1 Cuban solenodon	1·25	1·25
3567	$1 *Papilio thersites* (butterfly)	1·25	1·25
3568	$1.50 Montserrat oriole	2·00	2·00
3569	$1.80 *Leptotes perkinsae* (butterfly)	2·50	2·50
3548/69 *Set of 22*		26·00	26·00
MS3570 Two sheets, each 110×85 mm. (a) $6 Olive Ridley Turtle. (b) $6 Margay *Set of 2 sheets*		11·00	12·00

Nos. 3550/8 and 3559/67 were each printed together, *se-tenant*, in sheetlets of 9 with the backgrounds forming composite designs.

(Litho B.D.T.)

2002 (11 June). 50th Anniv of Community Players. T **480** and similar multicoloured designs showing scenes from various productions. P 13½.

3571	20c. Type **480**	35	30
3572	25c. Men in suits with women in long dresses	35	30
3573	30c. In *Pirates of Penzance*	40	30
3574	75c. Female choir	75	50
3575	90c. In Mexican dress	90	55
3576	$1.50 Members at a reception	1·25	1·50
3577	$1.80 Production in the open air	1·50	2·00
3571/7 *Set of 7*		5·00	5·00
MS3578 Two sheets, each 76×84 mm. (a) $4 Mrs. Edie Hill-Thibou. (former President) (*vert*). (b) $4 Miss Yvonne Maginley (Acting President and Director of Music) (*vert*). P 14 *Set of 2 sheets*		7·00	8·00

(Des Anna Singer. Litho Cartor)

2002 (15 July). International Year of Mountains. T **481** and similar vert designs. Multicoloured. P 13½.

3579	$2 Type **481**	1·50	1·50
	a. Sheetlet. Nos. 3579/81	4·00	4·00
3580	$2 Machu Picchu, Peru	1·50	1·50
3581	$2 The Matterhorn, Switzerland	1·50	1·50
3579/81 *Set of 3*		4·00	4·00

Nos. 3579/81 were printed together, *se-tenant*, in sheetlets of 3 with an enlarged illustrated top margin.

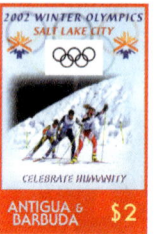

482 Cross-country Skiing

483 Amerigo Vespucci wearing Skullcap

(Litho Cartor)

2002 (15 July). Winter Olympic Games, Salt Lake City. T **482** and similar vert design. Multicoloured. P 13½.

3582	$2 Type **482**	1·75	2·00
3583	$2 Pairs figure skating	1·75	2·00
MS3584 84×114 mm. Nos. 3582/3		3·50	4·00

(Des H. Friedman. Litho Cartor)

2002 (15 July). 500th Anniv of Amerigo Vespucci's Third Voyage. T **483** and similar multicoloured designs. P 13½.

3585	$2.50 Type **483**	2·50	2·50
	a. Sheetlet. Nos. 3585/7	6·75	6·75
3586	$2.50 Vespucci as an old man	2·50	2·50
3587	$2.50 16th-century map	2·50	2·50
3585/7 *Set of 3*		6·75	6·75
MS3588 49×68 mm. $5 Vespucci holding dividers (*vert*)		4·50	5·00

Nos. 3585/7 were printed together, *se-tenant*, in sheetlets of 3 with an enlarged illustrated top margin.

484 *Spirit of St. Louis* and Charles Lindbergh (pilot)

ANTIGUA AND BARBUDA

(Des J. Iskowitz. Litho Cartor)

2002 (15 July). 75th Anniv of First Solo Transatlantic Flight. T **484** and similar horiz designs. Multicoloured. P 13½.

3589	$2.50 Type **484**	2·50	2·50
	a. Sheetlet. Nos. 3589/91	6·75	6·75
3590	$2.50 *Spirit of St. Louis* at Le Bourget, Paris, 1927	2·50	2·50
3591	$2.50 Charles Lindbergh in New York ticker-tape parade, 1927	2·50	2·50
3589/91	*Set of 3*	6·75	6·75
MS3592	80×110 mm. $6 Charles Lindbergh wearing flying helmet	4·50	5·00

Nos. 3589/91 were printed together, *se-tenant*, in sheetlets of 3 with an enlarged illustrated top margin.

485 Princess Diana

(Des M. Friedman. Litho B.D.T.)

2002 (29 July). 5th Death Anniv of Diana, Princess of Wales. T **485** and similar vert designs. Multicoloured. P 14.

3593	$1.80 Type **485**	1·40	1·40
	a. Sheetlet. Nos. 3593/8	7·50	7·50
3594	$1.80 Princess Diana in tiara (looking left)	1·40	1·40
3595	$1.80 Wearing hat	1·40	1·40
3596	$1.80 Princess Diana wearing pearl drop earrings and black dress	1·40	1·40
3597	$1.80 Wearing tiara (facing front)	1·40	1·40
3598	$1.80 Princess Diana wearing pearl drop earrings	1·40	1·40
3593/8	*Set of 6*	7·50	7·50
MS3599	91×106 mm. $6 Princess Diana	4·50	5·00

Nos. 3593/8 were printed together, *se-tenant*, in sheetlets of 6 with an enlarged illustrated right margin.

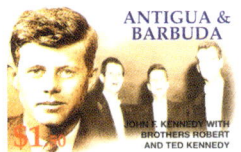

486 Kennedy Brothers

(Des J. Iskowitz. Litho B.D.T.)

2002 (29 July). Presidents John F. Kennedy and Ronald Reagan Commemoration. T **486** and similar multicoloured designs. P 14.

3600	$1.50 Type **486**	1·60	1·60
	a. Sheetlet. Nos. 3600/5	8·50	8·50
3601	$1.50 John Kennedy with Danny Kaye (American entertainer)	1·60	1·60
3602	$1.50 Delivering Cuban Blockade speech, 1962	1·60	1·60
3603	$1.50 With Jacqueline Kennedy	1·60	1·60
3604	$1.50 Meeting Bill Clinton (future president)	1·60	1·60
3605	$1.50 Family at John Kennedy's funeral	1·60	1·60
3606	$1.50 President and Mrs. Reagan with Pope John Paul II, 1982	1·60	1·60
	a. Sheetlet. Nos. 3606/11	8·50	8·50
3607	$1.50 As George Gipp in *Knute Rockne – All American*, 1940	1·60	1·60
3608	$1.50 With General Matthew Ridgeway, Bitburg Military Cemetery, Germany, 1985	1·60	1·60
3609	$1.50 With George. H. Bush and Secretary Mikhail Gorbachev of USSR., 1988	1·60	1·60
3610	$1.50 Presidents Reagan, Ford, Carter and Nixon at the White House, 1981	1·60	1·60
3611	$1.50 Horse riding with Queen Elizabeth, Windsor, 1982	1·60	1·60
3600/11	*Set of 12*	17·00	17·00
MS3612	Two sheets, each 88×122 mm. (a) $6 President Kennedy at press conference (*vert*). (b) $6 President Reagan (*vert*) *Set of 2 sheets*	11·00	12·00

Nos. 3600/5 (Kennedy) and 3606/11 (Reagan) were each printed together, *se-tenant*, in sheetlets of 6 showing further portraits in the enlarged illustrated right margins.

No. 3609 is inscribed "GORBACHOV" in error.

487 Red-billed Tropicbird

(Des Katie McConnachie. Litho B.D.T.)

2002 (12 Aug). Endangered Species of Antigua. T **487** and similar horiz designs. Multicoloured. P 14.

3613	$1.50 Type **487**	2·00	2·00
	a. Sheetlet. Nos. 3613/21	16·00	16·00
3614	$1.50 Brown pelican	2·00	2·00
3615	$1.50 Magnificent frigatebird	2·00	2·00
3616	$1.50 Ground lizard	2·00	2·00
3617	$1.50 West Indian whistling duck	2·00	2·00
3618	$1.50 Antiguan racer snake	2·00	2·00
3619	$1.50 Spiny lobster	2·00	2·00
3620	$1.50 Hawksbill turtle	2·00	2·00
3621	$1.50 Queen conch	2·00	2·00
3613/21	*Set of 9*	16·00	16·00

Nos. 3613/21 were printed together, *se-tenant*, in sheetlets of 9 with inscribed margins.

488 Elvis Presley **489** Cheerleader Teddy

(Litho Questa)

2002 (20 Aug). 25th Death Anniv of Elvis Presley (American entertainer). P 13½×14.

3622	**488**	$1 multicoloured	1·75	1·40

No. 3622 was printed in sheetlets of 9 with an enlarged left margin repeating the stamp design.

(Des Esther Ainspan. Litho Questa)

2002 (26 Aug). Centenary of the Teddy Bear. Girl Teddies. T **489** and similar vert designs. Multicoloured. P 13½×14.

3623	$2 Type **489**	1·25	1·40
	a. Sheetlet. Nos. 3623/6	4·50	5·00
3624	$2 Figure skater	1·25	1·40
3625	$2 Ballet dancer	1·25	1·40
3626	$2 Aerobics instructor	1·25	1·40
3623/6	*Set of 4*	4·50	5·00

Nos. 3623/6 were printed together, *se-tenant*, in sheetlets of 4 die-cut in the shape of a teddy bear.

490 "Croconaw No. 159" **491** Charlie Chaplin

(Litho Questa)

2002 (26 Aug). Pokémon (children's cartoon series). T **490** and similar vert designs. Multicoloured. P 13½×14.

3627	$1.50 Type **490**	90	90
	a. Sheetlet. Nos. 3627/32	4·75	4·75
3628	$1.50 "Mantine No. 226"	90	90
3629	$1.50 "Feraligatr No. 160"	90	90

95

3630	$1.50 "Qwilfish No. 211"		90	90
3631	$1.50 "Remoraid No. 223"		90	90
3632	$1.50 "Quagsire No. 195"		90	90
3627/32 Set of 6			4·75	4·75
MS3633 80×106 mm. $6 "Chinchou No. 170"			3·25	3·50

Nos. 3627/32 were printed together, *se-tenant*, in sheetlets of 6 with an enlarged illustrated top margin.

(Des Esther Ainspan. Litho B.D.T.)

2002 (16 Sept). 25th Death Anniv of Charlie Chaplin (British actor). T **491** and similar vert designs. Each black, bluish grey and brownish grey. P 14.

3634	$1.80 Type **491**	1·75	1·75
	a. Sheetlet. Nos. 3634/9	9·50	9·50
3635	$1.80 Wearing waistcoat and spotted bow-tie	1·75	1·75
3636	$1.80 In top hat	1·75	1·75
3637	$1.80 Wearing coat and bowler hat	1·75	1·75
3638	$1.80 Charlie Chaplin in old age	1·75	1·75
3639	$1.80 With finger on chin	1·75	1·75
3634/9 Set of 6		9·50	9·50
MS3640 90×105 mm. $6 Charlie Chaplin as The Tramp		4·50	4·75

Nos. 3634/9 were printed together, *se-tenant* in sheetlets of 6 with further portraits in the enlarged margins.

492 Bob Hope   **493** Lee Strasberg

(Des Esther Ainspan. Litho B.D.T.)

2002 (16 Sept). Bob Hope (American entertainer) Commemoration. T **492** and similar vert designs showing him entertaining American troops. Multicoloured. P 14.

3641	$1.50 Type **492**	1·50	1·50
	a. Sheetlet. Nos. 3641/6	8·00	8·00
3642	$1.50 Wearing bush hat, Vietnam, 1972	1·50	1·50
3643	$1.50 On board USS *John F. Kennedy* (aircraft carrier)	1·50	1·50
3644	$1.50 With hawk badge on sleeve, Berlin, 1948	1·50	1·50
3645	$1.50 Wearing desert fatigues	1·50	1·50
3646	$1.50 In white cap and stars on collar	1·50	1·50
3641/6 Set of 6		8·00	8·00

Nos. 3641/6 were printed together, *se-tenant*, in sheetlets of 6 with an enlarged illustrated left margin.

(Des Esther Ainspan. Litho B.D.T.)

2002 (16 Sept). 20th Death Anniv of Lee Strasberg (pioneer of "Method Acting"). P 14.

3647	**493** $1 black and stone	1·00	1·00

No. 3647 was printed in sheetlets of 9 with an enlarged right margin repeating the stamp design.

494 Marlene Dietrich   **495** Ferrari 801, 1957

(Des Esther Ainspan. Litho B.D.T.)

2002 (16 Sept). Tenth Death Anniv of Marlene Dietrich (actress and singer). T **494** and similar vert designs. Each black and grey. P 14.

3648	$1.50 Type **494**	90	90
	a. Sheetlet. Nos. 3648/53	4·75	4·75
3649	$1.50 Wearing top hat	90	90
3650	$1.50 In chiffon dress	90	90
3651	$1.50 Resting chin on left hand	90	90
3652	$1.50 In cloche hat	90	90
3653	$1.50 Wearing black evening gloves	90	90
3648/53 Set of 6		4·75	4·75
MS3654 83×108 mm. $6 Marlene Dietrich wearing chiffon scarf		3·25	3·75

Nos. 3648/53 were printed together, *se-tenant*, in sheetlets of 6 with an enlarged illustrated left margin.

(Litho B.D.T.)

2002 (14 Oct). Ferrari Racing Cars. T **495** and similar horiz designs. Multicoloured. P 14.

3655	20c. Type **495**	30	30
3656	25c. Ferrari 256, 1959	30	30
3657	30c. Ferrari 246 P, 1960	35	30
3658	90c. Ferrari 246, 1966	85	55
3659	$1 Ferrari 312 B2, 1971	95	70
3660	$1.50 Ferrari 312, 1969	1·40	1·40
3661	$2 Ferrari F310 B, 1997	1·75	2·00
3662	$4 Ferrari F2002, 2002	3·00	3·50
3655/62 Set of 8		8·00	8·00

496 Antigua & Barbuda Flag   **497** Juan Valeron (Spain)

(Litho B.D.T.)

2002 (31 Oct). 21st Anniv of Independence. T **496** and similar multicoloured designs. P 14.

3663	25c. Type **496**	50	35
3664	30c. Antigua & Barbuda coat of arms (*vert*)	50	35
3665	$1.50 Mount St. John's Hospital under construction	1·75	1·75
3666	$1.80 Parliament Building, St. John's	2·00	2·25
3663/6 Set of 4		4·25	4·25
MS3667 Two sheets, each 77×81 mm. (a) $6 Sir Vere Bird (Prime Minister 1967–94) (38×51 mm). (b) $6 Lester Bird (Prime Minister since 1994) (38×51 mm) Set of 2 sheets		10·00	11·00

(Litho Questa)

2002 (4 Nov). World Cup Football Championship, Japan and Korea. T **497** and similar vert designs. Multicoloured. P 13½.

3668	$1.65 Type **497**	1·00	1·00
	a. Sheetlet. Nos. 3668/73	6·00	6·00
3669	$1.65 Iker Casillas (Spain)	1·00	1·00
3670	$1.65 Fernando Hierro (Spain)	1·00	1·00
3671	$1.65 Gary Kelly (Ireland)	1·00	1·00
3672	$1.65 Damien Duff (Ireland)	1·00	1·00
3673	$1.65 Matt Holland (Ireland)	1·00	1·00
3674	$1.65 Pyo Lee (South Korea)	1·00	1·00
	a. Sheetlet. Nos. 3674/9	6·00	6·00
3675	$1.65 Ji Sung Park (South Korea)	1·00	1·00
3676	$1.65 Jung Hwan Ahn (South Korea)	1·00	1·00
3677	$1.65 Filippo Inzaghi (Italy)	1·00	1·00
3678	$1.65 Paolo Maldini (Italy)	1·00	1·00
3679	$1.65 Dammiano Tommasi (Italy)	1·00	1·00
3668/79 Set of 12		11·00	11·00
MS3680 Four sheets, each 82×82 mm. (a) $3 Jose Camacho (Spanish coach); $3 Raul Gonzales Blanco (Spain). (b) $3 Robbie Keane (Ireland); $3 Mick McCarthy (Irish coach). (c) $3 Guus Hiddink (South Korean coach); $3 Chul Sang Yoo (South Korea). (d) $3 Francesco Totti (Italy); $3 Giovanni Trapattoni (Italian coach) Set of 4 sheets		13·00	14·00

Nos. 3668/73 and 3674/9 were each printed together, *se-tenant*, in sheetlets of 6 with inscribed margins.

No. **MS**3680a is inscribed "Carlos Gamarra" in error.

498 "Coronation of the Virgin" (Domenico Ghirlandaio)

ANTIGUA AND BARBUDA

(Litho B.D.T.)

2002 (18 Nov). Christmas. Religious Paintings. T **498** and similar multicoloured designs. P 14.

3681	25c. Type **498**	40	20
3682	45c. "Adoration of the Magi" (detail) (D. Ghirlandaio)	60	25
3683	75c. "Annunciation" (Simone Martini) (*vert*)	1·00	45
3684	90c. "Adoration of the Magi" (different detail) (D. Ghirlandaio)	1·25	55
3685	$5 "Madonna and Child" (Giovanni Bellini)	5·00	6·00
3681/5 Set of 5		7·50	6·75
MS3686 76×110 mm $6 "Madonnna and Child" (S. Martini)		5·00	6·00

499 Antiguan Racer Snake Head

2002 (25 Nov). Endangered Species. Antiguan Racer Snake. T **499** and similar horiz designs. Multicoloured. Litho. P 14.

3687	$1 Type **499**	1·25	1·25
	a. Strip of 4. Nos. 3687/90	4·50	4·50
3688	$1 Coiled Antiguan racer snake with tail at right	1·25	1·25
3689	$1 Antiguan racer snake with pebbles and leaves	1·25	1·25
3690	$1 Coiled Antiguan racer snake with tail at left	1·25	1·25
3687/90 Set of 4		4·50	4·50

Nos. 3687/90 were printed together, *se-tenant* horizontally and vertically, in sheetlets of 16.

500 Magnificent Frigate Bird

501 Dr. Margaret O'garro

(Des Jennifer Toombs. Litho B.D.T.)

2002 (25 Nov). Fauna and Flora. T **500** and similar horiz designs. Multicoloured. P 14.

3691	$1.50 Type **500**	1·75	1·75
	a. Sheetlet. Nos. 3691/6	9·50	9·50
3692	$1.50 Sooty tern	1·75	1·75
3693	$1.50 Bananaquit	1·75	1·75
3694	$1.50 Yellow-crowned night heron	1·75	1·75
3695	$1.50 Greater flamingo	1·75	1·75
3696	$1.50 Belted kingfisher	1·75	1·75
3697	$1.50 Killer whale	1·75	1·75
	a. Sheetlet. Nos. 3697/702	9·50	9·50
3698	$1.50 Sperm whale	1·75	1·75
3699	$1.50 Minke whale	1·75	1·75
3700	$1.50 Blainville's beaked whale	1·75	1·75
3701	$1.50 Blue whale	1·75	1·75
3702	$1.50 Cuvier's beaked whale	1·75	1·75
3703	$1.80 *Epidendrum fragans*	1·75	1·75
	a. Sheetlet. Nos. 3703/8	9·50	9·50
3704	$1.80 *Dombeya wallichii*	1·75	1·75
3705	$1.80 *Tabebuia serratifolia*	1·75	1·75
3706	$1.80 *Cryptostegia grandiflora*	1·75	1·75
3707	$1.80 *Hylocereus undatus*	1·75	1·75
3708	$1.80 *Rodriguezia lanceolata*	1·75	1·75
3709	$1.80 *Diphthera festiva*	1·75	1·75
	a. Sheetlet. Nos. 3709/14	9·50	9·50
3710	$1.80 *Hypocrita dejanira*	1·75	1·75
3711	$1.80 *Eupseudosoma involutum*	1·75	1·75
3712	$1.80 *Composia credula*	1·75	1·75
3713	$1.80 *Citherania magnifica*	1·75	1·75
3714	$1.80 *Divana diva*	1·75	1·75
3691/714 Set of 24		38·00	38·00
MS3715 Four sheets, each 75×45 mm. (a) $5 Snowy egret. (b) $5 *Rothschildia orizaba* (moth). (c) $6 Humpback whale. (d) $6 *Ionopsis utricularioides* (flower) Set of 4 sheets		22·00	23·00

Nos. 3691/6 (birds), 3697/702 (whales), 3703/8 (moths) and 3709/14 (flowers) were each printed together, *se-tenant*, in sheetlets of 6 with the backgrounds forming composite designs.

2002 (2 Dec). Centenary of Pan American Health Organization. Health Professionals. T **501** and similar vert designs. Multicoloured. Litho. P 14.

3716	$1.50 Type **501**	1·40	1·40
	a. Sheetlet. Nos. 3716/18	3·75	3·75
3717	$1.50 Ineta Wallace (nurse)	1·40	1·40
3718	$1.50 Vincent Edwards (public health official)	1·40	1·40
3716/18 Set of 3		3·75	3·75

Nos. 3716/18 were printed together, *se-tenant*, as a sheetlet of three with an enlarged, inscribed top margin.

502 Antiguan Brownie

2002 (12 Dec). 20th World Scout Jamboree, Thailand. T **502** and similar designs, each slate-lilac and chestnut (Nos. 3719/21) or multicoloured (others). Litho. P 14.

3719	$3 Type **502**	3·00	3·00
	a. Sheetlet. Nos. 3719/21	8·00	8·00
3720	$3 Brownie with badge on cap	3·00	3·00
3721	$3 Brownie without badge on cap	3·00	3·00
3722	$3 Robert Baden-Powell on horseback, 1896 (*horiz*)	3·00	3·00
	a. Sheetlet. Nos. 3722/4	8·00	8·00
3723	$3 Ernest Thompson Seton (founder, Boy Scouts of America), 1910, and American scout badge (*horiz*)	3·00	3·00
3724	$3 First black scout troop, Virginia, 1928 (*horiz*)	3·00	3·00
3719/24 Set of 6		16·00	16·00
MS3725 Two sheets. (a) 80×113 mm. $6 Ernest Thompson Seton. (b) 110×83 mm. $6 Scout salute Set of 2 sheets		11·00	12·00

Nos. 3719/31 and 3722/4 were each printed together, *se-tenant*, in sheetlets of three with enlarged, illustrated top margins, the backgrounds of Nos. 3719/21 forming a composite design.

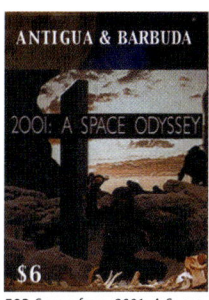

503 Scene from *2001: A Space Odyssey* (Arthur C. Clarke)

504 "Goat and Kids" (Liu Jiyou)

(Des J. Iskowitz. Litho Questa)

2002 (12 Dec). Famous Science Fiction Authors. Three sheets, each 150×108 mm, containing vert designs as T **503**. Multicoloured. P 13½.

MS3726 Three sheets. (a) $6 Type **503**. (b) $6 Scene from *The Monuments of Mars* (Richard C. Hoagland). (c) $6 Nostradamus with globe .... 13·00 14·00

(Des Yuan Lee. Litho Questa)

2003 (10 Feb). Chinese New Year ("Year of the Goat"). P 14.
3727 **504** $1.80 multicoloured .... 1·60 1·60

No. 3727 was printed in sheetlets of four with inscribed margins.

505 "Lucretia"

(Litho BDT)

2003 (30 Apr). 450th Death Anniv of Lucas Cranach the Elder (artist). T **505** and similar vert designs. Multicoloured. P 14.

3728	75c. Type **505**	75	55
3729	90c. "Venus and Cupid" (detail)	90	65
3730	$1 "Judith with the Head of Holofernes" (c. 1530)	1·00	1·00
3731	$1.50 "Portrait of a Young Lady" (detail)	1·25	1·75
3728/31	Set of 4	3·50	3·50
MS3732	152×188 mm. $2 "Portrait of the Wife of a Jurist"; $2 "Portrait of a Jurist"; $2 "Johannes Cuspinian"; $2 "Portrait of Anna Cuspinian"	4·75	5·50
MS3733	120×100 mm. $6 "Judith with the Head of Holofernes" (c. 1532)	4·75	5·50

506 "A High Class Maid training in a Samurai Household"

(Litho BDT)

2003 (30 Apr). Japanese Art of Taiso Yoshitoshi. T **506** and similar vert designs. Multicoloured. P 14.

3734	25c. Type **506**	35	20
3735	50c. "A Castle-Toppler known as a Keisei"	55	30
3736	$1 "Stylish Young Geisha battling a Snowstorm on her Way to Work"	90	65
3737	$5 "A Lady in Distress being treated with Moxa"	3·50	4·25
3734/7	Set of 4	4·75	4·75
MS3738	178×140 mm. $2 "A Lady of the Imperial Court wearing Four Layers of Robes"; $2 "Young Mother adoring her Infant Son"; $2 "Lady-in-Waiting looking amused over a Veranda in the Household of a Great Lord"; $2 A High Ranking Courtesan Known as an "Oiran", waiting for a Private Assignation"	5·50	6·50
MS3739	135×67 mm. $6 "A Girl teasing her Cat"	4·50	5·00

507 "Boats at Martigues"

(Litho BDT)

2003 (30 Apr). 50th Death Anniv of Raoul Dufy (artist). T **507** and similar multicoloured designs. P 14.

3740	90c. Type **507**	75	45
3741	$1 "Harvesting"	90	60
3742	$1.80 "Sailboats in the Port of Le Havre"	1·40	1·40
3743	$5 "The Big Bather" (vert)	4·00	4·50
3740/3	Set of 4	6·25	6·25
MS3744	173×124 mm. $2 "The Beach and the Pier at Trouville"; $2 "Port with Sailing Ships"; $2 "Black Cargo"; $2 "Nice, The Bay of Anges"	5·50	6·00
MS3745	Two sheets, each 95×76 mm. (a) $6 "Vence". (b) $6 "The Interior with an Open Window". Both imperf	8·50	9·50

508 Queen Elizabeth II at Trooping the Colour

509 Prince William

(Des R. Rundo. Litho)

2003 (14 May). 50th Anniv of Coronation. T **508** and similar vert designs. Multicoloured. P 14.

MS3746	155×93 mm. $3 Type **508**; $3 Queen wearing fawn beret with single feather; $3 Queen wearing feathered hat	8·50	9·00
MS3747	105×75 mm. $6 Princess Elizabeth	5·00	5·50

2003 (14 May). 21st Birthday of Prince William of Wales. T **509** and similar vert designs. Multicoloured. Litho. P 14.

MS3748	147×77 mm. $3 Type **509**; $3 Prince William wearing polo helmet; $3 Wearing blue T-shirt	8·00	8·50
MS3749	67×97 mm. $6 As teenager holding bouquet	4·75	5·00

510 Tamarind Tree, Parham

511 First Anglican Scout Troop, 1931

(Litho BDT)

2003 (19 May). Centenary of Salvation Army in Antigua. T **510** and similar multicoloured designs. P 14.

3750	30c. Type **510**	60	30
3751	90c. Salvation Army pre-school	1·25	55
3752	$1 Meals on wheels (horiz)	1·40	80
3753	$1.50 St. John Citadel band (horiz)	1·75	1·75
3754	$1.80 Salvation Army Citadel (horiz)	2·00	2·50
3750/4	Set of 5	6·25	5·50
MS3755	146×78 mm. $6 As Type **510** but without badge and centenary inscription	5·50	6·00

(Litho De La Rue)

2003 (9 June). 90th Anniv of Antigua and Barbuda Scouts Association. T **511** and similar multicoloured (except No. 3756) designs. P 14.

3756	30c. Type **511** (black and grey-brown)	50	30
3757	$1 National Scout Camp, 2002	1·25	80
3758	$1.50 Woodbadge Training Course, 2000 (horiz)	1·60	1·60
3759	$1.80 Visitors to National Camp, 1986 (horiz)	1·90	2·25
3756/9	Set of 4	4·75	4·50
MS3760	136×96 mm. 90c. Edris George; 90c. Theodore George; 90c. Edris James (all Deputy Commissioners)	3·00	3·25
MS3761	74×101 mm. $6 Scout leader demonstrating semaphore	5·00	5·50

ANTIGUA AND BARBUDA

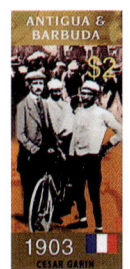

512 Cesar Garin (1903)

513 Frigate Bird and Emblem

2003 (9 June). Centenary of Tour de France Cycle Race. T **512** and similar vert designs showing past winners. Multicoloured. Litho. P 13½.
MS3762 160×100 mm. $2 Type **512**; $2 Caricature of Henri Cornet (1904); $2 Louis Trousselier (1905); $2 René Pottier (1906)		8·00	8·00
MS3763 160×100 mm. $2 Lucien Petit-Breton (1907); $2 Lucien Petit-Breton (1908); $2 François Faber (1909); $2 Octave Lapize (1910)		8·00	8·00
MS3764 160×100 mm. $2 Gustave Garrigou (1911); $2 Odile Defraye (1912); $2 Phillipe Thys (1913); $2 Philippe Thys (1914)		8·00	8·00
MS3765 Three sheets, each 100×70 mm. (a) $6 Henri Desgranges (editor of "L'Auto"). (b) $6 Pierre Giffard (editor of "Le Vélo"). (c) Le Compte de Dion (sponsor) *Set of 3 sheets*		13·00	14·00

(Litho Questa)

2003 (4 July). 30th Anniv of CARICOM. P 14.
3766	**513**	$1 multicoloured	1·25	1·00

514 Cadillac Eldorado Convertible (1955)

(Des T. Wood and R. Rundo. Litho BDT)

2003 (14 July). Centenary of General Motors Cadillac. T **514** and similar horiz designs. Multicoloured. P 13½.
MS3767 110×150 mm. $2 Type **514**; $2 Cadillac Series 60 (1937); $2 Cadillac Eldorado (1959); $2 Cadillac Eldorado (2002)		6·00	6·50
MS3768 102×76 mm. $6 Cadillac Eldorado (1953)		3·75	4·00

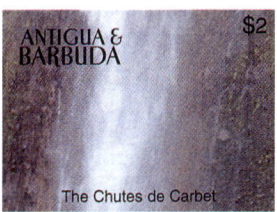

515 Chutes de Carbet Waterfall, Guadeloupe

2003 (14 July). International Year of Freshwater. T **515** and similar multicoloured designs. Litho. P 13½.
MS3769 94×180 mm. $2 Type **515**; $2 Foot of Chutes de Carbet waterfall; $2 Rapids at foot of Chutes de Carbet waterfall		4·50	4·75
MS3770 96×67 mm. $6 Waterfall, Ocho Rios, Jamaica (vert)		4·50	4·75

516 Corvette Convertible (1954)

2003 (14 July). 50th Anniv of General Motors Chevrolet Corvette. T **516** and similar horiz designs. Multicoloured. Litho. P 13½.
MS3771 110×151 mm. $2 Type **516**; $2 Corvette Sting Ray (1964); $2 Corvette Sting Ray Convertible (1964); $2 Corvette Convertible (1998)		6·00	6·50
MS3772 102×74 mm. $6 Corvette Convertible (1956)		3·75	4·00

517 *Flyer I* (first manned powered flight), 1903

2003 (28 July). Centenary of Powered Flight. T **517** and similar horiz designs. Multicoloured. Litho. P 14.
MS3773 176×106 mm. $2 Type **517**; $2 Paul Cornu's helicopter on first helicopter flight, 1907; $2 E. B. Ely's biplane making first landing on ship, 1911; $2 Curtiss A-1 (first seaplane), 1911		8·00	8·00
MS3774 176×106 mm. $2 Bell X-5 research aircraft with variable wings, 1951; $2 Convair XFY-1 vertical take-off and landing; $2 North American X-15 rocket aircraft, 1959; $2 Alexei Leonov on first spacewalk, 1965		8·00	8·00
MS3775 176×106 mm. $2 Concorde, 1969; $2 Martin X-24 Lifting Body Vehicle Pre-Space Shuttle, 1969; $2 Apollo-Soyuz, 1975; $2 Viking Robot Mars Expedition, 1976		8·00	8·00
MS3776 Three sheets, each 106×76 mm. (a) $6 Boeing Model 200 Monomail with retractable landing gear, 1930. (b) $6 Bell XS-1 rocket plane breaking sound barrier, 1947. (c) $6 Grumman X-29 with forward swept wings, 1984 *Set of 3 sheets*		13·00	14·00

(Litho BDT)

2003 (11 Aug). As Nos. 2067/81 but "ANTIGUA.BARBUDA" smaller (13½ mm long) and bird inscriptions in English only. Multicoloured. P 15×14.
3777	$5 *Montezuma oropendola*	4·50	5·00
3778	$10 *Green jay*	8·50	9·50

518 *Psychopsis papilio*

519 Bull Shark

2003 (12 Aug). Orchids. T **518** and similar multicoloured designs. Litho. P 13½.
MS3779 96×138 mm. $2.50 Type **518**; $2.50 *Amesiella philippinensis*; $2.50 *Maclellanara* "Pagan Dove Song"; $2.50 *Phalaenopsis* "Little Hal"		8·00	8·00
MS3780 205×124 mm. $2.50 *Daeliocattleya* "Amber Glow"; $2.50 *Hygrochilus parishii*; $2.50 *Dendrobium crystallinum*; $2.50 *Disa* hybrid (*all horiz*)		8·00	8·00
MS3781 98×68 mm. $5 *Cattleya deckeri* (*horiz*)		5·00	5·00

2003 (12 Aug). Sharks. T **519** and similar horiz designs. Multicoloured. Litho. P 13½.
MS3782 128×128 mm. $2 Type **519**; $2 Grey reef shark; $2 Black tip shark; $2 Leopard shark		8·00	8·00
MS3783 88×88 mm. $5 Great white shark		5·00	5·00

520 Esmeralda

ANTIGUA AND BARBUDA

2003 (12 Aug). Butterflies. T **520** and similar horiz designs. Multicoloured. Litho. P 13½.
MS3784 105×86 mm. $2 Type **520**; $2 Tiger pierid; $2 Blue night butterfly; $2 *Charaxes nobilis* .... 8·00 8·00
MS3785 205×132 mm. $2.50 Orange-barred sulphur; $2.50 Scarce bamboo page; $2.50 *Charaxes latona*; $2.50 Hewitson's blue hairstreak .... 8·00 8·00
MS3786 98×68 mm. $5 *Diaethia merdionalis* .... 5·00 5·00

521 Apes

522 "Madonna and Child" (detail) (Bartolommeo Vivarini)

(Des Irina Lyampe. Litho Cartor)

2003 (1 Sept). Centenary of Circus Clowns. T **521** and similar vert designs. Multicoloured. Litho. P 14.
MS3787 119×195 mm. $1.80 Type **521**; $1.80 Mo Lite; $1.80 Gigi; $1.80 "Buttons" M. C. Bride .... 4·75 5·50
MS3788 145×218 mm. $1.80 Chun Group; $1.80 Casselly Sisters (acrobats); $1.80 Oliver Groszer; $1.80 Keith Nelson (sword swallower) .... 4·75 5·50
No. **MS**3787 is cut in the shape of a clown on a bicycle and No. **MS**3788 in the shape of a circus elephant.

(Litho BDT)

2003 (10 Nov). Christmas. T **522** and similar vert designs. Multicoloured. P 14.

3789	25c. Type **522**	35	20
3790	30c. "Holy Family" (detail) (Pompeo Girolano Batoni)	35	20
3791	45c. "Madonna and Child" (detail) (Benozzo Gozzoli)	50	25
3792	50c. "Madonna and Child" (detail) (Benozzo Gozzoli), Calci Parish Church	50	30
3793	75c. "Madonna and Child giving Blessings" (Benozzo Gozzoli)	75	50
3794	90c. "Madonna and Child" (detail) (Master of the Female Half-Figures)	90	55
3795	$2.50 "The Benois Madonna" (detail) (da Vinci)	2·50	3·25
3789/95	Set of 7	5·25	4·75

MS3796 70×110 mm. $6 "The Virgin and Child with Angels" (Rosso Fiorentino) .... 5·50 6·00

523 Blue and Yellow Macaw ("Blue and Gold Macaw")

524 Diana Monkey

2003 (8 Dec). Birds. T **523** and similar multicoloured designs. Litho. P 13½.
MS3797 96×137 mm. $2.50 Type **523**; $2.50 Green-winged macaw; $2.50 Rainbow lory ("Green-naped Lorikeet"); $2.50 Lesser sulphur-crested cockatoo..... 8·50 8·50
MS3798 205×133 mm. $2.50 Chestnut-fronted macaw ("Severe Macaw"); $2.50 Blue-headed parrot; $2.50 Budgerigar; $2.50 Sun conure (*all horiz*) .... 8·50 8·50
MS3799 98×68 mm. $5 Waldrapp ("Bald Ibis") (*horiz*) .. 5·50 5·50

2004 (19 Jan). Chinese New Year ("Year of the Monkey"). T **524** and similar vert designs. Multicoloured. Litho. P 14.
MS3800 152×95 mm. $1.50 Type **524**; $1.50 Mandrill; $1.50 Lar gibbon; $1.50 Red howler monkey .... 4·50 4·75

525 Mountain Landscape

2004 (16 Feb). Hong Kong 2004 International Stamp Exhibition. Paintings by Ren Xiong. T **525** and similar vert designs. Multicoloured. Litho. P 13½.
MS3801 131×138 mm. $1.50 Type **525**; $1.50 "Myriad Bamboo in Misty Rain"; $1.50 Winter landscape; $1.50 House and tree .... 4·50 4·75
MS3802 170×137 mm. $1.50 "Myriad Sceptres worshipping Heaven"; $1.50 Misty mountain landscape; $1.50 Myriad cherry trees; $1.50 Mountain landscape with two streams; $1.50 "Myriad Valleys with competing Streams"; $1.50 Myriad lights .... 5·50 6·00
MS3803 74×153 mm. $2.50 Bird singing from flowering cherry branch; $2.50 Bird in maple tree ... 3·75 4·00
Nos. **MS**3801/2 show paintings from *The Ten Myriads* album and No. **MS**3803 paintings from *Album after the Poems of Yao Xie*.

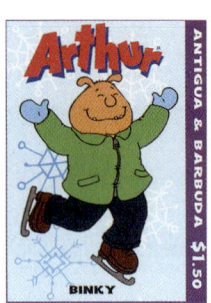

526 Binky skating

2004 (16 Feb). Arthur the Aardvark by Marc Brown (children's books and TV programme). T **526** and similar vert designs. Multicoloured. Litho. P 13½.
MS3804 150×183 mm. $1.50 Type **526**; $1.50 Buster skating; $1.50 Francine skating; $1.50 D.W.; $1.50 Sue Ellen; $1.50 Muffy skating .... 6·00 6·50
MS3805 150×183 mm. $1.80 Binky in baseball game; $1.80 Muffy with bat; $1.80 Francine running; $1.80 Buster catching ball .... 5·00 5·50
MS3806 150×183 mm. $2.50 Arthur hitting ball; $2.50 Sue Ellen with bat; $2.50 Binky holding bat; $2.50 Arthur with bat raised .... 5·00 5·50
No. **MS**3804 shows Arthur characters skating and **MS**3805/6 show them playing baseball.

527 "Freedom of Speech"

528 "Woman with a Flower"

2004 (8 Mar). 25th Death Anniv of Norman Rockwell (artist) (2003). T **527** and similar vert designs. Multicoloured. Litho. P 14.
MS3807 135×145 mm. $2 Type **527**; $2 "Freedom to Worship"; $2 "Freedom from Want"; $2 "Freedom from Fear" .... 6·00 6·50

MS3808 62×82 mm. $6 "Do Unto Others as you would have them Do Unto You". Imperf................... 6·00 6·50

No. **MS**3807 shows a series of posters and **MS**3808 a painting for Saturday Evening Post cover, 1961.

2004 (8 Mar). 30th Death Anniv of Pablo Picasso (artist). T **528** and similar vert designs. Multicoloured. P 14.

MS3809 177×127 mm. $2 Type **528**; $2 "Marie-Thérèse Seated"; $2 The Red Armchair (Marie-Thérèse Seated); $2 "The Dream (Marie-Thérèse) Seated".. 6·00 6·50

MS3810 58×69 mm. $5 "Bust of a Girl (Marie-Thérèse)". Imperf... 4·50 4·75

529 "The Smile of Flaming Wings, 1953"

(Litho BDT)

2004 (8 Mar). 20th Death Anniv of Joan Miró (artist). T **529** and similar multicoloured designs. P 14.

3811	75c. Type **529**..	70	45
3812	90c. "The Bird's Song in the Dew of the Moon, 1955"...	85	50
3813	$1 "Dancer II, 1957" (vert)...................	90	70
3814	$4 "Painting, 1954" (vert).....................	3·50	4·50
3811/14	Set of 4...	5·50	5·50

MS3815 Sheet 181×152 mm containing four different $2 designs, each entitled "Painting Based on a Collage, 1933".. 6·50 7·00

MS3816 Two sheets. (a) 102×83 mm. $5 "Bather, 1932". (b) 83×102 mm. $6 "Flame in Space and Nude Woman, 1932. Both imperf Set of 2 sheets....... 8·50 9·50

530 "Vaite Goupil"  **531** Felípe de Borbón and Letízia Ortíz

(Litho BDT)

2004 (8 Mar). Death Centenary of Paul Gauguin (2003) (artist). T **530** and similar multicoloured designs. P 14.

3817	25c. Type **530**..	40	25
3818	30c. "Autoportrait. Près du Golgotha"...............	40	25
3819	75c. "Le Moulin David À Pont-Aven" (horiz)..	85	60
3820	$2.50 "Moisson en Bretagne".........................	2·75	3·25
2817/20	Set of 4...	4·00	4·00

MS3821 77×62 mm. $4 "Cavaliers sur la Plage". Imperf.. 4·25 4·50

(Litho BDT)

2004 (21 May). Marriage of Crown Prince Felípe de Borbón and Letízia Ortíz. T **531** and similar multicoloured designs. P 13.

3822	30c. Type **531**..	40	25
3823	50c. Felípe de Borbón and Letízia Ortíz in gardens...	55	30
3824	75c. Letízia Ortíz..	80	55
3825	90c. Felípe de Borbón..................................	1·00	60
3826	$1 Felípe de Borbón and Letízia Ortíz wearing dark coats.................................	1·10	85
3827	$5 Felípe de Borbón and Letízia Ortíz at social function...	4·00	5·00
3822/7	Set of 6...	7·00	6·75

MS3828 190×174 mm. $1.80 Family photo; $1.80 Felípe de Borbón swearing allegiance to the Flag; $1.80 Felípe de Borbón with father and grandfather; $1.80 With King Juan Carlos I and Queen Sofia (horiz); $1.80 As No. 3824; $1.80 As No. 3825.. 9·00 10·00

MS3829 Six sheets, each 138×123 mm. (a) $5 Family photo. (b) $5 Felípe de Borbón with father and grandfather. (c) $5 Felípe de Borbón and Letízia Ortíz laughing. (d) $6 With King Juan Carlos I and Queen Sofia (horiz). (e) $6 Felípe de Borbón swearing allegiance to the Flag. (f) $6 Letízia Ortíz reading news Set of 6 sheets................................... 26·00 29·00

532 Dove carrying Olive Branch

2004 (17 June). United Nations International Year of Peace. Sheet 146×86 mm containing T **532** and similar horiz designs. Multicoloured. Litho. P 14.

MS3830 $3 Type **532**; $3 Dove with olive branch and globe; $3 Dove with olive branch and United Nations emblem.. 6·00 7·00

533 King Class 4-6-0

2004 (17 June). Bicentenary of Steam Locomotives. Six sheets containing T **533** and similar multicoloured designs. Litho. P 14.

MS3831 Three sheets. (a) 147×175 mm. $1 Type **533**; $1 Argentinian 11B Class 2-8-0; $1 Baldwin Mikado; $1 Track signal; $1 Signal block instrument; $1 Forders Sidings signal box; $1 Signal on line; $1 Signal in snow; $1 Interior of signal box; $1 Two light signals. (b) 147×176 mm. $1 Class 2-4-0T, Douglas-Port Erin line; $1 Class 4-8-2S, South African; $1 Class 2-8-2, China; $1 St. Pancras Station; $1 Ulverston Station; $1 Bolton Station; $1 Liverpool Street Station; $1 Cannon Street Station; $1 Malvern Station. (c) 146×177 mm. $1 Evening Star (horiz); $1 Indian Railways XC Pacific (horiz); $1 German Kreigslokomotive (horiz); $1 Bullied Light Pacific and Corfe Castle (horiz); $1 Copper cap chimney (horiz); $1 Tallylyn Railway (horiz); $1 Preservation volunteers (horiz); $1 Class Y7 0-4-0T (horiz); $1 Asmara Locoshed and Breda 0-4-0, Eritrea (horiz) Set of 3 sheets.. 26·00 28·00

MS3832 Three sheets, each 97×67 mm. (a) $5 Settle-Carlisle line (horiz). (b) $6 Lake Egridir (horiz). (c) $6 Douro Valley railway (horiz) Set of 3 sheets............ 16·00 17·00

534 Pope John Paul II and Mother Teresa

(Des Irina Lyamphe. Litho)

2004 (17 June). 25th Anniv of the Pontificate of Pope John Paul II. Sheet 162×152 mm containing T **534** and similar horiz designs. Multicoloured. P 14.

MS3833 $1.80 Type **534**; $1.80 At the Wailing Wall; $1.80 With Pres. George W. Bush; $1.80 Waving with left hand; $1.80 Waving with right hand........... 13·00 13·00

ANTIGUA AND BARBUDA

535 Poster of 1964 Olympic Games, Tokyo

536 Milan Galic (Yugoslav player)

(Litho BDT)

2004 (17 June). Olympic Games, Athens. T **535** and similar multicoloured designs. P 14.

3834	$1 Type **535**	1·00	60
3835	$1.65 Commemorative medal of 1964 Olympic Games, Tokyo	1·50	1·25
3836	$1.80 Fencing (*horiz*)	1·60	1·60
3837	$2 Pankration (wrestling, Greek art) (*horiz*)	1·75	2·25
3834/7	Set of 4	5·25	5·25

(Des M. Servin. Litho)

2004 (17 June). European Football Championship 2004, Portugal. Commemoration of First European Football Championship (1960). T **536** and similar multicoloured designs. P 14.

MS3838 147×86 mm. $2 Type **536**; $2 Slava Metreveli (USSR player); $2 Igor Netto (USSR player); $2 Parc des Princes stadium .... 6·50 7·00

MS3839 98×85 mm. $6 USSR football team, 1960 (50×37 *mm*) .... 4·50 4·75

537 Derrick Tysoe (Durham Light Infantry)

(Litho BDT)

2004 (26 July). 60th Anniv of D-Day Landings. T **537** and similar horiz designs. P 14.

3840	30c. multicoloured	50	30
3841	45c. multicoloured	65	30
3842	$1.50 multicoloured	1·75	1·75
3843	$3 multicoloured	3·00	3·75
3840/3	Set of 4	5·50	5·50

MS3844 Two sheets, each 177×107 mm. (a) $2 deep dull purple, dull mauve and black; $2 multicoloured; $2 deep reddish purple; $2 deep reddish-lilac and black. (b) $2 deep blue and black; $2 deep blue and black; $2 slate violet and black; $2 slate-violet and black *Set of 2 sheets* .... 17·00 17·00

MS3845 Two sheets, each 100×69 mm. (a) $6 dull purple and black. (b) $6 purple brown and black *Set of 2 sheets* .... 13·00 13·00

Designs:—No. 3840 Type **537**; No. 3841 Lt. Gen. Walter Bedell Smith; No. 3842 Les Perry, 1st Battalion, Suffolk Regiment; No. 3843 Major Gen. Percy Hobart; **MS**3844 (a) $2 Tiger II tank; $2 Kurt Meyer and tactics; $2 Canadian infantry; $2 British infantry; (b) $2 Hamilcar and Tetrarch tank; $2 Horsa Glider and soldiers; $2 Beachheads; $2 Soldiers and civilians; **MS**3845 (a) $6 Mulberry Harbour; (b) $6 Sherman tank Nos. 3840/3 were printed with accompanying *se-tenant* stamp-sized label at foot.

538 Queen Juliana

2004 (6 Sept). Queen Juliana of the Netherlands. Sheet, 170×180 mm, containing T **538** and similar horiz designs. Multicoloured. Litho. P 13½.

MS3846 $2 Type **538**; $2 With Prince Bernhard; $2 With Princess Beatrix; $2 With Princess Irene; $2 With Princess Margriet; $2 With Princess Christina ... 12·00 12·00

539 Mike Bibby

541 George Herman "Babe" Ruth

540 Zinedine Zidane (France)

2004 (8 Nov). National Basketball Association, China. Sheet, 204×140 mm, containing T **539** and similar vert designs. Multicoloured. Litho. P 12.

MS3847 $1.50 Type **539**; $1.50 Jim Jackson; $1.50 Tracy McGrady; $1.50 Chris Webber; $1.50 Peja Stojakovic; $1.50 Yao Ming .... 12·00 12·00

2004 (8 Nov). Centenary of FIFA (Fédération Internationale de Football Association). T **540** and similar horiz designs. Multicoloured. Litho. P 12½.

MS3848 193×97 mm. $2 Type **540**; $2 Roberto Baggio (Italy); $2 Franz Beckenbauer (Germany); $2 Ossie Ardiles (Argentina) .... 6·00 6·50

MS3849 108×87 mm. $6 Jimmy Greaves (England) ...... 5·00 5·50

2004 (22 Nov). Centenary of Baseball World Series. Sheet 127×118 mm containing T **541** and similar vert designs showing portraits of George Herman Ruth Jr ("Babe Ruth"). Multicoloured. Litho. P 14.

MS3850 $1.80,Type 541; $1.80 Wearing crown; $1.80 Wearing striped cap; $1.80 Holding baseball bat over shoulder .... 4·50 5·00

542 John Denver

543 "If you had wider shoulders–"

2004 (22 Nov). John Denver Commemoration. Sheet 117×107 mm containing T **542** and similar vert designs. Multicoloured. Litho. P 14.

MS3851 $1.50 Type **542**; $1.50 John Denver (wearing pale waistcoat); $1.50 Wearing dark waistcoat; $1.50 Facing left .... 4·50 4·75

2004 (22 Nov). The Family Circus (cartoon). T **543** and similar vert designs. Multicoloured. Litho. P 13½.

MS3852 115×176 mm. $2 Type **543**; $2 "Billy attacked me too hard!" (red border); $2 "Who tee-peed the mummies?"; $2 "Looking out there makes me realize its indeed the little things that count" .... 6·00 6·50

MS3853 115×176 mm. $2 "Billy attacked me too hard!" (purple border); $2 "His ears came from where his eyes are"; $2 "Tennessee!"; $2 "One candy, or one bowl?" .... 6·00 6·50
MS3854 176×115 mm. $2 "Someday I might travel to another planet, but I'm not sure why"; $2 "Adam and Eve were lucky. They didn't have any history to learn"; $2 "My backpack is too full. Will somebody help me to stand up?"; $2 "I tripped because one foot tried to hug the other foot" .... 6·00 6·50
MS3855 176×115 mm. $2 "If you don't put enough stamps on it the mailman will only take it part way"; $2 "Gee, Grandma, you have a lot of thoughts on your wall"; $2 "Shall I play for you, pa-rum-pa-rum-pummm–"; $2 "You have to do that when you're married" .... 6·00 6·50
MS3856 192×105 mm. $2 Billy; $2 Jeffy; $2 PJ; $2 Dolly. P 14½ .... 6·00 6·50

544 People holding Balloons forming AIDS Ribbon

(Litho BDT)

2004 (1 Dec). World AIDS Day. P 14.
3857 **544** $2 multicoloured .... 2·00 2·00

545 "Madonna in Floral Wreath" (Bruegel the Elder with Rubens)

546 Santa on Skis

2004 (6 Dec). Christmas. Multicoloured. P 12½×12.
*(a) Vert designs as T **545**.*
3858	20c. Type **545**	30	25
3859	25c. "Madonna and Child" (detail) (Mabuse (Jan Gossaert))	30	25
3860	$1 "Floral Wreath with Virgin and Child" (detail) (Daniel Seghers)	1·00	75
3861	$1.80 "Madonna and Child" (detail) (Andrea Mantegna)	1·75	2·00
3858/61 Set of 4		3·00	3·00

MS3862 70×100 mm. $6 "Madonna in a Floral Wreath" (Daniel Seghers) .... 5·50 6·00

*(b) Vert designs as T **546**.*
3863	30c. Type **546**	30	25
3864	45c. Santa ornament with arms raised	50	25
3865	50c. Santa on chimney	55	35
2863/5 Set of 3		1·25	75

547 American Pit (inscr "Pitt") Bull Terrier

548 Yellowtail Damselfish

2005 (23 May). Cats and Dogs. T **547** and similar multicoloured designs. Litho. P 13.
3866	30c. Type **547**	50	30
3867	75c. Golden Persian	90	50
3868	90c. Maltese (dog)	1·10	55
3869	$1 Calico Shorthair (cat)	1·25	80
3870	$1.50 Siamese	1·40	1·60
3871	$1.50 Rottweiler	1·40	1·60
3872	$3 Tabby Persian	2·75	3·50
3873	$3 Australian Terrier	2·75	3·50
3866/73 Set of 8		11·00	11·00

MS3874 Two sheets, each 100×70 mm. (a) $5 Turkish Cat. (b) $5 German Shepherd Dog (*horiz*) Set of 2 sheets .... 10·00 11·00

2005 (23 May). Tropical Sea Life. T **548** and similar horiz designs. Multicoloured. Litho. P 13.
MS3875 143×84 mm. $2 Type **548**; $2 French Angelfish; $2 Horseshoe Crab; $2 Emerald Mithrax Crab .... 8·00 8·00
MS3876 100×70 mm. $6 Spanish Hogfish .... 5·50 6·00
The stamps within No. **MS**3875 form a composite design of a coral reef.

549 Figure-of-eight Butterfly

2005 (23 May). Insects. T **549** and similar multicoloured designs. Litho. P 13.
MS3877 143×83 mm. $2 Type **549**; $2 Honey Bee; $2 Migratory Grasshopper; $2 Hercules Beetle .... 8·00 8·00
MS3878 100×70 mm. $5 Cramer's Mesene butterfly (*vert*) .... 5·00 5·50

550 Mammuthus imperator

2005 (23 May). Prehistoric Animals. T **550** and similar horiz designs. Multicoloured. Litho. P 13.
MS3879 Three sheets, each 140×110 mm. (a) $2 Mammuthus imperator; $2 Brontops; $2 Hyracotherium; $2 Propaleotherium. (b) $2.50 Ceratosaurs; $2.50 Coelurosaurs; $2.50 Ornitholestes; $2.50 Baryonyx. (c) $3 Plateosaurus; $3 Yangchuanosaurus; $3 Ceolophysis; $3 Lystrosaurus Set of 3 sheets .... 25·00 27·00
MS3880 Three sheets, each 98×70 mm. (a) $4 Triceratops. (b) $5 Stegosaurus. (c) $6 Coelodonta Set of 3 sheets .... 12·00 13·00
The stamps within Nos. **MS**3879a/c each form composite background designs.

551 Uruguay Team, 1930

2005 (15 June). 75th Anniv of First World Cup Football Championship, Uruguay. T **551** and similar horiz designs. Multicoloured. Litho. P 14½.
3881	$2.50 Type **551**	2·00	2·00
	a. Sheetlet. Nos. 3881/4	7·25	7·25
3882	$2.50 Hector Castro scoring goal against Argentina, World Cup final, 1930	2·00	2·00
3883	$2.50 Estadio Centenario	2·00	2·00
3884	$2.50 Hector Castro	2·00	2·00
3881/4 Set of 4		7·25	7·25

ANTIGUA AND BARBUDA

MS3885 111×86 mm. $6 Players after victory of Uruguay, 1930 .... 5·00 6·00
Nos. 3881/4 were printed together, *se-tenant*, in sheetlets of four stamps with enlarged illustrated top and right margins.

552 Bust of Von Schiller (C. L. Richter), Central Park, New York

553 *Misterio en la Isla de los Monstruos*, 1961

2005 (15 June). Death Bicentenary of Friedrich von Schiller (poet and dramatist). T **552** and similar horiz designs. Multicoloured. Litho. P 14.
3886	$3 Type **552**	2·50	2·50
	a. Sheetlet. Nos. 3886/8	6·75	6·75
3887	$3 Modern performance of *Kabale und Liebe*	2·50	2·50
3888	$3 Von Schiller's birthplace, Marbach, Germany	2·50	2·50
3886/8	*Set of 3*	6·75	6·75

MS3889 66×95 mm. $6 Von Schiller and statue, Lincoln Park, Chicago .... 4·75 5·50
Nos. 3886/8 were printed together, *se-tenant*, in sheetlets of three stamps with enlarged illustrated left margins.

2005 (15 June). Death Centenary of Jules Verne (writer). T **553** and similar multicoloured designs showing posters from films of Jules Verne's novels. Litho. P 14.
3890	$2 Type **553**	2·25	2·25
	a. Sheetlet. Nos. 3890/3	8·00	8·00
3891	$2 *Journey to the Centre of the Earth*, 1961	2·25	2·25
3892	$2 *From the Earth to the Moon*, 1956	2·25	2·25
3893	$2 *Los Diablos del Mar*, 1961	2·25	2·25
3890/3	*Set of 4*	8·00	8·00

MS3894 103×97 mm. $5 Michael Strogoff (56×41 mm) 5·00 5·00
Nos. 3890/3 were printed together, *se-tenant*, in sheetlets of four stamps with enlarged illustrated margins.

554 British attempting to Board Spanish Ship *Santisima Trinidad*

2005 (15 June). Bicentenary of the Battle of Trafalgar. T **554** and similar horiz designs. Multicoloured. Litho. P 14½.
3895	90c. Type **554**	1·75	1·00
3896	$1 Sailors clinging to wreckage and HMS *Royal Sovereign*, *Santa Ana*, HMS *Mars*, *Fouguex* and HMS *Temeraire*	2·00	1·25
3897	$1.50 HMS *Britannia* firing on crippled French *Bucentaure*	2·50	2·50
3898	$1.80 French *Redoubtable* and HMS *Victory*	3·00	3·50
3895/8	*Set of 4*	8·25	7·50

MS3899 90×122 mm. $6 Crew of HMS *Victory* firing during battle .... 8·00 8·00

555 Ronald Reagan

556 Defeated German Soldiers, Red Square, 9 May 1945

2005 (15 June). Ronald Reagan (US President 1981–9) Commemoration. Litho. P 14.
3900 **555** $1.50 multicoloured .... 1·25 1·50
No. 3900 was printed in sheetlets of six stamps with enlarged illustrated right margins.

2005 (15 June). 60th Anniv of Victory in Europe Day. T **556** and similar vert designs. Multicoloured. Litho. P 14.
3901	$1.50 Type	2·00	2·00
	a. Sheetlet. Nos. 3901/4	7·25	7·25
3902	$1.50 General Montgomery	2·00	2·00
3903	$1.50 Marshal Zhukov	2·00	2·00
3904	$1.50 General Bradley	2·00	2·00
3901/4	*Set of 4*	7·25	7·25

Nos. 3901/4 were printed together, *se-tenant*, in sheetlets of four stamps with enlarged illustrated top margins.

557 Churchill, Roosevelt and Stalin at Yalta Summit, 1945

2005 (15 June). 60th Anniv of Victory in Japan Day. T **557** and similar horiz designs. Multicoloured. Litho. P 14.
3905	$2 Type **557**	2·50	2·50
	a. Sheetlet. Nos. 3905/8	9·00	9·00
3906	$2 US troops raising flag on Mt. Suribachi	2·50	2·50
3907	$2 Gen. McArthur signing Japanese surrender documents	2·50	2·50
3908	$2 Surrendering Japanese officials, 2 September 1945	2·50	2·50
3095/8	*Set of 4*	9·00	9·00

Nos. 3905/8 were printed together, *se-tenant*, in sheetlets of four stamps with enlarged illustrated top margins.

558 "Mother Hen and her Brood" (Wang Ning)

2005 (15 June). Chinese New Year ("Year of the Rooster"). T **558** and similar horiz design. Multicoloured. Litho. P 14½.
3909 $1 Type **558** .... 1·25 1·25
MS3910 75×105 mm. $4 "Mother Hen and her Brood" (Wang Ning) .... 3·50 4·00
No. 3909 is printed in sheetlets of four stamps with an enlarged illustrated right margin. It depicts a portion of the painting and MS3910 shows the whole painting.

559 Dwight Howard, Orlando Magic

2005 (22 Aug). US National Basketball Association Players. T **559** and similar vert designs. Multicoloured. Litho. P 14.
3911	75c. Type **559**	1·25	90
3912	75c. Lucious Harris, Cleveland Cavaliers	1·25	90
3913	75c. Emeka Okafor, Charlotte Bobcats	1·25	90
3914	75c. Antonio McDyess, Detroit Pistons	1·25	90

3915	75c. Ray Allen, Seattle Supersonics		1·25	90
3911/15	Set of 5		5·50	4·00

Nos. 3911/15 were each printed in sheetlets of 12 stamps.

560 Pope John Paul II with Rabbi Meir Lau (Chief Rabbi of Israel, 1993–2003)

561 Italy 1979 World Rotary Congress Stamp

2005 (10 Oct). Pope John Paul II Commemoration. Litho. P 13½.
3916	560	$3 multicoloured	3·75	3·50

No. 3916 was printed in sheetlets of six stamps with enlarged illustrated right margins.

2005 (10 Oct). Centenary of Rotary International. T **561** and similar multicoloured designs. Litho. P 13½.
3917	$3 Type **561**	2·25	2·25
	a. Sheetlet. Nos. 3917/19	6·00	6·00
3918	$3 Paul Harris medallion and "Sow the Seeds of Love"	2·25	2·25
3919	$3 Paul Harris (founder), Tokyo, 1935	2·25	2·25
3917/19	Set of 3	6·00	6·00
MS3920	100×70 mm. $6 Young African children (horiz)	4·75	5·00

Nos. 3917/19 were printed together, se-tenant, in sheetlets of three stamps.

562 Albert Einstein

2005 (10 Oct). 50th Death Anniv of Albert Einstein (physicist). T **562** and similar horiz designs. Multicoloured. Litho. P 13½.
3921	$3 Type **562**	2·50	2·50
	a. Sheetlet. Nos. 3921/3	6·75	6·75
3922	$3 On bicycle	2·50	2·50
3923	$3 Albert Einstein (violet-grey background)	2·50	2·50
3921/3	Set of 3	6·75	6·75

Nos. 3921/3 were printed together, se-tenant, in sheetlets of three stamps with enlarged illustrated margins.

563 Hans Christian Andersen

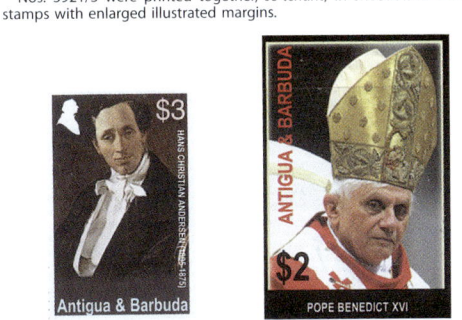

564 Pope Benedict XVI

2005 (10 Oct). Birth Bicentenary of Hans Christian Andersen (writer). T **563** and similar vert designs. Multicoloured. Litho. P 13½.
3924	$3 Type **563**	2·25	2·25
	a. Sheetlet. Nos. 3924/6	6·00	6·00
3925	$3 Statue in Central Park, New York	2·25	2·25
3926	$3 Tombstone	2·25	2·25
3924/6	Set of 3	6·00	6·00
MS3927	100×70 mm. $6 Hans Christian Andersen seated in chair	4·50	5·00

Nos. 3924/6 were printed together, se-tenant, in sheetlets of three stamps with enlarged illustrated margins.

2005 (21 Nov). Election of Pope Benedict XVI. Litho. P 14×13½.
3928	**564**	$2 multicoloured	2·50	2·50

No. 3928 was printed in sheetlets of four stamps with enlarged illustrated margins.

565 Gilbert's Memorial Methodist Church

2005 (19 Dec). Christmas. Churches. T **565** and similar multicoloured designs. Litho. P 13.
3929	25c. Type **565**	35	20
3930	30c. The People's Church, Barbuda	40	30
3931	30c. Tyrell's Roman Catholic Church	40	30
3932	45c. St. Barnabas Anglican Church	55	25
3933	50c. St. Peter's Anglican Church	60	35
3934	75c. Spring Gardens Moravian Church	75	75
3935	75c. St. Steven's Anglican Church	75	75
3936	90c. Pilgrim Holiness Church (vert)	90	90
3937	90c. Holy Family Catholic Cathedral	90	90
3938	$1 Ebenezer Methodist Church	1·00	1·00
3929/38	Set of 10	6·00	5·25
MS3939	Two sheets, each 100×70 mm. (a) $5 St. John's Cathedral. (b) $5 Service at Spring Gardens Moravian Church (vert) Set of 2 sheets	8·50	9·50

566 The Joiners Loft, Nelson's Dockyard

(Litho BDT)

2006 (9 Jan). National Parks of Antigua. T **566** and similar multicoloured designs. P 14.
3940	20c. Type **566**	30	30
3941	20c. Pay Office, Nelson's Dockyard (vert)	30	30
3942	30c. Bakery, Nelson's Dockyard	45	45
3943	30c. Admirals House Museum, Nelson's Dockyard	45	45
3944	75c. Devil's Bridge National Park	80	80
3945	75c. View from Shirley Heights Lookout, Nelson's Dockyard National Park	80	80
3946	90c. Green Castle Hill National Park	95	95
3947	90c. Fort Berkeley, Nelson's Dockyard National Park	95	95
3948	$1.50 Pigeon Point Beach, Nelson's Dockyard National Park	1·50	1·75
3949	$1.50 Half Moon Bay National Park	1·50	1·75
3950	$1.80 Cannon at Fort Berkeley	1·75	2·00
3940/50	Set of 11	8·75	9·50
MS3951	Two sheets. (a) 96×67 mm. $5 Frigate birds nesting at Codrington Lagoon National Park, Barbuda. (b) 65×96 mm. $5 Cannon and Admirals House Museum, Nelson's Dockyard (vert) Set of 2 sheets	10·00	11·00

567 Yellowstone National Park

2006 (9 Jan). National Parks of the USA. T **567** and similar horiz designs. Multicoloured. Litho. P 14½.
3952	$1.50 Type **567**	1·40	1·40
	a. Sheetlet. Nos. 3952/7	7·50	7·50
3953	$1.50 Olympic National Park	1·40	1·40
3954	$1.50 Glacier National Park	1·40	1·40
3955	$1.50 Grand Canyon National Park	1·40	1·40
3956	$1.50 Yosemite National Park	1·40	1·40

ANTIGUA AND BARBUDA

3957	$1.50 Great Smoky Mountains National Park..	1·40	1·40
3952/7 Set of 6		7·50	7·50
MS3958 95×70 mm. $6 Mount Rainier National Park (42×28 mm). P 14		4·75	5·50

Nos. 3952/7 were printed together, *se-tenant*, in sheetlets of six stamps with enlarged illustrated margins.

A $20 gold stamp with a multicoloured illustration was issued on 30 January 2006 for the 70th Birth Anniversary of Elvis Presley.

568 Bishop John Ephraim Knight

2006 (3 Apr). 250th Anniv of Moravian Church in Antigua. Moravian Church Antigua Conference. T **568** and similar multicoloured designs. Litho. P 13.

3959	30c. Type **568**	35	20
3960	$1 John Andrew Buckley (minister 1856–79)	1·00	85
3961	$1.50 Old Spring Gardens Moravian Church, 1854–1963 (*horiz*)	1·40	1·75
3959/61 Set of 3		2·50	2·50

MS3962 Three sheets, each 95×60 mm. (a) $5 Westerby Memorial, St. John's. (b) $5 Sandbox Tree (site of beginnings of antigua Moravian Church). (c) $5 Spring Gardens Teachers College, 1854–1958 (*horiz*) Set of 3 sheets................ 12·00 13·00

569 Princess Elizabeth  **570** Marilyn Monroe

2006 (10 Apr). 80th Birthday of Queen Elizabeth II. T **569** and similar vert designs. Multicoloured. Litho. P 13½.

3963	$2 Type **569**	2·25	2·25
	a. Sheetlet. Nos. 3963/6	8·00	8·00
3964	$2 Princess Elizabeth wearing cream dress and pearl necklace	2·25	2·25
3965	$2 Princess Elizabeth wearing white blouse	2·25	2·25
3966	$2 Queen Elizabeth II wearing diadem and red dress	2·25	2·25
3963/6 Set of 4		8·00	8·00

MS3967 120×120 mm. $6 Queen Elizabeth II wearing diadem and drop earrings.................. 6·00 6·00

Nos. 3963/6 were printed together, *se-tenant*, in sheetlets of four stamps with enlarged illustrated left margins.

2006 (10 Apr). 80th Birth Anniv of Marilyn Monroe (actress). Litho. P 13½.

3968	**570**	$3 multicoloured	2·50	2·50

No. 3968 was printed in sheetlets of four stamps with enlarged illustrated margins.

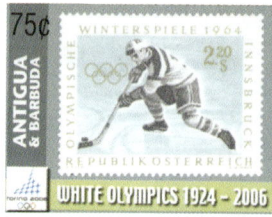

571 Austria 1964 Winter Olympics 2s.20 Ice Hockey Stamp

(Litho BDT)

2006 (11 May). Winter Olympic Games, Turin. T **571** and similar multicoloured designs. P 14½.

3969	75c. Type **570**	75	65
3970	75c. Poster for Winter Olympic Games, Sapporo, 1972 (*vert*)	75	65
3971	90c. Japan 1972 Winter Olympics 20y. skiing stamp (*vert*)	85	65
3972	90c. Austria 1964 Winter Olympics 1s.80, Figure skating stamp	85	65
3973	$2 Austria 1964 Winter Olympics 4s. Bobsleighing stamp	1·75	2·00
3974	$3 Poster for Winter Olympic Games, Innsbruck, 1964 (*vert*)	2·75	3·25
3969/74 Set of 6		7·00	7·00

572 Benjamin Franklin  **573** Mozart's Viola

2006 (29 May). Washington 2006 International Stamp Exhibition. T **572** and similar multicoloured designs showing Benjamin Franklin. Litho. P 11½ or imperf.

MS3975 Two sheets, each 140×152 mm. (a) $3×4 Type **572**; Wearing red in oval portrait in gold frame (84×93 *mm*) (imperf); USA 1847 5c. stamp; Close-up portrait. (b) $3×3 Round portraits in gold frames: Wearing red; Sitting at desk; In close-up Set of 2 sheets.................. 17·00 19·00

The imperf stamp has a red printed stamp frame with red printed "perforations" on the vertical sides.

2006 (3 July). 250th Birth Anniv of Wolfgang Amadeus Mozart (composer). T **573** and similar vert designs. Multicoloured. Litho. P 13.

3976	$3 Type **573**	3·50	3·00
	a. Sheetlet. Nos. 3976/9	12·50	11·00
3977	$3 Mozart aged eleven	3·50	3·00
3978	$3 Young Mozart	3·50	3·00
3979	$3 Mozart in Verona, 1770	3·50	3·00
3976/9 Set of 4		12·50	11·00

Nos. 3976/9 were printed together, *se-tenant*, in sheetlets of four stamps with enlarged illustrated right margins.

574 Elvis Presley in *Charro!*  **575** Leaders after Garbage Collection Race, 2002

2006 (12 July). 50th Anniv of Elvis Presley's Film Debut. Sheet 190×127 mm containing T **574** and similar vert designs showing film posters. Multicoloured. Litho. P 13½.

3980	$3 Type **574**	2·50	2·50
	a. Sheetlet. Nos. 3980/3	9·00	9·00
3981	$3 Follow That Dream	2·50	2·50
3982	$3 G I Blues	2·50	2·50
3983	$3 Blue Hawaii	2·50	2·50
3980/3 Set of 4		9·00	9·00

Nos. 3980/3 were printed together, *se-tenant*, in sheetlets of four stamps.

2006 (17 July). 75th Anniv of Antigua and Barbuda Girl Guides. T **575** and similar multicoloured designs. Litho. P 13.

3984	25c. Type **575**	35	20
3985	30c. Girl guides colour party (*horiz*)	35	20
3986	45c. Uniformed and non-uniformed members.	55	25
3987	50c. Girl guides marching band (*horiz*)	60	30

3988	$1 Leeward Islands leaders training camp, 1946 (*horiz*)	1·00	1·25
3984/8	Set of 5	2·50	2·00
MS3989	Three sheets, each 100×70 mm. (a) $5 Enrolment ceremony, 2006 (*horiz*). (b) $5 Girl guides gathering at Fort James, 1935 (*horiz*). (c) $5 Lisa Simon, Assistant Commissioner *Set of 3 sheets*	12·00	13·00

576 HS-748 Hawker Siddely Avro

2006 (2 Oct). 50th Anniv of LIAT (Leeward Islands Air Transport) Airline. T **576** and similar multicoloured designs. Litho. P 14.

3990	30c. Type **576**	50	25
3991	50c. BN2 Islanders on ground	70	70
3992	50c. BN2 Norman Islander	70	70
3993	50c. Beechcraft Twin Bonanza (*vert*)	70	70
3994	$1.50 BAC111-orange and HS748-pink/lilac on ground	2·00	2·00
3995	$2.50 Present brand DH8-300 51 seater de Havilland on ground	3·25	3·50
3990/5	Set of 6	7·00	7·00
MS3996	70×100 mm. $5 Sir Frank Delisle (founder) and first Beechcraft Twin Bonanza N9614R (*vert*)	5·50	6·00

577 Magnificent Frigate Bird

2006 (30 Oct). 25th Anniv of Independence. T **577** and similar horiz designs. Multicoloured. Litho. P 13.

3997	25c. Type **577**	50	50
	a. Sheetlet. Nos. 3997/4000	1·75	1·75
3998	25c. Fallow deer hinds	50	50
3999	25c. Fallow deer stag on beach	50	50
4000	25c. Magnificent frigate birds in flight and on nest	50	50
4001	30c. Pineapple	50	20
4002	$1 National flag	1·50	1·00
4003	$1.50 Coat of Arms	1·75	2·00
3997/4003	Set of 7	4·75	4·75
MS4004	100×70 mm. $5 New Parliament building (38×49 *mm*). P 12	4·50	5·00

Nos. 3997/4000 were printed together, *se-tenant*, in sheetlets of four stamps with enlarged illustrated margins.

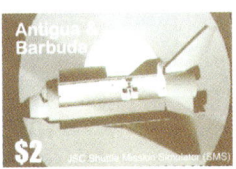

578 JSC Shuttle Mission Simulator (SMS)

579 Dalai Lama (Tibetan leader)

2006 (15 Nov). Space Anniversaries. T **578** and similar horiz designs. Multicoloured. Litho. P 13.

(a) 25th Anniv of First Flight of Space Shuttle Columbia.

4005	$2 Type **578**	2·25	2·25
	a. Sheetlet. Nos. 4005/10	12·00	12·00
4006	$2 STS-1 prime crew during classroom session	2·25	2·25
4007	$2 STS-1 *Columbia* on launch pad	2·25	2·25
4008	$2 STS-1 *Columbia* blast-off	2·25	2·25
4009	$2 Pre-touchdown landing of *Columbia* at Edwards AFB, California	2·25	2·25
4010	$2 Space shuttle *Columbia* landing at Edwards Air Force Base	2·25	2·25
4005/10	Set of 6	12·00	12·00

Nos. 4005/10, 4011/14 and 4015/18 were each printed together, *se-tenant*, in sheetlets of six or four stamps.

(b) 40th Anniv of Luna 9 Moon Landing

4011	$3 Molniya 8K78M rocket on launch vehicle	3·00	3·00
	a. Sheetlet. Nos. 4011/14	11·00	11·00
4012	$3 Luna 9 flight apparatus	3·00	3·00
4013	$3 Image of Moon's surface transmitted by Luna 9	3·00	3·00
4014	$3 Luna 9 capsule	3·00	3·00
4011/14	Set of 4	11·00	11·00

(c) 30th Anniv (2005) of Apollo-Soyuz Test Project

4015	$3 Apollo crew boarding transfer van	3·00	3·00
	a. Sheetlet. Nos. 4015/18	11·00	11·00
4016	$3 Handshake after Apollo-Soyuz linkup	3·00	3·00
4017	$3 Display of ASTP commemorative plaque	3·00	3·00
4018	$3 Recovery of ASTP Apollo command module	3·00	3·00
4015/18	Set of 4	11·00	11·00
MS4019	Three sheets, each 100×70 mm. (a) $6 Calipso satellite. (b) $6 SS *Atlantis* docking on Space Station MIR. (c) $6 Artist's concept of a NASA spaceship to orbit the Moon *Set of 3 sheets*	16·00	16·00

2006 (20 Nov). Civil Rights. T **579** and similar square designs. Multicoloured. Litho. P 12½ (Nos. 4024/6) or 12 (others).

4020	$2 Type **579**	2·75	2·75
	a. Horiz strip of 4. Nos. 4020/3	10·00	10·00
4021	$2 Abraham Lincoln (slavery abolitionist)	2·75	2·75
4022	$2 Susan Anthony (women's suffragist)	2·75	2·75
4023	$2 Harriet Tubman (slave liberator)	2·75	2·75
4024	$2 Mahatma Gandhi (Indian leader)	2·75	2·75
	a. Sheetlet. Nos. 4024/6	7·50	7·50
4025	$2 Nelson Mandela (anti-apartheid leader)	2·75	2·75
4026	$2 Rosa Parks (civil rights activist)	2·75	2·75
4020/6	Set of 7	17·00	17·00
MS4027	70×100 mm. $5 Martin Luther King (civil rights leader)	4·50	5·00

Nos. 4020/3 were printed together, *se-tenant*, in horizontal strips of four stamps throughout the sheet. Nos. 4024/6 were printed together, *se-tenant*, in sheetlets of three stamps.

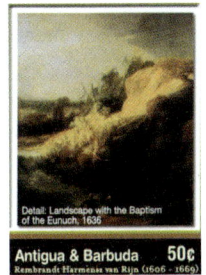

580 "Landscape with the Baptism of the Eunuch" (detail)

581 Bauble

2006 (18 Dec). 400th Birth Anniv of Rembrandt Harmenszoon van Rijn (artist). T **580** and similar vert designs. Multicoloured. Litho. P 12 (Nos. 4028/31) or 13½ (4032/9).

4028	50c. Type **580**	60	30
4029	75c. "Landscape with a Coach" (detail)	1·00	55
4030	$1 "River Landscape with Ruins" (detail)	1·10	80
4031	$2 "Landscape with a Castle" (detail)	1·75	1·75
4032	$2 "Samson Posing the Riddle to the Wedding Guests" (detail, Samson's bride)	1·75	1·75
	a. Sheetlet. Nos. 4032/5	6·25	6·25
4033	$2 "Samson Posing the Riddle to the Wedding Guests" (detail, two men)	1·75	1·75
4034	$2 "Samson Posing the Riddle to the Wedding Guests" (detail, two guests listening)	1·75	1·75
4035	$2 "Samson Posing the Riddle to the Wedding Guests" (detail, woman)	1·75	1·75
4036	$2 "The Holy Family (detail, man sitting at table)	1·75	1·75
	a. Sheetlet. Nos. 4036/9	6·25	6·25
4037	$2 "The Good Samaritan arriving at the Inn" (detail)	1·75	1·75
4038	$2 "Rebecca Taking Leave of her Family" (detail)	1·75	1·75
4039	$2 "The Holy Family" (detail, man sitting)	1·75	1·75
4028/39	Set of 12	16·00	16·00
MS4040	Two sheets, each 70×100 mm. (a) $5 "Self-Portrait". (b) $5 "Rembrandt's Mother". Both imperf *Set of 2 sheets*	8·00	9·00

Nos. 4032/5 and 4036/9 were each printed together, *se-tenant*, in sheetlets of four stamps.

ANTIGUA AND BARBUDA

2006 (23 Dec). Christmas. T **581** and similar vert designs. Multicoloured. Litho. P 13½.

4041	30c. Type **581**	40	20
4042	90c. Gold star	1·10	55
4043	$1 Red bell	1·25	75
4044	$1.50 Miniature tree	1·75	2·00
4041/4	Set of 4	4·00	3·25
MS4045	100×150 mm. $2×4 As Nos. 4041/4	8·00	9·00
MS4046	100×70 mm. $6 Santa on beach with wrapped presents	4·75	5·00

Nos. 4041/5 show Christmas tree decorations. Stamps from **MS**4045 are in similar designs to Nos. 4041/4 but have the country inscription at top and no coloured panel at the foot of the stamp.

The background of **MS**4045 forms a composite design showing a decorated Christmas tree.

582 Betty Boop

2006 (30 Dec). Betty Boop. T **582** and similar multicoloured designs. Litho. P 14.

4047	$1.50 Type	1·00	1·00
	a. Sheetlet. Nos. 4047/52	6·00	6·00
4048	$1.50 Leaning forward	1·00	1·00
4049	$1.50 Holding mirror	1·00	1·00
4050	$1.50 Holding microphone	1·00	1·00
4051	$1.50 Seated, looking over shoulder	1·00	1·00
4052	$1.50 Wearing red heart garter	1·00	1·00
4047/52	Set of 6	6·00	6·00
MS4053	70×100 mm. $3 "BETTY BOOP"; $3 With yellow fur stole	3·50	4·00

Nos. 4047/52 were printed together, *se-tenant*, in sheetlets of six stamps with enlarged illustrated margins.

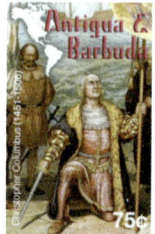

583 Columbus landing in New World

2007 (15 Jan). 500th Death Anniv of Christopher Columbus. T **583** and similar vert designs. Multicoloured. Litho. P 13½.

4054	75c. Type **583**	1·00	60
4055	90c. Christopher Columbus	1·10	65
4056	$2 Columbus (portrait in oval frame)	2·00	2·00
4057	$3 Columbus (in profile)	2·75	3·25
4054/7	Set of 4	6·00	6·00
MS4058	100×70 mm. $6 *Nina*, *Pinta* and *Santa Maria*	5·50	6·00

584 National Flags forming Knot

2007 (18 Jan). Centenary of World Scout Movement. T **584** and similar horiz design. Multicoloured. Litho. P 13½.

4059	$4 Type **584**	4·00	4·25
MS4060	110×80 mm. $6 National flags forming knot	5·50	6·00

No. 4059 is printed in sheetlets of three stamps with enlarged illustrated left margins.

585 Ensign Kennedy    **586** *Alamanda*

2007 (18 Jan). 90th Birth Anniv of John F. Kennedy (president of USA 1960–3). T **585** and similar vert designs. Multicoloured. Litho. P 13½.

4061	$3 Type **585**	2·50	2·50
	a. Sheetlet. Nos. 4061/4	9·00	9·00
4062	$3 Kennedy and crew	2·50	2·50
4063	$3 Kennedy at the USS *PT-109*	2·50	2·50
4064	$3 Kennedy in the South Pacific	2·50	2·50
4065	$3 Campaigning on crutches	2·50	2·50
	a. Sheetlet. Nos. 4065/8	9·00	9·00
4066	$3 "The New Congressman"	2·50	2·50
4067	$3 John F Fitzgerald, Joseph Kennedy and John F. Kennedy	2·50	2·50
4068	$3 "Celebrating Victory"	2·50	2·50
4061/8	Set of 8	18·00	18·00

Nos. 4061/4 (showing John Kennedy in the Navy, 1941–5) and 4065/8 (showing his election to the House of Representatives, 1947–53) were each printed together, *se-tenant*, in sheetlets of four stamps with enlarged illustrated left margins.

2007 (2 Apr). Flowers. T **586** and similar multicoloured designs. Litho. P 14½×14 (vert) or 14×14½ (horiz).

4069	75c. Type **586**	90	50
4070	90c. *Bidens sulphurea*	1·00	50
4071	$1 *Alstroemeria caryophyllacea*	1·10	80
4072	$2 *Canna limbata* (horiz)	2·00	2·00
	a. Sheetlet. Nos. 4072/5	7·00	7·00
4073	$2 *Gazania rigens* (horiz)	2·00	2·00
4074	$2 *Gloriosa rothschildiana* (horiz)	2·00	2·00
4075	$2 *Hibiscus sinensis* (horiz)	2·00	2·00
4076	$4 *Bougainvillea*	3·50	4·00
4069/76	Set of 8	13·00	12·50
MS4077	100×70 mm. $6 *Caesalpinia pulcherrima*	5·50	6·00

Nos. 4072/5 were printed together, *se-tenant*, in sheetlets of four stamps with enlarged illustrated margins.

587 *Callicore maimuna* (figure-of-eight butterfly)    **588** *Cantharellus cibarius*

2007 (2 Apr). Butterflies of the Caribbean. T **587** and similar vert designs. Multicoloured. Litho. P 14½×14.

4078	75c. Type **587**	1·00	60
4079	90c. *Dismorphia amphione* (tiger pierid)	1·25	65
4080	$1 *Eryphanis polyxena* (purple mort bleu)	1·40	90
4081	$4 *Colobura dirce* (mosaic butterfly)	4·75	5·50
4078/81	Set of 4	7·50	7·00
MS4082	130×108 mm. $2×4 Type **588**; *Actinote pellenea* (small lacewing); *Anteos clorinde* (clorinde); *Morpho peleides* (common morpho); *Anartia jatrophae* (white peacock)	8·00	8·00
MS4083	70×99 mm. $5 *Catonephele numilia* (Grecian shoemaker)	5·00	5·00

The stamps and margins of No. **MS**4082 form a composite design of palm tree foliage.

2007 (2 Apr). Mushrooms of the Caribbean. T **588** and similar vert designs. Multicoloured. Litho. P 14.

MS4084	131×108 mm. $2×4 Type **588**; *Auricularia auricula-judae*; *Mycena acicula*; *Peziza vesiculosa*	8·00	8·00
MS4085	100×70 mm. $6 *Pleurotus djamor*	6·00	6·00

The stamps and margins of No. **MS**4084 form a composite design.

ANTIGUA AND BARBUDA

589 Oncidium flexuosum

590 Kenneth Benjamin

2007 (2 Apr). Orchids. T **589** and similar multicoloured designs. Litho. P 14×14½ (horiz) or 14½×14 (vert).

4086	$3 Type **589**	3·00	3·00
	a. Sheetlet. Nos. 4086/9	11·00	11·00
4087	$3 Paphiopedilum Pinocchio	3·00	3·00
4088	$3 Cattleyopsis lindenii	3·00	3·00
4089	$3 Cattleyopsis cubensis	3·00	3·00
4086/9	Set of 4	11·00	11·00
MS4090	100×70 mm. $6 Osmoglossum pulchellum (vert)	6·00	6·00

Nos. 4086/9 were printed together, *se-tenant*, in sheetlets of four stamps with enlarged illustrated margins.

2007 (5 Apr). World Cup Cricket, West Indies. Famous West Indian Cricketers. T **590** and similar vert designs. Multicoloured. Litho. P 13.

4091	25c. Type **590**	50	30
4092	30c. Anderson Roberts	50	30
4093	90c. Ridley Jacobs	1·25	60
4094	$1 Curtly Ambrose	1·40	1·00
4095	$1.50 Richard (Richie) Richardson	2·25	2·50
4091/6	Set of 5	5·40	4·25
MS4096	117×90 mm. $5 Sir Vivian Richards	7·00	7·00

591 Princess Elizabeth and Duke of Edinburgh

2007 (1 May). Diamond Wedding of Queen Elizabeth II and Duke of Edinburgh. T **591** and similar horiz design. Multicoloured. Litho. P 14.

4097	$1.50 Type **591**	1·50	1·50
	a. Sheetlet. Nos. 4097/8, each ×3	8·00	8·00
4098	$1.50 Wedding shoes	1·50	1·50
MS4099	101×70 mm. $6 On wedding day with family (vert)	5·50	6·00

Nos. 4097/8 were printed together, *se-tenant*, in sheetlets of six stamps with enlarged illustrated margins, containing three of each design.

592 Camellias and Butterfly

2007 (1 May). 50th Death Anniv of Qi Baishi (artist). Paintings on Fans. T **592** and similar multicoloured designs. Litho. P 14½.

4100	$1.50 Type **592**	1·25	1·25
	a. Sheetlet. Nos. 4100/5	6·75	6·75
4101	$1.50 Two shrimps and arrowhead leaves	1·25	1·25
4102	$1.50 Gourd and ladybug	1·25	1·25
4103	$1.50 Bird	1·25	1·25
4104	$1.50 Landscape	1·25	1·25
4105	$1.50 Five shrimps	1·25	1·25
4100/5	Set of 6	6·75	6·75
MS4106	(a) 102×72 mm. $3 Chrysanthemums; $3 Maple leaves (*both vert*). (b) 72×102 mm. $6 Wisteria (*vert*)	10·00	12·00

Nos. 4100/5 were printed together, *se-tenant*, in sheetlets of six stamps with enlarged illustrated margins.

593 Ferrari 365 GTS4, 1969

2007 (4 June). Ferrari Classic Cars. T **593** and similar horiz designs. Multicoloured. Litho. P 13½.

4107	$1.40 Type **593**	1·10	1·10
	a. Sheetlet. Nos. 4107/14	8·00	8·00
4108	$1.40 Superamerica, 2005	1·10	1·10
4109	$1.40 F1 90, 1990	1·10	1·10
4110	$1.40 400 Automatic, 1976	1·10	1·10
4111	$1.40 250 GT Coupé, 1954	1·10	1·10
4112	$1.40 156 F2, 1960	1·10	1·10
4113	$1.40 312 P, 1972	1·10	1·10
4114	$1.40 D 50, 1956	1·10	1·10
4107/14	Set of 8	8·00	8·00

Nos. 4107/14 were printed together, *se-tenant*, in sheetlets of eight stamps.

594 Concorde 01 rolled out, Filton, 20 Sept 1971

2007 (20 June). Concorde. T **594** and similar horiz designs. Multicoloured. Litho. P 13.

4115	$1.50 Type **594**	1·50	1·50
	a. Sheetlet. Nos. 4115/20	8·00	8·00
4116	$1.50 Concorde 01 (G-AXDN) in flight (yellowish green border)	1·50	1·50
4117	$1.50 As Type **594** (bluish violet border)	1·50	1·50
4118	$1.50 As No. 4116 (deep magenta border)	1·50	1·50
4119	$1.50 As Type **594** (yellowish green border)	1·50	1·50
4120	$1.50 As No. 4116 (bluish violet border)	1·50	1·50
4121	$1.50 Concorde and London Eye (yellow-green inscr)	1·50	1·50
	a. Sheetlet. Nos. 4121/6	8·00	8·00
4122	$1.50 Concorde and Sydney Opera House (black inscr)	1·50	1·50
4123	$1.50 As No. 4121 (bright magenta inscr)	1·50	1·50
4124	$1.50 As No. 4122 (reddish-orange inscr)	1·50	1·50
4125	$1.50 As No. 4121 (black inscr)	1·50	1·50
4126	$1.50 As No. 4122 (greenish blue inscr)	1·50	1·50
4115/26	Set of 12	16·00	16·00

Nos. 4115/20 and 4121/6 were each printed together, *se-tenant*, in sheetlets of six stamps with enlarged illustrated margins. Nos. 4115/20 show Concorde 01, the first pre-production aircraft.

Nos. 4121/6 commemorate the London to Sydney flight record set on 13 February 1985. The colours given for Nos. 4121/6 are those of the country inscription 'ANTIGUA & BARBUDA'.

595 NH-90 Helicopter

2007 (20 June). Centenary of the Helicopter. T **595** and similar multicoloured designs. Litho. P 13.

4127	$1.50 Type **595**	2·25	2·00
	a. Sheetlet. Nos. 4127/32	12·00	11·00
4128	$1.50 BO 105 helicopter carrying pipes	2·25	2·00
4129	$1.50 NH-90 helicopter on ground	2·25	2·00
4130	$1.50 AS-61 helicopter 6-15 over sea	2·25	2·00
4131	$1.50 BO 105 helicopter and lighthouse	2·25	2·00
4132	$1.50 AS-61 helicopter 6-26	2·25	2·00
4127/32	Set of 6	12·00	11·00
MS4133	$1.50 100×71 mm. $6 Bell UH-1 Iroquois 'Huey' troop carrier (*vert*)	7·50	7·00

Nos. 4127/32 were printed together, *se-tenant*, in sheetlets of six stamps with enlarged illustrated margins.

109

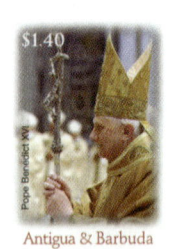

ANTIGUA AND BARBUDA

596 Pope Benedict XVI
597 Elvis Presley 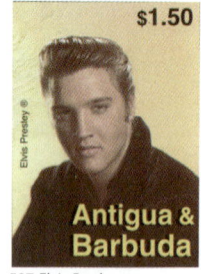

2007 (30 July). 80th Birthday of Pope Benedict XVI. Litho. P 13½.
4134	**596**	$1.40 multicoloured	2·00	2·00

No. 4134 was printed in sheetlet of eight stamps with enlarged illustrated left margins.

2007 (30 July). 30th Death Anniv of Elvis Presley. T **597** and similar vert designs. Multicoloured. Litho. P 13½.
4135	$1.50 Type **597**	1·40	1·40
	a. Sheetlet. Nos. 4135/40	7·50	7·50
4136	$1.50 Wearing striped shirt, seen in profile	1·40	1·40
4137	$1.50 Holding guitar, wearing jacket and bow tie	1·40	1·40
4138	$1.50 Wearing striped shirt, smiling	1·40	1·40
4139	$1.50 Wearing red shirt	1·40	1·40
4140	$1.50 Holding guitar, seen in half-profile	1·40	1·40
4135/40 Set of 6		7·50	7·50

Nos. 4135/40 were printed together, *se-tenant*, in sheetlets of six stamps with enlarged illustrated right margins.

598 Diana, Princess of Wales

2007 (30 July). Tenth Death Anniv of Diana, Princess of Wales. T **598** and similar vert designs. Litho. P 13½.
4141	$2 Type **598**	1·75	1·75
	a. Sheetlet. Nos. 4141/4	6·25	6·25
4142	$2 Wearing pale mauve and drop earrings	1·75	1·75
4143	$2 Wearing purple jacket with black edging on collar	1·75	1·75
4144	$2 Wearing brownish grey and white dress and hat	1·75	1·75
4141/4 Set of 4		6·25	6·25
MS4145 70×100 mm. $6 Wearing headscarf		4·50	4·75

Nos. 4141/4 were printed together, *se-tenant*, in sheetlets of four stamps with enlarged illustrated margins.

599 *Strelitzia parvifolia* (bird of paradise)

(Litho Cardon Enterprise, Taiwan)

2007 (1 Oct). Plants and Trees. T **599** and similar multicoloured designs. P 12½×13½ (vert) or 13½×12½ (horiz).
4146	15c. Type **599**	20	20
4147	20c. *Thespesia populnea* (seaside mahoe)	25	20
4148	30c. *Hibiscus rosa sinensis*	30	20
4149	50c. *Agave karatto*	45	20
4150	70c. *Barringtonia asiatica*	65	35
4151	75c. *Cocos nucifera* (coconut)	70	40
4152	90c. *Prosopis chilensis* (mesquite) (*horiz*)	85	45
4153	$1 *Tamarindus indica*	1·00	55
4154	$1.50 *Capparis cynophallophora* (black willow) (*horiz*)	1·25	75
4155	$1.80 *Baobab* (*horiz*)	1·50	1·10
4156	$2 *Petrea volubilis*	1·75	1·50
4157	$2.50 *Opuntia cochenillifera* (cactus) (*horiz*)	2·00	2·00
4158	$5 *Hymenaea courbaril* (locust fruit) (*horiz*)	3·25	3·50
4159	$10 *Caesalpinia ciliata* (Barbuda black warri)	5·50	6·00
4160	$20 *Ricinus communis* (castor oil plant)	10·00	11·00
4146/60 Set of 15		26·00	25·00

600 John W. Ashe, Antigua & Barbuda
601 Antigua and Barbuda on Bauble 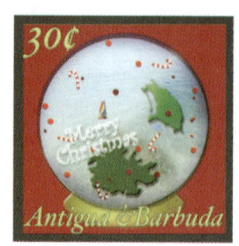

2007 (25 Oct). Holocaust Remembrance. T **600** and similar vert designs. Multicoloured. Litho. P 13½.
4161	$1.40 Type **600**	1·50	1·50
	a. Sheetlet. Nos. 4161/8	9·00	9·00
4162	$1.40 Alfred Capelle, Marshall Islands	1·50	1·50
4163	$1.40 Masao Nakayama, Micronesia	1·50	1·50
4164	$1.40 Gilles Noghes, Monaco	1·50	1·50
4165	$1.40 Baatar Choisuren, Mongolia	1·50	1·50
4166	$1.40 Filipe Chiduma, Mozambique	1·50	1·50
4167	$1.40 Marlene Moses, Nauru	1·50	1·50
4168	$1.40 Franciscus Majoor, Netherlands	1·50	1·50
4161/8 Set of 8		9·00	9·00

Nos. 4161/8 were printed together, *se-tenant*, in sheetlets of eight stamps with enlarged illustrated margins.

(Litho BDT)

2007 (5 Nov). Christmas. T **601** and similar square designs. Multicoloured. P 15×14.
4169	30c. Type **601**	40	20
4170	90c. Decorated palm tree and parade dancers on beach	90	50
4171	$1 Cake decorations	1·00	70
4172	$1.50 Parade costume	1·40	1·40
4169/72 Set of 4		3·25	2·50

602 Hands
603 King Court (Prince Klaas), 1691–1736 

2007 (27 Dec). World Hospice and Palliative Care Day. T **602** and similar horiz design. Multicoloured. Litho. P 13½.
4173	30c. Type **602**	50	50
4174	30c. Clock	50	50

2008 (7 Mar). National Heroes. T **603** and similar vert designs. Multicoloured. Litho. P 13.
4175	90c. Type **603**	85	80
4176	90c. Dame Georgiana E. (Nellie) Robinson, 1880–1972	85	85
4177	$1 Sir Vivian Richards	1·50	1·50
4178	$1.50 Sir V. C. Bird Snr, 1909–99	1·50	1·75
4175/78 Set of 4		4·25	4·00

603a Field Marshal William 'Bill' Slim

ANTIGUA AND BARBUDA

2008 (7 Mar). Field Marshal William 'Bill' Slim Commemoration. P 14.
4178a   603a $1.20 multicoloured ....   1·50   1·50

604 Americas Cup Yachts

605 Pierre de Coubertin (founder of modern Olympics), 1896

2008 (25 Mar). 32nd Americas Cup Yachting Championship, Valencia, Spain. T **604** and similar horiz designs. Multicoloured. Litho. P 12½.
4179	$1.20 Type **604**	1·25	1·50
	a. Block of 4. Nos. 4179/82	8·00	8·75
4180	$1.80 Two yachts, yellow-hulled *Lladro* at right	1·60	1·75
4181	$3 Two yachts	2·25	2·50
4182	$5 Five yachts	3·75	4·00
4179/82	Set of 4	8·00	8·75

Nos. 4179/82 were printed together, *se-tenant*, as blocks of four stamps in sheetlets of 16.

2008 (25 Mar). Olympic Games, Beijing. T **605** and similar vert designs. Multicoloured. Litho. P 13.
4183	$1.40 Type **605**	1·50	1·50
	a. Sheetlet. Nos. 4183/6	5·50	5·50
4184	$1.40 Poster for first modern Olympic Games, Athens, 1896	1·50	1·50
4185	$1.40 Spiridon Louis of Greece, marathon gold medallist, 1896	1·50	1·50
4186	$1.40 Paul Masson of France, cycling gold medallist, 1896	1·50	1·50
4183/6	Set of 4	5·50	5·50

Nos. 4183/6 were printed together, *se-tenant*, in sheetlets of four stamps with enlarged illustrated margins.

606 King's Garden, Walls of Old City and Al-Aqsa Mosque, Jerusalem (Illustration reduced. Actual size 110×100 mm)

2008 (14 May). Israel 2008 World Stamp Championship. Sheet 110×100 mm. Litho. Imperf.
MS4187   **606** $6 multicoloured ....   6·00   6·50

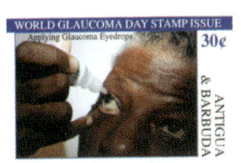

607 Applying Glaucoma Eye Drops

2008 (18 June). World Glaucoma Day. T **607** and similar horiz designs. Multicoloured. P 13½.
4188	30c. Type **607**	45	30
4189	50c. Normal and glaucomatous optic nerves	70	35
4190	$1 Using braille typewriter	1·40	1·40
4188/90	Set of 3	2·25	1·75

608 Pope Benedict XVI

2008 (18 June). First Visit of Pope Benedict XVI to the United States. Litho. P 13½.
4191   **608** $2 multicoloured ....   2·25   2·25

No. 4191 was printed in sheetlets of four stamps with enlarged illustrated margins.

609 Elvis Presley

610 *Vanguard I*, 1958

2008 (18 June). 50th Anniv of Elvis Presley's Induction into the US Army. Sheet 160×130 mm containing T **609** and similar vert designs. Multicoloured. P 13½.
MS4192 $2×4 Type **609**; In light grey uniform; In dark grey uniform; In light grey uniform with cap ...   6·50   7·00

The stamps within **MS**4192 share a composite background design.

2008 (29 July). 50 Years of Space Exploration and Satellites. T **610** and similar multicoloured designs. Litho. P 13½.
4193	$1.50 Type **610**	1·50	1·50
	a. Sheetlet. Nos. 4193/5, each ×2	8·00	8·00
4194	$1.50 *Vanguard I* (green and white background)	1·50	1·50
4195	$1.50 *Vanguard I* (sphere and base)	1·50	1·50
4196	$1.50 *Explorer III*, 1958	1·50	1·50
	a. Sheetlet. Nos. 4196/8, each ×3	8·00	8·00
4197	$1.50 *Explorer III* orbiting Earth	1·50	1·50
4198	$1.50 Van Allen radiation belt (discovered by *Explorer* programme)	1·50	1·50
4199	$2 *Vanguard I* and Moon	2·00	2·00
	a. Sheetlet. Nos. 4199/200, each×2	7·00	7·00
4200	$2 *Vanguard I* orbiting Earth at sunrise	2·00	2·00
4201	$2 *Explorer III* (deep brown-red and light green background)	2·00	2·00
	a. Sheetlet. Nos. 4201/2, each ×2	7·00	7·00
4202	$2 *Explorer III*	2·00	2·00
4193/4202	Set of 10	15·00	15·00

MS4203 Two sheets, each 100×70 mm. (a) $6 *Vanguard I* above Earth (*horiz*). (b) $6 *Explorer III* and Earth (*horiz*) ....   12·00   12·00

611 Capt. Kirk and Mr. Spock

2008 (29 Sept). *Star Trek*. T **611** and similar horiz designs. Multicoloured. Litho. P 11½ ($1.50) or 13½ ($2).
4204	$1.50 Type **611**	1·50	1·50
	a. Sheetlet. Nos. 4204/9	8·00	8·00
4205	$1.50 Mr. Spock, Capt. Kirk, Dr. Leonard McCoy and Lt. Cmdr Scott	1·50	1·50
4206	$1.50 Mr. Spock and Lt. Uhura	1·50	1·50

111

ANTIGUA AND BARBUDA

4207	$1.50 Enterprise crew in alien city............	1·50	1·50
4208	$1.50 Lt. Uhura (Nichelle Nichols) on bridge of Enterprise..................................	1·50	1·50
4209	$1.50 Lt. Cmdr Scott (James Doohan)............	1·50	1·50
4210	$2 Dr. Leonard McCoy (DeForest Kelley) (50×37 mm)..	2·00	2·00
	a. Sheetlet. Nos. 4210/13.......................	7·00	7·00
4211	$2 Mr. Spock (Leonard Nimoy) (50×37 mm)..	2·00	2·00
4212	$2 Captain Kirk (William Shatner) (50×37 mm)...	2·00	2·00
4213	$2 Hikaru Sulu (George Takei) (50×37 mm)..	2·00	2·00
4204/13 Set of 10		15·00	15·00

Nos. 4204/9 and 4210/13 were each printed together, *se-tenant*, in sheetlets of six or four stamps with enlarged illustrated margins.

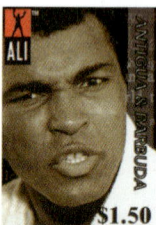

612 Muhammad Ali

613 John F. Kennedy (in profile)

2008 (29 Sept). Muhammad Ali (world heavyweight boxing champion, 1964, 1974–8). T **612** and similar vert designs. Multicoloured. Litho. P 11½ ($1.50) or 13½ ($2).

4214/19	$1.50×6 Type **612** and similar designs showing Muhammad Ali speaking		
	a. Sheetlet. Nos. 4214/19...................	7·50	8·50
4220/3	$2×4 Hitting punchbag; Wearing white robe, speaking; With white robe over back of shoulders; Wearing helmet (all 37×50 mm).................	6·50	7·50

Nos. 4214/19 and 4220/3 were each printed together, *se-tenant*, in sheetlets of six or four stamps with enlarged illustrated margins.

2008 (18 Dec). John F. Kennedy (US President 1960-3) Commemoration. Sheet 100×130 mm containing T **613** and similar vert designs showing President Kennedy. Multicoloured. Litho. P 13.

MS4224	$2×4 Type **613**; Facing straight ahead; Head turned to left; With hand raised to chin................	7·50	8·00

614 Marilyn Monroe

615 Holy Family

2008 (18 Dec). Marilyn Monroe Commemoration. Sheet 100×140 mm containing T **614** and similar horiz designs. Multicoloured. Litho. P 13½.

MS4225	$2×4 Type **614**; Head turned to left; Wearing deep orange; Wearing mauve sweater...........	7·00	8·00

2009 (2 Jan). Christmas. T **615** and similar multicoloured designs showing stained glass windows. Litho. P 14½×14.

4226	30c. Type **615**	35	20
4227	90c. Baby Jesus in manger............................	90	55
4228	$1 Mary and infant Jesus with hands held together in prayer (*vert*)..................	1·10	80
4229	$1.50 Mary and infant Jesus standing on her lap (*vert*)...	1·50	1·75
4226/9 Set of 4		3·50	3·00

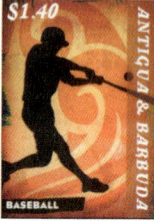

616 Baseball

617 First Inaugural Address of Pres. Lincoln, 4 March 1861

2009 (5 Jan). Olympic Games, Beijing (2008). Sports of the Summer Games. Sheet 130×94 mm containing T **616** and similar vert designs. Multicoloured. Litho. P 11½.

MS4230	$1·40×4 Type **616**; Beach volleyball; Gymnastics; Judo.......................................	4·50	5·00

2009 (5 Jan). Birth Bicentenary of Abraham Lincoln (US President 1861–5). Sheet 130×100 mm containing T **617** and similar horiz designs. Multicoloured. Litho. P 11½.

MS4231	$2×4 Type **617**; Abraham Lincoln; Crowd at his second inaugural address, 4 March 1865; Crowd and Abraham Lincoln.......................	6·50	7·50

The stamps and margins of No. **MS**4231 form composite designs.

618 Pres. Barack Obama (in profile)

619 Ox

2009 (20 Jan). Inauguration of President Barack Obama. T **618** and similar vert design. Multicoloured. Litho. P 12×11½ (**MS**4232) or 13 (**MS**4233).

MS4232	130×100 mm. $2.75 Type **618**×4.................	6·50	7·50
MS4232a	100×70 mm. $10 Pres. Obama (in front of US flag) (37×50 mm)................................	8·00	8·50

2009 (26 Jan). Chinese New Year. Year of the Ox. Sheet 190×78 mm. Litho. P 11½×12.

MS4233	$1 Type **619**×4 multicoloured.......................	4·50	4·75

620 Xian

621 Emperor Quin Shi Huang

2009 (2 Jan). China 2009 World Stamp Exhibition, Luoyang (1st issue). Sites and Scenes of China. T **620** and similar horiz designs. Multicoloured. Litho. P 12.

MS4234	100×145 mm. $1.40×4 Type **620**; Harbin; Chongqing; Tianjin...................................	3·75	4·00

2009 (2 Jan). China 2009 World Stamp Exhibition, Luoyang (2nd issue). First Emperor Quin Shi Huang (221–210BC) and his Terracotta Army. T **621** and similar horiz designs. Multicoloured. Litho. P 12½.

MS4235	120×150 mm. $1.40×4 Type **621**; Horses; Warriors; Excavation with army in columns.........	3·75	4·00

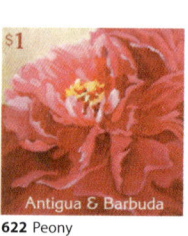

622 Peony

623 Elvis Presley

2009 (10 Apr). China 2009 World Stamp Exhibition, Luoyang (3rd issue). Peonies. T **622** and similar multicoloured design. Litho. P 13.

4236	$1 Type **622**...	1·25	1·25
MS4237	100×70 mm. $5 Black and dull pink peony design (triangular 35×30 mm).....................	4·75	5·00

No. 4236 was printed in sheetlets of eight stamps with enlarged illustrated margins.

ANTIGUA AND BARBUDA

2009 (14 Apr). Elvis Presley Commemoration. T **623** and similar vert designs. Multicoloured. Litho. P 14.
MS4238 185×125 mm. $1.50×6 Type **623**; Wearing jacket and tie (orange background); Standing with hands on hips; Wearing pale orange jacket with white stripe; Playing guitar, wearing lei; Wearing jacket and tie (sky background) .... 5·50 6·00

624
625 Labrador Retriever 

2009 (9 July). National Stamp Day. Litho. P 14×14½.
4239 **624** $4 multicoloured .... 3·75 4·00
No. 4239 was issued in large sheets and also in sheetlets of eight stamps and eight blank labels.

2009 (13 Aug). 125th Anniv of the American Kennel Club. Two sheets, each 100×120 mm, containing T **625** and similar horiz designs showing Labrador Retriever puppies (MS4240) or Dachshunds (MS4241). Multicoloured. P 12.
MS4240 $2·50×4 Type **625**; Two golden labrador puppies; Black and golden labrador puppies carrying stick; Golden labrador puppy in tub .... 12·00 12·00
MS4241 $2·50×4 Black and tan dachshund pawing case; Tan dachshund in green wooden crate; Two dachshund puppies in wooden trug; Wire-haired dachshund .... 12·00 12·00

626 Michael Jackson
627 Flypast of Fighter Jets 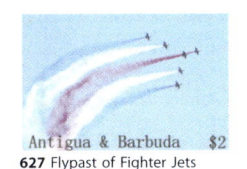

2009 (30 Sept). Michael Jackson Commemoration. T **626** and similar vert designs. Multicoloured. Litho. P 11½ (MS4242) or 12×11½ (MS4243) MS4244 13½.
MS4242 158×112 mm. $2·50×4 Type **626**; Wearing black with gold crossbelts and waistband; Wearing orange-red with black diagonal band; Wearing silver jacket with eagle design .... 9·75 9·75
MS4243 130×100 mm. $2·50×4 Wearing plain white shirt; Wearing white jacket with black armbands....... 9·75 9·75
MS4244 150×110 mm. $6 Wearing white T-shirt (38×51 mm).. 4·75 4·75

2009 (2 Nov). Centenary of Chinese Aviation and Aeropex 2009 Exhibition, Beijing. T **627** and similar horiz designs. Multicoloured. Litho. P 14.
MS4245 145×95 mm. $2×4 Type **627**; Jet fighters flying to right; Jet fighters flying to left; Jet fighters flying in fan formation.. 7·50 7·50
MS4246 120×80 mm. $6 J–7GB fighter jet (50×38 mm).. 6·00 6·00

628 Pres. Barack Obama
629 Apollo 11 Emblem 

2009 (4 Nov). Meeting of US President Barack Obama and Pope Benedict XVI, Vatican, 10 July 2009. T **628** and similar multicoloured designs. Litho. P 11½ (MS4247) or 11½×12 (MS4248).
MS4247 150×100 mm. $2·75×2 Type **628**; Pope Benedict XVI; Michelle Obama............................ 7·50 7·50

MS4248 110×90 mm. $6 Pope Benedict XVI and Pres. Barack Obama (horiz).. 6·50 6·50

2009 (13 Nov). 40th Anniv of First Manned Moon Landing and International Year of Astronomy. T **629** and similar horiz designs. Multicoloured. Litho. P 12½ (MS4249) or 13 (MS4250).
MS4249 151×100 mm. $2·50×4 Type **629**; Lunar Module *Eagle*; Passive Seismic Experiment Package; Apollo 11... 9·75 9·75
MS4250 101×71 mm. $6 Apollo 11 orbiting Moon....... 5·75 5·75

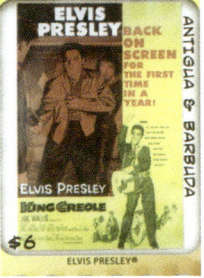

630 Poster for *King Creole*, 1958
631 Candles and Wreath 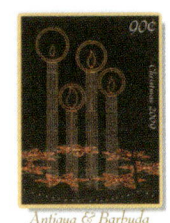

2009 (26 Nov). Elvis Presley in Film *King Creole*. T **630** and similar multicoloured designs. Litho. P 13½.
MS4251 125×90 mm. $6 Type **630**................................. 4·50 4·50
MS4252 90×125 mm. $6 Elvis Presley playing guitar..... 4·50 4·50
MS4253 90×125 mm. $6 Elvis Presley with arms raised (horiz)... 4·50 4·50
MS4254 125×90 mm. $6 Elvis Presley playing guitar (horiz)... 4·50 4·50

2009 (3 Dec). Christmas. T **631** and similar multicoloured designs showing Christmas lights. Litho. P 14×14½ (vert) or 14½×14 (horiz).
4255 90c. Type **631** .... 1·00 85
4256 $1 Gold, red and green lights.......................... 1·10 90
4257 $1.80 Three bells and tree branches .... 2·00 1·75
4258 $3 Nativity .... 3·00 3·50
4255/8 Set of 4... 6·25 65·25

632 Pair of Caribbean Coot
633 Sir Vere Cornwall Bird 

2009 (3 Dec). Endangered Species. Caribbean Coot (*Fulica caribaea*). T **632** and similar horiz designs. Multicoloured. Litho. P 13½.
4259 $2.65 Type **632** .... 3·00 3·00
       a. Strip of 4. Nos. 4259/62 .... 11·00 11·00
4260 $2.65 Pair landing .... 3·00 3·00
4261 $2.65 Pair with chick...................................... 3·00 3·00
4262 $2.65 Adult feeding chick............................... 3·00 3·00
4259/62 Set of 4... 11·00 11·00
MS4263 112×165 mm. Nos. 4259/62, each ×2............. 20·00 20·00
Nos. 4259/62 were printed together, *se-tenant*, as horizontal and vertical strips of four in sheetlets of 16.
No. MS4263 contained two blocks of Nos. 4259/62 separated by a horizontal gutter.

2009 (8 Dec). Birth Centenary of Rt. Honourable Dr. Sir Vere Cornwall Bird Sr. (first Chief Minister, Premier and Prime Minister of Antigua and Barbuda). T **633** and similar vert designs. Multicoloured. Litho. P 12×11½ (MS4269) or 11½ (others).
4264 30c. Type **633** 40 25
4265 75c. Sir V. C. Bird (Antigua flag in background)... 85 75
4266 90c. Wearing red jacket and hat...................... 1·00 85
4267 $1.50 Sir V. C. Bird (black and white photo).... 1·50 1·75
4264/7 Set of 4... 3·25 3·25
MS4268 160×110 mm. $2·50×4 As Nos. 4265/7 .... 9·75 9·75
MS4269 100×70 mm. $6 Sir V. C. Bird (Antigua flag and outline map in background)........................... 6·50 6·50

ANTIGUA AND BARBUDA

634 Glossy Ibis (*Plegadis falcinellus*)

635 Risso's Dolphin (*Grampus griseus*)

2009 (8 Dec). Birds of Antigua and Barbuda. T **634** and similar multicoloured designs. Litho. P 11½ (Nos. 4270/3) or 11½×12 (MS4274/5).

4270	$1.20 Type **634**............	1·75	1·25
4271	$1.80 Green-winged teal (*Anas carolinensis*)............	2·25	1·75
4272	$3 California clapper rail (*Rallus longirostris obsoletus*)............	3·50	3·50
4273	$5 Cattle egret (*Bubulcus ibis*) (vert)............	5·50	6·50
4270/3	Set of 4............	11·50	11·50

MS4274 90×90 mm. $2.50×4 Green heron (*Butorides virescens*); Common ground dove (*Columbina passerina*); White-tailed hawk (*Buteo albicaudatus*); Black-faced grassquit (*Tiaris bicolor*)............ 10·00 10·00

MS4275 70×100 mm. $3×2 Bananaquit (*Coereba flaveola*); Osprey (*Pandion haliaetus*)............ 8·00 8·00

(Litho)

2010 (4 Jan). Sharks of the Caribbean. T **634a** and similar horiz designs. Multicoloured. P 14 (Nos. 4275a/d) or 14½×14 (MS4275e).

4275a	$1.20 Type **634a**............	1·75	1·25
4275b	$1.80 Caribbean reef shark (*Carcharhinus perezi*)............	2·25	1·75
4275c	$3 Tiger Shark (*Galeocerdo cuvier*)............	3·50	3·50
4275d	$5 Whale shark (*Rhincodon typus*)............	5·50	6·50
4275a/d	Set of 4............	11·50	11·50

MS4275e $2.75×4 170×100 mm. $2.75×4 Caribbean sharpnose shark (*Rhizoprionodon porosus*); Blacktip shark (*Carcharhinus limbatus*); Oceanic whitetip shark (*Carcharhinus longimanus*); Bull shark (*Carcharhinusleucas*)............ 11·00 11·00

The stamps and margins of **MS**4275e form a composite design.

(Litho)

2010 (4 Jan). Chinese Lunar Calendar. 30th Anniv of Chinese Zodiac Stamps. Sheet 150×120 mm containing T **634b** and similar horiz designs. Multicoloured. P 12.

MS4275f 60c.×12 Type **634b**; Ox; Tiger; Rabbit; Dragon; Snake; Horse; Ram; Monkey; Rooster; Dog; Pig............ 4·75 5·50

(Litho)

2010 (4 Jan). Chinese New Year. Year of the Tiger. Sheet 120×90 mm. Multicoloured. P 11½×12.

MS4275g $5 Type **634c**; $5 Bronze tiger, Shang Dynasty, China............ 5·50 6·00

(Litho)

2010 (23 Feb). Whales and Dolphins of the Caribbean. T **635** and similar horiz designs. Multicoloured. P 12.

4276	$1.20 Type **635**............	1·75	1·25
4277	$1.80 Common dolphin (*Delphinus delphis*)............	2·25	1·75
4278	$3 Humpback whale (*Megaptera novaeangliae*)............	3·50	3·50
4279	$5 Sperm whale (*Physeter macrocephalus*)............	5·50	6·50
4276/9	Set of 4............	11·50	11·50

MS4280 100×140 mm. $2×6 Shortsnout dolphin (*Lagenodelphis hosei*); Spotted dolphin (*Stenella frontalis*); Cuvier's beaked whale (*Ziphius cavirostris*); Shortfin pilot whale (*Globicephala macrorhynchus*); Gulf Stream beaked whale (*Mesoplodon europaeus*); Rough-toothed dolphin (*Stenobredanensis*)............ 13·00 13·00

636 Diana, Princess of Wales

637 Airfoil of Ferrari 312 F1-68, 1968

(Litho)

2010 (23 Feb). Diana, Princess of Wales Commemoration. Sheet 130×90 mm containing T **636** and similar vert designs. Multicoloured. Litho. P 12×11½.

MS4281 $2×4 Type **636**; Wearing pink; Wearing pale mauve; Wearing pale green............ 7·00 7·50

(Litho)

2010 (22 Mar). Ferrari Cars. T **637** and similar horiz designs. Multicoloured. P 12. P 12×11½.

4282	$1.25 Type **637**............	1·25	1·25
	a. Sheetlet. Nos. 4282/3, each×4............	9·00	9·00
4283	$1.25 Ferrari 312 F1-68, 1968............	1·25	1·25
	a. Sheetlet. Nos. 4282/3, each×4............	9·00	9·00
4284	$1.25 Engine of Ferrari 246 P F1, 1960............	1·25	1·25
	a. Sheetlet. Nos. 4284/5, each×4............	9·00	9·00
4285	$1.25 Ferrari 246 P F1, 1960 (car no. 34)............	1·25	1·25
	a. Sheetlet. Nos. 4284/5, each×4............	9·00	9·00
4286	$1.25 Interior of Ferrari 365 P Speciale, 1966............	1·25	1·25
	a. Sheetlet. Nos. 4286/7, each ×4............	9·00	9·00
4287	$1.25 Ferrari 365 P Speciale, 1966............	1·25	1·25
	a. Sheetlet. Nos. 4286/7, each ×4............	9·00	9·00
4288	$1.25 Engine of Ferrari 158 F1, 1964............	1·25	1·25
	a. Sheetlet. Nos. 4288/9, each ×4............	9·00	9·00
4289	$1.25 Ferrari 158 F1, 1964 (car no. 20)............	1·25	1·25
	a. Sheetlet. Nos. 4288/9, each ×4............	9·00	9·00
4282/89	Set of 8............	9·00	9·00

638 Common Buckeye (*Junonia coenia*)

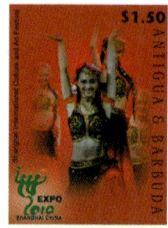

639 Dancers, Shanghai International Culture and Art Festival

(Litho)

2010 (14 Apr). Butterflies of the Caribbean. T **638** and similar horiz designs. Multicoloured. P 14 (Nos. 4290/3) or 14½×14 (**MS**4294).

4290	$1.20 Type **638**............	1·75	1·25
4291	$1.80 Red postman (*Heliconius erato*)............	2·25	1·75
4292	$3 Red admiral (*Vanessa atalanta*)............	3·50	3·50
4293	$5 Zebra longwing (*Heliconius charithonia*)............	5·50	6·50
4290/93	Set of 4............	11·50	11·50

MS4294 140×100 mm. $2×6 Orange sulphur (inscr 'sulfur') (*Colias eurytheme*); Blue morpho (*Morpho peleides*); Queen butterfly (*Danaus gilippus*); Zebra swallowtail (*Eurytides marcellus*); Malachite (*Siproata stelenes*); Gatekeeper butterfly (*Pyronia tithonus*)............ 10·00 11·00

The stamps and margins of **MS**4294 form a composite background design of a flowering plant.

(Litho)

2010 (10 May). Expo 2010, Shanghai, China. Sheet 148×135 mm containing T **639** and similar vert designs. Multicoloured. P 11½.

MS4295 $1.50×4 Type **639**; China National Grand Theatre, Beijing; Green rice terrace, Guangxi Province, China; Dance performance, Beijing (yellow background)............ 4·25 4·50

640 Mother Teresa with Princess Diana, New York

(Litho)

2010 (10 May). Birth Centenary of Mother Teresa. Sheet 160×139 mm containing T **640** and similar horiz designs. Multicoloured. P 11½×12.

MS4296 $2.50×4 Type **640**; Receiving Order of Merit from Queen Elizabeth II, India; Receiving Medal of Freedom from Pres. Reagan; With Pope John Paul II, Calcutta, India............ 11·00 11·00

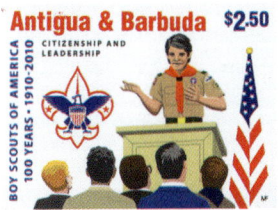

641 Scout giving Lecture ('Citizenship and Leadership')

(Des Michael Feigenbaum. Litho)
2010 (10 May). Centenary of Boy Scouts of America. Two sheets, each 160×160 mm, containing T **641** and similar horiz designs. Multicoloured. P 13½.
MS4297 $2.50 Type **641**×2; $2.50 Two scouts in kayak ('Aquatic sport adventures')×2 .... 7·50 8·50
MS4298 $2.50 Statue of Liberty giving Scout salute×2; $2.50 Two scouts ('Navigation with map and compass')×2 .... 7·50 8·50

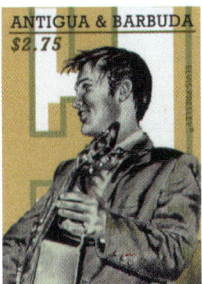

642 Elvis Presley **643** Pres. Obama holding Nobel Peace Prize

(Litho)
2010 (10 May). 75th Birth Anniv of Elvis Presley. Artwork by Betty Harper. Two sheets, each 180×140 mm, containing T **642** and similar vert designs. Multicoloured. P 13.
MS4299 $2.75×4 Type **642**; Facing forward, singing; Facing left, guitar strap over face; Three images of Elvis Presley .... 7·50 8·00
MS4300 $2.75×4 Wearing white with pattern; Wearing open neck shirt; Two images of Elvis Presley; Wearing white jacket with dark piping .... 7·50 8·00

(Litho)
2010 (10 May). Pres. Barack Obama's Nobel Peace Prize (2009). Sheet, 140×100 mm, containing T **643** and similar vert designs. Multicoloured. P 12×11½.
MS4301 $2.75×4 Type **643**; Speaking (side view); Speaking from podium; Holding Nobel Peace Prize, smiling .... 7·50 8·00

644 Princess Diana on Visit to Hindu Mission, UK  **645** Rainbows

(Litho)
2010 (10 May). Princess Diana Commemoration. Two sheets, each 150×105 mm, containing T **644** and similar vert designs. Multicoloured. P 12×11½.
MS4302 $2.75×4 Type **644**; Visit to Pakistan; Visit to Dubai; Visit to Japan .... 7·50 8·00
MS4303 $2.75×4 Wearing tiara with pearls and pearl drop earrings; Wearing tiara with sapphire and diamond earrings; Wearing tiara and pearl drop earrings; Wearing tiara and white jacket with stand-up collar .... 7·50 8·00

(Litho)
2010 (10 May). Centenary of Girlguiding. T **645** and similar horiz designs. Multicoloured. P 11½×12 (**MS**4304) or 11½ (**MS**4305).
MS4304 150×100 mm. $2.75×4 Type **645**; Brownies in kayaks; Three guides; Three Senior Section guides hiking .... 7·50 8·00
MS4305 70×100 mm. $6 Guides .... 4·75 5·50

646 Abraham Lincoln  **647** Pope John Paul II

(Litho)
2010 (10 May). Birth Bicentenary (2009) of Abraham Lincoln (US President 1861–5). Two sheets, each 138×184 mm, containing T **646** and similar vert designs showing portraits. Multicoloured. 11½.
MS4306 $2.75×4 Type **646**; With beard, facing forward; With beard, looking to left; Profile, facing left .... 7·50 8·00
MS4307 $2.75×4 Type **646**; With beard, facing forward; With beard, looking to left; Profile, facing left .... 7·50 8·00

(Litho)
2010 (10 May). Pope John Paul II Commemoration. Multicoloured. P 11½.
4308 $2.75 Type **647** .... 2·50 2·50

648 Pres. John F. Kennedy  **649** The Three Stooges

(Litho)
2010 (10 May). 50th Anniv of Election of Pres. John F. Kennedy. Sheet 145×83 mm. Multicoloured. P 11½.
MS4309 $2.75×4 Type **648**; Pres. John F. Kennedy; Seated in chair (bookcase in background); Speaking .... 7·50 8·00

(Litho)
2010 (27 Sep). The Three Stooges. T **649** and similar horiz designs. Multicoloured. P 11½.
MS4310 $2.50×4 Type **649**; The Three Stooges as decorators, Curly holding cloth to Moe's neck; The Three Stooges as doctors and patient, Larry holding scissors to Curly's nose; Larry and Moe with Curly's head in guillotine .... 6·50 7·00

650 Maximiliano Pereira (Uruguay)  **651** California Spangled Cat

(Litho)
2010 (18 Oct). World Cup Football Championship, South Africa. T **650** and similar vert designs. Multicoloured. P 12.
MS4311 130×150 mm. $1.50×6 Type **650**; John Heitinga (Netherlands); Edinson Cavani (Uruguay); Mark Van Bommel (Netherlands); Martin Caceres (Uruguay); Giovanni van Bronckhorst (Netherlands) .... 8·00 8·00

ANTIGUA AND BARBUDA

MS4312	85×90 mm. $3.50 Oscar Tabarez (Uruguay coach); $3.50 Uruguay flag on football................	5·50	5·50
MS4313	85×90 mm. $3.50 Bert van Marwijk (Dutch coach); $3.50 Dutch flag on football................	5·50	5·50

(Litho)

2010 (20 Dec). Cats of the World. T **651** and similar vert designs. Multicoloured. P 12 (**MS**4314) or 12½ (**MS**4315).

MS4314	150×100 mm. $2.50×6 Type **651**; Siamese; British shorthair; Norwegian forest; Egyptian mau; American curl longhair................	9·00	9·00
MS4315	100×70 mm. $6 Manx cat................	5·00	5·00

652 Henri Dunant and Nurses with Wounded Soldiers

653 Pope Benedict XVI

(Litho)

2010 (20 Dec). Death Centenary of Henri Dunant (instigator of Red Cross). T **652** and similar horiz designs, each showing inset portrait of Henri Dunant and scenes from Battle of Solferino, 1859. Multicoloured. P 12.

MS4316	150×100 mm. $2.50×4 Type **652**; Wounded laying on battlefield; Cavalry; Cavalry and soldiers................	8·00	8·00
MS4317	70×100 mm. $6 Battle of Solferino................	5·00	5·00

(Litho)

2010 (20 Dec). Fifth Anniv of Papacy of Pope Benedict XVI. T **653** and similar vert design showing Pope on visit to synagogue of Rome. Multicoloured. P 12.

MS4318	142×153 mm. $2.75 Type **653**×4................	9·75	9·75
MS4319	171×113 mm. $2.75 Pope Benedict XVI (facing left)×4................	9·75	9·75

The stamps within **MS**4318 differ slightly in the background markings at the foot of the stamps.

654 Rabbit

(Litho)

2011 (3 Jan). Chinese New Year. Year of the Rabbit. Sheet 131×82 mm containing T **654** and similar horiz design, both carmine-red. P 12.

MS4320	$4 Type **654**; $4 Chinese rabbit symbol	6·00	6·00

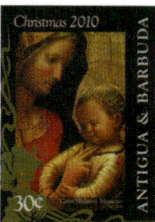

655 Giant Panda

656 Casini Madonna (Masaccio)

(Litho)

2011 (3 Jan). Beijing 2010 International Stamp and Coin Exposition. Giant Panda. T **655** and similar horiz designs. Multicoloured. P 12.

MS4321	170×95 mm. $2×4 Type **655**; Close-up of face; Panda with bamboo plant; Panda eating leaves (side view)................	6·00	6·00
MS4322	62×90 mm. $5 Giant panda (facing right)......	4·00	4·00

(Litho)

2011 (17 Jan). Christmas. T **656** and similar vert designs. Multicoloured. P 12½.

4323	30c. Type **656**................	30	25
4324	75c. *Madonna of the Stars* (Tintoretto)........	70	70
4325	90c. Wall mosaic showing magi from Basilica of Sant Apollinan, Nuovo, Italy.	90	85
4326	$1.50 *The Annunciation* (Fra Angelico)........	1·40	1·50
4323/26	Set of 4	3·00	3·00

657 Prince William and Miss Catherine Middleton

658 Mahatma Gandhi

(Litho)

2011 (14 Feb). Royal Engagement. T **657** and similar multicoloured design. P 13 (with one elliptical hole on each vert (4327/9) or horiz (**MS**4330/1) side).

4327	$2.50 Type **657**................	2·50	2·50
4328	$2.50 Prince William................	2·50	2·50
4329	$2.50 Miss Catherine Middleton................	2·50	2·50
4327/29	Set of 3	6·75	6·75
MS4330	120×70 mm. $6 Prince William (smiling).....	5·00	5·00
MS4331	120×70 mm. $6 Prince William (speaking).....	5·00	5·00

No. 4327 was printed in sheetlets of four stamps with enlarged illustrated margins.

Nos. 4328/9 were printed together, *se-tenant*, in sheetlets of four stamps containing two of each design.

(Litho)

2011 (1 Mar). Indipex 2011 World Philatelic Exhibition, Delhi. Mahatma Gandhi. Two sheets, each 150×101 mm containing T **658** and similar horiz designs. Multicoloured. P 12.

MS4332	$2.75×4 Type **658**; Gandhi and Asokan capital; Gandhi and towers and gateway; Gandhi and Taj Mahal, India................	10·00	10·00
MS4333	$2.75×4 Gandhi (in profile, wearing white) and crowd; Gandhi (facing forward) and crowd; Gandhi (in profile, looking down) and crowd; Gandhi (looking to right) and crowd................	10·00	10·00

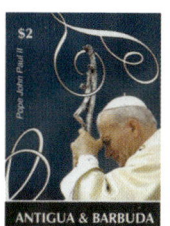

659 Pope John Paul II praying

660 Stephen Mallory, Lt-Commander Murray and Warships of Atlantic Blockading Squadron

(Litho)

2011 (4 Apr). Beatification of Pope John Paul II. T **659** and similar vert designs. Multicoloured. P 13 (with one elliptical hole on each horiz side).

MS4334	176×91 mm. $2 Type **659**×3; $2 Pope John Paul II wearing red cape×3................	10·00	10·00
MS4335	100×70 mm. $6 Pope John Paul II................	10·00	10·00

(Litho)

2011 (4 Apr). 150th Anniv of the American Civil War. Three sheets, each 150×100 mm, containing T **660** and similar horiz designs. Multicoloured. P 12.

MS4336	$2.50×4 Type **660**; Stephen Mallory (Confederate Secretary of Navy), Union Lt. Commander Alexander Murray and flotilla of Union warships; Mallory, Murray and Confederate privateers near Delaware Bay; Mallory, Murray and flagship USS *Minnesota*................	10·00	10·00
MS4337	$2.50×4 Confederate General Henry Jackson, Union General Joseph Reynolds and map of battle of Greenbriar River by A. T. McRae of the Quitman Guards; Jackson, Reynolds and skirmish along the Greenbriar River; Jackson, Reynolds and Union forces assembling near Greenbriar River; Jackson, Reynolds and battle of Greenbriar River	10·00	10·00

MS4338 $2.50×4 Confederate Brigadier General Richard Anderson, Union Colonel Harvey Brown and Fort Pickens; Anderson, Brown and battle at Santa Rosa Island; Anderson, Brown and Union ships cutting off Confederate dispatch galley; Anderson, Brown and Colonel Brown in command of 3rd US Infantry .... 10·00 10·00

661 *Tylopilus potamogeton*

662 Princess Diana in Barbuda, April 1997

(Litho)

2011 (9 May). Mushrooms of the Caribbean. T **661** and similar vert designs. Multicoloured. P 12.
MS4339 170×100 mm. $2×6 Type **661**; *Amanita campinaranae*; *Cantharellus atratus*; *Tylophilus orsonianus*; *Boletellus ananas*; *Amanita craseoderma*... 10·00 10·00
MS4340 170×100 mm. $2.50×4 *Amanita cyanopus*; *Phyllobolites miniatus*; *Chroogomphus jamaicensis*; *Coltricia cf. montagnei* .... 9·00 9·00
MS4341 170×100 mm. $2.50×4 *Amanita cyanopus*; *Phyllobolites miniatus*; *Chroogomphus jamaicensis*; *Coltricia cf. montagnei* .... 9·00 9·00
MS4342 101×70 mm. $6 *Austroboletus rostrupii* .... 6·00 6·00

2011 (12 Jul). 50th Birth Anniv of Princess Diana. T **662** and similar multicoloured designs. P 12.
MS4343 150×100 mm. $10 Type **662**×6 .... 10·00 10·00
MS4344 150×100 mm. $10 Princess Diana, Prince William and Prince Harry in Barbuda, April 1997×5 . 10·00 10·00
MS4345 101×70 mm. $50 Princess Diana wearing red dress and beach (*horiz*) .... 22·00 22·00

663 Pope Benedict XVI and Church

(Litho)

2011 (3 Aug). Pope Benedict XVI visits Germany. Two sheets, each 140×151 mm containing T **663** and similar horiz designs. Multicoloured. P 12.
MS4346 $3×3 Type **663**; Pope Benedict XVI and church with blue roof; Pope Benedict XVI and Brandenburg Gate, Berlin.. 10·50 10·50
MS4347 $3×3 Pope Benedict XVI and St. Mary's Cathedral and Church of St. Severus, Erfurt; Pope Benedict XVI and church with turquoise roof; Pope Benedict XVI and Bavarian houses and bell tower ... 10·50 10·50

664 Duke and Duchess of Cambridge

665 Bleeding Tooth Nerite (*Nerita peloronta*)

2011 (15 Aug). Royal Wedding. T **664** and similar horiz designs showing Duke and Duchess of Cambridge on their wedding day. Multicoloured. P 13 (**MS**4348/9) or 12 (**MS**4350)
MS4348 100×134 mm. $2.50 Type **664**×2; $2.50 Prince William (in profile); $2.50 Duchess of Cambridge (in profile) .... 9·00 9·00
MS4349 100×134 mm. $2.50 Prince William waving; $2.50 Duke and Duchess of Cambridge kissing×2; $2.50 Duchess of Cambridge .... 9·00 9·00
MS4350 100×106 mm. $6 Duke and Duchess of Cambridge .... 7·00 7·00

(Litho)

2011 (15 Aug). Shells of the Caribbean. T **665** and similar multicoloured designs. P 13.
MS4351 100×150 mm. $2×6 Type **665**; Pen shell (*Atrina rigida*); Banded tulip shell (*Fasciolaria lillium*); Chank shell (*Turbinella pyrum*); Flame helmet (*Cassis flammea*); Atlantic partridge tun (*Tonna maculosa*) .... 10·00 10·00
MS4352 101×131 mm. $2.75×4 Pink conch (*Strombusgigas*); Sunrise tellin (*Tellina radiata*); Flamingo tongue (*Cyphomagibbosum*); Queen's helmet (*Cassis madagascariensis*) .... 10·00 10·00
MS4353 101×101 mm. $6 King's helmet (*Cassis tuberosa*) . 6·00 6·00
MS4354 101×101 mm. $6 Triton's trumpet (*Charonia tritonis*) (*horiz*) .... 6·00 6·00

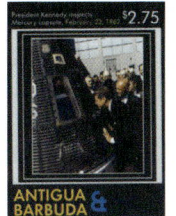

666 Pres. Kennedy inspects Mercury Capsule, 23 February 1962

667 Elvis Presley

(Litho)

2011 (9 Sep). 50th Anniv of Inauguration of Pres. John F. Kennedy. T **666** and similar multicoloured designs. P 12 (**MS**4355) or 12½ (**MS**4356).
MS4355 150×110 mm. $2.75×4 Type **666**; Cape Canaveral tour, 16 November 1963; Saturn rocket briefing, 16 November 1963; Pres. Kennedy at Cape Canaveral, 16 November 1963 .... 10·00 10·00
MS4356 100×100 mm. $6 Pres. John F. Kennedy (51×38 *mm*).. 6·00 6·00

(Litho)

2011 (9 Sep). Elvis Presley Commemoration. T **667** and similar multicoloured designs. P 13 (with one elliptical hole in each vert side (**MS**4357) or one elliptical hole in each horiz side (others)) .
MS4357 90×140 mm. $2×3 Type **667**; Wearing white suit, boarding train; On motorbike .... 10·00 10·00
MS4358 138×80 mm. $2.75×4 Elvis Presley in army uniform: Head and shoulders portrait; Leaning on railing; Wearing overalls; Reading letter (*all vert*)....... 10·00 10·00
MS4359 176×124 mm. $2.75×4 In concert: Wearing red shirt; Wearing blue jacket and white shirt; Wearing white jacket with silver studs; Wearing white jacket with patterned collar (*all vert*) .... 10·00 10·00
MS4360 140×90 mm. $3 On stage, wearing black; $3 Wearing sweater with two shoulder stripes (*both vert*).. 10·00 10·00

668 Pres. Barack Obama

(Litho)

2011 (9 Sep). Pres. Barack Obama. T **668** and similar vert designs. Multicoloured. P 13 (with one elliptical perforation in each horiz side).
MS4361 150×110 mm. $2.75×4 Type **668**; Pres. Obama facing forward, speaking; Facing forward; Facing left .. 10·00 10·00
MS4362 100×70 mm. $6 Pres. Barack Obama .... 10·00 10·00

ANTIGUA AND BARBUDA / Barbuda

669 Liftoff of Vostok 1, 1961

(Litho)
2011 (9 Sep). 50th Anniv of the First Man in Space. T **669** and similar horiz designs. Multicoloured. P 12.

MS4363	150×100 mm. $2.75×4 Type **669**; Kosmonaut Yuri Gagarin (tracking ship), 1970-91; Vostok 1 mission logo; Alan Shepard (first American astronaut) and Freedom 7, 1961	10·00	10·00
MS4364	150×100 mm. $2.75×4 Globe showing flightpath of Yuri Gagarin; Vostok 8K72K rocket; Yuri Gagarin in space; US astronaut Virgil Gus Grissom and rocket	10·00	10·00
MS4365	100×71 mm. $6 Vostok 1 orbiting Earth	6·00	6·00
MS4366	100×71 mm. $6 Yuri Gagarin	6·00	6·00

670 Princess Diana

671 Queen Angelfish (*Holacanthus ciliaris*)

(Litho)
2011 (9 Sep). 50th Birth Anniv of Princess Diana. T **670** and similar multicoloured designs. P 12 (MS4367) or 12½ (MS4368).

MS4367	150×100 mm. $2.75×4 Type **670**; Princess Diana wearing beige top with white lapels and beige pleated skirt; Wearing white; On honeymoon with Prince Charles at Balmoral, 1981	10·00	10·00
MS4368	101×101 mm. $6 Princess Diana wearing pale mauve and white patterned dress (51×38 mm)	10·00	10·00

(Litho)
2011 (30 Sep). Tropical Fish. T **671** and similar multicoloured designs. P 12.

MS4369	161×100 mm. $3.50×4 Type **671**; Ocean surgeonfish (*Acanthurus bahianus*); Rock beauty (*Holacanthus tricolor*); Gray angelfish (*Pomacanthus arcuatus*)	11·00	11·00
MS4370	161×100 mm. $3.50×4 Foureye butterflyfish (*Chaetodon capistratus*); French grunt (*Haemulon flavolineatum*); French angelfish (*Pomacanthus paru*); Spotfin butterflyfish (*Chaetodon ocellatus*)	11·00	11·00
MS4371	121×81 mm. $9 Great barracuda (*Sphyraena barracuda*) (80×30 mm)	14·00	14·00
MS4372	121×81 mm. $9 Banded butterflyfish (*Chaetodon striatus*) (40×40 mm)	14·00	14·00

STAMP BOOKLETS

1968 (2 Oct). Blue cover. Stitched.
SB1 $1.20 booklet containing 5c., 10c. and 15c. (Nos. 185, 187, 188) in blocks of 4 .... 8·50

1977 (26 Sept). Silver Jubilee. Blue, silver and sepia cover, 165×82 mm showing the Royal Family. Stitched.
SB2 $8 booklet containing pane of 6 (No. 532a) and pane of 1 (No. 533a) .... 3·25

1978 (2 June). 25th Anniv of Coronation. Multicoloured cover, 165×92 mm, showing Coronation Coach. Stitched.
SB3 $7.25 booklet containing pane of 6 (No. 587a) and pane of 1 (No. 589a) .... 2·75

1981 (23 June). Royal Wedding. Multicoloured cover, 165×92 mm, showing Prince Charles and Lady Diana Spencer on front and Prince Charles on back. Stitched.
SB4 $11.50 booklet containing pane of 6 (No. 706a) and pane of 1 (No. 712a) .... 2·50

BARBUDA
DEPENDENCY OF ANTIGUA

PRICES FOR STAMPS ON COVER TO 1945
Nos. 1/11   from × 5

BARBUDA
(**1**)

1922 (13 July). Stamps of Leeward Islands optd with T **1**. All Die II. Chalk-surfaced paper (3d. to 5s.).

(a) Wmk Mult Script CA

1	**11**	½d. deep green	1·50	12·00
2		1d. bright scarlet	1·50	12·00
		x. Wmk reversed	£850	£900
3	**10**	2d. slate-grey	1·50	7·00
		x. Wmk reversed	90·00	
4	**11**	2½d. bright blue	1·50	7·50
		w. Wmk inverted	38·00	£110
5		6d. dull and bright purple	2·00	18·00
6	**10**	2s. purple and blue/*blue*	14·00	55·00
7		3s. bright green and violet	35·00	80·00
8		4s. black and red (R.)	42·00	80·00

(b) Wmk Mult Crown CA

9	**10**	3d. purple/*pale yellow*	1·75	13·00
10	**12**	1s. black/*emerald* (R.)	1·50	8·00
11		5s. green and red/*pale yellow*	65·00	£130
1/11 Set of 11			£150	£375
1s/11s Optd "SPECIMEN" Set of 11			£225	

Examples of all values are known showing a forged Barbuda postmark of "JU 1 23".

Stocks of the overprinted stamps were exhausted by October 1925 and issues of Antigua were then used in Barbuda until 1968.
The following issues for Barbuda were also valid for use in Antigua

(New Currency. 100 cents = 1 Eastern Caribbean dollar)

2 Map of Barbuda

3 Greater Amberjack

(Des R. Granger Barrett. Litho Format)
1968 (19 Nov)–**70**. Designs as T **2**/**3**. P 14.

12		½c. brown, black and pink	45	3·25
13		1c. orange, black and flesh	1·25	35
14		2c. blackish brown, rose-red and rose	2·25	1·25
15		3c. blackish brown, orange-yellow and lemon	1·25	55
16		4c. black, bright green and apple-green	3·00	3·25
17		5c. blue-green, black and pale blue-green	2·25	20
18		6c. black, bright purple and pale lilac	1·25	3·25
19		10c. black, ultramarine and cobalt	1·75	1·25
20		15c. black, blue-green and turquoise-green	2·00	3·75
20a		20c. multicoloured (22.7.70)	1·50	2·00
21		25c. multicoloured (6.2.69)	1·00	25
22		35c. multicoloured (5.2.69)	3·00	25
23		50c. multicoloured (5.2.69)	1·00	1·50
24		75c. multicoloured (5.2.69)	1·00	80
25		$1 multicoloured (6.3.69)	50	1·50
26		$2.50 multicoloured (6.3.69)	55	2·00
27		$5 multicoloured (6.3.69)	65	2·25
12/27 Set of 17			22·00	25·00

Designs: ½ to 15c. Type **2**. Horiz as T **3**—20c. Great Barracuda; 35c. French Angelfish; 50c. Porkfish; 75c. Princess Parrotfish; $1, Long-spined Squirrelfish; $2.50, Bigeye; $5, Blue Chromis.

10 Sprinting and Aztec Sun-stone

(Des R. Granger Barrett. Litho Format)

1968 (20 Dec). Olympic Games, Mexico. T **10** and similar horiz designs. Multicoloured. P 14.

28		25c. Type **10**	50	30
29		35c. High-jumping and Aztec statue	55	30
30		75c. Dinghy-racing and Aztec lion mask	60	1·10
28/30	Set of 3		1·50	1·50
MS31	85×76 mm. $1 Football and engraved plate		2·00	3·25

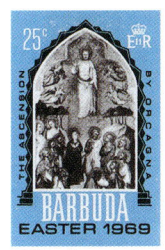

14 "The Ascension" (Orcagna)

(Des R. Granger Barrett. Litho Format)

1969 (24 Mar). Easter Commemoration. P 14.

32	**14**	25c. black and light blue	15	45
33		35c. black and deep carmine	15	50
34		75c. black and bluish lilac	15	55
32/34	Set of 3		40	1·40

15 Scout Enrolment Ceremony

18 "Sistine Madonna" (Raphael)

(Des R. Granger Barrett. Litho Format)

1969 (7 Aug). Third Caribbean Scout Jamboree. T **15** and similar horiz designs. Multicoloured. P 14.

35	25c. Type **15**	35	55
36	35c. Scouts around camp fire	45	65
37	75c. Sea Scouts rowing boat	55	1·40
35/37	Set of 3	1·25	2·40

(Des R. Granger Barrett. Litho Format)

1969 (20 Oct). Christmas. P 14.

38	**18**	½c. multicoloured	10	30
39		25c. multicoloured	10	15
40		35c. multicoloured	10	20
41		75c. multicoloured	20	35
38/41	Set of 4		30	90

19 William I (1066–87) **(20)**

(Des R. Granger Barrett. Litho Format (Nos. 42/9) or Questa (others))

1970–71. English Monarchs. T **19** and similar vert designs. Multicoloured. P 14½×14.

42	35c. Type **19** (16.2.70)	30	15
43	35c. William II (2.3.70)	10	15
44	35c. Henry I (16.3.70)	10	15
45	35c. Stephen (1.4.70)	10	15
46	35c. Henry II (15.4.70)	10	15
47	35c. Richard I (1.5.70)	10	15
48	35c. John (15.5.70)	10	15
49	35c. Henry III (1.6.70)	10	15
50	35c. Edward I (15.6.70)	10	15
51	35c. Edward II (1.7.70)	10	15
52	35c. Edward III (15.7.70)	10	15
53	35c. Richard II (1.8.70)	10	15
54	35c. Henry IV (15.8.70)	10	15
55	35c. Henry V (1.9.70)	10	15
56	35c. Henry VI (15.9.70)	10	15
57	36c. Edward IV (1.10.70)	10	15
58	35c. Edward V (15.10.70)	10	15
59	35c. Richard III (2.11.70)	10	15
60	35c. Henry VII (16.11.70)	35	15
61	35c. Henry VIII (1.12.70)	35	15
62	35c. Edward VI (15.12.70)	35	15
63	35c. Lady Jane Grey (2.1.71)	35	15
64	35c. Mary I (15.1.71)	35	15
65	35c. Elizabeth I (1.2.71)	35	15
66	35c. James I (15.2.71)	35	15
67	35c. Charles I (1.3.71)	35	15
68	35c. Charles II (15.3.71)	35	15
69	35c. James II (1.4.71)	35	15
70	35c. William III (15.4.71)	35	15
71	35c. Mary II (1.5.71)	35	15
72	35c. Anne (15.5.71)	35	15
73	35c. George I (1.6.71)	35	15
74	35c. George II (15.6.71)	35	15
75	35c. George III (1.7.71)	35	15
76	35c. George IV (15.7.71)	35	15
77	35c. William IV (2.8.71)	35	60
78	35c. Victoria (16.8.71)	35	60
42/78	Set of 37	7·50	6·00

Further values in this series were issued in 1984.

1970 (26 Feb). No. 12 surch with T **20**.

79	**2**	20c. on ½c. brown, black and pink	20	20
		a. Surch inverted	60·00	
		b. Surch double	55·00	

21 "The Way to Calvary" (Ugolino)

22 Oliver is introduced to Fagin (*Oliver Twist*)

(Des R. Granger Barrett. Litho Questa)

1970 (16 Mar). Easter Paintings. T **21** and similar vert designs. Multicoloured.

80		25c. Type **21**	15	30
		a. Horiz strip of 3. Nos. 80/2	40	85
81		35c. "The Deposition from the Cross" (Ugolino)	15	30
82		75c. Crucifix (The Master of St. Francis)	15	35
80/82	Set of 3		40	85

Nos. 80/2 were printed together, *se-tenant*, in horizontal strips of 3 throughout the sheet.

(Des R. Granger Barrett. Litho Questa)

1970 (10 July). Death Centenary of Charles Dickens. T **22** and similar horiz design. Multicoloured. P 14.

83	20c. Type **22**	45	25
84	75c. Dickens and Scene from *The Old Curiosity Shop*	80	75

23 "Madonna of the Meadow" (Bellini)

24 Nurse with Patient in Wheelchair

(Des R. Granger Barrett. Litho Questa)

1970 (15 Oct). Christmas. T **23** and similar horiz designs. Multicoloured. P 14.

85	20c. Type **23**	10	25

86	50c. "Madonna, Child and Angels" (from Wilton diptych)	15	30
87	75c. "The Nativity" (della Francesca)	15	35
85/7 Set of 3		30	80

(Des R. Granger Barrett. Litho Questa)

1970 (21 Dec). Centenary of British Red Cross. T **24** and similar multicoloured designs. P 14.

88	20c. Type **24**	15	30
89	35c. Nurse giving patient magazines (*horiz*)	20	40
90	75c. Nurse and mother weighing baby (*horiz*)	25	70
88/90 Set of 3		55	1·25

25 Angel with Vases **26** Martello Tower

(Des R. Granger Barrett. Litho Questa)

1971 (7 Apr). Easter. Details of the "Mond" Crucifixion by Raphael. T **25** and similar vert designs. Multicoloured. P 14.

91	35c. Type **25**	15	85
	a. Horiz strip of 3. Nos. 91/3	40	2·50
92	50c. Christ crucified	15	95
93	75c. Angel with vase	15	1·00
91/3 Set of 3		40	2·50

Nos. 91/3 were issued horizontally *se-tenant* within the sheet.

(Des R. Granger Barrett. Litho Questa)

1971 (10 May). Tourism. T **26** and similar horiz designs. Multicoloured. P 14.

94	20c. Type **26**	15	35
95	25c. "Sailfish" dinghy	25	40
96	50c. Hotel bungalows	25	45
97	75c. Government House and Mystery Stone	25	55
94/7 Set of 4		80	1·60

27 "The Granducal Madonna" (Raphael) **(28)**

(Des R. Granger Barrett. Litho Questa)

1971 (4 Oct). Christmas. T **27** and similar vert designs. Multicoloured. P 14.

98	½c. Type **27**	10	10
99	35c. "The Ansidei Madonna" (Raphael)	10	20
100	50c. "The Madonna and Child" (Botticelli)	15	25
101	75c. "The Madonna of the Trees" (Bellini)	15	30
98/101 Set of 4		35	65

The contract with the agency for the distribution of Barbuda stamps was cancelled by the Antiguan Government on 15 August 1971 but the above issue was duly authorised. Four stamps (20, 35, 50 and 70c.) were prepared to commemorate the 500th anniversary of the birth of Albrecht Dürer but the issue was not authorised.

Barbuda ceased to have separate stamps issues in 1972 but again had stamps of her own on 14 November 1973 with the following issue.

1973 (14 Nov). Royal Wedding. Nos. 370/1 of Antigua optd with T **28**.

102	35c. multicoloured	3·25	2·00
	a. Opt inverted	£100	
103	$2 multicoloured	1·25	1·25
	a. Opt inverted	£120	

No. **MS**372 of Antigua also exists with this overprint, but was not placed on sale at post offices. Examples of this sheet are known with "Specimen" overprint (*Price* £120).

BARBUDA (29) (30) (30a) (31)

1973 (26 Nov)–**74**. T **92** etc. of Antigua optd with T **29**.

(a) On Nos. 270 etc. W w 12 (sideways)

104	1c. Columbus and *Nina*	15	30
105	2c. Sir Thomas Warner's emblem and *Concepcion*	25	30
106	4c. Sir George Rodney and H.M.S. *Formidable*	30	30
107	5c. Nelson and H.M.S. *Boreas*	40	40
108	6c. William IV and H.M.S. *Pegasus*	40	40
109	10c. "Blackbeard" and pirate ketch	45	45
110	20c. Nelson and H.M.S. *Victory*	55	60
111	25c. *Solent I* (paddle-steamer)	55	60
112	35c. George V (when Prince George) and H.M.S. *Canada* (screw corvette)	55	70
113	50c. H.M.S. *Renown* (battle cruiser)	55	70
114	75c. *Federal Maple* (freighter)	55	70
115	$2.50 H.M.S. *London* (destroyer) (18.2.74)	75	1·50

(b) On Nos. 323 etc. W w 12 (upright). White paper

116	½c. Type **92** (11.12.73)	15	20
117	3c. Viscount Hood and H.M.S. *Barfleur* (11.12.73)	25	25
	w. Wmk inverted	35·00	
118	15c. Captain Collingwood and H.M.S. *Pelican* (11.12.73)	45	50
119	$1 *Sol Quest* (yacht) and class emblem (11.12.73)	55	70
120	$2.50 H.M.S. *London* (destroyer) (18.2.74)	9·00	13·00
121	$5 *Pathfinder* (tug) (26.11.73)	1·10	2·50
104/21 Set of 18		15·00	21·00

1973 (26 Nov). Commemorative stamps of Antigua optd.

*(a) Nos. 353, 355 and 357/8 optd with T **30***

122	½c. Private, Zacharia Tiffin's Regt of Foot, 1701	10	10
123	20c. Light Company Officer, 35th Regt of Foot, 1828	15	10
	aw. Wmk Crown to right of CA	7·00	
	b. Optd with T **30a**	60	70
	bw. Wmk Crown to right of CA	6·00	
124	75c. Sergeant, 49th Regt, 1858	40	15
122/4 Set of 3		55	25
MS125	127×145 mm. Nos. 353/7 of Antigua	2·00	3·50

*(b) Nos 360/3 optd with T **31**, in red*

126	20c. Carnival street scene	10	10
127	35c. Carnival troupe	10	10
	a. Opt inverted	30·00	
128	75c. Carnival Queen	20	25
126/8 Set of 3		30	40
MS129	134×95 mm. Nos. 359/62 of Antigua	1·00	2·25
	a. Albino opt		
	b. Opt double	£275	

Type **30a** is a local overprint, applied by typography.

BARBUDA (32) (33) (34) (35)

1973 (11 Dec). Christmas. Nos. 364/9 of Antigua optd with T **32**.

130	3c. Type **105** (Sil.)	10	10
	a. Opt inverted	24·00	
	b. "BABRUDA" (R.4/2)	5·50	5·50
131	5c. "Adoration of the Magi" (Stomer) (Sil.)	10	10
	a. "BABRUDA" (R.4/2)	7·00	7·00
132	20c. "Granducal Madonna" (Raphael) (Sil.)	10	10
	a. "BABRUDA" (R.4/2)	9·00	9·00

ANTIGUA AND BARBUDA / Barbuda

133	35c. "Nativity with God the Father and Holy Ghost" (Battista) (R.)		15	15
134	$1 "Madonna and Child" (Murillo) (R.)		30	30
	a. Opt inverted		45·00	
130/4 Set of 5			60	60
MS135 130×128 mm. Nos. 130/4 (Sil.)			2·25	9·00

1973 (15 Dec). Honeymoon Visit of Princess Anne and Capt. Phillips. Nos. 373/5 of Antigua further optd with T **33**.

136	35c. multicoloured		30	20
	a. Type **33** double, one albino		65·00	
	b. Optd on Antigua No. 373a			
137	$2 multicoloured		70	60
	a. Type **33** double, one albino		†	—
	b. Optd on Antigua No. 374a			
MS138 78×100 mm. Nos. 136/7			1·10	1·00

1974 (18 Feb). 25th Anniv of University of West Indies. Nos. 376/9 of Antigua optd with T **34**.

139	5c. Coat of arms		10	10
	a. Opt double, one albino		†	—
140	20c. Extra-mural art		10	10
141	35c. Antigua campus		15	15
	a. Opt double			
142	75c. Antigua Chancellor		15	15
139/42 Set of 4			30	30

No. 139a has only been seen used on first day cover. It shows the "normal" impression misplaced and very faint.

1974 (1 May). Military Uniforms. Nos. 380/4 of Antigua optd with T **35**.

143	½c. Officer, 59th Foot, 1797		10	10
144	10c. Gunner, Royal Artillery, 1800		20	10
	a. Horiz pair, left-hand stamp without opt		£130	
145	20c. Private, 1st West India Regt, 1830		30	10
	a. Horiz pair, left-hand stamp without opt		£130	
146	35c. Officer, 92nd Foot, 1843		35	10
	a. Opt inverted		50·00	
147	75c. Private, 23rd Foot, 1846		50	25
	a. Horiz pair, left-hand stamp without opt			
143/7 Set of 5			1·25	45

Nos. 144a, 145a and 147a come from sheets on which the overprint was so misplaced as to miss the first vertical row completely. Other stamps in these sheets show the overprint at left instead of right.

No. **MS**385 of Antigua also exists with this overprint, but was not placed on sale at post offices.

BARBUDA 13 JULY 1922 (36)

BARBUDA 15 SEPT. 1874 G.P.U. (37 "General Postal Union")

BARBUDA (38)

1974 (15 July). Centenary of Universal Postal Union (1st issue). Nos. 386/92 of Antigua optd with T **36** (Nos. 148, 150, 152, 154, 156, 158 and 160) or T **37** (others), in red.

148	½c. English postman, mailcoach and Westland Dragonfly helicopter		10	10
149	½c. English postman, mailcoach and Westland Dragonfly helicopter		10	10
150	1c. Bellman, mail steamer *Orinoco* and satellite		10	10
151	1c. Bellman, mail steamer *Orinoco* and satellite		10	10
152	2c. Train guard, post-bus and hydrofoil		20	15
153	2c. Train guard, post-bus and hydrofoil		20	15
154	5c. Swiss messenger, Wells Fargo coach and Concorde		50	15
155	5c. Swiss messenger, Wells Fargo coach and Concorde		50	15
156	20c. Postillion, Japanese postmen and carrier pigeon		40	70
157	20c. Postillion, Japanese postmen and carrier pigeon		40	70
158	35c. Antiguan postman, Sikorsky S-38 flying boat and tracking station		80	1·50
159	35c. Antiguan postman, Sikorsky S-38 flying boat and tracking station		80	1·50
160	$1 Medieval courier, American express train and Boeing 747-100		1·75	4·00
161	$1 Medieval courier, American express train and Boeing 747-100		1·75	4·00
148/61 Set of 14			6·50	12·00
MS162 141×164 mm. No. **MS**393 of Antigua overprinted with T **38**, in red			3·50	6·00
	a. Albino opt			

Nos. 148/9, 150/1, 152/3, 154/5 156/7, 158/9 and 160/1 were each printed together, *se-tenant*, in horizontal pairs throughout the sheet.

See also Nos. 177/80.

1974 (14 Aug). Antiguan Steel Bands. Nos. 394/8 of Antigua optd with T **38**.

163	5c. rose-red, carmine and black		10	10
164	20c. brown-ochre, chestnut and black		10	10
165	35c. light sage-green, blue-green and black		10	10
166	75c. dull blue, dull ultramarine and black		20	20
163/6 Set of 4			35	35
MS167 115×108 mm. Nos. 163/6			65	80

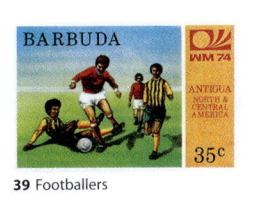

39 Footballers

(40)

(Des G. Drummond. Litho Format)

1974 (2 Sept). World Cup Football Championship (1st issue). Various horiz designs as T **39** each showing footballers in action. P 14.

168	**39** 35c. multicoloured		10	10
169	$1.20 multicoloured		25	35
170	$2.50 multicoloured		35	50
168/70 Set of 3			60	75
MS171 70×128 mm. Nos. 168/70			85	90

Nos. 168/71 exist imperforate from stock dispersed by the liquidator of Format International Security Printers Ltd.

The stamps are also known, perforated and imperforate, with match scores included within the designs.

1974 (23 Sept). World Cup Football Championship (2nd issue). Nos. 399/403 of Antigua optd with T **40**.

172	5c. multicoloured		10	10
173	35c. multicoloured		20	10
174	75c. multicoloured		25	15
175	$1 multicoloured		25	25
172/5 Set of 4			70	45
MS176 135×130 mm. Nos. 172/5			75	1·25

41 Ship Letter of 1833

42 Greater Amberjack

(Des G. Drummond. Litho Format)

1974 (30 Sept). Centenary of Universal Postal Union (2nd issue). T **41** and similar vert designs. Multicoloured. P 13½.

177	35c. Type **41**		10	10
178	$1.20 Stamps and postmark of 1922		25	50
179	$2.50 Britten Norman Islander mailplane over map of Barbuda		35	75
177/9 Set of 3			60	1·25
MS180 128×97 mm. Nos. 177/9			1·00	2·00

Nos. 177/80 exist imperforate from stock dispersed by the liquidator of Format International Security Printers Ltd.

(Des G. Drummond. Litho Format)

1974 (15 Oct)–**75**. Multicoloured designs as T **42**. P 14×14½ (½c. to 3c., 25c.), 14½×14 (4c. to 20c., 35c.), 14 (50c., to $1) or 13½ (others).

181	½c. Oleander, Rose Bay (6.1.75)		10	40
182	1c. Blue Petrea (6.1.75)		15	40
183	2c. Poinsettia (6.1.75)		15	40
184	3c. Cassia tree (6.1.75)		15	40
185	4c. Type **42**		1·75	40
186	5c. Holy Trinity School		15	15
187	6c. Snorkeling		15	30
188	10c. Pilgrim Holiness Church		15	20
189	15c. New Cottage Hospital		15	20
190	20c. Post Office and Treasury		15	20
191	25c. Island jetty and boats		30	30
192	35c. Martello Tower		30	30
193	50c. Warden's House (6.1.75)		30	30
194	75c. Britten Norman Islander aircraft		3·50	1·00

ANTIGUA AND BARBUDA / Barbuda

195	$1 Tortoise (6.1.75)	70	80
196	$2.50 Spiny lobster (6.1.75)	80	1·75
197	$5 Magnificent Frigate Bird (6.1.75)	4·00	2·50
	a. Perf 14×14½ (24.7.75)*	9·00	18·00
197b	$10 Hibiscus (19.9.75)	1·50	4·50
181/976 Set of 18		13·00	13·00

*See footnote below Nos. 227/8.
The 50c. to $1 are larger, 39×25 mm; the $2.50 and $5 are 45×29 mm; the $10 is 34×48 mm and the ½c. to 3c. 25c. and $10 are vert designs.

1974 (15 Oct). Birth Centenary of Sir Winston Churchill (1st issue). Nos. 408/12 of Antigua optd with T **38** in red.

198	5c. Churchill as schoolboy, and school college building, Harrow	15	10
	a. Opt inverted	65·00	
199	35c. Churchill and St. Paul's Cathedral	25	15
200	75c. Coat of arms and catafalque	40	45
201	$1 Churchill, "reward" notice and South African escape route	75	70
	a. Opt inverted	65·00	
198/201 Set of 4		1·40	1·25
MS202 107×82 mm. Nos. 198/201		7·00	14·00

43 Churchill making Broadcast

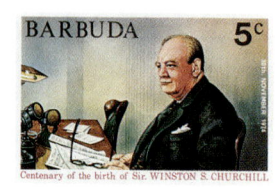

BARBUDA (**44**)

(Des G. Drummond. Litho Questa)

1974 (20 Nov). Birth Centenary of Sir Winston Churchill (2nd issue). T **43** and similar horiz designs. Multicoloured. P 13½×14.

203	5c. Type **43**	10	10
204	35c. Churchill and Chartwell	10	10
205	75c. Churchill painting	20	20
206	$1 Churchill making "V" sign	25	30
203/6 Set of 4		55	60
MS207 146×95 mm. Nos. 203/6		75	2·50

1974 (25 Nov). Christmas. Nos. 413/21 of Antigua optd with T **33**.

208	½c. Bellini	10	10
	a. Opt inverted	48·00	
209	1c. Raphael	10	10
210	2c. Van der Weyden	10	10
211	3c. Giorgione	10	10
212	5c. Mantegna	10	10
213	20c. Vivarini	10	10
214	35c. Montagna	15	15
215	75c. Lorenzo Costa	30	30
208/15 Set of 8		60	60
MS216 139×126 mm. Nos. 208/15		80	1·40

1975 (17 Mar). Nelson's Dockyard. Nos. 427/32 of Antigua optd with T **44**.

217	5c. Carib war canoe, English Harbour, 1300	15	15
218	15c. Ship of the line, English Harbour, 1770	35	25
219	35c. H.M.S. *Boreas* at anchor, and Lord Nelson, 1787	40	35
220	50c. Yachts during "Sailing Week", 1974	45	50
221	$1 Yacht Anchorage, Old Dockyard, 1970	50	80
217/21 Set of 5		1·60	1·75
MS222 130×134 mm. As Nos. 217/21, but in larger format; 43×28 mm		1·75	2·75

45 Battle of the Saints, 1782

(Des G. Vasarhelyi. Litho Format)

1975 (30 May). Sea Battles. T **45** and similar horiz designs showing scenes from the Battle of the Saints, 1782. Multicoloured. P 13½.

223	35c. Type **45**	40	65
224	50c. H.M.S. *Ramillies*	40	75
225	75c. *Bonhomme Richard* (American frigate) firing broadside	50	90
226	95c. *L'Orient* (French ship of the line) burning	50	1·25
223/6 Set of 4		1·60	3·25

(**46**)

1975 (24 July). "Apollo-Soyuz" Space Project. No. 197a optd with T **46** and similar ("Soyuz") opt.

227	$5 Magnificent Frigate Bird ("Apollo")	3·25	6·00
	a. *Se-tenant* strip of 3. Nos. 227/8 and 197a	14·00	24·00
228	$5 Magnificent Frigate Bird ("Soyuz")	3·25	6·00

Nos. 227/8 were issued together *se-tenant* in sheets of 25 (5×5), with the "Apollo" opts in the first and third vertical rows and the "Soyuz" opts in the second and fourth vertical rows, the fifth vertical row comprising five unoverprinted stamps (No. 197a).

47 Officer, 65th Foot, 1763

30TH ANNIVERSARY UNITED NATIONS 1945 — 1975 (**48**)

(Des G. Drummond. Litho Questa)

1975 (17 Sept). Military Uniforms. T **47** and similar vert designs. Multicoloured. P 13½.

229	35c. Type **47**	60	60
230	50c. Grenadier, 27th Foot, 1701–10	75	75
231	75c. Officer, 21st Foot, 1793–6	80	80
232	95c. Officer, Royal Regt of Artillery, 1800	90	90
229/32 Set of 4		2·75	3·75

1975 (24 Oct). 30th Anniv of United Nations. Nos. 203/6 optd with T **48**.

233	5c. Churchill making broadcast	10	10
234	35c. Churchill and Chartwell	10	15
235	75c. Churchill painting	15	20
236	$1 Churchill making "V" sign	20	30
233/6 Set of 4		40	60

BARBUDA (**49**) **BARBUDA** (**50**)

1975 (17 Nov). Christmas. Nos. 457/65 of Antigua optd with T **49**.

237	½c. Correggio	10	15
238	1c. El Greco	10	15
239	2c. Dürer	10	15
240	3c. Antonello	10	15
241	5c. Bellini	10	15
242	10c. Dürer	10	15
243	25c. Bellini	15	20
244	$2 Dürer	60	1·00
237/44 Set of 8		95	1·90
MS245 138×119 mm. Nos. 241/4		1·10	2·25

1975 (15 Dec). World Cup Cricket Winners. Nos. 466/8 of Antigua optd with T **50**.

246	5c. Vivian Richards	1·50	1·75
247	35c. Andy Roberts	2·75	2·00
248	$2 West Indies team	4·25	5·50
246/8 Set of 3		7·75	8·25

51 "Surrender of Cornwallis at Yorktown" (Trumbull)

(Des G. Vasarhelyi. Litho Format)

1976 (8 Mar). Bicentenary of American Revolution. T **51** and similar horiz designs. Multicoloured. P 13½×13.

249	15c. Type **51**	10	15
250	15c. Type **51**	10	15
251	15c. Type **51**	10	15

252	35c. "The Battle of Princeton"	10	15
253	35c. "The Battle of Princeton"	10	15
254	35c. "The Battle of Princeton"	10	15
255	$1 "Surrender of General Burgoyne at Saratoga" (W. Mercer)	15	25
256	$1 "Surrender of General Burgoyne at Saratoga" (W. Mercer)	15	25
257	$1 "Surrender of General Burgoyne at Saratoga" (W. Mercer)	15	25
258	$2 "The Declaration of Independence" (Trumbull)	25	40
259	$2 "The Declaration of Independence" (Trumbull)	25	40
260	$2 "The Declaration of Independence" (Trumbull)	25	40
249/60 Set of 12		1·50	2·50
MS261 140×70 mm. Nos. 249/54 and 255/60 (two sheets)		1·40	9·00

The three designs of each value were printed horizontally se-tenant within the sheet to form the composite designs listed. Type **51** shows the left-hand stamp of the 15c. design.

52 Bananaquits

(Des G. Drummond. Litho Format)

1976 (30 June). Birds. T **52** and similar horiz designs. Multicoloured. P 13½.

262	35c. Type **52**	20	25
263	50c. Blue-hooded Euphonia	20	40
264	75c. Royal Tern	20	50
265	95c. Killdeer	25	55
266	$1.25 Common Cowbird	25	70
267	$2 Purple Gallinule	30	85
262/7 Set of 6		1·25	3·00

1976 (12 Aug). Royal Visit to the U.S.A. As Nos. 249/60 but redrawn and inscr at top "H.M. QUEEN ELIZABETH ROYAL VISIT 6TH JULY 1976 H.R.H. DUKE OF EDINBURGH".

268	15c. As Type **51**	10	15
269	15c. As Type **51**	10	15
270	15c. As Type **51**	10	15
271	35c. As Nos. 252/4	10	20
272	35c. As Nos. 252/4	10	20
273	35c. As Nos. 252/4	10	20
274	$1 As Nos. 255/7	15	50
275	$1 As Nos. 255/7	15	50
276	$1 As Nos. 255/7	15	50
277	$2 As Nos. 258/60	25	70
278	$2 As Nos. 258/60	25	70
279	$2 As Nos. 258/60	25	70
268/79 Set of 12		1·50	4·25
MS280 143×81 mm. Nos. 268/73 and 274/9 (two sheets)		1·50	9·00

The three designs of each value were printed horizontally se-tenant, imperf between.

BARBUDA
(53)

1976 (2 Dec). Christmas. Nos. 514/18 of Antigua optd with T **53**.

281	8c. The Annunciation	10	10
282	10c. The Holy Family	10	10
283	15c. The Magi	10	10
284	50c. The Shepherds	15	15
285	$1 Epiphany scene	25	30
281/5 Set of 5		45	55

BARBUDA
(54)

1976 (28 Dec). Olympic Games, Montreal. Nos. 495/502 of Antigua optd with T **54**.

286	½c. High jump	10	10
287	1c. Boxing	10	10
288	2c. Pole-vault	10	10
289	15c. Swimming	10	10
290	30c. Running	10	10
291	$1 Cycling	20	20
292	$2 Shot put	35	35
286/92 Set of 7		60	60
MS293 88×138 mm. Nos. 289/92		1·75	2·40

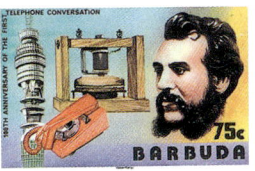

55 Post Office Tower, Telephones and Alexander Graham Bell

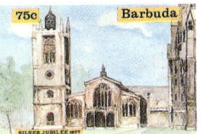

56 St. Margaret's Church, Westminster

(Des G. Vasarhelyi. Litho Format)

1977 (31 Jan). Telephone Centenary (1976). T **55** and similar horiz designs. Multicoloured. P 13½.

294	75c. Type **55**	15	35
295	$1.25 Dish aerial and television	20	55
296	$2 Globe and satellites	30	75
294/6 Set of 3		60	1·50
MS297 96×144 mm. Nos. 294/6. P 15		70	2·00

1977 (7 Feb). Silver Jubilee (1st issue). T **56** and similar horiz designs. Multicoloured. Litho. P 13½×13.

298	75c. Type **56**	10	15
299	75c. Entrance, Westminster Abbey	10	15
300	75c. Westminster Abbey	10	15
301	$1.25 Household Cavalry	15	20
302	$1.25 Coronation Coach	15	20
303	$1.25 Team of Horses	15	20
298/303 Set of 6		65	90
MS304 148×83 mm. As Nos. 298/303, but with silver borders. P 15		75	1·50

Nos. 298/300 and 301/3 were printed horizontally se-tenant, forming composite designs.

See also Nos. 323/30 and 375/8.

1977 (4 Apr). Nos. 469A/86A of Antigua optd with T **54**.

305	½c. Antillean Crested Hummingbird	1·00	75
306	1c. Imperial Amazon	1·00	75
307	2c. Zenaida Dove	1·00	75
308	3c. Loggerhead Kingbird	1·00	75
309	4c. Red-necked Pigeon	1·00	75
310	5c. Rufous-throated Solitaire	1·00	75
311	6c. Orchid Tree	50	50
312	10c. Bougainvillea	30	20
313	15c. Geiger Tree	30	25
314	20c. Flamboyant	30	25
315	25c. Hibiscus	30	25
316	35c. Flame of the Wood	35	30
317	50c. Cannon at Fort James	40	40
318	75c. Premier's Office	40	40
319	$1 Potworks Dam	50	60
320	$2.50 Irrigation scheme	75	1·60
321	$5 Government House	1·25	3·25
322	$10 Coolidge Airport	3·50	7·50
305/22 Set of 18		13·00	17·00

BARBUDA (57)   BARBUDA (58)   BARBUDA (59)

1977 (4 Apr–20 Dec). Silver Jubilee (2nd issue).

(a) Sheet stamps. Nos. 526/31 of Antigua optd with T **57**

323	10c. Royal Family	10	15
	a. Opt double	45·00	
324	30c. Royal Visit, 1966	10	20
325	50c. Queen enthroned	15	30
326	90c. Queen after Coronation	15	40
327	$2.50 Queen and Prince Charles	45	1·25
323/7 Set of 5		85	2·10
MS328 116×78 mm. $5 Queen Elizabeth and Prince Philip		80	1·25
	a. Error. Imperf	£600	
	b. Opt albino	25·00	
	c. Opt double		

(b) Booklet stamps. Nos. 532/3 of Antigua optd with T **58** in silver (50c.) or T **59** in gold ($5) (20 Dec)

329	50c. Queen after Coronation	40	70
	a. Booklet pane of 6	2·25	
330	$5 The Queen and Prince Philip	3·00	9·00
	a. Booklet pane of 1	3·00	

BARBUDA
(60)

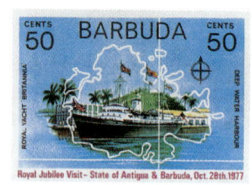

61 Royal Yacht *Britannia*

1977 (13 June). Caribbean Scout Jamboree, Jamaica. Nos. 534/41 of Antigua optd with T **60**.

331	½c. Making camp	10	10
332	1c. Hiking	10	10
333	2c. Rock-climbing	10	10
334	10c. Cutting logs	10	10
335	30c. Map and sign reading	25	40
336	50c. First aid	25	65
337	$2 Rafting	55	2·25
331/37 *Set of 7*		1·10	3·00
MS338 127×114 mm. Nos. 335/7		1·75	4·00

1977 (12 Aug). 21st Anniv of Carnival. Nos. 542/7 of Antigua optd with T **60**.

339	10c. Carnival costume	10	10
340	30c. Carnival Queen	10	10
341	50c. Butterfly costume	15	20
342	90c. Queen of the band	20	35
343	$1 Calypso King and Queen	25	45
339/43 *Set of 5*		65	1·00
MS344 140×120 mm. Nos. 339/43		1·00	1·75

(Des G. Drummond. Litho Format)

1977 (27 Oct). Royal Visit (1st issue). T **61** and similar horiz designs. Multicoloured. P 14½.

345	50c. Type **61**	10	20
346	$1.50 Jubilee emblem	25	35
347	$2.50 Union Jack and flag of Antigua	35	55
345/7 *Set of 3*		60	1·00
MS348 77×124 mm. Nos. 345/7		85	2·25

BARBUDA (62) BARBUDA (63)

1977 (28 Nov–20 Dec). Royal Visit (2nd issue). Nos. 548/53 of Antigua optd.

A. With T **57**. P 14 (28 Nov).

349A	10c. Royal Family	35	35
350A	30c. Royal Visit, 1966	90	95
351A	50c. Queen enthroned	2·75	1·90
352A	90c. Queen after Coronation	5·00	3·50
353A	$2.50 Queen and Prince Charles	11·00	9·50
349A/53A *Set of 5*		80	2·00
MS354A 116×78 mm. $5 Queen and Prince Philip		1·50	4·00

B. With T **62**. P 11½×12 (20 Dec)

349B	10c. Royal Family	10	10
	a. Blue opt	35	35
350B	30c. Royal Visit, 1966	10	15
	a. Blue opt	90	95
351B	50c. Queen enthroned	15	20
	a. Blue opt	2·75	1·90
352B	90c. Queen after Coronation	20	30
	a. Blue opt	5·00	3·50
353B	$2.50 Queen and Prince Charles	45	80
	a. Blue opt	11·00	9·50
349B/53B *Set of 5*		85	1·40

Nos. 349B/53B were each printed in small sheets of 6 including one se-tenant stamp-size label.

1977 (28 Nov). Christmas. Nos. 554/61 of Antigua optd with T **63**. "Virgin and Child" paintings by the artists given.

355	½c. Tura	10	10
356	1c. Crivelli	10	10
357	2c. Lotto	10	10
358	8c. Pontormo	10	10
359	10c. Tura	10	10
360	25c. Lotto	15	10
361	$2 Crivelli	45	45
355/61 *Set of 7*		70	65
MS362 144×118 mm. Nos. 358/61		1·00	1·75

64 Airship LZ-1

(Des I. Oliver. Litho Format)

1977 (29 Dec). Special Events, 1977. T **64** and similar horiz designs. Multicoloured. P 14.

363	75c. Type **64**	30	30
	a. Nos. 363/6 in *se-tenant* block	1·10	1·10
364	75c. German battleship and naval airship L-31	30	30
365	75c. Airship LZ-127 *Graf Zeppelin* in hangar	30	30
366	75c. Gondola of military airship	30	30
367	95c. "Sputnik 1"	35	35
	a. Nos. 367/70 in *se-tenant* block	1·25	1·25
368	95c. "Vostok"	35	35
369	95c. "Voskhod"	35	35
370	95c. Space walk	35	35
371	$1.25 Fuelling for flight	40	45
	a. Nos. 371/4 in *se-tenant* block	1·40	1·60
372	$1.25 Leaving New York	40	45
373	$1.25 Ryan NYP Special *Spirit of St. Louis*	40	45
374	$1.25 Welcome in France	40	45
375	$2 Lion of England	50	70
	a. Nos. 375/8 in *se-tenant* block	1·75	2·50
376	$2 Unicorn of Scotland	50	70
377	$2 Yale of Beaufort	50	70
378	$2 Falcon of Plantagenets	50	70
379	$5 "Daniel in the Lion's Den" (Rubens)	50	1·25
380	$5 Different detail of painting	50	1·25
381	$5 Different detail of painting	50	1·25
382	$5 Different detail of painting	50	1·25
	a. Nos. 379/82 in *se-tenant* block	1·75	4·50
363/82 *Set of 20*		6·00	11·00
MS383 132×156 mm. Nos. 363/82		6·00	17·00

Events:—75c. 75th Anniv of Navigable Airships; 95c. 20th Anniv of U.S.S.R. Space Programme; $1.25, 50th Anniv of Lindbergh's Transatlantic Flight; $2 Silver Jubilee of Queen Elizabeth II; $5 400th Birth Anniv of Rubens.

Nos. 363/66, 367/70, 371/74, 375/78 and 379/82 were printed in *se-tenant* blocks of four within the sheet.

Nos. 363/83 exist imperforate from stock dispersed by the liquidator of Format International Security Printers Ltd.

BARBUDA (65)

66 "Pieta" (sculpture) (detail)

1978 (15 Feb). Tenth Anniv of Statehood. Nos. 562/7 of Antigua optd with T **65**.

384	10c. Pineapple	10	10
385	15c. State flag	15	10
386	50c. Police band	1·25	80
387	90c. Premier V. C. Bird	20	40
388	$2 State Coat of Arms	40	1·00
384/8 *Set of 5*		1·75	2·25
MS389 126×99 mm. Nos. 385/88. P 14		7·00	4·00

(Des G. Vasarhelyi. Litho Format)

1978 (23 Mar). Easter. Works by Michelangelo. T **66** and similar horiz designs. Multicoloured. P 13½×14.

390	75c. Type **66**	15	15
391	95c. "The Holy Family" (painting)	15	20
392	$1.25 "Libyan Sibyl" from Sistine Chapel, Rome	15	35
393	$2 "The Flood" from Sistine Chapel	20	45
390/3 *Set of 4*		60	1·00
MS394 117×85 mm. Nos. 390/3		1·90	2·00

Nos. 390/4 exist imperforate from stock dispersed by the liquidator of Format International Security Printers Ltd.

BARBUDA (67)

68 St. Edward's Crown

1978 (28 Mar). 75th Anniv of Powered Flight. Nos. 568/75 of Antigua optd with T **67**.

395	½c. Wright Glider III, 1902	10	10
396	1c. Wright *Flyer I*, 1903	10	10

ANTIGUA AND BARBUDA / Barbuda

397	2c. Launch system and engine	10	10
398	10c. Orville Wright	10	10
399	50c. Wright *Flyer III*, 1905	25	20
400	90c. Wilbur Wright	35	25
401	$2 Wright Type B, 1910	60	45
395/401 Set of 7		1·25	1·00
MS402 90×75 mm. $2.50, Wright *Flyer I* on launch system		1·50	2·50

1978 (22 May). Sailing Week. Nos. 576/80 of Antigua optd with T **67**.

403	10c. Sunfish regatta	20	10
404	50c. Fishing and work boat race	40	25
405	90c. Curtain Bluff race	55	35
406	$2 Power boat rally	85	75
403/6 Set of 4		1·75	1·25
MS407 110×77 mm. $2.50, Guadeloupe–Antigua race		1·25	1·60
a. Albino opt		†	—

(Des J. Cooter. Litho Format)

1978 (2 June). 25th Anniv of Coronation (1st issue). T **68** and similar vert designs. Multicoloured. P 15.

408	75c. Type **68**	15	20
409	75c. Imperial State Crown	15	20
410	$1.50 Queen Mary's Crown	20	30
411	$1.50 Queen Mother's Crown	20	30
412	$2.50 Queen Consort's Crown	35	50
413	$2.50 Queen Victoria's Crown	35	50
408/413 Set of 6		1·10	1·75
MS414 123×117 mm. Nos. 408/13. P 14½		1·10	1·75

The two designs for each value were issued as two *se-tenant* pairs, together with 2 labels, in small sheets of 6.

Examples of the 75c. and $2.50 values exist in separate miniature sheets of four exist from stock dispersed by the liquidator of Format International Security Printers Ltd, as do imperforate examples of No. **MS**414.

1978 (2 June–12 Oct). 25th Anniv of Coronation (2nd issue).

*(a) Sheet stamps. Nos. 581/6 of Antigua optd with T **67**. P 14 (2.6)*

415	10c. Queen Elizabeth and Prince Philip	10	10
416	30c. Crowning	10	10
417	50c. Coronation procession	10	15
418	90c. Queen seated in St. Edward's Chair	15	20
a. Opt triple		85·00	
419	$2.50 Queen wearing Imperial State Crown	30	60
415/19 Set of 5		60	1·00
MS420 114×103 mm. $5 Queen and Prince Philip (17.7)		1·00	1·50
a. Albino opt		£250	

(b) Booklet stamps. Horiz designs as Nos. 587/9 of Antigua but additionally inscr "BARBUDA". Multicoloured. Roul 5×imperf*. Self-adhesive (12.10)

421	25c. Glass Coach	30	70
a. Booklet pane. Nos. 421/2×3		1·60	
422	50c. Irish State Coach	30	70
423	$5 Coronation Coach	1·00	2·25
a. Booklet pane of 1		1·00	
421/3 Set of 3		1·75	3·25

*The 25 and 50c. values were separated by various combinations of rotary knife (giving a straight edge) and roulette. The $5 value exists only with straight edges.

Nos. 415/19 also exist perf 12 (*Price for set of 5 55p mint or used*) from additional sheetlets of three stamps and one label, issued 12 October 1978. These stamps have different background colours from Nos. 415/19.

1978 (12 Sept). World Cup Football Championship, Argentina. Nos. 590/3 of Antigua optd with T **67**.

424	10c. Player running with ball	10	10
425	15c. Players in front of goal	10	10
426	$3 Referee and player	1·25	1·25
424/6 Set of 3		1·25	1·25
MS427 126×88 mm. 25c. Player crouching with ball; 30c. Players heading ball; 50c. Players running with ball; $2 Goalkeeper diving		80	90

(69)

70 Black-barred Soldierfish

1978 (20 Nov). Flowers. Nos. 594/8 of Antigua optd with T **69**.

428	25c. Petrea	15	20
429	50c. Sunflower	25	40
430	90c. Frangipani	35	45
431	$2 Passion Flower	60	90
428/31 Set of 4		1·25	1·75
MS432 118×85 mm. $2.50, Hibiscus		1·00	1·50

1978 (20 Nov). Christmas. Paintings. Nos. 599/602 optd with T **69** in silver.

433	8c. "St. Ildefonso receiving the Chasuble from the Virgin"	10	10
434	25c. "The Flight of St. Barbara"	15	15
435	$2 "Madonna and Child, with St. Joseph, John the Baptist and Donor"	60	1·25
433/5 Set of 3		75	1·25
MS436 170×113 mm. $4 "The Annunciation"		1·00	2·25

(Litho Format)

1978 (20 Nov). Flora and Fauna. T **70** and similar horiz designs. Multicoloured. P 14½.

437	25c. Type **70**	75	1·50
438	50c. *Cynthia cardui* (butterfly)	1·50	2·25
439	75c. Dwarf Poinciana	80	2·25
440	95c. *Heliconius charithonia* (butterfly)	1·50	2·50
441	$1.25 Bougainvillea	90	2·50
437/41 Set of 5		5·00	10·00

71 Footballers and World Cup

72 Sir Rowland Hill

(Des J. Cooter. Litho Format)

1978 (29 Dec). Anniversaries and Events. T **71** and similar multicoloured designs. P 14.

442	75c. Type **71**	30	30
443	95c. Wright brothers and *Flyer I* (*horiz*)	30	40
444	$1.25 Balloon *Double Eagle II* and map of Atlantic (*horiz*)	55	45
445	$2 Prince Philip paying homage to the newly crowned Queen	55	60
442/5 Set of 4		1·50	1·60
MS446 122×90 mm. Nos. 442/5. Imperf		5·00	6·00

Events:—75c. Argentina—Winners of World Cup Football Championship; 95c. 75th anniversary of powered flight; $1.25 1st Atlantic crossing by balloon; $2 25th anniversary of Coronation.

(Des J. Cooter. Litho Format)

1979 (4 Apr). Death Centenary of Sir Rowland Hill (1st issue) T **72** and similar multicoloured designs. P 14.

447	75c. Type **72**	25	45
448	95c. Mail coach, 1840 (*horiz*)	25	50
449	$1.25 London's first pillar box, 1855 (*horiz*)	30	60
450	$2 Mail leaving St. Martin's Le Grand Post Office, London	45	85
447/50 Set of 4		1·10	2·25
MS451 129×104 mm. Nos. 447/50 Imperf		1·40	2·25

Nos. 447/50 were each printed in small sheets of 4 including one *se-tenant* stamp-size label.

(73)

74 Passengers alighting from Boeing 747-200

1979 (4 Apr). Death Centenary of Sir Rowland Hill (2nd issue). Nos. 603/7 of Antigua optd with T **73** in black (No. **MS**456) or blue (others). P 14.

452	25c. Antigua 1863 1d. stamp	15	15
453	50c. Penny Black stamp	20	20
454	$1 Stage-coach and woman posting letter, *circa* 1840	35	30
455	$2 Modern mail transport	80	60
452/5 Set of 4		1·40	1·10
MS456 108×82 mm. $2.50, Sir Rowland Hill		75	80

Nos. 452/5 also exist perf 12 (*Price for set of 4 £1.75 mint or used*) from additional sheetlets of four stamps and one label, issued 28 December 1979.

1979 (12 Apr). Easter. Works by Dürer. Nos. 608/11 of Antigua optd with T **67**.

457	10c. multicoloured	10	10
458	50c. multicoloured	20	20
459	$4 black, magenta and greenish yellow	90	1·10
457/9 Set of 3		1·00	1·25
MS460 114×99 mm. $2.50, multicoloured		55	75

(Litho Format)

1979 (24 May). 35th Anniv of International Civil Aviation Organisation. T **74** and similar horiz designs. Multicoloured. P 13½×14.

461	75c. Type **74**	25	50
	a. Block of 4. Nos. 461/3 plus label	65	1·40
462	95c. Air traffic control	25	50
463	$1.25 Ground crew-man directing Douglas DC-8 on runway	25	50
461/3 Set of 3		65	1·40

Nos. 461/3 were either printed in separate sheets, or together with a stamp-size label, *se-tenant*, in blocks of 4, each block divided in the sheet by margins.

1979 (24 May). International Year of the Child (1st issue). Nos. 612/16 of Antigua optd with T **67**.

464	25c. Yacht	20	15
465	50c. Rocket	30	25
466	90c. Car	40	35
467	$2 Train	80	60
464/7 Set of 4		1·50	1·25
MS468 80×112 mm. $5 Aeroplane		1·10	1·10

BARBUDA (75)   **BARBUDA** (76)

1979 (1 Aug). Fish. Nos. 617/21 of Antigua optd with T **75**.

469	30c. Yellow Jack	20	15
470	50c. Blue-finned Tuna	25	20
471	90c. Sailfish	30	30
472	$3 Wahoo	65	1·10
469/72 Set of 4		1·25	1·60
MS473 122×75 mm. $2.50, Great Barracuda (overprinted with T **73**)		1·00	1·25
a. Albino opt			

1979 (1 Aug). Death Bicentenary of Captain Cook. Nos. 622/6 of Antigua optd with T **76**.

474	25c. Cook's Birthplace, Marton	25	25
475	50c. H.M.S. *Endeavour*	70	35
476	90c. Marine chronometer	70	40
477	$3 Landing at Botany Bay	1·50	1·00
474/7 Set of 4		2·75	1·75
MS478 110×85 mm. $2.50, H.M.S. *Resolution* (overprinted with T **82**)		1·25	1·50
a. Albino opt			

77 "Virgin with the Pear"   **BARBUDA** (78)

(Des G. Vasarhelyi. Litho Format)

1979 (24 Sept). International Year of the Child (2nd issue). Details of Paintings by Dürer showing the infant Jesus. T **77** and similar vert designs. Multicoloured. P 14×13½.

479	25c. Type **77**	15	15
480	50c. "Virgin with the Pink"	20	25
481	75c. "Virgin with the Pear" (*different*)	25	30
482	$1.25 "Nativity"	25	40
479/82 Set of 4		75	1·00
MS483 86×118 mm. Nos. 479/82		1·00	1·75

1979 (21 Nov). Christmas. Nos. 627/31 of Antigua optd with T **78**.

484	8c. The Holy Family	10	10
485	25c. Virgin and Child on Ass	15	10
486	50c. Shepherd and star	25	15
487	$4 Wise Men with gifts	85	80
484/7 Set of 4		1·10	1·00
MS488 113×94 mm. $3 Angel with trumpet		80	1·10

1980 (18 Mar). Olympic Games, Moscow. Nos. 632/6 of Antigua optd with T **67**.

489	10c. Javelin throwing	10	10
490	25c. Running	15	10
491	$1 Pole vaulting	35	20
492	$2 Hurdling	55	40
489/92 Set of 4		1·00	65
MS493 127×96 mm. $3 Boxing		70	1·10

LONDON 1980

(79)   80 "Apollo 11" Crew Badge

1980 (6 May). "London 1980" International Stamp Exhibition. As Nos. 452/5 optd with T **79** in blue. P 12.

494	25c. Antigua 1863 1d. stamp	35	20
495	50c. Penny Black stamp	45	40
496	$1 Mail coach and woman posting letter, *circa* 1840	85	65
497	$2 Modern mail transport	2·75	1·50
494/7 Set of 4		4·00	2·50

(Litho Format)

1980 (21 May). Tenth Anniv of Moon Landing. T **80** and similar horiz designs. Multicoloured. P 13½×14.

498	75c. Type **80**	60	25
499	95c. Plaque left on Moon	60	30
500	$1.25 Rejoining mother ship	70	50
501	$2 Lunar Module	90	75
498/501 Set of 4		2·50	1·60
MS502 118×84 mm. Nos. 498/501		1·60	2·50

81 American Wigeon

(Litho Questa)

1980 (16 June). Birds. Multicoloured designs as T **81**. P 14.

503	1c. Type **81**	70	1·50
504	2c. Snowy Plover	70	80
505	4c. Rose-breasted Grosbeak	75	80
506	6c. Mangrove Cuckoo	75	80
507	10c. Adelaide's Warbler	75	70
508	15c. Scaly-breasted Thrasher	80	70
509	20c. Yellow-crowned Night Heron	80	70
510	25c. Bridled Quail Dove	80	70
511	35c. Carib Grackle	85	1·50
512	50c. Pintail	90	55
513	75c. Black-whiskered Vireo	1·00	55
514	$1 Blue-winged Teal	1·25	80
515	$1.50 Green-throated Carib (*vert*)	1·50	80
516	$2 Red-necked Pigeon (*vert*)	2·25	1·25
517	$2.50 Wied's Crested Flycatcher (*vert*)	2·75	1·50
518	$5 Yellow-bellied Sapsucker (*vert*)	3·50	3·75
519	$7.50 Caribbean Elaenia (*vert*)	4·00	6·50
520	$10 Great Egret (*vert*)	4·00	5·00
503/20 Set of 18		25·00	26·00

1980 (29 July). Famous Works of Art. Nos. 651/7 of Antigua optd with T **67**.

521	10c. "David" (statue, Donatello)	10	10
522	30c. "The Birth of Venus" (painting, Sandro Botticelli)	15	15
523	50c. "Reclining Couple" (sarcophagus, Cerveteri)	15	20
524	90c. "The Garden of Earthly Delights" (painting, Hieronymus Bosch)	20	25
525	$1 "Portinari Altarpiece" (painting, Hugo van der Goes)	20	25
526	$4 "Eleanora of Toledo and her Son Giovanni de' Medici" (painting, Agnolo Bronzino)	60	80
521/6 Set of 6		1·25	1·50

ANTIGUA AND BARBUDA / Barbuda

MS527	99×124 mm. $5 "The Holy Family" (painting, Rembrandt)	1·50	1·75

1980 (8 Sept). 75th Anniv of Rotary International. Nos. 658/62 of Antigua optd with T **67**.

528	30c. Rotary anniversary emblem and headquarters, U.S.A.	15	15
529	50c. Rotary anniversary emblem and Antigua Rotary Club banner	20	20
530	90c. Map of Antigua and Rotary emblem	25	25
531	$3 Paul P. Harris (founder) and Rotary emblem	65	65
528/31	Set of 4	1·10	1·10
MS532	102×77 mm. $5 Antigua flags and Rotary emblems	1·50	2·25

BARBUDA (82)   BARBUDA (83)

1980 (6 Oct). 80th Birthday of Queen Elizabeth the Queen Mother. Nos. 663/5 of Antigua optd with T **82**.

533	10c. multicoloured	50	15
	a. Opt inverted	38·00	
	b. Opt double	30·00	
534	$2.50 multicoloured	1·25	1·50
MS535	68×88 mm. $3 multicoloured	2·00	1·75

1980 (8 Dec). Birds. Nos. 666/70 of Antigua optd with T **83**.

536	10c. Ringed Kingfisher	3·25	1·00
537	30c. Plain Pigeon	3·75	1·10
538	$1 Green-throated Carib	5·00	3·00
539	$2 Black-necked Stilt	6·00	6·00
536/9	Set of 4	16·00	10·00
MS540	73×73 mm. $2.50, Roseate Tern	6·50	2·75

1981 (26 Jan). Sugar Cane Railway Locomotives. Nos. 681/5 of Antigua optd with T **67**.

541	25c. Diesel Locomotive No. 15	1·00	25
542	50c. Narrow-gauge steam locomotive	1·25	35
543	90c. Diesel locomotives Nos. 1 and 10	1·75	45
544	$3 Steam locomotive hauling sugar cane	3·25	1·40
541/4	Set of 4	6·50	2·25
MS545	82×111 mm. $2.50, Antigua sugar factory, railway yard and sheds	1·50	1·75

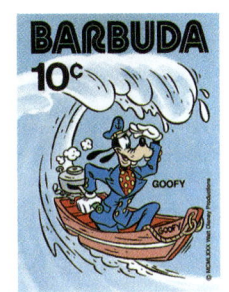

84 Florence Nightingale   **85** Goofy in Motor-boat

(Litho Format)

1981 (9 Mar). Famous Women. T **84** and similar vert. designs. P 14×13½.

546	50c. multicoloured	15	30
547	90c. multicoloured	40	55
548	$1 multicoloured	35	60
549	$4 black, yellow-brown and rose-lilac	50	1·75
546/9	Set of 4	1·25	2·75

Designs:—90c. Marie Curie; $1 Amy Johnson; $4 Eleanor Roosevelt.
Nos. 546/9 exist imperforate from stock dispersed by the liquidator of Format International Security Printers Ltd.

(Litho Format)

1981 (15 May). Walt Disney Cartoon Characters. T **85** and similar vert designs showing characters afloat. Multicoloured. P 13½.

550	10c. Type **85**	90	15
551	20c. Donald Duck reversing car into sea	1·25	20
552	25c. Mickey Mouse asking tug-boat to take on more than it can handle	1·40	30
553	30c. Porpoise turning the tables on Goofy	1·40	35
554	35c. Goofy in sailing boat	1·40	35
555	40c. Mickey Mouse and boat being lifted out of water by fish	1·40	40
556	75c. Donald Duck fishing for flying-fish with butterfly net	2·00	60
557	$1 Minnie Mouse in brightly decorated sailing boat	2·00	80
558	$2 Chip and Dale on floating ship-in-bottle	2·50	1·40
550/8	Set of 9	13·00	4·00
MS559	127×101 mm. $2.50, Donald Duck	4·50	3·00

BARBUDA (86)

1981 (9 June). Birth Centenary of Picasso. Nos. 697/701 of Antigua optd with T **86**.

560	10c. "Pipes of Pan"	10	10
561	50c. "Seated Harlequin"	25	15
562	90c. "Paulo as Harlequin"	35	30
563	$4 "Mother and Child"	90	1·00
560/3	Set of 4	1·50	1·50
MS564	115×140 mm. $5 "Three Musicians" (detail)	1·40	1·40

87 Buckingham Palace   **88**

(Des G. Drummond. Litho Format)

1981 (27 July). Royal Wedding (1st issue). Buildings. T **87/8** and similar horiz designs. Each bicoloured*. P 11½×11½.

565	$1 Type **87**	25	40
566	$1 Type **88**	25	40
	a. Sheetlet. Nos. 565/70	2·00	
	b. Booklet pane. Nos. 565/6×2 in imperf between horiz pairs	2·00	
567	$1.50 Caernarvon Castle	30	50
568	$1.50 Caernarvon Castle	30	50
	b. Booklet pane. Nos. 567/8×2 in imperf between horiz pairs	2·25	
569	$4 Highgrove House	55	90
570	$4 Highgrove House	55	90
	b. Booklet pane. Nos. 569/70×2 in imperf between horiz pairs	2·50	
565/70	Set of 6	2·00	3·25
MS571	75×90 mm. $5 black and olive-yellow (St. Paul's Cathedral—26×32 mm). P 11½×11	80	1·25

*Nos. 565/70 each exist printed in black with three different background colours, turquoise-green and lavender.
No. 566b was printed only in black and rose-pink. No. 568b black and turquoise-green and No. 570b black and lavender.
Nos. 565/70 were printed together, se-tenant, in sheetlets of 6, the two versions of each value forming a composite design.
Nos. 565/70 exist imperforate from stock dispersed by the liquidator of Format International Security Printers Ltd.

1981 (14 Aug). Royal Wedding (2nd issue). Nos. 702/5 of Antigua optd with T **86**.

572	25c. Prince Charles and Lady Diana Spencer	15	15
573	50c. Glamis Castle	25	25
	a. Opt double	25·00	
574	$4 Prince Charles skiing	75	1·00
	a. Error. Optd on unissued Uganda 20s. showing Prince Charles at Balmoral	60·00	
	ab. Opt double		
572/4	Set of 3	1·10	1·25
MS575	95×85 mm. $5 Glass Coach	90	90

Nos. 572/4 exist perforated 12 (Price for set of 3 £1.10 mint or used) from additional sheetlets of five stamps and one label. These stamps have changed background colours. One sheetlet of the 25c. is known with the overprint inverted.

89 "Integration and Travel"

(Litho Format)

1981 (14 Sept). International Year for Disabled Persons (1st issue). T **89** and similar horiz designs. P 14.

576	50c. multicoloured	25	20
577	90c. black, red-orange and blue-green	25	25
578	$1 black, light blue and bright green	30	30

127

ANTIGUA AND BARBUDA / Barbuda

579		$4 black, yellow-ochre and orange-brown	45	85
576/9	Set of 4		1·10	1·40

Designs:—90c. Braille and sign language; $1 "Helping hands"; $4 "Mobility aids for disabled".

Nos. 576/9 exist imperforate from stock dispersed by the liquidator of Format International Security Printers Ltd.

See also Nos. 603/7.

BARBUDA
(90)

1981 (12 Oct). Royal Wedding (3rd issue). Nos. 706/12 of Antigua optd with T **90** in silver.

580		25c. Prince of Wales at Investiture, 1969	40	70
		a. Booklet pane. Nos. 580/5	3·00	
581		25c. Prince Charles as baby, 1948	40	70
582		$1 Prince Charles at R.A.F. College, Cranwell, 1971	50	85
583		$1 Prince Charles attending Hill House School, 1956	50	85
584		$2 Prince Charles and Lady Diana Spencer	75	1·00
585		$2 Prince Charles at Trinity College, 1967	75	1·00
586		$5 Prince Charles and Lady Diana	4·25	6·50
		a. Booklet pane of 1	4·25	
580/6	Set of 7		7·75	10·50

1981 (1 Nov). Independence. Nos. 686B/96B of Antigua additionally optd with T **86**.

587		6c. Orchid Tree	50	15
588		10c. Bougainvillea	55	15
589		20c. Flamboyant	70	20
590		25c. Hibiscus	80	25
591		35c. Flame of the Wood	90	30
592		50c. Cannon at Fort James	1·10	45
593		75c. Premier's Office	1·25	75
594		$1 Potworks Dam	1·50	80
595		$2.50 Irrigation scheme, Diamond Estate	2·50	2·75
596		$5 Government House	2·75	3·75
597		$10 Coolidge International Airport	4·50	6·00
587/97	Set of 11		15·00	14·00

BARBUDA
(91)

BARBUDA
(92)

1981 (14 Dec). 50th Anniv of Antigua Girl Guide Movement. Nos. 713/17 of Antigua optd with T **83** (No. MS602) or T **91** (others).

598		10c. Irene Joshua (founder)	55	10
599		50c. Campfire sing-song	1·25	30
600		90c. Sailing	1·75	45
601		$2.50 Animal tending	3·00	1·40
598/601	Set of 4		6·00	2·00
MS602	110×85 mm. $5 Raising the flag		3·50	3·50

1981 (14 Dec). International Year for Disabled Persons (2nd issue). Nos. 728/32 of Antigua optd with T **83** (No. MS607) or T **91** (others).

603		10c. Swimming	15	15
604		50c. Discus throwing	20	25
605		90c. Archery	45	45
606		$2 Baseball	60	1·50
603/6	Set of 4		1·25	2·10
MS607	108×84 mm. $4 Basketball		2·00	1·75

1981 (22 Dec). Christmas. Paintings. Nos. 723/7 of Antigua optd with T **92**.

608		8c. "Holy Night" (Jacques Stella)	10	10
609		30c. "Mary with Child" (Julius Schnorr von Carolfeld)	20	20
610		$1 "Virgin and Child" (Alonso Cano) (S.)	40	40
611		$3 "Virgin and Child" (Lorenzo di Credi)	1·10	1·10
608/11	Set of 4		1·60	1·60
MS612	77×111 mm. $5 "Holy Family" (Pieter van Avon)		1·75	2·25

93 Princess of Wales

S. Atlantic Fund + 50c.
(94)

(Des G. Drummond. Litho Format)

1982 (21 June). Birth of Prince William of Wales (1st issue). T **93** and similar vert portraits. W w **15**. P 14.

613		$1 multicoloured	75	50
		w. Wmk inverted	75	
614		$2.50 multicoloured	1·00	1·10
		a. Reddish violet (top inscr) omitted	£180	
		w. Wmk inverted	1·10	
615		$5 multicoloured	1·60	1·75
		w. Wmk inverted	2·40	
613/15	Set of 3		3·00	3·00
MS616	88×108 mm. $4 multicoloured. No wmk		2·00	2·10

Nos. 613/15 were issued in sheets of 10 stamps with 2 undenominated black prints, in positions 9 and 13, and 9 blank labels. These sheets exist in two different formats, with all stamps upright or with 6 stamps and one black print inverted.

1982 (28 June). South Atlantic Fund. Nos. 580/6 surch as T **94** and similar.

617		25c.+50c. Prince of Wales at Investiture, 1969	30	50
		a. Booklet Pane. Nos. 617/22	2·50	
		b. Surch double	20·00	
618		25c.+50c. Prince Charles as baby, 1948	30	50
		b. Surch double	20·00	
619		$1+50c. Prince Charles at R.A.F. College, Cranwell, 1971	50	75
		b. Surch double	20·00	
620		$1+50c. Prince Charles attending Hill House School, 1956	50	75
		b. Surch double	20·00	
621		$2+50c. Prince Charles and Lady Diana Spencer	75	1·10
		b. Surch double	20·00	
622		$2+50c. Prince Charles at Trinity College, 1967	75	1·10
		b. Surch double	20·00	
623		$5+50c. Prince Charles and Lady Diana	3·00	4·25
		a. Booklet pane of 1	3·00	
		b. Surch double	£150	
617/23	Set of 7		5·50	8·00

(Des G. Drummond. Litho Format)

1982 (1 July). 21st Birthday of Princess of Wales (1st issue). As Nos. 613/16 but inscribed "Twenty First Birthday Greetings to H.R.H. The Princess of Wales". W w **15**. P 14.

624		$1 multicoloured	1·50	45
		w. Wmk inverted	1·50	
625		$2.50 multicoloured	2·25	1·25
		w. Wmk inverted	2·25	
626		$5 multicoloured	3·00	2·40
		w. Wmk inverted	3·00	
624/6	Set of 3		6·00	3·75
MS627	88×108 mm. $4 multicoloured. No wmk		2·75	2·25

See note beneath Nos. 613/16.

BARBUDA MAIL
(95)

BARBUDA MAIL
(96)

1982 (30 Aug). 21st Birthday of Princess of Wales (2nd issue). Nos. 748/51 of Antigua optd as T **95**, in silver (No. 629) or black (others).

628		90c. Queen's House, Greenwich	80	45
629		$1 Prince and Princess of Wales	1·25	50
630		$4 Princess of Wales	3·00	1·50
628/30	Set of 3		4·00	2·25
MS631	102×75 mm. $5 Princess of Wales (different)		1·75	2·00

The overprint on No. MS631 measures 18×6 mm. Nos. 628/30 also exist from additional sheetlets of 5 stamps and 1 label overprinted with a larger overprint, 18×6 mm long (price for set of 3 £4 mint or used). On the $1 and $4 values the second line of overprint aligns to left.

1882 (12 Oct). Birth of Prince William of Wales (2nd issue). Nos. 757/60 of Antigua further optd with T **95**, in silver ($1, $4) or black (others).

632		90c. Queen's House, Greenwich	80	45
633		$1 Prince and Princess of Wales	1·50	50
634		$4 Princess of Wales	3·25	2·00
632/4	Set of 3		5·00	2·75
MS635	102×75 mm. $5 Princess of Wales (different)		4·50	2·50

The overprint on No. MS635 measures 18×6 mm.

1982 (6 Dec). Birth Centenary of Franklin D. Roosevelt (Nos. 636, 638, 640/2) and 250th Birth Anniv of George Washington (others). Nos. 761/8 of Antigua optd as T **95** (second line ranged left on No. MS642).

636		10c. Roosevelt in 1940	10	10
637		25c. Washington as blacksmith	15	15
638		45c. Churchill, Roosevelt and Stalin at Yalta conference	2·00	25

639	60c. Washington crossing the Delaware	20	25
640	$1 "Roosevelt Special" train	2·00	40
641	$3 Portrait of Roosevelt	60	90
636/41 Set of 6		4·50	1·75
MS642 92×87 mm. $4 Roosevelt and wife		1·00	1·75
MS643 92×87 mm. $4 Portrait of Washington		1·00	1·75

1982 (6 Dec). Christmas. Religious Paintings by Raphael. Nos. 769/73 of Antigua optd with T **96**.

644	10c. "Annunciation"	10	10
645	30c. "Adoration of the Magi"	15	15
646	$1 "Presentation at the Temple"	40	40
647	$4 "Coronation of the Virgin"	1·00	1·00
644/7 Set of 4		1·50	1·50
MS648 95×124 mm. $5 "Marriage of the Virgin"		1·25	2·00

1983 (14 Mar). 500th Birth Anniv of Raphael. Details from "Galatea" Fresco. Nos. 774/8 of Antigua optd as T **95** (45, 50c. and larger (18×6 mm) on **MS**653) or T **96** (others).

649	45c. Tritons and Dolphins	20	20
650	50c. Sea Nymph carried off by Triton	20	20
651	60c. Winged angel steering Dolphins (*horiz*)	25	25
652	$4 Cupids shooting arrows (*horiz*)	1·00	1·00
649/52 Set of 4		1·50	1·50
MS653 101×126 mm. $5 Galatea pulled along by Dolphins		1·25	2·00

1983 (14 Mar). Commonwealth Day. Nos. 779/82 of Antigua optd as T **96**.

654	25c. Pineapple produce	45	55
655	45c. Carnival	55	70
656	60c. Tourism	70	1·25
657	$3 Airport	1·50	3·50
654/7 Set of 4		3·00	5·50

1983 (12 Apr). World Communications Year. Nos. 783/7 of Antigua optd as T **96** (Nos. 658/61) or as T **95** with second line ranged left (No. **MS**662).

658	15c. T.V. satellite coverage of Royal Wedding	2·00	25
659	50c. Police communications	5·00	90
660	60c. House-to-train telephone call	3·00	90
661	$3 Satellite earth station with planets Jupiter and Saturn	4·25	2·50
658/61 Set of 4		13·00	4·00
MS662 100×90 mm. $5 "Comsat" satellite over West Indies		1·50	2·25
	a. Albino opt	30·00	

97 Vincenzo Lunardi's Balloon Flight, London, 1785   (**98**)

(Des G. Drummond. Litho)

1983 (13 June). Bicentenary of Manned Flight (1st issue). T **97** and similar vert designs. Multicoloured. P 14.

663	$1 Type **97**	35	35
664	$1.50 Montgolfier brothers' balloon flight, Paris, 1783	50	55
665	$2.50 Blanchard and Jeffries' Cross-Channel balloon flight, 1785	70	90
663/5 Set of 3		1·40	1·60
MS666 111×111 mm. $5 Maiden flight of Airship LZ-127 *Graf Zeppelin*, 1928		2·00	2·75

See also Nos. 672/6.

1983 (4 July). Whales. Nos. 788/92 of Antigua optd as T **95** (Nos. 667/70) or larger, 17×5½ mm (No. **MS**671), each with the second line ranged left.

667	15c. Bottle-nosed Dolphin	1·25	40
668	50c. Fin Whale	4·00	1·60
669	60c. Bowhead Whale	4·50	1·75
670	$3 Spectacled Porpoise	5·50	4·25
667/70 Set of 4		14·00	7·25
MS671 122×101 mm. $5 Narwhal		6·00	4·50

1983 (12 Sept). Bicentenary of Manned Flight (2nd issue). Nos. 811/15 of Antigua optd as T **96**.

672	30c. Dornier Do-X flying boat	1·50	35
673	50c. Supermarine S6B seaplane	1·75	60
674	60c. Curtiss F-9C Sparrowhawk biplane and airship U.S.S. *Akron*	2·25	70
675	$4 Hot-air balloon *Pro Juventute*	5·50	4·00
672/5 Set of 4		10·00	5·00
MS676 80×105 mm. $5 Airship LZ-127 *Graf Zeppelin*		3·75	4·25

1983 (21 Oct). Nos. 565/70 surch as T **98**. P 11×11½.

677	45c. on $1 Type **87**	25	45
	a. Sheetlet. Nos. 677/82	1·40	
	b. Perf 14½	1·25	2·50
	ba. Sheetlet. Nos. 677b/82b	6·50	
	bb. Error 50c. on $1	4·50	
	bc. Surch omitted	35·00	
678	45c. on $1 Type **88**	25	45
	b. Perf 14½	1·25	2·50
	bb. Error 50c. on $1	4·50	
	bc. Surch omitted	35·00	
679	50c. on $1.50 Caernarvon Castle (left)	25	45
	b. Perf 14½	1·25	2·50
	bb. Error 45c. on $1.50	4·50	
	bc. Surch omitted	35·00	
680	50c. on $1.50 Caernarvon Castle (right)	25	45
	b. Perf 14½	1·25	2·50
	bb. Error. 45c. on $1.50	4·50	
	bc. Surch omitted	35·00	
681	60c. on $4 Highgrove House (left)	25	45
	b. Perf 14½	1·25	2·50
	bc. Surch omitted	35·00	
682	60c. on $4 Highgrove House (right)	25	45
	b. Perf 14½	1·25	2·50
	bc. Surch omitted	35·00	
677/82 Set of 6		1·40	2·50

Nos. 677bb, 678bb, 679bb and 680bb occur on the 14½ perforated sheetlets with rose-pink background.

Examples of No. 677a, and also of the errors, imperforate exist from stock dispersed by the liquidator of Format International Security Printers Ltd.

1983 (28 Oct). Nos. 793/810 of Antigua optd with T **96**.

683	1c. Cashew Nut	10	40
684	2c. Passion Fruit	15	40
685	3c. Mango	15	40
686	5c. Grapefruit	15	40
687	10c. Pawpaw	20	30
688	15c. Breadfruit	40	20
689	20c. Coconut	50	30
690	25c. Oleander	50	20
691	30c. Banana	55	20
692	40c. Pineapple	65	25
693	45c. Cordia	70	30
694	50c. Cassia	80	30
695	60c. Poui	80	30
696	$1 Frangipani	1·10	50
697	$2 Flamboyant	1·75	1·50
698	$2.50 Lemon	2·00	2·00
699	$5 Lignum Vitae	3·00	3·25
700	$10 National flag and coat of arms	4·50	6·00
683/700 Set of 18		16·00	15·00

BARBUDA MAIL

(**99**)   **100** Edward VII

1983 (28 Oct). Christmas. 500th Birth Anniv of Raphael. Nos. 816/20 of Antigua optd with T **99** or slightly smaller (29×4 mm) (**MS**705).

701	10c. multicoloured	10	10
702	30c. multicoloured	10	20
703	$1 multicoloured	30	50
704	$4 multicoloured	1·00	1·50
701/4 Set of 4		1·25	2·00
MS705 101×131 mm. $5 multicoloured		1·40	2·50

1983 (14 Dec). Bicentenary of Methodist Church (1984). Nos. 821/4 of Antigua optd with T **95** (in silver on 15c. and 50c.).

706	15c. John Wesley (founder)	20	15
707	50c. Nathaniel Gilbert (founder in Antigua)	30	25
708	60c. St. John Methodist Church steeple	30	30
709	$3 Ebenezer Methodist Church, St. John's	80	1·00
706/9 Set of 4		1·40	1·50

ANTIGUA AND BARBUDA / Barbuda

(Des G. Drummond. Litho Format)

1984 (14 Feb). Members of British Royal Family. T **100** and similar vert portraits. Multicoloured. P 14½.

710	$1 Type **100**	70	1·50
711	$1 George V	70	1·50
712	$1 George VI	70	1·50
713	$1 Elizabeth II	70	1·50
714	$1 Charles, Prince of Wales	70	1·50
715	$1 Prince William	70	1·50
710/15 Set of 6		3·75	8·00

1984 (26 Apr). Olympic Games, Los Angeles (1st issue). Nos. 825/9 of Antigua optd as T **99** (23×3 mm in size on Nos. 716/19).

716	25c. Discus	25	20
717	50c. Gymnastics	40	40
718	90c. Hurdling	50	60
719	$3 Cycling	2·75	1·50
716/19 Set of 4		3·50	2·40
MS720 82×67 mm. $5 Volleyball		2·00	3·25

1984 (12 July). Ships. Nos. 830/4 of Antigua optd with T **95** (MS725) or T **99** (others).

721	45c. Booker Vanguard (freighter)	1·50	45
722	50c. Canberra (liner)	1·50	50
723	60c. Yachts	1·75	60
724	$4 Fairwind (cargo liner)	4·25	2·75
721/4 Set of 4		8·00	3·75
MS725 107×80 mm. $5 18th-century British man-o-war (vert)		4·50	4·25

1984 (12 July). Universal Postal Union Congress, Hamburg. Nos. 835/9 of Antigua optd with T **95**.

726	15c. Chenille	25	15
727	50c. Shell Flower	30	30
728	60c. Anthurium	40	40
729	$3 Angels Trumpet	75	1·25
726/9 Set of 4		1·50	1·90
MS730 100×75 mm. $5 Crown of Thorns		2·00	2·50

101 Olympic Stadium, Athens, 1896

(Litho Format)

1984 (27 July). Olympic Games, Los Angeles (2nd issue). T **101** and similar horiz designs. Multicoloured. P 13½.

731	$1.50 Type **101**	40	90
732	$2.50 Olympic stadium, Los Angeles, 1984	60	1·50
733	$5 Athlete carrying Olympic torch	95	2·25
731/3 Set of 3		1·75	4·25
MS734 121×95 mm. No. 733. P 15		1·50	2·50

1984 (1 Oct). Presidents of the United States of America. Nos. 856/63 of Antigua optd with T **95** (in silver on 10, 90c., $1.10 and $1.50).

735	10c. Abraham Lincoln	10	10
736	20c. Harry Truman	15	15
737	30c. Dwight Eisenhower	20	25
738	40c. Ronald Reagan	25	30
739	90c. Gettysburg Address, 1863	40	55
740	$1.10 Formation of N.A.T.O., 1949	40	65
741	$1.50 Eisenhower during Second World War	45	70
742	$2 Reagan and Caribbean Basin Initiative	50	1·00
735/42 Set of 8		2·25	3·50

1984 (1 Oct). 150th Anniv of Abolition of Slavery. Nos. 864/8 of Antigua optd with T **96** (Nos. 743/6) or as T **95**, but 18×6½ mm (No. **MS**747).

743	40c. View of Moravian Mission	30	30
744	50c. Antigua Courthouse, 1823	40	40
745	60c. Planting sugar-cane, Monks Hill	45	45
746	$3 Boiling house, Delaps' Estate	1·40	1·40
743/6 Set of 4		2·25	2·25
MS747 95×70 mm. $5 Loading sugar, Willoughby Bay		2·00	2·50

1984 (21 Nov). Songbirds. Nos. 869/74 of Antigua optd with T **95** or larger (18×7 mm) (No. **MS**753).

748	40c. Rufous-sided Towhee	2·25	55
749	50c. Parula Warbler	2·25	70
750	60c. House Wren	2·25	75
751	$2 Ruby-crowned Kinglet	3·25	2·00
752	$3 Common Flicker	3·50	2·75
748/52 Set of 5		10·00	4·75
MS753 76×76 mm. $5 Yellow-breasted Chat		4·00	4·50

1984 (21 Nov). 450th Death Anniv of Correggio (painter). Nos. 878/82 of Antigua optd with T **95** or larger (18×7 mm) No. **MS**758), all in silver.

754	25c. "The Virgin and Infant with Angels and Cherubs"	15	20
755	60c. "The Four Saints"	40	45
756	90c. "St. Catherine"	50	55
757	$3 "The Campori Madonna"	1·25	1·75
754/7 Set of 4		2·10	2·75
MS758 90×60 mm. $5 "St. John the Baptist"		1·75	3·25

1984 (30 Nov). "Ausipex" International Stamp Exhibition, Melbourne. Australian Sports. Nos. 875/7 of Antigua optd with T **95** or larger (18×7 mm) (No. **MS**761).

759	$1 Grass-skiing	50	40
760	$5 Australian Football	1·50	2·25
MS761 108×78 mm. $5 Boomerang-throwing		1·50	2·75

1984 (30 Nov). 150th Birth Anniv of Edgar Degas (painter). Nos. 883/7 of Antigua optd with T **95** (Nos. 762/5) or T **99** (No. **MS**766), all in silver.

762	15c. "The Blue Dancers"	10	10
763	50c. "The Pink Dancers"	30	40
764	70c. "Two Dancers"	45	55
765	$4 "Dancers at the Bar"	1·25	3·50
762/5 Set of 4		1·75	4·00
MS766 90×60 mm. $5 "The Folk Dancers" (40×27 mm)		1·75	2·75

BARBUDA MAIL

(**102**)

1985 (18 Feb). Famous People. Nos. 888/96 of Antigua optd with T **102** (horizontally on Nos. 771/5).

767	60c. Winston Churchill	7·00	3·00
768	60c. Mahatma Gandhi	7·00	3·00
769	60c. John F. Kennedy	7·00	3·00
770	60c. Mao Tse-tung	7·00	3·00
771	$1 Churchill with General De Gaulle, Paris, 1944 (horiz)	7·00	3·00
772	$1 Gandhi leaving London by train, 1931 (horiz)	7·00	3·00
773	$1 Kennedy with Chancellor Adenauer and Mayor Brandt, Berlin, 1963 (horiz)	7·00	3·00
774	$1 Mao Tse-tung Lin Piao, Peking, 1969 (horiz)	7·00	3·00
767/74 Set of 8		50·00	22·00
MS775 114×80 mm. $5 Flags of Great Britain, India, the United States and China		12·00	8·50

103 Lady Elizabeth Bowes-Lyon, 1907, and Camellias

104 Roseate Tern

(Des G. Drummond. Litho Format)

1985 (26 Feb). Life and Times of Queen Elizabeth the Queen Mother (1st issue). T **103** and similar vert designs. Multicoloured. P 14×14½.

776	15c. Type **103**	35	20
777	45c. Duchess of York, 1926, and "Elizabeth of Glamis" roses	45	25
778	50c. The Queen Mother after the Coronation, 1937	45	25
779	60c. In Garter robes, 1971, and Dog Roses	45	30
780	90c. Attending Royal Variety show, 1967, and red Hibiscus	60	45
781	$2 The Queen Mother in 1982, and blue Plumbago	75	1·10
782	$3 Receiving 82nd birthday gifts from children, and Morning Glory	95	2·50
776/82 Set of 7		3·50	4·50

Nos. 776/82 exist imperforate from stock dispersed by the liquidator of Format International Security Printers Ltd.

See also Nos. 826/9.

ANTIGUA AND BARBUDA / Barbuda

(Des G. Drummond. Litho Format)

1985 (4 Apr). Birth Bicentenary of John J. Audubon (ornithologist) (1st issue). T **104** and similar vert designs showing original paintings. Multicoloured. P 14.

783	45c. Type **104**	20	30
784	50c. Mangrove Cuckoo	20	30
785	60c. Yellow-crowned Night Heron	20	40
786	$5 Brown Pelican	80	3·50
783/6 Set of 4		1·25	4·00

Nos. 783/6 exist imperforate from stock dispersed by the liquidator of Format International Security Printers Ltd.
See also Nos. 794/8 and 914/17.

1985 (10 May). Centenary of the Statue of Liberty (1986) (1st issue). Nos. 907/13 of Antigua optd horizontally with T **102**.

787	25c. Torch from Statue in Madison Square Park, 1885	20	20
788	30c. Statue of Liberty and scaffolding ("Restoration and Renewal") (vert)	20	20
789	50c. Frederic Bartholdi (sculptor) supervising construction, 1876	30	30
790	90c. Close-up of Statue	55	55
791	$1 Statue and sailing ship ("Operation Sail", 1976) (vert)	80	60
792	$3 Dedication ceremony, 1886 (vert)	1·75	1·75
787/92 Set of 6		3·50	3·00
MS793 110×80 mm. $5 Port of New York		5·75	4·75

See also Nos. 987/96.

BARBUDA MAIL (105)   BARBUDA MAIL (106)   4TH AUG 1900–1985 (107)

1985 (18 July). Birth Bicentenary John J. Audubon (ornithologist) (2nd issue). Nos. 924/8 of Antigua optd with T **105**.

794	90c. Slavonian Grebe	10·00	4·25
795	$1 British Storm Petrel	10·00	4·50
796	$1.50 Great Blue Heron	11·00	8·50
797	$3 Double-crested Cormorant	16·00	13·00
794/7 Set of 4		42·00	27·00
MS798 103×72 mm. $5 White-tailed Tropic Bird (vert)		28·00	11·00

1985 (18 July). Butterflies. Nos. 929/33 of Antigua optd with T **106**.

799	25c. Anaea cyanea	7·00	1·25
800	60c. Leodonta dysoni	9·00	2·00
801	90c. Junea doraete	10·00	2·50
802	$4 Prepona pylene	19·00	19·00
799/802 Set of 4		40·00	22·00
MS803 132×105 mm. $5 Caerois gerdtrudtus		17·00	9·00

1985 (2 Aug). Centenary of the Motorcycle. Nos. 919/23 of Antigua optd with T **106**.

804	10c. Triumph 2hp "Jap", 1903	1·25	40
805	30c. Indian "Arrow", 1949	1·75	45
806	60c. BMW "R100RS", 1976	2·25	70
807	$4 Harley-Davidson "Model II", 1916	5·75	5·00
804/7 Set of 4		10·00	6·00
MS808 90×93 mm. $5 Laverda "Jota", 1975		7·00	4·00

1985 (2 Aug). 85th Birthday of Queen Elizabeth the Queen Mother. Nos. 776/82 optd with T **107**.

809	15c. Type **103**	75	50
	a. Red (frame, flowers, etc) omitted	32·00	
810	45c. Duchess of York, 1926, and "Elizabeth of Glamis" roses	1·10	60
811	50c. The Queen Mother after the Coronation, 1937	1·10	60
812	60c. In Garter robes, 1971, and Dog Roses	1·25	1·00
813	90c. Attending Royal Variety show, 1967, and red Hibiscus	1·25	1·25
814	$2 The Queen Mother in 1982, and blue Plumbago	1·40	3·75
815	$3 Receiving 82nd birthday gifts from children, and Morning Glory	1·50	3·75
809/15 Set of 7		7·50	10·00

The 45c. exists with the yellow omitted from stock dispersed by the liquidator of Format International Security Printers Ltd.

1985 (30 Aug). Native American Artefacts. Nos. 914/18 of Antigua optd horizontally with T **102**.

816	15c. Arawak pot sherd and Indians making clay utensils	15	10
817	50c. Arawak body design and Arawak Indians tattooing	25	25
818	60c. Head of the god "Yocahu" and Indians harvesting manioc	35	35
819	$3 Carib war club and Carib Indians going into battle	1·25	1·50
816/19 Set of 4		1·75	1·90
MS820 97×68 mm. $5 Taino Indians worshipping stone idol		2·00	3·00

1985 (30 Aug). 40th Anniv of International Civil Aviation Organization. Nos. 934/8 of Antigua optd with T **106**.

821	30c. Cessna 172D Sky hawk	2·75	75
822	90c. Fokker D.VII	3·75	1·25
823	$1.50 SPAD VII	4·75	6·00
824	$3 Boeing 747	6·50	9·00
821/4 Set of 4		16·00	15·00
MS825 97×83 mm. de Havilland DHC-6 Twin Otter		3·25	3·50

1985 (8 Nov). Life and Times of Queen Elizabeth the Queen Mother (2nd issue). Nos. 946/9 of Antigua optd with T **95** (in silver on Nos. 826/7 and MS829).

826	$1 The Queen Mother attending church	6·00	2·50
827	$1.50 Watching children playing in London garden	7·00	3·00
828	$2.50 The Queen Mother in 1979	8·00	3·50
826/8 Set of 3		19·00	8·00
MS829 56×85 mm. $5 With Prince Edward at Royal Wedding, 1981		17·00	11·00

Nos. 826/7 also exist with black and No. 828 with silver overprints (Price for set of 3 £50 mint).
The stamps from the sheetlets mentioned beneath Antigua No. MS949 also exist overprinted with Type **95**.

1985 (25 Nov). 850th Birth Anniv of Maimonides (physician, philosopher and scholar). Nos. 939/40 of Antigua optd with T **95**.

830	$2 bright green	4·50	4·50
MS831 70×84 mm. $5 reddish brown		4·25	4·50

1985 (25 Nov). Marine Life. Nos. 950/4 of Antigua optd with T **95** (in silver on 15c. and $3).

832	15c. Magnificent Frigate Bird	7·00	1·25
833	45c. Brain Coral	7·00	80
834	60c. Cushion Star	7·00	1·25
835	$3 Spotted Moray	15·00	5·50
832/5 Set of 4		32·00	8·00
MS836 110×80 mm. $5 Elkhorn Coral		18·00	6·50

1986 (17 Feb). International Youth Year. Nos. 941/5 of Antigua optd with T **95**.

837	25c. Young farmers with produce	15	15
838	50c. Hotel management trainees	25	30
839	60c. Girls with goat and boys with football ("Environment")	30	35
840	$3 Windsurfing ("Leisure")	1·50	1·60
837/40 Set of 4		2·00	2·10
MS841 102×72 mm. $5 Young people with Antiguan flags		2·75	3·25

1986 (17 Feb). Royal Visit. Nos. 965/8 of Antigua optd with T **106**.

842	60c. Flags of Great Britain and Antigua	3·75	50
843	$1 Queen Elizabeth II (vert)	3·00	65
844	$4 Royal Yacht Britannia	8·50	2·50
842/4 Set of 3		13·75	3·25
MS845 110×83 mm $5 Map of Antigua		12·00	4·00

1986 (10 Mar). 75th Anniv of Girl Guide Movement. Nos. 955/9 of Antigua optd with T **95**.

846	15c. Girl Guides nursing	1·50	80
847	45c. Open-air Girl Guide meeting	2·75	1·75
848	60c. Lord and Lady Baden-Powell	2·75	2·50
849	$3 Girl Guides gathering flowers	7·50	9·50
846/9 Set of 4		13·00	13·00
MS850 67×96 mm. $5 Barn Swallow (Nature study)		35·00	23·00

1986 (10 Mar). 300th Birth Anniv of Johann Sebastian Bach (composer). Nos. 960/4 of Antigua optd with T **95**.

851	25c. multicoloured	3·50	70
852	50c. multicoloured	3·75	1·40
853	$1 multicoloured	5·00	2·00
854	$3 multicoloured	8·50	9·00
851/4 Set of 4		19·00	11·50
MS855 104×73 mm. $5 black and brownish grey		27·00	12·00

1986 (4 Apr). Christmas. Religious Paintings. Nos. 985/9 of Antigua optd with T **106**.

856	10c. "Madonna and Child" (De Landi)	40	30
857	25c. "Madonna and Child" (Berlinghiero)	80	50

ANTIGUA AND BARBUDA / Barbuda

858	60c. "The Nativity" (Fra Angelico)	1·50	1·00
859	$4 "Presentation in the Temple" (Giovanni di Paolo)	4·00	7·00
856/9 Set of 4		6·00	8·00
MS860 113×81 mm. $5 "The Nativity" (Antoniazzo Romano)		4·25	5·50

108 Queen Elizabeth II meeting Members of Legislature

(Litho Format)

1986 (21 Apr). 60th Birthday of Queen Elizabeth II (1st issue). T **108** and similar horiz designs. Multicoloured. P 15.

861	$1 Type **108**	50	1·00
862	$2 Queen with Headmistress of Liberta School	60	1·10
863	$2.50 Queen greeted by Governor-General of Antigua	60	1·25
861/3 Set of 3		1·50	3·00
MS864 95×75 mm. $5 Queen Elizabeth in 1928 and 1986 (33×27 mm). P 13½×14		6·50	8·50

Nos. 861/3 exist imperforate from stock dispersed by the liquidator of Format International Security Printers Ltd.

See also Nos. 872/5.

109 Halley's Comet over Barbuda Beach

(Des and litho Format)

1986 (10 July). Appearance of Halley's Comet (1st issue). T **109** and similar multicoloured designs. P 15.

865	$1 Type **109**	60	1·25
866	$2.50 Early telescope and dish aerial (vert)	80	2·25
867	$5 Comet and World map	1·40	3·75
865/7 Set of 3		2·50	6·50

Nos. 865/7 exist imperforate from stock dispersed by the liquidator of Format International Security Printers Ltd.

1986 (12 Aug). 40th Anniv of United Nations Organization. Nos. 981/4 of Antigua optd with T **96** (Nos. 868/70) or T **95** (No. MS871).

868	40c. Benjamin Franklin and U.N. (New York) 1953 U.P.U. 5c. stamp	1·50	1·00
869	$1 George Washington Carver (agricultural chemist) and 1982 Nature Conservation 28c. stamp	2·25	2·25
870	$3 Charles Lindbergh (aviator) and 1978 I.C.A.O 25c. stamp	4·00	5·00
868/70 Set of 3		7·00	7·50
MS871 101×77 mm. $5 Marc Chagall (artist) (vert)		13·00	14·00

1986 (12 Aug). 60th Birthday of Queen Elizabeth II (2nd issue). Nos. 1005/8 of Antigua optd with T **95** in black (No. MS875) or silver (others).

872	60c. black and yellow	2·50	1·25
873	$1 multicoloured	3·00	2·00
874	$4 multicoloured	4·75	4·50
872/4 Set of 3		9·25	7·00
MS875 120×85 mm. $5 black and grey-brown		8·00	9·00

1986 (28 Aug). World Cup Football Championship, Mexico. Nos. 995/9 of Antigua optd with T **96** (30c., $4) or T **95** (others).

876	30c. Football, boots and trophy	4·00	1·00
877	60c. Goalkeeper (vert)	5·50	2·00
878	$1 Referee blowing whistle (vert)	6·00	2·25
879	$4 Ball in net	13·00	7·00
876/9 Set of 4		26·00	25·00
MS880 87×76 mm. $5 Two players competing for ball		24·00	15·00

1986 (28 Aug). "Ameripex '86" International Stamp Exhibition, Chicago. Famous American Trains. Nos. 1014/18 of Antigua optd with T **106**.

881	25c. "Hiawatha" express	2·00	1·50
882	50c. "Grand Canyon" express	2·75	2·25
883	$1 "Powhattan Arrow" express	3·50	3·00
884	$3 "Empire State" express	6·00	7·00
881/4 Set of 4		13·00	12·00
MS885 116×87 mm $5 Southern Pacific "Daylight" express		9·00	9·50

1986 (22 Sept). Appearance of Halley's Comet (2nd issue). Nos. 1000/4 of Antigua optd with T **96** (Nos. 886/9) or T **95** (MS890).

886	5c. Edmond Halley and Old Greenwich Observatory	2·75	1·00
887	10c. Messerschmitt Me 163B Komet (fighter aircraft), 1944	2·75	1·00
888	60c. Montezuma (Aztec Emperor) and Comet in 1517 (from "Historias de las Indias de Neuva Espana")	3·75	2·00
889	$4 Pocahontas saving Capt. John Smith and Comet in 1607	13·00	8·00
886/9 Set of 4		20·00	11·00
MS890 101×70 mm. $5 Halley's Comet over English Harbour, Antigua		7·00	5·00

1986 (22 Sept). Royal Wedding. Nos. 1019/22 of Antigua optd with T **95** in silver.

891	45c. Prince Andrew and Miss Sarah Ferguson	75	50
892	60c. Prince Andrew	90	65
893	$4 Prince Andrew with Prince Philip	3·50	4·00
891/3 Set of 3		4·75	4·75
MS894 88×88 mm. $5 Prince Andrew and Miss Sarah Ferguson (different)		8·00	8·00

1986 (10 Nov). Sea Shells. Nos. 1023/7 of Antigua optd with T **106** (in silver on 15c. to $3).

895	15c. Fly-specked Cerith	2·50	2·00
896	45c. Smooth Scotch Bonnet	2·75	2·25
897	60c. West Indian Crown Conch	3·50	2·75
898	$3 Ciboney Murex	8·00	12·00
895/8 Set of 4		15·00	17·00
MS899 109×75 mm. $5 Colourful Atlantic Moon (horiz)		20·00	18·00

1986 (10 Nov). Flowers. Nos. 1028/36 of Antigua optd with T **106**.

900	10c. Nymphaea ampla (water lily)	50	50
901	15c. Queen of the Night	60	50
902	50c. Cup of Gold	1·00	70
903	60c. Beach Morning Glory	1·10	70
904	70c. Golden Trumpet	1·25	90
905	$1 Air Plant	1·50	90
906	$3 Purple Wreath	3·00	4·00
907	$4 Zephyr Lily	3·50	4·25
900/7 Set of 8		11·00	11·50
MS908 Two sheets, each 102×72 mm. (a) $4 Dozakie. (b) $5 Four O'Clock Flower Set of 2 sheets		27·00	24·00

1986 (28 Nov). Mushrooms. Nos. 1042/6 of Antigua optd with T **106**.

909	10c. Hygrocybe occidentalis var. scarletina	90	50
910	50c. Trogia buccinalis	3·25	1·75
911	$1 Collybia subpruinosa	4·75	2·75
912	$4 Leucocoprinus brebissonii	9·50	8·00
909/12 Set of 4		16·00	11·50
MS913 102×82 mm. $5 Pyrrhoglossum pyrrhum		27·00	18·00

1986 (1 Dec). Birth Bicentenary of John J. Audubon (ornithologist) (3rd issue). Nos. 990/3 of Antigua optd with T **96** (in silver on 60, 90c.).

914	60c. Mallard	7·50	2·50
915	90c. North American Black Duck	9·50	2·75
916	$1.50 Pintail	13·00	8·50
917	$3 American Wigeon	19·00	14·00
914/17 Set of 4		45·00	25·00

1987 (12 Jan). Local Boats. Nos. 1009/13 of Antigua optd with T **95**.

918	30c. Tugboat	1·50	1·50
919	60c. Game fishing boat	1·75	80
920	$1 Yacht	2·25	1·25
921	$4 Lugger with auxiliary sail	4·50	6·00
918/21 Set of 4		9·00	7·75
MS922 108×78 mm. $5 Boats under construction		24·00	17·00

1987 (12 Jan). Centenary of First Benz Motor Car. Nos. 1052/60 of Antigua optd with T **95** (No. MS931) or T **96** (others).

923	10c. Auburn "Speedster" (1933)	1·25	45
924	15c. Mercury "Sable" (1986)	1·50	50
925	50c. Cadillac (1959)	2·00	70
926	60c. Studebaker (1950)	2·00	70
927	70c. Lagonda "V-12" (1939)	2·00	1·00
928	$1 Adler "Standard" (1930)	2·50	1·00
929	$3 DKW (1956)	3·25	4·00
930	$4 Mercedes "500K" (1936)	3·25	4·00
923/30 Set of 8		16·00	11·00
MS931 Two sheets, each 99×70 mm. (a) $5 Daimler (1896). (b) $5 Mercedes "Knight" (1921) Set of 2 sheets		27·00	15·00

ANTIGUA AND BARBUDA / Barbuda

1987 (10 Mar). World Cup Football Championship Winners, Mexico. Nos. 1037/40 of Antigua optd with T **95** (60c., $1) or T **96** (30c., $4).

932	30c. Football, boots and trophy	4·50	1·00
933	60c. Goalkeeper (*vert*)	5·00	1·50
934	$1 Referee blowing whistle (*vert*)	6·00	2·25
935	$4 Ball in net	13·00	12·00
932/5 Set of 4		26·00	15·00

1987 (23 Apr). America's Cup Yachting Championship. Nos. 1072/6 of Antigua optd horizontally as T **102**.

936	30c. *Canada I* (1981)	90	40
937	60c. *Gretel II* (1970)	1·25	50
938	$1 *Sceptre* (1958)	1·60	80
939	$3 *Vigilant* (1893)	2·25	3·50
936/9 Set of 4		5·50	4·75
MS940 113×84 mm. $5 *Australia II* defeating *Liberty* (1983) (*horiz*)		4·75	5·00

1987 (1 July). Marine Life. Nos. 1077/85 of Antigua optd with T **95** (No. **MS**949) or T **96** (others).

941	15c. Bridled Burrfish	7·00	1·50
942	30c. Common Noddy	12·00	1·50
943	40c. Nassau Grouper	9·00	1·50
944	50c. Laughing Gull	14·00	2·25
945	60c. French Angelfish	10·00	1·75
946	$1 Porkfish	10·00	2·50
947	$2 Royal Tern	22·00	10·00
948	$3 Sooty Tern	22·00	11·00
941/8 Set of 8		95·00	29·00
MS949 Two sheets, each 120×94 mm. (a) $5 Banded Butterflyfish. (b) $5 Brown Booby Set of 2 sheets		60·00	24·00

1987 (28 July). Milestones of Transportation. Nos. 1100/9 of Antigua optd with T **106**.

950	10c. *Spirit of Australia* (fastest powerboat), 1978	3·50	1·50
951	15c. Werner von Siemens's electric locomotive, 1879	4·50	1·25
952	30c. U.S.S. *Triton* (first submerged circumnavigation), 1960	4·50	1·25
953	50c. Trevithick s steam carriage (first passenger-carrying vehicle), 1801	5·00	2·00
954	60c. U.S.S. *New Jersey* (battleship), 1942	6·50	2·00
955	70c. Draisine bicycle, 1818	7·50	2·75
956	90c. *United States* (liner) (holder of Blue Riband), 1952	7·50	2·25
957	$1.50 Cierva C. 4 (first autogyro), 1923	7·50	7·00
958	$2 Curtiss NC-4 (first translantic flight), 1919	8·00	8·00
959	$3 *Queen Elizabeth 2* (liner), 1969	12·00	10·00
950/9 Set of 10		60·00	35·00

110 Shore Crab

(Litho Format)

1987 (15 Sept). Marine Life. T **110** and similar multicoloured designs. P 15.

960	5c. Type **110**	10	20
961	10c. Sea Cucumber	10	20
962	15c. Stop-light Parrotfish	10	20
963	25c. Banded Coral Shrimp	15	20
964	35c. Spotted Drum	15	20
965	60c. Thorny Starfish	20	40
966	75c. Atlantic Trumpet Triton	20	60
967	90c. Feather Star and Yellow Beaker Sponge	20	65
968	$1 Blue Gorgonian (*vert*)	20	65
969	$1.25 Slender Filefish (*vert*)	20	85
970	$5 Barred Hamlet (*vert*)	45	3·50
971	$7.50 Royal Gramma ("Fairy Basslet") (*vert*)	60	4·50
972	$10 Fire Coral and Banded Butterflyfish (*vert*)	75	5·00
960/72 Set of 13		2·75	15·00

Nos. 960/72 exist imperforate from stock dispersed by the liquidator of Format International Security Printers Ltd.

1987 (12 Oct). Olympic Games, Seoul (1988). Nos. 1086/90 of Antigua optd with T **95** (No. **MS**977) or T **96** in silver (others).

973	10c. Handball	1·00	50
974	60c. Fencing	2·25	80
975	$1 Gymnastics	2·75	1·40
976	$3 Football	4·50	5·50
973/6 Set of 4		9·50	7·50
MS977 100×72 mm. $5 Boxing gloves		9·00	4·75

1987 (12 Oct). Birth Centenary of Marc Chagall (artist). Nos. 1091/9 of Antigua optd as T **95** (in silver on Nos. 983, **MS**986b).

978	10c. "The Profile"	25	40
979	30c. "Portrait of the Artist's Sister"	35	20
980	40c. "Bride with Fan"	40	30
981	60c. "David in Profile"	45	30
982	90c. "Fiancee with Bouquet"	60	50
983	$1 "Self Portrait with Brushes"	70	55
984	$3 "The Walk"	2·00	2·50
985	$4 "Three Candles"	2·25	2·75
978/85 Set of 8		6·25	6·75
MS986 Two sheets, each 110×95 mm. (a) $5 "Fall of Icarus" (104×89 *mm*). (b) $5 "Myth of Orpheus" (104×89 *mm*) Set of 2 sheets		7·00	8·00

1987 (5 Nov). Centenary of Statue of Liberty (1986) (2nd issue). Nos 1110/19 of Antigua optd with T **95** (15, 30, 45, 50c., $1, $2, $5) or T **96** (60, 90c., $3), in black (50c., $3) or silver (others).

987	15c. Lee Iacocca at unveiling of restored Statue	20	20
988	30c. Statue at sunset (side view)	30	20
989	45c. Aerial view of head	45	25
990	50c. Lee Iacocca and torch	50	30
991	60c. Workmen inside head of Statue (*horiz*)	55	30
992	90c. Restoration work (*horiz*)	70	50
993	$1 Head of Statue	80	75
994	$2 Statue at Sunset (front view)	1·25	1·75
995	$3 Inspecting restoration work (*horiz*)	1·60	2·50
996	$5 Statue at night	2·50	3·50
987/96 Set of 10		8·00	9·00

1987 (5 Nov). Entertainers. Nos. 1120/7 of Antigua optd with T **95** (in silver on $3).

997	15c. Grace Kelly	2·00	70
998	30c. Marilyn Monroe	5·00	1·25
999	45c. Orson Welles	2·00	75
1000	50c. Judy Garland	2·00	1·00
1001	60c. John Lennon	15·00	2·50
1002	$1 Rock Hudson	2·75	1·75
1003	$2 John Wayne	4·50	3·50
1004	$3 Elvis Presley	26·00	11·00
997/1004 Set of 8		55·00	20·00

1987 (5 Nov). "Capex '87" International Stamp Exhibition, Toronto. Reptiles and Amphibians. Nos. 1133/7 of Antigua optd with T **95** (No. **MS**1009) or T **96** (others).

1005	30c. Whistling Frog	7·00	2·00
1006	60c. Croaking Lizard	8·00	2·00
1007	$1 Antiguan Anole	9·00	3·00
1008	$3 Red-footed Tortoise	18·00	17·00
1005/8 Set of 4		38·00	22·00
MS1009 106×76 mm. $5 Ground Lizard		30·00	12·00

1988 (12 Jan). Christmas. Religious Paintings. Nos. 1144/8 of Antigua optd with T **95**.

1010	45c. "Madonna and Child" (Bernardo Daddi)	2·00	30
1011	60c. "St. Joseph" (detail, "The Nativity") (Sano di Pietro)	2·00	55
1012	$1 "Virgin Mary" (detail, "The Nativity") (Sano di Pietro)	2·25	1·25
1013	$4 "Music-making Angel" (Melozzo da Forli)	6·50	8·50
1010/13 Set of 4		11·50	9·50
MS1014 99×70 mm. $5 "The Flight into Egypt" (Sano di Pietro)		9·00	6·50

1988 (25 Mar). Salvation Army's Community Service. Nos. 1163/71 of Antigua optd with T **106**.

1015	25c. First aid at daycare centre, Antigua	2·25	1·00
1016	30c. Giving penicillin injection, Indonesia	2·25	1·00
1017	40c. Children at daycare centre, Bolivia	2·25	1·00
1018	45c. Rehabilitation of the handicapped, India	2·25	1·00
1019	50c. Training blind man, Kenya	2·75	1·50
1020	60c. Weighing baby, Ghana	2·75	1·50
1021	$1 Training typist, Zambia	3·25	2·50
1022	$2 Emergency food kitchen, Sri Lanka	3·75	4·00
1015/22 Set of 8		19·00	12·00
MS1023 152×83 mm. $5 General Eva Burrows		28·00	25·00

1988 (6 May). Bicentenary of U.S. Constitution. Nos. 1139/43 of Antigua optd with T **95** ($4, $5) or T **96** (others), all in silver.

1024	15c. House of Burgesses, Virginia ("Freedom of Speech")	10	15
1025	45c. State Seal, Connecticut	20	25
1026	60c. State Seal, Delaware	25	40
1027	$4 Gouverneur Morris (Pennsylvania delegate) (*vert*)	1·75	3·25

1024/7 Set of 4		2·10	3·50
MS1028 105×75 mm. $5 Roger Sherman (Connecticut delegate) (vert)		2·75	3·25

1988 (4 July). Royal Ruby Wedding. Nos. 1149/53 of Antigua optd with T **95**.

1029	25c. deep brown, black and bright new blue	2·75	40
1030	60c. multicoloured	3·25	65
1031	$2 deep brown, black and light green	7·00	2·50
1032	$3 multicoloured	8·00	3·00
	a. Opt triple	†	
1029/32 Set of 4		19·00	6·00
MS1033 102×77 mm. $5 multicoloured		17·00	6·50

No. 1032a is known used on mail from the Philatelic Bureau in 1995.

1988 (4 July). Birds of Antigua. Nos. 1154/62 of Antigua optd with T **95** (10c., $1, $5) or T **96** (others).

1034	10c. Great Blue Heron	4·00	1·75
1035	15c. Ringed Kingfisher (horiz)	4·25	1·75
1036	50c. Bananaquit (horiz)	6·00	1·75
1037	60c. Purple Gallinule (horiz)	6·00	1·75
1038	70c. Blue-hooded Euphonia (horiz)	6·50	2·75
1039	$1 Brown-throated Conure ("Caribbean Parakeet")	7·50	2·75
1040	$3 Troupial (horiz)	13·00	8·50
1041	$4 Purple-throated Carib (horiz)	13·00	8·50
1034/41 Set of 8		55·00	26·00
MS1042 Two sheets, each 115×86 mm. (a) $5 Greater Flamingo. (b) $5 Brown Pelican Set of 2 sheets		40·00	19·00

1988 (25 July–8 Dec). 500th Anniv of Discovery of America by Columbus (1992) (1st issue). Nos. 1172/80 of Antigua optd with T **96** (Nos. 1043/50) or T **95** (No. **MS**1051).

1043	10c. Columbus' second fleet, 1493	3·50	1·00
1044	30c. Painos Indian village and fleet	3·50	80
1045	45c. Santa Mariagalante (flagship) and Painos village	4·25	80
1046	60c. Painos Indians offering Columbus fruit and vegetables	3·00	85
1047	90c. Painos Indian and Columbus with Scarlet Macaw	7·50	1·75
1048	$1 Columbus landing on island	6·00	1·75
1049	$3 Spanish soldier and fleet	7·50	4·50
1050	$4 Fleet under sail	7·50	4·50
1043/50 Set of 8		38·00	14·50
MS1051 Two sheets, each 110×80 mm. (a) $5 Queen Isabella's cross (b) $5 Gold coin of Ferdinand and Isabella (8 Dec) Set of 2 sheets		20·00	14·00

See also Nos. 1112/16, 1177/85, 1285/93, 1374/80 and 1381/2.

1988 (25 July). 500th Birth Anniv of Titian. Nos. 1181/9 of Antigua optd with T **96** (Nos. 1052/9) or T **95** (No. **MS**1060), all in silver.

1052	30c. "Bust of Christ"	1·00	20
1053	40c. "Scourging of Christ"	1·25	25
1054	45c. "Madonna in Glory with Saints"	1·25	25
1055	50c. "The Averoldi Polyptych" (detail)	1·40	30
1056	$1 "Christ Crowned with Thorns"	2·00	55
1057	$2 "Christ Mocked"	2·75	1·50
1058	$3 "Christ and Simon of Cyrene"	3·25	2·75
1059	$4 "Crucifixion with Virgin and Saints"	3·25	3·00
1052/9 Set of 8		14·50	8·00
MS1060 Two sheets, each 110×95 mm. (a) $5 "Ecce Homo" (detail). (b) $5 "Noli me Tangere" (detail) Set of 2 sheets		11·00	8·00

1988 (25 Aug). 16th World Scout Jamboree, Australia. Nos. 1128/32 of Antigua optd with T **95** (No. **MS**1064) or T **96** (others).

1061	10c. Scouts around camp fire and Red Kangaroo	2·50	1·00
1062	60c. Scouts canoeing and Blue-winged Kookaburra	8·50	1·50
1063	$1 Scouts on assault course and Ring-tailed Rock Wallaby	4·00	1·75
1064	$3 Field kitchen and Koala	7·50	6·50
1061/4 Set of 4		20·00	9·75
MS1065 103×78 mm. $5 Flags of Antigua, Australia and Scout Movement		10·00	6·50

1988 (25 Aug–8 Dec). Sailing Week. Nos. 1190/4 of Antigua optd with T **95** (No. **MS**1070) or T **96** (others).

1066	30c. Two yachts rounding buoy	60	35
1067	60c. Three yachts	1·00	70
1068	$1 British yacht under way	1·25	1·10
1069	$3 Three yachts (different)	2·25	2·75
1066/9 Set of 4		4·50	4·50
MS1070 103×92 mm. $5 Two yachts (8 Dec)		7·50	4·50

1988 (16 Sept). Flowering Trees. Nos. 1213/21 of Antigua optd with T **95**.

1071	10c. Jacaranda	15	20
1072	30c. Cordia	30	20
1073	50c. Orchid Tree	40	25
1074	90c. Flamboyant	60	45
1075	$1 African Tulip Tree	70	60
1076	$2 Potato Tree	1·25	1·50
1077	$3 Crepe Myrtle	1·50	2·00
1078	$4 Pitch Apple	1·75	2·50
1071/8 Set of 8		6·00	7·00
MS1079 Two sheets, each 106×76 mm. (a) $5 Cassia. (b) $5 Chinaberry Set of 2 sheets		6·00	6·50

1988 (16 Sept). Olympic Games, Seoul. Nos. 1222/6 of Antigua optd with T **95** (Nos. 1080/1, **MS**1084) or T **96** (Nos. 1082/3).

1080	40c. Gymnastics	1·50	40
1081	60c. Weightlifting	1·75	55
1082	$1 Water polo (horiz)	2·00	1·00
1083	$3 Boxing (horiz)	2·75	3·00
1080/3 Set of 4		7·00	4·50
MS1084 114×80 mm. $5 Runner with Olympic torch		3·00	2·40

BARBUDA MAIL
(111)

1988 (8 Dec)–90. Caribbean Butterflies. Nos. 1227/44a of Antigua optd with T **96** (Nos. 1085/1102) or T **111** (No. 1102a).

1085	1c. Danaus plexippus	50	1·00
1086	2c. Greta diaphanus	50	1·00
1087	3c. Calisto archebates	60	1·00
1088	5c. Hamadryas feronia	60	1·00
1089	10c. Mestra dorcas	75	1·00
1090	15c. Hypolimnas misippus	1·00	60
1091	20c. Dione juno	1·25	60
1092	25c. Heliconius charithonia	1·25	60
1093	30c. Eurema pyro	1·25	60
1094	40c. Papilio androgeus	1·50	60
1095	45c. Anteos maerula	1·50	60
1096	50c. Aphrissa orbis	1·75	85
1097	60c. Astraptes xagua	1·75	70
1098	$1 Heliopetes arsalte	2·50	1·00
1099	$2 Polites baracoa	4·25	4·25
1100	$2.50 Phocides pigmalion	4·50	4·75
1101	$5 Prepona amphitoe	6·00	7·00
1102	$10 Oarisma nanus	9·00	10·00
1102a	$20 Parides lycimenes (4.5.90)	16·00	17·00
1085/102a Set of 19		50·00	48·00

BARBUDA MAIL
(112)

BARBUDA MAIL
(113)

1989 (28 Apr). 25th Death Anniv of John F. Kennedy (American statesman). Nos. 1245/53 of Antigua optd with T **96** (Nos. 1103/10) or T **112** (No. **MS**1111).

1103	1c. President Kennedy and family	10	75
1104	2c. Kennedy commanding PT 109	10	75
1105	3c. Funeral cortege	10	75
1106	4c. In motorcade, Mexico City	10	75
1107	30c. As 1c.	1·50	50
1108	60c. As 4c.	3·50	60
1109	$1 As 3c.	3·50	1·50
1110	$4 As 2c.	9·00	11·00
1103/10 Set of 8		16·00	15·00
MS1111 105×75 mm. $5 Kennedy taking presidential oath of office		4·50	6·00

1989 (24 May). 500th Anniv of Discovery of America by Columbus (1992) (2nd issue). Pre-Columbian Arawak Society. Nos. 1267/71 of Antigua optd with T **113**.

1112	$1.50 Arawak warriors	4·50	4·50
	a. Horiz strip of 4. Nos. 1112/15	17·00	17·00
1113	$1.50 Whip dancers	4·50	4·50
1114	$1.50 Whip dancers and chief with pineapple	4·50	4·50
1115	$1.50 Family and campfire	4·50	4·50
1112/15 Set of 4		17·00	17·00
MS1116 71×84 mm. $6 Arawak chief		5·50	6·50

1989 (29 June). 50th Anniv of First Jet Flight. Nos. 1272/80 of Antigua optd with T **111**.

1117	10c. Hawker Siddeley Comet 4 airliner	3·50	2·00
1118	30c. Messerschmitt Me 262 fighter	4·50	1·50
1119	40c. Boeing 707 airliner	4·75	2·25
1120	60c. Canadair CL-13 Sabre ("F-86 Sabre") fighter	6·00	1·25
1121	$1 Lockheed F-104 Starfighter	7·00	2·50
1122	$2 Douglas DC-10 airliner	9·00	8·00
1123	$3 Boeing 747-300/400 airliner	10·00	11·00
1124	$4 McDonnell Douglas F-4 Phantom II fighter	10·00	11·00
1117/24 Set of 8		50·00	35·00

BARBUDA
MAIL
(114)

BARBUDA
MAIL
(115)

1989 (18 Sept). Caribbean Cruise Ships. Nos. 1281/9 of Antigua optd as T **114**, but with lines spaced (No. **MS**1134b). or with T **111** (others).

1126	25c. *Festivale*	4·00	1·50
1127	45c. *Southward*	4·25	1·50
1128	50c. *Sagafjord*	4·25	1·75
1129	60c. *Daphne*	4·25	1·75
1130	75c. *Cunard Countess*	4·50	2·75
1131	90c. *Song of America*	4·50	2·75
1132	$3 *Island Princess*	12·00	10·00
1133	$4 *Galileo*	12·00	10·00
1126/33 Set of 8		45·00	29·00

MS1134 (a) 113×87 mm. $6 *Norway*. (b) 111×82 mm. $6 *Oceanic* Set of 2 sheets .... 55·00 38·00

1989 (14 Dec). Japanese Art. Paintings by Hiroshige. Nos. 1290/8 of Antigua optd with T **114**.

1135	25c. "Fish swimming by Duck half-submerged in Stream"	4·50	1·00
1136	45c. "Crane and Wave"	5·50	1·00
1137	50c. "Sparrows and Morning Glories"	5·50	1·50
1138	60c. "Crested Blackbird and Flowering Cherry"	5·50	1·50
1139	$1 "Great Knot sitting among Water Grass"	6·50	1·75
1140	$2 "Goose on a Bank of Water"	8·50	4·25
1141	$3 "Black Paradise Flycatcher and Blossoms"	10·00	5·00
1142	$4 "Sleepy Owl perched on a Pine Branch"	11·00	5·50
1135/42 Set of 8		50·00	19·00

MS1143 Two sheets, each 102×75 mm. (a) $5 "Bullfinch flying near a Clematis Branch". (b) $5 "Titmouse on a Cherry Branch" Set of 2 sheets .... 50·00 23·00

1989 (20 Dec). World Cup Football Championship, Italy (1990). Nos. 1308/12 of Antigua optd with T **115**.

1144	15c. Goalkeeper	2·00	65
1145	25c. Goalkeeper moving towards ball	2·00	65
1146	$1 Goalkeeper reaching for ball	5·00	2·00
1147	$4 Goalkeeper saving goal	8·00	10·00
1144/7 Set of 4		15·00	12·00

MS1148 Two sheets, each 75×105 mm. (a) $5 Three players competing for ball (*horiz*). (b) $5 Ball and players' legs (*horiz*) Set of 2 sheets .... 38·00 32·00

1989 (20 Dec). Christmas. Paintings by Raphael and Giotto. Nos. 1351/9 of Antigua optd with T **114**.

1149	10c. "The Small Cowper Madonna" (Raphael)	40	30
1150	25c. "Madonna of the Goldfinch" (Raphael)	50	20
1151	30c. "The Alba Madonna" (Raphael)	50	20
1152	50c. Saint (detail, "Bologna Altarpiece") (Giotto)	80	30
1153	60c. Angel (detail, "Bologna Altarpiece") (Giotto)	85	45
1154	70c. Angel slaying serpent (detail, "Bologna Altarpiece") (Giotto)	90	60
1155	$4 Evangelist (detail, "Bologna Altarpiece") (Giotto)	3·00	4·50
1156	$5 "Madonna of Foligno" (Raphael)	3·00	4·50
1149/56 Set of 8		9·00	10·00

MS1157 Two sheets, each 71×96 mm. (a) $5 "The Marriage of the Virgin" (detail) (Raphael). (b) $5 Madonna and Child (detail, "Bologna Altarpiece") (Giotto) Set of 2 sheets .... 13·00 15·00

1990 (21 Feb). Fungi. Nos. 1313/21 of Antigua optd with T **111**.

1158	10c. *Mycena pura*	2·50	1·50
1159	25c. *Psathyrella tuberculata* (*vert*)	2·75	65
1160	50c. *Psilocybe cubensis*	3·25	1·00
1161	60c. *Leptonia caeruleocapitata* (*vert*)	3·25	1·00
1162	75c. *Xeromphalina tenuipes* (*vert*)	3·25	1·40
1163	$1 *Chlorophyllum molybdites* (*vert*)	3·50	1·40
1164	$3 *Marasmius haematocephalus*	6·00	7·50
1165	$4 *Cantharellus cinnabarinus*	6·00	7·50
1158/65 Set of 8		27·00	20·00

MS1166 Two sheets, each 88×62 mm. (a) $6 *Leucopaxillus gracillimus* (*vert*). (b) $6 *Volvariella volvacea* Set of 2 Sheets .... 38·00 23·00

BARBUDA MAIL
(116)

1990 (30 Mar). Local Fauna. Nos. 1322/6 of Antigua optd with T **116** (vertically on 60c., $4).

1167	25c. Desmarest's Hutia	1·00	60
1168	45c. Caribbean Monk Seal	2·50	1·25
1169	60c. Mustache Bat (*vert*)	1·75	1·25
1170	$4 American Manatee (*vert*)	4·25	6·50
1167/70 Set of 4		8·50	8·75

MS1171 113×87 mm. $5 West Indies Giant Rice Rat.... 22·00 22·00

1990 (30 Mar). 20th Anniv of First Manned Landing on Moon. Nos. 1346/50 of Antigua optd with T **116** (vertically on 10, 45c. and $5).

1172	10c. Launch of "Apollo 11"	3·25	1·50
1173	45c. Aldrin on Moon	6·00	80
1174	$1 Module *Eagle* over Moon (*horiz*)	7·50	2·75
1175	$4 Recovery of "Apollo 11" crew after splashdown (*horiz*)	13·00	13·00
1172/5 Set of 4		27·00	16·00

MS1176 107×77 mm. $5 Astronaut Neil Armstrong........ 24·00 23·00

1990 (6 June). 500th Anniv of Discovery of America by Columbus (1992) (3rd issue). New World Natural History – Marine Life. Nos. 1360/8 of Antigua optd as T **114**, but with lines spaced.

1177	10c. Star-eyed Hermit Crab	1·75	1·75
1178	20c. Spiny Lobster	2·25	1·75
1179	25c. Magnificent Banded Fanworm	2·25	1·75
1180	45c. Cannonball Jellyfish	3·25	1·00
1181	60c. Red-spiny Sea Star	3·50	1·00
1182	$2 Peppermint Shrimp	4·75	5·00
1183	$3 Coral Crab	5·00	6·00
1184	$4 Branching Fire Coral	5·00	6·00
1177/84 Set of 8		25·00	22·00

MS1185 Two sheets, each 101×69 mm. (a) $5 Common Sea Fan. (b) $5 Portuguese Man-of-war Set of 2 sheets.. 28·00 27·00

1990 (12 July). "EXPO 90" International Garden and Greenery Exhibition, Osaka. Orchids. Nos. 1369/77 of Antigua optd as T **114**, but with lines spaced.

1186	15c. *Vanilla mexicana*	2·00	80
1187	45c. *Epidendrum ibaguense*	2·50	80
1188	50c. *Epidendrum secundum*	2·50	90
1189	60c. *Maxillaria conferta*	2·75	1·10
1190	$1 *Oncidium altissimum*	3·00	1·75
1191	$2 *Spiranthes lanceolata*	5·00	5·00
1192	$3 *Tonopsis utricularioides*	5·50	6·50
1193	$5 *Epidendrum nocturnum*	7·00	8·50
1186/93 Set of 8		27·00	23·00

MS1194 Two sheets, each 101×69 mm. (a) $6 *Octomeria graminifolia*. (b) $6 *Rodriguezia lanceolata* Set of 2 sheets .... 38·00 23·00

1990 (14 Aug). Reef Fish. Nos. 1386/94 of Antigua optd with T **111**.

1195	10c. Flamefish	2·50	1·75
1196	15c. Coney	2·50	1·75
1197	50c. Long-spined Squirrelfish	3·50	1·50
1198	60c. Sergeant Major	3·50	1·50
1199	$1 Yellow-tailed Snapper	4·25	2·50
1200	$2 Rock Beauty	7·00	7·00
1201	$3 Spanish Hogfish	9·00	10·00
1202	$4 Striped Parrotfish	9·00	10·00
1195/1202 Set of 8		38·00	32·00

MS1203 Two sheets, each 99×70 mm. (a) $5 Black-barred Soldierfish. (b) $5 Four-eyed Butterflyfish Set of 2 sheets .... 38·00 32·00

$5.00

1st Anniversary
Hurricane Hugo
16th September, 1989-1990

(117)

1990 (17 Sept). First Anniv of Hurricane Hugo. Nos. 971/2 surch as T **117**.

1204	$5 on $7.50 Fairy Basslet (*vert*)	12·00	15·00
1205	$7.50 on $10 Fire Coral and Butterfly Fish (*vert*)	13·00	17·00

1990 (12 Oct). 90th Birthday of Queen Elizabeth the Queen Mother. Nos. 1415/19 of Antigua optd as T **114**, but with lines spaced.

1206	15c. multicoloured	8·00	1·75
1207	35c. multicoloured	11·00	1·50
1208	75c. multicoloured	17·00	3·25

1209	$3 multicoloured	30·00	19·00
1206/9	Set of 4	60·00	23·00
MS1210	67×98 mm. $6 multicoloured	55·00	26·00

BARBUDA MAIL

(118)

1990 (14 Dec). Achievements in Space. Nos. 1395/1414 of Antigua optd with T **118** in silver.

1211	45c. "Voyager 2" passing Saturn	3·75	3·25
	a. Sheetlet. Nos. 1211/30	65·00	60·00
1212	45c. "Pioneer 11" photographing Saturn	3·75	3·25
1213	45c. Astronaut in transporter	3·75	3·25
1214	45c. Space shuttle *Columbia*	3·75	3·25
1215	45c. "Apollo 10" command module on parachutes	3·75	3·25
1216	45c. "Skylab" space station	3·75	3·25
1217	45c. Astronaut Edward White in space	3·75	3·25
1218	45c. "Apollo" spacecraft on joint mission	3·75	3·25
1219	45c. "Soyuz" spacecraft on joint mission	3·75	3·25
1220	45c. "Mariner 1" passing Venus	3·75	3·25
1221	45c. "Gemini 4" capsule	3·75	3·25
1222	45c. "Sputnik 1"	3·75	3·25
1223	45c. Hubble space telescope	3·75	3·25
1224	45c. North American X-15	3·75	3·25
1225	45c. Bell XS-1 airplane	3·75	3·25
1226	45c. "Apollo 17" astronaut and lunar rock formation	3·75	3·25
1227	45c. Lunar Rover	3·75	3·25
1228	45c. "Apollo 14" lunar module	3·75	3·25
1229	45c. Astronaut Buzz Aldrin on Moon	3·75	3·25
1230	45c. Soviet "Lunokhod" lunar vehicle	3·75	3·25
1211/30	Set of 20	65·00	60·00

1990 (14 Dec). Christmas. Paintings by Renaissance Masters. Nos. 1457/65 of Antigua optd with T **111**.

1231	25c. "Madonna and Child with Saints" (detail, Sebastiano del Piombo)	2·25	60
1232	30c. "Virgin and Child with Angels" (detail, Grünewald) (*vert*)	2·25	60
1233	40c. "The Holy Family and a Shepherd" (detail, Titian)	2·25	60
1234	60c. "Virgin and Child" (detail, Lippi) (*vert*)	3·00	1·10
1235	$1 "Jesus, St. John and Two Angels" (Rubens)	3·75	1·50
1236	$2 "Adoration of the Shepherds" (detail, Vincenzo Catena)	5·50	6·00
1237	$4 "Adoration of the Magi" (detail, Giorgione)	8·50	9·50
1238	$5 "Virgin and Child adored by Warrior" (detail, Vincenzo Catena)	8·50	9·50
1231/8	Set of 8	32·00	23·00

MS1239 Two sheets, each 71×101 mm. (a) $6 "Allegory of the Blessings of Jacob" (detail, Rubens) (*vert*). (b) $6 "Adoration of the Magi" (detail, Fra Angelico) (*vert*) *Set of 2 sheets* .... 27·00 28·00

1991 (4 Feb). 150th Anniv of the Penny Black. Nos. 1378/81 of Antigua optd with T **116**.

1240	45c. blue-green	5·00	1·00
1241	60c. magenta	5·00	1·10
1242	$5 ultramarine	15·00	15·00
1240/2	Set of 3	23·00	16·00
MS1243	102×80 mm. $6 blackish purple	20·00	15·00

1991 (4 Feb). "Stamp World London 90" International Stamp Exhibition. Nos. 1382/5 of Antigua optd with T **116**.

1244	50c. deep grey-green and scarlet-vermilion	5·00	1·00
1245	75c. purple-brown and scarlet-vermilion	5·00	1·50
1246	$4 deep ultramarine and scarlet-vermilion	15·00	15·00
1244/6	Set of 3	23·00	16·00
MS1247	104×81 mm. $6 brownish black and scarlet-vermilion	22·00	23·00

119 Troupial

(Des G. Drummond. Litho Questa)

1991 (25 Mar). Wild Birds. T **119** and similar vert designs. Multicoloured. P 14.

1248	60c. Type **119**	2·25	65
1249	$2 Adelaide's Warbler ("Christmas Bird")	3·75	3·00
1250	$4 Rose-breasted Grosbeak	5·50	6·50
1251	$7 Wied's Crested Flycatcher	7·50	11·00
1248/51	Set of 4	17·00	19·00

1991 (23 Apr). Olympic Games, Barcelona (1992). Nos. 1429/33 of Antigua optd as T **114**, but with lines spaced.

1252	50c. Men's 20 kilometres walk	2·75	90
1253	75c. Triple jump	3·00	1·00
1254	$1 Men's 10,000 metres	3·25	1·75
1255	$5 Javelin	12·00	14·00
1252/5	Set of 4	19·00	16·00

MS1256 100×70 mm. $6 Athlete lighting Olympic flame at Los Angeles Olympics .... 16·00 18·00

1991 (23 Apr). Birds. Nos. 1448/56 of Antigua optd with T **116** diagonally.

1257	10c. Pearly-eyed Thrasher	3·00	1·75
1258	25c. Purple-throated Carib	4·00	1·00
1259	50c. Yellowthroat	5·00	1·25
1260	60c. American Kestrel	5·00	1·25
1261	$1 Yellow-bellied Sapsucker	5·50	2·00
1262	$2 Purple Gallinule	7·50	7·00
1263	$3 Yellow-crowned Night Heron	8·00	9·00
1264	$4 Blue-hooded Euphonia	8·00	9·00
1257/64	Set of 8	42·00	29·00

MS1265 Two sheets, each 76×60 mm. (a) $6 Brown Pelican. (b) $6 Magnificent Frigate Bird *Set of 2 sheets* .... 32·00 25·00

1991 (21 June). 350th Death Anniv of Rubens. Nos. 1466/74 of Antigua optd with T **111**.

1266	25c. "Rape of the Daughters of Leucippus" (detail)	2·50	80
1267	45c. "Bacchanal" (detail)	3·00	80
1268	50c. "Rape of the Sabine Women" (detail)	3·00	85
1269	60c. "Battle of the Amazons" (detail)	3·25	90
1270	$1 "Rape of the Sabine Women" (different detail)	3·75	1·75
1271	$2 "Bacchanal" (different detail)	6·00	6·50
1272	$3 "Rape of the Sabine Women" (different detail)	8·50	10·00
1273	$4 "Bacchanal" (different detail)	8·50	10·00
1266/73	Set of 8	35·00	28·00

MS1274 Two sheets, each 101×71 mm. (a) $6 "Rape of Hippodameia" (detail). (b) $6 "Battle of the Amazons" (different detail) *Set of 2 sheets* .... 30·00 32·00

1991 (25 July). 50th Anniv of Second World War. Nos. 1475/84 of Antigua optd diagonally with T **116**.

1275	10c. U.S. troops cross into Germany, 1944	3·25	2·25
1276	15c. Axis surrender in North Africa, 1943	3·75	2·00
1277	25c. U.S. tanks invade Kwajalein, 1944	4·00	1·50
1278	45c. Roosevelt and Churchill meet at Casablanca, 1943	12·00	2·50
1279	50c. Marshall Badoglio, Prime Minister of Italian anti-fascist government, 1943	3·75	1·75
1280	$1 Lord Mountbatten, Supreme Allied Commander South-east Asia, 1943	15·00	4·75
1281	$2 Greek victory at Koritza, 1940	10·00	10·00
1282	$4 Anglo-Soviet mutual assistance pact, 1941	12·00	13·00
1283	$5 Operation Torch landings, 1942	13·00	13·00
1275/83	Set of 9	70·00	45·00

MS1284 Two sheets, each 108×80 mm. (a) $6 Japanese attack on Pearl Harbor, 1941. (b) $6 U.S.A.A.F. daylight raid on Schweinfurt, 1943 *Set of 2 sheets* .... 60·00 40·00

1991 (26 Aug). 500th Anniv of Discovery of America by Columbus (1992) (4th issue). History of Exploration. Nos. 1503/11 of Antigua optd with T **111**.

1285	10c. multicoloured	2·25	2·00
1286	15c. multicoloured	2·50	2·00
1287	45c. multicoloured	3·50	1·00
1288	60c. multicoloured	3·75	1·25
1289	$1 multicoloured	4·00	2·00
1290	$2 multicoloured	6·50	6·00
1291	$4 multicoloured	10·00	11·00
1292	$5 multicoloured	10·00	11·00
1285/92	Set of 8	38·00	32·00

MS1293 Two sheets, each 106×76 mm. (a) $6 black and Indian red. (b) $6 black and Indian red *Set of 2 sheets* .... 35·00 28·00

1991 (18 Oct). Butterflies. Nos. 1494/502 of Antigua optd with T **116** diagonally.

1294	10c. *Heliconius charithonia*	3·25	2·25

1295	35c. *Marpesia petreus*	4·50	1·25
1296	50c. *Anartia amathea*	5·00	1·40
1297	75c. *Siproeta stelenes*	6·00	2·25
1298	$1 *Battus polydamas*	6·00	2·50
1299	$2 *Historis odius*	9·00	8·50
1300	$4 *Hypolimnas misippus*	11·00	12·00
1301	$5 *Hamadryas feronia*	11·00	12·00
1294/1301	Set of 8	50·00	38·00

MS1302 Two sheets. (a) 73×100 mm. $6 *Vanessa cardui* caterpillar (*vert*). (b) 100×73 mm. $6 *Danaus plexippus* caterpillar (*vert*) Set of 2 sheets .... 40·00 35·00

BARBUDA MAIL
(120)

1991 (18 Nov). 65th Birthday of Queen Elizabeth II. Nos. 1534/8 of Antigua optd with T **120**.

1303	15c. Queen Elizabeth and Prince Philip in 1976	6·00	1·50
1304	20c. Queen and Prince Philip in Portugal, 1985	6·00	1·50
1305	$2 Queen Elizabeth II	17·00	8·00
1306	$4 The Queen and Prince Philip at Ascot, 1986	26·00	17·00
1303/6	Set of 4	50·00	25·00

MS1307 68×90 mm. $4 The Queen at National Theatre, 1986, and Prince Philip .... 50·00 20·00

1991 (18 Nov). Tenth Wedding Anniv of Prince and Princess of Wales. Nos. 1539/43 of Antigua optd with T **120**.

1308	10c. Prince and Princess of Wales at party, 1986	5·50	2·50
1309	40c. Separate portraits of Prince, Princess and sons	11·00	1·75
1310	$1 Prince Henry and Prince William	13·00	4·50
1311	$5 Princess Diana in Australia and Prince Charles in Hungary	27·00	19·00
1308/11	Set of 4	50·00	25·00

MS1312 68×90 mm. $4 Prince Charles in Hackney and Princess and sons in Majorca, 1987 .... 50·00 20·00

1991 (24 Dec). Christmas. Religious Paintings by Fra Angelico. Nos. 1595/602 of Antigua optd with T **120**.

1313	10c. "The Annunciation"	2·50	1·50
1314	30c. "Nativity"	3·00	70
1315	40c. "Adoration of the Magi"	3·00	70
1316	60c. "Presentation in the Temple"	3·75	70
1317	$1 "Circumcision"	5·00	1·75
1318	$3 "Flight into Egypt"	8·50	9·00
1319	$4 "Massacre of the Innocents"	8·50	10·00
1320	$5 "Christ teaching in the Temple"	8·50	10·00
1313/20	Set of 8	38·00	30·00

1992 (20 Feb). Death Centenary of Vincent van Gogh (artist) (1990) Nos. 1512/24 of Antigua optd with T **120**.

1321	5c. "Camille Roulin"	2·00	2·00
1322	10c. "Armand Roulin"	2·25	2·00
1323	15c. "Young Peasant Woman with Straw Hat sitting in the Wheat"	2·50	2·00
1324	25c. "Adeline Ravoux"	2·50	2·00
1325	30c. "The Schoolboy"	2·50	1·25
1326	40c. "Doctor Gachet"	2·75	1·50
1327	50c. "Portrait of a Man"	2·75	1·75
1328	75c. "Two Children"	4·25	2·25
1329	$2 "The Postman Joseph Roulin"	8·00	7·50
1330	$3 "The Seated Zouave"	9·00	9·00
1331	$4 "L'Arlésienne"	9·50	10·00
1332	$5 "Self-Portrait, November/December 1888"	9·50	10·00
1321/32	Set of 12	50·00	45·00

MS1333 Three sheets, each 102×76 mm. (a) $5 "Farmhouse in Provence" (*horiz*). (b) $5 "Flowering Garden" (*horiz*). (c) $6 "The Bridge at Trinquetaille" (*horiz*). Imperf Set of 3 sheets .... 45·00 42·00

1992 (7 Apr). Birth Centenary of Charles de Gaulle (French statesman). Nos. 1562/70 of Antigua optd with T **111** (10c., $1, $2, $4, $6) or T **114** (others).

1334	10c. Presidents De Gaulle and Kennedy, 1961	3·00	2·00
1335	15c. General De Gaulle with Pres. Roosevelt, 1915 (*vert*)	3·00	2·00
1336	45c. Pres. De Gaulle with Chancellor Adenauer, 1962 (*vert*)	3·75	80
1337	60c. De Gaulle at Arc de Triomphe, Liberation of Paris, 1944 (*vert*)	4·00	1·00
1338	$1 General De Gaulle crossing the Rhine, 1945	4·75	2·25
1339	$2 General De Gaulle in Algiers, 1944	8·00	8·00
1340	$4 Presidents De Gaulle and Eisenhower, 1960	10·00	13·00
1341	$5 De Gaulle returning from Germany, 1968 (*vert*)	10·00	13·00
1334/41	Set of 8	42·00	38·00

MS1342 Two sheets, (a) 76×106 mm. $6 De Gaulle with crowd. (b) 106×76 mm. $6 De Gaulle and Churchill at Casablanca, 1943 Set of 2 sheets .... 42·00 35·00

1992 (16 Apr). Easter. Religious Paintings. Nos. 1627/35 of Antigua optd with T **111**.

1343	10c. "Supper at Emmaus" (Caravaggio)	1·75	1·50
1344	15c. "The Vision of St. Peter" (Zurbarán)	2·00	1·50
1345	30c. "Christ driving the Money-changers from the Temple" (Tiepolo)	2·25	80
1346	40c. "Martyrdom of St. Bartholomew" (detail) (Ribera)	2·25	80
1347	$1 "Christ driving the Money-changers from the Temple" (detail) (Tiepolo)	4·00	2·25
1348	$2 "Crucifixion" (detail) (Altdorfer)	6·00	6·50
1349	$4 "The Deposition" (detail) (Fra Angelico)	8·50	10·00
1350	$5 "The Deposition" (different detail) (Fra Angelico)	8·50	10·00
1343/50	Set of 8	32·00	30·00

MS1351 Two sheets. (a) 102×71 mm. $6 "The Last Supper" (detail) (Masip). (b) 71×102 mm. $6 "Crucifixion" (detail) (*vert*) (Altdorfer) Set of 2 sheets ... 30·00 27·00

1992 (19 June). Anniversaries and Events. Nos. 1573/83 of Antigua optd as T **114**, but with lines spaced (Nos. 1358 and MS1362b) or with T **111** (others).

1352	25c. Germans celebrating Reunification	1·00	70
1353	75c. Cubs erecting tent	2·25	1·50
1354	$1.50 *Don Giovanni* and Mozart	12·00	4·25
1355	$2 Chariot driver and Gate at night	3·00	3·50
1356	$2 Lord Baden-Powell and members of the 3rd Antigua Methodist cub pack (*vert*)	3·00	3·50
1357	$2 Lilienthal's signature and glider *Flugzeug Nr. 5*	3·00	3·50
1358	$2.50 Driver in Class P36 steam locomotive (*vert*)	9·00	4·50
1359	$3 Statues from podium	3·00	4·50
1360	$3.50 Cubs and camp fire	4·50	5·50
1361	$4 St. Peter's Cathedral, Salzburg	15·00	11·00
1352/61	Set of 10	50·00	38·00

MS1362 Two sheets. (a) 100×72 mm. $4 Detail of chariot and helmet. (b) 89×117 mm. $5 Antiguan flag and Jamboree emblem (*vert*) Set of 2 sheets ...... 45·00 35·00

1992 (12 Aug). 50th Anniv of Japanese Attack on Pearl Harbor. Nos. 1585/94 of Antigua optd as T **111**, but with lines spaced.

1364	$1 *Nimitz* class carrier and *Ticonderoga* class cruiser	7·00	4·00
	a. Sheetlet. Nos. 1364/73	65·00	35·00
1365	$1 Tourist launch	7·00	4·00
1366	$1 U.S.S. *Arizona* memorial	7·00	4·00
1367	$1 Wreaths on water and aircraft	7·00	4·00
1368	$1 White Tern	7·00	4·00
1369	$1 Mitsubishi A6M Zero-Sen fighters over Pearl City	7·00	4·00
1370	$1 Mitsubishi A6M Zero-Sen fighters attacking	7·00	4·00
1371	$1 Battleship Row in flames	7·00	4·00
1372	$1 U.S.S. *Nevada* (battleship) underway	7·00	4·00
1373	$1 Mitsubishi A6M Zero-Sen fighters returning to carriers	7·00	4·00
1364/73	Set of 10	65·00	35·00

1992 (12 Oct). 500th Anniv of Discovery of America by Columbus (5th issue). World Columbian Stamp "Expo '92", Chicago. Nos. 1654/60 of Antigua optd with T **111**.

1374	15c. Memorial cross and huts, San Salvador	1·25	1·25
1375	30c. Martin Pinzon with telescope	1·50	90
1376	40c. Christopher Columbus	2·50	1·00
1377	$1 *Pinta*	7·00	3·00
1378	$2 *Nina*	9·00	8·00
1379	$4 *Santa Maria*	13·00	15·00
1374/9	Set of 6	30·00	26·00

MS1380 Two sheets, each 108×76 mm. (a) $6 Ship and map of West Indies. (b) $6 Sea monster Set of 2 sheets.. 35·00 38·00

1992 (12 Oct). 500th Anniv of Discovery of America by Columbus (6th issue). Organization of East Caribbean States. Nos. 1670/1 of Antigua optd with T **111**.

1381	$1 Columbus meeting Amerindians	3·50	2·50
1382	$2 Ships approaching island	8·50	9·50

1992 (29 Oct). Postage Stamp Mega Event, New York. No. MS1690 of Antigua optd with T **111**.

MS1383 $6 multicoloured .... 15·00 17·00

1992 (3 Nov). 40th Anniv of Queen Elizabeth II's Accession. Nos. 1604/8 of Antigua optd with T **111**.

1384	10c. Queen Elizabeth II and bird sanctuary	8·00	2·25
1385	30c. Nelson's Dockyard	9·00	1·25

ANTIGUA AND BARBUDA / Barbuda

1386	$1 Ruins on Shirley Heights	13·00	2·75
1387	$5 Beach and palm trees	26·00	17·00
1384/7	Set of 4	50·00	21·00

MS1388 Two sheets, each 75×98 mm. (a) $6 Beach. (b) $6 Hillsie foliage *Set of 2 sheets* ... 55·00 29·00

1992 (8 Dec). Prehistoric Animals. Nos. 1618/26 of Antigua optd with T **120** (sideways on Nos. 1391/2 and **MS**1397).

1389	10c. Pteranodon	2·25	2·00
1390	15c. Brachiosaurus	2·75	2·00
1391	30c. Tyrannosaurus Rex	3·25	1·50
1392	50c. Parasaurolophus	3·25	2·50
1393	$1 Deinonychus (*horiz*)	4·00	2·50
1394	$2 Triceratops (*horiz*)	6·50	6·00
1395	$4 Protoceratops hatching (*horiz*)	7·50	9·50
1396	$5 Stegosaurus (*horiz*)	7·50	9·50
1389/96	Set of 8	32·00	32·00

MS1397 Two sheets, each 100×70 mm. (a) $6 Apatosaurus (*horiz*). (b) $6 Allosaurus (*horiz*) *Set of 2 sheets* ... 45·00 38·00

1992 (8 Dec). Christmas. Nos. 1691/9 of Antigua. optd with T **111**.

1398	10c. "Virgin and Child with Angels" (School of Piero della Francesca)	2·00	1·25
1399	25c. "Madonna Degli Alberelli" (Giovanni Bellini)	2·00	1·00
1400	30c. "Madonna and Child with St. Anthony Abbot and St. Sigismund" (Neroccio)	2·00	85
1401	40c. "Madonna and the Grand Duke" (Raphael)	2·25	85
1402	60c. "The Nativity" (George de la Tour)	2·50	1·00
1403	$1 "Holy Family" (Jacob Jordaens)	3·25	1·50
1404	$4 "Madonna and Child Enthroned" (Magarione)	7·50	9·50
1405	$5 "Madonna and Child on a Curved Throne" (Byzantine school)	7·50	9·50
1398/405	Set of 8	26·00	23·00

MS1406 Two sheets, each 76×102 mm. (a) $6 "Madonna and Child" (Domenco Ghirlando). (b) $6 "The Holy Family" (Pontormo) *Set of 2 sheets* ... 27·00 30·00

1993 (25 Jan). Fungi. Nos. 1645/53 of Antigua optd with T **120**.

1407	10c. *Amanita caesarea*	1·75	1·75
1408	15c. *Collybia fusipes*	2·00	1·75
1409	30c. *Boletus aereus*	2·25	1·50
1410	40c. *Laccaria amethystina*	2·25	1·50
1411	$1 *Russula virescens*	3·25	2·00
1412	$2 *Tricholoma equestre* ("*Tricholoma auratum*")	4·50	4·00
1413	$4 *Calocybe gambosa*	5·50	7·00
1414	$5 *Lentinus tigrinus* ("*Panus tigrinus*")	5·50	7·00
1407/14	Set of 8	24·00	24·00

MS1415 Two sheets, each 100×70 mm. (a) $6 *Clavariadelphus truncatus*. (b) $6 *Auricularia auricula-judae* *Set of 2 sheets* ... 28·00 26·00

1993 (22 Mar). "Granada '92" International Stamp Exhibition, Spain. Spanish Paintings. Nos. 1636/44 of Antigua optd diagonally with T **116**.

1416	10c. "The Miracle at the Well" (Alonzo Cano)	1·50	1·50
1417	15c. "The Poet Luis de Goingora y Argote" (Velázquez)	1·75	1·50
1418	30c. "The Painter Francisco Goya" (Vincente López Portana)	2·00	1·00
1419	40c. "Maria de las Nieves Michaela Fourdinier" (Luis Paret y Alcázar)	2·00	1·00
1420	$1 "Carlos III eating before his Court" (Alcázar) (*horiz*)	3·50	2·25
1421	$2 "Rain Shower in Granada" (Antonio Munoz Degrain) (*horiz*)	5·50	5·50
1422	$4 "Sarah Bernhardt" (Santiago Ruisnol i Prats)	7·50	9·00
1423	$5 "The Hermitage Garden" (Joaquim Mir Trinxet)	7·50	9·00
1416/23	Set of 8	28·00	28·00

MS1424 Two sheets, each 120×95 mm. (a) $6 "The Ascent of Monsieur Boucle's Montgolfier Balloon in the Gardens of Aranjuez" (Antonio Carnicero) (112×87 *mm*). (b) $6 "Olympus: Battle with the Giants" (Francisco Bayeu y Subias) (112×87 *mm*). Imperf *Set of 2 sheets* ... 22·00 25·00

1993 (10 May). "Genova '92" International Thematic Stamp Exhibition. Hummingbirds and Plants. Nos. 1661/9 of Antigua optd with T **120**.

1425	10c. Antillean Crested Hummingbird and Wild Plantain	2·75	2·00
1426	25c. Green Mango and Parrot's Plantain	3·00	1·50
1427	45c. Purple-throated Carib and Lobster Claws	3·50	1·25
1428	60c. Antillean Mango and Coral Plant	3·50	1·50
1429	$1 Vervain Hummingbird and Cardinal's Guard	4·50	2·25
1430	$2 Rufous-breasted Hermit and Heliconia	6·00	5·50
1431	$4 Blue-headed Hummingbird and Red Ginger	7·50	9·00
1432	$5 Green-throated Carib and Ornamental Banana	7·50	9·00
1425/32	Set of 8	35·00	29·00

MS1433 Two sheets, each 100×70 mm. (a) $6 Bee Hummingbird and Jungle Flame. (b) $6 Western Streamertail and Bignonia *Set of 2 sheets* ... 35·00 25·00

1993 (29 June). Inventors and Inventions. Nos. 1672/80 of Antigua optd with T **111**.

1434	10c. Ts'ai Lun and paper	65	1·10
1435	25c. Igor Sikorsky and *Bolshoi Baltiskii* (first four-engined airplane)	4·00	1·00
1436	30c. Alexander Graham Bell and early telephone	1·50	80
1437	40c. Johannes Gutenberg and early printing press	1·50	80
1438	60c. James Watt and stationary steam engine	11·00	2·25
1439	$1 Anton van Leeuwenhoek and early microscope	3·50	2·75
1440	$4 Louis Braille and hands reading braille	10·00	11·00
1441	$5 Galileo and telescope	10·00	11·00
1434/41	Set of 8	38·00	28·00

MS1442 Two sheets, each 100×71 mm. (a) $6 Edison and Latimer's phonograph. (b) $6 *Clermont* (first commercial paddle-steamer) *Set of 2 sheets* ... 32·00 35·00

1993 (16 Aug). Anniversaries and Events. Nos. 1700/14 of Antigua optd with T **111** (Nos. 1450/1) or as T **114**, but with lines spaced (others).

1443	10c. Russian cosmonauts	2·00	1·75
1444	40c. Airship LZ-127 *Graf Zeppelin*, 1929	3·50	1·00
1445	45c. Bishop Daniel Davis	1·00	70
1446	75c. Konrad Adenauer making speech	1·25	1·00
1447	$1 Bus Mosbacher and *Weatherly* (yacht)	2·50	1·75
1448	$1.50 Rain Forest	3·50	3·25
1449	$2 Tiger	12·00	6·00
1450	$2 National flag, plant and emblem (*horiz*)	7·00	4·00
1451	$2 Members of Community Players company (*horiz*)	4·00	4·00
1452	$2.25 Women carrying pots	4·00	4·25
1453	$3 Lions Club emblem	4·25	4·75
1454	$4 Chinese rocket on launch tower	7·00	8·00
1455	$4 West German and N.A.T.O. flags	7·00	8·00
1456	$6 Hugo Eckener (airship pioneer)	7·50	8·50
1443/56	Set of 14	60·00	50·00

MS1457 Four sheets, each 100×71 mm. (a) $6 Projected European space station. (b) $6 Airship LZ-129 *Hindenburg*, 1936. (c) $6 Brandenburg Gate on German flag. (d) $6 *Danaus plexippus* (butterfly) *Set of 4 sheets* ... 60·00 45·00

1993 (21 Sept). Flowers. Nos. 1733/40 of Antigua optd with T **114**, but with lines spaced (Nos. 1458/65) or T **111** (No. **MS**1466).

1458	15c. Cardinal's Guard	1·75	1·25
1459	25c. Giant Grandadilla	1·90	1·10
1460	30c. Spider Flower	2·00	1·25
1461	40c. Gold Vine	2·25	1·40
1462	$1 Frangipani	3·50	2·25
1463	$2 Bougainvillea	4·50	4·50
1464	$4 Yellow Oleander	6·00	7·00
1465	$5 Spicy Jatropha	6·00	7·00
1458/65	Set of 8	25·00	23·00

MS1466 Two sheets, each 100×70 mm. (a) $6 Bird Lime Tree. (b) $6 Fairy Lily *Set of 2 sheets* ... 32·00 32·00

WORLD BIRDWATCH
9-10 OCTOBER 1993
(121)

1993 (9 Oct). World Bird Watch. Nos. 1248/51 optd as T **121** (horiz opt on $2, $4).

1467	60c. Type **119**	4·00	1·75
1468	$2 Adelaide's Warbler	7·00	4·50
1469	$4 Rose-breasted Grosbeak	9·50	10·00
1470	$7 Wied's Crested Flycatcher	12·00	13·00
1467/70	Set of 4	29·00	26·00

1993 (11 Nov). Endangered Species. Nos. 1759/71 of Antigua optd with T **111**.

1471	$1 St. Lucia Amazon	5·50	4·00
	a. Sheetlet. Nos. 1471/82	60·00	42·00
1472	$1 Cahow	5·50	4·00
1473	$1 Swallow-tailed Kite	5·50	4·00
1474	$1 Everglade Kite	5·50	4·00
1475	$1 Imperial Amazon	5·50	4·00
1476	$1 Humpback Whale	5·50	4·00
1477	$1 Plain Pigeon	5·50	4·00

1478	$1 St. Vincent Amazon	5·50	4·00
1479	$1 Puerto Rican Amazon	5·50	4·00
1480	$1 Leatherback Turtle	5·50	4·00
1481	$1 American Crocodile	5·50	4·00
1482	$1 Hawksbill Turtle	5·50	4·00
1471/82	Set of 12	60·00	42·00

MS1483 Two sheets, each 100×70 mm. (a) $6 As No. 1476. (b) $6 West Indian Manatee *Set of 2 sheets* .... 50·00 35·00

1994 (6 Jan). Bicentenary of the Louvre, Paris. Paintings by Peter Paul Rubens. Nos. 1742/9 and **MS**1758 of Antigua optd with T **120**.

1484	$1 "The Destiny of Marie de Medici" (upper detail)	4·75	3·50
	a. Sheetlet. Nos. 1484/91	35·00	25·00
1485	$1 "The Birth of Marie de Medici"	4·75	3·50
1486	$1 "The Education of Marie de Medici"	4·75	3·50
1487	$1 "The Destiny of Marie de Medici" (lower detail)	4·75	3·50
1488	$1 "Henry VI receiving the Portrait of Marie"	4·75	3·50
1489	$1 "The Meeting of the King and Marie de Medici"	4·75	3·50
1490	$1 "The Marriage by Proxy"	4·75	3·50
1491	$1 "The Birth of Louis XIII"	4·75	3·50
1484/91	Set of 8	35·00	25·00

MS1492 70×100 mm. $6 "Helene Fourment with a Coach" (52×85 *mm*) .... 22·00 23·00

1994 (3 Mar). World Cup Football Championship 1994, U.S.A. (1st issue). Nos. 1816/28 of Antigua optd with T **114**, but with lines spaced (Nos. 1493/1504) or T **111** (No. **MS**1505).

1493	$2 Paul Gascoigne	3·50	2·50
1494	$2 David Platt	3·50	2·50
1495	$2 Martin Peters	3·50	2·50
1496	$2 John Barnes	3·50	2·50
1497	$2 Gary Lineker	3·50	2·50
1498	$2 Geoff Hurst	3·50	2·50
1499	$2 Bobby Charlton	3·50	2·50
1500	$2 Bryan Robson	3·50	2·50
1501	$2 Bobby Moore	3·50	2·50
1502	$2 Nobby Stiles	3·50	2·50
1503	$2 Gordon Banks	3·50	2·50
1504	$2 Peter Shilton	3·50	2·50
1493/1504	Set of 12	38·00	27·00

MS1505 Two sheets, each 135×109 mm. (a) $6 Bobby Moore holding World Cup. (b) $6 Gary Lineker and Bobby Robson *Set of 2 sheets* .... 30·00 23·00

See also Nos. 1573/9.

1994 (21 Apr). Anniversaries and Events. Nos. 1829/38, 1840 and 1842/7 of Antigua optd with T **111**.

1506	10c. Grand Inspector W. Heath	5·00	2·50
1507	15c. Rodnina and Oulanov (U.S.S.R.) (pairs figure skating) (*horiz*)	2·00	2·00
1508	30c. Present Masonic Hall, St. John's (*horiz*)	6·50	2·50
1509	30c. Willy Brandt with Helmut Schmidt and George Leber (*horiz*)	1·50	1·50
1510	30c. "Cat and Bird" (Picasso) (*horiz*)	1·50	1·50
1511	40c. Previous Masonic Hall, St. John's (*horiz*)	6·50	2·50
1512	40c. "Fish on a Newspaper" (Picasso) (*horiz*)	1·50	1·50
1513	40c. Early astronomical equipment	1·50	1·50
1514	40c. Prince Naruhito and engagement photographs (*horiz*)	1·50	1·50
1515	60c. Grand Inspector J. Jeffery	7·50	2·50
1516	$3 Masako Owada and engagement photographs (*horiz*)	3·00	4·25
1517	$4 Willy Brandt and protest march (*horiz*)	4·50	5·50
1518	$4 Galaxy	4·50	5·50
1519	$5 Alberto Tomba (Italy) (giant slalom) (*horiz*)	4·50	5·50
1520	$5 "Dying Bull" (Picasso) (*horiz*)	4·50	5·50
1521	$5 Pres. Clinton and family (*horiz*)	4·50	5·50
1506/21	Set of 16	55·00	45·00

MS1522 Six sheets. (a) 106×75 mm. $5 Copernicus. (b) 106×75 mm. $6 Womens' 1500 metre speed skating medallists (*horiz*). (c) 106×75 mm. $6 Willy Brandt at Warsaw Ghetto Memorial (*horiz*). (d) 106×75 mm. $6 "Woman with a Dog" (detail) (Picasso) (*horiz*). (e) 106×75 mm. $6 Masako Owada. (f) 106×75 mm. $6 Pres. Clinton taking the Oath (42½×57 *mm*) *Set of 6 sheets* .... 60·00 55·00

1994 (15 June). Aviation Anniversaries. Nos. 1848/55 of Antigua optd with T **111** (vertically reading down on No. 1526).

1523	30c. Hugo Eckener and Dr. W. Beckers with Airship LZ-127 *Graf Zeppelin* over Lake George, New York	3·25	1·75
1524	40c. Chicago World's Fair from *Graf Zeppelin*	3·25	1·75
1525	40c. Gloster Whittle E28/39, 1941	3·25	1·75
1526	40c. George Washington writing balloon mail letter (*vert*)	3·25	1·75
1527	$4 Pres. Wilson and Curtiss JN-4 "Jenny"	10·00	11·00
1528	$5 Airship LZ-129 *Hindenburg* over Ebbets Field baseball stadium, 1937	10·00	11·00
1529	$5 Gloster Meteor in dogfight	10·00	11·00
1523/9	Set of 7	38·00	35·00

MS1530 Three sheets. (a) 86×105 mm. $6 Hugo Eckener (*vert*). (b) 105×86 mm. $6 Consolidated Catalina PBY-5 flying boat (57×42½ *mm*). (c) 105×86 mm. $6 Alexander Hamilton, Washington and John Jay watching Blanchard's balloon, 1793 (*horiz*) *Set of 3 sheets* .... 42·00 35·00

1994 (15 June). Centenaries of Henry Ford's First Petrol Engine (Nos. 1531, 1533, **MS**1535a) and Karl Benz's First Four-wheeled Car (others). Nos. 1856/60 of Antigua optd with T **111**.

1531	30c. Lincoln Continental	2·50	1·50
1532	40c. Mercedes racing car, 1914	2·50	1·50
1533	$4 Ford "GT40", 1966	7·50	8·50
1534	$5 Mercedes Benz "gull-wing" coupe, 1954	7·50	8·50
1531/4	Set of 4	18·00	18·00

MS1535 Two sheets. (a) 114×87 mm. $6 Ford's Mustang emblem. (b) 87×114 mm. $6 Germany 1936 12pf. Benz and U.S.A. 1968 12c. Ford stamps *Set of 2 sheets* .... 24·00 21·00

1994 (18 Aug). Famous Paintings by Rembrandt and Matisse. Nos. 1881/9 of Antigua optd with T **111**.

1536	15c. "Hannah and Samuel" (Rembrandt)	2·50	2·00
1537	15c. "Guitarist" (Matisse)	2·50	2·00
1538	30c. "The Jewish Bride" (Rembrandt)	2·75	1·10
1539	40c. "Jacob wrestling with the Angel" (Rembrandt)	2·75	1·10
1540	60c. "Interior with a Goldfish Bowl" (Matisse)	3·25	1·25
1541	$1 "Mlle. Yvonne Landsberg" (Matisse)	4·00	1·75
1542	$4 "The Toboggan" (Matisse)	8·00	9·00
1543	$5 "Moses with the Tablets of the Law" (Rembrandt)	8·00	9·00
1536/43	Set of 8	30·00	24·00

MS1544 Two sheets. (a) 124×99 mm. $6 "The Blinding of Samson by the Philistines" (detail) (Rembrandt). (b) 99×124 mm. $6 "The Three Sisters" (detail) (Matisse) *Set of 2 sheets* .... 23·00 23·00

1994 (21 Sept). "Polska '93" International Stamp Exhibition Poznan. Nos. 1839, 1841 and **MS**1847f of Antigua optd with T **114**, but with lines spaced (sideways on $1, $3).

1545	$1 "Woman Combing her Hair" (W. Slewinski) (*horiz*)	5·00	2·50
1546	$3 "Artist's Wife with Cat" (Konrad Kryzanowski) (*horiz*)	9·00	10·00

MS1547 70×100 mm. $6 "General Confusion" (S. I. Witkiewicz) .... 10·00 12·00

1994 (21 Sept). Orchids. Nos. 1948/56 of Antigua optd with T **114**, but with lines spaced (Nos. 1548/55) or T **111** (No. **MS**1556).

1548	10c. *Spiranthes lanceolata*	3·50	2·25
1549	20c. *Ionopsis utriculariodes*	4·50	2·25
1550	30c. *Tetramicra canaliculata*	5·00	1·50
1551	50c. *Oncidium picturatum*	5·50	1·50
1552	$1 *Epidendrum difforme*	6·50	2·50
1553	$2 *Epidendrum ciliare*	8·00	6·50
1554	$4 *Epidendrum ibaguense*	9·00	10·00
1555	$5 *Epidendrum nocturnum*	9·00	10·00
1548/55	Set of 8	45·00	32·00

MS1556 Two sheets, each 100×73 mm. (a) $6 *Rodriguezia lanceolata*. (b) $6 *Encyclia cochleata* Set of 2 sheets .... 35·00 27·00

1994 (3 Nov). Centenary of Sierra Club (environmental protection society) (1992). Endangered Species. Nos. 1907/22 of Antigua optd with T **114**, but lines spaced (Nos. 1557/71) or T **111** (No. **MS**1572).

1557	$1.50 Sumatran Rhinoceros lying down	3·00	2·50
	a. Sheetlet. Nos. 1557/64	20·00	17·00
1558	$1.50 Sumatran Rhinoceros feeding	3·00	2·50
1559	$1.50 Ring-tailed Lemur on ground	3·00	2·50
1560	$1.50 Ring-tailed Lemur on branch	3·00	2·50
1561	$1.50 Red-fronted Brown Lemur on branch	3·00	2·50
1562	$1.50 Head of Red-fronted Brown Lemur	3·00	2·50
1563	$1.50 Head of Red-fronted Brown Lemur in front of trunk	3·00	2·50
1564	$1.50 Sierra Club Centennial emblem	1·75	1·60
	a. Sheetlet. Nos. 1564/71	20·00	17·00
1565	$1.50 Head of Bactrian Camel	3·00	2·50
1566	$1.50 Bactrian Camel	3·00	2·50
1567	$1.50 African Elephant drinking	3·00	2·50
1568	$1.50 Head of African Elephant	3·00	2·50
1569	$1.50 Leopard sitting upright	3·00	2·50
1570	$1.50 Leopard in grass (emblem at right)	3·00	2·50
1571	$1.50 Leopard in grass (emblem at left)	3·00	2·50
1557/71	Set of 15	40·00	32·00

ANTIGUA AND BARBUDA / Barbuda

MS1572 Four sheets. (a) 100×70 mm. $1.50, Sumatran Rhinoceros (*horiz*). (b) 70×100 mm. $1.50, Ring-tailed Lemur (*horiz*). (c) 70×100 mm. $1.50, Bactrian Camel (*horiz*). (d) 100×70 mm. $1.50, African Elephant (*horiz*) *Set of 4 sheets* 22·00 20·00

1995 (12 Jan). World Cup Football Championship, U.S.A. (2nd issue). Nos. 2039/45 of Antigua optd with T **116** diagonally in silver.

1573 15c. Hugo Sanchez (Mexico) 2·25 1·25
1574 35c. Jürgen Klinsmann (Germany) 2·75 1·25
1575 65c. Antiguan player 3·00 1·25
1576 $1.20 Cobi Jones (U.S.A.) 4·00 2·75
1577 $4 Roberto Baggio (Italy) 8·00 8·50
1578 $5 Bwalya Kalusha (Zambia) 8·00 8·50
1573/8 *Set of 6* 25·00 21·00
MS1579 Two sheets. (a) 72×105 mm. $6 Maldive Islands player (*vert*). (b) 107×78 mm. $6 World Cup trophy (*vert*) *Set of 2 sheets* 22·00 17·00

1995 (12 Jan). Christmas. Religious Paintings. Nos. 2058/66 of Antigua optd with T **111**.

1580 15c. "Virgin and Child by the Fireside" (Robert Campin) 1·75 1·00
1581 35c. "The Reading Madonna" (Giorgione) 2·25 70
1582 40c. "Madonna and Child" (Giovanni Bellini) 2·25 70
1583 45c. "The Litta Madonna" (Da Vinci) 2·25 70
1584 65c. "The Virgin and Child under the Apple Tree" (Lucas Cranach the Elder) 2·75 1·00
1585 75c. "Madonna and Child" (Master of the Female Half-lengths) 2·75 1·25
1586 $1.20 "An Allegory of the Church" (Alessandro Allori) 4·25 4·00
1587 $5 "Madonna and Child wreathed with Flowers" (Jacob Jordaens) 8·50 13·00
1580/7 *Set of 8* 24·00 20·00
MS1588 Two sheets. (a) 123×88 mm. $6 "Madonna and Child with Commissioners" (detail) (Palma Vecchio). (b) 88×123 mm. $6 "The Virgin Enthroned with Child" (detail) (Bohemian master) *Set of 2 sheets* 20·00 18·00

1995 (24 Feb). "Hong Kong '94" International Stamp Exhibition (1st issue). Nos. 1890/1 of Antigua optd with T **111**.

1589 40c. Hong Kong 1981 $1 Golden Threadfin Bream stamp and sampans, Shau Kei Wan 4·00 2·50
a. Horiz pair. Nos. 1589/90 8·00 5·00
1590 40c. Antigua 1990 $2 Rock Beauty stamp and sampans, Shau Kei Wan 4·00 2·50

1995 (24 Feb). "Hong Kong '94" International Stamp Exhibition (2nd issue). Nos. 1892/7 of Antigua. optd with T **111**.

1591 40c. Terracotta warriors 1·25 1·00
a. Sheetlet. Nos. 1591/6 6·50 5·50
1592 40c. Cavalryman and horse 1·25 1·00
1593 40c. Warriors in armour 1·25 1·00
1594 40c. Painted bronze chariot and team 1·25 1·00
1595 40c. Pekingese dog 1·25 1·00
1596 40c. Warriors with horses 1·25 1·00
1591/6 *Set of 6* 6·50 5·50

1995 (24 Feb). Centenary of International Olympic Committee. Nos. 1990/2 of Antigua optd with T **114** but with lines spaced.

1597 50c. Edwin Moses (U.S.A.) (400 metres hurdles), 1984 1·00 75
1598 $1.50 Steffi Graf (Germany) (tennis), 1988 8·50 4·25
MS1599 79×110 mm. $6 Johann Olav Koss (Norway) (500, 1500 and 10,000 metre speed skating), 1994 10·00 11·00

1995 (4 Apr). Dogs of the World. Chinese New Year ("Year of the Dog"). Nos. 1923/47 of Antigua optd with T **111**.

1600 50c. West Highland White Terrier 1·60 1·10
a. Sheetlet. Nos. 1600/11 18·00 12·00
1601 50c. Beagle 1·60 1·10
1602 50c. Scottish Terrier 1·60 1·10
1603 50c. Pekingese 1·60 1·10
1604 50c. Dachshund 1·60 1·10
1605 50c. Yorkshire Terrier 1·60 1·10
1606 50c. Pomeranian 1·60 1·10
1607 50c. Poodle 1·60 1·10
1608 50c. Shetland Sheepdog 1·60 1·10
1609 50c. Pug 1·60 1·10
1610 50c. Shih Tzu 1·60 1·10
1611 50c. Chihuahua 1·60 1·10
1612 50c. Mastiff 1·60 1·10
a. Sheetlet. Nos. 1612/23 18·00 12·00
1613 50c. Border Collie 1·60 1·10
1614 50c. Samoyed 1·60 1·10
1615 50c. Airedale Terrier 1·60 1·10
1616 50c. English Setter 1·60 1·10
1617 50c. Rough Collie 1·60 1·10
1618 50c. Newfoundland 1·60 1·10
1619 50c. Weimarana 1·60 1·10
1620 50c. English Springer Spaniel 1·60 1·10
1621 50c. Dalmatian 1·60 1·10
1622 50c. Boxer 1·60 1·10
1623 50c. Old English Sheepdog 1·60 1·10
1600/23 *Set of 24* 35·00 24·00
MS1624 Two sheets, each 93×58 mm. (a) $6 Welsh Corgi. (b) $6 Labrador Retriever *Set of 2 sheets* 35·00 23·00

1995 (18 May). Centenary of First English Cricket Tour to the West Indies (1995). Nos. 1994/7 of Antigua optd with T **114**, but with lines spaced.

1625 35c. Mike Atherton (England) and Wisden Trophy 4·00 1·50
1626 75c. Viv Richards (West Indies) (*vert*) 6·00 2·75
1627 $1.20 Richie Richardson (West Indies) and Wisden Trophy 8·00 4·75
1625/7 *Set of 3* 16·00 8·00
MS1628 80×100 mm. $3 English team, 1895 (black and grey-brown) 13·00 11·00

1995 (18 May–12 July). "Philakorea' 94" International Stamp Exhibition (1st issue). Nos. 1998/2009 of Antigua optd with T **114**, but with lines spaced (Nos. 1629 and 1638/40) or T **111** (others).

1629 40c. Entrance bridge, Songgwangsa Temple (12 July) 1·00 80
1630 75c. Long-necked Bottle 1·25 1·50
a. Sheetlet. Nos. 1630/7 9·00 11·00
1631 75c. Punch'ong ware jar with floral decoration 1·25 1·50
1632 75c. Punch'ong ware jar with blue dragon pattern 1·25 1·50
1633 75c. Ewer in shape of bamboo shoot 1·25 1·50
1634 75c. Punch'ong ware green jar 1·25 1·50
1635 75c. Pear-shaped bottle 1·25 1·50
1636 75c. Porcelain jar with brown dragon pattern 1·25 1·50
1637 75c. Porcelain jar with floral pattern 1·25 1·50
1638 90c. Song-op Folk Village, Cheju (12 July) 1·25 1·25
1639 $3 Port Sogwipo (12 July) 3·00 3·75
1629/39 *Set of 11* 12·50 15·00
MS1640 104×71 mm. $4 Ox herder playing flute (*vert*) 4·75 6·50

1995 (18 May). First Recipients of Order of the Caribbean Community. Nos. 2046/8 of Antigua optd with T **111**.

1641 65c. Sir Shridath Ramphal 60 75
1642 90c. William Demas 90 1·00
1643 $1.20 Derek Walcott 4·50 4·25
1641/3 *Set of 3* 5·50 5·50

1995 (12 July–29 Sept). 25th Anniv of First Moon Landing Nos. 1977/89 of Antigua optd with T **114**, but with lines spaced (vertically reading upward on Nos. 1644/55).

1644 $1.50 Edwin Aldrin (astronaut) 4·25 2·75
a. Sheetlet. Nos. 1644/49 23·00 15·00
1645 $1.50 First lunar footprint 4·25 2·75
1646 $1.50 Neil Armstrong (astronaut) 4·25 2·75
1647 $1.50 Aldrin stepping onto Moon 4·25 2·75
1648 $1.50 Aldrin and equipment 4·25 2·75
1649 $1.50 Aldrin and U.S.A. flag 4·25 2·75
1650 $1.50 Aldrin at Tranquility Base 4·25 2·75
a. Sheetlet. Nos. 1650/55 23·00 15·00
1651 $1.50 Moon plaque 4·25 2·75
1652 $1.50 *Eagle* leaving Moon 4·25 2·75
1653 $1.50 Command module in lunar orbit 4·25 2·75
1654 $1.50 First day cover of U.S.A. 1969 10c. First Man on Moon stamp 4·25 2·75
1655 $1.50 Pres. Nixon and astronauts 4·25 2·75
1644/55 *Set of 12* 45·00 30·00
MS1656 72×162 mm. $6 Armstrong and Aldrin with postal official (29 Sept) 23·00 16·00

1995 (12 July). International Year of the Family. No. 1993 of Antigua optd with T **114**, but with lines spaced.

1657 90c. Antiguan family 1·75 1·50

1995 (29 Sept). 50th Anniv of D-Day. Nos. 2010/13 of Antigua optd as T **113**, but with lines spaced.

1658 40c. Short S.25 Sunderland flying boat 4·50 1·25
1659 $2 Lockheed P-38 Lightning fighters attacking train 13·00 6·50
1660 $3 Martin B-26 Marauder bombers 13·00 8·00
1658/60 *Set of 3* 27·00 14·00
MS1661 108×78 mm. $6 Hawker Typhoon fighter bomber 21·00 19·00

For a full range of Stanley Gibbons catalogues, please visit **www.stanleygibbons.com**

122 Queen Elizabeth the Queen Mother (95th birthday)

(Des G. Vasarhelyi. Litho B.D.T.)

1995 (13–27 Nov). Anniversaries. T **122** and similar multicoloured designs. P 13.
1662	$7.50 Type **122** (20 Nov)	12·00	13·00
1663	$8 German bombers over St. Paul's Cathedral, London (*horiz*) (50th anniv of end of Second World War)	27·00	18·00
1664	$8 New York skyline with U.N. and national flags (*horiz*) (50th anniv of United Nations) (27 Nov)	16·00	18·00
1662/4 *Set of 3*		50·00	45·00

HURRICANE RELIEF + $1
(**123**)

BARBUDA MAIL
(**124**)

1995 (13 Nov). Hurricane Relief. Nos. 1662/4 surch with T **123** in silver.
1665	$7.50+$1 Type **122** (90th birthday) (20 Nov)	8·00	11·00
1666	$8+$1 German bombers over St. Paul's Cathedral, London (*horiz*) (50th anniv of end of Second World War)	20·00	16·00
1667	$8+$1 New York skyline with U.N. and national flags (*horiz*) (50th anniv of United Nations) (27 Nov)	8·00	11·00
1665/7 *Set of 3*		32·00	35·00

1996 (22 Jan). Marine Life. Nos. 1967/76 of Antigua optd as T **114**, but with lines spaced.
1668	50c. Bottlenose Dolphin	1·50	1·50
	a. Sheetlet. Nos. 1668/76	12·00	12·00
1669	50c. Killer Whale	1·50	1·50
1670	50c. Spinner Dolphin	1·50	1·50
1671	50c. Oceanic Sunfish	1·50	1·50
1672	50c. Caribbean Reef Shark and Short Fin Pilot Whale	1·50	1·50
1673	50c. Copper-banded Butterflyfish	1·50	1·50
1674	50c. Mosaic Moray	1·50	1·50
1675	50c. Clown Triggerfish	1·50	1·50
1676	50c. Red Lobster	1·50	1·50
1668/76 *Set of 9*		12·00	12·00
MS1677	Two sheets, each 106×76 mm. (a) $6 Seahorse. (b) $6 Swordfish ("Blue Marlin") (*horiz*) *Set of 2 sheets*	21·00	21·00

1996 (22 Jan). Christmas. Religious Paintings. Nos. 2267/73 of Antigua optd with T **111**.
1678	15c. "Rest on the Flight into Egypt" (Paolo Veronese)	65	60
1679	35c. "Madonna and Child" (Van Dyck)	75	50
1680	65c. "Sacred Conversation Piece" (Veronese)	1·00	70
1681	75c. "Vision of St. Anthony" (Van Dyck)	1·25	80
1682	90c. "Virgin and Child" (Van Eyck)	1·40	90
1683	$6 "The Immaculate Conception" (Giovanni Tiepolo)	4·75	9·00
1678/83 *Set of 5*		9·00	11·00
MS1684	Two sheets. (a) 101×127 mm. $5 "Christ appearing to his Mother" (detail) (Van der Weyden). (b) 127×101 mm. $6 "The Infant Jesus and the Young St. John" (Murillo) *Set of 2 sheets*	18·00	20·00

1996 (14 Feb). Stars of Country and Western Music. Nos. 2014/38 of Antigua optd with T **114**, but with lines spaced.
1685	75c. Travis Tritt	80	80
	a. Sheetlet. Nos. 1685/92	5·50	5·50
1686	75c. Dwight Yoakam	80	80
1687	75c. Billy Ray Cyrus	80	80
1688	75c. Alan Jackson	80	80
1689	75c. Garth Brooks	80	80
1690	75c. Vince Gill	80	80
1691	75c. Clint Black	80	80
1692	75c. Eddie Rabbit	80	80
1693	75c. Patsy Cline	80	80
	a. Sheetlet. Nos. 1693/1700	5·50	5·50
1694	75c. Tanya Tucker	80	80
1695	75c. Dolly Parton	80	80
1696	75c. Anne Murray	80	80
1697	75c. Tammy Wynette	80	80
1698	75c. Loretta Lynn	80	80
1699	75c. Reba McEntire	80	80
1700	75c. Skeeter Davis	80	80
1701	75c. Hank Snow	80	80
	a. Sheetlet. Nos. 1701/8	5·50	5·50
1702	75c. Gene Autry	80	80
1703	75c. Jimmie Rodgers	80	80
1704	75c. Ernest Tubb	80	80
1705	75c. Eddy Arnold	80	80
1706	75c. Willie Nelson	80	80
1707	75c. Johnny Cash	80	80
1708	75c. George Jones	80	80
1685/1708 *Set of 24*		16·00	16·00
MS1709	Three sheets. (a) 100×70 mm. $6 Hank Williams Jr. (b) 100×70 mm. $6 Hank Williams Snr. (c) 70×100 mm. $6 Kitty Wells (*horiz*) *Set of 3 sheets*	17·00	17·00

1996 (14 Feb). Birds. Nos. 2067/81 of Antigua optd with T **124**.
1710	15c. Magnificent Frigate Bird	1·50	1·25
1711	25c. Blue-hooded Euphonia	1·60	1·25
1712	35c. Eastern Meadowlark	1·75	1·00
1713	40c. Red-billed Tropic Bird	1·75	1·00
1714	45c. Greater Flamingo	1·75	1·00
1715	60c. Yellow-faced Grassquit	2·00	1·50
1716	65c. Yellow-billed Cuckoo	2·00	1·50
1717	70c. Purple-throated Carib	2·00	2·00
1718	75c. Bananaquit	2·00	1·25
1719	90c. Painted Bunting	2·25	1·25
1720	$1.20 Red-legged Honeycreeper	2·50	2·25
1721	$2 Northern Jacana	3·50	3·50
1722	$5 Greater Antillean Bullfinch	5·50	7·50
1723	$10 Caribbean Elaenia	8·50	13·00
1724	$20 Brown Trembler	13·00	19·00
1710/24 *Set of 15*		45·00	50·00

1996 (2 Apr). Birds. Nos. 2050, 2052, 2054 and 2056/7 of Antigua optd with T **111**.
1725	15c. Bridled Quail Dove	2·00	1·50
1726	40c. Purple-throated Carib (*vert*)	2·50	1·00
1727	$1 Broad-winged Hawk (*vert*)	3·75	2·50
1728	$4 Yellow Warbler	6·00	8·00
1725/8 *Set of 4*		13·00	11·50
MS1729	Two sheets. (a) 70×100 mm. $6 Female Magnificent Frigate Bird (*vert*). (b) 100×70 mm. $6 Black-billed Whistling Duck ducklings *Set of 2 sheets*	17·00	18·00

1996 (13 June). Prehistoric Animals. Nos. 2082/100 of Antigua optd with T **114**, but with lines spaced (Nos. 1730/2 and 1745/7) or T **111** (others).
1730	15c. Head of Pachycephalosaurus	2·00	2·00
1731	20c. Head of Afrovenator	2·00	2·00
1732	65c. Centrosaurus	2·00	2·00
1733	75c. Kronosaurus (*horiz*)	2·00	2·00
	a. Sheetlet. Nos. 1733/44	22·00	22·00
1734	75c. Ichthyosaurus (*horiz*)	2·00	2·00
1735	75c. Plesiosaurus (*horiz*)	2·00	2·00
1736	75c. Archelon (*horiz*)	2·00	2·00
1737	75c. Pair of Tyrannosaurus (*horiz*)	2·00	2·00
1738	75c. Tyrannosaurus (*horiz*)	2·00	2·00
1739	75c. Parasaurolophus (*horiz*)	2·00	2·00
1740	75c. Pair of Parasaurolophus (*horiz*)	2·00	2·00
1741	75c. Oviraptor (*horiz*)	2·00	2·00
1742	75c. Protoceratops with eggs (*horiz*)	2·00	2·00
1743	75c. Pteranodon and Protoceratops (*horiz*)	2·00	2·00
1744	75c. Pair of Protoceratops (*horiz*)	2·00	2·00
1745	90c. Pentaceratops drinking	2·25	1·50
1746	$1.20 Head of Tarbosaurus	2·75	2·00
1747	$5 Head of Styracosaurus	6·50	7·50
1730/47 *Set of 18*		38·00	38·00
MS1748	Two sheets, each 101×70 mm. (a) $6 Head of Corythosaurus (*horiz*) (b) $6 Head of Carnotaurus (*horiz*) *Set of 2 sheets*	20·00	23·00

1996 (16 July). Olympic Games, Atlanta. Previous Gold Medal Winners. Nos. 2101/7 of Antigua optd diagonally with T **116**.
1749	15c. Al Oerter (U.S.A.) (discus – 1956, 1960, 1964, 1968)	1·50	1·00
1750	20c. Greg Louganis (U.S.A.) (diving – 1984, 1988)	1·50	1·00
1751	65c. Naim Suleymanoglu (Turkey) (weightlifting – 1988)	2·00	1·00
1752	90c. Louise Ritter (U.S.A.) (high jump – 1988)	2·50	1·25
1753	$1.20 Nadia Comaneci (Rumania) (gymnastics – 1976)	4·00	2·75
1754	$5 Olga Boldarenko (Russia) (10,000 metres – 1988)	6·00	8·50
1749/54 *Set of 6*		16·00	14·00

ANTIGUA AND BARBUDA / Barbuda

MS1755 Two sheets, 106×76 mm. (a) $6 United States crew (eight-oared shell – 1964). (b) $6 Lutz Hessilch (Germany) (cycling – 1988) (*vert*). *Set of 2 sheets* 18·00 16·00

1996 (10 Sept). 18th World Scout Jamboree, Netherlands. Tents. Nos. 2203/9 of Antigua optd with T **116** diagonally.

1756	$1.20 The Explorer Tent	1·25	1·50
	a. Horiz strip of 3. Nos. 1756/8	3·25	4·00
1757	$1.20 Camper tent	1·25	1·50
1758	$1.20 Wall tent	1·25	1·50
1759	$1.20 Trail tent	1·25	1·50
	a. Horiz strip of 3. Nos. 1759/61	3·25	4·00
1760	$1.20 Miner's tent	1·25	1·50
1761	$1.20 Voyager tent	1·25	1·50
1756/61	*Set of 6*	6·50	8·00

MS1762 Two sheets, each 76×106 mm. (a) $6 Scout and camp fire. (b) $6 Scout with back pack (*vert*) *Set of 2 sheets* 8·00 10·00

1996 (25 Oct). Centenary of Nobel Prize Trust Fund. Nos. 2226/44 of Antigua optd with T **120**.

1763	$1 Dag Hammarskjold (1961 Peace)	1·60	1·25
	a. Sheetlet. Nos. 1763/71	13·00	10·00
1764	$1 Georg Wittig (1979 Chemistry)	1·60	1·25
1765	$1 Wilhelm Ostwold (1909 Chemistry)	1·60	1·25
1766	$1 Robert Koch (1905 Medicine)	1·60	1·25
1767	$1 Karl Ziegler (1963 Chemistry)	1·60	1·25
1768	$1 Alexander Fleming (1945 Medicine)	1·60	1·25
1769	$1 Hermann Staudinger (1953 Chemistry)	1·60	1·25
1770	$1 Manfred Eigen (1967 Chemistry)	1·60	1·25
1771	$1 Arno Penzias (1978 Physics)	1·60	1·25
1772	$1 Shumal Agnon (1966 Literature)	1·60	1·25
	a. Sheetlet. Nos. 1772/80	13·00	10·00
1773	$1 Rudyard Kipling (1907 Literature)	1·60	1·25
1774	$1 Aleksandr Solzhenitsyn (1970 Literature)	1·60	1·25
1775	$1 Jack Steinburger (1988 Physics)	1·60	1·25
1776	$1 Andrei Sakharov (1975 Peace)	1·60	1·25
1777	$1 Otto Stern (1943 Physics)	1·60	1·25
1778	$1 John Steinbeck (1962 Literature)	1·60	1·25
1779	$1 Nadine Gordimer (1991 Literature)	1·60	1·25
1780	$1 William Faulkner (1949 Literature)	1·60	1·25
1763/80	*Set of 18*	26·00	20·00

MS1781 Two sheets, each 100×70 mm. (a) $6 Elie Wiesel (1986 Peace) (*vert*). (b) $6 Dalai Lama (1989 Peace) (*vert*) *Set of 2 sheets* 14·00 17·00

1996 (14 Nov). 70th Birthday of Queen Elizabeth II. Nos. 2355/8 of Antigua optd with T **111**.

1782	$2 Queen Elizabeth II in blue dress	3·25	2·75
	a. Strip of 3. Nos. 1782/4	8·75	7·50
1783	$2 With bouquet	3·25	2·75
1784	$2 In Garter robes	3·25	2·75
1782/4	*Set of 3*	8·75	7·50

MS1785 96×111 mm. $6 Wearing white dress 8·50 7·50

1997 (28 Jan). Christmas. Religious Paintings by Filippo Lippi. Nos. 2377/83 of Antigua optd with T **111**.

1786	60c. "Madonna Enthroned"	60	35
1787	90c. "Adoration of the Child and Saints"	85	55
1788	$1 "The Annunciation"	1·00	80
1789	$1.20 "Birth of the Virgin"	1·25	1·10
1790	$1.60 "Adoration of the Child"	1·60	2·00
1791	$1.75 "Madonna and Child"	1·75	2·25
1786/91	*Set of 6*	3·75	3·75

MS1792 Two sheets, each 76×106 mm. (a) $6 "Madonna and Child" (*different*). (b) $6 "The Circumcision" *Set of 2 sheets* 12·00 15·00

1997 (24 Feb). 50th Anniv of Food and Agriculture Organization. Nos. 2121/4 of Antigua optd with T **114**, but with lines spaced.

1793	75c. Woman buying produce from market	1·00	1·00
	a. Horiz strip of 3. Nos. 1793/5	3·25	3·50
1794	90c. Women shopping	1·10	1·10
1795	$1.20 Women talking	1·40	1·75
1793/5	*Set of 3*	3·25	3·50

MS1796 100×70 mm. $6 Tractor 5·50 7·00

1997 (24 Feb). 90th Anniv of Rotary International (1995). Nos. 2125/6 of Antigua optd with T **114**, but with lines spaced.

1797	$5 Beach and rotary emblem	3·25	4·25

MS1798 74×104 mm. $6 National flag and emblem 4·50 5·50

1997 (4 Apr). 50th Anniv of End of Second World War in Europe and the Pacific. Nos. 2108/16 and 2132/8 of Antigua optd with T **114** but with lines spaced (No. **MS**1813b) or with T **111** (others).

1799	$1.20 Map of Berlin showing Russian advance	1·50	1·50
	a. Sheetlet. Nos. 1799/1806	9·50	9·50
1800	$1.20 Russian tank and infantry	1·50	1·50
1801	$1.20 Street fighting in Berlin	1·50	1·50
1802	$1.20 German tank exploding	1·50	1·50
1803	$1.20 Russian air raid	1·50	1·50
1804	$1.20 German troops surrendering	1·50	1·50
1805	$1.20 Hoisting the Soviet flag on the Reichstag	1·50	1·50
1806	$1.20 Captured German standards	1·50	1·50
1807	$1.20 Gen. Chiang Kai-shek and Chinese guerrillas	1·50	1·50
	a. Sheetlet. Nos. 1807/12	9·50	9·50
1808	$1.20 Gen. Douglas MacArthur and beach landing	1·50	1·50
1809	$1.20 Gen. Claire Chennault and U.S. fighter aircraft	1·50	1·50
1810	$1.20 Brig. Orde Wingate and supply drop	1·50	1·50
1811	$1.20 Gen. Joseph Stilwell and U.S. supply plane	1·50	1·50
1812	$1.20 Field-Marshal Bill Slim and loading cow onto plane	1·50	1·50
1799/1812	*Set of 14*	19·00	19·00

MS1813 Two sheets, each 100×70 mm. (a) $3 Admiral Nimitz and aircraft carrier. (b) $6 Gen. Konev (*vert*). *Set of 2 sheets* 14·00 15·00

1997 (4 Apr). Bees. Nos. 2172/6 of Antigua optd with T **111**.

1814	90c. Mining Bees	1·00	50
1815	$1.20 Solitary Bee	1·25	80
1816	$1.65 Leaf-cutter Bee	1·60	1·75
1817	$1.75 Honey Bees	1·75	2·00
1814/17	*Set of 4*	5·00	4·50

MS1818 110×80 mm. $6 Solitary Mining Bee 5·50 6·50

1997 (4 Apr). Flowers. Nos. 2177/89 of Antigua optd with T **111** (No. **MS**1831) or T **114**, but with lines spaced (others).

1819	75c. Narcissus	75	85
	a. Sheetlet. Nos. 1819/30	8·00	9·25
1820	75c. Camellia	75	85
1821	75c. Iris	75	85
1822	75c. Tulip	75	85
1823	75c. Poppy	75	85
1824	75c. Peony	75	85
1825	75c. Magnolia	75	85
1826	75c. Oriental Lily	75	85
1827	75c. Rose	75	85
1828	75c. Pansy	75	85
1829	75c. Hydrangea	75	85
1830	75c. Azaleas	75	85
1819/30	*Set of 12*	8·00	9·25

MS1831 80×110 mm. $6 Calla Lily 6·50 8·00

1997 (4 Apr). Cats. Nos. 2190/202 of Antigua optd with T **111**.

1832	45c. Somali	70	70
	a. Sheetlet. Nos. 1832/43	7·50	7·50
1833	45c. Persian and butterflies	70	70
1834	45c. Devon Rex	70	70
1835	45c. Turkish Angora	70	70
1836	45c. Himalayan	70	70
1837	45c. Maine Coon	70	70
1838	45c. Ginger non-pedigree	70	70
1839	45c. American Wirehair	70	70
1840	45c. British Shorthair	70	70
1841	45c. American Curl	70	70
1842	45c. Black non-pedigree and butterfly	70	70
1843	45c. Birman	70	70
1832/43	*Set of 12*	7·50	7·50

MS1844 104×74 mm. $6 Siberian kitten (*vert*) 9·00 10·00

1997 (25 Apr). 95th Birthday of Queen Elizabeth the Queen Mother. Nos. 2127/31 of Antigua optd with T **111**.

1845	$1.50 orange-brown, pale brown and black	5·00	3·50
	a. Sheetlet. Nos. 1845/8×2	18·00	12·50
1846	$1.50 multicoloured	5·00	3·50
1847	$1.50 multicoloured	5·00	3·50
1848	$1.50 multicoloured	5·00	3·50
1845/8	*Set of 4*	18·00	12·50

MS1849 102×27 mm. $6 multicoloured 14·00 11·00

1997 (25 Apr). 50th Anniv of United Nations. Nos. 2117/20 optd with T **114** but with lines spaced.

1850	75c. Signatures and Earl of Halifax	80	80
	a. Horiz strip of 3. Nos. 1850/2	2·75	3·00
1851	90c. Virginia Gildersleeve	90	90
1852	$1.20 Harold Stassen	1·25	1·50
1850/53	*Set of 3*	2·75	3·00

MS1853 100×70 mm. $6 Pres. Franklin D. Roosevelt 4·50 6·00

1997 (30 May). Trains of the World. Nos. 2210/25 of Antigua optd with T **114**, but with lines spaced (No. **MS**1869) or with T **111** (others).

1854	35c. Trans-Gabon diesel-electric train	90	30
1855	65c. Canadian Pacific diesel-electric train	1·00	40
1856	75c. Santa Fe Railway diesel-electric locomotive, U.S.A.	1·00	50
1857	90c. High Speed Train, Great Britain	1·00	60
1858	$1.20 TGV express train, France	1·00	1·25
1859	$1.20 Diesel-electric locomotive, Australia	1·00	1·25
	a. Sheetlet. Nos. 1859/67	8·00	10·00

1860	$1.20 Pendolino "ETR 450" electric train, Italy		1·00	1·25
1861	$1.20 Diesel-electric locomotive, Thailand		1·00	1·25
1862	$1.20 Pennsylvania Railroad steam locomotive, U.S.A.		1·00	1·25
1863	$1.20 Beyer-Garratt steam locomotive, East African Railways		1·00	1·25
1864	$1.20 Natal Govt steam locomotive		1·00	1·25
1865	$1.20 Rail gun, American Civil War		1·00	1·25
1866	$1.20 Locomotive *Lion* (red livery), Great Britain		1·00	1·25
1867	$1.20 William Hedley's *Puffing Billy* (green livery), Great Britain		1·00	1·25
1868	$6 Amtrak high-speed diesel locomotive, U.S.A.		3·50	4·50
1854/68 *Set of 15*			16·00	17·00
MS1869 Two sheets, each 110×80 mm. (a) $6 Locomotive *Iron Rooster*, China (*vert*). (b) $6 "Indian-Pacific" diesel-electric locomotive, Australia (*vert*) *Set of 2 sheets*			13·00	16·00

Golden Wedding of H.M. Queen Elizabeth II and H.R.H. Prince Phillip 1947 - 1997
(125)

1997 (25 July). Golden Wedding of Queen Elizabeth II and Prince Philip (1st issue). Nos. 1662/3 optd with T **125** in gold.

1870	$7.50 Type **122**	7·50	8·00
1871	$8 German bombers over St. Paul's Cathedral, London (*horiz*)	9·50	10·00

1997 (16 Sept). Fungi. Nos. 2274/82 of Antigua optd with T **114** but with lines spaced.

1872	75c. *Hygrophoropsis aurantiaca*	1·50	1·50
	a. Horiz strip of 4. Nos. 1872/5	5·75	5·75
1873	75c. *Hygrophorus bakerensis*	1·50	1·50
1874	75c. *Hygrophorus conicus*	1·50	1·50
1875	75c. *Hygrophorus miniatus* (*Hygrocybe miniata*)	1·50	1·50
1876	75c. *Suillus brevipes*	1·50	1·50
	a. Horiz strip of 4. Nos. 1876/9	5·75	5·75
1877	75c. *Suillus luteus*	1·50	1·50
1878	75c. *Suillus granulatus*	1·50	1·50
1879	75c. *Suillus caerulescens*	1·50	1·50
1872/9 *Set of 8*		11·00	11·00
MS1880 Two sheets, each 106×76 mm. (a) $6 *Conocybe filaris*. (b) $6 *Hygrocybe flavescens Set of 2 sheets*		13·00	15·00

1997 (16 Sept). Birds. Nos. 2140/64 of Antigua optd with T **114** with lines spaced (Nos. 1881/904) or T **111** (No. **MS**1905).

1881	75c. Purple-throated Carib	90	90
	a. Sheetlet. Nos. 1850/61	9·75	9·75
1882	75c. Antillean Crested Hummingbird	90	90
1883	75c. Bananaquit	90	90
1884	75c. Mangrove Cuckoo	90	90
1885	75c. Troupial	90	90
1886	75c. Green-throated Carib	90	90
1887	75c. Yellow Warbler	90	90
1888	75c. Blue-hooded Euphonia	90	90
1889	75c. Scaly-breasted Thrasher	90	90
1890	75c. Burrowing Owl	90	90
1891	75c. Carib Grackle	90	90
1892	75c. Adelaide's Warbler	90	90
1893	75c. Ring-necked Duck	90	90
	a. Sheetlet. Nos. 1893/904	9·75	9·75
1894	75c. Ruddy Duck	90	90
1895	75c. Green-winged Teal	90	90
1896	75c. Wood Duck	90	90
1897	75c. Hooded Merganser	90	90
1898	75c. Lesser Scaup	90	90
1899	75c. Black-billed Whistling Duck	90	90
1900	75c. Fulvous Whistling Duck	90	90
1901	75c. Bahama Pintail	90	90
1902	75c. Shoveler	90	90
1903	75c. Masked Duck	90	90
1904	75c. American Wigeon	90	90
1881/904 *Set of 24*		19·00	19·00
MS1905 Two sheets, each 104×74 mm. (a) $6 Head of Purple Gallinule. (b) $6 Heads of Blue-winged Teals *Set of 2 sheets*		14·00	13·00

1997 (3 Nov). Sailing Ships. Nos. 2283/301 of Antigua optd with T **116** diagonally.

1906	15c. H.M.S. *Resolution* (Cook)	1·25	1·00
1907	25c. *Mayflower* (Pilgrim Fathers)	1·00	50
1908	45c. *Santa Maria* (Columbus)	1·25	60
1909	75c. *Aemilia* (Dutch galleon)	1·00	60
1910	75c. *Sovereign of the Seas* (English galleon)	1·00	60
1911	90c. H.M.S. *Victory* (Nelson)	1·25	1·00
1912	$1.20 As No. 1909	1·25	1·25
	a. Sheetlet. Nos. 1912/17	6·50	6·50
1913	$1.20 As No. 1910	1·25	1·25
1914	$1.20 *Royal Louis* (French galleon)	1·25	1·25
1915	$1.20 H.M.S. *Royal George* (ship of the line)	1·25	1·25
1916	$1.20 *Le Protecteur* (French frigate)	1·25	1·25
1917	$1.20 As No. 1911	1·25	1·25
1918	$1.50 As No. 1908	1·25	1·40
	a. Sheetlet. Nos. 1887/92	6·50	6·50
1919	$1.50 *Vitoria* (Magellan)	1·25	1·40
1920	$1.50 *Golden Hind* (Drake)	1·25	1·40
1921	$1.50 As No. 1907	1·25	1·40
1922	$1.50 *Griffin* (La Salle)	1·25	1·40
1923	$1.50 As No. 1906	1·25	1·40
1906/23 *Set of 18*		18·00	18·00
MS1924 (a) 102×72 mm. $6 U.S.S. *Constitution* (frigate). (b) 98×67 mm. $6 *Grande Hermine* (Cartier) *Set of 2 sheets*		10·00	12·00

1997 (3 Nov). Golden Wedding of Queen Elizabeth and Prince Philip (2nd issue). Nos. 2474/80 of Antigua optd with T **111**.

1925	$1 Queen Elizabeth II	2·50	2·00
	a. Sheetlet. Nos. 1925/30	13·50	
1926	$1 Royal coat of arms	2·50	2·00
1927	$1 Queen Elizabeth and Prince Philip at reception	2·50	2·00
1928	$1 Queen Elizabeth and Prince Philip in landau	2·50	2·00
1929	$1 Balmoral	2·50	2·00
1930	$1 Prince Philip	2·50	2·00
1894/9 *Set of 6*		13·50	11·00
MS1931 100×71 mm. $6 Queen Elizabeth with Prince Philip in naval uniform		14·00	13·00

1997 (24 Dec). Christmas. Religious Paintings. Nos. 2566/72 of Antigua optd with T **116** diagonally.

1932	15c. "The Angel leaving Tobias and his Family" (Rembrandt)	80	60
1933	25c. "The Resurrection" (Martin Knoller)	90	60
1934	60c. "Astronomy" (Raphael)	1·25	75
1935	75c. "Music-making Angel" (Melozzo da Forli)	1·40	1·25
1936	90c. "Amor" (Parmigianino)	1·60	1·25
1937	$1.20 "Madonna and Child with Saints" (Rosso Fiorentino)	1·75	2·00
1932/7 *Set of 6*		7·00	5·75
MS1938 Two sheets, each 105×96 mm. (a) $6 "The Wedding of Tobias" (Gianantonio and Francesco Guardi) (*horiz*). (b) $6 "The Portinari Altarpiece" (Hugo van der Goes) (*horiz*) *Set of 2 sheets*		9·00	11·00

1998 (16 Feb). Sea Birds. Nos. 2325/33 of Antigua optd with T **111**.

1939	75c. Black Skimmer	1·50	1·50
	a. Vert strip of 4. Nos. 1939/42	5·50	5·50
1940	75c. Black-capped Petrel	1·50	1·50
1941	75c. Sooty Tern	1·50	1·50
1942	75c. Royal Tern	1·50	1·50
1943	75c. Pomarine Skua ("Pomarine Jaegger")	1·50	1·50
	a. Vert strip of 4. Nos. 1943/6	5·50	5·50
1944	75c. White-tailed Tropic Bird	1·50	1·50
1945	75c. Northern Gannet	1·50	1·50
1946	75c. Laughing Gull	1·50	1·50
1939/46 *Set of 8*		11·00	11·00
MS1947 Two sheets, each 105×75 mm. (a) $5 Great Frigate Bird. (b) $6 Brown Pelican *Set of 2 sheets*		9·00	11·00

1998 (25 Mar). Centenary of Radio. Entertainers. Nos. 2372/6 of Antigua optd with T **111**.

1948	65c. Kate Smith	90	65
1949	75c. Dinah Shore	1·00	85
1950	90c. Rudy Vallee	1·25	90
1951	$1.20 Bing Crosby	1·50	2·25
1948/51 *Set of 4*		4·25	4·25
MS1952 72×104 mm. $6 Jo Stafford (28×42 mm)		5·50	7·50

1998 (25 Mar). Olympic Games, Atlanta (2nd issue). Previous Medal Winners. Nos. 2302/24 of Antigua optd with T **111** (Nos. 1954/5, 1974 and **MS**1975a) or with T **114**, but with lines spaced (others).

1953	65c. Florence Griffith Joyner (U.S.A.) (Gold – track, 1988)	85	75
1954	75c. Olympic Stadium, Seoul (1988) (*horiz*)	85	75
1955	90c. Allison Jolly and Lynne Jewell (U.S.A.) (Gold – yachting, 1988) (*horiz*)	1·00	1·00
1956	90c. Wolfgang Nordwig (Germany) (Gold – pole vaulting, 1972)	1·00	1·00
	a. Sheetlet. Nos. 1956/64	8·00	8·00
1957	90c. Shirley Strong (Great Britain) (Silver – 100 metres hurdles, 1984)	1·00	1·00
1958	90c. Sergei Bubka (Russia) (Gold – pole vault, 1988)	1·00	1·00
1959	90c. Filbert Bayi (Tanzania) (Silver – 3000 metres steeplechase, 1980)	1·00	1·00
1960	90c. Victor Saneyev (Russia) (Gold – triple jump, 1968, 1972, 1976)	1·00	1·00

1961	90c. Silke Renk (Germany) (Gold – javelin, 1992)	1·00	1·00
1962	90c. Daley Thompson (Great Britain) (Gold – decathlon, 1980,1984)	1·00	1·00
1963	90c. Robert Richards (U.S.A.) (Gold – pole vault, 1952, 1956)	1·00	1·00
1964	90c. Parry O'Brien (U.S.A) (Gold – shot put, 1952, 1956)	1·00	1·00
1965	90c. Ingrid Kramer (Germany) (Gold – Women's platform diving, 1960)	1·00	1·00
	a. Sheetlet. Nos. 1965/73	8·00	8·00
1966	90c. Kelly McCormick (U.S.A.) (Silver – Women's springboard diving, 1984)	1·00	1·00
1967	90c. Gary Tobian (U.S.A.) (Gold – Men's springboard diving, 1960)	1·00	1·00
1968	90c. Greg Louganis (U.S.A.) (Gold – Men's diving, 1984 and 1988)	1·00	1·00
1969	90c. Michelle Mitchell (U.S.A.) (Silver – Women's platform diving, 1984 and 1988)	1·00	1·00
1970	90c. Zhou Jihong (China) (Gold – Women's platform diving, 1984)	1·00	1·00
1971	90c. Wendy Wyland (U.S.A.) (Bronze – Women's platform diving, 1984)	1·00	1·00
1972	90c. Xu Yanmei (China) (Gold – Women's platform diving, 1988)	1·00	1·00
1973	90c. Fu Mingxia (China) (Gold – Women's platform diving, 1992)	1·00	1·00
1974	$1.20 2000 metre tandem cycle race (*horiz*)	3·25	3·00
1953/74	Set of 21	21·00	21·00

MS1975 Two sheets each 106×76 mm. (a) $5 Bill Toomey (U.S.A.) (Gold – decathlon, 1968) (*horiz*). (b) $6 Mark Lenzi (U.S.A.) (Gold – Men's springboard diving, 1992) *Set of 2 sheets* ...... 9·00 11·00

1998 (12 May). World Cup Football Championship, France. Nos. 2525/39 of Antigua optd with T **114**.

1976	60c. multicoloured	75	60
1977	75c. multicoloured	75	60
1978	90c. multicoloured	80	65
1979	$1 agate	80	80
	a. Sheetlet. Nos. 1979/86 and central label	5·50	5·50
1980	$1 agate	80	80
1981	$1 agate	80	80
1982	$1 grey-black	80	80
1983	$1 agate	80	80
1984	$1 agate	80	80
1985	$1 agate	80	80
1986	$1 agate	80	80
1987	$1.20 multicoloured	1·00	1·10
1988	$1.65 multicoloured	1·25	1·40
1989	$1.75 multicoloured	1·40	1·60
1976/89	Set of 14	11·00	11·00

MS1990 Two sheets, each 102×127 mm. (a) $6 multicoloured. (b) $6 multicoloured *Set of 2 sheets* . 9·00 11·00

1998 (4 June). Cavalry through the Ages. Nos. 2359/63 of Antigua optd with T **111** (Nos. 1991/4) or T **114** (No. **MS**1995).

1991	60c. Ancient Egyptian cavalryman	1·50	1·25
	a. Block of 4. Nos. 1991/4	5·50	4·50
1992	60c. 13th-century English knight	1·50	1·25
1993	60c. 16th-century Spanish lancer	1·50	1·25
1994	60c. 18th-century Chinese cavalryman	1·50	1·25
1991/4	Set of 4	5·50	4·50

MS1995 100×70 mm. $6 19th-century French cuirassier (*vert*) .... 6·50 8·00

1998 (20 July). 50th Anniv of U.N.I.C.E.F. Nos. 2364/7 of Antigua optd with T **114**.

1996	75c. Girl in red sari	90	90
1997	90c. South American mother and child	1·10	1·10
1998	$1.20 Nurse with child	1·40	2·00
1996/8	Set of 3	3·00	3·50

MS1999 114×74 mm. $6 Chinese child .... 4·75 6·50

1998 (20 July). 3000th Anniv of Jerusalem. Nos. 2368/71 of Antigua optd with T **111**.

2000	75c. Tomb of Zachariah and *Verbascum sinuatum*	2·00	1·10
2001	90c. Pool of Siloam and *Hyacinthus orientalis*	2·25	1·10
2002	$1.20 Hurva Synagogue and *Ranunculus asiaticus*	2·50	2·75
2000/2	Set of 3	6·00	4·50

MS2003 66×80 mm. $6 Model of Herod's Temple and *Cercis siliquastrum* .... 7·00 7·00

1998 (31 Aug). Diana, Princess of Wales Commemoration. Nos. 2573/85 of Antigua optd with T **114**, but with lines spaced.

2004	$1.65 Diana, Princess of Wales	1·25	1·10
	a. Sheetlet. Nos. 2004/9	6·75	6·00
2005	$1.65 Wearing hoop earrings (rose-carmine and black)	1·25	1·10
2006	$1.65 Carrying bouquet	1·25	1·10
2007	$1.65 Wearing floral hat	1·25	1·10
2008	$1.65 With Prince Harry	1·25	1·10
2009	$1.65 Wearing white jacket	1·25	1·10
2010	$1.65 In kitchen	1·25	1·10
	a. Sheetlet. Nos. 2010/15	6·75	6·00
2011	$1.65 Wearing black and white dress	1·25	1·10
2012	$1.65 Wearing hat (orge-brown & black)	1·25	1·10
2013	$1.65 Wearing floral print dress (lake-brown and black)	1·25	1·10
2014	$1.65 Dancing with John Travolta	1·25	1·10
2015	$1.65 Wearing white hat and jacket	1·25	1·10
2004/15	Set of 12	13·50	12·00

MS2016 Two sheets, each 70×100 mm. (a) $6 Wearing red jumper. (b) $6 Wearing black dress for Papal audience (lake-brown and black) *Set of 2 sheets* .... 9·00 11·00

1998 (12 Oct). Broadway Musical Stars. Nos. 2384/93 of Antigua optd with T **111**.

2017	$1 Robert Preston (*The Music Man*)	1·50	1·50
	a. Sheetlet. Nos. 2017/25	12·00	12·00
2018	$1 Michael Crawford (*Phantom of the Opera*)	1·50	1·50
2019	$1 Zero Mostel (*Fiddler on the Roof*)	1·50	1·50
2020	$1 Patti Lupone (*Evita*)	1·50	1·50
2021	$1 Raul Julia (*Threepenny Opera*)	1·50	1·50
2022	$1 Mary Martin (*South Pacific*)	1·50	1·50
2023	$1 Carol Channing (*Hello Dolly*)	1·50	1·50
2024	$1 Yul Brynner (*The King and I*)	1·50	1·50
2025	$1 Julie Andrews (*My Fair Lady*)	1·50	1·50
2017/25	Set of 9	12·00	12·00

MS2026 106×76 mm. $6 Mickey Rooney (*Sugar Babies*).. 7·00 8·50

1998 (12 Oct). 20th Death Anniv of Charlie Chaplin (film star). Nos. 2404/13 of Antigua optd with T **111**.

2027	$1 Charlie Chaplin as young man	1·50	1·50
	a. Sheetlet. Nos. 2027/35	12·00	12·00
2028	$1 Pulling face	1·50	1·50
2029	$1 Looking over shoulder	1·50	1·50
2030	$1 In cap	1·50	1·50
2031	$1 In front of star	1·50	1·50
2032	$1 In *The Great Dictator*	1·50	1·50
2033	$1 With movie camera and megaphone	1·50	1·50
2034	$1 Standing in front of camera lens	1·50	1·50
2035	$1 Putting on make-up	1·50	1·50
2027/35	Set of 9	12·00	12·00

MS2036 76×106 mm. $6 Charlie Chaplin .... 9·00 10·00

1998 (23 Nov). Butterflies. Nos. 2414/36 of Antigua. optd with T **114**, but with lines spaced.

2037	90c. *Charaxes porthos*	1·00	70
2038	$1.10 *Charaxes protoclea protocleon*	1·00	1·00
	a. Sheetlet. Nos. 2038/46	8·00	8·00
2039	$1.10 *Byblia ilithyia*	1·00	1·00
2040	$1.10 Black-headed Bush Shrike ("Tchagra") (bird)	1·00	1·00
2041	$1.10 *Charaxes nobilis*	1·00	1·00
2042	$1.10 *Pseudacraea boisduvali trimeni*	1·00	1·00
2043	$1.10 *Charaxes smaragdalis*	1·00	1·00
2044	$1.10 *Charaxes lasti*	1·00	1·00
2045	$1.10 *Pseudacraea poggei*	1·00	1·00
2046	$1.10 *Graphium colonna*	1·00	1·00
2047	$1.10 Carmine Bee Eater (bird)	1·00	1·00
	a. Sheetlet. Nos. 2047/55	8·00	8·00
2048	$1.10 *Pseudacraea eurytus*	1·00	1·00
2049	$1.10 *Hypolimnas monteironis*	1·00	1·00
2050	$1.10 *Charaxes anticlea*	1·00	1·00
2051	$1.10 *Graphium leonidas*	1·00	1·00
2052	$1.10 *Graphium illyris*	1·00	1·00
2053	$1.10 *Nephronia argia*	1·00	1·00
2054	$1.10 *Graphium policenes*	1·00	1·00
2055	$1.10 *Papilio dardanus*	1·00	1·00
2056	$1.20 *Aethiopana honorius*	1·00	1·10
2057	$1.60 *Charaxes hadrianus*	1·25	1·40
2058	$1.75 *Precis westermanni*	1·40	1·60
2037/58	Set of 21	20·00	20·00

MS2059 Three sheets, each 106×76 mm. (a) $6 *Charaxes lactitinctus* (*horiz*). (b) $6 *Eupheadra neophron*. (c) $6 *Euxanthe tiberius* (*horiz*) *Set of 3 sheets* .... 19·00 22·00

BARBUDA MAIL
(126)

BARBOUDA MAIL
(127)

1998 (23 Dec). Christmas. Dogs. Nos. 2771/8 of Antigua optd with T **126** diagonally.

2060	15c. Border Collie	65	60
2061	25c. Dalmatian	75	60

ANTIGUA AND BARBUDA / Barbuda

2062	65c. Weimaraner	1·40	80
2063	75c. Scottish Terrier	1·40	85
2064	90c. Long-haired Dachshund	1·50	85
2065	$1.20 Golden Retriever	1·75	1·75
2066	$2 Pekingese	2·25	2·75
2060/6 Set of 7		8·75	7·50
MS2067 Two sheets, each 75×66 mm. (a) $6 Dalmatian. (b) $6 Jack Russell Terrier Set of 2 sheets		13·00	12·00

1999 (25 Jan). Lighthouses of the World. Nos. 2612/20 of Antigua optd with T **111**.

2068	45c. Europa Point Lighthouse, Gibraltar	1·50	65
2069	65c. Tierra del Fuego, Argentina (*horiz*)	1·75	75
2070	75c. Point Loma, California, U.S.A. (*horiz*)	1·75	90
2071	90c. Groenpoint, Cape Town, South Africa	1·75	90
2072	$1 Youghal, Cork, Ireland	1·75	1·25
2073	$1.20 Launceston, Tasmania, Australia	1·90	1·50
2074	$1.65 Point Abino, Ontario, Canada (*horiz*)	2·25	2·75
2075	$1.75 Great Inagua, Bahamas (*horiz*)	2·25	2·75
2068/75 Set of 8		13·50	10·50
MS2076 99×70 mm. $6 Cape Hatteras, North Carolina, USA		11·00	11·00

1999 (1 Mar). Endangered Species. Nos. 2457/69 of Antigua optd with T **111**.

2077	$1.20 Red Bishop	2·00	2·00
	a. Sheetlet. Nos. 2077/82	11·00	11·00
2078	$1.20 Yellow Baboon	2·00	2·00
2079	$1.20 Superb Starling	2·00	2·00
2080	$1.20 Ratel	2·00	2·00
2081	$1.20 Hunting Dog	2·00	2·00
2082	$1.20 Serval	2·00	2·00
2083	$1.65 Okapi	2·25	2·25
	a. Sheetlet. Nos. 2083/8	12·00	12·00
2084	$1.65 Giant Forest Squirrel	2·25	2·25
2085	$1.65 Lesser Masked Weaver	2·25	2·25
2086	$1.65 Smalls spotted Genet	2·25	2·25
2087	$1.65 Yellow-billed Stork	2·25	2·25
2088	$1.65 Red-headed Agama	2·25	2·25
2077/88 Set of 12		23·00	23·00
MS2089 Three sheets, each 106×76 mm. (a) $6 South African Crowned Crane. (b) $6 Bat-eared Fox. (c) $6 Malachite Kingfisher Set of 3 sheets		19·00	22·00

1999 (4 May). "Pacific 97" International Stamp Exhibition, San Francisco. Death Centenary of Heinrich von Stephan (founder of the U.P.U.). Nos. 2481/4 of Antigua optd with T **114**.

2090	$1.75 dull blue	2·50	2·50
	a. Sheetlet. Nos. 2090/2	6·75	6·75
2091	$1.75 chestnut	2·50	2·50
2092	$1.75 deep magenta	2·50	2·50
2090/2 Set of 3		6·75	6·75
MS2093 82×119 mm. $6 violet		4·75	6·00

1999 (4 May). 175th Anniv of Brothers Grimm's Third Collection of Fairy Tales. Cinderella. Nos. 2485/8 of Antigua optd with T **111**.

2094	$1.75 The Ugly Sisters and their Mother	2·75	2·75
	a. Sheetlet. Nos. 2094/6	7·50	7·50
2095	$1.75 Cinderella and her Fairy Godmother	2·75	2·75
2096	$1.75 Cinderella and the Prince	2·75	2·75
2094/6 Set of 3		7·50	7·50
MS2097 124×96 mm. $6 Cinderella trying on slipper		6·00	7·50

1999 (24 June). Orchids of the World. Nos. 2502/24 of Antigua optd with T **111**, but vert reading upwards.

2098	45c. *Odontoglossum cervantesii*	1·50	45
2099	65c. *Phalaenopsis* Medford Star	1·75	35
2100	75c. *Vanda* Motes Resplendent	1·75	85
2101	90c. *Odontonia* Debutante	2·00	1·00
2102	$1 *Iwanagaara* Apple Blossom	2·25	1·10
2103	$1.65 *Cattleya* Sophia Martin	2·25	2·00
	a. Sheetlet. Nos. 2103/10	16·00	14·00
2104	$1.65 Dogface Butterfly	2·25	2·00
2105	$1.65 *Laeliocattleya* Mini Purple	2·25	2·00
2106	$1.65 *Cymbidium* Showgirl	2·25	2·00
2107	$1.65 *Brassolaeliocattleya* Dorothy Bertsch	2·25	2·00
2108	$1.65 *Disa blackii*	2·25	2·00
2109	$1.65 *Paphiopedilum leeanum*	2·25	2·00
2110	$1.65 *Paphiopedilum macranthum*	2·25	2·00
2111	$1.65 *Brassocattleya* Angel Lace	2·25	2·00
	a. Sheetlet. Nos. 2111/18	16·00	14·00
2112	$1.65 *Sophrolaeliocattleya* Precious Stones	2·25	2·00
2113	$1.65 Orange Theope Butterfly	2·25	2·00
2114	$1.65 *Promenaea xanthina*	2·25	2·00
2115	$1.65 *Lycaste macrobulbon*	2·25	2·00
2116	$1.65 *Amestella philippinensis*	2·25	2·00
2117	$1.65 *Masdevallia* Machu Picchu	2·25	2·00
2118	$1.65 *Phalaenopsis* Zuma Urchin	2·25	2·00
2119	$2 *Dendrobium victoria-reginae*	2·75	2·75
2098/119 Set of 22		42·00	30·00
MS2120 Two sheets, each 76×106 mm. (a) $6 *Miltonia* Seine. (b) $6 *Paphiopedilum gratrixanum* Set of 2 sheets		15·00	15·00

1999 (12 Aug). 50th Death Anniv of Paul Harris (founder of Rotary International). Nos. 2472/3 of Antigua optd with T **111**.

2121	$1.65 Paul Harris and James Grant	2·50	3·25
MS2122 78×107 mm. $6 Group study exchange, New Zealand		5·00	7·00

1999 (12 Aug). Royal Wedding. Nos. 2912/15 of Antigua optd with T **127**.

2123	$3 Sophie Rhys-Jones	2·50	2·75
	a. Sheetlet. Nos. 2123/5	6·75	7·50
2124	$3 Sophie and Prince Edward	2·50	2·75
2125	$3 Prince Edward	2·50	2·75
2123/5 Set of 3		6·75	7·50
MS2126 108×78 mm. $6 Prince Edward with Sophie Rhys-Jones and Windsor Castle		6·00	7·50

All examples of Nos. 2123/6 show the incorrect country overprint as above.

1999 (28 Sept). Fungi. Nos. 2489/501 of Antigua optd with T **111**.

2127	45c. *Marasmius rotula*	1·00	35
2128	65c. *Cantharellus cibarius*	1·25	55
2129	70c. *Lepiota cristata*	1·25	60
2130	90c. *Auricularia mesenterica*	1·40	70
2131	$1 *Pholiota alnicola*	1·40	1·00
2132	$1.65 *Leccinum aurantiacum*	1·40	1·75
2133	$1.75 *Entoloma serrulatum*	1·40	1·75
	a. Sheetlet. Nos. 2133/8	7·50	9·50
2134	$1.75 *Panaeolus sphinctrinus*	1·40	1·75
2135	$1.75 *Volvariella bombycina*	1·40	1·75
2136	$1.75 *Conocybe percincta*	1·40	1·75
2137	$1.75 *Pluteus cervinus*	1·40	1·75
2138	$1.75 *Russula foetens*	1·40	1·75
2127/38 Set of 12		14·00	14·00
MS2139 Two sheets, each 106×76 mm. (a) $6 *Amanita cothurnata*. (b) $6 *Panellus serotinus* Set of 2 sheets		12·00	14·00

1999 (28 Sept). 1st Death Anniv of Diana, Princess of Wales. No. 2753 of Antigua optd with T **111**.

2140	$1.20 Diana, Princess of Wales	1·50	1·50

1999 (30 Nov). Railway Locomotives of the World. Nos. 2553/65 of Antigua optd with T **111**.

2141	$1.65 Original drawing by Richard Trevithick, 1803	1·75	1·75
	a. Sheetlet. Nos. 2141/6	9·50	9·50
2142	$1.65 William Hedley's *Puffing Billy*, (1813–14)	1·75	1·75
2143	$1.65 Crampton locomotive of French Nord Railway, 1858	1·75	1·75
2144	$1.65 Lawrence Machine Shop locomotive, USA, 1860	1·75	1·75
2145	$1.65 Natchez and Hamburg Railway steam locomotive Mississippi, U.S.A., 1834	1·75	1·75
2146	$1.65 Bury "Coppernob" locomotive, Furness Railway, 1846	1·75	1·75
2147	$1.65 David Joy's *Jenny Lind*, 1847	1·75	1·75
	a. Sheetlet. Nos. 2147/52	9·50	9·50
2148	$1.65 Schenectady Atlantic locomotive, U.S.A., 1899	1·75	1·75
2149	$1.65 Kitson Class 1800 tank locomotive, Japan, 1881	1·75	1·75
2150	$1.65 Pennsylvania Railroad express freight	1·75	1·75
2151	$1.65 Karl Gölsdorf's 4 cylinder locomotive, Austria	1·75	1·75
2152	$1.65 Series "E" locomotive, Russia, 1930	1·75	1·75
2141/52 Set of 12		19·00	19·00
MS2153 Two sheets, each 72×100 mm. (a) $6 George Stephenson's "Patentee" type locomotive, 1843. (b) $6 Brunel's trestle bridge over River Lynher, Cornwall Set of 2 sheets		11·00	12·00

1999 (30 Nov). 175th Anniv of Cedar Hall Moravian Church. Nos. 2605/11 of Antigua optd with T **128** diagonally.

2154	20c. First Church and Manse, 1822–40	45	50
2155	45c. Cedar Hall School, 1840	55	40
2156	75c. Hugh A King, minister 1945–53	75	60
2157	90c. Present Church building	85	60
2158	$1.20 Water tank, 1822	1·25	1·25
2159	$2 Former Manse, demolished 1978	1·75	3·00
2154/9 Set of 6		5·00	5·75
MS2160 100×70 mm. $6 Present church building (*different*) (50×37 mm)		4·75	6·50

BARBUDA MAIL

(**128**)

1999 (15 Dec). Christmas. Religious Paintings. Nos. 2945/51 of Antigua optd with T **111**.

2161	15c. multicoloured	35	40
2162	25c. black, stone and yellow	40	40
2163	45c. multicoloured	55	30
2164	60c. multicoloured	80	35
2165	$2 multicoloured	1·75	2·50
2166	$4 black, stone and yellow	2·75	4·50
2161/6 *Set of 6*		6·00	7·75
MS2167 76×106 mm. $6 multicoloured		4·50	6·00

1999 (15 Dec). Centenary of Thomas Oliver Robinson Memorial School. Nos. 2634/40 of Antigua optd with T **128** diagonally.

2168	20c. brown-olive and black	35	40
2169	45c. multicoloured	55	30
2170	65c. brown-olive and black	75	45
2171	75c. multicoloured	80	65
2172	90c. multicoloured	90	65
2173	$1.20 red-brown, brown-olive and black	1·10	1·50
2168/73 *Set of 6*		4·00	3·50
MS2174 106×76 mm. $6 olive-brown		4·50	6·00

2000 (25 Jan). Cats and Dogs. Nos. 2540/52 of Antigua optd with T **111**.

2175	$1.65 Scottish fold kitten	2·25	2·25
	a. Sheetlet. Nos. 2175/80	12·00	12·00
2176	$1.65 Japanese bobtail	2·25	2·25
2177	$1.65 Tabby Manx	2·25	2·25
2178	$1.65 Bicolor American shorthair	2·25	2·25
2179	$1.65 Sorel Abyssinian	2·25	2·25
2180	$1.65 Himalayan blue point	2·25	2·25
2181	$1.65 Dachshund	2·25	2·25
	a. Sheetlet. Nos. 2181/6	12·00	12·00
2182	$1.65 Staffordshire terrier	2·25	2·25
2183	$1.65 Shar-pei	2·25	2·25
2184	$1.65 Beagle	2·25	2·25
2185	$1.65 Norfolk terrier	2·25	2·25
2186	$1.65 Golden retriever	2·25	2·25
2175/86 *Set of 12*		24·00	24·00
MS2187 Two sheets, each 107×77 mm. (a) $6 Red tabby (vert). (b) $6 Siberian husky (vert) *Set of 2 sheets*		15·00	17·00

2000 (29 Feb). Fish. Nos. 2586/604 of Antigua optd with T **128** diagonally.

2188	75c. Yellow damselfish	75	50
2189	90c. Barred hamlet	80	55
2190	$1 Yellow-tailed damselfish ("Jewelfish")	90	70
2191	$1.20 Blue-headed wrasse	1·10	1·00
2192	$1.50 Queen angelfish	1·25	1·25
2193	$1.65 Jackknife-fish	1·25	1·25
	a. Sheetlet. Nos. 2193/8	6·75	6·75
2194	$1.65 Spot-finned hogfish	1·25	1·25
2195	$1.65 Sergeant major	1·25	1·25
2196	$1.65 Neon goby	1·25	1·25
2197	$1.65 Jawfish	1·25	1·25
2198	$1.65 Flamefish	1·25	1·25
2199	$1.65 Rock beauty	1·25	1·25
	a. Sheetlet. Nos. 2199/204	6·75	6·75
2200	$1.65 Yellow-tailed snapper	1·25	1·25
2201	$1.65 Creole wrasse	1·25	1·25
2202	$1.65 Slender filefish	1·25	1·25
2203	$1.65 Long-spined squirrelfish	1·25	1·25
2204	$1.65 Royal gramma ("Fairy Basslet")	1·25	1·25
2205	$1.75 Queen triggerfish	1·40	1·40
2188/205 *Set of 18*		19·00	18·00
MS2206 Two sheets, each 80×110 mm. (a) $6 Porkfish. (b) $6 Black-capped basslet *Set of 2 sheets*		20·00	20·00

2000 (29 Feb). Ships of the World. Nos. 2679/85 of Antigua optd with T **111**.

2207	$1.75 Savannah (paddle-steamer)	1·75	1·75
	a. Sheetlet. Nos. 2207/9	4·75	4·75
2208	$1.75 Viking longship	1·75	1·75
2209	$1.75 Greek galley	1·75	1·75
2210	$1.75 Sailing clipper	1·75	1·75
	a. Sheetlet. Nos. 2210/12	4·75	4·75
2211	$1.75 Dhow	1·75	1·75
2212	$1.75 Fishing catboat	1·75	1·75
2207/12 *Set of 6*		9·50	9·50
MS2213 Three sheets, each 100×70 mm. (a) $6 13th-century English warship (41×22 mm). (b) $6 Sailing dory (22×41 mm). (c) $6 Baltimore clipper (41×22 mm) *Set of 3 sheets*		14·00	16·00

2000 (4 Apr). Modern Aircraft. Nos. 2700/12 of Antigua optd with T **111**.

2214	$1.65 Lockheed-Boeing General Dynamics Yf-22	1·75	1·75
	a. Sheetlet. Nos. 2214/9	9·50	9·50
2215	$1.65 Dassault-Breguet Rafale BO 1	1·75	1·75
2216	$1.65 MiG 29	1·75	1·75
2217	$1.65 Dassault-Breguet Mirage 2000D	1·75	1·75
2218	$1.65 Rockwell B-1B "Lancer"	1·75	1·75
2219	$1.65 McDonnell-Douglas C-17A	1·75	1·75
2220	$1.65 Space Shuttle	1·75	1·75
	a. Sheetlet. Nos. 2220/25	9·50	9·50
2221	$1.65 SAAB "Grippen"	1·75	1·75
2222	$1.65 Eurofighter EF-2000	1·75	1·75
2223	$1.65 Sukhoi SU 27	1·75	1·75
2224	$1.65 Northrop B-2	1·75	1·75
2225	$1.65 Lockheed F-117 "Nighthawk"	1·75	1·75
2214/25 *Set of 12*		19·00	19·00
MS2226 Two sheets, each 110×85 mm. (a) $6 F18 Hornet. (b) $6 Sukhoi SU 35 *Set of 2 sheets*		13·00	15·00

BARBUDA MAIL   BARBUDA MAIL
(129)   (130)

2000 (8 May). Classic Cars. Nos. 2687/98 of Antigua optd with T **129** and No. **MS**2699 of Antigua optd with T **130**.

2227	$1.65 Ford (1896)	1·75	1·75
	a. Sheetlet. Nos. 2227/32	9·50	9·50
2228	$1.65 Ford A (1903)	1·75	1·75
2229	$1.65 Ford T (1928)	1·75	1·75
2230	$1.65 Ford T (1922)	1·75	1·75
2231	$1.65 Ford Blackhawk (1929)	1·75	1·75
2232	$1.65 Ford Sedan (1934)	1·75	1·75
2233	$1.65 Torpedo (1911)	1·75	1·75
	a. Sheetlet. Nos. 2233/8	9·50	9·50
2234	$1.65 Mercedes 22 (1913)	1·75	1·75
2235	$1.65 Rover (1920)	1·75	1·75
2236	$1.65 Mercedes Benz (1956)	1·75	1·75
2237	$1.65 Packard V-12 (1934)	1·75	1·75
2238	$1.65 Opel (1924)	1·75	1·75
2227/38 *Set of 12*		19·00	19·00
MS2239 Two sheets, each 70×100 mm. (a) $6 Ford (1908) (60×40 mm). (b) $6 Ford (1929) (60×40 mm). P 14×14½ *Set of 2 sheets*		12·00	13·00

2000 (8 May). 19th World Scout Jamboree, Chile. Nos. 2739/**MS**2742 of Antigua optd with T **111**.

2240	90c. Scout handshake	1·50	1·00
2241	$1 Scouts hiking	1·75	1·25
2242	$1.20 Scout salute	2·25	2·50
2240/2 *Set of 3*		5·00	4·25
MS2243 68×98 mm. $6 Lord Baden-Powell		7·50	8·50

2000 (16 June). 50th Anniv of Organisation of American States (1998). No. 2730 of Antigua optd with T **111**.

2244	$1 Stylised Americas	1·25	1·50

BARBUDA MAIL
(131)   (132)

2000 (16 June). International Year of the Ocean (1998). Nos. 2641/77 of Antigua optd with T **131** and No. **MS**2678a/b of Antigua optd with T **111**.

2245/69	40c.× 25 Spotted eagle ray; Manta ray; Hawksbill turtle; Jellyfish; Queen angelfish; Octopus; Emperor angelfish; Regal angelfish; Porkfish; Racoon butterflyfish; Atlantic barracuda; Sea horse; Nautilus; Trumpetfish; White tip shark; Sunken Spanish galleon; Black tip shark; Long-nosed butterflyfish; Green moray eel; Captain Nemo; Treasure chest; Hammerhead shark; Divers; Lionfish; Clownfish		
	a. Sheetlet. Nos. 2245/69	14·00	17·00
2270/81	75c× 12 Maroon-tailed conure; Cocoi heron; Common tern; Rainbow lorikeet; Saddleback butterflyfish; Goatfish and cat shark; Blue shark and stingray; Majestic snapper; Nassau grouper; Black-cap gramma and blue tang; Stingrays; Stingray and giant starfish		
	a. Sheetlet. Nos. 2270/8	18·00	22·00
MS2282 Two sheets, each 68×98 mm. (a) $6 Humpback whale. (b) 98×68 mm. $6 Fiddler ray *Set of 2 sheets*		15·00	16·00

Nos. 2245/69 and 2270/81 were each printed together, *se-tenant*, in sheetlets of 25 or 12 stamps, with the backgrounds forming composite designs.

2000. Olympic Games, Sydney. Nos. 3109/12 of Antigua optd with T **132**.

2283	$2 Marcus Latimer Hurley (cycling), St Louis (1904)	4·50	3·75
	a. Sheetlet. Nos. 2283/6	16·00	13·50
2284	$2 Diving	4·50	3·75
2285	$2 Flaminio Stadium, Rome (1960) and Italian flag	4·50	3·75
2286	$2 Ancient Greek javelin thrower	4·50	3·75
2283/6	Set of 4	16·00	13·50

Nos. 2283/6 were printed together, *se-tenant*, in sheetlets of 4 (2×2), with the horizontal rows separated by a gutter margin showing Sydney landmarks and athlete carrying Olympic Torch.

2000. West Indies Cricket Tour and 100th Test Match at Lord's. Nos. 3113/MS3115 of Antigua optd with T **132**.

2287	90c. Richie Richardson	2·25	1·60
2288	$5 Viv Richards	8·00	9·00
MS2289	121×104 mm. $6 Lord's Cricket Ground	9·00	10·00

2000. Satellites and Spacecraft. Nos. 2835/40 and **MS**2847b of Antigua optd with T **111**.

2290	$1.65 "Luna 2" moon probe	2·50	2·50
	a. Sheetlet. Nos. 2290/5	13·50	13·50
2291	$1.65 "Mariner 2" space probe	2·50	2·50
2292	$1.65 Giotto space probe	2·50	2·50
2293	$1.65 Rosat satellite	2·50	2·50
2294	$1.65 International Ultraviolet Explorer	2·50	2·50
2295	$1.65 Ulysses space probe	2·50	2·50
2290/5	Set of 6	13·50	13·50
MS2296	106×76 mm. $6 "MIR" space station	8·50	9·50

Nos. 2297/312 are left for the 60th anniv of Battle of Britain sheetlets (Nos. 3217/32 of Antigua optd BARBUDA MAIL).

2000 (16 Oct). 60th Anniv of Battle of Britain. No. **MS**3233 of Antigua optd with T **111**.

MS2313	Two sheets, each 90×60 mm. (a) $6 Junkers 87B (dive bomber). (b) $6 Supermarine Spitfires at dusk *Set of 2 sheets*	17·00	18·00

STAMP BOOKLETS

1977 (20 Dec). Silver Jubilee. No. SB2 of Antigua with cover optd "BARBUDA".

SB1	$8 booklet containing pane of 6 (No. 329a) and pane of 1 (No. 330a)	5·00

1978 (12 Oct). 25th Anniv of Coronation. No. SB3 of Antigua with cover optd "BARBUDA".

SB2	$7.25 booklet containing pane of 6 (No. 421a) and pane of 1 (No. 423a)	2·50

1981 (27 July). Royal Wedding (1st issue). Cover printed in grey, 98×63 mm, showing crown, bells and inscription. Stitched.

SB3	$26 booklet containing panes of four (Nos. 566b, 568b, 570b)	6·00

The panes in this booklet each consist of two imperforate-between horizontal pairs.

1981 (12 Oct). Royal Wedding (3rd issue). No. SB4 of Antigua with cover optd "BARBUDA" in silver.

SB4	$11.50 booklet containing pane of 6 (No. 580a) and pane of 1 (No. 586a)	6·50

1982 (28 June). South Atlantic Fund. No. SB4 with contents surcharged.

SB5	$15 booklet containing pane of 6 (No. 617a) and pane of 1 (No. 623a)	5·00

REDONDA

DEPENDENCY OF ANTIGUA

Appendix

The following stamps were issued in anticipation of commercial and tourist development, philatelic mail being handled by a bureau in Antigua. Since at the present time the island is uninhabited, we do not list or stock these items. It is understood that the stamps are valid for the prepayment of postage in Antigua. Miniature sheets, imperforate stamps etc., are excluded from this section.

1979

Antigua 1976 definitive issue optd "REDONDA". 3, 5,10, 25, 35, 50, 75c., $1, $2.50, $5, $10.
Antigua Coronation Anniversary issue optd "REDONDA". 10, 30, 50, 90c., $2.50.
Antigua World Cup Football Championship issue optd "REDONDA". 10, 15c., $3.
Death Centenary of Sir Rowland Hill. 50, 90c., $2.50, $3.
International Year of the Child. 25, 50c., $1, $2.
Christmas. Paintings. 8, 50, 90c., $3.

1980

Marine Life. 8, 25, 50c., $4.
75th Anniv of Rotary International. 25, 50c., $1, $2.
Birds of Redonda. 8, 10, 15, 25, 30, 50c., $1, $2, $5.
Olympic Medal Winners, Lake Placid and Moscow. 8, 25, 50c., $3.
80th Birthday of Queen Elizabeth the Queen Mother. 10c., $2.50.
Christmas. Paintings. 8, 25, 50c., $4.

1981

Royal Wedding 25, 55c., $4.
Christmas. Walt Disney Cartoon Characters. ½, 1, 2, 3, 4, 5, 10c., $2.50, $3.
World Cup Football Championship, Spain (1982). 30c.×2, 50c.×2, $1×2, $2×2.

1982

Boy Scout Anniversaries. 8, 25, 50c., $3, $5.
Butterflies. 8, 30, 50c., $2.21st Birthday of Princess of Wales. $2, $4.
Birth of Prince William of Wales. Optd on 21st Birthday of Princess of Wales issue. $2, $4.
Christmas. Walt Disney's "One Hundred and One Dalmatians". ½, 1, 2, 3, 4, 5,10c., $2.50, $3.

1983

Easter. 500th Birth Anniv of Raphael. 10, 50, 90c., $4.
Bicentenary of Manned Flight. 10, 50, 90c., $4.
Christmas. Walt Disney Cartoon Characters. "Deck the Halls". ½, 1, 2, 3, 4, 5, 10c., $2.50, $3.

1984

Easter. Walt Disney Cartoon Characters. ½, 1, 2, 3, 4, 5, 10c., $2, $4.
Olympia Games, Los Angeles. 10, 50, 90c., $2.50.
Christmas. 50th Birthday of Donald Duck. 45, 60, 90c., $2, $4.

1985

Birth Bicentenary of John J. Audubon (ornithologist) (1st issue). 60, 90c., $1, $3.
Life and Times of Queen Elizabeth the Queen Mother. $1, $1.50, $2.50.
Royal Visit. 45c., $1, $4.
150th Birth Anniv of Mark Twain (author). 25, 50c., $1.50, $3.
Birth Bicentenaries of Grimm Brothers (folklorists). Walt Disney Cartoon Characters. 30, 60, 70c., $4.

1986

Birth Bicentenary of John J. Audubon (ornithologist) (2nd issue). 90c., $1, $1.50, $3.
Appearance of Halley's Comet. 5, 15, 55c., $4.
Centenary of Statue of Liberty (1st issue). 5, 15, 25, 30c., $4.
60th Birthday of Queen Elizabeth II. 50, 60c., $4.
Royal Wedding. 60c., $1, $4.
Christmas (1st issue). Disney characters in Hans Andersen Stories. 30, 60, 70c., $4.
Christmas (2nd issue). "Wind in the Willows" (Kenneth Grahame). 25, 50c., $1.50, $3.

1987

"Capex '87" International Stamp Exhibition, Toronto. Disney characters illustrating Art of Animation. 25, 30, 50, 60, 70c., $1.50, $3, $4.
Birth Centenary of Marc Chagall (artist). 10, 30, 40, 60, 90c., $1, $3, $4.
Centenary of Statue of Liberty (2nd issue). 10, 15, 25, 30, 40, 60, 70, 90c., $1, $2, $3, $4.
250th Death Anniv of Sir Isaac Newton (scientist). 20c., $2.50.
750th Anniv of Berlin. $1, $4.
Bicentenary of U.S. Constitution. 30c., $3.
16th World Scout Jamboree, Australia. 10c., $4.

1988

500th Anniv of Discovery of America by Columbus (1992) (1st issue). 15, 30, 45, 60, 90c., $1, $2, $3.
"Finlandia '88" International Stamp Exhibition, Helsinki. Disney characters in Finnish scenes. 1, 2, 3, 4, 5, 6c., $5, $6.
Olympic Games, Seoul. 25, 60c., $1.25, $3.
500th Birth Anniv of Titian. 10, 25, 40, 70, 90c., $2, $3, $4.

1989

20th Anniv of First Manned Landing on Moon. Disney characters on Moon. ½, 1, 2, 3, 4, 5c., $5, $6.
500th Anniv Discovery of America by Columbus (1992) (2nd issue). Pre-Columbian Societies. 15, 45, 45, 50c., $2, $2, $3, $3.
Christmas. Disney characters and Cars of 1950's. 25, 35, 45, 60c., $1, $2, $3, $4.

1990

Christmas. Disney characters and Hollywood Cars. 25, 35, 40, 60c., $1, $2, $4, $5.

1991

Nobel Prize Winners. 5, 15, 25, 40, 50c., $1, $2, $4.

British Virgin Islands

CROWN COLONY

Apart from the 1951 Legislative Council issue, the word "BRITISH" did not appear regularly on the stamps until 1968 when it was introduced to avoid confusion with the nearby Virgin Islands of the United States (the former Danish West Indies).

Most mail from the early years of the islands' history was sent via the Danish island of St. Thomas.

It is not known exactly when the first post office, or agency, was established on Tortola, but an entry in a G.P.O. account book suggest that it was operating by 1787 and the earliest letter postmarked "TORTOLA" dates from June of that year. The stamps of Great Britain were used from 1858 to May 1860, when the colonial authorities assumed responsibility for the overseas mails from the British G.P.O.

TORTOLA
CROWNED-CIRCLE HANDSTAMPS

CC1	CC **1**	TORTOLA (R.) (15.12.1842).......	Price on cover	£6500
CC2	CC **5**	TORTOLA (R.) (21.6.1854).......	Price on cover	£22000

No. CC2 is known used as an Official Paid mark during the years 1900 to 1918. *Price on cover* £950.

Stamps of GREAT BRITAIN cancelled "A 13"
1858–60.
Z1	1d. rose-red (1857), perf 14.................	£4000
Z2	4d. rose (1857)....................................	£5000
Z3	6d. lilac (1856)....................................	£1600
Z4	1s. green (1856)..................................	

PRICES FOR STAMPS ON COVER TO 1945	
Nos. 1/7	from × 30
Nos. 8/9	from × 40
No. 10	—
No. 11	from × 10
No. 12	from × 30
No. 13	—
Nos. 14/b	from × 10
Nos. 15/17	from × 30
Nos. 18/19	from × 40
No. 20	—
Nos. 21/b	from × 20
Nos. 22/b	from × 30
Nos. 24/31	from × 25
Nos. 32/4	from × 50
Nos. 35/7	from × 30
Nos. 38/41	from × 15
No. 42	from × 30
Nos. 43/50	from × 8
Nos. 54/77	from × 6
Nos. 78/81	from × 6
Nos. 82/101	from × 3
Nos. 103/6	from × 4
Nos. 107/9	from × 6
Nos. 110/21	from × 2

1 St. Ursula   **2** St. Ursula

(Litho Nissen & Parker from original dies by Waterlow)
1866 (Dec). No wmk. P 12.

(a) White wove paper
1	**1**	1d. green...............................	45·00	60·00
2		1d. deep green.....................	55·00	65·00
3	**2**	6d. rose...............................	90·00	£110
		a. Large "V" in "VIRGIN" (R. 2/1).......	£375	£475
4		6d. deep rose......................	£130	£140
		a. Large "V" in "VIRGIN" (R. 2/1).......	£425	£500

(b) Toned paper
5	**1**	1d. green...............................	48·00	60·00
		a. Perf 15×12........................	£5500	£7000
6		1d. deep green.....................	£100	£120
7	**2**	6d. rose-red.........................	60·00	90·00
		a. Large "V" in "VIRGIN" (R. 2/1).......	£275	£375

The above were printed in sheets of 25.
6d. stamps showing part of the papermaker's watermark ("A. Cowan & Sons Extra Superfine A. C. & S.") are worth 50% more.
Beware of fakes of No. 5a made from perf 12 stamps.

3   **4**

Normal   Variety

1s. Long-tailed "S" in "ISLANDS" (R. 3/1)
(Litho and typo (figure of the Virgin) (1s.) or litho (others) Nissen and Parker from original dies by Waterlow)
1867–70. No wmk. P 15. 1s. with double-lined frame.

(a) White wove paper
8	**1**	1d. yellow-green (1868)..........	80·00	80·00
9		1d. blue-green (1870)............	65·00	70·00
10	**2**	6d. pale rose........................	£600	£600
11	**4**	1s. black and rose-carmine.....	£275	£375
		a. Long-tailed "S".................	£900	£1100

(b) Greyish (No. 14) or toned paper (others)
12	**1**	1d. yellow-green (1868)..........	85·00	80·00
13	**2**	6d. dull rose (1868)...............	£300	£350
14	**4**	1s. black & rose-carmine (*greyish paper*).......	£275	£375
		a. Long-tailed "S".................	£900	£1100
14b		1s. black and rose-carmine (*toned paper*).....	£325	£375
		ba. Long-tailed "S"...............	£900	£1100

(c) Pale rose paper
15	**3**	4d. lake-red.........................	50·00	70·00

(d) Buff paper
16	**3**	4d. lake-red.........................	42·00	60·00
17		4d. lake-brown.....................	42·00	60·00

The thin lines of the frame on the 1s. are close together and sometimes merge into one.

The 1d. from the 1868 printing was in sheets of 20 (5×4) with narrow margins between the stamps. Later printings were in sheets of 12 (3×4) with wider margins. The 4d. was in sheets of 25; and the remaining two values in sheets of 20 (5×4).

The greyish paper used for Nos. 14 and 20 often shows traces of blue.

1867. Nos. 11 and 14/b with crimson frames superimposed extending into margins. P 15.
18	**4**	1s. black and rose-carmine (*white paper*)......	85·00	95·00
		a. Long-tailed "S".................	£275	£325
		b. Figure of Virgin omitted....	£150000	
19		1s. black and rose-carmine (*toned paper*)......	70·00	80·00
		a. Long-tailed "S".................	£200	£250
20		1s. black and rose-carmine (*greyish paper*)....	£750	£900
		a. Long-tailed "S".................	£2000	£2250

1868. Nos. 11 and 14b with frame lines retouched so as to make them single lines. Margins remain white. P 15.
21	**4**	1s. black and rose-carmine (*white paper*)......	£150	£180
		a. Long-tailed "S".................	£475	£550
21b		1s. black and rose-carmine (*toned paper*)......	£150	£180
		ba. Long-tailed "S"...............	£450	£550

(Litho D.L.R.)
1878. Wmk Crown CC (sideways). P 14.
22	**1**	1d. green...............................	80·00	£100
		a. Yellow-green.....................	£170	£130
		b. Wmk upright.....................	95·00	£130

6 (Die I)   **(7)**   **4D**

BRITISH VIRGIN ISLANDS

(Typo D.L.R.)

1879–**80**. Wmk Crown CC. P 14.
24	**6**	1d. emerald-green (1880)	75·00	90·00
25		2½d. red-brown	£110	£130

1883 (June)–**84**. Wmk Crown CA. P 14.
26	**6**	½d. yellow-buff	85·00	85·00
		x. Wmk reversed		
27		½d. dull green (*shades*) (11.83)	6·50	13·00
		b. Top left triangle detached	£325	£400
29		1d. pale rose (15.9.83)	38·00	40·00
		a. Deep rose (1884)	60·00	65·00
31		2½d. ultramarine (9.84)	2·75	16·00
		b. Top left triangle detached	£300	
		w. Wmk inverted	£180	

For illustration of "top left triangle detached" variety see above No. 21 of Antigua.

(Litho D.L.R.)

1887–**89**. Wmk Crown CA. P 14.
32	**1**	1d. red (5.89)	3·75	9·00
		x. Wmk reversed	£180	
33		1d. rose-red	3·25	8·50
34		1d. rose	5·50	14·00
35	**3**	4d. chestnut	35·00	65·00
		x. Wmk reversed	£250	
36		4d. pale chestnut	35·00	65·00
37		4d. brown-red	45·00	70·00
38	**2**	6d. dull violet	19·00	50·00
39		6d. deep violet	19·00	50·00
40	**4**	1s. sepia (2.89)	80·00	£100
41		1s. brown *to* deep brown	45·00	70·00
34s/40s Optd "SPECIMEN" Set of 4			£300	

The De La Rue transfers of T **1** to **4** are new transfers and differ from those of Messrs. Nissen and Parker, particularly T **4**.

1888 (July). Nos. 18/19. Surch with T **7**, in violet, in Antigua.
42	**4**	4d. on 1s. black and rose-car (*toned paper*)	£130	£160
		a. Surch double	£8500	
		b. Surch inverted (in pair with normal)	£55000	
		c. Long-tailed "S"	£500	£600
42d		4d. on 1s. black and rose-car (*white paper*)	£180	£225
		dc. Long-tailed "S"	£600	£750

The special issues for Virgin Islands were superseded on 31 October 1890, by the general issue for Leeward Islands. In 1899, however, a new special issue, Nos. 43/50, appeared; it did not supersede the general issue for Leeward Islands, but was used concurrently, as were all subsequent issues, until 1 July 1956 when the general Leeward Islands stamps were withdrawn.

(Recess D.L.R.)

1899 (Jan). Wmk Crown CA. P 14.
43	**8**	½d. yellow-green	3·75	55
		a. Error. "HALFPENNY" (R. 10/1)	85·00	£120
		b. Error. "HALFPENNY" (R. 8/2)	85·00	£120
		c. Imperf between (horiz pair)	£13000	
44		1d. brick-red	5·00	2·50
45		2½d. ultramarine	12·00	2·75
46		4d. brown	4·00	18·00
		a. Error "FOURPENCF" (R.10/3)	£750	£1100
47		6d. dull violet	6·50	3·00
48		7d. deep green	12·00	6·00
49		1s. brown-yellow	22·00	35·00
50		5s. indigo	75·00	85·00
43/50 Set of 8			£130	£140
43s/50s Optd "SPECIMEN" Set of 8			£180	

Nos. 43a/b and 46a were corrected after the first printing.

(Typo D.L.R.)

1904 (1 June). Wmk Mult Crown CA. P 14.
54	**9**	½d. dull purple and green	1·00	40
55		1d. dull purple and scarlet	2·50	35
56	**10**	2d. dull purple and ochre	7·50	3·50
57	**9**	2½d. dull purple and ultramarine	3·25	2·00
58	**10**	3d. dull purple and black	4·25	2·50
59	**9**	6d. dull purple and brown	3·50	2·50
60	**10**	1s. green and scarlet	6·00	5·00
61		2s.6d. green and black	35·00	55·00
62	**9**	5s. green and blue	48·00	70·00
54/62 Set of 9			£100	£130
54s/62s Optd "SPECIMEN" Set of 9			£160	

(Typo D.L.R.)

1913 (Feb)–**19**. Die I. Chalk-surfaced paper (3d. to 5s.). Wmk Mult Crown CA. P 14.
69	**11**	½d. green	3·75	6·00
		a. Yellow-green (8.16)	4·50	14·00
		b. Blue-green and deep green (3.19)	1·25	6·00
70		1d. deep red	8·50	11·00
		a. Deep red and carmine (10.17)	2·25	14·00
		b. Scarlet (10.17)	2·25	14·00
		c. Carmine-red (3.19)	48·00	27·00
71	**12**	2d. grey	5·50	28·00
		a. Slate-grey (1919)	6·00	38·00
72	**11**	2½d. bright blue	7·00	9·00
73	**12**	3d. purple/*yellow*	2·75	6·50
74	**11**	6d. dull and bright purple	8·00	17·00
75	**12**	1s. black/*blue-green*	3·25	9·00
76		2s.6d. black and red/*blue*	50·00	55·00
77	**11**	5s. green and red/*yellow*	45·00	£130
69/77 Set of 9			£110	£250
69s/77s Optd "SPECIMEN" Set of 9			£200	

Stock of the original printing of the ½d., No. 69 was exhausted by January 1916 and Leeward Islands ½d. stamps were used until the yellow-green printing, No. 69a, arrived in August 1916.

WAR STAMP

(13)

1916 (20 Oct)–**19**. Optd with T **13**.
78	**11**	1d. carmine	1·75	21·00
		a. Watermark sideways	£1100	
		b. Pale red/bluish	50	7·00
		bw. Wmk inverted	75·00	
		by. Wmk inverted and reversed		
		c. Scarlet (11.3.19)	1·75	3·75
		d. Short opt (right pane R.10/1)	25·00	
79	**12**	3d. purple/*yellow*	4·50	26·00
		a. Purple/lemon (12.3.17)	4·00	18·00
		b. Purple/buff-yellow (11.3.19)	6·00	25·00
		bw. Wmk inverted	10·00	48·00
		by. Wmk inverted and reversed		
		c. Short opt (right pane R. 10/1)	50·00	
78s/9s Optd "SPECIMEN" Set of 2			70·00	

Nos. 78d and 79c show the overprint 2 mm high instead of 2½ mm. No. 78c is known with the "A" of the "CA" watermark sideways.

1921 (18 Nov). As 1913–19, but Die II and wmk Mult Script CA.
80	**11**	½d. green	9·50	48·00
		w. Wmk inverted		
81		1d. scarlet and deep carmine	6·50	30·00
80s/1s Optd "SPECIMEN" Set of 2			80·00	

(Typo D.L.R.)

1922 (Mar)–**28**. P 14.

(a) Wmk Mult Crown CA. Chalk surfaced paper
82	**14**	3d. purple/*pale yellow* (15.6.22)	65	17·00
83		1s. black/*emerald* (15.6.22)	75	14·00
84		2s.6d. black and red/*blue* (15.6.22)	5·50	11·00
85		5s. green and red/*pale yellow* (15.6.22)	40·00	£100
82/5 Set of 4			42·00	£130
82s/5s Optd "SPECIMEN" Set of 4			95·00	

(b) Wmk Mult Script CA. Chalk-surfaced paper (5d. to 5s.)
86	**14**	½d. dull green	85	2·75
87		1d. rose-carmine	60	60
88		1d. bright violet (1.27)	1·25	5·00
89		1d. scarlet (12.28)	23·00	14·00
90		1½d. carmine-red (1.27)	1·75	2·50
91		1½d. Venetian red (11.28)	2·00	1·50
92		2d. grey	1·25	6·00
93		2½d. pale bright blue	3·50	20·00
94		2½d. dull orange (1.9.23)	1·25	1·75
95		2½d. bright blue (1.27)	11·00	3·50
96		3d. purple/*pale yellow* (2.28)	2·25	11·00
97		5d. dull purple and olive (6.22)	5·50	45·00
98		6d. dull and bright purple (6.22)	1·75	6·50
99		1s. black/*emerald* (2.28)	2·50	15·00
100		2s.6d. black and red/*blue* (2.28)	19·00	48·00

149

BRITHISH VIRGIN ISLANDS

101	5s. green and red/*yellow* (1.9.23)	19·00	70·00
86/101 *Set of* 16		85·00	£225
86s/101s Optd or Perf (Nos. 89, 91) "SPECIMEN" *Set of* 16			£325

In the 1½d. stamps the value is in colour on a white ground.

Kite and vertical log (Plate "2A" R. 10/6)

Kite and horizontal log (Plate "2B" R. 10/6)

Bird by turret (Plate "7" R. 1/5)

1935 (6 May). Silver Jubilee. As Nos. 91/4 of Antigua but printed by Waterlow. P 11×12.

103	1d. deep blue and scarlet	1·25	8·00
	k. Kite and vertical log	£140	
	l. Kite and horizontal log	£140	£250
104	1½d. ultramarine and grey	1·25	7·00
	k. Kite and vertical log	£150	
	l. Kite and horizontal log	£150	£250
	m. "Bird" by turret	£190	£225
105	2½d. brown and deep blue	3·75	6·50
	k. Kite and vertical log	£170	
	l. Kite and horizontal log	£180	£250
106	1s. slate and purple	19·00	35·00
	k. Kite and vertical log	£375	
	l. Kite and horizontal log	£350	£450
103/6 *Set of* 4		23·00	50·00
103s/6s Perf "SPECIMEN" *Set of* 4		£140	

1937 (12 May). Coronation. As Nos. 95/7 of Antigua. P 11×11½.

107	1d. carmine	1·00	3·25
108	1½d. yellow-brown	75	3·00
109	2½d. blue	60	1·50
107/9 *Set of* 3		2·10	7·00
107s/9s Perf "SPECIMEN" *Set of* 3		£100	

15 King George VI and Badge of Colony  **16** Map

(Photo Harrison)

1938 (1 Aug)–**47**. Chalk-surfaced paper. Wmk Mult Script CA. P 14.

110	**15**	½d. green	3·00	3·75
		a. Ordinary paper (10.43)	1·50	1·00
111		1d. scarlet	5·00	2·25
		a. Ordinary paper (10.43)	2·50	1·75
112		1½d. red-brown	6·00	7·50
		a. Ordinary paper (10.43)	2·75	1·75
		w. Wmk inverted	†	£1600
113		2d. grey	5·50	2·75
		a. Ordinary paper (10.43)	2·75	1·75
114		2½d. ultramarine	4·50	1·75
		a. Ordinary paper (10.43)	3·50	2·75
115		3d. orange	7·00	1·25
		a. Ordinary paper (10.43)	2·25	1·00
116		6d. mauve	11·00	2·75
117		a. Ordinary paper (10.43)	6·00	2·25
		1s. olive-brown	20·00	4·75
		a. Ordinary paper (8.42)	4·00	2·25
118		2s.6d. sepia	65·00	10·00
		a. Ordinary paper (8.42)	17·00	5·50
119		5s. carmine	65·00	12·00
		a. Ordinary paper (8.42)	17·00	6·50
120		10s. blue (1.12.47)	8·50	9·50
121		£1 black (1.12.47)	10·00	24·00
110a/21 *Set of* 12			70·00	55·00
110s/21s Perf "SPECIMEN" *Set of* 12			£325	

The ordinary paper, used as a substitute for the chalk-surfaced for printings between 1942 and 1945, is thick, smooth and opaque.

1946 (1 Nov). Victory. As Nos. 110/11 of Antigua.

122	1½d. lake-brown	10	10
123	3d. orange	10	60
122s/3s Perf "SPECIMEN" *Set of* 2		85·00	

1949 (3 Jan). Royal Silver Wedding. As Nos. 112/13 of Antigua.

124	2½d. ultramarine	10	10
125	£1 black	16·00	21·00

1949 (10 Oct). 75th Anniv of U.P.U. As Nos. 114/17 of Antigua.

126	2½d. ultramarine	30	2·25
127	3d. orange	1·50	2·50
128	6d. magenta	45	40
129	1s. olive	35	50
126/9 *Set of* 4		2·40	5·00

(New Currency. 100 cents = 1 B.W.I. dollar)

1951 (16 Feb–10 Apr). Inauguration of B.W.I. University College. As Nos. 118/19 of Antigua.

130	3c. black and brown-red (10 Apr)	40	2·50
131	12c. black and reddish violet	60	1·75

Issue of the 3c. value was delayed when the supplies were sent to Puerto Rico by mistake.

(Recess Waterlow)

1951 (2 Apr). Restoration of Legislative Council. Wmk Mult Script CA. P 14½×14.

132	**16**	6c. orange	50	1·50
133		12c. purple	1·00	50
134		24c. olive	70	1·00
135		$1.20 carmine	2·25	1·00
132/5 *Set of* 4			4·00	3·50

17 Sombrero Lighthouse

18 Map of Jost Van Dyke

19 Sheep industry

20 Map of Anegada

21 Cattle industry

22 Map of Virgin Gorda

23 Map of Tortola

24 Badge of the Presidency

BRITISH VIRGIN ISLANDS

25 Dead Man's Chest
26 Sir Francis Drake Channel 
27 Road Town 
28 Map of Virgin Islands 

(Recess D.L.R.)

1952 (15 Apr). T **17/28**. Wmk Mult Script CA. P 12½×13 (vert) or 13×12½ (horiz.).

136	**17**	1c. black	80	3·50
137	**18**	2c. deep green	70	30
138	**19**	3c. black and brown	80	2·50
139	**20**	4c. carmine-red	70	2·75
140	**21**	5c. claret and black	1·50	50
141	**22**	8c. bright blue	1·00	2·00
142	**23**	12c. dull violet	1·00	2·00
143	**24**	24c. deep brown	70	50
144	**25**	60c. yellow-green and blue	5·00	11·00
145	**26**	$1.20 black and bright blue	5·50	12·00
146	**27**	$2.40 yellowish green and red-brown	16·00	17·00
147	**28**	$4.80 bright blue and carmine	18·00	20·00
136/47	Set of 12		45·00	65·00

1953 (2 June). Coronation. As No. 120 of Antigua.

148		2c. black and green	30	1·25

29 Map of Tortola 
30 Virgin Islands sloop 
31 Nelthrop Red Poll bull 
32 Road Harbour 
33 Mountain travel 
34 Badge of the Presidency 
35 Beach scene 
36 *New Idea* (sloop) under construction 
37 White Cedar tree 
38 Skipjack Tuna ("Bonito")

39 Coronation celebrations, Treasury Square
40 Brown Pelican 
41 Magnificent Frigate Bird 

(Recess D.L.R.)

1956 (1 Nov)–**62**. T **29/41**. Wmk Mult Script CA. P 13×12½ (½c. to $1.20) or 12×11½ ($2.40 and $4.80).

149	**29**	½c. black and reddish purple	1·25	30
		a. Black and deep reddish purple (19.4.60)	3·25	4·00
150	**30**	1c. turquoise-blue and slate	1·50	1·25
		a. Turquoise and slate-violet (26.11.62)	22·00	20·00
151	**31**	2c. vermilion and black	30	10
152	**32**	3c. blue and deep olive	30	30
153	**33**	4c. deep brown and turquoise-green	70	30
154	**34**	5c. grey-black	50	10
155	**35**	8c. yellow-orange and deep blue	2·00	40
156	**36**	12c. ultramarine and rose-red	4·00	75
157	**37**	24c. myrtle-green and brown-orange	1·00	65
158	**38**	60c. indigo and yellow-orange	8·50	8·00
159	**39**	$1.20 deep yellow-green and carmine-red	4·00	9·50
160	**40**	$2.40 lemon and deep dull purple	42·00	13·00
161	**41**	$4.80 blackish brown and turquoise-blue	42·00	13·00
149/61	Set of 13		95·00	42·00

(New Currency. 100 cents = 1 U.S. dollar)

(**42**)

1962 (10 Dec). As Nos. 149/53 and 155/61, but W w **12**, surch in U.S. currency as T **42** by D.L.R.

162	1c. on ½c. black and deep reddish purple	30	10
163	2c. on 1c. turquoise and slate-violet	1·75	10
164	3c. on 2c. vermilion and black	70	10
165	4c. on 3c. black and deep olive	30	10
166	5c. on 4c. deep brown and turquoise-green	30	10
167	8c. on 8c. yellow-orange and deep blue	30	10
168	10c. on 12c. ultramarine and rose-red	2·00	10
169	12c. on 24c. myrtle-green and brown-orange	30	10
170	25c. on 60c. indigo and yellow-orange	2·75	45
171	70c. on $1.20 deep yellow-green and carmine-red	35	45
	a. Stop to right of C in surcharge instead of beneath it (in pair with normal)	6·50	4·00
172	$1.40 on $2.40 lemon and deep dull purple	9·50	4·50
173	$2.80 on $4.80 blackish brown and turquoise-blue	9·50	4·50
162/73	Set of 12	25·00	9·50

No. 171a occurs on the first stamp on Rows 1 to 10.

1963 (4 June). Freedom from Hunger. As No. 146 of Antigua.

174	25c. reddish violet	20	10

1963 (2 Sept). Red Cross Centenary. As Nos. 147/8 of Antigua.

175	2c. red and black	15	20
176	25c. red and blue	50	20

1964 (23 Apr). 400th Birth Anniv of William Shakespeare. As No. 164 of Antigua.

177	10c. bright blue	20	10

43 Skipjack Tuna
44 Soper's Hole

BRITISH VIRGIN ISLANDS

45 Brown Pelican
46 Dead Man's Chest 
47 Road Harbour 
48 Fallen Jerusalem 
49 The Baths, Virgin Gorda 
50 Map of Virgin Islands 
51 Youth of Tortola, Tortola-St. Thomas ferry 
52 The Towers, Tortola 
53 Beef Island Airfield 
54 Map of Tortola 
55 Virgin Gorda 
56 Yachts at anchor 
57 Badge of the Colony 

(Des and recess D.L.R.)

1964 (2 Nov)–**68**. T **43**/**57**. W w **12**. P 11½×12 ($2.80), 13×13½ (70c., $1, $1.40), or 13×12½ (others).

178	43	1c. blue and olive-green	30	2·00
179	44	2c. yellow-olive and rose-red	15	30
180	45	3c. sepia and turquoise-blue	4·75	2·25
181	46	4c. black and carmine-red	80	3·00
182	47	5c. black and deep bluish green	1·75	2·25
183	48	6c. black and brown-orange	30	85
184	49	8c. black and magenta	30	50
185	50	10c. lake and deep lilac	6·00	1·00
		a. Bright lake and reddish lilac (26.11.68)	20·00	3·75
186	51	12c. deep bluish green and deep violet-blue	2·50	3·25
187	52	15c. yellow-green and grey-black	1·50	2·75
188	53	25c. green and purple	11·00	2·50
189	54	70c. black and yellow-brown	4·25	8·50
190	55	$1 yellow-green and chestnut	3·00	2·00
191	56	$1.40 light blue and rose	24·00	11·00
192	57	$2.80 black and bright purple	26·00	12·00
178/92		Set of 15	75·00	48·00

1965 (17 May). I.T.U. Centenary. As Nos. 166/7 of Antigua.

193		4c. yellow and turquoise	20	10
194		25c. light blue and orange-buff	45	20

1965 (25 Oct). International Cooperation Year. As Nos. 168/9 of Antigua.

195		1c. reddish purple and turquoise-green	10	15
196		25c. deep bluish green and lavender	30	15

1966 (24 Jan). Churchill Commemoration. As Nos. 170/3 of Antigua.

197		1c. new blue	10	40
198		2c. deep green	35	40
199		10c. brown	75	10
200		25c. bluish violet	1·40	25
197/200		Set of 4	2·25	1·00

1966 (22 Feb). Royal Visit. As Nos. 174/5 of Antigua.

201		4c. black and ultramarine	40	10
202		70c. black and magenta	1·40	45

58 Atrato I (paddle-steamer), 1866

(Des R. Granger Barrett. Litho B.W.)

1966 (25 Apr). Stamp Centenary. T **58** and similar horiz designs. W w **12** (sideways). P 13.

203		5c. black, red, yellow and emerald	35	10
204		10c. black, green and rose-red/cream	35	10
205		25c. black, rose-red and blue/pale green	55	10
206		60c. black, red and green/pale blue	1·00	2·50
203/6		Set of 4	2·00	2·50

Design:—10c. 1d. and 6d. stamps of 1866; 25c. Air mail transport, Beef Island, and 6d. stamp of 1866; 60c. Landing mail at Roadtown, 1866 and 1d. stamp of 1866.

50c.

=

(**62**)

1966 (15 Sept). As Nos. 189 and 191/2 but wmk sideways, surch as T **62**.

207		50c. on 70c. black and yellow-brown	1·25	90
208		$1.50 on $1.40 light blue and rose	2·25	2·00
209		$3 on $2.80 black and bright purple	2·25	2·75
207/9		Set of 3	5·00	5·00

1966 (1 Dec). 20th Anniv of U.N.E.S.C.O. As Nos. 196/8 of Antigua.

210		2c. slate-violet, red, yellow and orange	10	10
211		12c. orange-yellow, violet and deep olive	30	10
212		60c. black, bright purple and orange	1·00	45
210/12		Set of 3	1·25	60

63 Map of Virgin Islands

BRITISH VIRGIN ISLANDS

(Des G. Vasarhelyi. Photo Harrison)
1967 (18 Apr). New Constitution. W w **12**. P 14½.

213	**63**	2c. multicoloured	10	10
214		10c. multicoloured	15	10
		w. Wmk inverted	19·00	
215		25c. multicoloured	15	10
		w. Wmk inverted	9·00	
216		$1 multicoloured	55	40
213/16	*Set of 4*		75	55

64 *Mercury* (cable ship) and Bermuda-Tortola Link

(Des G. Drummond, Photo Harrison)
1967 (14 Sept). Inauguration of Bermuda-Tortola Telephone Service. T **64** and similar horiz designs. Multicoloured. W w **12**. P 14½.

217	4c. Type **64**	30	10
218	10c. Chalwell Telecommunications Station	20	10
219	50c. *Mercury* (cable ship)	60	30
217/19	*Set of 3*	1·00	40

67 Blue Marlin

(Des V. Whiteley. Photo Enschedé)
1968 (2 Jan). Game Fishing. T **67** and similar horiz designs. W w **12** (sideways). P 12½×12.

220	2c. multicoloured	10	1·00
221	10c. multicoloured	25	10
222	25c. black, blue and bright violet	55	10
223	40c. multicoloured	85	85
220/3	*Set of 4*	1·60	1·75

Designs—10c. Cobia; 25c. Wahoo; 40c. Fishing launch and map.

1968 INTERNATIONAL YEAR FOR HUMAN RIGHTS
(**71**)

72 Dr. Martin Luther King, Bible, Sword and Armour Gauntlet

1968 (29 July). Human Rights Year. Nos. 185 and 188 optd with T **71**.

224	10c. lake and deep lilac	20	10
225	25c. green and purple	30	40

29 July was the date of issue in the islands. The Crown Agents supplies went on sale in London on 1 July, the local consignment being delayed in transit.

(Des V. Whiteley. Litho Format)
1968 (15 Oct). Martin Luther King Commemoration. W w **12** (sideways). P 14.

226	**72**	4c. multicoloured	25	20
227		25c. multicoloured	40	40

73 de Havilland DHC-6 Twin Otter 100

77 Long John Silver and Jim Hawkins

(Des R. Granger Barrett. Litho Format)
1968 (16 Dec). Opening of Beef Island Airport Extension. T **73** and similar horiz designs. Multicoloured. P 14.

228	2c. Type **73**	25	1·25
229	10c. Hawker Siddeley H.S.748 airliner	40	10
230	25c. De Havilland D.H.114 Heron 2	45	10
231	$1 Royal Engineers cap badge	50	2·00
228/31	*Set of 4*	1·40	3·00

78 Jim Hawkins escaping from the Pirates

(Des Jennifer Toombs. Photo Enschedé)
1969 (18 Mar). 75th Death Anniv of Robert Louis Stevenson. Scenes from *Treasure Island*. T **77/8** and similar designs. W w **12** (sideways on 10c., $1). P 13½×13 (4c., 40c.) or 13×13½ (others).

232	4c. indigo, pale yellow and carmine-red	20	15
233	10c. multicoloured	20	10
234	40c. brown, black and blue	25	30
235	$1 multicoloured	45	1·00
232/5	*Set of 4*	1·00	1·40

Designs: *Vert*—40c. The fight with Israel Hands. *Horiz*—$1 Treasure trove.

82 Yachts in Road Harbour, Tortola

(Des J. Cooter, Litho P.B.)
1969 (20 Oct). Tourism. T **82** and similar multicoloured designs. W w **12** (sideways on 2c., $1). P 12½.

236	2c. Tourist and Yellow-finned Grouper (fish) (*vert*)	15	50
237	10c. Type **82**	30	10
238	20c. Sun-bathing at Virgin Gorda National Park	40	20
239	$1 Tourist and Pipe Organ Cactus at Virgin Gorda (*vert*)	90	1·50
236/9	*Set of 4*	1·60	2·00

85 Carib Canoe

(Des and litho J.W.)
1970 (16 Feb)–**74**. Horiz designs as T **85**. W w **12** (sideways*). P 14.

240	½c. buff, red-brown and sepia	10	1·50
241	1c. new blue, apple-green and chalky blue	15	75
	a. Perf 13½ (12.11.74)	1·25	2·00
242	2c. yellow-orange, red-brown and slate	40	1·00
243	3c. orange-red, cobalt and sepia	30	1·25
244	4c. greenish blue, chalky blue and bistre-brown	30	50
	w. Wmk Crown to right of CA	£150	
245	5c. emerald, pink and black	30	10
246	6c. reddish violet mauve and myrtle-green	40	2·25
247	8c. apple-green, greenish yellow and sepia	50	6·00
248	10c. greenish blue, yellow-brown and red-brown	50	15
	a. Perf 13½ (12.11.74)	2·50	2·25
249	12c. yellow, crimson and brown	65	1·50
	a. Perf 13½ (12.11.74)	2·50	3·25
250	15c. turquoise-green, orange and bistre-brown	6·00	85
	a. Perf 13½ (12.11.74)	3·50	3·25
251	25c. grey-green, steel-blue and plum	4·00	1·75
252	50c. magenta, dull green and purple-brown	3·25	1·50

153

253	$1 salmon, olive-green and red-brown		4·00	3·75
254	$2 buff, slate and grey		8·00	7·00
255	$3 ochre, deep blue and sepia		2·75	4·50
256	$5 violet and grey		2·75	5·00
240/56	Set of 17		30·00	35·00

Designs:—1c. *Santa Maria.* (Columbus' flagship); 2c. *Elizabeth Bonaventure* (Drake's flagship); 3c. Dutch Buccaneer, circa 1660; 4c. *Thetis*, 1827 (after etching by E. W. Cooke); 5c. Henry Morgan's ship (17th century); 6c. H.M.S. *Boreas* (Captain Nelson, 1784); 8c. H.M.S. *Eclair*, 1804; 10c. H.M.S. *Formidable*, 1782; 12c. H.M.S. *Nymph*, 1778; 15c. *Windsor Castle* (sailing packet) engaging *Jeune Richard* (French brig), 1807; 25c. H.M.S. *Astrea*, 1808; 50c. Wreck of R.M.S. *Rhone*, 1867; $1 Tortola sloop; $2 H.M.S. *Frobisher*; $3 *Booker Viking* (cargo liner), 1967; $5 Hydrofoil *Sun Arrow*.

*The normal sideways watermark shows Crown to left of CA, as seen from the back of the stamp.

The ½c., 3c., 4c., 5c., 10c., and 12c. were reissued in 1973 with W w **12** upright.

102 *A Tale of Two Cities*

(Des W. G. Brown. Litho D.L.R.)

1970 (4 May). Death Centenary of Charles Dickens. T **102** and similar horiz designs showing original book illustrations. W w **12** (sideways). P 14.

257	5c. black, light rose and grey	25	1·00
258	10c. black, light blue and pale green	35	10
259	25c. black, light green and pale yellow	50	25
257/9	Set of 3	1·00	1·00

Designs:—10c. *Oliver Twist*; 25c. *Great Expectations*.

103 Hospital Visit **104** Mary Read

(Des R. Granger Barrett. Litho Questa)

1970 (10 Aug). Centenary of British Red Cross. T **103** and similar horiz designs. Multicoloured. W w **12** (sideways*). P 14.

260	4c. Type **103**	20	45
261	10c. First Aid Class	20	10
262	25c. Red Cross and Coat of Arms	50	55
	w. Wmk Crown to right of CA	65·00	
260/2	Set of 3	1·00	1·00

*The normal sideways watermark shows Crown to left of CA, as seen from the back of the stamp.

(Des and litho J. W.)

1970 (16 Nov). Pirates. T **104** and similar vert designs. Multicoloured. W w **12**. P 14×14½.

263	½c. Type **104**	10	15
264	10c. George Lowther	30	10
265	30c. Edward Teach (Blackbeard)	60	25
266	60c. Henry Morgan	80	1·00
263/6	Set of 4	1·50	1·40

(Des L. Curtis. Litho Format)

1971 (13 Dec). 25th Anniv of UNICEF. W w **12** (sideways). P 13½×14.

267	**105** 15c. multicoloured	10	10
268	30c. multicoloured	20	25

VISIT OF H.R.H. THE PRINCESS MARGARET
1972   1972

(**106**)

1972 (7 Mar). Royal Visit of Princess Margaret. Nos. 244 and 251 optd with T **106**.

269	4c. greenish blue, chalky blue and bistre-brown	40	15
270	25c. grey-green, steel-blue and plum	60	45

107 Seaman of 1800 **108** Sailfish and *Sir Winston Churchill* (cadet schooner)

(Des J.W. Litho Questa)

1972 (17 Mar). "Interpex" Stamp Exhibition, New York. T **107** and similar vert designs showing Naval Uniforms. Multicoloured. W w **12** (sideways*). P 13½.

271	½c. Type **107**	10	40
	w. Wmk Crown to left of CA	1·75	
272	10c. Boatswain, 1787–1807	35	10
273	30c. Captain, 1795–1812	85	55
274	60c. Admiral, 1787–95	1·25	2·75
271/4	Set of 4	2·25	3·25

*The normal sideways watermark shows Crown to right of CA, as seen from the back of the stamp.

(Des from photograph by D. Groves) and photo Harrison)

1972 (24 Nov). Royal Silver Wedding. Multicoloured; background colour given. W w **12**. P 14×14½.

275	**108** 15c. bright blue	25	15
276	25c. turquoise-blue	25	15
	a. Blue omitted*	£500	
	w. Wmk inverted	35·00	

*The omission of the blue colour results in the Duke's suit appearing sepia instead of deep blue.

109 Blue Marlin

(Des G. Drummond. Litho Questa)

1972 (12 Dec). Game Fish. T **109** and similar horiz designs. Multicoloured. W w **12**. P 13½.

277	½c. Type **109**	15	1·40
	a. Pair. Nos. 277/8	30	2·75
278	½c. Wahoo	15	1·40
279	15c. Yellow-finned Tuna ("Allison Tuna")	65	25
280	25c. White Marlin	75	30
281	50c. Sailfish	1·25	1·50
282	$1 Dolphin	2·00	2·50
277/82	Set of 6	4·50	6·75
MS283	194×158 mm. Nos. 277/82	8·50	8·50

Nos. 277/8 were printed horizontally and vertically *se-tenant* within the sheet.

110 J. C. Lettsom **111** Green-throated Carib and Antillean Crested Hummingbird

BRITISH VIRGIN ISLANDS

(Des J. Cooter. Litho Questa)

1973 (9 Mar). Interpex 1973 (Quakers). T **110** and similar multicoloured designs. W w **12** (sideways on ½c. and 15c.). P 13½.

284	½c. Type **110**	10	15
285	10c. Lettsom House (*horiz*)	15	10
286	15c. Dr. W. Thornton	20	10
287	30c. Dr. Thornton and Capitol, Washington (*horiz*)	25	20
288	$1 William Penn (*horiz*)	60	1·10
284/8 Set of 5		1·10	1·50

(Des G. Drummond. Litho Questa)

1973 (30 June). First Issue of Coinage. T **111** and similar horiz designs showing coins and local scenery. Multicoloured. W w **12**. P 14.

289	1c. Type **111**	10	30
290	5c. Zenaida Dove	60	10
291	10c. Ringed Kingfisher	75	10
292	25c. Mangrove Cuckoo	95	15
293	50c. Brown Pelican	1·10	1·00
294	$1 Magnificent Frigate Bird	1·40	2·00
289/94 Set of 6		4·50	3·25

1973 (17 Oct). As Nos. 240, 243/5 and 248/9, but W w **12** upright.

295	½c. buff, red-brown and sepia	50	7·00
296	3c. orange-red, cobalt and sepia	1·25	2·50
297	4c. greenish blue, chalky blue and bistre-brown	1·25	6·00
298	5c. emerald, pink and black	1·25	2·50
299	10c. greenish blue, yellow-brown and red-brown	1·50	2·00
	w. Wmk inverted		
300	12c. yellow, dull crimson and light brown	2·00	3·50
295/300 Set of 6		7·00	21·00

1973 (14 Nov). Royal Wedding. As T **47** of Anguilla. Centre multicoloured. W w **12** (sideways). P 13½.

301	5c. brown-ochre	10	10
302	50c. light turquoise-blue	20	20

112 "The Virgin and Child" (Pintoricchio)

113 Crest of the *Canopus* (French)

(Des G. Drummond. Litho Questa)

1973 (7 Dec). Christmas. T **112** and similar vert designs. Multicoloured. W w **12**. P 14.

303	½c. Type **112**	10	10
304	3c. "Virgin and Child" (Lorenzo di Credi)	10	10
305	25c. "Virgin and Child" (Crivelli)	15	10
306	50c. "Virgin and Child with St. John" (Luini)	30	40
303/6 Set of 4		55	60

(Des J. Cooter. Litho Questa)

1974 (22 Mar). "Interpex 1974" (Naval Crests). T **113** and similar vert designs. Multicoloured. W w **12**. P 14.

307	5c. Type **113**	15	10
308	18c. U.S.S. *Saginaw*	25	25
309	25c. H.M.S. *Rothesay*	25	30
310	50c. H.M.C.S. *Ottawa*	45	60
307/10 Set of 4		1·00	1·10
MS311 196×128 mm. Nos. 307/10		1·25	4·50

114 Christopher Columbus

115 Atlantic Trumpet Triton (*Charonia variegata*)

(Des J. W. Litho Format)

1974 (19 Aug). Historical Figures. T **114** and similar vert designs. W w **12**. P 14.

312	5c. orange and black	20	10
	w. Wmk inverted	2·25	
313	10c. greenish blue and black	20	10
314	25c. reddish violet and black	25	25
315	40c. yellow-brown and sepia	45	75
312/15 Set of 4		1·00	1·00
MS316 84×119 mm. Nos. 312/15		1·00	2·25

Portraits: –10c. Sir Walter Raleigh; 25c. Sir Martin Frobisher; 40c. Sir Francis Drake.

(Des G. Drummond. Litho Harrison)

1974 (30 Sept). Seashells. T **115** and similar horiz designs. Multicoloured. W w **12**. P 13×13½.

317	5c. Type **115**	30	15
	a. Wmk T **53** of Lesotho (sideways)	£120	
	w. Wmk inverted	85·00	
318	18c. West Indian Murex (*Murex brevifrons*)	50	30
319	25c. Bleeding Tooth (*Nerita peloranta*)	60	35
320	75c. Virgin Islands Latirus (*Latirus virginensis*)	1·25	2·25
317/20 Set of 4		2·25	2·75
MS321 146×95 mm. Nos. 317/20		3·00	6·50
	a. Printed on the gummed side	£600	
	w. Wmk inverted	32·00	

116 Churchill and St. Mary, Aldermanbury, London

117 H.M.S. *Boreas*

(Des J.W. Litho Questa)

1974 (30 Nov). Birth Centenary of Sir Winston Churchill. T **116** and similar horiz design. Multicoloured. W w **14** (sideways*). P 14.

322	10c. Type **116**	15	10
	w. Wmk Crown to right of CA	2·25	2·75
323	50c. St. Mary, Fulton, Missouri	35	50
MS324 141×108 mm. Nos. 322/3		80	1·40

*The normal sideways watermark shows Crown to left of CA, *as seen from the back of the stamp*.

(Des J. Cooter. Litho J.W.)

1975 (14 Mar). Interpex 1975 Stamp Exhibition, New York. Ships' Figureheads. T **117** and similar vert designs. Multicoloured. W w **12**. P 13.

325	5c. Type **117**	20	10
326	18c. *Golden Hind*	50	15
327	40c. H.M.S. *Superb*	50	25
328	85c. H.M.S. *Formidable*	1·00	1·50
325/8 Set of 4		1·50	1·75
MS329 192×127 mm. Nos. 325/8 (Wmk inverted). P 14		1·75	8·00
	w. Wmk upright	90·00	

118 Rock Beauty

(Des C. Abbott. Litho Questa)

1975 (16 June-15-Aug). Fish. Horiz designs as T **118**. Multicoloured. W w **14** (sideways*). P 14.

330	½c. Type **118**	15	50
	w. Wmk Crown to right of CA	3·50	
331	1c. Long-spined Squirrelfish	40	2·75
332	3c. Queen Triggerfish	1·00	2·75
333	5c. Blue Angelfish	30	20
334	8c. Stoplight Parrotfish	30	25
335	10c. Queen Angelfish	30	25
336	12c. Nassau Grouper	40	30
337	13c. Blue Tang	40	30

BRITISH VIRGIN ISLANDS

338	15c. Sergeant Major	40	35
339	18c. Spotted Jewfish	80	1·50
340	20c. Bluehead Wrasse	60	80
	w. Wmk Crown to right of CA	70·00	
341	25c. Grey Angelfish	1·00	60
342	60c. Glass-eyed Snapper	1·25	2·25
343	$1 Blue Chromis	1·75	1·75
	w. Wmk Crown to right of CA	3·75	
344	$2.50 French Angelfish	2·00	4·50
345	$3 Queen Parrotfish	2·50	4·50
346	$5 Four-eyed Butterfyfish (15.8)	2·75	6·00
330/46 Set of 17		14·50	26·00

*The normal sideways watermark shows Crown to left of CA, *as seen from the back of the stamp*.

Imprint dates: "1975", Nos. 330/46; "1977", Nos. 330, 333/8, 340.

The imprints on all the stamps show the designer's name as "Abbot".

119 St. George's Parish School (First meeting-place, 1950)

(Des R. Granger Barrett. Litho Questa)

1975 (27 Nov). 25th Anniv of Restoration of Legislative Council. T **119** and similar horiz designs. Multicoloured. W w **14** (sideways). P 14.

347	5c. Type **119**	10	10
348	25c. Legislative Council Building	20	10
349	40c. Mace and gavel	25	15
350	75c. Commemorative scroll	35	65
347/50 Set of 4		75	80

120 Copper Mine Point

(Des PAD Studio. Litho Walsall)

1976 (12 Mar). Historic Sites. T **120** and similar horiz designs. Multicoloured. W w **14** (sideways). P 14½.

351	5c. Type **120**	10	10
352	18c. Pleasant Valley	20	10
353	50c. Callwood Distillery	40	30
354	75c. The Dungeon	60	65
351/4 Set of 4		1·10	1·00

121 Massachusetts Brig *Hazard*

(Des J. W. Litho Questa)

1976 (29 May). Bicentenary of American Revolution. T **121** and similar horiz designs. Multicoloured. W w **14** (sideways). P 14.

355	8c. Type **121**	30	15
356	22c. American Privateer *Spy*	45	20
357	40c. *Raleigh* (American frigate)	55	60
358	75c. Frigate *Alliance* and H.M.S. *Trepassy*	80	1·25
355/8 Set of 4		1·90	2·00
MS359 114×89 mm. Nos. 355/8		2·25	11·00

122 Government House, Tortola

(Des Walsall. Litho Questa)

1976 (29 Oct). Fifth Anniv of Friendship Day with U.S. Virgin Is. T **122** and similar multicoloured designs. W w **14** (sideways on 8 and 75c.). P 14.

360	8c. Type **122**	10	10
361	15c. Government House, St. Croix (*vert*)	10	10
362	30c. Flags (*vert*)	15	10
363	75c. Government seals	50	40
360/3 Set of 4		55	60

123 Royal Visit, 1966

(Des J. Cooter. Litho Walsall)

1977 (7 Feb). Silver Jubilee. T **123** and similar vert designs (inscr "SILVER JUBILEE" at top). Multicoloured. W w **14**. P 13½.

364	8c. Type **123**	10	10
365	30c. The Holy Bible	15	15
366	60c. Presentation of Holy Bible	25	40
364/6 Set of 3		40	50

For stamps with different inscription, see Nos. 371/3.

The imprint at the stamp's foot gives the designer (wrongly) as "Waddington Studio".

124 Chart of 1739

(Des J. Cooter. Litho Walsall)

1977 (13 June). 18th-Century Maps. T **124** and similar horiz designs. Multicoloured. W w **14**. P 13½.

367	8c. Type **124**	40	10
368	22c. French Map, 1758	55	30
369	30c. Map from English and Danish surveys, 1775	65	65
370	75c. Map of 1779	85	1·50
367/70 Set of 4		2·25	2·25

1977 (26 Oct). Royal Visit. Designs as Nos. 364/6 but inscr "SILVER JUBILEE ROYAL VISIT" at top, and face-values changed.

371	5c. Type **123**	10	10
372	25c. The Holy Bible	20	10
373	50c. Presentation of Holy Bible	35	25
	w. Wmk inverted	6·00	6·50
371/3 Set of 3		55	35

The above also differ from Nos. 364/6 in having the silver frame removed and the silver lettering replaced by white. The imprint at foot now has the designer's name correctly given as "J. E. Cooter".

125 Divers checking Equipment

126 Fire Coral

BRITISH VIRGIN ISLANDS

(Des J.W. Litho Rosenbaum Bros, Vienna)

1978 (10 Feb). Tourism. T **125** and similar vert designs. Multicoloured. W w **14**. P 13½.

374	½c. Type **125**		10	10
	w. Wmk inverted		9·00	
375	5c. Cup coral on wreck of *Rhone*		20	10
	w. Wmk inverted		1·00	
376	8c. Sponge formation on wreck of *Rhone*		25	10
	w. Wmk inverted		1·00	
377	22c. Cup coral and sponges		45	15
	w. Wmk inverted		1·00	
378	30c. Sponges inside cave		60	20
	w. Wmk inverted		1·25	
379	75c. Marine life		90	85
	w. Wmk inverted		2·00	
374/9 Set of 6			2·25	1·25

(Des G. Drummond. Litho Harrison)

1978 (27 Feb). Corals. T **126** and similar horiz designs. Multicoloured. W w **14** (sideways). P 14.

380	8c. Type **126**	25	15
381	15c. Staghorn coral	40	30
382	40c. Brain coral	75	85
383	75c. Elkhorn coral	1·50	1·60
380/3 Set of 4		2·50	2·50

127 Iguana

(Des Jennifer Toombs. Litho Questa)

1978 (2 June). 25th Anniv of Coronation. T **127** and similar vert designs. P 15.

384	50c. brown-ochre, green and silver	20	40
	a. Sheetlet. Nos. 384/6×2	1·00	2·00
385	50c. multicoloured	20	40
386	50c. brown-ochre, green and silver	20	40
384/6 Set of 3		55	1·10

Designs:—No. 384, Plantagenet Falcon; No. 385, Queen Elizabeth II; No. 386, Type **127**.

128 Lignum Vitae

(Des and litho J.W.)

1978 (4 Sept). Flowering Trees. T **128** and similar horiz designs. Multicoloured. W w **14** (sideways*). P 13.

387	8c. Type **128**	15	10
388	22c. Ginger Thomas	20	15
389	40c. Dog Almond	30	20
390	75c. White Cedar	45	70
387/90 Set of 4		1·00	1·00
MS391 131×95 mm. Nos. 387/90. P 14		1·00	3·00
	w. Wmk Crown to left of CA	65·00	

*The normal sideways watermark shows Crown to right of CA, as seen from the back of the stamp.

129 *Eurema lisa*

(Des G. Hutchins. Litho Questa)

1978 (4 Dec). Butterflies. T **129** and similar horiz designs. Multicoloured. W w **14** (sideways). P 14.

392	5c. Type **129**	25	10
393	22c. *Agraulis vanillae*	40	20
394	30c. *Heliconius charithonia*	1·10	30
395	75c. *Hemiargus hanno*	1·40	1·25
392/5 Set of 4		2·75	1·60
MS396 159×113 mm. No. 392×6 and 393×3		2·00	5·50

130 Spiny Lobster

(Des Picton Print. Litho Harrison)

1979 (10 Feb). Wildlife Conservation. T **130** and similar multicoloured designs. W w **14** (sideways on 5 and 22c.). P 14.

397	5c. Type **130**	15	10
398	15c. Large Iguana (*vert*)	25	10
399	22c. Hawksbill Turtle	40	15
400	75c. Black Coral (*vert*)	75	90
397/400 Set of 4		1·40	1·10
MS401 130×153 mm. Nos. 397/400 (wmk sideways)		1·40	3·75

131 Strawberry Cactus   **132** West Indian Girl

(Des BG Studio. Litho Format)

1979 (7 May). Cacti. T **131** and similar vert designs. Multicoloured. W w **14**. P 14.

402	½c. Type **131**	10	10
403	5c. Snowy Cactus	15	10
404	13c. Barrel Cactus	20	20
405	22c. Tree Cactus	25	35
406	30c. Prickly Pear	30	40
407	75c. Dildo Cactus	40	1·00
402/7 Set of 6		1·10	1·90

(Des R. Granger Barrett. Litho Questa)

1979 (9 July). International Year of the Child. T **132** and similar vert designs. Multicoloured. W w **14** (inverted). P 14½×14.

408	5c. Type **132**	10	10
409	10c. African boy	10	10
410	13c. Asian girl	10	10
411	$1 European boy	50	85
408/11 Set of 4		65	1·00
MS412 91×114 mm. Nos. 408/11		70	1·50

133 1956 Road Harbour 3c. Definitive Stamp   **134** Pencil Urchin

(Des J.W. Photo Heraclio Fournier)

1979 (1 Oct). Death Centenary of Sir Rowland Hill. T **133** and similar designs showing stamps. P 13½.

413	5c. deep blue, new blue and brown-olive	10	10
414	13c. deep blue and claret	10	10
415	75c. deep blue and bright purple	45	50
413/15 Set of 3		55	60

157

BRITISH VIRGIN ISLANDS

MS416 37×91 mm. $1 deep blue & carmine-red.
P 131 .... 70 1·25
Designs: (39×27 mm)—13c. 1889 2½d.; 75c. Great Britain unissued 1910 2d. Tyrian plum. (40×28 mm)—$1. 1867 1s. "Missing Virgin" error.

(Des BG Studio. Litho Questa)

1979 (17 Dec)–82. Marine Life. Vert designs as T **134**. Multicoloured. W w **14**. Ordinary paper. P 14.

417	½c. Calcified Algae (1.4.80)	40	2·75
418	1c. Purple-tipped Sea Anemone (1.4.80)	55	2·75
419	3c. Common Starfish (1.4.80)	1·00	2·75
420	5c. Type **134**	1·25	2·25
	a. Chalk-surfaced paper (27.8.82)	75	60
421	8c. Atlantic Trumpet Triton (*Charonia variegata*)	1·25	1·75
	a. Chalk-surfaced paper (27.8.82)	1·25	60
422	10c. Christmas Tree Worms	30	1·25
423	13c. Flamingo Tongue (*Cyphoma gibbosus*) (1.4.80)	1·50	2·75
	a. Chalk-surfaced paper (27.8.82)	1·50	75
424	15c. Spider Crab	40	1·00
	a. Chalk-surfaced paper (27.8.82)	1·50	55
425	18c. Sea Squirts (1.4.80)	2·00	4·25
426	20c. True Tulip (*Fasciolaria tulipa*)	55	1·50
	a. Chalk-surfaced paper (27.8.82)	1·25	65
427	25c. Rooster-tail Conch (*Strombus gallus*)	1·25	4·00
	w. Wmk inverted		
428	30c. West Indian Fighting Conch (*Strombus pugilis*) (1.4.80)	2·50	1·50
	a. Chalk-surfaced paper (27.8.82)	2·00	1·00
429	60c. Mangrove Crab (1.4.80)	1·50	3·00
430	$1 Coral Polyps (1.4.80)	1·25	4·25
431	$2.50 Peppermint Shrimp	1·25	4·00
432	$3 West Indian Murex (*Murex brevifrons*)	1·25	4·50
433	$5 Carpet Anemone (1.4.80)	1·75	5·50
417/33 Set of 17		17·00	42·00

Imprint dates: "1979", Nos. 420/2, 424, 426/7, 431/2; "1980", Nos. 417/19, 423, 425, 428/30, 433; "1982", Nos. 420a/1a, 423a/4a, 426a, 428a.

135 Rotary Athletics Meeting, Tortola

136 Brown Booby

(Des J.W. Litho Enschedé)

1980 (23 Feb). 75th Anniv of Rotary International. T **135** and similar horiz designs. Multicoloured. W w **14** (sideways). P 13½×14.

434	8c. Type **135**	10	10
435	22c. Paul P. Harris (founder) and Rotary emblem	15	10
436	60c. "Creation of a National Park", Mount Sage, Tortola	30	40
437	$1 Rotary anniversary emblem	55	75
434/7 Set of 4		1·00	1·25
MS438 149×148 mm. Nos. 434/7		1·00	3·75

(Des K. Penny. Litho Secura, Singapore)

1980 (6 May). "London 1980" International Stamp Exhibition. Birds. T **136** and similar horiz designs. Multicoloured. W w **14** (sideways*). P 13½.

439	20c. Type **136**	20	20
	aw. Wmk Crown to right of CA		
	b. Wmk upright	40	50
	bw. Wmk inverted	50	60
440	25c. Magnificent Frigate Bird	25	25
	b. Wmk upright	1·25	2·00
	bw. Wmk inverted	1·75	2·00
441	50c. White-tailed Tropic Bird	40	40
	b. Wmk upright	65	75
	bw. Wmk inverted	80	90
442	75c. Brown Pelican	55	55
	w. Wmk Crown to right of CA	5·00	
439/42 Set of 4		1·25	1·25
MS443 152×130 mm. Nos. 439/42		1·25	2·25
	w. Wmk Crown to left of CA	16·00	

*The normal sideways watermark shows Crown to left of CA on the sheet stamps and to right of CA on the miniature sheet; *both as seen from the back*. Singles of Nos. 439aw and 442w cannot be identified as the listed variety unless part of the sheet margin is attached to distinguish them from stamps originating in No. **MS**443.

(**137**)

138 Sir Francis Drake

1980 (7 July). Caribbean Commonwealth Parliamentary Association Meeting, Tortola. Nos. 414/15 optd wth T **137**.

444	13c. deep blue and claret	15	10
445	75c. deep blue and bright blue	40	40

(Des Franklin Mint. Litho Questa)

1980 (26 Sept). Sir Francis Drake Commemoration. T **138** and similar vert designs. Multicoloured. W w **14** (inverted on 75c.). P 14×14½.

446	8c. Type **138**	60	10
447	15c. Queen Elizabeth I	80	15
448	30c. Drake receiving knighthood	1·00	30
449	75c. *Golden Hind* and coat of arms	1·90	1·25
446/9 Set of 4		3·75	1·60
MS450 171×121 mm. Nos. 446/9. Wmk inverted		3·75	6·50
	a. 75c. value in miniature sheet imperf	£225	
	b. 30c. value in miniature sheet imperf	£225	

139 Jost van Dyke

(Des Jennifer Toombs. Litho Rosenbaum Bros, Vienna)

1980 (1 Dec). Island Profiles. T **139** and similar horiz designs. Multicoloured. W w **14** (sideways*). P 13½.

451	2c. Type **139**	10	10
	w. Wmk Crown to right of CA	10	10
452	5c. Peter Island	10	10
	w. Wmk Crown to right of CA	10	10
453	13c. Virgin Gorda	15	10
	w. Wmk Crown to right of CA	20	20
454	22c. Anegada	20	10
	w. Wmk Crown to right to CA	30	30
455	30c. Norman Island	25	15
	w. Wmk Crown to right of CA	45	45
456	$1 Tortola	70	1·00
	w. Wmk Crown to right of CA	1·10	1·10
451/6 Set of 6		1·25	1·10
MS457 95×88 mm. No. 456 (wmk upright)		85	1·50
	a. Error. Imperf	£750	
	b. Gold and black omitted	£750	
	w. Wmk inverted	1·25	

The normal sideways watermark shows Crown to left of CA, *as seen from the back of the stamp*.

140 Dancing Lady

141 Wedding Bouquet from British Virgin Islands

BRITISH VIRGIN ISLANDS

(Des C. Abbott. Litho Walsall)

1981 (3 Mar). Flowers. T **140** and similar vert designs. Multicoloured. W w **14** (sideways). P 11.
458	5c. Type **140**	10	10
459	20c. Love in the Mist	15	15
460	22c. *Pitcairnia angustifolia*	15	15
461	75c. Dutchman's Pipe	35	65
462	$1 Maiden Apple	35	80
458/62	Set of 5	1·00	1·60

(Des J.W. Litho Harrison)

1981 (22 July). Royal Wedding. T **141** and similar vert designs. Multicoloured. W w **14**. P 14.
463	10c. Type **141**	10	10
	w. Wmk inverted	2·50	
464	35c. Prince Charles and Queen Elizabeth the Queen Mother in Garter robes	20	15
	w. Wmk inverted	3·00	
465	$1.25 Prince Charles and Lady Diana Spencer	60	80
463/5	Set of 3	80	90

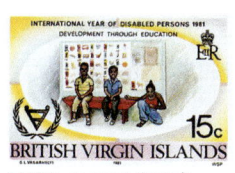

142 Stamp Collecting

143 "Development through Education"

(Des BG Studio. Litho Questa)

1981 (10 Oct). 25th Anniv of Duke of Edinburgh Award Scheme. T **142** and similar vert designs. Multicoloured. W w **14**. P 14.
466	10c. Type **142**	10	10
467	15c. Athletics	10	10
468	50c. Camping	25	25
469	$1 Duke of Edinburgh	40	45
466/9	Set of 4	65	80

(Des G. Vasarhelyi. Litho Walsall)

1981 (19 Oct). International Year for Disabled Persons. T **143** and similar horiz designs. Multicoloured. W w **14** (sideways). P 14.
470	15c. Type **143**	15	15
471	20c. Fort Charlotte Children's Centre	15	20
472	30c. "Developing cultural awareness"	20	30
473	$1 Fort Charlotte Children's Centre (*different*)	60	1·25
470/3	Set of 4	1·00	1·75

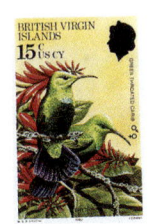

144 Detail from "The Adoration of the Shepherds" (Rubens)

145 Green-throated Caribs and Erythrina

(Des J. W. Litho Questa)

1981 (30 Nov). Christmas. T **144** and similar designs showing details from "The Adoration of the Shepherds" by Rubens. W w **14**. P 14.
474	5c. multicoloured	15	10
475	15c. multicoloured	25	10
476	30c. multicoloured	45	15
477	$1 multicoloured	1·10	1·10
474/7	Set of 4	1·75	1·25
MS478	117×90 mm. 50c. multicoloured (*horiz*) (wmk sideways)	2·00	1·00

(Des Walsall. Litho Format)

1982 (5 Apr). Hummingbirds. T **145** and similar vert designs. Multicoloured. W w **14**. P 14×14½.
479	15c. Type **145**	50	15
480	30c. Green-throated Carib and Bougainvillea	60	45
481	35c. Antillean Crested Hummingbirds and *Granadilla passiflora*	70	55
482	$1.25 Antillean Crested Hummingbird and Hibiscus	1·75	3·00
479/82	Set of 4	3·25	3·75

146 "People caring for People"

147 Princess at Victoria and Albert Museum, November 1981

(Des Harrison. Litho Format)

1982 (3 May). Tenth Anniv of Lions Club of Tortola. T **146** and similar horiz designs. Multicoloured. W w **14** (sideways). P 13½×14.
483	10c. Type **146**	15	10
484	20c. Tortola Headquarters	20	15
485	30c. "We Serve"	25	15
486	$1.50 "Lions" symbol	60	1·00
483/6	Set of 4	1·10	1·25
MS487	124×102 mm. Nos. 483/6	1·75	4·25

(Des C. Abbott. Litho Harrison)

1982 (2 July*). 21st Birthday of Princess of Wales. T **147** and similar vert designs. Multicoloured. W w **14**. P 14½×14.
488	10c. British Virgin Islands coat of arms	15	10
489	35c. Type **147**	25	15
490	50c. Bride and groom proceeding into Vestry	35	35
491	$1.50 Formal portrait	80	1·10
488/91	Set of 4	1·40	1·50

*This is the local release date. The Crown Agents released the stamps on 1 July.

148 Douglas DC-3

(Des A. Theobald. Litho Questa)

1982 (10 Sept). Tenth Anniv of Air BV1. T **148** and similar horiz designs. Multicoloured. W w **14** (sideways). P 14.
492	10c. Type **148**	45	15
493	15c. Britten Norman Islander	60	20
494	60c. Hawker Siddeley H.S.748	1·10	75
495	75c. Runway scene	1·25	90
492/5	Set of 4	3·00	1·75

149 Scouts raising Flag

(Des R. Vigurs. Litho Questa)

1982 (18 Nov). 75th Anniv of Boy Scout Movement ($1) and 50th Anniv of Scouting in B.V.I. (others). T **149** and similar horiz designs. Multicoloured. W w **14** (sideways*). P 14.
496	8c. Type **149**	20	10
497	20c. Cub Scout	30	25
498	50c. Sea Scout	40	55
	w. Wmk Crown to right of CA	15·00	
499	$1 First camp, Brownsea Island, and portrait of Lord Baden-Powell	70	1·50
	w. Wmk Crown to right of CA	15·00	
496/9	Set of 4	1·40	2·10

*The normal sideways watermark shows Crown to left of CA, *as seen from the back of the stamp.*

BRITISH VIRGIN ISLANDS

150 Legislature in Session
151 Florence Nightingale 

(Des G. Vasarhelyi. Litho Enschedé)

1983 (10 Mar). Commonwealth Day. T **150** and similar horiz designs. Multicoloured. W w **14** (sideways). P 13×13½.

500	10c. Type **150**		10	10
501	30c. Tourism		25	20
502	35c. Satellite view of Earth showing Virgin Islands		25	25
503	75c. B.V.I. and Commonwealth flags		70	90
500/3	Set of 4		1·10	1·25

(Des L. Curtis. Litho Questa)

1983 (9 May). Nursing Week. T **151** and similar multicoloured designs. W w **14** (sideways on 60c. and 75c.). P 14.

504	10c. Type **151**	60	15
505	30c. Staff nurse and assistant nurse	1·00	45
506	60c. Public Health nurses testing blood pressure (*horiz*)	1·90	1·25
507	75c. Peebles Hospital (*horiz*)	1·90	1·75
504/7	Set of 4	4·75	3·25

152 Frame Construction

(Des R. Burnett. Litho Harrison)

1983 (25 July). Traditional Boat-building. T **152** and similar horiz designs. Multicoloured. W w **14** (sideways). P 14.

508	15c. Type **152**	25	25
509	25c. Planking	30	45
510	50c. Launching	50	80
511	$1 Maiden voyage	65	1·75
508/11	Set of 4	1·50	3·00
MS512	127×101 mm. Nos. 508/11	1·50	3·75

153 Grumman G-21 Goose Amphibian
154 "Madonna and Child with the Infant Baptist" 

(Des Walsall. Litho Questa)

1983 (15 Sept). Bicentenary of Manned Flight. T **153** and similar horiz designs. Multicoloured. W w **14** (sideways). P 14.

513	10c. Type **153**	20	15
514	30c. Riley Turbo Skyliner	45	45
515	60c. Embraer EMB-110 Bandeirante	65	85
516	$1.25 Hawker Siddeley H.S.748	90	1·60
513/16	Set of 4	2·00	2·75

(Des M. Joyce. Litho Questa)

1983 (7 Nov). Christmas. 500th Birth Anniv of Raphael. T **154** and similar vert designs showing details of different paintings. Multicoloured. W w **14**. P 14½×14.

517	8c. Type **154**	10	10
518	15c. "Belle Jardinière"	20	15
519	50c. "Madonna Del Granduca"	50	60
520	$1 "The Terranuova Madonna"	90	1·10
517/20	Set of 4	1·50	1·75
MS521	108×101 mm. Nos. 517/20	2·25	3·50

155 Local Tournament
156 Port Purcell 

(Des L. Curtis. Litho Questa)

1984 (20 Feb). 60th Anniv of World Chess Federation. T **155** and similar multicoloured designs. W w **14** (sideways on 10c. and $1, inverted on 35c.). P 14.

522	10c. Type **155**	1·00	40
523	35c. Staunton chess pieces (*vert*)	2·00	1·50
524	75c. Karpov's winning position, 1980 Chess Olympiad (*vert*)	3·75	4·25
525	$1 B.V.I. Gold Medal won by Bill Hook at 1980 Chess Olympiad	4·25	5·50
522/5	Set of 4	10·00	10·50

(Des L. Curtis. Litho Questa)

1984 (16 Apr). 250th Anniv of *Lloyd's List* (newspaper). T **156** and similar vert designs. Multicoloured. W w **14**. P 14½×14.

526	15c. Type **156**	35	30
527	25c. Boeing 747-100	60	50
528	50c. Wreck of *Rhone* (mail steamer), 1867	1·00	95
529	$1 *Booker Viking* (cargo liner)	1·75	1·60
526/9	Set of 4	3·25	3·00

157 Mail Ship *Boyne*, Boeing 747-100 and UPU Logo

(Des L. Curtis. Litho Walsall)

1984 (16 May). Universal Postal Union Congress, Hamburg. Sheet 90×69 mm. W w **14** (sideways). P 14.

MS530	**157** $1 pale blue and black	2·25	2·50

158 Running
159 Steel Band 

(Des R. Granger Barrett. Litho Walsall)

1984 (3 July). Olympic Games, Los Angeles. T **158** and similar horiz designs. Multicoloured. W w **14** (sideways*). P 14.

531	15c. Type **158**	40	40
	a. Pair. Nos. 531/2	80	80
	aw. Wmk Crown to right of CA	6·00	
532	15c. Runner	40	40
533	20c. Wind-surfing	40	45
	a. Pair. Nos. 533/4	80	90
534	20c. Surfer	40	45
535	30c. Sailing	45	65
	a. Pair. Nos. 535/6	90	1·25
536	30c. Yacht	45	65
531/6	Set of 6	2·25	2·75
MS537	97×69 mm. $1 Torch bearer. Wmk upright	1·50	1·90

*The normal sideways watermark shows Crown to left of CA, *as seen from the back of the stamp*.

Nos. 531/2, 533/4 and 535/6 were printed together, *se-tenant*, in horizontal and vertical pairs throughout the sheets.

160

BRITISH VIRGIN ISLANDS

(Des D. Miller. Litho Format)

1984 (14 Aug). 150th Anniv of Abolition of Slavery. T **159** and similar vert designs showing various aspects of Emancipation Festival. Multicoloured. W w **14**. P 14.

538	10c. Type **159**	30	35
	a. Horiz strip of 5. Nos. 538/42	1·40	1·60
539	10c. Dancing girls	30	35
540	10c. Men in traditional costumes	30	35
541	10c. Girl in traditional costume	30	35
542	10c. Festival Queen	30	35
543	30c. Green and yellow dinghies	45	50
	a. Horiz strip of 5. Nos. 543/7	2·00	2·25
544	30c. Blue and red dinghies	45	50
545	30c. White and blue dinghies	45	50
546	30c. Red and yellow dinghies	45	50
547	30c. Blue and white dinghies	45	50
538/47 Set of 10		3·25	3·75

Nos. 538/42 and 543/7 were each printed together, *se-tenant*, in horizontal strips of 5 throughout the sheet, forming composite designs. On Nos. 543/7 the sail colours of the dinghies are described to assist identification.

160 Sloop

(Des R. Burnett. Litho J.W.)

1984 (15 Nov). Boats. T **160** and similar horiz designs. Multicoloured. W w **14** (sideways). P 13×13½.

548	10c. Type **160**	40	20
549	35c. Fishing boat	60	65
550	60c. Schooner	75	1·25
551	75c. Cargo boat	75	1·60
548/51 Set of 4		2·25	3·25
MS552 125×90 mm. Nos. 548/51. P 14		1·50	4·00

161 One Cent Coin and Aerial View

162 Red-billed Tropic Bird

(Litho Walsall)

1985 (15 Jan). New Coinage. T **161** and similar horiz designs showing coins and local scenery. Multicoloured. W w **14** (sideways). P 14½.

553	1c. Type **161**	10	10
554	5c. Five cent coin and boulders on beach	10	10
555	10c. Ten cent coin and scuba diving	20	20
556	25c. Twenty-five cent coin and yachts	45	50
557	50c. Fifty cent coin and jetty	90	1·25
558	$1 One dollar coin and beach at night	1·75	2·25
553/8 Set of 6		3·00	4·00
MS559 103×156 mm. Nos. 553/8		3·00	7·00

A set of stamps, 55c. and $1.50 each×2, showing Michael Jackson the entertainer was prepared in 1985, but was never released for postal use. Samples of the $1.50 values were, however, distributed for publicity purposes and both values exist from stock dispersed by the liquidator of Format International Security Printers Ltd.

(Des N. Arlott. Litho Questa)

1985 (3 July). Birds of the British Virgin Islands. T **162** and similar vert designs. Multicoloured. W w **14**. "1985" imprint date. P 14.

560	1c. Type **162**	1·25	2·50
561	2c. Yellow-crowned Night Heron	1·25	2·50
562	5c. Mangrove Cuckoo	1·75	2·00
563	8c. Northern Mockingbird	1·75	3·00
564	10c. Grey Kingbird	2·00	75
565	12c. Red-necked Pigeon	2·25	1·50
566	15c. Least Bittern	2·75	1·00
567	18c. Smooth-billed Ani	3·00	3·50
568	20c. Clapper Rail	2·75	1·00
569	25c. American Kestrel	3·25	1·75
570	30c. Pearly-eyed Thrasher	2·75	1·75
571	35c. Bridled Quail Dove	3·25	1·75
572	40c. Green Heron	3·25	1·75
573	50c. Scaly-breasted Ground Dove	3·50	3·50
574	60c. Little Blue Heron	4·00	5·00
575	$1 Audubon's Shearwater	5·50	5·50
576	$2 Blue-faced Booby	5·50	8·50
577	$3 Cattle Egret	7·50	13·00
578	$5 Zenaida Dove	9·00	15·00
560/78 Set of 19		55·00	65·00

For these stamps watermarked w **16** see Nos. 647/60.

IMPERFORATES AND MISSING COLOURS. Various issues between Nos. 579 and 609 exist either imperforate or with colours omitted. Many originate from stock dispersed by the liquidator of Format International Security Printers Ltd. Such items are not listed as there is no evidence that they fulfil the criteria outlined on page x of this catalogue.

163 The Queen Mother at Festival of Remembrance

164 Seaside Sparrow

(Des Maxine Marsh. Litho Format)

1985 (26 Aug). Life and Times of Queen Elizabeth the Queen Mother. Various vertical portraits as T **163**. Multicoloured. P 12½.

*A. W w **15** (sideways).*

579A	10c. Type **163**	5·50	5·50
	a. Horiz pair. Nos. 579A/80A	20	40
580A	10c. At Victoria Palace Theatre, 1984	10	20
581A	25c. At the engagement of the Prince of Wales, 1981	5·50	5·50
	a. Horiz pair. Nos. 581A/2A	30	80
582A	25c. Opening Celia Johnson Theatre, 1985	15	40
583A	50c. The Queen Mother on her 82nd birthday	6·50	6·50
	a. Horiz pair. Nos. 583A/4A	40	1·40
584A	50c. At the Tate Gallery, 1983	20	70
585A	75c. At the Royal Smithfield Show, 1983	6·50	6·50
	a. Horiz pair. Nos. 585A/6A	50	2·00
586A	75c. Unveiling Mountbatten statue, 1983	25	1·00
579A/86A Set of 8		1·25	4·25
MS587A 85×114 mm. $1 At Columbia University; $1 At a Wedding, St Margaret's Westminster, 1983		85	4·00

B. No wmk.

579B	10c. Type **163**	2·75	2·75
	a. Horiz pair. Nos. 579B/80B	5·50	5·50
580B	10c. At Victoria Palace Theatre, 1984	2·75	2·75
581B	25c. At the engagement of the Prince of Wales, 1981	2·75	2·75
	a. Horiz pair. Nos. 581B/2B	5·50	5·50
582B	25c. Opening Celia Johnson Theatre, 1985	2·75	2·75
583B	50c. The Queen Mother on her 82nd birthday	3·25	3·25
	a. Horiz pair. Nos. 583B/4B	6·50	6·50
584B	50c. At the Tate Gallery, 1983	3·25	3·25
585B	75c. At the Royal Smithfield Show, 1983	3·25	3·25
	a. Horiz pair. Nos. 585B/6B	6·50	6·50
586B	75c. Unveiling Mountbatten statue, 1983	3·25	3·25
579B/86B Set of 8		22·00	22·00

The two designs of each value were issued, *se-tenant*, in horizontal pairs within the sheets.

Each *se-tenant* pair shows a floral pattern across the bottom of the portraits which stops short of the lefthand edge on the left-hand stamp and of the right-hand edge on the right-hand stamp.

Sets of four miniature sheets, containing the two designs of each value, were prepared, but not issued. Examples exist from stock dispersed by the liquidator of Format International Security Printers Ltd.

Designs as Nos. 583/4 and 585/6, but with face values of $2.50×2 and $1×2, also exist in additional miniature sheets from a restricted printing issued 18 December 1985.

(Des R. Vigurs. Litho Format)

1985 (17 Dec). Birth Bicentenary of John J. Audubon (ornithologist). T **164** and similar vert designs, showing original paintings. Multicoloured. P 15.

588	5c. Type **164**	30	20
589	30c. Passenger Pigeon	40	70

161

BRITISH VIRGIN ISLANDS

590	50c. Yellow-breasted Chat	45	1·75
591	$1 American Kestrel	50	2·75
588/91 Set of 4		1·50	4·75

165 S.V. *Flying Cloud*

(Des G. Drummond. Litho Format)

1986 (27 Jan). Visiting Cruise Ships. T **165** and similar horiz designs. Multicoloured. W w **15**. P 15.

592	35c. Type **165**	80	85
	w. Wmk inverted	10·00	
593	50c. M.V. *Newport Clipper*	1·10	1·50
	w. Wmk inverted	9·00	
594	75c. M.V. *Cunard Countess*	1·10	2·50
595	$1 M.V. *Sea Goddess*	1·25	3·00
	w. Wmk inverted	17·00	
592/5 Set of 4		3·75	7·00

INAUGURAL FLIGHT
(166)

1986 (17 Apr). Inaugural Flight of Miami–Beef Island Air Service. Nos. 581/2 and 585/6 optd with T **166**.

A. W w **15** *(sideways).*

596A	25c. At the engagement of the Prince of Wales, 1981	4·00	6·00
	a. Horiz pair. Nos. 596A/7A	80	1·00
597A	25c. Opening Celia Johnson Theatre, 1985	40	50
598A	75c. At the Royal Smithfield Show, 1983	4·50	8·00
	a. Horiz pair. Nos. 598A/9A	2·50	3·00
599A	75c. Unveiling Mountbatten statue, 1983	1·25	1·50
596A/9A Set of 4		3·00	3·50

B. No wmk.

596B	25c. At the engagement of the Prince of Wales, 1981	2·00	3·00
	a. Horiz pair. Nos. 596B/7B	4·00	6·00
597B	25c. Opening Celia Johnson Theatre, 1985	2·00	3·00
598B	75c. At the Royal Smithfield Show, 1983	2·25	4·00
	a. Horiz pair. Nos. 598B/9B	4·50	8·00
599B	75c. Unveiling Mountbatten statue, 1983	2·25	4·00
596B/9B Set of 4		7·50	12·50

167 Queen Elizabeth II in 1958

(Des Court House Studio. Litho Format)

1986 (21 Apr). 60th Birthday of Queen Elizabeth II. T **167** and similar multicoloured designs. P 12½.

600	12c. Type **167**	15	20
	a Wmk w 15 (sideways)		
601	35c. At a Maundy Service	20	45
	a. Wmk w **15** (sideways)	2·00	
602	$1.50 Queen Elizabeth	45	1·75
	a. Wmk w **15** (sideways)	3·25	
603	$2 During a visit to Canberra, 1982 (*vert*)	60	2·25
600/3 Set of 4		1·25	4·25
MS604 85×115 mm $3 Queen with bouquet		3·50	6·00

Examples of the 12c., 35c. and $1.50 values with the blue (ribbons and frame) omitted are from stock dispersed by the liquidator of Format International Security Printers Ltd.

Unissued sets of five miniature sheets, each containing one value, come from the same source.

168 Miss Sarah Ferguson

(Des Court House Studio. Litho Format)

1986 (23-15 July-Oct). Royal Wedding. T **168** and similar multicoloured designs. P 12½.

605	35c. Type **168**	30	70
	a. Pair. Nos. 605/6	60	1·40
	b. Wmk w **15**	2·00	
	ba. Pair. Nos. 605/6b	4·00	
606	35c. Prince Andrew and Miss Sarah Ferguson	30	70
	b. Wmk w **15**	2·00	
607	$1 Prince Andrew in morning dress (*horiz*)	50	1·25
	a. Pair. Nos. 607/8	1·00	2·50
608	$1 Miss Sarah Ferguson (*different*) (*horiz*)	50	1·25
605/8 Set of 4		1·40	3·50
MS609 115×85 mm. $4 Duke and Duchess of York in carriage after wedding (*horiz*) (15.10.86)		2·00	6·00

Nos. 605/6 and 607/8 were each printed together, *se-tenant*, in horizontal and vertical pairs throughout the sheets.

Nos. 605/8 imperforate come from souvenir stamp booklets.

Nos. 605/8 overprinted "Congratulations to T.R.H. The Duke & Duchess of York" were not issued.

169 Harvesting Sugar Cane

(Des Toni Lance. Litho Questa)

1986 (30 July). History of Rum Making. T **169** and similar horiz designs. Multicoloured. W w **15**. P 14.

610	12c. Type **169**	1·50	45
611	40c. Bringing sugar cane to mill	1·75	1·25
612	60c. Rum distillery	2·25	3·50
613	$1 Delivering barrels of rum to ship	5·50	6·50
610/13 Set of 4		10·00	10·50
MS614 115×84 mm. $2 Royal Navy rum issue. Wmk sideways		6·50	8·50

170 C.S. *Sentinel* **171** Statue of Liberty at Sunset

(Des Court House Studio. Litho Format)

1986 (28 Oct). 20th Anniv of Cable and Wireless Caribbean Headquarters, Tortola. T **170** and similar horiz designs. Multicoloured. W w **15**. P 12½.

615	35c. Type **170**	60	80
	a. Vert pair. Nos. 615/16	1·10	1·60
616	35c. C.S. *Retriever* (1961)	60	80

162

BRITISH VIRGIN ISLANDS

617	60c. C.S. *Cable Enterprise* (1964)	75	1·50
	a. Vert pair. Nos. 617/18	1·50	3·00
618	60c. C.S. *Mercury* (1962)	75	1·50
619	75c. C.S. *Recorder* (1955)	75	1·75
	a. Vert pair. Nos. 619/20	1·50	3·50
620	75c. C.S. *Pacific Guardian* (1984)	75	1·75
621	$1 S.S. *Great Eastern* (1860's)	80	2·00
	a. Vert pair. Nos. 621/2	1·60	4·00
622	$1 C.S. *Cable Venture* (1977)	80	2·00
615/22 Set of 8		5·00	11·00

MS623 Four sheets, each 102×131 mm. (a) 40c.×2 As 35c. (b) 50c.×2 As 60c. (c) 80c.×2 As 75c. (d) $1.50×2 As $1 Set of 4 sheets .... 5·00 12·00

The two designs of each value were printed, *se-tenant*, in vertical pairs throughout the sheets.

(Des Court House Studio. Litho Format)

1986 (15 Dec). Centenary of Statue of Liberty. T **171** and similar vert views of Statue in separate miniature sheets. Multicoloured. P 14×13½.

MS624 Nine sheets, each 85×115 mm. 50c.; 75c.; 90c.; $1; $1.25; $1.50; $1.75; $2; $2.50 Set of 9 sheets .... 4·25 11·00

172 18th-century Spanish Galleon

173 Outline Map and Flag of Montserrrat

(Des J. Batchelor. Litho Questa)

1987 (15 Apr). Shipwrecks. T **172** and similar horiz designs. Multicoloured. W w **15**. P 14.

625	12c. Type **172**	2·50	55
626	35c. H.M.S. *Astrea* (frigate), 1808	3·75	1·40
627	75c. *Rhone* (mail steamer), 1867	5·50	4·50
628	$1.50 *Captain Rokos* (freighter), 1929	8·00	11·00
625/8 Set of 4		17·00	15·00
MS629 86×65 mm. $1.50, *Volvart*, 1819		16·00	15·00

(Des R. Burnett. Litho Walsall)

1987 (28 May). 11th Meeting of Organization of Eastern Caribbean States. T **173** and similar vert designs, each showing outline map and flag. Multicoloured. W w **16**. P 14.

630	10c. Type **173**	70	70
631	15c. Grenada	80	75
632	20c. Dominica	85	80
633	25c. St. Kitts-Nevis	90	1·00
634	35c. St. Vincent and Grenadines	1·40	1·00
635	50c. British Virgin Islands	2·00	2·50
636	75c. Antigua and Barbuda	2·25	3·25
637	$1 St. Lucia	2·75	3·50
630/7 Set of 8		10·50	12·00

174 Spider Lily

175 Early Mail Packet and 1867 1s. Stamp

(Des Jennifer Toombs. Litho Questa)

1987 (20 Aug). Opening of Botanical Gardens. T **174** and similar vert designs. Multicoloured. W w **16**. P 14.

638	12c. Type **174**	80	35
639	35c. Barrel Cactus	1·75	1·00
640	$1 Wild Plantain	2·75	3·25
641	$1.50 Little Butterfly Orchid	8·00	8·50
638/41 Set of 4		12·00	12·00
MS642 139×104 mm. $2.50, White Cedar		3·75	6·00

1987 (28 Oct). As Nos. 564, 566, 568/9, 571, 575 and 577 but W w **16**. "1987" imprint date. P 14.

647	10c. Grey Kingbird	1·00	1·25
649	15c. Least Bittern	2·75	1·50
651	20c. Clapper Rail	2·75	1·75
652	25c. American Kestrel	2·75	1·75
654	35c. Bridled Quail Dove	2·75	1·25
658	$1 Audubon's Shearwater	5·00	6·00
660	$3 Cattle Egret	6·50	13·00
647/60 Set of 7		21·00	24·00

(Des and litho Walsall)

1987 (17 Dec). Bicentenary of Postal Services. T **175** and similar horiz designs, each including stamp and cancellation. Multicoloured. W w **16** (sideways). P 14½.

662	10c. Type **175**	1·75	80
663	20c. Map and 1899 1d.	2·50	1·40
664	35c. Road Town Post Office and Customs House, 1913, and 1867 4d.	2·50	1·75
665	$1.50 Piper PA-23 Apache mail plane and 1964 25c. definitive	8·00	11·00
662/5 Set of 4		13·00	13·50
MS666 70×60 mm. $2.50, Mail ship, 1880's, and 1880 1d.		6·00	9·50

(Litho Questa)

1988 (11 Aug). 500th Birth Anniv of Titian (artist). Vert designs as T **238** of Antigua. Multicoloured. P 13½×14.

667	10c. "Salome"	65	55
668	12c. "Man with the Glove"	70	60
669	20c. "Fabrizio Salvaresio"	90	80
670	25c. "Daughter of Roberto Strozzi"	1·00	90
671	40c. "Pope Julius II"	1·60	2·00
672	50c. "Bishop Ludovico Beccadelli"	1·75	2·00
673	60c. "King Philip II"	1·90	2·50
674	$1 "Empress Isabella of Portugal"	2·50	2·75
667/74 Set of 8		10·00	11·00

MS675 Two sheets, each 110×95 mm. (a) $2 "Emperor Charles V at Muhlberg" (detail). (b) $2 "Pope Paul III and his Grandsons" (detail) Set of 2 sheets .... 17·00 14·00

176 de Havilland DHC-5 over Sir Francis Drake Channel and Staunton Pawn

177 Hurdling

(Des B. Bundock. Litho Questa)

1988 (25 Aug). First British Virgin Islands Open Chess Tournament. T **176** and similar horiz designs. Multicoloured. P 14.

676	35c. Type **176**	4·75	1·50
677	$1 Jose Capablanca (former World Champion) and Staunton king	9·50	8·50
MS678 109×81 mm. $2 Chess match		10·00	11·00

(Des L. Fried. Litho B.D.T.)

1988 (8 Sept). Olympic Games, Seoul. T **177** and similar horiz designs. Multicoloured. P 14.

679	12c. Type **177**	35	25
680	20c. Windsurfing	60	45
681	75c. Basketball	3·75	3·25
682	$1 Tennis	3·75	3·75
679/82 Set of 4		7·50	7·00
MS683 71×102 mm. $2 Athletics		3·00	4·50

178 Swimmer ("Don't Swim Alone")

(Des I. Arbell. Litho Questa)

1988 (26 Sept). 125th Anniv of International Red Cross. T **178** and similar designs. P 14.

684	12c. black, bright scarlet and cobalt	1·75	40
685	30c. black, bright scarlet and cobalt	2·50	80
686	60c. black, bright scarlet and cobalt	3·75	3·00
687	$1 black, bright scarlet and cobalt	4·50	4·00
684/7 Set of 4		11·00	7·50
MS688 68×96 mm. 50c.×4 black and bright scarlet		5·00	6·50

BRITISH VIRGIN ISLANDS

Designs: *Horiz*—30c. Swimmers ("No swimming during electrical storms"); 60c. Beach picnic ("Don't eat before swimming"); $1 Boat and equipment ("Proper equipment for boating"). *Vert*—50c.×4 Recovery position; clearing airway; mouth-to-mouth resuscitation; cardiac massage.

179 Princess Alexandra

(Litho Questa)

1988 (9 Nov). Visit of Princess Alexandra. T **179** and similar vert designs showing different portraits. P 14.

689	40c. multicoloured	2·75	75
690	$1.50 multicoloured	6·00	4·75
MS691	102×98 mm. $2 multicoloured	5·50	6·50

180 Brown Pelican in Flight

181 Anegada Rock Iguana

(Des S. Barlowe. Litho Questa)

1988 (30 Nov). Wildlife (1st series). Aquatic Birds. T **180** and similar multicoloured designs. P 14.

692	10c. Type **180**	1·60	50
693	12c. Brown Pelican perched on post	1·60	55
694	15c. Brown Pelican	1·75	1·10
695	35c. Brown Pelican swallowing fish	2·75	3·00
692/5 Set of 4		7·00	4·75
MS696 106×76 mm. $2 Common Shoveler (*horiz*)		12·00	9·00

No. **MS**696 is without the WWF logo.

(Des S. Barlowe. Litho Questa)

1988 (15 Dec). Wildlife (2nd series). Endangered Species. T **181** and similar multicoloured designs. P 14.

697	20c. Type **181**	1·50	75
698	40c. Virgin Gorda Dwarf Gecko	1·75	1·40
699	60c. Hawksbill Turtle	2·75	3·50
700	$1 Humpback Whale	7·50	8·00
697/700 Set of 4		12·00	12·00
MS701 106×77 mm. $2 Trunk Turtle (*vert*)		7·00	8·50

182 Yachts at Start

183 "Apollo 11" Emblem

(Des D. Miller. Litho Questa)

1989 (7 Apr). Spring Regatta. T **182** and similar multicoloured designs. P 14.

702	12c. Type **182**	45	40
703	40c. Yacht tacking (*horiz*)	1·00	1·00
704	75c. Yachts at sunset	1·60	2·50
705	$1 Yachts rounding buoy (*horiz*)	2·00	2·75
702/5 Set of 4		4·50	6·00
MS706 83×69 mm. $2 Yacht under full sail		5·50	7·00

(Des D. Miller. Litho Questa)

1989 (8 May). 500th Anniv of Discovery of America by Columbus (1992) (1st issue). Pre-Columbian Arawak Society. Multicoloured designs as T **247** of Antigua, but horiz. P 14.

707	10c. Arawak in hammock	70	45
708	20c. Making fire	1·00	50
709	25c. Making implements	1·00	60
710	$1.50 Arawak family	4·50	7·00
707/10 Set of 4		6·50	7·75
MS711 85×70 mm. $2 Religious ceremony		9·00	11·00

See also Nos. 741/5, 793/7 and 818/26.

(Des W. Hanson. Litho Questa)

1989 (28 Sept). 20th Anniv of First Manned Landing on Moon. T **183** and similar multicoloured designs. P 14.

712	15c. Type **183**	1·25	60
713	30c. Edwin Aldrin deploying scientific experiments	2·25	1·00
714	65c. Aldrin and U.S. flag on Moon	3·00	4·00
715	$1 "Apollo 11" capsule after splashdown	4·00	4·25
712/15 Set of 4		8·50	8·50
MS716 102×77 mm. $2 Neil Armstrong (38×50 *mm*). P 13½×14		9·50	10·50

184 Black Harry and Nathaniel Gilbert preaching to Slaves

185 Player tackling

(Des R. Vigurs. Litho Questa)

1989 (24 Oct). Bicentenary of Methodist Church in British Virgin Islands. T **184** and similar multicoloured designs. P 14.

717	12c. Type **184**	1·00	50
718	25c. Methodist school exercise book	1·40	75
719	35c. East End Methodist Church, 1810	1·60	85
720	$1.25 Revd John Wesley (founder of Methodism) and church youth choir	3·25	6·50
717/20 Set of 4		6·50	7·75
MS721 100×69 mm. $2 Dr. Thomas Coke		4·75	9·00

(Des R. Vigurs. Litho Questa)

1989 (6 Nov). 1990 World Cup Football Championship, Italy, 1990. T **185** and similar vert designs. Multicoloured. P 14.

722	5c. Type **185**	80	80
723	10c. Player dribbling ball	80	80
724	20c. Two players chasing ball	1·50	80
725	$1.75 Goalkeeper diving for ball	7·00	7·50
722/5 Set of 4		9·00	9·00
MS726 100×70 mm. $2 British Virgin Islands team captain		8·50	11·00

186 Princess Alexandra and Sunset House

(Litho Questa)

1990 (3 May). Stamp World London 90 International Stamp Exhibition. Royal Visitors. T **186** and similar horiz designs. Multicoloured. P 14.

727	50c. Type **186**	4·50	4·50
	a. Sheetlet. Nos. 727/30	16·00	16·00
728	50c. Princess Margaret and Government House	4·50	4·50
729	50c. Hon. Angus Ogilvy and Little Dix Bay Hotel	4·50	4·50
730	50c. Princess Diana with Princes William and Harry and Necker Island Resort	4·50	4·50
727/30 Set of 4		16·00	16·00
MS731 89×80 mm. $2 Royal Yacht *Britannia*		15·00	15·00

Nos. 727/30 were printed together, *se-tenant*, in sheetlets of four.

BRITISH VIRGIN ISLANDS

187 Audubon's Shearwater

188 Queen Elizabeth the Queen Mother

191 Tree-fern, Sage Mountain National Park

192 Haiti Haiti

(Litho Questa)

1990 (15 May). Birds. T **187** and similar multicoloured designs showing birds and eggs. P 14.

732	5c. Type **187**	1·75	1·75
733	12c. Red-necked Pigeon	2·25	60
734	20c. Moorhen ("Common Gallinule")	2·50	60
735	25c. Green Heron	2·50	60
736	40c. Yellow Warbler	2·75	1·50
737	60c. Smooth-billed Ani	3·00	2·75
738	$1 Antillean Crested Hummingbird	3·00	3·25
739	$1.25 Black-faced Grassquit	3·00	4·50
732/9	Set of 8	19·00	14·00
MS740	Two sheets, each 98×70 mm. (a) $2 Royal Tern egg (*vert*). (b) $2 Red-billed Tropic bird egg (*vert*) Set of 2 sheets	11·00	7·00

(Des Mary Walters. Litho Questa)

1990 (18 June). 500th Anniv of Discovery of America by Columbus (1992) (2nd issue). New World Natural History Fishes. Multicoloured designs as T **260** of Antigua, but horiz. P 14.

741	10c. Blue Tang	1·50	60
742	35c. Glass-eyed Snapper	2·50	70
743	50c. Slippery Dick	3·00	3·50
744	$1 Porkfish	4·50	4·75
741/4	Set of 4	10·00	8·50
MS745	100×70 mm. $2 Yellow-tailed Snapper	5·00	6·50

(Litho Questa)

1990 (30 Aug). 90th Birthday of Queen Elizabeth the Queen Mother. T **188** and similar vert designs showing recent photographs. P 14.

746	12c. multicoloured	50	25
747	25c. multicoloured	90	55
748	60c. multicoloured	1·75	2·25
749	$1 multicoloured	2·00	2·50
746/9	Set of 4	4·50	5·00
MS750	75×75 mm. $2 multicoloured	2·75	2·75

189 Footballers

190 Judo

(Litho Questa)

1990 (10 Dec). World Cup Football Championship, Italy. T **189** and similar vert designs showing footballers. P 14.

751	12c. multicoloured	60	40
752	20c. multicoloured	90	50
753	50c. multicoloured	1·75	2·00
754	$1.25 multicoloured	2·50	3·75
751/4	Set of 4	5·25	6·00
MS755	91×76 mm. $2 multicoloured	4·50	4·50

(Litho Questa)

1990 (20 Dec). Olympic Games, Barcelona (1992). T **190** and similar horiz designs. Multicoloured. P 14.

756	12c. Type **190**	1·50	45
757	40c. Yachting	2·25	1·60
758	60c. Hurdling	2·75	3·75
759	$1 Showjumping	4·50	4·50
756/9	Set of 4	10·00	9·25
MS760	78×105 mm. $2 Windsurfing	4·50	4·00

(Litho Questa)

1991 (1 Mar). 30th Anniv of National Parks Trust. T **191** and similar multicoloured designs. P 14.

761	10c. Type **191**	1·00	1·25
762	25c. Coppermine ruins, Virgin Gorda (*horiz*)	1·75	80
763	35c. Ruined windmill, Mount Healthy	1·75	80
764	$2 The Baths (rock formation), Virgin Gorda (*horiz*)	9·50	12·00
761/4	Set of 4	12·50	13·50

(Des Wendy Smith-Griswold. Litho Questa)

1991 (1 May)–**95**. Flowers. T **192** and similar vert designs. Multicoloured. Without imprint date. P 14.

765	1c. Type **192**	20	1·50
766	5c. Lobster Claw	20	1·50
767	5c. Frangipani	20	1·50
768	10c. Autograph Tree	60	1·00
769	12c. Yellow Allamanda	40	30
770	15c. Lantana	70	80
771	20c. Jerusalem Thorn	50	30
772	25c. Turk's Cap	55	40
773	30c. Swamp Immortelle	80	80
774	35c. White Cedar	90	90
775	40c. Mahoe Tree	75	65
776	45c. Pinguin	1·25	1·25
777	50c. Christmas Orchid	2·75	1·75
	a. Perf 12 (8.95)	5·50	3·50
778	70c. Lignum Vitae	1·10	2·00
779	$1 African Tulip Tree	1·25	2·00
	a. Perf 12 (8.95)	5·00	4·50
780	$2 Beach Morning Glory	4·00	6·00
	a. Perf 12 (8.95)	9·00	10·00
781	$3 Organ Pipe Cactus	4·00	7·00
	a. Perf 12½×11½(8.95)	9·00	10·00
782	$5 Tall Ground Orchid	12·00	15·00
783	$10 Ground Orchid (1.5.92)	17·00	22·00
765/83	Set of 19	45·00	60·00

No. 781a shows a larger hole on every sixth perforation, both vertically and horizontally.

Nos. 777a, 779a and 780a/1a are known to have been sold for postal purposes by the B.V.I. post offices.

For some of these designs watermarked w **14** (sideways) and with imprint date see Nos. 887/901.

193 Phoebis sennae

194 Agaricus bisporus

(Litho Questa)

1991 (28 June). Butterflies. T **193** and similar multicoloured designs. P 14.

784	5c. Type **193**	1·00	1·50
785	10c. *Dryas iulia*	1·25	1·50
786	15c. *Junonia evarete*	1·75	75
787	20c. *Dione vanillae*	1·75	1·00
788	25c. *Battus polydamus*	1·75	1·00
789	30c. *Eurema lisa*	1·90	1·00
790	35c. *Heliconius charitonius*	1·90	1·10
791	$1.50 *Siproeta stelenes*	4·75	7·00
784/91	Set of 8	14·00	13·50
MS792	Two sheets. (a) 77×117 mm. $2 *Danaus plexippus* (*horiz*). (b) 117×77 mm. $2 *Biblis hyperia* (*horiz*) Set of 2 sheets	14·00	15·00

BRITISH VIRGIN ISLANDS

(Des T. Agans. Litho Questa)

1991 (20 Sept). 500th Anniv of Discovery of America by Columbus (1992) (3rd issue). History of Exploration. Designs as T **277** of Antigua. P 14.

793	12c. multicoloured	2·00	50
794	50c. multicoloured	3·75	2·00
795	75c. multicoloured	4·50	3·25
796	$1 multicoloured	5·00	4·00
793/6 Set of 4		14·00	9·00
MS797 105×76 mm. $2 black and red-orange		9·50	9·50

Designs: *Horiz*—12c. *Vitoria* in Pacific (Magellan, 1519–21); 50c. La Salle on the Mississippi, 1682 75c. John Cabot landing in Nova Scotia, 1497–98; $1 Cartier discovering the St Lawrence, 1534. *Vert*—$2 *Santa Maria* (woodcut).

(Litho B.D.T.)

1991 (1 Nov). Death Centenary of Vincent van Gogh (artist) (1990). Multicoloured designs as T **278** of Antigua. P 13.

798	15c. "Cottage with Decrepit Barn and Stooping Woman" (*horiz*)	1·25	50
799	30c. "Paul Gauguin's Armchair"	1·75	80
800	75c. "Breton Women" (*horiz*)	3·00	3·00
801	$1 "Vase with Red Gladioli"	3·50	3·50
798/801 Set of 4		8·50	7·00
MS802 103×81 mm. $2 "Dance Hall in Arles" (detail) (*horiz*)		13·00	14·00

(Litho Walsall)

1991 (12 Dec). Christmas. Religious Paintings by Quinten Massys. Vert designs as T **291** of Antigua. Multicoloured. P 12.

803	15c. "The Virgin and Child Enthroned" (detail)	1·25	25
804	30c. "The Virgin and Child Enthroned" (different detail)	2·00	50
805	60c. "Adoration of the Magi" (detail)	3·50	3·75
806	$1 "Virgin in Adoration"	3·75	4·00
803/6 Set of 4		9·50	7·75
MS807 Two sheets, each 102×127 mm. (a) $2 "The Virgin standing with Angels"; (b) $2 "The Adoration of the Magi". P 14×14½ Set of 2 sheets		16·00	18·00

(Litho Questa)

1992 (15 Jan). Fungi. T **194** and similar multicoloured designs. P 14.

808	12c. Type **194**	1·50	55
809	30c. *Lentinula edodes* (*horiz*)	2·25	85
810	45c. *Hygrocybe acutoconica*	2·25	1·00
811	$1 *Gymnopilus chrysopellus* (*horiz*)	4·00	6·00
808/11 Set of 4		9·00	7·50
MS812 94×68 mm. $2 *Pleurotus ostreatus* (*horiz*)		12·00	13·00

(Des D. Miller. Litho Questa)

1992 (12 Mar). 40th Anniv of Queen Elizabeth II's Accession. Horiz designs as T **288** of Antigua. Multicoloured. P 14.

813	12c. Little Dix Bay, Virgin Gorda	1·25	30
814	45c. Deadchest Bay, Peter Island	2·75	90
815	60c. Pond Bay, Virgin Gorda	2·75	2·50
816	$1 Cane Garden Bay, Tortola	3·00	3·00
813/16 Set of 4		8·75	5·50
MS817 75×97 mm. $2 Long Bay, Beef Island		9·50	10·00

195 Queen Isabella of Spain

196 Basketball

(Des W. Hanson. Litho B.D.T.)

1992 (26 May). 500th Anniv of Discovery of America by Columbus (4th issue). T **195** and similar multicoloured designs. P 14.

818	10c. Type **195**	90	1·00
819	15c. Fleet of Columbus (*horiz*)	1·60	1·00
820	20c. Arms awarded to Columbus	1·60	1·25
821	30c. Landing Monument, Watling Island and Columbus' signature (*horiz*)	1·60	1·00
822	45c. Christopher Columbus	2·25	1·40
823	50c. Landing in New World and Spanish royal standard (*horiz*)	2·25	2·25
824	70c. Convent at La Rabida	2·50	3·50
825	$1.50 Replica of *Santa Maria* and Caribbean Pavilion, New York World's Fair (*horiz*)	3·75	5·50
818/25 Set of 8		15·00	15·00

MS826 Two sheets. (a) 116×86 mm. $2 Ships of second voyage at Virgin Gorda (*horiz*). (b) 86×116 mm. $2 De la Cosa's map of New World (*horiz*) Set of 2 sheets........ 15·00   17·00

(Litho Questa)

1992 (26 Oct). Olympic Games, Barcelona. T **196** and similar vert designs. Multicoloured. P 14.

827	15c. Type **196**	2·50	75
828	30c. Tennis	2·50	90
829	60c. Volleyball	2·75	3·00
830	$1 Football	3·00	3·75
827/30 Set of 4		9·50	7·50
MS831 100×70 mm. $2 Olympic flame		12·00	14·00

197 Issuing Social Security Cheque

(Litho Questa)

1993 (14 May). 25th Anniv of Ministerial Government. T **197** and similar horiz designs. Multicoloured. P 14.

832	12c. Type **197**	40	40
833	15c. Map of British Virgin Islands	1·25	70
834	45c. Administration building	80	70
835	$1.30 International currency abbreviations	2·25	4·25
832/5 Set of 4		4·25	5·50

198 Cruising Yacht and Swimmers, The Baths, Virgin Gorda

(Litho Questa)

1993 (23 July). Tourism. T **198** and similar multicoloured designs. P 14.

836	15c. Type **198**	1·50	50
837	30c. Cruising yacht under sail (*vert*)	1·75	60
838	60c. Scuba diving	2·50	2·75
839	$1 Cruising yacht at anchor and snorklers (*vert*)	2·75	3·25
836/9 Set of 4		7·50	6·25
MS840 79×108 mm. $1 Promenade (trimaran) (*vert*); $1 Scuba diving (*different*) (*vert*)		7·50	8·50

(Des Kerri Schiff. Litho Questa)

1993 (27 Aug). 40th Anniv of Coronation. Vert designs as T **307** of Antigua. P 13½×14.

841	12c. multicoloured	90	1·25
	a. Sheetlet. Nos. 841/4×2	9·50	
842	45c. multicoloured	1·25	1·50
843	60c. bluish grey and black	1·40	1·75
844	$1 multicoloured	1·60	1·90
841/4 Set of 4		4·75	5·75

Designs:—12c. Queen Elizabeth II at Coronation (photograph by Cecil Beaton); 45c. Orb; 60c. Queen with Prince Philip, Queen Mother and Princess Margaret, 1953; $1 Queen Elizabeth II on official visit.

Nos. 841/4 were printed in sheetlets of 8, containing two *se-tenant* blocks of 4.

A $2 miniature sheet showing "Queen Elizabeth II" (Sir Herbert James) was prepared, but not issued in British Virgin Islands.

200 Columbus with King Ferdinand and Queen Isabella

(Des G. Vasarhelyi. Litho Questa)

1993 (24 Sept). 500th Anniv of Discovery of Virgin Islands by Columbus. T **200** and similar horiz designs. Multicoloured. P 14.

846	3c. Type **200**	25	80

847	12c. Columbus's ship leaving port	70	40
848	15c. Blessing the fleet	75	45
849	25c. Arms and flag of B.V.I.	85	60
850	30c. Columbus and *Santa Maria*	1·00	70
851	45c. Ships of second voyage	1·25	95
852	60c. Columbus in ship's boat	1·75	2·50
853	$1 Landing of Columbus	2·25	2·75
846/53 Set of 8		8·00	8·25

MS854 Two sheets, each 120×80 mm. (a) $2 Amerindians sighting fleet. (b) $2 Christopher Columbus and ships *Set of 2 sheets* .... 13·00 14·00

201 Library Services Publications **202** Anegada Ground Iguana

1993 (20 Dec). 50th Anniv of Secondary Education and Library Services. T **201** and similar multicoloured designs. Litho. P 14×13½ (horiz) or 13½×14 (vert).

855	5c. Type **201**	65	1·50
856	10c. Secondary school sports	3·00	1·50
857	15c. Stanley Nibbs (school teacher) (*vert*)	1·25	80
858	20c. Mobile library	1·75	80
859	30c. Dr. Norwell Harrigan (adminstrator and lecturer) (*vert*)	1·75	80
860	35c. Children in library	1·75	80
861	70c. Commemorative inscription on book	2·50	3·50
862	$1 B.V.I. High School	2·75	3·50
855/62 Set of 8		14·00	12·00

(Litho Questa)

1994 (18 Mar). Endangered Species. Anegada Ground Iguana. T **202** and similar vert designs showing iguanas. P 14.

863	5c. multicoloured	90	1·25
864	10c. multicoloured	90	1·25
865	15c. multicoloured	1·00	75
866	45c. multicoloured	1·60	1·50
863/6 Set of 4		4·00	4·25
MS867 106×77 mm. $2 multicoloured		5·00	6·50

No. **MS**867 does not carry the WWF Panda emblem.

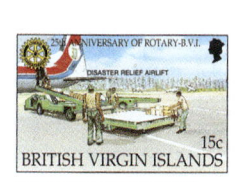

203 Loading Disaster Relief Aircraft **204** Argentina v Netherlands, 1978

(Litho Questa)

1994 (3 June). Centenary of Rotary International in B.V.I. T **203** and similar horiz designs. Multicoloured. P 14.

868	15c. Type **203**	35	35
869	45c. Training children in marine safety	85	85
870	50c. Donated operating table	90	1·00
871	90c. Paul Harris (founder and emblem)	1·60	2·50
868/71 Set of 4		3·25	4·25

(Des W. Hanson. Litho Questa)

1994 (30 Sept). 25th Anniv of First Moon Landing. Horiz designs as T **326** of Antigua. Multicoloured. P 14.

872	50c. Anniversary logo	2·00	2·25
	a. Sheetlet. Nos. 872/7	11·00	12·00
873	50c. Lunar landing training vehicle	2·00	2·25
874	50c. Launch of "Apollo 11"	2·00	2·25
875	50c. Lunar module *Eagle* in flight	2·00	2·25
876	50c. Moon's surface	2·00	2·25
877	50c. Neil Armstrong (astronaut) taking first step	2·00	2·25
872/7 Set of 6		11·00	12·00

MS878 106×76 mm. $2 Signatures and mission logo		14·00	14·00

Nos. 872/7 were printed together, *se-tenant*, in sheetlets of 6.

(Des J. Iskowitz. Litho Questa)

1994 (16 Dec). World Cup Football Championship, U.S.A. Previous Winners. T **204** and similar multicoloured designs. P 14.

879	15c. Type **204**	1·25	50
880	35c. Italy v West Germany, 1982	2·00	70
881	50c. Argentina v West Germany, 1986	2·75	2·25
882	$1.30 West Germany v Argentina, 1990	4·50	6·50
879/82 Set of 4		9·50	9·00
MS883 74×101 mm. $2 US flag and World Cup trophy (*horiz*)		12·00	14·00

1995 (1 June). As Nos. 768, 770, 773/4, 776/7, 780 and 782, but W w **14** (sideways) and with "1995" imprint date. P 14.

887	10c. Autograph Tree	50	1·40
889	15c. Lantana	65	40
892	30c. Swamp Immortelle	70	50
893	35c. White Cedar	85	55
895	45c. Pinguin	95	80
896	50c. Christmas Orchid	2·25	2·00
899	$2 Beach Morning Glory	3·00	5·50
901	$5 Tall Ground Orchid	8·50	13·00
887/901 Set of 8		16·00	22·00

204a Peugeot P4 all-purpose Field cars

(Des A. Theobald. Litho Questa)

1995 (24 Oct). 50th Anniv of United Nations. Horiz designs as T **204a**. Multicoloured. W w **16** (sideways). P 14.

903	15c. Type **204a**	45	40
904	30c. Foden medium road tanker	75	60
905	45c. SISU all-terrain vehicle	1·00	90
906	$2 Westland Lynx AH7 helicopter	3·75	5·50
903/6 Set of 4		5·50	6·75

205 Pair of Juvenile Flamingos **206** "Tortola House with Christmas Tree" (Maureen Walters)

(Des N. Arlott. Litho Cartor)

1995 (15 Nov). Anegada Flamingos Restoration Project. T **205** and similar vert designs. Multicoloured. W w **14**. P 13×13½.

907	15c. Type **205**	85	50
908	20c. Pair of adults	85	55
909	60c. Adult feeding	1·40	2·00
910	$1.45 Adult feeding chick	2·50	4·00
907/10 Set of 4		5·00	6·25
MS911 80×70 mm. $2 Chicks. P 13		6·50	7·00

(Adapted G. Vasarhelyi. Litho Walsall)

1995 (1 Dec). Christmas. Children's Paintings. T **206** and similar horiz designs. Multicoloured. W w **16** (sideways). P 13½×14.

912	12c. Type **206**	1·75	30
913	50c. "Father Christmas in Rowing Boat" (Collin Collins)	3·00	1·40
914	70c. "Christmas Tree and Gifts" (Clare Wassell)	3·25	2·75
915	$1.30 "Peace Dove" (Nicholas Scott)	4·50	6·50
912/15 Set of 4		11·00	12·00

207 Seine Fishing

BRITISH VIRGIN ISLANDS

(Des G. Vasarhelyi. Litho Cartor)

1996 (14 Feb). Island Profiles (1st series). Jost Van Dyke. T **207** and similar horiz designs. Multicoloured. W w **14** (sideways). P 13½×13.

916	15c. Type **207**	1·50	40
917	35c. Sandy Spit	1·75	55
918	90c. Map	4·00	3·50
919	$1.50 Foxy's Regatta	4·25	6·50
916/19 Set of 4		10·00	9·75

See also Nos. 1003/7.

207a Goverment House, Tortola
208 Hurdling

(Des D. Miller. Litho Cartor)

1996 (22 Apr). 70th Birthday of Queen Elizabeth II. Vert designs as T **207a**, each incorporating a different photograph of the Queen. Multicoloured. W w **14**. P 13½×14.

920	10c. Type **207a**	30	20
921	30c. Legislative Council Building	65	55
922	45c. Liner in Road Harbour	1·50	70
923	$1.50 Map of British Virgin Islands	3·25	5·00
920/3 Set of 4		5·00	5·75
MS924 63×65 mm. $2 Queen Elizabeth II. P 13×13½		3·00	3·75

(Des S. Noon. Litho Cartor)

1996 (22 May). Centenary of Modern Olympic Games. T **208** and similar horiz designs. Multicoloured. W w **14** (sideways). P 13.

925	20c. Type **208**	45	30
926	35c. Volleyball	70	60
927	50c. Swimming	1·10	1·75
928	$1 Yachting	2·00	2·75
925/8 Set of 4		3·75	4·75

209 Mercedes-Benz "500 K A", 1934

(Des R. Watton. Litho B.D.T.)

1996 (8 June). CAPEX '96 International Stamp Exhibition, Toronto. Early Motor Cars. T **209** and similar horiz designs. Multicoloured. W w **14** (sideways*). P 13½.

929	15c. Type **209**	45	30
930	40c. Citröen "12", 1934	1·00	70
931	60c. Cadillac "V-8 Sport Phaeton", 1932	1·25	1·75
	w. Wmk Crown to right of CA	2·75	
932	$1.35 Rolls Royce "Phantom II", 1934	2·75	4·00
	w. Wmk Crown to right of CA	2·75	
929/32 Set of 4		5·00	6·00
MS933 79×62 mm. $2 Ford "Sport Coupé", 1932		3·25	4·25

*The normal sideways watermark shows Crown to left of CA, *as seen from the back of the stamp*.

210 Children with Computer

(Des R. Watton. Litho Cot Printery Ltd, Barbados)

1996 (16 Sept). 50th Anniv of U.N.I.C.E.F. T **210** and similar horiz designs. Multicoloured. W w **14** (sideways). P 14×14½.

934	10c. Type **210**	40	40
935	15c. Carnival costume	50	50
936	30c. Children on Scales of Justice	80	80
937	45c. Children on beach	1·25	1·25
934/7 Set of 4		2·75	2·75

211 Young Rainbows in Art Class

(Des G. Vasarhelyi. Litho Cartor)

1996 (30 Dec). 75th Anniv of Guiding in the British Virgin Islands. T **211** and similar horiz designs. Multicoloured. W w **14** (sideways). P 13½.

938	10c. Type **211**	20	20
939	15c. Brownies serving meals	30	25
940	30c. Guides around campfire	50	45
941	45c. Rangers on parade	65	60
942	$2 Lady Baden-Powell	2·75	4·00
938/42 Set of 5		4·00	5·00

212 Spanish Mackerel

(Des A. Robinson. Litho Walsall)

1997 (6 Jan). Game Fishes. T **212** and similar horiz designs. Multicoloured. W w **16** (sideways). P 14.

943	1c. Type **212**	10	50
944	10c. Wahoo	25	80
945	15c. Great Barracuda	55	40
946	20c. Tarpon	90	40
947	25c. Tiger Shark	90	50
948	35c. Sailfish	90	40
949	40c. Dolphin	1·50	75
950	50c. Black-finned Tuna	1·50	90
951	60c. Yellow-finned Tuna	1·50	90
952	75c. King Mackerel ("Kingfish")	1·75	1·25
953	$1.50 White Marlin	3·25	3·25
954	$1.85 Amberjack	4·00	3·50
955	$2 Atlantic Bonito	4·50	4·50
956	$5 Bonefish	9·00	10·00
957	$10 Blue Marlin	16·00	19·00
943/57 Set of 15		42·00	42·00

(Des D. Miller. Litho Questa)

1997 (3 Feb). HONG KONG '97 International Stamp Exhibition. Sheet 130×90 mm, containing design as No. 953, but with "1997" imprint date. Multicoloured. W w **14** (inverted). P 14.

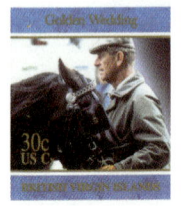

MS958 $1.50 White Marlin ... 2·00 2·75

212a Prince Phillip with Horse

(Des N. Shewring (No. **MS**965), D. Miller (others). Litho Questa (No. **MS**965), Cartor (others))

1997 (10 July). Golden Wedding of Queen Elizabeth and Prince Philip. Multicoloured designs as T **212a**. W w **14**. P 13.

959	30c. Type **212a**	70	1·00
	a. Horiz pair. Nos. 959/60	1·40	2·00
960	30c. Queen Elizabeth at Windsor, 1989	70	1·00
961	45c. Queen in phaeton, Trooping the Colour	90	1·25
	a. Horiz pair. Nos. 91/2	1·75	2·50
962	45c. Prince Philip in Scots Guards uniform	90	1·25

963	70c. Queen Elizabeth and Prince Philip at the Derby, 1993	1·25	1·60
	a. Horiz pair. Nos. 963/4	2·50	3·00
964	70c. Prince Charles playing polo, Mexico, 1993	1·25	1·60
959/64 Set of 6		5·00	7·00
MS965 110×70 mm. $2 Queen Elizabeth and Prince Philip in landau (*horiz*). Wmk sideways. P 14×14½		3·25	4·00

Nos. 959/60, 961/2 and 963/4 were each printed together, *se-tenant*, in horizontal pairs throughout the sheets with the backgrounds forming composite designs.

213 Fiddler Crab

(Des Jennifer Toombs. Litho Cartor)

1997 (11 Sept). Crabs. T **213** and similar horiz designs. Multicoloured. W w **14** (sideways). P 13.

966	12c. Type **213**	65	50
967	15c. Coral Crab	70	50
968	35c. Blue Crab	1·10	60
969	$1 Giant Hermit Crab	2·00	3·00
966/9 Set of 4		4·00	4·25
MS970 76×67 mm. $2 Arrow Crab		3·50	4·50

214 *Psychilis macconnelliae*

(Des I. Loe. Litho Cot Printery Ltd, Barbados)

1997 (26 Nov). Orchids of the World. T **214** and similar multicoloured designs. W w **14** (sideways). P 14.

971	20c. Type **214**	1·25	1·25
	a. Horiz strip of 4. Nos. 971/4	5·00	5·00
972	50c. *Tolumnia prionochila*	1·40	1·40
973	60c. *Tetramicra canaliculata*	1·40	1·40
974	75c. *Liparis elata*	1·50	1·50
971/4 Set of 4		5·00	5·00
MS975 59×79 mm. $2 *Dendrobium crumenatum* (*vert*). Wmk upright		3·25	4·25

Nos. 971/4 were printed together, *se-tenant*, in horizontal strips of four throughout the sheet.

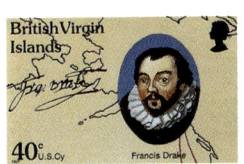

215 Sir Francis Drake and Signature

(Des E. Nisbet. Litho Questa)

1997 (13 Dec). 420th Anniv of Drake's Circumnavigation of the World. T **215** and similar horiz designs. Multicoloured. W w **14** (sideways). P 14½.

976	40c. Type **215**	1·75	1·75
	a. Sheetlet. Nos. 976/87	19·00	19·00
977	40c. Drake's coat of arms	1·75	1·75
978	40c. Queen Elizabeth I and signature	1·75	1·75
979	40c. Christopher and *Marigold*	1·75	1·75
980	40c. Golden Hind	1·75	1·75
981	40c. Swan	1·75	1·75
982	40c. *Cacafuego* (Spanish galleon)	1·75	1·75
983	40c. Elizabeth	1·75	1·75
984	40c. *Maria* (Spanish merchant ship)	1·75	1·75
985	40c. Drake's astrolabe	1·75	1·75
986	40c. Golden Hind's figurehead	1·75	1·75
987	40c. Compass rose	1·75	1·75
976/87 Set of 12		19·00	19·00
MS988 96×76 mm. $2 *Sir Francis Drake* (ketch)		3·75	4·50

Nos. 976/87 were printed together, *se-tenant*, in sheetlets of 12 with the backgrounds forming a composite map of Drake's route.

215a Princess Diana, 1992

(Des D. Miller. Litho Questa)

1998 (31 Mar). Diana, Princess of Wales Commemoration. Sheet, 145×70 mm, containing vert designs as T **215a**. Multicoloured. W w **14** (sideways). P 14½×14.

MS989 15c. Type **215a** 45c. Holding child, 1991; 70c. Laughing, 1991; $1 Wearing high-collared blouse, 1986 (*sold at $2.30+20c. charity premium*)	2·50	4·00

215b Fairey 111F (seaplane)

(Des A. Theobald. Litho Enschedé)

1998 (1 Apr). 80th Anniv of Royal Air Force. Horiz designs as T **215b**. Multicoloured. W w **14** (sideways). P 13½×14.

990	20c. Type **215b**	60	40
991	35c. Supermarine Scapa (flying boat)	85	50
992	50c. Westland Sea King H.A.R.3 (helicopter)	1·40	1·10
993	$1.50 BAe Harrier GR7	2·50	3·25
990/3 Set of 4		4·75	4·75
MS994 110×77 mm. 75c. Curtiss H.16 (flying boat); 75c. Curtiss JN-4A; 75c. Bell Airacobra; 75c. Boulton-Paul Defiant		6·50	7·00

216 Fingerprint Cyphoma    **217** "Carnival Reveller" (Rebecca Peck)

(Des Odile and J. Scheiner. Litho Questa)

1998 (20 May). Marine Life. T **216** and similar horiz designs. Multicoloured. W w **16** (sideways). P 14×14½.

995	15c. Type **216**	1·00	50
996	30c. Long-spined Sea Urchin	1·25	55
997	45c. Split Crown Feather Duster Worm	1·60	70
998	$1 Upside Down Jelly	2·50	3·75
995/8 Set of 4		5·75	5·00
MS999 77×56 mm. $2 Giant Anemone		4·75	5·00

(Adapted G. Vasarhelyi. Litho Cot Printery, Barbados)

1998 (25 Aug). Festival. Children's Paintings. T **217** and similar multicoloured designs. W w **14** (sideways on $1.30, inverted on others). P 14.

1000	30c. Type **217**	1·25	50
1001	45c. "Leader of a Troupe" (Jehiah Maduro)	1·50	65
1002	$1.30 "Steel Pans" (Rebecca McKenzie) (*horiz*)	3·50	5·00
1000/2 Set of 3		5·50	5·50

218 Salt Pond

BRITISH VIRGIN ISLANDS

(Des G. Vasarhelyi. Litho Cot Printery Ltd, Barbados)

1998 (28 Oct). Island Profiles (2nd series). Salt Island. T **218** and similar horiz designs. Multicoloured. W w **14** (sideways). P 14.

1003	12c. Type **218**	1·50	70
1004	30c. Wreck of *Rhone* (mail steamer)	2·00	75
1005	70c. Traditional house	1·75	2·25
1006	$1.45 Salt Island from the air	3·25	4·50
1003/6 Set of 4		7·75	7·50
MS1007 119×78 mm. $2 Collecting salt		7·00	8·00

219 Business Studies, Woodwork and Technology Students

(Des N. Shewring. Litho Questa)

1998 (14 Dec). Anniversaries. T **219** and similar horiz designs. Multicoloured. W w **16** (sideways). P 14.

1008	5c. Type **219**	25	75
1009	15c. Comprehensive school band	45	40
1010	30c. Chapel, Mona Campus, Jamaica	60	50
1011	45c. Anniversary plaque and University arms	75	70
1012	50c. Dr. John Coakley Lettsom and map of Little Jost Van Dyke	1·00	1·25
1013	$1 The Medical Society of London building and arms	1·50	2·50
1008/13 Set of 6		4·25	5·50

Events:—5, 15c, 30th anniv of Comprehensive Education in B.V.I.; 30, 45c, 50th anniv of University of West Indies; 50c., $1, 250th anniv of Medical Society of London.

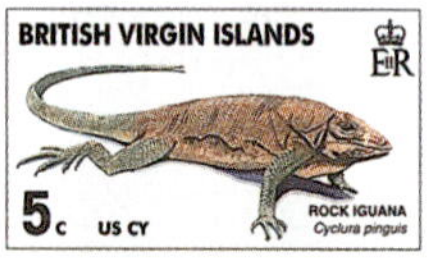

220 Rock Iguana

220a Prince Edward and Miss Sphie Rhys Jones

(Des R. Watton. Litho Enschedé)

1999 (30 Apr). Lizards. T **220** and similar horiz designs. Multicoloured. W w **14** (sideways). P 15×14.

1014	5c. Type **220**	30	65
1015	35c. Pygmy Gecko	85	45
1016	60c. Slippery Back Skink	1·50	1·50
1017	$1.50 Wood Slave Gecko	2·25	3·50
1014/17 Set of 4		4·50	5·50
MS1018 100×70 mm. 75c. Doctor Lizard; 75c. Yellow-bellied Lizard; 75c. Man Lizard; 75c. Ground Lizard		5·00	6·00

(Des D. Miller. Litho Walsall)

1999 (15 June). Royal Wedding. Vert designs as T **220a**. Multicoloured. W w **16**. P 14.

1019	20c. Type **220a**	1·00	40
1020	$3 Engagement photograph	4·75	6·00

220b "Apollo" on launch Pad

(Des N. Shewring. Litho Walsall)

1999 (20 July). 30th Anniv of first Manned Landing on Moon. Multicoloured designs as T **220b**. W w **16**. P 14×13½.

1021	10c. Type **220b**	45	60
1022	40c. Firing of second stage rockets	1·00	65
1023	50c. Lunar module on Moon	1·10	1·00
1024	$2 Astronauts transferring to command module	3·00	4·50
1021/4 Set of 4		5·00	6·00
MS1025 90×80 mm. $2.50, Earth as seen from Moon (*circular, 40 mm diam*). Wmk sideways. P 14		3·75	4·50

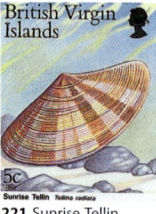

221 Sunrise Tellin

222 Zion Hill Methodist Church

(Litho Questa)

1999 (1 Nov). Sea Shells. T **221** and similar vert designs. W w **14** (sideways). Multicoloured. P 14½.

A. Without imprint date at bottom right (from se-tenant sheets of 60).

1026A	5c. Type **221**	65	90
	a. Horiz strip of 6. Nos. 1026A/31A	5·00	6·25
1027A	10c. King Helmet	65	90
1028A	25c. Measle Cowrie	80	1·00
1029A	35c. West Indian Top Shell	85	1·00
1030A	75c. Zigzag Scallop	1·25	1·50
1031A	$1 West Indian Fighting Conch	1·25	1·50
1026A/31A Set of 6		5·00	6·25

B. With "1999" imprint date at bottom right (from individual sheets of 100).

1028B	25c. Measle Cowrie	75	60
1029B	35c. West Indian Top Shell	1·00	60
1030B	75c. Zigzag Scallop	1·75	2·00
1031B	$1 West Indian Fighting Conch	2·25	2·50
1028B/31B Set of 4		5·25	5·25

Nos. 1026A/31A were printed together, *se-tenant*, in horizontal strips of 6 throughout the sheet with the backgrounds forming a composite design.

(Des Jennifer Toombs. Litho Cartor)

1999 (16 Dec). Christmas. Church Buildings. T **222** and similar horiz designs. Multicoloured. W w **14** (sideways). P 13½×13.

1032	20c. Type **222**	45	35
1033	35c. Seventh Day Adventist Church, Fat Hogs Bay, 1982	60	45
1034	50c. Ruins of St. Phillip's Anglican Church, Kingstown	85	1·00
1035	$1 St. William's Catholic Church, Road Town	1·60	2·75
1032/5 Set of 4		3·25	4·00

223 King Henry VII

223a Prince William as Baby

(Litho Walsall)

2000 (29 Feb). Stamp Show 2000 International Stamp Exhibition, London. Kings and Queens of England. T **223** and similar vert designs. Multicoloured. W w **14**. P 14.

1036	60c. Type **223**	1·10	1·25
	a. Sheetlet. Nos. 1036/41	6·00	6·75
1037	60c. Lady Jane Grey	1·10	1·25
1038	60c. King Charles I	1·10	1·25
1039	60c. King William III	1·10	1·25
1040	60c. King George III	1·10	1·25
1041	60c. King Edward VII	1·10	1·25
1036/41 Set of 6		6·00	6·75

Nos. 1036/41 were printed together, *se-tenant*, in sheetlets of 6 with an enlarged illustrated right-hand margin.

BRITISH VIRGIN ISLANDS

(Des A. Robinson. Litho Questa)

2000 (21 June). 18th Birthday of Prince William. Multicoloured designs as T **223a**. W w **14** (sideways on 40c. and 50c.). P 14½×14 (horiz) or 14×14½ (vert).

1042	20c. Type **223a**...		60	35
1043	40c. Prince William playing with ball, 1984 (vert)...		90	60
1044	50c. Skiing in British Columbia, 1998 (vert)..		1·25	1·00
1045	$1 In evening dress, 1997		2·00	2·75
1042/5	Set of 4		4·25	4·25
MS1046	175×95 mm. 60c. Prince William in 1999 (horiz) and Nos. 1042/5. Wmk sideways. P 14½.........		8·50	8·50

224 Duchess of York, 1920s

(Litho Questa)

2000 (4 Aug). Queen Elizabeth the Queen Mother's 100th Birthday. T **224** and similar square designs. Multicoloured. W w **14** (sideways). P 14.

1047	15c. Type **224**	50	25
1048	35c. As Queen Mother in 1957	1·00	1·50
1049	70c. In evening dress, 1970	1·50	1·75
1050	$1·50 With family on 99th birthday................	2·50	3·25
1047/50	Set of 4	5·00	6·00

225 Red Hibiscus

226 Sunday Morning Well (site of Emancipation Proclamation)

(Des I. Loe. Litho Enschedé)

2000 (7 Sept). Flowers. T **225** and similar vert designs. Multicoloured. W w **14** (sideways). P 13½×14.

1051	10c. Type **225**...	40	50
1052	15c. Pink Oleander.......................................	45	50
1053	35c. Yellow Bell...	1·00	55
1054	50c. Yellow and White Frangipani..................	1·25	1·00
1055	75c. Flamboyant...	1·75	2·25
1056	$2 Bougainvillea..	3·50	5·00
1051/6	Set of 6...	7·50	9·00

(Des G. Vasarhelyi. Litho Questa)

2000 (16 Nov). New Millennium. T **226** and similar multicoloured designs. W w **14** (sideways). P 14.

1057	5c. Type **226**..	15	50
1058	20c. Nurse Mary Louise Davies M.B.E.	45	35
1059	30c. Cheyney University, U.S.A......................	60	45
1060	45c. Enid Leona Scatliffe (former chief education officer)..	80	70
1061	50c. H. Lavity Stoutt Community College.......	90	1·00
1062	$1 Sir J. Olva Georges	1·60	2·25
1057/62	Set of 6..	4·00	4·50
MS1063	69×59 mm. $2 Private Samuel Hodge's Victoria Cross (vert)...	3·75	4·50

227 Dr. Q. William Osborne and Arnando Scatliffe

(Des G. Vasarhelyi. Litho Questa)

2000 (22 Nov). 50th Anniv of Restoration of Legislative Council. T **227** and similar horiz designs. Multicoloured. W w **14** (sideways). P 14.

1064	10c. Type **227**	25	50
1065	15c. H. Robinson O'Neal and A. Austin Henley.	35	50
1066	20c. Wilfred W. Smith and John C. Brudenell-Bruce................................	45	50
1067	35c. Howard R. Penn and I. G. Fonseca	65	55
1068	50c. Carlton L. de Castro and Theodohr H. Faulkner..................................	90	1·00
1069	60c. Willard W. Wheatley (Chief Minister, 1971–79)..	1·25	1·50
1070	$1 H. Lavity Stoutt (Chief Minister, 1967–71, 1979–83 and 1986–95)...................	1·60	2·25
1064/70	Set of 7...	5·00	6·00

228 White-crowned Dove

(Des T. Thackeray and A. Robinson. Litho Questa)

2001 (1 Feb). HONG KONG 2001 Stamp Exhibition. Sheet 150×90 mm containing T **228** and similar horiz design showing dove. Multicoloured. W w **14** (sideways). P 14.

MS1071	50c. Type **41**; 50c. Bar-tailed Cuckoo Dove.....	3·50	4·50

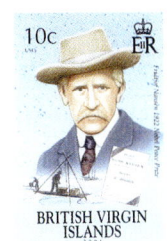

229 HMS *Wistaria* (minesweeping trawler), 1939–46

230 Fridtjof Nansen (Peace Prize, 1922)

(Des J. Batchelor. Litho Enschedé)

2001 (28 Sept). Royal Navy Ships connected to British Virgin Islands. T **229** and similar horiz designs. Multicoloured. W w **14** (sideways). P 14.

1072	35c. Type **229**	1·50	55
1073	50c. HMS *Dundee* (sloop), 1934–35	1·75	90
1074	60c. HMS *Eurydice* (frigate), 1787	1·75	1·60
1075	75c. HMS *Pegasus* (frigate), 1787	2·00	1·90
1076	$1 HMS *Astrea* (frigate), 1807	2·75	2·75
1077	$1·50 Royal Yacht *Britannia*, 1966	4·00	5·00
1072/7	Set of 6..	12·00	11·50

(Des N. Shewring. Litho Enschedé)

2001 (5 Oct). Centenary of Nobel Prize. T **230** and similar vert designs. Multicoloured. W w **14** (inverted). P 14.

1078	10c. Type **230**	70	1·00
1079	20c. Albert Einstein (Physics Prize,1921).........	80	60
1080	25c. Sir Arthur Lewis (Economic Sciences Prize, 1979)...	70	60
1081	40c. Saint-John Perse (Literature Prize, 1960)...	80	80
1082	70c. Mother Teresa (Peace Prize, 1979)	6·00	3·50
1083	$2 Christian Lous Lange (Peace Prize, 1921)...	3·75	5·00
1078/83	Set of 6...	11·50	10·50

230a Princess Elizabeth in ATS Uniform, changing Wheel

(Des A. Robinson. Litho Questa)

2002 (6 Feb). Golden Jubilee. T **230a** and similar designs. W w **14** (sideways). P 14½.

1084	15c. agate, deep mauve and gold...................	70	25
1085	50c. multicoloured......................................	1·25	1·00
1086	60c. multicoloured......................................	1·25	1·40
1087	75c. multicoloured......................................	1·50	1·75

171

BRITISH VIRGIN ISLANDS

1084/7 Set of 4	4·25	4·00

MS1088 162×95 mm. Nos. 1084/7 and $1 multicoloured. P 13½ ($1) or 14½ (others) ... 8·00 9·00

Designs: Horiz (as Type **230a**)–50c. Queen Elizabeth in fur hat, 1977; 60c. Queen Elizabeth carrying bouquet; 75c. Queen Elizabeth at banquet, Prague, 1996. Vert (38×51 mm)–$1 Queen Elizabeth after Annigoni.

Designs as Nos. 1084/7 in No. **MS**1088 omit the gold frame around each stamp and the "Golden Jubilee 1952–2002" inscription.

231 Estuarine Crocodile

(Litho Cartor)

2002 (21 June). Reptiles. T **231** and similar horiz designs. Multicoloured. W w **14** (sideways). P 13.

1089	5c. Type **231**	30	75
	a. Sheetlet. Nos. 1089/94	8·00	9·00
1090	20c. Reticulated Python	60	45
1091	30c. Komodo Dragon	80	50
1092	40c. Boa Constrictor	95	70
1093	$1 Dwarf Caiman	2·25	2·50
1094	$2 *Sphaerodactylus parthenopion* (gecko)	4·00	5·00
1089/94 Set of 6		8·00	9·00

MS1095 89×68 mm. $1.50 Head of *Sphaerodactylus parthenopion* on finger ... 3·75 4·50

Nos. 1089/94 were printed in individual sheets of 20 and also as a *se-tenant* sheetlet of 6 with the enlarged right hand margin showing details of associated Guinness World Records.

231a Duchess of York, 1920s

(Des A. Robinson. Litho Questa)

2002 (5 Aug). Queen Elizabeth the Queen Mother Commemoration. T **231a** and similar vert designs. W w **14**. P 14×14½.

1096	20c. blackish brown, gold and purple	45	30
1097	60c. multicoloured	1·25	1·00
1098	$2 black, gold and purple	3·50	3·75
1099	$3 multicoloured	4·75	5·50
1096/9 Set of 4		9·00	9·50

MS1100 145×70 mm. Nos. 1098/9. Wmk sideways. P 14½×14 ... 8·50 9·50

Designs:—60c. Queen Mother at Somerset House, 2000; $2 Lady Elizabeth Bowes-Lyon, 1920; $3 Queen Mother inspecting guard of honour.

Designs as Nos. 1098/9 in No. **MS**1100 omit the "1900–2002" inscription and the coloured frame.

(Des G. Vasarhelyi. Litho B.D.T.)

2002 (30 Aug). Royal Navy Ships connected to British Virgin Islands (2nd series). Horiz designs as T **229**. Multicoloured. W w **14** (sideways). P 14.

1101	20c. H.M.S. *Invincible* (ship of the line) re-capturing HMS *Argo* (frigate), 1783	85	55
1102	35c. H.M.S. *Boreas* and HMS *Solebay* (sailing frigates)	1·50	60
1103	50c. H.M.S. *Coventry* (frigate)	1·75	1·25
1104	$3 H.M.S. *Argyll* (frigate)	7·50	9·00
1101/4 Set of 4		10·50	10·50

(Des G. Vasarhelyi. Litho B.D.T.)

2002 (13 Sept). Island Profiles (3rd series). Virgin Gorda. Horiz designs as T **218**. Multicoloured. W w **14** (sideways). P 14.

1105	5c. Spring Bay	30	75
1106	40c. Devils Bay	1·00	55
1107	60c. The Baths	1·40	1·00
1108	75c. St. Thomas Bay	1·50	1·50
1109	$1 Savannah and Pond Bay	1·75	2·00
1110	$2 Trunk Bay	3·50	5·00
1105/10 Set of 6		8·50	9·75

232 Young West Indian Whistling Duck and Nest

233 200 Metres Race

(Des R. Gorringe. Litho Questa)

2002 (13 Dec). Birdlife International, West Indian Whistling Duck (*Dendrocygna arborea*). T **232** and similar multicoloured designs. W w **14** (sideways on vert designs). P 14×13½ (horiz) or 13½×14 (vert).

1111	10c. Type **232**	40	65
1112	35c. Adult bird on rock (*vert*)	1·00	55
1113	40c. Adult bird landing on water (*vert*)	1·00	70
1114	70c. Two adult birds	1·50	2·00
1111/14 Set of 4		3·50	3·50

MS1115 175×80 mm. Nos. 1111/14 and $2 Head of duck. Wmk sideways. P 14½ ... 6·00 7·00

Examples of Nos. 1111/14 in No. **MS**1015 omit the frame and "2002" imprint date.

(Des R. Watton. Litho B.D.T.)

2003 (14 Mar). Anniversaries and Events. T **233** and similar horiz designs. Multicoloured. W w **14** (sideways). P 13½.

1116	10c. Type **233**	50	70
	a. Horiz pair. Nos. 1116/17	1·00	1·40
1117	10c. Indoor cycling	50	70
1118	35c. Laser class dinghy racing	75	75
	a. Horiz pair. Nos. 1118/19	1·50	1·50
1119	35c. Women's long-jumping	75	75
1120	50c. Bareboat class yachts	1·00	1·25
	a. Horiz pair. Nos. 1120/1	2·00	2·50
1121	50c. Racing Cruiser class yachts	1·00	1·25
1122	$1.35 Carlos and Esme Downing (founders)	2·00	2·25
	a. Horiz pair. Nos. 1122/3	4·00	4·50
1123	$1.35 Copies of newspaper and anniversary logo	2·00	2·25
1116/23 Set of 8		7·75	9·00

Anniversaries and Events:-10c. Commonwealth Games, 2002; 35c. 20th anniv of British Virgin Islands' admission to Olympic Games; 50c. 30th anniversary of Spring Regatta; $1.35 40th anniversary of *The Island Sun* (newspaper).

Nos. 1116/17, 1118/19, 1120/1 and 1122/3 were each printed together, *se-tenant*, as horizontal pairs throughout the sheets.

233a Queen Elizabeth II

(Des A. Robinson. Litho DLR)

2003 (2 June). 50th Anniv of Coronation. T **233a** and similar horiz designs. Multicoloured. W w **14** (sideways). P 14×14½.

1124	15c. Queen Elizabeth II	75	30
1125	$5 Queen and Royal Family on Buckingham Palace balcony	8·50	9·00

MS1126 95×115 mm. As Nos. 1124/5 ... 8·00 8·50

Nos. 1124/5 have scarlet frame; stamps from **MS**1126 have no frame and country name in mauve panel.

233b Queen Elizabeth II

(Des CASB Studio. Litho BDT)

2003 (13 June). W w **14**. P 14.

1127	**233b**	$5 black, bistre and light brown	5·25	6·00

172

233c Prince William at Tidworth and Beaufort Polo Clubs, 2002

233d Douglas DC-4

(Des A. Robinson. Litho DLR)

2003 (21 June). 21st Birthday of Prince William of Wales. Multicoloured. P 14½.

(a) T 233c and similar square design. W w 14 (sideways).

1128	50c. Type **233c**	1·00	75
	a. Horiz pair. Nos. 1128/9	5·00	5·00
1129	$2 Playing polo, 2002 and at Holyrood House, 2001	4·00	4·25

Nos. 1128/9 were printed together, *se-tenant*, as horizontal pairs in sheets of ten (2×5) with enlarged illustrated left-hand margins. Nos. 1130/1 were each printed in sheets of 20.

(b) As Nos. 1128/9 but with grey frame. W w 14.

1130	50c. As No. 1128	1·00	75
1131	$2 As No. 1129	4·00	4·25

(Des J. Batchelor. Litho Enschedé)

2003 (15 Nov). Centenary of Powered Flight. T **233d** and similar horiz designs. Multicoloured. W w **14** (sideways). P 13½×14.

1132	15c. Type **233d**	70	50
1133	20c. Boeing Stearman "Kaydet"	75	50
1134	35c. North American B-25 J Mitchell	1·00	50
1135	40c. McDonnell Douglas F-4B Phantom	1·10	60
1136	70c. Boeing-Vertol CH-47 Chinook helicopter	2·00	1·75
1137	$2 Hughes AH-64 Apache helicopter	4·25	5·50
1132/7 Set of 6		8·75	8·50

Nos. 1132/7 were each printed in sheets of 20 containing vertical rows of stamps alternated with rows of illustrated half stamp-size labels.

234 Townsmen under Arcades

235 Pomegranate

(Litho BDT)

2003 (15 Dec). Christmas. "Stories from the Life of St. Ursula: Arrival of the English Ambassadors" by Carpaccio. T **234** and similar vert designs. Multicoloured. W w **14**. P 13½.

1138	20c. Type **234**	60	25
1139	40c. English ambassadors	1·00	50
1140	$2.50 King Maurus of Brittany	4·50	6·00
1138/40 Set of 3		5·50	6·00
MS1141	172×87 mm. $1 King Maurus receiving English ambassadors (35×35 mm) and Nos. 1138/40. Wmk inverted	7·50	8·50

Nos. 1138/40 show details of the painting and No. **MS**1141 the complete painting.

2004 (1 July). Game Fish. Designs as Nos. 945/6 and 948/9. Self-adhesive. Size 23×19 mm. P 12½.

1142	15c. Great Barracuda	15	20
	a. Booklet pane. Nos. 1142 and 1144, each ×4	2·20	
1143	20c. Tarpon	25	30
	a. Booklet pane. No. 1143×4 and No. 1145×3, plus label	2·30	
1144	35c. Sailfish	40	45
1145	40c. Dolphin	45	50
1142/5 Set of 4		1·25	1·40

Nos. 1142/5 were only available from $2 stamp booklets, Nos. SB4/5, in which the surplus self-adhesive paper around each stamp is retained. Booklet panes 1142a and 1143a have the horizontal edges of the pane imperforate giving stamps imperforate either at top or at foot.

(Des D. Miller. Litho BDT)

2004 (20 July). Local Fruits. T **235** and similar vert designs. Multicoloured. W w **14**. P 13½.

1146	1c. Hog Plum (25.8.05)	10	30
1147	10c. Coco Plum (25.8.05)	20	30
1148	15c. Type **235**	30	30
1149	20c. Cashew	40	30
1150	25c. Sugar Apple (25.8.05)	60	45
1151	35c. Tamarind	70	45
1152	40c. Soursop	75	50
1153	50c. Mango	85	65
1154	60c. Papaya (25.8.05)	1·25	75
1155	75c. Custard Apple (25.8.05)	1·50	1·25
1156	$1 Otaheite Gooseberry (25.8.05)	2·00	2·00
1157	$1.50 Guava (25.8.05)	3·00	3·25
1158	$2 Tamarind	4·00	4·25
1159	$5 Mamee Apple	8·50	10·00
1160	$10 Passion Fruit (25.8.05)	15·00	17·00
1146/60 Set of 15		35·00	38·00

Nos. 1146, 1149, 1151, 1153 and 1158 were re-issued in June 2007 with "2007" imprint dates.

236 Festival Parade

237 Women's Football

(Des D. Miller. Litho Cartor)

2004 (26 Oct). Golden Jubilee of Island Festival. T **236** and similar square designs. Multicoloured. W w **14** (sideways). P 13½.

1161	10c. Type **236**	30	50
1162	60c. Horse racing	1·75	1·00
1163	$1 Canoeing	2·00	2·00
1164	$2 Festival queen	3·75	4·75
1161/4 Set of 4		7·00	7·50

(Des J. Vasarhelyi. Litho BDT)

2004 (30 Dec). Centenary of FIFA (Fédération Internationale de Football Association) and Olympic Games, Athens. T **237** and similar vert design. Multicoloured. W w **14**. P 14.

1165	75c. Type **237**	1·40	1·40
1166	$1 Sprinting	1·75	1·75

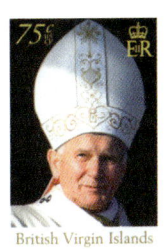

238 Black and White Warbler

238a Pope John Paul II

(Litho BDT)

2005 (8 July). Birdlife International (2nd series). Caribbean Endemic Bird Festival. T **238** and similar horiz designs. Multicoloured. W w **14** (sideways). P 14.

1167	5c. Type **238**	60	70
	a. Sheetlet. Nos. 1167/76	16·00	18·00
1168	10c. Prairie Warbler	80	1·50
1169	15c. Yellow-rumped Warbler	1·00	1·25
1170	25c. Worm-eating Warbler	1·25	50
1171	35c. Yellow Warbler	1·25	70
1172	40c. Black-throated Blue Warbler	1·50	2·00
1173	50c. Prothonotary Warbler	1·50	1·50
1174	60c. Cape May Warbler	2·25	3·00
1175	75c. Parula Warbler (inscr "Northern Parula")	2·50	3·25
1176	$2.75 Palm Warbler	5·50	6·50
1167/76 Set of 10		16·00	18·00

Nos. 1167/76 were printed together, *se-tenant*, in sheetlets of ten stamps. Nos. 1167, 1170, 1171 and 1173 were also printed in separate sheets.

(Des A. Robinson. Litho BDT)

2005 (18 Aug). Pope John Paul II Commemoration. W w **14** (inverted). P 14½×14.

1177	**238a**	75c. multicoloured	2·25	2·00

No. 1177 was printed in sheetlets of eight stamps with an enlarged illustrated right margin.

239 Virgin Islands Tree Boa

(Des R. Gorringe. Litho BDT)

2005 (15 Sept). Endangered Species. Virgin Islands Tree Boa (*Epicrates monensis granti*). T **239** and similar horiz designs. Multicoloured. W w **14** (sideways). P 14.

1178	20c. Type **239**	75	55
	a. Sheetlet. Nos. 1178/81, each ×2	12·00	
1179	30c. Boa in plant (facing left)	1·00	60
1180	70c. On leafy branch	2·00	2·00
1181	$1.05 In foliage (facing right)	2·75	3·50
1178/81	Set of 4	6·00	6·00

Nos. 1178/81 were printed in separate sheets of 20 and also in *se-tenant* sheetlets containing eight stamps, two of each value.

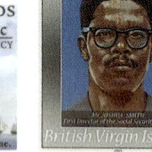

239a HMS *Colossus* in Action before breaking the Line

240 Mr. Joshua Smith (first director of Social Security)

(Des Pauline Gyles ($3) or J. Batcheler (others). Litho BDT)

2005 (18 Oct). Bicentenary of the Battle of Trafalgar. T **239a** and similar multicoloured designs. W w **14** (sideways). P 14×15.

1182	5c. Type **239a**	75	75
1183	25c. HMS *Boreas* off British Virgin Islands, 1787	1·75	75
1184	75c. "HMS *Victory*" (Francis Smitheman)	3·50	2·50
1185	$3 Admiral Lord Nelson (*vert*)	8·50	10·00
1182/5	Set of 4	13·00	12·50
MS1186	120×79 mm. $2.50 HMS *Colossus* firing (44×44 mm). P 13½	9·00	10·00

(Des D. Miller. Litho Enschedé)

2005 (16 Nov). Anniversaries. T **240** and similar vert designs. Multicoloured. W w **14**. P 14.

1187	20c. Type **240** (25th anniv of Social Security)	60	55
1188	40c. Transmitter on mast and world map (40th anniv of Radio Station ZBVI)	1·50	1·00
1189	50c. Control tower (25th anniv of Beef Island airstrip)	2·00	1·50
1190	$1 Emblem (Centenary of Rotary International)	2·50	3·50
1187/90	Set of 4	6·00	6·00

241 Decorated Century Plant

241a Princess Elizabeth in Girl Guide Uniform

(Des Jennifer Toombs. Litho BDT)

2005 (21 Nov). Christmas. Plants and Flowers. T **241** and similar multicoloured designs. W w **14** (sideways on 35c., $2.50). P 15×14 (vert) or 14×15 (horiz).

1191	15c. Type **241**	65	30
1192	35c. Poinsettia (*horiz*)	1·25	70
1193	60c. Decorated ink-berry in pot	1·75	1·25
1194	$2.50 Snow-on-the-mountain (*horiz*)	5·50	7·50
1191/4	Set of 4	8·25	8·75

(Litho BDT)

2006 (17 July). 80th Birthday of Queen Elizabeth II. T **241** and similar horiz designs. Multicoloured. W w **14** (sideways). P 14.

1195	15c. Type **241a**	75	30
1196	75c. Queen Elizabeth II wearing white hat and green and white jacket	2·00	1·25
1197	$1.50 Wearing drop earrings	3·50	4·25
1198	$2 Wearing pale mauve hat and jacket	4·75	6·00
1195/8	Set of 4	10·00	10·50
MS1199	144×75 mm. $1.50 As No. 1196; $2 As No. 1197	8·00	9·00

Stamps from No. **MS**1199 do not have white borders.

242 New Red Cross Headquarters, Virgin Gorda

(Litho BDT)

2007 (1 Aug). Red Cross Buildings. T **242** and similar horiz design. W w **14** (sideways). P 14.

1200	20c. Type **242**	75	80
1201	$3 Former Red Cross building	4·50	5·00

242a Supermarine Spitfire

(Litho BDT)

2008 (1 Apr). 90th Anniv of the Royal Air Force. Horiz designs as T **242a** and similar vert designs. Multicoloured. W w **14** (sideways). P 14.

1202	18c. Type **242a**	60	50
1203	20c. Avro Lancaster	75	50
1204	35c. Douglas C-47 Dakota	1·25	55
1205	60c. Handley Page Halifax	2·25	1·75
1206	$1.75 Westland Lysander	4·75	6·00
1202/6	Set of 5	8·75	8·50
MS1207	110×70 mm. $2.50 Spitfire patrolling D-Day beaches	6·00	6·50

Nos. 1202/6 were each printed in sheetlets of eight stamps with a central label showing anniversary emblem and enlarged illustrated bottom margins.

243 Diana, Princess of Wales

244 Shield

(Litho BDT)

2008 (7 Apr). Tenth Death Anniv of Diana, Princess of Wales. T **243** and similar vert design. Multicoloured. W w **14**. P 14.

1208	60c. Type **243**	1·00	1·00
MS1209	120×85 mm. $3.50 Wearing red sleeveless dress (42×57 mm). Wmk sideways	6·00	7·00

No. 1208 was printed in sheetlets of six stamps with enlarged illustrated left margins and also in sheets of 20 (2 panes 2×5).

BRITISH VIRGIN ISLANDS

(Litho BDT)

2008 (1 May). 300th Birth Anniv of Charles Wesley (2007). T **244** and similar vert designs. Multicoloured. W w **14**. P 14.

1210	20c. Type **244**	60	40
1211	50c. Rev. Charles Wesley	1·25	1·25
1212	$1.75 Rev. Charles Wesley (in half profile)	3·00	4·00
1210/12	Set of 3	4·25	5·00

245 Athlete running

(Richard Allen. Litho BDT)

2008 (1 Aug). Olympic Games, Beijing. T **245** and similar square designs. Multicoloured. W w **14** (sideways). P 13½.

1213	15c. Type **245**	30	30
1214	18c. Yachting	35	35
1215	20c. Athlete in race	40	40
1216	$1 Dinghy sailing	2·25	2·75
1213/16	Set of 4	3·00	3·50

246 Mace and Mace Head

(Litho BDT)

2008 (21 Aug). Ministerial Government. T **246** and similar horiz designs. Multicoloured. W w **14** (sideways). P 14×15.

1217	18c. Type **246**	35	25
1218	35c. Facade and entrance of House of Assembly	70	55
1219	60c. Henry O. Creque and Ivan Dawson (legislators)	1·40	1·50
1220	$2 Paul Wattley and Terrance B. Lettsome (legislators)	3·75	5·00
1217/20	Set of 4	5·50	6·50

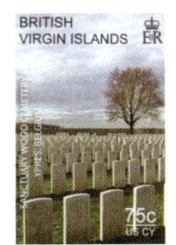

247 Sanctuary Wood Cemetery, Ypres, Belgium

248 Climbing Pandanus (*Freycinetia cumingiana*)

(Litho BDT)

2008 (16 Sept). 90th Anniv of the End of World War I. T **247** and similar multicoloured designs. W w **18** (inverted on 75c., $1, sideways on others). P 14.

1221	75c. Type **247**	1·60	1·75
1222	80c. Poppies growing on Somme Battlefield, France (*horiz*)	1·75	2·00
1223	90c. Lone Pine Cemetery, Gallipoli (*horiz*)	2·00	2·25
1224	$1 War Memorial, Vauquois, France	2·25	2·50
1225	$1.15 Thiepval Memorial, France (*horiz*)	2·50	2·75
1226	$1.25 Menin Gate, Ypres, Belgium (*horiz*)	2·50	2·75
1221/6	Set of 6	11·00	12·50
MS1227	110×70 mm. $2 UK Overseas Territories Wreath of Remembrance. Wmk inverted	4·00	4·50

Nos. 1221/6 were each printed in sheetlets of six stamps with enlarged illustrated bottom margins.

(Litho BDT)

2009 (27 Mar). J. R. O'Neal Botanic Gardens, Road Town, Tortola. T **248** and similar vert designs. Multicoloured. W w **14**. P 14.

1228	20c. Type **248**	50	45
1229	35c. True aloe (*Aloe vera*)	85	65
1230	50c. Crown of thorns (*Euphorbia milii*)	1·50	1·50
1231	$1 Red-eared slider (*Trachemys scripta elegans*) (terrapin)	2·25	2·75
1228/31	Set of 4	4·50	4·75
MS1232	64×90 mm. $2.50 Fountain and royal palms. Wmk inverted	4·50	5·50

248a HMS *Ark Royal* (English galleon)

(Des John Batchelor (Nos. 1233/8). Litho BDT)

2009 (26 June). Seafaring and Exploration. As T **248a** and similar horiz designs. W w **18** (sideways). Multicoloured. P 14.

1233	15c. Type **248a**	70	60
1234	20c. *Whydah* (three masted ship of galley design)	70	60
1235	60c. *Santa Maria* (Columbus)	1·75	1·40
1236	70c. RMS *Rhone* (steam packet)	1·90	1·90
1237	90c. *Golden Hind* (Drake)	2·50	2·25
1238	$1.95 HMY *Britannia* (royal yacht)	4·50	5·00
1233/8	Set of 6	11·00	10·50
MS1239	110×70 mm. $2 Christopher Columbus. Wmk inverted	8·00	8·00

Nos. 1233/8 were each printed in sheetlets of six stamps with enlarged illustrated margins.

249 Lt. Robert Hampton Gray, 9 August 1945

(Litho BDT)

2009 (30 June). Centenary of Naval Aviation. T **249** and similar horiz designs showing Victoria Cross holders and aircraft. Multicoloured. W w **18** (sideways). P 14.

1240	18c. Type **249**	60	60
1241	35c. Lt. Cdr. (A) Eugene Esmonde, 12 February 1942	1·25	1·00
1242	60c. Flt. SLt. Rex Warneford, 7 June 1915	2·25	2·25
1243	90c. Sqn. Cdr. Richard Bell Davies, 19 November 1915	3·00	3·75
1240/3	Set of 5	6·25	7·00
MS1244	110×70 mm. $2 Airplane on deck of HMS *Illustrious*, Taranto, 1940	5·50	6·00

Nos. 1240/3 were each printed in sheetlets of eight stamps with a central label and enlarged illustrated bottom margins.

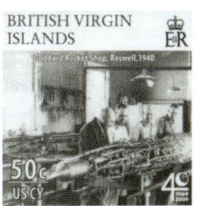

249a Goddard Rocket Shop, Roswell, 1940

(Litho Lowe-Martin Group)

2009 (20 July). International Year of Astronomy. 40th Anniv of First Moon Landing. As T **249a** and similar square designs. Multicoloured. W w **18** (sideways). P 13.

1245	50c. Type **249a**	1·50	1·75
1246	75c. Vertol VZ-2, 1960	1·75	2·00
1247	$1 Apollo 11, 1969	2·10	2·50
1248	$1.25 Space Transportation System 126, 2008	2·50	2·75

BRITISH VIRGIN ISLANDS

1249	$2.30 Docking procedure, International Space Station	3·00	3·50
1245/9	Set of 4	9·75	11·00
MS1250	100×80 mm. $3 Tuning in Earth (Dave Scott pointing antenna at Earth and Jim Irwin loading Lunar Rover) (Alan Bean) (39×59 mm). Wmk upright	6·00	7·00

Nos. 1245/49 were printed in separate sheets of six stamps with enlarged illustrated margins.

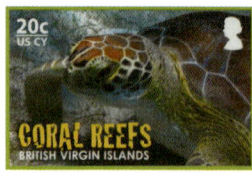

250 Turtle

(Litho Lowe-Martin Group)

2010 (29 Mar). Coral Reefs. T **250** and similar multicoloured designs. W w **18** (sideways on horiz, inverted on vert designs). P 12½.

1251	20c. Type **250**	50	50
1252	35c. Fish	65	55
1253	50c. Seahorse (vert)	1·50	1·50
1254	60c. Conch shell (vert)	1·60	1·60
1255	$1.50 Coral reef	3·75	4·50
1251/5	Set of 5	7·25	7·75

251 Mr. John E. George (sub-postmaster)

252 Church Bell

(Litho Lowe-Martin Group)

2010 (3 May). North Sound Post Office. T **251** and similar multicoloured designs. Multicoloured. W w **18** (inverted on 20c., sideways on others). P 12½.

1256	20c. Type **251**	90	90
1257	50c. New North Sound Sub Post Office (horiz)	1·60	1·60
1258	£2 Old North Sound Sub Post Office (horiz)	4·50	5·50
1256/58	Set of 3	6·25	7·25

(Litho Lowe-Martin Group)

2010 (3 May). Bicentenary of East End Methodist Church. T **252** and similar square designs. Multicoloured. W w **18** (sideways). P 13.

1259	20c. Type **252**	60	50
1260	50c. East End Methodist Church, 2010	1·75	1·60
1261	60c. East End Methodist Church, 1977	2·00	1·90
1262	60c. East End Methodist Church in early 19th century	5·00	6·00
1259/62	Set of 4	8·50	9·00

253 Dinghy Sailing

(Litho Lowe-Martin Group)

2011 (24 Feb). Sailability BVI (sailing programme for the disabled). T **253** and similar horiz designs. Multicoloured. W w **18** (sideways). P 12½.

1263	5c. Type **253**	15	25
1264	20c. Two sailors in dinghy with red sails	70	50
1265	25c. Two sailors in blue dinghy	75	65
1266	40c. Arrival of Geoff Holt (quadriplegic transatlantic sailor) in Tortola, 2010	1·40	1·25
1267	50c. Geoff Holt on board yacht Impossible Dream, arm raised in triumph	1·60	1·60
1268	$1.50 GGeoff Holt on board yacht Impossible Dream, arm raised in triump	4·00	5·00
1263/8	Set of 6	7·25	8·25

254 J24 Keel Boat Racing, 2000

(Litho Lowe-Martin Group)

2011 (1 May). 40th Anniv of British Virgin Islands Spring Regatta. T **254** and similar multicoloured designs. Multicoloured. W w **18** (sideways on horiz designs, inverted on vert designs). P 12½.

1269	15c. Type **254**	60	45
1270	35c. Mixed fleet (vert), 1980s	1·50	1·00
1271	50c. Yachts flying spinnakers, 1990s	1·90	1·90
1272	$2. Clubhouse and moored dinghies, 1970s	4·00	5·00
1269/72	Set of 4	7·25	7·50

255 Prince William and Miss Catherine Middleton

(Litho Lowe-Martin Group)

2011 (29 Apr). Royal Wedding. Sheet 118×90 mm. W w **18** (sideways). P 14½×14.

MS1273	**255** $5 multicoloured	7·50	8·00

STAMP BOOKLETS

1981 (22 July). Royal Wedding. Gold on blue cover, 75×50 mm, showing Royal coat of arms on front and St. Paul's Cathedral on back. Stapled.

SB1	$3.50 booklet containing 10c., 35c., $1.25 (Nos. 463/5), in pairs		2·25

No. SB1 was sold at a 10c. premium above the total face value of the stamps it contained.

1986 (23 July). Royal Wedding. Gold (No. SB2) or silver (No. SB3) on new blue covers. Stapled.

SB2	$4.20 booklet (Westminster Abbey cover) containing twelve 35c. (Nos. 605/6) in blocks of four		5·50
SB3	$5.40 booklet (State Coach cover) containing four 35c. (Nos. 605/6) and four $1 (Nos. 607/8), each in block of four		5·50

The stamps from No. SB3 are imperforate.

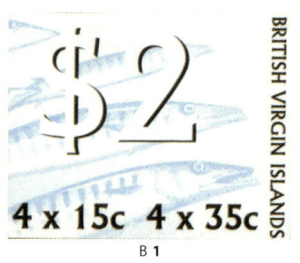

B 1

2004 (1 July). Game Fish. Pale blue and black cover (SB4) or light turquoise-green and black cover (SB5) as Type B **1**. Self-adhesive.

SB4	$2 booklet containing four 15c. and four 35c. (No. 1142a)		2·20

SB5	$2 booklet containing four 20c., three 40c. and one label (No. 1143a)......................		2·30

OFFICIAL STAMPS

OFFICIAL

(O **1**)

Two varieties of overprint:
Type I. Foot of "OFFICIAL" 15–16 mm from top of design. Light impression with little or no black outline to letters.
Type II. Foot of "OFFICIAL" 20 mm from top of design. Heavy impression with thick black outline to letters.

1985 (Feb). Nos. 418/19, 420a/1a, 423a/4a, 425, 426a, 427, 428a and 429/33 optd as Type *O* **1** in silver by Questa.

O1	1c. Purple-tipped Sea Anemone (I)..............	30	1·25
	a. Opt Type II..	55·00	65·00
O2	3c. Common Starfish (I)......................................	45	1·25
	a. Opt Type II..	60·00	70·00
O3	5c. Type **134** (I)...	45	45
O4	8c. Atlantic Trumpet Triton (*Charonia variegata*) (I)..	55	60
	a. Opt Type II..	£110	
O5	13c. Flamingo Tongue (*Cyphoma gibbosus*) (II)..	80	75
O6	15c. Spider Crab (I)..	85	70
O7	18c. Sea Squirts (I)..	90	1·75
	a. Opt Type II..	£120	
O8	20c. True Tulip (*Fasciolaria tulipa*) (I)................	90	80
O9	25c. Rooster-tail Conch (*Strombus gallus*) (I)..	1·25	2·00
	w. Wmk inverted..	15·00	
O10	30c. West Indian Fighting Conch (*Strombus pugilis*) (I)...	1·40	1·00
	a. Optd on No. 428..	5·00	11·00
O11	60c. Mangrove Crab (I)..	2·00	2·50
O12	$1 Coral Polyps (I)..	3·00	3·75
O13	$2.50 Peppermint Shrimp (I)................................	4·50	9·00
O14	$3 West Indian Murex (*Murex brevifrons*) (I)..	5·50	10·00
	a. Opt inverted..	£110	£130
O15	$5 Carpet Anemone (I).....................................	7·50	10·00
O1/15 *Set of* 15..		27·00	42·00

Examples of the ½c. and 10c. overprinted in silver and of all seventeen values overprinted in gold also exist, but were not issued in British Virgin Islands.

OFFICIAL   **OFFICIAL**

(O **2**)   (O **3**)

1988 (10 Feb–Sept). Nos. 560/78 optd with Type O **2** by Questa.

O16	1c. Type **162** (9.86)...	60	1·75
O17	2c. Yellow-crowned Night Heron...................	40	1·75
O18	5c. Mangrove Cuckoo (9.86).............................	1·25	2·00
O19	8c. Northern Mockingbird................................	55	2·75
O20	10c. Grey Kingbird (9.86).....................................	1·25	2·00
O21	12c. Red-necked Pigeon......................................	70	40
O22	15c. Least Bittern (9.86)......................................	1·50	40
O23	18c. Smooth-billed Ani.......................................	70	75
O24	20c. Clapper Rail (9.86).......................................	1·50	1·00
O25	25c. American Kestrel (9.86)..............................	1·50	1·00
O26	30c. Pearly-eyed Thrasher (9.86).......................	1·50	1·00
O27	35c. Bridled Quail Dove (9.86)............................	1·50	1·00
O28	40c. Green Heron...	1·25	1·00
O29	50c. Scaly-breasted Ground Dove.....................	1·40	1·75
O30	60c. Little Blue Heron..	1·50	2·50
O31	$1 Audubon's Shearwater................................	2·25	3·50
O32	$2 Blue-faced Booby..	2·50	4·00
O33	$3 Cattle Egret..	6·00	7·50
O34	$5 Zenaida Dove (9.86)...................................	8·00	10·00
O16/34 *Set of* 19..		32·00	40·00

1991 (1 Sept). Nos. 767/8, 771, 773/9 and 781 optd with Type O **3**.

O35	5c. Frangipani..	60	1·50
O36	10c. Autograph Tree..	60	1·50
O37	20c. Jerusalem Thorn..	80	65
O38	30c. Swamp Immortelle......................................	1·00	65
O39	35c. White Cedar...	1·00	65
O40	40c. Mahoe Tree...	1·25	85
O41	45c. Pinguin..	1·25	85
O42	50c. Christmas Orchid...	2·00	1·25
O43	70c. Lignum Vitae..	2·00	2·50
O44	$1 African Tulip Tree..	2·00	2·75
O45	$3 Organ Pipe Cactus.......................................	5·00	7·50
O35/45 *Set of* 11...		16·00	19·00

The same stamps, except for the 30c., exist overprinted with Type O **2**, but such overprints were not placed on sale in British Virgin Islands.

Leeward Islands

The Federal Colony of the Leeward Islands was constituted in 1871 formalising links between Antigua, British Virgin Islands, Dominica, Montserrat and St. Kitts-Nevis which stretched back to the 1670s. Issues for the individual islands were superseded by those inscribed "LEEWARD ISLANDS", but were in concurrent use with them from 1903 (British Virgin Islands from 1899). Dominica was transferred to the Windward Islands on 31 December 1939.

PRICES FOR STAMPS ON COVER TO 1945	
Nos. 1/8	from × 10
Nos. 9/16	from × 12
Nos. 17/19	from × 8
Nos. 20/8	from × 5
Nos. 29/35	from × 4
Nos. 36/45	from × 5
Nos. 46/57	from × 4
Nos. 58/87	from × 5
Nos. 88/91	from × 6
Nos. 92/4	from × 10
Nos. 95/114	from × 5

PRINTERS. All the stamps of Leeward Islands were typographed by De La Rue & Co, Ltd, London, *except where otherwise stated.*

4d. Damaged "S" (R. ?/6, left pane)

1890 (31 Oct). Name and value in second colour. Wmk Crown CA. P 14.

1	1	½d. dull mauve and green	3·50	1·25
2		1d. dull mauve and rose	7·50	20
3		2½d. dull mauve and blue	8·50	30
		w. Wmk inverted	£425	£200
4		4d. dull mauve and orange	10·00	9·00
		a. Damaged "S"	£190	
5		6d. dull mauve and brown	12·00	13·00
6		7d. dull mauve and slate	10·00	17·00
7	2	1s. green and carmine	23·00	55·00
8		5s. green and blue	£140	£300
1/8 Set of 8			£190	£350
1s/8s Optd "SPECIMEN" Set of 8			£275	

The colours of this issue are fugitive.

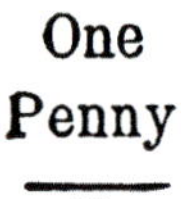

1897 (22 July) Queen Victoria's Diamond Jubilee. Handstamped with T **3**.

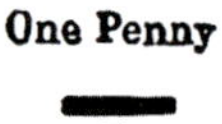

9	1	½d. dull mauve and green	7·00	22·00
		a. Opt double	£1400	
		b. Opt triple	£5500	
10		1d. dull mauve and rose	8·00	22·00
		a. Opt double	£1000	
		b. Opt triple	£5500	

11		2½d. dull mauve and blue	8·50	22·00
		a. Opt double	£1200	
12		4d. dull mauve and orange	55·00	80·00
		a. Opt double	£1300	
13		6d. dull mauve and brown	60·00	£130
		a. Opt double	£1700	
14		7d. dull mauve and slate	60·00	£130
		a. Opt double	£1700	
15	2	1s. green and carmine	£130	£275
		a. Opt double	£2250	
16		5s. green and blue	£450	£800
		a. Opt double	£6000	
9/16 Set of 8			£700	£1300

Beware of forgeries.

1902 (11 Aug). Nos. 4/6 surch locally.

17	4	1d. on 4d. dull mauve and orange	6·00	9·00
		a. Pair, one with tall narrow "O" in "One"	45·00	85·00
		b. Surch double	£6000	
		c. Damaged "S"	£160	
18		1d. on 6d. dull mauve and brown	8·00	15·00
		a. Pair, one with tall narrow "O" in "One"	65·00	£150
19	5	1d. on 7d. dull mauve and slate	6·50	12·00
17/19 Set of 3			18·00	32·00

The tall narrow "O" variety occurred on R. 1/1, 5/3, 5/5 and 7/4.

2½d. Wide "A" (R. 6/1 of both panes. Replaced in 1912)

1s. Dropped "R" (R.1/1 of both panes from Pl 2 (1st ptg only))

1902 (1 Sept–Oct). Wmk Crown CA. P 14.

20	6	½d. dull purple and green	6·00	1·00
21		1d. dull purple and carmine	8·00	20
22	7	2d. dull purple and ochre (Oct)	2·75	4·25
23	6	2½d. dull purple and ultramarine	6·00	2·25
		a. Wide "A" in "LEEWARD"	£275	£160
24	7	3d. dull purple and black (Oct)	8·00	7·50
25	6	6d. dull purple and brown	2·50	8·00
26	8	1s. green and carmine	7·50	25·00
		a. Dropped "R" in "LEEWARD"	£550	£800
27	7	2s.6d. green and black (Oct)	28·00	75·00
28	8	5s. green and blue	65·00	90·00
20/8 Set of 8			£120	£190
20s/8s Optd "SPECIMEN" Set of 9			£180	

1905 (Apr)–**08**. Wmk Mult Crown CA. Ordinary paper (½d., 3d.) or chalk-surfaced paper (others).

29	6	½d. dull purple and green (2.06)	3·75	2·00
		a. Chalk-surfaced paper (25.7.08)	32·00	19·00
30		1d. dull purple and carmine (29.8.06)	9·00	80
31	7	2d. dull purple and ochre (25.7.08)	10·00	23·00
32	6	2½d. dull purple and ultramarine (23.7.06)	75·00	50·00
		a. Wide "A" in "LEEWARD"	£800	£500
33	7	3d. dull purple and black	21·00	55·00
		a. Chalk-surfaced paper (18.4.08)	60·00	95·00
34	6	6d. dull purple and brown (15.7.08)	55·00	85·00
35	8	1s. green and carmine (15.7.08)	48·00	£130
29/35 Set of 7			£200	£300

1907 (14 Apr)–**11**. Wmk Mult Crown CA. Chalk-surfaced paper (3d. to 5s.). P 14.

36	7	¼d. brown (7.8.09)	2·75	1·75
37		½d. dull green	4·00	1·25
38		1d. bright red (7.07)	11·00	80
		a. Rose-carmine (1910)	42·00	3·50
39	7	2d. grey (3.8.11)	4·20	9·00
40	6	2½d. bright blue (5.07)	8·00	4·25
		a. Wide "A" in "LEEWARD"	£300	£180
41	7	3d. purple/*yellow* (28.10.10)	3·50	7·50
42	6	6d. dull and bright purple (3.8.11)	9·00	7·50

43	8	1s. black/green (3.8.11)	7·00	21·00
44	7	2s.6d. black and red/blue (15.9.11)	42·00	55·00
45	8	5s. green and red/yellow (21.11.10)	48·00	65·00
36/45 Set of 10			£130	£150
36s/45s Optd "SPECIMEN" Set of 10			£275	

10  **11**

12  **13**

1912 (23 Oct)–**22**. Die I (¼d. to 3d., 6d., 1s., 2s.6d. 5s.) or Die II (4d., 2s.). Wmk Mult Crown CA. Chalk-surfaced paper (3d. to 5s.). P 14.

46	10	¼d. brown	1·75	1·00
		a. Pale brown	4·00	2·50
47	11	½d. yellow-green (12.12)	5·50	2·00
		a. Deep green (1916)	5·50	1·50
48		1d. red	5·00	1·00
		a. Bright scarlet (8.15)	11·00	1·00
49	10	2d. slate-grey (9.1.13)	4·00	5·50
50	11	2½d. bright blue	3·25	7·00
		a. Deep bright blue (1914)	5·50	4·00
51	10	3d. purple/yellow (9.1.13)	2·00	19·00
		a. White back (11.13)	90·00	£180
		as. Optd "SPECIMEN"	50·00	
		b. On lemon (11.14)	6·50	21·00
		c. On buff (1920)	35·00	50·00
		cs. Optd "SPECIMEN"	45·00	
		d. On orange-buff (1920)	7·00	22·00
		dw. Wmk inverted	£475	
52		4d. black and red/pale yellow (Die II) (12.5.22)	6·00	22·00
53	11	6d. dull and bright purple (9.1.13)	3·50	8·50
54	12	1s. black/green (9.1.13)	3·00	8·00
		a. White back (11.13)	80·00	38·00
		as. Optd "SPECIMEN"	50·00	
		b. On blue-green, olive back (1917)	13·00	8·00
		bs. Optd "SPECIMEN"	70·00	
55	10	2s. purple and blue/blue (Die II) (12.5.22)	17·00	65·00
56		2s.6d. black and red/blue (11.13)	20·00	55·00
57	12	5s. green and red/yellow (9.14)	65·00	£120
		a. White back (11.13)	55·00	90·00
		as. Optd "SPECIMEN"	60·00	
		b. On lemon (1915)	45·00	85·00
		c. On orange-buff (1920)	£120	£200
46/57b Set of 12			£100	£250
46s/57s Optd "SPECIMEN" Set of 12			£275	

Nos. 51a, 54a and 57a were only on sale from Montserrat.

1d., 1s. "D I" shaved at foot 1d. R. 7/3 of left pane (printings from Sept 1947 until corrected during first printing in green in Oct 1948). 1s. R. 9/6 of right pane (all ptgs between 1932 and 1938).

1921 (Oct)–**32**. Wmk Mult Script CA or Mult Crown CA (£1). Chalk-surfaced paper (3d. to £1). P 14.

(a) Die II (1921–29)

58	10	¼d. brown (1.4.22)	2·25	1·00
59	11	½d. blue-green	1·25	75
60		1d. carmine-red	2·25	55
61		1d. bright violet (21.8.22)	2·25	1·00
62		1d. bright scarlet (1929)	13·00	2·25
63	10	1½d. carmine-red (10.9.26)	5·00	2·00
64		1½d. red-brown (1929)	1·25	10
65		2d. slate-grey (6.22)	2·50	80
		w Wmk inverted	†	£325
		x. Wmk reversed		
66	11	2½d. orange-yellow (22.9.23)	10·00	60·00
67		2½d. bright blue (1.3.27)	3·50	1·25
68	10	3d. light ultramarine (22.9.23)	12·00	29·00
		a. Deep ultramarine (1925)	60·00	60·00
69		3d. purple/yellow (1.7.27)	5·00	6·50
70		4d. black and red/pale yellow (2.24)	3·25	21·00
71		5d. dull purple and olive-green (12.5.22)	2·50	4·25
72	11	6d. dull and bright purple (17.7.23)	16·00	40·00
73	12	1s. black/emerald (17.7.23)	10·00	8·00
74	10	2s. purple and blue/blue (12.5.22)	22·00	45·00
		a. Red-purple and blue/blue (1926)	8·50	48·00
		aw. Wmk inverted	£400	
75		2s.6d. black and red/blue (17.7.23)	8·50	23·00
76		3s. bright green and violet (12.5.22)	12·00	35·00
77		4s. black and red (12.5.22)	18·00	42·00
78	12	5s. green and red/pale yellow (17.7.23)	48·00	85·00
79	13	10s. green and red/green (1928)	80·00	£130
		a. Break in scroll	£300	
		b. Broken crown and scroll	£300	
		c. Nick in top right scroll	£300	
		e. Break in lines below left scroll	£300	
		f. Damaged leaf at bottom right	£300	
80		£1 purple and black/red (1928)	£225	£275
		a. Break in scroll	£550	
		b. Broken crown and scroll	£550	
		e. Break in lines below left scroll	£550	
		f. Damaged leaf at bottom right	£550	
58/80 Set of 23			£425	£700
58s/80s Optd or Perf (1d. bright scarlet, 1½d. red-brown, 10s. £1) "SPECIMEN" Set of 23			£600	

(b) Reversion to Die I (Plate 23) (1931–32)

81	10	¼d. brown	13·00	20·00
82	11	½d. blue-green	27·00	55·00
83		1d. bright scarlet	45·00	1·00
84	10	1½d. red-brown	4·25	2·75
85	11	2½d. bright blue	7·00	3·50
86		6d. dull and bright purple	29·00	95·00
87	12	1s. black/emerald	60·00	85·00
		a. "D I" flaw	£600	
		b. "A" of "CA" missing from wmk	—	£2250
81/7 Set of 7			£170	£225

No. 66 was issued in Montserrat and 68a in St. Kitts-Nevis.

Nos. 59, 62 and 82/3 exist in coils, constructed from normal sheets. No. 82 was only issued in this form.

For illustrations of varieties on Nos. 79/80 see above No. 51b of Bermuda.

Nos. 81/7 result from the use, in error, of Die I which had previously been "retired" in late 1920, to produce Plate 23.

1935 (6 May). Silver Jubilee. As Nos. 91/4 of Antigua, but printed by Waterlow. P 11×12.

88		1d. deep blue and scarlet	1·90	3·00
89		1½d. ultramarine and grey	2·75	1·25
90		2½d. brown and deep blue	4·25	4·50
91		1s. slate and purple	25·00	35·00
		k. Kite and vertical log	£500	
		l. Kite and horizontal log	£500	
88/91 Set of 4			30·00	40·00
88s/91s Perf "SPECIMEN" Set of 4			£130	

1937 (12 May). Coronation. As Nos. 95/7 of Antigua, but printed by D.L.R.

92		1d. scarlet	80	1·00
93		1½d. buff	80	1·50
94		2½d. bright blue	90	1·50
92/4 Set of 3			2·25	3·50
92s/4s Perf "SPECIMEN" Set of 3			£110	

14  **15**

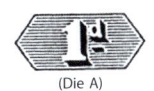

(Die A) 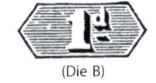 (Die B)

In Die B the figure "1" has a broader top and more projecting serif.

LEEWARD ISLANDS

½d. "ISl.ANDS" flaw (R. 1/2 of right pane) (Pl 2 ptg of May 1944)

6d. Broken second "E" in "LEEWARD" (R. 4/1 of right pane) (Pl 2 and 3 ptgs from November 1942 until corrected in June 1949) (The similar variety on the 5s. shows traces of the top bar)

5s. Damaged value tablet (R. 3/5 of left pane, first printing only)

Broken top right scroll (R. 5/11) (1942 ptg of 10s. only. Corrected on £1 value from same period)

Broken lower right scroll (R. 5/12. 1942 ptgs only)

Missing pearl (R. 5/1. 1944 ptgs only)

Gash in chin (R. 2/5. 1942 ptgs only)

1938 (25 Nov)–**51**. T **14** (and similar type, but shaded value tablet, ½d., 1d., 2½d., 6d.) and **15** (10s., £1). Chalk-surfaced paper (3d. to £1). P 14.

(a) Wmk Mult Script CA

95	¼d. brown		60	1·50
	a. Chalk-surfaced paper. *Deep brown* (13.6.49)		30	1·75
96	½d. emerald		1·00	70
	a. "ISIANDS" flaw		£140	
97	½d. slate-grey (*chalk-surfaced paper*) (1.7.49)		2·00	1·50
98	1d. scarlet (Die A)		10·00	2·50
99	1d. scarlet (*shades*) (Die B) (1940)		2·25	1·75
	a. "D I" flaw (9.47)		£200	
	b. Carmine (9.42)		2·00	11·00
	c. Red (13.9.48)		6·00	6·00
	ca. "D I" flaw		£200	
100	1d. blue-green (*chalk-surfaced paper*) (1.7.49)		55	15
	a. "D I" flaw		£200	£180
101	1½d. chestnut		1·00	50
102	1½d. yellow-orange and black (*chalk-surfaced paper*) (1.7.49)		1·50	40
103	2d. olive-grey		3·25	2·25
	a. *Slate-grey* (11.42)		6·50	3·75
104	2d. scarlet (*chalk-surfaced paper*) (1.7.49)		1·40	1·25
105	2½d. bright blue		28·00	4·00
	a. *Light bright blue* (11.42)		80	1·25
106	2½d. black and purple (*chalk-surfaced paper*) (1.7.49)		80	15
107	3d. orange		35·00	2·75
	a. Ordinary paper. *Pale orange* (3.42)		50	85
108	3d. bright blue (1.7.49)		80	15
109	6d. deep dull purple and bright purple		25·00	7·00
	a. Ordinary paper (3.42)		10·00	3·50
	ab. Broken "E"		£550	£400
	b. *Purple and deep magenta* (29.9.47)		14·00	5·00
	ba. Broken "E"		£700	£450
110	1s. black/emerald		16·00	2·00
	a. "D I" flaw		£650	
	b. Ordinary paper (3.42)		4·25	1·00
	ba. *Grey and black/emerald* (8.42)		21·00	3·50
	bb. *Black and grey/emerald* (11.42)		£130	13·00
111	2s. reddish purple and blue/*blue*		27·00	3·00
	a. Ordinary paper (3.42)		12·00	2·00
	ab. *Deep purple and blue/blue* (29.9.47)		12·00	2·50
112	5s. green and red/*yellow*		50·00	22·00
	a. Broken "E" (R. 4/3 of left pane)		£1700	£900
	ab. Damaged value tablet		£1700	£900
	b. Ordinary paper (12.43)		35·00	15·00
	ba. Broken "E" (R. 4/3 of left pane)		£1200	
	c. *Bright green and red/yellow* (24.10.51)		60·00	£100
113	10s. bluish green and deep red/*green*		£200	£130
	a. Ordinary paper. *Pale green and dull red/green* (26.6.44*)		£800	£375
	ad. Broken top right scroll		£6500	
	ae. Broken lower right scroll		£6500	£4500
	af. Gash in chin		£6500	£4500
	b. Ordinary paper. *Green and red/green* (22.2.45*)		£150	90·00
	c. Ordinary paper. *Deep green and deep vermilion/green* (15.10.47*)		£120	£100
	ca. Missing pearl		£1700	

(b) Wmk Mult Crown CA

114	£1 brown-purple and black/*red*		£375	£375
	a. *Purple and black/carmine* (21.9.42*)		90·00	55·00
	ad. Broken top right scroll			
	ae. Broken lower right scroll		£2000	£1100
	af. Gash in chin		£2250	£1100
	b. *Brown-purple and black/salmon* (5.2.45*)		45·00	28·00
	ba. Missing pearl		£1600	£1100
	c. Perf 13. *Violet and black/scarlet* (4.1.52*)		35·00	38·00
	ca. Wmk sideways		£6000	
	cw. Wmk inverted		£6000	
95/114b	Set of 19		£200	£140
95s/114s	Perf "SPECIMEN" Set of 13		£650	

*Dates quoted for Nos. 113a/14c are earliest known postmark dates. Nos. 113a and 114a were despatched to the Leeward Islands in March 1942, No. 113b in December 1943, No. 113c in June 1944 and No. 114c on 13 December 1951.

Nos. 96, 98 and 99 exist in coils constructed from normal sheets.

Printings of the 10s. in March 1942 (No. 113a) and of the £1 in February and October 1942 (No. 114a) were made by Williams Lea & Co. Ltd. following bomb damage to the De La Rue works in 1940.

For illustrations of Nos. 99a, 99ca, 100a and 110a see above No. 58.

1946 (1 Nov). Victory. As Nos. 110/11 of Antigua.

115	1½d. brown		15	75
116	3d. red-orange		15	75
115s/16s	Perf "SPECIMEN" Set of 2		£100	

1949 (2 Jan). Royal Silver Wedding. As Nos. 112/13 of Antigua.

117	2½d. ultramarine		10	10
118	5s. green		7·00	7·00

1949 (10 Oct). 75th Anniv of Universal Postal Union. As Nos. 114/17 of Antigua.

119	2½d. blue-black		15	2·50
120	3d. deep blue		2·00	2·50
121	6d. magenta		15	2·50
122	1s. blue-green		15	2·50
119/22	Set of 4		2·25	9·00

(New Currency. 100 cents = 1 B.W.I. dollar)

1951 (16 Feb). Inauguration of B.W.I. University College. As Nos. 118/19 of Antigua.

123	3c. orange and black		30	2·00
124	12c. rose-carmine and reddish violet		70	2·00

1953 (2 June). Coronation. As No. 120 of Antigua.

125	3c. black and green		1·00	2·25

ARE YOU LOOKING TO SELL ALL OR PART OF YOUR COLLECTION?

Contact Stanley Gibbons Auctions on **020 7836 8444** for more information

16 Queen Elizabeth II

1954 (22 Feb). Chalk-surfaced paper. Wmk Mult Script CA. P 14 (T **16**) or 13 (T **17**).

126	**16**	½c. brown	10	60
127		1c. grey	1·25	1·25
128		2c. green	1·75	10
129		3c. yellow-orange and black	2·50	1·00
130		4c. rose-red	1·75	10
131		5c. black and brown-purple	2·25	1·00
132		6c. yellow-orange	2·25	60
133		8c. ultramarine	2·50	10
134		12c. dull and reddish purple	2·00	10
135		24c. black and green	2·00	20
136		48c. dull purple and ultramarine	8·00	2·75
137		60c. brown and green	6·00	2·25
138		$1.20 yellow-green and rose-red	7·00	3·50
139	**17**	$2.40 bluish green and red	11·00	6·00
140		$4.80 brown-purple and black	15·00	11·00
126/40 *Set of* 15			60·00	27·00

The 3c., 4c., 6c., 8c., 24c., 48c., 60c. and $1.20 have their value tablets unshaded.

The stamps of Leeward Islands were withdrawn and invalidated on 1 July 1956 when the federal colony was dissolved.

Montserrat

A local post office operated on Montserrat from 1702, although the first recorded postal marking does not occur until 1791. A branch of the British G.P.O. was established at Plymouth, the island capital, in 1852.

The stamps of Great Britain were used from 1858 until the overseas postal service reverted to local control on 1 April 1860.

In the interim period between 1860 and the introduction of Montserrat stamps in 1876 No. CC1 and a similar "uncrowned" handstamp were again used.

PLYMOUTH
CROWNED-CIRCLE HANDSTAMPS

CC1 C **1** MONTSERRAT (R.) (15.7.1852).........*Price on cover* £4500

No. CC1 was used as an emergency measure, struck in black, during 1886.

Stamps of GREAT BRITAIN cancelled "A 08"
1858 (8 May)–**60**.
Z1		1d. rose-red (1857), perf 14	£1300
Z2		4d. rose (1857)	
Z3		6d. lilac (1856)	£550
Z4		1s. green (1856)	£2750

PRICES FOR STAMPS ON COVER TO 1945	
Nos. 1/2	from × 50
No. 3	†
Nos. 4/5	from × 10
Nos. 6/13	from × 12
Nos. 14/22	from × 4
No. 23	—
Nos. 24/33	from × 4
Nos. 35/47	from × 3
No. 48	—
Nos. 49/59	from × 3
Nos. 60/2	from × 15
Nos. 63/83	from × 3
Nos. 84/93	from × 4
Nos. 94/7	from × 3
Nos. 98/100	from × 8
Nos. 101/12	from × 5

1   (**2**)   **3** (Die I)

(T **1** recess D.L.R.)

1876 (Aug)–**83**. Stamps of Antigua optd with T **2**. Wmk Crown CC. P 14.
1	**1**	1d. red	26·00	17·00
		a. Bisected (½d.) (1883) (on cover)	†	£1400
		b. Inverted "S"	£1000	£750
		w. Wmk inverted	50·00	45·00
		x. Wmk reversed	30·00	22·00
		y. Wmk inverted and reversed	50·00	60·00
2		6d. green	70·00	45·00
		a. Trisected (used as 2d.) (12.83) (on cover)	†	£6000
		b. Inverted "S"	£1900	£1200
		x. Wmk reversed	—	£100
3		6d. blue-green	£1300	
		a. Inverted "S"	£13000	

Nos. 1/3 were overprinted either from a setting of 120 (12×10) or from a setting of 60 (6×10) applied twice to each sheet. This setting of 60 had an inverted "S" on R. 2/3. The same setting was subsequently used for some sheets of Nos. 6 and 8.

No. 1 was bisected and used for a ½d. in 1883. This bisected stamp is found surcharged with a small "½" in *black* and also in *red*; both were unofficial and they did not emanate from the Montserrat P.O. (*Price on cover, from* £500).

The 6d. in blue-green is only known unused.

(T **3** typo D.L.R.)

1880 (Jan). Wmk Crown CC. P 14.
4	**3**	2½d. red-brown	£250	£180
5		4d. blue	£150	40·00
		w. Wmk inverted	—	£225
		x. Wmk reversed	£500	

1883 (Mar). Wmk Crown CA. P 12.
6	**1**	1d. red	75·00	60·00
		a. Inverted "S"	£2000	£1300
		b. Bisected (½d.) (on cover)	†	£1600
		x. Wmk reversed	—	55·00

Top left triangle detached (Pl 2 R. 3/3 of right pane)

1884–85. Wmk Crown CA. P 14.
7	**3**	½d. dull green	1·00	11·00
		a. Top left triangle detached	£190	
8	**1**	1d. red	25·00	16·00
		a. Inverted "S"	£1000	£1000
		bx. Wmk reversed	—	26·00
		c. *Rose-red* (1885)	26·00	13·00
		ca. Bisected vert (½d.) (on cover)	†	£1300
		cb. Inverted "S"	£1100	£1000
		cx. Wmk reversed	29·00	21·00
9	**3**	2½d. red-brown	£275	65·00
10		2½d. ultramarine (1885)	26·00	21·00
		a. Top left triangle detached	£550	£450
		w. Wmk inverted	£140	
11		4d. blue	£1800	£250
12		4d. mauve (1885)	5·50	3·00
		a. Top left triangle detached	£350	
10s, 12s Optd "SPECIMEN" *Set of* 2			£475	

The stamps for Montserrat were superseded by the general issue for Leeward Islands in November 1890, but the following issues were in concurrent use with the stamps inscribed "LEEWARD ISLANDS" until 1 July 1956, when Leeward Islands stamps were withdrawn and invalidated.

4 Device of the Colony   **5**

(Typo D.L.R.)

1903 (Aug).

(a) Wmk Crown CA. P 14
14	**4**	½d. grey-green and green	75	19·00
15		1d. grey-black and red	75	40
		w. Wmk inverted	£250	
16		2d. grey and brown	5·50	50·00
17		2½d. grey and blue	1·50	1·75
18		3d. dull orange and deep purple	6·00	50·00
19		6d. dull purple and olive	10·00	60·00
20		1s. green and bright purple	10·00	21·00
21		2s. green and brown-orange	35·00	22·00
22		2s.6d. green and black	25·00	50·00

(b) Wmk Crown CC. P 14
23	**5**	5s. black and scarlet	£160	£225
14/23 *Set of* 10			£225	£450
14s/23s Optd "SPECIMEN" *Set of* 10			£200	

1904–08. Ordinary paper (½d., 2d., 3d., 6d.) or chalk-surfaced paper (others). Wmk Mult Crown CA. P 14.
24	**4**	½d. grey-green and green	9·50	2·75
		a. Chalk-surfaced paper (3.06)	1·00	1·25

25		1d. grey-black and red (11.07)	17·00	24·00
26		2d. grey and brown	1·50	10·00
		a. Chalk-surfaced paper (5.06)	2·25	1·25
27		2½d. grey and blue (12.05)	2·50	6·50
28		3d. dull orange and deep purple	8·00	8·00
		a. Chalk-surfaced paper (5.08)	10·00	2·50
29		6d. dull purple and olive	7·50	35·00
		a. Chalk-surfaced paper (5.08)	12·00	5·50
30		1s. green and bright purple (5.08)	12·00	7·00
31		2s. green and orange (5.08)	55·00	45·00
32		2s.6d. green and black (5.08)	60·00	55·00
33	**5**	5s. black and red (9.07)	£150	£160
24/33 *Set of* 10			£275	£275

1908 (June)–**14**. Ordinary paper (½d. to 2½d.) or chalk-surfaced paper (3d. to 5s.). Wmk Mult Crown CA. P 14.

35	**4**	½d. deep green (4.10)	8·50	1·00
36		1d. rose-red	1·40	30
38		2d. greyish slate (9.09)	1·75	20·00
39		2½d. blue	2·25	3·50
40		3d. purple/*yellow* (9.09)	1·00	18·00
		a. White back (1.14)	4·00	38·00
		as. Optd "SPECIMEN"	30·00	
43		6d. dull and deep purple (9.09)	10·00	55·00
		a. Dull and bright purple (1914)	14·00	55·00
44		1s. black/*green* (9.09)	8·50	45·00
45		2s. purple and bright blue/*blue* (9.09)	48·00	55·00
46		2s.6d. black and red/*blue* (9.09)	35·00	75·00
47	**5**	5s. red and green/*yellow* (9.09)	65·00	75·00
35/47 *Set of* 10			£160	£300
35s/47s Optd "SPECIMEN" *Set of* 10			£250	

Examples of most values are known showing forged Montserrat postmarks dated "OC 16 1909" or "NO 26 1910".

7

8

WAR STAMP

(**9**)

(T **7**/**8** typo D.L.R.)

1914. Chalk-surfaced paper. Wmk Mult Crown CA. P 14.

48	**7**	5s. red and green/*yellow*	85·00	£140
		s. Optd "SPECIMEN"	80·00	

1916 (10 Oct)–**22**. Ordinary paper (½d. to 2½d.) or chalk-surfaced paper (3d. to 5s.). Wmk Mult Crown CA. P 14.

49	**8**	½d. green	30	2·50
50		1d. scarlet	1·75	75
		a. Carmine-red	30·00	9·00
51		2d. grey	2·00	4·00
52		2½d. bright blue	1·75	26·00
53		3d. purple/*yellow*	1·25	22·00
		a. On pale yellow (13.7.22)	1·00	19·00
		as. Optd "SPECIMEN"	28·00	
54		4d. grey-black and red/*pale yellow* (13.7.22)	6·50	38·00
55		6d. dull and deep purple	3·00	29·00
56		1s. black/*blue-green* (*olive back*)	3·00	35·00
57		2s. purple and blue/*blue*	17·00	50·00
58		2s.6d. black and red/*blue*	32·00	85·00
59		5s. green and red/*yellow*	55·00	85·00
49/59 *Set of* 11			£110	£325
49s/59s Optd "SPECIMEN" *Set of* 11			£225	

1917 (8 Oct)–**18**. No. 49 optd with T **9**.

60	**8**	½d. green (R.)	10	1·50
		a. Short opt (right pane R. 10/1)	11·00	
		y. Wmk inverted and reversed	65·00	
61		½d. green (Blk.) (5.18)	3·25	5·00
		a. Short opt (right pane R. 10/1)	35·00	
		b. Deep green (10.18)	15	1·75
		ba. "C" and "A" missing from wmk	£1200	
		bb. Short opt (right pane R. 10/1)	11·00	
		w. Wmk inverted	£130	

Nos. 60a, 61a, and 61bb show the overprint 2 mm high instead of 2½ mm.

No. 61ba shows the "C" omitted from one impression and the "A" missing from the next. The price quoted is for a horizontal pair.

1919 (4 Mar). T **8**. Special printing in orange. Value and "WAR STAMP" as T **9** inserted in black at one printing.

62		1½d. black and orange	10	30
60s/2s Optd "SPECIMEN" *Set of* 3			£100	

1922 (13 July)–**29**. Ordinary paper (¼d. to 3d.) (No. 73) or chalk-surfaced paper (others). Wmk Mult Script CA. P 14.

63	**8**	¼d. brown	15	5·50
64		½d. green (5.4.23)	30	30
65		1d. bright violet (5.4.23)	30	60
66		1d. carmine (1929)	75	1·50
67		1½d. orange-yellow	1·75	9·50
68		1½d. carmine (5.4.23)	45	5·50
69		1½d. red-brown (1929)	3·00	50
70		2d. grey	50	2·00
71		2½d. deep bright blue	8·50	16·00
		a. Pale bright blue (17.8.26)	70	90
		as. Optd "SPECIMEN"	38·00	
72		2½d. orange-yellow (5.4.23)	1·25	19·00
73		3d. dull blue (5.4.23)	75	16·00
74		3d. purple/*yellow* (2.1.27)	1·10	5·00
75		4d. black and red/*pale yellow* (5.4.23)	75	13·00
76		5d. dull purple and olive	4·00	10·00
77		6d. pale and bright purple (5.4.23)	3·00	7·50
78		1s. black/*emerald* (5.4.23)	3·00	7·00
79		2s. purple and blue/*blue*	7·00	18·00
80		2s.6d. black and red/*blue* (5.4.23)	12·00	60·00
81		3s. green and violet	12·00	19·00
82		4s. black and scarlet	15·00	42·00
83		5s. green and red/*pale yellow* (6.23)	32·00	60·00
63/83 *Set of* 21			90·00	£275
63s/83s Optd or Perf (Nos. 66s, 69s) "SPECIMEN" *Set of* 21			£350	

10 Plymouth

(Recess D.L.R.)

1932 (18 Apr). 300th Anniv of Settlement of Montserrat. Wmk Mult Script CA. P 14.

84	**10**	½d. green	75	13·00
85		1d. scarlet	75	5·50
86		1½d. red-brown	1·25	2·50
87		2d. grey	1·50	21·00
88		2½d. ultramarine	1·25	18·00
89		3d. orange	1·50	21·00
90		6d. violet	2·25	38·00
91		1s. olive-brown	12·00	50·00
92		2s.6d. purple	48·00	80·00
93		5s. chocolate	£110	£180
84/93 *Set of* 10			£160	£375
84s/93s Perf "SPECIMEN" *Set of* 10			£250	

Examples of all values are known showing a forged G.P.O. Plymouth postmark dated "MY 13 32".

1935 (6 May). Silver Jubilee. As Nos. 91/4 of Antigua, but ptd by Waterlow & Sons. P 11×12.

94		1d. deep blue and scarlet	85	3·25
95		1½d. ultramarine and grey	2·25	3·50
96		2½d. brown and deep blue	2·25	4·50
97		1s. slate and purple	4·00	17·00
94/7 *Set of* 4			8·50	25·00
94s/7s Perf "SPECIMEN" *Set of* 4			£110	

1937 (12 May). Coronation. As Nos. 95/7 of Antigua, but printed by D.L.R. P 14.

98		1d. scarlet	35	1·50
99		1½d. yellow-brown	1·00	40
100		2½d. bright blue	60	1·50
98/100 *Set of* 3			1·75	3·00
98s/100s Perf "SPECIMEN" *Set of* 3			80·00	

11 Carr's Bay

12 Sea Island cotton

13 Botanic Station

MONTSERRAT

3d. "Tower" on hill (R. 2/2)

1s. Plate scratch (R. 10/5)

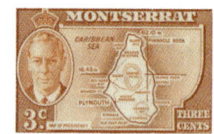

16 Map of colony **17** Picking tomatoes

17a St Anthony's Church **18** Badge of Presidency

19 Sea Island cotton: ginning **19a** Government House

(Recess D.L.R.)

1938 (2 Aug)–**48**. Wmk Mult Script CA. P 12 (10s., £1) or 13 (others).

101	**11**	½d. blue-green	4·50	2·00
		a. Perf 14 (1942)	15	20
102	**12**	1d. carmine	4·25	40
		a. Perf 14 (1943)	1·25	30
103		1½d. purple	24·00	1·25
		a. Perf 14 (1942)	1·00	50
		ab. "A" of "CA" missing from wmk	£1200	
104	**13**	2d. orange	24·00	1·00
		a. Perf 14 (1942)	1·50	70
105	**12**	2½d. ultramarine	3·50	1·50
		a. Perf 14 (1943)	50	30
106	**11**	3d. brown	8·00	2·00
		a. Perf 14. *Red-brown* (1942)	2·25	40
		ab. *Deep brown* (1943)	1·75	7·50
		ac. "Tower" on hill	£120	£200
107	**13**	6d. violet	24·00	1·25
		a. Perf 14 (1943)	3·50	60
108	**11**	1s. lake	25·00	1·25
		aa. Plate scratch	£180	38·00
		a. Perf 14 (1942)	2·25	30
109	**13**	2s.6d. slate-blue	45·00	1·00
		a. Perf 14 (1943)	24·00	3·00
110	**11**	5s. rose-carmine	48·00	10·00
		a. Perf 14 (1942)	29·00	3·00
111	**13**	10s. pale blue (1.4.70)	19·00	22·00
112	**11**	£1 black (1.4.48)	24·00	40·00
101a/12 *Set of 12*			95·00	60·00
101s/12s Perf "SPECIMEN" *Set of 12*			£325	

Nos. 101/2 exist in coils constructed from normal sheets.

1946 (1 Nov). Victory. As Nos. 110/11 of Antigua.

113		1½d. purple	15	15
114		3d. chocolate	15	15
113s/14s Perf "SPECIMEN" *Set of 2*			80·00	

1949 (3 Jan). Royal Silver Wedding. As Nos. 112/13 of Antigua.

115		2½d. ultramarine	10	10
116		5s. carmine	4·75	13·00

1949 (10 Oct). 75th Anniv of U.P.U. As Nos. 114/17 of Antigua.

117		2½d. ultramarine	15	1·25
118		3d. brown	1·75	1·25
119		6d. purple	30	1·25
120		1s. purple	30	1·25
117/20 *Set of 4*			2·25	4·50

(New Currency. 100 cents = 1 West Indies, later Eastern Caribbean dollar)

1951 (16 Feb). Inauguration of B.W.I. University College. As Nos. 118/19 of Antigua.

121		3c. black and purple	20	1·25
122		12c. black and violet	20	1·25

14 Government House  **15** Sea Island cotton: cultivation

(Recess B.W.)

1951 (17 Sept). T **14/19a**. Wmk Mult Script CA. P 11½×11.

123	**14**	1c. black	10	2·75
124	**15**	2c. green	15	1·00
125	**16**	3c. orange-brown	40	70
126	**17**	4c. carmine	30	2·75
127	**17a**	5c. reddish violet	30	1·00
128	**18**	6c. olive-brown	30	30
129	**19**	8c. deep blue	2·75	20
130	**17a**	12c. blue and chocolate	1·00	30
131	**17**	24c. carmine and yellow-green	1·25	30
132	**19**	60c. black and carmine	9·00	5·00
133	**15**	$1.20 yellow-green and blue	7·00	7·50
134	**19a**	$2.40 black and green	16·00	21·00
135	**18**	$4.80 black and purple	30·00	30·00
123/135 *Set of 13*			60·00	65·00

In the 4c. and 5c. the portrait is on the left and on the 12c. and 24c. it is on the right.

1953 (2 June). Coronation. As No. 120 of Antigua.

136		2c. black and deep green	60	40

20 Government House

Two Types of ½c., 3c., 6c. and $4.80: I. Inscr "PRESIDENCY". II. Inscr "COLONY".

1953 (15 Oct)–**62**. As King George VI issue, but with portrait of Queen Elizabeth II as in T **20**. Wmk Mult Script CA. P 11½×11.

136a	**16**	½c. deep violet (I) (3.7.56)	50	10
136b		½c. deep violet (II) (1.9.58)	80	10
137	**20**	1c. black	10	10
138	**15**	2c. green	15	10
139	**16**	3c. orange-brown (I)	50	10
139a		3c. orange-brown (II) (1.9.58)	80	2·00
140	**17**	4c. carmine-red (1.6.55)	30	20
141	**17a**	5c. reddish lilac (1.6.55)	30	1·00
142	**18**	6c. deep bistre-brown (I) (1.6.55)	30	10
142a		6c. deep bistre-brown (II) (1.9.58)	55	15
		ab. *Deep sepia-brown* (30.7.62)	12·00	6·50
143	**19**	8c. deep bright blue (1.6.55)	1·00	10
144	**17a**	12c. blue and red-brown (1.6.55)	1·50	10
145	**17**	24c. carmine-red and green (1.6.55)	1·50	20
145a	**15**	48c. yellow-olive and purple (15.10.57)	13·00	5·00
146	**19**	60c. black and carmine (1.6.55)	9·00	2·25
147	**15**	$1.20 green and greenish blue (1.6.55)	18·00	11·00
148	**19a**	$2.40 black and bluish green (1.6.55)	18·00	22·00
149	**18**	$4.80 black and deep purple (I) (1.6.55)	5·00	10·00
149a		$4.80 black and deep purple (II) (1.9.58)	25·00	10·00
136a/49 *Set of 15*			60·00	45·00

See also No. 157.

1958 (22 Apr). Inauguration of British Caribbean Federation. As Nos. 135/7 of Antigua.

150		3c. deep green	60	20
151		6c. blue	80	75
152		12c. scarlet	1·00	15
150/2 *Set of 3*			2·25	1·00

1963 (8 July). Freedom from Hunger. As No. 146 of Antigua.
153   12c. reddish violet 30   15

1963 (2 Sept). Red Cross Centenary. As Nos. 147/8 of Antigua.
154   4c. red and black 15   20
155   12c. red and blue 35   50

1964 (23 Apr). 400th Birth Anniv of William Shakespeare. As No. 164 of Antigua.
156   12c. indigo 35   10

1964 (29 Oct). As No. 138 but wmk w **12**.
157   2c. green 60   20

1965 (17 May). I.T.U. Centenary. As Nos. 166/7 of Antigua.
158   4c. vermilion and violet 15   10
159   48c. light emerald and carmine 30   20

21 Pineapple    **22** Avocado

(Des Sylvia Goaman. Photo Harrison)

1965 (16 Aug). T **21/2** and similar vert designs showing vegetables, fruit or plants. Multicoloured. W w **12** (upright). P 15×14.
160   1c. Type **21** 10   10
      w. Wmk inverted .... 1·00   1·50
161   2c. Type **22** 10   10
162   3c. Soursop 10   10
163   4c. Pepper 10   10
164   5c. Mango 10   10
165   6c. Tomato 10   10
166   8c. Guava 10   10
167   10c. Ochro 10   10
168   12c. Lime 50   40
      w. Wmk inverted .... —   38·00
169   20c. Orange 30   10
170   24c. Banana 20   10
171   42c. Onion 75   60
172   48c. Cabbage .... 2·00   75
173   60c. Pawpaw .... 3·00   1·10
174   $1.20 Pumpkin .... 2·00   5·00
175   $2.40 Sweet potato .... 7·50   8·50
176   $4.80 Egg plant .... 7·50   11·00
160/76 Set of 17 .... 22·00   25·00
See also Nos. 213/22.

1965 (25 Oct). International Co-operation Year. As Nos. 168/9 of Antigua.
177   2c. reddish purple and turquoise-green 10   20
178   12c. deep bluish green and lavender 25   10

1966 (26 Jan). Churchill Commemoration. As Nos. 170/3 of Antigua.
179   1c. new blue 10   2·00
      a. Cerise (sky) omitted £650
180   2c. deep green 25   20
181   24c. brown 80   10
182   42c. bluish violet 90   1·00
179/82 Set of 4 .... 1·75   3·00

1966 (4 Feb). Royal Visit. As No. 174 of Antigua.
183   14c. black and ultramarine .... 1·00   15
184   24c. black and magenta .... 1·50   15

1966 (20 Sept). Inauguration of W.H.O. Headquarters, Geneva. As Nos. 178/9 of Antigua.
185   12c. black, yellow-green and light blue 20   25
186   60c. black, light purple and yellow-brown 55   75

1966 (1 Dec). 20th Anniv of U.N.E.S.C.O. As Nos. 196/8 of Antigua.
187   4c. slate-violet, red, yellow and orange 10   10
      a. Orange omitted £130
188   60c. orange-yellow, violet and deep olive ... 55   20
189   $1.80 black, bright purple and orange ...... 1·75   85
187/9 Set of 3 .... 2·10   1·00
On No. 187a the omission of the orange only affects the squares of the lower case letters so that they appear yellow, the same as the capital squares.

25 Yachting

(Des and photo Harrison)

1967 (29 Dec). International Tourist Year. T **25** and similar multicoloured designs. W w **12** (sideways on 15c.). P 14.
190   5c. Type **25** 10   10
191   15c. Waterfall near Chance Mountain (vert)... 15   10
192   16c. Fishing, skin-diving and swimming 20   70
193   24c. Playing golf .... 1·25   45
190/3 Set of 4 .... 1·50   1·25

$1.00

(26)

1968 (6 May). Nos. 168, 170, 172 and 174/6 surch as T **26**. W w **12** (upright).
194   15c. on 12c. Lime 20   15
195   25c. on 24c. Banana 25   15
196   50c. on 48c. Cabbage 45   15
197   $1 on $1.20 Pumpkin .... 1·10   40
198   $2.50 on $2.40 Sweet potato .... 1·10   4·25
199   $5 on $4.80 Egg plant .... 1·10   4·25
194/9 Set of 6 .... 3·75   8·50
See also Nos. 219 etc.

27 Sprinting 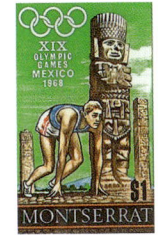   **28** Sprinting, and Aztec Pillars

(Des G. Vasarhelyi. Photo Harrison)

1968 (31 July). Olympic Games, Mexico. T **27/8** and similar designs. W w **12** (sideways on $1). P 14.
200   15c. deep claret, emerald and gold 10   10
201   25c. blue, gold and green 15   10
202   50c. green, red and gold 25   15
203   $1 multicoloured 35   30
200/3 Set of 4 75   55
Designs: Horiz as T **27**—25c. Weightlifting; 50c. Gymnastics.

31 Alexander Hamilton

(Des and photo Harrison)

1968 (6 Dec*). Human Rights Year. T **31** and similar horiz designs. Multicoloured. W w **12**. P 14×14½.
204   5c. Type **31** 10   10
205   15c. Albert T. Marryshow 10   10
206   25c. William Wilberforce 10   10
207   50c. Dag Hammarskjöld 10   15
208   $1 Dr. Martin Luther King 25   30
204/8 Set of 5 60   65
*Although first day covers were postmarked 2 December, these stamps were not put on sale in Montserrat until 6 December.

32 "The Two Trinities" (Murillo)    **33** "The Adoration of the Kings" (detail, Botticelli)

MONTSERRAT

(Des and photo Harrison)

1968 (16 Dec). Christmas. W w **12** (sideways). P 14½×14.

209	**32**	5c. multicoloured	10	10
210	**33**	15c. multicoloured	10	10
211	**32**	25c. multicoloured	10	10
212	**33**	50c. multicoloured	25	25
209/12 Set of 4			50	45

1969–70. As Nos. 160/4, 167, 167 and 194/6 but wmk w **12** sideways*.

213		1c. Type **21** (24.6.69)	10	10
214		2c. Type **22** (23.4.70)	1·25	85
215		3c. Soursop (24.6.69)	30	15
		w. Wmk Crown to right of CA	24·00	
216		4c. Pepper (24.6.69)	60	15
217		5c. Mango (23.4.70)	2·50	85
218		10c. Ochro (24.6.69)	50	15
		w. Wmk Crown to right of CA	90·00	
219		15c. on 12c. Lime (24.6.69)	60	20
220		20c. Orange (17.3.69)	75	20
221		25c. on 24c. Banana (24.6.69)	1·00	25
222		50c. on 48c. Cabbage (24.6.69)	7·00	12·00
213/22 Set of 10			13·00	13·50

*The normal sideways watermark shows Crown to left of CA, *as seen from the back of the stamp*.

The 1c., 3c., 4c., 10c., 15c. and 20c. exist with PVA gum as well as gum arabic, but the 2c. and 5c. exist with PVA gum only.

34 Map showing "CARIFTA" Countries

35 "Strength in Unity"

(Des J. Cooter. Photo Harrison)

1969 (27 May). First Anniv of CARIFTA (Caribbean Free Trade Area). W w **12** (sideways* on T **34**). P 14.

223	**34**	15c. multicoloured	10	10
224		20c. multicoloured	10	10
		w. Wmk Crown to right of CA	1·25	
225	**35**	35c. multicoloured	10	20
226		30c. multicoloured	15	20
223/6 Set of 4			40	55

*The normal sideways watermark shows Crown to left of CA, *as seen from the back of the stamp*.

36 Telephone Receiver and Map of Montserrat

40 Dolphin (fish)

(Des R. Reid, adapted by V. Whiteley. Litho P.B.)

1969 (29 July). Development Projects. T **36** and similar vert designs. Multicoloured. W w **12**. P 13½.

227		15c. Type **36**	10	10
228		25c. School symbols and map	10	10
229		50c. Hawker Siddeley H.S.748 aircraft and map	15	20
230		$1 Electricity pylon and map	25	75
227/30 Set of 4			55	1·00

(Des Harrison. Photo Enschedé)

1969 (1 Nov). Game Fish. T **40** and similar horiz designs. Multicoloured. P 13×13½.

231		5c. Type **40**	35	10
232		15c. Atlantic Sailfish	50	10
233		25c. Black-finned Tuna	60	10
234		40c. Spanish Mackerel	80	55
231/4 Set of 4			2·00	75

41 King Caspar before the Virgin and Child (detail) (Norman 16th-cent stained glass window)

42 "Nativity" (Leonard Limosin)

(Des J. Cooter. Litho D.L.R.)

1969 (10 Dec). Christmas. Paintings multicoloured; frame colours given. W w **12** (sideways on 50c.). P 13.

235	**41**	15c. black, gold and violet	10	10
236		25c. black and vermilion	10	10
237	**42**	50c. black, ultramarine and yellow-orange	15	15
235/7 Set of 3			30	30

43 "Red Cross Sale"

(Des and litho J. W.)

1970 (13 Apr). Centenary of British Red Cross. T **43** and similar horiz designs. Multicoloured. W w **12** (sideways). P 14½×14.

238		3c. Type **43**	15	25
239		4c. School for deaf children	15	25
240		15c. Transport services for disabled	20	20
241		20c. Workshop	20	60
238/41 Set of 4			65	1·10

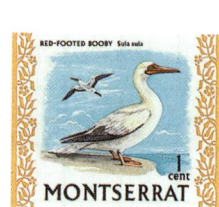

44 Red-footed Booby

45 "Madonna and Child with Animals" (Brueghel the Elder, after Dürer)

(Des V. Whiteley. Photo Harrison)

1970 (2 July)–**74**. Birds. T **44** and similar multicoloured designs. W w **12** (sideways* on vert designs and upright on horiz designs). Glazed ordinary paper ($10) or chalk-surfaced paper (others). P 14×14½ (horiz) or 14½×14 (vert).

242		1c. Type **44**	10	10
		w. Wmk inverted	19·00	
243		2c. American Kestrel (*vert*)	15	15
		a. Glazed, ordinary paper (22.1.71)	1·25	3·00
244		3c. Magnificent Frigate Bird (*vert*)	15	15
		w. Wmk Crown to right of CA		
245		4c. Great Egret (*vert*)	2·00	15
246		5c. Brown Pelican (*vert*)	2·50	10
		aw. Wmk Crown to right of CA	2·50	
		b. Glazed, ordinary paper (22.1.71)	1·50	2·00
		bw. Wmk Crown to right of CA		
247		10c. Bananaquit (*vert*)	40	10
		a. Glazed, ordinary paper (22.1.71)	1·50	2·00
248		15c. Smooth-billed Ani	30	15
		a. Glazed, ordinary paper (22.1.71)	4·50	5·00
		aw. Wmk inverted	4·50	
249		20c. Red-billed Tropic Bird	35	15
		a. Glazed, ordinary paper (22.1.71)	1·50	2·00
250		25c. Montserrat Oriole	50	50
		a. Glazed, ordinary paper (22.1.71)	5·00	6·00
251		50c. Green-throated Carib (*vert*)	5·50	1·50

MONTSERRAT

252	a. Glazed, ordinary paper (22.1.71)		4·00	4·50
	$1 Antillean Crested Hummingbird		10·00	1·00
	aw. Wmk inverted		26·00	
	b. Glazed, ordinary paper (22.1.71)		4·25	5·00
253	$2.50 Little Blue Heron (vert)		5·50	12·00
	a. Glazed, ordinary paper (22.1.71)		8·00	10·00
254	$5 Purple-throated Carib		7·50	19·00
	a. Glazed, ordinary paper (22.1.71)		13·00	18·00
254c	$10 Forest Thrush (30.10.74)		18·00	20·00
242/54c Set of 14			40·00	45·00

*The normal sideways watermark shows Crown to left of CA, *as seen from the back of the stamp.*

Eight values in this set were subsequently reissued with the watermark sideways on horizontal designs and upright on vertical designs.

(Des G. Drummond. Litho D.L.R.)

1970 (1 Oct*). Christmas. T **45** and similar multicoloured design. W w **12**. P 13½×14.

255	5c. Type **45**	10	10
	w. Wmk inverted	28·00	
256	15c. "The Adoration of the Shepherds" (Domenichino)	10	10
257	20c. Type **45**	10	10
	w. Wmk inverted	4·00	
258	$1 As 15c.	35	1·50
255/8 Set of 4		60	1·60

*This was the local date of issue but the stamps were released by the Crown Agents on 21 September.

46 War Memorial

47 Girl Guide and Badge

(Des V. Whiteley. Litho J.W.)

1970 (30 Nov). Tourism. T **46** and similar horiz designs. Multicoloured. W w **12** (sideways*). P 14½×14.

259	5c. Type **46**	10	10
260	15c. Plymouth from Fort St. George	10	10
261	25c. Carr's Bay	15	15
262	50c. Golf Fairway	1·00	2·25
	w. Wmk Crown to right of CA	7·00	
259/62 Set of 4		1·25	2·40
MS263 135×109 mm. Nos. 259/62		2·50	2·25

*The normal sideways watermark shows Crown to left of CA, *as seen from the back of the stamp.*

(Des V. Whiteley. Litho Questa)

1970 (31 Dec). Diamond Jubilee of Montserrat Girl Guides. T **47** and similar vert design. Multicoloured. W w **12**. P 14.

264	10c. Type **47**	10	10
265	15c. Brownie and Badge	10	10
266	25c. As 15c.	15	15
267	40c. Type **47**	20	80
264/7 Set of 4		50	1·00

48 "Descent from the Cross" (Van Hemessen)

49 D.F.C. and D.F.M. in Searchlights

(Des J.W. Photo Enschedé)

1971 (22 Mar). Easter. T **48** and similar vert design. Multicoloured. W w **12**. P 13½.

268	5c. Type **48**	10	10
269	15c. "Noli me tangere" (Orcagna)	10	10
270	20c. Type **48**	10	10
271	40c. As 15c.	15	85
268/71 Set of 4		40	1·00

(Des Col. A. Maynard. Litho Questa)

1971 (8 July). Golden Jubilee of Commonwealth Ex-Services League. T **49** and similar vert designs. Multicoloured. W w **12**. P 14.

272	10c. Type **49**	15	10
273	20c. M.C., M.M. and jungle patrol	20	10
274	40c. D.S.C., D.S.M. and submarine action	20	15
275	$1 V.C. and soldier attacking bunker	30	80
272/5 Set of 4		75	1·00

50 "The Nativity with Saints" (Romanino)

51 Piper PA-23 Apache

(Des G. Drummond. Litho Questa)

1971 (16 Sept). Christmas. T **50** and similar vert design. Multicoloured. W w **12**. P 14×13½.

276	5c. Type **50**	10	10
277	15c. "Choir of Angels" (Simon Marmion)	10	10
278	20c. Type **50**	10	10
279	$1 As 15c.	35	40
276/9 Set of 4		55	60

(Des and litho J.W.)

1971 (16 Dec). 14th Anniv of Inauguration of L.I.A.T. (Leeward Islands Air Transport). T **51** and similar horiz designs. Multicoloured. W w **12** (sideways). P 13½.

280	5c. Type **51**	10	10
281	10c. Beech 50 Twin Bonanza	15	15
282	15c. de Havilland DH.114 Heron 2	30	15
283	20c. Britten Norman Islander	35	15
284	40c. de Havilland DHC-6 Twin Otter 100	50	45
285	75c. Hawker Siddeley H.S.748	1·40	2·25
280/5 Set of 6		2·50	3·00
MS286 203×102 mm. Nos. 280/5		7·00	13·00

52 "Chapel of Christ in Gethsemane", Coventry Cathedral

(Des G. Drummond. Litho A. & M.)

1972 (9 Mar). Easter. T **52** and similar horiz design. Multicoloured. W w **12**. P 13.

287	5c. Type **52**	10	10
288	10c. "The Agony in the Garden" (Bellini)	10	10
289	20c. Type **52**	10	10
290	75c. As 10c.	35	1·25
287/90 Set of 4		55	1·40

53 Lizard

MONTSERRAT

(Des G. Drummond. Litho Questa)

1972 (20 July). Reptiles. T **53** and similar multicoloured designs. W w **12** (sideways on 40c. and $1). P 14½.

291	15c. Type **53**	15	10
292	20c. Mountain Chicken (frog)	20	10
293	40c. Iguana (*horiz*)	35	20
294	$1 Tortoise (*horiz*)	1·00	1·00
291/4 Set of 4		1·50	1·25

1972 (21 July)–**74**. As No. 242 etc., but W w **12**, sideways* on horiz designs (1, 15, 20, 25c.) and upright on vert designs (others). Glazed, ordinary paper.

295	1c. Type **44**	3·00	75
	a. Chalk-surfaced paper (4.2.74)	1·00	45
296	2c. American Kestrel	4·50	2·00
	aw. Wmk inverted	10·00	
	b. Chalk-surfaced paper (4.2.74)	3·75	45
297	3c. Magnificent Frigate Bird	15·00	13·00
298	4c. Great Egret (*chalk-surfaced paper*) (4.2.74)	1·00	3·00
	w. Wmk inverted	6·00	
299	5c. Brown Pelican (8.3.73)	2·75	30
	a. Chalk-surfaced paper (4.2.74)	75	55
300	15c. Smooth-billed Ani (8.3.73)	50	45
	a. Chalk-surfaced paper (2.10.73)	85	1·00
	aw. Wmk Crown to left of CA (17.5.74)	2·75	2·25
301	20c. Red-billed Tropic Bird (*chalk-surfaced paper*) (2.10.73)	1·40	1·50
302	25c. Montserrat Oriole (*chalk-surfaced paper*) (17.5.74)	3·25	3·50
295a/302 Set of 8		24·00	20·00

*The normal sideways watermark shows Crown to left of CA on 1c and 20c., and to right on 15c and 25c., *as seen from the back of the stamp*.

In 1973–74, during shortages of the 5c. value, letters can be found posted unstamped and franked with a "postage paid" mark. Other covers exist with the word "paid" in manuscript.

54 "Madonna of the Chair" (Raphael)

(Des J. Cooter. Litho Format)

1972 (18 Oct). Christmas. T **54** and similar horiz designs. Multicoloured. W w **12**. P 13½.

303	10c. Type **54**	10	10
304	35c. 'Virgin and Child with Cherub" (Fungai)	15	10
305	50c. "Madonna of the Magnificat" (Botticelli)	20	30
306	$1 "Virgin and Child with St. John and an Angel" (Botticelli)	30	65
303/6 Set of 4		65	1·00

55 Lime, Tomatoes and Pawpaw

56 *Passiflora herbertiana*

(Des (from photographs by D. Groves) and photo Harrison)

1972 (20 Nov). Royal Silver Wedding. Multicoloured; background colour given. W w **12**. P 14x14½.

307	**55** 35c. rose	10	10
308	$1 bright blue	20	20
	w. Wmk inverted	40·00	

(Des J. Cooter. Litho Walsall)

1973 (9 Apr). Easter. T **56** and and similar vert designs showing passion-flowers. Multicoloured. W w **12**. P 13½.

309	20c. Type **56**	20	10
310	35c. *P. vitifolia*	25	10
311	75c. *P. amabilis*	35	75
312	$1 *P.alata-caerulea*	50	80
309/12 Set of 4		1·10	1·60

Nos. 309/12 are inscribed on the reverse with information about the passion-flower.

57 Montserrat Monastery, Spain

58 "Virgin and Child" (School of Gerard David)

(Des J. Cooter. Litho Format)

1973 (9 July). 480th Anniv of Columbus's Discovery of Montserrat. T **57** and similar horiz designs. Multicoloured. W w **12**. P 13½.

313	10c. Type **57**	15	10
314	35c. Columbus sighting Montserrat	30	15
315	60c. *Santa Maria* off Montserrat	70	60
316	$1 Colony badge and map of voyage	80	70
313/16 Set of 4		1·75	1·40
MS317 126×134 mm. Nos. 313/16. Wmk inverted		9·00	13·00
w. Wmk upright		80·00	

(Des J. Cooter. Litho Questa)

1973 (22 Oct). Christmas. T **58** and similar vert designs. Multicoloured. W w **12** (sideways). P 13½.

318	20c. Type **58**	15	10
319	35c. The Holy Family with St. John" (Jordaens)	20	10
320	50c. "Virgin and Child" (Bellini)	25	30
321	90c. "Virgin and Child with Flowers" (Dolci)	50	70
318/21 Set of 4		1·00	1·00

58a Princess Anne and Captain Mark Phillips

59 Steel Band

(Des PAD Studio. Litho Questa)

1973 (14 Nov). Royal Wedding. Centre multicoloured. W w **12** (sideways). P 13½.

322	**58a** 35c. sage-green	10	10
323	$1 violet-blue	20	20

(Des J.W. Litho Questa)

1974 (8 Apr). 25th Anniv of University of West Indies. T **59** and similar designs. Multicoloured. W w **12** (sideways on 20c., $1 and **MS**328).

324	20c. Type **59**	15	10
325	35c. Masqueraders (*vert*)	15	10
326	60c. Student weaving (*vert*)	25	45
	w. Wmk inverted	†	£110
327	$1 University Centre, Montserrat	30	55
324/7 Set of 4		75	1·00
MS328 130×89 mm. Nos. 324/7		1·75	6·00

60 Hands with Letters

(Des P. Powell. Litho Walsall)

1974 (3 July). Centenary of Universal Postal Union. T **60** and similar horiz design. W w **12**. P 14½×14.

329	**60**	1c. multicoloured	10	10
330	–	2c. light rose-red, orange-vermilion and black	10	10
331	**60**	3c. multicoloured	10	10

332	–	5c. light yellow-orange, reddish orange and black	10	10
333	60	50c. multicoloured	20	20
334	–	$1 pale blue, turquoise-blue and black	40	65
329/34 Set of 6			70	1·00

Designs:—2c., 5c., $1 Figures from U.P.U. Monument.

02¢
(61)

1974 (2 Oct). Various stamps surch as T **61**.

335		2c. on $1 (No. 252b)	1·00	2·75
		w. Wmk inverted	42·00	
336		5c. on 50c. (No. 333)	30	60
337		10c. on 60c. (No. 326)	65	1·75
		a. Surch double		
338		20c. on $1 (No. 252b)	30	2·50
		a. "2" with serifs (Pl 1B R. 3/1)	14·00	
		b. Bottom bar of surch omitted (Pl 1B R. 5/1-5)	4·75	
339		35c. on $1 (No. 334)	40	1·25
335/9 Set of 5			2·40	8·00

62 Churchill and Houses of Parliament

63 Carib "Carbet"

(Des R. Granger Barrett. Litho D.L.R.)

1974 (30 Nov). Birth Centenary of Sir Winston Churchill. T **62** and similar vert design. Multicoloured. No wmk. P 13×13½.

340	35c. Type **62**		15	10
341	70c. Churchill and Blenheim Palace		20	20
MS342 81×85 mm. Nos. 340/1			50	70

(Des C. Abbott. Litho Walsall)

1975 (3 Mar). Carib Artefacts. T **63** and similar horiz designs.

(a) W w 12 (sideways). From sheets. P 14

343	5c. lake-brown, yellow and black		10	10
344	20c. black, lake-brown and yellow		10	10
345	35c. black, yellow and lake-brown		15	10
346	70c. yellow, lake-brown and black		45	40
343/6 Set of 4			70	60

(b) No wmk. Self-adhesive with advertisements on the reverse. From booklets. Rouletted

347	5c. lake-brown, yellow and black		15	25
	a. Booklet pane. Nos. 347/50 se-tenant		90	
348	20c. black, lake-brown and yellow		15	25
	a. Booklet pane. Nos. 348×3 and No. 349×3		90	
349	35c. black, yellow and lake-brown		15	25
350	70c. yellow, lake-brown and black		55	80
347/50 Set of 4			90	1·40

Designs:—20c. "Caracoli"; 35c. Club or mace; 70c. Canoe.

64 One-Bitt Coin

(Des J. Cooter. Litho Questa)

1975 (1 Sept). Local Coinage, 1785–1801. T **64** and similar diamond-shaped designs. W w **14** (sideways). P 13½.

351	5c. black, light violet-blue and silver		10	10
352	10c. black, salmon and silver		15	10
353	35c. black, light blue-green and silver		20	15
354	$2 black, bright rose and silver		70	1·50
351/4 Set of 4			1·00	1·60
MS355 142×142 mm. Nos. 351/4			1·25	2·75

Designs:—10c. Eighth dollar; 35c. Quarter dollar; $2 One dollar.

No. MS355 has details of the coins depicted printed on the reverse side, beneath the gum.

65 1d. and 6d. Stamps of 1876

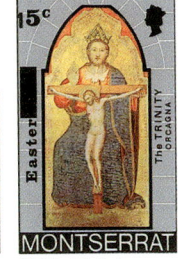

66 "The Trinity"

(Des J. Cooter. Litho J.W.)

1976 (5 Jan). Centenary of First Montserrat Postage Stamp. T **65** and similar horiz designs. W w **12** (sideways). P 13.

356	5c. deep carmine, yellowish green and black		15	10
357	10c. light yellow-ochre, scarlet and black		20	10
358	40c. multicoloured		40	40
359	55c. deep mauve, yellowish green and black		50	50
360	70c. multicoloured		60	70
361	$1.10 yellowish green, bright blue and grey-black		80	1·00
356/61 Set of 6			2·40	2·50
MS362 170×159 mm. Nos. 356/61. P 13½			2·50	5·50

Designs:—10c. G.P.O. and bisected 1d. stamp; 40c. Bisects on cover; 55c. G.B. 6d. used in Montserrat and local 6d. of 1876; 70c. Stamps for 2½d. rate, 1876; $1.10, Packet boat *Antelope* and 6d. stamp.

(Des J. Cooter. Litho Questa)

1976 (5 Apr). Easter. Unissued stamps prepared for Easter 1975 with values and date obliterated by black bars. T **66** and similar vert designs showing paintings by Orcagna. Multicoloured. W w **14**. P 13½.

363	15c. on 5c. Type **66**		10	10
	a. Surch omitted		40·00	
364	40c. on 35c. "The Resurrection"		20	15
	a. Surch omitted		40·00	
365	55c. on 70c. "The Ascension"		20	15
	a. Surch omitted		40·00	
366	$1.10 on $1 "Pentecost"		35	40
	a. Surch omitted		40·00	
363/6 Set of 4			70	65
MS367 160×142 mm. Nos. 363/6			1·50	2·25
	a. Surch omitted		£160	

For No. 363 the "1" was added to the original 5c. to make 15c.

2¢
(67)

1976 (12 Apr). Nos. 244 and 246/7 surch as T **67**.

368	2c. on 5c. Brown Pelican		10	1·25
369	30c. on 10c. Bananaquit		30	30
370	45c. on 3c. Magnificent Frigate Bird		40	50
	a. Surch triple			
	b. Surch double		32·00	
368/70 Set of 3			70	1·90

68 White Frangipani

(Des J. Cooter. Litho Questa)

1976 (5 July)–**80**. Various horiz designs showing Flowering Trees as T **68**. Multicoloured. Ordinary paper. W w **14** (sideways*). P 13½.

371	1c. Type **68**		10	10
372	2c. Cannon-ball Tree		10	10
	w. Wmk Crown to right of CA		70·00	

MONTSERRAT

373	3c. Lignum vitae		10	10
374	5c. Malay apple		15	10
	w. Wmk Crown to right of CA		27·00	
375	10c. Jacaranda		30	10
376	15c. Orchid Tree		50	10
	a. Chalk-surfaced paper (8.80)		1·25	2·00
377	20c. Manjak		30	10
	a. Chalk-surfaced paper (8.80)		1·25	2·00
378	25c. Tamarind		60	75
379	40c. Flame of the Forest		30	30
380	55c. Pink Cassia		40	40
381	70c. Long John		40	30
382	$1 Saman		50	80
383	$2.50 Immortelle		75	1·50
384	$5 Yellow Poui		1·10	2·25
	w. Wmk Crown to right of CA		10·00	
385	$10 Flamboyant		1·50	4·25
371/85 Set of 15			6·25	10·00

*The normal sideways watermark shows Crown to left of CA, *as seen from the back of the stamp.*

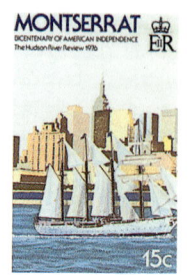

69 Mary and Joseph   **70** Hudson River Review, 1976

(Des L. Curtis. Litho Format)

1976 (4 Oct). Christmas. T **69** and similar vert designs. Multicoloured. W w **14**. P 14.

386	15c. Type **69**		10	15
387	20c. The Shepherds		10	15
388	55c. Mary and Jesus		15	15
389	$1.10 The Magi		30	70
386/9 Set of 4			50	1·00
MS390 95×135 mm. Nos. 386/9			60	2·25

(Des and litho J.W.)

1976 (13 Dec). Bicentenary of American Revolution. T **70** and similar vert designs. Multicoloured. W w **14**. P 13.

391	15c. Type **70**		65	50
	a. Horiz pair. Nos. 391 and 394		1·60	1·40
392	40c. *Raleigh* (American frigate), 1777*		80	70
	a. Horiz pair. Nos. 392/3		1·60	1·40
393	75c. H.M.S. *Druid* (frigate), 1777*		80	70
394	$1.25 Hudson River Review		1·00	90
391/4 Set of 4			3·00	2·50
MS395 95×145 mm. Nos. 391/4. P 13½			2·50	2·75

*The date is wrongly given on the stamps as "1776".

Nos. 392/3 and 391 with 394 were each printed in horizontal *se-tenant* pairs throughout the sheets, the pairs forming composite designs.

71 The Crowning   **72** *Ipomoea alba*

(Des G. Vasarhelyi. Litho J.W.)

1977 (7 Feb). Silver Jubilee. T **71** and similar horiz designs. Multicoloured. W w **14** (sideways). P 13.

396	30c. Royal Visit, 1966		10	10
397	45c. Cannons firing salute		15	10
398	$1 Type **71**		25	50
396/8 Set of 3			45	60

(Des J. Cooter. Litho Questa)

1977 (1 June). Flowers of the Night. T **72** and similar multicoloured designs. W w **14** (sideways on 40 and 55c.). P 14.

399	15c. Type **72**		15	10
400	40c. *Epiphyllum hookeri* (horiz)		25	30
401	55c. *Cereus hexagonus* (horiz)		25	30
402	$1.50 *Cestrum nocturnum*		60	1·40
399/402 Set of 4			1·10	1·90
MS403 126×130 mm. Nos. 399/402. Wmk sideways			1·25	3·50

73 Princess Anne laying Foundation Stone of Glendon Hospital

(Des BG Studio. Litho Questa)

1977 (3 Oct). Development. T **73** and similar horiz designs. Multicoloured. W w **14** (sideways*). P 14½×14.

404	20c. Type **73**		30	10
405	40c. Statesman (freighter) at Plymouth		35	15
406	55c. Glendon Hospital		35	20
	w. Wmk Crown to right of CA		38·00	
407	$1.50 Jetty at Plymouth Port		1·00	1·50
404/7 Set of 4			1·75	1·75
MS408 146×105 mm. Nos. 404/7			1·75	3·00

*The normal sideways watermark shows Crown to left of CA, *as seen from the back of the stamp.*

$1.00
SILVER JUBILEE 1977
ROYAL VISIT
TO THE CARIBBEAN
(**74**)

1977 (28 Oct). Royal Visit. Nos. 380/1 and 383 surch locally with T **74**.

409	$1 on 55c. Pink Cassia		25	45
410	$1 on 70c. Long John		25	45
411	$1 on $2.50 Immortelle		25	45
	a. Surch double			
	b. Surch omitted (top stamp of vert pair)			
409/11 Set of 3			65	1·25

On No. 411b the lower stamp in the pair also shows the surcharge bars omitted.

75 The Stable at Bethlehem   **76** Four-eyed Butterflyfish

(Des L. Curtis. Litho Walsall)

1977 (14 Nov). Christmas. T **75** and similar vert designs. Multicoloured. W w **14**. P 14×14½.

412	5c. Type **75**		10	10
413	40c. The Three Kings		10	10
414	55c. Three Ships		15	10
415	$2 Three Angels		40	2·00
412/15 Set of 4			65	2·00
MS416 119×115 mm. Nos. 412/15			1·00	2·25

(Des J.W. Litho Walsall)

1978 (15 Mar). Fish. T **76** and similar horiz designs. Multicoloured. W w **14** (sideways). P 14.

417	30c. Type **76**		45	10
418	40c. French Angelfish		50	15
419	55c. Blue Tang		60	15
420	$1.50 Queen Triggerfish		90	1·25
417/20 Set of 4			2·25	1·50
MS421 152×102 mm. Nos. 417/20			3·00	3·00

MONTSERRAT

77 St. Paul's Cathedral
78 *Alpinia speciosa*

(Des G. Drummond. Litho J.W.)

1978 (2 June). 25th Anniv of Coronation. T **77** and similar horiz designs. Multicoloured. W w **14** (sideways). P 13.

422	40c. Type **77**		10	10
423	55c. Chichester Cathedral		10	10
424	$1 Lincoln Cathedral		20	25
425	$2.50 Llandaff Cathedral		40	50
422/5 Set of 4			65	75
MS426 130×102 mm. Nos. 422/5. P 13½×14			70	1·25

Nos. 422/5 were each printed in sheets including two *se-tenant* stamp-size labels.

(Des J. Cooter. Litho J.W.)

1978 (18 Sept). Flowers. T **78** and similar vert designs. Multicoloured. W w **14**. P 13½×13.

427	40c. Type **78**		20	10
428	55c. *Allamanda cathartica*		20	15
429	$1 *Petrea volubilis*		35	45
430	$2 *Hippeastrum puniceum*		55	80
427/30 Set of 4			1·10	1·40

79 Private, 21st (Royal North British Fusiliers), 1796

80 Cub Scouts

(Des J.W. Litho Questa)

1978 (20 Nov). Military Uniforms (1st series). T **79** and similar vert designs showing soldiers from British infantry regiments. Multicoloured. W w **14**. P 14×14½.

431	30c. Type **79**		15	15
432	40c. Corporal, 86th (Royal County Down), 1831		20	15
433	55c. Sergeant, 14th (Buckinghamshire) 1837		25	15
434	$1.50 Officer, 55th (Westmorland), 1784		50	80
431/4 Set of 4			1·25	1·10
MS435 140×89 mm. Nos. 431/4			1·50	2·75

See also Nos. 441/5.

(Des J.W. Litho Walsall)

1979 (2 Apr). 50th Anniv of Boy Scout Movement on Montserrat. T **80** and similar multicoloured designs. W w **14** (sideways on 40 and 55c.). P 14.

436	40c. Type **80**		20	10
437	55c. Scouts with signalling equipment		20	15
438	$1.25 Camp fire (*vert*)		35	60
439	$2 Oath ceremony (*vert*)		45	1·00
436/9 Set of 4			1·10	1·75
MS440 120×110 mm. Nos. 436/9			1·25	2·25

(Des J.W. Litho Questa)

1979 (4 June). Military Uniforms (2nd series). Vert designs as T **79** showing soldiers from infantry regiments. Multicoloured. W w **14**. P 14×14½.

441	30c. Private, 60th (Royal American), 1783		15	15
442	40c. Private, 1st West India, 1819		20	15
443	55c. Officer, 5th (Northumberland), 1819		20	15
444	$2.50 Officer, 93rd (Sutherland Highlanders), 1830		60	1·25
441/4 Set of 4			1·00	1·50
MS445 139×89 mm. Nos. 441/4			1·25	2·50

81 Child reaching out to Adult

(Des G. Vasarhelyi. Litho Questa)

1979 (17 Sept). International Year of the Child. W w **14** (sideways). P 13½×14.

446	**81**	$2 black, orange-brown and flesh	50	55
MS447 85×99 mm. No. 446			50	1·10

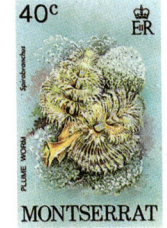

82 Sir Rowland Hill with Penny Black and Montserrat 1876 1d. Stamp
83 Plume Worm

(Des G. Vasarhelyi. Litho Questa)

1979 (1 Oct). Death Centenary of Sir Rowland Hill and Centenary of U.P.U. Membership. T **82** and similar horiz designs. Multicoloured. W w **14** (sideways). P 14.

448	40c. Type **82**		20	10
449	55c. U.P.U. emblem and notice announcing Leeward Islands entry into Union		20	15
450	$1 1883 Letter following U.P.U. membership		30	50
451	$2 Great Britain Post Office Regulations notice and Sir Rowland Hill		40	1·50
448/51 Set of 4			1·00	2·00
MS452 135×154 mm. Nos. 448/51			1·00	2·25

(Des G. Drummond. Litho Walsall)

1979 (26 Nov). Marine Life. T **83** and similar vert designs. Multicoloured. W w **14**. P 14.

453	40c. Type **83**		30	15
454	55c. Sea Fans		40	20
455	$2 Coral and Sponge		1·00	2·50
453/5 Set of 3			1·50	2·50

84 Tree Frog

(Des J. Cooter. Litho Rosenbaum Bros, Vienna)

1980 (4 Feb). Reptiles and Amphibians. T **84** and similar horiz designs. Multicoloured. W w **14** (sideways*). P 13½.

456	40c. Type **84**		15	15
	w. Wmk Crown to right of CA		20	
457	55c. Tree Lizard		15	15
	w. Wmk Crown to right of CA		30	
458	$1 Crapaud		30	50
	w. Wmk Crown to right of CA		55	
459	$2 Wood Slave		50	1·00
	w. Wmk Crown to right of CA		90	
456/9 Set of 4			1·00	1·60

*The normal sideways watermark shows Crown to left of CA, *as seen from the back of the stamp*.

85 *Marquess of Salisbury* and 1838 Handstamps

75th Anniversary of Rotary International
(**86**)

191

MONTSERRAT

(Des BG Studio. Litho Questa)

1980 (14 Apr). London 1980 International Stamp Exhibition. T **85** and similar horiz designs. Multicoloured. W w **14** (sideways). P 14.

460	40c. Type **85**	20	15
461	55c. Hawker Siddeley H.S.748 aircraft and 1976 55c. definitive	25	25
462	$1.20 *La Plata* (liner) and 1903 5s. stamp	30	55
463	$1.20 *Lady Hawkins* (packet steamer) and 1932 Tercentenary 5s. commemorative	30	55
464	$1.20 *Avon* (paddle-steamer) and Penny Red stamp with "A 08" postmark	30	55
465	$1.20 Aeronca Champion 17 airplane and 1953 $1.20 definitive	30	55
460/5 Set of 6		1·50	2·00
MS466 115×110 mm. Nos. 460/5. P 12		1·25	2·25

Nos. 460/5 were each printed in sheets of 4 stamps and two *se-tenant* stamp-size labels.

Some sheets of No. 462 showed the red colour omitted from the map in the right-hand label.

1980 (7 July). 75th Anniv of Rotary International. No. 383 optd with T **86**.

467	$2.50 Immortelle	55	85

87 Greek, French and U.S.A. Flags   **(88)** XX 5¢

(Des A. Theobald. Litho Questa)

1980 (7 July). Olympic Games, Moscow. T **87** and similar horiz designs. Multicoloured. W w **14** (sideways). P 13½×14.

468	40c. Type **87**	20	60
469	55c. Union, Swedish and Belgian flags	20	60
470	70c. French, Dutch and U.S.A flags	25	75
471	$1 German, Union and Finnish flags	30	75
472	$1.50 Australian Italian and Japanese flags	35	1·00
473	$2 Mexican, West German and Canadian flags	40	1·00
474	$2.50 "The Discus Thrower" (sculpture by Miron)	40	1·10
468/74 Set of 7		1·90	5·25
MS475 150×100 mm. Nos. 468/74		1·50	3·50
a. Bottom row of stamps in miniature sheet imperf on 3 sides		£550	

Nos. 468/74 were each printed in small sheets of 4 including one *se-tenant* stamp-size label.

No. **MS**475a shows the three stamps in the bottom row of the miniature sheet imperforate vertically and with no perforations between the stamps and the bottom margin.

1980 (30 Sept). Nos. 371, 373, 376 and 379 such as T **88**.

476	5c. on 3c. Lignum vitae	10	10
	a. Surch double, one inverted	38·00	
477	35c. on 1c. Type **68**	15	15
	a. Surch omitted (in pair with normal)	38·00	
478	35c. on 3c. Lignum vitae	15	15
479	35c. on 15c. Orchid Tree	15	15
	a. Surch double	38·00	
	b. Surch omitted (in vert pair with normal)	38·00	
480	55c. on 40c. Flame of the Forest	15	15
	a. Surch inverted	55·00	
481	$5 on 40c. Flame of the Forest	60	2·00
476/81 Set of 6		1·10	2·40

For 30c. on 15c. and $2.50 on 40c. see Nos. O33a and O39a.

89 *Lady Nelson*, 1928   **90** *Heliconius charithonia*

(Des J.W. Litho Walsall)

1980 (3 Nov). Mail Packet Boats (1st series). T **89** and similar horiz designs. Multicoloured. W w **14** (sideways). P 14.

482	40c. Type **89**	30	15
483	55c. *Chignecto*, 1913	30	15
484	$1 *Solent II*, 1878	50	65
485	$2 *Dee*, 1841	70	1·25
482/5 Set of 4		1·60	2·00

See also Nos. 615/19.

(Des J.W. Litho Questa)

1981 (2 Feb). Butterflies. T **90** and similar square designs. Multicoloured. W w **14** (inverted). P 14.

486	50c. Type **90**	50	40
	w. Wmk upright	1·75	
487	65c. *Pyrgus oileus*	60	45
488	$1.50 *Phoebis agarithe*	70	1·00
489	$2.50 *Danaus plexippus*	1·00	1·50
486/9 Set of 4		2·50	3·00

Nos. 486/9 were each printed in sheets including two *se-tenant* stamp-size labels.

91 Atlantic Spadefish   **92** Fort St. George

(Des G. Drummond. Litho J.W.)

1981 (20 Mar). Fish. Vert designs as T **91**. Multicoloured. W w **14**. No imprint date. P 13½×13.

490	5c. Type **91**	70	60
491	10c. Hogfish and Neon Goby	70	30
492	15c. Creole Wrasse	80	30
493	20c. Three-spotted Damselfish	1·00	30
494	25c. Sergeant Major	90	60
495	35c. Fin-spot Wrasse	80	30
496	45c. Schoolmaster	80	40
497	55c. Striped Parrotfish	1·10	45
498	65c. Bigeye	80	60
499	75c. French Grunt	80	60
	w. Wmk inverted	8·00	
500	$1 Rock Beauty	1·00	70
501	$2 Blue Chromis	1·50	1·10
502	$3 Royal Gramma ("Fairy Basslet") and Blueheads	1·50	1·75
503	$5 Cherub Angelfish	1·50	2·75
	w. Wmk inverted	13·00	
504	$7.50 Long jawed Squirrelfish	2·00	4·75
505	$10 Caribbean Long-nosed Butterflyfish	2·00	6·50
490/505 Set of 16		16·00	20·00

For stamps watermarked with W w **15** see Nos. 555/70.

(Des J. Cooter. Litho Format)

1981 (18 May). Montserrat National Trust. T **92** and similar horiz designs. Multicoloured. W w **14** (sideways). P 13½×14.

506	50c. Type **92**	25	20
507	65c. Bird sanctuary, Fox's Bay	45	35
508	$1.50 Museum	50	65
509	$2.50 Bransby Point Battery, *circa* 1780	60	1·10
506/9 Set of 4		1·60	2·10

92a Charlotte

92b Prince Charles and Lady Diana Spencer

(Des D. Shults. Litho Questa)

1981 (17-19 July-Nov). Royal Wedding. Horiz designs as T **92a**, showing Royal Yachts, and T **92b**. Multicoloured.

(a) W w **15**. P 14.

510	90c. Type **92a**	25	25
	aw. Wmk inverted	9·00	

MONTSERRAT

		b. Sheetlet. No. 510×6 and No. 511	2·10	
		bw. Wmk inverted	70·00	
511		90c. Type **92b**	85	85
		aw. Wmk inverted	25·00	
512		$3 *Portsmouth*	60	60
		aw. Wmk inverted	5·50	
		b. Sheetlet. No. 512×6 and No. 513	4·50	
		bw. Wmk inverted	48·00	
513		$3 Type **92b**	1·50	1·50
		aw. Wmk inverted	20·00	
514		$4 *Britannia*	75	75
		aw. Wmk inverted	8·00	
		b. Sheetlet. No. 514×6 and No. 515	5·50	
		bw. Wmk inverted	65·00	
515		$4 Type **92b**	1·75	1·75
		aw. Wmk inverted	25·00	
510/15 Set of 6			5·25	5·25
MS516 120×109 mm. $5 As No. 511. Wmk sideways. P 12 (19 Nov)			1·00	1·00

(b) Booklet stamps. No wmk. P 12 (19 Nov)

517		90c. Type **92a**	30	45
		a. Booklet pane. No. 517×4 with margins all round	1·10	
518		$3 Type **92b**	1·40	1·75
		a. Booklet pane. No. 518×2 with margins all round	2·75	

Nos. 510/15 were printed in sheetlets of seven stamps of the same face value, each containing six of the "Royal Yacht" design and one of the larger design showing Prince Charles and Lady Diana.

Nos. 517/18 come from $13.20 stamp booklets.

93 H.M.S. *Dorsetshire* and Fairey IIIF Firefly Seaplane

94 Methodist Church, Bethe I

(Des Court House Advertising Ltd. Litho Questa)

1981 (31 Aug). 50th Anniv of Montserrat Airmail Service. T **93** and similar horiz designs. Multicoloured. W w **14** (sideways). P 14.

519		50c. Type **93**	30	30
520		65c. Beech 50 Twin Bonanza	40	30
521		$1.50 de Havilland DH.89 Dragon Rapide *Lord Shaftesbury*	60	1·75
522		$2.50 Hawker Siddeley H.S.748 and maps of Montserrat and Antigua	80	3·00
519/22 Set of 4			1·90	4·75

(Des J. Cooter. Litho Walsall)

1981 (16 Nov). Christmas. Churches. T **94** and similar vert designs. Multicoloured. W w **14**. P 14×13½.

523		50c. Type **94**	15	15
524		65c. St George's Anglican Church, Harris	15	15
525		$1.50 St Peter's Anglican Church, St Peters	30	60
526		$2.50 St Patrick's R.C. Church, Plymouth	50	1·00
523/6 Set of 4			1·00	1·75
MS527 176×120 mm. Nos. 523/6			1·40	3·00

95 Rubiaceae (*Rondeletia buxifolia*)

(Des local artist. Litho Questa)

1982 (18 Jan). Plant Life. T **95** and similar multicoloured designs. W w **14** (sideways on 65c. and $2.50). P 14½.

528		50c. Type **95**	20	30
529		65c. Boraginacrge (*Heliotropium ternatum*) (horiz)	20	40
530		$1.50 Siarubaceae (*Picramnia pentandra*)	40	85
531		$2.50 Ebanaceae (*Diospyrus revoluta*) (horiz)	55	1·25
528/31 Set of 4			1·25	2·50

96 Plymouth

(Litho Format)

1982 (17 Apr). 350th Anniv of Settlement of Montserrat by Sir Thomas Warner. W w **14** (sideways). P 14½.

532	**96**	40c. green	20	30
533		55c. red	20	35
534		65c. chestnut	20	50
535		75c. olive-grey	20	60
536		85c. bright blue	20	75
537		95c. bright orange	20	80
538		$1 bright reddish violet	20	80
539		$1.50 brown-olive	25	1·25
540		$2 deep claret	30	1·50
541		$2.50 bistre-brown	35	1·50
532/41 Set of 10			2·10	7·50

Nos. 532/41 are based on the 1932 Tercentenary set.

97 Catherine of Aragon, Princess of Wales, 1501

98 Local Scout

(Des D. Shults and J. Cooter. Litho Format)

1982 (16 June). 21st Birthday of Princess of Wales. T **97** and similar vert designs. Multicoloured. W w **15**. P 13½×14.

542		75c. Type **97**	15	15
543		$1 Coat of arms of Catherine of Aragon	15	15
		w. Wmk inverted	11·00	
544		$5 Diana, Princess of Wales	80	1·25
542/4 Set of 3			1·00	1·40

(Des D. Shults. Litho Format)

1982 (13 Sept). 75th Anniv of Boy Scout Movement. T **98** and similar vert design. Multicoloured. W w **15**. P 14.

545		$1.50 Type **98**	50	50
546		$2.50 Lord Baden-Powell	60	75

Nos. 545/6 exist imperforate from stock dispersed by the liquidator of Format International Security Printers Ltd.

99 Annunciation

(Des Jennifer Toombs. Litho Walsall)

1982 (18 Nov). Christmas. T **99** and similar horiz designs. Multicoloured. W w **14** (sideways). P 14.

547		35c. Type **99**	15	15
548		75c. Shepherd's Vision	25	35
549		$1.50 The Stable	45	85
550		$2.50 Flight into Egypt	55	1·10
547/50 Set of 4			1·25	2·25

MONTSERRAT

100 *Lepthemis vesiculosa*

101 Blue-headed Hummingbird

(Des J. Cooter. Litho Walsall)

1983 (19 Jan). Dragonflies. T **100** and similar horiz designs. Multicoloured. W w **14** (sideways). P 13½×14.

551	50c. Type **100**	65	20
552	65c. *Orthemis ferruginea*	75	25
553	$1.50 *Triacanthagyna trifida*	1·40	1·75
554	$2.50 *Erythrodiplax umbrata*	1·90	3·25
551/4	Set of 4	4·25	5·00

1983 (12 Apr). As Nos. 490/505, but W w **15** and imprint date "1983" added. P 13½×13.

555	5c. Type **91**	20	10
556	10c. Hagfish and Neon Goby	25	10
559	25c. Sergeant Major	35	20
560	35c. Fin-spot Wrasse	45	30
564	75c. French Grunt	75	55
565	$1 Rock Beauty	85	65
568	$5 Cherub Angelfish	2·00	3·00
570	$10 Caribbean Long-nosed Butterflyfish	2·00	6·00
555/70	Set of 8	6·00	9·75

(Des G. Drummond. Litho Format)

1983 (24 May). Hummingbirds. T **101** and similar vert designs. Multicoloured. W w **14**. P 14.

571	35c. Type **101**	1·50	35
572	75c. Green-throated Carib	1·75	85
573	$2 Antillean Crested Hummingbird	2·75	2·75
574	$3 Purple-throated Carib	3·00	3·75
571/4	Set of 4	8·00	7·00

102 Montserrat Emblem

(103)

(Litho Harrison)

1983 (25 July). W w **14**. P 14½.

575	**102**	$12 royal blue and rose	2·50	5·00
576		$30 rose and royal blue	5·50	12·00

1983 (15 Aug). Various stamps surch as T **103**.

(a) Nos. 491, 498, 501 (all W w **14**), 559, 564 (both W w **15**).

577	40c. on 25c. Sergeant Major (No. 559)	30	35
	a. Surch inverted	15·00	
	b. Surch on No. 494	4·00	9·00
	c. Error. Surch on 10c. (No. 491)	11·00	
	d. Surch double	40·00	
578	70c. on 10c. Hogfish and Neon Goby (No. 491)	45	50
	a. Surch inverted	14·00	
	b. Surch on No. 556	24·00	24·00
	c. Surch omitted (in pair with normal)	£130	
	d. Surch double	24·00	
579	90c. on 65c. Bigeye (No. 498)	55	70
	a. Error. Surch on 10c. (No. 491)	80·00	
	b. Error. Surch on 75c. (No. 499)	80·00	
	c. Surch double	40·00	
580	$1.15 on 75c. French Grunt (No. 564)	65	80
	a. Surch on No. 499	9·50	11·00
	b. Error. Surch on 25c. (No. 559)	40·00	
	c. Surch inverted	25·00	
581	$1.50 on $2 Blue Chromis (No. 501)	85	1·00
	a. Surch inverted	60·00	
	b. Error. Surch on 75c. (No. 499)	80·00	
	c. Error. Surch on 75c. (No. 564)	80·00	

(b) Nos. 512/15.

582	70c. on $3 *Portsmouth*	50	1·00
	aw. Wmk inverted	15·00	
	b. Sheetlet. No. 582×6 and No. 583	3·00	
	bw. Wmk inverted	£120	
	c. Surch double	5·00	
	d. Surch inverted	17·00	
	e. Surch inverted (horiz pair)	35·00	
583	70c. on $3 Prince Charles and Lady Diana Spencer	1·50	2·75
	aw. Wmk inverted	55·00	
	b. Surch double	32·00	
	c. Surch inverted	90·00	
584	$1.15 on $4 *Britannia*	65	1·50
	aw. Wmk inverted	15·00	
	b. Sheetlet. No. 584×6 and No. 585	3·75	
	bw. Wmk inverted	£120	
	c. Surch double	20·00	
	d. Surch inverted	11·00	
	e. Surch inverted (horiz pair)	2·00	
	f. Error. Surch on $3 (No. 512)	5·50	
585	$1.15 on $4 As No. 583	1·75	3·25
	aw. Wmk inverted	55·00	
	b. Surch double	30·00	
	c. Surch inverted	65·00	
	f. Error. Surch on $3 (No. 513)	70·00	
577/85	Set of 9	6·50	10·50

Nos. 582e and 584e show the long surcharge intended for Nos. 583 or 585 inverted across horizontal pairs of the smaller design. Nos. 583c and 585c show two examples of the smaller surcharge inverted.

104 Montgolfier Balloon, 1783

105 Boys dressed as Clowns

(Des A. Theobald. Litho Format)

1983 (19 Sept). Bicentenary of Manned Flight. T **104** and similar multicoloured designs. W w **14** (sideways* on 75c. to $2). P 14.

586	35c. Type **104**	15	15
587	75c. de Havilland DHC-6 Twin Otter 200/300 (*horiz*)	25	30
588	$1.50 Lockheed Vega V (*horiz*)	40	75
	w. Wmk Crown to right of CA	35·00	
589	$2 Beardmore airship R-34 (*horiz*)	60	1·25
586/9	Set of 4	1·25	2·25
MS590	109×145 mm. Nos. 586/9. Wmk sideways	1·25	2·75

*The normal sideways watermark shows Crown to left of CA, *as seen from the back of the stamp*.

Nos. 586/9 were re-issued on 15 December 1983 overprinted "INAUGURAL FLIGHT Montserrat-Nevis-St. Kitts". It is understood that all but approximately 100 sets were used on Flown First Flight/Day Covers (*Price for set of 4 on First Flight Cover* £30).

(Des Jennifer Toombs. Litho Format)

1983 (18 Nov). Christmas. Carnival. T **105** and similar horiz designs. Multicoloured. W w **15** (sideways). P 14.

591	55c. Type **105**	10	10
592	90c. Girls dressed as silver star bursts	15	20
593	$1.15 Flower girls	20	35
594	$2 Masqueraders	35	1·25
591/4	Set of 4	70	1·75

106 Statue of Discus-thrower

107 Cattle Egret

MONTSERRAT

(Des Court House Studio. Litho Questa)

1984 (26 Mar). Olympic Games, Los Angeles. T **106** and similar vert designs. Multicoloured. W w **15** (sideways*). P 14.

595	90c. Type **106**	30	35
	w. Wmk POST OFFICE reading upwards	2·50	
596	$1 Olympic torch	35	45
	w. Wmk POST OFFICE reading upwards	4·50	
597	$1.15 Olympic Stadium, Los Angeles	40	50
	w. Wmk POST OFFICE reading upwards	4·50	
598	$2.50 Olympic and American flags	65	1·00
	w. Wmk POST OFFICE reading upwards	4·50	
595/8 Set of 4		1·50	2·10
MS599 110×110 mm. Nos. 595/8. Wmk upright		1·50	2·25
	w. Wmk inverted	16·00	

*The normal sideways watermark shows "POST OFFICE" reading downwards.

(Des G. Drummond. Litho Walsall)

1984 (28 May). Birds of Montserrat. T **107** and similar multicoloured designs. W w **15** (sideways* on 5c. to 90c.). P 14.

600	5c. Type **107**	30	50
601	10c. Carib Grackle	30	50
	a. Printed on the gummed side	80·00	
602	15c. Moorhen ("Common Gallinule")	30	50
	w. Wmk POST OFFICE reading upwards	3·50	
603	20c. Brown Booby	40	50
604	25c. Black-whiskered Vireo	40	50
605	40c. Scaly-breasted Thrasher	60	60
606	55c. Laughing Gull	75	40
607	70c. Glossy Ibis	90	45
608	90c. Green Heron	1·00	60
609	$1 Belted Kingfisher (*vert*)	1·25	70
	a. Imperf (pair)		
610	$1.15 Bananaquit (*vert*)	1·50	1·40
	w. Wmk inverted	4·50	
611	$3 American Kestrel ("Sparrow Hawk") (*vert*)	3·25	5·50
612	$5 Forest Thrush (*vert*)	4·50	7·50
613	$7.50 Black-crowned Night Heron (*vert*)	5·00	13·00
614	$10 Bridled Quail Dove (*vert*)	5·50	13·00
600/14 Set of 15		23·00	40·00

*The normal sideways watermark shows "POST OFFICE" reading downwards.

(Des J.W. Litho Format)

1984 (9 July). Mail Packet Boats (2nd series). Multicoloured designs as T **89**. W w **15** (sideways*). P 14.

615	55c. *Tagus II*, 1907	20	40
	w. Wmk POST OFFICE reading upwards	11·00	
616	90c. *Cobequid*, 1913	30	50
	w. Wmk POST OFFICE reading upwards	11·00	
617	$1.15 *Lady Drake*, 1942	40	70
618	$2 *Factor*, 1948	60	1·75
615/18 Set of 4		1·40	3·00
MS619 152×100 mm. Nos. 615/18		1·50	5·00

*The normal sideways watermark shows "POST OFFICE" reading downwards.

No. **MS**619 also commemorates the 250th anniversary of *Lloyd's List* (newspaper).

108 Hermit Crab and West Indian Top Shell (*Cittarium pica*)

(Des G. Drummond. Litho Questa)

1984 (24 Sept). Marine Life. T **108** and similar horiz designs. Multicoloured. W w **15** (sideways). P 14.

620	90c. Type **108**	1·50	1·00
621	$1.15 Rough File Shell (*Lima scabra*)	1·75	1·40
622	$1.50 True Tulip (*Fasciolaria tulipa*)	2·50	3·25
623	$2.50 Queen or Pink Conch (*Strombus gigas*)	3·25	5·00
620/3 Set of 4		8·00	9·50

109 "Bull Man"

(Des Jennifer Toombs. Litho Questa)

1984 (12 Nov). Christmas. Carnival Costumes. T **109** and similar horiz designs. Multicoloured. W w **15** (sideways). P 14.

624	55c. Type **109**	50	25
625	$1.15 Masquerader Captain	1·50	1·25
626	$1.50 "Fantasy" Carnival Queen	1·75	2·50
627	$2.30 "Ebony and Ivory" Carnival Queen	2·50	4·25
624/7 Set of 4		5·75	7·50

110 Mango

(Des G. Drummond. Litho Format)

1985 (8 Feb). National Emblems. T **110** and similar vert designs. Multicoloured. W w **15**. P 14.

628	$1.15 Type **110**	30	60
629	$1.50 Lobster Claw	40	1·00
630	$3 Montserrat Oriole	60	3·75
628/30 Set of 3		1·10	3·50

IMPERFORATES AND MISSING COLOURS. Various issues between Nos. 631 and 695 exist either imperforate or with colours omitted. Such items are not listed as there is no evidence that they fulfil the criteria outlined on page x of this catalogue.

111 *Oncidium urophyllum*

112 Queen Elizabeth the Queen Mother

(Des J. Cooler. Litho Format)

1985 (9 May). Orchids of Montserrat. T **111** and similar vert designs. Multicoloured. W w **15**. P 14.

631	90c. Type **111**	40	55
632	$1.15 *Epidendrum difforme*	40	80
633	$1.50 *Epidendrum ciliare*	45	1·25
634	$2.50 *Brassavola cucullata*	55	2·75
631/4 Set of 4		1·60	4·75
MS635 120×140 mm. Nos. 631/4		3·75	7·00

(Des D. Ewart ($2), Maxine Marsh (others). Litho Format)

1985 (7 Aug). Life and Times of Queen Elizabeth the Queen Mother. Various vertical portraits as T **112**. P 12½.

636	55c. multicoloured	25	45
	a. Horiz pair. Nos. 636/7	50	90
637	55c. multicoloured	25	45
638	90c. multicoloured	25	55
	a. Horiz pair. Nos. 638/9	50	1·10
639	90c. multicoloured	25	55
640	$1.15 multicoloured	25	60
	a. Horiz pair. Nos. 640/1	50	1·10
641	$1.15 multicoloured	25	60
642	$1.50 multicoloured	30	70
	a. Horiz pair. Nos. 642/3	60	1·10
643	$1.50 multicoloured	30	70
636/43 Set of 8		1·90	4·00
MS644 85×113 mm. $2 multicoloured; $2 multicoloured.		65	1·90

The two designs of each value were issued, *se-tenant*, in horizontal pairs within the sheets. Each *se-tenant* pair shows a floral pattern across the bottom of the portraits which stops short of the left-hand edge on the left-hand stamp and of the right-hand edge on the right-hand stamp.

Designs as Nos. 636/7 and 642/3 but with face values of $6×2 and $3.50×2, also exist in additional miniature sheets from a restricted printing issued 10 January 1986.

Nos. 636/43 and an unissued 15c. also exist in separate miniature sheets, combining the two designs for each value, from stock dispersed by the liquidator of Format International Security Printers Ltd.

MONTSERRAT

113 Cotton Plants

(Des G. Drummond. Litho Format)

1985 (18 Oct). Montserrat Sea Island Cotton Industry. T **113** and similar horiz designs. Multicoloured. W w **15**. P 15.

645	90c. Type **113**...	25	45
646	$1 Operator at carding machine...............	25	50
647	$1.15 Threading loom.......................................	25	65
648	$2.50 Weaving with hand loom.......................	50	2·75
645/8 Set of 4..		1·10	3·75
MS649 148×103 mm. Nos. 645/8. Wmk sideways...........		3·00	3·75

114 CARIBBEAN ROYAL VISIT 1985

115 Black-throated Blue Warbler

1985 (25 Oct). Royal Visit. Nos. 514/15, 543, 587/8 and 640/1 optd as T **114** or surch also.

650	75c. multicoloured (No. 587)..........................	3·00	2·50
651	$1 multicoloured (No. 543).............................	4·50	3·50
652	$1.15 multicoloured (No. 640)........................	4·25	6·50
	a. Horiz pair. Nos. 652/3...........................	8·50	13·00
653	$1.15 multicoloured (No. 641).......................	4·25	6·50
654	$1.50 multicoloured (No. 588).......................	7·00	7·00
655	$1.60 on $4 multicoloured (No. 514)...........	2·00	4·25
	a. Sheetlet. No. 655×6 and No. 656.........	27·00	
	ab. Sheetlet. No. 655×6 and No. 656a......	25·00	
	abw. Sheetlet. Wmk inverted		
656	$1.60 on $4 multicoloured (No. 515) (surch $1.60 only).........	20·00	25·00
	a. Additionally optd "CARIBBEAN ROYAL VISIT–1985".............	18·00	26·00
650/6 Set of 7...		40·00	50·00

No. 656 shows a new face value only; "CARIBBEAN ROYAL VISIT" being omitted from the surcharge. No. 656a is the corrected version issued subsequently.

(Des R. Vigurs. Litho Format)

1985 (29 Nov). Leaders of the World. Birth Bicentenary of John J. Audubon (ornithologist). T **115** and similar vert designs showing original paintings. Multicoloured. P 12½.

657	15c. Type **115**..	15	40
	a. Horiz pair. Nos. 657/8..........................	30	80
658	15c. Palm Warbler..	15	40
659	30c. Bobolink..	15	40
	a. Horiz pair. Nos. 659/60........................	30	80
660	30c. Lark Sparrow...	15	40
661	55c. Chipping Sparrow...................................	20	40
	a. Horiz pair. Nos. 661/2...........................	40	80
662	55c. Northern Oriole.......................................	20	40
663	$2.50 American Goldfinch...............................	40	1·40
	a. Horiz pair. Nos. 663/4...........................	80	2·75
664	$2.50 Blue Grosbeak..	40	1·40
657/64 Set of 8..		1·60	4·50

Nos. 657/8, 659/60, 661/2 and 663/4 were printed together, se-tenant, in horizontal pairs throughout the sheets.

116 Herald Angel appearing to Goatherds

(Des Jennifer Toombs. Litho Format)

1985 (2 Dec). Christmas. T **116** and similar horiz designs showing a Caribbean Nativity. Multicoloured. P 15.

665	70c. Type **116**..	20	15
666	$1.15 Three Wise Men following the Star...........	30	40
667	$1.50 Carol singing around War Memorial, Plymouth..	40	85
668	$2.30 Praying to "Our Lady of Montserrat" Church of Our Lady, St. Patrick's Village.	50	2·00
665/8 Set of 4...		1·25	3·00

117 Lord Baden-Powell

(Des G. Vasarhelyi. Litho Format)

1986 (11 Apr). 50th Anniv of Montserrat Girl Guide Movement. T **117** and similar vert designs. Multicoloured. W w **15** (sideways). P 15.

669	20c. Type **117**..	15	60
	a. Horiz pair. Nos. 669/70........................	30	1·10
670	20c. Girl Guide saluting.................................	15	60
671	75c. Lady Baden-Powell................................	25	75
	a. Horiz pair. Nos. 671/2...........................	50	1·50
672	75c. Guide assisting in old people's home	25	75
673	90c. Lord and Lady Baden-Powell...............	30	75
	a. Horiz pair. Nos. 673/4...........................	60	1·50
674	90c. Guides serving meal in old people's home	30	75
675	$1.15 Girl Guides of 1936.................................	40	80
	a. Horiz pair. Nos. 675/6...........................	80	1·60
676	$1.15 Two Guides saluting...............................	40	80
669/76 Set of 8...		2·00	5·25

Nos. 669/70, 671/2, 673/4 and 675/6 were each printed together, se-tenant, in horizontal pairs throughout the sheets.

(Des Court House Studio. Litho Format)

1986 (21 Apr). 60th Birthday of Queen Elizabeth II. Multicoloured designs as T **167** of British Virgin Islands. P 12½.

677	10c. Queen Elizabeth II.................................	10	10
	a Wmk w 15 (sideways)...........................	15·00	
678	$1.50 Princess Elizabeth in 1928.....................	25	50
679	$3 In Antigua, 1977......................................	40	1·25
	w Wmk inverted...	15·00	
680	$6 In Canberra, 1982 (vert)........................	65	2·25
677/80 Set of 4...		1·25	3·75
MS681 85×115 mm. $8 Queen with bouquet.................		3·25	5·50

The 10c., $1.50 and $3 also exist watermarked w **16** (sideways), but no examples of these used from Montserrat have been seen.

Nos. 677/80 also exist in individual miniature sheets from stock dispersed by the liquidator of Format International Security Printers Ltd.

118 King Harold and Halley's Comet, 1066 (from Bayeux Tapestry)

(Des Court House Studio. Litho Format)

1986 (9 May). Appearance of Halley's Comet. T **118** and similar horiz designs. Multicoloured. P 14×13½.

682	35c. Type **118**..	20	25
683	50c. Comet of 1301 (from Giotto's "Adoration of the Magi")................................	25	30
684	70c. Edmond Halley and Comet of 1531........	25	40
685	$1 Comets of 1066 and 1910.....................	25	40
686	$1.15 Comet of 1910...	30	50
687	$1.50 E.S.A. *Giotto* spacecraft and Comet.......	30	80
688	$2.30 U.S. Space Telescope and Comet	40	1·75
689	$4 Computer reconstruction of 1910 Comet.	50	3·25
682/9 Set of 8...		2·25	6·75
MS690 Two sheets, each 140×115 mm. (a) 40c. Type **118**; $1.75, As No. 683; $2 As No. 684; $3 As Nos. 685. (b) 55c. As No. 686; 60c. As No. 687; 80c. As No. 688; $5 As No. 689 *Set of 2 sheets*..........		3·00	9·00

196

MONTSERRAT

(Des Court House Studio. Litho Format)

1986 (23 July-15 Oct). Royal Wedding (1st issue). Multicoloured designs as T **168** of British Virgin Islands. P 12½.

691	70c. Prince Andrew	25	40
	a. Pair. Nos. 691/2	50	80
692	70c. Miss Sarah Ferguson	25	40
693	$2 Prince Andrew wearing stetson (*horiz*)...	40	90
	a. Pair. Nos. 693/4	80	1·75
694	$2 Miss Sarah Ferguson on skiing holiday (*horiz*)	40	90
691/4 Set of 4		1·10	2·25
MS695 115×85 mm. $10 Duke and Duchess of York on Palace balcony after wedding (*horiz*) (15.10)		3·25	6·00

Nos. 691/2 and 693/4 were printed together, *se-tenant*, in horizontal and vertical pairs throughout the sheets.

Nos. 691/4 imperforate come from souvenir stamp booklets. See also Nos. 705/8.

A set of eight was prepared for the 1986 World Cup Football Championships, but was not issued. Examples exist from stock dispersed by the liquidator of Format International Security Printers Ltd.

119 *Antelope* being attacked by *L'Atalante*

120 Radio Montserrat Building, Dagenham

(Des T. Hadler. Litho Questa)

1986 (29 Aug). Mail Packet Sailing Ships. T **119** and similar horiz designs. Multicoloured. W w **15**. P 14.

696	90c. Type **119**	2·00	1·50
697	$1.15 *Montagu* (1810)	2·25	2·00
698	$1.50 *Little Catherine* being pursued by *L'Etoile* (1813)	2·75	2·75
699	$2.30 *Hinchingbrook* I (1813)	3·50	5·00
696/9 Set of 4		9·50	10·00
MS700 165×123 mm. Nos. 696/9, Wmk sideways		10·00	11·00

(Des G. Vasarhelyi. Litho Questa)

1986 (29 Sept). Communications. T **120** and similar horiz designs. Multicoloured. W w **15**. P 14.

701	70c. Type **120**	1·00	70
702	$1.15 Radio Gem dish aerial, Plymouth	1·00	1·50
703	$1.50 Radio Antilles studio, O'Garro's	1·75	2·25
704	$2.30 Cable and Wireless building, Plymouth	2·25	4·25
701/4 Set of 4		5·50	8·00

(**121**)

1986 (14 Nov). Royal Wedding (2nd issue). Nos. 691/4 optd as T **121** in silver.

705	70c. Prince Andrew	90	1·50
	a. Pair. Nos. 705/6	1·75	3·00
706	70c. Miss Sarah Ferguson	90	1·50
707	$2 Prince Andrew wearing stetson (*horiz*)	1·25	2·00
	a. Pair. Nos. 707/8	2·50	4·00
708	$2 Miss Sarah Ferguson on skiing holiday (*horiz*)	1·25	2·00
705/8 Set of 4		3·75	6·25

121a Statue of Liberty

(Des Court House Studio. Litho Format)

1986 (18 Nov). Centenary of Statue of Liberty. Vert views of Statue as T **121a** in separate miniature sheets. Multicoloured. P 14×13½.
MS709 Three sheets, each 85×115 mm. $3; $4.50; $5
Set of 3 sheets .... 3·75 9·00

122 Sailing and Windsurfing    **123** Christmas Rose

(Des J. Cooter. Litho Format)

1986 (10 Dec). Tourism. T **122** and similar horiz designs. Multicoloured. P 15.

710	70c. Type **122**	40	70
711	$1.15 Golf	70	1·50
712	$1.50 Plymouth market	70	2·00
713	$2.30 Air Recording Studios	80	3·00
710/13 Set of 4		2·25	6·50

(Des Jennifer Toombs. Litho Questa)

1986 (12 Dec). Christmas. Flowering Shrubs. T **123** and similar vert designs. Multicoloured. P 14.

714	70c. Type **123**	70	40
715	$1.15 Candle Flower	95	85
716	$1.50 Christmas Tree Kalanchoe	1·50	1·50
717	$2.30 Snow on the Mountain	2·00	4·50
714/17 Set of 4		4·75	6·50
MS718 150×110 mm. Nos. 714/17. P 12		8·00	9·00

124 Tiger Shark   (**125**)

(Des M. Hillier. Litho Questa)

1987 (2 Feb). Sharks. T **124** and similar horiz designs. Multicoloured. W w **15**. P 14.

719	40c. Type **124**	1·50	55
720	90c. Lemon Shark	2·50	1·50
721	$1.15 Great White Shark	2·75	2·00
722	$3.50 Whale Shark	5·50	8·00
719/22 Set of 4		11·00	11·00
MS723 150×102 mm. Nos. 719/22. Wmk sideways. P 12		13·00	15·00

1987 (6 Apr). Nos. 601, 603, 607/8 and 611 surch as T **125**.

724	5c. on 70c. Glossy Ibis	60	3·25
725	$1 on 20c. Brown Booby	2·00	1·50
726	$1.15 on 10c. Carib Grackle	2·25	1·50
727	$1.50. on 90c Green Heron	2·50	2·75
728	$2.30 on $3 American Kestrel (*vert*)	3·50	9·00
724/8 Set of 5		9·75	16·00

(**126**)   **127** *Phoebis trite*

1987 (13 June). "Capex '87" International Stamp Exhibition, Toronto. No. **MS**690 optd with T **126** in black and red.
MS729 Two sheets. As No. **MS**690 Set of 2 sheets .... 4·00 10·00

No. **MS**729 also carries an overprint commemorating the exhibition on the lower sheet margins.

No. **MS**729 exists imperforate from stock dispersed by the liquidator of Format International Security Printers Ltd.

(Des M. Hillier. Litho Questa)

1987 (10 Aug). Butterflies. T **127** and similar square designs. Multicoloured. W w **15**. P 14.

730	90c. Type **127**	2·00	1·10
731	$1.15 *Biblis hyperia*	2·50	1·60
732	$1.50 *Polygonus leo*	3·00	2·50
733	$2.50 *Hypolimnas misippus*	4·50	6·50
730/3 Set of 4		11·00	10·50

MONTSERRAT

128 *Oncidium variegatum*

(Des R. Vigurs. Litho Questa)

1987 (13 Nov). Christmas. Orchids. T **128** and similar multicoloured designs. P 14×13½ (90c., $1.50) or 13½×14 (others).

734	90c. Type **128**	60	45
735	$1.15 *Vanilla planifolia* (horiz)	85	55
736	$1.50 *Gongora quinquenervis*	1·10	1·10
737	$3.50 *Brassavola nodosa* (horiz)	2·00	5·00
734/7 Set of 4		4·00	6·25
MS738 100×75 mm. $5 *Oncidium lanceanum* (horiz)		12·00	14·00

(**129**)

130 Free-tailed Bat

1987 (29 Nov-18 Dec). Royal Ruby Wedding. Nos. 601, 604/5 and 608 surch as T **129**.

A. Surch "Edingburgh".

739A	5c. on 90c. Green Heron	2·50	4·00
740A	$1.15 on 10c. Carib Grackle	6·00	4·25
741A	$2.30 on 25c. Black-whiskered Vireo	10·00	9·00
742A	$5 on 40c. Scaly-breasted Thrasher	13·00	15·00
739A/42A Set of 4		28·00	29·00

B. Surch "Edinburgh" (18 Dec).

739B	5c. on 90c. Green Heron	30	1·00
740B	$1.15 on 10c. Carib Grackle	1·00	1·00
741B	$2.30 on 25c. Black-whiskered Vireo	1·75	2·25
742B	$5 on 40c. Scaly-breasted Thrasher	3·50	5·50
739B/42B Set of 4		6·00	8·75

Nos. 739A/42A were from the first printing using Type **129**. After the spelling mistake was noticed it was corrected on sheets subsequently surcharged.

(Des M. Pollard. Litho Questa)

1988 (8 Feb). Bats. T **130** and similar vert designs. Multicoloured. W w **15** (sideways). P 14.

743	55c. Type **130**	80	40
744	90c. *Chiroderma improvisum* (fruit bat)	1·25	90
745	$1.15 Fisherman Bat	1·60	1·50
746	$2.30 *Brachyphylla cavernarum* (fruitbat)	3·00	5·50
743/6 Set of 4		6·00	7·50
MS747 133×110 mm. $2.50, Funnel-eared Bat. Wmk upright		6·50	8·00

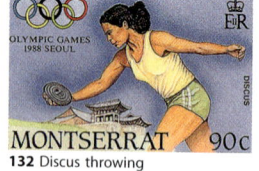

131 Magnificent Frigate Bird

132 Discus throwing

(Des R. Vigurs. Litho Questa)

1988 (2 Apr). Easter. Birds. T **131** and similar vert designs. Multicoloured. P 14×13½.

748	90c. Type **131**	60	45
749	$1.15 Caribbean Elaenia	80	75
750	$1.50 Glossy Ibis	1·00	1·50
751	$3.50 Purple-throated Carib	2·00	4·00
748/51 Set of 4		4·00	6·00
MS752 100×75 mm. $5 Brown Pelican		2·50	3·50

(Des R. Vigurs. Litho Questa)

1988 (29 July). Olympic Games, Seoul. T **132** and similar horiz designs. Multicoloured. P 13½×14.

753	90c. Type **132**	80	50
754	$1.15 High jumping	90	55
755	$3.50 Athletics	2·25	3·25
753/5 Set of 3		3·50	3·75
MS756 103×77 mm. $5 Rowing		3·00	3·00

133 Golden Tulip (*Pleuroploca aurantiaca*)

(Des R. Vigurs. Litho Questa)

1988 (30 Aug). Sea Shells. T **133** and similar horiz designs. Multicoloured. P 14.

757	5c. Type **133**	45	75
758	10c. Little Knobbed Scallop (*Chlamys imbricata*)	60	75
759	15c. Sozoni's Cone (*Conus delessertii*)	60	75
760	20c. Globular Coral Shell (*Coralliophila aberrans*)	70	40
761	25c. American or Common Sundial (*Architectonica nobilis*)	70	50
762	40c. King Helmet (*Cassis tuberosa*)	85	50
763	55c. Channelled Turban (*Turbo canaliculatus*)	1·00	50
764	70c. True Tulip (*Fasciolaria tulipa*)	1·25	75
765	90c. Music Volute (*Voluta musica*)	1·50	75
766	$1 Flame Auger (*Terebra taurina*)	1·60	80
767	$1.15 Rooster-tail Conch (*Strombus gallus*)	1·75	90
768	$1.50 Queen or Pink Conch (*Strombus gigas*)	1·75	1·40
769	$3 Teramchis Slit Shell (*Perotrochus teramachii*)	2·75	4·50
770	$5 Common or Florida Crown Conch (*Melongena corona*)	3·50	7·00
771	$7.50 Beau's Murex (*Murex beauii*)	4·25	12·00
772	$10 Atlantic Trumpet Triton (*Charonia variegata*)	4·50	12·00
757/72 Set of 16		25·00	40·00

134 University Crest

(Des R. Vigurs. Litho Questa)

1988 (14 Oct). 40th Anniv of University of West Indies. P 14×13½.

773	**134** $5 multicoloured	2·75	3·50

(**135**)

1988 (10 Nov). Princess Alexandra's Visit. Nos. 763, 766 and 769/70 surch as T **135**.

774	40c. on 55c. Channelled Turban (*Turbo canaliculatus*)	75	45
775	90c. on $1 Flame Auger (*Terebra taurina*)	1·25	80
776	$1.15 on $3 Teramachi's Slit Shell (*Perotrochus teromachii*)	1·50	95
	a. Surch double	60·00	
777	$1.50 on $5 Common or Florida Crown Conch (*Melongena corona*)	1·75	1·75
774/7 Set of 4		4·75	3·50

It was intended that Nos. 774/7 were to be issued on 4 November, but the day before it was found that the surcharge contained the error "ALEXANDRIA". The issue was postponed until 10 November to allow replacements to be printed, but examples of the error exist from pre-release stock sent to dealers overseas.

136 Spotted Sandpiper

(Des R. Vigurs. Litho Questa)

1988 (4 Dec). Christmas. Sea Birds. T **136** and similar horiz designs. Multicoloured. P 13½×14.

778	90c. Type **136**..	70	55
779	$1.15 Turnstone..	85	70
780	$3.50 Red-footed Booby....................................	2·00	3·75
778/80 Set of 3...		3·25	4·50
MS781 105×79 mm. $5 Audubon's Shearwater............		2·75	4·00

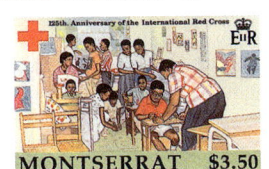

137 Handicapped Children in Classroom

(Des R. Vigurs. Litho Questa)

1988 (16 Dec). 125th Anniv of International Red Cross. P 13½×14.
782	**137** $3.50 multicoloured........................	1·50	2·25

138 Drum Major in Ceremonial Uniform

139 Amazon Lily

(Des R. Vigurs. Litho Questa)

1989 (24 Feb). 75th Anniv of Montserrat Defence Force (1988). Uniforms. T **138** and similar vert designs. Multicoloured. P 14×13½.

783	90c. Type **138**..	90	50
784	$1.15 Field training uniform................................	1·00	75
785	$1.50 Cadet in ceremonial uniform....................	1·50	2·00
786	$3.50 Gazetted Police Officer in ceremonial uniform	4·00	4·50
783/6 Set of 4...		6·75	7·00
MS787 102×76 mm. $5 Island Girl Guide Commissioner and Brownie		3·50	4·25

(Litho Questa)

1989 (21 Mar). Easter. Lilies. T **139** and similar multicoloured designs. P 13½×14 (90c.) or 14×13½ (others).

788	90c. Type **139**..	50	50
789	$1.15 Salmon Blood Lily (vert)............................	70	70
790	$1.50 Amaryllis (*Hippeastrum vittatum*) (vert) ..	85	1·25
791	$3.50 Amaryllis (*Hippeastrum* hybrid) (vert)......	1·90	3·00
788/91 Set of 4...		3·50	5·00
MS792 103×77 mm. $5 Resurrection Lily (vert)		4·75	7·00

140 *Morning Prince* (schooner), 1942

(Des R. Vigurs. Litho Questa)

1989 (30 June). Shipbuilding in Montserrat. T **140** and similar horiz designs. Multicoloured. P 13½×14.

793	90c. Type **140**..	1·40	60
794	$1.15 *Western Sun* (inter-island freighter)..........	1·90	1·10
795	$1.50 *Kim G* (inter-island freighter) under construction...	2·25	2·25
796	$3.50 *Romaris* (island ferry), c. 1942.................	3·50	5·50
793/6 Set of 4...		8·00	8·50

141 The Scarecrow

(Litho Questa)

1989 (22 Sept). 50th Anniv of *The Wizard of Oz* (film). T **141** and similar multicoloured designs. P 14.

797	90c. Type **141**..	40	45
798	$1.15 The Lion...	55	60
799	$1.50 The Tin Man...	70	85
800	$3.50 Dorothy...	1·60	2·50
797/800 Set of 4...		3·00	4·00
MS801 113×84 mm. $5 Characters from film (*horiz*)		2·40	3·75

Hurricane Hugo Relief Surcharge $2.50

(**142**)

1989 (20 Oct). Hurricane Hugo Relief Fund. Nos. 795/6 surch with T **142**.

802	$1.50 +$2.50 *Kim G* (inter-island freighter) under construction.....................................	2·25	4·00
803	$3.50 +$2.50 *Romaris* (island ferry), c. 1942......	2·50	5·00

143 "Apollo 11" above Lunar Surface

(Litho Questa)

1989 (19 Dec). 20th Anniv of First Manned Landing on Moon. T **143** and similar multicoloured designs. P 13½×14.

804	90c. Type **143**..	45	40
805	$1.15 Astronaut alighting from lunar module *Eagle*	55	50
806	$1.50 *Eagle* and astronaut conducting experiment	75	80
807	$3.50 Opening "Apollo 11" hatch after splashdown	1·60	2·50
804/7 Set of 4...		3·00	3·75
MS808 101×76 mm. $5 Astronaut on Moon. P 14×13½ .		5·00	6·00

144 *Yamato* (Japanese battleship) 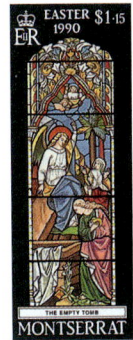   **145** The Empty Tomb

MONTSERRAT

(Litho Questa)

1990 (12 Feb). World War II Capital Ships. T **144** and similar horiz designs. Multicoloured. P 14.

809	70c. Type **144**.	3·25	70
810	$1.15 U.S.S. *Arizona* at Pearl Harbor	3·75	95
811	$1.50 *Bismarck* (German battleship) in action	4·75	2·75
812	$3.50 H.M.S. *Hood* (battle cruiser)	7·00	10·00
809/12	Set of 4	17·00	13·00
MS813	118×90 mm. $5 *Bismarck* and map of North Atlantic	15·00	15·00

(Des R. Vigurs. Litho Questa)

1990 (12 Apr). Easter. T **145** and similar vert designs showing stained glass windows from St. Michael's Parish Church, Bray, Berkshire. Multicoloured. P 14×15.

814	$1.15 Type **145**	2·25	2·50
	a. Horiz strip of 3. Nos. 814/16	6·50	7·50
815	$1.50 The Ascension	2·25	2·50
816	$3.50 The Risen Christ with Disciples	2·75	3·25
814/16	Set of 3	6·50	7·50
MS817	65×103 mm. $5 The Crucifixion	5·00	6·50

Nos. 814/16 were printed together, *se-tenant*, in sheets of 6 (3×2).

1990 (3 May). Stamp World London 90 International Stamp Exhibition. Nos. 460/4 surch as T **146** in bright purple.

818	70c. on 40c. Type **85**	80	80
819	90c. on 55c. Hawker Siddeley H.S.748 aircraft and 1976 55c. definitive	1·00	1·00
820	$1 on $1.20 *La Plata* (liner) and 1903 5s. stamp	1·25	1·40
821	$1.15 on $1.20 *Lady Hawkins* (packet steamer) and 1932 Tercentrary 5s. commemorative	1·40	1·50
822	$1.50 on $1.20 *Avon* (paddle-steamer) and Penny Red stamp with "A08" postmark	1·75	2·00
818/22	Set of 5	5·50	6·00

Nos. 818/22 also show the "Stamp World London 90" emblem overprinted on one of the *se-tenant* labels.

(Litho Questa)

1990 (1 June). 150th Anniv of the Penny Black. T **147** and similar multicoloured designs. P 13½×14 (horiz) or 14×13½ (vert).

823	90c. Type **147**	65	65
824	$1.15 Sorting letters and Montserrat 1d. stamp of 1876 (*vert*)	85	90
825	$1.50 Posting letters and Penny Black (*vert*)	1·25	1·75
826	$3.50 Postman delivering letters and 1840 Twopence Blue	3·00	4·50
823/6	Set of 4	5·25	7·00
MS827	102×75 mm. $5 Montserrat soldier's letter of 1836 and Penny Black	8·50	10·00

(Litho Questa)

1990 (8 July). World Cup Football Championship, Italy. T **148** and similar multicoloured designs. P 14.

828	90c. Type **148**	65	55
829	$1.15 U.S.A .v. Trinidad match	85	75
830	$1.50 Montserrat team	1·25	1·50
831	$3.50 West Germany v. Wales match	2·25	3·50
828/31	Set of 4	4·50	5·50
MS832	77×101 mm. $5 World Cup trophy (*vert*)	6·00	7·50

149 Spinner Dolphin

(Des Jennifer Toombs. Litho Questa)

1990 (25 Sept). Dolphins. T **149** and similar horiz designs. Multicoloured. P 14.

833	90c. Type **149**	1·50	85
834	$1.15 Common Dolphin	1·75	1·25
835	$1.50 Striped Dolphin	2·50	2·50
836	$3.50 Atlantic Spotted Dolphin	3·75	5·00
833/6	Set of 4	8·50	8·75
MS837	103×76 mm. $5 Atlantic White-sided Dolphin	8·50	9·50

150 Spotted Goatfish (**151**)

(Litho Questa)

1991 (7 Feb). Tropical Fish. T **150** and similar horiz designs. Multicoloured. P 13½×14.

838	90c. Type **150**	1·50	95
839	$1.15 Cushion Star	1·75	1·25
840	$1.50 Rock Beauty	2·50	2·75
841	$3.50 French Grunt	3·75	5·50
838/41	Set of 4	8·50	9·50
MS842	103×76 mm. $5 Buffalo Trunkfish	6·50	8·00

1991 (27 Feb). Nos. 760/1, 768 and 771 surch as T **151**.

843	5c. on 20c. Globular Coral Shell (*Coralliophila aberrans*)	65	2·25
844	5c. on 25c. American or Common Sundial (*Architectonica nobilis*)	65	2·25
845	$1.15 on $1.50 Queen or Pink Conch (*Strombus gigas*)	2·75	3·25
846	$1.15 on $7.50 Beau's Murex (*Murex beauii*)	2·75	3·25
843/6	Set of 4	6·00	10·00

152 Duck

153 *Panaeolus antillarum*

(Des K. West. Litho Questa)

1991 (29 May). Domestic Birds. T **152** and similar horiz designs. Multicoloured. P 14.

847	90c. Type **152**	60	60
848	$1.15 Hen and chicks	80	90
849	$1.50 Red Junglefowl	1·10	1·50
850	$3.50 Helmet Guineafowl	2·40	3·50
847/50	Set of 4	4·50	5·75

(Des M. Pollard. Litho Questa)

1991 (13 June). Fungi. T **153** and similar square designs. P 14.

851	90c. olive-grey	1·50	1·00
852	$1.15 rosine	1·75	1·25
853	$1.50 yellow-brown	2·50	2·25
854	$2 maroon	2·75	3·50
855	$3.50 dull ultramarine	4·00	6·00
851/5	Set of 5	11·00	12·50

Designs:—$1.15, *Cantharellus cinnabarinus*; $1.50, *Gymnopilus chrysopellus*; $2, *Psilocybe cubensis*; $3.50, *Leptonia caeruleocapitata*.

MONTSERRAT

154 Red Water Lily
155 Tree Frog 

(Des M. Pollard. Litho Questa)

1991 (8 Aug). Lilies. T **154** and similar vert designs. Multicoloured. P 14.

856	90c. Type **154**...	65	65
857	$1.15 Shell Ginger.......................................	75	85
858	$1.50 Early Day Lily....................................	1·00	1·60
859	$3.50 Anthurium...	2·50	3·75
856/9	Set of 4..	4·50	6·00

(Des M. Pollard. Litho B.D.T.)

1991 (9 Oct). Frogs and Toad. T **155** and similar multicoloured designs. P 14.

860	$1.15 Type **155**..	3·75	1·25
861	$2 Crapaud Toad..	5·00	5·00
862	$3.50 Mountain Chicken (frog)..................	8·50	9·50
860/2	Set of 3..	15·00	14·00
MS863 110×110 mm. $5 Tree Frog, Crapaud Toad and Mountain Chicken (76½×44 mm). P 15×14................		13·00	14·00

156 Black British Shorthair Cat

(Des M. Pollard. Litho B.D.T.)

1991 (5 Dec). Cats. T **156** and similar horiz designs. Multicoloured. P 14.

864	90c. Type **156**...	2·00	90
865	$1.15 Seal Point Siamese..........................	2·25	1·10
866	$1.50 Silver Tabby Persian.......................	2·75	2·25
867	$2.50 Birman Temple Cat.........................	3·50	4·50
868	$3.50 Egyptian Mau....................................	5·00	7·00
864/8	Set of 5..	14·00	14·00

157 Navigational Instruments
158 Runner with Olympic Flame 

(Des M. Pollard. Litho Questa)

1992 (16 Jan). 500th Anniv of Discovery of America by Columbus. T **157** and similar horiz designs. Multicoloured. P 14.

869	$1.50 Type **157**..	1·75	1·90
	a. Sheetlet. Nos. 869/75..........................	11·00	12·00
870	$1.50 Columbus and coat of arms...........	1·75	1·90
871	$1.50 Landfall on the Bahamas...............	1·75	1·90
872	$1.50 Petitioning Queen Isabella.............	1·75	1·90
873	$1.50 Tropical birds...................................	1·75	1·90
874	$1.50 Tropical fruits..................................	1·75	1·90
875	$3 Ships of Columbus (81×26 mm)..........	2·00	2·25
869/75	Set of 7..	11·00	12·00

Nos. 869/75 were printed together, *se-tenant*, in sheetlets of 7 with decorative margins.

For these designs, some with different face values, inscr "500TH ANNIVERSARY DISCOVERY OF MONTSERRAT", see Nos. 915/21.

(Des M. Pollard. Litho B.D.T.)

1992 (10 Apr). Olympic Games, Barcelona. T **158** and similar square designs. Multicoloured. P 14.

876	$1 Type **158**..	1·00	60
877	$1.15 Montserrat, Olympic and Spanish flags..	2·25	1·00
878	$2.30 Olympic flame on map of Montserrat......	3·25	3·50
879	$3.60 Olympic events................................	3·25	5·50
876/9	Set of 4..	8·75	9·50

159 Tyrannosaurus

(Des M. Pollard. Litho Questa)

1992 (1 May). Death Centenary of Sir Richard Owen (zoologist). T **159** and similar multicoloured designs. P 14.

880	$1 Type **159**..	2·00	1·25
881	$1.15 Diplodocus..	2·25	1·40
882	$1.50 Apatosaurus.....................................	2·75	2·75
883	$3.45 Dimetrodon.......................................	5·50	8·00
880/3	Set of 4..	11·00	12·00
MS884 114×84 mm. $4.60, Sir Richard Owen and dinosaur bone (*vert*).............................		8·50	10·00

160 Male Montserrat Oriole

(Des R. Vigurs. Litho Questa)

1992 (30 June). Montserrat Oriole. T **160** and similar horiz designs. Multicoloured. P 14.

885	$1 Type **160**..	1·10	1·10
886	$1.15 Male and female Orioles.................	1·40	1·40
887	$1.50 Female Oriole with chicks..............	1·75	2·00
888	$3.60 Map of Montserrat and male Oriole......	3·50	5·00
885/8	Set of 4..	7·00	8·50

161 *Psophus stridulus* (grasshopper)

(Des M. Pollard. Litho B.D.T.)

1992 (20 Aug). Insects. T **161** and similar horiz designs. Multicoloured. P 15×14.

889	5c. Type **161**..	40	70
890	10c. *Gryllus campestris* (field cricket)..........	50	70
891	15c. *Lepthemis vesiculosa* (dragonfly)..........	60	70
892	20c. *Orthemis ferruginea* (red skimmer)......	65	75
893	25c. *Gerris lacustris* (pond skater)...............	65	75
894	40c. *Bycticus betulae* (leaf weevil)...............	80	75
895	55c. *Atta texana* (leaf-cutter ants)................	85	40
896	70c. *Polistes fuscatus* (paper wasp)............	1·00	60
897	90c. *Sparmopolius fulvus* (bee fly)...............	1·25	60
898	$1 *Chrysopa carnea* (lace wing)..................	1·75	65
899	$1.15 *Phoebis philea* (butterfly).................	2·25	90
900	$1.50 *Cynthia cardui* (butterfly).................	2·50	1·75
901	$3 *Utetheisa bella* (moth)...........................	3·25	4·50
902	$5 *Alucita pentadactyla* (moth)...................	4·50	6·50
903	$7.50 *Anartia jatropha* (butterfly)...............	6·50	9·50
904	$10 *Heliconius melpomene* (butterfly).........	6·50	9·50
889/904	Set of 16..	30·00	35·00

162 Adoration of the Magi

(Des M. Pollard. Litho Questa)

1992 (26 Nov). Christmas. T **162** and similar horiz design. Multicoloured. P 13½×14.

905	$1.15 Type **162**..	2·00	75
906	$4.60 Appearance of angel to shepherds..........	4·50	6·50

MONTSERRAT

163 $1 Coin and $20 Banknote

(Des R. Vigurs. Litho Questa)

1993 (10 Feb). East Caribbean Currency. T **163** and similar vert designs. Multicoloured. P 14.

907	$1 Type **163**	90	70
908	$1.15 10c. and 25c. coins with $10 bank note	1·25	85
909	$1.50 5c. coin and $5 banknote	1·75	2·00
910	$3.60 1c. and 2c. coins with $1 banknote	4·00	6·00
907/10 Set of 4		7·00	8·50

164 Columbus meeting Amerindians

(Des M. Pollard. Litho Questa)

1993 (10 Mar). Organization of East Caribbean States. 500th Anniv of Discovery of America by Columbus. T **164** and similar square design. Multicoloured. P 14.

911	$1 Type **164**	1·25	1·00
912	$2 Ships approaching island	2·25	3·00

165 Queen Elizabeth II on Montserrat with Chief Minister W. H. Bramble, 1966

(Des M. Pollard. Litho Questa)

1993 (2 June). 40th Anniv of Coronation. T **165** and similar horiz design. Multicoloured. P 14.

913	$1.15 Type **165**	1·50	75
914	$4.60 Queen Elizabeth II in State Coach, 1953	4·50	5·50

1993 (5 Oct). 500th Anniv of Discovery of Montserrat. Designs as Nos. 869/75, some with new values, some showing "500th ANNIVERSARY DISCOVERY OF MONTSERRAT" at foot and with additional historical inscr across the centre. P 14.

915	$1.15 multicoloured (As Type **157**)	2·25	2·50
	a. Sheetlet. Nos. 915/21	16·00	18·00
916	$1.15 multicoloured (As No. 870)	2·25	2·50
917	$1.15 multicoloured (As No. 871)	2·25	2·50
918	$1.50 multicoloured (As No. 872)	2·50	2·75
919	$1.50 multicoloured (As No. 873)	2·50	2·75
920	$1.50 multicoloured (As No. 874)	2·50	2·75
921	$3.45 multicoloured (As No. 875)	3·75	4·25
915/21 Set of 7		16·00	18·00

Additional inscriptions:—No. 915, "PRE-COLUMBUS CARIB NAME OF ISLAND ALLIOUGANA"; No. 916, "COLUMBUS NAMED ISLAND SANTA MARIA DE MONTSERRATE"; No. 917, "COLUMBUS SAILED ALONG COASTLINE 11th NOV. 1493"; No. 918, "ISLAND OCCUPIED BY FRENCH BRIEFLY IN 1667"; No. 919, "ISLAND DECLARED ENGLISH BY TREATY OF BREDA 1667"; No. 920, "AFRICAN SLAVES BROUGHT IN DURING 1600's "; No. 921, "IRISH CATHOLICS FROM ST. KITTS AND VIRGINIA SETTLED ON ISLAND BETWEEN 1628–1634".

Nos. 915/21 were printed together, *se-tenant*, in sheetlets of 7, with decorative margins.

166 Boeing E-3 Sentry, 1993

(Des A. Theobald. Litho Questa)

1993 (17 Nov). 75th Anniv of Royal Air Force. T **166** and similar horiz designs. Multicoloured. W w **14** (sideways). P 14.

922	15c. Type **166**	45	20
923	55c. Vickers Valiant B Mk 1, 1962	65	40
924	$1.15 Handley Page H.P.67 Hastings C Mk 2, 1958	1·25	75
925	$3 Lockheed PV-1 Ventura, 1943	2·50	4·25
922/5 Set of 4		4·25	5·00
MS926 117×78 mm. $1.50, Felixstowe F5, 1921; $1.50, Armstrong Whitworth Atlas, 1934; $1.50, Fairey Gordon, 1935; $1.50, Boulton & Paul Overstrand, 1936		4·50	6·00

167 Ground Beetle   **168** *Gossypium barbadense*

(Des M. Pollard. Litho B.D.T.)

1994 (21 Jan). Beetles. T **167** and similar horiz designs. Multicoloured. P 15×14.

927	$1 Type **167**	65	65
928	$1.15 Click Beetle	80	80
929	$1.50 Harlequin Beetle	1·25	1·50
930	$3.45 Leaf Beetle	3·00	4·50
927/30 Set of 4		5·25	6·75
MS931 68×85 mm. $4.50, Scarab Beetle		3·50	4·00

(Des R. Vigurs. Litho Questa)

1994 (22 Mar). Flowers. T **168** and similar vert designs. Multicoloured. P 14×13½.

932	90c. Type **168**	1·25	80
933	$1.15 *Hibiscus sabdariffa*	1·50	1·00
934	$1.50 *Hibiscus esculentus*	1·75	1·75
935	$3.50 *Hibiscus rosa-sinensis*	3·75	6·00
932/5 Set of 4		7·50	8·50

169 Coaching Young Players and Logo   **170** Elasmosaurus

(Litho Questa)

1994 (20 Apr). World Cup Football Championship, U.S.A. T **169** and similar horiz designs. Multicoloured. P 14×14½.

936	90c. Type **169**	1·90	2·25
	a. Vert strip of 4. Nos. 936/9	7·75	9·25
937	$1 United States scoring against England, 1950	1·90	2·25
938	$1.15 Rose Bowl stadium, Los Angeles, and trophy	1·90	2·25
939	$3.45 German players celebrating with trophy, 1990	3·00	3·50
936/9 Set of 4		7·75	9·25
MS940 114×85 mm. $2 Jules Rimet (founder) and Jules Rimet Trophy, $2 Bobby Moore (England) holding trophy, 1966; $2 Lew Jaschin (U.S.S.R.); $2 Sepp Herberger (Germany) and German players celebrating, 1990		7·00	9·00

202

Nos. 936/9 were printed together, *se-tenant*, in vertical strips of 4, each sheet containing two such strips separated by a gutter of 4 stamp-size labels showing Montserrat flag, championship mascot and logos.

(Des M. Pollard. Litho B.D.T.)

1994 (6 May). Aquatic Dinosaurs. T **170** and similar horiz designs. Multicoloured. P 15×14.

941	$1 Type **170**...	2·25	2·25
	a. Horiz strip of 4. Nos. 941/4............	9·75	10·50
942	$1.15 Plesiosaurus....................................	2·25	2·25
943	$1.50 Nothosaurus....................................	2·75	2·75
944	$3.45 Mosasaurus.....................................	3·50	4·25
941/4 *Set of 4*..		9·75	10·50

Nos. 941/4 were printed together, *se-tenant*, in horizontal strips of 4 throughout the sheet.

Space Anniversaries
Columbia
First Space Shuttle
April 12, 1981
$2·30

(**171**)

1994 (20 July). Space Anniversaries. Nos. 804/7 surch in black and red or optd in red only as T **171**, each including "Space Anniversaries".

945	40c. on 90c. Type **143**............................	1·75	80
946	$1.15 Astronaut alighting from lunar module *Eagle*.................................	2·50	1·50
947	$1.50 *Eagle* and astronaut conducting experiment...........................	3·00	3·00
948	$2.30 on $3.50 Opening "Apollo 11" hatch after splashdown........................	4·75	7·00
945/8 *Set of 4*..		10·50	11·00

Surcharges and overprints:—No. 945, "Juri Gagarin First man in space April 12, 1961"; No. 946, "First Joint US Soviet Mission July 15, 1975"; No. 947, "25th Anniversary First Moon Landing Apollo XI–July 20, 1994".

Nos. 945 and 948 show the face value obliterated in black and the rest of the surcharge in red.

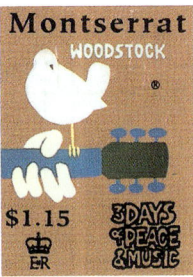

172 1969 Festival Logo

(Des A. Skolnick and Barbara Pensoy. Litho The Mansfield Press)

1994 (20 Oct). 25th Anniv of Woodstock Music Festival. T **172** and similar vert design. Multicoloured. P 12½.

949	$1.15 Type **172**...	1·00	1·00
950	$1.50 1994 anniversary festival logo....	1·25	1·25

173 Sea Fan

(Des M. Pollard. Litho B.D.T.)

1995 (14 Feb). Marine Life. T **173** and simlar vert designs. Multicoloured. P 14×15.

951	$1 Type **173**..	60	50
952	$1.15 Sea Lily...	70	60
953	$1.50 Sea Pen..	90	1·00
954	$3.45 Sea Fern...	2·00	3·00
951/4 *Set of 4*..		3·75	4·50
MS955 88×96 mm. $4.50, Sea Rose...................		3·00	4·00

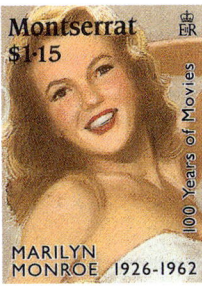

174 Marilyn Monroe

175 Jesse Owens (U.S.A.)

(Des S. Bickel (No. **MS**965), Lisa Egeli (others). Litho)

1995 (13 June). Centenary of Cinema. T **174** and similar vert designs showing portraits of Marilyn Monroe (film star). Multicoloured. P 12½.

956	$1.15 Type **174**...	60	85
	a. Sheetlet. Nos. 956/64.......................	4·75	7·00
957	$1.15 Puckering lips..................................	60	85
958	$1.15 Laughing in brown evening dress and earrings...............................	60	85
959	$1.15 Wearing red earrings......................	60	85
960	$1.15 In brown dress without earrings...	60	85
961	$1.15 With white boa................................	60	85
962	$1.15 In red dress......................................	60	85
963	$1.15 Wearing white jumper....................	60	85
964	$1.15 Looking over left shoulder..............	60	85
956/64 *Set of 9*..		4·75	7·00
MS965 102×132 mm. $6 With Elvis Presley (50×56 mm)..		3·75	5·00

Nos. 956/64 were printed together, *se-tenant*, in sheetlets of 9.

(Des M. Morck. Litho B.D.T.)

1995 (3 Aug). Fifth International Amateur Athletic Federation Games, Göteborg. Sheet 181×103 mm, containing T **175** and similar vert designs. P 14.

MS966 $1.50, black and pink (Type **175**); $1.50, black and pale orange (Eric Lemming (Sweden), $1.50, black and chrome-yellow (Rudolf Harbig (Germany)); $1.50, black and bright yellow-green (young Montserrat athletes)...	4·50	6·00

176 Atmospheric Sounding Experiments using V2 Rockets

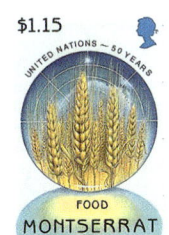

177 Ears of Wheat ("Food")

(Des M. Pollard. Litho Cot Printery Ltd, Barbados)

1995 (15 Aug). 50th Anniv of End of Second World War. Scientific Achievements. T **176** and similar horiz designs. Multicoloured. P 14.

967	$1.15 Type **176**...	1·00	1·25
	a. Horiz pair. Nos. 967/8.......................	2·00	2·50
968	$1.15 American Space Shuttle *Challenger*........	1·00	1·25
969	$1.15 Nuclear experiment, Chicago, 1942..	1·00	1·25
	a. Horiz pair. Nos. 969/70.....................	2·00	2·50
970	$1.15 Calder Hall Atomic Power Station, 1956	1·00	1·25
971	$1.50 Radar-equipped Ju 88G 7a night-fighter..	1·90	2·00
	a. Horiz pair. Nos. 971/2.......................	3·75	4·00
972	$1.50 Boeing E6 A.W.A.C.S. aircraft........	1·90	2·00
973	$1.50 Gloster G.41 Meteor Mk III jet fighter......	1·90	2·00
	a. Horiz pair. Nos. 973/4.......................	3·75	4·00
974	$1.50 Concorde (airliner)..........................	1·90	2·00
967/74 *Set of 8*..		10·00	11·00

Nos. 967/8, 969/70, 971/2 and 973/4 were each printed together, *se-tenant*, in horizontal pairs throughout the sheets.

MONTSERRAT

(Des M. Pollard. Litho Cot Printery Ltd, Barbados)

1995 (14 Sept). 50th Anniv of United Nations. T **177** and similar vert designs. Multicoloured. P 14.

975	$1.15 Type **177**	90	75
976	$1.50 Open book ("Education")	1·25	1·00
977	$2.30 P.T. class ("Health")	1·75	2·25
978	$3 Dove ("Peace")	2·25	3·50
975/8 Set of 4		5·50	6·75
MS979 105×75 mm. $6 Scales ("Justice")		3·75	6·00

(177a)   **178** Headquarters Building

1995 (Nov ?). Nos. 892 and 895/6 surch as T **177a**.

979a	5c. on 55c. *Atta texana* (leaf-cutter ants)	
979b	5c. on 70c. *Polistes fuscatus* (paper wasp)	
979c	10c. on 20c. *Orthemis ferruginea* (red skimmer)	

Nos. 979a/c were emergency surcharges issued following the eruption of the Soufrière Hills Volcano in July and August 1995.

(Litho Cot Printery Ltd, Barbados)

1995 (15 Nov). 25th Anniv of Montserrat National Trust. T **178** and similar multicoloured designs. P 14.

980	$1.15 Type **178**	80	75
981	$1.50 17th-century cannons, Brans by Point	1·25	1·00
982	$2.30 Impression of Galways Sugar Mill (*vert*)	2·25	2·50
983	$3 Great Alps Falls (*vert*)	5·00	6·00
980/3 Set of 4		8·50	9·25

(179)

1995 (29 Dec). 25th Anniv of Air Recording Studios. No. 713 surch with T **179** in red.

984	$2.30 +$5 Air Recording Studios	3·50	5·50

The $5 premium on No. 984 was for relief following a volcanic eruption.

180 Bull Shark

(Des M. Pollard. Litho B.D.T.)

1996 (14 Feb). Scavengers of the Sea. T **180** and similar horiz designs. Multicoloured. P 15×14.

985	$1 Type **180**	80	70
986	$1.15 Sea Mouse	90	80
987	$1.50 Bristleworm	1·25	1·50
988	$3.45 Prawn *Xiphocaris*	2·50	3·50
985/8 Set of 4		5·00	6·00
MS989 69×95 mm. $4.50 Man of War Fish		3·00	4·00

181 Marconi and Radio Equipment, 1901

(Des M. Pollard. Litho Cot Printery Ltd, Barbados)

1996 (19 Mar). Centenary of Radio. T **181** and similar horiz designs. Multicoloured. P 14.

990	$1.15 Type **181**	90	80
991	$1.50 Marconi's steam yacht *Elettra*	1·25	1·00
992	$2.30 Receiving first Transatlantic radio message, Newfoundland, 1901	1·75	2·25
993	$3 Imperial Airways airplane at Croydon Airport, 1920	2·25	3·50
990/3 Set of 4		5·50	6·75
MS994 74×105 mm. $4.50, Radio telescope, Jodrell Bank		3·00	4·00

182 Paul Masson (France) (Cycling)

(Litho B.D.T.)

1996 (24 June). Olympic Games, Atlanta. Gold Medal Winners of 1896. T **182** and similar diamond-shaped designs. Multicoloured. P 14.

995	$1.15 Type **182**	1·25	80
996	$1.50 Robert Garrett (U.S.A.) (Discus)	1·25	1·00
997	$2.30 Spyridon Louis (Greece) (Marathon)	1·50	1·75
998	$3 John Boland (Great Britain) (Tennis)	2·00	3·25
995/8 Set of 4		5·50	6·00

183 James Dean   **184** Leprechaun

(Des T. Kelly. Litho)

1996 (28 June). James Dean (film star) Commemoration. T **183** and similar designs. Multicoloured. P 12½.

999	$1.15 Type **183**	60	80
	a. Sheetlet. Nos. 999/1007	4·75	6·50
1000	$1.15 Wearing stetson facing right	60	80
1001	$1.15 Wearing blue sweater	60	80
1002	$1.15 Wearing black sweater	60	80
1003	$1.15 Full face portrait wearing stetson	60	80
1004	$1.15 Wearing fawn jacket	60	80
1005	$1.15 Wearing red wind-cheater	60	80
1006	$1.15 Smoking a cigarette	60	80
1007	$1.15 In open-necked shirt and green jumper	60	80
999/1007 Set of 9		4·75	6·50
MS1008 169×133 mm. $6 As No. 1000 (51×57 *mm*)		4·00	6·00

Nos. 999/1007 were printed together, *se-tenant*, in sheetlets of 9.

(Litho Cot Printery Ltd, Barbados)

1996 (15 Aug). Mythical Creatures. T **184** and similar vert designs. Multicoloured. P 14.

1009	5c. Type **184**	10	30
1010	10c. Pegasus	10	30
1011	15c. Griffin	15	30
1012	20c. Unicorn	20	30
1013	25c. Gnomes	25	30
1014	40c. Mermaid	40	40
1015	55c. Cockatrice	50	30
1016	70c. Fairy	65	40
1017	90c. Goblin	80	50
1018	$1 Faun	90	55
1019	$1.15 Dragon	1·00	65
1020	$1.50 Giant	1·25	85
1021	$3 Elves	2·00	2·50
1022	$5 Centaur	3·25	3·75
1023	$7.50 Phoenix	4·75	6·00
1024	$10 Erin	5·50	6·50
1009/24 Set of 16		20·00	21·00

MONTSERRAT

185 Blue and Green Teddybears

186 Turkey Vulture

1996 (21 Oct). Jerry Garcia and the Grateful Dead (rock group) Commemoration. T **185** and similar vert designs. Multicoloured. Litho. P 12½.
1025	$1.15 Type **185**..	1·00	1·00
	a. Horiz strip of 3. Nos. 1025/7........................	2·75	2·75
1026	$1.15 Green and yellow teddybears................	1·00	1·00
1027	$1.15 Brown and pink teddybears..................	1·00	1·00
1028	$6 Jerry Garcia (37×50 *mm*)...........................	5·50	5·50
1025/8 Set of 4..		7·75	7·75

Nos. 1025/7 were printed together, *se-tenant*, in horizontal strips of 3 throughout the sheet, each strip forming a composite design.

(Des M. Pollard. Litho B.D.T.)

1997 (28 Jan). Scavengers of the Sky. T **186** and similar horiz designs. Multicoloured. P 15×14.
1029	$1 Type **186**...	85	70
1030	$1.15 American Crow..	1·00	70
1031	$1.50 Great Skua...	1·50	1·50
1032	$3.45 Kittiwake..	2·50	4·00
1029/32 Set of 4...		5·25	6·25
MS1033 74×95 mm. $4.50, King Vulture		3·50	4·50

HONG KONG '97
(**187**)

(Litho Cambridge Security Press Ltd)

1997 (26 Mar). HONG KONG '97 International Stamp Exhibition. Nos. 1025/7 overprinted with T **187** in deep blue across horizontal strips of three.
1034	$1.15 Type **185**...	70	1·00
	a. Horiz strip of 3. Nos. 1034/6.....................	1·90	2·75
1035	$1.15 Green and yellow teddy bears................	70	1·00
1036	$1.15 Brown and pink teddy bears..................	70	1·00
1034/6 Set of 3...		1·90	2·75

Type **187** falls across the three stamps with "HO" on No. 1034, "NG KONG" on No. 1035 and "'97" on No. 1036.

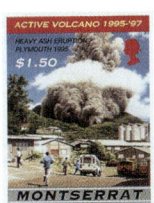

(**188**)

189 Heavy Ash Eruption over Plymouth, 1995

(Des M. Pollard. Litho Cot Printery, Barbados)

1997 (2 June). Pacific '97 International Stamp Exhibition, San Francisco. Nos. 999/1007 optd with T **188** with each impression falling across two stamps.
1037	$1.15 Type **183**...	60	80
	a. Sheetlet. Nos. 1037/45...............................	4·75	6·50
1038	$1.15 Wearing stetson facing right...................	60	80
1039	$1.15 Wearing blue sweater..............................	60	80
1040	$1.15 Wearing black sweater............................	60	80
1041	$1.15 Full-face portrait wearing stetson............	60	80
1042	$1.15 Wearing fawn jacket................................	60	80
1043	$1.15 Wearing red wind-cheater.......................	60	80
1044	$1.15 Smoking a cigarette.................................	60	80
1045	$1.15 In open-necked shirt and green jumper ..	60	80
1037/45 Set of 9..		4·75	6·50

(Des M. Pollard. Litho Cot Printery, Barbados)

1997 (23 June). Eruption of Soufriere Volcano. T **189** and similar vert designs. Multicoloured. P 14½×14.
1046	$1.50 Type **189**...	1·40	1·60
	a. Sheetlet. Nos. 1046/54...............................	11·00	13·00
1047	$1.50 Burning rock flow entering sea...............	1·40	1·60
1048	$1.50 Double venting at Castle Peak................	1·40	1·60
1049	$1.50 Mangrove Cuckoo...................................	1·40	1·60
1050	$1.50 Lava flow at night, 1996.........................	1·40	1·60
1051	$1.50 Antillean Crested Hummingbird.............	1·40	1·60
1052	$1.50 Ash cloud over Plymouth........................	1·40	1·60
1053	$1.50 Lava spine, 1996.....................................	1·40	1·60
1054	$1.50 Burning rock flows forming new land	1·40	1·60
1046/54 Set of 9...		11·00	13·00

Nos. 1046/54 were printed together, *se-tenant*, in sheetlets of 9.

No. 1046a was reissued on 29 December 1997 overprinted "MUSIC FOR / IN AID OF THE VICTIMS OF SOUFRIERE HILLS VOLCANO / ROYAL ALBERT HALL LONDON / 15th SEPTEMBER 1997" in black on top, left and right margins.

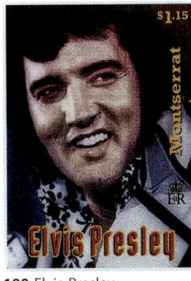

190 Elvis Presley

191 Untitled Painting by Frama

(Litho Cambridge Security Press Ltd)

1997 (29 Aug). Rock Legends. T **190** and similar vert designs. Multicoloured. P 12½.
1055	$1.15 Type **190**..	1·75	1·40
1056	$1.15 Jimi Hendrix	1·75	1·40
1057	$1.15 Jerry Garcia..	1·75	1·40
1058	$1.15 Janis Joplin..	1·75	1·40
1055/8 Set of 4..		6·25	5·00

Nos. 1055/8 were each printed in sheets of 8 containing two blocks of four separated by a vertical gutter.

(Litho Cambridge Security Press Ltd)

1997 (29 Aug). Frama Exhibition at Guggenheim Museum, New York. P 12½.
1059	**191**	$1.50 multicoloured..	1·00	1·25
		a. Sheetlet. No. 1059×8................................	7·00	

No. 1059 was printed in sheetlets of 8 stamps, containing two blocks of four separated by an illustrated margin.

(**192**)

193 Prickly Pear

194 Eva and Juan Peron (Argentine politicians)

1997 (21 Nov). No. 1028 surch with T **192** in black on gold by Benjies Printery, Antigua.
1060	$1.50 on $6 Jerry Garcia (37×50 *mm*)	2·25	2·50

(Des M. Pollard. Litho Questa)

1998 (30 Mar). Medicinal Plants. T **193** and similar vert designs. Multicoloured. P 15×14½.
1061	$1 Type **193**..	65	50
1062	$1.15 Pommie Coolie..	70	55
1063	$1.50 Aloe...	85	90
1064	$3.45 Bird Pepper...	1·75	2·50
1061/4 Set of 4..		3·50	4·00

(Litho Cambridge Security Press)

1998 (18 May). Famous People of the 20th Century. T **194** and similar multicoloured designs. P 12½.
1065	$1.15 Type **194**..	1·50	1·50
	a. Sheetlet of 4..	5·50	
1066	$1.15 Pablo Picasso (painter)............................	1·50	1·50
	a. Sheetlet of 4..	5·50	
1067	$1.15 Wernher von Braun (space scientist)........	1·50	1·50
	a. Sheetlet of 4..	5·50	
1068	$1.15 David Ben Gurion (Israeli states man).....	1·50	1·50
	a. Sheetlet of 4..	5·50	
1069	$1.15 Jean Henri Dunant (founder of Red Cross)	1·50	1·50
	a. Sheetlet of 4..	5·50	
1070	$1.15 Dwight Eisenhower (President of U.S.A.)	1·50	1·50
	a. Sheetlet of 4..	5·50	

MONTSERRAT

1071	$1.15 Mahatma Gandhi (leader of Indian Independence movement)...............	1·50	1·50
	a. Sheetlet of 4................................	5·50	
1072	$1.15 King Leopold III and Queen Astrid of Belgium...	1·50	1·50
	a. Sheetlet of 4................................	5·50	
1073	$1.15 Grand Duchess Charlotte and Prince Felix of Luxembourg..........................	1·50	1·50
	a. Sheetlet of 4................................	5·50	
1074	$1.50 Charles Augustus Lindbergh (pioneer aviator).......................................	1·50	1·50
	a. Sheetlet of 4................................	5·50	
1075	$1.50 Mao Tse-tung (Chinese communist leader)...	1·50	1·50
	a. Sheetlet of 4................................	5·50	
1076	$1.50 Earl Mountbatten (last Viceroy of India).	1·50	1·50
	a. Sheetlet of 4................................	5·50	
1077	$1.50 Konrad Adenauer (German statesman)..	1·50	1·50
	a. Sheetlet of 4................................	5·50	
1078	$1.50 Anne Frank (Holocaust victim)...............	1·50	1·50
	a. Sheetlet of 4................................	5·50	
1079	$1.50 Queen Wilhelmina of the Netherlands...	1·50	1·50
	a. Sheetlet of 4................................	5·50	
1080	$1.50 King George VI of Great Britain.............	1·50	1·50
	a. Sheetlet of 4................................	5·50	
1081	$1.50 King Christian X of Denmark.................	1·50	1·50
	a. Sheetlet of 4................................	5·50	
1082	$1.50 King Haakon VII and Crown Prince Olav of Norway............................	1·50	1·50
	a. Sheetlet of 4................................	5·50	
1083	$1.50 King Alfonso XIII of Spain.......................	1·50	1·50
	a. Sheetlet of 4................................	5·50	
1084	$1.50 King Gustavus V of Sweden...................	1·50	1·50
	a. Sheetlet of 4................................	5·50	
1065/84 Set of 20..		27·00	27·00
MS1085 115×63 mm. $3 John F. Kennedy (President of U.S.A.) (50×32 mm)................................		2·00	2·75

Nos. 1065/84 were each printed in sheetlets of 4 with enlarged illustrated right margins.

195 Jerry Garcia

(Litho Cambridge Security Press Ltd)
1998 (6 Aug). Rock Music Legends. T **195** and similar vert designs. Multicoloured. P 12½.

(a) Jerry Garcia.

1086	$1.15 In long-sleeved blue shirt................	1·10	1·25
	a. Sheetlet. Nos. 1086/94................	9·00	10·00
1087	$1.15 With drum kit in background..........	1·10	1·25
1088	$1.15 Type **195**...	1·10	1·25
1089	$1.15 Wearing long-sleeved black t-shirt	1·10	1·25
1090	$1.15 Close-up with left hand in foreground...	1·10	1·25
1091	$1.15 With purple and black background.........	1·10	1·25
1092	$1.15 Holding microphone...............................	1·10	1·25
1093	$1.15 In short-sleeved blue t-shirt...................	1·10	1·25
1094	$1.15 In sunglasses with cymbal in background...	1·10	1·25

(b) Bob Marley. Predominant colour for each design given

1095	$1.15 Pointing (green).......................................	1·10	1·25
	a. Sheetlet. Nos. 1095/1102, and 1 central label...	8·00	9·00
1096	$1.15 Wearing neck chain (green)...................	1·10	1·25
1097	$1.15 Singing into microphone (green)...........	1·10	1·25
1098	$1.15 Singing with eyes closed (yellow)..........	1·10	1·25
1099	$1.15 Facing audience (yellow).......................	1·10	1·25
1100	$1.15 In striped t-shirt with fingers on chin (red)..	1·10	1·25
1101	$1.15 In Rastafarian hat (red)..........................	1·10	1·25
1102	$1.15 In striped t-shirt with hand closed (red)..	1·10	1·25
1086/1102 Set of 17...		17·00	19·00
MS1103 152×101 mm. $5 Jerry Garcia (50×75 mm).......		3·00	3·75

Nos. 1086/94 and 1095/102 were each printed together, *se-tenant*, in sheetlets of 9 or 8 stamps and one label.

196 Ash Eruption from Soufriere Hills Volcano

(Litho Cambridge Security Press Ltd)
1998 (21 Sept). Total Eclipse of the Sun on 26 February. T **196** and similar multicoloured designs. P 12½.

1104	$1.15 Type **196**...	2·00	1·50
1105	$1.15 Volcano emitting black cloud..............	2·00	1·50
1106	$1.15 Village below volcano.........................	2·00	1·50
1107	$1.15 Lava flow and wrecked house............	2·00	1·50
1104/7 Set of 4..		7·00	5·50
MS1108 152×102 mm. $6 Solar eclipse (*vert*)................		8·00	8·50

Nos. 1104/7 were each printed in small sheets of 4.

197 Princess Diana on Wedding Day, 1981   (198)

(Des M. Pollard. Litho Cambridge Security Press Ltd)
1998 (23 Nov). Diana, Princess of Wales Commemoration. T **197** and similar horiz designs. Multicoloured. P 12½.

1109	$1.15 Type **197**...	1·50	70
1110	$1.50 Accepting bouquet from children............	1·75	1·10
1111	$3 At Royal Ascot...	3·00	4·00
1109/11 Set of 3..		5·50	5·25
MS1112 133×100 mm. $6 Diana and "Princess of Wales" rose (50×37 mm)...		5·50	5·50

1998 (29 Dec). 19th World Scout Jamboree, Chile. Nos. 669/72 optd with T **198** in red.

1113	20c. Type **117**...	30	40
	a. Horiz pair. Nos. 1113/14...................	60	80
1114	20c. Girl Guide saluting...............................	30	40
1115	75c. Lady Baden-Powell...............................	70	1·00
	a. Horiz pair. Nos. 1115/16...................	1·40	2·00
1116	75c. Guide assisting in old people's home	70	1·00
1113/16 Set of 4..		1·75	2·50

199 Jerry Garcia

(Litho Cambridge Security Press Ltd)
1999 (9-7 Apr-May). Jerry Garcia (rock musician) Commemoration. T **199** and similar multicoloured designs. P 12½.

1117	$1.15 Type **199**...	90	1·00
	a. Sheetlet. Nos. 1117/19, each×3........	7·00	8·00
1118	$1.15 In front of drum kit (bluish violet background)...	90	1·00
1119	$1.15 Singing into microphone......................	90	1·00
1120	$1.15 Playing guitar, facing right (*vert*).........	90	1·00
	a. Sheetlet. Nos. 1120/2, each×3.........	7·00	8·00
1121	$1.15 Singing with eyes closed (*vert*)...........	90	1·00
1122	$1.15 Singing in white spotlight (*vert*)..........	90	1·00
1123	$1.15 In front of drum kit (deep turquoise green background) (7 May)...................	90	1·00
	a. Sheetlet. Nos. 1123/5, each×3.........	7·00	8·00
1124	$1.15 In long-sleeved black shirt (7 May).........	90	1·00
1125	$1.15 In red shirt (7 May)..............................	90	1·00
1126	$1.15 In short-sleeved black t-shirt (without frame) (*vert*) (7 May)...............................	90	1·00

MONTSERRAT

		a. Sheetlet. Nos. 1126/8, each×3	7·00	8·00
1127		$1.15 In blue t-shirt (oval frame) (vert) (7 May)	90	1·00
1128		$1.15 In short-sleeved black t-shirt (oval frame) (vert) (7 May)	90	1·00
1117/28 Set of 12			9·75	11·00
MS1129 Two sheets. (a) 115×153 mm. $6 Jerry Garcia in concert (50×75 mm). (b) 153×115 mm. $6 Singing into microphone (75×50 mm) (7 May) Set of 2 sheets			8·00	10·00

Nos. 1117/19, 1120/2, 1123/5 and 1126/8 were each printed together, se-tenant, in sheetlets of 9 containing three of each design.

(200)   201 Mango

1999 (27 Apr). "iBRA '99" International Stamp Exhibition, Nuremberg. Nos. 975/6 optd with T **200**.

1130	$1.15 Type **200**	2·25	1·75
1131	$1.50 Open book ("Education")	2·25	2·50

(Des M. Pollard. Litho Cambridge Security Press Ltd)

1999 (5 July). Tropical Caribbean Fruits. T **201** and similar square designs. Multicoloured. P 12½.

1132	$1.15 Type **201**	85	70
1133	$1.50 Breadfruit	1·00	85
1134	$2.30 Papaya	1·60	1·60
1135	$3 Lime	2·00	2·50
1136	$6 Akee	3·75	6·00
1132/6 Set of 5		8·25	10·00
MS1137 134×95 mm. Nos. 1132/6		10·00	12·00

202 Yorkshire Terrier   203 Pupil's Equipment and World Map

(Des M. Pollard. Litho Cambridge Security Press Ltd)

1999 (27 Sept). Dogs. T **202** and similar square designs. Each black. P 12½.

1138	70c. Type **202**	1·75	80
1139	$1 Welsh Corgi	2·00	90
1140	$1.15 King Charles Spaniel	2·25	90
1141	$1.50 Poodle	2·50	1·50
1142	$3 Beagle	4·50	7·00
1138/42 Set of 5		11·50	10·00
MS1143 133×95 mm. Nos. 1138/42		11·50	12·00

(Des M. Pollard. Litho Cambridge Security Press Ltd)

1999 (5 Oct). World Teachers' Day. T **203** and similar square designs. Multicoloured. P 12½.

1144	$1 Type **203**	2·00	90
1145	$1.15 Teacher and class	2·00	90
1146	$1.50 Emblems of vocational training	2·25	1·50
1147	$5 Scientific equipment	6·50	8·50
1144/7 Set of 4		11·50	11·00

204 Great Hammerhead Shark

(Des R. Walton. Litho Impressor)

1999 (29 Nov). Endangered Species. Great Hammerhead Shark. T **204** and similar horiz designs. Multicoloured. P 13½.

1148	50c. Type **204**	85	90
	a. Strip of 4. Nos. 1148/51	3·00	3·25
1149	50c. Two Hammerhead Sharks among fish	85	90
1150	50c. Two Hammerhead Sharks on sea-bed	85	90
1151	50c. Three Hammerhead Sharks	85	90
1148/51 Set of 4		3·00	3·25

Nos. 1148/51 were printed together, se-tenant, both horizontally and vertically, in sheets of 16.

205 Flowers   206 Alfred Valentine

(Des R. Watton. Litho Impressor)

2000 (1 Jan). New Millennium. P 13½.

1152	**205**	$1.50 multicoloured	2·75	2·75

(Des A. Melville-Brown. Litho Cartor)

2000 (5 May). West Indies Cricket Tour and 100th Test Match at Lord's. T **206** and similar multicoloured designs. P 13½.

1153	$1 Type **206**	2·50	1·00
1154	$5 George Headley	5·50	6·50
MS1155 119×101 mm. $6 Lord's Cricket Ground (horiz)		8·00	9·00

207 Spitfire Squadron taking-off

(Des J. Batchelor. Litho Questa)

2000 (22 May). "The Stamp Show 2000" International Stamp Exhibition, London. 60th Anniv of Battle of Britain. T **207** and similar horiz designs. Multicoloured. W w **14** (sideways). P 14.

1156	70c. Type **207**	1·00	50
1157	$1.15 Overhauling Hurricane Mk 1	1·25	65
1158	$1.50 Hurricane Mk I attacking	1·50	1·25
1159	$5 Flt. Lt. Frank Howell's Spitfire Mk IA	3·50	5·50
1156/9 Set of 4		6·50	7·00
MS1160 110×87 mm. $6 Hawker Hurricane		4·50	5·50

208 Statue of Liberty and Carnival Scene

(Des R. Vigurs. Litho Cartor)

2000 (3 July). New Millennium. Landmarks. T **208** and similar horiz designs, each including carnival scene. Multicoloured. P 13½.

1161	90c. Type **208**	75	50
1162	$1.15 Great Wall of China	95	60
1163	$1.50 Eiffel Tower	1·25	1·25
1164	$3.50 Millennium Dome	2·50	4·00
1161/4 Set of 4		5·00	5·75

209 Queen Elizabeth the Queen Mother and W.H. Bramble Airport

(Des. N. Shewring. Litho Cartor)

2000 (4 Aug). Queen Elizabeth the Queen Mother's 100th Birthday. T **209** and similar horiz designs each showing different portrait. Multicoloured. P 13½×13.

1165	70c. Type **209**	85	40
1166	$1.15 Government House	1·25	65
1167	$3 Court House	2·50	3·00

MONTSERRAT

1168	$6 War Memorial Clock Tower		4·50	6·00
1165/8 Set of 4			8·25	9·00
MS1169 120×75 mm. Nos. 1165/8			8·00	9·50

210 Three Wise Men following Star

211 Golden Swallow

(Des M. Pollard. Litho B.D.T.)

2000 (29 Nov). Christmas. T **210** and similar vert designs. Multicoloured. P 14×15.

1170	$1 Type **210**	1·00	55
1171	$1.15 Cavalla Hill Methodist Church	1·10	65
1172	$1.50 Shepherds with flocks	1·25	85
1173	$3 Mary and Joseph arriving at Bethlehem	2·25	3·75
1170/3 Set of 4		5·00	5·00
MS1174 105×75 mm. $6 As $3		4·50	6·00

(Des R. Vigurs. Litho Cartor)

2001 (26 Mar). Caribbean Birds. T **211** and similar multicoloured designs. P 13½.

1175	$1 Type **211**	1·25	65
1176	$1.15 Crested quail dove (horiz)	1·40	75
1177	$1.50 Red-legged thrush (horiz)	1·50	1·10
1178	$5 Fernandina's flicker	4·25	6·00
1175/8 Set of 4		7·50	7·75
MS1179 95×68 mm. $8 St. Vincent amazon (horiz)		9·00	9·50

212 Edward Stanley Gibbons, Charles J. Phillips and 391 Strand Shop

(Des R. Vigurs. Litho Cartor)

2001 (30 Apr). Famous Stamp Personalities. T **212** and similar horiz designs. Multicoloured. P 13½.

1180	$1 Type **212**	1·40	75
1181	$1.15 John Lister and Montserrat stamps	1·50	75
1182	$1.50 Theodore Champion and French postilion	1·60	1·25
1183	$3 Thomas De La Rue and De La Rue's stand at Great Exhibition, 1851	3·00	4·50
1180/3 Set of 4		6·75	6·50
MS1184 95×68 mm. $8 Sir Rowland Hill and Bruce Castle		6·50	8·50

213 Princess Elizabeth at International Horse Show, 1950

214 Look Out Village

(Des. R Vigurs. Litho Cartor)

2001 (22 June). Queen Elizabeth II's 75th Birthday. T **213** and similar vert designs. Multicoloured. P 13½.

1185	90c. Type **213**	1·25	60
1186	$1.15 Queen Elizabeth II, 1986	1·40	75
1187	$1.50 Queen Elizabeth II, 1967	1·60	1·40
1188	$5 Queen Elizabeth, 1976	4·75	5·50
1185/8 Set of 4		8·00	7·50
MS1189 90×68 mm. $6 Queen Elizabeth, 2000		7·00	8·00

(Des J. Lister. Litho Cartor)

2001 (15 Aug). Reconstruction. T **214** and similar horiz designs. Multicoloured. P 13½.

1190	70c. Type **214**	80	60
1191	$1 St John's Hospital	1·00	65
1192	$1.15 Tropical Mansions Suites Hotel	1·10	70
1193	$1.50 Montserrat Secondary School	1·40	1·25
1194	$3 Golden Years Care Home	3·00	4·50
1190/4 Set of 4		6·50	7·00

215 West Indian Cherry

(Des R. Vigurs. Litho Cartor)

2001 (10 Oct). Caribbean Fruits. T **215** and similar horiz designs. Multicoloured. P 13½.

1195	5c. Type **215**	40	70
1196	10c. Mammee Apple	40	70
1197	15c. Lime	45	70
1198	20c. Grapefruit	45	70
1199	25c. Orange	45	70
1200	40c. Passion Fruit	60	50
1201	55c. Banana	70	40
1202	70c. Pawpaw	90	50
1203	90c. Pomegranate	1·00	70
1204	$1 Guava	1·10	75
1205	$1.15 Mango	1·25	75
1206	$1.50 Sugar Apple	1·50	1·10
1207	$3 Cashew	2·75	3·00
1208	$5 Soursop	4·50	5·50
1209	$7.50 Watermelon	7·00	9·00
1210	$10 Pineapple	8·00	9·50
1195/210 Set of 16		28·00	32·00

216 Common Long-tail Skipper (butterfly)

(Des R. Vigurs. Litho Cartor)

2001 (20 Dec). Caribbean Butterflies. T **216** and similar horiz designs. Multicoloured. P 13½.

1211	$1 Type **216**	1·10	60
1212	$1.15 Straight-line sulphur	1·25	70
1213	$1.50 Giant hairstreak	1·50	1·25
1214	$3 Monarch	2·50	4·00
1211/14 Set of 4		5·75	6·00
MS1215 115×115 mm. $10 Painted lady		8·50	11·00

The overall design of No. **MS**1215 is butterfly-shaped.

217 Alpine Ski-ing

(Des R. Vigurs. Litho Cartor)

2002 (12 Mar). Winter Olympic Games, Salt Lake City. T **217** and similar horiz design. Multicoloured. P 13½.

1216	$3 Type **217**	2·25	2·75
	a. Horiz pair. Nos 1216/17	5·50	7·00
1217	$5 Four man bobsleigh	3·25	4·25

Nos. 1216/17 were printed together, *se-tenant*, as horizontal pairs throughout the sheet.

MONTSERRAT

218 Sergeant Major (fish)

(Litho Cartor)

2002 (24 July). Fish of the Caribbean. T **218** and similar horiz designs. Multicoloured. P 13½×13.

1218	$1 Type **218**	1·25	60
1219	$1.15 Mutton snapper	1·40	70
1220	$1.50 Lantern bass	1·75	1·25
1221	$5 Shy Hamlet	6·00	7·50
1218/21	Set of 4	9·50	9·00
MS1222	102×70 mm. $8 Queen angelfish	9·00	10·00

(**219**)

2002 (23 Sept). Queen Elizabeth the Queen Mother Commemoration. Nos. 1165/8 optd with T **219**.

1223	70c. Type **219**	70	55
1224	$1.15 Government House	1·00	70
1225	$3 Court House	2·75	3·00
1226	$6 War Memorial Clock Tower	4·75	6·00
1223/6	Set of 4	8·25	9·25

220 *Allamanda cathartica*

221 Queen Elizabeth II wearing Imperial State Crown and Coronation Robes

(Des R. Vigurs. Litho Cartor)

2002 (29 Nov). Wild Flowers. T **220** and similar horiz designs. Multicoloured. P 13½.

1227	70c. Type **220**	85	55
1228	$1.15 *Lantana camara*	1·25	70
1229	$1.50 *Leonotis nepetifolia*	1·50	1·25
1230	$5 *Plumeria rubra*	5·00	6·50
1227/30	Set of 4	7·75	8·00
MS1231	105×75 mm. $8 *Alpinia purpurata*	8·00	9·50

(Des T. Wood. Litho DLR)

2003 (30 Apr). 50th Anniv of Coronation. Two sheets containing vert designs as T **221**. Multicoloured. P 14.

MS1232	153×85 mm. $3 Type **219**; $3 St. Edward's Crown; $3 Queen wearing diadem and blue sash	7·00	8·00
MS1233	105×75 mm. $6 Queen wearing Imperial State Crown and Coronation robes	4·50	5·00

222 Wright Flyer II (blue)

223 Prince William

(Litho DLR)

2003 (30 June). Centenary of Powered Flight. T **222** and similar horiz designs. Multicoloured. P 14.

MS1234	116×125 mm. $2 Type **222**; $2 *Wright Flyer II* (brown); $2 Orville and Wilbur Wright; $2 *Wright Flyer I*.	5·50	6·00
MS1235	106×76 mm. $6 *Wright Flyer II*	5·50	6·00

(Litho BDT)

2003 (20 Aug). 21st Birthday of Prince William of Wales. T **223** and similar vert designs showing different portraits. Multicoloured. P 14.

MS1236	155×85 mm. $3 Type **223**; $3 Prince William (frame incomplete at bottom left); $3 Prince William (frame complete at bottom left)	7·00	8·00
MS1237	106×76 mm. $6 Prince William	4·75	5·50

224 Piping Frog

(Litho BDT)

2003 (28 Nov). Animals of the Caribbean. T **224** and similar horiz designs. Multicoloured. P 14.

MS1238	145×90 mm. $1.50 Type **224**; $1.50 Land hermit crab; $1.50 Spix's pinche; $1.50 Dwarf gecko; $1.50 Green sea turtle; $1.50 Small Indian mongoose	7·00	8·00
MS1239	92×66 mm. $6 Sally lightfoot crab	6·00	6·00

225 *Lactarius trivialis*

(Litho BDT)

2003 (28 Nov). Mushrooms of the World. T **225** and similar horiz designs. Multicoloured. P 14.

MS1240	145×90 mm. $1.50 Type **225**; $1.50 *Gomphidius roseus*; $1.50 *Lycoperdonpyriforme*; $1.50 *Hygrophorus coccineus*; $1.50 *Russula xerampelina*; $1.50 *Gomphusfloccosus*	8·00	9·00
MS1241	92×66 mm. $6 *Amanita muscaria*	5·50	6·00

226 Belted Kingfisher

227 Olympic Poster, Los Angeles, 1932

(Litho BDT)

2003 (22 Dec). Birds of the Caribbean. T **226** and similar horiz designs. Multicoloured. P 14.

1242	90c. Type **226**	1·40	75
1243	$1.15 Yellow warbler	1·60	95
1244	$1.50 Hooded warbler	1·90	1·50
1245	$5 Cedar waxwing	7·00	8·50
1242/5	Set of 4	11·00	10·50
MS1246	145×90 mm. $1.50 Roseate spoonbill; $1.50 Laughing gull; $1.50 White-tailed tropic bird; $1.50 Bare-eyed thrush; $1.50 Glittering-throated emerald; $1.50 Carib grackle ("Lesser Antillean Grackle")	8·00	9·00
MS1247	92×68 mm. $6 Bananaquit	6·50	6·50

(Litho Cartor)

2004 (30 June). Olympic Games, Athens. T **227** and similar multicoloured designs. P 13½.

1248	90c. Type **227**	1·25	70

MONTSERRAT

1249	$1.15 Olympic pin, Munich, 1972	1·50	80
1250	$1.50 Olympic poster, Montreal, 1976	1·75	1·50
1251	$5 Greek art depicting Pankration (*horiz*)	4·00	6·00
1248/51	Set of 4	7·75	8·00

228 Singapura

229 Lace Wing

(Litho BDT)

2004 (23 Aug). Cats. T **228** and similar vert designs. Multicoloured. P 14.

1252	$1.15 Type **228**	1·50	90
1253	$1.50 Burmese	1·75	1·25
1254	$2 Abyssinian	2·25	2·00
1255	$5 Norwegian	5·50	7·00
1252/5	Set of 4	10·00	10·00
MS1256	92×68 mm. $6 Russian blue	6·50	7·50

(Litho BDT)

2004 (23 Aug). Butterflies. T **229** and similar horiz designs. Multicoloured. P 14.

MS1257	125×88 mm. $2.30 Type **229**; $2.30 Swallowtail; $2.30 Shoemaker; $2.20 White peacock	7·00	7·50
MS1258	70×96 mm. $6 Flashing astraptes	5·00	5·50

230 Blue-girdled Angelfish

(Litho BDT)

2004 (30 Sept). Fish. T **230** and similar horiz designs. Multicoloured. P 14.

MS1259	122×93 mm. $2.30 Type **230**; $2.30 Regal angelfish; $2.30 Emperor angelfish; $2.30 Blotch-eye soldierfish	7·00	7·50
MS1260	70×96 mm. $6 Banded butterflyfish	5·00	5·50

231 Austerity Steam Locomotive

232 AIDS Ribbon

(Litho SNP Sprint, Australia)

2004 (29 Oct). Bicentenary of Steam Locomotives. T **231** and similar horiz designs. Multicoloured. P 14½ ($1.50) or 14½×14 (others).

MS1261	159×120 mm. $1.50 Type **231**; $1.50 Deli Vasut No. 109.109; $1.50 Class 424 No. 424.247/287; $1.50 L1646; $1.50 No. 324.1564; $1.50 Class 204	7·00	7·50
MS1262	119×159 mm. $2 375.562 Old Class TV; $2 Class Va 7111; $2 Class 424 No. 424.009; $2 Class III No. 269	6·00	6·50
MS1263	92×106 mm. $6 Class QR1 No. 3038	5·00	5·50

(Des. M. Servin. Litho Cartor)

2004 (1 Dec). World AIDS Day. Sheet 123×95 mm. P 13½.

MS1264	**232** $3×4 multicoloured	8·00	10·00

233 National Football Team

(Des M. Servin. Litho State Ptg Wks, Beijing)

2004 (24 Dec). Centenary of FIFA (Fédération Internationale de Football Association). P 12.

1265	**233** $6 multicoloured	5·00	6·50

234 Start of Air Assault

(Des R. Rundon. Litho BDT)

2004 (24 Dec). 60th Anniv of D-Day Landings. T **234** and similar horiz designs. Multicoloured. P 14.

1266	$1.15 Type **234**	1·75	1·00
1267	$1.50 Soldiers landing on Normandy beaches	2·25	1·50
1268	$2 Field Marshall Montgomery	2·75	2·75
1269	$5 HMS *Belfast*	7·00	8·50
1266/9	Set of 4	12·00	12·00

THE VISIT OF HRH THE PRINCESS ROYAL FEBRUARY 2005

(**235**)

2005 (21 Feb). Royal Visit. Nos. 1190/4 optd with T **235**.

1270	70c. Look Out Village	1·25	85
1271	$1 St John's Hospital	1·75	1·25
1272	$1.15 Tropical Mansions Suites Hotel	1·75	1·25
1273	$1.50 Montserrat Secondary School	2·25	1·75
1274	$3 Golden Years Care Home	4·00	5·50
1271/4	Set of 4	10·00	9·50

236 *Cattleya lueddemanniana*

(Litho Cartor)

2005 (25 Apr). Orchids. T **236** and similar horiz designs. Multicoloured. P 13½.

MS1275	140×105 mm. $2.30×4, Type **236**; *Cattleya luteola*; *Cattleya trianaei*; *Cattleya mossiae*	7·50	8·00
MS1276	100×70 mm. $6 *Cattleya mendelii*	5·50	6·00

237 Brown Pelican

238 *Liguus virgineus*

MONTSERRAT

(Litho Cartor)

2005 (25 Apr). Seabirds. T **237** and similar horiz designs. Multicoloured. P 13½.

MS1277	140×105 mm. $2.30×4, Type **237**; Red-billed tropic bird; Galapagos Island cormorant; Waved albatross	7·50	8·00
MS1278	100×70 mm. $6 Common tern	6·50	7·00

(Litho Cartor)

2005 (1 June). Molluscs. T **238** and similar multicoloured designs. P 13½.

1279	$1.15 Type **238**	1·75	1·00
1280	$1.50 *Liguus fasciatus testudineus*	2·25	1·50
1281	$2 *Liguus fasciatus*	2·75	2·75
1282	$5 *Cerion striatella*	7·00	8·50
1279/82	Set of 4	12·00	12·00
MS1283	70×100 mm. $6 *Liguus fasciatus* (vert)	8·00	9·00

239 Soufrière Hills Volcano

(Litho BDT)

2005 (18 July). Tenth Anniv of the Eruption of Soufrière Hills Volcano. Sheet 146×116 mm containing T **239** and similar horiz designs. Multicoloured. P 14.

MS1284	$2×9, Type **239**; Explosion; Tar River Delta; Belham River; Montserrat Volcano Observatory building; Pyroclastic flow; Blackburne airport, destroyed in 1997; Maintenance and monitoring helicopter; Instruments used for monitoring volcano	19·00	22·00

240 Shamrock

241 Napoleon Bonaparte

(Litho State Ptg Wks, Beijing)

2005 (12 Sept). Centenary of Rotary International. T **240** and similar multicoloured designs. P 13.

1285	$1 Type **240**	1·50	90
1286	$1.15 *Heliconia* (national flower)	1·75	1·00
1287	$1.50 The lady and the harp	2·25	2·00
1288	$5 Map of Montserrat	6·50	8·00
1285/8	Set of 4	11·00	11·00
MS1289	100×70 mm. $6 Immunising children (horiz)	6·50	8·50

(Litho State Ptg Wks, Beijing)

2005 (4 Nov). Bicentenary of the Battle of Trafalgar. T **241** and similar vert designs. Multicoloured. P 12.

1290	$2 Type **241**	3·50	3·50
	a. Sheetlet. Nos. 1290/3	12·50	12·50
1291	$2 Admiral Lord Nelson (seated)	3·50	3·50
1292	$2 Battle of the Nile, 1798	3·50	3·50
1293	$2 Battle of Trafalgar, 1805	3·50	3·50
1290/3	Set of 4	12·50	12·50
MS1294	109×70 mm. $6 Admiral Lord Nelson	11·00	12·00

Nos. 1290/3 were printed together, *se-tenant*, in sheetlets of four stamps.

242 Patricia Griffin (voluntary social worker)

(Litho State Ptg Wks, Beijing)

2005 (5 Dec). Local Personalities. T **242** and similar horiz designs. Multicoloured. P 13.

1295	$1.15 Type **242**	1·25	1·50
1296	$1.15 Michael Simmons Osborne (merchant/parliamentarian)	1·25	1·50
1297	$1.15 Lilian Cadogan (nurse)	1·25	1·50
1298	$1.15 Samuel Aymer (folk musician)	1·25	1·50
1299	$1.15 William Henry Bramble (first Chief Minister)	1·25	1·50
1300	$1.15 Robert William Griffith (trade union pioneer)	1·25	1·50
1295/300	Set of 6	6·75	8·00
MS1301	100×115 mm. Nos. 1295/1300	6·75	8·00

243 Thumbelina

(Litho State Ptg Wks, Beijing)

2005 (23 Dec). Birth Bicentenary of Hans Christian Andersen (writer). T **243** and similar horiz designs. Multicoloured. P 13.

1302	$3 Type **243**	2·75	3·50
	a. Sheetlet. Nos. 1302/4	7·50	9·50
1303	$3 The Flying Trunk	2·75	3·50
1304	$3 The Buckwheat	2·75	3·50
1302/4	Set of 3	7·50	9·50
MS1305	100×70 mm. $6 The Little Mermaid (49×38 mm)	6·00	7·00

30th ANNIVERSARY OF THE PHILATELIC BUREAU 1976-2006
(244)

2006 (1 Apr). 30th Anniv of the Philatelic Bureau. Nos. 1175, 1212/13, 1227 and 1230 optd as Type **244**.

1306	70c. Type **220**	75	55
1307	$1 Type **211**	1·00	85
1308	$1.15 Straight-line sulphur	1·25	90
1309	$1.50 Giant hairstreak	1·50	1·50
1310	$5 *Plumeria rubra*	5·00	6·50
1306/10	Set of 5	8·50	9·25

The overprint on No. 1307 is smaller, 25 mm wide, and in four lines.

245 Cecropia Moth

246 Giant Caribbean Anemone

(Litho Beijing Stamp Printing House)

2006 (2 May). Moths and Butterflies of the World. T **245** and similar square designs. Multicoloured. P 12.

1311	$2.30 Type **245**	3·75	4·00
	a. Sheetlet. Nos. 1311/14	13·00	14·00
1312	$2.30 Madagascan sunset moth	3·75	4·00
1313	$2.30 Peacock butterfly	3·75	4·00
1314	$2.30 Zodiac moth	3·75	4·00
1311/14	Set of 4	13·00	14·00
MS1315	96×76 mm. $6 White-lined sphinx moth	7·00	8·00

Nos. 1311/14 were printed together, *se-tenant*, in sheetlets of four stamps with enlarged illustrated margins.

No. 1313 is wrongly inscr "GREAT PEACOCK MOTH *Saturnia pyri*".

(Litho Beijing Stamp Printing House)

2006 (2 May). Caribbean "Sea Flowers". T **246** and similar square designs. Multicoloured. P 12.

1316	$2.30 Type **246**	2·75	3·50
	a. Sheetlet. Nos. 1316/19	10·00	12·00
1317	$2.30 Beadlet anemone	2·75	3·50
1318	$2.30 Golden crinoid	2·75	3·50
1319	$2.30 Oval cup coral	2·75	3·50
1316/19	Set of 4	10·00	12·00
MS1320	96×78 mm. $6 Tube-dwelling anemone	6·50	8·00

Nos. 1316/19 were printed together, *se-tenant*, in sheetlets of four stamps with enlarged illustrated margins.

MONTSERRAT

247 Doberman (inscr Rottweiller)
248 "Mountain Chicken" 

(Litho Beijing Stamp Printing House)

2006 (2 May). Dogs. T **247** and similar square designs. Multicoloured. P 12.
1321	$1.15 Type **247**................................	2·00	1·00
1322	$1.50 Boxer..	2·25	1·50
1323	$2 Corgi...	3·00	2·75
1324	$5 Great Dane....................................	6·00	7·00
1321/4 Set of 4..		12·00	11·00
MS1325 96×78 mm. $6 St. Bernard................		7·50	8·50

(Litho Beijing Stamp Printing House)

2006 (16 Aug). Endangered Species. "Mountain Chicken" (frog *Leptodactylus fallax*). T **248** and similar horiz designs. Multicoloured. P 13½.
1326	70c. Type **248**...................................	55	75
	a. Strip of 4. Nos. 1326/9.................	3·25	4·00
1327	$1 In close-up....................................	80	1·00
1328	$1.15 Back view.................................	95	1·25
1329	$1.50 Facing left................................	1·25	1·40
1326/9 Set of 4..		3·25	4·00
MS1330 102×152 mm. Nos. 1326/9, each ×2..........		6·50	8·00

Nos. 1326/9 were printed together, *se-tenant*, as horizontal and vertical strips of four stamps in sheetlets of 16.

249 World Cup Stadium, Hanover, Germany, 2006

(Litho Beijing Stamp Printing House)

2006 (31 Aug). World Cup Football Championship, Germany. Sheet 127×102 mm containing T **249** and similar horiz designs. Multicoloured. P 12.
MS1331 $1.15 Type **249**; $1.50 Sir Stanley Matthews; $2 Sir William Ralph "Dixie" Dean; $3 Bobby Moore .... 8·50 9·50

250 Queen Elizabeth II at Coronation, 1953
251 Replica of Columbus's Fleet 

(Litho CEC Security Printers Ltd)

2006 (2 Oct). 80th Birthday of Queen Elizabeth II. T **250** and similar vert designs. Multicoloured. P 13½.
1332	$2.30 Type **250**................................	1·75	2·00
	a. Sheetlet. Nos. 1332/5...................	6·25	7·25
1333	$2.30 Queen Elizabeth wearing crown, c. 1977	1·75	2·00
1334	$2.30 Wearing tiara, c. 1980............	1·75	2·00
1335	$2.30 Wearing tiara, c. 2002............	1·75	2·00
1332/5 Set of 4..		6·25	7·25
MS1336 120×120 mm. $8 Wearing tiara and pearl drop earrings, c. 2002		6·00	7·50

Nos. 1332/5 were printed together, *se-tenant*, in sheetlets of four stamps with enlarged illustrated margins.

(Des M. Servin Litho Beijing Stamp Printing House)

2006 (27 Oct). 500th Death Anniv of Christopher Columbus. T **251** and similar multicoloured designs. P 13.
1337	$1.15 Type **251**................................	1·75	1·00
1338	$1.50 Columbus and map showing voyage to New World	2·50	1·50
1339	$2 Sailing ships, globe and Columbus.........	3·00	2·75
1340	$5 Christopher Columbus (*vert*).......	6·00	7·50
1337/40 Set of 4.....................................		12·00	11·50
MS1341 100×70 mm. $6 Columbus and his crew in New World (*vert*)		6·50	7·50

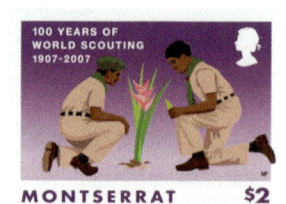

252 Boy Scouts and Bird of Paradise Flower

(Litho Cardon Enterprises, Taiwan)

2007 (9 Mar). Centenary of Scouting. T **252** and similar multicoloured designs. P 13½.
1342	$2 Type **252**.....................................	1·60	1·60
	a. Sheetlet. Nos. 1342/7...................	8·75	8·75
1343	$2 Scouts working in damaged building......	1·60	1·60
1344	$2 Scouts sailing dinghy...................	1·60	1·60
1345	$2 Scout bottle-feeding kid..............	1·60	1·60
1346	$2 Scout gathering firewood............	1·60	1·60
1347	$2 Scouts putting up bird nestbox	1·60	1·60
1342/7 Set of 6..		8·75	8·75
MS1348 100×70 mm. $6 Lord Baden-Powell (founder) (*vert*)		4·75	4·75

Nos. 1342/7 were printed together, *se-tenant*, in sheetlets of six stamps.

253 Montserrat Flag and Outline Map
254 *Euphorbia pulcherrima* (poinsettia) 

(Litho Cardon Enterprises, Taiwan)

2007 (30 Mar). World Cup Cricket, West Indies. T **253** and similar multicoloured design. P 13½.
1349	$3 Type **253**.....................................	2·25	2·25
1350	$5 Cricket team (*horiz*)....................	4·00	4·00
MS1351 117×90 mm. $8 World Cup Cricket emblem		6·35	6·25

(Litho Cardon Enterprises, Taiwan)

2007 (14 May). Flowers. T **254** and similar vert designs. Multicoloured. P 12½.
1352	10c. Type **254**...................................	20	25
1353	30c. *Catharanthus roseus* (periwinkle)............	45	50
1354	35c. *Bougainvillea glabra*	50	50
1355	50c. *Ixora macrothyrsa*	70	50
1356	70c. *Heliconia humilis*	90	65
1357	80c. *Ipomoea learii* (morning glory)	1·00	70
1358	90c. *Delonix regia* (poinciana).........	1·00	75
1359	$1 *Solandra nitida* (cup of gold).....	1·10	85
1360	$1.10 *Acalypha hispida* (chenille plant)..........	1·25	90
1361	$1.50 *Nerium oleander*	1·75	1·40
1362	$2.25 *Hibiscus rosa-sinensis*...........	2·25	2·25
1363	$2.50 *Plumeria acuminata* (frangipani)	2·50	2·75
1364	$2.75 *Strelitzia reginae* (bird of paradise flower)...............	2·75	3·00
1365	$5 *Stephanotis floribunda* (Madagascar jasmine).........	4·50	4·75
1366	$10 *Tabebuia serratifolia* (yellow poui)	8·00	9·00
1367	$20 *Rosa 'Bucbi'*..............................	14·00	16·00
1352/67 Set of 16....................................		38·00	40·00

MONTSERRAT

255 Hawksbill Turtle

256 Diana, Princess of Wales

(Litho Cartor)

2007 (8 Aug). Turtles of Montserrat. T **255** and similar horiz designs. Multicoloured. P 13½.

MS1368	130×100 mm. $3.40×4 Type **255**; Green turtle; Leatherback turtle; Loggerhead turtle	10·50	10·50
MS1369	100×70 mm. $7 Kemp's Ridley sea turtle	6·50	7·50

The stamps and margins of No. **MS**1368 form a composite design.

(Litho Cardon Enterprises, Taiwan)

2007 (31 Aug). Tenth Death Anniv of Diana, Princess of Wales. T **256** and similar vert designs. Multicoloured. P 13½.

1370	$3.40 Type **256**	3·75	3·75
	a. Sheetlet. Nos. 1370/3	13·50	13·50
1371	$3.40 Wearing black dress	3·75	3·75
1372	$3.40 Wearing white dress	3·75	3·75
1373	$3.40 Wearing white jacket with stand-up collar	3·75	3·75
1370/3 Set of 4		13·50	13·50
MS1374	100×70 mm. $7 Black/white photograph	7·00	8·00

Nos. 1370/3 were printed together, *se-tenant*, in sheetlets of four stamps with enlarged illustrated margins

257 *Hippeastrum puniceum*

(Litho Cartor)

2007 (11 Oct). Lilies of Montserrat. T **257** and similar multicoloured designs. P 13½.

MS1375	130×100 mm.$3.40×4 Type **257**; *Hymenocallis caribaea*; *Zephyranthespuertoricensis*; *Belamcanda chinensis*	10·00	11·00
MS1376	100×70 mm. $7 *Crinum erubescens* (vert)	8·00	8·50

The stamps and margins of No. **MS**1375 form a composite background design of lily foliage

258 Green-winged Macaw

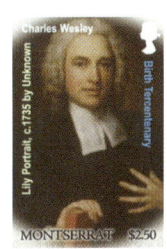

259 Charles Wesley

(Litho Cartor)

2007 (11 Oct). Parrots of the Caribbean. T **258** and similar vert designs. Multicoloured. P 13½.

1377	$3.40 Type **258**	3·75	3·75
	a. Sheetlet. Nos. 1377/80	13·50	13·50
1378	$3.40 Mitred conure	3·75	3·75
1379	$3.40 Sun conure	3·75	3·75
1380	$3.40 Blue-and-yellow macaw	3·75	3·75
1377/80 Set of 4		13·50	13·50
MS1381	100×70mm. $7 Hyacinth macaw	8·00	9·00

Nos. 1377/80 were printed together, *se-tenant*, in sheetlets of four stamps with enlarged illustrated margins.

(Litho Cardon Enterprises, Taiwan)

2007 (18 Dec). 300th Birth Anniv of Charles Wesley (founder of Methodism). T **259** and similar vert designs. Multicoloured. P 13½.

1382	$2.50 Type **259**	2·50	2·75
	a. Sheetlet. Nos. 1382/5	9·00	10·00
1383	$2.50 Charles Wesley (hands at left)	2·50	2·75
1384	$2.50 Charles Wesley with Bible	2·50	2·75
1385	$2.50 Bethany Methodist Church	2·50	2·75
1382/5 Set of 4		9·00	9·00

Nos. 1382/5 were printed together, *se-tenant*, in sheetlets of four stamps with enlarged illustrated margins

260 Sperm Whale

(Litho Beijing Stamp Printing House)

2008 (2 May). Whales of the World. T **260** and similar horiz designs. Multicoloured. P 13.

MS1386	130×100 mm. $3.55×4 Type **260**; Minke whale; Cuvier's beaked whale; Humpback whale	12·00	12·00
MS1387	100×70 mm. $7 Blue whale	7·50	7·50

The stamps and margins of No. **MS**1386 form a composite background design.

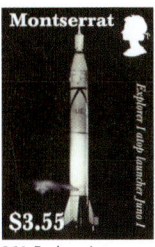

261 *Explorer I* atop Launcher *Juno I*, 1958

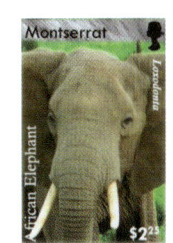

262 African Elephant

(Litho Cardon Enterprises, Taiwan)

2008 (29 May). 50 Years of Space Exploration and Satellites. T **261** and similar multicoloured designs. P 13½.

1388	$3.55 Type **261**	3·50	3·75
	a. Sheetlet. Nos. 1388/91	12·50	13·50
1389	$3.55 Dr. James Van Allen and *Explorer I*	3·50	3·75
1390	$3.55 *Explorer I*	3·50	3·75
1391	$3.55 Drs. William Pickering, James Van Allen and Wernher von Braun with *Explorer I* model	3·50	3·75
1388/91 Set of 4		12·50	13·50
MS1392	100×70 mm. $7 *Explorer I* (horiz)	7·00	8·00

Nos. 1388/91 were printed together, *se-tenant*, in sheetlets of four stamps with enlarged illustrated margins.

(Litho Cardon Enterprises, Taiwan)

2008 (3 July). Endangered Animals of the World. T **262** and similar multicoloured designs. P 13½.

1393	$2.25 Type **262**	3·00	3·00
	a. Sheetlet. Nos. 1393/8	16·00	16·00
1394	$2.25 Bald eagle	3·00	3·00
1395	$2.25 Sumatran tiger	3·00	3·00
1396	$2.25 Hawksbill turtle	3·00	3·00
1397	$2.25 Indian rhinoceros	3·00	3·00
1398	$2.25 Western gorilla	3·00	3·00
1393/8 Set of 6		16·00	16·00
MS1399	100×70 mm. $7 Rock iguana (horiz)	7·00	8·00

Nos. 1393/8 were printed together, *se-tenant*, in sheetlets of six stamps with enlarged illustrated margins.

263 First Caribbean Stamp and *Lady McLeod* (early packet ship)

(Litho Cardon Enterprises, Taiwan)

2008 (31 July). Early Postal History. T **263** and similar horiz designs. Multicoloured. P 13½.

1400	$2.75 Type **263**	3·25	3·25
	a. Sheetlet. Nos. 1400/5	18·00	18·00

MONTSERRAT

1401	$2.75 Early Montserrat postcard..................		3·25	3·25
1402	$2.75 Great Britain Mulready envelopes...........		3·25	3·25
1403	$2.75 Great Britain Penny Black and Sir Rowland Hill............		3·25	3·25
1404	$2.75 Antigua 1d. red and 6d. green stamps overprinted Montserrat, 1876........		3·25	3·25
1405	$2.75 Montserrat fleuron and crowned circle handstamps and 'A08' cancellation........		3·25	3·25
1400/5 Set of 6........			18·00	18·00

Nos. 1400/5 were printed together, *se-tenant*, in sheetlets of six stamps with enlarged illustrated margins.

264 English Electric Lightning F3

(Litho Cardon Enterprises, Taiwan)

2008 (5 Sept). 90th Anniv. of the Royal Air Force. T **264** and similar horiz designs. Multicoloured. P 13½.

1406	$3.55 Type **264**........		4·50	4·50
	a. Sheetlet. Nos. 1406/9........		16·00	16·00
1407	$3.55 Hurricane IIC........		4·50	4·50
1408	$3.55 Jet Provost T3A........		4·50	4·50
1409	$3.55 Jaguar TR3A........		4·50	4·50
1410	$3.55 Westland Sea King HAR.3 helicopter........		4·50	4·50
	a. Sheetlet. Nos. 1410/13........		16·00	16·00
1411	$3.55 Gloster Javelin FAW9........		4·50	4·50
1412	$3.55 P-66 Pembroke C1........		4·50	4·50
1413	$3.55 Chinook HC2 helicopter........		4·50	4·50
1406/13 Set of 8........			32·00	32·00

Nos. 1406/9 and 1410/13 were each printed together, *se-tenant*, in sheetlets of four stamps with enlarged illustrated margins.

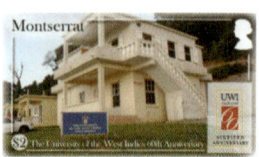

265 University of the West Indies Centre, Montserrat

(Litho Cardon Enterprises)

2008 (30 Sept). 60th Anniv. of the University of the West Indies. T **265** and similar horiz design. Multicoloured. Litho. P 13½.

1414	$2 Type **265**........		2·75	2·75
1415	$5 Scroll........		4·25	4·25

266 Common Dolphin

267 *Cattleya labiata*

(Litho Beijing Stamp Printing House)

2008 (27 Nov). Dolphins of the World. T **266** and similar horiz designs. Multicoloured. Litho. P 13.

1416	$3.55 Type **266**........		3·50	3·50
	a. Sheetlet. Nos. 1416/19........		12·50	12·50
1417	$3.55 Bottlenose dolphin........		3·50	3·50
1418	$3.55 Pantropical spotted dolphin........		3·50	3·50
1419	$3.55 Long-snouted spinner dolphin........		3·50	3·50
1416/19 Set of 4........			12·50	12·50
MS1420 100×70 mm. $7 Risso's dolphin........			8·50	9·00

Nos. 1416/19 were printed together, *se-tenant*, in sheetlets of four stamps with enlarged illustrated margins.

(Litho Cardon Enterprises, Taiwan)

2008 (27 Nov). Orchids of the Caribbean. T **267** and similar horiz designs. Multicoloured. P 13½.

1421	$2.75 Type **267**........		3·75	3·75
	a. Sheetlet. Nos. 1421/4........		13·50	13·50
1422	$2.75 *Phalaenopsis* cultivar........		3·75	3·75
1423	$2.75 *Cymbidium annabelle*........		3·75	3·75
1424	$2.75 *Phalaenopsis taisuco*........		3·75	3·75
1424a	$2.75 *Phalaenopsis amabilis*........		3·75	3·75
	ab. Sheetlet. Nos. 1424a/d........			
1424b	$2.75 *Cattleya aurantiaca*........		3·75	3·75
1424c	$2.75 *Phalaenopsis* cultivar........		3·75	3·75
1424d	$2.75 *Dendrobium nobile*........		3·75	3·75
142/24d Set of 8........			27·00	27·00

268 Ox

(Litho Beijing Stamp Printing House)

2009 (2 Feb). Chinese New Year. Year of the Ox. T **268** and similar horiz designs. Multicoloured, outline colours given. P 12½.

MS1425 Type **268**; Ox (black) (facing left); Ox (purple-brown); Ox (white) (facing left)........			15·00	16·00

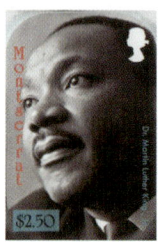

269 Martin Luther King

(Litho Cardon Enterprises, Taiwan)

2009 (26 Feb). 80th Birth Anniv of Dr. Martin Luther King (civil rights leader). Two sheets, 130×100 mm, containing T **269** and similar multicoloured designs. P 13½.

MS1426 Type **269**; Sitting in chair; Wearing hat; Mrs. Coretta Scott King........			9·00	10·00
MS1427 Crowd of marchers ('March on Washington for Jobs and Freedom'); Martin Luther King meeting Malcolm X, 1964; With Pres. John F. Kennedy and Civil Rights leaders; Waving to crowd ('March on Washington for Jobs and Freedom') (*all horiz*)........			9·00	10·00

270 Smooth-billed Ani (*Crotophaga ani*)

(Litho Cardon Enterprises, Taiwan)

2009 (1 Apr). Birds of Montserrat. T **270** and similar horiz designs. Multicoloured. P 13½.

MS1428 100×130 mm. $2.75×4 Type **270**; American kestrel (*Falco sparverius*); Common moorhen (*Gallinula chloropus*); Cattle egret (*Bubulcus ibis*)........			17·00	18·00
MS1429 70×100 mm. $7 Male Montserrat oriole (*Icterus oberi*)........			9·00	9·50

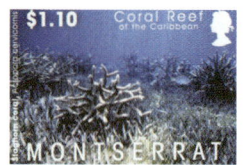

271 Staghorn Coral (*Actopora cervicornis*)

(Litho Cardon Enterprises, Taiwan)

2009 (29 Apr). Coral Reef of the Caribbean. T **271** and similar horiz designs. Multicoloured. P 13.

1430	$1.10 Type **271**........		1·75	1·25
1431	$2.25 Zoanthid coral (*Palythoa caesia*)........		2·50	2·50
1432	$2.50 Blade fire coral (*Millepora complanata*)........		2·75	3·00
1433	$2.75 Brain coral (*Diploria strigosa*)........		3·00	3·75

1430/3 Set of 4	9·00	9·50
MS1434 100×70 mm. $7 Orange tube coral (*Tubastrea aurea*)	8·00	8·50

272 Charles Darwin

273 Green Iguana (*Iguana iguana*)

(Litho Cardon Enterprises, Taiwan)

2009 (28 July). Birth Bicentenary of Charles Darwin (evolutionary theorist). T **272** and similar multicoloured designs. P 13½.

MS1435 Type **272**; Soldier crab (*Coenobita clypeatus*); Tree lizard (*Anolis lividus*); Endemic orchid (*Epidendrum montserratense*)	15·00	16·00
MS1436 70×100 mm. $7 Charles Darwin and Montserrat Centre Hills Project emblem (*horiz*)	9·00	9·50

(Litho Cardon Enterprises, Taiwan)

2009 (25 Sept). Rain Forest Animals of Montserrat. T **273** and similar horiz designs. Multicoloured. P 13½.

MS1437 100×80 mm. $1.10 Type **273**; $2.25 Galliwasp (*Diploglossus montserrati*); $2.50 Black snake (*Alsophis antillensis manselli*); $2.75 Common agouti (*Dasyprocta leporina*)	12·00	13·00
MS1438 100×70 mm. $5 Yellow-shouldered bat (*Sturnira thomasi vulcanensis*)	6·50	7·00

274 Tamarind Tree (*Tamarindus indica*)

275 HMS *Ark Royal II*

(Litho BDT)

2009 (30 Oct). Tropical Trees. T **274** and similar vert designs. Multicoloured. P 14×14½.

1439	$1.10 Type **274**	1·75	1·25
1440	$2.25 Dwarf coconut tree (*Cocos nucifera*)	2·50	2·00
1441	$2.50 Breadfruit tree (*Artocarpus altilis*)	2·75	2·50
1442	$2.75 Calabash tree (*Crescentia cujete*)	3·00	3·00
1443	$5 Geiger tree (*Cordia sebestena*)	5·00	6·00
1439/43 Set of 5		13·50	13·50

(Litho Cardon Enterprises, Taiwan)

2009 (4 Dec). Centenary of Naval Aviation. Aircraft Carriers. Sheet 160×134 mm containing T **275** and similar horiz designs. Multicoloured. P 11½.

MS1444 70c. Type **275**; $1.10 HMS *Furious*; $2.25 HMS *Argus*; $2.50 HMS *Illustrious*; $2.75 HMS *Ark Royal IV*; $5 HMS *Invincible*	16·00	16·00

276 Snowflake (*Euphorbia leucocephala*)

277 Basket Star

(Litho Beijing Stamp Printing House)

2009 (18 Dec). Christmas. T **276** and similar multicoloured designs. P 12½.

1445	$1.10 Type **276**	1·25	70
1446	$2.25 Carnival troupe	1·75	1·25
1447	$2.50 Masquerade	2·00	1·75
1448	$2.75 St. Patrick's Roman Catholic Church	2·25	3·00
1445/8 Set of 4		6·50	6·00
MS1449 100×70 mm. $6 Nativity (*vert*)		5·00	6·00

(Litho BDT)

2010 (12 Feb). Marine Life. T **277** and simiilar multicoloured designs. P 14.

1450	$1.10 Type **277**	1·75	1·25
1451	$2.25 Spiny lobster	2·50	2·00
1452	$2.50 Spotted drum	2·75	2·50
1453	$2.75 Sea anemone (*vert*)	3·00	3·00
1454	$5 Batwing coral crab	5·00	6·00
1450/4 Set of 5		13·50	13·50

278 Jin Mao Tower at Night, Shanghai, China

(Litho BDT)

2010 (19 Apr). Expo 2010, Shanghai, China. Sites and Scenes of the World. Two sheets, each 130×100 mm, containing T **278** and similar horiz designs. Multicoloured. P 14.

MS1455 $1.10 Type **278**; $2.25 Montserrat Cultural Centre, Little Bay; $2.50 Assumption Cathedral, Kremlin, Russia; $2.75 Brooklyn Bridge, New York	9·00	10·00
MS1456 $1.10 Fishing village in Shanghai, Hong Kong Island, China; $2.25 Camelot Villa, Montserrat; $2.50 Zaanse Schans Windmill, Zaandam, Holland; $2.75 Reichstag German Parliament, Berlin, Germany	9·00	10·00

279 Michael Jackson

(Cardon Enterprises, Taiwan)

2010 (25 Jun). Michael Jackson Commemoration. Two sheets, each 130×100 mm, containing T **279** and similar horiz designs. Multicoloured. P 13½.

MS1457 $2.50×4 Type **279**; Wearing red jacket and white T shirt; In close-up, singing, wearing silver jacket; In profile, facing left, wearing red and gold jacket	10·00	11·00
MS1458 $2.50×4 Wearing white jacket and black shirt, in profile facing right; Wearing black jacket, holding microphone, facing left; Wearing white T shirt and black leather jacket; Wearing black shirt and white jacket, facing forwards	10·00	11·00

280 Wild Marigold (*Wedelia calycina*)

281 Reddish Egret

(Litho Cardon Enterprises, Taiwan)

2010 (18 Apr). Wild Flowers of Montserrat. T **280** and similar vert designs. Multicoloured. P 13½.

1459	$1.10 Type **280**	1·00	1·00
1460	$2.25 Shrubby toothedthread (*Odontonema nitidum*)	2·10	2·10
1461	$2.50 Wild sweet pea (*Crotalaria retusa*)	2·40	2·40
1462	$2.75 Rosy periwinkle (*Catharanthus roseus*)	3·00	3·00
1463	$5 Measle bush (*Lantana camara*)	6·00	6·00
1459/63 Set of 5		13·00	13·00
MS1464 100×70 mm. $7 Pribby (*Rondeletia buxifolia*)		8·00	9·00

MONTSERRAT

(Litho Cardon Enterprises, Taiwan)

2010 (29 Oct). Endangered Species. Reddish Egret (*Egretta rufescens*). T **281** and similar horiz designs. Multicoloured. P 13½.
1465	$1.10 Type **281**	2·25	2·25
	a. Strip of 4. Nos. 1465/8	9·75	9·75
1466	$2.25 White phase and dark phase egrets in flight	2·75	2·75
1467	$2.25 Reddish egret (dark phase) preening	2·75	2·75
1468	$2.75 White phase egret taking off from wetland	3·00	3·00
1465/68 Set of 4		9·75	9·75
MS1469 100×139 mm. Nos. 1465/8, each ×2		16·00	16·00

Nos. 1465/8 were printed together, *se-tenant*, as horizontal and vertical strips of four stamps in sheetlets of 16.

282 Giant Panda

(Litho C and C Printing)

2010 (22 Nov). Beijing 2010 International Stamp and Coin Exhibition. Giant Panda (*Ailuropoda melanoleuca*). T **282** and similar horiz designs. Multicoloured. P 12.
MS1470 160×95 mm. $2.50×4 Type **282**; Panda laying between rock and tree trunk; Panda eating bamboo; Panda looking down (side view of head, shoulders and foreleg)	9·50	9·50
MS1471 90×62 mm. $7 Panda looking down (side view of head and shoulders)	7·00	7·50

283 Beaded Periwinkle (*Tectarius muricatus*)

284 Anise (*Pimpinella anisum*)

(Litho C and C Printing)

2011 (10 Jan). Seashells. T **283** and similar multicoloured designs. P 13 (with one elliptical hole on each vert (Nos. 1472/6) or horiz (**MS**1477) side).
1472	$1.10 Type **283**	1·75	1·25
1473	$2.25 Green star shell (*Astraea tuber*)	2·75	2·25
1474	$2.50 Smooth Scotch bonnet (*Phalium cicatricosum*)	3·00	2·75
1475	$2.75 Calico scallop (*Aequipecten gibbus*)	3·50	3·50
1476	$5 Hawk wing conch (*Strombus raninus*)	5·00	6·00
1472/6 Set of 5		14·50	14·50
MS1477 100×80 mm. $7 Atlantic partridge tun (*Tonna maculosa*) (vert)		8·00	8·50

(Litho Cardon Enterprises)

2011 (15 Mar). Medicinal Plants. Sheet 100×130 mm containing T **284** and similar vert designs. Multicoloured. P 12×11½.
MS1478 $2.25×6 Type **284**; Lemon grass (*Cymbopogon citratus*); Vervain (*Stachytarpheta jamaicenis*); Ram goat bush (*Eryngium foetidum*); Rosemary (*Rosmarinus officinalis*); Inflammation bush (*Peperomia pellucida*)	16·00	16·00

285 Prince William and Miss Catherine Middleton

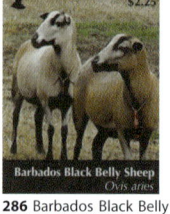

286 Barbados Black Belly Sheep (*Ovis aries*)

(Litho Cardon Enterprises)

2011 (31 Mar). Royal Engagement. T **285** and similar vert designs. Multicoloured. P 13½.
MS1479 100×130 mm. $2.75×4 Type **285**; Miss Catherine Middleton waring black hat with white curled feather; Prince William; Prince William and Miss Catherine Middleton (gold framed painting in background)	12·00	12·00
MS1480 80×110 mm. $5 Miss Catherine Middleton; $5 Prince William	10·00	10·00

(Litho C and C Printing)

2011 (6 Jun). Animals of Montserrat. T **286** and similar vert designs. Multicoloured. P 12.
1481	$2.25 Type **286**	2·75	2·25
1482	$2.50 Boer goat (*Capra aegagrus hircus*)	3·00	2·75
1483	$2.75 Black donkey (*Equus africanus asinus*)	3·50	3·50
1484	$5 Red cattle (*Bos primigenius*)	5·00	6·00
1481/84 Set of 4		13·00	13·00
MS1485 100×100 mm. $7 Arabian horse (*Equus caballus*)		8·00	8·00

287 Prince William

288 Washington Square, New York, 14 September 2001

(Litho Beijing Stamp Printing House)

2011 (29 Jun). Royal Wedding. T **287** and similar horiz designs showing Duke and Duchess of Cambridge on wedding day. Multicoloured. P 13.
MS1486 ×6 Type **287**; Leaving Westminster Abbey after wedding; Duchess of Cambridge; Prince William (no cap); Duke and Duchess of Cambridge in carriage; Duchess of Cambridge (facing right)	16·00	16·00
MS1487 100×70 mm. $7 Duke and Duchess of Cambridge kissing on Buckingham Palace balcony	8·00	8·50

(Litho C and C Printing)

2011 (11 Sep). Tenth Anniv of Attack on World Trade Center, New York. T **288** and similar vert designs. Multicoloured. P 12.
MS1488 100×130 mm. $2.75×4 Type **288**; US flag and 'God Bless the Memory of those Lost' banner; 'Love' and 'No War Peace' messages, Union Square, New York, 13 September 2001; US flag and memorial cross, Stoneycreek township, Pennsylvania	12·00	12·00
MS1489 100×70 mm. $6 Keithroy Maynard, 1971-2001 (Montserrat born New York firefighter)	5·50	6·50

289 Alphonsus Cassell

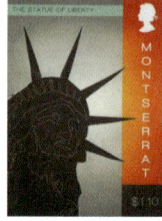

290 Statue of Liberty

(Litho C and C Printing)

2011 (15 Oct). Alphonsus Cassell 'Mighty Arrow' (soca musician) Commemoration. T **289** and similar multicoloured designs. P 14 (1490/1) or 12 (**MS**1492).
1490	$2.25 Type **289**	2·75	2·25
1491	$2.50 Alphonsus Cassell (wearing red and black jacket)	3·00	2·75
MS1492 130×100 mm. $2.75×4 Alphonsus Cassell (wearing white jacket); Wearing headphones; Wearing tasselled sleeveless top; Wearing patterned V-neck top (*all horiz*)		12·00	12·00

(Litho C and C Printing)

2011 (28 Oct). 125th Anniv of Statue of Liberty. T **290** and similar vert designs. Multicoloured. P 12.
MS1493 100×131 mm. $1.10 Type **290**; $1.10 Torch; $2.25 Head of Statue of Liberty; $2.25 Book; $2.50 Statue of Liberty; $2.50 Back of Statue's head and book	5·00	4·00

MS1494 70×100 mm. $6 Statue of Liberty and base (30×80 *mm*) .... 5·00 6·00

291 Purple Heron (*Ardea purpurea*)

292 The Choral Group Voices

(Litho Beijing Stamp Printing House)

2011 (11 Nov). China 2011 27th Asian International Stamp Exhibition, Wuxi. Fauna and Flora of China. Two sheets, 150×100 mm, containing T **291** and similar square designs. Multicoloured. P 12.
MS1495 Type **291**; $2.25 Indian elephant (*Elephas maximus indicus*); $2.50 Snub-nosed monkey (*Rhinopithecus roxellana*); $2.75 Royal Bengal tiger (*Panthera tigris tigris*) .... 10·00 8·75
MS1496 Chinese plum (*Prunus mume*); $2.25 Opium poppy (*Papaver somniferum*); $2.50 Japanese camellia (*Camellia japonica*); $2.75 Pomegranate (*Punica granatum*) .... 10·00 8·75

(Litho C and C Printing)

2011 (6 Dec). Christmas. T **292** and similar horiz designs. Multicoloured. P 14.
1497	$2.25 Type **292**	2·50	2·00
1498	$2.50 Emerald Community Singers	2·75	2·50
1499	$2.75 Volpanics Steel Band	3·00	3·00
1500	$5 New Ebenezer SDA Church	5·00	6·00
1497/1500	Set of 4	12·00	12·00

STAMP BOOKLETS

1975 (3 Mar). Carib Artefacts. Multicoloured cover. Stitched.
SB1 $2.95 booklet containing *se-tenant* panes of 4 and 6 (Nos. 347a/8a) .... 1·90

1977 (7 Feb). Silver Jubilee. Black on white cover. Stapled.
SB2 $7 booklet containing 30c., 45c. and $1 (Nos. 396/8), each in block of 4 .... 4·50

1978 (2 June). 25th Anniv of Coronation. Multicoloured cover, 82×52 mm, showing Coronation ceremony on the front and Westminster Abbey on the reverse. Stapled.
SB3 $8.90 booklet containing 40c., 55c., $1 and $2.50 (Nos. 422/5), each in pair .... 1·25

1981. Black and blue cover, 102×64 mm, showing stylized fishes design. Stitched.
SB4 $5.80 booklet containing 35c., 45c. and 65c. (Nos. 495/6, 498), each in block of 4 .... 4·00

1981 (19 Nov). Royal Wedding. Multicoloured cover, 105×65 mm, showing The Charlotte. Stitched.
SB5 $13.20 booklet containing eight 90c. in panes of 4 (No. 517a) and two $3 in pane of 2 (No. 518a) .... 4·25

1986 (23 July). Royal Wedding. Gold (No. SB6) or silver (No. SB7) on greenish yellow covers. Stapled.
SB6 $8.40 booklet (Westminster Abbey) containing twelve 70c. (Nos. 691/2) in block of 4 .... 3·50
SB7 $10.80 booklet (State Coach) containing 70c. and $2 (Nos. 691/4, but imperf), each value in block of 4 .... 4·75

OFFICIAL STAMPS

O.H.M.S. (O **1**) **O.H.M.S.** (O **2**)

1976 (12 Apr). Various stamps, some already surcharged, optd locally with Type O **1**.
O1	5c. multicoloured (No. 246)		†	70
O2	10c. multicoloured (No. 247)		†	1·00
	a. Opt double		†	14·00
	b. Horiz pair, one stamp without opt		†	£300
O3	30c. on 10c. multicoloured (No. 369)		†	1·50
	a. Opt double		†	45·00
	w. Wmk Crown to right of CA		†	25·00
O4	45c. on 3c. multicoloured (No. 370)		†	2·00
O5	$5 multicoloured (No. 254)		†	£110
O6	$10 multicoloured (No. 254c)		†	£650
O1/6	Set of 6		†	£700

These stamps were issued for use on mail from the Montserrat Philatelic Bureau. They were not available for sale in either unused or used condition.

1976 (1 Oct)–**80**. Nos. 374/8, 380/2 and 384/5 optd with Type O **2** locally.
O7	5c. Malay Apple	†	15
	a. Opt inverted	†	80·00
	b. Missing stop after "S"	†	1·50
O8	10c. Jacaranda	†	20
	a. Missing stop after "S"	†	1·50
O9	15c. Orchid Tree	†	25
	a. Opt inverted	†	75·00
	b. Missing stop after "S"	†	1·75
	w. Wmk Crown to right of CA	†	25·00
O10	20c. Manjak	†	30
	a. Opt inverted	†	70·00
	b. Missing stop after "S"	†	1·75
	c. Chalk-surfaced paper (1980)	†	—
O11	25c. Tamarind	†	35
	a. Missing stop after "S"	†	1·75
O12	55c. Pink Cassia	†	40
	a. Opt inverted	†	£100
	b. Opt double	†	—
	c. Missing top after "S"	†	2·50
O13	70c. Long John	†	45
	a. Missing stop after "S"	†	3·50
O14	$1 Saman	†	55
	a. Opt inverted	†	—
	b. Missing stop after "S"	†	5·00
O15	$5 Yellow Poui	†	1·50
	a. Missing stop after "S"	†	11·00
	w. Wmk Crown to right of CA	†	10·00
O16	$10 Flamboyant (14.4.80)	†	3·75
	a. Missing stop after "S"	†	25·00
O7/16	Set of 10	†	7·00

Nos. O7/16 were not available in an unused condition, but were sold to the public cancelled-to-order.
The missing stop after "S" variety occurs on R. 1/3 and 3/5.

O.H.M.S. (O **3**) **O.H.M.S.** (O **4**) **O.H.M.S. 45¢** (O **5**)

1980 (7 July). Nos. 374/8, 380/2 and 384/5 optd with Type O **3** in Great Britain.
O17	5c. Malay Apple	†	10
	a. Opt double	†	60·00
O18	10c. Jacaranda	†	10
O19	15c. Orchid Tree	†	10
O20	20c. Manjak	†	10
	a. Opt double	†	70·00
O21	25c. Tamarind	†	15
O22	55c. Pink Cassia	†	35
		†	11·00
O23	70c. Long John	†	45
O24	$1 Saman	†	60
O25	$5 Yellow Poui	†	1·50
O26	$10 Flamboyant	†	2·50
O17/26	Set of 10	†	5·25

Nos. O17/26 were not available in an unused condition, but were sold to the public cancelled-to-order. At least two values, the 20c. and $1 are, however, known uncancelled.
These stamps were originally intended for issue on 3 November 1980, but certain values were placed on sale from 7 July onwards to meet shortages. Bulk supplies did not arrive on the island until early December 1980.

O.H. M.S.
Spaced "H" and "M" (R. 3/4)

1980 (30 Sept). Nos. 374/82, 384/5 and 476, together with surcharges on Nos. 372, 376 and 379, optd as Type O **4** locally.
O27	5c. Malay Apple	†	30
O28	5c. on 3c. Lignum vitae	†	20
	a. Surch double	†	38·00
O29	10c. Jacaranda	†	30
O30	15c. Orchid Tree	†	30
	a. Opt double	†	—
O31	20c. Manjak	†	40
	a. Opt double	†	11·00
O32	25c. Tamarind	†	40
O33	30c. on 15c. Orchid Tree	†	30
	a. "O.H.M.S." opt omitted	†	£110
O34	35c. on 2c. Cannon-ball Tree	†	30

MONTSERRAT

		a. Spaced "H" and "M"	†	3·50
		b. Surch omitted (in vert with normal)	†	£120
O35		40c. Flame of the Forest	†	40
O36		55c. Pink Cassia	†	45
O37		70c. Long John	†	60
O38		$1 Saman	†	60
O39		$2.50 on 40c. Flame of the Forest	†	2·00
		a. "O.H.M.S." opt omitted	£180	
O40		$5 Yellow Poui	†	2·00
O41		$10 Flamboyant	†	3·00
		a. Opt double	†	80·00
O27/41	Set of 15		†	10·50

Nos. O27/41 were not available in an unused condition, but were sold to the public cancelled-to-order: No. O39a was, however, found amongst supplies of the postage series.

1981 (20 Mar). Nos. 490/4, 496, 498, 500, 502/3 and 505 optd with Type O **4**.

O42	5c. Type **91**		10	10
	a. Opt inverted		15·00	
	b. Horiz pair, one without opt		45·00	
O43	10c. Hogfish and Neon Goby		10	10
	a. Horiz pair, one without opt		45·00	
O44	15c. Creole Wrasse		10	10
	a. Opt double		†	85·00
	b. Horiz pair, one without opt		45·00	
O45	20c. Three-spotted Damselfish		15	15
	a. Horiz pair, one without opt		45·00	
O46	25c. Sergeant Major		15	15
	a. Vert pair, one without opt		45·00	
O47	45c. Schoolmaster		25	20
	a. Opt double		16·00	
	ab. Opt double, one on reverse		11·00	
	b. Opt inverted		20·00	
O48	65c. Bigeye		35	30
	a. Opt inverted		70·00	
	b. Horiz pair, one without opt		45·00	
O49	$1 Rock Beauty		65	65
O50	$3 Royal Gramma ("Fairy Basslet") and Blueheads		1·50	1·75
O51	$5 Cherub Angelfish		2·00	2·25
	w. Wmk inverted		30·00	
O52	$10 Caribbean Long-nosed Butterflyfish		3·00	2·25
	w. Wmk inverted		32·00	
O42/52	Set of 11		7·50	7·25

1982 (17 Nov). Nos. 510/15 surch as Type O **5** (in one line on Nos. O54, O56 and O58).

O53	45c. on 90c. Charlotte		20	30
	a. Sheetlet. No. O53×6 and No. O54		1·60	
	b. Surch double		18·00	
	c. Surch inverted		12·00	
	d. Surch inverted (horiz pair)		32·00	
	e. Horiz pair, one without surch		70·00	
O54	45c. on 90c. Prince Charles and Lady Diana Spencer		60	1·00
	b. Surch double		70·00	
	c. Surch inverted		50·00	
O55	75c. on $3 Portsmouth		25	35
	aw. Wmk inverted		6·00	
	b. Sheetlet. No. O55×6 and No. O56		2·25	
	bw. Wmk inverted		60·00	
	c. Surch double		27·00	
	d. Surch inverted		13·00	
	e. Surch inverted (horiz pair)		23·00	
	f. Horiz pair, one without surch		70·00	
	g. Error. Surch on $4 (No. 514)		12·00	
	ga. Sheetlet. No. O55g×6 and No. O56g		£130	
O56	75c. on $3 Prince Charles and Lady Diana Spencer		90	1·40
	aw. Wmk inverted		30·00	
	c. Surch double		75·00	
	d. Surch inverted		22·00	
	g. Error. Surch on $4 (No. 515)		70·00	
O57	$1 on $4 Britannia		35	50
	aw. Wmk inverted		7·00	
	b. Sheetlet. No. O57×6 and No. O58		2·75	
	bw. Wmk inverted		65·00	
	c. Surch double		32·00	
	d. Surch inverted		7·50	
	e. Surch inverted (horiz pair)		21·00	
	f. Horiz pair, one without surch			
O58	$1 on $4 Prince Charles and Lady Diana Spencer		1·00	1·50
	aw. Wmk inverted		32·00	
	c. Surch double		80·00	
	d. Surch inverted		23·00	
O53/8	Set of 6		3·00	4·50

Nos. O53d, O55e and O57e show the long surcharge, intended for Nos. O54, O56 or O58, inverted across horizontal pairs of the smaller design. Nos. O54c, O56d and O58d show two examples as Type O **5** inverted on the same stamp.

O.H.M.S.
(O **6**)

O H M S
(O **7**)

O H M S
(O **8**)

1983 (19 Oct). Nos. 542/4 surch as Type O **6** or optd only ($1).

O59	70c. on 75c. Type **97**		60	40
O60	$1 Coat of Arms of Catherine of Aragon		70	50
	a. Opt inverted		32·00	
O61	$1.50 on $5 Diana, Princess of Wales		1·00	80
O59/61	Set of 3		2·10	1·50

1985 (12 Apr). Nos. 600/12 and 614 opt with Type O **7** (horizontally on Nos. O71/5).

O62	5c. Type **107**		1·25	1·25
O63	10c. Carib Grackle		1·25	1·00
O64	15c. Moorhen		1·50	1·00
O65	20c. Brown Booby		1·50	1·00
O66	25c. Black-whiskered Vireo		1·50	1·00
O67	40c. Scaly-breasted Thrasher		2·00	70
	a. Opt double		†	
O68	55c. Laughing Gull		2·25	70
O69	70c. Glossy Ibis		2·50	90
O70	90c. Green Heron		2·75	90
O71	$1 Belted Kingfisher		2·75	70
O72	$1.15 Bananaquit		3·00	1·00
O73	$3 American Kestrel		4·50	2·50
O74	$5 Forest Thrush		5·50	2·50
O75	$10 Bridled Quail Dove		7·00	2·50
O62/75	Set of 14		35·00	16·00

1989 (9 May). Nos. 757/70 and 772 nptd with Type O **8**.

O76	6c. Type **133**		40	75
O77	10c. Little Knobbed Scallop (Chlamys imbricata)		40	75
O78	15c. Sozoni s Cone (Conus delessertii)		50	1·00
O79	20c. Globular Coral Shell (Coralliophila aberrans)		55	1·00
O80	25c. American or Common Sundial (Architectonica nobilis)		55	50
O81	40c. King Helmet (Cassia tuberosa)		60	55
O82	55c. Channelled Turban (Turbo canaliculatus)		70	70
O83	70c. True Tulip (Fasciolaria tulipa)		90	1·25
	a. Horiz pair, left-hand stamp without opt			
O84	90c. Music Volute (Voluta musica)		1·00	90
O85	$1 Flame Auger (Terebra taurina)		1·00	80
O86	$1.15 Rooster-tail Conch (Strombus gallus)		1·25	1·00
O87	$1.50 Queen or Pink Conch (Strombus gigas)		1·40	1·60
O88	$3 Teramachi's Slit Shell (Perotrochus teramachii)		2·00	2·50
O89	$5 Common or Florida Crown Conch (Melongena corona)		3·25	3·25
O90	$10 Atlantic Trumpet Triton (Charonia variegata)		5·50	5·50
O76/90	Set of 15		18·00	20·00

OHMS
(O **9**)

70¢
(O **10**)

1989 (26 May). Nos. 578 and 580/1 optd with Type O **9** and surch as Type O9a.

O91	70c. on 10c. Hogfish and Neon Goby		2·25	1·75
	a. "OHMS" inverted			
O92	$1.15 on 75c. French Grunt		3·00	1·75
O93	$1.50 on $2 Blue Chromis		3·00	3·00
O91/3	Set of 3		7·50	6·00

1992 (3 July–Nov). Nos. 838/41, 847/50 and 856/9 surch or optd only as Type O **10** ("OHMS" vert on Nos. O96, O98/9, O102/3 and O105) by Benjies Printery, Antigua.

O94	70c. on 90c. Type **150**		1·40	1·40
O95	70c. on 90c. Type **152**		1·40	1·40
	a. Vert opt (11.92)		9·50	
O96	70c. on 90c. Type **154**		1·40	1·40
O97	70c. on $3.50 French Grunt		1·40	1·40
O98	$1 on $3.50 Helmet Guineafowl		1·50	1·50
O99	$1 on $3.50 Anthurium		1·50	1·50

O100	$1.15 Cushion Star	1·50	1·75
	a. Vert opt (11.92)	1·50	1·75
O101	$1.15 Hen and Chicks	1·50	1·75
O102	$1.15 Shell Ginger	1·50	1·75
O103	$1.50 Rock Beauty	1·60	2·00
O104	$1.50 Red Junglefowl	1·60	2·00
O105	$1.50 Early Day Lily	1·60	2·00
O94/105 Set of 12		16·00	18·00

OHMS O. H. M. S.
(O **11**)   (O **12**)

1993 (14 Apr). Nos. 889/902 and 904 optd with Type O **11** in red.

O106	5c. Type **161**	70	1·25
O107	10c. *Gryllus campestris* (field cricket)	70	1·25
O108	15c. *Lepthemis vesiculosa* (dragonfly)	80	1·25
O109	20c. *Orthemis ferruginea* (Red Skimmer)	80	1·25
O110	25c. *Gerris lacustris* (pond skater)	80	1·25
O111	40c. *Byctiscus betulae* (leaf weevil)	1·25	60
O112	55c. *Atta texana* (Leaf-cutter Ants)	1·40	60
O113	70c. *Polistes fuscatus* (Paper Wasp)	1·60	1·25
O114	90c. *Sparmopolius fulvus* (Bee Fly)	1·75	1·00
O115	$1 *Chrysopa carnea* (lace wing)	1·75	1·00
O116	$1.15 *Phoebis philea* (butterfly)	2·25	1·75
O117	$1.50 *Cynthia cardui* (butterfly)	2·75	2·50
O118	$3 *Utetheisa bella* (moth)	4·00	4·50
O119	$5 *Alucita pentodactyla* (moth)	5·50	6·00
O120	$10 *Heliconius melpomene* (butterfly)	8·00	9·00
O106/20 Set of 15		30·00	30·00

1997 (21 Nov). Nos. 1009/22 and 1024 optd with Type O **12** in red.

O121	5c. Type **184**	15	70
O122	10c. Pegasus	25	70
O123	15c. Griffin	35	1·00
O124	20c. Unicorn	35	1·00
O125	25c. Gnomes	15	50
O126	40c. Mermaid	50	70
O127	55c. Cockatrice	60	70
O128	70c. Fairy	70	70
O129	90c. Goblin	90	1·00
O130	$1 Faun	1·00	70
O131	$1.15 Dragon	1·25	70
O132	$1.50 Giant	1·40	1·00
O133	$3 Elves	2·50	2·75
O134	$5 Centaur	4·00	5·50
O135	$10 Erin	6·00	8·50
O121/35 Set of 15		18·00	24·00

2002 (14 June). Nos. 1195/1208 and 1210 optd with Type O **11**.

O137	5c. Type **215**	30	1·00
O138	10c. Mammee apple	35	80
O139	15c. Lime	50	1·00
O140	20c. Grapefruit	55	1·00
O141	25c. Orange	55	1·00
O142	40c. Passion fruit	75	45
O143	55c. Banana	90	65
O144	70c. Pawpaw	1·25	1·00
O145	90c. Pomegranate	1·50	1·00
O146	$1 Guava	1·50	75
O147	$1.15 Mango	1·75	1·00
O148	$1.50 Sugar apple	2·00	1·25
O149	$3 Cashew	3·50	3·50
O150	$5 Soursop	5·00	6·00
O151	$10 Pineapple	7·50	8·50
O137/51 Set of 15		25·00	26·00

STANLEY GIBBONS

Commonwealth Department

Recently offered St Christopher from our ever changing stock

SG 22a, 23b

1885 registered cover at 6d rate, including four ½d on 1d bisects showing surcharge inverted

If you would like to receive our bi-monthly illustrated list, contact
Pauline MacBroom on 020 7557 4450 or by email at pmacbroom@stanleygibbons.com
or Brian Lucas on 020 7557 4418 or by email at blucas@stanleygibbons.com

Stanley Gibbons Limited, 399 Strand, London WC2R 0LX
Tel: 020 7836 8444 Fax: 020 7557 4499

To view all of our stock 24 hours a day visit **www.stanleygibbons.com**

# St. Kitts-Nevis

ST. CHRISTOPHER

From 1760 the postal service for St. Christopher was organised by the Deputy Postmaster General on Antigua. It was not until May 1779 that the first postmaster was appointed to the island and the use of postmarks on outgoing mail commenced.

Stamps of Great Britain were used between May 1858 and the end of March 1860 when control of the postal services passed to the local authorities. In the years which followed, prior to the introduction of St. Christopher stamps in April 1870, a circular "PAID" handstamp was used on overseas mail.

BASSETERRE

Stamps of GREAT BRITAIN cancelled "A 12".

1858–60.

Z1	1d. rose-red (1857), perf 14	£700
Z2	2d. blue (1858) (Plate No. 7)	£1300
Z3	4d. rose (1857)	£450
Z4	6d. lilac (1856)	£200
Z5	1s. green (1856)	£2250

PRICES FOR STAMPS ON COVER	
Nos. 1/9	from × 25
Nos. 11/21	from × 30
Nos. 22/6	from × 25
No. 27	—
No. 28	from × 30
Nos. R1/6	—

1 Halfpenny

Distorted "E" (R. 2/1)

1870 (1 Apr)–**79.** Wmk Crown CC.

(a) P 12½

1	**1**	1d. dull rose		90·00	50·00
		a. Wmk sideways		£225	£160
		w. Wmk inverted			
2		1d. magenta (*shades*) (1871)		80·00	32·00
		a. Wmk sideways		†	£800
		w. Wmk inverted		£160	80·00
		x. Wmk reversed			
4		6d. yellow-green		£120	19·00
		w. Wmk inverted			
5		6d. green (1871)		£120	7·50
		w. Wmk inverted		—	£130

(b) P 14

6	**1**	1d. magenta (*shades*) (1875)		75·00	7·00
		a. Bisected diag or vert (½d.) (on cover) (3.82)		†	£2500
		w. Wmk inverted			
7		2½d. red-brown (11.79)		£190	£250
8		4d. blue (11.79)		£200	15·00
		a. Wmk sideways		£1600	£200
		w. Wmk inverted		£400	55·00
9		6d. green (1876)		55·00	5·00
		a. Imperf between (pair)			
		b. Wmk sideways		£900	£200
		w. Wmk inverted		—	£130
		x. Wmk reversed		£325	

The magenta used for the 1d. was a fugitive colour which reacts to both light and water.

No. 6a was authorised for use between March and June 1882 to make up the 2½d. letter rate and for ½d. book post.

1882 (June)–**90.** Wmk Crown CA. P 14.

11	**1**	½d. dull green		4·75	2·50
		a. Wmk sideways		£300	
		x. Wmk reversed		£400	
12		1d. dull magenta		£550	70·00
		a. Bisected diagonally (½d.) (on cover)		†	
13		1d. carmine-rose (2.84)		2·50	2·25
		a. Bisected (½d.) (on cover)		†	—
		b. Distorted "E"		26·00	
		x. Wmk reversed			
14		2½d. pale red-brown		£180	60·00
15		2½d. deep red-brown		£190	65·00
16		2½d. ultramarine (2.84)		4·25	1·50
17		4d. blue		£550	20·00
		w. Wmk inverted			
18		4d. grey (10.84)		1·50	1·00
		w. Wmk inverted		£150	
19		6d. olive-brown (3.90)		90·00	£400
		w. Wmk inverted			
20		1s. mauve (6.86)		£100	65·00
		w. Wmk inverted		—	£180
21		1s. bright mauve (1890)		90·00	£180
19s/20s Optd "SPECIMEN" Set of 2				£120	

FOUR PENCE
(2)

1884 (Dec). No. 9 surch with T **2** by The Advertiser Press.

22	**1**	4d. on 6d. green		65·00	50·00
		a. Full stop after "PENCE"		65·00	50·00
		b. Surch double		—	£2750

No. 22a occurred on alternate stamps.

Halfpenny
(3)

1885 (Mar). No. 13 bisected and each half diagonally surch with T **3**.

23	**1**	½d. on half of 1d. carmine-rose		29·00	42·00
		a. Unsevered pair		£120	£120
		ab. Ditto, one surch inverted		£400	£275
		b. Surch inverted		£225	£110
		ba. Ditto, unsevered pair		£1000	
		c. Surch double			

ONE PENNY.   4d.
(4)   (5)

1886 (June). No. 9 surch with T **4** or **5** each showing a manuscript line through the original value.

24	**1**	1d. on 6d. green		20·00	40·00
		a. Surch inverted		£9000	
		b. Surch double		—	£1500
25		4d. on 6d. green		60·00	95·00
		a. No stop after "d"		£225	£300
		b. Surch double		£2500	£2750

No. 24b is only known penmarked with dates between 21 July and 3 August 1886, or with violet handstamp.

1887 (May). No. 11 surch with T **4** showing a manuscript line through the original value.

26	**1**	1d. on ½d. dull green		48·00	55·00

ONE PENNY.
(7)

1888 (May). No. 16 surch.

*(a) With T **4**. Original value unobliterated.*

27	**1**	1d. on 2½d. ultramarine		£21000	£14000

*(b) With T **7** showing a manuscript line through the original value*

28	**1**	1d. on 2½d. ultramarine		70·00	70·00
		a. Surch inverted		£25000	£11000

The 1d. of Antigua was used provisionally in St. Christopher between January and March 1890 during a shortage of 1d. stamps. Such use can be distinguished by the postmark, which is "A 12" in place of "A02" (*price from* £130 *used*).

REVENUE STAMPS USED FOR POSTAGE

Saint Christopher

(R 1)

1883. Nos. F6 and F8 of Nevis optd with Type R **1**, in violet. Wmk Crown CA. P 14.

R1		1d. lilac-mauve		£375	
R2		6d. green		£120	£160

SAINT KITTS NEVIS

REVENUE
(R 2)

ST. KITTS-NEVIS / St. Christopher, Nevis

1885. Optd with Type R **2**. Wmk Crown CA. P 14.

R3	**1**	1d. rose	2·75	18·00
		a. Distorted "E"	25·00	
R4		3d. mauve	16·00	65·00
R5		6d. orange-brown	16·00	50·00
R6		1s. olive	3·25	42·00

Other fiscal stamps with overprints as above also exist, but none of these were ever available for postal purposes.

The stamps for St. Christopher were superseded by the general issue for Leeward Islands on 31 October 1890.

NEVIS

Little is known concerning the early postal affairs of Nevis, although several covers exist from the island in the 1660s. It is recorded that the British G.P.O. was to establish a branch office on the island under an Act of Parliament of 1710, although arrangements may not have been finalised for a number of years afterwards. Nevis appears as "a new office" in the P.O. Accounts of 1787.

Stamps of Great Britain were used on the island from May 1858 until the colonial authorities assumed control of the postal service on 1 May 1860. Between this date and the introduction of Nevis stamps in 1862 No. CC1 was again used on overseas mail.

CHARLESTOWN
CROWNED-CIRCLE HANDSTAMPS

CC 1

CC1	CC **1** NEVIS (R.) (9.1852)	*Price on cover*		£4500

No. CC1, struck in black or red (1882) was later used on several occasions up to 1882 when there were shortages of adhesive stamps.

Stamps of GREAT BRITAIN cancelled "A 09"
1858–60.

Z1	1d. rose-red (1857), perf 14		£650
Z2	2d. blue (1858) (Plate Nos. 7, 8)		£2000
Z3	4d. rose (1857)		£450
Z4	6d. lilac (1856)		£300
Z5	1s. green (1856)		£2500

PRICES FOR STAMPS ON COVER	
Nos. 5/22	from × 20
Nos. 23/4	from × 10
Nos. 25/34	from × 20
Nos. 35/6	from × 10
Nos. F1/8	from × 30

1 2
3 4

The designs on the stamps refer to a medicinal spring on the island

(Recess Nissen & Parker, London)

1862 (19 July). Greyish paper. P 13.

5	**1**	1d. dull lake	£100	55·00
		a. On blued paper	£300	£120
6	**2**	4d. rose	£150	70·00
		a. On blued paper	£850	£170
7	**3**	6d. grey-lilac	£150	60·00
		a. On blued paper	£700	£225
8	**4**	1s. green	£350	80·00
		a. On blued paper	£1000	£200

Nos. 5/8 and later printings of Types **1/4** were in sheets of 12 (3×4).

Crossed lines on hill

1866–76. White paper. P 15.

9	**1**	1d. pale red	60·00	50·00
10		1d. deep red	60·00	50·00
11	**2**	4d. orange	£140	23·00
12		4d. deep orange	£140	23·00
13	**4**	1s. blue-green	£300	40·00
14		1s. yellow-green (1876)	£850	£110
		a. Vertically laid paper	£21000	£6000
		b. No. 9 on sheet with crossed lines on hill	£3500	£500
		c. Ditto. On laid paper	†	£16000

Examples of the 4d. exist showing part of a papermakers watermark reading "A. COWAN & SONS EXTRA SUPERFINE".

(Lithographed by transfer from the engraved plates Nissen and Parker, London)

1876–78.

(a) P 15

15	**1**	1d. pale rose-red	28·00	21·00
		a. Imperf (pair)	£1600	
16		1d. deep rose-red	42·00	27·00
17		1d. vermilion-red	38·00	38·00
		a. Bisected (½d.) (on cover)	†	£3000
18	**2**	4d. orange-yellow (1878)	£170	38·00
		a. Imperf between (vert pair)	£11000	
19	**3**	6d. grey (1878)	£225	£200
20	**4**	1s. pale green (1878)	90·00	£110
		a. Imperf		
		b. Imperf between (horiz strip of three)	£16000	
		c. No. 9 on sheet with crossed lines on hill	£250	
21		1s. deep green	£110	£150
		c. No. 9 on sheet with crossed lines on hill	£950	

(b) P 11½

22	**1**	1d. vermilion-red (1878)	60·00	55·00
		a. Bisected (½d.) (on cover)	†	£3000
		b. Imperf (pair)	£800	
		c. Imperf between (horiz pair)		

No. 21c occurs on a small part of the deep green printing only.

RETOUCHES. 1d. Lithograph.

i. No. 1 on sheet. Top of hill over kneeling figure redrawn by five thick lines and eight small slanting lines	£150	£160
ii. No. 1 on sheet. Another retouch. Three series of short vertical strokes behind the kneeling figure	£150	£160
iii. No. 3 on sheet. Right upper corner star and border below star retouched	£150	£160
iv. No. 9 on sheet. Retouch in same position as on No. 3 but differing in detail	£170	£180
v. No. 12 on sheet. Dress of standing figure retouched by a number of horizontal and vertical lines	£150	£160

5 (Die I)   (6)

(Typo D.L.R.)

1879–80. Wmk Crown CC. P 14.

23	**5**	1d. lilac-mauve (1880)	80·00	50·00
		a. Bisected (½d.) (on cover)	†	£1000
		w. Wmk inverted		
24		2½d. red-brown	£140	90·00

1882–90. Wmk Crown CA. P 14.

25	**5**	½d. dull green (11.83)	11·00	22·00
		a. Top left triangle detached	£375	
26		1d. lilac-mauve	£110	42·00
		a. Bisected (½d.) on cover (1883)	†	£700
27		1d. dull rose (11.83)	38·00	26·00
		a. Carmine (1884)	17·00	17·00
		ab. Top left triangle detached	£475	

28		2½d. red-brown	£120	50·00	
29		2½d. ultramarine (11.83)	20·00	24·00	
		a. Top left triangle detached	£700		
30		4d. blue	£350	50·00	
31		4d. grey (1884)	22·00	8·00	
		a. Top left triangle detached	£700	£425	
32		6d. green (11.83)	£450	£350	
33		6d. chestnut (10.88)	24·00	65·00	
		a. Top left triangle detached	£800		
34		1s. pale violet (3.90)	£110	£200	
		a. Top left triangle detached	£1600		
33s/4s Optd "SPECIMEN" Set of 2				£110	

For illustration of the "top left triangle detached" variety, which occurs on Plate 2 R. 3/3 of the right pane, see above No. 21 of Antigua.

1883 (4 Sept). No. 26 bisected vertically and surch with T **6**, reading upwards or downwards.

35		½d. on half 1d. lilac-mauve (V.)	£900	55·00	
		a. Surch double	—	£325	
		b. Surch on half "REVENUE" stamp No. F6	—	£550	
36		½d. on half 1d. lilac-mauve	£1100	50·00	
		a. Surch double	—	£325	
		b. Unsevered pair	£6500	£750	
		c. Surch on half "REVENUE" stamp No. F6	—	£550	

FISCALS USED FOR POSTAGE

Revenue (F **1**)   REVENUE (F **2**)

1882.

*(a) Stamps of 1876–78 optd with Type F **1** by Nissen & Parker, London*

F1	1	1d. bright red		80·00	60·00
F2	2	1d. rose		80·00	38·00
F3		4d. orange		£140	
F4	3	6d. grey		£250	
F5	4	1s. green		£275	
		a. No. 9 on sheet with crossed lines on hill			

*(b) Nos. 26, 30 and 32 optd with Type F **2** by D.L.R.*

F6	5	1d. lilac-mauve		65·00	55·00
		a. Bisected (½d.) (on cover)		†	—
F7		4d. blue		50·00	60·00
F8		6d. green		29·00	65·00

Nos. F1/5 were produced from fresh transfers. Similar "REVENUE" handstamps, both with and without stop, were also applied to postage issues.

The stamps of Nevis were superseded by the general issue for Leeward Islands on 31 October 1890.

ST. KITTS-NEVIS

CROWN COLONY

Stamps for the combined colony were introduced in 1903, and were used concurrently with the general issues of Leeward Islands until the latter were withdrawn on 1 July 1956.

PRICES FOR STAMPS ON COVER TO 1945	
Nos. 1/9	from × 3
No. 10	—
Nos. 11/20	from × 3
No. 21	—
Nos. 22/3	from × 15
Nos. 24/34	from × 3
Nos. 35/6	—
Nos. 37/47	from × 2
Nos. 47a/b	—
Nos. 48/57	from × 2
Nos. 58/60	—
Nos. 61/4	from × 2
Nos. 65/7	from × 5
Nos. 68/77	from × 2

1 Christopher Columbus   **2** Medicinal Spring

(Typo D.L.R.)

1903. Wmk Crown CA. P 14.

1	1	½d. dull purple and deep green	1·75	70
2	2	1d. grey-black and carmine	4·75	20
3	1	2d. dull purple and brown	2·75	11·00
4		2½d. grey-black and blue	19·00	4·25
5	2	3d. deep green and orange	19·00	30·00
6	1	6d. grey-black and bright purple	5·50	42·00
7		1s. grey-green and orange	7·50	11·00
8	2	2s. grey-black and grey-black	12·00	20·00
9	1	2s.6d. grey-black and violet	18·00	42·00
10	2	5s. dull purple and sage-green	65·00	55·00
1/10 Set of 10			£140	£190
1s/10s Optd "SPECIMEN" Set of 10			£140	

1905–18. Chalk-surfaced paper (1d. (No. 13), 5s.) or ordinary paper (others). Wmk Mult Crown CA. P 14.

11	1	½d. dull purple and deep green	12·00	6·00
12		½d. grey-green (1907)	1·00	60
		a. Dull blue-green (1916)	50	2·75
13	2	1d. grey-black and carmine (1906)	6·00	25
14		1d. carmine (1907)	2·25	15
		a. Scarlet (1916)	1·00	20
15	1	2d. dull purple and brown	11·00	8·00
		a. Chalk-surfaced paper (1906)	6·50	8·00
16		2½d. grey-black and blue (1907)	26·00	4·25
17		2½d. bright blue (1907)	2·50	50
18	2	3d. deep green and orange	22·00	15·00
		a. Chalk-surfaced paper (1906)	3·00	2·75
19	1	6d. grey-black and deep violet	30·00	55·00
		a. Chalk-surfaced paper. Grey-black and deep purple (1908)	22·00	25·00
		ab. Grey-black and bright purple (1916)	8·50	30·00
20		1s. grey-green and orange (1909)	40·00	60·00
		a. Chalk-surfaced paper	3·50	35·00
21	2	5s. dull purple and sage-green (11.18)	38·00	95·00
11/21 Set of 11			95·00	£160
12s, 14s, 17s Optd "SPECIMEN" Set of 3			70·00	

WAR TAX   WAR STAMP
(**3**)   (**3a**)

1916 (Oct). Optd with T **3**. Wmk Mult Crown CA. P 14.

22	1	½d. dull blue-green (No. 12a)	2·00	50
		a. Deep green	1·00	50
		s. Optd "SPECIMEN"	50·00	
		x. Wmk reversed	45·00	

No. 22a was a special printing produced for this overprint.

1918 (26 July). Optd with T **3a**. Wmk Mult Crown CA. P 14.

23	1	1½d. orange	1·25	80
		a. Short opt (right pane R. 10/1)	21·00	
		s. Optd "SPECIMEN"	55·00	

No. 23 was a special printing produced for this overprint.
No. 23a shows the overprint 2 mm high instead of 2½ mm.

4   **5**

(Typo D.L.R.)

1920–22. Ordinary paper (½d. to 2½d.) or chalk-surfaced paper (others). Wmk Mult Crown CA (sideways*). P 14.

24	4	½d. blue-green	3·75	5·50
25	5	1d. scarlet	2·25	6·00
26	4	1½d. orange-yellow	1·25	1·75
		x. Wmk sideways reversed	£120	
		y. Wmk sideways inverted and reversed		
27	5	2d. slate-grey	3·00	4·50
28	4	2½d. ultramarine	5·50	9·00
		a. "A" of "CA" missing from wmk	£600	
29	5	3d. purple/*yellow*	1·75	11·00
30	4	6d. dull purple and bright mauve	3·50	11·00
31	5	1s. grey and black/*green*	3·50	4·00
32	4	2s. dull purple and blue/*blue*	17·00	38·00
		x. Wmk sideways reversed	£300	
33	5	2s.6d. grey and red/*blue*	5·00	40·00
		x. Wmk sideways reversed	£325	
		y. Wmk sideways inverted and reversed	£300	
34		5s. green and red/*pale yellow*	5·00	40·00
		x. Wmk sideways reversed	£200	
35	5	10s. green and red/*green*	12·00	48·00
36	4	£1 purple and black/*red* (1922)	£275	£350
24/36 Set of 13			£300	£500
24s/36s Optd "SPECIMEN" Set of 13			£350	

*The normal sideways watermark shows Crown to left of CA, *as seen from the back of the stamp*.

Examples of most values are known showing a forged St. Kitts postmark dated "8 DE 23".

1921–29. Chalk-surfaced paper (2½d. (No. 44), 3d. (No. 45*a*) and 6d. to 5s.) or ordinary paper (others). Wmk Mult Script CA (sideways*).

37	**4**	½d. blue-green	2·50	1·50
		a. Yellow-green (1922)	2·50	80
38	**5**	1d. rose-carmine	65	15
		sa. Perf "SPECIMEN" (1929)	70·00	
39		1d. deep violet (1922)	7·00	1·00
		a. Pale violet (1929)	9·00	1·50
40	**4**	1½d. red (1925)	5·00	1·50
40*a*		1½d. red-brown (1929)	1·00	30
41	**5**	2d. slate-grey (1922)	60	60
42	**4**	2½d. pale bright blue (1922)	3·25	2·00
43		2½d. brown (1922)	3·25	9·50
44		2½d. ultramarine (1927)	1·50	1·00
45	**5**	3d. dull ultramarine (1922)	1·00	4·25
45*a*		3d. purple/*yellow* (1927)	75	2·75
46	**4**	6d. dull and bright purple (1924)	5·50	6·00
		aw. Wmk Crown to right of CA	4·50	6·00
46*b*	**5**	1s. black/*green* (1929)	3·75	3·25
47	**4**	2s. purple and blue/*blue* (1922)	9·50	28·00
47a	**5**	2s.6d. black and red/*blue* (1927)	17·00	29·00
47b	**4**	5s. green and red/*yellow* (1929)	48·00	90·00
37/47b *Set of 16*			95·00	£160
37s/47bs Optd or Perf (1½d. red-brown, 1s., 5s.) "SPECIMEN" *Set of 16*			£400	

*The normal watermark shows Crown to left of CA, *as seen from the back of the stamp.*

6 Old Road Bay and Mount Misery

(Typo D.L.R.)

1923. Tercentenary of Colony. Chalk-surfaced paper. P 14.

		(a) Wmk Mult Script CA (sideways)		
48	**6**	½d. black and green	2·25	7·00
49		1d. black and bright violet	4·50	1·50
50		1½d. black and scarlet	4·50	10·00
51		2d. black and slate-grey	3·75	1·50
52		2½d. black and brown	6·00	32·00
53		3d. black and ultramarine	3·75	15·00
54		6d. black and bright purple	9·50	32·00
55		1s. black and sage-green	14·00	32·00
56		2s. black and blue/*blue*	50·00	75·00
57		2s.6d. black and red/*blue*	50·00	90·00
58		10s. black and red/*emerald*	£300	£475
		(b) Wmk Mult Crown CA (sideways)		
59	**6**	5s. black and red/*pale yellow*	90·00	£200
60		£1 black and purple/*red*	£800	£1600
48/60 *Set of 13*			£1200	£2250
48s/60s Optd "SPECIMEN" *Set of 13*			£800	

Examples of all values are known showing a forged St. Kitts postmark dated "8 DE 23".

1935 (6 May). Silver Jubilee. As Nos. 91/4 of Antigua, but ptd by Waterlow. P 11×12.

61	1d. deep blue and scarlet	1·00	70
	k. Kite and vertical log	£150	£160
	l. Kite and horizontal log	£190	£190
62	1½d. ultramarine and grey	75	1·00
	k. Kite and vertical log	£120	£130
63	2½d. brown and deep blue	1·00	1·00
64	1s. slate and purple	11·00	16·00
	k. Kite and vertical log	£425	
	l. Kite and horizontal log	£425	£475
61/4 *Set of 4*		12·50	17·00
61s/4s Perf "SPECIMEN" *Set of 4*		£100	

For illustrations of plate varieties see British Virgin Islands.

1937 (12 May). Coronation. As Nos. 95/7 of Antigua, but ptd by D.L.R. P 14.

65	1d. scarlet	30	25
66	1½d. buff	40	10
67	2½d. bright blue	60	1·60
65/7 *Set of 3*		1·10	1·75
65s/7s Perf "SPECIMEN" *Set of 3*		85·00	

Nos. 61/7 are inscribed "ST. CHRISTOPHER AND NEVIS".

7 King George VI

8 King George VI and Medicinal Spring

9 King George VI and Christopher Columbus

10 King George VI and Anguilla Island

Break in value tablet (R. 12/5) (1947 ptg only)

6d. Break in oval (R. 12/1) (1938 ptg only)

Break in value tablet frame (R. 3/2)

Break in value tablet frame (R. 12/3) (ptgs between 1941 and 1945)

5s. Break in frame above ornament (R. 2/4) (ptgs between 1941 and 1950)

5s. Break in oval at foot (R. 12/5) (ptgs between 1941 and 1945 only). Sometimes touched-in by hand painting

5s. Break in oval at left (R. 7/1) (ptgs between 1941 and 1945 only)

(Typo; centre litho (T **10**). D.L.R.)

1938 (15 Aug)–**50**. Chalk-surfaced paper (10s., £1). Wmk Mult Script CA (sideways on T **8** and **9**). P 14 (T **7** and **10**) or 13×12 (T **8**/**9**).

68	**7**	½d. green	4·25	20
		a. Blue-green (5.4.43)	10	10
69		1d. scarlet	6·50	70
		a. Carmine (5.43)	2·00	50
		b. Carmine-pink (4.47)	65·00	16·00
		c. Rose-red (7.47)	2·00	80
70		1½d. orange	20	30
71	**8**	2d. scarlet and grey	29·00	2·75
		a. Chalk-surfaced paper. *Carmine and deep grey* (18.2.41*)	55·00	12·00
		b. Perf 14. *Scarlet and pale grey* (6.43*)	1·25	1·25
		ba. *Scarlet and deep grey* (6.42*)	27·00	2·25
		c. Perf 14. Chalk-surfaced paper. *Scarlet and pale grey* (2.50*)	6·50	4·50
72	**7**	2½d. ultramarine	8·00	30
		a. Bright ultramarine (5.4.43)	70	30
73	**8**	3d. dull reddish purple and scarlet	25·00	7·50
		a. Chalk-surfaced paper. *Brown-purple and carmine-red* (1940)	30·00	10·00
		b. Perf 14. Chalk-surfaced paper. *Dull reddish purple and carmine-red* (6.43*)	42·00	5·50
		c. Perf 14. Ordinary paper. *Reddish lilac and scarlet* (8.46*)	3·75	38·00
		d. Perf 14. Ordinary paper. *Purple and bright scarlet* (1.46*)	26·00	17·00
		da. Break in value tablet	£300	
		e. Perf 14. Chalk-surfaced paper. *Deep purple and scarlet* (12.47*)	95·00	38·00

ST. KITTS-NEVIS / St. Christopher, Nevis, Anguilla

		f. Perf 14. Ordinary paper. *Rose-lilac and bright scarlet* (1.49*)	20·00	14·00
		g. Perf 14. Chalk-surfaced paper. *Deep reddish purple and bright scarlet* (8.50*)	11·00	11·00
74	9	6d. green and bright purple	7·00	3·00
		a. Break in oval	£180	
		b. Perf 14. Chalk-surfaced paper. *Green and deep claret* (17.5.43*)	55·00	13·00
		c. Perf 14. Ordinary paper. *Green and purple* (10.44*)	9·00	1·50
		d. Perf 14. Chalk-surfaced paper. *Green and purple* (11.48*)	8·50	5·50
75	8	1s. black and green	12·00	1·50
		a. Break in value tablet frame	£250	
		b. Perf 14 (8.43*)	4·00	85
		ba. Break in value tablet frame	£140	85·00
		c. Perf 14. Chalk-surfaced paper (7.50*)	13·00	8·00
		ca. Break in value tablet frame	£225	
76		2s.6d. black and scarlet	32·00	9·00
		a. Perf 14. Chalk-surfaced paper (12.43*)	23·00	6·00
		ab. Ordinary paper (5.45*)	12·00	4·50
77	9	5s. grey-green and scarlet	65·00	23·00
		a. Perf 14. Chalk-surfaced paper (25.10.43*)	£140	48·00
		ab. Break in value tablet frame	£800	£400
		ac. Break in frame above ornament	£800	£400
		ad. Break in oval at foot	£800	£400
		ae. Break in oval at left	£800	£400
		b. Perf 14. Ordinary paper. *Bluish green and scarlet* (7.11.45*)	25·00	12·00
		ba. Break in value tablet frame	£350	£190
		bb. Break in frame above ornament	£350	£190
		bc. Break in oval at foot	£350	£190
		bd. Break in oval at left	£350	£190
		c. Perf 14. Chalk-surfaced paper. *Green and scarlet-vermilion* (10.50*)	55·00	70·00
		cb. Break in frame above ornament	£475	
77e	10	10s. black and ultramarine (1.9.48)	14·00	19·00
77f		£1 black and brown (1.9.48)	15·00	23·00
68a/77f Set of 12			75·00	60·00
68s/77fs Perf "SPECIMEN" Set of 10			£275	

*Earliest postmark date. Many printings were supplied to St. Kitts-Nevis considerably earlier. Details of many of the dates are taken, with permission, from *A Study of the King George VI Stamps of St. Kitts-Nevis* by P. L. Baldwin (2nd edition 1997).

1946 (1 Nov). Victory. As Nos. 110/11 of Antigua.

78		1½d. red-orange	10	10
79		3d. carmine	10	30
78s/9s Perf "SPECIMEN" Set of 2			85·00	

1949 (3 Jan). Royal Silver Wedding. As Nos. 112/13 of Antigua.

80		2½d. ultramarine	10	50
81		5s. carmine	9·50	7·00

1949 (10 Oct). 75th Anniv of U.P.U. As Nos. 114/17 of Antigua.

82		2½d. ultramarine	15	30
83		3d. carmine-red	2·10	2·50
84		6d. magenta	20	1·75
85		1s. blue-green	20	40
		a. "A" of "CA" missing from wmk	—	£700
82/5 Set of 4			2·40	4·50

ANGUILLA

TERCENTENARY 1650-1950 (11)
TERCENTENARY 1650—1950 (12)

1950 (10 Nov). Tercentenary of British Settlement in Anguilla. Nos. 69c, 70 and 72a (perf 14) optd as T **11** and new ptgs of T **8/9** on chalk-surfaced paper perf 13×12½ optd as T **12**.

86	7	1d. rose-red	10	20
87		1½d. orange	10	50
		a. Error. Crown missing, W **9a**	£3000	
		b. Error. St. Edward's Crown, W **9b**	£1300	
88		2½d. bright ultramarine	25	20
89	8	3d. dull purple and scarlet	60	75
90	9	6d. green and bright purple	45	20
91	8	1s. black and green (R.)	1·40	25
		a. Break in value tablet frame	19·00	19·00
86/91 Set of 6			2·50	1·90

Nos. 87a/b occur on a row in the watermark, in which the crowns and letters "CA" alternate.

(New Currency. 100 cents = 1 West Indian dollar)

1951 (16 Feb). Inauguration of B.W.I. University College. As Nos. 118/19 of Antigua.

92		3c. black and yellow-orange	30	15
93		12c. turquoise-green and magenta	30	2·00

ST. CHRISTOPHER, NEVIS AND ANGUILLA

LEGISLATIVE COUNCIL

13 Bath House and Spa, Nevis

14 Warner Park

15 Map of the Islands

16 Brimstone Hill

17 Nevis from the Sea, North

18 Pinney's Beach

19 Sir Thomas Warner's Tomb

20 Old Road Bay

21 Sea Island Cotton

22 The Treasury

23 Salt Pond, Anguilla

24 Sugar Factory

(Recess Waterlow)

1952 (14 June). T **13/24**. Wmk Mult Script CA. P 12½.

94	13	1c. deep green and ochre	15	2·50
95	14	2c. green	1·00	1·00
96	15	3c. carmine-red and violet	30	1·25
97	16	4c. scarlet	20	20
98	17	5c. bright blue and grey	30	10
99	18	6c. ultramarine	30	15
100	19	12c. deep blue and reddish brown	1·25	10
101	20	24c. black and carmine-red	30	10
102	21	48c. olive and chocolate	2·75	4·50
103	22	60c. ochre and deep green	2·25	4·50
104	23	$1.20 deep green and ultramarine	7·50	4·50
105	24	$4.80 green and carmine	13·00	18·00
94/105 Set of 12			26·00	32·00

1953 (2 June). Coronation. As No. 120 of Antigua.

106		2c. black and bright green	30	30

ST. KITTS-NEVIS / St. Christopher, Nevis, Anguilla

25 Sombrero Lighthouse

26 Map of Anguilla and Dependencies

(Recess Waterlow (until 1961), then D.L.R.)

1954 (1 Mar)–**63**. Designs previously used for King George VI issue, but with portrait of Queen Elizabeth II as in T **25/6** or new values and designs (½c., 8c., $2.40). Wmk Mult Script CA. P 12½.

106a	23	½c. deep olive (3.7.56)	30	10
107	13	1c. deep green and ochre	20	10
		a. Deep green and orange-ochre (13.2.62)	1·25	3·25
		b. Imperf vert (horiz strip of three)	†	£8000
108	14	2c. green	50	10
		a. Yellow-green (31.7.63)	4·50	6·50
109	15	3c. carmine-red and violet	65	10
		a. Carmine and deep violet (31.7.63)	4·50	7·00
110	16	4c. scarlet	15	10
111	17	5c. bright blue and grey	15	10
112	18	6c. ultramarine	70	10
		a. Blue (19.2.63)	1·25	30
112b	25	8c. grey-black (1.2.57)	3·00	25
113	19	12c. deep blue and red-brown	15	10
114	20	24c. black and carmine-red (1.12.54)	15	10
115	21	48c. olive-bistre and chocolate (1.12.54)	1·25	60
116	22	60c. ochre and deep green (1.12.54)	5·50	7·50
117	23	$1.20 deep green and ultramarine (1.12.54)	18·00	2·75
		a. Deep green and violet-blue (19.2.63)	50·00	14·00
117b	26	$2.40 black and red-orange (1.2.57)	16·00	13·00
118	24	$4.80 green and carmine (1.12.54)	21·00	11·00
106a/18		Set of 15	60·00	32·00

27 Alexander Hamilton and View of Nevis

(Des Eva Wilkin. Recess Waterlow)

1957 (11 Jan). Birth Bicentenary of Alexander Hamilton. Wmk Mult Script CA. P 12½.

119	27	24c. green and deep blue	60	25

1958 (22 Apr). Inauguration of British Caribbean Federation. As Nos. 135/7 of Antigua.

120		3c. deep green	60	15
121		6c. blue	90	2·50
122		12c. scarlet	1·00	35
120/2		Set of 3	2·25	2·75

MINISTERIAL GOVERNMENT

28 One Penny Stamp of 1861

(Recess Waterlow)

1961 (15 July). Nevis Stamp Centenary. T **28** and similar horiz designs. W w **12**. P 14.

123		2c. red-brown and green	20	20
124		8c. red-brown and blue	25	10
125		12c. black and carmine-red	30	15
126		24c. deep bluish green and red-orange	35	15
123/6		Set of 4	1·00	55

Designs:—8c. Fourpence stamp of 1861; 12c. Sixpence stamp of 1861; 24c. One shilling stamp of 1861.

1963 (2 Sept). Red Cross Centenary. As Nos. 147/8 of Antigua.

127	3c. red and black	10	10
128	12c. red and blue	20	40

32 New Lighthouse, Sombrero

33 Loading Sugar Cane, St. Kitts

(Des V. Whiteley. Photo Harrison)

1963 (20 Nov)–**69**. Vert designs as T **32** (2, 3, 15, 25, 60c., $1, $5) or horiz as T **33** (others) in sepia and light blue (½ c.), greenish yellow and blue ($1) or multicoloured (others). W w **12** (upright). P 14.

129	½c. Type **32**	10	10
	w. Wmk inverted	£225	
130	1c. Type **33**	10	10
131	2c. Pall Mall Square, Basseterre	10	10
	a. Yellow omitted (White fountain and church)	£275	
	w. Wmk inverted	†	£110
132	3c. Gateway, Brimstone Hill Fort, St. Kitts	10	10
	w. Wmk inverted	†	£100
133	4c. Nelson's Spring, Nevis	10	10
	w. Wmk inverted		
134	5c. Grammar School, St. Kitts	3·50	10
135	6c. Crater, Mt Misery, St. Kitts	10	10
	w. Wmk inverted (19.12.69)	30	30
136	10c. Hibiscus	15	10
137	15c. Sea Island cotton, Nevis	70	10
	w. Wmk inverted		
138	20c. Boat building, Anguilla	30	10
139	25c. White-crowned Pigeon (turquoise-blue background)	2·25	10
	a. Turquoise-green background (13.4.65)	8·00	1·75
	w. Wmk inverted	—	80·00
140	50c. St. George's Church Tower, Basseterre	60	25
141	60c. Alexander Hamilton	1·00	30
142	$1 Map of St. Kitts-Nevis	2·50	40
143	$2.50 Map of Anguilla	2·50	3·00
144	$5 Arms of St. Christopher, Nevis and Anguilla	7·00	7·50
129/44	Set of 16	19·00	11·00

The 1, 4, 5, 6, 10 and 20c. values exist with PVA gum as well as gum arabic.

See also Nos. 166/71.

ARTS FESTIVAL ST KITTS 1964

(48)

49 Festival Emblem

1964 (14 Sept). Arts Festival. Nos. 132 and 139 optd as T **48**.

145	3c. Gateway, Brimstone Hill Fort, St. Kitts	10	15
	a. Opt double	£375	
146	25c. White-crowned Pigeon	20	15
	a. "FESTIVAI" (R. 1/10)	70·00	
	w. Wmk inverted	—	8·00

1985 (17 May). I.T.U. Centenary. As Nos. 166/7 of Antigua.

147	2c. bistre-yellow and rose-carmine	10	10
148	50c. turquoise-blue and yellow-olive	40	50

1965 (15 Oct). International Co-operation Year. As Nos. 168/9 of Antigua.

149	2c. reddish purple and turquoise-green	10	20
150	25c. deep bluish green and lavender	50	10

1966 (24 Jan). Churchill Commemoration. As Nos. 170/3 of Antigua.

151	½c. new blue	10	2·75
	a. Value omitted	£425	
	b. Value at left instead of right	£110	

ST. KITTS-NEVIS / St. Christopher, Nevis, Anguilla

152		3c. deep green	35	10
153		15c. brown	80	20
154		25c. bluish violet	85	20
151/4	Set of 4		1·75	3·00

1966 (4 Feb). Royal Visit. As Nos. 174/5 of Antigua.

155		3c. black and ultramarine	25	30
156		25c. black and magenta	55	30

1966 (1 July). World Cup Football Championship. As Nos. 176/7 of Antigua.

157		6c. violet, yellow-green, lake and yellow-brown	40	20
158		25c. chocolate, blue-green, lake and yellow-brown	60	10

(Photo Harrison)

1966 (15 Aug). Arts Festival. P 14×14½.

159	**49**	3c. black, buff, emerald-green and gold	10	10
160		25c. black, buff, emerald-green and silver	20	10

1966 (20 Sept). Inauguration of W.H.O. Headquarters, Geneva. As Nos. 178/9 of Antigua.

161		3c. black, yellow-green and light blue	10	10
162		40c. black, light purple and yellow-brown	30	20

1966 (1 Dec). 20th Anniv of U.N.E.S.C.O. As Nos. 196/8 of Antigua.

163		3c. slate-violet, red, yellow and orange	10	10
164		6c. orange-yellow, violet and deep olive	10	10
165		40c. black, bright purple and orange	30	35
163/5	Set of 3		45	50

ASSOCIATED STATEHOOD

1967–69. As Nos. 129, 131/2, 137, 139 and 142 but wmk sideways.

166	**20**	½c. sepia and light blue (9.1.69)	20	2·50
167	–	2c. multicoloured (27.6.67)	1·75	10
168	–	3c. multicoloured (16.7.68)	20	10
169	–	15c. multicoloured (16.7.68)	70	30
170	–	25c. multicoloured (16.7.68)	2·50	20
171	–	$1 greenish yellow and blue (16.7.68)	5·00	4·00
		a. Greenish yellow and ultramarine-blue (19.12.69)	12·00	6·00
166/71	Set of 6		9·25	6·50

The 2c. and $1 values exist with PVA gum as well as gum arabic. Nos. 172/81 vacant.

50 Government Headquarters, Basseterre
53 John Wesley and Cross 

(Des V. Whiteley. Photo Harrison)

1967 (1 July). Statehood. T **50** and similar horiz designs. Multicoloured. W w **12**. P 14½×14.

182		3c. Type **50**	10	10
183		10c. National flag	10	10
		w. Wmk inverted	24·00	
184		25c. Coat of arms	15	15
182/4	Set of 3		30	30

(Litho D.L.R.)

1967 (1 Dec). West Indies Methodist Conference. T **53** and similar vert designs. P 13×13½.

185		3c. black, cerise and reddish violet	10	10
186		25c. black, light greenish blue and blue	15	10
187		40c. black, yellow and orange	15	15
185/7	Set of 3		35	30

Designs:—25c. Charles Wesley and Cross; 40c. Thomas Coke and Cross.

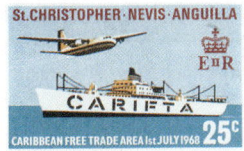

56 Handley Page H.P.R.7 Dart Herald Aircraft over *Jamaica Producer* (freighter)

(Des and litho D.L.R.)

1968 (30 July). Caribbean Free Trade Area. W w **12** (sideways). P 13.

188	**56**	25c. multicoloured	40	10
189		50c. multicoloured	40	20

57 Dr. Martin Luther King

(Des G. Vasarhelyi. Litho Enschedé)

1968 (30 Sept). Martin Luther King Commemoration. W w **12**. P 12×12½.

190	**57**	50c. multicoloured	15	10

58 "Mystic Nativity" (Botticelli)
60 Tarpon Snook 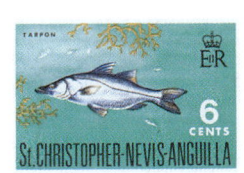

(Des and photo Harrison)

1968 (27 Nov). Christmas. Paintings. T **58** and similar vert design. Multicoloured. W w **12** (sideways). P 14½×14.

191		12c. Type **58**	10	10
192		25c. "The Adoration of the Magi" (Rubens)	10	10
193		40c. Type **58**	15	10
194		50c. As 25c.	15	10
191/4	Set of 4		45	35

(Des G. Drummond. Photo Harrison)

1969 (25 Feb). Fish. T **60** and similar horiz designs. W w **12**. P 14×14½.

195		6c. multicoloured	10	10
196		12c. black, turquoise-green and greenish blue	15	10
197		40c. multicoloured	25	10
198		50c. multicoloured	30	15
195/8	Set of 4		70	40

Designs:—12c. Needlefish; 40c. Horse-eyed Jack; 50c. Blackfinned Snapper.

64 The Warner Badge and Islands
67 "The Adoration of the Kings" (Mostaert) 

(Des V. Whiteley. Litho Format)

1969 (1 Sept). Sir Thomas Warner Commemoration. T **64** and similar horiz designs. Multicoloured. W w **12** (sideways). P 13½×14.

199		20c. Type **64**	10	10
200		25c. Sir Thomas Warner's tomb	10	10
201		40c. Charles I's commission	15	15
199/201	Set of 3		30	30

(Des Enschedé. Litho B.W.)

1969 (17 Nov). Christmas. Paintings. T **67** and similar vert design. Multicoloured. W w **12** (sideways). P 13½.

202		10c. Type **67**	10	10

ST. KITTS-NEVIS / St. Christopher, Nevis, Anguilla

203	25c. Type **67**	10	10
204	40c. "The Adoration of the Kings" (Geertgen)	10	10
205	50c. As 40c.	10	10
202/5	Set of 4	35	35

73 Portuguese Caravels (16th cent)

(Des and litho J.W.)

1970 (2 Feb)–**74**. Designs as T **73** in black, pale orange and emerald (½c.) or multicoloured (others). W w **12** (upright on vert designs, sideways* on horiz designs). P 14.

206	½c. Pirates and treasure at Frigate Bay (vert)	10	10
	w. Wmk inverted (15.3.71)	20	20
207	1c. English two-decker warship, 1650 (vert)	30	10
208	2c. Naval flags of colonising nations (vert)	15	10
209	3c. Rapier hilt (17th-century) (vert)	15	10
210	4c. Type **73**	20	10
	w. Wmk Crown to right of CA (24.7.74)	55	15
211	5c. Sir Henry Morgan and fireships, 1669	60	40
	w. Wmk Crown to right of CA (24.7.74)	40	60
212	6c. L'Ollonois and pirate carrack (16th century)	30	10
	w. Wmk Crown to right of CA (24.7.74)	40	50
213	10c. 17th-century smugglers' ship	30	10
	w. Wmk Crown to right of CA (24.7.74)	40	15
214	15c. "Piece-of-eight" (vert) (I)	2·50	40
214a	15c. "Piece-of-eight" (vert) (II) (8.9.70)	5·00	10
215	20c. Cannon (17th-century)	35	10
	w. Crown to right of CA (24.7.74)	50	20
216	25c. Humphrey Cole's Astrolabe, 1574 (vert)	40	10
217	50c. Flintlock pistol (17th-century)	85	80
	w. Wmk Crown to right of CA (24.7.74)	1·25	80
218	60c. Dutch flute (17th-century) (vert)	1·50	70
219	$1 Captain Bartholomew Roberts and his crew's death warrant (vert)	1·50	75
220	$2.50 Railing piece (16th-century)	1·25	5·00
	w. Wmk Crown to right of CA (24.7.74)	2·00	5·00
221	$5 Drake, Hawkins and sea battle	1·50	4·50
	w. Wmk Crown to right of CA (24.7.74)	3·25	5·00
206/21	Set of 17	15·00	11·50

Nos. 214/a. Type I, coin inscribed "HISPANIANUM"; Type II corrected to "HISPANIARUM". No. 214a also differs considerably in shade from No. 214.
*The normal sideways watermark shows Crown to left of CA, as seen from the back of the stamp.

Values from this set were subsequently reissued with W w **12** sideways on vertical designs and upright on horizontal designs (Nos. 269/80). Later values were issued on paper watermarked W w **14** (Nos. 322/31).

85 Graveyard Scene (Great Expectations)

(Des Jennifer Toombs. Litho B. W.)

1970 (1 May). Death Centenary of Charles Dickens. T **85** and similar designs. W w **12** (sideways on horiz designs). P 13.

222	4c. bistre-brown, gold and deep blue-green	10	80
223	20c. bistre-brown, gold and reddish purple	10	20
224	25c. bistre-brown, gold and olive-green	10	20
225	40c. bistre-brown, gold and ultramarine	15	35
222/5	Set of 4	40	1·40

Designs: Horiz—20c. Miss Havisham and Pip (Great Expectations). Vert—25c. Dickens's Birthplace; 40c. Charles Dickens.

86 Local Steel Band

(Des V. Whiteley. Litho Enschedé)

1970 (1 Aug). Festival of Arts. T **86** and similar horiz designs. Multicoloured. W w **12** (sideways). P 13½.

226	20c. Type **86**	10	10
227	25c. Local String Band	10	10
228	40c. Scene from A Midsummer Night's Dream	15	15
226/8	Set of 3	30	30

87 1d. Stamp of 1870 and Post Office, 1970

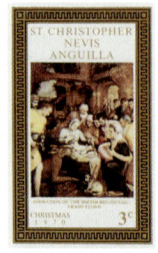

88 "Adoration of the Shepherds" (detail) (Frans van Floris)

(Des J. Cooter. Litho J.W.)

1970 (14 Sept). Stamp Centenary. T **87** and similar horiz designs. W w **12** (sideways). P 14½.

229	½c. green and rose	10	10
230	20c. deep blue, green and rose	10	10
231	25c. brown-purple, green and rose	10	10
232	50c. scarlet, green and black	30	45
229/32	Set of 4	55	65

Designs:—20c., 25c., 1d. and 6d. Stamps of 1870; 50c., 6d. Stamp of 1870 and early postmark.

(Des Enschedé. Litho Format)

1970 (16 Nov). Christmas. T **88** and similar vert design. Multicoloured. W w **12**. P 14.

233	3c. Type **88**	10	10
234	20c. "The Holy Family" (Van Dyck)	10	10
235	25c. As 20c.	10	10
236	40c. Type **88**	15	50
235/6	Set of 4	40	70

89 Monkey Fiddle

(Des Sylvia Goaman. Litho Format)

1971 (1 Mar). Flowers. T **89** and similar horiz designs. Multicoloured. W w **12** (sideways*). P 14½.

237	½c. Type **89**	10	40
	w. Wmk Crown to right of CA	75	
238	20c. Tropical Mountain Violet	15	10
239	30c. Trailing Morning Glory	15	15
240	50c. Fringed Epidendrum	30	1·00
237/40	Set of 4	60	1·50

*The normal sideways watermark shows Crown to left of CA, as seen from the back of the stamp.

90 Royal Poinciana

(Des Enschedé. Litho J.W.)

1971 (1 June). Phillipe de Poincy Commemoration. T **90** and similar multicoloured designs. W w **12** (sideways on 20 and 30c.). P 13½.

241	20c. Type **90**	10	10
242	30c. Chateau de Poincy	10	10
243	50c. De Poincy's badge (vert)	20	15
241/3	Set of 3	35	30

ST. KITTS-NEVIS / St. Christopher, Nevis, Anguilla

91 The East Yorks

(Des V. Whiteley. Litho Walsall)

1971 (1 Sept). Siege of Brimstone Hill, 1782. T **91** and similar horiz designs. Multicoloured. W w **12** (sideways*). P 14½.
244	½c. Type **91**		10	10
	w. Wmk Crown to right of CA		75	
245	20c. Royal Artillery		30	10
246	30c. French infantry		30	10
247	50c. The Royal Scots		40	20
244/7 Set of 4			90	45

*The normal sideways watermark shows Crown to left of CA, as seen from the back of the stamp.

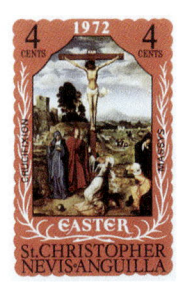

92 "Crucifixion" (Massys)

(Des J. Cooter. Litho J.W.)

1972 (1 Apr). Easter. W w **12**. P 14×13½.
248	**92**	4c. multicoloured	10	10
249		20c. multicoloured	10	20
250		30c. multicoloured	10	25
251		40c. multicoloured	10	25
248/51 Set of 4			35	70

93 "Virgin and Child" (Borgognone)

(Des J. Cooter. Litho J.W.)

1972 (2 Oct). Christmas. T **93** and similar multicoloured designs. W w **12** (sideways on vert designs). P 14.
252	3c. Type **93**		10	10
253	20c. "Adoration of the Kings" (J. Bassano) (horiz)		15	10
254	25c. "Adoration of the Shepherds" (Domenichino)		15	10
255	40c. "Virgin and Child" (Fiorenzo di Lorenzo)		20	10
252/5 Set of 4			50	35

94 Brown Pelicans

(Des (from photograph by D. Groves) and photo Harrison)

1972 (20 Nov). Royal Silver Wedding. Multicoloured; background colour given. W w **12**. P 14×14½.
256	**94** 20c. carmine	35	20
	w. Wmk inverted	—	42·00
257	25c. bright blue	35	20

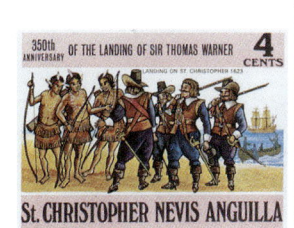

95 Landing on St. Christopher, 1623
96 "The Last Supper" (Titian)

(Des J.W. Litho Quests)

1973 (28 Jan). 350th Anniv of Sir Thomas Warner's landing on St. Christopher. T **95** and similar horiz designs. Multicoloured. W w **12**. P 13½.
258	4c. Type **95**	15	10
259	25c. Growing tobacco	15	10
	w. Wmk inverted	1·00	
260	40c. Building fort at Old Road	20	10
261	$2.50 Concepcion	80	1·10
258/61 Set of 4		1·10	1·25

(Des J. Cooter. Litho Walsall)

1973 (16 Apr). Easter. T **96** and similar multicoloured designs showing paintings of The Last Supper by the artists listed. W w **12** (sideways on $2.50). P 13½×14 ($2.50) or 14×13½ (others).
262	4c. Type **96**	10	10
263	25c. Ascr to Roberti	10	10
264	$2.50 Juan de Juanes (horiz)	70	60
262/4 Set of 3		75	60

VISIT OF
H. R. H. THE PRINCE OF WALES 1973
(**97**)

1973 (31 May). Royal Visit. Nos. 258/61 optd with T **97** by Questa.
265	4c. Type **95**	10	15
266	25c. Growing tobacco	10	15
267	40c. Building fort at Old Road	15	15
268	$2.50 Concepcion	45	50
265/8 Set of 4		65	85

(Des J.W. Litho Harrison ($10), J.W. (others))

1973 (12 Sept)–**74**. As Nos. 206, 208/9, 211/13, 214a/17, 219 and new horiz design ($10), but W w **12** (sideways on vert designs, upright on horiz designs).
269	½c. Pirates and treasure at Frigate Bay	10	2·00
270	2c. Naval flags of colonizing nations	20	2·00
271	3c. Rapier hilt	20	1·50
272	5c. Sir Henry Morgan and fireships, 1669	35	1·75
273	6c. L'Ollonois and pirate carrack (16th-century)	35	80
274	10c. 17th-century smugglers' ship	40	80
275	15c. "Piece-of-eight" (II)	65	85
276	20c. Cannon (17th-century)	75	1·40
277	25c. Humphrey Cole's Astrolabe, 1574	80	1·75
278	50c. Flintlock pistol (17th-century)	1·10	1·75
279	$1 Captain Bartholomew Roberts and his crew's death warrant	2·75	3·75
280	$10 "The Apprehension of Blackbeard" (Edward Teach) (16.11.74)	15·00	13·00
269/80 Set of 12		20·00	28·00

Nos. 281/4 are vacant.

99 Harbour Scene and 2d. Stamp of 1903

ST. KITTS-NEVIS / St. Christopher, Nevis, Anguilla

(Des V. Whiteley Studio. Litho Enschedé)

1973 (1 Oct). 70th Anniv of First St. Kitts–Nevis Stamps. T **99** and similar horiz designs. Multicoloured. W w **12** (sideways). P 13×13½.

285	4c. Type **99**	10	10
286	25c. Sugar-mill and 1d. stamp of 1903	15	10
287	40c. Unloading boat and ½d. stamp of 1903	35	10
288	$2.50 Rock-carvings and 3d. stamp of 1903	1·00	1·00
285/8	Set of 4	1·40	1·10
MS289	144×95 mm. Nos. 285/8	1·50	4·50

1973 (14 Nov). Royal Wedding. As Nos. 322/3 of Montserrat.

290	25c. light emerald	15	10
291	40c. brown-ochre	15	10

100 "Madonna and Child" (Murillo)

101 "Christ carrying the Cross" (S. del Piombo)

(Des J. Cooter. Litho Format)

1973 (1 Dec). Christmas. T **100** and similar multicoloured designs showing 'The Holy Family" by the artists listed. W w **12** (sideways on $1). P 13½.

292	4c. Type **100**	10	10
293	40c. Mengs	15	10
294	60c. Sassoferrato	20	15
295	$1 Filippino Lippi (*horiz*)	25	30
292/5	Set of 4	55	50

(Des J. Cooter. Litho D.L.R.)

1974 (8 Apr). Easter. T **101** and similar multicoloured designs. W w **12** (sideways on $2.50). P 13½.

296	4c. Type **101**	10	10
297	25c. "The Crucifixion" (Goya)	15	10
298	40c. "The Trinity" (Ribera)	15	10
299	$2.50 "The Deposition" (Fra Bartolomeo) (*horiz*)	1·00	1·00
296/9	Set of 4	1·25	1·00

102 University Centre, St. Kitts

103 Hands reaching for Globe

(Des G. Drummond. Litho Questa)

1974 (1 June). 25th Anniv of University of West Indies. T **102** and similar horiz design. Multicoloured. W w **12** (sideways*). P 13½.

300	10c. Type **102**	10	10
301	$1 As Type **102** but showing different buildings	20	25
MS302	99×95 mm. Nos. 300/1	35	65
	w. Wmk Crown to right of CA	32·00	

*The normal sideways watermark shows Crown to left of CA, *as seen from the back of the stamp.*

(Des Jennifer Toombs. Litho Questa)

1974 (5 Aug). Family Planning. T **103** and similar designs. W w **12** (sideways on 25c. and $2.50). P 14.

303	4c. orange-brown, new blue and black	10	10
304	25c. multicoloured	10	10
305	40c. multicoloured	10	10
306	$2.50 multicoloured	35	55
303/6	Set of 4	50	65

Designs: *Horiz*—25c. Instruction by nurse; $2.50, Emblem and globe on scales. *Vert*—40c. Family group.

104 Churchill as Army Lieutenant

105 Aeroplane and Map

(Des PAD Studio. Litho Questa)

1974 (30 Nov). Birth Centenary of Sir Winston Churchill. T **104** and similar vert designs. Multicoloured. W w **12**. P 13½.

307	4c. Type **104**	10	10
308	25c. Churchill as Prime Minister	15	10
309	40c. Churchill as Knight of the Garter	15	10
310	60c. Churchill's statue, London	25	15
307/10	Set of 4	50	30
MS311	99×148 mm. Nos. 307/10	75	1·25

(Des J.W. Litho Questa)

1974 (16 Dec). Opening of Golden Rock Airport, St. Kitts. Sheets 98×148 mm. W w **12**. P 13½.

MS312	**105** 40c. multicoloured	20	40
MS313	45c. multicoloured	20	40

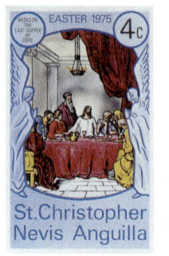

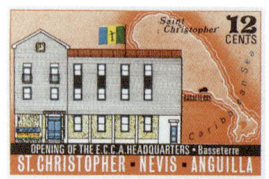

106 "The Last Supper" (Doré)

107 E.C.C.A. H.Q. Buildings, Basseterre

(Des PAD Studio. Litho Questa)

1975 (24 Mar). Easter. T **106** and similar vert designs showing paintings by Doré. Multicoloured. W w **12**. P 14½.

314	4c. Type **106**	10	10
315	25c. "Christ Mocked"	10	10
316	40c. "Jesus falling beneath the Cross"	10	10
317	$1 "The Erection of the Cross"	25	30
314/17	Set of 4	40	40

(Des J. Cooter. Litho Enschedé)

1975 (2 June*). Opening of East Caribbean Currency Authority Headquarters. T **107** and similar horiz designs. W w **14** (sideways). P 13×13½.

318	12c. multicoloured	10	10
319	25c. multicoloured	10	10
320	40c. light vermilion, silver and grey-black	15	10
321	45c. multicoloured	15	15
	a. Silver omitted	£110	
318/21	Set of 4	30	30

Designs:—25c. Specimen one-dollar banknote; 40c. Half-dollar of 1801 and current 4-dollar coin; 45c. Coins of 1801 and 1960.

*This is the local date of issue; the Crown Agents released the stamps on 28 april.

†This affects the dull silver coin on the left which on No. 321a appears in tones of the black plate.

1975 (11 June)–77. As Nos. 207, 209/13, 214a/15 and 218/19 but W w **14** (sideways* on 4, 5, 6,10,20 and 60c.). Cream, chalk-surfaced paper (1c., $1) or white, ordinary paper (others). P 14.

322	1c. English two-decker warship, 1650 (17.5.77)	40	30
323	3c. Rapier hilt (17th-century) (11.6.76)	60	10
	a. Cream, chalk-surfaced paper (17.5.77)	2·75	3·00
324	4c. Type **73** (11.6.76)	20	10
	a. Cream, chalk-surfaced paper (17.5.77)	2·75	3·00
325	5c. Sir Henry Morgan and fireships, 1669	30	60
	a. Cream, chalk-surfaced paper (16.8.77)	14·00	12·00
326	6c. L'Ollonois and pirate carrack (16th century)	1·50	10

ST. KITTS-NEVIS / St. Christopher, Nevis, Anguilla

	a. Cream, chalk-surfaced paper (17.5.77)	1·00	2·25
	aw. Wmk Crown to right of CA (16.8.77)	8·50	8·50
327	10c. 17th-century smugglers' ship (11.6.76)	45	15
	a. Cream, chalk-surfaced paper (17.5.77)	1·50	2·50
328	15c. "Piece-of-eight" (II) (11.6.76)	55	15
	a. Cream, chalk-surfaced paper (16.8.77)	11·00	9·50
329	20c. Cannon (17th-century)	2·75	8·00
	a. Cream, chalk-surfaced paper (17.5.77)	2·00	9·00
330	60c. Dutch lute (17th-century) (11.6.76)	9·50	2·00
331	$1 Captain Bartholomew Roberts and his crew's death warrant (16.8.77)	12·00	3·00
322/31 Set of 10		24·00	13·00

*The normal sideways watermark shows Crown to left of CA on No. 326a and to right of CA on the others, *as seen from the back of the stamp.*

The cream, chalk-surfaced paper stamps appear thicker, with white gum. The ordinary paper stamps have slightly bluish gum.

Nos. 332/7 are vacant.

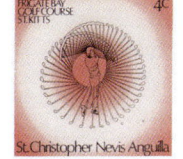

108 Evangeline Booth (Salvation Army General) **109** Golfer

(Des Jennifer Toombs. Litho Questa)

1975 (15 Sept). International Women's Year. T **108** and similar vert designs. Multicoloured. W w **12**. P 14.

338	4c. Type **108**	30	10
339	25c. Sylvia Pankhurst	35	10
340	40c. Marie Curie	2·50	80
341	$2.50 Lady Annie Allen (teacher and guider)	1·50	4·25
338/41 Set of 4		4·25	4·75

(Des Sue Lawes. Litho Questa)

1975 (1 Nov). Opening of Frigate Bay Golf Course. W w **14** (sideways). P 13½.

342	**109**	4c. black and rose-red	80	10
343		25c. black and greenish yellow	1·10	10
344		40c. black and light emerald	1·40	20
345		$1 black and new blue	1·90	2·75
342/5 Set of 4			4·75	2·75

110 "St. Paul" (Pier Francesco Sacchi) **111** "Crucifixion" (detail)

(Des J.W. Litho Questa)

1975 (1 Dec). Christmas. T **110** and similar vert designs showing details from paintings in the National Gallery, London. Multicoloured. W w **14**. P 13½.

346	25c. Type **110**	25	10
347	40c. "St. James" (Bonifazio di Pitati)	30	10
348	45c. "St. John the Baptist" (Mola)	30	10
349	$1 "St. Mary" (Raphael)	80	2·25
346/9 Set of 4		1·50	2·25

(Des J. Cooter. Litho Questa)

1976 (14 Apr). Easter. Stained-glass Windows. T **111** and similar vert designs. Multicoloured. W w **14**. P 14×13½ (4c.) or 14 (others).

350	4c. Type **111**	10	50
	a. Strip of 3. Nos. 350/2	20	1·40
351	4c. "Crucifixion"	10	50
352	4c. "Crucifixion"	10	50
353	25c. "Last Supper"	35	10
354	40c. "Last Supper" (*different*)	40	10
355	$1 "Baptism of Christ"	70	80
350/5 Set of 6		1·60	2·25

Nos. 350/2 were printed horizontally *se-tenant*, together forming a composite design, No. 350 being the left-hand stamp.

Nos. 353/5 are smaller, 27×35 mm.

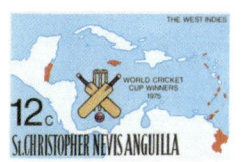

111a Map of the Caribbean

(Des PAD Studio. Litho Questa)

1976 (8 July). West Indian Victory in World Cricket Cup. T **111a** and similar design. No wmk. P 14.

356	12c. multicoloured	60	20
357	40c. black and magenta	1·40	50
MS358 95×80 mm. Nos. 356/7		4·25	3·75

Design Vert–40c. Prudential Cup.

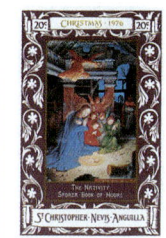

112 Crispus Attucks and the Boston Massacre **113** "The Nativity" (Sforza Book of Hours)

(Des J.W. Litho Questa)

1976 (26 July). Bicentenary of American Revolution. T **112** and similar horiz designs. Multicoloured. W w **14** (sideways). P 13½.

359	20c. Type **112**	20	10
360	40c. Alexander Hamilton and Battle of Yorktown	25	10
361	45c. Jefferson and Declaration of Independence	25	10
362	$1 Washington and the Crossing of the Delaware	45	85
359/62 Set of 4		1·00	1·00

(Des Jennifer Toombs. Litho Questa)

1976 (1 Nov). Christmas. T **113** and similar vert designs. Multicoloured. W w **14**. P 14.

363	20c. Type **113**	10	10
364	40c. "Virgin and Child with St. John" (Pintoricchio)	15	10
365	45c. "Our Lady of Good Children" (Ford Maddox-Brown)	15	10
366	$1 "Little Hands Outstretched to Bless" (Margaret Tarrant)	35	50
363/6 Set of 4		65	70

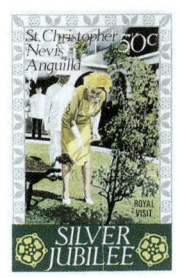

114 Royal Visit, 1966 **115** "Christ on the Cross" (Niccolo di Liberatore)

ST. KITTS-NEVIS / St. Christopher, Nevis, Anguilla

(Des J.W. Litho Questa)

1977 (7 Feb). Silver Jubilee. T **114** and similar vert designs. Multicoloured. W w **14**. P 13½.

367		50c. Type **114**	10	10
368		55c. The Sceptre	10	10
369		$1.50 Bishops paying homage	25	50
367/9 Set of 3			35	60

(Des G. Hutchins. Litho Questa)

1977 (14 Apr*). Easter. T **115** and similar designs showing paintings from the National Gallery, London. Multicoloured. W w **14** (sideways on 50c.). P 14.

370		25c. Type **115**	10	10
371		30c. "The Resurrection" (imitator of Mantegna)	10	10
372		50c. "The Resurrection" (Ugolino da Siena) (horiz)	15	10
373		$1 "Christ Rising from the Tomb" (Gaudenzio Ferrari)	25	30
370/3 Set of 4			55	55

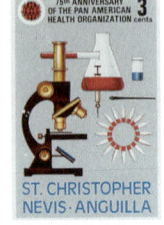

*This is the local release date; the Crown Agents released the stamps ten days earlier.

116 Estridge Mission

117 Laboratory Instruments

(Des Jennifer Toombs. Litho Cartor)

1977 (27 June). Bicentenary of Moravian Mission. T **116** and similar horiz designs. W w **14** (sideways*). P 12½.

374		4c. black, greenish blue and new blue	10	10
		w. Wmk Crown to left of CA	30	
375		20c. black, brightt mauve and bright reddish violet	10	10
		w. Wmk Crown to left of CA	40	
376		40c. black, yellow and yellow-orange	15	15
		w. Wmk Crown to left of CA	60	
374/6 Set of 3			30	30

Designs:—20c. Mission symbol; 40c. Basseterre Mission.
*The normal sideways watermark shows Crown to right of CA, as seen from the back of the stamp.

(Des G. Hutchins. Litho Questa)

1977 (11 Oct). 75th Anniv of Pan-Amerièan Health Organization. T **117** and similar vert designs. W w **14**. P 14.

377		3c. multicoloured	20	10
378		12c. multicoloured	35	60
379		20c. multicoloured	40	10
380		$1 red-brown, bright orange and black	1·00	1·40
377/80 Set of 4			1·75	2·00

Designs:—12c. Fat cells, blood cells and nerve cells; 20c. "Community participation in health"; $1 Inoculation.

118 "Nativity" (West Window)

119 Savanna Monkey with Vervet

(Des Jennifer Toombs. Litho Rosenbaum Bros, Vienna)

1977 (15 Nov). Christmas. Vert designs as T **118** showing stained glass windows from Chartres Cathedral. Multicoloured. W w **14** (inverted). P 13½.

381		4c. Type **118**	10	10
		w. Wmk upright	30	
382		6c. "Three Magi" (West window)	10	10
383		40c. "La Belle Verriere"	35	10
		w. Wmk upright	55	
384		$1 "Virgin and Child" (Rose window)	75	45
		w. Wmk upright	2·50	
381/4 Set of 4			1·10	65

(Des BG Studio. Litho Questa)

1978 (15 Apr). The Savanna ("Green") Monkey. T **119** and similar vert design. W w **14**. P 14½.

385	**119**	4c. yellow-brown, rosine and black	10	10
386	–	5c. multicoloured	10	10
387	**119**	55c. yellow-brown, apple-green and black	30	10
388	–	$1.50 multicoloured	75	60
385/8 Set of 4			1·10	80

Design:—5c., $1.50, Savanna Monkeys on branch.

120 Falcon of Edward III

121 Tomatoes

(Des C. Abbott. Litho Questa)

1978 (2 June). 25th Anniv of Coronation. T **120** and similar vert designs. P 15.

389		$1 olive-brown and vermilion	15	20
		a. Sheetlet. Nos. 389/91×2	75	1·00
390		$1 multicoloured	15	20
391		$1 olive-brown and vermilion	15	20
389/91 Set of 3			40	55

Designs:—No. 389, Type **120**; No. 390, Queen Elizabeth II; No. 391, Brown Pelican.

(Des BG Studio. Litho D.L.R.)

1978 (8 Sept). Horiz designs as T **121**. Multicoloured. W w **14** (sideways*). P 14½×14.

392		1c. Type **121**	10	20
393		2c. Defence Force band	10	20
394		5c. Radio and TV station	10	10
395		10c. Technical college	10	10
396		12c. TV assembly plant	10	75
		w. Wmk Crown to left of CA	3·50	
397		15c. Sugar cane harvesting	15	20
398		25c. Crafthouse (craft centre)	15	10
399		30c. *Europa* (liner)	1·50	1·50
400		40c. Lobster and sea crab	30	10
401		45c. Royal St. Kitts Hotel and golf course	2·75	1·25
		w. Wmk Crown to left of CA	8·00	
402		50c. Pinney's Beach, Nevis	30	10
403		55c. New runway at Golden Rock	1·25	10
404		$1 Cotton picking	35	30
405		$5 Brewery	75	1·25
406		$10 Pineapples and peanuts	1·00	1·75
		w. Wmk Crown to left of CA	55·00	
392/406 Set of 15			8·00	7·25

*The normal sideways watermark shows Crown to right of CA, as seen from the back of the stamp.

122 Investiture

123 Wise Man with Gift of Gold

(Des L. Curtis. Litho Rosenbaum Bros, Vienna)

1978 (9 Oct). 50th Anniv of Boy Scout Movement on St. Kitts and Nevis. T **122** and similar vert designs. Multicoloured. W w **14**. P 13½.

407		5c. Type **122**	10	35

ST. KITTS-NEVIS / St. Christopher, Nevis, Anguilla, St. Kitts

408	10c. Map reading		10	35
409	25c. Pitching tent		20	35
410	40c. Cooking		35	50
	w. Wmk inverted		15·00	
411	50c. First aid		40	60
	w. Wmk inverted		15·00	
412	55c. Rev W.A. Beckett (founder of scouting in St. Kitts)		45	65
	w. Wmk inverted		13·00	
407/12 Set of 6			1·40	2·50

(Des Jennifer Toombs. Litho Walsall)

1978 (1 Dec). Christmas. T **123** and similar vert designs. Multicoloured. W w **14**. P 13½.

413	5c. Type **123**	10	10
414	15c. Wise Man with gift of Frankincense	10	10
415	30c. Wise Man with gift of Myrrh	10	10
416	$2.25 Wise Men paying homage to the infant Jesus	35	50
413/16 Set of 4		55	70

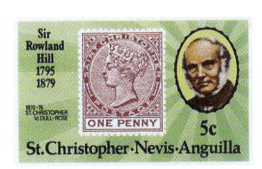

124 *Canna coccinea*   **125** St. Christopher 1870–76 1d. Stamp and Sir Rowland Hill

(Des Daphne Padden. Litho Questa)

1979 (19 Mar). Flowers (1st series). T **124** and similar vert designs. Multicoloured. W w **14**. P 14.

417	5c. Type **124**	10	10
418	30c. *Heliconia bihai*	25	20
419	55c. *Ruellia tuberosa*	30	30
420	$1.50 *Gesneria ventricosa*	50	1·60
417/20 Set of 4		1·00	2·00

See also Nos. 430/3.

(Des J.W. Litho Walsall)

1979 (2 July). Death Centenary of Sir Rowland Hill. T **125** and similar horiz designs showing stamps and portrait. Multicoloured. W w **14** (sideways). P 14½×14.

421	5c. Type **125**	10	10
422	15c. 1970 Stamp Centenary 50c. commemorative	10	10
423	50c. Great Britain 1841 2d.	30	35
424	$2.50 St. Kitts–Nevis 1923 300th Anniversary of Colony £1 commemorative	70	1·10
421/4 Set of 4		1·00	1·40

126 "The Woodman's Daughter"   **127** Nevis Lagoon

(Des BG Studio. Litho Format)

1979 (12 Nov). Christmas and International Year of the Child. Paintings by Sir John Millais. T **126** and similar vert designs. Multicoloured. W w **14**. P 13½.

425	5c. Type **126**	10	10
426	25c. "Cherry Ripe"	25	25
427	30c. "The Rescue"	25	25
428	55c. "Bubbles"	30	30
425/8 Set of 4		80	80
MS429 100×68 mm. $1 "Christ in the House of His Parents"		70	55

(Des J Cooter. Litho Questa)

1980 (4 Feb). Flowers (2nd series). Vert designs as T **124**. Multicoloured. W w **14** (inverted). P 14.

430	4c. *Clerodendrum aculeatum*	30	10
431	55c. *Inga laurina*	30	20
432	$1.50 *Epidendrum difforme*	1·40	1·75
433	$2 *Salvia serotina*	60	2·25
430/3 Set of 4		2·40	3·75

(Des and litho Secura, Singapore)

1980 (6 May). "London 1980" International Stamp Exhibition. T **127** and similar multicoloured designs. W w **14** (sideways* on 5 and 55c., inverted on 30c.). P 13.

434	5c. Type **127**	15	10
	w. Wmk Crown to right of CA	1·75	
435	30c. Fig Tree Church (*vert*)	25	10
436	55c. Nisbet Plantation	45	25
	w. Wmk Crown to right of CA	4·00	
437	$3 "Nelson" Fuger (*vert*)	1·75	1·60
	w. Wmk inverted	4·75	
434/7 Set of 4		2·25	1·75
MS438 107×77 mm. 75c. Detail of "Nelson Falling" (D. Dighton). P 13½×13		1·40	75
a. Wmk sideways		48·00	

*The normal sideways watermark shows Crown to left of CA, *as seen from the back of the stamp*.

OFFICIAL STAMPS

OFFICIAL

(O **1**)

1980 (3 Mar). Nos. 396, 398 and 400/6 optd with Type O **1**.

O1	12c. TV assembly plant	80	1·25
	w. Wmk Crown to left of CA	7·00	7·00
O2	25c. Crafthouse (craft centre)	15	20
O3	40c. Lobster and sea crab	40	50
O4	45c. Royal St. Kitts Hotel and golf course	2·50	2·00
	w. Wmk Crown to left of CA	10·00	
O5	50c. Pinney's Beach, Nevis	30	40
O6	55c. New runway at Golden Rock	1·25	50
O7	$1 Cotton picking	70	2·25
O8	$5 Brewery	80	2·50
O9	$10 Pineapples and peanuts	1·00	3·50
O1/9 Set of 9		7·00	11·50

From 23 June 1980 St. Kitts and Nevis had separate postal authorities, each with their own issues.

ST. KITTS

St. Kitts

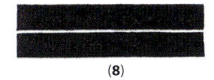

(**8**)

1980 (23 June). As Nos. 394/406 of St. Christopher, Nevis and Anguilla optd with T **8**. A. W w **14** (sideways*)

29A	5c. Radio and TV station	10	15
30A	10c. Technical college	10	15
	w. Wmk Crown to left of CA	48·00	
31A	12c. TV assembly plant	35	80
32A	15c. Sugar cane harvesting	10	15
33A	25c. Crafthouse (craft centre)	10	15
34A	30c. *Europa* (liner)	10	15
35A	40c. Lobster and sea crab	10	20
36A	45c. Royal St. Kitts Hotel and golf course	50	15
37A	50c. Pinney's Beach, Nevis	10	15
38A	55c. New runway at Golden Rock	15	15
39A	$1 Cotton picking	10	25
40A	$5 Brewery	30	1·00
41A	$10 Pineapples and peanuts	35	1·75
29A/41A Set of 13		1·90	4·75

B. *No wmk*

29B	5c. Radio and TV station	10	10
30B	10c. Technical college	10	10
32B	15c. Sugar cane harvesting	10	10
33B	25c. Crafthouse (craft centre)	10	10
34B	30c. *Europa* (liner)	10	10
35B	40c. Lobster and sea crab	10	15
38B	55c. New runway at Golden Rock	15	15
39B	$1 Cotton picking	25	25
40B	$5 Brewery	45	1·50
41B	$10 Pineapples and peanuts	70	2·50
29B/41B Set of 10		1·75	4·50

*The normal sideways watermark shows Crown to right of CA, *as seen from the back of the stamp*.

ST. KITTS-NEVIS / St. Kitts

9 H.M.S. *Vanguard*, 1762

10 Queen Elizabeth the Queen Mother at Royal Variety Performance, 1978

(Litho Secura, Singapore)

1980 (8 Aug). Ships. T **9** and similar horiz designs. Multicoloured. W w **14** (sideways*). P 13×13½.

42	4c. Type **9**...		10	10
	a. Opt omitted.....................................	18·00		
	c. No stop after "ST"...........................	75		
	w. Wmk Crown to right of CA............	10		
43	10c. H.M.S. *Boreas*, 1787........................		10	10
	a. Opt omitted.....................................	40·00		
	c. No stop after "ST"...........................	75		
	w. Wmk Crown to right of CA............	10		
44	30c. H.M.S. *Druid*, 1827.........................		15	10
	a. Opt omitted.....................................	40·00		
	c. No stop after "ST"...........................	1·00		
	w. Wmk Crown to right of CA............	25		
45	55c. H.M.S. *Winchester*, 1831.................		15	15
	a. Opt inverted...................................	75·00		
	b. Opt omitted.....................................	40·00		
	c. No stop after "ST"...........................	1·25		
	w. Wmk Crown to right of CA............	50		
46	$1.50 Harrison Line *Philosopher*, 1857....		30	35
	a. Opt omitted.....................................	40·00		
	c. No stop after "ST"...........................	1·50		
	w. Wmk Crown to right of CA............	80		
47	$2 Harrison Line *Contractor*, 1930........		35	45
	a. Opt double.......................................	60·00		
	b. Opt omitted.....................................	90·00		
	c. No stop after "ST"...........................	1·50		
	w. Wmk Crown to right of CA............	1·00		
42/7 Set of 6..			1·00	1·00

Nos. 42/7 are overprinted "ST. KITTS" and have the previous combined inscription obliterated.

*The normal sideways watermark shows Crown to left of CA, *as seen from the back of the stamp*.

The "no stop" variety occurs on R. 3/4 of the lower pane.

(Des and litho Format)

1980 (4 Sept). 80th Birthday of Queen Elizabeth the Queen Mother. W w **14**. P 13½.

48	**10**	$2 multicoloured..............................	25	60

No. 48 was printed in sheets containing two *se-tenant* stamp-size labels.

11 The Three Wise Men

(Des Walsall. Litho Questa)

1980 (10 Nov). Christmas. T **11** and similar horiz designs. Multicoloured. W w **14** (sideways). P 14½×14.

49	5c. Type **11**...	10	10
50	15c. The Shepherds................................	10	10
51	30c. Bethlehem.......................................	10	10
52	$4 Nativity scene..................................	50	60
49/52 Set of 4...		55	65

12 Purple-throated Carib

13 Bananaquit

(Des Jennifer Toombs. Litho Quests)

1981 (5 Feb)–**82**. Birds. Vert designs as T **12** (1 to 10c.) or horiz as T **13** (15c. to $10). Multicoloured. W w **14** (sideways on 1 to 10c.). P 13½×14 (1 to 10c.) or 14 (15c. to $10).

A. Without imprint date

53A	1c. Magnificent Frigate Bird (30.5.81).........	25	20
54A	4c. Wied's Crested Flycatcher (30.5.81).......	35	20
55A	5c. Type **12**...	30	20
56A	6c. Burrowing Owl (30.5.81).....................	60	30
57A	8c. Caribbean Martin (30.5.81)..................	45	30
58A	10c. Yellow-crowned Night Heron.............	30	20
59A	15c. Type **13**...	30	20
60A	20c. Scaly-breasted Thrasher.....................	30	20
61A	25c. Grey Kingbird..................................	30	20
62A	30c. Green-throated Carib........................	30	20
63A	40c. Turnstone.......................................	35	30
64A	45c. Black-faced Grassquit........................	35	30
65A	50c. Cattle Egret.....................................	40	30
66A	55c. Brown Pelican..................................	40	30
67A	$1 Lesser Antillean Bullfinch....................	60	60
68A	$2.50 Zenaida Dove.................................	1·25	2·25
69A	$5 American Kestrel................................	2·25	3·50
70A	$10 Antillean Crested Hummingbird..........	4·50	6·00
53A/70A Set of 18...................................		12·00	14·00

B. With imprint date at foot of design (8.6.82)

53B	1c. Magnificent Frigate Bird.....................	45	35
54B	4c. Wied's Crested Flycatcher...................	45	30
55B	5c. Type **12**...	55	30
56B	6c. Burrowing Owl...................................	65	40
57B	8c. Caribbean Martin...............................	70	30
58B	10c. Yellow-crowned Night Heron.............	70	30
59B	15c. Type **13**...	75	30
60B	20c. Scaly-breasted Thrasher.....................	80	30
61B	25c. Grey Kingbird..................................	80	30
62B	30c. Green-throated Carib........................	80	35
63B	40c. Turnstone.......................................	90	40
64B	45c. Black-faced Grassquit........................	1·00	45
65B	50c. Cattle Egret.....................................	1·10	50
66B	55c. Brown Pelican..................................	1·25	50
67B	$1 Lesser Antillean Bullfinch....................	2·00	80
68B	$2.50 Zenaida Dove.................................	3·25	3·00
69B	$5 American Kestrel................................	5·00	5·50
70B	$10 Antillean Crested Hummingbird..........	8·00	9·00
53B/70B Set of 18...................................		26·00	21·00

Imprint dates: "1982", Nos. 53B/70B; "1983", Nos. 59B/64B, 67B/8B.

14 Battalion Company Sergeant, 3rd Regt of Foot ("The Buffs"), circa 1801

15 Miriam Pickard (first Guide Commissioner)

(Des G. Vasarhelyi. Litho Format)

1981 (15 Mar). Military Uniforms (1st series). T **14** and similar vert designs. Multicolored. W w **14**. P 14½.

71	5c. Type **14**...	10	10
72	30c. Battalion Company Officer, 45th Regt of Foot, 1796–97..................................	15	10
73	55c. Battalion Company Officer, 9th Regt of Foot, 1790..	15	10
74	$2.50 Grenadier, 38th Regt of Foot, 1751.....	45	35
71/4 Set of 4..		70	55

See also Nos. 110/13 and 220/6.

(Des D. Shults. Litho Questa)

1981 (23–14 June). Royal Wedding. Horiz designs as T **92a/b** of Monserrat. Multicoloured.

(a) W w **14**. P 14.

75	55c. *Saudadoes*.......................................	10	10
	aw. Wmk inverted................................	18·00	
	b. Sheetlet. No. 75×6 and No. 76...........	1·10	
	bw. Wmk inverted...............................	£130	
76	55c. Prince Charles and Lady Diana Spencer...	40	40
	aw. Wmk inverted................................	65·00	
77	$2.50 *Royal George*................................	25	30
	aw. Wmk inverted................................	18·00	
	b. Sheetlet. No. 77×6 and No. 78...........	2·00	

ST. KITTS-NEVIS / St. Kitts

	bw. Wmk inverted	£130	
78	$2.50 As No. 76	70	70
	aw. Wmk inverted	65·00	
79	$4 Britannia	35	50
	a. Sheetlet. No. 79×6 and No. 80	2·50	
80	$4 As No. 76	75	1·00
75/80 Set of 6		2·25	2·75
MS81	120×109 mm. $5 As No. 76. Wmk sideways. P 12 (14 Dec)	1·00	1·00

(b) Booklet stamps. No wmk. P 12 (19 Nov)

82	55c. As No. 76	15	30
	a. Booklet pane. No. 82×4 with margins all round	55	
83	$2.50 As No. 78	65	1·25
	a. Booklet pane. No. 83×2 with margins all round		1·25

Nos. 75/80 were printed in sheetlets of seven stamps of the same face value, each containing six of the "Royal Yacht" design and one of the larger design showing Prince Charles and Lady Diana.

Nos. 82/3 come from $9.40 stamp booklets.

(Des Jennifer Toombs. Litho Walsall)

1981 (21 Sept). 50th Anniv of St. Kitts Girl Guide Movement. T **15** and similar vert designs. Multicoloured. W w **14**. P 14.

84	5c. Type **15**	10	10
85	30c. Lady Baden-Powell's visit, 1964	15	10
86	55c. Visit of Princess Alice, 1960	25	10
87	$2 Thinking-Day parade, 1980's	45	35
84/7 Set of 4		80	45

16 Stained-glass Windows

17 Admiral Samuel Hood

(Des Jennifer Toombs. Litho Format)

1981 (30 Nov). Christmas. T **16** and similar vert designs showing stained-glass windows. W w **14**. P 13×14.

88	5c. multicoloured	10	10
89	30c. multicoloured	10	10
90	55c. multicoloured	15	10
	w. Wmk inverted	22·00	
91	$3 multicoloured	50	50
88/91 Set of 4		75	60

(Des D. Shults. Litho Format)

1982 (15 Mar). Bicentenary of Brimstone Hill Siege. T **17** and similar horiz designs. W w **14** (sideways). P 14.

92	15c. multicoloured	10	10
93	55c. multicoloured	20	10
MS94	96×71 mm. $5 black, red-orange & yellow-brown	1·10	1·10

Designs:—55c. Marquis De Bouillé; $5 Battle scene.

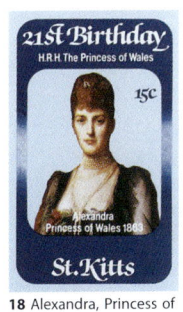

18 Alexandra, Princess of Wales, 1863

(19) ROYAL BABY

(Des D. Shults and J. Cooter. Litho Format)

1982 (22 June). 21st Birthday of Princess of Wales. T **18** and similar vert designs. Multicoloured. W w **14**. P 13½×14.

95	15c. Type **18**	10	10
	w. Wmk inverted	7·00	
96	55c. Coat of arms of Alexandra of Denmark	15	15
97	$6 Diana, Princess of Wales	55	80
	w. Wmk inverted	5·00	
95/7 Set of 3		70	85

1982 (12 July). Birth of Prince William of Wales. Nos. 95/7 optd with T **19**.

98	15c. Type **18**	10	10
	a. Opt inverted	7·00	
	b. Opt omitted (in pair with normal)	15·00	
	w. Wmk inverted	15·00	
99	55c. Coat of arms of Alexandra of Denmark	15	15
100	$6 Diana, Princess of Wales	55	80
	w. Wmk inverted	8·00	
98/100 Set of 3		70	85

The overprint which resulted in No. 986 was applied diagonally with most of the stamps in the sheet bearing partial overprints or parts of two overprints.

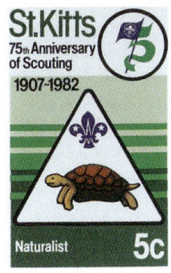

20 Naturalist Badge

21 Santa with Christmas Tree and Gifts

(Des Philatelists (1980) Ltd. Litho Questa)

1982 (18 Aug). 75th Anniv of Boy Scout Movement. T **20** and similar vert designs. Multicoloured. W w **14**. P 14×13½.

101	5c. Type **20**	10	10
102	55c. Rescuer badge	30	15
103	$2 First Aid badge	80	90
101/3 Set of 3		1·10	1·00

(Des Marcel Frazer (5c.), Sinclair Herbert (55c.), Marijka Grey ($1.10), Gary Bowrin ($3). Litho Format)

1982 (20 Oct). Christmas. Children's Paintings. T **21** and similar horiz designs. Multicoloured. W w **14** (sideways). P 14×13½.

104	5c. Type **21**	10	10
105	55c. The Inn	15	10
106	$1.10 Three Kings	20	15
107	$3 Annunciation	40	40
104/7 Set of 4		65	60

22 Cruise Ship *Stella Oceanis* at Basseterre

23 Sir William Smith (founder)

(Des G. Drummond. Litho Format)

1983 (14 Mar). Commonwealth Day. T **22** and similar horiz design. Multicoloured. W w **14** (sideways). P 14.

108	55c. Type **22**	15	10
109	$2 *Queen Elizabeth 2* at Basseterre	35	40

(Des G. Vasarhelyi. Litho Format)

1983 (25 May). Military Uniforms (2nd series). Vert designs as T **14**. Multicoloured. W w **14**. P 14½.

110	15c. Light Company Private, 15th Regt of Foot, *circa* 1814	20	10
111	30c. Battalion Company Officer, 15th Regt of Foot, *circa* 1780	30	15
112	55c. Light Company Officer, 5th Regt of Foot, *circa* 1822	30	20
113	$2.50 Battalion Company Officer, 11th Regt of Foot, *circa* 1804	60	1·60
110/13 Set of 4		1·25	1·75

ST. KITTS-NEVIS / St. Kitts

(Des J. Cooter. Litho Format)

1983 (27 July). Centenary of the Boys' Brigade. T **23** and similar vert designs. Multicoloured. W w **14**. P 13½.

114	10c. Type **23**	25	10
115	45c. BB members on steps of Sandy Point Methodist Church	30	10
116	50c. Brigade drummers	30	10
117	$3 Boys' Brigade badge	70	2·25
114/17 Set of 4		1·40	2·25

(24) (24a) **25** Montgolfier Balloon, 1783

1983 (19 Sept). Nos. 55, 59/63 and 66/70 optd as T **24** (horiz 20 mm long on Nos. 119/28).

A. Without imprint date

118A	5c. Type **12**	15	10
	c. Optd with T **24 a** (local opt)	7·00	9·00
	ca. Opt inverted (reading upwards)	25·00	
119A	15c. Type **13**	7·00	1·00
122A	30c. Green-throated Carib	25·00	25·00
124A	55c. Brown Pelican	50	50
125A	$1 Lesser Antillean Bullfinch	10·00	10·00
126A	$2.50 Zenaida Dove	2·00	2·00
127A	$5 American Kestrel	2·50	2·75
128A	$10 Antillean Crested Hummingbird	6·00	6·00
118A/28A Set of 8		42·00	42·00

B. With imprint date at foot of design

118B	5c. Type **12**	15	30
	a. Opt inverted	32·00	
	b. Pair, one without opt	80·00	
	c. Optd with T **24a** (local opt)	1·50	2·00
	ca. Opt inverted (reading upwards)	6·00	
119B	15c. Type **13**	30	10
	a. Opt double	7·00	
120B	20c. Scaly-breasted Thrasher	35	10
121B	25c. Grey Kingbird	40	10
	a. Opt inverted	12·00	
122B	30c. Green-throated Carib	45	15
123B	40c. Turnstone	50	20
124B	55c. Brown Pelican	55	30
	a. Opt inverted	8·50	
125B	$1 Lesser Antillean Bullfinch	1·00	75
126B	$2.50 Zenaida Dove	1·75	2·25
127B	$5 American Kestrel	2·75	4·00
128B	$10 Antillean Crested Hummingbird	4·00	6·00
118B/28B Set of 11		11·00	12·50

Imprint dates: "1982", Nos. 118B/19B, 121B/2B, 127B; "1983", Nos. 119B/28B.

(Des A. Theobald. Litho Format)

1983 (28 Sept). Bicentenary of Manned Flight. T **25** and similar multicoloured designs. W w **15** (sideways on Nos. 130/3). P 14.

129	10c. Type **25**	10	10
130	45c. Sikorsky *Russky Vityaz* biplane (*horiz*)	15	10
131	50c. Lockheed L-1011 TriStar 500 *Flamingo* (*horiz*)	15	15
132	$2.50 Bell XS-1 (*horiz*)	1·00	90
129/32 Set of 4		1·25	1·10
MS133 108×145 mm. Nos. 129/32		1·25	1·25

26 Star over West Indian Town

27 Parrot in Tree

(Des Jennifer Toombs. Litho Format)

1983 (7 Nov). Christmas. T **26** and similar horiz designs. Multicoloured. W w **15** (sideways*). P 14.

134	15c. Type **26**	10	10
135	30c. Shepherds watching Star	15	10
	w. Wmk POST OFFICE reading upwards	24·00	
136	55c. Mary and Joseph	15	10
137	$2.50 The Nativity	30	40
134/7 Set of 4		60	60
MS138 130×130 mm. Nos. 134/7. Wmk upright		60	1·10
	w. Wmk inverted	75·00	

*The normal sideways watermark shows "POST OFFICE" reading downwards.

(Des Court House Studio. Litho Format)

1984 (30 Jan). Batik Designs (1st series). T **27** and similar vert designs. W w **15**. P 14×13½.

139	45c. multicoloured	15	10
	w. Wmk inverted	14·00	
140	50c. multicoloured	15	10
	w. Wmk inverted	15·00	
141	$1.50 new blue, bistre-yellow and & bright magenta	40	70
142	$3 multicoloured	65	1·75
	w. Wmk inverted	30·00	
139/42 Set of 4		1·25	2·40

Designs:—50c. Man under coconut tree; $1.50, Women with fruit; $3 Butterflies.

See also Nos. 169/72.

28 Cushion Star

(Des G. Drummond. Litho J.W.)

1984 (4 July). Marine Wildlife. T **28** and similar multicoloured designs. W w **15** (sideways* on 5c. to 75c.). P 14.

143	5c. Type **28**	30	40
	w. Wmk POST OFFICE reading downwards	1·00	
144	10c. Rough File shell (*Lima scabra*)	35	40
	w. Wmk POST OFFICE reading downwards	1·00	
145	15c. Red-lined Cleaning Shrimp	35	15
146	20c. Bristleworm	35	15
147	25c. Flamingo Tongue (*Cyphoma gibbosus*)	40	15
148	30c. Christmas Tree Worm	40	20
149	40c. Pink-tipped Anemone	55	25
150	50c. Smallmouth Grunt	55	30
151	60c. Glass-eyed Snapper	1·25	75
152	75c. Reef Squirrelfish	90	70
153	$1 Sea Fans and Flamefish (*vert*)	1·00	60
154	$2.50 Reef Butterflyfish (*vert*)	2·25	3·50
155	$5 Black-barred Soldierfish (*vert*)	4·50	14·00
	w. Wmk inverted	15·00	
156	$10 Cocoa Damselfish (*vert*)	6·00	14·00
	w. Wmk inverted	15·00	
143/56 Set of 14		17·00	32·00

*The normal sideways watermark shows "POST OFFICE" reading upwards.

For 10c., 60c., $5 and $10 with watermark w **16** and imprint dates see Nos. 194/206.

29 Agriculture

(Des G. Vasarhelyi. Litho Questa)

1984 (15 Aug). 25th Anniv of 4-H Organisation. T **29** and similar horiz designs. Multicoloured. W w **15** (sideways). P 14.

157	30c. Type **29**	15	10
158	55c. Animal husbandry	20	15
159	$1.10 The 4-H Pledge	35	60
160	$3 On parade	65	1·25
157/60 Set of 4		1·25	1·90

IMPERFORATES. Issues between Nos. 161 and 184 exist imperforate. Such items are not listed as there is no evidence that they fulfil the criteria outlined on page x of this catalogue.

30 Construction of Royal St. Kitts Hotel

(Des K. Tatem (15c.), Tessa Wattley (30c.), Myrna Elcock and L. Freeman ($1.10), A. Williams ($3), adapted Jennifer Toombs. Litho Format)

1984 (18 Sept). First Anniv of Independence of St. Kitts–Nevis. T **30** and similar multicoloured designs. W w **15** (sideways on 15, 30c.). P 14.

161	15c. Type **30**	15	10
162	30c. Independence celebrations	20	15
163	$1.10 National Anthem and aerial view (*vert*)	40	60
164	$3 "Dawn of a New Day" (*vert*)	1·00	1·40
161/4 *Set of 4*		1·60	2·00

31 Opening Presents

(Des Jennifer Toombs. Litho Questa)

1984 (1 Nov). Christmas. T **31** and similar horiz designs. Multicoloured. W w **15** (sideways). P 14.

165	15c. Type **31**	15	10
166	60c. Singing carols	45	35
167	$1 Nativity play	75	60
168	$2 Leaving church on Christmas Day	1·40	1·10
165/8 *Set of 4*		2·50	1·90

(Des Court House Studio. Litho Format)

1985 (6 Feb). Batik Designs (2nd series). Horiz designs as T **27**. W w **15** (sideways). P 13½×14.

169	15c. black, bright green and light green	15	10
170	40c. black, bright greenish blue and bright new blue	30	15
171	60c. black, orange-vermilion and vermilion	45	25
172	$3 black, lake-brown and orange-brown	1·25	2·25
169/72 *Set of 4*		1·90	2·50

Designs:—15c. Country bus; 40c. Donkey cart; 60c. Rum shop and man on bicycle; $3 *Polynesia* (cruise schooner).

32 Container Ship *Tropic Jade*

33 James Derrick Cardin (leading Freemason)

(Des J. Cooter. Litho Format)

1985 (27 Mar). Ships. T **32** and similar horiz designs. Multicoloured. W w **15** (sideways). P 13½×14.

173	40c. Type **32**	1·00	30
174	$1.20 *Atlantic Clipper* (schooner)	2·00	1·50
175	$2 *Mandalay* (schooner)	2·25	2·50
176	$2 *Cunard Countess* (liner)	2·25	2·50
173/6 *Set of 4*		6·75	6·00

(Des G. Vasarhelyi. Litho Format)

1985 (9 Nov). 150th Anniv of Mount Olive S.C. Masonic Lodge. T **33** and similar multicoloured designs. W w **15** (sideways on 15, 75c., and $3). P 15.

177	15c. Type **33**	65	30
178	75c. Banner of Mount Olive Lodge	1·40	1·25
179	$1.20 Masonic symbols (*horiz*)	1·40	3·00
180	$3 Lodge Charter (1835)	1·75	5·00
177/80 *Set of 4*		4·75	8·50

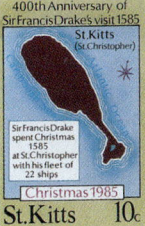

34 Map of St. Kitts

35 Queen Elizabeth and Prince Philip on St. Kitts

(Des. J. Cooter. Litho Format)

1985 (27 Nov). Christmas. 400th Anniv of Sir Francis Drake's Visit. T **34** and similar vert designs. Multicoloured. P 15.

181	10c. Type **34**	30	15
182	40c. *Golden Hind*	60	35
183	60c. Sir Francis Drake	60	50
184	$3 Drake's heraldic shield	75	4·25
181/4 *Set of 4*		2·00	4·75

(Des D. Miller. Litho B.D.T.)

1986 (9 July). 60th Birthday of Queen Elizabeth II. T **35** and similar vert designs. Multicoloured. P 13½.

185	10c. Type **35**	20	10
186	20c. Queen Elizabeth on St. Kitts	30	15
187	40c. At Trooping the Colour	60	30
188	$3 In Sweden	2·00	3·25
185/8 *Set of 4*		2·75	3·25

35a Prince Andrew and Miss Sarah Ferguson

(Des D. Miller. Litho Walsall)

1986 (23 July). Royal Wedding. T **35a** and similar square design. Multicoloured. W w **16**. P 14½×14.

189	15c. Type **35a**	15	10
190	$2.50 Prince Andrew	1·00	2·00

36 Family on Smallholding

(37)

(Des K. Tatem (15c.), A. Williams ($1.20), adapted G. Vasarhelyi. Litho Questa)

1986 (18 Sept). Agriculture Exhibition. T **36** and similar horiz design. Multicoloured. W w **16** (sideways). P 13½×14.

191	15c. Type **36**	20	10
192	$1.20 Hands holding people, computers and crops	1·25	1·60

(Litho Questa)

1986 (5 Nov)–**88**. As Nos. 144, 151 and 155/6 but W w **16** (sideways on 10, 60c.). With imprint date. P 14.

194	10c. Rough File Shell	1·25	85
201	60c. Glass-eyed Snapper (17.8.88)	2·50	1·60
205	$5 Black-barred Soldierfish (*vert*) (17.8.88)	6·00	10·00
206	$10 Cocoa Damselfish (*vert*) (17.8.88)	11·00	15·00
194/206 *Set of 4*		19·00	25·00

Imprint dates: "1986", No. 194; "1988", Nos. 194, 201, 205/6.

1986 (12 Nov). 40th Anniv of United Nations Week. Nos. 185/8 optd with T **37** in gold.

207	10c. Type **35**	15	15
208	20c. Queen Elizabeth on St. Kitts	25	20

ST. KITTS-NEVIS / St. Kitts

209	40c. At Troopping the Colour		30	30
210	$3 In Sweden		1·00	3·25
	a. Opt triple 75			
207/10 Set of 4			1·50	3·50

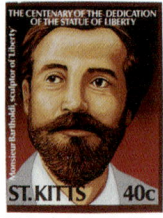

38 Adult Green Monkey with Young

39 Frederic Bartholdi (sculptor)

(Des Doreen McGuinness. Litho Walsall)

1986 (1 Dec). Endangered Species. Green Monkeys on St. Kitts. T **38** and similar vert designs. Multicoloured. W w **16**. P 14×13½.

211	15c. Type **38**	3·00	50
212	20c. Adult on ground	3·25	50
213	60c. Young monkey in tree	6·50	2·50
214	$1 Adult grooming young monkey	6·50	4·50
211/14 Set of 4		17·00	7·25

(Des D. Miller. Litho Format)

1986 (17 Dec). Centenary of Statue of Liberty. T **39** and similar multicoloured designs. W w **16** (sideways on 60c., $1.50). P 14.

215	40c. Type **39**	30	30
216	60c. Torch (1876) and head (1878) on exhibition (*horiz*)	40	60
217	$1.50 *Isere* (French warship) carrying Statue (*horiz*)	1·00	1·75
218	$3 Statue of Liberty, Paris, 1884	1·25	3·00
215/18 Set of 4		2·75	5·00
MS219 70×85 mm. $3.50, Head of Statue of Liberty		2·00	3·50

40 Officer, 9th Regt (East Norfolk), 1792

41 Sugar Cane Warehouse

(Des C. Collins. Litho Format)

1987 (25 Feb). Military Uniforms (3rd series). T **40** and similar vert designs. Multicoloured. W w **16**. P 14½.

220	15c. Type **40**	40	30
221	15c. Officer, Regt de Neustrie, 1779	40	30
222	40c. Sergeant, 3rd Regt ("The Buffs"), 1801	65	45
223	40c. Officer, French Artillery, 1812	65	45
224	$2 Light Company Private, 5th Regt, 1778	1·25	3·00
225	$2 Grenadier of the Line, 1796	1·25	3·00
220/5 Set of 6		4·00	6·75
MS226 121×145 mm. Nos. 220/5		6·75	8·00

The two designs for each value were printed in sheets of 50 containing two panes 5×5 with the British uniform depicted on the left-hand pane and the French on the right.

(Des G. Vasarhelyi. Litho Format)

1987 (15 Apr). Sugar Cane Industry. T **41** and similar vert designs. Multicoloured (colour of panel behind "ST. KITTS" given). W w **16**. P 14.

227	15c. greenish yellow (Type **41**)	20	30
	a. Horiz strip of 5. Nos. 227/31	90	1·50
228	15c. cinnamon	20	30
229	15c. lilac	20	30
230	15c. azure	20	30
231	15c. pale greenish blue	20	30
232	75c. bright green	25	85
	a. Horiz strip of 5. Nos. 232/6	1·10	3·75
233	75c. lilac	25	85
234	75c. dull green	25	85
235	75c. orange-yellow	25	85
236	75c. greenish blue	25	85
227/36 Set of 10		2·00	5·25

Designs:—Nos. 227/31, Sugar cane factory; Nos. 232/6, Loading sugar train.

Nos. 227/31 and 232/6 were each printed together, *se-tenant*, in horizontal strips of five throughout the sheets, each strip forming a composite design.

42 B.W.I.A. L-1011 TriStar 500

43 *Hygrocybe occidentalis*

(Des T. Hadler. Litho Format)

1987 (24 June). Aircraft visiting St. Kitts. T **42** and similar horiz designs. Multicoloured. W w **14** (sideways). P 14.

237	40c. Type **42**	75	30
238	60c. LIAT Hawker Siddeley Super 748	95	60
239	$1.20 WIA de Havilland DHC-6 Twin Otter 300	1·50	3·00
240	$3 American Eagle Aerospatiale/Aeritalia ATR 42	2·75	5·00
237/40 Set of 4		5·25	8·00

(Des I. Loe. Litho Questa)

1987 (26 Aug). Fungi. T **43** and similar vert designs. Multicoloured. W w **16**. P 14.

241	15c. Type **43**	80	20
242	40c. *Marasmius haematocephalus*	1·25	40
243	$1.20 *Psilocybe cubensis*	2·75	2·75
	w. Wmk inverted	12·00	
244	$2 *Hygrocybe acutoconica*	3·50	3·50
245	$3 *Boletellus cubensis*	4·00	4·50
241/5 Set of 5		11·00	10·00

44 Carnival Clown

(Des Rose Cameron-Smith. Litho Format)

1987 (28 Oct). Christmas. T **44** and similar square designs showing different clowns. Multicoloured. W w **16** (sideways). P 14½.

246	15c. multicoloured	25	15
247	40c. multicoloured	55	30
248	$1 multicoloured	1·25	1·40
249	$3 multicoloured	2·50	4·50
246/9 Set of 4		4·00	5·75

See also Nos. 266/9.

45 Ixora

(Des Josephine Martin. Litho Questa)

1988 (20 Jan). Flowers. T **45** and similar vert designs. Multicoloured. W w **16**. P 14½×14.

250	15c. Type **45**	30	15
251	40c. Shrimp Plant	55	30
252	$1 Poinsettia	1·00	1·40
253	$3 Honolulu Rose	2·50	4·50
250/3 Set of 4		4·00	5·75

ST. KITTS-NEVIS / St. Kitts

46 Fort Thomas Hotel

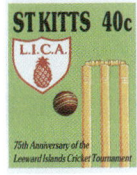

47 Ball, Wicket and Leeward Islands Cricket Association Emblem

(Des L. Curtis. Litho Walsall)

1988 (20 Apr). Tourism (1st series). Hotels. T **46** and similar horiz designs. Multicoloured. W w **14** (sideways). P 14×14½.
254	60c. Type **46**.......................................		70	70
255	60c. Fairview Inn.......................................		70	70
256	60c. Frigate Bay Beach Hotel....................		70	70
257	60c. Ocean Terrace Inn.............................		70	70
258	$3 The Golden Lemon.............................		2·25	2·75
259	$3 Royal St. Kitts Casino and Jack Tar Village..		2·25	2·75
260	$3 Rawlins Plantation Hotel and Restaurant.		2·25	2·75
254/60	Set of 7...		8·50	10·00

See also Nos. 270/5.

(Des Joan Thompson. Litho Walsall)

1988 (13 July). 75th Anniv of Leeward Islands Cricket Tournament. T **47** and similar vert design. Multicoloured. W w **14**. P 13×13½.
261	40c. Type **47**.....................................	2·25	30
262	$3 Cricket match at Warner Park.............	4·50	4·50

48 Flag of St. Kitts-Nevis

49 Red Cross Nurse with Hospital Patient

(Des L. Curtis. Litho Questa)

1988 (19 Sept). Fifth Anniv of Independence. T **48** and similar vert designs. Multicoloured. W w **16**. P 14½×14.
263	15c. Type **48**.....................................	1·25	30
264	60c. Arms of St. Kitts.............................	1·25	95
MS265	61×53 mm. $5 Princess Margaret presenting Constitutional Instrument to Prime Minister Kennedy Simmonds, 1983. W w **16**......................	4·00	4·25

(Des Rose Cameron-Smith. Litho Format)

1988 (2 Nov). Christmas. Square designs as T **44** showing carnival masqueraders. W w **14** (sideways). P 14½.
266	15c. multicoloured.................................	10	10
267	40c. multicoloured.................................	20	25
268	80c. multicoloured.................................	40	55
269	$3 multicoloured...................................	1·25	2·50
266/9	Set of 4..	1·75	3·00

(Des L. Curtis. Litho Format)

1989 (25 Jan). Tourism (2nd series). Colonial Architecture. Horiz designs as T **46**. Multicoloured. W w **16** (sideways). P 14.
270	20c. Georgian house.............................	20	20
271	20c. Colonial-style house.......................	20	20
272	$1 Romney Manor.................................	50	90
273	$1 Lavington Great House......................	50	90
274	$2 Government House...........................	70	1·75
275	$2 Treasury Building..............................	70	1·75
270/5	Set of 6..	2·50	5·00

For a redrawn version of No. 275 in a miniature sheet, see No. MS400.

(Des C. Collins. Litho Format)

1989 (8 May). 125th Anniv of International Red Cross. T **49** and similar vert designs. Multicoloured. W w **16**. P 14×14½.
276	40c. multicoloured.................................	30	30
277	$1 multicoloured...................................	65	75
278	$3 orange-vermilion and black...............	1·75	3·25
276/8	Set of 3..	2·40	3·75

Designs:—$1 Loading patient into ambulance; $3 125th anniversary logo.

50 Battle on the Champ-de-Mars

(Des D. Miller. Litho B.D.T.)

1989 (7 July). Philexfrance 89 International Stamp Exhibition, Paris. Sheet 115×99 mm. W w **16**. P 14.
MS279	**50** $5 multicoloured............................	3·25	3·75

50a Lunar Rover on Moon

(Des A. Theobald ($5), D. Miller (others). Litho Questa)

1989 (20 July). 20th Anniv of First Manned Landing on Moon. T **50a**. W w **16** (sideways on 20c., $1). P 14×13½ (10c., $2) or 14 (others).
280	10c. Lunar rover on Moon......................	10	10
281	20c. Crew of "Apollo 13" (30×30 mm).....	10	10
282	$1 "Apollo 13" emblem (30×30 mm).....	45	65
283	$2 "Apollo 13" splashdown, South Pacific..	95	1·50
280/3	Set of 4..	1·40	2·00
MS284	100×83 mm. $5 Aldrin leaving "Apollo 11" lunar module. Wmk inverted. P 14×13½...........	3·50	4·00

51 Outline Map of St. Kitts

(Des D. Miller. Litho B.D.T.)

1989 (25 Oct). W w **16**. P 15×14.
285	**51**	10c. deep mauve and black...............	20	30
286		15c. bright carmine and black............	25	10
287		20c. yellow-orange and black............	25	10
288		40c. yellow and black.......................	40	20
289		60c. bright blue and black.................	60	50
290		$1 yellow-green and black................	90	1·40
285/90	Set of 6..		2·40	2·25

52 *Santa Mariagallante* passing St. Kitts, 1493

(Des L. Curtis. Litho Questa)

1989 (8 Nov). 500th Anniv of Discovery of America (1992) by Columbus (1st issue). T **52** and similar horiz designs. Multicoloured. W w **16** (sideways). P 14.
291	15c. Type **52**.....................................	2·25	30
292	80c. Arms of Columbus and map of fourth voyage, 1502–04...............................	3·75	1·75

ST. KITTS-NEVIS / St. Kitts

293	$1 Navigation instruments, c. 1500		3·75	1·75
294	$5 Columbus and map of second voyage, 1493–96		11·00	12·00
291/4 Set of 4			19·00	14·00

See also Nos. 359/60.

53 Poinciana Tree

54 *Junonia evarete*

(Des G. Vasarhelyi. Litho Walsall)

1989 (17 Nov). World Stamp Expo '89 International Stamp Exhibition, Washington. T **53** and similar horiz designs. Multicoloured. W w **14** (sideways). P 14.

295	15c. Type **53**	50	10
296	40c. Fort George Citadel, Brimstone Hill	90	30
297	$1 Private, Light Company, 5th Foot, 1778	2·50	1·40
298	$3 St. George's Anglican Church	3·25	5·00
295/8 Set of 4		6·50	6·00

(Des I. Loe. Litho B.D.T.)

1990 (6 June). Butterflies. T **54** and similar horiz designs. Multicoloured. W w **14** (sideways). P 13½×14.

299	15c. Type **54**	1·00	40
300	40c. *Anartia jatrophae*	1·75	40
301	60c. *Heliconius charitonia*	1·75	80
302	$3 *Biblis hyperia*	3·75	6·00
299/302 Set of 4		7·50	7·00

(55)   **56** Brimstone Hill

1990 (6 June). EXPO 90 International Garden and Greenery Exhibition, Osaka. Nos. 299/302 optd with T **55**.

303	15c. Type **54**	1·25	50
304	40c. *Anartia jatrophae*	2·00	50
305	60c. *Heliconius charitonia*	2·00	85
306	$3 *Biblis hyperia*	4·25	6·50
303/6 Set of 4		8·50	7·50

(Des D. Miller. Litho Questa)

1990 (30 June). 300th Anniv of English Bombardment of Brimstone Hill. T **56** and similar horiz designs. Multicoloured. W w **16** (sideways). P 14.

307	15c. Type **56**	45	20
308	40c. Restored Brimstone Hill fortifications	70	30
309	60c. 17th-century English marine and Fort Charles under attack	1·25	1·60
	a. Horiz pair. Nos. 309/10	4·75	6·50
310	$3 English sailors firing cannon	3·50	5·25
307/10 Set of 4		5·50	6·50

Nos. 307/9 were printed in complete sheets, each containing one value. No. 309 also exists *se-tenant*, as a horizontal pair, with No. 310. Each pair shows a composite design across the two stamps with no margin at the left of the 60c. or at the right of the $3.

57 Supermarine Spitfire Mk Vb *St. Kitts Nevis I*, 71 Squadron

(Des A. Theobald. Litho B.D.T.)

1990 (15 Sept). 50th Anniv of Battle of Britain. Sheet 103×76 mm, containing T **57** and similar horiz design. Multicoloured. W w **16** (sideways). P 14.

MS311	$3 Type **57**; $3 Supermarine Spitfire Mk Vb *St. Kitts Nevis II*, 345 Squadron	16·00	16·00

58 *Romney* (freighter)

(Des S. Williams. Litho B.D.T.)

1990 (10 Oct). Ships. T **58** and similar horiz designs. Multicoloured. W w **14** (sideways). P 14.

312	10c. Type **58**	70	50
313	15c. *Baralt* (freighter)	1·00	35
314	20c. *Wear* (mail steamer)	1·00	30
315	25c. *Sunmount* (freighter)	1·00	30
316	40c. *Inanda* (cargo liner)	1·25	30
317	50c. *Alcoa Partner* (freighter)	1·25	30
318	60c. *Dominica* (freighter)	1·40	35
319	80c. *C.G.M Provence* (container ship)	1·50	55
320	$1 *Director* (freighter)	1·50	80
321	$1.20 Barque	2·00	1·75
322	$2 *Chignecto* (packet steamer)	3·00	3·00
323	$3 *Berbice* (mail steamer)	3·25	4·25
324	$5 *Vamos* (freighter)	4·50	6·50
325	$10 *Federal Maple* (freighter)	7·00	10·00
312/25 Set of 14		27·00	26·00

For 10c. watermarked w **16** (sideways) see No. 413.
For miniature sheet containing the $3 see No. MS472.

59 Single Fork Game

(Des G. Vasarhelyi. Litho Questa)

1990 (14 Nov). Christmas. Traditional Games. T **59** and similar horiz designs. Multicoloured. W w **16** (sideways). P 14.

326	10c. Type **59**	15	10
327	15c. Boulder breaking	15	10
328	40c. Double fork	30	30
329	$3 The run up	1·75	4·00
326/9 Set of 4		2·10	4·00

60 White Periwinkle

(Des Annette Robinson. Litho Cartor)

1991 (8 May). Flowers. T **60** and similar multicoloured designs. W w **14** (sideways on 10, 40c.). P 14×13½ (10, 40c.) or 13½×14 (others).

330	10c. Type **60**	70	20
331	40c. Pink Oleander	1·40	30
332	60c. Pink Periwinkle (*vert*)	1·90	70
333	$2 White Oleander (*vert*)	3·25	4·75
330/3 Set of 4		6·50	5·50

61 Census Logo

(Des G. Vasarbelyi, Litho B.D.T)

1991 (13 May). National Census. W w **16**. P 14.

334	**61**	15c. multicoloured	30	15

ST. KITTS-NEVIS / St. Kitts

335	$2.40 multicoloured	2·50	3·25

The $2.40 differs from Type **61** by showing "ST. KITTS" in a curved panel.

61a Prince Philip
62 Nassau Grouper

(Des D. Miller. Litho Quests)

1991 (17 June). 65th Birthday of Queen Elizabeth II and 70th Birthday of Prince Philip. T **61a** and similar vert designs. W w **16** (sideways). P 14½×14.

336	$1.20 T**61**a	1·00	1·25
	a. Horiz pair. Nos. 336/7 separated by label	2·00	2·50
337	$1.80 Queen holding bouquet of flowers	1·00	1·25

Nos. 336/7 were printed together *se-tenant*, is sheetlets of 10 (2×5) with designs alternating and the vertical rows separated by inscribed labels.

(Des G. Drummond. Litho Questa)

1991 (28 Aug). Fish. T **62** and similar horiz designs. Multicoloured. W w **14** (sideways). P 14.

338	10c. Type **62**	50	20
339	60c. Hogfish	1·25	50
340	$1 Red Hind	2·00	1·50
341	$3 Porkfish	3·50	5·50
338/41 Set of 4		6·50	7·00

63 School of Continuing Studies, St. Kitts, and Chancellor Sir Shridath Ramphal

(Des G. Vasarhelyi. Litho Questa)

1991 (28 Sept). 40th Anniv of University of West Indies. T **63** and similar horiz designs. Multicoloured. W w **16** (sideways). P 14.

342	15c. Type **63**	40	15
343	50c. Administration Building, Barbados	70	40
344	$1 Engineering Building, Trinidad and Tobago	1·25	1·40
345	$3 Mona Campus, Jamaica, and Sir Shridath Ramphal	3·00	5·00
342/5 Set of 4		4·75	6·25

64 Whipping The Bull

(Des Marijka Grey and G. Vasarhelyi. Litho Walsall)

1991 (6 Nov). Christmas. "The Bull" (Carnival play). T **64** and similar horiz designs. Multicoloured. W w **14** (sideways). P 14.

346	10c. Type **64**	40	10
347	15c. Death of The Bull	40	10
348	60c. Cast of characters and musicians	1·25	60
349	$3 The Bull in procession	3·00	5·00
346/9 Set of 4		4·50	5·00

64a St. Kitts Coastline

(Des D. Miller. Litho Questa ($3), Leigh-Mardon Ltd, Melbourne (others))

1992 (6 Feb). 40th Anniv of Queen Elizabeth II's Accession. T **64a** and similar horiz designs Multicoloured. W w **14** (sideways) ($3) or w **16** (sideways) (others). P 14.

350	10c. Type **64a**	40	10
351	40c. Warner Park Pavilion	2·00	50
352	60c. Brimstone Hill	75	40
353	$1 Three portraits of Queen Elizabeth	1·00	1·00
354	$3 Queen Elizabeth II	1·90	2·75
350/4 Set of 5		5·50	4·25

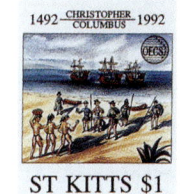

65 Map of St. Kitts-Nevis
66 Columbus meeting Amerindians

(Des L. Curtis. Litho Enschedé)

1992 (8 May). 50th Anniv of St. Kitts–Nevis Red Cross Society. T **65** and similar horiz designs. Multicoloured. W w **14** (sideways). P 14½×14.

355	10c. Type **65**	1·50	60
356	20c. St. Kitts-Nevis flag	2·25	45
357	50c. Red Cross House, St. Kitts	1·50	80
358	$2.40 Henri Dunant	3·50	5·50
355/8 Set of 4		7·75	6·50

(Adapted G. Vasarhelyi. Litho Cartor)

1992 (6 July). Organization of East Caribbean States. 500th Anniv of Discovery of America by Columbus (2nd issue). T **66** and similar vert design. Multicoloured. W w **14**. P 13.

359	$1 Type **66**	1·75	1·25
360	$2 Ships approaching island	3·50	4·00

67 Fountain, Independence Square
68 Joseph and Mary travelling to Bethlehem

(Des D. Miller. Litho Enschedé)

1992 (19 Aug). Local Monuments. T **67** and similar vert designs. Multicoloured. W w **14**. P 12½×13.

361	25c. Type **67**	25	20
362	50c. Berkeley Memorial drinking fountain	35	35
363	80c. Sir Thomas Warner's tomb	55	65
364	$2 War memorial	1·10	2·50
361/4 Set of 4		2·00	3·25

(Des L. Curtis. Litho Questa)

1992 (28 Oct). Christmas. T **68** and similar vert designs. Multicoloured. W w **16**. P 14½.

365	20c. Type **68**	30	20
366	25c. Shepherds and star	30	20
367	80c. Wise Men with gifts	65	55
368	$3 Mary, Joseph and Holy Child	1·75	4·00
365/8 Set of 4		2·75	4·50

(Des A. Theobald. Litho Questa)

1993 (1 Apr). 75th Anniv of Royal Air Force. Aircraft. Horiz designs as T **166** of Montserrat. Multicoloured. W w **14** (sideways). P 14.

369	25c. Short Singapore III	85	20
370	50c. Bristol Type **152** Beaufort Mk II	1·40	30
371	80c. Westland Whirlwind Series 3HAR10 helicopter	3·00	1·50
372	$1.60 English Electric Canberra T11	3·00	3·50
369/72 Set of 4		7·50	5·00
MS373	110×78 mm. $2 Handley Page 0/400; $2 Fairey Long Range monoplane; $2 Vickers Wellesley; $2 Sepecat Jaguar G.R.1	11·00	11·00

241

ST. KITTS-NEVIS / St. Kitts

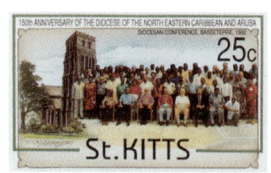

69 Members of Diocesan Conference, Basseterre, 1992

70 1953 Coronation 2c. Stamp and Ampulla

(Des G. Vasarhelyi. Litho Walsall)

1993 (21 May). 150th Anniv of Anglican Diocese of Northeastern. Caribbean and Aruba. T **69** and similar multicoloured designs. W w **16** (sideways on 25c., 80c.). P 13½×14 (horiz) or 14×13½ (vert).

374	25c. Type **69**	15	10
375	50c. Cathedral of St. John the Divine (*vert*)	40	35
376	80c. Coat of arms and motto	70	85
377	$2 The Right Revd. Daniel Davis (first bishop) (*vert*)	1·50	3·00
374/7	*Set of* 4	2·50	3·75

(Des D. Miller. Litho Walsall)

1993 (2 June). 40th Anniv of Coronation. T **70** and similar vert designs. Multicoloured. W w **16**. P 14½×14.

378	10c. Type **70**	40	20
379	25c. 1977 Silver Jubilee $1.50 stamp and anointing spoon	50	20
380	80c. 1977 Silver Jubilee 55c stamp and tassels	1·00	1·25
381	$2 1978 25th Anniv of Coronation stamps and sceptre	2·00	3·50
378/81	*Set of* 4	3·50	4·75

71 Flags of Girls Brigade and St. Kitt-Nevis

(Des G. Vasarhelyi. Litho Walsall)

1993 (1 July). Centenary of Girls Brigade. T **71** and similar horiz design. Multicoloured. W w **16** (sideways). P 13½×14.

382	80c. Type **71**	2·50	1·00
383	$3 Girls Brigade badge and coat of arms	4·00	4·50

72 Aspects of St. Kitts on Flag

73 *Hibiscus sabdariffa*

(Des Ruth Vaughan (20c.), S. Richards (80c.) P. Maynard ($3), adapted D. Miller. Litho B.D.T.)

1993 (10 Sept). Tenth Anniv of Independence. T **72** and similar horiz designs. Multicoloured. W w **14** (sideways). P 14.

384	20c. Type **72**	1·00	15
385	80c. Coat of arms and Independence anniversary logo	1·25	80
386	$3 Coat of arms and map	4·25	5·00
384/6	*Set of* 3	5·75	5·50

(Des Jennifer Toombs. Litho Cartor)

1993 (16 Nov). Christmas. Flowers. T **73** and similar vert designs. Multicoloured. W w **14**. P 13½×14.

387	25c. Type **73**	25	10
388	50c. *Euphorbia pulcherrima*	60	45
389	$1.60 *Euphorbia leucocephala*	1·75	3·00
387/9	*Set of* 3	2·40	3·25

74 Mesosaurus

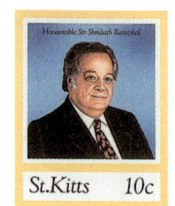

(**74a**)

75 Sir Shridath Ramphal

(Des N. Shewring. Litho B.D.T.)

1994 (18 Feb). Prehistoric Aquatic Reptiles. T **74** and similar vert designs. Multicoloured. W w **16**. P 14.

390	$1.20 Type **74**	1·40	1·75
	a. Horiz strip of 5. Nos. 390/4	6·25	7·75
391	$1.20 Placodus	1·40	1·75
392	$1.20 Liopleurodon	1·40	1·75
393	$1.20 Hydrotherosaurus	1·40	1·75
394	$1.20 Caretta	1·40	1·75
390/4	*Set of* 5	6·25	7·75

Nos. 390/4 were printed together, *se-tenant*, in horizontal strips of 5 throughout the sheet with the background forming a composite design.

1994 (18 Feb). Hong Kong '94 International Stamp Exhibition. Nos. 390/4 optd as T **74a**.

395	$1.20 Type **74**	1·90	2·25
	a. Horiz strip of 5. Nos. 395/9	8·50	10·00
396	$1.20 Placodus	1·90	2·25
397	$1.20 Liopleurodon	1·90	2·25
398	$1.20 Hydrotherosaurus	1·90	2·25
399	$1.20 Caretta	1·90	2·25
395/9	*Set of* 5	8·50	10·00

(Des L. Curtis and G. Vasarhelyi. Litho B.D.T.)

1994 (21 Mar). Centenary of Treasury Building. Sheet 73×58 mm. containing horiz design as No. 275, but with redrawn frame and inscriptions. W w **14** (sideways). P 13½.

MS400	$10 multicoloured	7·50	8·50

(Des D. Miller. Litho Questa)

1994 (13 July). First Recipients of Order of the Caribbean Community. T **75** and similar vert designs. Multicoloured. W w **14**. P 14½×14.

401	10c. Type **75**	30	50
	a. Horiz strip of 5. Nos. 401, 402×2, 403/4	1·10	1·90
402	10c. Star of Order	20	30
403	10c. Derek Walcott	30	50
404	10c. William Demas	30	50
405	$1 Type **75**	1·25	1·40
	a. Horiz strip of 5. Nos. 405, 406×2, 407/8	5·00	5·50
406	$1 As No. 402	1·00	1·00
407	$1 As No. 403	1·25	1·40
408	$1 As No. 404	1·25	1·40
401/8	*Set of* 8	5·25	6·25

Nos. 401/4 and 405/8 were printed together, *se-tenant*, in horizontal strips of 5 throughout the sheets with examples of Nos. 402 or 406 in the second and fourth positions in each strip.

76 Family singing Carols

(Des Jennifer Toombs. Litho B.D.T.)

1994 (31 Oct). Christmas. International Year of the Family. T **76** and similar horiz designs. Multicoloured. W w **14** (sideways). P 13½.

409	25c. Type **76**	15	10
410	25c. Family unwrapping Christmas presents	15	10

411	80c. Preparing for Christmas carnival		60	60
412	$2.50 Nativity		1·90	3·25
409/12	Set of 4		2·50	3·50

1995 (13 Jan). As No. 312, but W w **16** (sideways). P 14.

413	10c. Type **58**		75	1·00

77 Green Turtle swimming

(Des A. Robinson. Litho B.D.T.)

1995 (27 Feb). Endangered Species. Green Turtle. T **77** and similar horiz designs. Multicoloured. W w **14** (sideways). P 14.

427	10c. Type **77**		40	50
	a. Strip of 4. Nos. 427/30		2·10	2·40
428	40c. Turtle crawling up beach		55	60
429	50c. Burying eggs		60	60
430	$1 Young heading for sea		75	1·00
427/30	Set of 4		2·10	2·40

In addition to separate sheets of 50 Nos. 427/30 were also available in small sheets of 16 containing four strips, *se-tenant* both vertically and horizontally.

78 St. Christopher 1d. Stamps of 1870

(Des D. Miller. Litho Cartor)

1995 (10 Apr). 125th Anniv of St. Kitts Postage Stamps. T **78** and similar horiz designs, each including the St. Christopher 1870 1d. W w **14** (sideways). P 13½.

431	25c. Type **78**		15	15
432	80c. St. Kitts-Nevis 1935 Silver Jubilee 1d		45	50
433	$2.50 St. Kitts-Nevis 1946 Victory 1½d		1·75	2·50
434	$3 St. Christopher Nevis Anguilla 1953 Coronation 2c		2·00	2·75
431/4	Set of 4		4·00	5·50

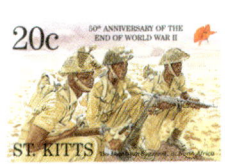

78a Caribbean Regiment Patrol, North Africa

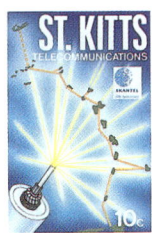

79 Telecommunication Links between Islands

(Des R. Walton. Litho Cartor (Nos. 435/8) or Questa (Nos. **MS**439))

1995 (8 May). 50th Anniv of End of Second World War. T **78a** and similar multicoloured designs . W w **14** (sideways). P 13½.

435	20c. Type **78a**		15	15
436	50c. Grumman TBF Avengers (bombers)		35	35
437	$2 Supermarine Spitfire Mk Vb (fighter)		1·25	1·50
438	$8 US Navy destroyer escort		5·00	6·50
435/8	Set of 4		6·00	7·75
MS439	75×85 mm. $3 Reverse of 1939–45 War Medal (*vert*). Wmk upright. P 14		1·50	2·00

(Des D. Miller. Litho Enschedé)

1995 (27 Sept). Tenth Anniv of SKANTEL (telecommunications company). T **79** and similar vert designs. Multicoloured. W w **14**. P 13×14½.

440	10c. Type **79**		25	10
441	25c. Payphone and computer link		30	15
442	$2 Telecommunications tower and dish aerial		2·25	2·75
443	$3 Silhouette of dish aerial at sunset		2·50	3·75
440/3	Set of 4		4·75	6·00

80 Water Treatment Works

81 F.A.O. Emblem and Vegetables

(Des D. Miller. Litho Cartor)

1995 (24 Oct). 50th Anniv of United Nations. T **80** and similar horiz designs. Multicoloured. W w **14** (sideways). P 13½×13.

444	40c. Type **80**		55	25
445	50c. Beach		50	30
446	$1.60 Dust cart		1·75	2·25
447	$2.50 Forest		2·75	3·75
444/7	Set of 4		4·75	6·00

(Des G. Vasarhelyi. Litho Cartor)

1995 (13 Nov). 50th Anniv of Food and Agriculture Organization. T **81** and similar horiz designs. Multicoloured. W w **14** (sideways). P 13½.

448	25c. Type **81**		20	10
449	50c. Glazed carrots and West Indian peas with rice		35	30
450	80c. Tanis, and Cassava plants		50	60
451	$1.50 Waterfall, Green Hill Mountain		2·50	3·00
448/51	Set of 4		3·25	3·50

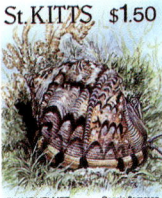

82 Flame Helmet

83 L.M.S. No. 45614 *Leeward Islands* Steam Locomotive in Green Livery

(Des G. Drummond. Litho Cartor)

1996 (10 Jan). Sea Shells. T **82** and similar vert designs. Multicoloured. W w **14**. P 13.

452	$1.50 Type **82**		95	1·10
	a. Horiz strip of 5. Nos. 452/6		4·25	5·00
453	$1.50 Tritons Trumpet		95	1·10
454	$1.50 King Helmet		95	1·10
455	$1.50 True Tulip		95	1·10
456	$1.50 Queen Conch		95	1·10
452/6	Set of 5		4·25	5·00

Nos. 452/6 were printed together, *se-tenant*, in horizontal strips of 5 throughout the sheet.

(Des A. Theobald. Litho Enschedé)

1996 (1 May). CAPEX '96 International Stamp Exhibition, Toronto. T **83** and similar horiz design. Multicoloured. W w **14** (sideways). P 13½×14.

457	10c. Type **83**		75	60
MS458	110×80 mm. $10 L.M.S. No. 5614 *Leeward Islands* steam locomotive in red livery (48×31½ mm). P 14×14½		7·50	7·50

84 Athlete and National Flag

85 Volunteer Rifleman, 1896

(Des R. Watton. Litho Walsall)

1996 (30 June). Centennial Olympic Games, Atlanta. T **84** and similar vert designs. Multicoloured. W w **16**. P 14.

459	10c. Type **84**		15	15
460	25c. High jumper and U.S.A. flag		20	20

ST. KITTS-NEVIS / St. Kitts

461	80c. Athlete and Olympic flag	50	55
462	$3 Poster for 1896 Olympic Games, Athens	1·75	2·50
459/62 Set of 4		2·40	3·00
MS463 70×64 mm. $6 Olympic torch		3·25	3·50

(Des W. Cribbs. Litho Cot Printery Ltd, Barbados)

1996 (1 Nov). Centenary of Defence Force. T **85** and similar vert designs. Multicoloured. W w **14**. P 14.

464	10c. Type **85**	15	15
465	50c. Mounted infantryman, 1911	35	35
466	$2 Drummer, 1940–60	1·25	1·75
467	$2.50 Ceremonial uniform, 1996	1·40	2·00
464/7 Set of 4		2·75	3·75

86 "Holy Virgin and Child" (A. Colin)

(Des D. Miller. Litho Questa)

1996 (29 Nov). Christmas. Religious Paintings. T **86** and similar vert designs. Multicoloured. W w **14**. P 14½.

468	15c. Type **86**	20	10
469	25c. "Holy Family" (after Rubens)	25	10
470	50c. "Madonna with the Goldfinch" (Krause after Raphael)	45	40
471	80c. "Madonna on Throne with Angels" (17th-cent Spanish)	75	1·25
468/71 Set of 4		1·50	1·60

(Des D. Miller. Litho Quests)

1997 (3 Feb). "HONG KONG '97" International Stamp Exhibition. Sheet 130×90 mm, containing No. 323. W w **14** (sideways). P 14.

MS472 $3 *Berbice* (mail steamer)		1·60	2·00

87 Princess Parrotfish

(Des G. Vasarhelyi. Litho Cartor)

1997 (24 Apr). Fish. T **87** and similar horiz designs. Multicoloured. P 13½.

473	$1 Type **87**	80	90
	a. Sheetlet. Nos. 473/84	8·50	
474	$1 Yellow-bellied Hamlet	80	90
475	$1 Coney	80	90
476	$1 Fin-spot Wrasse	80	90
477	$1 Doctor Fish	80	90
478	$1 Squirrelfish	80	90
479	$1 Queen Angelfish	80	90
480	$1 Spanish Hogfish	80	90
481	$1 Red Hind	80	90
482	$1 Red Grouper	80	90
483	$1 Yellow-tailed Snapper	80	90
484	$1 Mutton Hamlet	80	90
473/84 Set of 12		8·50	9·50

Nos. 473/84 were printed together, *se-tenant*, in sheetlets of 12.

(Des N. Shewring (No. **MS**491), D. Miller (others). Litho Questa (No. **MS**491), B.D.T. (others))

1997 (10 July). Golden Wedding of Queen Elizabeth and Prince Philip. Multicoloured designs as T **212a** of British Virgin Islands. W w **14**. P 13½.

485	10c. Queen Elizabeth in evening dress	70	1·00
	a. Horiz pair. Nos. 485/6	1·40	2·00
486	10c. Prince Philip and Duke of Kent at Trooping the Colour	70	1·00
487	25c. Queen Elizabeth in phaeton at Trooping the Colour	90	1·10
	a. Horiz pair. Nos. 487/8	1·75	2·10
488	25c. Prince Philip in naval uniform	90	1·10
489	$3 Queen Elizabeth and Prince Philip	2·50	2·75
	a. Horiz pair. Nos. 489/90	5·00	5·50
490	$3 Peter Phillips on horseback	2·50	2·75
485/90 Set of 6		7·25	8·75
MS491 110×70 mm. $6 Queen Elizabeth and Prince Philip in landau (*horiz*). Wmk sideways. P14×14½		5·50	6·50

Nos. 485/6, 487/8 and 489/90 were each printed together, *se-tenant*, in horizontal pairs throughout the sheets with the backgrounds forming composite designs.

88 C. A. Paul Southwell (first Chief Minister)

89 Wesley Methodist Church

(Des G. Vasarhelyi. Litho Cartor)

1997 (16 Sept). National Heroes Day. T **88** and similar multicoloured designs. W w **14** (sideways on $3). P 13½.

492	25c. Type **88**	15	25
493	25c. Sir Joseph France (trade union leader)	15	25
494	25c. Robert Bradshaw (first Prime Minister)	15	25
495	$3 Sir Joseph France, Robert Bradshaw and C. A. Paul Southwell (*horiz*)	1·75	2·50
492/5 Set of 4		2·00	3·00

(Des D. Miller. Litho Walsall)

1997 (31 Oct). Christmas. Churches. T **89** and similar multicoloured designs. W w **16** (sideways on horiz designs). P 13½×14 (horiz) or 14×13½ (vert).

496	10c. Type **89**	10	10
497	10c. Zion Moravian Church	10	10
498	$1.50 St. George's Anglican Church (*vert*)	1·00	1·00
499	$15 Co-Cathedral of the Immaculate Conception (*vert*)	8·50	12·00
496/9 Set of 4		8·75	12·00

90 Common Long-tail Skipper

COT PRINTINGS. Overall design size 34×27 mm. Country inscription and face value as Type A (on 10c. "c" only half the height of the figures) with gap between "St." and "Kitts". Species name in light type.

QUESTA PRINTINGS. Overall design size 35×27½ mm. Country inscription and face value as Type B (on 10c. "c" is three-quarters the height of the figures) without gap between "St." and "Kitts". Species name in heavy type.

(Des I. Loe)

1997 (29 Dec). Butterflies. T **90** and similar horiz designs. Multicoloured. W w **14** (sideways). P 14×14½.

(a) Litho Cot Printery Ltd, Barbados

500	10c. Type **90**	20	30
501	15c. White Peacock	30	30
502	25c. Caribbean Buckeye	40	40
503	30c. The Red Rim	40	30
504	40c. Cassius Blue	45	40
505	50c. The Flambeau	50	40
506	60c. Lucas's Blue	65	45
507	90c. Cloudless Sulphur	1·00	70
508	$1 The Monarch	1·10	75
509	$1.20 Fiery Skipper	1·25	1·00
510	$1.60 The Zebra	1·40	1·40
511	$3 Southern Dagger Tail	2·50	3·25
512	$5 Polydamas Swallowtail	3·50	5·00
513	$10 Tropical Chequered Skipper	6·50	10·00
500/13 Set of 14		18·00	22·00

(b) Litho Questa (28.12.2000)

500a	10c. Type **90**	40	60
511a	$3 Southern Dagger Tail	3·50	4·00

512a		$5 Polydamas Swallowtail	5·50	6·50
513a		$10 Tropical Chequered Skipper	9·00	11·00
500a/13a	Set of 4		17·00	20·00

No. 512 is incorrectly inscribed "Polydamus". This is corrected on No. 512a.

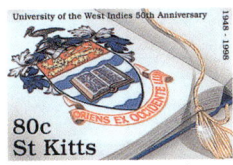

91 University Arms on Book

(Des D. Miller. Litho Questa)

1998 (31 Mar). Diana Princess of Wales Commemoration. Vert designs as T **215a** of British Virgin Islands. Multicoloured. W w **16** (30c). P 14½×14.

514		30c. Wearing hat	30	30
MS515	145×70 mm. $1.60, As 30c.; $1.60, Wearing red jacket; $1.60, Wearing white jacket; $1.60, Carrying bouquets. W w **14** (sideways) (*sold at $6.40+90c. charity premium*)		2·25	3·25

(Des D. Miller. Litho Cartor)

1998 (20 July). 50th Anniv of University of West Indies. T **91** and similar horiz design. Multicoloured. W w **14** (sideways). P 13½×13.

516		80c. Type **91**	45	40
517		$2 University arms and mortar-board	95	1·40

92 Santa at Carnival
93 Launching Rowing Boat 

(Des R. Watton. Litho Cot Printery Ltd, Barbados)

1998 (30 Oct). Christmas. T **92** and similar horiz design. Multicoloured. W w **14** (sideways). P 14.

518		80c. Type **92**	45	40
519		$1.20 Santa with two carnival dancers	65	1·00

(Des adapted D. Miller. Litho B.D.T.)

1999 (5 Mar). 125th Anniv of Universal Postal Union. T **93** and similar vert design. Multicoloured. W w **16**. P 13½.

520		30c. Type **93**	25	20
521		90c. Pictorial map of St. Kitts	1·00	1·00

94 Caribbean Martin

(Des I. Loe. Litho B.D.T.)

1999 (27 Apr). Birds of the Eastern Caribbean. T **94** and similar horiz designs. Multicoloured. W w **14** (sideways). P 13½×14.

522		80c. Type **94**	60	70
	a.	Sheetlet. Nos. 522/37	8·50	10·00
523		80c. Spotted Sandpiper	60	70
524		80c. Sooty Tern	60	70
525		80c. Red-tailed Hawk	60	70
526		80c. Brown Trembler	60	70
527		80c. Belted Kingfisher	60	70
528		80c. Black-billed Whistling Duck	60	70
529		80c. Yellow Warbler	60	70
530		80c. Blue-headed Hummingbird	60	70
531		80c. Blue-headed Euphonia ("Antillean Euphonia")	60	70
532		80c. Fulvous Whistling Duck	60	70
533		80c. Mangrove Cuckoo	60	70
534		80c. Carib Grackle	60	70
535		80c. Caribbean Elaenia	60	70
536		80c. Scaly-breasted Ground Dove ("Common Ground Dove")	60	70
537		80c. Forest Thrush	60	70
522/37	Set of 16		8·50	10·00

Nos. 522/37 were printed together, *se-tenant*, in sheetlets of 16 which show the "IBRA '99" International Stamp Exhibition, Nuremberg, emblem on the sheet margins.

(Des N. Shewring. Litho Walsall)

1999 (20 July). 30th Anniv of First Manned Landing on Moon. Multicoloured designs as T **220b** of British Virgin Islands. W w **16**. P 14×13½.

538		80c. Lift-off	60	40
539		90c. In Moon orbit	70	65
540		$1 Buzz Aldrin on Moon's surface	80	85
541		$1.20 Heat shields burning during re-entry	90	1·25
538/41	Set of 4		2·75	2·75
MS542	90×80 mm. $10 Earth as seen from Moon (*circular, 40 mm diam*). Wmk sideways. P 14		4·75	5·00

95 Local Quartet

(Des Jennifer Toombs. Litho Questa)

1999 (29 Oct). Christmas. Musicians. T **95** and similar horiz designs. Multicoloured. W w **14** (sideways). P 13½×14.

543		10c. Type **95**	20	10
544		30c. Trio	30	20
545		80c. Sextet	60	45
546		$2 Quartet in green jerseys	1·10	2·25
543/6	Set of 4		2·00	2·75

96 "Rockets, Saturn and Earth" (A. Taylor)
97 Carnival Celebrations 

(Adapted D. Miller. Litho Questa)

1999 (29 Dec). New Millennium. Children's Paintings. T **96** and similar horiz designs. Multicoloured. W w **14** (sideways). P 14.

547		10c. Type **96**	30	15
548		30c. "Y2K, computer and Earth weeping" (T. Liburd)	45	25
549		50c. "Alien destroying computer" (D. Moses)	55	45
550		$1 "Technology past, present and future" (P. Liburd)	90	1·50
547/50	Set of 4		2·00	2·10

(Adapted G. Vasarhelyi. Litho cot Printery Ltd, Barbados)

2000 (30 Aug). "Carifesta VII" Arts Festival. T **97** and similar multicoloured designs. W w **14** (sideways on 30c. and 90c., inverted on $1.20). P 14.

551		30c. Type **97**	30	20
552		90c. Carifesta logo	75	75
553		$1.20 Stylised dancer with streamer (*vert*)	1·00	1·50
551/3	Set of 3		1·75	2·25

98 Steam Locomotive No. 133, U.S. Military Railroad, 1864

(Des J. Iskowitz. Litho Questa)

2001 (19 Feb). Railways in the American Civil War. T **98** and similar horiz designs. Multicoloured (except for Nos. **MS**578a and c). P 14.

554		$1.20 Type **98**	1·40	1·40
	a.	Sheetlet. Nos. 554/9	7·50	7·50

555	$1.20 Locomotive *Quigley*, Louisville and Nashville Railroad, 1860		1·40	1·40
556	$1.20 Locomotive *Colonel Holobird*, New Orleans, Opelousas and Great Western Railroad, 1865		1·40	1·40
557	$1.20 Locomotive No. 150, U.S. Military Railroad, 1864		1·40	1·40
558	$1.20 Locomotive *Doctor Thompson*, Atlanta and West Point Railroad, 1860		1·40	1·40
559	$1.20 Locomotive No. 156, U.S. Military Railroad, 1856		1·40	1·40
560	$1.20 Locomotive *Governor Nye*, U.S. Military Railroad, 1863		1·40	1·40
	a. Sheetlet. Nos. 560/5		7·50	7·50
561	$1.20 Locomotive No. 31, Illinois Central Railroad, 1856		1·40	1·40
562	$1.20 Locomotive *CA Henry*, Memphis, Clarksville and Louisville Line, 1863		1·40	1·40
563	$1.20 Locomotive No. 152, Illinois Central Railroad, 1856		1·40	1·40
564	$1.20 Locomotive No. 116, U.S. Military Railroad, 1863		1·40	1·40
565	$1.20 Locomotive *Job Terry* (shown as No. 111 of the Wilmington and Weldon Railroad, 1890)		1·40	1·40
566	$1.60 Locomotive *Dover*, U.S. Military Railroad, 1856		1·40	1·40
	a. Sheetlet. Nos. 566/71		7·50	7·50
567	$1.60 Locomotive *Scout*, Richmond to Gordonsville Line, 1861		1·40	1·40
568	$1.60 Baltimore & Ohio Railroad Locomotive, 1861		1·40	1·40
569	$1.60 Locomotive *John M Forbes*, Philadelphia, Wilmington and Baltimore Railroad, 1861		1·40	1·40
570	$1.60 Locomotive *Edward Kidder*, Wilmington and Weldon Railroad, 1866		1·40	1·40
571	$1.60 Locomotive *William W Wright*, U.S. Military Railroad, 1863		1·40	1·40
572	$1.60 Locomotive No. 83, Illinois Central Railroad, 1856		1·40	1·40
	a. Sheetlet. Nos. 572/7		7·50	7·50
573	$1.60 Locomotive *The General*, Western and Atlantic Railroad 1855		1·40	1·40
574	$1.60 Locomotive No. 38, Louisville and Nashville Railroad, 1860		1·40	1·40
575	$1.60 Locomotive *Texas*, Western and Atlantic Railroad, 1856		1·40	1·40
576	$1.60 Locomotive No. 162, U.S. Military Railroad, 1864		1·40	1·40
577	$1.60 Locomotive *Christopher Adams Jr.*, Memphis and Littlerock Line, 1853		1·40	1·40
554/77 Set of 24			30·00	30·00

MS578 Four sheets, each 99×78 mm. (a) $5 Brigadier-general Herman Haupt (Federal railway chief) (purple-brown and black) (*vert*). (b) $5 General George B. McClellan (*vert*). (c) $5 General Ulysses S. Grant (purple-brown, grey and black) (*vert*). (d) $5 General Robert E. Lee (*vert*) Set of 4 sheets ... 27·00 30·00

Nos. 554/9, 560/5, 566/71 and 572/7 were each printed together, *se-tenant*, in sheetlets of 6 as two horizontal rows separated by an inscribed margin. No. 577 is inscribed "Chritopher" in error.

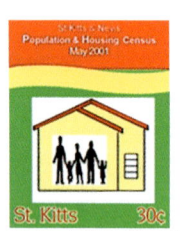

99 Bananaquit

100 Symbolic Family and House

(Des T. Wood. Litho Questa)

2001 (12 Mar). Caribbean Flora and Fauna. T **99** and similar multicoloured designs. P 14.

579	$1.20 Type **99**		1·25	1·25
	a. Sheetlet. Nos. 579/84		6·50	6·50
580	$1.20 Anthurium (face value in white)		1·25	1·25
581	$1.20 Common dolphin		1·25	1·25
582	$1.20 Horse mushroom		1·25	1·25
583	$1.20 Green anole		1·25	1·25
584	$1.20 Monarch butterfly		1·25	1·25
585	$1.20 Heliconia		1·25	1·25
	a. Sheetlet. Nos. 585/90		6·50	6·50
586	$1.20 Anthurium (black face value)		1·25	1·25
587	$1.20 *Oncidium splendidum*		1·25	1·25
588	$1.20 Trumpet creeper		1·25	1·25
589	$1.20 Bird of paradise		1·25	1·25
590	$1.20 Hibiscus		1·25	1·25
591	$1.60 Beaugregory		1·25	1·25
	a. Sheetlet. Nos. 591/6		6·50	6·50
592	$1.60 Banded butterflyfish		1·25	1·25
593	$1.60 Cherubfish		1·25	1·25
594	$1.60 Rock beauty		1·25	1·25
595	$1.60 Red snapper		1·25	1·25
596	$1.60 Leatherback turtle		1·25	1·25
597	$1.60 Figure-of-eight butterfly		1·25	1·25
	a. Sheetlet. Nos. 597/602		6·50	6·50
598	$1.60 Banded king shoemaker		1·25	1·25
599	$1.60 Orange theope		1·25	1·25
600	$1.60 Grecian shoemaker		1·25	1·25
601	$1.60 Clorinde		1·25	1·25
602	$1.60 Small lace-wing		1·25	1·25
603	$1.60 Laughing gull		1·25	1·25
	a. Sheetlet. Nos. 603/8		6·50	6·50
604	$1.60 Sooty tern		1·25	1·25
605	$1.60 White-tailed tropicbird		1·25	1·25
606	$1.60 Painted bunting		1·25	1·25
607	$1.60 Belted kingfisher		1·25	1·25
608	$1.60 Yellow-bellied sapsucker		1·25	1·25
579/608 Set of 30			32·00	32·00

MS609 Five sheets, each 82×112 mm. (a) $5 Iguana (*horiz*). (b) $5 *Leochiluscarinatus* (orchid). (c) $5 Redband parrotfish (*horiz*). (d) $5 Common morpho (butterfly) (*horiz*). (e) $5 Ruby-throated hummingbird (*horiz*) Set of 5 sheets ... 22·00 25·00

Nos. 579/84, 585/90 (flowers), 591/6 (fish), 597/602 (butterflies) and 603/8 (birds) were each printed together, *se-tenant*, in sheetlets of 6 with inscribed margins.

No. 608 is inscribed "Yello-bellied" in error.

(Litho Questa)

2001 (18 Apr). Population and Housing Census. T **100** and similar vert design. P 14×14½.

610	30c. Type **100**		30	15
611	$3 People with Census symbol		2·00	2·75

101 Coronation of Queen Victoria

102 Mao Tse-tung, 1926

(Des R. Sauber. Litho Questa)

2001 (16 July). Death Centenary of Queen Victoria. T **101** and similar vert designs. Multicoloured (except No. **MS**616). P 14.

612	$2 Type **101**		1·50	2·00
	a. Sheetlet Nos. 612/15		5·50	7·25
613	$2 Wedding of Queen Victoria and Prince Albert		1·50	2·00
614	$2 Royal Family with Crimean War veterans		1·50	2·00
615	$2 Queen Victoria with Prince Albert		1·50	2·00
612/15 Set of 4			5·50	7·25

MS616 88×113 mm. $5 Queen Victoria as Empress of India (43×52 mm) (black) ... 3·75 5·00

Nos. 612/15 were printed together, *se-tenant*, in sheetlets of 4, with an enlarged illustrated bottom margin.

(Des R. Sauber. Litho Questa)

2001 (16 July). 25th Death Anniv of Mao Tse-tung (Chinese leader). T **102** and similar vert designs. Multicoloured. P 13½.

617	$2 Type **102**		1·50	2·00
	a. Sheetlet. Nos. 617/19		4·00	5·50
618	$2 Mao Tse-tung, 1945 (face value at top left)		1·50	2·00
619	$2 Mao Tse-tung, 1945 (face value at bottom left)		1·50	2·00
617/19 Set of 3			4·00	5·50

MS620 160×142 mm. $3 Mao Tse-tung in blue jacket ... 2·50 3·25

Nos 617/19 were printed together, *se-tenant*, in sheetlets of 3, with an inscribed top margin carrying a quotation.

ST. KITTS-NEVIS / St. Kitts

103 "On the Coast at Trouville" (Monet)

(Litho Questa)

2001 (16 July). 75th Death Anniv of Claude-Oscar Monet (French painter). T **103** and similar multicoloured designs. P 13½.
621	$2 Type **103**	2·00	2·50
	a. Sheetlet Nos. 621/4	7·25	9·00
622	$2 "Vétheuil in Summer"	2·00	2·50
623	$2 "Yellow Iris near Giverny"	2·00	2·50
624	$2 "Coastguard's Cottage at Varengeville"	2·00	2·50
621/4 Set of 4		7·25	9·00
MS625 137×111 mm. $5 "Poplars on Banks of Epte" (vert)		4·25	5·00

Nos. 621/4 were printed together, *se-tenant*, in sheetlets of 4, with an enlarged top margin showing a photograph of the artist.

104 Queen Elizabeth carrying Bouquet

(Litho Questa)

2001 (16 July). 75th Birthday of Queen Elizabeth II. T **104** and similar vert designs. Multicoloured. P 14.
626	$2 Type **104**	1·50	2·00
	a. Sheetlet Nos. 626/9	5·50	7·25
627	$2 Wearing cream floral hat	1·50	2·00
628	$2 Wearing blue coat and hat	1·50	2·00
629	$2 Queen in beige hat and dress	1·50	2·00
626/9 Set of 4		5·50	7·25
MS630 80×109 mm. $5 Queen Elizabeth riding		3·75	4·25

Nos. 626/9 were printed together, *se-tenant*, in sheetlets of 4, with an enlarged left margin showing Queen Elizabeth at State Opening of Parliament.

105 French Dragoons from *Sicilian Vespers* (opera)

(Des R. Sauber. Litho Questa)

2001 (16 July). Death Centenary of Giuseppe Verdi (Italian composer). T **105** and similar vert designs showing Sicilian Vespers (opera). Multicoloured. P 14.
631	$2 Type **105**	2·00	2·25
	a. Sheetlet. Nos. 631/4	7·25	8·00
632	$2 French dragoons, drinking round table	2·00	2·25
633	$2 Original costume design	2·00	2·25
634	$2 Inhabitants of Palermo	2·00	2·25
631/4 Set of 4		7·25	8·00
MS635 80×108 mm. $5 Montserrat Caballe as Elena		5·50	6·00

Nos. 631/4 were printed together, *se-tenant*, in sheetlets of 4, with enlarged illustrated top and bottom margins.

Nos. 631/2 are inscribed "FREWNCH" and **MS**635 "MOUNTSERRAT", all in error.

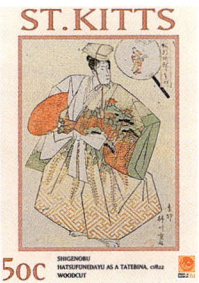

106 "Hatsufunedayu as a Tatebina" (Shigenobu)

108 *Maxillaria cucullata* (orchid)

107 Submarine "A1", 1902

(Litho Walsall)

2001 (16 July). Philanippon 01 International Stamp Exhibition, Tokyo. Japanese Woodcuts. T **106** and similar vert designs. Multicoloured. P 12.
636	50c. Type **106**	40	30
637	80c. "Samurai Kodenji as Tsuyu No Mae" (Kiyonobu I)	60	50
638	$1 "Nakamura Senya as Tokonatsu" (Kiyomasu I)	75	65
639	$1.60 "Sunida River" (Shunsho)	1·10	1·40
640	$2 "Kuemon Yoba the Wrestler" (Shune I)	1·50	2·00
641	$3 "Two actors" (Kiyonobu I/Tori I)	2·00	3·00
636/41 Set of 6		5·75	7·00
MS642 78×78 mm. $5 "Actor with swords" (Shune I)		3·75	4·25

(Des E. Nisbet. Litho Questa)

2001 (16 July). Centenary of Royal Navy Submarine Service. T **107** and similar multicoloured designs. P 14.
643	$1.50 Type **107**	2·25	2·25
	a. Sheetlet. Nos. 643/8	12·00	12·00
644	$1.50 HMS *Dreadnought* (battleship), 1906	2·25	2·25
645	$1.50 HMS *Amethyst* (cruiser), 1903	2·25	2·25
646	$1.50 HMS *Barham* (battleship), 1914	2·25	2·25
647	$1.50 HMS *Exeter* (cruiser), 1929	2·25	2·25
648	$1.50 HMS *Eagle* (aircraft carrier), 1918	2·25	2·25
643/8 Set of 6		12·00	12·00
MS649 129×90 mm. $5 HMS *Dreadnought* (nuclear submarine), 1960 (43×57 mm)		9·00	9·00

Nos. 643/8 were printed together, *se-tenant*, in sheetlets of 6, containing two horizontal rows of three, separated by an illustrated gutter.

Nos. 644 and **MS**649 are inscribed "DREADNAUGHT" and No. 646 "BARNHAM", all in error.

(Des T. Wood. Litho Questa)

2001 (18 Sept). Caribbean Flora and Fauna. T **108** and similar multicoloured designs. P 14.
650	$1.20 Type **108**	1·00	1·00
	a. Sheetlet. Nos. 650/5	5·50	5·50
651	$1.20 *Cattleya dowiana*	1·00	1·00
652	$1.20 *Rossioglossum grande*	1·00	1·00
653	$1.20 *Aspasia epidendroides*	1·00	1·00
654	$1.20 *Lycaste skinneri*	1·00	1·00
655	$1.20 *Cattleya percivaliana*	1·00	1·00
656	$1.20 Trembler	1·00	1·00
	a. Sheetlet. Nos. 656/61	5·50	5·50
657	$1.20 White-tailed tropic bird	1·00	1·00
658	$1.20 Red-footed booby	1·00	1·00
659	$1.20 Red-legged thrush	1·00	1·00
660	$1.20 Painted bunting	1·00	1·00
661	$1.20 Bananaquit	1·00	1·00
662	$1.60 Killer whale (horiz)	1·00	1·00
	a. Sheetlet. Nos. 662/7	5·50	5·50
663	$1.60 Cuvier's beaked whale (horiz)	1·00	1·00
664	$1.60 Humpback whale (horiz)	1·00	1·00
665	$1.60 Sperm whale (horiz)	1·00	1·00
666	$1.60 Blue whale (horiz)	1·00	1·00
667	$1.60 Whale shark (horiz)	1·00	1·00
668	$1.60 *Pholiota spectabilis*	1·00	1·00
	a. Sheetlet. Nos. 668/73	5·50	5·50
669	$1.60 *Flammula penetrans*	1·00	1·00
670	$1.60 *Ungulina marginata*	1·00	1·00

ST. KITTS-NEVIS / St. Kitts

671	$1.60 Collybia iocephala	1·00	1·00
672	$1.60 Amanita muscaria	1·00	1·00
673	$1.60 CoprinU.S. comatus	1·00	1·00
674	$1.60 Orange-barred sulphur	1·00	1·00
	a. Sheetlet. Nos. 674/9	5·50	5·50
675	$1.60 Giant swallowtail	1·00	1·00
676	$1.60 Orange theope butterfly	1·00	1·00
677	$1.60 Blue night butterfly	1·00	1·00
678	$1.60 Grecian shoemaker	1·00	1·00
679	$1.60 Cramer's mesene	1·00	1·00
650/79 Set of 30		26·00	26·00

MS680 Five sheets, each 99×69 mm (No. **MS**680c) or 69×99 mm (others) (a) $5 *Psychilis atropurpurea* (orchid). (b) $5 Ruby-throated hummingbird. (c) $5 Sei whale (horiz). (d) $5 *Lepiota procera* (fungus). (e) $5 Figure-of-eight butterfly *Set of 5 sheets* .... 22·00 24·00

Nos. 650/5 (orchids), 656/61 (birds), 662/7 (whales), 668/73 (fungi) and 674/9 (butterflies), were each printed together, *se-tenant*, in sheetlets of 6, with illustrated margins. No. 672 is inscribed "Aminita" and No. 673 "Corinus", both in error.

109 Christmas Tree and Angel

110 Coronation Coach

(Litho B.D.T.)

2001 (12 Dec). Christmas and Carnival. T **109** and similar vert designs. Multicoloured. P 14.

681	10c. Type **109**	35	15
682	30c. Fireworks	50	15
683	80c. Christmas wreath	1·50	60
684	$2 Steel drums	2·75	3·50
681/4 Set of 4		4·50	4·00

(Des D. Miller. Litho Questa)

2002 (6 Feb). Golden Jubilee (2nd issue). T **110** and similar square designs. Multicoloured. P 14½.

685	$2 Type **110**	1·60	1·75
	a. Sheetlet. Nos. 685/9	5·75	6·75
686	$2 Prince Philip after polo	1·60	1·75
687	$2 Queen Elizabeth and the Queen Mother in evening dress	1·60	1·75
688	$2 Queen Elizabeth in evening dress	1·60	1·75
685/8 Set of 4		5·75	6·75

MS689 76×108 mm. $5 Queen Elizabeth presenting Prince Philip with polo trophy. P 14 .... 4·75 5·50

Nos. 685/9 were printed together, *se-tenant*, in sheetlets of 4, with an illustrated left margin.

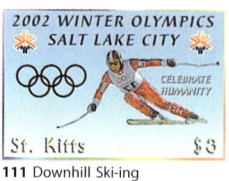

111 Downhill Ski-ing

112 Xiong Nu Tribesman and Dog

(Litho Cartor)

2002 (17 June). Winter Olympic Games, Salt Lake City. T **111** and similar horiz design. Multicoloured. P 13½.

690	$3 Type **111**	2·00	2·50
691	$3 Cross country ski-ing	2·00	2·50
MS692 82×102 mm. Nos. 690/1		4·00	5·00

(Des Y. Lee. Litho Cartor)

2002 (17 June). Chinese New Year ("Year of the Horse"). "Wen-Gi's Return to Han" (Chang Yu). T **112** and similar square designs. Multicoloured. P 12½.

693	$1.60 Type **112**	1·00	1·25
	a. Sheetlet. Nos. 693/6	3·50	4·50
694	$1.60 Group of Xiong Nu tribesmen	1·00	1·25
695	$1.60 Wen-Gi (Chinese noblewoman)	1·00	1·25
696	$1.60 Standard bearer	1·00	1·25
693/6 Set of 4		3·50	4·50

Nos. 693/4 were printed together, *se-tenant*, in sheetlets of 4 with inscribed upper and lower margins.

113 World Cup Poster, Spain, 1982

114 Policeman's Cap, Fireman's Helmet with U.S. and St. Kitts Flags

(Des G. Bibby. Litho Cartor)

2002 (17 June). World Cup Football Championship, Japan and Korea (2002). T **113** and similar multicoloured designs. P 13½.

697	$1.65 Type **113**	1·00	1·10
	a. Sheetlet. Nos. 697/701	6·75	7·50
698	$1.65 Just Fontaine, (France)	1·00	1·10
699	$1.65 American footballer	1·00	1·10
700	$1.65 Swedish footballer	1·00	1·10
701	$6 Daegu Stadium, Korea (56×42 *mm*)	3·50	4·00
697/701 Set of 5		6·75	7·50

MS702 51×73 mm. $6 Roger Milla (Cameroun), Italy, 1990 .... 3·75 4·00

Nos. 697/701 were printed together, *se-tenant*, in sheetlets of 5 with an enlarged illustrated right margin.

(Des T. Wood. Litho Cartor)

2002 (17 June). "United We Stand". Support for Victims of 11 September 2001 Terrorist Attacks. P 13½.
703 **114** 80c. multicoloured .... 1·00 1·00

No. 703 was printed in sheetlets of 4 with an inscribed bottom margin.

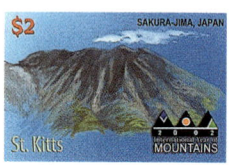

115 Sakura-jima Volcano, Kyushu, Japan

(Des R. Rundo. Litho Cartor)

2002 (17 June). International Year of Mountains. T **115** and similar horiz designs. Multicoloured. P 13½.

704	$2 Type **115**	1·25	1·50
	a. Sheetlet. Nos. 704/7	4·50	5·50
705	$2 Mount Assiniboine, Alberta, Canada	1·25	1·50
706	$2 Mount Asgard, Baffin Island, Canada	1·25	1·50
707	$2 Bugaboo Spire, British Columbia, Canada	1·25	1·50
704/7 Set of 4		4·50	5·50

MS708 75×57 mm. $6 Mount Owen, Wyoming, U.S.A. .... 3·75 5·00

Nos. 704/7 were printed together, *se-tenant*, in sheetlets of 4 with an inscribed top margin.

116 Scout saluting

(R. Rundo. Litho Cartor)

2002 (17 June). 20th World Scout Jamboree, Thailand. T **116** and similar multicoloured designs. P 13½.

709	$2 Type **116**	1·25	1·50
	a. Sheetlet. Nos. 709/12	4·50	5·50
710	$2 Silver Award 2 badge	1·25	1·50
711	$2 Illinois Scout badge	1·25	1·50
712	$2 Scout with ceremonial sword	1·25	1·50
709/12 Set of 4		4·50	5·50

MS713 78×84 mm. $6 Environmental Merit badge (*vert*).. 3·75 5·00

Nos. 709/12 were printed together, *se-tenant*, in sheetlets of 4 with an enlarged inscribed top margin.

ST. KITTS-NEVIS / St. Kitts

117 Amerigo Vespucci

118 Kim Collins running

(Des H. Friedman. Litho Cartor)

2002 (17 June). 500th Anniv of Amerigo Vespucci's Third Voyage. T **117** and similar multicoloured designs. P 13½.
714	$3 Type **117**	2·00	2·50
	a. Sheetlet. Nos. 714/16	5·50	6·75
715	$3 Map of the World by Waldseemüller, 1507	2·00	2·50
716	$3 Vespucci with globe	2·00	2·50
714/16 Set of 3		5·50	6·75
MS717 55×76 mm. $6 Vespucci as an old man (*vert*)		3·75	5·00

Nos. 714/16 were printed together, *se-tenant*, in sheetlets of 3 with an enlarged illustrated left margin.

(Litho B.D.T.)

2002 (2 July). Kim Collins (Commonwealth Games gold medallist) Commemoration. T **118** and similar vert design. Multicoloured. P 14.
718	30c. Type **118**	50	20
719	90c. Collins with World Championship bronze medal	1·10	1·10

119 Charles Lindbergh

120 Sour Sop

(Des Akemi Etheridge (No. MS725) or J. Iskowitz (others). Litho Questa)

2002 (18 Nov). Famous People of the 20th Century. T **119** and similar vert designs. P 14.

(a) 75th Anniv of First Solo Transatlantic Flight. Sheet 130×145 mm.
MS720 $1.50 Type **119** (black, slate-violet and scarlet-vermilion); $1.50 Lindbergh holding propellor of Ryan NYP Special *Spirit of St. Louis* (maroon, bluish violet and scarlet-vermilion); $1.50 Lindbergh (purple-brown, bluish violet and scarlet-vermilion); $1.50 Lindbergh and *Spirit of St. Louis* (maroon and scarlet-vermilion); $1.50 Lindbergh wearing flying helmet (brown-purple, bluish violet and scarlet-vermilion); $1.50 Lindbergh (deep claret, bluish violet and scarlet-vermilion)	8·00	10·00

(b) Life and Times of President John F. Kennedy. Two sheets, each 132×145 mm. Multicoloured
MS721 $2 John Kennedy in Solomon Islands, 1942; $2 Torpedo boat commander, 1942; Naval ensign, 1941; Receiving medal for gallantry, 1944	4·00	5·00
MS722 $2 President Kennedy forming Peace Corps; $2 Promoting Space Programme; $2 With Civil Rights leaders; $2 Signing Nuclear Disarmament Treaty with Soviet Union	6·00	7·00

(c) Fifth Death Anniv of Diana, Princess of Wales. Two sheets, each 132×145 mm. Multicoloured
MS723 $2 Princess Diana wearing jacket with mauve edged collar; $2 Wearing dress with frilled neckline; $2 Wearing pink dress; $2 Wearing mauve dress	5·00	6·00
MS724 $2 Wearing protective vest; $2 Wearing turquoise jacket; $2 Wearing yellow blouse; $2 Wearing red dress	5·00	6·00

(d) Queen Elizabeth the Queen Mother Commemoration. Sheet 200×143 mm, containing two of each design. Multicoloured
MS725 $2×2 Duchess of York; $2×2 Queen Mother	5·50	6·50

(Litho BDT)

2002 (15 Dec). Christmas. Island Fruits. T **120** and similar vert designs. Multicoloured. P 14.
726	10c. Type **120**	30	15
727	80c. Passion fruit	1·00	35
728	$1 Sugar apple	1·25	80
729	$2 Custard apple	2·00	3·00
726/9 Set of 4		4·00	3·75

121 Ram

122 Pelican and Emblem

2003 (27 Jan). Chinese New Year ("Year of the Ram"). T **121** and similar vert designs. Multicoloured. Litho. P 14.
MS730 110×122 mm. $1×2 Type **121**; $1×2 Brown and white ram with spiral horns; $1×2 Brown ram with long horns	4·25	5·50

(Litho Questa)

2003 (23 June). 30th Anniv of CARICOM. P 14.
731	**122**	30c. multicoloured	1·00	65

123 Queen Victoria Bear

124 Queen Elizabeth II

(Des R. Rundo. Litho Questa)

2003 (1 July). Centenary of the Teddy Bear. T **123** and similar vert designs. Multicoloured. P 13½×14.
MS732 135×156 mm. $2 Type **123**; $2 Teddy Roosevelt bear; $2 George Washington bear; $2 General Patton bear	5·00	6·00
MS733 90×113 mm. $5 Buffalo Bill bear	3·50	4·25

(Des M. Servin. Litho Questa)

2003 (1 July). 50th Anniv of Coronation. T **124** and similar vert designs. Multicoloured. P 14.
MS734 156×94 mm. $3 Type **124**; $3 Queen wearing tiara and pink sash; $3 Wearing tiara and blue sash	6·50	7·50
MS735 106×76 mm. $6 Wearing tiara and blue robes	3·75	4·25

125 Prince William as Toddler

126 Voisin LA5

(Des R. Rundo. Litho Questa)

2003 (1 July). 21st Birthday of Prince William. T **125** and similar vert designs. Multicoloured. P 14.
MS736 156×96 mm. $3 Type **125**; $3 As schoolboy; $3 As adult	6·50	7·50
MS737 106×76 mm. $5 As young boy, waving from carriage	3·50	4·00

ST. KITTS-NEVIS / St. Kitts

(Des R. Rundo. Litho Questa)

2003 (1 July). Centenary of Powered Flight. T **126** and similar horiz designs. Multicoloured. P 14.

MS738	185×106 mm. $2 Type **126**; $2 Gotha G.V.; $2 Polikarpov I-16; $2 Bell YFM-1	5·50	7·00
MS739	106×76 mm. $5 Bristol Type **142** Blenheim Mk I	3·50	4·00

127 Miguel Induráin (1991–95)

128 "Child with Wooden Horse (Claude)"

(Des J. Iskowitz. Litho Questa)

2003 (1 July). Centenary of Tour de France. T **127** and similar vert designs showing past winners. Multicoloured. P 13½×13.

MS740	166×106 mm. $2 Type **127**; $2 Miguel Induráin (1995); $2 Bjarne Riis (1996); $2 Jan Ullrich (1997)	5·50	6·50
MS741	105×75 mm. $5 Miguel Induráin (1991–5)	3·50	4·00

2003 (18 Aug). 30th Death Anniv of Pablo Picasso (artist). T **128** and similar vert designs. Multicoloured. Litho. P 14.

MS742	178×103 mm. $1.60 Type **128**; $1.60 "Child with a Ball (Claude)"; $1.60 "The Butterfly Catcher"; $1.60 "Boy with a Lobster"; $1.60 "Baby wearing Polka-Dot Dress"; $1.60 "El Bobo" (after Murillo)	6·50	7·50
MS743	68×86 mm. $5 Woman with baby (63×80 mm). Imperf.	3·50	4·00

129 Scout and Seaman with Globe (1937)

130 "Tokiwa Gozen with her Son in the Snow"

(Shunkyokusai Hokumei)

2003 (18 Aug). 25th Death Anniv of Norman Rockwell (artist). T **129** and similar vert designs showing illustrations from scout calendars. Multicoloured. Litho. P 14.

MS744	141×180 mm. $2 Type **129**; $2 Scouts hiking (1937); $2 Boy and dog at window (1968); $2 Scout and statue (1932)	5·50	6·50
MS745	60×83 mm. $5 Scout with cub scout (1950)	3·50	4·00

2003 (18 Aug). Japanese Art. T **130** and similar vert designs. Multicoloured. Litho. P 14.

746	90c. Type **130**	70	55
747	$1 "Courtesan and Asahina" (attrib. Eshosai Choki)	75	60
748	$1.50 "Parody of Sugawara no Michizane seated on an Ox" (Utagawa Toyokuni)	1·10	1·40
749	$3 "Visiting a Flower Garden" (detail) (Utagawa Kunisada)	2·00	3·00
746/9 Set of 4		4·00	5·00
MS750	147×147 mm. $2 "Akugenta Yoshihira" holding crossbow; $2 Holding painting; $2 As woman, with hand outstretched; $2 Holding sword	5·50	6·50
MS751	86×115 mm. $6 "The Courtesan Katachino under a Cherry Tree" (Utagawa Toyoharu)	3·75	4·25

No. **MS750** shows a set of four prints of "Akugenta Yoshihira" by Utagawa Kunisada.

131 "A Family Group" (detail)

(Giuseppe Castiglione)

2003 (18 Aug). Rembrandt (artist) Commemoration. T **131** and similar multicoloured designs. P 14.

752	50c. Type **131**	50	40
753	$1 "Portrait of Cornelis Claesz Anslo and Aeltje Gerritsdr Schouten" (horiz)	75	65
754	$1.60 "Portrait of a Young Woman"	1·25	1·50
755	$3 "Man in Military Costume"	2·00	3·00
752/5 Set of 4		4·00	5·00
MS756	181×172 mm. $2 "An Old Woman Reading"; $2 "Hendrickje Stoffels"; $2 "Rembrandt's Mother"; $2 "Saskia"	5·50	6·50
MS757	152×117 mm. $5 "Judas returning the Thirty Pieces of Silver"	3·50	4·00

132 "White Gibbon"

133 Jiri Guth Jarkovsky

(Des Y. Lee)

2004 (15 Jan). Chinese New Year ("Year of the Monkey"). Litho. P 13½.

MS758	156×141 mm. **132** $1.60×4 multicoloured	4·25	4·75
MS759	158×92 mm. **132** $3 multicoloured (30×37 mm)	2·50	2·75

(Des R. Rundo. Litho BDT)

2004 (21 Sept). Olympic Games, Athens. T **133** and similar multicoloured designs. P 14½.

760	50c. Type **133**	40	35
761	90c. Olympic poster, Munich (1972)	65	55
762	$1 Medal and Eiffel Tower, Paris (1900)	75	65
763	$3 Wrestling (Greek bronze statue) (horiz)	2·00	3·00
760/3 Set of 4		3·50	4·00

134 12th SP Panzer Division and Map

135 Pope John Paul II

2004 (21 Sept). 60th Anniv of D-Day Landings. T **134** and similar designs. P 14.

MS764	Two sheets. (a) 178×106 mm. $2×4 multicoloured; blackish purple; maroon; dull purple and blackish purple. (b) 100×68 mm. $5 multicoloured	12·00	12·00

Designs:—**MS764** (a) $2×4 Type **134**; German heavy tank; Soldier aiming weapon; Soldiers and tank. (b) $5 Allied cemetery, Normandy.

250

2004 (21 Sept). 25th Anniv of the Pontificate of Pope John Paul II. Sheet, 147×105 mm, containing T **135** and similar vert designs. Multicoloured. P 14.
MS765 $2×4 Type **135**; Walking in gardens; Standing with hands crossed; Holding Pastoral Staff .... 8·50 9·00

136 Berti Vogts

137 Deng Xiaoping

(Des M. Servin. Litho Cartor)

2004 (21 Sept). European Football Championship 2004, Portugal. Commemoration of Match between Germany and Czech Republic (1996). T **136** and similar multicoloured designs. P 14.
MS766 Two sheets (a) 147×86 mm. $2×4 Type **136**; Patrik Berger; Oliver Bierhoff; Empire Stadium. (b) 97×86 mm. $5 German team (1996) (51×48 *mm*)..... 8·50 11·00

2004 (21 Sept). Birth Centenary of Deng Xiaoping (Chinese leader, 1978–89). Litho. P 14.
MS767 **137** $5 multicoloured .... 3·50 4·00

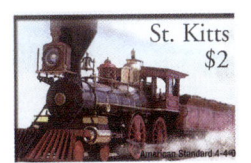

138 American Standard 4-4-0

2004 (21 Sept). Bicentenary of Steam Trains. T **138** and similar multicoloured designs. Litho. P 13½.

768	$2 Type **138**	1·60	1·60
	a. Sheetlet. Nos. 768/71	5·75	5·75
769	$2 New South Wales Government Class "79" 4-4-0	1·60	1·60
770	$2 Johnson Midland Single 4-2-2	1·60	1·60
771	$2 Union Pacific FEF-3 Class 4-8-4 ..	1·60	1·60
772	$2 Northumbrian 0-2-2	1·60	1·60
	a. Sheetlet. Nos. 772/5	5·75	5·75
773	$2 Prince Class 2-2-2	1·60	1·60
774	$2 Adler 2-2-2	1·60	1·60
775	$2 London and North Western Railway Webb Compound 2-4-0	1·60	1·60
776	$2 Italian State Railways Class 685 2-6-2 ..	1·60	1·60
	a. Sheetlet. Nos. 776/9	5·75	5·75
777	$2 Swiss Federal Railways 4-6-0	1·60	1·60
778	$2 British Engineering Standards Association Class 4-6-0	1·60	1·60
779	$2 Great Western City Class 4-4-0 ..	1·60	1·60
768/79 Set of 12		16·00	16·00

MS780 Three sheets. (a) 98×68 mm. $5 CN Class U-2 4-8-4. (b) 98×68 mm. $5 Crampton 4-2-0. (c) 68×98 mm. $5 Baldwin 2-8-2 Set of 3 sheets .... 12·00 14·00
Nos. 768/71, 772/5 and 776/9 were each printed together, *se-tenant*, in sheetlets of 4 stamps with enlarged, illustrated margins.

139 Demetrio Albertini

2004 (8 Nov). Centenary of FIFA (Fédération Internationale de Football Association). T **139** and similar horiz designs. Multicoloured. Litho. P 13×12½.
MS781 193×97 mm. $2×4, Type **139**; Romario; Gerd Muller; Danny Blanchflower .... 5·00 6·00
MS782 107×87 mm. $5 Gianfranco Zola .... 3·25 3·75

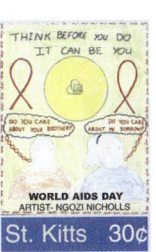

140 Couple with Thought Bubbles and AIDS Ribbons (Ngozi Nicholls)

141 Hen and Three Chicks

(Litho BDT)

2004 (1 Dec). World AIDS Day. T **140** and similar multicoloured designs. P 14.

783	30c. Type **140**	50	20
784	80c. Man in shackles, fire, top of globe and characters dancing (Travis Liburd)	1·00	60
785	90c. Flag inscribed with "AIDS or LIFE" (Darren Kelly) (horiz)	1·10	90
786	$1 Red "AIDS", syringe and smiley condom (Shane Berry)	1·40	1·60
783/6 Set of 4		3·50	3·00

2005 (7 Feb). Chinese New Year ("Year of the Rooster"). T **141** and similar vert design. Multicoloured. Litho. P 12.
787   $1.60 Type **414** .... 1·25 1·60
MS788 70×100 mm. $5 As No. 787 but design enlarged 3·25 3·75
No. 787 was printed in sheetlets of 4 with an enlarged illustrated right margin.

142 Papilio demoleus

143 Bahama ("White-cheeked") Pintail

2005 (7 Feb). Butterflies. T **142** and similar multicoloured designs. Litho. P 13.
MS789 127×151 mm. $2×4, Type **142**; Ephemeroptera; Hamadryas februa; Aphyllacaraiba.... 6·00 7·00
MS790 100×70 mm. $5 Lycaenidae cupido minimus...... 4·00 4·50

2005 (7 Feb). Ducks. T **143** and similar horiz designs. Multicoloured. Litho. P 13.

791	25c. Type **143**	75	60
792	$1 Fulvous whistling duck.................	1·25	85
793	$2 White-faced whistling duck.........	2·00	2·25
794	$3 Red-billed ("Black-bellied") whistling duck	2·75	3·50
791/4 Set of 4		6·00	6·50

144 Ocelot

145 Australian King Parrot

2005 (7 Feb). Wildcats. T **144** and similar multicoloured designs. Litho. P 13.
MS795 128×152 mm. $2×4, Type **144**; Bengal leopard; Tiger; Leopard .... 6·00 7·00
MS796 101×70 mm. $5 Sumatran tiger...................... 5·50 6·00

ST. KITTS-NEVIS / St. Kitts

2005 (7 Feb). Parrots. T **145** and similar multicoloured designs. Litho. P 13.
MS797	128×152 mm. $2×4, Type **145**; Rose-breasted cockatoo; Pale-headed rosella; Eastern rosella...........		6·50	7·00
MS798	101×70 mm. $5 Two rainbow lorikeets (*horiz*)........		4·75	5·50

146 Triceratops

2005 (7 Feb). Prehistoric Animals. T **146** and similar multicoloured designs. Litho. P 13.
MS799 Three sheets, each 150×84 mm. (a) $3×3, Type **146**; Deinonychus; Apatosaurus. (b) $3×3, Sabre-toothed Tiger; Edmontosaurus; Tyrannosaurus Rex. (c) $3×3, Dimetroden; Homalocephale; Stegosaurus *Set of 3 sheets* .... 19·00 23·00
MS800 Three sheets, each 100×70 mm. (a) $5 Brontosaurus (*vert*). (b) $5 Andrewsarchus. (c) $5 Woolly Mammoth (*vert*) *Set of 3 sheets*....................... 11·00 12·00

147 Montagne

2005 (11 May). Bicentenary of the Battle of Trafalgar. T **147** and similar vert designs. Multicoloured. Litho. P 13.
801	50c. Type **147**.......................................	1·00	55
802	90c. *San Jose*...	1·25	75
803	$2 *Impérieuse*..	2·25	2·50
804	$3 *San Nicolas*......................................	2·75	3·50
801/4 *Set of 4*		6·50	6·50
MS805	69×99 mm. $5 British Navy gun crew aboard HMS *Victory*	5·50	6·50

148 Beijing Rotary

149 U.S. Navy Hudson PBO-1 Patrol Bombers

2005 (11 May). Centenary of Rotary International. T **148** and similar horiz designs. Multicoloured. Litho. P 13.
806	$3 Type **148**...	2·25	2·75
	a. Sheetlet. Nos. 806/8...................	6·00	7·50
807	$3 Man lying against pillow.................	2·25	2·75
808	$3 Man in hospital..................................	2·25	2·75
806/8 *Set of 3*		6·00	7·50

Nos. 806/8 were printed together, *se-tenant*, in sheetlets of 3 stamps with enlarged, illustrated right and bottom margins.

2005 (11 May). 60th Anniv of Victory in Europe. T **149** and similar vert designs. Multicoloured. Litho. P 13.
809	$2 Type **149**...	2·25	2·25
	a. Sheetlet. Nos. 809/13.....................	10·00	10·00
810	$2 Soldiers...	2·25	2·25
811	$2 General Dwight D. Eisenhower..............	2·25	2·25
812	$2 German Prisoners of War.................	2·25	2·25
813	$2 Newspaper headline..........................	2·25	2·25
809/13 *Set of 5*...		10·00	10·00

Nos. 809/13 were printed together, *se-tenant*, in sheetlets of 5 stamps with an enlarged, illustrated margin at top.

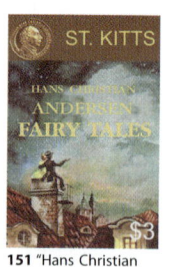

150 Jules Verne

151 "Hans Christian Anderson Fairy Tales"

2005 (11 May). Death Centenary of Jules Verne (writer). T **150** and similar designs. Multicoloured. Litho. P 13.
814	$2 reddish-brown and bistre-brown............	2·00	2·00
	a. Sheetlet. Nos. 814/17.....................	7·25	7·25
815	$2 deep turquoise-blue................................	2·00	2·00
816	$2 multicoloured..	2·00	2·00
817	$2 multicoloured..	2·00	2·00
814/17 *Set of 4*		7·25	7·25
MS818	99×70 mm. $5 multicoloured....................	5·50	6·00

Designs:—No. 814, Type **150**; No. 815, Sea monster attack; No. 816, Rouquayrol (breathing apparatus); No. 817, Modern aqualung; No. MS818, Atomic submarine.

2005 (11 May). Birth Bicentenary of Hans Christian Andersen (artist and children's writer). T **151** and similar vert designs. Multicoloured. Litho. P 13.
MS819 115×172 mm. $3×3, Type **151**, The *Emperor's New Clothes; The Nutcracker* .... 6·00 7·50
MS820 70×101 mm. $5 Characters and Banner (The *Emperor's New Clothes*)... 3·50 4·00

152 USS *Arizona*

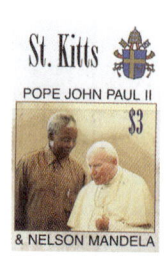

153 Pope John Paul II and Nelson Mandela

2005 (11 May). 60th Anniv of Victory in Japan. T **152** and similar vert designs. Multicoloured. Litho. P 13.
821	$2 Type **152**..	2·25	2·25
	a. Sheetlet. Nos. 821/5........................	10·00	10·00
822	$2 Captain Franklin van Valkenburgh	2·25	2·25
823	$2 Hiroshima...	2·25	2·25
824	$2 Marker of first atomic bomb loading pit on Tinian Island...............................	2·25	2·25
825	$2 Memorial cenotaph at Hiroshima Peace Park...	2·25	2·25
821/5 *Set of 5*...		10·00	10·00

Nos. 821/5 were printed together, *se-tenant*, in sheetlets of 5 stamps with an enlarged, illustrated margin at top.

2005 (19 July). Pope John Paul II Commemoration. Litho. P 13½.
826   **153** $3 multicoloured.......................... 3·50 3·75

No. 826 was printed in sheetlets of four stamps with an enlarged, illustrated left margin.

154 Junk

2005 (19 Aug). TAIPEI 2005 International Stamp Exhibition. T **154** and similar horiz designs. Multicoloured. Litho. P 14.
827	$2 Type **154**...	1·50	2·00
	a. Sheetlet. Nos. 827/30.....................	5·50	7·25
828	$2 Junk with yellow sails..........................	1·50	2·00
829	$2 Junk with dark orange sails	1·50	2·00
830	$2 Junk with white sails...........................	1·50	2·00
827/30 *Set of 4*..		5·50	7·25

Nos. 827/30 were printed together, *se-tenant*, in sheetlets of four stamps with illustrated margins.

155 "Virgin and Child" (detail) (Gerard David)

2005 (6 Dec). Christmas. T **155** and similar vert. designs. Multicoloured. Litho. P 14×13½.
831	30c. Type **155**	50	15
832	50c. "Virgin and Child" (detail) (*different*) (Gerard David)	85	35
833	90c. "Virgin and Child" (detail) (*different*) (Gerard David)	1·40	80
834	$2 "Virgin and Child" (detail) (Bartolomeo Suardi Bramentine)	3·25	4·00
831/4 Set of 4		5·50	4·75
MS835 67×97 mm. $5 "The Nativity" (Martin Schongauer)		7·00	7·50

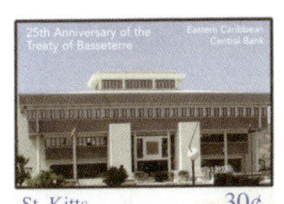

156 Eastern Caribbean Central Bank, Basseterre, St. Kitts

2006 (11 Sept). 25th Anniv of the Treaty of Basseterre (established Organisation of Eastern Caribbean States). T **156** and similar multicoloured designs. Litho. P 13.
836	30c. Type **156**	30	15
837	90c. Flags of member countries	1·40	1·00
MS838 100×75 mm. $2.50 Inset portraits of OECS heads of government (*vert*). P 12		1·75	2·00

157 "Bathsheba with King David's Letter" (detail)

158 "Mary in Adoration before the Sleeping Infant" (detail)

2006 (15 Nov). 400th Birth Anniv of Rembrandt Harmenszoon van Rijn (artist). T **157** and similar multicoloured designs showing paintings. Litho. P 12.
839	50c. Type **157**	40	25
840	80c. "Isaac and Rebecca (The Jewish Bride)" (detail of bride)	60	40
841	90c. "Isaac and Rebecca (The Jewish Bride)" (detail of groom)	65	45
842	$1 "Samson threatening his Father-in-Law" (detail of father-in-law)	70	55
843	$1.60 "Samson threatening his Father-in-Law" (detail of Samson)	1·25	1·25
844	$2 "Equestrian Portrait" (detail)	1·50	1·75
839/44 Set of 6		4·50	4·25
MS845 100×70 mm. $6 "Landscape with a Stone Bridge" (detail). Imperf		4·00	4·25

2006 (27 Dec). Christmas. T **158** and similar vert designs showing paintings by Peter Paul Rubens. Multicoloured. Litho. P 13½.
846	25c. Type **158**	35	15
847	60c. "The Holy Family under the Apple Tree" (detail, Mary and Jesus)	70	30
848	$1 "The Holy Family under the Apple Tree" (detail, Infant John the Baptist)	85	45
849	$1.20 "St. Francis of Assisi Receives the Infant JesU.S. from Mary" (detail, Mary and Jesus)	90	60
850	$2 Type **158**	1·40	1·75
	a. Sheetlet. Nos. 850/3	5·00	6·25
851	$2 As No. 847	1·40	1·75
852	$2 As No. 848	1·40	1·75
853	$2 As No. 849	1·40	1·75
846/53 Set of 8		7·50	8·00

Nos. 850/3 were printed together, *se-tenant*, in sheetlets of four stamps with enlarged illustrated margins.

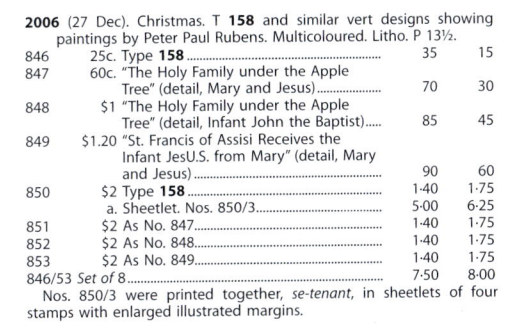

159 Queen Elizabeth II

160 Christopher Columbus

2007 (3 Jan). 80th Birthday of Queen Elizabeth II. T **159** and similar vert designs. Multicoloured. Litho. P 13½.
854	$2 Type **159**	1·40	2·00
	a. Sheetlet. Nos. 854/7	5·00	7·25
855	$2 Wearing tiara and Order of the Garter	1·40	2·00
856	$2 At Trooping the Colour	1·40	2·00
857	$2 On throne, wearing crown	1·40	2·00
854/7 Set of 4		5·00	7·25
MS858 120×120 mm. $5 Seated at desk		4·00	4·25

Nos. 854/7 were printed together, *se-tenant*, in sheetlets of four stamps with enlarged illustrated margins.

2007 (3 Jan). 500th Death Anniv (2006) of Christopher Columbus. Sheet 100×70 mm. Litho. P 13½.
MS859 **160** $6 multicoloured		4·00	4·50

161 Dove, Emblem and Ribbon of Flags

2007 (3 Jan). Centenary of World Scouting. T **161** and similar multicoloured design. P 13½.
860	$3 Type **161**	2·25	2·50
MS861 110×80 mm. $5 Dove, emblem, and ribbon of flags (*horiz*)		3·25	3·50

No. 860 is printed in sheetlets of four stamps with enlarged illustrated left margins.

162 Pre-Launch Tests at the Kourou Launch Site

ST. KITTS-NEVIS / St. Kitts

2007 (3 Jan). Space Anniversaries. T **162** and similar multicoloured designs. Litho. P 13½.

(a) 20th Anniv of Giotto Comet Probe

862	$1.60 Type **162**	1·40	1·40
	a. Sheetlet. Nos. 862/7	7·50	7·50
863	$1.60 Halley's Comet (black background)	1·40	1·40
864	$1.60 Halley's Comet (seen from Earth's surface)	1·40	1·40
865	$1.60 *Giotto* Comet Probe	1·40	1·40
866	$1.60 *Giotto* Spacecraft mounted on Rocket Ariane	1·40	1·40
867	$1.60 Halley's Comet (blue background)	1·40	1·40

(b) 40th Anniv of Luna 9 Moon Landing

868	$2 Molniya rocket on launch vehicle (*vert*)	1·50	1·50
	a. Sheetlet. Nos. 868/71	5·50	5·50
869	$2 Luna 9 flight apparatus (*vert*)	1·50	1·50
870	$2 Luna 9 soft lander (*vert*)	1·50	1·50
871	$2 Image of "Ocean of Storms" on Moon's surface (*vert*)	1·50	1·50
862/71 Set of 10		13·00	13·00
MS872	100×70 mm. $5 Space Station MIR, 1986–2001	3·75	4·25

Nos. 862/7 and 868/71 were each printed together, *se-tenant*, in sheetlets of six or four stamps with enlarged illustrated margins.

163 John Kennedy shaking hands with Peace Corps Volunteers

2007 (3 Jan). 90th Birth Anniv of John F. Kennedy (president of USA 1960–3). T **163** and similar horiz designs. Multicoloured. Litho. P 13½.

873	$2 Type **163**	2·00	2·00
	a. Sheetlet. Nos. 873/6	7·25	7·25
874	$2 Volunteer Ida Shoatz running school lunch programme in the Peruvian Andes	2·00	2·00
875	$2 R. Sargent Shriver, Director, Peace Corps	2·00	2·00
876	$2 John Kennedy greeting Peace Corps volunteers	2·00	2·00
877	$2 John Kennedy and map showing Guatemala, El Salvador and Honduras	2·00	2·00
	a. Sheetlet. Nos. 877/80	7·25	7·25
878	$2 John Kennedy and South American mother and daughter	2·00	2·00
879	$2 John Kennedy and map showing Colombia	2·00	2·00
880	$2 Map showing Venezuela, Guyana, Suriname and French Guiana	2·00	2·00
873/80 Set of 8		14·50	14·50

Nos. 873/6 (showing Peace Corps volunteers) and 877/80 (showing "Alliance for Progress" for economic co-operation between North and South America) were each printed together, *se-tenant*, in sheetlets of four stamps.

164 Betty Boop

165 Marilyn Monroe

2007 (8 Jan). Betty Boop. T **164** and similar vert designs. Multicoloured, background colours given. Litho. P 13½.

881	$1.60 Type **164**	90	1·00
	a. Sheetlet. Nos. 881/6	4·75	5·50
882	$1.60 With microphone (emerald)	90	1·00
883	$1.60 With hat and cane (white)	90	1·00
884	$1.60 With arms raised (reddish violet)	90	1·00
885	$1.60 With arms outstretched to side (new blue)	90	1·00
886	$1.60 Seated, with right leg raised (greenish yellow)	90	1·00
881/6 Set of 6		4·75	5·50
MS887	100×70 mm. $3 Wearing red dress with white flower design (green heart background); $3 With right hand held out (inverted purple heart background)	3·25	3·50

Nos. 881/6 were printed together, *se-tenant*, in sheetlets of six stamps with enlarged illustrated margins.

2007 (15 Feb). 80th Birth Anniv (2006) of Marilyn Monroe (actress). T **165** and similar vert designs. Multicoloured. Litho. P 13½.

888	$2 Type **165**	1·60	1·60
	a. Sheetlet. Nos. 888/91	5·75	5·75
889	$2 Wearing spectacles, hair wrapped in towel	1·60	1·60
890	$2 Facing forwards, bare shoulders	1·60	1·60
891	$2 Facing left, hand on chin	1·60	1·60
888/91 Set of 4		5·75	5·75

Nos. 888/91 were printed together, *se-tenant*, in sheetlets of four stamps with enlarged illustrated margins.

166 Elvis Presley

167 Two Tiger Sharks

2007 (15 Feb). 30th Death Anniv of Elvis Presley. T **166** and similar vert design. Multicoloured. Litho. P 14.

892	$2 Type **166** (inscr in new blue)	1·60	1·60
	a. Sheetlet. Nos. 892/5	7·25	7·25
893	$2 As Type **166** (inscr in bright magenta)	1·60	1·60
894	$2 As Type **166** (inscr in brownish-black)	1·60	1·60
895	$2 As Type **166** (inscr in lavender)	1·60	1·60
896	$2 Elvis Presley playing guitar and signature	1·60	1·60
892/6 Set of 5		7·25	7·25

Nos. 892/5 were printed together, *se-tenant*, in sheetlets of four stamps with enlarged illustrated right margins.

No. 896 was printed in sheetlets of four stamps with enlarged illustrated right margins.

(Des Owen Bell. Litho)

2007 (18 June). Endangered Species. Tiger Shark (*Galeocerdo cuvier*). T **167** and similar horiz designs. Multicoloured. P 13.

897	$1.20 Type **167**	1·00	1·00
	a. Strip of 4. Nos. 897/900	3·50	3·50
898	$1.20 Two sharks, foreground shark with mouth open	1·00	1·00
899	$1.20 Tiger shark	1·00	1·00
900	$1.20 Three tiger sharks, showing spotted markings	1·00	1·00
897/900 Set of 4		3·50	3·50
MS901	115×168 mm. Nos. 897/900	3·50	3·75

Nos. 897/900 were printed together, *se-tenant*, as horizontal and vertical strips of four stamps in sheets of 16.

The stamps within **MS**901 are arranged in two blocks of Nos. 897/900 separated by a gutter.

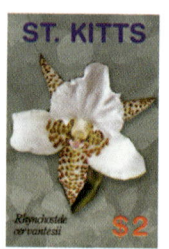

168 *Rhynchostele cervantesii*

2007 (18 June). Orchids. T **168** and similar vert designs. Multicoloured. Litho. P 13.

MS902	131×109 mm. $2×4 Type **168**; *Oerstedella wallisii*; *Disa uniflora*; *Pleioneformosana* 6	7·50	7·50
MS903	70×100 mm. $6 *Dendrobium bracteosum*	5·50	5·50

The stamps and margins of No. **MS**902 form a composite background design of white orchids.

ST. KITTS-NEVIS / St. Kitts

169 Brown Noddy

170 Cherries

2007 (18 June). Seabirds of the World. T **169** and similar multicoloured designs. Litho. P 13.
904	$2 Type **169**	2·25	2·25
	a. Sheetlet. Nos. 904/7	8·00	8·00
905	$2 Royal albatross	2·25	2·25
906	$2 Masked booby	2·25	2·25
907	$2 Great cormorant	2·25	2·25
904/7 Set of 4		8·00	8·00
MS908 70×100 mm. $6 Rock cormorant (*vert*)		6·50	6·50

On 16 August 2007 a set of four imperforate pairs of $8 silver stamps with the margins inscribed "NBA ALL-STARS International Basketball Players" was issued. Each pair contained two multicoloured $8 stamps showing basketball player and team emblem. The stamps depict Steve Nash and Phoenix Suns, Yao Ming and Houston Rockets, Shaquille O?Neal and Miami Heat and Dwyane Wade and Miami Heat.

(Litho Cardon Enterprise, Taiwan)

2007 (16 Oct). Fruit. T **170** and similar horiz designs. Multicoloured. Litho. P 13½×12½.
909	10c. Type **170**	10	15
910	15c. Coconut	15	15
911	30c. Watermelon	25	20
912	40c. Pineapple	35	25
913	50c. Guava	40	30
914	60c. Sugar apple	50	35
915	80c. Passion fruit	65	45
916	90c. Star apple	75	50
917	$1 Tangerines	90	60
918	$5 Noni fruit	4·50	5·00
919	$10 Papaya	8·00	10·00
909/19 Set of 11		15·00	16·00

171 Elvis Presley

172 Pope Benedict XVI

2007 (26 Oct). 30th Death Anniv of Elvis Presley (2nd issue). T **171** and similar horiz designs. Multicoloured. Litho. P 13½.
920	$1.60 Type **171**	1·25	1·25
	a. Sheetlet. Nos. 920/5	6·75	6·75
921	$1.60 Wearing white jacket with black eagle design	1·25	1·25
922	$1.60 Wearing black shirt	1·25	1·25
923	$1.60 Wearing blue shirt	1·25	1·25
924	$1.60 Wearing white shirt and red waistcoat	1·25	1·25
925	$1.60 Wearing white leather jacket	1·25	1·25
920/5 Set of 6		6·75	6·75

Nos. 920/5 were printed together, *se-tenant*, in sheetlets of six stamps with enlarged illustrated right margins.

2007 (26 Nov). 80th Birthday of Pope Benedict XVI. Litho. P 13½.
926	**172**	$1.10 multicoloured	1·75	1·75

No. 926 was printed in sheetlets of eight stamps with enlarged illustrated margins.

173 Queen Elizabeth II

2007 (26 Nov). Diamond Wedding of Queen Elizabeth II and Prince Philip. T **173** and similar horiz designs. Multicoloured. Litho. P 13½.
927	$1.60 Type **173**	1·25	1·25
	a. Sheetlet. Nos. 927/8, each ×3	6·75	6·75
928	$1.60 Princess Elizabeth and Prince Philip on wedding day, 1949	1·25	1·25
MS929 100×70 mm. $6 Queen Elizabeth and Prince Philip in recent years		6·50	7·00

Nos. 927/8 were printed together, *se-tenant*, in sheetlets of six stamps with enlarged illustrated margins containing three of each design.

174 Concorde in Flight

2007 (26 Nov). Concorde. T **174** and similar horiz designs. Multicoloured. Litho. P 13½.
930	$1.60 Type **174**	1·25	1·25
	a. Sheetlet. Nos. 930/1, each ×3	6·75	6·75
931	$1.60 Concorde in flight (side view)	1·25	1·25
932	$1.60 Concorde over Singapore (panel yellow-olive at left, bright yellow-green at right)	1·25	1·25
	a. Sheetlet. Nos. 932/7	6·75	6·75
933	$1.60 Concorde at Melbourne Airport, Australia ('Austria' in panel)	1·25	1·25
934	$1.60 As No. 932	1·25	1·25
935	$1.60 As No. 933 ('Spain' at left of panel)	1·25	1·25
936	$1.60 As No. 932 (bright yellow-green (Italy) in centre of panel)	1·25	1·25
937	$1.60 As No. 933 (bright yellow-green at left and yellow-olive (Black Sea) at right of panel)	1·25	1·25
930/7 Set of 8		9·00	9·00

Nos. 930/2 were printed together, *se-tenant*, in sheetlets of six stamps with enlarged illustrated margins containing three of each design.

Nos. 932/7 were printed together, *se-tenant*, in sheetlets of six stamps with enlarged illustrated margins showing map of Europe. The panels at the foot of the stamps show parts of this map of Europe.

175 Diana, Princess of Wales

2007 (26 Nov). Tenth Death Anniv of Diana, Princess of Wales. T **175** and similar vert designs. Multicoloured. Litho. P 13½.
938	$2 Type **175**	1·75	2·00
	a. Sheetlet. Nos. 938/41	6·25	7·25
939	$2 Diana, Princess of Wales (pale chestnut background)	1·75	2·00
940	$2 Wearing pearl necklace	1·75	2·00
940*a*	$2 Wearing white and mauve brimmed hat	1·75	2·00
938/940*a* Set of 4		6·25	7·25
MS941 70×100 mm. $6 As No. 940		5·00	5·50

Nos. 938/40 were printed together, *se-tenant*, in sheetlets of four stamps with enlarged illustrated margins.

176 Door Wreath with Mauve Ribbons

2007 (3 Dec). Christmas. T **176** and similar square designs showing Christmas door wreaths. Multicoloured. Litho. P 12½.
942	10c. Type **176**	30	20

255

ST. KITTS-NEVIS / St. Kitts

943	30c. Wreath with cherries and red bow		55	25
944	60c. Wreath with holly and red ribbon		90	70
945	$1 Holly leaves and berries and yellow ribbon		1·25	1·50
942/5 Set of 4			2·75	2·40

177 Paris World's Fair, 1900

178 Bethel Chapel

2008 (18 June). Olympic Games, Beijing. T **177** and similar vert designs. Multicoloured. Litho. P 13.

946	$1.40 Type **177**	1·25	1·25
	a. Sheetlet. Nos. 946/9	4·50	4·50
947	$1.40 Poster for Olympic Games, Paris, 1900	1·25	1·25
948	$1.40 Charlotte Cooper (Britain), tennis gold medallist, 1900	1·25	1·25
949	$1.40 Alvin Kraenzlein (USA), quadruple athletics gold medallist, 1900	1·25	1·25
946/9 Set of 4		4·50	4·50

Nos. 946/9 were printed together, *se-tenant*, in sheetlets of four stamps with enlarged illustrated margins.

2008 (19 Sept). 230th Anniv of the Moravian Church in St. Kitts. T **178** and similar multicoloured designs. Litho. P 11½.

950	10c. Type **178**	30	20
951	$3 Zion Chapel	2·50	2·50
952	$10 Bethesda Chapel (*vert*)	6·00	7·50
950/2 Set of 3		8·00	9·00

179 University of the West Indies Centre, St. Kitts

2008 (19 Sept). 60th Anniv of the University of the West Indies. T **179** and similar designs. Litho. P 11½.

953	**179**	30c. multicoloured	40	25
954		90c. bright scarlet, yellow and black	1·25	90
955		$5 bright scarlet, yellow and black	4·00	5·00
953/5 Set of 3			5·00	5·50

Designs: *Vert*—90c. Anniversary emblem. *Horiz*—$5 Anniversary emblem.

180

2008 (19 Sept). 25th Anniv of Independence of St. Kitts-Nevis. T **180** and similar multicoloured designs showing winners of stamp design competition. P 11½.

956	30c. Type **180** (Davern Johnson)	40	25
957	$1 Produce of St. Kitts (Yvado Simmonds)	1·25	95
958	$5 Sailing ship with national flag as sail ('Sailing Towards Our Future') (Richard Browne) (*vert*)	4·50	4·50
958*a*	$25 '25' and lifebelt ('Riding the Waves') (Dennis Richards) (*vert*)	12·00	14·00
958*b*	$30 Angel and St. Kitts Landscape ('Past and Present') (Melvin Maynard)	13·00	15·00
958*c*	$50 Mrs. Ada May Edwards (*vert*)	21·00	25·00
956/58*c* Set of 6		45·00	55·00

Nos. 956/8*b* show winning designs from stamp design competition.

181 Elvis Presley

2008 (26 Sept). 40th Anniv of Elvis Presley's '68 Special' (TV programme). T **181** and similar horiz designs. Multicoloured. P 13½.

959	$1.60 Type **181**	1·50	1·50
	a. Sheetlet. Nos. 959/64	8·00	8·00
960	$1.60 In profile, wearing black leather jacket	1·50	1·50
961	$1.60 Wearing red shirt and black waistcoat	1·50	1·50
962	$1.60 Wearing blue shirt	1·50	1·50
963	$1.60 Wearing beige shirt	1·50	1·50
964	$1.60 Wearing white shirt and red tie	1·50	1·50
959/64 Set of 6		8·00	8·00

Nos. 959/64 were printed together, *se-tenant*, in sheetlets of six stamps with enlarged illustrated margins.

182 Pope Benedict XVI and Statue of Virgin Mary

2008 (26 Sept). 150th Anniv of the Apparition of the Virgin Mary to St. Bernadette and Visit of Pope Benedict XVI to Lourdes. Sheet 127×178 mm containing T **182** and similar horiz designs. Litho. P 13½.

MS965	$2×4 multicoloured	9·00	9·00

The four stamps within **MS**965 are as Type **182** but all have slightly different backgrounds of the church building showing in the backgrounds of the stamps.

183 R. L. Bradshaw

2008 (15 Dec). 75th Anniv of the St. Kitts Labour Party. P 11½.

966	**183**	10c. multicoloured	30	30

184 Palm Trees with Christmas Baubles

2008 (29 Dec). Christmas. T**184** and similar vert designs. Multicoloured. Litho. P 14×14½.

967	10c. Type **184**	30	20
968	50c. Palm trees and beach house on stilts	55	40
969	60c. Palm trees and star	65	55
970	$1 Baubles on Christmas tree	1·25	1·50
967/70 Set of 4		2·50	2·40

185 Pres. Barack Obama
186 Princess Diana

2009 (24 Feb). Inauguration of President Barack Obama. T **185** and similar multicoloured design. Litho. P 12×11½ (**MS**971) or 13½ (**MS**972).
MS971 133×100 mm. $3 Type **185**×4 .... 14·00 15·00
MS972 80×110 mm. $10 Pres. Obama (37×37 *mm*, circular) .... 10·00 11·00

2009 (7 July). Princess Diana Commemoration. Sheet 150×100 mm containing T **186** and similar vert designs. Multicoloured. Litho. P 13.
MS973 $2×4 Type **186**; Wearing mauve dress; Wearing white strapless dress; Wearing blue off the shoulder dress with ruffle .... 8·00 9·00

187 *Freewinds* lit at Night

2009 (20 July). 20th Anniv of *Freewinds* (cruise ship) calling at St. Kitts. T **187** and similar multicoloured designs. Litho. P 13½ (**MS**974) or 11½×12 (**MS**975).
MS974 112×135 mm. 30c. Type **187**; 90c. *Freewinds* and sailing ship at St. Kitts; $3 Bow of *Freewinds* with crew on decks (42×56 *mm*) .... 4·00 4·25
MS975 144×100 mm. $2 *Freewinds* with crew on decks (79×59 *mm*) .... 2·00 2·25

188 Brimstone Hill Fortress

2009 (7 Dec). Tenth Anniv of Inscription of Brimstone Hill Fortress, St. Kitts on UNESCO World Heritage List. Litho. P 13½.
976 **188** 90c. multicoloured .... 1·25 1·25

189 Michael Jackson
190 John Kennedy jr. as Child

2009 (15 Dec). Michael Jackson Commemoration. T **189** and similar multicoloured designs. Litho. P 11½.
MS977 127×178 mm. $2.50×4 Type **189** (green inscriptions); Wearing blue shirt with white jacket, tie and hat (green inscriptions); As Type **189** (blue inscriptions); Wearing blue shirt with white jacket, tie and hat (blue inscriptions) .... 6·50 7·00
MS978 178×127 mm. $2.50×4 Wearing red jacket×2; With python×2 .... 6·50 7·00
The stamps from No. **MS**978 differ in the amount of yellow light in the red background.

2009 (15 Dec). Tenth Death Anniv of John F. Kennedy Jr. Sheet 130×100 mm containing T **190** and similar vert designs. Multicoloured. Litho. P 11½.
MS979 $2.50×4 Type **190**; With his parents; With his mother on horseback; As adult .... 7·00 7·50

191 Saturn 5 Rocket

2009 (30 Dec). 40th Anniv of the First Manned Moon Landing. International Year of Astronomy. T **191** and similar horiz designs. Multicoloured. Litho. P 11½×12.
MS980 150×100 mm. $2.50×4 Type **191**; Astronaut's bootprint on Moon; Bald Eagle, Pres. John F. Kennedy and Earth seen from Moon; Apollo 11 Command Module above Moon .... 8·00 8·00
MS981 100×70 mm. $6 Command Module in space ..... 5·50 5·50

192 St. Kitts & Nevis Flag and 'MERRY CHRISTMAS'
193 Elvis Presley

(Litho BDT)
2009 (30 Dec). Christmas. T **192** and similar horiz designs. Multicoloured. Litho. P 14½×14.
982   10c. Type **192** 25   15
983   30c. Candy canes 50   25
984      $1.20 Outline map of St. Kitts-Nevis with Christmas trees .... 1·40 1·00
985      $3 St. Kitts & Nevis flag as cake decorated with candles and Christmas tree .... 3·25 3·75
982/5 Set of 4 .... 4·75 4·75

2010 (8 Jan). 75th Birth Anniv of Elvis Presley. Sheet 120×194 mm containing T **193** and similar vert designs. Multicoloured. Litho. P 11½.
MS986 $2×6 Type **193**; Wearing jacket and tie; Wearing white jacket; Looking to left; Wearing jacket and shirt; Wearing dark zipped jacket .... 8·50 8·50

194 Scarlet Peacock (*Anartia amathea*)

(Litho)
2010 (15 Mar). Butterflies of the Caribbean. T **194** and similar horiz designs. Multicoloured. Litho. P 12.
987   30c. Type **194** 50   25
988   90c. Gulf fritillary (*Agraulis vanillae*) .... 1·40 95
989      $3 White peacock (*Anartia jatrophae*) .... 3·00 3·00
990      $5 Painted lady (*Vanessa virginiensis*) .... 5·00 5·50
987/90 Set of 4 .... 9·00 8·75
MS991 Ruddy daggerwing (*Marpesia petreus*); Danaid eggfly (*Hypolimnas misippus*); Mangrove buckeye (*Junonia evarete*); Black swallowtail (*Papilio polyxenes*) . 6·50 7·00
MS992 $3 Owl butterfly (*Caligo memnon*); $3 Giant swallowtail (*Papilio cresphontes*) .... 6·50 7·00
The stamps and margins of Nos. **MS**991/2 form composite designs.

195 Solitary Sandpiper (*Tringa solitaria*)

2010 (22 Mar). Birds of the Caribbean. T **195** and similar multicoloured designs. Litho. P 12.

993	30c. Type **195**		60	30
994	90c. Piping plover (*Charadrius melodus*)		1·50	1·00
995	$3 Prairie warbler (*Dendroica discolor*)		3·50	3·50
996	$5 Western sandpiper (*Calidris* or *Erolia mauri*)		5·50	6·00
993/6	Set of 4		10·00	10·00

MS997 150×100 mm. $2.50×4 Masked booby (*Sula dactylatra*); Sooty tern (*Onychoprion fuscatus*); Brown booby (*Sula leucogaster*); Black noddy (*Anous minutus*) . 7·00 7·50

MS998 110×80 mm. $3 Long-billed dowitcher (*Limnodromus scolopaceus*); $3 Willet (*Tringa semipalmata*) 6·50 7·00

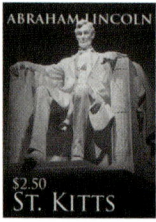

196 Statue of Abraham Lincoln Lincoln Memorial, Washington D.C.

197 Red Lionfish (*Pterois volitans*)

(Litho)

2010 (7 June). Birth Bicentenary of Abraham Lincoln (US President 1861–5). Sheet 160×105 mm. P 12.
MS999 $2.50×4 Type **196** 7·00 8·00

(Litho)

2010 (7 June). Reef Fish of the Caribbean. T **197** and similar horiz designs. Multicoloured. P 14½×14.

1000	30c. Type **197**		45	20
1001	90c. Stoplight parrotfish (*Sparisoma viride*)		1·25	90
1002	$3 Black Jack (*Caranx lugubris*)		3·50	3·50
1003	$5 Bermuda blue angelfish (*Holacanthus bermudensis*)		5·00	5·50
1000/30	Set of 4		9·00	9·50

MS1004 100×140 mm. $2.50×4 Banggai cardinalfish (*Pterapognon kauderni*); Barrier reef anemonefish (*Amphiprion akindynos*); Crevelle Jack (*Caranx hippos*); Lookdown fish (*Selene vomer*) 7·00 8·00

MS1005 100×70 mm. $3 Red Sea clownfish (*Amphiprion bicinctus*); $3 Saddleback clownfish (*Amphiprion polymnus*) 6·50 6·50

Although titled "Tropical Reef of the Caribbean", some of the fish shown are not indigenous to the region.

198 Alboleptonia stylophora

(Litho)

2010 (7 June). Fungi of the Caribbean. T **198** and similar multicoloured designs. P 14½×14 ((MS1010) or 14×14½ (others).

1006	25c. Type **198**		0·45	0·30
1007	80c. *Cantharellus cibarius*		1·25	75
1008	$1 *Armillaria puiggarii*		1·40	1·00
1009	$5 *Armillaria puiggarii*		5·00	5·50
1006/9	Set of 4		7·25	6·75

MS1010 106×140 mm. $2×6 *Cantharellus cinnabarinus*; *Collybia aurata*; *Collybia biformis*; *Amanita ocreata*; *Calocybe cyanea*; *Chroogomphus rutilus* (all horiz) 9·00 9·50
No. **MS**1010 was inscr "ANTVERPIA 2010 09–12/04/2010 NATIONAL".

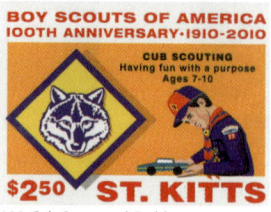

199 Cub Scout and Emblem

(Litho)

2010 (30 June). Centenary of Boy Scouts of America. Two sheets, each 170×112 mm, containing T **199** and similar horiz designs. Multicoloured. P 13½.
MS1011 $2.50×4 Type **199**; Scout cooking over campfire and emblem; Varsity scouts playing basketball and emblem; Venture scout kayaking and emblem 7·00 8·00
MS1012 $2.50×4 Scouts of 1910 and 2010 and emblem; Boy using pickaxe and Order of the Arrow emblem; Man painting with roller and Alpha Phi Omega emblem; Eagle scout handing out voting forms and emblem 7·00 8·00

200 Ermine

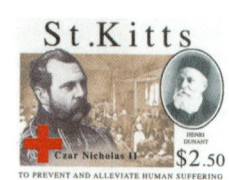

201 Czar Nicholas II

(Litho)

2011 (4 Aug). Arctic Animals. T **200** and similar vert designs. Multicoloured. P 11½.
MS1013 120×124 mm. $2×6 Type **200**; Arctic fox; Harp seal pup; Arctic wolf; Arctic hare; Snowy owl.. 8·00 8·00
MS1014 100×70 mm. $6 Polar bear 4·75 5·00

(Litho)

2011 (1 Sep). Death Centenary of Henri Dunant (founder of Red Cross). T **201** and similar horiz designs, each showing inset portrait of Henri Dunant. Multicoloured. P 11½×12 (MS1015) or 11½ (MS1016).
MS1015 150×100 mm. $2.50×4 Type **201**; Henri Dufour; Frédéric Passy; Victor Hugo 7·00 7·50
MS1016 70×100 mm. $6 Early Red Cross nurse 4·75 5·00

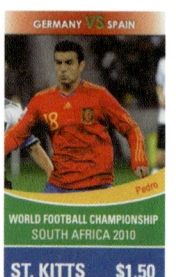

202 Pedro (Spain)

203 Poster for *Blue Hawaii*

(Litho)

2011 (6 Oct). World Cup Africa. T **202** and similar vert designs. Multicolured. P 12.
MS1017 130×155 mm. $1.50×6 Germany vs. Spain: Type **202**; Miroslav Klose (Germany); Xavi (Spain); Piotr Trochowski (Germany); Carlos Puyol (Spain); Philipp Lahm (Germany) 6·00 7·00
MS1018 $3.50 Joachim Loew (coach, Germany); $3.50 German flag on football 4·75 5·50
MS1019 $3.50 German flag on football 2·50 2·75

ST. KITTS-NEVIS / St. Kitts

(Litho)

2011 (6 Oct). Elvis Presley in Film *Blue Hawaii*, 1961. T **203** and similar vert designs. Multicoloured. P 13½.

MS1020	125×90 mm. $6 Type **203**............................	4·75	5·50
MS1021	90×125 mm. $6 Wearing swimming trunks....	4·75	5·50
MS1022	90×125 mm. $6 Playing guitar......................	4·75	5·50
MS1023	125×90 mm. $6 Wearing lei and playing guitar...	4·75	5·50

204 Princess Diana

205 *Journey of the Magi* (Fra Angelico)

(Litho)

2011 (8 Dec). Princess Diana Commemoration. T **204** and similar vert designs. Multicoloured. P 12.

MS1024	170×130 mm. $2×6 Type **204**×2; Wearing pearl drop earrings, pearl necklace and white strapless dress×2; Wearing tiara×2................	7·50	8·00
MS1025	90×120 mm. $2·75×4 Wearing lilac hat with white band and pearl choker×2; In profile, wearing cream hat and coat×2	7·50	8·00

(Litho)

2011 (2 Feb). Christmas. T **205** and similar vert designs. Multicoloured. P 11½.

1026	10c. Type **205**	15	15
1027	25c. *Madonna Worshipping the Child and an Angel* (Biagio d'Antonio)	20	20
1028	30c. *The Nativity* (Master of Vyšší Brod)..........	25	25
1029	90c. *The Journey of the Magi* (James Tissot)..	90	90
1030	$1·80 *Worship of the Shepherds* (Agnolo di Cosimo)..	1·40	1·40
1031	$3 *Madonna with Child* (Carlo Crivelli)	1·75	1·75
1026/31	Set of 6...	4·00	4·00

206 *Giovanna Albizi with Venus and the Graces*

(Litho)

2011 (21 Feb). 500th Death Anniv (2010) of Sandro Botticelli (artist). T **206** and similar multicoloured designs. P 12 (**MS**1032) or 13 (with one elliptical hole in each vert side) (**MS**1033).

MS1032	150×95 mm. $2·50×4 Type **206**; Lemmi frescoes from the villa near Florence; *Portrait of a Young Woman*; *St. Sebastian*...............................	5·50	5·50
MS1033	70×100 mm. $6 *The Last Communion of St. Jerome* (horiz)...	4·75	4·75

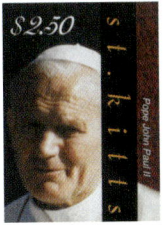

207 Pope John Paul II

(Litho)

2011 (21 Feb). Fifth Death Anniv (2010) of Pope John Paul II. Two sheets, 150×110 mm, containing T **207** and similar vert design. Multicoloured. P 12.

MS1034	Type **207**×4...	5·50	5·50
MS1035	$2·50 Pope John Paul II praying ×4...................	2·50	2·50

208 Pres. Barack Obama

209 Prince William and Miss Catherine Middleton

(Litho)

2011 (21 Feb). Pres. Barack Obama. T **208** and similar vert design. Multicoloured. P 12.

MS1036	175×113 mm. $2·50 Type **208**×4........................	2·50	5·50
MS1037	113×174 mm. $2·50 Pres. Obama (blue lower border with "THE OFFICE" inscription)×4..........	5·50	5·50

(Litho)

2011 (21 Feb). Royal Engagement (2010). T **209** and similar multicoloured designs. P 12 (**MS**1038/9) or 13 (with one elliptical hole on each horiz side) (**MS**1040/1).

MS1038	170×130 mm. $2·50×4 Type **209**; Prince William; Miss Catherine Middleton; Prince William and Miss Catherine Middleton (all horiz with blue frame)...............	5·50	5·50
MS1039	1170×130 mm. $2·50×4 Prince William and Miss Catherine Middleton (door in background); Prince William; Miss Catherine Middleton; Prince William and Miss Catherine Middleton (gold picture frame in background) (all horiz with red frame)..........	5·50	5·50
MS1040	135×95 mm. $6 Prince William and Miss Catherine Middleton (vert, blue frame)...................	4·75	4·75
MS1041	135×95 mm. $6 Prince William and Miss Catherine Middleton (vert, red frame)...................	4·75	4·75

210 Pantropical Spotted Dolphin

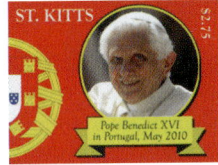

211 Pope Benedict XVI and Arms of Portugal

(Litho)

2011 (21 Feb). Caribbean Dolphins. T **210** and similar horiz designs. Multicoloured. P 13 (with one elliptical hole on each vert side) (**MS**1042) or 12 (**MS**1043/4).

MS1042	150×101 mm. $2·50×4 Type **210**; Killer whale (*Orcinus orca*); Tucuxi (*Sotalia fluviatilis*); Clymene dolphin (*Stenella clymene*).....................	5·50	5·50
MS1043	100×70 mm. $6 Bottlenose dolphin (*Tursiops truncatus*)...	4·75	4·75
MS1044	100×70 mm. $6 Rough-toothed dolphin (*Steno bredanensis*)...	4·75	4·75

(Litho)

2011 (21 Feb). Pope Benedict XVI visits Portugal. T **211** and similar horiz designs. Multicoloured. P 13.

MS1045	170×111 mm. $2·75 Type **211**; $2·75 Portrait as Type **211** but green background and arms at right×3..	5·00	5·00
MS1046	191×110 mm. $2·75 Pope Benedict XVI and Portuguese city×4..	6·75	6·75

212 Ricky Ponting (Australia)

259

ST. KITTS-NEVIS / St. Kitts

(Litho)

2011 (2 Apr). Cricket World Cup. Maestros of Cricket. T **212** and similar circular designs. Multicoloured. P 13.

MS1047 212×150 mm. $1.90×14 Type **212**; Shakib Al Hasan (Bangladesh) (wrongly inscr 'Shahid Afridi'); Ashish Bagai (Canada); Mahendra Singh Dhoni (India); Andrew Strauss (England) (wrongly inscr 'Ricky Ponting'); William Porterfield (Ireland); Maurice Ouma (Kenya); Daniel Vettori (New Zealand); Shahid Afridi (Pakistan); Graeme Smith (South Africa); Kumar Sangakkara (Sri Lanka); Peter Borren (Netherlands); Elton Chigumbura (Zimbabwe); Darren Sammy (West Indies) .... 15·00 15·50

MS1048 212×150 mm. $1.90×14 As **MS**1047 but corrected inscriptions on stamps depicting Shakib Al Hasan and Andrew Strauss .... 15·00 15·50

213 Mt. Fuji, Japan

(Litho)

2011 (18 May). Philanippon 2011 World Stamp Exhibition, Yokohama. Sites and Scenes of Japan. Three sheets, each 125×55 mm, containing T **213** and similar horiz designs. Multicoloured. P 11½.

MS1049 Type **213** .... 4·75 5·00
MS1050 Okinawa, Japan .... 4·75 4·75
MS1051 Tokyo, Japan .... 4·75 5·00

214 St. Kitts-Nevis-Anguilla National Bank, Basseterre, St. Kitts

215 Mother Teresa with Ronald and Nancy Reagan

(Litho)

2011 (18 May). 40th Anniv of St. Kitts-Nevis-Anguilla National Bank. T **214** and similar multicoloured design. P 14½×14 (10c.) or 14×14½ ($3).

1052   10c. Type **214** 10 10
1053 $3 40th anniversary emblem (*vert*) .... 2·50 2·50

(Litho)

2011 (5 July). Mother Teresa Commemoration. T **215** and similar horiz designs. Multicoloured. P 13 (with one elliptical hole in each vert side).

MS1054 150×100 mm. $2.75×4 Type **215**; Mother Teresa and nun inside convent; Mother Teresa with children; Mother Teresa with Mayor Jacques Chirac .... 7·50 8·00
MS1055 101×100 mm. $2.75×4 Mother Teresa in close-up); With Prince Charles; Holding baby; With mother and baby .... 7·50 8·00

216 Princess Diana

217 Gen. Robert Lee, Gen. George Meade and Union Positions near Cemetery Ridge

(Litho)

2011 (14 July). 50th Birth Anniv of Princess Diana. T **216** and similar multicoloured desgns. P 13 (**MS**1056) or 12½ (**MS**1057).

MS1056 131×80 mm. $2.75×4 Type **216**; Holding baby Prince William; Wearing red dress with white collar; Wearing check jacket, on honeymoon at Balmoral, 1981 .... 7·00 7·50
MS1057 101×70 mm. $6 Princess Diana wearing white jacket and red top (51×38 *mm*) .... 4·75 5·50

(Litho)

2011 (14 July). 150th Anniv of the American Civil War. Three sheets, each 150×100 mm, containing T **217** and similar horiz designs. Multicoloured. P 13 (with one elliptical hole in each vert side).

MS1058 ×4 each showing inset portraits of Gen. Robert E. Lee and Gen. George G. Meade: Type **217**; Union artillery Hazlitt's Battery in action; Union positions near Cemetery Ridge; Union Artillery Cemetery Hill in the distance .... 7·00 7·50
MS1059 ×4 all with inset portraits of Lt. General James Longstreet and Maj. General Oliver O. Howard: Behind the breastworks on Culp's Hill; Jubal Early's attack on East Cemetery Hill; CSA 2nd Maryland Infantry at Culp's Hill; Confederate pickets at Culp's Hill .... 7·00 7·50
MS1060 ×4 all with inset portraits of Lt. General Richard S. Ewell and Brigadier General George S. Greene: Cavalry engagement at Gettysburg; Battle of Gettysburg; Hand to hand combat at Gettysburg; Battery A, 1st Rhode Island, Cemetery Ridge .... 7·00 7·50

218 Duchess of Cambridge

(Litho)

2011 (14 July). Royal Wedding. T **218** and similar multicoloured designs. P 11½ (**MS**1061), 12½×12 (**MS**1062) or 13½ (**MS**1063).

MS1061 150×100 mm. $2 Type **218**; $2 Prince William; $2 Duke and Duchess of Cambridge; $2 Duke (hand raised) and Duchess of Cambridge; $4 Miss Catherine Middleton arriving at Westminster Abbey (40×60 *mm*) .... 11·00 12·00
MS1062 150×100 mm. $2.75×4 Duke and Duchess of Cambridge (side view, Abbey wall background); Duke and Duchess of Cambridge (Abbey wall background); Duke and Duchess of Cambridge (carriage horse in background); Duke and Duchess of Cambridge (side view, carriage horse in background) .... 7·50 8·00
MS1063 70×100 mm. $6 Duke and Duchess of Cambridge (51×37 *mm*) .... 4·75 5·00

219 Bird of Paradise Flower (*Strelitzia reginae*)

(Litho)

2011 (14 July). Exotic Flowers. T **219** and similar multicoloured designs. P 12.

MS1064 141×140 mm. $2×6 Type **219**; Gardenia jasminoides; Dutch amaryllis (*Amaryllis hippeastrum*); Ginger flower (*Etlingera elatior*); Lobster claw (*Heliconia rostrata*); Bleeding heart (*Dicentra spectabilis*) .... 9·50 11·00
MS1065 140×100 mm. $2.75×4 Cockscomb (*Celosia spicata*); Passion flower (*Passiflora caerulea*); Prairie Blue Eyes daylily (*Hemerocallis*); Blue water lily (*Nymphaea caerulea*) (all 30×40 *mm*) .... 9·50 11·00
MS1066 101×70 mm. $6 Painted feather (*Vriesia carinata*) (30×40 *mm*) .... 7·50 8·50
MS1067 101×70 mm. $6 Cuban lily (*Scilla peruviana*) (40×30 *mm*) .... 4·57 5·00

220 Elvis Presley

ST. KITTS-NEVIS / St Kitts, Nevis

(Litho)

2011 (14 July). 75th Birth Anniv (2010) of Elvis Presley (2nd issue). T **220** and similar multicoloured designs. P 12½.

MS1068	154×174 mm. $3×4 Type **220**; Elvis Presley playing guitar; Holding microphone, seen from back; Holding microphone, side view	9·50	11·00
MS1069	154×190 mm. $3×4 Wearing white jacket with gold design on back; In profile, blue background; In close-up with microphone; Wearing black leather jacket, arms raised (*all vert*)	9·50	11·50

STAMP BOOKLETS

1981 (19 Nov). Royal Wedding. Multicoloured cover, 105×65 mm, showing The Saudadoes. Stitched.

SB1	$9.40 booklet containing eight 55c. in panes of 4 (No. 82a) and $2.50 in pane of 2 (No. 83a)		2·10

OFFICIAL STAMPS

1980 (23 June). Nos. 32/41 additionally optd with Type O **1** of St. Christopher, Nevis and Anguilla.

*A. W w **14** (sideways)*

O1A	15c. Sugar cane harvesting	10	10
O2A	25c. Crafthouse (craft centre)	10	10
O3A	30c. *Europa* (liner)	10	10
O4A	40c. Lobster and sea crab	10	15
O5A	45c. Royal St. Kitts Hotel and golf course	15	15
O6A	50c. Pinney's Beach, Nevis	15	15
O7A	55c. New runway at Golden Rock	15	15
	a. Opt inverted	22·00	
O8A	$1 Cotton picking	25	25
O9A	$5 Brewery	80	1·50
O10A	$10 Pineapples and peanuts	1·00	2·50
	a. Opt inverted	£110	
O1A/10A	Set of 10	2·50	4·50

B. No wmk

O2B	25c. Crafthouse (craft centre)	25	15
O3B	30c. *Europa* (liner)	50	35
O4B	40c. Lobster and sea crab	9·00	12·00
O7B	55c. New runway at Golden Rock	60	1·00
O8B	$1 Cotton picking	1·00	2·00
O9B	$5 Brewery	3·00	6·50
O10B	$10 Pineapples and peanuts	3·50	8·50
O2B/10B	Set of 7	16·00	27·00

OFFICIAL
(O **1**)

1981 (5 Feb). Nos. 59A/70A optd with Type O **1**.

O11	15c. Type **13**	20	10
O12	20c. Scaly-breasted Thrasher	20	10
O13	25c. Grey Kingbird	25	10
O14	30c. Green-throated Carib	25	10
O15	40c. Turnstone	35	15
O16	45c. Black-faced Grassquit	40	20
O17	50c. Cattle Egret	40	20
O18	55c. Brown Pelican	50	25
O19	$1 Lesser Antillean Bullfinch	75	45
O20	$2.50 Zenaida Dove	1·60	1·00
O21	$5 American Kestrel	2·75	2·00
O22	$10 Antillean Crested Hummingbird	5·00	4·25
O11/22	Set of 12	11·50	8·00

1983 (2 Feb). Nos. 75/80 optd with Type O **1** (55c.) or surch also (others).

O23	45c. on $2.50 *Royal George* (New Blue)	15	15
	a. Sheetlet. No. O23×6 and No. O24	1·00	
	b. Surch double	16·00	
	c. Albino surch	7·00	
	f. Deep ultramarine surch	50	
	fd. Surch inverted	3·00	
	fe. Surch inverted (horiz pair)	12·00	
	g. Black opt		
O24	45c. on $2.50 Prince Charles and Lady Diana Spencer (New Blue)	25	25
	b. Surch double	60·00	
	c. Albino surch	25·00	
	f. Deep ultramarine surch	75	
	fd. Surch inverted	20·00	
	g. Black opt		
O25	55c. *Saudadoes* (New Blue)	15	15
	a. Sheetlet. No. O25×6 and No. O26	1·10	
	b. Opt double	18·00	
	c. Albino opt	7·00	
	d. Opt inverted	6·00	
	e. Opt inverted (horiz pair)	18·00	
	f. Block of 3 containing No. O25×2 without opt and No. O26 with two opts		
	g. Deep ultramarine opt	60	
	gd. Opt inverted	4·00	
	ge. Opt inverted (horiz pair)	15·00	
O26	55c. Prince Charles and Lady Diana Spencer (New Blue)	30	30
	b. Opt double	60·00	
	c. Albino opt	27·00	
	d. Opt inverted	23·00	
	f. Deep ultramarine opt	90	
	fd. Opt inverted	19·00	
O27	$1.10 on $4 *Britannia* (Blk.)	30	40
	a. Sheetlet. No. O27×6 and No. O28	2·25	
	b. Surch double	15·00	
	c. Decimal point omitted from surch (R 3/2)	60	
	f. Deep ultramarine surch	2·25	
	fc. Decimal point omitted from surch (R. 3/2)	4·50	
	fd. Surch inverted		
	fe. Surch inverted (horiz pair)		
O28	$1.10 on $4 Prince Charles and Lady Diana Spencer (Blk.)	60	70
	b. Surch double	45·00	
	f. Deep ultramarine surch	25·00	
	fd. Surch inverted		
O23/8	Set of 6	1·60	1·75

Nos. O23fe, O25e, O25ge and O27fe show the surcharge or overprint intended for the large design, inverted and struck across a horizontal pair of the smaller. Nos. O24fd, O26d, O26fd and O28fd each show two inverted surcharges or overprints intended for a horizontal pair of the smaller design.

1984 (4 July). Nos. 145/56 optd with Type O **1**.

O29	15c. Red-lined Cleaning Shrimp	70	1·50
O30	20c. Bristleworm	80	1·75
O31	25c. Flamingo Tongue (*Cyphoma gibbosus*)	80	1·75
O32	30c. Christmas Tree Worm	90	1·75
O33	40c. Pink-tipped Anemone	1·00	1·75
O34	50c. Small-mouthed Grunt	1·00	1·75
O35	60c. Glass-eyed Snapper	1·25	2·25
O36	75c. Reef Squirrelfish	1·50	2·75
O37	$1 Sea Fans and Flamefish (*vert*)	2·00	2·75
O38	$2.50 Reef Butterflyfish (*vert*)	3·75	6·50
O39	$5 Black-barred Soldierfish (*vert*)	5·50	3·00
O40	$10 Cocoa Damselfish (*vert*)	8·50	6·00
O29/40	Set of 12	25·00	30·00

NEVIS

(**7**)   **8** Nevis Lighter

1980 (23 June). Nos. 394/406 of St. Christopher, Nevis and Anguilla optd with T **7**.

37	5c. Radio and TV station	10	10
38	10c. Technical college	10	10
	w. Wmk Crown to left of CA	30·00	
39	12c. TV assembly plant	10	30
40	15c. Sugar cane harvesting	10	10
41	25c. Crafthouse (craft centre)	10	10
	a. No wmk	1·00	1·75
42	30c. *Europa* (liner)	20	15
43	40c. Lobster and sea crab	20	40
44	45c. Royal St. Kitts Hotel and golf course	80	70
45	50c. Pinney's Beach, Nevis	20	30
46	55c. New runway at Golden Rock	40	15
47	$1 Picking cotton	15	30
	a. No wmk	2·50	5·00
48	$5 Brewery	30	75
49	$10 Pineapples and peanuts	40	1·00
37/49	Set of 13	2·50	3·75

1980 (4 Sept). 80th Birthday of Queen Elizabeth the Queen Mother. As T **10** of St. Kitts, but inscr "NEVIS".

50	$2 multicoloured	20	30

No. 50 was printed in sheets including two *se-tenant* stamp-size labels.

(Des Jennifer Toombs. Litho Questa)

1980 (8 Oct). Boats. T **8** and similar multicoloured designs. W w **14** (sideways on 5, 30 and 55c.). P 14.

51	5c. Type **8**	10	10
52	30c. Local fishing boat	15	10
53	55c. *Caona* (catamaran)	15	10

STANLEY GIBBONS

Commonwealth Department
Recently offered Nevis
from our ever changing stock

SG 18

1876-78 4d litho printing. Lovely complete sheet. Ex Jaffé.

If you would like to receive our bi-monthly illustrated list, contact
Pauline MacBroom on 020 7557 4450 or by email at pmacbroom@stanleygibbons.com
or Brian Lucas on 020 7557 4418 or by email at blucas@stanleygibbons.com

Stanley Gibbons Limited, 399 Strand, London WC2R 0LX
Tel: 020 7836 8444   Fax: 020 7557 4499

To view all of our stock 24 hours a day visit **www.stanleygibbons.com**

54	$3 *Polynesia* (cruise schooner) (39×53 *mm*)	40	40
	a. Perf 12 (booklets)	30	60
	ab. Booklet pane of 3	80	
	aw. wmk inverted	30	
	ab. Booklet pane of 3	80	
51/4 Set of 4		65	60

No. 54a comes from $12.30 stamp booklets containing No. 53×6 and one pane as No. 54ab. In this pane each stamp is surrounded by white margins, the pane being divided in three by vertical roulettes.

9 Virgin and Child

(Des Jennifer Toombs. Litho Format)

1980 (20 Nov). Christmas. T **9** and similar vert designs. Multicoloured. W w **14**. P 14.

55	5c. Type **9**	10	10
56	30c. Angel	10	10
57	$2.50 The Three Wise Men	20	30
55/7 Set of 3		20	35

Nos. 55/7 were each printed in sheets of 8 stamps and 1 label.

10 Charlestown Pier    **11** New River Mill

(Des Jennifer Toombs. Litho Questa)

1981 (5 Feb)–**82**. Horiz designs as T **10** (5, 10c.) or T **11** (15c. to $10). Multicoloured. W w **14**. P 14×13½ (5, 10c.) or 14 (others).

A. Without imprint date

58A	5c. Type **10**	10	10
59A	10c. Court House and Library	10	10
60A	15c. Type **11**	10	10
61A	20c. Nelson Museum	10	10
62A	25c. St. James' Parish Church	15	15
63A	30c. Nevis Lane	15	15
64A	40c. Zetland Plantation	20	20
65A	45c. Nisbet Plantation	20	25
66A	50c. Pinney's Beach	25	25
67A	55c. Eva Wilkin's Studio	25	30
68A	$1 Nevis at dawn	30	45
69A	$2.50 Ruins of Fort Charles	35	80
70A	$5 Old Bath House	40	1·00
71A	$10 Beach at Nisbet's	50	1·50
58A/71A Set of 14		2·50	4·50

B. With imprint date at foot (9.6.82)

58B	5c. Type **10** (*wmk inverted*)	40	30
59B	10c. Court House and Library (*wmk inverted*)	40	30
60B	15c. Type **11**	15	10
61B	20c. Nelson Museum	15	10
62B	25c. St James' Parish Church	20	15
63B	30c. Nevis Lane	20	15
64B	40c. Zetland Plantation	25	20
65B	45c. Nisbet Plantation	25	25
66B	50c. Pinney's Beach	30	25
67B	55c. Eva Wilkin's Studio	30	30
68B	$1 Nevis at dawn	45	45
69B	$2.50 Ruins of Fort Charles	70	80
70B	$5 Old Bath House	90	1·00
71B	$10 Beach at Nisbet's	1·25	2·00
58B/71B Set of 14		5·50	5·00

Imprint dates: "1982", Nos. 58/71B; "1983", Nos. 61B/7B, 69B.

(Des D. Shults. Litho Questa)

1981 (23 June–14 Dec). Royal Wedding. Horiz designs as T **26/27** of kiribati. Multicloured.

*(a) W w **14**. P 14.*

72	55c. *Royal Caroline*	15	15
	a. Sheetlet. No. 72×6 and No. 73	1·10	
73	55c. Prince Charles and Lady Diana Spencer	40	40
74	$2 *Royal Sovereign*	30	30
	aw. Wmk inverted	8·00	
	b. Sheetlet. No. 74×6 and No. 75	2·40	
	bw. Wmk inverted	70·00	
75	$2 As No. 73	80	1·25
	aw. Wmk inverted	35·00	
76	$5 *Britannia*	45	80
	aw. Wmk inverted	4·00	
	b. Sheetlet. No. 76×6 and No. 77	3·25	
	bw. Wmk inverted	35·00	
77	$5 As No. 73	1·00	2·00
	aw. Wmk inverted	17·00	
72/7 Set of 6		2·75	4·50
MS78 120×109 mm. $4.50, As No. 73, Wmk sideways. P 12 (14 Dec)		1·10	1·25

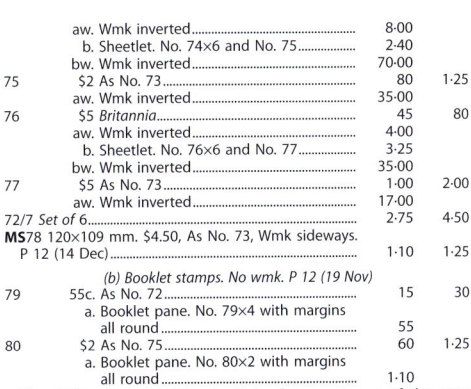

(b) Booklet stamps. No wmk. P 12 (19 Nov)

79	55c. As No. 72	15	30
	a. Booklet pane. No. 79×4 with margins all round	55	
80	$2 As No. 75	60	1·25
	a. Booklet pane. No. 80×2 with margins all round	1·10	

Nos. 72/7 were printed in sheetlets of seven stamps of the same face value, each containing six of the "Royal Yacht" design and one of the larger design showing Prince Charles and Lady Diana.

Nos. 79/80 come from $8.40 stamp booklets.

12 *Heliconius charithonia*    **13** Caroline of Brunswick, Princess of Wales, 1793

(Des Jennifer Toombs. Litho Questa)

1982 (16 Feb). Butterflies (1st series). T **12** and similar horiz designs. Multicoloured. W w **14** (sideways). P 14.

81	5c. Type **12**	10	10
82	30c. *Siproeta stelenes*	20	15
83	55c. *Marpesia petreus*	25	15
84	$2 *Phoebis agarithe*	60	80
81/4 Set of 4		1·00	1·00

See also Nos. 105/8.

(Des D. Shults and J. Cooter. Litho Format)

1982 (22 June). 21st Birthday of Princess of Wales. T **13** and similar vert designs. Multicoloured. W w **14**. P 13½×14.

85	30c. Type **13**	10	10
86	55c. Coat of arms of Caroline of Brunswick	15	15
87	$5 Diana, Princess of Wales	60	1·00
85/7 Set of 3		75	1·10

1982 (12 July). Birth of Prince William of Wales. Nos. 85/7 optd with T **19** of St. Kitts.

88	30c. Type **13**	10	10
89	55c. Coat of arms of Caroline of Brunswick	15	15
	a. Opt triple	25·00	
90	$5 Diana, Princess of Wales	60	1·00
88/90 Set of 3		75	1·10

14 Cyclist

(Des Philatelists (1980) Ltd. Litho Questa)

1982 (18 Aug). 75th Anniv of Boy Scout Movement. T **14** and similar horiz designs. Multicoloured. W w **14** (sideways). P 13½×14.

91	5c. Type **14**	20	10
92	30c. Athlete	25	10
93	$2.50 Camp cook	50	65
91/3 Set of 3		85	70

15 Santa Claus
16 Tube Sponge

(Des Eugene Seabrookes (15c.), Kharenzabeth Glasgow (30c.) Davia Grant ($1.50), Leonard Huggins ($2.50); adapted Jennifer Toombs. Litho Format)

1982 (20 Oct). Christmas. Children's Paintings. T **15** and similar multicoloured designs. W w **14** (sideways on $1.50 and $2.50). P 13½×14 (15c., 30c.) or 14×13½ (others).

94	15c. Type **15**	10	10
95	30c. Carollers	10	10
96	$1.50 Decorated house and local band (*horiz*)	15	25
97	$2.50 Adoration of the Shepherds (*horiz*)	25	40
94/7	Set of 4	45	65

(Des G. Drummond. Litho Format)

1983 (12 Jan). Corals (1st series). T **16** and similar vert designs. Multicoloured. W w **14**. P 14.

98	15c. Type **16**	10	10
99	30c. Stinging coral	15	10
100	55c. Flower coral	15	10
101	$3 Sea Rod and Red Fire Sponge	50	90
98/101	Set of 4	75	1·00
MS102	82×115 mm. Nos. 98/101	1·60	3·00

See also Nos. 423/6.

17 H.M.S. *Boreas* off Nevis

(Des G. Drummond. Litho Format)

1983 (14 Mar). Commonwealth Day. T **17** and similar horiz design. Multicoloured. W w **14** (sideways). P 14.

103	55c. Type **17**	15	10
104	$2 Capt Horatio Nelson and H.M.S. *Boreas* at anchor	45	60

(Des Jennifer Toombs. Litho Format)

1983 (8 June). Butterflies (2nd series). Multicoloured designs as T **12**. W w **14** (sideways* on 30c. and $2). P 14.

105	30c. *Pyrgus oileus*	25	10
	w. Wmk Crown to right of CA	16·00	
106	55c. *Junonia evarete* (*vert*)	25	10
107	$1.10 *Urbanus proteus* (*vert*)	40	40
108	$2 *Hypolimnas misippus*	50	75
	w. Wmk Crown to right of CA	17·00	
105/8	Set of 4	1·25	1·25

*The normal sideways watermark shows Crown to left of CA, as seen from the back of the stamp.

INDEPENDENCE 1983 (**18**)	INDEPENDENCE 1983 (**18a**)

1983 (19 Sept). Nos. 58 and 60/71 optd as T **18** (Nos. 110/21).

A. Without imprint date.

109Ab	5c. Type **10** (optd locally with T **18a**)	15·00	11·00
110A	15c. Type **11**	40·00	40·00
111A	20c. Nelson Museum	5·50	5·50
112A	25c. St. James' Parish Church	5·50	5·50
113A	30c. Nevis Lane	11·00	90
114A	40c. Zetland Plantation	75	75
117A	55c. Eva Wilkin's Studio	12·00	75
118A	$1 Nevis at dawn	75	75
119A	$2.50 Ruins of Fort Charles	1·10	1·10
120A	$5 Old Bath House	1·90	2·25
121A	$10 Beach at Nisbet's	60·00	4·25
	a. Opt inverted	60·00	
109Ab/21A	Set of 11	65·00	65·00

B. With imprint date at foot

109B	5c. Type **10**	1·00	2·00
	a. Vert pair, lower stamp without opt	32·00	
	b. Optd with T **18a** (local opt)	1·00	2·00
	ba. Opt T **18a** inverted	32·00	
110B	15c. Type **11**	10	10
111B	20c. Nelson Museum	10	10
112B	25c. St. James' Parish Church	10	15
113B	30c. Nevis Lane	15	15
	a. Opt inverted	11·00	
114B	40c. Zetland Plantation	15	20
115B	45c. Nisbet Plantation	15	25
116B	50c. Pinney's Beach	15	25
117B	55c. Eva Wilkin's Studio	15	30
	a. Opt double	12·00	
118B	$1 Nevis at dawn	15	30
119B	$2.50 Ruins of Fort Charles	25	45
120B	$5 Old Bath House	30	55
121B	$10 Beach at Nisbet's	40	70
109B/21B	Set of 13	2·00	3·00

Imprint dates: "1982", Nos. 109B/10B; "1983", Nos. 110B/21B.

19 Montgolfier Balloon, 1783

(Des A. Theobald. Litho Format)

1983 (28 Sept). Bicentenary of Manned Flight. T **19** and similar multicoloured designs. W w **15** (sideways* on 45c. to $2.50). P 14.

122	10c. Type **19**	10	10
123	45c. Sikorsky S-38 flying boat (*horiz*)	25	10
124	50c. Beech 50 Twin Bonanza (*horiz*)	25	10
125	$2.50 Hawker Siddeley Sea Harrier (*horiz*)	55	1·25
122/5	Set of 4	1·00	1·40
MS126	118×145 mm. Nos. 122/5. Wmk sideways	75	1·25
	w. Wmk POST OFFICE reading downwards	55·00	

*The normal sideways watermark shows "POST OFFICE" reading downwards on Nos. 122/5 and upwards on No. **MS**126.

20 Mary praying over Holy Child

(Des Jennifer Toombs. Litho Format)

1983 (7 Nov). Christmas. T **20** and similar horiz designs. Multicoloured. W w **15** (sideways). P 14.

127	5c. Type **20**	10	10
128	30c. Shepherds with flock	10	10
129	55c. Three Angels	10	10
130	$3 Boy with two girls	30	60
127/30	Set of 4	45	70
MS131	135×149 mm. Nos. 127/30	85	2·00

IMPERFORATES AND MISSING COLOURS. Various issues between Nos. 134 and 422 exist either imperforate or with colours omitted. Such items are not listed as there is no evidence that they fulfil the criteria outlined on page x of this catalogue.

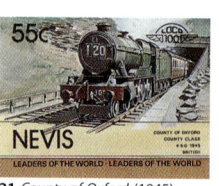

21 *County of Oxford* (1945)
22 Boer War

ST. KITTS-NEVIS / Nevis

(Des J.W. Litho Format)

1983 (10 Nov). Leaders of the World. Railway Locomotives (1st series). T **21** and similar horiz designs, the first in each pair showing technical drawings and the second the locomotive at work. P 12½.

132	55c. multicoloured	10	20
	a. Vert pair. Nos. 132/3	15	40
133	55c. multicoloured	10	20
134	$1 bright crimson, new blue and black	10	20
	a. Vert pair. Nos. 134/5	20	40
135	$1 multicoloured	10	20
136	$1 magenta, new blue and black	10	20
	a. Vert pair. Nos. 136/7	20	40
137	$1 multicoloured	10	20
138	$1 bright crimson, black and greenish yellow	10	20
	a. Vert pair. Nos. 138/9	20	40
139	$1 multicoloured	10	20
140	$1 multicoloured	10	20
	a. Vert pair. Nos. 140/1	20	40
141	$1 multicoloured	10	20
142	$1 greenish yellow, black and new blue	10	20
	a. Vert pair. Nos. 142/3	20	40
143	$1 multicoloured	10	20
144	$1 greenish yellow, black & bright magenta	10	20
	a. Vert pair. Nos. 144/5	20	40
145	$1 multicoloured	10	20
146	$1 multicoloured	10	20
	a. Vert pair. Nos. 146/7	20	40
147	$1 multicoloured	10	20
132/47 Set of 16		1·40	2·75

Designs:—Nos. 132/3, *County of Oxford*, Great Britain (1945); 134/5, *Evening Star*, Great Britain (1960); 136/7, Stanier Class 5 No. 44806, Great Britain (1934); 138/9, *Pendennis Castle*, Great Britain (1924); 140/1, *Winston Churchill*, Great Britain (1946); 142/3, *Mallard*, Great Britain (1938) (inscr "1935" in error); 144/5, *Britannia*, Great Britain (1951); 146/7, *King George V*, Great Britain (1927).

Nos. 132/3, 134/5, 136/7, 138/9, 140/1, 142/3, 144/5 and 146/7 were printed together, *se-tenant*, in vertical pairs throughout the sheets.

See also Nos. 219/26, 277/84, 297/308, 352/9 and 427/42.

(Des Court House Studio. Litho Format)

1984 (11 Apr). Leaders of the World. British Monarchs (1st series). T **22** and similar vert designs. Multicoloured. P 12½.

148	5c. Type **22**	10	10
	a. Horiz pair. Nos. 148/9	10	10
149	5c. Queen Victoria	10	10
150	50c. Queen Victoria at Osborne House	10	30
	a. Horiz pair. Nos. 150/1	20	60
151	50c. Osborne House	10	30
152	60c. Battle of Dettingen	10	30
	a. Horiz pair. Nos. 152/3	20	60
153	60c. George II	10	30
154	75c. George II at the Bank of England	10	30
	a. Horiz pair. Nos. 154/5	20	60
155	75c. Bank of England	10	30
156	$1 Coat of Arms of George II	10	30
	a. Horiz pair. Nos. 156/7	20	60
157	$1 George II (*different*)	10	30
158	$3 Coat of Arms of Queen Victoria	20	50
	a. Horiz pair. Nos. 158/9	40	1·00
159	$3 Queen Victoria (*different*)	20	50
148/59 Set of 12		1·10	3·00

Nos. 148/9, 150/1, 152/3, 154/5, 156/7 and 158/9 were printed together, *se-tenant* in horizontal pairs throughout the sheet.

See also Nos. 231/6.

23 Golden Rock Inn

24 Early Seal of Colony

(Des Jennifer Toombs. Litho J.W.)

1984 (16 May). Tourism. (1st series). T **23** and similar horiz designs. Multicoloured. W w **15** (sideways). P 14.

160	55c. Type **23**	25	20
161	55c. Rest Haven Inn	25	20
162	55c. Cliffdwellers Hotel	25	20
163	55c. Pinney's Beach Hotel	25	20
160/3 Set of 4		90	70

See also Nos. 245/8.

(Des G. Drummond. Litho Format)

1984 (8 June). W w **15** (sideways). P 14.

164	**24**	$15 dull scarlet	1·10	4·00

25 Cadillac

(Des J.W. Litho Format)

1984 (25 July). Leaders of the World. Automobiles (1st series). T **25** and similar horiz designs, the first in each pair showing technical drawings and the second paintings. P 12½.

165	1c. greenish yellow, black and magenta	10	10
	a. Vert pair. Nos. 65/6	10	10
166	1c. multicoloured	10	10
167	5c. new blue, magenta and black	10	10
	a. Vert pair. Nos. 167/8	10	10
168	5c. multicoloured	10	10
169	15c. multicoloured	10	15
	a. Vert pair. Nos. 169/70	10	30
170	15c. multicoloured	10	15
171	35c. magenta, greenish yellow and black	10	25
	a. Vert pair. Nos. 171/2	10	50
172	35c. multicoloured	10	25
173	45c. new blue, magenta and black	10	25
	a. Vert pair. Nos. 173/4	10	50
174	45c. multicoloured	10	25
175	55c. multicoloured	10	25
	a. Vert pair. Nos. 175/6	10	50
176	55c. multicoloured	10	25
177	$2.50 magenta, black and greenish yellow	20	40
	a. Vert pair. Nos. 177/8	40	80
178	$2.50 multicoloured	20	40
179	$3 new blue, greenish yellow and black	20	40
	a. Vert pair. Nos. 179/80	40	80
180	$3 multicoloured	20	40
165/80 Set of 16		1·10	3·25

Designs:—Nos. 165/6, Cadillac "V16 Fleetwood Convertible" (1932); 167/8, Packard "Twin Six Touring Car" (1916); 169/70, Daimler, "2 Cylinder" (1886); 171/2, Porsche "911 S Targa" (1970); 173/4, Benz "Three Wheeler" (1885); 175/6, M.G. "TC" (1947); 177/8, Cobra "Roadster 289" (1966); 179/80, Aston Martin DB6 Hardtop" (1966).

Nos. 165/6, 167/8, 169/70, 171/2, 173/4, 175/6, 177/8 and 179/80 were printed together, *se-tenant*, in vertical pairs throughout the sheet.

See also Nos. 203/10, 249/64, 326/37, 360/71 and 411/22.

26 Carpentry

27 Yellow Bell

(Des Jennifer Toombs. Litho Questa)

1984 (1 Aug). Tenth Anniv of Culturama. Celebrations. T **26** and similar horiz designs. Multicoloured. W w **15** (sideways*). P 14.

181	30c. Type **26**	10	10
182	55c. Grass mat and basket-making	10	10
	w. Wmk POST OFFICE reading upwards	3·50	
183	$1 Pottery-firing	15	25
184	$3 Culturama Queen and dancers	40	55
181/4 Set of 4		65	85

*The normal sideways watermark shows "POST OFFICE" reading downwards.

(Des Jennifer Toombs, Litho Format)

1984 (8 Aug)–86. Flowers. T **27** and similar vert designs. Multicoloured. W w **15**. P 14.

A. Without imprint date.

185A	5c. Type **27**	10	10
186A	10c. Plumbago	10	10
187A	15c. Flamboyant	10	10
188A	20c. Eyelash Orchid	60	15
189A	30c. Bougainvillea	10	15
190A	40c. Hibiscus *sp.*	50	25
191A	50c. Night-blooming Cereus	10	20
192A	55c. Yellow Mahoe	10	25
193A	60c. Spider-lily	10	25

ST. KITTS-NEVIS / Nevis

194A	75c. Scarlet Cordia	15	30
195A	$1 Shell-ginger	15	40
196A	$3 Blue Petrea	20	1·10
197A	$5 Coral Hibiscus	40	2·00
198A	$10 Passion Flower	70	3·50
185A/98A Set of 14		3·00	8·00

B. With imprint date ("1986") at foot of design (23.7.86)

188B	20c. Eyelash Orchid	60	30
190B	40c. Hibiscus sp.	30	30

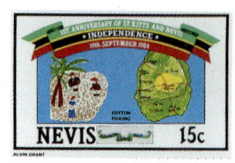

28 Cotton-picking and Map  **29** C. P. Mead

(Des A. Grant (15c.), Tracy Watkins (55c.), C. Manners ($1.10), D. Grant ($3), adapted Court House Advertising. Litho Format)

1984 (18 Sept). First Anniv of Independence of St. Kitts-Nevis. T **28** and similar horiz designs. Multicoloured. W w **15** (sideways). P 14.

199	15c. Type **28**	10	10
200	55c. Alexander Hamilton's birthplace	10	10
201	$1.10 Local agricultural produce	20	40
202	$3 Nevis Peak and Pinneys Beach	50	1·00
199/202 Set of 4		75	1·40

(Des J.W. Litho Format)

1984 (23 Oct). Leaders of the World. Automobiles (2nd series). Horiz designs as T **25**, the first in each pair showing technical drawings and the second paintings. P 12½.

203	5c. black, pale new blue and yellow-brown	10	10
	a. Vert pair. Nos. 203/4	10	10
204	5c. multicoloured	10	10
205	30c. black, pale turquoise-green and lake-brown	15	15
	a. Vert pair. Nos. 205/6	30	30
206	30c. multicoloured	15	15
207	50c. black, pale drab and red-brown	15	15
	a. Vert pair. Nos. 207/8	30	30
208	50c. multicoloured	15	15
209	$3 black, grey-brown and dull green	30	45
	a. Vert pair. Nos. 209/10	60	90
210	$3 multicoloured	30	45
203/10 Set of 8		1·10	1·40

Designs:—Nos. 203/4, Lagonda "Speed Model" touring car (1929); 205/6, Jaguar "E-Type" 4.2 litre (1967); 207/8, Volkswagen "Beetle" (1947); 209/10, Pierce Arrow "V12" (1932).

Nos. 203/10 were issued in a similar sheet format to Nos. 165/80.

(Des Court House Studio. Litho Format)

1984 (23 Oct). Leaders of the World. Cricketers (1st series). T **29** and similar vert designs, the first in each pair showing a head portrait and the second the cricketer in action. P 12½.

211	5c. multicoloured	10	10
	a. Horiz pair. Nos. 211/12	15	15
212	5c. multicoloured	10	10
213	25c. multicoloured	20	30
	a. Horiz pair. Nos. 213/14	40	60
214	25c. multicoloured	20	30
215	55c. multicoloured	30	40
	a. Horiz pair. Nos. 215/16	60	80
216	55c. multicoloured	30	40
217	$2.50 multicoloured	50	1·25
	a. Horiz pair. Nos. 217/18	1·00	2·50
218	$2.50 multicoloured	50	1·25
211/18 Set of 8		2·00	3·50

Designs:—Nos. 211/12, C. P. Mead; 213/14, J. B. Statham; 215/16, Sir Learie Constantine; 217/18, Sir Leonard Hutton.

Nos. 211/12, 213/14, 215/16 and 217/18 were printed together, *se-tenant*, in horizontal pairs throughout the sheets.

See also Nos. 237/44.

(Des J. W. Litho Format)

1984 (29 Oct). Leaders of the World. Railway Locomotives (2nd series). Horiz designs as T **21** the first in each pair showing technical drawings and the second the locomotive at work. P 12½.

219	5c. multicoloured	10	10
	a. Vert pair. Nos. 219/20	10	10
220	5c. multicoloured	10	10
221	10c. multicoloured	10	10
	a. Vert pair. Nos. 221/2	10	15
222	10c. multicoloured	10	10
223	60c. multicoloured	15	25
	a. Vert pair. Nos. 223/4	30	50
224	60c. multicoloured	15	25
225	$2.50 multicoloured	50	70
	a. Vert pair. Nos. 225/6	1·00	1·40
226	$2.50 multicoloured	50	70
219/26 Set of 8		1·25	1·75

Designs:—Nos. 219/20, Class EF81 electric locomotive, Japan (1968); 221/2, Class 5500 electric locomotive, France (1927); 223/4, Class 240P, France (1940); 225/6, "Hikari" express train, Japan (1964).

Nos. 219/26 were issued in a similar sheet format to Nos. 132/47.

30 Fifer and Drummer from Honeybees Band

(Des Jennifer Toombs. Litho Questa)

1984 (2 Nov). Christmas. Local Music. T **30** and similar horiz designs. Multicoloured. W w **15** (sideways). P 14.

227	15c. Type **30**	15	10
228	40c. Guitar and "barhow" players from Canary Birds Band	25	10
229	60c. Shell All Stars steel band	30	10
230	$3 Organ and choir, St. John's Church, Fig Tree	1·25	1·00
227/30 Set of 4		1·75	1·10

(Des Court House Studio. Litho Format)

1984 (20 Nov). Leaders of the World. British Monarchs (2nd series). Vert designs as T **22**. Multicoloured. P 12½.

231	5c. King John and Magna Carta	10	10
	a. Horiz pair. Nos. 231/2	10	10
232	5c. Barons and King John	10	10
233	55c. King John	10	15
	a. Horiz pair. Nos. 233/4	20	30
234	55c. Newark Castle	10	15
235	$2 Coat of arms	25	40
	a. Horiz pair. Nos. 235/6	50	80
236	$2 King John (*different*)	25	40
231/6 Set of 6		65	1·00

Nos. 231/6 were issued in a similar sheet format to Nos. 148/59.

(Des Court House Studio. Litho Format)

1984 (20 Nov). Leaders of the World. Cricketers (2nd series). Vert designs as T **29**, the first in each pair listed showing a head portrait and the second the cricketer in action. P 12½.

237	5c. multicoloured	10	10
	a. Horiz pair. Nos. 237/8	10	15
238	5c. multicoloured	10	10
239	15c. multicoloured	10	15
	a. Horiz pair. Nos. 239/40	15	30
240	15c. multicoloured	10	15
241	55c. multicoloured	15	20
	a. Horiz pair. Nos. 241/2	30	40
242	55c. multicoloured	15	20
243	$2.50 multicoloured	40	60
	a. Horiz pair. Nos. 243/4	80	1·10
244	$2.50 multicoloured	40	60
237/44 Set of 8		1·25	1·75

Designs:—Nos. 237/8, J. D. Love; 239/40, S. J. Dennis; 241/2, B. W. Luckhurst; 243/4, B. L. D'Oliveira.

Nos. 237/44 were issued in a similar sheet format to Nos. 211/18.

(Des Jennifer Toombs, Litho Format)

1985 (12 Feb). Tourism (2nd series). Horiz designs as T **23**. Multicoloured. W w **15** (sideways). P 14.

245	$1.20 Croney's Old Manor Hotel	15	25
246	$1.20 Montpelier Plantation Inn	15	25
247	$1.20 Nisbet's Plantation Inn	15	25
248	$1.20 Zetland Plantation Inn	15	25
245/8 Set of 4		55	90

(Des G. Turner (10c.), J.W. (others). Litho Format)

1985 (20 Feb). Leaders of the World. Automobiles (3rd series). Horiz designs as T **25**, the first in each pair showing technical drawings and the second paintings. P 12½.

249	1c. black, light green and pale green	10	10
	a. Vert pair. Nos. 249/50	10	10
250	1c. multicoloured	10	10
251	5c. black, cobalt and pale violet-blue	10	10
	a. Vert pair. Nos. 251/2	10	10

ST. KITTS-NEVIS / Nevis

252	5c. multicoloured	10	10
253	10c. black, grey-olive and pale green	10	10
	a. Vert pair. Nos. 253/4	10	10
254	10c. multicoloured	10	10
255	50c. black, sage-green and pale cinnamon	10	10
	a. Vert pair. Nos. 255/6	10	20
256	50c. multicoloured	10	10
257	60c. black, dull yellowish green and pale blue..	10	10
	a. Vert pair. Nos. 257/8	10	20
258	60c. multicoloured	10	10
259	75c. black, dull vermilion and pale orange	10	10
	a. Vert pair. Nos. 259/60	15	20
260	75c. multicoloured	10	10
261	$2.50 black, light green and azure	20	30
	a. Vert pair. Nos. 261/2	40	60
262	$2.50 multicoloured	20	30
263	$3 black, bright yellow-green and pale green	20	30
	a. Vert pair. Nos. 263/4	40	60
264	$3 multicoloured	20	30
249/64 Set of 16		1·00	1·75

Designs:—Nos. 249/50 Delahaye "Type 35 Cabriolet" (1935); 251/2a Ferrari "Tests Rossa" (1958) 253/4 Voisin "Aerodyne" (1934); 255/6, Buick "Riviera" (1963); 257/8, Cooper "Climax" (1960); 259/60, Ford "999" (1904); 261/2, MG "M-Type Midget" (1930); 263/4, Rolls-Royce "Corniche" (1971).

Nos. 249/64 were issued in a similar sheet format to Nos. 165/80.

31 Broad-winged Hawk

(Des Jennifer Toombs. Litho Format)

1985 (19 Mar). Local Hawks and Herons. T **31** and similar horiz designs. Multicoloured. W w **15** (sideways). P 14.

265	20c. Type **31**	1·25	20
266	40c. Red-tailed Hawk	1·40	30
267	60c. Little Blue Heron	1·40	40
268	$3 Great Blue Heron (white phase)	2·75	1·90
265/8 Set of 4		6·00	2·50

No. 268 was re-issued on 24 May 1990 overprinted "40th Anniversary C.S.S." to mark the fortieth anniversary of Charlestown Secondary School. This overprint was only available on First Day Covers.

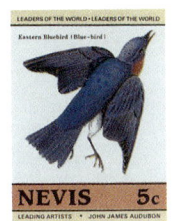

32 Eastern Bluebird

(Des R. Vigurs. Litho Format)

1985 (25 Mar). Leaders of the World. Birth Bicentenary of John J. Audubon (ornithologist) (1st issue). T **32** and similar vert designs. Multicoloured. P 12½.

269	5c. Type **32**	10	10
	a. Horiz pair. Nos. 269/70	20	20
270	5c. Common Cardinal	10	10
271	55c. Belted Kingfisher	20	55
	a. Horiz pair. Nos. 271/2	40	1·10
272	55c. Mangrove Cuckoo	20	55
273	60c. Yellow Warbler	20	55
	a. Horiz pair. Nos. 273/4	40	1·10
274	60c. Cerulean Warbler	20	55
275	$2 Burrowing Owl	60	1·25
	a. Horiz pair. Nos. 275/6	1·10	2·50
276	$2 Long-eared Owl	60	1·25
269/76 Set of 8		2·00	4·50

Nos. 269/70, 271/2, 273/4 and 275/6 were printed together, se-tenant, in horizontal pairs throughout the sheets.

See also Nos. 285/92.

(Des J.W. Litho Format)

1985 (26 Apr). Leaders of the World. Railway Locomotives (3rd series). Horiz designs as T **21**, the first in each pair showing technical drawings and the second the locomotive at work. P 12½.

277	1c. multicoloured	10	10
	a. Vert pair. Nos. 277/8	10	10
278	1c. multicoloured	10	10
279	60c. multicoloured	20	20
	a. Vert pair. Nos. 279/80	40	40
280	60c. multicoloured	20	20
281	90c. multicoloured	25	25
	a. Vert pair. Nos. 281/2	50	50
282	90c. multicoloured	25	25
283	$2 multicoloured	40	60
	a. Vert pair. Nos. 283/4	80	1·10
284	$2 multicoloured	40	60
277/84 Set of 8		1·50	1·75

Designs:—Nos. 277/8, Class "Wee Bogie", Great Britain (1882); 279/80, *Comet*, Great Britain (1851); 281/2, Class 8H No. 6173, Great Britain (1908); 283/4, Class A No. 23, Great Britain (1866).

Nos. 277/84 were issued in a similar sheet format to Nos. 132/47.

(Des R. Vigurs. Litho Format)

1985 (3 June). Leaders of the World. Birth Bicentenary of John J. Audubon (ornithologist) (2nd issue). Vert designs as T **32** showing original paintings. Multicoloured. P 12½.

285	1c. Painted Bunting	10	10
	a. Horiz pair. Nos. 285/6	10	10
286	1c. Golden-crowned Kinglet	10	10
287	40c. Common Flicker	25	40
	a. Horiz pair. Nos. 287/8	50	80
288	40c. Western Tanager	25	40
289	60c. Varied Thrush ("Sage Thrasher")	25	45
	a. Horiz pair. Nos. 289/90	50	90
290	60c. Evening Grosbeak	25	45
291	$2.50 Blackburnian Warbler	50	80
	a. Horiz pair. Nos. 291/2	1·00	1·60
292	$2.50 Northern Oriole	50	80
285/92 Set of 8		1·75	3·00

Nos. 285/92 were issued in a similar sheet format to Nos. 269/76.

Nos. 285/92 exist with yellow omitted from stock dispersed by the liquidator of Format International Security Printers Ltd.

33 Guides and Guide Headquarters

34 The Queen Mother at Garter Ceremony

(Des G. Vasarhelyi. Litho Format)

1985 (17 June). 75th Anniv of Girl Guide Movement. T **33** and similar multicoloured designs. W w **15** (inverted on 60c., sideways on 15c.). P 14.

293	15c. Type **33**	10	10
294	60c. Girl Guide uniforms of 1910 and 1985 (*vert*)	15	25
295	$1 Lord and Lady Baden-Powell (*vert*)	20	40
296	$3 Princess Margaret in Guide uniform (*vert*)	50	1·25
293/6 Set of 4		75	1·75

(Des T. Hadler (75c., $1, $2.50), J.W. (others). Litho Format)

1985 (26 July). Leaders of the World. Railway Locomotives (4th series). Horiz designs as T **21**, the first in each pair showing technical drawings and the second the locomotive at work. P 12½.

297	5c. multicoloured	10	10
	a. Vert pair. Nos. 297/8	10	10
298	5c. multicoloured	10	10
299	30c. multicoloured	10	15
	a. Vert pair. Nos. 299/300	15	30
300	30c. multicoloured	10	15
301	60c. multicoloured	10	20
	a. Vert pair. Nos. 301/2	20	40
302	60c. multicoloured	10	20
303	75c. multicoloured	10	25
	a. Vert pair. Nos. 303/4	20	50
304	75c. multicoloured	10	25
305	$1 multicoloured	10	25
	a. Vert pair. Nos. 305/6	20	50
306	$1 multicoloured	10	25
307	$2.50 multicoloured	20	60
	a. Vert pair. Nos. 307/8	40	1·10
308	$2.50 multicoloured	20	60
297/308 Set of 12		1·10	2·50

Designs:—Nos. 297/8, *Snowdon Ranger*, Great Britain (1878); 299/300, Large Belpaire locomotive, Great Britain (1904); 301/2, Class "County" No. 3821, Great Britain (1904); 303/4, *L'Outrance*, France (1877); 305/6, Class PB-15, Australia (1899); 307/8, Class 64, Germany (1928).

Nos. 297/308 were issued in a similar sheet format to Nos. 132/47.

ST. KITTS-NEVIS / Nevis

(Des Court House Studio. Litho Format)

1985 (31 July). Leaders of the World. Life and Times of Queen Elizabeth the Queen Mother. Various vertical portraits as T **34**. P 12½.

309	45c. multicoloured		10	15
	a. Horiz pair. Nos. 309/10		20	30
310	45c. multicoloured		10	15
311	75c. multicoloured		10	20
	a. Horiz pair. Nos. 311/12		20	40
312	75c. multicoloured		10	20
313	$1.20 multicoloured		15	35
	a. Horiz pair. Nos. 313/14		30	70
314	$1.20 multicoloured		15	35
315	$1.50 multicoloured		20	40
	a. Horiz pair. Nos. 315/16		40	80
316	$1.50 multicoloured		20	40
309/16 Set of 8			1·00	2·00
MS317	85×114 mm. $2 multicoloured; $2 multicoloured		50	1·40

The two designs of each value were issued, *se-tenant*, in horizontal pairs within the sheets.

Each *se-tenant* pair shows a floral pattern across the bottom of the portraits which stops short of the left-hand edge on the left-hand stamp and of the right-hand edge on the right-hand stamp.

Nos. 309/16 exist in unissued miniature sheets, one for each value, from stock dispersed by the liquidator of Format International Security Printers Ltd.

Designs as Nos. 309/10 and 315/16, but with face values of $3.50×2 and $6×2 also exist in additional miniature sheets from a restricted printing issued 27 December 1985.

35 Isambard Kingdom Brunel

36 St. Pauls Anglican Church, Charlestown

(Des Tudor Art Agency. Litho Format)

1985 (31 Aug). 150th Anniv of the Great Western Railway. T **35** and similar vert designs showing railway engineers and their achievements. Multicoloured. P 12½.

318	25c. Type **35**		15	35
	a. Horiz pair. Nos. 318/19		30	70
319	25c. Royal Albert Bridge, 1859		15	35
320	50c. William Dean		20	45
	a. Horiz pair. Nos. 320/1		40	90
321	50c. Locomotive *Lord of the Isles*, 1895		20	45
322	$1 Locomotive *Lode Star*, 1907		20	65
	a. Horiz pair. Nos. 322/3		40	1·25
323	$1 G. J. Churchward		20	65
324	$2.50 Locomotive *Pendennis Castle*, 1924		30	80
	a. Horiz pair. Nos. 324/5		60	1·60
325	$2.50 C. B. Collett		30	80
318/25 Set of 8			1·50	4·00

Nos. 318/19, 320/1, 322/3 and 324/5 were printed together, *se-tenant*, in horizontal pairs throughout the sheets, each pair forming a composite design.

(Des J.W. Litho Format)

1985 (4 Oct). Leaders of the World. Automobiles (4th series). Horiz designs as T **25**, the first in each pair showing technical drawings and the second paintings. P 12½.

326	10c. black, azure and brown-red		10	10
	a. Vert pair. Nos. 326/7		10	15
327	10c. multicoloured		10	10
328	35c. black, pale turquoise-green & greenish blue		10	25
	a. Vert pair. Nos. 328/9		10	50
329	35c. multicoloured		10	25
330	75c. black, bright green and light purple-brown		10	40
	a. Vert pair. Nos. 330/1		15	80
331	75c. multicoloured		10	40
332	$1.15 black, pale cinnamon and olive-green		15	45
	a. Vert pair. Nos. 332/3		30	90
333	$1.15 multicoloured		15	45
334	$1.50 black, pale blue and carmine		15	50
	a. Vert pair. Nos. 334/5		30	1·00
335	$1.50 multicoloured		15	50
336	$2 black, rose-lilac and reddish violet		20	60
	a. Vert pair. Nos. 336/7		40	1·10
337	$2 multicoloured		20	60
326/37 Set of 12			1·10	4·00

Designs:—Nos. 326/7, Sunbeam "Coupe de l'Auto" (1912); 328/9, Cisitalia "Pininfarina Coupe" (1948); 330/1, Porsche "928 S" (1980); 332/3 MG "K3 Magnetic" (1933); 834/5, Lincoln "Zephyr", (1937); 336/7, Pontiac 2 Door (1926).

Nos 326/37 were issued in a similar sheet format to Nos. 165/80.

1985 (23 Oct). Royal Visit. Nos. 76/7, 83, 86, 92/3, 98/9 and 309/10 optd as T **114** of Montserrat or surch also.

338	**16**	15c. multicoloured	75	1·25
339	–	30c. multicoloured (No. 92)	2·25	2·25
340	–	30c. multicoloured (No. 99)	75	1·25
341	–	40c. multicoloured (No. 86)	2·25	3·50
342	**34**	45c. on 55c. multicoloured	1·50	3·50
		a. Horiz pair. Nos. 342/3	3·00	7·00
343	–	45c. multicoloured (No. 310)	1·50	3·50
344	–	55c. multicoloured (No. 83)	1·75	1·25
345	–	$1.50 on $5 multicoloured (No. 76)	2·25	3·50
		aw. Wmk inverted		
		b. Sheetlet. No. 345×6 and No. 346	19·00	
		bw. Wmk inverted		
		c. Error. (Surch $1.60)	1·40	2·25
		ca. Sheetlet. No. 345c×6 and No. 346c	13·00	
346	–	$1.50 on $5 multicoloured (No. 77)	13·00	19·00
		aw. Wmk inverted		
		c. Error. (Surch $1.60)	6·50	11·00
347	–	$2.50 multicoloured (No. 93)	2·50	4·00
338/47 Set of 10			26·00	38·00

Nos. 345c/ca and 346c had the surcharge intended for similar St. Vincent sheetlets applied by mistake.

(Des G. Drummond. Litho Format)

1985 (5 Nov). Christmas. Churches of Nevis (1st series). T **36** and similar horiz designs. Multicoloured. W w **15**. P 15.

348	10c. Type **36**		15	10
349	40c. St. Theresa Catholic Church, Charlestown		35	30
350	60c. Methodist Church, Gingerland		40	50
351	$3 St. Thomas Anglican Church, Lowland		80	2·75
348/51 Set of 4			1·50	3·25

See also Nos. 462/5.

(Des T. Hadler. Litho Format)

1986 (30 Jan). Leaders of the World. Railway Locomotives (5th series). Horiz designs as T **21**, the first in each pair showing technical drawings and the second the locomotive at work. P 12½.

352	30c. multicoloured		15	25
	a. Vert pair. Nos. 352/3		30	50
353	30c. multicoloured		15	25
354	75c. multicoloured		25	50
	a. Vert pair. Nos. 354/5		50	1·00
355	75c. multicoloured		25	50
356	$1.50 multicoloured		40	70
	a. Vert pair. Nos. 356/7		80	1·40
357	$1.50 multicoloured		40	70
358	$2 multicoloured		50	80
	a. Vert pair. Nos. 358/9		1·00	1·60
359	$2 multicoloured		50	80
352/9 Set of 8			2·40	4·00

Designs:—Nos. 352/3, *Stourbridge Lion*, U.S.A. (1829); 354/5, EP-2 Bi-Polar, electric locomotive, U.S.A. (1919); 356/7, Gas turbine, No. 59, U.S.A. (1953); 358/9, Class FL9 diesel locomotive No. 2039, U.S.A. (1955).

Nos. 352/9 were issued in a similar sheet format to Nos. 132/47.

(Des G. Turner (60c.), J.W. (others). Litho Format)

1986 (30 Jan). Leaders of the World. Automobiles (5th series). Horiz designs as T **25** the first in each pair showing technical drawings and the second paintings. P 12½.

360	10c. black, pale cinnamon and yellow-olive		10	10
	a. Vert pair. Nos. 360/1		10	20
361	10c. multicoloured		10	10
362	60c. black, salmon and bright scarlet		15	25
	a. Vert pair. Nos. 362/3		30	50
363	60c. multicoloured		15	25
364	75c. black, pale cinnamon and cinnamon		15	25
	a. Vert pair. Nos. 364/5		30	50
365	75c. multicoloured		15	25
366	$1 black, lavender-grey and violet-grey		15	30
	a. Vert pair. Nos. 366/7		30	60
367	$1 multicoloured		15	30
368	$1.50 black, pale olive-yellow & olive-green		20	35
	a. Vert pair. Nos. 368/9		40	70
369	$1.50 multicoloured		20	35
370	$3 black, azure and cobalt		30	65
	a. Vert pair. Nos. 370/1		60	1·25
371	$3 multicoloured		30	65
360/71 Set of 12			1·75	3·25

Designs:—No. 360/1, Adler "Trumpf" (1936); 362/3, Maserati "Tipo 250F" (1957); 364/5, Oldsmobile "Limited" (1910); 366/7, Jaguar "C-Type" (1951); 368/9, ERA "1.5L B Type" (1937); 370/1, Chevrolet "Corvette" (1953).

Nos. 360/71 were issued in a similar sheet format to Nos. 165/80.

37 Supermarine Spitfire Prototype, 1936

(Des J. Batchelor. Litho Format)

1986 (5 Mar). 50th Anniv of the Spitfire (fighter aircraft). T **37** and similar horiz designs. Multicoloured. P 12½.

372	$1 Type **37**	30	50
373	$2.50 Supermarine Spitfire Mk 1A in Battle of Britain, 1940	35	90
374	$3 Supermarine Spitfire Mk XII over convoy, 1944	35	90
375	$4 Supermarine Spitfire Mk XXIV, 1948	35	1·40
372/5 Set of 4		1·25	3·25
MS376	114×86 mm. $6 Supermarine Seafire Mk III on escort carrier H.M.S. *Hunter*	1·10	3·75

38 Head of Amerindian
39 Brazilian Player 

(Litho Format)

1986 (11 Apr). 500th Anniv of Discovery of America (1992) (1st issue). T **38** and similar vert designs. Multicoloured. P 12½.

377	75c. Type **38**	85	1·00
	a. Horiz pair. Nos. 377/8	1·60	2·00
378	75c. Exchanging gifts for food from Amerindians	85	1·00
379	$1.75 Columbus's coat of arms	1·40	2·00
	a. Horiz pair. Nos. 379/80	2·75	4·00
380	$1.75 Breadfruit plant	1·40	2·00
381	$2.50 Columbus's fleet	1·40	2·25
	a. Horiz pair. Nos. 381/2	2·75	4·50
382	$2.50 Christopher Columbus	1·40	2·25
377/82 Set of 6		5·50	9·50
MS383	95×84 mm. $6 Christopher Columbus (*different*)	6·50	10·00

The two designs of each value were printed together, *se-tenant*, in horizontal pairs throughout the sheets. Each pair forms a composite design showing charts of Columbus's route in the background.

Miniature sheets, each containing $2×2 stamps in the above designs, also exist from a restricted printing and from stock dispersed by the liquidator of Format International Security Printers Ltd.

See also Nos. 546/54, 592/600, 678/84 and 685/6.

(Des Court House Studio. Litho Format)

1986 (21 Apr). 60th Birthday of Queen Elizabeth II. Multicoloured designs as T **167** of British Virgin Islands. P 12½.

384	5c. Queen Elizabeth in 1976	10	10
385	75c. Queen Elizabeth in 1953	15	25
386	$2 In Australia	20	60
387	$8 In Canberra, 1982 (*vert*)	75	2·00
384/7 Set of 4		1·10	2·75
MS388	85×115 mm. $10 Queen Elizabeth II	4·50	7·50

The 5c., 75c. and $2 values exist with PVA gum as well as gum arabic.

No. 387 also exists watermarked w **15** (inverted), but no examples have been reported used from Nevis.

Nos. 384/7 exist in separate miniature sheets from unissued stock dispersed by the liquidator of Format International Security Printers Ltd.

(Des Court House Studio. Litho Format)

1986 (16 May). World Cup Football Championship, Mexico. T **39** and similar multicoloured designs. P 12½ (75c., $1, $1.75 $6) or 15 (others).

389	1c. Official World Cup mascot (*horiz*)	10	10
390	2c. Type **39**	10	10
391	5c. Danish player	10	10
392	10c. Brazilian player (*different*)	10	10
393	20c. Denmark v Spain	20	20
394	30c. Paraguay v Chile	30	30
395	60c. Italy v West Germany	40	55
396	75c. Danish team (56×36 *mm*)	40	65
397	$1 Paraguayan team (56×36 *mm*)	40	70
398	$1.75 Brazilian team (56×36 *mm*)	50	1·25
399	$3 Italy v England	60	1·90
400	$6 Italian team (56×36 *mm*)	85	3·00
389/400 Set of 12		3·50	8·00
MS401	Five sheets, each 85×115 mm. (a) $1.50, As No. 398. (b) $2 As No. 393. (c) $2 As No. 400. (d) $2.50, As No. 395. (e) $4 As No. 394 Set of 5 sheets.	12·00	16·00

40 Clothing Machinist
41 Gorgonia 

(Des G. Vasarhelyi. Litho Questa)

1986 (18 July). Local Industries. T **40** and similar horiz designs. Multicoloured. W w **15**. P 14.

402	15c. Type **40**	20	15
403	40c. Carpentry/joinery workshop	45	30
404	$1.20 Agricultural produce market	1·25	1·60
405	$3 Fishing boats landing catch	2·50	3·50
402/5 Set of 4		4·00	4·75

(Des Court House Studio. Litho Format)

1986 (23 July-15 Oct). Royal Wedding (1st issue). Multicoloured designs as T **168** of British Virgin Islands. P 12½.

406	60c. Prince Andrew in midshipman's uniform.	15	25
	a. Pair. Nos. 406/7	30	50
407	60c. Miss Sarah Ferguson	15	25
408	$2 Prince Andrew on safari in Africa (*horiz*)	40	60
	a. Pair. Nos. 408/9	80	1·10
409	$2 Prince Andrew at the races (*horiz*)	40	60
406/9 Set of 4		1·00	1·50
MS410	115×85 mm. $10 Duke and Duchess of York on Palace balcony after wedding (*horiz*) (15.10.86)	2·50	5·00

Nos. 406/7 and 408/9 were each printed together, *se-tenant*, in horizontal and vertical pairs throughout the sheets.

Nos. 406/9 imperforate come from souvenir stamp booklets.

Nos. 408/9 exist in *tête-bêche* pairs from unissued stock dispersed by the liquidator of Format International Security Printers Ltd.

See also Nos. 454/7.

(Litho Format)

1986 (15 Aug). Automobiles (6th series). Horiz designs as T **25**, the first in each pair showing technical drawings and the second paintings. P 12½.

411	15c. multicoloured	10	10
	a. Vert pair. Nos. 411/12	20	20
412	15c. multicoloured	10	10
413	45c. black, light blue and grey-blue	20	25
	a. Vert pair. Nos. 413/14	40	50
414	45c. multicoloured	20	25
415	60c. multicoloured	20	30
	a. Vert pair. Nos. 415/16	40	60
416	60c. multicoloured	20	30
417	$1 black, yellow-green and dull green	25	40
	a. Vert pair. Nos. 417/18	50	80
418	$1 multicoloured	25	40
419	$1.75 black, pale reddish lilac and deep lilac.	30	50
	a. Vert pair. Nos. 419/20	60	1·00
420	$1.75 multicoloured	30	50
421	$3 multicoloured	50	90
	a. Vert pair. Nos. 421/2	1·00	1·75
422	$3 multicoloured	50	90
411/22 Set of 12		2·75	4·25

Designs:—Nos. 411/12 Riley, "Brooklands Nine" (1930); 413/14, Alfa Romeo "GTA" (1966); 415/16, Pierce Arrow "Type 66" (1913); 417/18, Willys-Knight "66 A" (1928); 419/20, Studebaker "Starliner" (1953); 421/2, Cunningham "V8" (1919).

Nos. 411/22 were issued in a similar sheet format to Nos. 165/80.

(Des G. Drummond. Litho Format)

1986 (8 Sept). Corals (2nd series). T **41** and similar vert designs. Multicoloured. W w **15** (sideways). P 15.

423	15c. Type **41**	25	15
424	60c. Fire Coral	45	55

ST. KITTS-NEVIS / Nevis

425	$2 Elkhorn Coral	75	2·00
426	$3 Vase Sponge and Feather Star	80	2·50
423/6 Set of 4		2·00	4·75

(Des Court House Studio. Litho Format)

1986 (1 Oct). Railway Locomotives (6th series). Horiz designs as T **21**, the first in each pair showing technical drawings and the second the Locomotive at work. P 12½.

427	15c. multicoloured	10	10
	a. Vert pair. Nos. 427/8	10	20
428	15c. multicoloured	10	10
429	45c. multicoloured	15	25
	a. Vert pair. Nos. 429/30	30	50
430	45c. multicoloured	15	25
431	60c. multicoloured	20	30
	a. Vert pair. Nos. 431/2	40	60
432	60c. multicoloured	20	30
433	75c. multicoloured	20	40
	a. Vert pair. Nos. 433/4	40	80
434	75c. multicoloured	20	40
435	$1 multicoloured	20	50
	a. Vert pair. Nos. 435/6	40	1·00
436	$1 multicoloured	20	50
437	$1.50 multicoloured	25	60
	a. Vert pair. Nos. 437/8	50	1·10
438	$1.50 multicoloured	25	60
439	$2 multicoloured	30	65
	a. Vert pair. Nos. 439/40	60	1·25
440	$2 multicoloured	30	65
441	$3 multicoloured	35	80
	a. Vert pair. Nos. 441/2	70	1·60
442	$3 multicoloured	35	80
427/42 Set of 16		3·00	6·50

Designs:—Nos. 427/8, Connor Single Class, Great Britain (1859); 429/30, Class P2 *Cock o' the North*, Great Britain (1934); 431/2, Class 7000 electric locomotive, Japan (1926); 433/4, Class P3, Germany (1897); 435/6, *Dorchester*, Canada (1836); 437/8, Class "Centennial" diesel locomotive, U.S.A. (1969); 439/40, *Lafayette*, U.S.A. (1837); 441/2, Class C-16 No. 222, U.S.A. (1882).

Nos. 427/42 were issued in a similar sheet format to Nos. 132/47.

(Des Court House Studio. Litho Format)

1986 (28 Oct). Centenary of Statue of Liberty. Multicoloured designs as T **121a** of Montserrat. P 13½×14 ($1, $2) or 14×13½ (others).

443	15c. Statue of Liberty and World Trade Centre, Manhattan	20	15
444	25c. Sailing ship passing Statue	30	20
445	40c. Statue in scaffolding	30	25
446	60c. Statue (side view) and scaffolding	30	30
447	75c. Statue and regatta	40	40
448	$1 Tall Ships parade passing Statue (*horiz*)	40	45
449	$1.50 Head and arm of Statue above scaffolding	40	60
450	$2 Ships with souvenir flags (*horiz*)	55	80
451	$2.50 Statue and New York waterfront	60	90
452	$3 Restoring Statue	80	1·25
443/52 Set of 10		3·75	4·75
MS453 Four sheets, each 85×115 mm. (a) $3.50, Statue at dusk. (b) $4 Head of Statue. (c) $4.50, Statue and lightning. (d) $5 Head and torch at sunset *Set of 4 sheets*		3·00	11·00

1986 (17 Nov). Royal Wedding (2nd issue). Nos. 406/9 optd as T **121** of Montserrat in silver.

454	60c. Prince Andrew in midshipman's uniform	15	40
	a. Pair. Nos. 454/5	30	80
455	60c. Miss Sarah Ferguson	15	40
456	$2 Prince Andrew on safari in Africa (*horiz*)	40	1·00
	a. Pair. Nos. 456/7	80	2·00
457	$2 Prince Andrew at the races (*horiz*)	40	1·00
454/7 Set of 4		1·00	2·50

42 Dinghy sailing

(Des G. Vasarhelyi. Litho Questa)

1986 (21 Nov). Sports. T **42** and similar horiz designs. Multicoloured. P 14.

458	10c. Type **42**	20	10
459	25c. Netball	35	15
460	$2 Cricket	3·25	2·75
461	$3 Basketball	4·00	3·25
458/61 Set of 4		7·00	5·50

43 St. George's Anglican Church, Gingerland

44 Constitution Document, Quill and Inkwell

(Des J. Cooter. Litho Questa)

1986 (8 Dec). Christmas. Churches of Nevis (2nd series). T **43** and similar horiz designs. Multicoloured. P 14.

462	10c. Type **43**	15	10
463	40c. Trinity Methodist Church, Fountain	30	25
464	$1 Charlestown Methodist Church	60	65
465	$5 Wesleyan Holiness Church, Brown Hill	2·75	4·00
462/5 Set of 4		3·50	4·50

(Des Maxine Marsh. Litho Questa)

1987 (11 Jan). Bicentenary of U.S. Constitution and 230th Birth Anniv of Alexander Hamilton (U.S. statesman). T **44** and similar vert designs. Multicoloured. P 14.

466	15c. Type **44**	10	10
467	40c. Alexander Hamilton and Hamilton House	20	25
468	60c. Alexander Hamilton	25	35
469	$2 Washington and his Cabinet	90	1·40
466/9 Set of 4		1·25	1·90
MS470 70×82 mm. $5 Model ship *Hamilton* on float, 1788		6·50	8·00

America's Cup 1987 Winners 'Stars & Stripes'

(**45**)

1987 (20 Feb). Victory of Stars and Stripes in America's Cup Yachting Championship. No. 54 optd with T **45**.

471	$3 Windjammer's S.V. *Polynesia*	1·10	1·60

46 Fig Tree Church

(Des Maxine Marsh. Litho Questa)

1987 (11 Mar). Bicentenary of Marriage of Horatio Nelson and Frances Nisbet. T **46** and similar horiz designs. Multicoloured. W w **15**. P 14.

472	15c. Type **46**	20	10
473	60c. Frances Nisbet	50	30
474	$1 H.M.S. *Boreas* (frigate)	1·90	1·25
475	$3 Captain Horatio Nelson	3·00	4·00
472/5 Set of 4		5·00	5·00
MS476 102×82 mm. $3 As No. 473; $3 No. 475		5·00	6·50

47 Queen Angelfish

(Des C. Abbott. Litho Format)

1987 (6 July). Coral Reef Fishes. T **47** and similar triangular designs. Multicoloured. P 14½.

477	60c. Type **47**	30	60
	a. Vert pair. Nos. 477/8	60	1·10
478	60c. Blue Angelfish	30	60
479	$1 Stoplight Parrotfish (male)	30	80

	a. Vert pair. Nos. 479/80	60	1·60
480	$1 Stoplight Parrotfish (female)	30	80
481	$1.50 Red Hind	35	90
	a. Vert pair. Nos. 481/2	70	1·75
482	$1.50 Rock Hind	35	90
483	$2.50 Coney (bicoloured phase)	35	1·50
	a. Vert pair. Nos. 483/4	70	3·00
484	$2.50 Coney (red-brown phase)	35	1·50
477/84 Set of 8		2·40	6·75

Nos. 477/8, 479/80, 481/2 and 483/4 were each printed together, *se-tenant*, in pairs throughout the sheets. The second design for each value is in the form of an inverted triangle.

Nos. 477/84 exist imperforate from stock dispersed by the liquidator of Format International Security Printers Ltd.

48 *Panaeolus antillarum*    **49** Rag Doll

(Des J. Cooter. Litho Format)

1987 (16 Oct). Fungi (1st series). T **48** and similar vert designs. Multicoloured. W w **16**. P 14.

485	15c. Type **48**	70	30
486	50c. *Pycnoporus sanguineus*	1·25	80
487	$2 *Gymnopilus chrysopellus*	2·25	3·25
488	$3 *Cantharellus cinnabarinus*	2·50	4·50
485/8 Set of 4		6·00	8·00

See also Nos. 646/54.

(Des J.W. Litho Walsall)

1987 (4 Dec). Christmas. Toys. T **49** and similar horiz designs. Multicoloured. W w **16** (sideways). P 14½.

489	10c. Type **49**	10	10
490	40c. Coconut boat	20	25
491	$1.20 Sandbox cart	55	60
492	$5 Two-wheeled cart	1·75	4·00
489/92 Set of 4		2·25	4·50

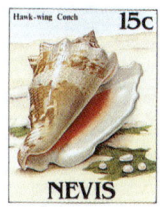

50 Hawk-wing Conch

(Des Josephine Martin. Litho Questa)

1988 (15 Feb). Seashells and Pearls. T **50** and similar vert designs. Multicoloured. W w **16**. P 14½×14.

493	15c. Type **50**	20	15
494	40c. Rooster-tail Conch	30	20
495	60c. Emperor Helmet	50	40
496	$2 Queen or Pink Conch	1·40	2·00
497	$3 King Helmet	1·50	2·25
493/7 Set of 5		3·50	4·50

51 Visiting Pensioners at Christmas

(Des L. Curtis. Litho Walsall)

1988 (20 June). 125th Anniv of International Red Cross. T **51** and similar horiz designs. Multicoloured. W w **16** (sideways). P 14×14½.

498	15c. Type **51**	10	10
499	40c. Teaching children first aid	15	20
500	60c. Providing wheelchairs for the disabled.	25	35
501	$5 Helping cyclone victim	2·10	3·50
498/501 Set of 4		2·25	3·75

52 Athlete on Starting Blocks    **53** Outline Map and Arms of St. Kitts Nevis

(Des G. Vasarhelyi. Litho Format)

1988 (26 Aug). Olympic Games, Seoul. T **52** and similar vert designs. Multicoloured. W w **16**. P 14.

502	10c. Type **52**	10	35
	a. Horiz strip of 4. Nos. 502/5	2·40	3·50
503	$1.20 At start	50	85
504	$2 During race	85	1·25
505	$3 At finish	1·25	1·50
502/5 Set of 4		2·40	3·50
MS506	137×80 mm. As Nos. 502/5, but each size 24×36 mm. Wmk sideways	2·50	3·75

Nos. 502/5 were printed together, *se-tenant*, in horizontal strips of 4 throughout the sheet, each strip forming a composite design showing an athlete from start to finish of race.

(Des L. Curtis. Litho Questa)

1988 (19 Sept). Fifth Anniv of Independence. W w **14**. P 14½×14.

507	**53**	$5 multicoloured	2·10	3·00

53a House of Commons passing Lloyd's Bill, 1871

(Des D. Miller (15c., $2.50), E. Nisbet and D. Miller (60c., $3). Litho Questa)

1988 (31 Oct). 300th Anniversary of Lloyd's of London. T **53aa** and simlar multicoloured designs. W w **16** (sideways on 60c., $2.50). P 14.

508	15c. Type **53a**	25	10
509	60c. *Cunard Countess* (liner) (*horiz*)	1·75	65
510	$2.50 Space shuttle deploying satellite (*horiz*)	2·75	3·00
511	$3 *Viking Princess* (cargo liner) on fire, 1966	3·50	3·00
508/11 Set of 4		7·50	6·00

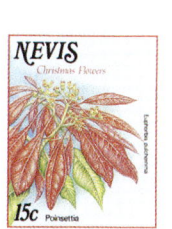

54 Poinsettia    **55** British Fleet off St. Kitts

(Des I. Loe. Litho Questa)

1988 (7 Nov). Christmas. Flowers. T **54** and similar vert designs. Multicoloured. W w **16**. P 14½×14.

512	15c. Type **54**	10	10
513	40c. Tiger Claws	15	20

ST. KITTS-NEVIS / Nevis

514	60c. Sorrel Flower		25	30
515	$1 Christmas Candle		40	60
516	$5 Snow Bush		1·60	3·75
512/16	Set of 5		2·25	4·50

(Des Jane Hartley. Litho Format)

1989 (17 Apr). Philexfrance 89 International Stamp Exhibition, Paris. Battle of Frigate Bay, 1782. T **55** and similar vert designs. Multicoloured. W w **16**. P 13½×14 ($3) or 14 (others).

517	50c. Type **55**		1·40	1·75
	a. Horiz strip of 3. Nos. 517/19		4·50	6·00
518	$1.20 Battle off Nevis		1·60	2·25
519	$2 British and French fleets exchanging broadsides		2·00	2·50
520	$3 French map of Nevis, 1764		2·50	3·00
517/20	Set of 4		6·75	8·50

Nos. 517/19 were printed together, *se-tenant*, in horizontal strips of 3 throughout the sheet, each strip forming a composite design.

56 Cicada

57 Queen or Pink Conch feeding

(Des I. Loe. Litho Questa)

1989 (15 May). "Sounds of the Night". T **56** and similar vert designs. Multicoloured. W w **16**. P 14.

521	10c. Type **56**		20	15
522	40c. Grasshopper		40	35
523	60c. Cricket		55	50
524	$5 Tree frog		3·75	5·50
521/4	Set of 4		4·50	6·00
MS525	135×81 mm. Nos. 521/4		5·50	7·00

(Des A. Theobald ($6), D. Miller (others). Litho Questa)

1989 (20 July). 20th Anniv of First Manned Landing on Moon. Multicoloured designs as T **50a** of St. Kitts. W w **16** (sideways on 40c., $2). P 14×13½ (15c., $3) or 14 (others).

526	15c. Vehicle Assembly Building, Kennedy Space Centre		15	10
527	40c. Crew of "Apollo 12" (30×30 *mm*)		20	20
528	$2 "Apollo 12" emblem (30×30 *mm*)		1·00	1·75
529	$3 "Apollo 12" astronaut on Moon		1·40	2·00
	w. Wmk inverted		32·00	
526/9	Set of 4		2·50	3·75
MS530	100×83 mm. $6 Aldrin undertaking lunar seismic experiment. P 14×13½		2·50	3·50

(Des Deborah Dudley Max. Litho Questa)

1990 (31 Jan). Queen or Pink Conch. T **57** and similar horiz designs. Multicoloured. P 14.

531	10c. Type **57**		60	30
532	40c. Queen or Pink Conch from front		90	40
533	60c. Side view of shell		1·25	90
534	$1 Back and flare		1·60	2·00
531/4	Set of 4		4·00	3·25
MS535	72×103 mm. $5 Underwater habitat		3·50	4·50

58 Wyon Medal Portrait

59

(Des M. Pollard. Litho B.D.T.)

1990 (3 May). 150th Anniv of the Penny Black. T **58** and similar vert designs. P 14×15.

536	15c. black and brown		20	10
537	40c. black and deep blue-green		40	25
538	60c. black		55	55
539	$4 black and ultramarine		2·50	3·25
536/9	Set of 4		3·25	3·75

MS540	114×84 mm. $5 black, brown-lake and pale buff	4·00	5·00

Designs:—40c. Engine-turned background; 60c. Heath's engraving of portrait; $4 Essay with inscriptions; $5 Penny Black.

No. **MS**540 also commemorates "Stamp World London 90" International Stamp Exhibition.

(Des S. Pollard. Litho B.D.T.)

1990 (3 May). 500th Anniv of Regular European Postal Services. T **59** and similar square designs with different corner emblems. P 13½.

541	15c. brown		20	15
542	40c. deep dull green		35	25
543	60c. bright reddish violet		55	65
544	$4 ultramarine		2·75	3·75
541/4	Set of 4		3·50	4·25
MS545	110×82 mm. $5 brown-lake, pale buff and pale grey		4·00	5·00

Nos. 541/5 commemorate the Thurn and Taxis postal service and the designs are loosely based on those of the initial 1852–58 series.

60 Sand Fiddler Crab

60a Duchess of York with Corgi

(Des Mary Walters. Litho Questa)

1990 (25 June). 500th Anniv of Discovery of America by Columbus (1992) (2nd issue). New World Natural History– Crabs. T **60** and similar horiz designs. Multicoloured. P 14.

546	5c. Type **60**		10	10
547	15c. Great Land Crab		15	15
548	20c. Blue Crab		15	15
549	40c. Stone Crab		30	30
550	60c. Mountain Crab		45	45
551	$2 Sargassum Crab		1·40	1·75
552	$3 Yellow Box Crab		1·75	2·25
553	$4 Spiny Spider Crab		2·25	3·00
546/53	Set of 8		6·00	7·25
MS554	Two sheets, each 101×70 mm. (a) $5 Sally Lightfoot. (b) $5 Wharf Crab Set of 2 sheets		9·50	11·00

(Des Young Phillips Studio. Litho Questa)

1990 (5 July). 90th Birthday of Queen Elizabeth the Queen Mother. Vert designs as T **60a** and similar designs showing portraits, (1930–39). P 14.

555	$2 brownish black, magenta and pale buff		1·40	1·60
	a. Strip of 3. Nos. 555/7		3·75	4·25
556	$2 brownish black, magenta and pale buff		1·40	1·60
557	$2 brownish black, magenta and pale buff		1·40	1·60
555/7	Set of 3		3·75	4·25
MS558	90×75 mm. $6 chestnut, magenta and black		3·50	4·25

Designs:—No. 555, Type **60a**; No. 556, Queen Elizabeth in Coronation robes, 1937; No. 557, Duchess of York in garden; No. **MS**558, Queen Elizabeth in Coronation robes, 1937 (*different*).

Nos. 555/7 were printed together, horizontally and vertically *se-tenant*, in sheetlets of 9 (3×3).

61 MaKanaky, Cameroons

62 *Cattleya deckeri*

(Des Young Phillips Studio. Litho Questa)

1990 (1 Oct). World Cup Football Championship, Italy. Star Players. T **61** and similar vert designs. Multicoloured. P 14.

559	10c. Type **61**		40	10
560	25c. Chovanec, Czechoslovakia		45	15
561	$2.50 Robson, England		2·75	3·25

ST. KITTS-NEVIS / Nevis

562	$5 Voller, West Germany	3·75	5·00
559/62	Set of 4	6·50	7·50

MS563 Two sheets, each 90×75 mm. (a) $5 Maradona, Argentina. (b) $5 Gordillo, Spain *Set of 2 sheets* .... 6·75 8·00

(Des Mary Walters. Litho B.D.T.)

1990 (19 Nov). Christmas. Native Orchids. T **62** and similar vert designs. Multicoloured. P 14.

564	10c. Type **62**	55	20
565	15c. *Epidendrum ciliare*	55	20
566	20c. *Epidendrum fragrans*	65	20
567	40c. *Epidendrum ibaguense*	85	25
568	60c. *Epidendrum latifolium*	1·10	50
569	$1.20 *Maxillaria conferta*	1·40	1·75
570	$2 *Epidendrum strobiliferum*	1·75	2·75
571	$3 *Brassavola cucullata*	2·00	3·00
564/71	Set of 8	8·00	8·00

MS572 102×71 mm. $5 *Rodriguezia lanceolata* .... 7·00 8·00

(Des T. Agans. Litho Questa)

1991 (14 Jan). 350th Death Anniv of Rubens. Multicoloured designs as T **273** of Antigua but vert, showing details from *The Feast of Achelous*. P 13½×14.

573	10c. Two jugs (*vert*)	55	15
574	40c. Woman at table (*vert*)	1·00	30
575	60c. Two servants with fruit (*vert*)	1·25	45
576	$4 Achelous (*vert*)	3·25	6·00
573/6	Set of 4	5·50	6·25

MS577 101×71 mm. $5 The *Feast of Achelous*. P 14×13½ .... 4·50 6·00

63 *Agraulis vanillae*

64 "Viking Mars Lander", 1976

(Des L. Nelson. Litho Questa)

1991 (1 Mar)–**92**. Butterflies. T **63** and similar horiz designs. Multicoloured. P 14.

A. Without imprint date.

578A	5c. Type **63**	40	60
579A	10c. *Historis odius*	40	50
580A	15c. *Marpesia corinna*	50	30
581A	20c. *Anartia amathea*	60	30
582A	25c. *Junonia evarete*	60	30
583A	40c. *Heliconius charithonia*	70	40
584A	50c. *Marpesia petreus*	70	50
585A	60c. *Dione juno*	75	50
586A	75c. *Heliconius doris*	85	80
587A	$1 *Hypolimnas misippus*	90	80
588A	$3 *Danaus plexippus*	2·00	2·75
589A	$5 *Heliconius sara*	2·75	4·00
590A	$10 *Tithorea harmonia*	5·00	8·00
591A	$20 *Dryas julia*	9·50	13·00
578A/91A	Set of 14	23·00	29·00

B. With imprint date (1.3.92).

578B	5c. Type **63**	40	60
579B	10c. *Historis odius*	40	50
580B	15c. *Marpesia corinna*	50	20
581B	20c. *Anartia amathea*	60	30
582B	25c. *Junonia evarete*	60	30
583B	40c. *Heliconius charithonia*	70	30
584B	50c. *Marpesia petreus*	70	35
586B	75c. *Heliconius doris*	80	60
586cB	80c. As 60c.	80	60
587B	$1 *Hypolimnas misippus*	1·00	80
588B	$3 *Danaus plexippus*	2·50	3·25
589B	$5 *Heliconius sara*	3·25	4·50
590B	$10 *Tithorea harmonia*	6·00	8·50
591B	$20 *Dryas julia*	11·00	14·00
578B/91B	Set of 14	26·00	32·00

Nos. 579A/B are inscribed "Historis osius", Nos. 581A/B "Anartia amathea", Nos. 583A/B "Heliconius charitonius", Nos. 587AB "Hypolimanas misippus" and Nos. 591A/B "Dryas iulia" all in error.

Imprint dates: "1992", Nos. 578B/84B, 586B/91B; "1994", Nos. 578B/9B, 582B, 584B, 586cB.

(Des T. Agans. Litho Questa)

1991 (23 Apr). 500th Anniv of Discovery of America by Columbus (1992) (3rd issue). History of Exploration. T **64** and similar multicoloured designs. P 14.

592	15c. Type **64**	20	20
593	40c. "Apollo 11", 1969	30	25
594	60c. "Skylab", 1973	45	45
595	75c. "Salyut 6", 1977	55	55
596	$1 "Voyager 1", 1977	65	65
597	$2 "Venera 7", 1970	1·25	1·60
598	$4 "Gemini 4", 1965	2·50	3·25
599	$5 "Luna 3", 1959	2·75	3·25
592/9	Set of 8	7·75	9·00

MS600 Two sheets, each 105×76 mm. (a) $6 Bow of Santa Maria (*vert*). (b) $6 Christopher Columbus (*vert*) *Set of 2 sheets* .... 8·00 9·00

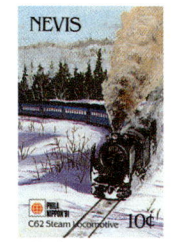

65 Magnificent Frigate Bird

65b Class C62 Steam Locomotive

(Des Jennifer Toombs. Litho Questa)

1991 (28 May). Island Birds. T **65** and similar horiz designs. Multicoloured. P 14.

601	40c. Type **65**	90	75
	a. Sheetlet. Nos. 601/20	16·00	13·00
602	40c. Roseate Tern	90	75
603	40c. Red-tailed Hawk	90	75
604	40c. Zenaida Dove	90	75
605	40c. Bananaquit	90	75
606	40c. American Kestrel	90	75
607	40c. Grey Kingbird	90	75
608	40c. Prothonotary Warbler	90	75
609	40c. Blue-hooded Euphonia	90	75
610	40c. Antillean Crested Hummingbird	90	75
611	40c. White-tailed Tropic Bird	90	75
612	40c. Yellow-bellied Sapsucker	90	75
613	40c. Green-throated Carib	90	75
614	40c. Purple-throated Carib	90	75
615	40c. Red-billed Whistling Duck ("Black-bellied Tree-duck")	90	75
616	40c. Ringed Kingfisher	90	75
617	40c. Burrowing Owl	90	75
618	40c. Turnstone	90	75
619	40c. Great Blue Heron	90	75
620	40c. Yellow-crowned Night-heron	90	75
601/20	Set of 20	16·00	13·00

MS621 76×59 mm. $6 Great Egret .... 11·00 12·00

Nos. 601/20 were printed together, *se-tenant*, in sheetlets of 20, forming a composite design.

(Des D. Miller. Litho Walsall)

1991 (5 July). 65th Birthday of Queen Elizabeth II. Horiz designs as T **280** of Antigua. Multicoloured. P 14.

622	15c. Queen Elizabeth at polo match with Prince Charles	40	20
623	40c. Queen and Prince Philip on Buckingham Palace balcony	50	35
624	$2 In carriage at Ascot, 1986	1·75	1·75
625	$4 Queen Elizabeth II at Windsor polo match, 1989	3·00	3·75
622/5	Set of 4	5·00	5·50

MS626 68×90 mm. $5 Queen Elizabeth and Prince Philip ...... 4·25 5·00

(Des D. Miller. Litho Walsall)

1991 (5 July). Tenth Wedding Anniv of Prince and Princess of Wales. Horiz designs as T **280** of Antigua. Multicoloured. P 14.

627	10c. Prince Charles and Princess Diana	85	20
628	50c. Prince of Wales and family	90	30
629	$1 Prince William and Prince Harry	1·40	1·00
630	$5 Prince and Princess of Wales	4·50	4·00
627/30	Set of 4	6·75	5·00

MS631 68×90 mm. $5 Prince and Princess of Wales in Hungary, and young princes at Christmas .... 6·00 6·00

(Litho Quests)

1991 (12 Aug). Phila Nippon '91 International Stamp Exhibition, Tokyo. Japanese Railway Locomotives. T **65b** and similar multicoloured designs. P 14.

632	10c. Type **65b**	90	30
633	15c. Class C56 steam locomotive (*horiz*)	1·00	30
634	40c. Class C55 streamlined steam locomotive (*horiz*)	1·50	50
635	60c. Class 1400 steam locomotive (*horiz*)	1·60	80
636	$1 Class 485 diesel train	1·90	1·00

273

ST. KITTS-NEVIS / Nevis

637	$2 Class C61 steam locomotive	3·00	2·50
638	$3 Class 485 diesel train (*horiz*)	3·25	3·00
639	$4 Class 7000 electric train (*horiz*)	3·50	3·75
632/9	Set of 8	15·00	11·00

MS640 Two sheets, each 108×72 mm. (a) $5 Class D51 steam locomotive (*horiz*). (b) $5 "Hikari" express train (*horiz*) Set of 2 sheets .... 8·50 9·00

65c "Mary being Crowned by an Angel"

66 *Marasmius haemtocephalus*

(Litho B.D.T.)

1991 (20 Dec). Christmas. Drawings by Albrecht Dürer. T **65c** and similar vert designs. P 13.

641	10c. black and apple-green	15	10
642	40c. black and yellow-orange	30	25
643	60c. black and new blue	35	30
644	$3 black and bright mauve	1·40	3·00
641/4	Set of 4	2·00	3·25

MS645 Two sheets, each 96×124 mm. (a) $6 black. (b) $6 black Set of 2 sheets .... 5·50 6·25

Designs:—10c.Type **65c**; 40c. "Mary with the Pear"; 60c. "Mary in a Halo"; $3 "Mary with Crown of Stars and Sceptre"; $6 (No. **MS**645a) "The Holy Family" (detail); $6 (No. **MS**645b) "Mary at the Yard Gate" (detail).

(Des D. Miller. Litho B.D.T.)

1991 (20 Dec). Fungi (2nd series). T **66** and similar multicoloured designs. P 14.

646	15c. Type **66**	30	20
647	40c. *Psilocybe cubensis*	40	30
648	60c. *Hygrocybe acutoconica*	50	40
649	75c. *Hygrocybe occidentalis*	60	60
650	$1 *Boletellus cubensis*	70	70
651	$2 *Gymnopilus chrysopellus*	1·00	1·50
652	$4 *Cantharellus cinnabarinus*	2·00	2·75
653	$5 *Chlorophyllum molybdites*	2·00	2·75
646/53	Set of 8	6·75	8·25

MS654 Two sheets, each 70×58 mm. (a) $6 *Psilocybe cubensis*, *Hygrocybe acutoconica* and *Boletellus cubensis* (*horiz*). (b) $6 *Hygrocybe occidentalis*, *Marasmius haematocephalus* and *Gymnopilus chrysopellus* (*horiz*) Set of 2 sheets .... 9·00 9·50

(Des D. Miller. Litho Questa)

1992 (26 Feb). 40th Anniv of Queen Elizabeth II's Accession. Horiz designs as T **288** of Antigua. Multicoloured. P 14.

655	10c. Charlestown from the sea	50	10
656	40c. Charlestown square	70	25
657	$1 Mountain scenery	1·25	60
658	$5 Early cottage	3·25	3·75
655/8	Set of 4	5·00	4·25

MS659 Two sheets, each 74×97 mm. (a) $6 Queen or Pink Conch on beach. (b) $6 Nevis sunset Set of 2 sheets .... 9·50 9·00

67 Monique Knol (cycling), Netherlands

68 "Landscape" (Mariano Fortuny i Marsal)

(Des R. Sauber. Litho B.D.T.)

1992 (7 May). Olympic Games, Barcelona. Gold Medal Winners of 1988. T **67** and similar vert designs. Multicoloured. P 14.

660	20c. Type **67**	1·25	50
661	25c. Roger Kingdom (hurdles), U.S.A	60	40
662	50c. Yugoslavia (men's waterpolo)	1·00	50
663	80c. Anja Fichtel (foil), West Germany	1·10	70
664	$1 Said Aouita, (mid-distance running), Morocco	1·25	80
665	$1.50 Yuri Sedykh (hammer throw), U.S.S.R	1·40	1·60
666	$3 Shushunova (women's gymnastics), U.S.S.R	2·50	3·00
667	$5 Valimir Artemov (men's gymnastics), U.S.S.R	2·75	3·50
660/7	Set of 8	10·50	10·00

MS668 Two sheets, each 103×73 mm. (a) $6 Niam Suleymanoglu (weightlifting), Turkey. (b) $6 Florence Griffith-Joyner (women's 100 metres), U.S.A. Set of 2 sheets .... 5·50 7·00

No. 660 is inscribed "FRANCE" in error.

(Litho B.D.T.)

1992 (1 June). Granada '92 International Stamp Exhibition, Spain. Spanish Paintings. T **68** and similar multicoloured designs. P 13×13½ (vert) or 13½×13 (horiz).

669	20c. Type **68**	40	30
670	25c. "Dona Juana laLoca" (Francisco Pradilla Ortiz) (*horiz*)	40	30
671	50c. "Idyll" (Fortuny i Marsal)	60	50
672	80c. "Old Man Naked in the Sun" (Fortuny i Marsal)	80	70
673	$1 "The Painter's Children in the Japanese Salon" (detail) (Fortuny i Marsal)	90	80
674	$2 "The Painter's Children in the Japanese Salon" (different detail) (Fortuny i Marsal)	1·40	1·40
675	$3 "Still Life: Sea Bream and Oranges" (Luis Eugenio Meléndez) (*horiz*)	2·25	2·75
676	$5 "Still Life: Box of Sweets, Pastry and Other Objects" (Meléndez)	2·75	3·50
669/76	Set of 8	8·50	9·25

MS677 Two sheets, each 121×95 mm. (a) $6 "Bullfight" (Fortuny i Marsal) (111×86 *mm*). (b) $6 "Moroccans" (Fortuny i Marsal) (111×86 *mm*). Imperf Set of 2 sheets .... 5·50 6·50

69 Early Compass and Ship

69a Empire State Building

(Des L. Fried. Litho Questa)

1992 (6 July). 500th Anniv of Discovery of America by Columbus (4th issue) and "World Columbian Stamp Expo '92", Chicago. T **69** and similar multicoloured designs. P 14.

678	20c. Type **69**	75	25
679	50c. Manatee and fleet	1·25	50
680	80c. Green Turtle and *Santa Maria*	1·50	80
681	$1.50 *Santa Maria* and arms	2·25	1·75
682	$3 Queen Isabella of Spain and commission	2·50	3·25
683	$5 Pineapple and colonists	3·00	4·50
678/83	Set of 6	10·00	10·00

MS684 Two sheets, each 101×70 mm. (a) $6 British Storm Petrel and town (*horiz*). (b) $6 Peppers and Carib canoe (*horiz*) Set of 2 sheets .... 12·00 13·00

(Des F. Paul ($1), J. Esquino ($2). Litho Questa)

1992 (24 Aug). 500th Anniv of Discovery of America by Columbus (5th issue). Organization of East Caribbean States. Vert designs as Nos. 911/12 of Montserrat. Multicoloured. P 14½.

685	$1 Columbus meeting Amerindians	50	50
686	$2 Ships approaching island	1·25	1·40

(Des Kerri Schiff. Litho Questa)

1992 (28 Oct). Postage Stamp Mega Event, New York. Sheet 100×70 mm T **69a**. P 14.

MS687 multicoloured $6 .... 5·00 5·50

70 Minnie Mouse

70a "The Virgin and Child between Two Saints" (Giovanni Bellini)

(Des Walt Disney Co. Litho Questa)

1992 (9 Nov). Mickey's Portrait Gallery. T **70** and similar multicoloured designs. P 13½×14.

688	10c. Type **70**		50	20
689	16c. Mickey Mouse		50	20
690	40c. Donald Duck		70	30
691	80c. Mickey Mouse, 1930		90	70
692	$1 Daisy Duck		1·00	80
693	$2 Pluto		1·75	1·50
694	$4 Goofy		2·75	3·00
695	$5 Goofy, 1932		2·75	3·00
688/95 *Set of 8*			9·75	8·75

MS696 Two sheets. (a) 102×128 mm. $6 Mickey in armchair (*horiz*). (b) 128×102 mm. $6 Mickey and Minnie in airplane (*horiz*). P 13½ *Set of 2 sheets* .... 10·00 11·00

(Litho Questa)

1992 (16 Nov). Christmas. Religious Paintings. T **70a** and similar vert designs. Multicoloured. P 13½.

697	20c. Type **70a**		55	15
698	40c. "The Virgin and Child surrounded by Four Angels" (Master of the Castello Nativity)		70	25
699	50c. "Virgin and Child surrounded by Angels with St. Frediano and St. Augustine" (detail) (Filippo Lippi)		75	30
700	80c. "The Virgin and Child between St. Peter and St. Sebastian" (Bellini)		1·00	70
701	$1 "The Virgin and Child with St. Julian and St. Nicholas of Myra" (Lorenzo di Credi)		1·40	80
702	$2 "St. Bernadino and a Female Saint presenting a Donor to Virgin and Child" (Francesco Bissolo)		2·25	1·50
703	$4 "Madonna and Child with Four Cherubs" (ascr Barthel Bruyn)		3·25	3·75
704	$5 "The Virgin and Child" (Quentin Metsys)		3·50	3·75
697/704 *Set of 8*			12·00	10·00

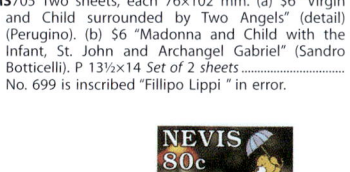

MS705 Two sheets, each 76×102 mm. (a) $6 "Virgin and Child surrounded by Two Angels" (detail) (Perugino). (b) $6 "Madonna and Child with the Infant, St. John and Archangel Gabriel" (Sandro Botticelli). P 13½×14 *Set of 2 sheets* .... 7·50 9·00

No. 699 is inscribed "Fillipo Lippi " in error.

71 Care Bear and Butterfly

(Des T.C.F.C. Inc. Litho Questa)

1993 (14 Jan). Ecology. T **71** and similar vert design showing Care Bear cartoon characters. Multicoloured. P 14.

706	80c. Type **71**		60	60

MS707 71×101 mm. $2 Care Bear on beach .... 2·50 3·75

(Litho Walsall)

1993 (14 Jan). Bicentenary of the Louvre, Paris. Vert designs as T **305** of Antigua. Multicoloured. P 12.

708	$1 "The Card Cheat" (left detail) (La Tour)		85	85
	a. Sheetlet. Nos. 708/15		6·00	6·00
709	$1 "The Card Cheat" (centre detail) (La Tour)		85	85
710	$1 "The Card Cheat" (right detail) (La Tour)		85	85
711	$1 "St. Joseph, the Carpenter" (La Tour)		85	85
712	$1 "St. Thomas" (La Tour)		85	85
713	$1 "Adoration of the Shepherds" (left detail) (La Tour)		85	85
714	$1 Adoration of the Shepherds" (right detail) (La Tour)		85	85
715	$1 "Mary Magdalene with a Candle" (La Tour)		85	85
708/15 *Set of 8*			6·00	6·00

MS716 70×100 mm. $6 "Archangel Raphael leaving the Family of Tobius" (Rembrandt) (52×85 *mm*). P 14½ .... 4·25 4·75

Nos. 708/15 were printed together, *se-tenant*, in sheetlets of 8 stamps and one centre label.

71b Elvis Presley

(Des A. Nahigian. Litho Questa)

1993 (14 Jan). 15th Death Anniv of Elvis Presley (singer). T **71b** and similar vert designs. Multicoloured. P 14.

717	$1 Type **71b**		1·40	1·00
	a. Strip of 3. Nos. 717/19		3·75	2·75
718	$1 Elvis with guitar		1·40	1·00
719	$1 Elvis with microphone		1·40	1·00
717/19 *Set of 3*			3·75	2·75

Nos. 717/19 were printed together, horizontally and vertically *se-tenant*, in sheetlets of 9 (3×3).

72 Japanease Launch Vehicle H-11

(Des W. Wright and L. Fried (Nos. 720, 731, **MS**734a), W. Wright and W. Hanson (Nos. 721, 732, **MS**734b), J. Genzo (Nos. 728, **MS**734e), W. Wright (others). Litho B.D.T.)

1993 (14 Jan). Anniversaries and Events. T **72** and similar multicoloured designs. P 14.

720	15c. Type **72**		60	30
721	50c. Airship LZ-129 *Hindenburg* on fire, 1937 (*horiz*)		1·25	65
722	75c. Konrad Adenauer and Charles de Gaulle (*horiz*)		65	65
723	80c. Red Cross emblem and map of Nevis (*horiz*)		1·75	1·00
724	80c. *Resolute* (yacht), 1920		1·50	1·00
725	80c. Nelson Museum and map of Nevis (*horiz*)		1·75	1·00
726	80c. St. Thomas's Church (*horiz*)		70	1·00
727	$1 Blue Whale (*horiz*)		2·50	1·50
728	$3 Mozart		3·25	3·00
729	$3 Graph and U.N. emblems (*horiz*)		1·75	2·50
730	$3 Lions Club emblem		1·75	2·50
731	$5 Soviet "Energia" launch vehicle SL-17		3·50	4·00
732	$5 Lebaudy-Juillot airship No. 1 *La Jaune*, 1903 (*horiz*)		3·50	4·00
733	$5 Adenauer and Pres. Kennedy (*horiz*)		3·50	4·00
720/33 *Set of 14*			25·00	24·00

MS734 Five sheets. (a) 104×71 mm. $6 Astronaut. (b) 104×71 mm. $6 Zeppelin LZ-5, 1909 (*horiz*). (c) 100×70 mm. $6 Konrad Adenauer (*horiz*). (d) 75×103 mm. $6 *America 3* (yacht), 1992 (*horiz*). (e) 98×66 mm. $6 Masked reveller from *Don Giovanni* (*horiz*) *Set of 5 sheets* .... 19·00 20·00

Anniversaries and Events:—Nos. 720, 731, **MS**734a, International Space Year; Nos. 721, 732, **MS**734b, 75th death anniv of Count Ferdinand von Zeppelin (airship pioneer); Nos. 722, 733, **MS**734c, 25th death anniv of Konrad Adenauer (German statesman); No. 723, 50th anniv of St. Kitts-Nevis Red Cross; Nos. 724, **MS**734d, Americas Cup Yachting Championship; No. 725, Opening of Nelson Museum; No. 726, 150th anniv of Anglican Diocese of North-eastern Caribbean and Aruba; No. 727, Earth Summit '92, Rio; Nos. 728, **MS**734e, Death bicent of Mozart; No. 729, International Conference on Nutrition, Rome; No. 730, 75th anniv of International Association of Lions Clubs.

73 *Plumeria rubra*

74 Antillean Blue (male)

(Des Mary Walters. Litho Questa)

1993 (26 Mar). West Indian Flowers. T **73** and similar vert designs. Multicoloured. P 14.

735	10c. Type **73**	75	30
736	25c. *Bougainvillea*	95	30
737	50c. *Allamanda cathartica*	1·10	50
738	80c. *Anthurium audraeanum*	1·50	70
739	$1 *Ixora coccinea*	1·75	75
740	$2 *Hibiscus rosa-sinensis*	2·75	2·25
741	$4 *Justicia brandegeeana*	4·00	4·75
742	$5 *Antigonon leptopus*	4·00	4·75
735/42 Set of 8		15·00	13·00

MS743 Two sheets, each 100×70 mm. (a) $6 *Lantana camara*. (b) $6 *Petrea volubilis* Set of 2 sheets .... 7·50 8·50

(Des T. Muse. Litho Questa)

1993 (17 May). Butterflies. T **74** and similar horiz designs. Multicoloured. P 14.

744	10c. Type **74**	60	40
745	25c. Cuban Crescentspot (female)	75	40
746	50c. Ruddy Daggerwing	1·00	50
747	80c. Little Yellow (male)	1·25	75
748	$1 Atala	1·25	90
749	$1.50 Orange-barred Giant Sulphur	2·00	2·25
750	$4 Tropic Queen (male)	3·25	4·50
751	$5 Malachite	3·25	4·50
744/51 Set of 8		12·00	12·50

MS752 Two sheets, each 76×105 mm. (a) $6 Polydamus Swallwtail (male). (b) $6 West Indian Buckeye Set of 2 sheets .... 10·00 11·00

(Des Kerri Schiff. Litho Questa)

1993 (2 June). 40th Anniv of Coronation. T **307** of Antigua. P 13½×14.

753	10c. multicoloured	15	20
	a. Sheetlet. Nos. 753/6×2	6·50	
754	80c. deep chocolate and black	45	55
755	$2 multicoloured	1·10	1·40
756	$4 multicoloured	2·00	2·25
753/6 Set of 4		3·25	4·00

MS757 71×101 mm. $6 multicoloured. P 14 .... 3·00 3·50

Designs: (38×47 *mm*)—10c. Queen Elizabeth II at Coronation (photograph by Cecil Beaton); 80c. Queen wearing Imperial State Crown; $2 Crowning of Queen Elizabeth II; $4 Queen and Prince Charles at polo match. (28½×42½ *mm*)—$6 "Queen Elizabeth II, 1977" (detail) (Susan Crawford).

Nos. 753/6 were printed together in sheetlets of 8 containing two *se-tenant* blocks of 4.

75 Flag and National Anthem

75a Imre Garaba (Hungary) and Michael Platini (France)

(Des Jennifer Toombs. Litho B.D.T.)

1993 (19 Sept). Tenth Anniv of Independence of St. Kitts-Nevis. T **75** and similar vert design. Multicoloured. P 13½.

758	25c. Type **75**	1·50	50
759	80c. Brown Pelican and map of St.- Kitts Nevis	1·75	1·50

(Des Rosemary DeFiglio. Litho Cartor)

1993 (9 Nov). World Cup Football Championship, 1994, U.S.A. T **75a** and similar multicoloured designs. P 14×13½.

760	10c. Type **75a**	70	30
761	25c. Diego Maradona (Argentina) and Giuseppe Bergomi (Italy)	85	30
762	50c. Luis Fernandez (France) and Vasily Rats (Russia)	1·10	45
763	80c. Victor Munez (Spain)	1·50	65
764	$1 Preben Elkjaer (Denmark) and Andoni Goicoechea (Spain)	1·75	85
765	$2 Elzo Coelho (Brazil) and Jean Tigana (France)	2·75	2·25
766	$3 Pedro Troglio (Argentina) and Sergei Alejnikov (Russia)	3·00	3·25
767	$5 Jan Karas (Poland) and Antonio Luiz Costa (Brazil)	3·75	4·75
760/7 Set of 8		14·00	11·50

MS768 Two sheets. (a) 100×70 mm. $5 Belloumi (Algeria). (b) 70×100 mm. $5 Trevor Steven (England) (*vert*). P 13 Set of 2 sheets .... 11·00 11·00

76 "Annunciation of Mary" (Dürer)

(Litho Cartor)

1993 (30 Nov). Christmas. Religious Paintings. T **76** and similar designs. Black, pale lemon and red (Nos. 769/73, 776, **MS**777a) or multicoloured (others). P 13.

769	20c. Type **76**	50	15
770	40c. "The Nativity" (drawing) (Dürer)	70	30
771	50c. "Holy Family on a Grassy Bank" (Dürer)	80	30
772	80c. "The Presentation of Christ in the Temple" (Dürer)	1·00	55
773	$1 "Virgin in Glory on the Crescent" (Dürer)	1·25	70
774	$1.60 "The Nativity (painting) (Dürer)	2·00	2·25
775	$3 "Madonna and Child" (Dürer)	2·50	3·25
776	$5 "The Presentation of Christ in the Temple" (detail) (Dürer)	3·25	4·75
769/76 Set of 8		11·00	11·00

MS777 Two sheets, each 105×130 mm. (a) $6 "Mary, Child and the Long-tailed Monkey" (detail) (Dürer). (b) $6 "The Rest on the Flight into Egypt" (detail) (Jean-Honore Fragonard) (*horiz*) Set of 2 sheets .... 8·50 9·50

77 Mickey Mouse playing Basketball

ST. KITTS-NEVIS / Nevis

(Litho Questa)

1994 (15 Feb). Sports and Pastimes. T **77** and similar multicoloured designs showing Walt Disney cartoon characters. P 14×13½ (horiz) or 13½×14 (vert).

778	10c. Type **77**...	40	30
779	25c. Minnie Mouse sunbathing (vert)...	50	20
780	50c. Mickey playing volleyball...	70	40
781	80c. Minnie dancing (vert)...	80	60
782	$1 Mickey playing football...	1·00	70
783	$1.50 Minnie hula hooping (vert)...	1·75	2·00
784	$4 Minnie skipping (vert)...	2·75	3·50
785	$5 Mickey wrestling Big Pete...	2·75	3·50
778/85 Set of 8...		9·50	10·00

MS786 Two sheets. (a) 127×102 mm. $6 Mickey, Donald Duck and Goofy in tug of war (black, bright rosine and blue-green). (b) 102×127 mm. $6 Mickey using Test your Strength machine Set of 2 sheets... 9·00 10·00

(Litho Questa)

1994 (18 Feb). Hong Kong '94 International Stamp Exhibition. No. **MS**752 optd with "HONG KONG '94" logo on sheet margins.
MS787 Two sheets, each 76×105 mm. (a) $6 Polydamas Swallowtail (male). (b) $6 West Indian Buckeye" Set of 2 sheets... 6·00 8·00

77a Girl with Umbrella    **79** Beekeeper collecting Wild Nest

(Litho Questa)

1994 (6 Apr). Hummel Figurines. T **77a** and similar vert designs. P 14.

788	5c. Type**77a**...	15	40
789	25c. Boy holding beer mug and parsnips...	45	15
790	50c. Girl sitting in tree...	65	35
791	80c. Boy in hat and scarf...	85	60
792	$1 Boy with umbrella...	1·00	70
793	$1.60 Girl with bird...	1·75	1·75
794	$2 Boy on sledge...	2·00	2·00
795	$5 Boy sitting in apple tree...	2·75	3·75
788/95 Set of 8...		8·50	8·75

MS796 Two sheets, each 94×125 mm. (a) Nos. 788 and 792/4. (b) Nos. 789/91 and 795 Set of 2 sheets. 6·50 7·50

(Des R. Vigurs. Litho Questa)

1994 (13 June). Beekeeping. T **79** and similar horiz designs. Multicoloured. P 14.

797	50c. Type **79**...	65	30
798	80c. Beekeeping club...	90	40
799	$1.60 Extracting honey from frames...	1·75	1·75
800	$3 Keepers placing queen in hive...	2·75	3·75
797/800 Set of 4...		5·50	5·50

MS801 100×70 mm. $6 Queen and workers in hive and mechanical honey extractor... 5·00 5·50

80 Blue Point Himalayan    **81** Black Coral

(Des R. Sauber. Litho Questa)

1994 (20 July). Persian Cats. T **80** and similar horiz designs. Multicoloured. P 14.

802	80c. Type **80**...	1·10	90
	a. Sheetlet. Nos. 802/9...	8·00	6·50
803	80c. Black and White Persian...	1·10	90
804	80c. Cream Persian...	1·10	90
805	80c. Red Persian...	1·10	90
806	80c. Persian...	1·10	90
807	80c. Persian Black Smoke...	1·10	90
808	80c. Chocolate Smoke Persian...	1·10	90
809	80c. Black Persian...	1·10	90
802/9 Set of 8...		8·00	6·50

MS810 Two sheets, each 100×70 mm. (a) $6 Silver Tabby Persian. (b) $6 Brown Tabby Persian Set of 2 sheets... 12·00 12·00

Nos. 802/9 were printed together, se-tenant, in sheetlets of 8.

(Des P. Chinelli. Litho Questa)

1994 (25 July). Endangered Species. Black Coral. T **81** and similar vert designs showing forms of coral. P 14.

811	25c. multicoloured...	60	75
	a. Horiz strip of 4. Nos. 811/14...	2·50	3·00
812	40c. multicoloured...	70	80
813	50c. multicoloured...	70	80
814	80c. multicoloured...	80	90
811/14 Set of 4...		2·50	3·00

Nos. 811/14 were printed in small sheets of 12 containing three horizontal se-tenant strips of 4 with each horizontal row starting with a different value.

82 Striped Burrfish

(Des P. Chinelli. Litho Questa)

1994 (25 July). Fish. T **82** and similar multicoloured designs. P 14.

815	10c. Type **82**...	50	50
816	50c. Flame-backed Angelfish...	55	55
	a. Sheetlet. Nos. 816/23...	4·00	4·00
817	50c. Reef Bass...	55	55
818	50c. Long-finned Damselfish ("Honey Gregory")...	55	55
819	50c. Saddle Squirrelfish...	55	55
820	50c. Cobalt Chromis...	55	55
821	50c. Genie's Neon Goby...	55	55
822	50c. Slender-tailed Cardinalfish...	55	55
823	50c. Royal Gramma...	55	55
824	$1 Blue-striped Grunt...	75	75
825	$1.60 Blue Angelfish...	1·00	1·25
826	$3 Cocoa Damselfish...	1·50	1·75
815/26 Set of 12...		7·25	7·75

MS827 Two sheets, each 100×70 mm. (a) $6 Blue Marlin. (b) $6 Sailfish (vert) Set of 2 sheets... 8·00 8·50

Nos. 816/23 were printed together, se-tenant, in sheetlets of 8 with the backgrounds forming a composite design.

No. 824 is inscribed "BLUESRIPED GRUNT" in error.

Nos. 816a was re-issued on 16 August 1994 showing the "Philakorea '94" International Stamp Exhibition logo on each corner of the sheetlet margins. The stamps show no listable differences.

83 Symbol 1. Turtles and Cloud

(Litho Questa)

1994 (16 Aug). Philakorea '94 International Stamp Exhibition, Seoul. T **93** and similar vert designs showing longevity symbols. Multicoloured. P 13½×14.

828	50c. Type **83**...	45	50
	a. Sheetlet. Nos. 828/35...	3·25	3·50
829	50c. Symbol 2. Cranes and bamboo...	45	50
830	50c. Symbol 3. Deer and bamboo...	45	50
831	50c. Symbol 4. Turtles and Sun...	45	50
832	50c. Symbol 5. Cranes under tree...	45	50
833	50c. Symbol 6. Deer and tree...	45	50

ST. KITTS-NEVIS / Nevis

834	50c. Symbol 7. Turtles and rock	45	50
835	50c. Symbol 8. Cranes above tree	45	50
828/35 Set of 8		3·25	3·50

Nos. 828/35 were printed together, *se-tenant*, in sheetlets of 8.

84 Twin-roofed House with Veranda

(Des R. Vigurs. Litho Questa)

1994 (22 Aug). Island Architecture. T **84** and similar horiz designs. Multicoloured. P 14.

836	25c. Type **84**	70	20
837	50c. Two-storey house with outside staircase	95	30
838	$1 Government Treasury	1·40	1·10
839	$5 Two-storey house with red roof	4·00	6·00
836/9 Set of 4		6·25	6·75
MS840 102×72 mm. $6 Raised bungalow with veranda		3·75	5·00

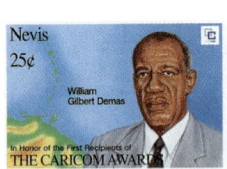

85 William Demas

86 "The Virgin Mary Queen of Heaven" (detail) (Jan Provost)

(Litho Questa)

1994 (1 Sept). First Recipients of Order of Caribbean Community. T **85** and similar horiz designs. Multicoloured. P 14.

841	25c. Type **85**	30	10
842	50c. Sir Shridath Ramphal	50	45
843	$1 Derek Walcott	2·50	1·50
841/3 Set of 3		3·00	1·75

(Litho Questa)

1994 (1 Dec). Christmas. Religious Paintings. T **86** and similar vert designs. Multicoloured. P 14.

844	20c. Type **86**	20	10
845	40c. "The Virgin Mary as Queen of Heaven" (different detail) (Provost)	35	25
846	50c. "The Virgin Mary as Queen of Heaven" (different detail) (Provost)	40	30
847	80c. "Adoration of the Magi" (detail) (Circle of Van der Goes)	60	40
848	$1 "Adoration of the Magi" (different detail) (Circle of Van der Goes)	70	50
849	$1.60 "Adoration of the Magi" (different detail) (Circle of Van der Goes)	1·25	1·50
850	$3 "Adoration of the Magi" (different detail) (Circle of Van der Goes)	1·75	2·50
851	$5 "The Virgin Mary as Queen of Heaven" (different detail) (Provost)	2·50	3·75
844/51 Set of 8		7·00	7·75
MS852 Two sheets, each 96×117 mm. (a) $5 "The Virgin Mary as Queen of Heaven" (different detail) (Provost). (b) $6 "Adoration of the Magi" (different detail) (Circle of Van der Goes) Set of 2 sheets		7·50	8·50

87 Mickey and Minnie Mouse

(Des Alvin White Studio. Litho Questa)

1995 (14 Feb). Disney Sweethearts (1st series). T **87** and similar multicoloured designs showing Walt Disney cartoon characters. P 14×13½.

853	10c. Type **87**	20	20
854	25c. Donald and Daisy Duck	35	20
855	50c. Pluto and Fifi	50	35
856	80c. Clarabelle Cow and Horace Horsecollar	70	50
857	$1 Pluto and Figaro	85	65
858	$1.50 Polly and Peter Penguin	1·25	1·50
859	$4 Prunella Pullet and Hick Rooster	2·50	3·25
860	$5 Jenny Wren and Cock Robin	2·50	3·25
853/60 Set of 8		8·00	9·00
MS861 Two sheets, each 133×107 mm. (a) $6 Daisy Duck (vert). (b) $6 Minnie Mouse (vert). P 13½×14 Set of 2 sheets		7·50	9·00

See also Nos. 998/1007.

88 Rufous-breasted Hermit

(Des Mary Walters (Nos. 862/73), Marilyn Abramowitz (others). Litho Questa).

1995 (30 Mar). Birds. T **88** and similar vert designs. Multicoloured. P 14.

862	50c. Type **88**	50	50
	a. Sheetlet. Nos. 862/73	6·00	6·00
863	50c. Purple-throated Carib	50	50
864	50c. Green Mango	50	50
865	50c. Bahama Woodstar	50	50
866	50c. Hispaniolan Emerald	50	50
867	50c. Antillean Crested Hummingbird	50	50
868	50c. Green-throated Carib	50	50
869	50c. Antillean Mango	50	50
870	50c. Vervain Hummingbird	50	50
871	50c. Jamaican Mango	50	50
872	50c. Cuban Emerald	50	50
873	50c. Blue-headed Hummingbird	50	50
874	50c. Hooded Merganser	50	50
875	80c. Green-backed Heron	70	50
876	$2 Double-crested Cormorant	1·25	1·40
877	$3 Ruddy Duck	1·50	1·75
862/77 Set of 16		9·00	9·00
MS878 Two sheets, each 100×70 mm. (a) $6 Black Skimmer. (b) $6 Snowy Plover Set of 2 sheets		8·00	8·50

Nos. 862/73 were printed together, *se-tenant*, in sheetlets of 12.
No. 870 is inscribed "VERVIAN" in error.

89 Pointer

(Des D. Miller. Litho B.D.T.)

1995 (23 May). Dogs. T **89** and similar horiz designs. Multicoloured. P 14.

879	25c. Type **89**	30	20
880	50c. Old Danish Pointer	50	50
881	80c. Irish Setter	65	65
	a. Sheetlet. Nos. 881/9	5·00	5·00
882	80c. Weimaraner	65	65
883	80c. Gordon Setter	65	65
884	80c. Brittany Spaniel	65	65
885	80c. American Cocker Spaniel	65	65
886	80c. English Cocker Spaniel	65	65
887	80c. Labrador Retriever	65	65
888	80c. Golden Retriever	65	65
889	80c. Flat-coated Retriever	65	65
890	$1 German Short-haired Pointer	75	75
891	$2 English Setter	1·40	1·40
879/91 Set of 13		8·00	7·75

ST. KITTS-NEVIS / Nevis

MS892 Two sheets, each 72×58 mm. (a) $6 German Shepherds. (b) $6 Bloodhounds *Set of 2 sheets*............ 8·00 8·50

Nos. 881/9 were printed together, *se-tenant*, in sheetlets of 9. "POINTER" is omitted from the inscription on No. 890. No. **MS**892a is incorrectly inscribed "SHEPHARD".

90 *Schulembergera truncata*

(Des Mary Walters. Litho Questa)

1995 (20 June). Cacti. T **90** and similar vert designs. Multicoloured. P 14.

893	40c. Type **90**...	30	20
894	50c. *Echinocereus pectinatus*.......................	40	25
895	80c. *Mammillaria zeilmanniana alba*............	65	40
896	$1.60 *Lobivia hertriehiana*...........................	1·10	1·25
897	$2 *Hammatocactus setispinus*......................	1·40	1·50
898	$3 *Astrophytum myriostigma*......................	1·60	2·00
893/8 *Set of 6*		5·00	5·00

MS899 Two sheets, each 106×76 mm. (a) $6 *Opuntia robusta*. (b) $6 *Rhipsalidopsis gaertneri Set of 2 sheets*.. 7·00 7·50

91 Scouts backpacking

(Des B. Hargreaves. Litho Questa)

1995 (20 July). 18th World Scout Jamboree, Netherlands. T **91** and similar multicoloured designs. P 14.

900	$1 Type **91**...	1·00	1·10
	a. Horiz strip. Nos. 900/2........................	4·00	4·50
901	$2 Scouts building aerial rope way............	1·50	1·75
902	$4 Scout map reading................................	2·00	2·25
900/2 *Set of 3*		4·00	4·50

MS903 101×71 mm. $6 Scout in canoe (*vert*).............. 4·00 4·50

Nos. 900/2 were printed together in sheets of 9 containing three *se-tenant* horizontal strips of 3, each forming a composite design.

91a Clark Gable and Aircraft

(Des J. Iskowitz. Litho Questa)

1995 (20 July). 50th Anniv of End of Second World War in Europe. T **91a** and similar multicoloured designs. P 14.

904	$1.25 Type **91a**..	1·00	1·00
	a. Sheetlet. Nos. 904/11..........................	7·25	7·25
905	$1.25 Audie Murphy and machine-gunner......	1·00	1·00
906	$1.25 Glenn Miller playing trombone.............	1·00	1·00
907	$1.25 Joe Louis and infantry........................	1·00	1·00
908	$1.25 Jimmy Doolittle and U.S.S. *Hornet* (aircraft carrier)...................................	1·00	1·00
909	$1.25 John Hersey and jungle patrol............	1·00	1·00
910	$1.25 John F. Kennedy in patrol boat...........	1·00	1·00
911	$1.25 James Stewart and bombers..............	1·00	1·00
904/11 *Set of 8*		7·25	7·25

MS912 101×71 mm. $6 Jimmy Doolittle (*vert*)............. 4·00 4·50

Nos. 904/11 were printed together, *se-tenant*, in sheetlets of 8 with the stamps arranged in two horizontal strips of 4 separated by a gutter showing ticker-tape parade and U.S. sailor kissing nurse in New York.

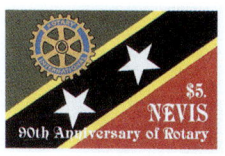

92 Oriental and African People

93 Rotary Emblem on Nevis Flag

(Des J. Iskowitz. Litho Questa)

1995 (20 July). 50th Anniv of United Nations. T **92** and similar vert designs, each pale lilac and black or multicoloured (No. **MS**916). P 14.

913	$1.25 Type **92**..	55	80
	a. Horiz strip of 3. Nos. 913/15...............	2·50	3·00
914	$1.60 Asian people.......................................	75	1·10
915	$3 American and European people	1·40	1·60
913/15 *Set of 3*..		2·50	3·00

MS916 105×75 mm. $6 Pres. Nelson Mandela of South Africa... 2·75 3·25

Nos. 913/15 were printed together in sheets of 9 containing three *se-tenant* horizontal strips of 3, each forming a composite design.

(Des J. Iskowitz. Litho Questa)

1995 (20 July). 50th Anniv of Food and Agriculture Organization. Vert designs as T **92**. Multicoloured. P 14.

917	40c. Woman wearing yellow headdress.........	15	60
	a. Horiz strip of 3. Nos. 917/19...............	2·00	3·00
918	$2 Babies and emblem................................	85	1·25
919	$3 Woman wearing blue headdress	1·25	1·60
917/19 *Set of 3*..		2·00	3·00

MS920 105×80 mm. $6 Man carrying hoe................. 2·75 3·75

Nos. 917/19 were printed together in sheets of 9 containing three *se-tenant* horizontal strips of 3, each forming a composite design.

No. **MS**920 is inscribed "1945–1955" in error.

(Des G. Bibby. Litho Questa)

1995 (20 July). 90th Anniv of Rotary International. T **93** and similar horiz design. Multicoloured. P 14.

921	$5 Type **93**..	2·50	3·25

MS922 95×66 mm. $6 Rotary emblem and beach........ 3·00 3·75

(Litho Questa)

1995 (20 July)–**2002**. 95th Birthday of Queen Elizabeth the Queen Mother. Vert designs as T **344** of Antigua. P 13½×14.

923	$1.50 orange-brown, pale brown and black...	2·25	1·75
	a. Sheetlet. Nos. 923/6×2........................	7·00	
	ab. Sheetlet. As No. 923a, but with top margin additionally inscr "IN MEMORIAM 1900-2002" (17.6.02).............	8·00	
924	$1.50 multicoloured.....................................	2·25	1·75
925	$1.50 multicoloured.....................................	2·25	1·75
926	$1.50 multicoloured.....................................	2·25	1·75
923/6 *Set of 4*		8·00	10·00

MS927 102×127 mm. $6 multicoloured...................... 4·75 5·00

a. Additionally inscr "IN MEMORIAM 1900-2002" on margin (17.6.02)................ 6·00 6·00

Designs:—No. 923, Queen Elizabeth the Queen Mother (pastel drawing); No. 924, Wearing pink hat; No. 925, At desk (oil painting); No. 926, Wearing blue hat; No. **MS**927, Wearing tiara.

Nos. 923/6 were printed together in sheetlets of 8, containing two *se-tenant* horizontal strips of 4.

Nos. 923a and **MS**927 were re-issued in 2002 with additional memorial inscription and black frames on the margins.

93b Grumman F4F Wildcat

(Des J. Batchelor. Litho Questa)

1995 (20 July). 50th Anniv of End of Second World War in the Pacific. United States Aircraft. T **93b** and similar horiz designs. Multicoloured. P 14.

928	$2 Type **93b**..	1·40	1·40
	a. Sheetlet. Nos. 928/33..........................	7·50	7·50
929	$2 Chance Vought F4U-1A Corsair	1·40	1·40
930	$2 Vought SB2U Vindicator.........................	1·40	1·40

279

ST. KITTS-NEVIS / Nevis

931	$2 Grumman F6F Hellcat	1·40	1·40
932	$2 Douglas SDB Dauntless	1·40	1·40
933	$2 Grumman TBF-1 Avenger	1·40	1·40
928/33	Set of 6	7·50	7·50
MS934	108×76 mm. $6 Chance Vought F4U-IA Corsair on carrier flight deck	5·50	6·50

Nos. 928/33 were printed together, *se-tenant*, in sheetlets of 6 with the stamps arranged in two horizontal strips of 3 separated by a gutter showing U.S.S. *Saratoga* (aircraft carrier).

94 Emil van Behring (1901 Medicine)
95 American Eagle Presidents' Club Logo 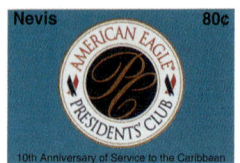

(Des R. Sauber. Litho Questa)

1995 (20 July). Centenary of Nobel Trust Fund. Past Prize Winners. T **94** and similar vert designs. Multicoloured. P 14.

935	$1.25 Type **94**	75	85
	a. Sheetlet. Nos. 935/43	6·00	7·00
936	$1.25 Wilhelm Röntgen (1901 Physics)	75	85
937	$1.25 Paul Heyse (1910 Literature)	75	85
938	$1.25 Le Duc Tho (1973 Peace)	75	85
939	$1.25 Yasunari Kawabata (1968 Literature)	75	85
940	$1.25 Tsung-dao Lee (1957 Physics)	75	85
941	$1.25 Werner Heisenberg (1932 Physics)	75	85
942	$1.25 Johannes Stark (1919 Physics)	75	85
943	$1.25 Wilhelm Wien (1911 Physics)	75	85
935/43	Set of 9	6·00	7·00
MS944	101×71 mm. $6 Kenzaburo Oe (1994 Literature)	3·25	3·75

Nos. 935/43 were printed together, *se-tenant*, in sheetlets of 9.

(Des Y. Lee. Litho Questa)

1995 (28 Aug). Tenth Anniv of American Eagle Air Services to the Caribbean. Sheet, 70×100 mm, containing T **95** and similar horiz design. Multicoloured. P 14.

MS945 80c. Type **95**; $3 Aircraft over Nevis beach ...... 2·40 2·50

96 Great Egrets
97 SKANTEL Engineer 

(Des Grace De Vito. Litho Questa)

1995 (1 Sept). Marine Life. T **96** and similar multicoloured designs. P 14.

946	50c. Type **96**	55	55
	a. Sheetlet. Nos. 946/61	8·00	8·00
947	50c. 17th-century galleon	55	55
948	50c. Galleon and Marlin	55	55
949	50c. Herring Gulls	55	55
950	50c. Nassau Groupers	55	55
951	50c. Spotted Eagleray	55	55
952	50c. Leopard Shark and Hammerhead	55	55
953	50c. Hourglass Dolphins	55	55
954	50c. Spanish Hogfish	55	55
955	50c. Jellyfish and Seahorses	55	55
956	50c. Angelfish and buried treasure	55	55
957	50c. Hawksbill Turtle	55	55
958	50c. Common Octopus	55	55
959	50c. Moray Eel	55	55
960	50c. Queen Angelfish and Butterflyfish	55	55
961	50c. Ghost Crab and Sea Star	55	55
946/61	Set of 16	8·00	8·00
MS962	Two sheets. (a) 106×76 mm. $5 Nassau Grouper. (b) 76×106 mm. $5 Queen Angelfish (*vert*) Set of 2 sheets	7·00	7·00

Nos. 946/61 were printed together, *se-tenant*, in sheetlets of 16, forming a composite design.

No. **MS**962 also commemorates the "Singapore '95" International Stamp Exhibition.

(Des M. Friedman. Litho Questa)

1995 (23 Oct). Tenth Anniv of SKANTEL (telecommunications company). T **97** and similar multicoloured designs. P 14.

963	$1 Type **97**	60	50
964	$1.50 SKANTEL sign outside Nevis office	80	1·25
MS965	76×106 mm. $5 St. Kitts SKANTEL office (*horiz*)	3·00	3·50

98 "Rucellai Madonna and Child" (detail) (Duccio)
99 View of Nevis Four Seasons Resort 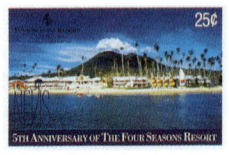

(Litho Questa)

1995 (1 Dec). Christmas. Religious Paintings by Duccio di Buoninsegna T **98** and similar vert designs. Multicoloured. P 13½×14.

966	20c. Type **98**	20	15
967	50c. "Angel from the Rucellai Madonna" (detail)	40	25
968	80c. "Madonna and Child" (*different*)	60	40
969	$1 "Angel from the Annunciation" (detail)	75	60
970	$1.60 "Madonna and Child" (*different*)	1·25	1·50
971	$3 "Angel from the Rucellai Madonna" (*different*)	1·90	2·75
966/71	Set of 6	4·50	5·00
MS972	Two sheets, each 102×127 mm. (a) $5 "Nativity with the Prophets Isaiah and Ezekiel" (detail). (b) $6 "The Crevole Madonna" (detail) Set of 2 sheets	6·50	7·50

(Des M. Friedman. Litho Questa)

1996 (14 Feb). Fifth Anniv of Four Seasons Resort, Nevis. T **99** and similar horiz designs. Multicoloured. P 14.

973	25c. Type **99**	15	20
974	50c. Catamarans, Pinney's Beach	25	30
975	80c. Robert Trent Jones II Golf Course	40	45
976	$2 Prime Minister Simeon Daniel laying foundation stone	1·00	1·40
973/6	Set of 4	1·60	2·10
MS977	76×106 mm. $6 Sunset over resort	3·00	3·50

100 Rat, Plant and Butterfly
101 Ancient Greek Boxers 

(Des Y. Lee. Litho Questa)

1996 (28 Feb). Chinese New Year ("Year of the Rat"). T **100** and similar vert designs. Multicoloured. P 14.

978	$1 Type **100**	60	60
	a. Block of 4. Nos. 978/81	2·25	2·25
979	$1 Rat with prickly plant	60	60
980	$1 Rat and bee	60	60
981	$1 Rat and dragonfly	60	60
978/81	Set of 4	2·25	2·25
MS982	74×104 mm. No. 978/81	2·25	2·50
MS983	74×104 mm. $3 Rat eating	2·25	2·50

Nos. 978/81 were printed together, *se-tenant*, in blocks of 4 throughout sheets of 16.

ST. KITTS-NEVIS / Nevis

(Des B. Durand. Litho B.D.T.)

1996 (28 May). Olympic Games, Atlanta. Previous Winners. T **101** and similar multicoloured designs. P 14.

			Medal
984	25c. Type **101**	30	20
985	50c. Mark Spitz (U.S.A.) (Gold–swimming, 1972)	40	30
986	80c. Siegbert Horn (East Germany) (Gold – single kayak slalom, 1972)	60	45
987	$1 Jim Thorpe on medal (U.&A.), 1912 (vert)	65	70
	a. Sheetlet. Nos. 987/95	4·50	5·00
988	$1 Glenn Morris on medal (U.S.A.), 1936 (vert)	65	70
989	$1 Bob Mathias on medal (U.S.A.), 1948 and 1952 (vert)	65	70
990	$1 Rater Johnson on medal (U.S.A.), 1960 (vert)	65	70
991	$1 Bill Toomey (U.S.A.), 1968 (vert)	65	70
992	$1 Nikolay Avilov (Russia), 1972 (vert)	65	70
993	$1 Bruce Jenner (U.S.A.), 1976 (vert)	65	70
994	$1 Daley Thompson (Great Britain), 1980 and 1984 (vert)	65	70
995	$1 Christian Schenk (East Germany), 1988 (vert)	65	70
996	$3 Olympic Stadium and Siegestor Arch, Munich (vert)	1·75	2·00
984/96 Set of 13		7·25	8·25

MS997 Two sheets, each 105×75 mm. (a) $5 Willi Holdorf (West Germany) (Gold–decathlon, 1964) (vert). (b) $5 Hans-Joachim Walde (West Germany) (Silver–decathlon, 1968) (vert) Set of 2 sheets .... 6·50 7·00

Nos. 987/95 were printed together, se-tenant, in sheetlets of 9 and depict decathlon gold medal winners.

(Des Alvin White Studios. Litho Questa)

1996 (17 June). Disney Sweethearts (2nd series). Horiz designs as T **87** showing Walt Disney cartoon characters. Multicoloured. P 14×13½.

998	$2 Pocahontas and John Smith	2·00	1·50
	a. Sheetlet. Nos. 998/1006	16·00	12·00
999	$2 Mowgli and the Girl	2·00	1·50
1000	$2 Belle and the Beast	2·00	1·50
1001	$2 Cinderella and Prince Charming	2·00	1·50
1002	$2 Pinocchio and the Dutch Girl	2·00	1·50
1003	$2 Grace Martin and Henry Coy	2·00	1·50
1004	$2 Snow White and the Prince	2·00	1·50
1005	$2 Aladdin and Jasmine	2·00	1·50
1006	$2 Pecos Bill and Slue Foot Sue	2·00	1·50
998/1006 Set of 9		16·00	12·00

MS1007 Two sheets, each 110×130 mm. (a) $6 Sleeping Beauty and Prince Phillip (vert). P 13½×14. (b) $6 Ariel and Eric. P 14×13½. Set of 2 sheets .... 10·00 11·00

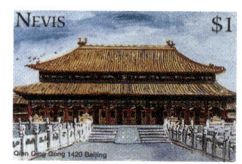

Nos. 998/1006 were printed together, se-tenant, in sheetlets of 9.

102 Qian Qing Gong, Peking

(Des Y. Lee. Litho Questa)

1996 (1 July). "CHINA '96" 9th Asian International Stamp Exhibition, Peking. Peking Pagodas. T **102** and similar multicoloured designs. P 14.

1008	$1 Type **102**	60	70
	a. Sheetlet. Nos. 1008/16	4·75	5·50
1009	$1 Temple of Heaven	60	70
1010	$1 Zhongnanhai	60	70
1011	$1 Da Zing Hall, Shehyang Palace	60	70
1012	$1 Temple of the Sleeping Buddha	60	70
1013	$1 Huang Qiong Yu, Altar of Heaven	60	70
1014	$1 The Grand Bell Temple	60	70
1015	$1 Imperial Palace	60	70
1016	$1 Pu Tu Temple	60	70
1008/16 Set of 9		4·75	5·50

MS1017 104×74 mm. $6 Summer Palace of Emperor Wan Yan-liang (vert) .... 3·00 3·50

Nos. 1008/16 were printed together, se-tenant, in sheetlets of 9.

(Litho Questa)

1996 (1 July). 70th Birthday of Queen Elizabeth II. Vert designs as T **364** of Antigua. Multicoloured. P 13½×14.

1018	$2 Queen Elizabeth II	1·25	1·40
	a. Strip of 3. Nos. 1018/20	3·25	3·75
1019	$2 Wearing evening dress	1·25	1·40
1020	$2 In purple hat and coat	1·25	1·40
1018/20 Set of 3		3·25	3·75

MS1021 125×103 mm. $6 Taking the salute at Trooping the Colour .... 4·25 4·50

Nos. 1018/20 were printed together, se-tenant, in horizontal and vertical strips of 3 throughout sheets of 9.

103 Children reading Book

(Des R. Sauber. Litho Questa)

1996 (1 July). 50th Anniv of U.N.I.C.E.F. T **103** and similar multicoloured designs. P 14.

1022	25c. Type **103**	40	20
1023	50c. Doctor and child	70	30
1024	$4 Children	2·75	3·75
1022/4 Set of 3		3·50	3·75

MS1025 75×105 mm. $6 Young girl (vert) .... 3·00 3·50

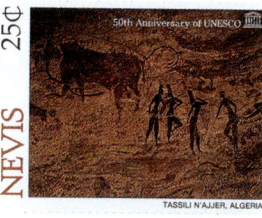

104 Cave Paintings, Tassili n'Ajjer, Algeria

(Des M. Friedman. Litho Questa)

1996 (1 July). 50th Anniv of U.N.E.S.C.O. T **104** and similar multicoloured designs. P 13½×14 ($2) or 14×13½ (others).

1026	25c. Type **104**	1·00	40
1027	$2 Temple, Tikai National Park, Guatemala (vert)	1·50	1·75
1028	$3 Temple of Hera, Samos, Greece	2·00	2·75
1026/8 Set of 3		4·00	4·25

MS1029 106×76 mm. $6 Pueblo, Taos, U.S.A. .... 3·00 3·50

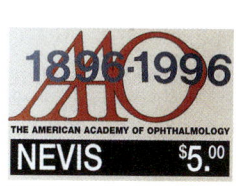

105 American Academy of Ophthalmology Logo

106 *Rothmannia longiflora*

(Des M. Friedman. Litho Questa)

1996 (1 July). Centenary of American Academy of Ophthalmology. P 14.

1030	**105**	$5 multicoloured	5·00	5·00

(Des T. Wood. Litho Questa)

1996 (24 Sept). Flowers. T **106** and similar vert designs. Multicoloured. P 14.

1031	25c. Type **106**	35	20
1032	50c. *Gloriosa simplex*	50	30
1033	$1 *Monodora myristica*	70	70
	a. Sheetlet. Nos. 1033/41	5·50	5·50
1034	$1 Giraffe	70	70
1035	$1 *Adansonia digitata*	70	70
1036	$1 *Ansellia gigantea*	70	70
1037	$1 *Geissorhiza rochensis*	70	70
1038	$1 *Arctotis venusta*	70	70
1039	$1 *Gladiotus cardinalis*	70	70
1040	$1 *Eucomis bicolor*	70	70
1041	$1 *Protea obtusifolia*	70	70
1042	$2 *Catharanthus roseus*	1·10	1·25
1043	$3 *Plumbago auriculata*	1·60	1·90
1031/43 Set of 13		8·75	9·00

MS1044 75×105 mm. $5 *Strelitzia reginae* .... 2·50 3·00

Nos. 1033/41 were printed together, se-tenant, in sheetlets of 9.

107 Western Meadowlark on Decoration

(Des R. Rundo. Litho B.D.T.)

1996 (2 Dec). Christmas. Birds. T **107** and similar multicoloured designs. P 14.
1045	25c. Type **107**	30	20
1046	50c. Bird (incorrectly inscr as "American Goldfinch") with decorations (*horiz*)	45	30
1047	80c. Santa Claus, sleigh and reindeer (*horiz*)	60	45
1048	$1 American Goldfinch on stocking	70	55
1049	$1.60 Mockingbird with snowman decoration	1·00	1·10
1050	$5 Yellow-rumped Cacique and bauble	2·75	4·00
1045/50	*Set of* 6	5·25	6·00

MS1051 Two sheets. (a) 106×76 mm. $6 Macaw (*horiz*). (b) 76×106 mm. $6 Vermilion Flycatcher (*horiz*) *Set of 2 sheets* .... 7·00 8·00

No. 1048 is inscribed "WESTERN MEADOWLARK" and No. 1050 "YELLOW-RUMPED CAIEQUE", both in error.

108 Ox (from "Five Oxen" by Han Huang)

(Des Y. Lee. Litho Questa)

1997 (16 Jan). Chinese New Year ("Year of the Ox"). T **108** and similar oxen from the painting by Han Huang. Sheet 230×93 mm. P 14×15.
MS1052 50c., 80c., $1.60, $2 multicoloured .... 3·50 3·75
The fifth ox appears on a small central label.

109 Giant Panda eating Bamboo Shoots
110 Elquemedo Willett 

(Des L. Fried. Litho Questa)

1997 (12 Feb). HONG KONG '97 International Stamp Exhibition. Giant Pandas. T **109** and similar vert designs. Multicoloured. P 14.
1053	$1.60 Type **109**	1·50	1·50
	a. Sheetlet. Nos. 1053/8	8·00	8·00
1054	$1.60 Head of Panda	1·50	1·50
1055	$1.60 Panda with new-born cub	1·50	1·50
1056	$1.60 Panda hanging from branch	1·50	1·50
1057	$1.60 Panda asleep on tree	1·50	1·50
1058	$1.60 Panda climbing trunk	1·50	1·50
1053/8	*Set of* 6	8·00	8·00

MS1059 73×103 mm. $5 Panda with cub .... 2·50 3·00

Nos. 1053/8 were printed together, *se-tenant*, in sheetlets of 6, with enlarged right-hand margin.

(Des M. Friedman. Litho B.D.T.)

1997 (1 May). Nevis Cricketers. T **110** and similar multicoloured designs. P 14.
1060	25c. Type **110**	45	25
1061	80c. Stuart Williams	80	50
1062	$2 Keith Arthurton	1·25	1·50
1060/2	*Set of* 3	2·25	2·00

MS1063 Two sheets, each 106×76 mm. (a) $5 Willett, Arthurton and Williams as part of the 1990 Nevis team (*horiz*). (b) $5 Williams and Arthurton as part of the 1994 West Indies team *Set of 2 sheets* .... 6·00 7·00

111 Crimson-speckled Moth

(Des Rinah Lyamph. Litho B.D.T.)

1997 (12 May). Butterflies and Moths. T **111** and similar horiz designs. Multicoloured. P 14.
1064	10c. Type **111**	20	30
1065	25c. Purple Emperor	35	20
1066	50c. Regent Skipper	45	30
1067	80c. Provence Burnet Moth	70	45
1068	$1 Common Wall Butterfly	70	80
1069	$1 Red-lined Geometrid	70	80
	a. Sheetlet. Nos. 1069/77	5·50	6·50
1070	$1 Boisduval's Autumnal Moth	70	80
1071	$1 Blue Pansy	70	80
1072	$1 Common Clubtail	70	80
1073	$1 Tufted Jungle King	70	80
1074	$1 Lesser Marbled Fritillary	70	80
1075	$1 Peacock Royal	70	80
1076	$1 Emperor Gum Moth	70	80
1077	$1 Orange Swallow-tailed Moth	70	80
1078	$4 Cruiser Butterfly	2·25	2·75
1064/78	*Set of* 15	9·75	11·00

MS1079 Two sheets. (a) 103×73 mm. $5 Great Purple ("*Saskiai charondal*"). (b) 73×103 mm. $5 Jersey Tiger Moth *Set of 2 sheets* .... 5·50 6·50

Nos. 1069/77 were printed together, *se-tenant*, in sheetlets of 9.
No. 1073 is inscribed "TUFTED JUNGLE QUEEN" in error.

112 Boy with Two Pigeons ("Two Pigeons")

(Des R. Rundo. Litho Questa)

1997 (29 May). 300th Anniv of Mother Goose Nursery Rhymes. Sheet 72×102 mm. P 14.
MS1080 **112** $5 multicoloured .... 2·75 3·50

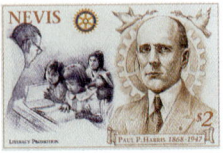

113 Paul Harris and Literacy Class

(Des J. Iskowitz. Litho Questa)

1997 (29 May). 50th Death Anniv of Paul Harris (founder of Rotary International). T **113** and similar horiz design. Multicoloured. P 14.
1081	$2 Type **113**	1·00	1·25

MS1082 78×108 mm. $5 Football coaching session, Chile 2·50 3·00

(Litho Questa)

1997 (29 May). Golden Wedding of Queen Elizabeth and Prince Philip. Horiz designs as T **378** of Antigua. Multicoloured. P 14.
1083	$1 Queen Elizabeth II	95	95
	a. Sheetlet. Nos. 1083/8	5·00	5·00
1084	$1 Royal coat of arms	95	95
1085	$1 Queen Elizabeth wearing red hat and coat with Prince Philip	95	95
1086	$1 Queen Elizabeth in blue coat and Prince Philip	95	95
1087	$1 Caernarvon Castle	95	95
1088	$1 Prince Philip in R.A.F. uniform	95	95

1083/8	Set of 6	5·00	5·00
MS1089	100×70 mm. $5 Queen Elizabeth at Coronation..	3·00	3·50

Nos. 1083/8 were printed together, *se-tenant*, in sheetlets of 6.

1997 (29 May). Pacific '97 International Stamp Exhibition, San Francisco. Death Centenary of Heinrich von Stephan. Horiz designs as T **379** of Antigua. P. 14.

1090	$1.60 turquoise-green	90	1·10
	a. Sheetlet. Nos. 1090/2	2·50	3·00
1091	$1.60 chestnut	90	1·10
1092	$1.60 deep blue	90	1·10
1090/2	Set of 3	2·50	3·00
MS1093	82×118 mm. $5 sepia	2·50	3·00

Designs:—No. 1090, Russian reindeer post, 1859; No. 1091, Von Stephan and Mercury; No. 1092, *City of Cairo* (paddle-steamer), Mississippi, 1800s; No. **MS**1093, Von Stephan and Bavarian postal messenger, 1640.

Nos. 1090/2 were printed together, *se-tenant*, in sheets of 3 with enlarged right-hand margin.

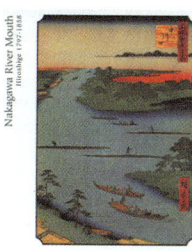

Nevis $1.60
113c "Scattered Pines, Tone River"

115 *Cantharellus cibarius*

114 Augusta National Course, U.S.A.

(Litho Questa)

1997 (29 May). Birth Bicentenary of Hiroshige (Japanese painter). "One Hundred Famous Views of Edo". T **113c** and similar vert designs. Multicoloured. P. 13½×14.

1094	$1.60 Type **113c**	1·25	1·25
	a. Sheetlet. Nos. 1094/9	6·75	6·75
1095	$1.60 "Mouth of Nakagawa River"	1·25	1·25
1096	$1.60 "Niijuku Ferry"	1·25	1·25
1097	$1.60 "Horie and Nekozane"	1·25	1·25
1098	$1.60 "Konodai and the Tone River"	1·25	1·25
1099	$1.60 "Maple Trees, Tekona Shrine and Bridge, Mama"	1·25	1·25
1094/9	Set of 6	6·75	6·75
MS1100	Two sheets, each 102×127 mm. (a) $6 "Mitsumata Wakarenofuchi". (b) $6 "Moto-Hachiman Shrine, Sunamura" Set of 2 sheets	7·00	7·50

Nos. 1094/9 were printed together, *se-tenant*, in sheetlets of 6.

(Des M. Friedman. Litho B.D.T.)

1997 (15 July). Golf Courses of the World. T **114** and similar horiz designs. Multicoloured. P. 14.

1101	$1 Type **114**	80	80
	a. Sheetlet. Nos. 1101/9	6·50	6·50
1102	$1 Cabo del Sol, Mexico	80	80
1103	$1 Cypress Point, U.S.A.	80	80
1104	$1 Lost City, South Africa	80	80
1105	$1 Moscow Country Club, Russia	80	80
1106	$1 New South Wales, Australia	80	80
1107	$1 Royal Montreal, Canada	80	80
1108	$1 St. Andrews, Scotland	80	80
1109	$1 Four Seasons Resort, Nevis	80	80
1101/9	Set of 9	6·50	6·50

Nos. 1101/9 were printed together, *se-tenant*, in sheetlets of 9.

(Des D. Miller. Litho Enschedé)

1997 (12 Aug). Fungi. T **115** and similar vert designs. Multicoloured. P. 13.

1110	25c. Type **115**	30	20
1111	50c. *Stropharia aeruginosa*	40	30
1112	80c. *Suillus hiteus*	60	65
	a. Sheetlet. Nos. 1112/17	3·25	3·50
1113	80c. *Amanita muscaria*	60	65
1114	80c. *Lactarius rufus*	60	65
1115	80c. *Amanita rubescens*	60	65
1116	80c. *Armillaria mellea*	60	65
1117	80c. *Russula sardonia*	60	65
1118	$1 *Boletus edulis*	65	70
	a. Sheetlet. Nos. 1118/23	3·50	3·75
1119	$1 *Pholiota lenta*	65	70
1120	$1 *Cortinarius bolaris*	65	70
1121	$1 *Coprinus picaceus*	65	70
1122	$1 *Amanita phalloides*	65	70
1123	$1 *Cystolepiota aspera*	65	70
1124	$3 *Lactarius turpis*	1·75	2·00
1125	$4 *Entoloma clypeatum*	2·25	2·50
1110/25	Set of 16	11·00	12·00
MS1126	Two sheets, each 98×68 mm. (a) $5 *Galerina mutabilis*. (b) $5 *Gymnopilus junonius* Set of 2 sheets..	6·00	6·50

Nos. 1112/17 and 1118/23 were each printed together, *se-tenant* in sheetlets of 6 with the backgrounds forming composite designs.

116 Diana, Princess of Wales

(Des Y. Lee. Litho Questa)

1997 (19 Sept). Diana, Princess of Wales Commemoration. T **116** and similar vert portraits. Multicoloured. P. 14.

1127	$1 Type **116**	1·00	90
	a. Sheetlet. Nos. 1127/35	8·00	7·25
1128	$1 Wearing white blouse	1·00	90
1129	$1 In wedding dress, 1981	1·00	90
1130	$1 Wearing turquoise blouse	1·00	90
1131	$1 Wearing tiara	1·00	90
1132	$1 Wearing blue blouse	1·00	90
1133	$1 Wearing pearl necklace	1·00	90
1134	$1 Wearing diamond drop earrings	1·00	90
1135	$1 Wearing sapphire necklace and earrings	1·00	90
1127/35	Set of 9	8·00	7·25

Nos. 1127/35 were printed together, *se-tenant*, in sheetlets of 9 with an illustrated right-hand margin.

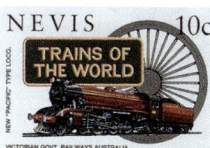

117 Victoria Govt Class S Pacific Locomotive, Australia

(Des D. Miller. Litho Questa)

1997 (29 Sept). Trains of the World. T **117** and similar horiz designs. Multicoloured. P. 14.

1136	10c. Type **117**	35	20
1137	50c. Express steam locomotive, Japan	55	30
1138	80c. L.M.S. steam-turbine locomotive, Great Britain	75	45
1139	$1 Electric locomotive, Switzerland	90	55
1140	$1.50 "Mikado" steam locomotive, Sudan	1·25	1·40
	a. Sheetlet. Nos. 1140/5	6·75	7·50
1141	$1.50 *Mohammed Ali el Kebir* steam locomotive, Egypt	1·25	1·40
1142	$1.50 Southern Region steam locomotive *Leatherhead*	1·25	1·40
1143	$1.50 Great Southern Railway Drumm battery-powered railcar, Ireland	1·25	1·40
1144	$1.50 Pacific locomotive, Germany	1·25	1·40
1145	$1.50 Canton–Hankow Railway Pacific locomotive, China	1·25	1·40
1146	$2 L.M.S. high-pressure locomotive, Great Britain	1·60	1·75
1147	$3 Great Northern Railway *Kestrel*, Ireland.	2·00	2·25
1136/47	Set of 12	12·00	12·50
MS1148	Two sheets, each 71×48 mm. (a) $5 L.M.S. high-pressure locomotive. (b) $5 G.W.R. *King George V* Set of 2 sheets	7·00	7·50

Nos. 1140/5 were printed together, *se-tenant*, in sheetlets of 6.

ST. KITTS-NEVIS / Nevis

118 "Selection of Angels" (detail) (Dürer)

119 Tiger (semi-circular character at top left)

(Litho Questa)

1997 (26 Nov). Christmas. Paintings. T **118** and similar multicoloured designs. P 14.

1149	20c. Type **118**	30	15
1150	25c. "Selection of Angels" (different detail) (Dürer)	35	20
1151	50c. "Andromeda and Perseus" (Rubens)	55	30
1152	80c. "Harmony" (detail) (Raphael)	75	45
1153	$1.60 "Harmony" (different detail) (Raphael)	1·40	1·50
1154	$5 Holy Trinity" (Raphael)	3·50	4·50
1149/54 Set of 6		6·00	6·25

MS1155 Two sheets, each 114×104 mm. (a) $5 "Study Muse" (Raphael) (horiz). (b) $5 "Ezekiel's Vision" (Raphael) (horiz) Set of 2 sheets .... 6·50 7·00

(Des Kan-chen Wang. Litho B.D.T.)

1998 (19 Jan). Chinese New Year ("Year of the Tiger"). T **119** and similar multicoloured designs showing symbolic tigers. P 14.

1156	80c. Type **119**	60	65
	a. Sheetlet. Nos. 1156/9	2·10	2·40
1157	80c. Oblong character at bottom right	60	65
1158	80c. Circular character at top left	60	65
1159	80c. Square character at bottom right	60	65
1156/9 Set of 4		2·10	2·40

MS1160 67×97 mm. $2 Tiger (vert) .... 1·40 1·60

Nos. 1156/9 were printed together, se-tenant, in sheetlets of 4.

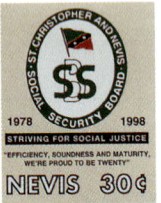

120 Social Security Board Emblem

121 Soursop

(Des M. Friedman. Litho Cartor)

1998 (2 Feb). 20th Anniv of Social Security Board. T **120** and similar multicoloured designs. P 13.

1161	30c. Type **120**	20	15
1162	$1.20 Opening of Social Security Building, Charlestown (horiz)	80	1·00

MS1163 100×70 mm. $6 Social Security staff (59×39 mm). P 13½×13 .... 3·50 4·00

(Des Zina Saunders. Litho Questa)

1998 (9 Mar)–**2000**. Fruits. T **121** and similar vert designs. Multicoloured. P 14.

A. Without imprint date at foot.

1164A	5c. Type **121**	10	30
1165A	10c. Carambola	15	30
1166A	25c. Guava	25	15
1167A	30c. Papaya	25	15
1168A	50c. Mango	35	25
1169A	60c. Golden Apple	40	30
1170A	80c. Pineapple	50	35
1171A	90c. Watermelon	60	40
1172A	$1 Bananas	70	50
1173A	$1.80 Orange	1·25	1·50
1174A	$3 Honeydew	1·75	2·25
1175A	$5 Cantaloupe	3·00	4·00
1176A	$10 Pomegranate	5·50	7·50
1177A	$20 Cashew	9·50	13·00
1164A/77A Set of 14		22·00	28·00

B. With "2000" imprint date at foot (22.3.2000)

1165B	10c. Carambola	20	40
1167B	30c. Papaya	40	30
1170B	80c. Pineapple	75	60
1173B	$1.80 Orange	1·75	2·00
1175B	$5 Cantaloupe	4·50	6·00
1176B	$10 Pomegranate	8·00	10·00
1165B/76B Set of 6		14·00	17·00

122 African Fish Eagle

123 Chaim Topol (Israeli actor)

(Des Zina Saunders. Litho Questa)

1998 (31 Mar). Endangered Species. T **122** and similar horiz designs. Multicoloured. P 14.

1178	30c. Type **122**	65	30
1179	80c. Summer Tanager at nest	1·00	55
1180	90c. Orang-utan and young	1·00	70
1181	$1 Young chimpanzee	80	90
	a. Sheetlet. Nos. 1181/9	6·50	7·25
1182	$1 Keel-billed Toucan	80	90
1183	$1 Chaco Peccary	80	90
1184	$1 Spadefoot Toad and insect	80	90
1185	$1 Howler Monkey	80	90
1186	$1 Alaskan Brown Bear	80	90
1187	$1 Koala bears	80	90
1188	$1 Brown Pelican	80	90
1189	$1 Iguana	80	90
1190	$1.20 Tiger cub	1·25	1·00
1191	$2 Cape Pangolin	1·40	1·75
1192	$3 Hoatzin	1·75	2·25
1178/92 Set of 15		13·00	13·00

MS1193 Two sheets, each 69×99 mm. (a) $5 Young Mandrill. (b) $5 Polar Bear cub Set of 2 sheets .... 7·00 7·50

Nos. 1181/9 were printed together, se-tenant, in sheetlets of 9.

No. 1185 is inscribed "MOWLER MONKEY" and No. 1192 "MOATZIN", both in error.

(Des G. Eichorn. Litho Cartor)

1998 (17 May). Israel 98 International Stomp Exhibition, Tel-Aviv. P 13½.

1194	**123** $1.60 multicoloured	1·75	1·75

No. 1194 was printed in sheets of 6 with enlarged illustrated right-hand margin.

124 Boeing 747 200B (U.S.A.)

(Des M. Servin. Litho Questa)

1998 (19 May). Aircraft. T **124** and similar horiz designs. Multicoloured. P 14.

1195	10c. Type **124**	40	40
1196	90c. Cessna 185 Skywagon (U.S.A.)	80	55
1197	$1 Northrop B-2 A (U.S.A.)	80	90
	a. Sheetlet. Nos. 1197/204	5·75	6·50
1198	$1 Lockheed SR-71A (U.S.A.)	80	90
1199	$1 Beechecraft T-44A (U.S.A.)	80	90
1200	$1 Sukhoi Su-27UB (U.S.S.R.)	80	90
1201	$1 Hawker Siddeley Harrier GR. Mk1 (Great Britain)	80	90
1202	$1 Boeing E-3A Sentry (U.S.A.)	80	90
1203	$1 Convair B-36H (U.S.A.)	80	90
1204	$1 IAI KFIR C2 (Israel)	80	90
1205	$1.80 McDonnell Douglas DC-9 SO (U.S.A.)	1·75	1·75
1206	$5 Airbus A-300 B4 (U.S.A.)	3·75	4·50
1195/206 Set of 12		12·00	13·00

MS1207 Two sheets, each 76×106 mm. (a) $5 Lockheed F-117A (U.S.A.) (56×42 mm). (b) $5 Concorde (Great Britain) (56×42 mm) Set of 2 sheets .... 7·50 7·50

Nos. 1197/204 were printed together, se-tenant, in sheetlets of 8 with enlarged left-hand margin.

NEVIS

125 Anniversary Logo

(Des M. Friedman. Litho Questa)
1998 (18 June). Tenth Anniv of "Voice of Nevis" Radio. T **125** and similar designs. P 14.

1208	20c. violet, bright reddish violet and black		40	35
1209	30c. multicoloured		40	25
1210	$1.20 multicoloured		1·40	1·60
1208/10	Set of 3		2·00	2·00
MS1211	110×85 mm. $5 multicoloured		3·25	3·50

Designs: *Horiz*—30c. Evered Herbert (Station Manager); $1.20, V.O.N. studio; $5 Merritt Herbert (Managing Director).

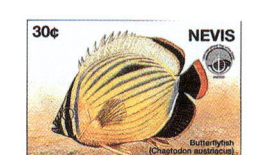

126 Butterflyfish

(Litho Questa)
1998 (18 Aug). International Year of the Ocean. T **126** and similar multicoloured designs. P 14.

1212	30c. Type **126**	30	15
1213	80c. Bicolor Cherub	65	35
1214	90c. Copperbanded Butterflyfish (*vert*)	70	80
	a. Sheetlet. Nos. 1214/22	5·50	6·50
1215	90c. Forcepsfish (*vert*)	70	80
1216	90c. Double-saddled Butterflyfish (*vert*)	70	80
1217	90c. Blue Surgeonfish (*vert*)	70	80
1218	90c. Orbiculate Batfish (*vert*)	70	80
1219	90c. Undulated Triggerfish (*vert*)	70	80
1220	90c. Rock Beauty (*vert*)	70	80
1221	90c. Flamefish (*vert*)	70	80
1222	90c. Queen Angelfish (*vert*)	70	80
1223	$1 Pyjama Cardinal Fish	70	80
	a. Sheetlet. Nos. 1223/31	5·50	6·50
1224	$1 Wimplefish	70	80
1225	$1 Long-nosed Filefish	70	80
1226	$1 Oriental Sweetlips	70	80
1227	$1 Blue-spotted Boxfish	70	80
1228	$1 Blue-stripe Angelfish	70	80
1229	$1 Goldrim Tang	70	80
1230	$1 Blue Chromis	70	80
1231	$1 Common Clownfish	70	80
1232	$1.20 Silver Badgerfish	80	80
1233	$2 Asfur Angelfish	1·40	1·50
1212/33	Set of 22	14·00	15·00
MS1234	Two sheets. (a) 76×106 mm. $5 Red-faced Batfish (*vert*). (b) 106×76 mm. $5 Longhorned Cowfish (*vert*) Set of 2 sheets	8·00	8·50

Nos. 1214/22 and 1223/31 were each printed together, *se-tenant*, in sheetlets of 9 with the backgrounds forming composite designs.
No. 1223 is inscribed "Pygama" in error.

127 Prime Minister Kennedy Simmonds receiving Constitutional Instruments from Princess Margaret, 1983

(Des M. Friedman. Litho Questa)
1998 (19 Sept). 15th Anniv of Independence. P 14.

1235	**127**	$1 multicoloured	85	1·00

128 Stylised "50"

(Des M. Friedman. Litho Questa)
1998 (15 Oct). 50th Anniv of Organization of American States. P 13½×14.

1236	**128**	$1 chalky blue, light new blue and black	75	1·00

129 365 "California"

(Des F. Rivera. Litho Questa)
1998 (15 Oct). Birth Centenary of Enzo Ferrari (car manufacturer). T **129** and similar horiz designs. Multicoloured. P 14.

1237	$2 Type **129**	1·60	1·60
	a. Sheetlet. Nos. 1237/9	4·25	4·25
1238	$2 Pininfarina's P6	1·60	1·60
1239	$2 250 LM	1·60	1·60
1237/9	Set of 3	4·25	4·25
MS1240	104×70 mm. $5 "Export Spyder" (91×34 mm). P 14×14½	4·50	4·75

Nos. 1237/9 were printed together, *se-tenant*, in sheetlets of 3.

130 Scouts of Different Nationalities

131 Gandhi in South Africa, 1914

(Des J. Iskowitz. Litho Questa)
1998 (15 Oct). 19th World Scout Jamboree, Chile. T **130** and similar horiz designs. Multicoloured. P 14.

1241	$3 Type **130**	2·00	2·25
	a. Sheetlet. Nos. 1241/3	5·50	6·00
1242	$3 Scout and Gettysburg veterans, 1913	2·00	2·25
1243	$3 First black scout troop, Virginia, 1928	2·00	2·25
1241/3	Set of 3	5·50	6·00

Nos. 1241/3 were printed together, *se-tenant*, in sheetlets of 3 with enlarged illustrated top and right margins.

(Des M. Leboeuf. Litho Questa)
1998 (15 Oct). 50th Death Anniv of Mahatma Gandhi. T **131** and similar vert design. Multicoloured. P 14.

1244	$1 Type **131**	1·25	1·00
	a. Sheetlet of 6	6·50	
1245	$1 Gandhi in Downing Street, London	1·25	1·00
	a. Sheetlet of 6	6·50	

Nos. 1244 and 1245 were each printed together, *se-tenant*, in sheetlets of 6.

132 Panavia Tornado F3
133 Princess Diana 

(Des D. Miller. Litho Questa)

1998 (15 Oct). 80th Anniv of Royal Air Force. T **132** and similar horiz designs. Multicoloured. P 14.

1246	$2 Type **132**	2·00	2·00
	a. Sheetlet. Nos. 1246/9	7·25	7·25
1247	$2 Panavia Tornado F3 firing Skyflash missile	2·00	2·00
1248	$2 Tristar Mk1 Tanker refuelling Tornado GR1	2·00	2·00
1249	$2 Panavia Tornado GR1 firing AIM-9L missile	2·00	2·00
1246/9 Set of 4		7·25	7·25

MS1250 Two sheets, each 91×68 mm. (a) $5 Bristol F2B Fighter and two falcons (birds). (b) $5 Wessex helicopter and EF-2000 Eurofighter Set of 2 sheets... 9·00 9·00

Nos. 1246/9 were printed together, se-tenant, in sheetlets of 4 with enlarged illustrated margins.

(Des G. Eichorn. Litho Questa)

1998 (15 Oct). First Death Anniv of Diana, Princess of Wales. P 14½.

1251	**133**	$1 multicoloured	75	75
		a. Sheetlet of 6	4·00	

No. 1251 was printed in sheetlets of 6 with enlarged illustrated margins.

134 Kitten and Santa Claus Decoration
135 Mickey Mouse 

(Des E. Moreiro. Litho B.D.T.)

1998 (24 Nov). Christmas. T **134** and similar multicoloured designs. P 14.

1252	25c. Type **134**	25	15
1253	60c. Kitten playing with bauble	40	30
1254	80c. Kitten in Christmas stocking (vert)	50	35
1255	90c. Fox Terrier puppy and presents	60	40
1256	$1 Angel with swallows	70	45
1257	$3 Boy wearing Santa hat (vert)	2·00	3·00
1252/7 Set of 6		4·00	4·25

MS1258 Two sheets. (a) 71×102 mm. $5 Two dogs. (b) 102×71 mm. $5 Family with dog (vert) Set of 2 sheets... 7·00 7·50

(Des Rosemary De Figlio. Litho Questa)

1998 (24 Dec). 70th Birthday of Mickey Mouse. T **135** and similar multicoloured designs showing Walt Disney cartoon characters playing basketball. P 13½×14.

1259	$1 Type **135**	95	85
	a. Sheetlet. Nos. 1259/66	7·00	6·00
1260	$1 Donald Duck bouncing ball	95	85
1261	$1 Minnie Mouse in green kit	95	85
1262	$1 Goofy wearing purple	95	85
1263	$1 Huey in green baseball cap	95	85
1264	$1 Goofy and Mickey	95	85
1265	$1 Mickey bouncing ball	95	85
1266	$1 Huey, Dewey and Louie	95	85
1267	$1 Mickey, in purple, shooting ball	95	85
	a. Sheetlet. Nos. 127/74	7·00	6·00
1268	$1 Goofy in yellow shorts and vest	95	85
1269	$1 Minnie in purple	95	85
1270	$1 Mickey in yellow vest and blue shorts	95	85
1271	$1 Minnie in yellow	95	85
1272	$1 Donald spinning ball on finger	95	85
1273	$1 Donald and Mickey	95	85
1274	$1 Dewey shooting for goal	95	85
1259/74 Set of 16		13·50	12·00

MS1275 Four sheets. (a) 127×105 mm. $5 Minnie wearing purple bow (horiz). (b) 105×127 mm. $5 Minnie wearing green bow (horiz). (c) 105×127 mm. $6 Mickey in yellow vest (horiz). (d) 105×127 mm. $6 Mickey in purple vest (horiz). P 14×13½ Set of 4 sheets. 15·00 15·00

Nos. 1259/66 and 1267/74 were each printed together, se-tenant, in sheetlets of 8.

136 Black Silver Fox Rabbits

(Des Y. Lee. Litho Questa)

1999 (4 Jan). Chinese New Year ("Year of the Rabbit"). T **136** and similar horiz designs. Multicoloured. P 14.

1276	$1·60 Type **136**	1·50	1·50
	a. Sheetlet. Nos. 1276/9	5·50	5·50
1277	$1·60 Dutch rabbits (brown with white "collar")	1·50	1·50
1278	$1·60 Dwarf rabbits (brown)	1·50	1·50
1279	$1·60 Netherlands Dwarf rabbits (white with brown markings)	1·50	1·50
1276/9 Set of 4		5·50	5·50

MS1280 106×76 mm. $5 Dwarf Albino Rabbit and young (57×46 mm)... 3·50 3·75

Nos. 1276/9 were printed together, se-tenant, in sheetlets of 4.

137 Laurent Blanc (France)

(Des Joanna Singh. Litho B.D.T.)

1999 (18 Jan). Leading Players of 1998 World Cup Football Championship, France. T **137** and similar horiz designs. Multicoloured. P 13½.

1281	$1 Type **137**	75	75
	a. Sheetlet. Nos. 1281/8	5·50	5·50
1282	$1 Dennis Bergkamp (Holland)	75	75
1283	$1 Davor Sukor (Croatia)	75	75
1284	$1 Ronaldo (Brazil)	75	75
1285	$1 Didier Deschamps (France)	75	75
1286	$1 Patrick Kluivert (Holland)	75	75
1287	$1 Rivaldo (Brazil)	75	75
1288	$1 Zinedine Zidane (France)	75	75
1281/8 Set of 8		5·50	5·50

MS1289 121×96 mm. $5 Zinedine Zidane (France)... 3·25 3·50

Nos. 1281/8 were printed together, se-tenant, in sheetlets of 8 with the backgrounds forming a composite design.

138 Kritosaurus
139 Emperor Haile Selassie of Ethiopia 

(Des R. Company. Litho Questa)

1999 (22 Feb). Australia '99 World Stamp Exhibition, Melbourne. Prehistoric Animals. T **138** and similar horiz designs. Multicoloured. P 14.

1290	30c. Type **138**	40	30
1291	60c. Oviraptor	50	45
1292	80c. Eustreptospondylus	60	50
1293	$1·20 Tenontosaurus	80	85
1294	$1·20 Edmontosaurus	80	85
	a. Sheetlet. Nos. 1294/9	4·25	4·50

ST. KITTS-NEVIS / Nevis

1295	$1.20 Avimimus		80	85
1296	$1.20 Minmi		80	85
1297	$1.20 Segnosaurus		80	85
1298	$1.20 Kentrosaurus		80	85
1299	$1.20 Deinonychus		80	85
1300	$1.20 Saltasaurus		80	85
	a. Sheetlet. Nos. 1300/5		4.25	4.50
1301	$1.20 Compsoganthus		80	85
1302	$1.20 Hadrosaurus		80	85
1303	$1.20 Tuojiangosaurus		80	85
1304	$1.20 Euoplocephalus		80	85
1305	$1.20 Anchisaurus		80	85
1306	$2 Ouranosaurus		1.40	1.75
1307	$3 Muttaburrasaurus		1.75	2.00
1290/1307	Set of 18		13.50	13.50
MS1308	Two sheets, each 110×85 mm. (a) $5 Triceratops. (b) $5 Stegosaurus *Set of 2 sheets*		7.00	7.50

Nos. 1294/9 and 1300/5 were each printed together, *se-tenant*, in sheetlets of 6 with the backgrounds forming composite designs.

(Des S. Stirnweis. Litho Questa)

1999 (8 Mar). Millennium Series. Famous People of the Twentieth Century. World Leaders. T **139** and similar multicoloured designs. P 14.

1309	90c. Type **139**		1.00	85
	a. Sheetlet. Nos. 1309/16		7.00	6.00
1310	90c. Haile Selassie and Ethiopian warriors (56×41 *mm*)		1.00	85
1311	90c. David Ben-Gurion, woman soldier and ancient Jewish prophet (56×41 *mm*)		1.00	85
1312	90c. David Ben-Gurion (Prime Minister of Israel)		1.00	85
1313	90c. President Franklin D Roosevelt of USA and Mrs Roosevelt		1.00	85
1314	90c. Franklin and Eleanor Roosevelt campaigning (56×41 *mm*)		1.00	85
1315	90c. Mao Tse-tung and the Long March, 1934 (56×41 *mm*)		1.00	85
1316	90c. Poster of Mao Tse-tung (founder of People's Republic of China)		1.00	85
1309/16	*Set of 8*		7.00	6.00
MS1317	Two sheets. (a) 76×105 mm. $5 President Nelson Mandela of South Africa. (b) 105×76 mm. $5 Mahatma Gandhi (leader of Indian Independence movement) *Set of 2 sheets*		8.00	8.50

Nos. 1309/16 were printed together, *se-tenant*, in sheetlets of 8 with enlarged illustrated margins.

140 Malachite Kingfisher   **141** *Phaius* hybrid

(Des R. Sauber. Litho B.D.T.)

1999 (10 May). Birds. T **140** and similar multicoloured designs. P 14.

1318	$1.60 Type **140**		1.00	1.10
	a. Sheetlet. Nos. 1318/23		5.50	6.00
1319	$1.60 Lilac-breasted Roller		1.00	1.10
1320	$1.60 Swallow-tailed Bee Eater		1.00	1.10
1321	$1.60 Jay		1.00	1.10
1322	$1.60 Black-collared Apalis		1.00	1.10
1323	$1.60 Grey-backed Camaroptera		1.00	1.10
1324	$1.60 Yellow Warbler		1.00	1.10
	a. Sheetlet. Nos. 1324/9		5.50	6.00
1325	$1.60 Common Yellowthroat		1.00	1.10
1326	$1.60 Painted Bunting		1.00	1.10
1327	$1.60 Belted Kingfisher		1.00	1.10
1328	$1.60 American Kestrel		1.00	1.10
1329	$1.60 Northern Oriole		1.00	1.10
1318/29	*Set of 12*		11.00	12.00
MS1330	Two sheets each 76×106 mm. (a) $5 Bananaquit. (b) $5 Groundscraper Thrush (*vert*) *Set of 2 sheets*		7.50	8.00

Nos. 1318/23 and 1324/9 were each printed together, *se-tenant*, in sheetlets of 6 stamps with enlarged illustrated margins.

(Des E. Moreino. Litho B.D.T.)

1999 (15 June). Orchids. T **141** and similar multicoloured designs. P 14.

1331	20c. Type **141**		30	30
1332	25c. *Cuitlauzina pendula*		30	30
1333	50c. *Bletilla striata*		45	40
1334	80c. *Cymbidium* "Showgirl"		60	55
1335	$1 *Cattleya intermedia*		70	75
	a. Sheetlet. Nos. 1335/42		5.00	5.50
1336	$1 *Cattleya* "Sophia Martin"		70	75
1337	$1 *Phalaenopsis* "Little Hal"		70	75
1338	$1 *Laeliocattleya alisal* "Rodeo"		70	75
1339	$1 *Laelia lucasiana fournieri*		70	75
1340	$1 *Cymbidium* "Red Beauty"		70	75
1341	$1 *Sobralia* sp.		70	75
1342	$1 *Promenaea xanthina*		70	75
1343	$1 *Cattleya pumpernickel*		70	75
	a. Sheetlet. Nos. 1343/50		5.00	5.50
1344	$1 *Odontocidium artur elle*		70	75
1345	$1 *Neostylis lou sneary*		70	75
1346	$1 *Phalaenopsis aphrodite*		70	75
1347	$1 *Arkundina graminieolia*		70	75
1348	$1 *Cymbidium* "Hunter's Point"		70	75
1349	$1 *Rhynchostylis coelestis*		70	75
1350	$1 *Cymbidium* "Elf's Castle"		70	75
1351	$1.60 *Zygopetalum crinitium* (*horiz*)		1.00	1.00
1352	$3 *Dendrobium nobile* (*horiz*)		1.90	2.50
1331/52	*Set of 22*		14.00	14.00
MS1353	Two sheets, each 106×81 mm. (a) $5 *Spathoglottis plicata* (*horiz*). (b) $5 *Arethusa bulbosa Set of 2 sheets*		9.00	9.00

Nos. 1335/42 and 1343/50 were each printed together, *se-tenant*, in sheetlets of 8.

142 Miss Sophie Rhys-Jones and Prince Edward   **143** Steelband

(Des J. Iskowitz. Litho Questa)

1999 (19 June). Royal Wedding. T **142** and similar multicoloured designs. P 14½×14.

1354	$2 Type **142**		1.40	1.40
	a. Sheetlet. Nos. 1354/7		5.00	5.00
1355	$2 Miss Sophie Rhys-Jones at Ascot		1.40	1.40
1356	$2 Miss Sophie Rhys-Jones smiling		1.40	1.40
1357	$2 Prince Edward smiling		1.40	1.40
1358	$2 Miss Sophie Rhys-Jones wearing black and white checked jacket		1.40	1.40
	a. Sheetlet. Nos. 1358/61		5.00	5.00
1359	$2 Prince Edward and Miss Sophie Rhys-Jones wearing sunglasses		1.40	1.40
1360	$2 Miss Sophie Rhys-Jones wearing black hat and jacket		1.40	1.40
1361	$2 Prince Edward wearing red-striped tie		1.40	1.40
1354/61	*Set of 8*		10.00	10.00
MS1362	Two sheets, each 83×66 mm. (a) $5 Prince Edward and Miss Sophie Rhys-Jones smiling (*horiz*). (b) $5 Prince Edward kissing Miss Sophie Rhys-Jones (*horiz*). P 14×14½ *Set of 2 sheets*		7.00	7.50

Nos. 1354/7 and 1358/61 were each printed together, *se-tenant*, in sheetlets of 4.

(Des R. Sauber. Litho Questa)

1999 (1 July). iBRA '99 International Stamp Exhibition, Nuremberg. Horiz designs as T **416** of Antigua. Multicoloured. P 14.

1363	30c. *Beuth* (railway locomotive) and Baden 1851 1k. stamp		30	25
1364	80c. *Beuth* and Brunswick 1852 1 sgr. stamp		50	45
1365	90c. *Kruzenshstern* (cadet barque) and Bergedorf 1861 ½s. and 1s. stamps		60	50
1366	$1 *Kruzenshstern* and Bremen 1855 3gr. stamp		70	70
1363/6	*Set of 4*		1.90	1.75
MS1367	134×90 mm. $5 1912 First Bavarian air flight label. P 14×14½		3.25	3.50

(Des R. Sauber. Litho Questa)

1999 (1 July). 150th Death Anniv of Katsushika Hokusai (Japanese artist). Multicoloured designs as T **417** of Antigua, but vert. P 13½×14.

1368	$1 "Women returning Home at Sunset" (women by lake)		70	80
	a. Sheetlet. Nos. 1368/73		3.75	4.25
1369	$1 "Blind Man" (without beard)		70	80
1370	$1 "Women returning Home at Sunset" (women descending hill)		70	80
1371	$1 "Young Man on a White Horse"		70	80
1372	$1 "Blind Man" (with beard)		70	80

ST. KITTS-NEVIS / Nevis

1373	$1 "Peasant crossing a Bridge"............	70	80
1374	$1.60 "Poppies" (one flower)................	1·00	1·10
	a. Sheetlet. Nos. 1374/9..................	5·50	6·00
1375	$1.60 "Blind Man" (with beard)............	1·00	1·10
1376	$1.60 "Poppies" (two flowers).............	1·00	1·10
1377	$1.60 "Abe No Nakamaro gazing at the Moon from a Terrace".......................	1·00	1·10
1378	$1.60 "Blind Man" (without beard).......	1·00	1·10
1379	$1.60 "Cranes on a Snowy Pine"..........	1·00	1·10
1368/79	Set of 12.......................................	9·00	10·00

MS1380 Two sheets, each 74×103 mm. (a) $5 "Carp in a Waterfall". (b) $5 "Rider in the Snow" *Set of 2 sheets*..... 7·00 7·50

Nos. 1368/73 and 1374/9 were each printed together, *se-tenant*, in sheetlets of 6.

(Des B. Pevsner. Litho Questa)

1999 (1 July). Philex France '99 International Stamp Exhibition, Paris. Two sheets, each 106×81 mm, containing horiz designs as T **420** of Antigua. Multicoloured. P 14×13½.

MS1381 (a) $5 First Class carriage, 1837. (b) $5 "141.R" Mixed Traffic steam locomotive *Set of 2 sheets*............ 8·50 9·00

(Litho B.D.T.)

1999 (1 July). 25th Culturama Festival. T **143** and similar horiz designs. Multicoloured. P 14.

1382	30c. Type **143**..................................	30	15
1383	80c. Clowns.......................................	60	35
1384	$1.80 Masqueraders with band............	1·40	1·10
1385	$5 Local string band..........................	3·25	4·00
1382/5	Set of 4..	5·00	5·00

MS1386 91×105 mm $5 Carnival dancers (50×37 mm)....... 3·25 3·75

(Litho Questa)

1999-2001 (4 Aug). "Queen Elizabeth the Queen Mother's Century". Vert designs as T **444** of Antigua. P 14.

1387	$2 black and gold.............................	1·75	1·50
	a. Sheetlet. Nos. 1387/90 (central label inscr "100th")...................................	6·00	5·50
	ab. Sheetlet. Nos. 1387/90 (central label inscr "101st") (13.12.01).....................	6·00	6·00
1388	$2 multicoloured................................	1·75	1·50
1389	$2 black and gold..............................	1·75	1·50
1390	$2 multicoloured................................	1·75	1·50
1387/90	Set of 4...	6·00	5·50

MS1391 153×157 mm. $6 multicoloured (embossed coat of arms)... 3·75 4·00
a. Inscr "Good Health and Happiness to Her Majesty the Queen Mother on her 101st Birthday" (13.12.01)................. 3·75 4·00

The sheetlet and miniature sheet were re-issued in 2001 with changed label and description (No. 1387ab), or bottom left of the miniature sheet replaced by a commemorative inscription for the Queen Mother's 101st birthday.

Designs: (As Type **444** of *Lesotho*)—No. 1387, Lady Elizabeth Bowes-Lyon on Wedding Day, 1923; No. 1388, Duchess of York with Princess Elizabeth, 1926; No. 1389, King George VI and Queen Elizabeth during Second World War; No. 1390, Queen Mother in 1983. (37×49 *mm*)—No. **MS**1391, Queen Mother in 1957.

Nos. 1387/90 were printed together, *se-tenant*, as a sheetlet of 4 stamps and central label with inscribed and embossed margins.
No. **MS**1391 also shows the Royal Arms embossed in gold.

144 "Adoration of the Magi (Dürer)

145 Flowers forming Top of Head

(Litho Questa)

1999 (12 Nov). Christmas. Religious Paintings. T **144** and similar multicoloured designs. P 14.

1392	30c. Type **144**..................................	35	15
1393	90c. "Canigiani Holy Family" (Raphael)............	70	40
1394	$1.20 "The Nativity" (Dürer)................	1·10	80
1395	$1.80 "Madonna and Child surrounded by Angels" (Rubens).................................	1·40	1·40
1396	$3 "Madonna and Child surrounded by Saints" (Rubens)..................................	2·50	3·25
1392/6	Set of 5..	5·50	5·50

MS1397 76×106 mm. $5 "Madonna and Child by a Window" (Dürer) (*horiz*).. 3·25 3·75

(Des R. Silvers. Litho Questa)

1999 (31 Dec). Faces of the Millennium: Diana, Princess of Wales. T **145** and similar vert designs showing collage of miniature flower photographs. Multicoloured. P 13½×14.

1398	$1 Type **145** (face value at left)..............	75	75
	a. Sheetlet. Nos. 1398/1405................	5·50	5·50
1399	$1 Top of head (face value at right)............	75	75
1400	$1 Ear (face value at left)...........................	75	75
1401	$1 Eye and temple (face value at right).......	75	75
1402	$1 Cheek (face value at left)......................	75	75
1403	$1 Cheek (face value at right)....................	75	75
1404	$1 Blue background (face value at left).......	75	75
1405	$1 Chin (face value at right).......................	75	75
1398/1405	Set of 8.....................................	5·50	5·50

Nos. 1398/1405 were printed together, *se-tenant*, in sheetlets of 8 with the stamps arranged in two vertical columns separated by a gutter also containing miniature photographs. When viewed as a whole, the sheetlet forms a portrait of Diana, Princess of Wales.

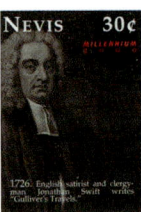

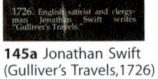

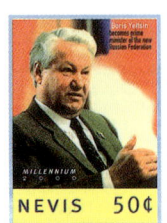

145a Jonathan Swift (Gulliver's Travels, 1726)

146 Boris Yeltsin (President of Russian Federation, 1991)

(Des Spotlight Designs. Litho Cartor)

2000 (4 Jan). New Millennium. People and Events of Eighteenth Century (1700–49). T **145a** and similar multicoloured designs. P 12½.

1406	30c. Type **145a**................................	50	40
	a. Sheetlet. Nos. 1406/22..................	7·75	6·00
1407	30c. Emperor Kangxi of China................	50	40
1408	30c. Bartolommeo Cristofori (invention of piano, 1709)......................................	50	40
1409	30c. Captain William Kidd hanging on gibbet, 1701.....................................	50	40
1410	30c. William Herschel (astronomer)........	50	40
1411	30c. King George I of Great Britain, 1714..	50	40
1412	30c. Peter the Great of Russia (trade treaty with China, 1720).............................	50	40
1413	30c. "Death" (bubonic plague in Austria and Germany, 1711)...........................	50	40
1414	30c. "Standing Woman" (Kaigetsudo Dohan (Japanese artist)).................................	50	40
1415	30c. Queen Anne of England, 1707.........	50	40
1416	30c. Anders Celsius (invention of centigrade thermometer, 1742)............................	50	40
1417	30c. Vitus Bering (discovery of Alaska and Aleutian Islands, 1741)..........................	50	40
1418	30c. Edmund Halley (calculation of Halley's Comet, 1705)....................................	50	40
1419	30c. John Wesley (founder of Methodist Church, 1729)....................................	50	40
1420	30c. Sir Isaac Newton (publication of *Optick Treatise*, 1704)...................................	50	40
1421	30c. Queen Anne (Act of Union between England and Scotland, 1707) (59×39 mm)..	50	40
1422	30c. Johann Sebastian Bach (composition of "The Well-tempered Clavier", 1722)....	50	40
1406/22	Set of 17.......................................	7·75	6·00

Nos. 1406/22 were printed together, *se-tenant*, in sheetlets of 17 including a central label (59×39 mm) and inscribed left margin.
No. 1418 is inscribed "cometis" in error.

(Des Spotlight Designs. Litho Cartor)

2000 (4 Jan). New Millennium. People and Events of Twentieth Century (1990–99). T **146** and similar multicoloured designs. P 12½.

1423	50c. Type **146**..................................	65	50
	a. Sheetlet. Nos. 1423/39..................	10·00	7·75
1424	50c. American soldiers and burning oil wells (Gulf War, 1991).......................	65	50
1425	50c. Soldiers (Bosnian Civil War, 1992)...........	65	50

ST. KITTS-NEVIS / Nevis

1426	50c. Pres. Clinton, Yitzchak Rabin and Yasser Arafat (Oslo Accords, 1993)	65	50
1427	50c. Prime Ministers John Major and Albert Reynolds (Joint Declaration on Northern Ireland, 1993)	65	50
1428	50c. Frederik de Klerk (end of Apartheid, South Africa, 1994)	65	50
1429	50c. Cal Ripkin (record number of consecutive baseball games, 1995)	65	50
1430	50c. Kobe from air (earthquake, 1995)	65	50
1431	50c. Mummified Inca girl preserved in ice, 1995	65	50
1432	50c. NASA's *Sojourner* on Mars, 1997	65	50
1433	50c. Dr. Ian Wilmat and cloned sheep, 1997	65	50
1434	50c. Death of Princess Diana, 1997	65	50
1435	50c. Fireworks over Hong Kong on its return to China, 1997	65	50
1436	50c. Mother with septuplets, 1998	65	50
1437	50c. Guggenheim Museum, Bilbao, 1998	65	50
1438	50c. "2000" and solar eclipse, 1999 (59×39 mm)	65	50
1439	50c. Pres. Clinton (impeachment in 1999)	65	50
1423/39 Set of 17		10·00	7·75

Nos. 1423/39 were printed together, *se-tenant*, in sheetlets of 17 including a central label (59×39 mm) and inscribed left margin.
No. 1423 incorrectly identifies his office as "Prime Minister".

147 Dragon

(Des Y. Lee. Litho Questa)

2000 (5 Feb). Chinese New Year ("Year of the Dragon"). T **147** and similar multicoloured designs. P 14.

1440	$1.60 Type **147**	1·10	1·10
	a. Sheetlet. Nos. 1440/3	4·00	4·00
1441	$1.60 Dragon with open claws (face value bottom left)	1·10	1·10
1442	$1.60 Dragon holding sphere (face value bottom right)	1·10	1·10
1443	$1.60 Dragon looking up (face value bottom left)	1·10	1·10
1440/3 Set of 4		4·00	4·00
MS1444 76×106 mm. $5 Dragon (37×50 mm). P 13½×14		3·50	4·00

Nos. 1440/3 were printed together, *se-tenant*, in sheetlets of 4.

148 Spotted Scat

149 Miniature Pinscher

(Des D. Burkhart. Litho Walsall)

2000 (27 Mar). Tropical Fish. T **148** and similar horiz designs showing fish in spotlight. Multicoloured. P 14.

1445	30c. Type **148**	50	20
1446	80c. Delta Topsail Platy ("Platy Variatus")	75	45
1447	90c. Emerald Betta	80	50
1448	$1 Sail-finned Tang	90	90
	a. Sheetlet. Nos. 1448/55	6·50	6·50
1449	$1 Black-capped Basslet ("Black-capped Gramma")	90	90
1450	$1 Sail-finned Snapper ("Majestic Snapper")	90	90
1451	$1 Purple Fire Goby	90	90
1452	$1 Clown Triggerfish	90	90
1453	$1 Forceps Butterflyfish ("Yellow Long-nose")	90	90
1454	$1 Clown Wrasse	90	90
1455	$1 Yellow-headed Jawfish	90	90
1456	$1 Oriental Sweetlips	90	90
	a. Sheetlet. Nos. 1456/63	6·50	6·50
1457	$1 Royal Gramma	90	90
1458	$1 Thread-finned Butterflyfish	90	90
1459	$1 Yellow Tang	90	90
1460	$1 Bicoloured Angelfish	90	90
1461	$1 Catalina Goby	90	90
1462	$1 Striped Mimic Blenny ("False Cleanerfish")	90	90
1463	$1 Powder-blue Surgeonfish	90	90
1464	$4 Long-horned Cowfish	2·75	3·25
1445/64 Set of 20		17·00	17·00
MS1465 Two sheets, each 97×68 mm. (a) $5 Clown Killifish. (b) $5 Twin-spotted Wrasse ("Clown Coris") Set of 2 sheets		7·00	7·50

Nos. 1448/55 and 1456/63 were each printed together, *se-tenant*, in sheetlets of 8 with the backgrounds forming composite designs.

(Des T. Wood. Litho Questa)

2000 (1 May). Dogs of the World. T **149** and similar multicoloured designs. P 14.

1466	10c. Type **149**	20	30
1467	20c. Pyrenean Mountain Dog	25	30
1468	30c. Welsh Springer Spaniel	30	20
1469	80c. Alaskan Malamute	65	40
1470	90c. Beagle (*horiz*)	75	80
	a. Sheetlet. Nos. 1470/5	4·00	4·25
1471	90c. Bassett Hound (*horiz*)	75	80
1472	90c. St. Bernard (*horiz*)	75	80
1473	90c. Rough Collie (*horiz*)	75	80
1474	90c. Shih tzu (*horiz*)	75	80
1475	90c. American Bulldog (*horiz*)	75	80
1476	$1 Irish Red and White Setter (*horiz*)	75	80
	a. Sheetlet. Nos. 1476/81	4·00	4·25
1477	$1 Dalmatian (*horiz*)	75	80
1478	$1 Pomeranian (*horiz*)	75	80
1479	$1 Chihuahua (*horiz*)	75	80
1480	$1 English Sheepdog (*horiz*)	75	80
1481	$1 Samoyed (*horiz*)	75	80
1482	$2 Bearded Collie	1·40	1·50
1483	$3 American Cocker Spaniel	1·90	2·25
1466/83 Set of 18		12·50	13·00
MS1484 Two sheets. (a) 76×106 mm. $5 Leonberger Dog. (b) 106×76 mm. $5 Longhaired Miniature Dachshund (*horiz*) Set of 2 sheets		7·50	8·00

Nos. 1470/5 and 1476/81 were each printed together, *se-tenant*, in sheetlets of 6.

(Litho Questa)

2000 (21 June). 18th Birthday of Prince William. Vert designs as T **433** of Antigua. Multicoloured. P 14.

1485	$1.60 Prince William shaking hands	1·10	1·10
	a. Sheetlet. Nos. 1485/8	4·00	4·00
1486	$1.60 Wearing ski outfit	1·10	1·10
1487	$1.60 At airport	1·10	1·10
1488	$1.60 Wearing blue shirt and jumper	1·10	1·10
1485/8 Set of 4		4·00	4·00
MS1489 100×80 mm. $5 At official engagement (38×50 mm). P 13½		3·75	4·00

Nos. 1485/8 were printed together, *se-tenant*, in sheetlets of 4 with enlarged illustrated margins.

150 "Mariner 9"

(Des Lollini. Litho Questa)

2000 (1 Aug). EXPO 2000 World Stamp Exhibition, Anaheim, U.S.A. Exploration of Mars. T **150** and similar multicoloured designs. P 14.

1490	$1.60 Type **150**	1·10	1·10
	a. Sheetlet. Nos. 1490/5	6·00	6·00
1491	$1.60 "Mars 3"	1·10	1·10
1492	$1.60 "Mariner 4"	1·10	1·10
1493	$1.60 "Planet B"	1·10	1·10
1494	$1.60 "Mars Express Lander"	1·10	1·10
1495	$1.60 "Mars Express"	1·10	1·10
1496	$1.60 "Mars 4"	1·10	1·10
	a. Sheetlet. Nos. 1496/1501	6·00	6·00
1497	$1.60 "Mars Water"	1·10	1·10
1498	$1.60 "Mars 1"	1·10	1·10
1499	$1.60 "Viking"	1·10	1·10
1500	$1.60 "Mariner 7"	1·10	1·10
1501	$1.60 "Mars Surveyor"	1·10	1·10
1490/1501 Set of 12		12·00	12·00
MS1502 Two sheets, each 106×76 mm. (a) $5 "Mars Observer" (*horiz*). (b) $5 "Mars Climate Orbiter" Set of 2 sheets		7·50	8·00

Nos. 1490/5 and 1496/1501 were each printed together, *se-tenant*, in sheetlets of 6 with the backgrounds forming composite designs.

289

ST. KITTS-NEVIS / Nevis

(Des R. Sauber. Litho B.D.T.)

2000 (1 Aug). 50th Anniv of Berlin Film Festival. Vert designs as T **436** of Antigua showing actors, directors and film scenes. Multicoloured. P 14.

1503	$1.60 *Rani Radovi*, 1969	1·10	1·10
	a. Sheetlet. Nos. 1503/8	6·00	6·00
1504	$1.60 *Salvatore Giuliano* (director), 1962	1·10	1·10
1505	$1.60 *Schonzeit fur Fuches*, 1966	1·10	1·10
1506	$1.60 Shirley Maclaine (actress), 1971	1·10	1·10
1507	$1.60 Simone Signoret (actress), 1971	1·10	1·10
1508	$1.60 Tabejad Bijad (director), 1974	1·10	1·10
1503/8 *Set of 6*		6·00	6·00
MS1509 97×103 mm. $5 *Komissar*, 1988		3·50	4·00

Nos. 1503/8 were printed together, *se-tenant*, in sheetlets of 6 with an enlarged illustrated left margin showing the Berlin Bear Award.

(Des J. Iskowitz. Litho B.D.T.)

2000 (1 Aug). 175th Anniv of Stockton and Darlington Line (first public railway). Horiz designs as T **437** of Antigua. Multicoloured. P 14.

1510	$3 As Type **437** of Antigua	2·25	2·25
	a. Sheetlet. Nos. 1510/11	4·50	4·50
1511	$3 Original drawing of Richard Trevithick's locomotive, 1804	2·25	2·25

Nos. 1510/11 were printed together, *se-tenant*, in sheetlets of 2 with enlarged illustrated and inscribed top and left margins.

150d Johann Sebastian Bach

151 Albert Einstein

(Des R. Rundo. Litho B.D.T.)

2000 (1 Aug). 250th Death Anniv of Johann Sebastian Bach (German composer). Sheet, 76×88 mm. P 14.

MS1512 **150d** $5 multicoloured		3·75	4·00

(Des R. Sauber and H. Friedman. Litho Questa)

2000 (1 Aug). Election of Albert Einstein (mathematical physicist) as Time Magazine "Man of the Century". T **151** and similar horiz designs showing portraits with photographs in background. Multicoloured. P 14.

1513	$2 Type **151**	2·25	2·25
	a. Sheetlet Nos. 1513/15	6·00	6·00
1514	$2 Riding bicycle	2·25	2·25
1515	$2 Standing on beach	2·25	2·25
1513/15 *Set of 3*		6·00	6·00

Nos. 1513/15 were printed together, *se-tenant*, in sheetlets of 3 with enlarged illustrated and inscribed top and left margins.

151a LZ-129 *Hindenburg*, 1929

151c Elquemeda Willet

(Des G. Capasso. Litho B.D.T.)

2000 (1 Aug). Centenary of First Zeppelin Flight. T **151a** and similar horiz designs. P 14.

1516	$3 turquoise-green, bright purple and black	2·50	2·50
	a. Sheetlet. Nos. 1516/18	6·75	6·75
1517	$3 turquoise-green, bright purple and black	2·50	2·50
1518	$3 turquoise-green, bright purple and black	2·50	2·50
1516/18 *Set of 3*		6·75	6·75
MS1519 116×76 mm. $5 dull yellow-green, magenta and black		3·75	4·00

Designs: (38×24 *mm*)—No. 1516, Type **151a**; No. 1517, LZ-1, 1900; No. 1518, LZ-11 *Viktoria Luise*. (50×37 *mm*)—No. **MS**1519, LZ-127 *Graf Zeppelin*, 1928.

Nos. 1516/18 were printed together, *se-tenant*, in sheetlets of 3 with enlarged illustrated left margin.
No. 1516 is inscribed "Hindenberg" in error.

(Des J. Iskowitz and Zina Saunders. Litho B.D.T.)

2000 (1 Aug). Olympic Games, Sydney. Horiz designs as T **441** of Antigua. Multicoloured. P 14.

1520	$2 Gisela Mauermeyer (discus), Berlin (1936)	1·50	1·50
	a. Sheetlet. Nos. 1520/3	5·50	5·50
1521	$2 Gymnast on uneven bars	1·50	1·50
1522	$2 Wembley Stadium, London (1948) and Union Jack	1·50	1·50
1523	$2 Ancient Greek horseman	1·50	1·50
1520/3 *Set of 4*		5·50	5·50

Nos. 1520/3 were printed together, *se-tenant*, in sheetlets of 4 (2×2), with the horizontal rows separated by a gutter margin showing Sydney landmarks and athlete with Olympic Torch.

(Des A. Melville-Brown. Litho B.D.T.)

2000 (1 Aug). West Indies Cricket Tour and 100th Test Match at Lord's. T **151c** and similar designs. P 14.

1524	$2 Type **151c**	2·25	1·75
1525	$3 Keith Arthurton	3·00	3·00
MS1526 121×104 mm. $5 Lord's Cricket Ground (*horiz*)		4·00	4·50

152 King Edward III of England

153 Member of The Angels

(Des R. Sauber. Litho Questa)

2000 (1 Aug). Monarchs of the Millennium. T **152** and similar vert designs. P 13½×14.

1527	$1.60 brownish black, stone and chocolate	1·25	1·25
	a. Sheetlet. Nos. 152/32	6·75	6·75
1528	$1.60 multicoloured	1·25	1·25
1529	$1.60 multicoloured	1·25	1·25
1530	$1.60 brownish black, stone and chocolate	1·25	1·25
1531	$1.60 brownish black, stone and chocolate	1·25	1·25
1532	$1.60 dull purple, stone and chocolate	1·25	1·25
1527/32 *Set of 6*		6·75	6·75
MS1533 115×135 mm. $5 multicoloured		3·75	4·00

Designs:—No. 1528, Emperor Charles V (of Spain); No. 1529, King Joseph II of Hungary; No. 1530, Emperor Henry II of Germany; No. 1531, King Louis IV of France; No. 1532, King Ludwig II of Bavaria; No. **MS**1533, King Louis IX of France.

Nos. 1527/32 were printed together, *se-tenant*, in sheetlets of 6 with enlarged illustrated bottom margin.

(Des Y. Fagbahoun. Litho Questa)

2000 (10 Aug). Famous Girl Pop Groups. T **153** and similar vert designs. Multicoloured. P 14.

1534	90c. Type **153**	65	65
	a. Sheetlet. Nos. 1534/42	5·25	5·25
1535	90c. Member of The Angels with long hair	65	65
1536	90c. Member of The Angels with chin on hand	65	65
1537	90c. Member of The Dixie Cups (record at left)	65	65
1538	90c. Member of The Dixie Cups with shoulder-length hair	65	65
1539	90c. Member of The Dixie Cups with short hair and slide	65	65
1540	90c. Member of The Vandellas (record at left)	65	65
1541	90c. Member of The Vandellas ("Nevis" clear of hair)	65	65
1542	90c. Member of The Vandellas ("is" of "Nevis" on hair)	65	65
1534/42 *Set of 9*		5·25	5·25

Nos. 1534/42 were printed together, *se-tenant*, in sheetlets of 9 (3×3) with enlarged left margin. Each horizontal row depicts a different group with Nos. 1534/6 having green backgrounds, Nos. 1537/9 pale yellow and Nos. 1540/2 pale magenta.

154 Bob Hope in Ranger Uniform, Vietnam

155 David Copperfield

(Des D. Klein. Litho Questa)

2000 (10 Aug). Bob Hope (American entertainer). T **154** and similar vert designs. P 14.

1543	$1 black, grey and dull mauve	1·00	85
	a. Sheetlet. Nos. 1543/8	5·50	4·50
1544	$1 Indian red, grey and dull mauve	1·00	85
1545	$1 black, grey and dull mauve	1·00	85
1546	$1 multicoloured	1·00	85
1547	$1 black, grey and dull mauve	1·00	85
1548	$1 multicoloured	1·00	85
1543/8 Set of 6		5·50	4·50

Designs:—No. 1544, On stage with Sammy Davis Jnr.; No. 1545, With wife Dolores; No. 1546, Playing golf; No. 1547, Making radio broadcast; No. 1548, Visiting Great Wall of China.

Nos. 1543/8 were printed together, *se-tenant*, in sheetlets of 6 with enlarged illustrated margins.

(Des H. Liwag, Cathy Daly and C. Kenner. Litho Walsall)

2000 (10 Aug). David Copperfield (conjurer). P 14.

1549	**155**	$1.60 multicoloured	1·25	1·50
		a. Sheetlet of 4	4·50	

No. 1549 was printed in sheetlets of 4 with enlarged illustrated left margin.

156 Mike Wallace

(Litho Questa)

2000 (10 Aug). Mike Wallace (television journalist). Sheet 120×112 mm. P 14×13½.

MS1550	**156** $5 multicoloured	3·25	3·50

2000 (14 Aug). Second Caribbean Beekeeping Congress. No. **MS**801 optd "2nd Caribbean Beekeeping Congress August 14–18, 2000" on top margin.

MS1551 100×70 mm. $6 Queen and workers in hive and mechanical honey extractor	3·75	4·00

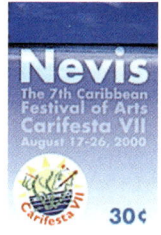

157 Beach Scene and Logo

158 Golden Elegance Oriental Lily

(Litho B.D.T.)

2000 (17 Aug). "Carifesta VII" Arts Festival. T **157** and similar vert designs. Multicoloured. P 14.

1552	30c. Type **157**	30	20
1553	90c. Carnival scenes	65	55
1554	$1.20 Stylized dancer with streamers	90	1·25
1552/4 Set of 3		1·60	1·75

(Des T. Wood. Litho Walsall)

2000 (30 Oct). Caribbean Flowers. T **158** and similar horiz designs. Multicoloured. P 14.

1555	30c. Type **158**	40	20
1556	80c. Frangipani	70	35
1557	90c. Star of the March	70	75
	a. Sheetlet. Nos. 1557/62	3·75	4·00
1558	90c. Tiger Lily	70	75
1559	90c. Mont Blanc Lily	70	75
1560	90c. Torch Ginger	70	75
1561	90c. Cattleya Orchid	70	75
1562	90c. St. John's Wort	70	75
1563	$1 Culebra	70	75
	a. Sheetlet. Nos. 1563/8	3·75	4·00
1564	$1 Rubellum Lily	70	75
1565	$1 Silver Elegance Oriental Lily	70	75
1566	$1 Chinese Hibiscus	70	75
1567	$1 Tiger Lily (*different*)	70	75
1568	$1 Royal Poincia	70	75
1569	$1.60 Epiphyte	70	75
	a. Sheetlet. Nos. 1569/74	5·50	6·00
1570	$1.60 Enchantment Lily	1·00	1·10
1571	$1.60 Glory Lily	1·00	1·10
1572	$1.60 Purple Granadilla	1·00	1·10
1573	$1.60 Jacaranda	1·00	1·10
1574	$1.60 Shrimp Plant	1·00	1·10
1575	$1.60 Garden Zinnia	1·00	1·10
1576	$5 Rose Elegance Lily	3·00	3·25
1555/76 Set of 22		17·00	19·00

MS1577 Two sheets. (a) 75×90 mm. $5 Bird of Paradise (plant). (b) 90×75 mm. $5 Dahlia *Set of 2 sheets* .... 7·00 8·00

Nos. 1557/62, 1563/8 and 1569/74 were each printed together, *se-tenant*, in sheetlets of 6 with the backgrounds forming composite designs. The three sheetlets and No. **MS**1577 include "The Stamp Show 2000" logo on the margins.

159 Aerial View of Resort

(Des M. Friedman. Litho Questa)

2000 (19 Nov). Re-opening of Four Seasons Resort. T **159** and similar horiz designs. Multicoloured. P 14×13½.

1578	30c. Type **159**	65	65
	a. Sheetlet. Nos. 1578/81	2·40	2·40
1579	30c. Palm trees on beach	65	65
1580	30c. Golf course	65	65
1581	30c. Couple at water's edge	65	65
1578/81 Set of 4		2·40	2·40

Nos. 1578/81 were printed together, *se-tenant*, in sheetlets of 4 with enlarged illustrated margins.

160 "The Coronation of the Virgin" (Velazquez)

(Litho B.D.T.)

2000 (4 Dec). Christmas. Religious Paintings. T **160** and similar multicoloured designs. P 13½.

1582	30c. Type **160**	40	20
1583	80c. "The Immaculate Conception" (Velazquez)	80	50
1584	90c. "Madonna and Child" (Titian) (*horiz*)	85	60
1585	$1.20 "Madonna and Child with St. John the Baptist and St. Catherine" (Titian) (*horiz*)	1·10	1·40
1582/5 Set of 4		2·75	2·40

MS1586 108×108 mm. $6 "Madonna and Child with St. Catherine" (Titian) (*horiz*). P 14 .... 4·00 4·50

Nos. 1584/5 are both inscribed "Titien" in error.

ST. KITTS-NEVIS / Nevis

161 Snake coiled around Branch

(Des Y. Lee. Litho Walsall)

2001 (4 Jan). Chinese New Year. Year of the Snake. T **161** and similar horiz designs. Multicoloured. P 14.
1587	$1.60 Type **161**	1·10	1·10
	a. Sheetlet. Nos. 1587/90	4·00	4·00
1588	$1.60 Snake in tree	1·10	1·10
1589	$1.60 Snake on path	1·10	1·10
1590	$1.60 Snake by rocks	1·10	1·10
1587/90 Set of 4		4·00	4·00
MS1591 70×100 mm. $5 Cobra at foot of cliff		3·25	3·50

Nos. 1587/90 were printed together, *se-tenant*, in sheetlets of 4.

162 Charlestown Methodist Church   **163** Two Giraffes

(Des M. Friedman. Litho B.D.T.)

2001 (23 Jan). Leeward Islands District Methodist Church Conference. T **162** and similar horiz designs. Multicoloured. P 14.
1592	50c. Type **162**	35	40
	a. Sheetlet. Nos. 1592/8	2·25	2·50
1593	50c. Jessups Methodist Church	35	40
1594	50c. Clifton Methodist Church	35	40
1595	50c. Trinity Methodist Church	35	40
1596	50c. Combermere Methodist Church	35	40
1597	50c. New River Methodist Church	35	40
1598	50c. Gingerland Methodist Church	35	40
1592/8 Set of 7		2·25	2·50

Nos. 1592/8 were printed together in sheetlets of 7 containing Nos. 1593/7, as a vertical *se-tenant* strip of 5, and Nos. 1592 and 1598 each perforated separately.

(Des J. Genzo. Litho Questa)

2001 (31 Jan). Wildlife from "The Garden of Eden". T **163** and similar multicoloured designs. P 14.
1599	$1.60 Type **163**	1·10	1·10
	a. Sheetlet. Nos. 1599/1604	6·00	6·00
1600	$1.60 Rainbow boa constrictor	1·10	1·10
1601	$1.60 Suffolk sheep and mountain cottontail hare	1·10	1·10
1602	$1.60 Bluebuck antelope	1·10	1·10
1603	$1.60 Fox	1·10	1·10
1604	$1.60 Box turtle	1·10	1·10
1605	$1.60 Red-crested woodpecker and unicorn	1·10	1·10
	a. Sheetlet. Nos. 1605/10	6·00	6·00
1606	$1.60 African elephant	1·10	1·10
1607	$1.60 Siberian tiger	1·10	1·10
1608	$1.60 Greater flamingo and Adam and Eve	1·10	1·10
1609	$1.60 Hippopotamus	1·10	1·10
1610	$1.60 Harlequin frog	1·10	1·10
1599/610 Set of 12		12·00	12·00
MS1611 Four sheets, each 84×69 mm. (a) $5 Toucan (vert). (b) $5 Bald eagle. (c) $5 Koala bear (vert). (d) $5 Blue and gold macaw (vert) Set of 4 *sheets*		14·00	15·00

Nos. 1599/1604 and 1605/10 were each printed together, *se-tenant*, in sheetlets of 6 with the backgrounds forming composite designs.

164 Zebra

(Des D. Burkhart. Litho Questa)

2001 (22 Mar). Butterflies of Nevis. T **164** and similar horiz designs. Multicoloured. P 14.
1612	30c. Type **164**	50	20
1613	80c. Julia	85	55
1614	$1 Ruddy dagger	90	90
	a. Sheetlet. Nos. 1614/19	4·75	4·75
1615	$1 Common morpho	90	90
1616	$1 Banded king shoemaker	90	90
1617	$1 Figure of eight	90	90
1618	$1 Grecian shoemaker	90	90
1619	$1 Mosaic	90	90
1620	$1 White peacock	90	90
	a. Sheetlet. Nos. 1620/5	4·75	4·75
1621	$1 Hewitson's blue hairstreak	90	90
1622	$1 Tiger pierid	90	90
1623	$1 Gold drop helicopsis	90	90
1624	$1 Cramer's mesene	90	90
1625	$1 Red-banded pereute	90	90
1626	$1.60 Small flambeau	1·40	1·40
1627	$5 Purple mort bleu	3·25	3·75
1612/27 Set of 16		14·00	14·00
MS1628 Two sheets, each 72×100 mm. (a) $5 Common mechanitis. (b) $5 Hewitson's pierella Set of 2 *sheets*		7·50	8·00

Nos. 1614/19 and 1620/5 were each printed together, *se-tenant*, in sheetlets of 6 with enlarged and inscribed margins.

165 *Clavulinopsis corniculata*

(Des D. Burkhart. Litho Walsall)

2001 (15 May). Caribbean Fungi. T **165** and similar vert designs. Multicoloured. P 14.
1629	20c. Type **165**	45	35
1630	25c. *Cantharellus cibarius*	45	35
1631	50c. *Chlorociboria aeruginascens*	70	45
1632	80c. *Auricularia auricula-judae*	85	55
1633	$1 *Entoloma incanum*	90	90
	a. Sheetlet. Nos. 1633/41	7·25	7·25
1634	$1 *Entoloma nitidum*	90	90
1635	$1 *Stropharia cyanea*	90	90
1636	$1 *Otidea onotica*	90	90
1637	$1 *Aleuria aurantia*	90	90
1638	$1 *Mitrula paludosa*	90	90
1639	$1 *Gyromitra esculenta*	90	90
1640	$1 *Helvella crispa*	90	90
1641	$1 *Morcella semilibera*	90	90
1642	$2 *Peziza vesiculosa*	1·60	1·75
1643	$3 *Mycena acicula*	2·25	2·75
1629/43 Set of 15		13·00	13·00
MS1644 Two sheets, each 110×85 mm. (a) $5 *Russula sardonia*. (b) $5 *Omphalotus olearius* Set of 2 *sheets*		7·50	8·00

Nos. 1633/41 were printed together, *se-tenant*, in sheetlets of 9.

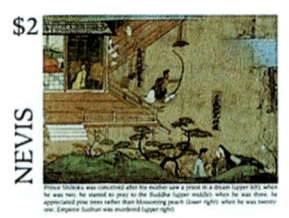

166 Early Life of Prince Shotoku

(Litho Questa)

2001 (31 May). Philanippon 01 International Stamp Exhibition, Tokyo. Prince Shotoku Pictorial Scroll. T **166** and similar horiz designs. Multicoloured. P 13½.
1645	$2 Type **166**	1·40	1·40
	a. Sheetlet. Nos. 645/8	5·00	5·00
1646	$2 With priests and nuns, and preaching	1·40	1·40
1647	$2 Subduing the Ezo	1·40	1·40
1648	$2 Playing with children	1·40	1·40
1649	$2 Passing through gate	1·40	1·40
	a. Sheetlet. Nos. 1649/52	5·00	5·00
1650	$2 Battle against Mononobe-no-Moriya	1·40	1·40
1651	$2 Yumedono Hall	1·40	1·40
1652	$2 Watching dog and deer	1·40	1·40
1645/52 Set of 8		10·00	10·00

Nos. 1645/8 and 1649/52 were each printed together, *se-tenant*, in sheetlets of 4 with enlarged illustrated and inscribed top, bottom and right margins.

167 Prince Albert

168 Queen Elizabeth II wearing Blue Hat

(Des Irina Lyampe. Litho Questa)

2001 (9 July). Death Centenary of Queen Victoria. T **167** and similar vert designs. Multicoloured. P 14.

1653	$1.20 Type **167**	90	90
	a. Sheetlet. Nos. 1653/8	4·75	4·75
1654	$1.20 Queen Victoria at accession	90	90
1655	$1.20 Queen Victoria as a young girl	90	90
1656	$1.20 Victoria Mary Louisa, Duchess of Kent (Queen Victoria's mother)	90	90
1657	$1.20 Queen Victoria in old age	90	90
1658	$1.20 Albert Edward, Prince of Wales as a boy	90	90
1653/8 Set of 6		4·75	4·75
MS1659 97×70 mm. $5 Queen Victoria at accession		3·25	3·75

Nos. 653/8 were printed together, *se-tenant*, in sheetlets of 6 (2×3), with the columns separated by an enlarged illustrated and inscribed gutter.

(Des J. Iskowitz. Litho Questa)

2001 (9 July). Queen Elizabeth II's 75th Birthday. T **168** and similar vert designs. Multicoloured. P 14.

1660	90c. Type **168**	80	80
	a. Sheetlet. Nos. 660/5	4·25	4·25
1661	90c. Wearing tiara	80	80
1662	90c. Wearing yellow hat	80	80
1663	90c. Wearing grey hat	80	80
1664	90c. Wearing red hat	80	80
1665	90c. Bare-headed and wearing pearl necklace	80	80
1660/5 Set of 6		4·25	4·25
MS1666 95×107 mm. $5 Wearing blue hat		4·00	4·25

Nos. 1660/5 were printed together, *se-tenant*, in sheetlets of 6 (2×3), with the columns separated by an enlarged illustrated and inscribed gutter margin.

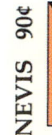

169 Christmas Candle (flower)

170 Flag of Antigua & Barbuda

(Des D. Burkhart. Litho Questa)

2001 (3 Dec). Christmas. Flowers. T **169** and similar multicoloured designs. P 14.

1667	30c. Type **169**	25	15
1668	90c. Poinsettia (*horiz*)	60	40
1669	$1.20 Snowbush (*horiz*)	85	75
1670	$3 Tiger claw	1·90	2·50
1667/70 Set of 4		3·25	3·50

(Litho Questa)

2001 (3 Dec). Flags of the Caribbean Community. T **170** and similar horiz designs. Multicoloured. P 14.

1671	90c. Type **170**	1·00	1·00
	a. Sheetlet. Nos. 1671/84	12·50	12·50
1672	90c. Bahamas	1·00	1·00
1673	90c. Barbados	1·00	1·00
1674	90c. Belize	1·00	1·00
1675	90c. Dominica	1·00	1·00
1676	90c. Grenada	1·00	1·00
1677	90c. Guyana	1·00	1·00
1678	90c. Jamaica	1·00	1·00
1679	90c. Montserrat	1·00	1·00
1680	90c. St. Kitts & Nevis	1·00	1·00
1681	90c. St. Lucia	1·00	1·00
1682	90c. Surinam	1·00	1·00
1683	90c. St. Vincent and the Grenadines	1·00	1·00
1684	90c. Trinidad & Tobago	1·00	1·00
1671/84 Set of 14		12·50	12·50

Nos. 1671/84 were printed together, *se-tenant*, in sheetlets of 14, with a centre label showing the Community flag.

No. 1675 shows the former flag of Dominica, superseded in 1990.

171 Maracana Football Stadium, Brazil 1950

172 Queen Elizabeth and Duke of Edinburgh in Reviewing Car

(Des D. Miller. Litho Questa)

2001 (10 Dec). World Cup Football Championship, Japan and Korea (2002). T **171** and similar vert designs. Multicoloured. P 14.

1685	$1.60 Type **171**	1·10	1·10
	a. Sheetlet. Nos. 1685/90	6·00	6·00
1686	$1.60 Ferenc Puskas (Hungary), Switzerland 1954	1·10	1·10
1687	$1.60 Luiz Bellini (Brazil), Sweden 1958	1·10	1·10
1688	$1.60 Mauro (Brazil), Chile 1962	1·10	1·10
1689	$1.60 West German cap, England 1966	1·10	1·10
1690	$1.60 Pennant, Mexico 1970	1·10	1·10
1691	$1.60 Passarella (Argentina), Argentina 1978	1·10	1·10
	a. Sheetlet. Nos. 1691/6	6·00	6·00
1692	$1.60 Dino Zoff (Italy), Spain 1982	1·10	1·10
1693	$1.60 Azteca Stadium, Mexico 1986	1·10	1·10
1694	$1.60 San Siro Stadium, Italy 1990	1·10	1·10
1695	$1.60 Dennis Bergkamp (Holland), U.S.A. 1994	1·10	1·10
1696	$1.60 Stade de France, France 1998	1·10	1·10
1685/96 Set of 12		12·00	12·00
MS1697 Two sheets, each 88×75 mm. (a) $5 Detail of Jules Rimet Trophy, Uruguay 1930. (b) $5 Detail of World Cup Trophy, Japan/Korea 2002 *Set of 2 sheets*		7·00	7·50

Nos. 1685/90 and 1691/6 were each printed together, *se-tenant*, in sheetlets of 6, with enlarged illustrated margins.

Nos. 1685 and 1687 are inscribed "Morocana" or "Luis", both in error.

(Des D. Miller. Litho Questa)

2002 (6 Feb). Golden Jubilee (2nd issue). T **172** and similar square designs. Multicoloured. P 14½.

1698	$2 Type **172**	1·75	1·75
	a. Sheetlet. Nos. 1698/701	6·25	6·25
1699	$2 Prince Philip	1·75	1·75
1700	$2 Queen Elizabeth wearing yellow coat and hat	1·75	1·75
1701	$2 Queen Elizabeth and horse at polo match	1·75	1·75
1698/701 Set of 4		6·25	6·25
MS1702 76×108 mm. $5 Queen Elizabeth with Prince Philip in naval uniform. P 14		5·00	5·00

Nos. 1698/1701 were printed together, *se-tenant*, in sheetlets of 4 with an illustrated left margin.

173 Chestnut and White Horse

(Des Y. Lee. Litho B.D.T.)

2002 (12 Feb). Chinese New Year. ("Year of the Horse"). Paintings by Ren Renfa. T **173** and similar horiz designs. Multicoloured. P 13×13½.

1703	$1.60 Type **173**	1·10	1·10
	a. Sheetlet. Nos. 1703/6	4·00	4·00
1704	$1.60 Bay horse	1·10	1·10

ST. KITTS-NEVIS / Nevis

1705	$1.60 Brown horse	1·10	1·10
1706	$1.60 Dappled grey horse	1·10	1·10
1703/6	Set of 4	4·00	4·00

Nos. 1703/6 were printed together, *se-tenant*, in sheetlets of 4 with an enlarged inscribed top margin.

174 Beechey's Bee

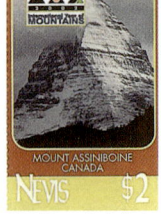

175 Mount Assiniboine, Canada

(Des R. Martin. Litho Walsall)

2002 (15 Aug). Fauna. T **174** and similar multicoloured designs. P 14.

1707	$1.20 Type **174**	1·00	1·00
	a. Sheetlet. Nos. 1707/12	5·50	5·50
1708	$1.20 Banded king shoemaker butterfly	1·00	1·00
1709	$1.20 Streaked sphinx caterpillar	1·00	1·00
1710	$1.20 Hercules beetle	1·00	1·00
1711	$1.20 South American palm weevil	1·00	1·00
1712	$1.20 Giant katydid	1·00	1·00
1713	$1.60 Roseate spoonbill	1·10	1·10
	a. Sheetlet. Nos. 1713/18	6·00	6·00
1714	$1.60 White-tailed tropicbird	1·10	1·10
1715	$1.60 Ruby-throated tropicbird	1·10	1·10
1716	$1.60 Black skimmer	1·10	1·10
1717	$1.60 Black-necked stilt	1·10	1·10
1718	$1.60 Mourning dove	1·10	1·10
1719	$1.60 Sperm whale and calf	1·10	1·10
	a. Sheetlet. Nos. 1719/24	6·00	6·00
1720	$1.60 Killer whale	1·10	1·10
1721	$1.60 Minke whales	1·10	1·10
1722	$1.60 Fin whale	1·10	1·10
1723	$1.60 Blaineville's beaked whale	1·10	1·10
1724	$1.60 Pygmy sperm whale	1·10	1·10
1707/24	Set of 18	17·00	17·00
MS1725	Three sheets, each 105×78 mm. (a) $5 Click beetle. (b) $5 Royal tern. (c) $5 Humpback whale (vert) Set of 3 sheets	11·00	12·00

Nos. 1707/12 (insects), 1713/18 (birds) and 1719/24 (whales) were each printed together, *se-tenant*, in sheetlets of 6 with the backgrounds forming composite designs that extend onto the sheetlet margins.

Nos. 1713/18 also show the "APS Stampshow 2002" logo on the margin.

(Des R. Sauber. Litho Questa)

2002 (26 Aug). International Year of Mountains. T **175** and similar vert designs. Multicoloured. P 14.

1726	$2 Type **175**	1·40	1·40
	a. Sheetlet. Nos. 1726/31	7·50	7·50
1727	$2 Mount Atitlan, Guatemala	1·40	1·40
1728	$2 Mount Adams, U.S.A.	1·40	1·40
1729	$2 The Matterhorn, Switzerland	1·40	1·40
1730	$2 Mount Dhaulagiri, Nepal	1·40	1·40
1731	$2 Mount Chamlang, Nepal	1·40	1·40
1726/31	Set of 6	7·50	7·50
MS1732	106×125 mm. $5 Mount Kvaenangen, Norway	3·25	3·75

Nos. 1726/31 were printed together, *se-tenant*, in sheetlets of 6 with enlarged illustrated margins.

Nos. 1727 and 1729 are inscribed "ATAILAN" and "MATTHERORN", both in error.

176 Horse-riders on Beach

(Des M. Servin. Litho Questa)

2002 (26 Aug). Year of Eco Tourism. T **176** and similar horiz designs. Multicoloured. P 14.

1733	$1.60 Type **176**	1·60	1·60
	a. Sheetlet. Nos. 1733/8	8·75	8·75
1734	$1.60 Windsurfing	1·60	1·60
1735	$1.60 Pinney's Beach	1·60	1·60
1736	$1.60 Hikers by beach	1·60	1·60
1737	$1.60 Robert T Jones Golf Course	1·60	1·60
1738	$1.60 Scuba diver and fish	1·60	1·60
1733/8	Set of 6	8·75	8·75
MS1739	115×90 mm $5 Snorkel diver on reef	3·50	3·75

Nos. 1733/8 were printed together, *se-tenant*, in sheetlets of 6 with an enlarged illustrated top margin.

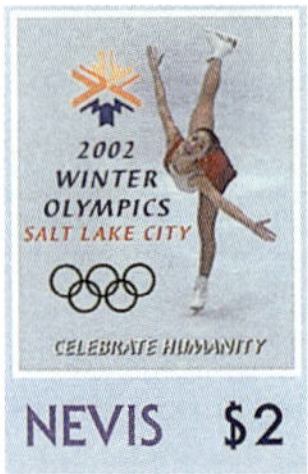

177 Women's Figure Skating

178 Two Scout Canoes in Mist

(Litho Questa)

2002 (26 Aug). Winter Olympic Games, Salt Lake City. T **177** and similar vert design. Multicoloured. P 14.

1740	$2 Type **177**	1·40	1·50
1741	$2 Aerial skiing	1·40	1·50
MS1742	88×119 mm. Nos. 1740/1	2·75	3·00

(Des R. Sauber. Litho Questa)

2002 (26 Aug). 20th World Scout Jamboree, Thailand. T **178** and similar vert designs. Multicoloured. P 14.

1743	$2 Type **178**	1·40	1·40
	a. Sheetlet. Nos. 1743/6	5·00	5·00
1744	$2 Canoe in jungle	1·40	1·40
1745	$2 Scout on rope-ladder	1·40	1·40
1746	$2 Scouts with inflatable boats	1·40	1·40
1743/6	Set of 4	5·00	5·00
MS1747	105×125 mm. $5 Scout painting	3·25	3·50

Nos. 1743/6 were printed together, *se-tenant*, in sheetlets of 4 with an enlarged illustrated left margin.

179 U.S. Flag as Statue of Liberty with Nevis Flag

180 "Nevis Peak with Windmill" (Eva Wilkin)

(Litho Questa)

2002 (26 Aug). "United We Stand". Support for Victims of 11 September 2001 Terrorist Attacks. P 14.

1748	**179** $2 multicoloured	1·40	1·40

No. 1748 was printed in sheetlets of 4 with an illustrated left margin.

(Litho B.D.T.)

2002 (21 Oct). Art. T **180** and similar multicoloured designs (except Nos. 1750/1). P 14×15 ($2) or 14 (others).

1749	$1.20 Type **180**	1·00	1·00
	a. Sheetlet. Nos. 1749/52	3·50	3·50
1750	$1.20 "Nevis Peak with ruined Windmill" (Eva Wilkin) (agate and black)	1·00	1·00
1751	$1.20 "Fig Tree Church" (Eva Wilkin) (agate and black)	1·00	1·00
1752	$1.20 "Nevis Peak with Blossom" (Eva Wilkin)	1·00	1·00
1753	$2 "Golden Pheasants and Loquat" (Kano Shoei) (30×80 *mm*)	1·50	1·50
	a. Sheetlet. Nos. 1753/6	5·50	5·50
1754	$2 "Flowers and Birds of the Four Seasons" (Winter) (Ikeda Koson) (30×80 *mm*)	1·50	1·50
1755	$2 "Pheasants and Azaleas" (Kano Shoei) (30×80 *mm*)	1·50	1·50
1756	$2 "Flowers and Birds of the Four Seasons" (Spring) (Ikeda Koson) (different) (30×80 *mm*)	1·50	1·50

1757	$3 "White Blossom" (Shikibu Terutada) (38×62 mm)		1·75	1·90
	a. Sheetlet. Nos. 1757/8		3·50	3·75
1758	$3 "Bird and Flowers" (Shikibu Terutada) (38×62 mm)		1·75	1·90
1759	$3 "Bird and Leaves" (Shikibu Terutada) (38×62 mm)		1·75	1·90
	a. Sheetlet. Nos. 1759/60		3·50	3·75
1760	$3 "Red and White Flowers" (Shikibu Terutada) (38×62 mm)		1·75	1·90
1761	$3 "Bird on Willow Tree" (Yosa Buson) (62×38 mm)		1·75	1·90
	a. Sheetlet. Nos. 1761/2		3·50	3·75
1762	$3 "Bird on Peach Tree" (Yosa Buson) (62×38 mm)		1·75	1·90
1749/62 Set of 14			18·00	18·00

MS1763 Two sheets, each 105×105 mm. (a) $5 "Golden Pheasants among Rhododendrons" (Yamamoto Baiitsu) (38×62 mm). (b) $5 "Musk Cat and Camellias" (Uto Gyoshi) (62×38 mm) Set of 2 sheets.. 7·50 8·00

Nos. 1749/52, 1753/6, 1757/8, 1759/60 and 1761/2 were each printed together, *se-tenant*, in sheetlets of 4 or 2 with inscribed margins.

The backgrounds on Nos. 1757/62 form composite designs that extend onto the sheetlet margins.

181 "Madonna and Child Enthroned with Saints" (Pietro Perugino)

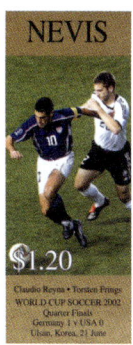

182 Claudio Reyna (U.S.A.) and Torsten Frings (Germany)

(Litho B.D.T.)

2002 (4 Nov). Christmas. Religious Art. T **181** and similar vert designs. Multicoloured. P 14.

1764	30c. Type **181**	35	15
1765	80c. "Adoration of the Magi" (Domenico Ghirlandaio)	70	35
1766	90c. "San Zaccaria Altarpiece" (Giovanni Bellini)	80	40
1767	$1.20 "Presentation at the Temple" (Bellini)	1·10	90
1768	$5 "Madonna and Child" (Simone Martini)	3·75	5·00
1764/8 Set of 5		6·00	6·00

MS1769 102×76 mm. $6 "Maesa" (Martini) .... 3·50 4·00

(Des D. Miller. Litho Cartor)

2002 (4 Nov). World Cup Football Championship, Japan and Korea. T **182** and similar vert designs. Multicoloured. P 13½.

1770	$1.20 Type **182**	95	95
	a. Sheetlet. Nos. 1770/5	5·25	5·25
1771	$1.20 Michael Ballack (Germany) and Eddie Pope (U.S.A.)	95	95
1772	$1.20 Sebastian Kehl (Germany) and Brian McBride (U.S.A.)	95	95
1773	$1.20 Carlos Puyol (Spain) and Eul Yong Lee (South Korea)	95	95
1774	$1.20 Jin Cheul Choi (South Korea) and Gaizka Mendieta (Spain)	95	95
1775	$1.20 Juan Valeron (Spain) and Jin Cheul Choi (South Korea)	95	95
1776	$1.60 Emile Heskey (England) and Edmilson (Brazil)	1·10	1·10
	a. Sheetlet. Nos. 1776/81	6·00	6·00
1777	$1.60 Rivaldo (Brazil) and Sol Campbell (England)	1·10	1·10
1778	$1.60 Ronaldinho (Brazil) and Nicky Butt (England)	1·10	1·10
1779	$1.60 Ilhan Mansiz (Turkey) and Omar Daf (Senegal)	1·10	1·10
1780	$1.60 Hasan Sas (Turkey) and Pape Bouba Diop (Senegal)	1·10	1·10
1781	$1.60 Lamine Diata (Senegal) and Hakan Sukur (Turkey)	1·10	1·10
1770/81 Set of 12		11·00	11·00

MS1782 Four sheets, each 82×82 mm. (a) $3 Sebastian Kehl (Germany); $3 Frankie Hejduk (U.S.A.). (b) $3 Hong Myung Bo (South Korea); $3 Gaizka Mendieta (Spain). (c) $3 David Beckham (England) and Roque Junior (Brazil); $3 Paul Scholes (England) and Rivaldo (Brazil). (d) $3 Alpay Ozalan (Turkey); $3 Khalilou Fadiga (Senegal) Set of 4 sheets   13·00   15·00

Nos. 1770/5 and 1776/81 were each printed together, *se-tenant*, in sheetlets of 6 with inscribed margins.

No. 1780 is inscribed "Papa" in error.

183 Ram and Two Ewes

184 Marlene Dietrich

(Des Yuan Lee. Litho Questa)

2003 (10 Feb). Chinese New Year. ("Year of the Ram"). P 14×13½.
1783   **183** $2 multicoloured... 1·75   1·75

No. 1783 was printed in sheetlets of four with inscribed margins.

(Des Esther Ainspan (**MS**1784/5), M. Friedman (**MS**1786), J. Iskowitz (**MS**1787/90). Litho Walsall)

2003 (10 Mar). Famous People of the 20th Century. T **184** and similar designs. P 14.

(a) Tenth Death Anniv of Marlene Dietrich. Multicoloured.
MS1784 127×165 mm. $1.60×2 Type **184**; $1.60×2 Wearing white coat and black hat; $1.60×2 Holding cigarette.. 5·50   6·00
MS1785 76×51 mm. $5 Marlene Dietrich .... 3·25   3·50

(b) 25th Death Anniv of Elvis Presley. Sheet 154×151 mm. Multicoloured. P 14.
MS1786 $1.60×6 Elvis Presley .... 7·00   7·50

(c) Life and Times of President John F. Kennedy. Two sheets, each 126×141 mm.
MS1787 $2 Taking Oath of Office, 1961 (brownish black, brown and rosine); $2 Watching swearing in of Cabinet Officers (black, purple-brown and rosine); $2 With Andrei Gromyko (Soviet Foreign Minister), 1963 (multicoloured); $2 Making speech during Cuban Missile Crisis, 1962 (black, deep violet and rosine)... 6·00   6·50
MS1788 $2 Robert and Ted Kennedy (brothers) (greenish slate, reddish violet and rosine); $2 John F. Kennedy (greenish slate, reddish violet and rosine); $2 John as boy with brother Joe Jnr (maroon, black and rosine); $2 With Robert Kennedy in Rose Garden of White House (multicoloured) .... 6·00   6·50

(d) 75th Anniv of First Solo Transatlantic Flight. Two sheets, each 142×126 mm. Multicoloured
MS1789 $2 Ryan Airlines crew attaching wing to fuselage of NYP Special *Spirit of St. Louis*; $2 Charles Lindbergh with Donald Hall and Mr. Mahoney (president of Ryan Airlines); $2 Lindbergh planning flight; $2 Donald Hall (chief engineer of Ryan Airlines) working on plans of aircraft............................ 6·00   6·50
MS1790 $2 Donald Hall and drawing of *Spirit of St. Louis*; $2 Charles Lindbergh; $2 *Spirit of St. Louis* being towed from factory; $2 *Spirit of St. Louis* at Curtis Field before flight... 6·00   6·50

185 Princess Diana

186 Abraham Lincoln Bear

ST. KITTS-NEVIS / Nevis

(Litho Walsall)

2003 (10 Mar). Fifth Death Anniv of Diana, Princess of Wales. T **185** and similar vert designs. Multicoloured. P 12.
MS1791 203×150 mm. $2 Type **185**; $2 Wearing white dress and four strings of pearls; $2 Wearing black sleeveless dress; $2 Wearing black and white hat....... 6·00 6·50
MS1792 95×116 mm. $5 Wearing pearl and sapphire choker... 3·50 3·75

(Des R. Rundo. Litho Cartor)

2003 (13 May). Centenary of the Teddy Bear. T **186** and similar vert designs. Multicoloured. P 13½.
MS1793 137×152 mm. $2 Type **186**; $2 Napolean bear; $2 Henry VIII bear; $2 Charlie Chaplin bear ..... 3·75 4·25
MS1794 100×70 mm. $5 Baseball bear .... 3·25 3·75

(Des J. Iskowitz. Litho)

2003 (13 May). Centenary of Tour de France Cycle Race. Vert designs as T **512** of Antigua showing past winners. Multicoloured. P 13½.
MS1795 160×100 mm. $2 Gustave Garrigou (1911); $2 Odile Defraye (1912); $2 Philippe Thys (1913); $2 Philippe Thys (1914).. 7·00 7·00
MS1796 100×70 mm. $5 François Faber .... 6·00 6·00

187 Cadillac 355-C V8 Sedan (1933)

(Des T. Wood. Litho Cartor)

2003 (13 May). Centenary of General Motors Cadillac. T **187** and similar horiz designs. Multicoloured. P 13½.
MS1797 120×170 mm. $2 Type **187**; $2 Eldorado (1953); $2 Coupe Deville (1977); $2 Seville Elegante (1980)........ 6·00 6·50
MS1798 84×120 mm. $5 Cadillac (1954)............................ 3·50 3·75

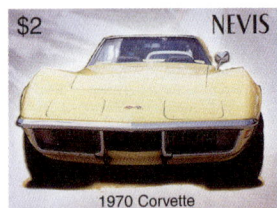

188 Corvette (1970)

(Des T. Wood. Litho Cartor)

2003 (13 May). 50th Anniv of General Motors Chevrolet Corvette. T **188** and similar horiz designs. Multicoloured. P 13½.
MS1799 120×140 mm. $2 Type **188**; $2 Corvette (1974); $2 Corvette (1971); $2 Corvette (1973)............ 6·00 6·50
MS1800 120×85 mm. $5 C5 Corvette (1997) .... 3·50 3·75

189 Queen Elizabeth II on Coronation Day

190 Prince William

(Des M. Servin. Litho Questa)

2003 (13 May). 50th Anniv of Coronation. T **189** and similar vert designs. Multicoloured. P 14.
MS1801 156×93 mm. $3 Type **189**; $3 Queen wearing Imperial State Crown (red background); $3 Wearing Imperial State Crown (in recent years)...... 8·50 8·50
MS1802 106×76 mm. $5 Wearing tiara and blue sash ...... 5·00 5·00

(Des M. Servin. Litho BDT)

2003 (13 May). 21st Birthday of Prince William of Wales. T **190** and similar vert designs. Multicoloured. P 14.
MS1803 147×86 mm. $3 Type **190**; $3 Wearing jacket and blue and gold patterned tie; $3 Wearing fawn sweater .... 8·50 8·50
MS1804 98×68 mm. $5 Prince William .... 5·00 5·00

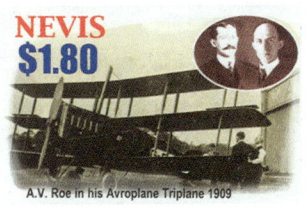

190a A. V. Roe's Triplane I, 1909

2003 (13 May). Centenary of Powered Flight. A. V. Roe (aircraft designer) Commemoration. T **190a** and similar horiz designs. Multicoloured. P 14.
MS1805 177×96 mm. $1.80, A. V. Roe's Triplane I, 1909; $1.80, Avro Type D biplane, 1911; $1.80, Avro Type F, 1912; $1.80, Avro 504 .... 6·00 6·50
MS1806 106×76 mm. $5 Avro No. 561, 1924.................. 3·75 4·00

191 *Phalaenopsis joline*

192 "Madonna of the Magnificat" (Botticelli)

(Des Ron Rundo. Litho BDT)

2003 (24 Oct). Orchids, Marine Life and Butterflies. T **191** and similar multicoloured designs. P 14.
1807	20c. Type **191**	45	35
1808	30c. Nassau grouper (fish)................................	50	40
1809	30c. *Perisama bonplandii* (butterfly) (*horiz*) ...	50	40
1810	80c. *Acropora* (coral).......................................	70	45
1811	90c. Doubletooth soldierfish (*horiz*)................	80	75
1812	90c. *Danaus formosa* (butterfly) (*horiz*)..........	80	75
1813	$1 *Amauris vasati* (butterfly) (*horiz*)..............	90	75
1814	$1.20 *Vanda thonglor* (orchid).........................	1·10	80
1815	$2 *Potinara* (orchid) (*horiz*)............................	1·90	1·90
1816	$3 *Lycaste aquila* (orchid) (*horiz*)..................	2·75	3·25
1817	$3 *Lycorea ceres* (butterfly) (*horiz*)...............	2·75	3·25
1818	$5 American manatee (*horiz*)..........................	3·50	4·00
1807/18 Set of 12..		15·00	15·00

MS1819 136×116 mm. $2 *Brassolaelia cattleya*; $2 *Cymbidium claricon*; $2 *Calantherestita*; $2 *Odontoglossum crispum* (orchids) (*all horiz*)............ 6·50 7·00
MS1820 116×136 mm. $2 Lionfish; $2 Copper-banded butterflyfish; $2 Honeycomb grouper; $2 Blue tang (*all horiz*).. 6·50 7·00
MS1821 136×116 mm. $2 *Kallima rumia*; $2 *Nessaea ancaeus*; $2 *Callicore cajetani*; $2 *Hamadryas guatemalena* (butterflies) (*all horiz*)......................... 6·50 7·00
MS1822 Three sheets, each 96×66 mm. (a) $5 *Odontioda brocade* (orchid). (b) $5 Blue-striped grunt (fish). (c) $5 *Euphaedra medon* (butterfly) (*all horiz*) ...... 11·00 12·00

(Litho BDT)

2003 (5 Nov). Christmas. T **192** and similar vert designs. Multicoloured. P 14.
1823	30c. Type **192**	35	20
1824	90c. "Madonna with the Long Neck" (detail) (Parmigianino)..	70	45
1825	$1.20 "Virgin and Child with St. Anne" (detail) (Da Vinci)...	1·10	70
1826	$5 "Madonna and Child and Scenes from the Life of St. Anne" (detail) (Filippo Lippi)	3·50	4·25
1823/6 Set of 4...		5·00	5·00

MS1827 96×113 mm. $6 "The Conestabile Madonna" (Raphael).. 3·75 4·25

ST. KITTS-NEVIS / Nevis

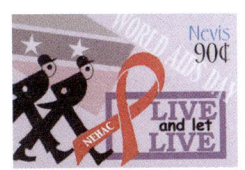

193 Two Stylised Men and AIDS Ribbon

(Des Mordechai Friedman. Litho BDT)

2003 (1 Dec). World AIDS Awareness Day. T **193** and similar horiz design. Multicoloured. P 14.
1828	90c. Type **193**	1·25	75
1829	$1.20 Nevis flag and map and ribbon	2·00	1·75

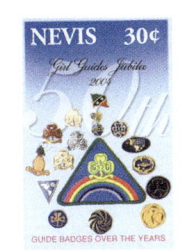

194 Monkey King

195 Guide Badges

(Des Y. Lee. Litho Cartor)

2004 (14 Feb). Chinese New Year ("Year of the Monkey"). T **194** and similar vert design. Grey, black and reddish-brown (**MS**1030) or multicoloured (**MS**1031). P 13½×13.
MS1830	102×130 mm. $1.60 Type **194**×4	4·50	4·75
MS1831	70×100 mm. $3 Monkey King (29×39 mm)	2·50	2·75

(Des Mordechai Friedman. Litho BDT)

2004 (22 Feb). 50th Anniv of Nevis Girl Guides. T **195** and similar multicoloured designs. P 14.
1832	30c. Type **195**	35	15
1833	90c. Mrs Gwendolyn Douglas-Jones and Miss Bridget Hunkins (past and present Commissioners) (*horiz*)	75	40
1834	$1.20 Lady Olave Baden Powell	1·00	70
1835	$5 Photographs of Girl Guides	3·50	4·25
1832/5	Set of 4	5·00	5·00

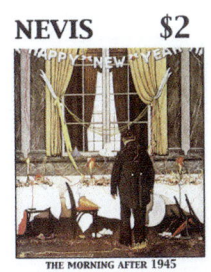

196 "The Morning After" (1945)

197 "Woman with a Hat" (1935)

(Litho Cartor)

2004 (4 Mar). 25th Death Anniv of Norman Rockwell (artist) (2003). T **196** and similar multicoloured designs. P 13½.
MS1836	150×180 mm. $2 Type **196**; $2 "Solitaire" (1950); $2 "Easter Morning" (1959); $2 "Walking to Church" (1953)	6·00	7·00
MS1837	90×98 mm. $5 "The Graduate" (1959) (*horiz*)	3·75	4·00

(Litho Cartor)

2004 (4 Mar). 30th Death Anniv of Pablo Picasso (2003) (artist). T **197** and similar vert designs. Multicoloured. P 13½.
MS1838 Two sheets each 133×168 mm. (a) $2 Type **197**; $2 "Seated Woman" (1937); $2 "Portrait of Nusch Eluard" (1937); $2 "Woman in a Straw Hat" (1936). (b) $2 "L'Arlésienne" (1937); $2 "The Mirror" (1932); $2 "Repose" (1932); $2 "Portrait of Paul Eluard" (1937)	11·00 12·00

MS1839 Two sheets. (a) 75×100 mm. $5 "Portrait of Nusch Eluard" (with green ribbon in hair) (1937). (b) 100×75 mm. $5 "Reclining Woman with a Book" (1939). Imperf *Set of 2 sheets*	7·50 8·00

198 "Still Life with a Drapery" (1899)

(Litho Cartor)

2004 (4 Mar). 300th Anniv of St. Petersburg. "Treasures of the Hermitage". T **198** and similar multicoloured designs. P 13½.
1840	30c. Type **198**	25	15
1841	90c. "The Smoker" (1895) (*vert*)	60	40
1842	$2 "Girl with a Fan" (1881) (*vert*)	1·40	1·40
1843	$5 "Grove" (1912) (*vert*)	3·25	5·00
1840/3	Set of 4	5·00	5·50
MS1844	94×74 mm. $5 "Lady in the Garden" (1867). Imperf	3·25	3·75

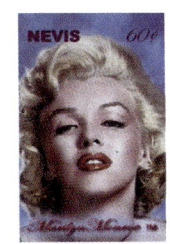

199 John Denver

200 Marilyn Monroe

(Des Ron Rundo. Litho Cartor)

2004 (17 June). John Denver (musician) Commemoration. Sheet 127×107 mm containing T **199** and similar vert designs. Multicoloured. P 13½.
MS1845	$1.20 Type **199**; $1.20 Wearing patterned shirt; $1.20 Wearing dark shirt; $1.20 Wearing white shirt	3·50	3·75

(Des Sarah Kleinstein. Litho Cartor)

2004 (17 June). Marilyn Monroe Commemoration. T **200** and similar vert designs. Multicoloured. P 13½.
1846	60c. Type **200**	1·00	75
MS1847	175×125 mm. $2 Pouting; $2 Laughing and looking left; $2 Laughing with head tilted back; $2 Smiling wearing drop earrings (37×50 *mm*)	5·00	6·00

No. 1846 was printed in sheetlets of 16 with an inscribed left margin.

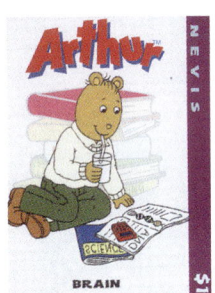

201 Brain

2004 (17 June). Arthur the Aardvark and Friends. T **201** and similar vert designs. Multicoloured. Litho. P 14.
MS1848 Three sheets, each 152×185. (a) $1×6, Type **201**; Sue Ellen; Buster; Francine; Muffy; Binky. (b) $2×4, Binky inside heart; Sue Ellen inside heart; Brain inside heart; Francine inside heart wearing red top. (c) $2×4, Arthur inside Heart; D.W. inside heart; Francine inside heart wearing pink top; Buster inside heart *Set of 3 sheets*	12·00 13·00

297

ST. KITTS-NEVIS / Nevis

202 HMCS *Penetang*

(Des Ron Rundo. Litho BDT)

2004 (7 Sept). 60th Anniv of D-Day Landings. T **202** and similar horiz designs. Multicoloured. P 14.
MS1849 Two sheets. (a) 136×122 mm. $1.20×6 Type **202**; Infantry disembarking from landing craft; Landing craft tank from above; Two landing craft tanks; Landing barge kitchen; Battleship *Texas*. (b) 96×76 mm. $6 H.M.S. *Scorpion* .... 14·00 14·00

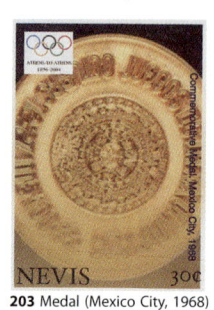

203 Medal (Mexico City, 1968)

(Des Ron Rundo. Litho BDT)

2004 (7 Sept). Olympic Games, Athens. T **203** and similar multicoloured designs. P 14½.
1850	30c. Type **203**	40	20
1851	90c. Pentathlon (Greek art)	75	50
1852	$1.80 Avery Brundage (International Olympic Committee, 1952–1972)	1·50	1·50
1853	$3 Tennis (Antwerp, 1920) (*horiz*)	2·25	3·00
1850/3	Set of 4	4·50	4·75

204 Deng Xiaoping  **205** Peace Dove carrying Olive Branch

(Des Irina Lyampe. Litho BDT)

2004 (7 Sept). Birth Centenary of Deng Xiaoping (leader of China, 1978–89). Sheet 96×66 mm. P 14.
MS1854 **204** $5 multicoloured .... 3·25 3·50

(Des Manuel Servin. Litho BDT)

2004 (7 Sept). United Nations International Year of Peace. Sheet 142×82 mm containing horiz designs as T **205**. Multicoloured. P 14.
MS1855 $3×3, Type **205**; Dove from front; Dove angled left .... 5·50 6·50

206 Elvis Presley

(Des Steven. Stines. Litho Cartor)

2004 (29 Nov). Elvis Presley Commemoration. T **206** and similar vert designs. Multicoloured. P 13½.
MS1856 Two sheets, each 146×103 mm. (a) $1.20×6, Type **206**×3; bright magenta background×3. (b) $1.20×6, bright scarlet sweater; orange-yellow sweater; new blue sweater; turquoise-blue sweater; bright purple sweater; apple green sweater .... 11·00 10·00

207 Nery Pumpido (Argentina)

(Des Derek Miller. Litho Beijing Stamp Printing House)

2004 (29 Nov) Centenary of FIFA (Féderation Internationale de Football Association). Type **207** and similar designs. P 12½.
MS1857 192×96 mm. $2×4, Type **207**; Gary Lineker (England); Thomas Hassler (Germany); Sol Campbell (England) .... 5·50 6·00
MS1857a 107×86 mm. $5 Michael Owen (England) .... 4·50 5·00

(Des Manuel Servin. Litho)

2004 (29 Nov) World Cup Football Championship, Germany. P 12
MS1858 90×115 mm. $5 Jason Berkley Joseph (Nevisian footballer) .... 4·50 5·00
No. MS1858 is inscribed in the border '100th Anniversary World Cup Soccer' (in error; World cup first staged in 1930)

208 "Santa's Good Boys"  **209** Steam Idyll, Indonesia

(Des Mordechai Friedman. Litho Beijing Stamp Printing House)

2004 (1 Dec). Christmas. Paintings by Norman Rockwell. T **208** and similar vert designs. Multicoloured. P 12.
1859	25c. Type **208**	35	15
1860	30c. "Ride 'em Cowboy"	40	20
1861	90c. "Christmas Sing Merrillie"	85	50
1862	$5 "The Christmas Newsstand"	3·50	4·25
1859/62	Set of 4	4·50	4·50
MS1863	63×72 mm. "Is He Coming". Imperf	3·50	3·75

(Des Mordechai Friedman. Litho Cartor)

2004 (13 Dec). Bicentenary of Steam Trains. T **209** and similar horiz designs. Multicoloured. P 13½.
1864	$3 Type **209**	2·75	2·75
	a. Sheetlet. Nos. 1864/7	10·00	10·00
1865	$3 2-8-2, Syria	2·75	2·75
1866	$3 Narrow Gauge Mallet 0-4-4-0, Portugal	2·75	2·75
1867	$3 Western Pacific Bo Bo Road Switcher, U.S.A.	2·75	2·75
1864/7	Set of 4	10·00	10·00
MS1868	100×70 mm. $5 LMS 5305, Great Britain	4·75	5·00

Nos. 1864/7 were printed together, *se-tenant*, in sheetlets of four stamps with an enlarged illustrated top margin.

210 Gekko Gecko

(Des Irina Lyampe. Litho BDT)

2005 (10 Jan). Reptiles and Amphibians. T **210** and similar horiz designs. Multicoloured. P 14.
1869	$1.20 Type **210**	1·00	1·25

		a. Sheetlet. Nos. 1869/72	3·50	4·50
1870	$1.20 Eyelash viper		1·00	1·25
1871	$1.20 Green iguana		1·00	1·25
1872	$1.20 Whistling frog		1·00	1·25
1869/72 Set of 4			3·50	4·50
MS1873 96×67 mm. $5 Hawksbill turtle			3·50	4·00

Nos. 1869/72 were printed together, *se-tenant*, in sheetlets of four stamps with an enlarged illustrated right margin.

211 Rufous Hummingbird

(Des Irina Lyampe. Litho BDT)

2005 (10 Jan). Hummingbirds. T **211** and similar horiz designs. Multicoloured. P 14.

1874	$2 Type **211**	3·00	2·75
	a. Sheetlet. Nos. 1874/7	11·00	10·00
1875	$2 Green-crowned brilliant	3·00	2·75
1876	$2 Ruby-throated hummingbird	3·00	2·75
1877	$2 Purple-throated carib	3·00	2·75
1874/7 Set of 4		11·00	10·00
MS1878 79×108 mm. $5 Rivoli's ("Magnificent") hummingbird		6·50	6·50

Nos. 1874/7 were printed together, *se-tenant*, in sheetlets of four stamps with an enlarged illustrated right margin.

212 *Xeromphalina campanella*

213 Hawksbill Turtle (Leon Silcott)

(Des Irina Lyampe. Litho BDT)

2005 (10 Jan). Mushrooms. T **212** and similar horiz designs. Multicoloured.

MS1879 137×127 mm. $2×4, Type **212**; *Calvatia sculpta*; *Mitrula elegans*; *Aleuriaaurantia*	7·00	7·50
MS1880 97×68 mm. $5 *Sarcoscypha coccinea*	4·50	4·75

(Des Irina Lyampe. Litho BDT)

2005 (10 Jan). Hawksbill Turtle. Children's Drawings. T **213** and similar horiz designs. Multicoloured. P 14.

1881	30c. Type **213**	35	20
1882	90c. Hawksbill turtle on sand (Kris Liburd)	85	40
1883	$1.20 Spotted hawksbill turtle (Alice Webber)	1·10	90
1884	$5 Hawksbill turtle in water (Jeuaunito Huggins)	3·75	4·50
1881/4 Set of 4		5·50	5·50

214 Zebra Shark

215 Rooster

(Des Ron Rundo. Litho BDT)

2005 (10 Jan). Sharks. T **214** and similar horiz designs. Multicoloured. P 14.

MS1885 99×137 mm. $2×4, Type **214**; Caribbean reef shark; Blue shark; Bronze whaler	6·00	6·50
MS1886 96×67 mm. $5 Blacktip reef shark	3·50	3·75

2005 (17 Jan). Chinese New Year. ("Year of the Rooster"). T **215** and similar square designs. Multicoloured. Litho. P 12.

1887	75c. Type **215**	70	70
	a. Sheetlet. Nos. 1887/90	2·50	2·50
1888	75c. Pink silhouette of rooster	70	70
1889	75c. Grey silhouette of rooster	70	70
1890	75c. Rooster on rose-lilac background	70	70
1887/90 Set of 4		2·50	2·50

Nos. 1887/90 were printed togther, *se-tenant*, in sheetlets of 4 stamps.

216 *Enola Gay* and Flight Crew

(Litho Beijing Stamp Printing House)

2005 (11 May). 60th Anniv of Victory in Japan. T **216** and similar horiz designs. Multicoloured. P 13.

1891	$2 Type **216**	2·50	2·50
	a. Sheetlet. Nos. 1891/95	11·00	11·00
1892	$2 Bomb exploding over Hiroshima	2·50	2·50
1893	$2 Souvenir of Japanese Surrender Ceremony	2·50	2·50
1894	$2 Japanese Delegation aboard USS *Missouri*	2·50	2·50
1895	$2 General Macarthur speaking	2·50	2·50
1891/5 Set of 5		11·00	11·00

Nos. 1891/95 were printed together, *se-tenant*, in sheetlets of 5 stamps with an enlarged, illustrated left margin.

217 Brazil Team, 1958

(Des Manuel Servin. Litho Beijing Stamp Printing House)

2005 (16 May). 75th Anniv of First World Cup Football Championship. T **217** and similar horiz designs. Multicoloured. P 12.

1896	$2 Type **217**	1·40	1·40
	a. Sheetlet. Nos. 1896/9	5·00	5·00
1897	$2 Brazil and Sweden	1·40	1·40
1898	$2 Rasunda Stadium, Stockholm	1·40	1·40
1899	$2 Edson Arantes do Nascimento (Pele)	1·40	1·40
1896/9 Set of 4		5·00	5·00
MS1900 115×89 mm. $5 Brazil celebrating with Swedish flag		3·25	3·50

Nos. 1896/9 were printed together, *se-tenant*, in sheetlets of 4 stamps with illustrated margins all round.

218 Friedrich von Schiller

219 Young Boy

(Litho Beijing Stamp Printing House)

2005 (16 May). Death Bicentenary of Friedrich von Schiller (poet and dramatist). T **218** and similar vert designs. Multicoloured. P 13.

1901	$3 Type **218**	1·75	1·90
	a. Sheetlet. Nos. 1901/3	4·75	5·00
1902	$3 Friedrich von Schiller (black and white portrait)	1·75	1·90
1903	$3 Birthplace of Friedrich von Schiller	1·75	1·90
1901/3 Set of 3		4·75	5·00
MS1904 100×70 mm. $5 Friedrich von Schiller statue, Chicago		3·25	3·50

(Des Irina Lyampe. Litho Beijing Stamp Printing House)

2005 (16 May). Centenary of Rotary International (humanitarian organisation). T **219** and similar multicoloured designs. P 13.

1905	$3 Type **219**	1·75	1·90
	a. Sheetlet. Nos. 1905/7	4·75	5·00
1906	$3 Immunising child	1·75	1·90
1907	$3 Boy with leg braces and crutches	1·75	1·90
1905/7 Set of 3		4·75	5·00
MS1908 103×70 mm. $5 Two children and adult (horiz).		3·25	3·50

Nos. 1905/7 were printed together, *se-tenant*, in sheetlets of 3 stamps with enlarged, illustrated margins all round.

ST. KITTS-NEVIS / Nevis

220 Admiral Sir William Cornwallis

(Des Joel Iskowitz. Litho Beijing Stamp Printing House)

2005 (16 May). Bicentenary of the Battle of Trafalgar. T **220** and similar horiz designs. Multicoloured. P 13.

1909	30c. Type **220**	70	30
1910	90c. Captain Maurice Suckling (Comptroller of the Navy)	1·25	70
1911	$1.20 Richard Earl Howe (First Lord of the Admiralty)	1·60	1·25
1912	$3 Sir John Jervis (First Earl of St Vincent)	3·75	4·25
1909/12	Set of 4	6·50	6·50
MS1913	83×119 mm. $5 Richard Earl Howe on quarterdeck of *Queen Charlotte*. P 12	6·00	6·50

Nos. 1909/12 were each printed with a *se-tenant* half stamp-sized label at foot inscribed with the details of the person depicted on the stamp.

221 General Charles de Gaulle

222 "The Little Mermaid" (sculpture)

(Litho Beijing Stamp Printing House)

2005 (16 May). 60th Anniv of Victory in Europe. T **221** and similar vert designs. P 13.

1914	$2 multicoloured	2·50	2·50
	a. Sheetlet. Nos. 1914/18	11·00	11·00
1915	$2 sepia and salmon-pink	2·50	2·50
1916	$2 brownish-black and greenish yellow	2·50	2·50
1917	$2 bistre-brown, stone and turquoise-blue	2·50	2·50
1918	$2 multicoloured	2·50	2·50
1914/18	Set of 5	11·00	11·00

Designs:—No. 1914, Type **221**; No. 1915, General George S. Patton; No. 1916, Field Marshall Bernhard Montgomery; No. 1917, Prisoners of War; No. 1918, "Germany Defeated!".

Nos. 1914/18 were printed together, *se-tenant*, in sheetlets of 5 stamps with an enlarged, illustrated margin at top.

(Litho Beijing Stamp Printing House)

2005 (16 May). Birth Bicentenary of Hans Christian Andersen (writer). T **222** and similar vert designs. Multicoloured. P 12½.

1919	$2 Type **222**	1·40	1·40
	a. Sheetlet. Nos. 1919/22	5·00	5·00
1920	$2 "Thumbelina"	1·40	1·40
1921	$2 "The Snow Queen"	1·40	1·40
1922	$2 "The Emperor's New Clothes"	1·40	1·40
1919/22	Set of 4	5·00	5·00
MS1923	100×75 mm. $6 Hans Christian Andersen	3·50	3·75

Nos. 1919/22 were printed together, *se-tenant*, in sheetlets of four stamps with an enlarged illustrated and inscribed left margin.

223 Tyrannosaurus Rex

224 Captain Nemo ("20,000 Leagues under the Sea")

(Litho Beijing Stamp Printing House)

2005 (7 June). Prehistoric Animals. T **223** and similar multicoloured designs. P 12½.

1924	30c. Type **223**	80	45
1925	$5 Hadrosaur	3·25	3·50
MS1926	Three sheets. (a) 104×128 mm. $1.20×6, Apatosaurus; Camarasaurus; Iguanodon; Edmontosaurus; Centrosaurus; Euoplocephalus. (b) 128×104 mm. $1.20×6 (*vert*), Deinotherium; Platybelodon; Palaeoloxodon; Arsinoitherium; Procoptodon; Macrauchenia. (c) 104×128 mm. $1.20×6, Ouranosaurus; Parasaurolophus; Psittacosaurus; Stegasaurus; Scelidosaurus; Hypsilophodon *Set of 3 sheets*	14·00	15·00
MS1927	Three sheets. (a) 97×77 mm. $5 Brontotherium. (b) 98×87 mm. $5 Daspletosaurus. (c) 98×92 mm. $5 Pliosaur *Set of 3 sheets*	11·00	12·00

The backgrounds of Nos. **MS**1926a/c form composite designs which bleed onto the sheet margins.

(Litho Beijing Stamp Printing House)

2005 (17 June). Death Centenary of Jules Verne (writer). T **224** and similar vert designs. Multicoloured. P 12½.

1928	$2 Type **224**	2·25	2·25
	a. Sheetlet. Nos. 1928/31	8·00	8·00
1929	$2 Michael Strogoff	2·25	2·25
1930	$2 Phileas Fogg (*Around the World in 80 Days*)	2·25	2·25
1931	$2 Captain Cyrus Smith (*Mysterious Island*)	2·25	2·25
1928/31	Set of 4	8·00	8·00
MS1932	78×100 mm. $5 Pat Boone (*Journey to the Centre of the Earth*)	4·50	4·75

Nos. 1928/31 were printed together, *se-tenant*, in sheetlets of four stamps with an enlarged illustrated and inscribed left margin.

No. 1930 is inscribed "Phinias Fogg".

225 No. SG69 of Vatican City optd with Type **69**

(Des Ron Rundo. Litho Beijing Stamp Printing House)

2005 (12 July). Pope John Paul II Commemoration. T **225** and similar multicoloured design. P 13×13½ (90c) or 13½ ($4).

1933	90c. Type **225**	1·50	70
1934	$4 Pope John Paul II (28×42 mm)	5·50	5·50

No. 1933 was printed in sheetlets of 12 stamps and No. 1934 in sheetlets of four stamps, both with enlarged, illustrated margins.

226 Shareef Abdur-Rahim (Portland Trail Blazers)

2005 (26 July). National Basketball Association. T **226** and similar vert designs. Multicoloured. Litho. P 14.

1935	$1 Type **226**	1·00	90
1936	$1 Vince Carter (New Jersey Nets)	1·00	90
1937	$1 Shaun Livingston (Los Angeles Clippers)	1·00	90
1938	$1 Theo Ratliff (Portland Trail Blazers)	1·00	90
	a. Sheetlet. Nos. 1938×10 and 1938b×2	11·00	
1938b	$1 Portland Trail Blazers emblem	1·00	90
1939	$1 Rasheed Wallace (Detroit Pistons)	1·00	90
1935/39	Set of 5	5·50	5·00

Nos. 1935/7 and 1939 were each printed in sheetlets of 12 stamps with the margins illustrated with a further photograph of each player and a table of their statistics.

Nos. 1938/b were printed together, *se-tenant*, in sheetlets containing ten of No. 1938 and two of No. 1938b with illustrated margins as the other sheetlets.

ST. KITTS-NEVIS / Nevis

227 Dr Sun Yat-Sen

228 "Madonna and the Angels" (detail) (Fra Angelico)

2005 (19 Aug). TAIPEI 2005 International Stamp Exhibition. 80th Death Anniv of Dr Sun Yat-Sen (Chinese revolutionary leader). T **227** and similar vert designs. Multicoloured. Litho. P 14.

1940	$2 Type **227**	1·40	1·40
	a. Sheetlet. Nos. 1940/3	5·00	5·00
1941	$2 Wearing jacket and tie	1·40	1·40
1942	$2 In front of statue	1·40	1·40
1943	$2 In front of building	1·40	1·40
1940/3 Set of 4		5·00	5·00

Nos. 1940/3 were printed together, *se-tenant*, in sheetlets of four stamps with an enlarged, illustrated bottom margin.

(Litho Cartor)

2005 (1 Dec). Christmas. T **228** and similar multicoloured designs. P 14×13½.

1944	25c. Type **228**	35	15
1945	30c. "Madonna and the Child" (detail) (Filippo Lippi)	40	20
1946	90c. "Madonna and Child" (detail) (Giotto)	90	60
1947	$4 "Madonna of the Chair" (detail) (Raphael)	3·25	4·00
1944/7 Set of 4		4·50	4·50
MS1948 67×97 mm. $5 "Adoration of the Magi" (Giovanni Batista Tiepolo) (*horiz*). P 13½×14		3·75	4·25

229 "A Dog" (Ren Xun)

(Des Yuan Lee. Litho Cardon Enterprises, Taiwan)

2006 (3 Jan). Chinese New Year ("Year of the Dog"). Litho. P 13½.

1949	**229** 75c. multicoloured	1·00	1·00

No. 1949 was printed in sheetlets of four stamps with enlarged margins.

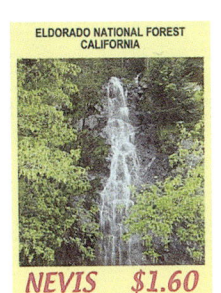

230 Eldorado National Forest, California

(Litho Cardon Enterprises, Taiwan)

2006 (3 Jan). Centenary of United States Forest Service (2005). T **230** and similar multicoloured designs. Litho. P 13½.

1950	$1.60 Type **230**	1·75	1·75
	a. Sheetlet. Nos. 1950/5	9·50	9·50
1951	$1.60 Pisgah National Forest, North Carolina	1·75	1·75
1952	$1.60 Chattahoochee-Oconee National Forests, Georgia	1·75	1·75
1953	$1.60 Nantahala National Forest, North Carolina	1·75	1·75
1954	$1.60 Bridger-Teton National Forest, Wyoming	1·75	1·75
1955	$1.60 Mount Hood National Forest, Oregon	1·75	1·75
1950/5 Set of 6		9·50	9·50
MS1956 Two sheets, each 104×70 mm. (a) $6 Klamath National Forest, California (*horiz*). (b) $6 The Source Rain Forest Walk, Nevis Set of 2 sheets		9·00	10·00

Nos. 1950/5 were printed together, *se-tenant*, in sheetlets of six stamps with enlarged illustrated margins.

231 Queen Elizabeth II wearing Garter Robes

(Litho CEC Security Printers)

2006 (20 Mar). 80th Birthday of Queen Elizabeth II. T **231** and similar vert designs. Multicoloured. P 13½.

1957	$2 Type **231**	2·00	2·00
	a. Sheetlet. Nos. 1957/60	7·25	7·25
1958	$2 Wearing white dress	2·00	2·00
1959	$2 Wearing tiara and evening dress	2·00	2·00
1960	$2 Waving, wearing white hat and gloves	2·00	2·00
1957/60 Set of 4		7·25	7·25
MS1961 120×120 mm. $5 Queen Elizabeth II, c. 1955		4·75	4·75

Nos. 1957/60 were printed together, *se-tenant*, in sheetlets of four stamps with enlarged illustrated margins.

232 Italy 1956 Winter Olympics 10l. Ski-jump Stamp

2006 (24 Apr). Winter Olympic Games, Turin. T **232** and similar multicoloured designs. Litho. P 14½ (25c., $1.20) or 13½ (others).

1962	25c. U.S.A. 1980 Winter Olympics 15c. downhill skiing stamp	35	25
1963	30c. Type **232**	35	25
1964	90c. Italy 1956 Winter Olympics 25l. ice stadium stamp	85	55
1965	$1.20 Emblem of Winter Olympic Games, Lake Placid, U.S.A., 1980	1·60	1·25
1966	$4 Italy 1956 Winter Olympics 60l. skating arena stamp	3·00	3·50
1967	$5 Emblem of Winter Olympic Games, Cortina d'Ampezzo, Italy 1956 (*vert*)	3·25	3·75
1963/7 Set of 4		8·50	8·50

233 Mahatma Gandhi

234 "The Anatomy Lesson of Dr. Tulp" (detail)

301

ST. KITTS-NEVIS / Nevis

(Litho CEC Security Printers)

2006 (27 May). Washington 2006 International Stamp Exhibition. Sheet 140×152 mm. P 11½.
1968 **233** $3 multicoloured .... 3·50 3·50

No. 1968 was printed in sheetlets of three stamps with enlarged illustrated margins.

(Litho Beijing Stamp Printing House)

2006 (23 June). 400th Birth Anniv of Rembrandt Harmenszoon van Rijn (artist). T **234** and similar vert designs. Multicoloured. P 13½.
1969	$2 Type **234**	1·50	1·50
	a. Sheetlet. Nos. 1969/72	5·50	5·50
1970	$2 "The Anatomy Lesson of Dr. Tulp" (detail of man leaning forward)	1·50	1·50
1971	$2 "The Anatomy Lesson of Dr. Tulp" (detail of man seen in profile)	1·50	1·50
1972	$2 "The Anatomy Lesson of Dr. Tulp" (detail)	1·50	1·50
1969/72 Set of 4		5·50	5·50
MS1973	70×100 mm. $6 "Bald-headed Old Man". Imperf	4·00	4·50

Nos. 1969/72 were printed together, *se-tenant*, in sheetlets of four stamps with enlarged illustrated margins.

235 Saturn 1B Launch KSC's from Launch Complex 39B

(Des Manuel Servin. Litho CEC Security Printers)

2006 (19 Sept). Space Anniversaries. T **235** and similar horiz designs. Multicoloured. P 13½.

(a) 30th Anniv (2005) of Apollo/Soyuz Test Project.
1974	$2 Type **235**	2·00	2·00
	a. Sheetlet. Nos. 1974/9	11·00	11·00
1975	$2 Astronaut Donald Slayton and cosmonaut Aleksey Leonov	2·00	2·00
1976	$2 Liftoff of Soyuz 19 from Baikonur Cosmodrome	2·00	2·00
1977	$2 Soyuz spacecraft seen from Apollo CM	2·00	2·00
1978	$2 American and Soviet crewmen	2·00	2·00
1979	$2 Apollo CSM with docking adapter seen from Soyuz	2·00	2·00
1974/9 Set of 6		11·00	11·00

(b) 30th Anniv of Viking 1 Landing on Mars
1980	$3 Titan/Centaur rocket lifting off from Cape Canaveral	2·50	2·50
	a. Sheetlet. Nos. 1980/3	9·00	9·00
1981	$3 Viking 1	2·50	2·50
1982	$3 Viking Lander	2·50	2·50
1983	$3 Global view of Mars taken from Viking 1	2·50	2·50
1980/3 Set of 4		9·00	9·00

Nos. 1974/9 and 1980/3 were each printed together, *se-tenant*, in sheetlets of six or four stamps with enlarged illustrated margins.

236 Christmas Tree, Charlestown Nevis

(Litho Cardon Enterprises, Taiwan)

2006 (8 Dec). Christmas. T **236** and similar multicoloured designs. Litho. P 13½.
1984	25c. Type **236**	40	25
1985	30c. Snowman and other decorations	40	25
1986	90c. Three white, Bath, Nevis reindeer and other decorations, Bath, Nevis	1·00	60
1987	$4 Decorated Christmas tree (*vert*)	4·25	5·00
1984/7 Set of 4		5·50	5·50
MS1988	100×70 mm. $6 Children meeting Santa	5·50	6·00

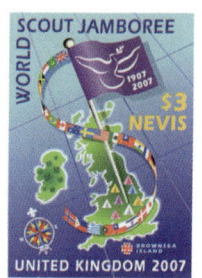

237 Map of United Kingdom and Centenary Flag

2007 (29 Jan). Centenary of World Scout Movement and 21st World Scout Jamboree, Chelmsford, England. T **237** and similar multicoloured design. Litho. P 13½.
1989	$3 Type **237**	2·25	2·50
MS1990	80×111 mm. $5 Centenary flag and streamer of national flags (*horiz*)	3·75	4·25

No. 1989 is printed in sheetlets of four stamps with enlarged illustrated right margins.

238 Marilyn Monroe

2007 (29 Jan). 80th Birth Anniv (2006) of Marilyn Monroe (actress). T **238** and similar vert designs. Multicoloured. Litho. P 13½.
1991	$2 Type **238**	1·40	1·50
	a. Sheetlet. Nos. 1991/4	5·00	5·50
1992	$2 Wearing necklace	1·40	1·50
1993	$2 Wearing pearl earrings	1·40	1·50
1994	$2 Wearing white dress	1·40	1·50
1991/4 Set of 4		5·00	5·50

Nos. 1991/4 were printed together, *se-tenant*, in sheetlets of four stamps with enlarged illustrated margins.

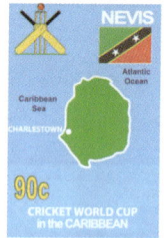

239 Outline Map of Nevis and Flag of St. Kitts and Nevis

240 Flame Helmet

(Des M. Brown. Litho BDT)

2007 (1 May). World Cup Cricket, West Indies. T **239** and similar vert designs. Multicoloured. P 14.
1995	90c. Type **239**	1·25	85
1996	$2 Runako Morton	2·75	3·00
MS1997	120×93 mm. $6 World Cup Cricket emblem ..	5·50	5·50

(Litho Cardon Enterprises)

2007 (5 July). Shells. T **240** and similar vert designs. Multicoloured. Litho. P 12½×13½.
1998	10c. Type **240**	10	15
1999	25c. Rooster tail conch	15	20
2000	30c. Three beaded periwinkles	15	20
2001	60c. Emperor helmet	35	40
2002	80c. Scotch bonnet	45	50
2003	90c. Milk conch	55	60
2004	$1 Beaded periwinkle	60	65
2005	$1.20 Alphabet cone	70	75
2006	$1.80 Measled cowrie	1·10	1·20

2007	$3 King helmet	1·75	1·90
2008	$5 Atlantic hairy triton	2·75	3·00
2009	$10 White lined mitre	5·00	5·50
2010	$20 Reticulated cowrie shell	11·25	11·50
1998/2010	Set of 14	22·00	23·00

241 *Pimenta racemosa* (wild cilliment)

242 *Battus zetides* (Zetides swallowtail)

2007 (23 July). Flowers of Nevis. T **241** and similar vert designs. Multicoloured. Litho. P 13½.
MS2011 108×131 mm. $2×4 Type **241**; *Abrus precatorius* (jumbie beads); *Lantanacamara* (wild sage); *Asclepias curassavica* (blood flower/milky-milky) .... 5·50 6·00
MS2012 70×100 mm. $6 *Tabebuia heterophylla* (pink trumpet) .... 3·75 4·00
The stamps and margins of No. MS2011 form a composite background design.

2007 (23 July). Butterflies of Nevis. T **242** and similar vert designs. Multicoloured. Litho. P 13½.
MS2013 131×108 mm. $2×4 Type **242**; *Parides hahnell* (Hahnel's amazon swallowtail); *Dismorphia spio* (Haitian mimic); *Hesperocharis graphites* (marbled white) .... 6·00 6·50
MS2014 100×70 mm. $6 *Papilio multicaudata* (three-tailed tiger swallowtail) .... 4·25 4·50
The stamps and margins of No. MS2013 form a composite background design.

243 Rainbow Parrotfish

2007 (23 July). Endangered Species. Rainbow Parrotfish (*Scarus guacamaia*). T **243** and similar horiz designs. Multicoloured. Litho. P 13½.
2015	$1.20 Type **243**	90	1·00
	a. Strip of 4. Nos. 2015/18	3·25	3·50
2016	$1.20 Pair	90	1·00
2017	$1.20 In close-up, facing to left	90	1·00
2018	$1.20 Facing to right	90	1·00
2015/18	Set of 4	2·50	2·75

MS2019 115×168 mm. Nos. 2015/18, each ×2............. 5·50 6·50
Nos. 2015/18 were printed together, *se-tenant*, as horizontal and vertical strips of four stamps in sheets of 16. The stamps within No. MS2019 are arranged in two blocks of Nos. 2015/18 separated by an illustrated gutter.

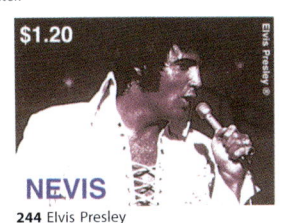

244 Elvis Presley

2007 (13 Aug). 30th Death Anniv of Elvis Presley. T **244** and similar horiz designs. Multicoloured. Litho. P 13½.
2020	$1.20 Type **244**	90	90
	a. Sheetlet. Nos. 2020/5	4·75	4·75
2021	$1.20 Wearing white jumpsuit, playing guitar	90	90
2022	$1.20 As No. 2021, but seen three-quarter length, spotlight at top right	90	90
2023	$1.20 Wearing black leather jacket	90	90
2024	$1.20 As No. 2023, seen three-quarter length	90	90
2025	$1.20 As Type **244**, seen in close-up	90	90
2020/2025	Set of 6	4·75	4·75

Nos. 2020/5 were printed together, *se-tenant*, in sheetlets of six stamps with enlarged illustrated top margins.

245 Concorde 02 on Ground

2007 (13 Aug). Concorde. T **245** and similar horiz designs. Multicoloured. Litho.P 13½.
2026	$1.20 Type **245**	1·10	1·10
	a. Sheetlet. Nos. 2026/31	6·00	6·00
2027	$1.20 Concorde 02 flying over snowy mountains (pale new blue inscriptions)	1·10	1·10
2028	$1.20 As Type **245** (lemon inscriptions)	1·10	1·10
2029	$1.20 As No. 2027 (lemon inscriptions)	1·10	1·10
2030	$1.20 As Type **245** (pale new blue inscriptions)	1·10	1·10
2031	$1.20 As No. 2027 (white inscriptions)	1·10	1·10
2026/31	Set of 6	6·00	6·00

MS2032 150×100 mm. $1.20×6 Concorde F-BTSD: Flying to right, dark blue background (over upper left part of globe); Flying to left, azure background (over map 'MERICA'); Flying right, dark blue background (over upper right part of globe); Flying left, azure background (over equator line); Flying right, dark blue background (over map of islands); Flying left, azure background (equator line at lower right) .... 7·00 7·00

Nos. 2026/31 were printed together, *se-tenant*, in sheetlets of six stamps with enlarged illustrated margins. They commemorate the Washington to Paris record flight of Concorde 02, the second pre-production aircraft, on September 26 1973. The stamps and margins of No. MS2032 form a composite background design showing a globe. No. MS2032 commemorates the eastbound round the world record of Concorde F-BTSD on August 15–16 1995.

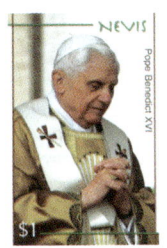

246 Diana, Princess of Wales

247 Pope Benedict XVI

2007 (13 Aug). Tenth Death Anniv of Diana, Princess of Wales. T **246** and similar vert designs. Multicoloured. Litho. P 13½.
2033	$2 Type **246**	1·50	1·50
	a. Sheetlet. Nos. 2033/6	5·50	5·50
2034	$2 Wearing black evening dress and choker	1·50	1·50
2035	$2 Wearing pale jacket and pearl necklace	1·50	1·50
2036	$2 Wearing white dress with narrow shoulder straps	1·50	1·50
2033/6	Set of 4	4·50	5·00

MS2037 70×100 mm. $6 Wearing blue and white jacket and hat .... 4·00 4·25
Nos. 2033/6 were printed together, *se-tenant*, in sheetlets of four stamps with enlarged illustrated left margins.

2007 (24 Oct). 80th Birthday of Pope Benedict XVI. Litho. P 13½.
2038	**247**	$1 multicoloured	1·40	1·40

No. 2038 was printed in sheetlets of eight stamps with enlarged illustrated margins.

248 Queen Elizabeth II and Prince Philip

303

ST. KITTS-NEVIS / Nevis

2007 (24 Oct). Diamond Wedding of Queen Elizabeth II and Prince Philip. T **248** and similar horiz designs. Multicoloured. Litho. P 13½.

2039	$1.20 Type **248**	2·00	2·00
	a. Sheetlet. Nos. 2039/44	11·00	11·00
2040	$1.20 Queen Elizabeth and Prince Philip waving	2·00	2·00
2041	$1.20 In Garter robes	2·00	2·00
2042	$1.20 Waving from Coronation coach at Golden Jubilee	2·00	2·00
2043	$1.20 Waving from carriage at Ascot	2·00	2·00
2044	$1.20 Waving from balcony	2·00	2·00
2039/44 Set of 6		11·00	11·00

Nos. 2039/44 were printed together, *se-tenant*, in sheetlets of six stamps with enlarged illustrated right margins.

249 *Begonias and Rock*

(Litho Cardon Enterprises, Taiwan)

2007 (28 Nov). 50th Death Anniv of Qi Baishi (artist). T **249** and similar vert designs showing paintings. Multicoloured. P 12½.

2045	$3 Type **249**	2·00	2·25
	a. Sheetlet. Nos. 2045/8	7·25	8·00
2046	$3 *Mother and Child 1*	2·00	2·25
2047	$3 *Fish and Bait 1*	2·00	2·25
2048	$3 *Solitary Hero* (bird)	2·00	2·25
2045/8 Set of 4		7·25	8·00
MS2049 100×70 mm. $6 *Chrysanthemums and Insects* (28×42 mm). P 13½		3·75	4·00

Nos. 2045/8 were printed together, *se-tenant*, in sheetlets of four stamps with enlarged illustrated margins.

250 *Westland Sea King Naval Helicopter*

(Litho Cardon Enterprises, Taiwan)

2007 (28 Nov). Centenary of the First Helicopter Flight. T **250** and similar multicoloured designs. P 13½.

MS2050	$3×4 Type **250**; Schweizer N330TT light utility helicopter; Sikorsky R-4/R-5 first production helicopter; PZL Swidnik W-3 Sokol	11·00	11·00
MS2051	100×70 mm. $6 MIL V-12 heavy transport helicopter	6·50	6·50

251 *Jacqueline Kennedy*

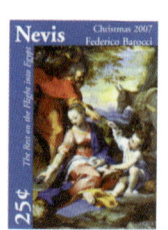

252 *The Rest on the Flight into Egypt* (Federico Barocci)

(Litho Cardon Enterprises, Taiwan)

2007 (28 Nov). 90th Birth Anniv of John F. Kennedy (US President 1960–3). T **251** and similar vert designs. Multicoloured. P 13½.

2052	$3 Type **251**	2·25	2·25
	a. Sheetlet. Nos. 2052/5	8·00	8·00
2053	$3 John F. Kennedy (in library)	2·25	2·25
2054	$3 John F. Kennedy (clapping)	2·25	2·25
2055	$3 Vice President Lyndon B. Johnson	2·25	2·25
2052/5 Set of 4		8·00	8·00

Nos. 2052/5 were printed together, *se-tenant*, in sheetlets of four stamps with enlarged illustrated margins.

(Litho Cardon Enterprises, Taiwan)

2007 (3 Dec). Christmas. Paintings. T **252** and similar vert designs. Multicoloured. P 11½.

2056	25c. Type **252**	30	25
2057	30c. *The Annunciation* (detail) (Federico Barocci)	30	25
2058	90c. *The Annunciation* (Cavalier d'Arpino)	80	65
2059	$4 *The Rest on the Flight into Egypt* (Francesco Mancini)	3·50	4·00
2056/9 Set of 4		4·50	4·75
MS2060 100×70 mm. $5 *The Virgin and Child between Saints Peter and Paul and the Twelve Magistrates of the Rota* (Antoniazzo Romano). P 13½		3·75	4·00

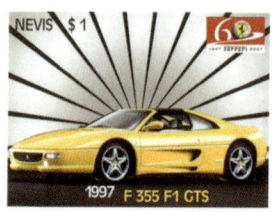

253 *F 355 F1 GTS, 1997*

2007 (10 Dec). 60th Anniv of Ferrari. T **253** and similar horiz designs. Multicoloured. Litho. P 13½.

2061	$1 Type **253**	80	80
	a. Sheetlet. Nos. 2061/8	5·75	5·75
2062	$1 412, 1985	80	80
2063	$1 158 F1, 1964	80	80
2064	$1 375 MM, 1953	80	80
2065	$1 330 P4, 1967	80	80
2066	$1 512 BB LM, 1978	80	80
2067	$1 312 B3-74, 197460	80	80
2068	$1 308 GTB Quattrovalvole, 1982	80	80
2061/8 Set of 8		5·75	5·75

Nos. 2061/8 were printed together, *se-tenant*, in sheetlets of eight stamps.

254 *Yacht*

255 *Cycling*

2007 (31 Dec). 32nd Americas Cup Yachting Championship, Valencia, Spain. T **254** and similar vert designs. Multicoloured. Litho. P 13½.

2069	$1.20 Type **254**	1·50	1·75
	a. Block of 4. Nos. 2069/72	8·50	9·50
2070	$1.80 White-hulled yacht	2·00	2·25
2071	$3 Yacht, 'T Systems' on sail	2·50	2·75
2072	$5 Yachts, sail with orange stripes in foreground	3·50	3·75
2069/72 Set of 4		8·50	9·50

Nos. 2069/723 were printed together, *se-tenant*, as blocks of four stamps in sheetlets of 16.

2008 (8 Mar). Olympic Games, Beijing. T **255** and similar vert designs. Multicoloured. Litho. P 13.

2073	$2 Type **255**	2·25	2·25
	a. Sheetlet. Nos. 2073/6	8·00	8·00
2074	$2 Kayaking	2·25	2·25
2075	$2 Yachting	2·25	2·25
2076	$2 Three-day eventing	2·25	2·25
2073/6 Set of 4		8·00	8·00

Nos. 2073/6 were printed together, *se-tenant*, in sheetlets of four stamps with enlarged illustrated margins.

ST. KITTS-NEVIS / Nevis

256 Mt. Masada
257 Elvis Presley 

2008 (21 May). Israel 2008 World Stamp Championship, Tel-Aviv. Natural Sites and Scenes of Israel. T **256** and similar horiz designs. Multicoloured. Litho. P 11½.

2077	$1.50 Type **256**	2·00	2·00
	a. Sheetlet. Nos. 2077/80	7·25	7·25
2078	$1.50 Red Sea and desert mountains	2·00	2·00
2079	$1.50 Dead Sea	2·00	2·00
2080	$1.50 Sea of Galilee	2·00	2·00
2077/80	Set of 4	5·00	5·50
MS2081	100×70 mm. $5 Mt. Hermon	6·00	6·00

Nos. 2077/80 were printed together, *se-tenant*, in sheetlets of four stamps with enlarged illustrated margins.

2008 (3 Sept). 40th Anniv of Elvis Presley's '68 Special'. T **257** and similar vert designs. Multicoloured. Litho. P 13½.

2082	$1.80 Type **257**	1·40	1·50
	a. Sheetlet. Nos. 2082/7	7·50	8·00
2083	$1.80 Wearing black leather, facing forward	1·40	1·50
2084	$1.80 Standing, seen three-quarter length (red background)	1·40	1·50
2085	$1.80 Wearing black leather, facing left	1·40	1·50
2086	$1.80 Wearing blue shirt	1·40	1·50
2087	$1.80 Wearing black leather, facing right	1·40	1·50
2082/7	Set of 6	7·50	8·00

Nos. 2082/7 were printed together, *se-tenant*, in sheetlets of six stamps with enlarged illustrated margins.

258 Muhammad Ali and Opponent
259 Pope Benedict XVI 

(Litho)

2008 (3 Sept). Muhammad Ali (world heavyweight boxing champion, 1964, 1974–8). T **258** and similar multicoloured designs. P 11½×12 ($1.80) or 13½ ($2).

2088	$1.80 Type **258**	1·40	1·50
	a. Sheetlet. Nos. 2088/93	7·50	8·00
2089	$1.80 In ring with fists raised, opponent at right	1·50	1·75
2090	$1.80 Punched by opponent	1·50	1·75
2091	$1.80 Seated by ring ropes	1·50	1·75
2092	$1.80 With arms raised in victory	1·50	1·75
2093	$1.80 Muhammad Ali and trophy	1·40	1·50
2094	$2 In profile, speaking (37×50 *mm*)	4·50	5·00
	a. Sheetlet. Nos. 2094/97	5·50	6·25
2095	$2 Seen full face, speaking (37×50 *mm*)	1·75	1·75
2096	$2 Looking towards left (37×50 *mm*)	1·75	1·75
2097	$2 Eyes looking to right, speaking (37×50 *mm*)	1·75	1·75
2088/97	Set of 10	13·00	14·00

Nos. 2088/93 and 2094/7 were each printed together, *se-tenant*, in sheetlets of six or four stamps with enlarged illustrated margins.

(Litho)

2008 (17 Sept). First Visit of Pope Benedict XVI to the United States. Sheet 178×127 mm containing T **259** and similar vert designs. P 13½.

MS2098	$2×4 multicoloured	7·25	7·25

The four stamps within No. MS2098 are as Type **259** but have slightly different backgrounds at the foot of the stamps, the middle two showing parts of the UN emblem.

260 Geothermal Well, Spring Hill, discovered June 2008
261 Voyager I 

(Litho)

2008 (19 Sept). 25th Anniv of Independence. P 11½×11.

2099	**260** $5 multicoloured	4·50	5·00

(Litho)

2008 (3 Dec). 50 Years of Space Exploration and Satellites. T **261** and similar vert designs. Multicoloured. P 13.

2100	$1.50 Type **261**	1·75	1·75
	a. Sheetlet. Nos. 2100/5	9·50	9·50
2101	$1.50 *Voyager I*, Io, and part of Ganymede and Callisto	1·75	1·75
2102	$1.50 *Voyager I*, Europa and part of Ganymede and Callisto	1·75	1·75
2103	$1.50 *Voyager I*	1·75	1·75
2104	$1.50 *Voyager I*, Dione and part of Titan	1·75	1·75
2105	$1.50 *Voyager I*, Enceladus and part of Titan	1·75	1·75
2106	$1.50 *Galileo* spacecraft	1·75	1·75
	a. Sheetlet. Nos. 2106/11	9·50	9·50
2107	$1.50 *Galileo* (without sun shields)	1·75	1·75
2108	$1.50 *Galileo* Probe	1·75	1·75
2109	$1.50 Technical drawing of *Galileo* Probe	1·75	1·75
2110	$1.50 *Galileo* passing Io	1·75	1·75
2111	$1.50 Technical drawing of *Galileo*	1·75	1·75
2112	$2 Van Allen radiation belt	1·75	1·75
	a. Sheetlet. Nos. 2112/15	6·25	6·25
2113	$2 Technical drawing of *Explorer I*	1·75	1·75
2114	$2 James Van Allen	1·75	1·75
2115	$2 *Explorer I* above Earth	1·75	1·75
2116	$2 Technical drawing of *Apollo 11* Command Module	1·75	1·75
	a. Sheetlet. Nos. 2116/19	6·25	6·25
2117	$2 Saturn V Apollo Programme Launcher	1·75	1·75
2118	$2 Edwin 'Buzz' Aldrin Jr. walking on Moon, 1969	1·75	1·75
2119	$2 Technical drawing of *Apollo 11* Lunar Module	1·75	1·75
2100/19	Set of 20	30·00	30·00

Nos. 2100/5, 2106/11, 2112/15 and 2116/19 were each printed together, *se-tenant*, in sheetlets of six or four stamps with enlarged illustrated margins.

262 Roast Pork
263 Pres. Barack Obama 

(Litho)

2008 (5 Dec). Christmas. T **262** and similar multicoloured designs. P 11½.

2120	25c. Type **262**	20	20
2121	30c. Fruit-topped sponge cake	25	20
2122	80c. Pumpkin pie	70	60
2123	90c. Sorrel drink	75	60
2124	$2 Fruit cake	1·90	2·50
2120/4	Set of 4	3·50	3·50
MS2125	100×70 mm. $6 Baked ham and turkey (*vert*)	5·00	5·50

(Litho Cardon Enterprises Taiwan)

2009 (20 Jan). Inauguration of President Barack Obama. Sheet 180×100 mm containing T **263** and similar horiz designs showing Pres. Obama. Multicoloured. P 11½×12.

MS2126	$3×4 Type **263**; US flag in background; White House garden in background; Black background	5·50	6·00

ST. KITTS-NEVIS / Nevis

264 Processed Agricultural Products

(Litho)

2009 (26 Mar). 15th Anniv of Agriculture Open Day. T **264** and similar horiz designs. Multicoloured. P 11½ (Nos. 2127/30) or 13 (**MS**2131).

2127	25c. Type **264**	25	20
2128	30c. Fruits	30	20
2129	90c. Goats	80	60
2130	$5 Plant propagation	4·50	5·00
2127/30	Set of 4	5·25	5·50
MS2131	100×70 mm. $6 Entertainment	5·00	5·50

265 Kangxi, Second Emperor of the Qing Dynasty

(Litho)

2009 (10 Apr). China 2009 World Stamp Exhibition, Luoyang (1st issue). Kangxi, Second Emperor of the Qing Dynasty (1654–1722). T **265** and similar vert designs. Multicoloured. P 12½.

MS2132 146×100 mm. $1.40×4 Type **265**; Wearing gold with blue armlets; Wearing gold with gold armlets; At desk writing......... 5·25 5·75
See also No. **MS**2133.

266 Shooting

(Litho)

2009 (10 Apr). China 2009 World Stamp Exhibition, Luoyang (2nd issue). Sports of the Summer Games. P 14×14½.

MS2133 137×98 mm. $1.40×4 Type **266**; Field hockey; Taekwondo; Softball......... 5·25 5·75

267 Marine Iguana (*Amblyrhynchus cristatus*)

268 Amazon River Dolphin (*Inia geoffrensis*)

(Litho)

2009 (15 June). Birth Bicentenary of Charles Darwin (naturalist and evolutionary theorist). T **267** and similar multicoloured designs. P 11½ (**MS**2134) or 13½ (**MS**2135).

MS2134 Type **267**; Statue of Charles Darwin, Shrewsbury, England; Platypus (*Ornithorhynchus anatinus*); Vampire bat (*Desmodus rotundus* incorrectly inscr *Desmodus d'Orbigny*); Portrait of Charles Darwin in late 1830s by George Richmond; Large ground-finch (*Geospiza magnirostris*)......... 10·00 11·00

MS2135 100×70 mm. $6 Charles Darwin (photograph), 1881 (37×50 mm)......... 4·75 5·50

(Litho)

2009 (15 June). Dolphins and Whales. T **268** and similar horiz designs. Multicoloured. Litho. P 13½.

MS2136 140×116 mm. $2×6 Type **268**; Indus river dolphin (*Platanista minor*); Atlantic white-sided dolphin (*Lagenorhynchus acutus*); La Plata dolphin; Peale's dolphin (*Lagenorhynchus australis*); White-beaked dolphin (*Lagenorhynchus albirostris*)......... 10·00 11·00

MS2137 100×70 mm. $3×2 Killer whale (*Orcinus orca*); Pygmy killer whale (*Feresa attenuata*)......... 5·00 5·00

MS2138 100×70 mm. $3×2 Long-finned pilot whale (*Globicephala melas*); Short-finned pilot whale (*Globicephala macrorhynchus*)......... 5·00 5·00

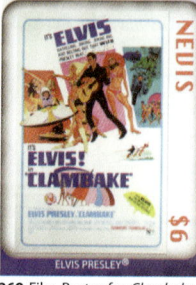

269 Film Poster for *Clambake*

270 Michael Jackson

(Litho)

2009 (15 June). Elvis Presley in Film *Clambake*. P 13.

MS2139 125×90 mm. $6 Type **269**......... 4·50 4·50
MS2140 90×125 mm. $6 Wearing black stetson and white jacket......... 4·50 4·50
MS2141 90×125 mm. $6 On motorcycle......... 4·50 4·50
MS2142 125×90 mm. $6 Wearing white jacket......... 4·50 4·50

(Litho)

2009 (20 Aug). Michael Jackson Commemoration. Two sheets, each 178×127 mm, containing T **270** and similar multicoloured designs. P 11½ (**MS**2143) or 11½×12 (**MS**2144).

MS2143 Wearing black: Type **270** (pale blue inscr); Three-quarter length (yellow inscr); Type **270** (lavender inscr); Three-quarter length (red inscr)......... 5·75 5·75

MS2144 Wearing white: With both hands raised to face; In profile; With microphone; With both arms raised......... 6·50 6·50

On No. **MS**2143 the colours given are for the country inscription 'NEVIS'.

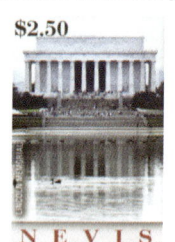

271 Lincoln Memorial

272 Moe, Curly and Larry

(Litho)

2009 (20 Aug). Birth Bicentenary of Abraham Lincoln (US President 1861–5). Sheet 175×136 mm containing T **271** and similar vert designs. Multicoloured. P 13.

MS2145 Type **271**; Statue of Abraham Lincoln; Head and upper body of statue; Lincoln Memorial from air......... 6·25 6·25

(Litho)

2009 (20 Aug). The Three Stooges. Sheet 130×150 mm containing T **272** and similar vert designs. Multicoloured. Litho. P 11½.

MS2146 Type **272**; Curly; Moe; Larry......... 6·25 6·25

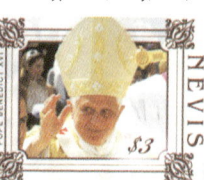

273 Pope Benedict XVI wearing Mitre

274 *Genipa americana*

ST. KITTS-NEVIS / Nevis

(Litho)

2009 (20 Aug). Visit of Pope Benedict XVI to Israel. Sheet 100×150 mm containing T **273** and similar horiz designs. Multicoloured. P 11½.

MS2147	Type **273**; As Type **273** (gold frame); Pope Benedict XVI wearing skull cap (brown frame); Pope wearing skull cap (gold frame)	8·00	8·00

(Litho)

2009 (1 Dec). Flowers of the Caribbean. T **274** and similar horiz designs. Multicoloured. P 13.

2148	25c. Type **274**	25	25
2149	30c. *Clusia rosea*	30	25
2150	80c. *Browallia americana*	85	70
2151	90c. *Bidens alba*	90	75
2152	$1 *Begonia odorata*	1·00	1·00
2153	$5 *Jatropha gossypiifolia*	4·50	4·75
2148/53	Set of 6	7·00	7·00
MS2154	150×100 mm. $2.50×4 *Crantzia cristata*; *Selaginella flabellata*; *Hibiscus tiliaceus*; *Heliconia psittacorum*	8·00	8·00

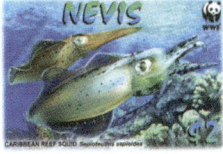

275 Caribbean Reef Squid

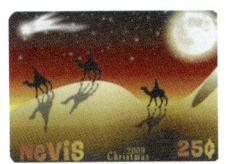

276 Journey of the Magi

(Des Owen Bell. Litho)

2009 (1 Dec). Endangered Species. Caribbean Reef Squid (*Sepioteuthis sepioidea*). T **275** and similar horiz designs. Multicoloured. P 13½.

2155	$2 Type **275**	1·75	1·75
	a. Strip of 4. Nos. 2155/8	6·25	6·25
2156	$2 One squid	1·75	1·75
2157	$2 One squid (body bent showing head and tail)	1·75	1·75
2158	$2 Two squid (foreground squid swimming to left)	1·75	1·75
2155/8	Set of 5	6·25	6·25
MS2159	112×165 mm. Nos. 2155/8, each ×2	12·00	12·00

Nos. 2155/8 were printed together, *se-tenant*, as horizontal and vertical strips of four in sheetlets of 16.

No. **MS**2159 contains two blocks of Nos. 2155/8 separated by an enlarged illustrated gutter.

(Litho)

2009 (7 Dec). Christmas. T **276** and similar horiz designs. Multicoloured. P 14½×14.

2160	25c. Type **276**	25	20
2161	30c. Nativity with magi on star	30	25
2162	90c. Magi and camel in stars	90	80
2163	$5 Nativity with angels	4·50	5·00
2160/63	Set of 4	5·50	5·75

277 Neil Armstrong and Saturn 5 Rocket

278 Engine of Dino 156. F2, 1957

(Litho)

2009 (30 Dec). 40th Anniv of First Manned Moon Landing. International Year of Astronomy. T **277** and similar horiz designs. Multicoloured. P 11½×12 (**MS**2164) or 11½ (**MS**2165).

MS2164	150×100 mm. $2.50×4 Type **277**; Lunar Module, Buzz Aldrin and Michael Collins; Command Module in Moon orbit; Lunar Module leaving the Moon	8·00	8·00
MS2165	100×70 mm. $6 Neil Armstrong and Lunar Module taking off	5·00	5·00

(Litho)

2010 (3 Mar). Ferrari Cars. T **278** and similar horiz designs. Multicoloured. P 12.

2166	$1.25 Type **278**	1·25	1·25
2167	$1.25 DINO 156 F2, 1957 (car no. 122)	1·25	1·25
2168	$1.25 Diagram of engine and chassis of 125 S, 1947	1·25	1·25
2169	$1.25 125 S, 1947 (car no. 56)	1·25	1·25
2170	$1.25 Exhaust pipes of 553 F2, 1953	1·25	1·25
2171	$1.25 553 F2, 1953	1·25	1·25
2172	$1.25 Engine of 500 F2, 1951	1·25	1·25
2173	$1.25 500 F2, 1951 (car no. 15)	1·25	1·25
2166/73	Set of 8	9·00	9·00

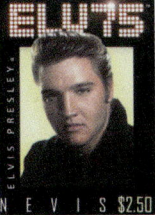

279 Elvis Presley

280 *Psilocybe guilartensis*

2010 (3 Mar). 75th Birth Anniv of Elvis Presley. Sheet 180×140 mm containing T **279** and similar vert designs. Multicoloured. P 12×11½.

MS2174	$2.50×4 Type **279**; Wearing brown jacket and tie; Wearing cream jacket; Wearing pale grey shirt	6·50	6·50

(Litho)

2010 (3 Mar). Fungi. T **280** and similar vert designs. Multicoloured. P 11½.

2175	25c. Type **280**	25	20
2176	80c. *Alboleptonia flavifolia*	80	75
2177	$1 *Agaricus* sp.	1·00	1·00
2178	$1 *Agaricus* sp.	1·00	1·00
2175/2178	Set of 4	2·75	2·75
MS2179	125×158 mm. $1.50×6 *Psilocybe portoricensis*; *Boletus ruborculus*; *Psilocybe plutonia* (one mushroom); *Alboleptonia largentii*; *Psilocybe plutonia* (three mushrooms); *Collybiaaurea*	5·50	5·50

281 Great Blue Heron (*Ardea herodias*)

282 John F. Kennedy

(Litho)

2010 (21 May). Birds of Nevis. T **281** and similar multicoloured designs. P 11½×12 (**MS**2185) or 11½ (others).

2180	30c. Type **281**	40	25
2181	90c. Magnificent frigatebird (*Fregata magnificens*)	1·00	75
2182	$1 Masked booby (*Sula dactylatra*)	1·10	1·00
2183	$5 Great egret (*Ardea alba*)	4·50	5·00
2180/83	Set of 4	6·25	6·25
MS2184	150×110 mm. $2×4 White-tailed tropicbird (*Phaethon lepturus*); Audubon's shearwater (*Puffinusl herminieri*); Red-billed tropicbird (*Phaethon aethereus*); Leach's storm-petrel (*Oceanodroma leucorhoa*) (all vert)	8·00	8·00
MS2185	120×80 mm. $3 Brown pelican (*Pelecanus occidentalis*); $3 Brown booby (*Sula leucogaster*)	8·00	8·00

(Litho)

2010 (21 May). 50th Anniv of Election of Pres. John F. Kennedy (1st issue). Two sheets, each 130×100 mm, containing T **282** and similar vert designs. Multicoloured. P 13½.

MS2186	$3×4 Type **282**; Nikita Khrushchev; Nikita Khrushchev seated; Pres. Kennedy seated)	6·50	6·50
MS2187	$3×4 Richard NIxon (Republican Candidate); John F. Kennedy (Democratic Candidate); John F. Kennedy (Democratic Candidate) (black/white photo); Richard Nixon (Republican Candidate) (black/white photo)	6·50	6·50

283 Four Brownies and Leader

284 Minke Whale (*Balaenoptera acutorostrata*)

ST. KITTS-NEVIS / Nevis

2010 (21 May). Centenary of Girlguiding. T **283** and similar multicoloured designs. P 11½×12 (**MS**2188) or 11½ (**MS**2189).

MS2188 150×100 mm. $3×4 Type **283**; Four guides; Guide abseiling; Three guides	7·00	7·00
MS2189 70×100 mm. $6 Four guides (*vert*)	5·00	5·00

(Litho)

2010 (14 July). Sea Mammals of the Caribbean. T **284** and similar horiz designs. Multicoloured. P 13.

2190	$1.20 Type **284**	1·75	1·25
2191	$1.80 Northern right whale (*Eubalaena glacialis*)	2·25	1·75
2192	$3 Fin whale (*Balaenoptera physalus*)	3·75	4·25
2193	$3 Sei whale (*Balaenoptera borealis*)	3·75	4·25
2190/2193 Set of 4		10·50	10·50
MS2194 101×70 mm. $3 Caribbean monk seal (*Monachus tropicalis*); $3 West Indian manatee (*Trichechus manatus*)		6·00	6·00
MS2195 99×70 mm. $6 Blue whale (*Balaenoptera musculus*)		6·00	6·00

285 "VOTE KENNEDY FOR PRESIDENT" Badge

286 Heart-lipped Brassavola (*Brassavola venosa*)

(Litho)

2010 (8 Sep). 50th Anniv of Election of Pres. John F. Kennedy (2nd issue). Campaign Badges. Sheet 182×122 mm. T **285** and similar circular designs. Multicoloured. P 14.

MS2196 $2×4 Type **285**; Portrait and "FOR PRESIDENT JOHN F. KENNEDY"; "KENNEDY JOHNSON"; Portraits and "AMERICA NEEDS KENNEDY JOHNSON"	7·00	7·00

(Litho)

2010 (8 Sep). Orchids of the Caribbean. T **286** and similar multicoloured designs. P 11½×12 (**MS**2197) or 11½ (**MS**2198).

MS2197 150×100 mm. $2×6 Type **286**; Waunakee Sunset (*Phragmepidium* Jason Fisher); Moss-loving Cranichis (*Cranichismuscosa*); Longclaw orchid (*Eltroplectris calcarata*); Golden yellow cattleya (*Cattleya aurea*); Fat cat (*Zygoneria* Adelaide Meadows)	10·00	10·00
MS2198 100×70 mm. $6 Von Martin's Brassavola (*Brassavola martiana*) (*vert*)	5·00	5·00

287 Bertha Von Suttner and Henri Dunant

288 *Annunciation* (Paolo Uccello), c. 1420

(Litho)

2010 (8 Sep). Death Centenary of Henri Dunant (founder of Red Cross). T **287** and similar horiz designs, each showing inset portrait of Henri Dunant. Multicoloured. P 13.

MS2199 151×100 mm. Type **287**; Victor Hugo; Charles Dickens; Harriet Beecher Stowe	2·25	2·25
MS2200 71×101 mm. $6 Abolition of slavery, Washington DC, 1862	5·00	5·00

(Litho)

2010 (6 Dec). Christmas. T **288** and similar vert designs. Multicoloured. P 12.

2201	30c. Type **288**	30	20
2202	90c. The Altarpiece of the Rose Garlands (Albrecht Dürer)	80	50
2203	$1.80 As 30c.	1·50	1·50
2204	$2 Sistine Madonna (Raffaello Sanzlo da Urbino), c. 1513	1·75	1·75
2205	$2.30 As $2	2·00	2·25
2206	$3 The Adoration of the Magi (Giotto di Bondone), c. 1305	2·75	3·25
2201/2206 Set of 6		8·25	8·50

289 Princess Diana

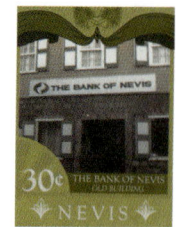

290 Bank of Nevis Building, Charlestown

(Litho)

2010 (6 Dec). Princess Diana Commemoration. T **289** and similar vert designs. Multicoloured. P 12.

MS2207 130×150 mm. $2×6 Type **289**×2; Wearing white jacket and tiara; Wearing white hat and jacket×2	9·50	9·50
MS2208 140×100 mm. $3 Wearing white sleeveless dress×4	2·50	2·50

(Litho)

2010 (9 Dec). 25th Anniv of the Bank of Nevis. T **290** and similar vert designs. Multicoloured. P 11½.

2209	30c. Type **290**	30	20
2210	$5 Projected new Bank of Nevis building	4·50	5·00

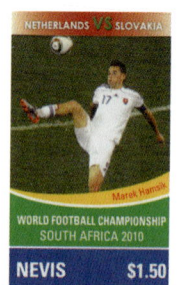

291 Marek Hamsik (Slovakia)

292 Abraham Lincoln

(Litho)

2010 (9 Dec). World Cup Football Championship, South Africa. T **291** and similar vert designs. Multicoloured. P 12.

MS2211 131×155 mm. $1.50×6 Netherlands vs. Slovakia: Type **291**; Giovanni Van Bronckhorst (Netherlands); Robert Vittek (Slovakia); Eljero Elia (Netherlands); Miroslav Stoch (Slovakia); Dirk Kuyt (Netherlands)	6·50	6·50
MS2212 130×155 mm. $1.50×6 Brazil vs. Chile: Lucio (Brazil); Alexis Sanchez (Chile); Dani Alves (Brazil); Arturo Vidal (Chile); Gilberto Silva (Brazil); Rodrigo Tello (Chile)	6·50	6·50
MS2213 130×155 mm. $1.50×6 Paraguay vs. Japan: Paulo Da Silva (Paraguay); Yoshito Okubo (Japan); Edgar Barreto (Paraguay); Yuichi Komano (Japan); Cristian Riveros (Paraguay); Yasuhito Endo (Japan)	6·50	6·50
MS2214 130×155 mm. $1.50×6 Spain vs. Portugal: Liedson (Portugal); Xavi Hernandez (Spain); Simao (Portugal); Jasper Juinen (Spain); Cristiano Ronaldo (Portugal); David Villa (Spain)	6·50	6·50
MS2215 85×90 mm. $1.50 Bert van Marwijk (Netherlands); $1.50 Joris Mathijsen	2·50	2·50
MS2216 85×90 mm. $1.50 Dunga (coach, Brazil); Kaka (Brazil)	2·50	2·50
MS2217 85×90 mm. $1.50 Gerardo Martino (coach, Paraguay); $1.50 Roque Santa Cruz	2·50	2·50
MS2218 85×90 mm. $1.50 Vicente del Bosque (coach, Spain); Sergio Ramos (Spain)	2·50	2·50

(Litho)

2010 (10 Dec). Birth Bicentenary (2009) of Abraham Lincoln (US President, 1861-5). T **292** and similar vert designs. Multicoloured. P 11½ (**MS**2219) or 12×11½ (**MS**2220).

MS2219 100×150 mm. $2 Type **292**×4	6·00	6·00
MS2220 110×150 mm. $2×4 Abraham Lincoln portraits: With sepia background; With grey background; Oval portrait with white background but facing forwards; Black background	6·00	6·00

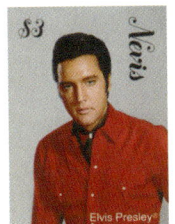

ST. KITTS-NEVIS / Nevis

293 Elvis Presley

(Litho)

2011 (10 Feb). Elvis Presley Commemoration. T **293** and similar vert design. Multicoloured. P 14×14½.
MS2221 100×168 mm. $3 Type **293**×4 .... 2·50 2·50
MS2222 167×100 mm. $3 Elvis Presley (wearing black jacket)×4 .... 2·50 2·50

294 Buckingham Palace

(Litho)

2010 (30 Dec). Royal Engagement. T **294** and similar multicoloured designs. P 11½.
MS2223 130×140 mm. $3×4 Type **294**; Miss Catherine Middleton (black/white photo); Coat of arms of Prince William of Wales (circular 38 mm diameter); Prince William (black/white photo) .... 2·50 2·50
MS2224 130×140 mm. $3×4 Prince William and Miss Catherine Middleton; Miss Catherine Middleton (wearing red jacket and black hat); Coat of arms of Prince William of Wales (circular 38 mm diameter); Prince William (colour photo) .... 3·25 3·25
MS2225 70×120 mm. $6 Prince William and Miss Catherine Middleton (40×30 mm) .... 5·00 5·00

Nos. MS2223/4 each contain a central circular stamp surrounded by three semi-circular stamps as T **294**.

295 Pres. Barack Obama and Mrs. Michelle Obama

296 Pope John Paul II

(Litho)

2010 (10 Dec). Visit of President Barack Obama to India. T **295** and similar multicoloured designs. P 14×14½ (MS2226) or 14½×14 (MS2227).
MS2226 157×100 mm. $3×4 Type **295**; Pres. Obama addressing Inidan students in Mumbai; Pres. Obama signing condolence book for Mumbai terror attack; Pres. Obama with Indian Prime Minister Singh .... 9·00 10·50
MS2227 70×100 mm. $6 Pres. Obama addressing Indian students in Mumbai (horiz) .... 4·75 5·00

(Litho)

2011 (10 Feb). Fifth Death Anniv of Pope John Paul II. T **296** and similar vert design. P 14×14½.
MS2228 110×170 mm. $3 Type **296**×4 .... 2·25 2·50
MS2229 110×170 mm. $4 Pope John Paul II wearing red brimmed hat×4 .... 3·25 3·25

297 Mahatma Gandhi    **298** Elvis Presley

(Litho)

2011 (30 Mar). Indipex 2011 International Stamp Exhibition, Delhi. Mahatma Gandhi. Two sheets, each 150×100 mm, containing T **297** and similar vert design. Multicoloured. P 12.
MS2230 $3 Type **297**×4 .... 2·50 2·50
MS2231 $3 Mahatma Gandhi (facing left)×4 .... 2·50 2·50

(Litho)

2011 (30 Mar). Elvis Presley Commemoration. Two sheets, each 130×170 mm, containing T **298** and similar multicoloured designs. P 13 (with one elliptical hole on each vert (MS2232) or horiz (MS2233) side).
MS2232 $3×4 Type **298**; Elvis Presley wearing cap; Head tilted to left; In profile .... 2·50 2·50
MS2233 $3×4 Elvis Presley smiling, wearing dark jacket; Singing, wearing white jacket and bow tie; Singing, wearing dark shirt; Smiling, wearing white (all vert) .... 2·50 2·50

299 Pope Benedict XVI

(Litho)

2011 (30 Mar). Pope Benedict XVI. T **299** and similar multicoloured designs. P 13.
MS2234 109×173 mm. $3×4 As Type **299** but with different backgrounds showing interior of Basilica: Type **299** (windows in dome); Top of pillar at bottom left; Pillars; Statue with cross at foot .... 2·50 2·50
MS2235 180×140 mm. $3 Pope Benedict XVI (in profile) (vert)×4 .... 2·50 2·50

300 Elvis Presley as Guy Lambert in *Double Trouble*, 1967   **301** Queen Elizabeth II

(Litho)

2011 (30 Mar). Elvis Presley in *Double Trouble*. T **300** and similar multicoloured designs. P 12½.
MS2236 90×125 mm. $6 Type **300** .... 5·00 5·00
MS2237 125×90 mm. $6 Poster for *Double Trouble* ...... 5·00 5·00
MS2238 90×125 mm. $6 Elvis Presley (wearing grey jacket and bow tie) (horiz) .... 5·00 5·00
MS2239 125×90 mm. $6 Elvis Presley playing guitar ... 5·00 5·00

(Litho)

2011 (4 Apr). 85th Birthday of Queen Elizabeth II and 90th Birthday of Prince Philip. Two sheets, each 149×100 mm, containing T **301** and similar vert designs. Multicoloured. P 12 (MS2240) or 13 (with one elliptical hole on each horiz side) (MS2241).
MS2240 $2 Type **301**×2 $2 Queen Elizabeth II (wearing mauve)×2 .... 3·50 3·50
MS2241 $2 Prince Philip×4 .... 3·50 3·50

309

ST. KITTS-NEVIS / Nevis

302 Meadow Argus (*Junonia villida*)

(Litho)

2011 (4 Apr). Butterflies of the World. T **302** and similar horiz designs. Multicoloured. P 13 (with one elliptical hole on each vert side) (**MS**2242) or 12 (**MS**2243).
MS2242 104×150 mm. $2×6 Type **302**; Gulf fritillary (*Agraulis vanillae*); Eastern tiger swallowtail (*Papilio glaucus*); Gabb's checkerspot (*Chlosyne gabbii*); Indian leafwing (*Kallima paralekta*); Blue diadem (*Hypolimnas salmacis*).. 10·00 10·00
MS2243 70×100 mm. $6 Monarch (*Danaus plexippus*).......... 5·00 5·00

303 Maine Coon 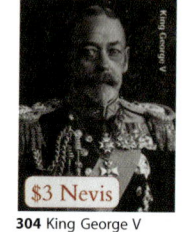   **304** King George V

(Litho)

2011 (4 Apr). Cats of the World. Two sheets, each 150×100 mm, containing T **303** and similar horiz designs. Multicoloured. P 12.
MS2244 $2.50×4 Type **303**; Norwegian forest cat; Ragdoll; Turkish angora... 8·50 8·50
MS2245 $2.50×4 Russian blue; Siamese; Abyssinian; Bombay... 8·50 8·50

(Litho)

2011 (4 Apr). Centenary of the Coronation of King George V. Sheet 150×101 mm. Multicoloured. P 13 (with one elliptical hole in each horiz side).
MS2246 $3 Type **304**×4...................................... 2·50 2·50

305 King George VI 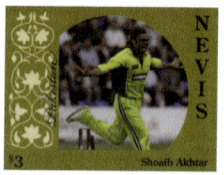   **306** Shoaib Akhtar (Pakistan)

(Litho)

2011 (4 Apr). 75th Anniv of the Accession of King George VI. Sheet 150×100 mm. Multicoloured. P 12.
MS2247 $3 Type **305**×4...................................... 2·50 2·50

(Litho)

2011 (4 Apr). Cricket World Cup, India, Sri Lanka and Bangladesh. Sheets, each 140×111 mm, containing T **306** and similar horiz designs. Multicoloured. P 12.
MS2248 $3×4 Type **306**; Shoaib Akhtar (head and shoulders); Pakistan team; Emblem (all with yellow-olive background)............................... 10·00 10·00
MS2249 $3×4 A. B. De Villiers batting; A. B. De Villiers; South Africa team; Emblem (all with orange-yellow backgrounds).. 10·00 10·00
MS2250 $3×4 A. B. De Villiers batting; A. B. De Villiers; South Africa team celebrating; Emblem (all with pale orange background)... 10·00 10·00
MS2251 $3×4 Chris Gayle on pitch; Chris Gayle; West Indies team; Emblem (all with brown-red background)... 10·00 10·00
MS2252 $3×4 A. B. De Villiers batting; A. B. De Villiers; South Africa team celebrating; Emblem (all with pale orange background)... 10·00 10·00

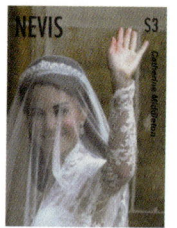

307 Miss Catherine Middleton on Wedding Day    **308** Princess Diana

(Litho)

2011 (29 Apr). Royal Wedding. T **307** and similar vert designs. Multicoloured. P 12.
MS2253 100×150 mm. $3 Type **307**×2; $3 Prince William (in profile)×2.................................. 7·50 7·50
MS2254 100×150 mm. $3 Duke and Duchess of Cambridge in carriage×2; $3 Duchess of Cambridge; $3 Prince William.......................... 7·50 7·50
MS2255 100×90 mm. $6 Duke and Duchess of Cambridge; $6 Duke and Duchess of Cambridge riding in carriage.. 7·50 7·50

(Litho)

2011 (20 Jun). 50th Birth Anniv of Princess Diana. T **308** and similar vert designs. Multicoloured.
MS2256 150×130 mm. $2×4 Type **308**; Wearing cap; Waving, in profile; Wearing dark purple and maroon hat... 6·50 6·50
MS2257 160×125 mm. $2×4 Princess Diana wearing bright mauve jacket; Wearing black and white hat and jacket; Wearing navy blue jacket and white top; Wearing red dress.................................. 6·50 6·50

309 Pres. Abraham Lincoln and "Government of the People by the People for the People shall not perish from the Earth"

(Litho)

2011 (20 Jun). 150th Anniv of the American Civil War. Two sheets, each 160×100 mm, containing T **309** and similar horiz designs. Multicoloured. P 13 (with one elliptical hole in each vert side).
MS2258 $2×4 all showing Pres. Abraham Lincoln and quotation: Type **309**; 'The best way to destroy an enemy is to make him a friend'; 'A house divided against itself cannot stand'; 'Avoid popularity if you would have peace'................... 6·50 6·50
MS2259 $2×4 Union Army soldier; Shield and Constitution ('The American Civil War'); Union Army soldiers in trenches; Pres. Abraham Lincoln.... 6·50 6·50

310 Blue Stripe Grunt (*Haemulon sciurus*)    **311** *Scaphella junonia*

(Litho)

2011 (25 Jul). Tropical Fish of the Caribbean. T **310** and similar multicoloured designs. P 12.
2260 10c. Type **310**.. 10 10
2261 30c. Red hind (*Cephalopholis miniatus*)........... 30 30
2262 40c. Red snapper (*Lutjanus campechanus*)........ 35 25
2263 $5 Old wife (*Enoplosus armatus*).................. 4·50 5·00

MS2264 102×123 mm. $2×6 Spotfin butterflyfish (*C. ocellatus*); Caribbean reef squid (*S. sepioidea*); Chubs (*K. bigibbus*); Surgeonfish (*A. olivaceus*); Blue-headed wrasse (*T. bifasciatum*); Long-spine porcupinefish (*D. holocanthus*) (all horiz) ...... 5·50 6·50
MS2265 100×71 mm. $6 Anemone fish (*Amphiprioninae*) (horiz) .... 5·00 5·00

(Litho)

2011 (25 Jul). Seashells of the Caribbean. T **311** and similar vert designs. Multicoloured. P 12 (2266/9) or 13 (with one elliptical hole in each horiz side) (others).
2266	20c. Type **311**	15	10
2267	30c. *Strombus gigas*	30	20
2268	$1.80 *Busycon contrarium*	1·50	1·50
2269	$5 *Arca zebra*	1·50	1·50

MS2270 150×101 mm. $2.50×4 *Charonia variegata*; *Cypraea aurantium*; *Cyphoma gibbosa*; *Chicoreus articulatus* .... 8·50 8·50
MS2271 100×71 mm. $6 *Thais deltoidea* .... 5·00 5·00
MS2272 100×71 mm. $6 *Thais deltoidea* .... 5·00 5·00

312 Pres. John F. Kennedy

313 Memorial, Staten Island, New York

(Litho)

2011 (29 Aug). 50th Anniv of the Inauguration of Pres. John F. Kennedy. T **312** and similar vert designs. Multicoloured. P 12.
MS2273 120×180 mm. $3×4 Type **312**; Pres. Kennedy in front of microphones; Facing microphones, in profile; Shaking hands .... 10·00 10·00
MS2274 90×100 mm. $6 Pres. Kennedy .... 5·00 5·00

(Litho)

2011 (29 Aug). Tenth Anniv of Attack on World Trade Center, New York. T **313** and similar vert designs. Each black and turquoise-green. P 12.
MS2275 161×100 mm. $2.75×4 Type **313**; Memorial, Bayonne, New Jersey; Memorial, The Pentagon; Memorial, Jerusalem .... 8·50 8·50
MS2276 100×100 mm. $6 Ground Zero Reflecting Pools ... 5·00 5·00

314 First Italian League, 1910

(Litho)

2011 (13 Sep). Juventus Football Club, Turin, Italy. Sheet, 173×135 mm, containing T **314** and similar horiz designs. Multicoloured. P 12½.
MS2277 $1.50×9 Type **314**; Giorgio Muggiani; Angelo Moratti; Helenio Herrera; Tim Cup, 2011; Giacinto Facchetti; Sandro Mazzola; Mario Corso; Luis Suarez.. 9·75 9·75

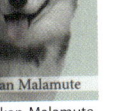

315 Alaskan Malamute

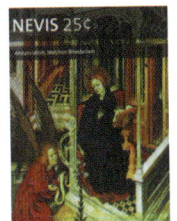

316 *Annunciation*

(Litho)

2011 (4 Oct). Dogs of the World. T **315** and similar vert designs. Multicoloured. P 13 (with one elliptical hole in each horiz side).
MS2278 140×100 mm. $2.75×4 Type **315**; Yorkshire terrier; Black labrador; Dachshund .... 8·50 8·50
MS2279 100×70 mm. $6 Beagle .... 5·00 5·00

(Litho)

2011 (7 Nov). Christmas. Paintings by Melchior Broederlam. T **316** and similar vert designs. Multicoloured. P 12.
2280	25c. Type **316**	20	15
2281	30c. *Visitation*	30	20
2282	90c. *Presentation in the Temple*	80	50
2283	$5 *Flight into Egypt*	2·75	3·25

317 Anegada Ground Iguana (*Cyclura pinguis*)

(Litho)

2011 (14 Nov). Reptiles of the Caribbean. T **317** and similar multicoloured designs. P 12 (MS2284) or 12½ (MS2285).
MS2284 150×100 mm. $3×4 Type **317**; Antilles racer (snake) (*Alsophis antillensis*); Brown anole (*Anolissagrei*); Lesser Antillean iguana (*Iguana delicatissima*) .... 2·50 2·50
MS2285 70×101 mm. $6 Anegada ground iguana (*Cyclura pinguis*) (51×38 mm) .... 2·50 2·50

318 Neptune

(Litho)

2011 (14 Nov). 50th Anniv of the First Man in Space. T **318** and similar multicoloured designs. P 12½×12 (MS2286) or 13 (MS2287).
MS2286 210×140 mm. $2×6 Type **318**; Uranus; Earth and Mars; Venus and Mercury; Jupiter; Saturn .... 5·00 5·00
MS2287 220×80 mm. $3×4 Full moon; Waxing gibbous moon; First quarter; Waxing crescent moon (all circular 35 mm diameter) .... 2·50 2·50

STAMP BOOKLETS

1980 (8 Oct). Boats. Multicoloured cover, 175×95 mm. Stitched.
SB1 $12.30 booklet containing 55c. (No. 53) in block of 6 and $3 in pane of 3 (No. 54ab) .... 1·60

1981 (19 Nov). Royal Wedding. Multicoloured cover, 105×65 mm, showing The Royal Charlotte. Stitched.
SB2 $8.40 booklet containing eight 55c. in panes of 4 (No. 79a) and $2 in pane of 2 (No. 80a) .... 2·00

1988 (23 July). Royal Wedding. Gold (No. SB3) or silver (No. SB4) on orange-red covers, 152×80 mm. Stapled.
SB3 $7.20 booklet (Westminster Abbey) containing twelve 60c. (Nos. 406/7) in blocks of 4 .... 3·00
SB4 $10.40 booklet (State Coach) containing 60c. and $2 (Nos. 406/9, but imperforate) in blocks of 4 ...... 3·50

OFFICIAL STAMPS

1980 (4 July*). Nos. 40/9 additionally optd with Type O **1** of St. Christopher, Nevis and Anguilla.
O1	15c. Sugar cane harvesting	10	10
O2	25c. Crafthouse (craft centre)	10	10
	a. "OFFICIAL" opt double	35·00	
	b. "OFFICIAL" opt omitted (in horiz pair with normal)	75·00	
	c. Optd on No. 41a	3·50	7·00
O3	30c. *Europa* (liner)	10	10

ST. KITTS-NEVIS / Nevis

O4	40c. Lobster and sea crab		15	15
O5	45c. Royal St. Kitts Hotel and golf course		20	20
	a. Opt inverted		13·00	
O6	50c. Pinney's Beach, Nevis		15	20
	a. Opt inverted		45·00	
O7	55c. New runway at Golden Rock		15	20
	a. Opt double		12·00	
O8	$1 Picking cotton		15	25
O9	$5 Brewery		45	55
	a. Opt inverted		70·00	
O10	$10 Pineapples and peanuts		70	90
O1/10	Set of 10		2·00	2·50

*Earliest known date of use.

1981 (1 Mar). Nos. 60A/71A optd with Type O **1** of St. Kitts.

O11	15c. New River Mill		10	10
O12	20c. Nelson Museum		10	10
O13	25c. St. James' Parish Church		10	15
O14	30c. Nevis Lane		15	15
O15	40c. Zetland Plantation		15	20
O16	45c. Nisbet Plantation		20	25
O17	50c. Pinney's Beach		20	25
O18	55c. Eva Wilkin's Studio		25	30
O19	$1 Nevis at dawn		30	30
O20	$2.50 Ruins of Fort Charles		40	50
O21	$5 Old Bath House		50	65
O22	$10 Beach at Nisbet's		80	1·00
O11/22	Set of 12		2·75	3·50

1983 (2 Feb). Nos. 72/7 optd with Type O **1** of St. Kitts (55c.) or surch also (others).

O23	45c. on $2 *Royal Sovereign* (New Blue)		10	15
	aw. Wmk inverted		10·00	
	b. Sheetlet. No. O23×6 and No. O24		70	
	bw. Wmk inverted		80·00	
	c. Surch inverted		6·00	
	d. Surch inverted (horiz pair)		30·00	
	e. Albino surch		6·50	
	ea. Albino surch inverted			
	f. Horiz pair, one without surch			
	g. Deep ultramarine surch		40	50
	gc. Surch inverted		5·00	
	gd. Surch inverted (horiz pair)		12·00	
	h. Black surch		40·00	
O24	45c. on $2 Prince Charles and Lady Diana Spencer (New Blue)		20	25
	aw. Wmk inverted		35·00	
	c. Surch inverted		20·00	
	e. Albino surch		15·00	
	g. Deep ultramarine surch		40	50
	gc. Surch inverted		12·00	
	h. Black surch		£110	
O25	55c. *Royal Caroline* (New Blue)		10	15
	b. Sheetlet. No. O25×6 and No. O26		75	
	e. Albino opt		7·00	
	ea. Albino opt inverted		10·00	
	eb. Albino opt inverted (horiz pair)		12·00	
	g. Deep ultramarine opt		75	
	gc. Opt inverted		5·00	
	gd. Opt inverted (horiz pair)		15·00	
	ge. Opt double		14·00	
	h. Black opt		40·00	
O26	55c. Prince Charles and Lady Diana Spencer (New Blue)		25	25
	e. Albino opt		15·00	
	ea. Albino opt inverted		20·00	
	g. Deep ultramarine opt		1·00	
	gc. Opt inverted		15·00	
	gd. Opt double		27·00	
	h. Black opt		£110	
O27	$1.10 on $5 *Britannia* (Blk.)		20	25
	aw. Wmk inverted		10·00	
	b. Sheetlet. No. O27×6 and No. O28		1·60	
	bw. Wmk inverted		80·00	
	e. Albino surch		7·50	
	f. Decimal point omitted from surch (R. 3/2)		55	
	g. Deep ultramarine surch		6·00	
	gc. Surch inverted		6·50	
	gd. Surch inverted (horiz pair)		32·00	
	gf. Decimal point omitted from surch (R. 3/2)		12·00	
O28	$1.10 on $5 Prince Charles and Lady Diana Spencer (Blk.)		55	60
	aw. Wmk inverted		35·00	
	e. Albino surch		22·00	
	g. Deep ultramarine surch		12·00	
	gc. Surch inverted		38·00	
O23/8	Set of 6		1·25	1·40

Nos. O23d, O23gd, O25eb, O25gd and O27gd show the surcharge or overprint intended for the large design inverted and struck across a horizontal pair of the smaller. Nos. O24c, O24gc, O26ea, O26gc and O28gc each show two inverted surcharges intended for a horizontal pair of the smaller design.

1985 (2 Jan). Nos. 187/98 optd with Type O **1** of St. Kitts.

O29	15c. Flamboyant		20	20
O30	20c. Eyelash Orchid		30	30
O31	30c. Bougainvillea		30	40
O32	40c. Hibiscus sp.		30	40
O33	50c. Night-blooming Cereus		35	40
O34	55c. Yellow Mahoe		35	45
O35	60c. Spider-lily		40	50
O36	75c. Scarlet Cordia		45	55
O37	$1 Shell-ginger		60	60
O38	$3 Blue Petrea		1·25	1·75
O39	$5 Coral Hibiscus		2·00	2·25
O40	$10 Passion Flower		3·00	2·50
O29/40	Set of 12		8·50	9·00

1993 (1 Mar). Nos. 578B/91B optd with Type O **1** of St. Kitts.

O41	5c. Type **63**		45	60
O42	10c. *Historis odius*		50	60
O43	15c. *Marpesia corinna*		60	50
O44	20c. *Anartia amathea*		60	40
O45	25c. *Junonia evarete*		60	40
O46	40c. *Heliconius charithonia*		75	45
O47	50c. *Marpesia petreus*		75	45
O48	75c. *Heliconius doris*		1·00	60
O49	80c. *Dione juno*		1·00	50
O50	$1 *Hypolimnas misippus*		1·00	80
O51	$3 *Danaus plexippus*		2·25	2·75
O52	$5 *Heliconius sara*		3·00	3·50
O53	$10 *Tithorea harmonia*		5·50	6·50
O54	$20 *Dryas julia*		11·00	12·00
O41/54	Set of 14		26·00	27·00

Imprint date: "1992", Nos. O41/54.

OFFICIAL

(O **1**)

1999 (22 Feb). Nos. 1166/77 optd with Type O **1**.

O55	25c. Guava		15	20
O56	30c. Papaya		15	20
O57	50c. Mango		25	30
O58	60c. Golden Apple		30	35
O59	80c. Pineapple		40	45
O60	90c. Watermelon		45	50
O61	$1 Bananas		50	55
O62	$1.80 Orange		90	95
O63	$3 Honeydew		1·50	1·60
O64	$5 Cantaloupe		2·50	2·75
O65	$10 Pomegranate		5·00	5·25
O66	$20 Cashew		10·00	10·50
O55/66	Set of 12		22·00	23·00